R I F L E S
O F   T H E
W O R L D

IN SERIES WITH THIS BOOK:
Military Small Arms of the 20th Century
SIXTH EDITION
Pistols of the World
THIRD EDITION

RIFLES
OF THE WORLD

THE DEFINITIVE
ILLUSTRATED GUIDE TO THE WORLD'S
CENTRE-FIRE RIFLES, FROM 1875 TO THE
PRESENT DAY

JOHN WALTER

ARMS AND
ARMOUR

To A.R.W. and A.D.W., with love.

Arms and Armour Press
A Cassell Imprint
Villiers House, 41–47 Strand, London WC2N 5JE

Distributed in Australia by
Capricorn Link (Australia) Pty, Ltd,
P.O. Box 665, Lane Cove, New South Wales 2066

© John Walter, 1993

British Library Cataloguing in Publication Data
A catalogue record for this book is available from the
British Library.

ISBN 1–85409–137–9

Every effort has been made to credit sources of
illustrations accurately, though some prints give no
clear indication of their origins. Unintentional
infringement of copyright will be acknowledged, if
appropriate, in future editions.

Title page illustrations
Top The 7·62mm Steyr-Mannlicher UIT
Match target rifle. STEYR-DAIMLER-PUCH AG
Centre The ·303 Martini-Enfield Mk I.
PATTERN ROOM COLLECTION
Bottom The standard 7·62mm FN FAL.
FN HERSTAL SA

Designed and produced by John Walter.
Typesetting by the Typesetting Bureau, Wimborne, Dorset.
Camerawork by Service Twenty Four Ltd, Brighton, East Sussex
Printed and bound in Great Britain by
The Bath Press, Bath, Avon

SUMMARY OF CONTENT

The major part of the book is
organised alphabetically. However,
should the required information be
absent from the directory or,
alternatively, filed under another
name (e.g., some Winchesters may
be found in the Browning section),
please consult either the brief
explanation of the directory
structure on page 12 or the
comprehensive index/minor gun
directory beginning on page 308.

Information:

DIMENSIONS: SOME OF THE MOST USEFUL IMPERIAL AND METRIC CONVERSION FACTORS

¶ To convert from grains to grams:
multiply by 0·0648.
¶ To convert from grains to
ounces: multiply by 0·0023
¶ To convert from grams to grains:
multiply by 15·432.
¶ To convert from grams to
ounces: multiply by 0·0353.
¶ To convert from kilograms to
pounds: multiply by 2·2046.
¶ To convert from ounces to
grains: multiply by 437·5.
¶ To convert from ounces to
grams: multiply by 28·35.
¶ To convert from pounds to
kilograms: multiply by 0·4536.
¶ To convert from feet to metres:
multiply by 0·3048.
¶ To convert from inches to
millimetres: multiply by 25·4.
¶ To convert from metres to feet:
multiply by 3·2808.
¶ To convert from metres to yards:
multiply by 1·0936.
¶ To convert from millimetres to
inches: multiply by 0·03937.
¶ To convert from yards to metres:
multiply by 0·9144.

When I first became seriously interested in firearms, as a schoolboy in the 1960s, I purchased a copy of the 1963 edition of Walter Smith's *The Book of Rifles*. The compact volume quickly became my indispensable companion. I marvelled at the scope of the information; at the breadth of coverage; and of the tremendous dedication it represented.

Twenty years of professional involvement with similar books has since done little to dim the regard in which I held *The Book of Rifles* : I still have my original copy. What interests me now is that a book originating as *The N.R.A. Book of Small Arms: Volume II, Rifles* as long ago as 1948 could still be regarded as authoritative.

It seems curious, too, that no effectual single-volume competitor has appeared in English in the last twenty years. I cannot suggest that nothing worthwhile has been achieved in this era—the bibliography proves otherwise—but I fear that ever-increasing specialisation of research (and the ever-rising cost of the books) may actually discourage the growth of a balanced interest amongst today's youngsters.

Though the interested reader may be able to discover the ultimate detail of Marlin trivia thanks to the late Bill Brophy's monumental 700-page study, he may not be able to discover the muzzle velocity of the rifles used in the Russo-Turkish War, nor what weapons were carried by secondary formations of the more obscure European armies in 1914. Even 'Smith' sometimes fails to provide these answers.

Twenty years ago, I became closely associated with production of the first edition of *Military Small Arms of the 20th Century* ; this was intended to compete with another of the well-established 'Smith' books, *Small Arms of the World*, which was then being prepared for its tenth edition and was widely regarded as an

enthusiasts' bible. *Military Small Arms* has now reached its sixth edition, whilst the third version of its series companion, *Pistols of the World*, appeared in 1992.

Unfortunately, the needs of the rifle enthusiast were largely overlooked during this period. I must confess that—despite producing detailed books on the Luger—I could never really understand the fascination for handguns at the expense of long arms. Handguns came in far less variety; were accompanied by far fewer accessories; and rarely had as interesting or convoluted a history. Rifles chambered a wider range of cartridges than pistols, and often accepted a range of bayonets sufficient to make a display in themselves. Most importantly, long arms often bore unit markings from which their service life could be reconstructed. This was rarely possible with an ordinary service pistol.

So it gives me particular pleasure to help the rifle enthusiast by drawing together as many facts as possible in one volume—a project that has been close to my heart for many years. I hope it provides the type of book I needed so badly when my initial interest began to grow.

Restrictions on content are explained on page 12.

I have inevitably drawn extensively on the work of others, which I hope to have credited satisfactorily, but I became increasingly conscious not only of the gaps in my own knowledge but also of many areas where too little information is available in English. And while I can truthfully claim to have gathered together enough material to fill some glaring gaps, I cannot, in all honesty, claim that none remain.

The work has been elating and depressing in turn, as each stroke of fortune was countered by the elusiveness of details. Had it not been for the continued love and support of my wife Alison and son

Adam, my parents and parents-in-law, the project would not have progressed as far as it has done.

I am particularly glad to acknowledge the help of Ian Hogg, who supplied most of the photographs of guns in the collections of the School of Infantry Museum and the Ministry of Defence Pattern Room (credited simply as 'Pattern Room'), and material concerning modern small-arms. Hans-Bert Lockhoven generously allowed me to plug gaps in coverage with excellent illustrations taken from his *Arms Archives* series, and the photographic archives of auctioneers Wallis & Wallis have also been most helpful. Most of the photographs are credited individually where appropriate.

Pietro Beretta SpA, the Browning Arms Company, the Marlin Firearms Company, O.F. Mossberg & Sons, Inc., Savage Arms Inc., and the US Repeating Arms Company (makers of the Winchesters) all responded to requests for assistance with particular alacrity. Among individual respondents, I would like to single out David Brown, for his help with the proof-reading; Anthony Carter of Tharston Press; Leslie E. Field; Joachim Görtz; Colin Greenwood, Editor of *Guns Review*; Victor Havlin, President of the National Mossberg Collectors Association; David Penn, Keeper of the Department of Exhibits and Firearms, Imperial War Museum; Karl Schäfer; Joseph J. Schroeder of Handgun Press; R. Blake Stevens of Collector Grade Publications; Ian Skennerton, who has done so much to advance the study of British military firearms; Major a.D. Hans-Rudolf von Stein; and Herbert Woodend, Custodian of the MOD Pattern Room, Nottingham.

I have tried to keep errors to a minimum but, as it is impossible to spread knowledge evenly across such a broad canvas, assistance that may improve a future edition will be gratefully accepted.

John Walter. Hove, England, 1993.

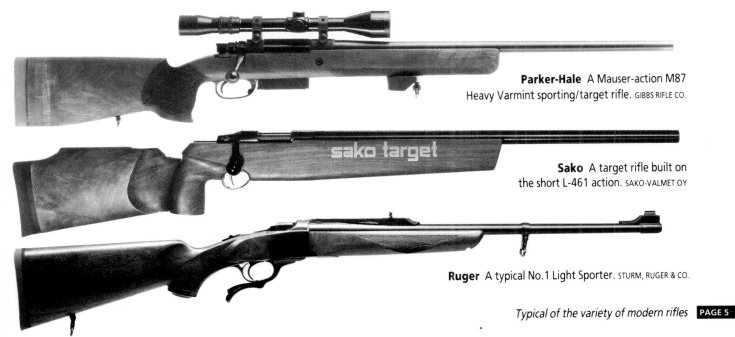

Parker-Hale A Mauser-action M87 Heavy Varmint sporting/target rifle. GIBBS RIFLE CO.

Sako A target rifle built on the short L-461 action. SAKO-VALMET OY

Ruger A typical No.1 Light Sporter. STURM, RUGER & CO.

Typical of the variety of modern rifles

Historical information and detail has been omitted from the directory text to concentrate on essentials. The list below is deliberately to confined to books—or reprints of books—that post-date 1960.

Anon.: *Treatise on Military Small Arms and Ammunition* ('With the Theory and Motion of a Rifle Bullet. A Text Book for the Army'). HMSO, London; 1888. Reprinted by Arms & Armour Press, 1971.

Barnes, Frank C.: *Cartridges of the World* ('The Book for Every Shooter, Collector and Handloader'). DBI Books, Inc., Northbrook, Illinois; fifth edition, 1985.

Brophy, Lt.-Col. William S.: *Marlin Firearms* ('A History of the Guns and the Company that Made Them'). Stackpole Books, Harrisburg, Pennsylvania; 1989.

Browning, John; and Gentry, Curt: *John M. Browning, American Gunmaker*. Doubleday & Company, New York; 1964.

Butler, David F.: *United States Firearms; The First Century, 1776–1875*. Winchester Press, New York; 1971.

Butler, David F.: *Winchester '73 & '76* ('The First Repeating Centerfire Rifles'). Winchester Press, New York; 1970.

Calvó, Juan L.: *Armamento Reglamentario y Auxiliar del Ejercito Español* ('Libro No.3. Modelos Portatiles de Retrocarga 1855–1922'). Published privately by the author. Barcelona; 1977.

Campbell, Clark S.: *The '03 Springfields*. Ray Riling Arms Books Co., Philadelphia, Pennsylvania; 1971.

Canfield, Bruce N.: *A Collector's Guide to the M1 Garand and the M1 Carbine*. Andrew Mowbray, Inc., Lincoln, Rhode Island; 1988.

De Haas, Frank: *Bolt Action Rifles*. DBI Books, Inc., Northfield, Illinois; 1971.

De Haas, Frank: *Single Shot Rifles & Actions*. DBI Books, Inc., Northfield, Illinois; 1969.

Dolleczek, Anton: *Monographie der k.u.k. österr.-ung. blanken und Handfeuer-Waffen...* ('seit Errichtung des stehendes Heeres bis zur Geganwart'). L.W. Seidel & Sohn, Vienna; 1896. Reprinted by Akademische Druck- und Verlagsanstalt, Graz, Austria; 1970.

Ezell, Edward C.: *Small Arms Today* ('Latest Reports on the World's Weapons and Ammunition'). Stackpole Books, Harrisburg, Pennsylvania, and Arms & Armour Press, London; second edition, 1988.

Fuller, Claud E.: *The Breech-Loader in the Service, 1816–1917* ('A History of All Standard and Experimental U.S. Breech-Loading and Magazine Shoulder Arms'). N. Flayderman & Company, New Milford, Connecticut; 1965.

Garavaglia, Louis; and Worman, Charles: *Firearms of the American West, 1866–1894*. University of New Mexico Press, Albuquerque, New Mexico; 1985.

Gianfranco, Simone; Belogi, Ruggero; and Grimaldi, Alessio: *Il 91* [the Mannlicher-Carcano rifle]. Editrice Ravizza, Milan; 1971.

Hatch, Alden: *Remington Arms in American History*. Remington Arms Company, Inc., Ilion, New York, USA; revised edition, 1972.

Hatcher, Major General Julian S.: *Book of the Garand*. National Rifle Association of America; 1948. Reprinted by The Gun Room Press, Highland Park, New Jersey, USA; 1977.

Hicks, Major James E.: *U.S. Military Firearms,*

1776–1956. James E. Hicks & Son, La Vineta, California; 1962.

Hogg, Ian V. [editor]: *Jane's Infantry Weapons*. Jane's Publishing Co. Ltd, London; revised annually.

Hogg, Ian V.; and Weeks, John S.: *Military Small Arms of the 20th Century* ('A comprehensive illustrated encyclopedia of the world's small-calibre firearms'). Arms & Armour Press, London; sixth edition, 1991.

Honeycutt, Fred L., Jr: *Military Rifles of Japan*. Julin Books, Lake Park, Florida, USA; 1982.

Hughes, James, B., Jr.: *Mexican Military Arms* ('The Cartridge Period, 1866–1967'). Deep River Armory, Houston, Texas; 1968.

Huon, Jean: *Un Siècle d'Armement Mondial* ('armes à feu d'infanterie de petit calibre'). Éditions Crépin-Leblond, Paris; six volumes, 1976–81.

Huovinen, Kalevi: *Sako, 1921–1971* ('jakso suomalaisen asesepän kehityskaarta' ['Finnish gunmakers for fifty years']). Published by the company, Riihimäki; 1971.

Kirkland, K.D.: *America's Premier Gunmakers*. Bison Books, London; 1990.

Korn, R.H.: *Mauser-Gewehre und Mauser-Patente* ('Als Beitrag zur Entwicklung der Handfeuerwaffen in den letzten vierzig Jahren'). Ecksteins biographischem Verlag, Berlin, 1908; reprinted by Akademische Druck- und Verlagsanstalt, Graz, Austria, 1971.

Kromar, Konrad Edeler von: *Repetier- und Automatische Handfeuerwaffen der Systeme Ferdinand Ritter von Mannlicher*. L.W. Seidel & Sohn, Vienna; 1900. Reprinted by Journal-Verlag Schwend GmbH, Schwäbisch Hall, Germany, 1976.

Lugs, Jaroslav: *Ruční palné zbrane*. Naše Vojsko, Prague, two volumes; 1956. Published in German as *Handfeuerwaffen* (Deutsche Militärverlag, Berlin, 1962) and in English as *Firearms Past and Present* (Ravenhill Publishing Company, London, c.1976).

Marquiset, Roger; and Lorain, Pierre: *Armes à Feu Françaises Modèles Réglementaires*. Published privately; several volumes, 1969–72.

Martin, Colonel Jean: *Armes à Feu de l'Armée Française, 1860 à 1940* ('Historiques des évolutions précédentes; comparaison avec les armes étrangères'). Éditions Crépin-Leblond, Paris; 1974.

Musgrave, Daniel D.; and Nelson, Thomas B.: *The World's Assault Rifles & Automatic Carbines*. TBN Enterprises, Alexandria, Virginia, USA; c.1966.

Olson, Ludwig: *Mauser Bolt Rifles*. F. Brownell & Son, Publishers, Inc., Montezuma, Iowa; third edition, 1976.

Otteson, Stuart; *The Bolt Action, A Design Analysis*. Winchester Press, New York; 1976.

Reynolds, Major E.G.B.: *The Lee-Enfield Rifle*. Herbert Jenkins Ltd, London; 1960.

Rubi, B. Barceló: *Armamento Portatil Español (1764–1939), una labor artillera*. Libreria Editorial San Martin, Madrid; 1976.

Sada, Plk Dr Miroslav: *Československé Ruční Palné Zbrane a Kulomety*. Naše Vojsko, Prague; 1971.

Sallaz, Kurt; and am Rhyn, Michael: *Handfeuerwaffen Gradzug-Systeme* (part four of 'Bewaffnung und Ausrüstung der Schweizer Armee seit 1817'). Verlag Stocker-Schmid, Dietikon-Zürich; 1978.

Schmidt, Rudolf: *Die Handfeuerwaffen*. B. Schwabe, Basel, Switzerland; two volumes, 1875–8. Reprinted by Akademische Druck- und Verlagsanstalt, Graz, 1968.

Schneider, Hugo; am Rhyn, Michael; Krebs, Oskar;

Reinhart, Christian; and Schiess, Robert: *Handfeuerwaffen System Vetterli* (part three of 'Bewaffnung und Ausrüstung der Schweizer Armee seit 1817'). Verlag Stocker-Schmid, Dietikon-Zürich; 1970.

Skennerton, Ian: *A Treatise on the Snider* ('The British Soldier's Firearm, 1866–c1880'). Published by the author, Margate, Queensland, Australia; 1977.

Skennerton, Ian: *British Small Arms of World War 2*. Published by the author, Margate, Queensland, Australia; 1988.

Skennerton, Ian: *The British Service Lee* ('Lee-Metford and Lee-Enfield Rifles and Carbines, 1880–1980'). Published by the author, Margate, Queensland, Australia, in association with Arms & Armour Press, London; 1982.

Smith, Walter H.B.: *The Book of Rifles*. The Stackpole Company, Harrisburg, Pennsylvania, USA; seventh edition, 1968.

Smith, Walter H.B.: *Mauser, Walther & Mannlicher Firearms*. The Stackpole Company, Harrisburg, Pennsylvania, USA; 1971.

Smith, Walter H.B. (Joseph E. Smith and Edward C. Ezell, revisers): *Small Arms of the World* ('A basic manual of small arms'). Stackpole Books, Harrisburg, Pennsylvania; eleventh edition, 1977.

Stevens, R. Blake: *North American FALs* ('NATO's Search for a Standard Rifle'). Collector Grade Publications, Inc., Toronto; 1979.

Stevens, R. Blake; and van Rutten, Jean E.: *The Metric FAL* ('The Free World's Right Arm'). Collector Grade Publications, Inc., Toronto; 1981.

Stevens, R. Blake: *UK and Commonwealth FALs*. Collector Grade Publications, Inc., Toronto; revised (second) edition, 1987.

Stevens, R. Blake: *US Rifle M14* ('From John Garand to the M21'). Collector Grade Publications, Inc., Toronto; 1983.

Stevens, R. Blake; and Ezell, Edward C.: *The Black Rifle. M16 Retrospective*. Collector Grade Publications, Inc., Toronto; 1987.

Sutherland, Robert Q.; and Wilson, R. L.: *The Book of Colt Firearms*. R.Q. Sutherland, Kansas City, Missouri; 1971.

Temple, B.A.; and Skennerton, I.D.: *A Treatise on the British Military Martini* ('The Martini-Henry, 1869–c.1900'). Published privately by B.A. Temple, Burbank, Queensland, Australia, and in Britain by Arms & Armour Press, London; 1983.

Temple, B.A.; and Skennerton, I.D.: *A Treatise on the British Military Martini* ('The ·40 and ·303 Martinis, 1880–c.1920'). Published privately by B.A. Temple, Burbank, Queensland, Australia, and in Britain by Greenhill Books, London; 1989.

Wahl, Paul: *Gun Trader's Guide*. Stoeger Publishing Company, South Hackensack, New Jersey; fourteenth edition (John E. Traister, reviser), 1990.

Walter, John D.: *The German Rifle* ('A comprehensive illustrated history of the standard bolt-action designs, 1871–1945'). Arms & Armour Press, London; 1979.

Walter, John D.: *The Rifle Book* ('The comprehensive one-volume guide to the world's shoulder guns'). Arms & Armour Press, London; 1990.

Watrous, George R.: *The History of Winchester Firearms, 1866–1966*. Winchester-Western Press, New Haven, Connecticut; third edition, 1966.

Accelerator A mechanism, usually consisting of a lever, which increases the rearward velocity of the recoiling bolt to separate it more effectually from a recoiling barrel. Accelerators are often found in machine-guns, where the goal is generally to increase the rate of fire. They may also be encountered in auto-loading rifles, often simply to increase the power of the operating stroke and enhance reliability.

Aiming Tube See 'sub-calibre adaptor'.

Auto-loading Also known as *self-loading* or *semi-automatic*. This is a mechanism which—through force generated on firing—unlocks the breech (if appropriate), extracts and ejects the empty case, then re-cocks the firing mechanism and re-loads so that the gun will fire when the trigger is pressed again. Strictly, all semi- and fully-automatic weapons are auto-loaders, though only guns in the latter group are *auto-firing*.

Automatic rifle A gun which will continue firing until either the trigger is released or the ammunition has been expended.

Automatic safety See 'mechanical safety'.

Azimuth adjustment Found on a back sight to move the point of impact laterally. Known in North America as 'windage'.

Barrel band Also known simply as 'band', this holds the barrel in the fore-end. It may be made in one piece or two, and retained by springs let into the fore-end (*sprung*) or by screws or threaded bolts (*screwed*).

Barrel extension A frame attached to the barrel to carry the bolt or breech-block; or, alternatively, the part of the barrel behind the breech into which the bolt or breech-block may lock.

Barrel rib A stiffener forged into the upper surface of the barrel, into which the front sight blade is formed or fixed, this is sometimes encountered in sporting guns (though much more common on shotguns). The object is to give the barrel rigidity without adding as much weight as would be required if it had been forged with a greater diameter. Half- and quarter-ribs will be encountered on sporting guns, usually to carry the sights rather than stiffen the barrel.

Bayonet A bladed weapon that can be attached to the muzzle of a rifle or musketoon, though not usually to a carbine. There are many differing types.

¶ A *socket bayonet* is an all-metal pattern with a short cylindrical socket, passing over the muzzle, and some method of locking the socket to the gun—a spring, a rotating collar or a sliding catch.

¶ A *knife bayonet* has a short straight blade, for the purposes of this book being defined as less than 25cm long; a *sword bayonet* is essentially similar to a knife pattern, but has a blade exceeding 25cm.

¶ A *sabre bayonet* is basically a sword pattern with a curved or recurved ('yataghan') blade.

¶ A *rod bayonet* usually slides in a channel beneath the muzzle, being carried on the gun at all times.

Belted case See 'cartridge case'.

Block action A mechanism relying on a block placed behind the chamber to seal the breech. It may be encountered in many differing guises.

¶ *Dropping* or *falling blocks* slide vertically downward through a mortise. The Farquharson, Sharps and Browning (Winchester) rifles are typical examples.

¶ *Rising blocks*—rarely encountered—should

invariably move vertically upward.

¶ *Swinging blocks* are common, though encountered in a variety of guises and difficult to categorise accurately. A few swing up and back. Some swing up and forward (e.g., Albini-Braendlin, Springfield-Allin). Some swing laterally backward (e.g., Restell) or forward (Milbank-Amsler). Many swing back and down (Remington Rolling Block, Spencer); others move down and back (Peabody, Martini). The Snider and similar breech blocks swing laterally on a longitudinal pin.

Blowback Alternatively classed as *case projection*, this is a system of operation in which closure of the breech is undertaken simply by the inertia of the breech block and pressure from the return spring. The breech is not locked at the moment of discharge and, therefore, is generally confined to low-power cartridges. Commonly encountered among pistols and submachine-guns, blowback is uncommon in auto-loading rifles other than rimfires and low-power centre-fire sporters (e.g, the Winchesters designed by Thomas Johnson). Attempts to chamber blowback rifles for military-pattern cartridge have always ended in failure, as some form of case lubrication is obligatory.

Blow-forward The reverse of blowback operation (see above), this relies on the barrel being projected forward by chamber pressure. The empty case is ejected before a spring returns the barrel to chamber a new cartridge. Though extraction and ejection are simplified, blow-forward has too many problems to attract rifle designers: the excessive weight of the moving parts disturbs aim too easily. SIG made a few AK-53 rifles in the early 1950s, but few other blow-forward rifles are known.

Bolt This closes the breech of a gun. Used on practically all military rifles made in 1890–1940, it usually comprises a cylindrical body containing the firing pin and firing-pin spring. Several differing types of bolt have been used, but most rely on lugs rotating into the receiver (or sometimes into the barrel extension) to lock the action securely. Some guns have the lugs on the bolt body; others have a detachable head. A few retract the lugs into the bolt during the opening stroke and others may have a pivoting bar or locking strut.

Bolt action A system of operation relying on a cylindrical bolt reciprocating to extract, eject, reload and cock the firing mechanism.

¶ *Straight-pull action* simply requires a handle to be pulled backward, usually transmitting a rotary motion to the bolt head by way of lugs and helical cam-tracks. Associated with the later Austro-Hungarian Mannlicher service rifles and the Swiss Schmidt(-Rubin), this system may be operated quickly when clean and properly lubricated but offers poor primary extraction.

¶ *Turning-bolt action* requires a handle to be lifted or the bolt-body rotated to disengage locking lugs before the backward movement can begin. Theoretically slower to operate than straight-pull systems, it offers more effectual primary extraction and is less likely to be affected by variations in cartridge dimensions.

Bolt carrier A component or assembly that carries the bolt, commonly encountered in auto-loaders. It may also control unlocking.

Bolt plug, sleeve or shroud A housing attached to the rear of the bolt, generally surrounding the cocking piece (q.v.).

Bolt way The portion of the receiver (q.v.) in which the bolt rides.

Bore The axial hole through the barrel, usually rifled to spin the projectile. *Bore diameter* measurements usually exclude the depth of the rifling.

Breech block Any non-cylindrical means of closing a breech. Breech blocks may take a wide variety of forms—e.g., sliding vertically, pivoting laterally, or tipping upward.

Breech The rear end of the action, containing the breech block and giving access to the chamber. See also 'receiver'.

Breech bolt See 'bolt', above.

Buckhorn See 'sights'.

Butt The part of the stock extending backward against the firer's shoulder. It may be integral with the fore-end (q.v.), forming a *one-piece stock*, or a separate component. The upper edge of the butt is known as the *comb* (q.v.), which terminates at the shoulder in the *heel*. The *toe* is the lower tip of the butt, and the *grip* (q.v.), *small* or *wrist* is the narrow portion immediately behind the action facilitating an effectual hand grip.

Butt or shoulder plate A fixture on the end of the butt, either to protect the wood or to ease the shock of firing on the firer's shoulder. The traditional metal pattern generally has a concave surface, known variously as *rifle type* or *crescentic*. Many sporting guns have been fitted with a straight or *shotgun type* plate, while others, especially recent ones, have had plates of rubber or injection-moulded plastic. The most powerful sporting guns have compressible butt plates, often of *ventilated* pattern. Target rifles invariably have hooked or adjustable butt plates.

Caliber, calibre An expression of the internal diameter of a gun barrel, generally measured across the lands, but sometimes across the grooves or even—as a compromise—from the bottom of one groove to the land diametrically opposite. A calibre dimension is often an approximation and may depend on marketing strategy. The term is commonly used as a synonym for 'chambering' (q.v.), but such misleading usage should be discouraged.

Carbine A short firearm with a barrel measuring less than 20–22in, usually—but not invariably—lacking a bayonet (cf., 'musketoon').

Cartridge case This contains the propellant and a means of igniting it. There are two major categories—*centre-fire* and *rimfire*, the former containing the primer centrally in the base of the case and the latter around the inside of the case-rim. Some cases are straight, others may be *necked* (or 'bottle-necked') in an attempt to increase propellant capacity without affecting the case length.

¶ *Belted cases* have a raised rib or 'belt' around the body, ahead of the extraction groove, to position the cartridge accurately in the chamber. Belted cases are often very strong, and are generally confined to those rounds that develop high chamber pressures.

¶ *Rimless cases* have an extraction groove in the base, the rim being the same diameter as the case-head. They feed well from magazines, owing to the absence of projecting rims, but must be indexed on the case mouth and are often affected by headspace problems.

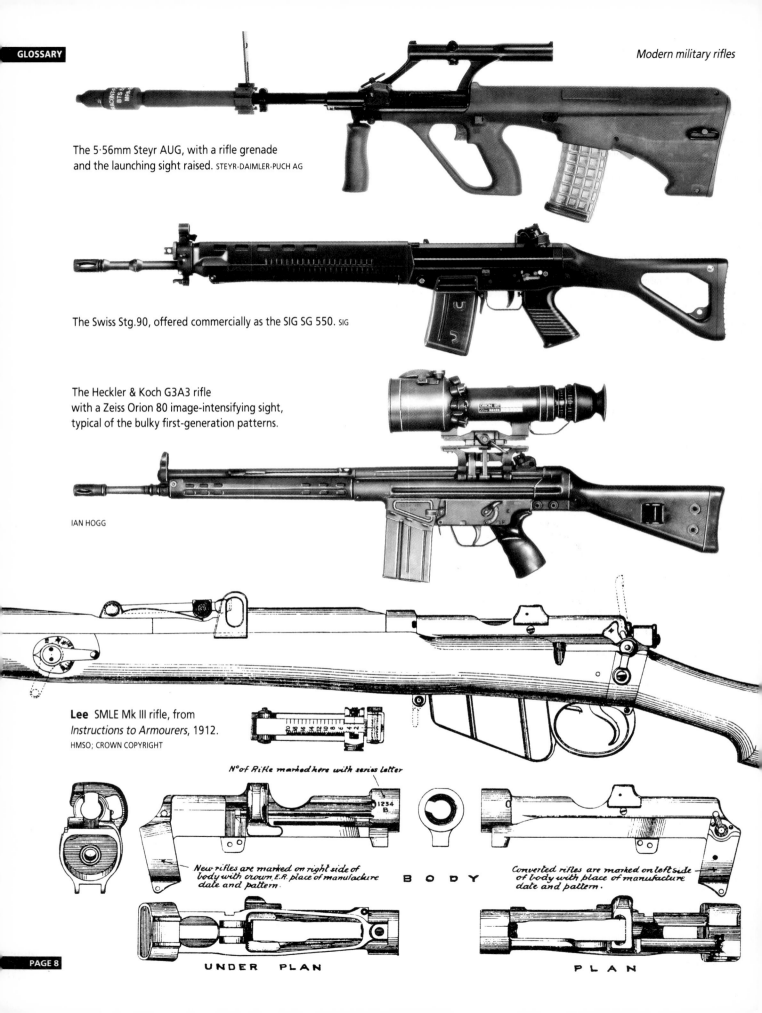

The 5·56mm Steyr AUG, with a rifle grenade and the launching sight raised. STEYR-DAIMLER-PUCH AG

The Swiss Stg.90, offered commercially as the SIG SG 550. SIG

The Heckler & Koch G3A3 rifle with a Zeiss Orion 80 image-intensifying sight, typical of the bulky first-generation patterns.

IAN HOGG

Lee SMLE Mk III rifle, from *Instructions to Armourers*, 1912.
HMSO; CROWN COPYRIGHT

Nº of Rifle marked here with series letter

New rifles are marked on right side of body with crown, E.R. place of manufacture date and pattern.

B O D Y

Converted rifles are marked on left side of body with place of manufacture date and pattern.

U N D E R   P L A N

P L A N

¶ *Rimmed cases* have a protruding rim at the base of the case, which abuts the chamber face to position the cartridge. Consequently, they index very well but are prone to rim-over-rim jams in the magazine.

¶ *Semi-rimmed cases* have an extraction groove like a rimless (q.v.) pattern, in addition to a rim offering slightly greater diameter than the case-head. Consequently, the rim can position the case correctly in the chamber but is small enough to avoid interference in the magazine.

Chamber The enlarged and shaped area of the interior of the gun barrel at the breech, into which the cartridge fits.

Chambering The act of cutting a chamber (q.v.) in the barrel. Alternatively, an indication of the cartridge a particular gun accepts—e.g., 'chambering ·30–30 Winchester Central Fire', 'chambered for 7·62 × 51mm NATO cartridges'. It should not be confused with calibre (q.v.); the ·30-calibre rifle chambering may be any of several alternatives. Thus the US Krag-Jørgensen M1892 (·30–40 Krag rimmed), Springfield M1903 (·30 M1903 or ·30 M1906 rimless) and Winchester M1894 (·30–30 rimmed) may share the same calibre, but accept entirely different cartridges.

Charger A device for loading a magazine firearm, very common in military weapons but much less popular on sporting guns. Cartridges are held in a special holder, usually made of sheet metal and often containing a spring. The action is opened, the cartridge-holder positioned at the entrance to the magazine, and the cartridges are pressed downward by the thumb. This strips them from the charger and into the magazine box. Chargers are confusingly known as 'clips' (q.v.) in North America, or sometimes as 'stripper clips' to avoid problems of communication.

Charger guides A method of positioning the charger (see above) to enable the firer to press cartridges into the magazine. Most charger-loading rifles have the guides on the front of the receiver bridge, though some early British Lee-Enfields had one guide on the bolt head and some Mausers have the left guide formed by an upward extension of the bolt-stop. Mauser is usually credited with the introduction of the charger-loaded magazine, but elements of the system may be seen in some early quick-loading devices.

Cheek piece Found on the side of the butt to help the firer position his eye behind the sights, this exists in several patterns. The classical design was a plain oval, but many modern rifles have a *Monte Carlo* type with a high comb suited to optical sights. The *Bavarian* cheek piece has a squared lower edge, while the *Tyrolean* pattern (often wrongly called 'Swiss') has a distinctive concave surface with a curved comb.

Clip A method of loading a magazine with several cartridges held in a special holder. The entire assembly is placed in the magazine, where a spring-loaded arm forces the cartridge upward until a fresh cartridge is pushed into the chamber each time the bolt or breech-block reciprocates. As the last cartridge is loaded, the clip falls (or is ejected) from the weapon. Many early Mannlichers, the M1 Garand and other rifles have been clip-loaded. The system is much less flexible than a charger, particularly in cases—such as the Garand—where the clip is essential to the action yet cannot be replenished with single rounds when in the magazine.

¶ The term 'clip' is widely used in North America to describe a 'charger'. It has also gained increasing—if exasperating—popularity among European sporting-rifle manufacturers to denote a detachable box magazine.

Cocking piece An attachment to the rear of the striker, carrying a knob or spur and the sear notches.

Comb The upper edge of the butt, extending backward from the grip (or wrist) to the heel. The classical comb is straight, but the popular *Monte Carlo* pattern curves upward at the heel—raising the line of sight—while the *Bavarian* (also known as 'Imperial' or ''Hog's Back'') comb has a noticeably convex curve from wrist to heel. A roll-over comb curves over the vertical toward the non-cheek side of the stock.

Compensator A device on the muzzle of a firearm which diverts some of the emerging gas upward, so developing a downward thrust to counteract the rise of the muzzle during rapid firing.

Cut-off Popular on early military rifles, this restricts them to single-shot firing while holding the contents of the magazine in reserve. A typical lever-type example merely depresses the cartridges in the magazine so that the returning bolt can pass over them.

Cycle of operation See 'operating cycle'.

Cyclic rate Also known as *rate of fire*, this is the theoretical continuous rate of fire of an automatic weapon, assuming an unlimited supply of ammunition—i.e., ignoring the need to reload or change magazines.

Delayed blowback This is a blowback (q.v.) mechanism in which an additional restraint or brake is placed on the bolt or similar breech closure to delay or slow the opening movement. There is no positive breech lock. The system is also sometimes known as *hesitation* or *retarded* blowback.

Disconnector A component in the trigger mechanism which disconnects the trigger from the remainder of the firing train after each shot; the firer must release the trigger and take a fresh pressure to fire again. This prevents the gun firing continuously for a single pressure on the trigger.

Double action A mechanism in which the hammer or striker is cocked and then released by pulling through on the trigger (cf., 'Self-cocking').

Doubling The firing of one or more shots for a single pull of the trigger, usually as a result of the disconnector (q.v.) failing.

Ejector A device to throw empty cases out of a gun. It is usually a fixed bar or blade which intercepts a spent case withdrawn from the breech by the extractor.

Elevation adjustment Found on sights, this makes alterations to vary the range—usually by raising or lowering the sight block. See also 'azimuth adjustment' and 'sights'.

Extractor This is customarily a claw, attached to the bolt or breech block, which engages the rim or groove to draw the cartridge case from the chamber before presenting it to the ejector.

Feed-way That part of a weapon where a cartridge, taken from the feed system, is positioned ready to be loaded into the chamber. Rarely seen in handguns, where the distance between the magazine and the chamber is generally very short, it is much more commonly encountered on rifles and machine-guns.

Fire selector See 'selective fire'.

Firing mechanism The trigger lever, sear(s), the hammer or striker, and all relevant pins, screws and springs.

Firing pin See 'striker'.

Flash-hider or suppressor A muzzle attachment designed to minimise the effects of propellant flash, generally by using prongs or a pierced tube. It may be combined with a muzzle brake (q.v.) but is rarely especially effectual.

Fluted chamber A chamber (q.v.) with longitudinal grooves extending into the bore, but not as far as the mouth. Propellant gas flows down these grooves to 'float' the case, counteracting pressure remaining inside the case. It is associated with actions in which the breech begins opening while the residual pressure is still high. If the chamber wall was plain, internal pressure would stick the body of the cartridge case firmly against the chamber; any rearward movement of the bolt would then tear the base off the cartridge. By floating the case, there is less resistance to movement and the bolt can begin opening without risk of premature damage. Fluted chambers are comparatively common in delayed-blowback military rifles (e.g., CETME, Heckler & Koch G3, Swiss Stgw.57).

Follower The mobile floor of the magazine which supports the cartridges.

Fore-end That part of the stock beneath the barrel. It may extend to the muzzle or, commonly in sporting patterns, only to half length. A fore-end that flares outward to provide a better grip is known as a *beaver-tail*. The fore-end tip may be rounded; have a pronounced downward curl (*schnabel tip*); or display a curious beak derived from a pattern introduced by Alexander Henry in the 1870s.

Gas operation A method of operating an auto-loader by tapping part of the propellant gas from the bore to unlock the breech and propel the bolt or breech-block backward. Most early gas-operated rifles relied on intermediate rods or levers to operate the breech (*indirect gas operation*) but, inspired by the ArmaLite series, many modern designs lead gas straight back to strike the bolt or bolt carrier (*direct gas operation*). The direct method is simpler, but more prone to fouling.

Grip (i) A part of the butt (q.v.) between the action and the comb, also known as the wrist. (ii) A separate hand grip, either behind the trigger or beneath the fore-end, commonly fitted either to compensate for the use of a straight-line stock or to improve control in automatic fire.

Hammerless Truly hammerless rifles rely on nothing but a striker to fire the primer cap; 'pseudo hammerless' designs may be similar externally, but have an unseen hammer inside the frame.

Hinged frame A gun in which the barrel forms a separate unit attached to the frame by a hinge bolt, so that by releasing a catch the barrel can be tipped down to expose the chambers. The barrel usually tips downward. Widely associated with shotguns and shotgun-type double rifles, the system is generally excluded from coverage in *Rifles of the World*.

Inertia firing pin See 'striker'.

Lands The raised portions of a gun-barrel bore between the grooves of the rifling.

Lever action A mechanism that relies on a lever or system of levers to open the breech, extract, eject, reload and then re-lock. The Winchester M1873 or Marlin M1895 are typical examples, but many differing patterns have been made. The term is now normally confined to magazine rifles (strictly, 'lever-action repeaters'); otherwise, it could be applied to many single-shot block-action guns.

Loaded-chamber indicator A pin, blade or other device—sometimes combined with the exractor—which gives visual and tactile indication of the presence of a cartridge in the chamber.

Lock time The period that elapses between pressing the trigger and the impact of the hammer, striker or firing-pin on the primer of a chambered cartridge. The shortest possible lock time is desirable to reduce the chance of a shift in aim during the period in which the striker is falling. Lock times as short as two milliseconds (·002 sec) will be encountered in bolt-action sporting rifles, which usually have a short light striker propelled very rapidly, to a ponderous ten milliseconds (·01 sec) for some military rifles where heavy cocking pieces—and sometimes even the safety catch—are attached directly to the striker.

¶ The fastest lock time of standard military rifles is generally regarded as the German Gew.98 at about five milliseconds, closely followed by the 1905-pattern Japanese Arisaka. Among the slowest are the US Krag-Jørgensen (about eight milliseconds), with the Gew.88 at nine milliseconds or worse.

Lock-work An expression covering the whole of the mechanism necessary to fire a weapon, from the trigger through to the hammer or striker.

Long recoil See 'recoil operation'.

Magazine The container in which the cartridges are held to permit continuous fire. Magazines take many differing forms. Among the earliest were tubes, usually contained in the fore-end beneath the barrel (e.g., Henry, Vetterli, Winchester) or, more rarely, in the butt (Chaffee-Reece, Hotchkiss). These were superseded by box patterns, credited—though not without dispute—to James Lee. Some boxes were *detachable*, others have been fixed. Fixed magazines are described here as *internal* if they are carried entirely inside the stock (introduced on the Spanish Mauser of 1893) and *fixed* or *integral* if they project externally but are part of the receiver or frame (e.g., most Mannlichers, Mosin-Nagant). Some of the earlier Mausers, such as the Argentine gun of 1891 have *semi-integral* magazines, which can be removed with the aid of a tool but are not genuinely readily detachable. Magazines described as *blind* are carried internally, but are not visible from the outside of the gun owing to the lack of a floor plate.

¶ Other patterns to have reached service status include a *pan* (lateral) magazine, featured by the Krag-Jørgensen, or the *spool* (rotary) mechanism embodied in Mannlicher-Schönauer and similar guns. Military magazines may be loaded from chargers or with clips (qq.v.).

Magazine safety A system ensuring that the firing mechanism will not function if the magazine is removed. The objective is to prevent a common accident where the magazine is removed, but a live round remains in the chamber. Magazine safeties are unpopular on military weapons, which would otherwise be prevented from firing single shots by the absence of a magazine.

Main spring The spring that propels the hammer or striker into the primer of a chambered cartridge.

Mechanical safety A method of ensuring that the action does not fire before the breech is properly closed. A mechanical safety is obligatory in an auto-loader, but is also present in most manually-operated rifles to ensure that the striker cannot reach the primer of a chambered round until the locking mechanism is engaged.

Musketoon A short-barrelled firearm, usually accepting a bayonet (cf., 'carbine').

Muzzle brake An attachment similar to a compensator, intended to turn the emerging gases and drive them rearward. This counteracts the recoil sensation by thrusting the muzzle forward. The effectiveness of muzzle brakes varies, as utility has to be balanced against the unpleasant consequences of directing gas-blast sideways.

Non-ejecting, non-ejector A class of gun unable to eject spent cartridges, generally confined to double rifles though many early military rifles lacked ejectors and some dropping-block patterns can be set to extract only partially. The feature is useful for those who do not want to lose spent cases or to have them damaged during ejection.

Nose cap The band or fitting nearest the muzzle. The term is usually applied to a military rifle, where the nose cap will often carry a lug for the bayonet and anchor the cleaning rod.

Operating cycle This is simply the complete routine required for the satisfactory functioning of an automatic weapon—firing, unlocking the breech, extracting, ejecting, cocking, feeding, chambering and breech-locking. (Note: not all functions may be present, some may overlap, and the order of their occurrence may vary.)

Proof mark Applied by an official body ('proof house') to certify that a gun is strong enough to withstand the rigours of continual use.

Pump action See 'slide action'.

Quick-loader A method of holding cartridges so that they are readily available for insertion in the chamber. The term is associated with single-shot rifles, though a charger and even a clip are quick-loaders of a particular form. A typical loader may take the form of a spring-clip attached to the breech, or a wooden block screwed to the fore-end.

Receiver A term applied to the frame of a rifle. The sides of a *solid bridge receiver* are connected above the bolt or breech block, while a *split-bridge receiver* allows the bolt or operating handle to pass through.

Recoil A force generated by firing, opposing the forward motion of the projectile.

Recoil bolt A transverse bolt through the stock, acting in concert with the recoil lug (below) to spread the force that may otherwise split or damage the woodwork.

Recoil lug A projection on the underside of the breech designed to spread the recoil force to a greater area of the stock than a bolt running up through the trigger guard, tang or magazine floor plate into the receiver.

Recoil operation The recoil (q.v.) force harnessed to operate an auto-loading action.

¶ *Long recoil* relies on the barrel and breech recoiling locked together for a distance at least as long as a complete unfired cartridge. At the end of this stroke, the bolt is unlocked and held while the barrel runs back to its forward position. During this movement, the cartridge case is extracted and ejected and a fresh round rises into the feedway. The bolt is then released, runs forward to chamber a round, locks, and the gun is ready to fire. Long recoil is uncommon, however.

¶ *Short recoil* is similar to long recoil, but the distance traversed by the components before unlocking occurs is less than the length of a complete unfired cartridge.

Recoil spring See 'return spring'.

Return spring The spring in an auto-loader which returns the bolt or breech-block after firing; sometimes less accurately called the 'recoil spring'.

Ribbed barrel See 'barrel rib'.

Rifling This is the means by which spin is imparted to a bullet in the period before it emerges from the muzzle. Rifling generally comprises *grooves* separated by *lands*, though the details vary appreciably; some early guns (e.g., the US ·45 M1873 Springfield) have three grooves, while others (such as modern Marlins) may have twenty or more.

¶ *Concentric rifling* has its grooves and lands cut on the basis of concentric circles.

¶ *Polygonal rifling* is formed of several equal sides and has no obvious grooves. British Metford-type polygonal rifling was seven-sided (heptagonal), though the British Whitworth and Danish Rasmussen patterns were six sided (hexagonal).

¶ *Ratchet rifling* is little more than a series of stepped arcs, being known as 'reverse ratchet' if it opposes the direction of twist.

¶ Patterns that fit none of these categories are classed here as *composite rifling*, though the term covers a multitude of differing styles.

¶ The direction of twist, when viewed from the breech to the muzzle, may be *left* (anti- or counter-clockwise) or *right* (clockwise). *Pitch* describes the rate at which the rifling turns about the axis of the bore: 'fast pitch' turns very rapidly, while 'slow pitch' barrels have rifling that turns so slowly that, in extreme cases, it may appear to be straight. *Progressive rifling* (also known as 'gain-twist') starts with a slow spiral and then quickens towards the muzzle; *progressive-depth rifling* is usually deeper at the breech than at the muzzle.

Rimless or rimmed case See 'cartridge case'.

Rocky Mountain Sight See 'sights'.

Schnabel tip See 'fore-end'. Occasionally rendered colloquially as 'snobble'.

Schuetzen, Schützen This term, which means 'marksmen' in German, is applied to a particular type of target shooting (and, by extension, target rifle) originating in central Europe and then popularised in the USA in the nineteenth century. The rifles usually have elaborate set triggers, palm rests beneath the fore-ends, exaggerated cheek pieces and combs, hooked butt plates, and fully adjustable sights.

Sealed Pattern Unique to the British Army and its colonial couterparts, this term denotes government acceptance. It arose from the attachment of a War Office (wax) seal—in the form of the Royal Arms—to guns and other stores approved or 'sealed' to guide manufacture. As a 'Sealed Pattern' gun was deemed to be dimensionally correct, all manufacturing patterns and gauges had to comply with it.

Sear An intermediate component or series of components ('sear train') linking the trigger with the hammer or firing pin, holding the latter back until released by trigger pressure.

Selective-fire A gun that may, when required, be set (with the 'selector') to fire single shots, multi-shot bursts or fully automatically. The selector is often combined with the manual safety catch.

Selector See 'selective fire'.

Self-cocking A firing mechanism in which the action of cocking the hammer or firing pin is performed automatically either by the breech mechanism or by pulling back the trigger (cf., 'double action'). Note that it is not released automatically, but instead requires an additional stimulus.

Self-loading See 'auto-loading'.

Semi-automatic rifle A gun that fires once for each pull on the trigger and reloads automatically, but requires the firer to release the trigger lever before another shot can be fired (cf., 'automatic rifle').

Semi-rimmed case See 'cartridge case'.

Set trigger A mechanism, commonly used on target guns, in which a lever or button 'sets' the trigger by taking up all the slack in the system; thereafter, a very slight pressure on the trigger is sufficient to fire. Set triggers come in many differing designs, some of which combine the function of the setting and trigger levers in a single component.

Short recoil See 'recoil operation'.

Sights Most rifles have sights at the muzzle (*front sight*) and at the breech (*back sight*). Front sights are usually blades, inverted-'V' blades (known as *barleycorn* patterns) or beads. Target rifles may offer exchangeable-element tunnel or globe sights, often with integral spirit levels and wind gauges.

¶ The simplest back sights are standing open notches. Popular in the North America, the leaf-and-elevator sight usually consists of a flat spring—bent into an open notch—with a sliding stepped plate controlling elevation; alternatively, a screw may raise the leaf. These were originally known as *Rocky Mountain Sights* when fitted with a buck-horn sighting notch.

¶ Other sights popular on sporting rifles include vertically sliding plates controlled by finger-wheels and the so-called *Express* sights, which had a rank of several folding leaves. The *Cape* sight (a useful, but apparently artificial designation) was a variant of the Express pattern with several small folding leaves and a large leaf-and-slider for longer ranges.

¶ The earliest military rifles retained the traditional *ramp-and-leaf sight* introduced on the rifle-muskets of the 1850s. A slider on the folding leaf acted in concert with ramps (stepped or continuously curved) to adjust the range for distances up to about 500 yards, whereafter the leaf was raised. A fixed 'battle sight' was usually cut into the leaf-pivot block. Variations of these sights, and simpler patterns without the stepped base, lasted until the First World War. They were replaced by the *tangent-leaf sight*, which relied on the slider and side-ramps for its entire range of adjustment, and then by a selection of aperture patterns. True *tangent sights* are rarely encountered, the most common taking the form of an arm pivoted on a quadrant block to adjust the range.

¶ Target rifles often have micrometer-adjustable back sights of the utmost sophistication on the barrel near the breech, on the breech itself, or on the upper tang behind the breech. Guns intended for long-range shooting in the supine position may have their back sight on the comb of the butt by the heel.

Silencer A device attached to the muzzle of a gun—or incorporated in its construction—whereby the gases emerging from the barrel are trapped, then circulated in expansion chambers to allow their temperature and pressure to drop before release to the atmosphere occurs. This prevents the usual noise of the muzzle blast. Silencers are rarely encountered on rifles, as the excessive muzzle velocity of most cartridges necessitates the use of special low-power subsonic ammunition.

Slide action An operating system relying on the reciprocal motion of a forward hand grip to unlock the breech, extract, eject, cock the firing mechanism, then reload and re-lock. The first successful method was developed by Christopher Spencer in the 1880s, but experiments had begun many years earlier.

Standing breech The fixed part of the frame that abuts the base of the cartridge in the firing position, carrying the firing pin or the firing-pin bush. The term is usually applied to single-shot dropping-block rifles.

Stock That part of the gun that contains or supports the barrel and action. It comprises the butt, grip and fore-end, but may be made in one piece or two. Originally wood, military stocks are now generally synthetic. Wood remains pre-eminent among the sporting patterns despite an ever-increasing challenge from fibreglass, Kevlar and other synthetics offering durability and warp resistance.

¶ A one-piece sporting stock extending to the muzzle is normally called a *Mannlicher* pattern, on no defensible authority; full-length stocks have been used almost since the dawn of gunsmithing era.

Striker Also known as the 'firing pin', this is driven by a spring to acquire sufficient energy to fire the cartridge primer. There is confusion over the terms 'striker' and 'firing pin', which are exchangeable. Two of many differing patterns are:

¶ *Inertia firing pin*. Strictly applied only to a floating pin that is struck forward by the hammer to reach the primer of a chambered round and then driven or cammed back to allow the breech to open, the term is now generally extended to include the spring-opposed or rebounding pattern.

¶ *Rebounding (or 'flying') firing pin*. This pin is shorter than the distance between the hammer and the primer of a chambered cartridge, being struck forward when required and then pushed back into the breech block or bolt by a small coil spring.

Sub-calibre adaptor (or liner) This may be inserted permanently into a barrel as a 'liner', generally to alter calibre, or to serve as an 'adaptor' when required—usually to permit training with low-cost rimfire ammunition. The adaptor was originally known as an 'Aiming Tube' in Britain, but then became a 'Morris Tube' after a particularly notable patentee.

Take-Down A North American term indicating that a gun may be instantaneously dismantled into major sub-assemblies for convenience. Most examples split into the barrel/fore-end and breech/butt.

Tang A rearward extension of the receiver, usually anchoring the butt to the receiver or frame.

Toggle lock A method of locking the bolt or breech-block by using a multiple-lever linkage to connect the locking block to the actuating mechanism by way of a hinge or intermediate link. The central hinge is placed so that any thrust generated on firing tends to keep the action closed. However, the breech opens with a minimum of effort when the strut-like resistance is broken. A feature of many early dropping-block rifles, where it was used to retain the block in its uppermost position, a rudimentary toggle-lock has been used in the Henry rifle of 1860 and all pre-1876 lever-action Winchesters. It is associated with the Maxim machine-gun and the Parabellum or Luger pistol, in conjunction with a locked breech, and also in the delayed-blowback Pedersen rifle. However, auto-loading toggle-locks demand accurate machining and consistent ammunition performance to operate satisfactorily. The machine-guns worked very well in an era in which high manufacturing costs and excessive weight were not regarded critically, but none of the auto-loading rifles (e.g., Heinemann, Pedersen) has been successful.

Ventilated rib A barrel rib (q.v.) in which the rib is held away from the barrel by a series of supports, allowing air to circulate beneath it. The objective is to cool the barrel and, by so doing, prevent heat rising from the barrel surface disturbing the sight line. Though widely used on thin-barrelled shotguns, ventilated ribs are much less common on sporting rifles.

Windage adjustment See 'azimuth adjustment'.
Wrist See 'butt'.

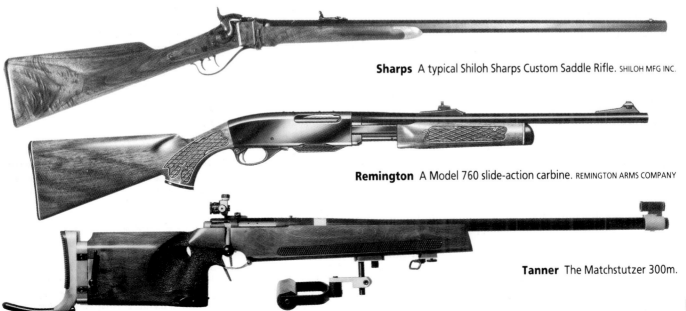

Sharps A typical Shiloh Sharps Custom Saddle Rifle. SHILOH MFG INC.

Remington A Model 760 slide-action carbine. REMINGTON ARMS COMPANY

Tanner The Matchstutzer 300m.

Coverage is restricted—at least for this edition—to the principal centre-fire military and sporting rifles used since 1875. Exceptions have been made for the Remington Rolling Blocks, the Swiss Vetterli and other rimfire rifles which remained in military service into the 1880s or later.

¶ In cases such as the British Snider conversions—adopted in the 1860s—gun-patterns that were *newly made* after 1875 will be found in the main directory. Guns that were *converted* after 1875, or had been made prior to 1875 but continued to serve thereafter, have usually been relegated to the combination index/minor gun directory.

¶ A painful decision was taken to exclude many of the fascinating, but often 'one off' prototype rifles from the main directory by applying a criterion that at least a hundred identical guns must have been made to qualify for inclusion. Unfortunately, it proved impossible to determine precisely how many examples of each rifle were made, nor even to decide which characteristics should be considered as salient—experimental guns were often produced in differing sub-patterns to be tested alongside one another. A broader range is included in the index, where the criterion is simply that a gun must have been tested militarily.

¶ There are undoubtedly many instances where the inclusion of particular guns could be argued. However, virtually any rule-of-inclusion proves to be unworkable if pursued too rigidly, so I have tried to be sensible. It is acknowledged that notoriety of particular designs—e.g., the British EM-2—often gives a prominence far in excess of paltry numbers, but this alone does not justify an entry in the directory at the expense of little-known trials guns whose production ran into thousands.

¶ Tremendous enthusiasm for specific makes of rifle, such as the lever-action Winchester, has led to great advances of scholarship. In many other cases, unfortunately, little work of consequence has yet been done. As a result, *Rifles of the World* can only reflect a patch-work overview.

¶ I have elected to concentrate on basic history; though mechanical descriptions are often very interesting, they are not always easy to follow and have been greatly curtailed. I have simply tried to list the salient points of each mechanism as briefly and clearly as possible, leaving the interested reader to pursue matters elsewhere. The books of Frank de Haas and Stuart Otteson—to name just two of many respected writers—will repay further study.

¶ *Rifles of the World* is organised alphabetically in sections. Each section is sub-divided, if necessary, into basic 'operating classes'; BROWNING, for example, contains information about auto-loading, block-action, bolt-action, and lever-action rifles.

¶ Each sub-section is divided, where appropriate, into military and sporting guns—categories that are then marshalled by country and, at the most basic level, by approximate date of introduction.

¶ To find details of the German Kar.98k short rifle, introduced in the mid 1930s, it is simply necessary to find the MAUSER section (beginning on page 161), then 2. THE BOLT-ACTION PATTERNS on page 162. Coverage of military guns also commences on this page, with the German entries running from 168 onward; the earliest German Mauser was the 1871 model (page 169), which was followed by a selection of rifles, carbines and short rifles until, finally, the Kar.98k was introduced. The relevant details commence on page 172.

¶ Most of the individual gun headings are accompanied by concise data summaries, giving official designations and the sub-variants included in the coverage. These are followed by a list of manufacturers, period of production and, if known with any degree of accuracy, the quantity made. Then come the principal dimensions, details of the magazine, and the style of back sight to aid identification. Brief details of performance are given, though alternative loads have often been made—particularly for sporting rifles. Thus the velocity figures may be qualified by the inclusion of bullet weight or a pattern designation, but should all be considered as representative rather than definitive.

¶ The data summaries are followed by historical information, organised chronologically to improve the ease with which specific details can be found. Dates qualified by asterisks (e.g., 1915*) are approximations.

¶ Most of the section-names are self-explanatory, though some guns are popularly known by the name of their manufacturers whilst others maintain the identity of the designer—particularly if more than one maker has been involved (e.g, the US ·30 M1 Garand).

¶ Prolific inventors such as John Browning or, more recently, Eugene Stoner have often licensed their guns to several manufacturers simultaneously. Attempts to devise rigid rules of classification fail in these instances; consequently, the original Browning-type Winchesters are discussed in the former section instead of the latter. The FN FAL has been listed under 'Saive', while the US ·30 M1 Carbine, widely credited to David M. Williams on doubtful authority, is regarded as a Winchester.

¶ I sincerely hope that this flexible approach to categorisation presents few serious problems, and that, in cases of doubt, the index will resolve confusion.

DIMENSIONS

The firearms used since 1875 have been manufactured in accordance with several differing systems of measurement, ranging from the Russian *Arshin* and Teutonic *Schritt* ('pace', generally about 27–30in or 68–76cm) to the metric method pioneered in France at the end of the eighteenth century.

¶ To avoid unnecessary repetition, most dimensions are given here either in Imperial (for British, US and some other guns) or metric units for the guns of most other countries. The most important Imperial/metric conversion factors will be found at the end of the contents list on page 4.

ArmaLite
A typical CAR-15, with a Davin Optics IRS-218 second-generation intensifying sight.
IAN HOGG

ACCURACY INTERNATIONAL

BRITAIN
~

This small-volume manufacturer promotes a purpose-built sniper rifle, adopted by the British Army after trials lasting several years.

L96A1

Sniper rifle: also known as Model 'PM'.
Made for Accuracy International Ltd, Portsmouth, Hampshire, 1986 to date.
7·62 × mm NATO, rimless.
Turning-bolt action, with three lugs on the bolt locking into the receiver.
44·25in overall, 14·33lb with sights and bipod.
25·75in barrel, 4-groove rifling; RH, concentric.
Detachable box magazine, 10 rounds.
Folding-leaf sight (optional).
2,825 ft/sec with standard ball ammunition.
No bayonet.
☆

1985: developed by a team led by Malcolm Cooper, the PM featured a bolt with a fully enclosed head and a 60° throw. The action allowed a trained firer to operate the gun with minimal disturbance of aim. The two-stage trigger was adjustable. Two 'stock sides', made of tough plastic with olive drab finish, bolted onto the aluminium chassis supporting the action to overcome warping in woodwork.

PM rifles could be seen with bipods and a small monopod or 'Quick Action Spike'. Four basic weapons were available: *Long Range*, fitted with Schmidt & Bender PM12 × 42 or Leupold 10 × /16 × M1 sights, and chambered for the 7mm Remington Magnum or ·300 Winchester Magnum rounds; *Counter-Terrorist*, in 7·62mm NATO, with Schmidt & Bender PM6 × 42 or PM2·5–10 × 56 sights; *Moderated*, with a PM6 × 42 optical sight and a full-length sound moderator suited to subsonic 7·62 × 51mm ammunition; and the 7·62mm *Infantry*, with a PM6 × 42 sight. Excepting the single-shot Long Range pattern, the rifles all had box magazines.

ALBINI

ITALY
~

This lifting-block action was designed by Augusto Albini, an Italian army officer, but perfected with the assistance of Francis Braendlin—associated with Albini in British patents of 1866-7. The gun was tested throughout Europe, but adopted only in Belgium. The essence of the breech was a locking bolt attached to the hammer-body. Rotating the hammer to half cock withdrew the bolt and allowed the breech-block handle to be lifted, extracting a spent case to be tipped from the feed way. Once the gun had been reloaded, the breech block was closed and the hammer thumbed back to full cock. Pressing the trigger allowed the hammer to fly forward, whereupon the locking bolt entered the back of the breech block and struck the firing pin.

After testing differing rifles, including the Remington, the Belgians selected the Albini-Braendlin breech owing to the ease with which existing rifle-muskets could be converted.

Model 1873

Infantry rifle: Fusil d'Infanterie Mle.1873.
Apparently made in Liége by Fabrique d'Armes de l'État, and possibly also by Henri Pieper & Co.
11 × 50mm, rimmed.
Action: as Mle.1867 rifle, above.
1,347mm overall, 4·49kg unladen.
882mm barrel, 4-groove rifling; RH, concentric.
Ramp-and-leaf sight graduated to 1,100 metres.
417 m/sec with Mle.1867 ball cartridges.
Mle.1867 socket bayonet.
☆

1873: this was simply a newly-made version of the Mle.1853/67 (see panel overleaf), with an improved extractor adapted from the Terssen conversions described in Part Two.
1880: Mle.1873 rifles (but not, apparently, the earlier conversions) were re-sighted for the Mle.1880 cartridge, which developed a higher muzzle velocity. A new back sight—its leaf

graduated to 1,400 metres—could be used for ranges up to 2,100 metres in conjunction with a sighting notch on the left side of the extended slider-block and a stud on the middle band.
1901: some surviving rifles ('Mle.1873/1901') were converted for rural gendarmerie.

Model 1873

Short rifle for the gendarmerie: Mousqueton Mle.1873.
Made in Liége by Dresse-Laloux & Co. and possibly Henri Piper & Co.
11 × 42mm, rimmed.
Action: as Mle.1867 rifle, above.
DATA FOR MLE.1873
1,145mm overall, 3·64kg unladen.
680mm barrel, 4-groove rifling; RH, concentric.
Ramp-and-leaf graduated to 500 metres.
352 m/sec with ball cartridges.
Socket bayonet.
☆

1874: this was a newly made short rifle, though conversions of ex-French muskets were also made (see panel). New guns had a cheek piece on the left side of the butt, and iron fittings instead of brass. The Mle 1873 also apparently had a sling ring on the wrist, which the Mle.1777/1873 lacked. Gendarmerie bayonets were basically diminutives of the Mle.1867, with shortened elbows and flattened blades.

ALLIN

UNITED STATES OF AMERICA
Also known as 'Trapdoor Springfield' or 'Springfield-Allin'
~

1864: advertisements were circulated in an attempt to find an effectual means of converting existing rifle-muskets. The Chief of Ordnance, General Dyer, asked Erskine Allin—then Master Armorer at the National Armory—to develop a gun on behalf of the Federal government.
1865: the first trials were completed by April, resulting in recommendation of the Spencer

Albini A typical Mle.1853/67 conversion.
WALLIS & WALLIS

Accuracy International
The PM Infantry Model (L96A1).
ACCURACY INTERNATIONAL

ALBINI-BRAENDLIN
BELGIAN CONVERSIONS

M1867 infantry rifle These were converted by Dresse-Laloux & Cie of Liége from Mle.1841 and Mle.1853 rifle-muskets, plus a few surviving Mle.1777 muskets (Fusils d'Infanterie Modèles 1841/67, 1853/67 et 1777/1867). The new barrel was copied from the Chassepot, with French-style rifling. The old Mle.1777 muskets, which had been acquired from France in the 1840s, had already been converted to cap-lock and had a typically Belgian back-action lock plate.

¶ A typical Mle.1853/67 rifle chambered an 11·4 × 50mm cartridge, measured 1,348mm overall and weighed 4·57kg. A ramp-and-leaf sight was graduated to 1,100 metres. The 883mm barrel was rifled with four grooves twisting to the right, muzzle velocity being about 417 m/sec with Mle.1867 ball cartridges. The Mle.1867 socket bayonet was standard.

¶ The guns all had one-piece stocks, with two sprung barrel bands and a large nose cap. Swivels lay under the middle band and ahead of the trigger guard. Mle.1777/1867 rifles were issued only to fortress artillerymen and reservists, newer guns serving line infantry and rifle regiments.

¶ Issue was extended in 1869 to the Garde Civique, but no guns had been delivered when the Comblain was substituted in 1871.

¶ In 1901, many surviving rifles were adapted for rural gendarmerie. Barrels and stocks were shortened, the nose cap was discarded, and barrel was smooth-bored to about 13·9mm for shot cartridges. A notch on the breech-block hinge sufficed as the back sight, with a blade on the barrel above the fore-end tip. Most 'Mle.1867/1901' adaptions had been withdrawn by 1910.

M1873 gendarmerie rifle The Mousqueton Mle.1777/1873 was another Dresse-Laloux conversion. It shared the action of the Mle.1867 rifle, but chambered a cartridge with a 42mm case and was merely 1,150mm overall. Converted from old French flint-lock muskets, it weighed about 3·75kg and had a 680mm barrel. The butt was plain and the mounts were brass.

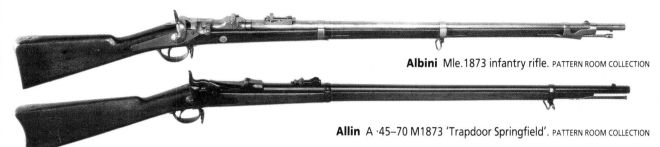

Albini Mle.1873 infantry rifle. PATTERN ROOM COLLECTION

Allin A ·45–70 M1873 'Trapdoor Springfield'. PATTERN ROOM COLLECTION

ALLIN-SPRINGFIELD
CONVERSIONS AND LESSER PATTERNS

The Allin or 'Trapdoor' Springfields shared a distinctive hinged-block breech, pushed up and forward to gain access to the chamber. Though details were improved during the weapons' service life, no basic changes were ever made. Virtually all guns were rifled with three grooves twisting to the right.

M1866 infantry rifle This was a simplification of the original rimfire M1865, with a U-spring extractor instead of the original ratchet mechanism. The ·58 barrels were successfully reamed out to ·64 to take a liner chambered for the ·50–70 centre-fire cartridge. Springfield was ordered to convert 25,000 guns on 26 July 1866. They were about 56in overall, had 36·60in barrels, and weighed 9·88lb. Aperture-leaf sights were graduated to 700 yards and the M1855 socket bayonet was to be mounted.

M1866 cadet rifle About 320 of these were made at Springfield, apparently for the US Military Academy at West Point. They incorporated more than a dozen new parts, were 54·81in long, had 34·63in barrels and weighed 8·5lb.

M1868 infantry rifle Changes made in this ·50–70 gun included the approval of a new barrel, and the ramrod was held by a stop inserted in the stock bearing on a shoulder on the rod about four inches from the tip. The receiver was a separate component into which the barrel screwed, much stronger than previous adaptions of existing barrels. Two bands were used instead of three, and a special long-range back sight was fitted.

¶ Small numbers were made in the National Armory, Springfield, in 1868–9. They were 52·00in long, had 32·63in barrels and weighed 9·25lb. The leaf sight was graduated to 1,000 yards, muzzle velocity was about 1,210 ft/sec with ·50–70–405 ball cartridges, and the standard M1855 socket bayonet was used.

M1869 cadet rifle Made in small quantities at Springfield in 1869–70, this was a diminutive ·50–70 rifle with a short barrel and only two bands. Minor variations will be encountered, the final pattern having a flat-face hammer. The earliest batches (sometimes identified as 'M1868') had a block-and-leaves back sight, but later guns had a ramp-and-leaf pattern graduated to 1,000 yards. They were 51·88in overall, had 29·50in barrels, and weighed 8·30lb. The M1855 socket bayonet was standard.

M1870 infantry rifle Made at Springfield in 1870–2, this was virtually identical with its immediate predecessor—the M1868—but the receiver was shortened and the breech block was relieved behind the hinge to open farther. This prevented the mechanism closing unexpectedly as a new cartridge was being loaded. The ramrod had a double shoulder, and sights were refined. The M1870 has often been regarded as semi-experimental. It chambered the regulation ·50–70 rimmed cartridge, was 51·75in overall and weighed 9·22lb. The barrel measured 32·50in and the leaf sight was graduated to 1,000 yards.

M1870 carbine Introduced in 1871, this incorporated the comparable rifle action, but was merely 41·38in overall and weighed 7·92lb. The barrel was 21·75in long.

M1875 officer's rifle Adapted from the contemporary 1873-pattern cadet rifle, this was sold to officers who wanted personal weapons of regulation pattern. The half stock had chequering on the butt-wrist and a fore-end with a German silver tip. Scroll engraving appeared on the lock, hammer, receiver, barrel band and butt plate. The globe-pattern front sight folded so that its pin could serve with the open buck-horn back sight. Most rifles had a Sharps aperture back sight folded onto the wrist. The trigger had a normal service-pattern pull, but could be 'set' by pushing it forward. The wooden ramrod had nickel-plated brass ferrules. About 290 guns were made in 1876–7. They were 47·38in long, had 26in barrels and weighed 9lb.

¶ Second-pattern rifles made after April 1877 had a detachable pistol-grip and an improved Springfield-pattern tang sight that folded closer to the wrist than the Sharps version. About 135 were made in 1877–9.

¶ A few guns—perhaps forty—were made in 1885 with proper pistol-grip stocks with an elongated schnabel tipped fore-end, improved sights, and a three-piece cleaning rod in a butt-trap. Total production in 1876–85 amounted to 477.

Long Range Rifle About 150 guns were made at National Armory, Springfield, in 1879; 24 more followed in 1881. The guns had full-length barrels and two spring-retained barrel bands. A typical ·45–70 example was 52·00in overall, weighed about 9·9lb, and had a 32·38in barrel. Muzzle velocity was 1,320 ft/sec with M1873 ball cartridges.

¶ The first version (later known as 'Pattern No.1') had a Hotchkiss-type butt plate, a full-length stock, a chequered fore-end, and a chequered wrist with a detachable pistol grip. A Sharps vernier back sight lay on the tang above the wrist, and the tunnel pattern front sight had an integral spirit level.

¶ Pattern No.2 shared the stock design of No.1, but its improved aperture tang sight was the work of Freeman Bull of Springfield Armory. An adjustable globe-pattern front sight was standard.

¶ Pattern No.3 had a Hotchkiss butt plate and a full-length stock, with a Bull back sight on the barrel and a standard front sight.

Marksman's Rifle In 1880, Springfield made nine ·45–80 guns with pistol-gripped half stocks. They had special vernier back sights on the tang behind the buck horn back sight on the barrel top. The tunnel-type front sights had spirit levels.

¶ The 26in cylindrical barrels had six-groove concentric rifling. A three-piece cleaning rod and the dismantling tool were carried in the butt trap, while the set-trigger mechanism was similar to that of the Officer's Model (q.v.). The engraved decoration also resembled the Officer's Model pattern, but was more ornate.

M1880 infantry rifle. Approved on 3 June 1880, this was the first Allin-type rifle to feature a triangular-section rod bayonet, carried under the barrel in what would normally have been the ramrod channel. The adoption of the rod bayonet—widely defended as saving weight and money—simply avoided producing new socket bayonets; those serving in 1880 had all been made before 1865, then bushed and re-bushed for the 1873-type rifles.

¶ About 1,100 M1880 rifles were made in Springfield in 1881. They were essentially similar to the preceding M1879, but had a special nose cap and two barrel bands.

M1882 short rifle In February 1882, the Board on Magazine Guns recommended development of a modified ·45 rifle with a short barrel, a full-length stock, and an improved lock with a shorter hammer fall. The goal was a rifle that could be issued to infantry and cavalrymen alike.

¶ The earliest M1882 short rifles—made only in small numbers—had swivels curved to fit the contours of the stock, facilitating the use of saddle-scabbards, but conventional swivels were soon substituted. The guns were 47·48in long, with 27·75in barrels, and weighed about 8·9lb. A few short rifles were subsequently fitted with triangular-section rod bayonets; and a trap in the butt was added to house the shell ejector and dismantling tool.

M1882 carbine Trials undertaken at Fort Leavenworth failed to persuade cavalrymen of the value of the M1882 short or 'universal' rifle. A few carbines were made at Springfield in 1883, amalgamating the action of the short rifle with a 23·75in barrel; the earliest guns were stocked almost to the muzzle—soon changed.

¶ The muzzle band was retained by a screw, instead of a spring, and a prominent web filled the space under the muzzle. Tools were carried in the butt-trap, and a large ring appeared on the left side of the breech. Later guns had heavy barrels, retained by a band behind the rounded stock tip. The band carried a curved swivel, with a standard flat pattern on the butt; the ring slid along a bar anchored in the left side of the stock, Buffington wind-gauge back sights were fitted, and the cleaning rod was carried in a butt-trap.

repeater and the single-shot Peabody. The end of the Civil War removed the need to act quickly, however, and nothing further was done.

The prototype Allin rifle appeared in the summer of 1865, performing well enough for substantial quantities to be ordered for field trials. About 5,000 ·58 rimfire rifles were made in the Springfield factory in 1865–6. They were adapted 1863-pattern cap-lock rifle-muskets with a new breech block hinged laterally at the front of the action. The block could be swung up to reveal the chamber, but the alteration was much too complicated; the ratchet-pattern extractor was weak and the cartridge performed poorly.

1866: just as the first M1865 Allin-type rifles were being issued for trials with the 12th Infantry, a Board of Officers convened in Washington to find a more effectual weapon. The M1865 was soon replaced by a gun with its barrel lined-down from ·58 to ·50. The extractor was greatly simplified and many detail changes were made. Trials still favoured the Berdan as the best conversion system, the Peabody being the best new rifle, but the ·50 Allin was controversially selected for production. The earliest conversions are listed in the accompanying panel.

Model 1873

Infantry rifle, cadet rifle and carbine.
Made by the National Armory, Springfield, Massachusetts, 1873–8.
·45–70, rimmed.
Lifting-block action, with a locking catch in the rear face of the block.
DATA FOR INFANTRY RIFLE
51·92in overall, 9·21lb unladen.
32·38in barrel, 3-groove rifling; RH, concentric.
Leaf sight graduated to 2,000 yards.
1,320 ft/sec with ·45–70–405 ball cartridges.
M1873 socket bayonet.
☆

1871: though experiments to reduce the calibre of the standard ·50 service cartridge and find a better breech-loader continued throughout the year, the Springfield-Allin was retained at the expense of Remington, Sharps, Ward-Burton and other designs.

1872: a Board of Officers, convened in the autumn, began trials with rifles chambering a new ·45–70–405 centre-fire cartridge.

1873: by January, more than a hundred submissions had been reduced to 21. The Martini-Henry and the Werndl were retained as a guide to the performance expected of foreign service weapons, the trials resolving as a contest between Elliot no.80, Freeman no.76, Peabody no.63, Remington no.86, Springfield no.69, Ward-Burton no.97 and the US government-sponsored Springfield no.99.

Springfield no.69 was similar to the standard Allin-type M1870 (tested as no.48), but had a lightened lock plate, a screw instead of the original main-spring bolster, a modified hammer, and a simpler stock. None of the trial guns was deemed effectual enough to challenge the major government entrant, and so the ·45 Springfield No.99 was immediately adopted. The purchase of a few Ward-Burton magazine rifles was recommended for the cavalry, but subsequently rejected by the Chief of Ordnance.

Formally approved on 5 May, the M1873 rifle was an improved form of the experimental Springfield no.99. As the Allin breech had cost the US Treasury more than $124,000 to settle patent-infringement claims, the government was reluctant to make wholesale changes. The new rifle was basically an M1870, but its lock plate was lightened—the edges being squared rather than bevelled—and the steel barrel had a smaller external diameter. The hammer body and most of the screws were rounded, while a screw replaced the trigger-guard swivel rivet. The top edges of the stock were rounded from the lock plate to the lower band, and the form of the ramrod was changed.

The M1873 rifle was to be accompanied by a trowel bayonet—an amalgam of Rice and Chillingworth designs with improvements made by Springfield Armory—but this was hastily abandoned in favour of a socket pattern.

Introduced some time after the infantry rifle, the M1873 carbine could be identified by its half-stock and short barrel. It was 41·31in overall, had a 21·88in barrel and weighed 7·9lb unladen; muzzle velocity with standard 1873 pattern ball cartridges was about 1,150 ft/sec. It lacked a butt-trap for the cleaning rods, but a stacking swivel was attached to the solitary barrel band. Bayonets did not accompany the cavalry carbines.

1874: a stacking swivel was adopted for the infantry rifle in the Spring. The first rifles were then issued to premier line infantry regiments in the late autumn.

Apparently adopted towards the end of the year, the M1873 cadet rifle was essentially similar to the infantry pattern, but lacked sling swivels and had a different stacking swivel on the upper band. It was 48·92in overall and had a 29·5in barrel.

1876: 1,008 rifles were made at Springfield with Metcalfe's Loader, eight cartridges being carried head upward in a detachable wooden block on the right side of the stock. (Note: as two prototypes had been made for army trials in 1874, it has been suggested that the guns made in 1876 may have been destined for militia instead of federal troops.)

Cavalrymen in Texas and 'Indian country' finally received their M1873 carbines in 1876. Consequently, men of the Seventh Cavalry fought the Battle of the Little Big Horn in June with brand-new firearms.

1877: the Model 1877 back sight was adopted in January, with differing graduations and an improved sighting notch.

1878: the back sight was altered again in May, without changing the designation. A base with curved wing plates replaced the original stepped design. The arch in the underside of the breech block was flattened from March, creating 'Low Arch' guns in a search for greater rigidity. At about the same time, the firing-pin spring and the corresponding shoulder on the firing pin were abandoned.

The widths of the breech block and receiver were increased in October; the gas-escape holes in the sides of the receiver were extended rearward at much the same time.

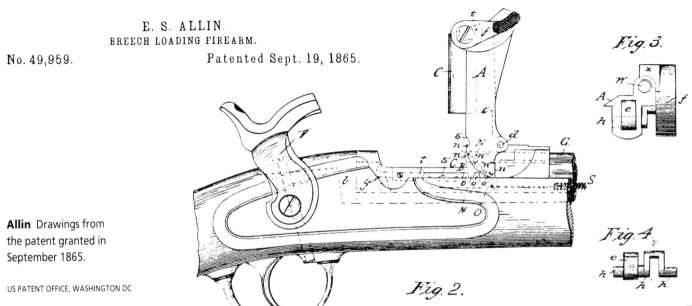

E. S. ALLIN.
BREECH LOADING FIREARM.
No. 49,959.   Patented Sept. 19, 1865.

Fig. 3.

Fig. 4.

Fig. 2.

Allin Drawings from the patent granted in September 1865.

Model 1879

Infantry rifle, cadet rifle and carbine.
Made by the National Armory, Springfield,
Massachusetts, 1879–81.
·45–70, rimmed.
Action: as M1873, above.
DATA FOR INFANTRY RIFLE
51·75in overall, 9·15lb unladen.
32·38in barrel, 3-groove rifling; RH, concentric.
Leaf graduated to 2,000 yards.
1,320 ft/sec with standard ·45–70–405
ball cartridges.
M1873 socket bayonet.
☆

1879: continual improvements in the 1873 pattern action led in January to this gun, sometimes known as the 'M1873 Improved' or 'M1873 with 1879 Improvements'. A standing plate with two projections (known as a 'buck-horn') improved the back sight picture. From April, a hole was bored up into the ramrod channel ahead of the trigger-guard to reduce fouling. The shape of the buck-horn plate was changed in October, when the distance between azimuth graduations became ·04in instead of ·02in. The upper surface of the leaf-hinge was flattened in November.

Approved in the middle of the year, the M1879 carbine was essentially similar to its 1873-pattern predecessor—though a rifle-type lower band replaced the special stacking-swivel band after December, and a bayonet could be mounted. Unlike the rifle, the carbine had a butt trap for the cleaning rod. The gun was 41·31in long and had a 21·88in barrel.

1880: a lip was added to the face of the hammer in January, and the notches in the buck-horn back sight were revised in July. The first M1879 cadet rifles were made at Springfield during 1880, but were little more than standard infantry rifles without sling swivels. However, they were only 48·75in long and had barrels measuring 29·5in.

1881: a heavy-pattern butt plate was formally approved in August.

1883: several changes were made to the rifle during the year. In January, the underside of the thumb piece was revised to prevent it striking the lock plate. A straight trigger-lever appeared in March 1883, and a detachable front-sight protector was approved in October.

Model 1884

Infantry rifle, cadet rifle and carbine.
Made by the National Armory, Springfield,
Massachusetts, 1884–9.
·45–70, rimmed.
Action: as M1873 rifle, above.
DATA FOR INFANTRY RIFLE
51·75in overall, about 9lb unladen.
32·38in barrel, 3-groove rifling; RH, concentric.
Leaf sight graduated to 2,000 yards, with a sliding
long-range extension.
1,320 ft/sec with ·45–70–405 ball cartridges.
M1873 socket bayonet.
☆

1884: the results of trials undertaken in 1883 failed to convince the US Army that magazine breech-loading rifles were acceptable. This Trap-door Springfield was approved as an expedient. Its Buffington-pattern wind-gauge back sight had an azimuth adjustment, the first to be approved for general service in the US Army, and the lower band was altered to accommodate the sight leaf. Cadet rifles (48·75in overall, 29·5in barrel) and carbines (41·31in overall, 21·88in barrel) were also made in small numbers. The Buffington sights distinguished them from the preceding 1879 models.

1885: alterations to the sear and tumbler were made in January. New front sights for rifles (·653 high) and carbines (·738) were approved to prevent guns shooting high at short ranges.

About a thousand 1884-type rifles with cylindrical rod bayonets and refined sights, authorised on 17 December 1884, were made at Springfield in 1885. They were unsuccessfully issued in the Spring of 1886 for trials with three artillery and ten infantry regiments.

1886: the issue of front-sight covers was approved in March, and improvements in the Buffington sight occurred in August. The heads of the wind gauge finger-screws were enlarged to improve grip, and to prevent the folded leaf moving laterally by projecting down over the edge of the sight-base. The design of the binding screw was revised, while the pivoting sight-base and slide were case-hardened.

1886: a lightweight aluminium-bronze firing pin replaced the original steel pattern in December in an effort to reduce lock time.

1887: the rear edge of the front-sight block (rifles only) was rounded from August onward.

1888: February brought the approval of an improved front-sight protector.

1890: a protector-band for the back sight was fitted to the carbine from October. The height of the carbine front sight was changed from ·738 to ·728 towards the end of the year. These carbines are often known as 'M1890', but were marked MODEL 1884 on the action.

Model 1889

Infantry rifle.
Made by the National Armory, Springfield,
Massachusetts, 1889–92.
·45–70, rimmed.
Otherwise generally as M1884 rifle, excepting for the
M1889 rod bayonet.
☆

1889: this was the last single-shot rifle to be approved for general issue in the US Army, though the authorities were well aware that production—a short-term expedient—would last only until a suitable magazine rifle had been perfected. The cylindrical rod bayonet was approved on 5 August, adoption of the finalised rifle and its accessories following on 16 August.

Note: Allin-pattern guns remained regulation US Army firearms until the introduction of the Krag-Jørgensen (q.v.) in the early 1890s. They were gradually withdrawn, serving the National Guard until about 1905, though many saw action in the brief Spanish-American War (1898). Any guns that remained on the official inventory after the end of the First World War were recalled to store, where they were held for the use of state militiamen until the early 1920s.

Allin The 1884-pattern infantry rifle, with an M1873 bayonet. WALLIS & WALLIS

Allin The H&R Model 174 Little Big Horn Commemorative Carbine.

ALPHA ARMS

UNITED STATES OF AMERICA

This company made a limited range of bolt action sporters designed by Homer Koon, based on a three-lug bolt mechanism with a 60° throw.

Alpha Sporting Rifle

Model 1, Alaskan, Custom and Grand Slam patterns.
Made by Alpha Arms, Inc., Dallas, Texas, 1982–9.
Chambering: see notes.
Turning-bolt action, with three lugs on the bolt head engaging the receiver.
DATA FOR A TYPICAL ALPHA MODEL
·338 Winchester Magnum, belted rimless.
About 43·50in overall, 6·85lb unladen.
24·00in barrel, 4-groove rifling; RH, concentric?
Internal box magazine, 3 rounds.
No sight.
2,700 ft/sec with 250-grain bullet.
☆

1982: the Alpha Model 1 appeared, in ·243 Winchester, 7mm–08 or ·308 Winchester. The medium-length action was accompanied by a four-round magazine and a 20in tapered barrel, which gave the rifle an overall length of about 39·5in and a weight averaging 6·3lb. It had a satin-finish stock with a Monte Carlo comb, but no cheek piece. An aluminium bedding-block system was used and the trigger guard/magazine floor-plate assembly was coated in Teflon.

1984: improved rifles were announced in three differing action-lengths (short, regular and Magnum). They were made to order with barrels of 20–24in, and could be chambered for virtually any cartridge the customer cared to specify from ·17 Remington to ·358 Winchester Magnum. In 1985, the standard Custom Model was being offered in ·243 Winchester, ·25–284, 7mm–08, ·284 Winchester or ·308 Winchester. It had a superbly grained oil-finished Claro walnut stock, with a straight comb and a metal Niedner cap on the pistol grip. The shoulder plate was hard rubber. Fore-end caps were

generally ebony, though rosewood patterns were sometimes substituted. The chequering panels on the grip and fore-end were invariably divided by sinuous ribands; quality was very high.

The Alaskan Model had a stainless-steel barrelled action, other metal parts being coated with Nitex. Stocks were usually laminated patterns, though a few synthetic examples were made. The Grand Slam Model duplicated the Custom pattern, but had a stock of AlphaWood (a composite of fibreglass and wood pulp).

The Alpha rifles were all made in right- or left-hand versions, but not in large quantities.

AMAC

UNITED STATES OF AMERICA

AMAC (American Military Arms Corporation) succeeded to the business of Iver Johnson in the early 1980s but continued to use the earlier tradename. AMAC still makes a copy of the ·30 M1 Carbine (see 'Winchester').

Model 5100 LRRS

Made by the American Military Arms Corporation, Jacksonville, Arkansas, 1987–9?
·338/416 Barrett or ·50 Browning, rimless.
Turning-bolt action, locked by two lugs on the bolt head engaging the barrel extension.
DATA FOR A TYPICAL EXAMPLE
·50 Browning, rimless.
About 53in overall, 28lb unladen.
32·50in barrel, 4-groove rifling; RH, concentric.
Optical sight.
2,800 ft/sec with M2 Ball ammunition.
No bayonet.
☆

1987: AMAC introduced a large-calibre heavy duty or sniper rifle chambered for the ·50 Browning Machine Gun cartridge. The single-shot gun had a free-floating fluted barrel with a muzzle brake, and a bipod attached to the tubular receiver extension. The variable-length butt, with an adjustable comb, slid on parallel

rods protruding behind the pistol grip. Barrett rounds gave better accuracy, while the ·50 pattern enhanced long-range striking capability.

ANSCHÜTZ

GERMANY

This bolt-action system was developed after the end of the Second World War and has since been incorporated successfully in a range of target and sporting guns. The basic Model 54 bolt—in varying forms—was used by all ·22 rimfire Anschütz rifles until the advent of the Model 64/Match 64 series, and also on ·22 Hornet and ·222 Remington guns. The M54 action relied on a simple breech lock, though it had twin extractors and offered impeccable quality.

Anschütz has also offered Models 1562, 1566 and 1568 built on the Savage 110 action, and Model 1574, on a Krico 700 action; these are covered in detail in the relevant sections. The Savage Arms Company handled Anschütz products in the USA (c.1965–81) before passing the agency to Precision Sales International, Inc.

Most guns were sold in North America under their original designations, but there have been exceptions: standard ·22 Hornet Model 1432 and ·222 Remington Model 1532 sporting rifles, for example, were promoted as the Savage-Anschütz 'Model 54 Sporter' and 'Model 153 Sporter' respectively. The standard European Models 1432 and 1532 are currently being sold in the USA as '1432 (or 1532) Custom'.

1430 series

1430 A, 1430 D, 1430 St, 1431 A, 1432 Bavarian, 1432 Classic, 1432 D, 1432 E, 1432 E D, 1432 E St, 1432 EK St, 1432 St, 1433 St Luxus, 1434 D and 1434 St patterns.
Made by J.G. Anschütz GmbH, Ulm/Donau.
·22 Hornet only.
Turning-bolt action, locked by a lug opposite the bolt handle engaging the receiver and the bolt-handle base turning down into its seat.

Anschütz The ·22 Hornet Model 1422 rifle. J.G. ANSCHÜTZ GMBH

Anschütz A typical ·22 Hornet Model 1430 rifle. J.G. ANSCHÜTZ GMBH

Anschütz The ·22 Hornet Model 1432 St rifle. J.G. ANSCHÜTZ GMBH

DATA FOR MODEL 1432 D
1,100mm overall, 3·05kg unladen.
610mm barrel, 4-groove rifling; RH, concentric.
Detachable box magazine, 5 rounds.
Folding-leaf sight.
820 m/sec with 2·9-gram bullet.

☆

1965: the Models 1430, 1431 and 1432 were introduced. The original guns had 59cm barrels and weighed about 3kg. The Model 1430 A was the basic model, with a plain hardwood stock with a Monte Carlo comb and a slab-sided fore-end with an obliquely cut tip. The Model 1431 A was similar, but apparently had a better quality walnut stock with a cheek piece and a roll-over comb. Double-bordered chequer panels appeared on the pistol grip and the fore-end. Neither rifle remained in production for more than a couple of years.

The Model 1432 had a walnut half-stock with a hog's back comb (a roll-over pattern was substituted about 1967) and a schnabel-tip fore-end. The pistol-grip was accompanied by a white spacer, skip-line chequering being used on the pistol grip and fore-end. Swivels lay on the underside of the fore-end and butt. A single-stage trigger was standard on the Model 1432 D, though a double set-trigger mechanism graced the otherwise identical Model 1432 St.

1972: the revised 1430 D (single trigger) and 1430 St (double set-trigger) appeared, sharing the action of the Model 1432 but displaying plainer stocks without chequering. The cheek piece was omitted, and the roll-over comb was replaced by a low Monte Carlo pattern. The fore-end tip was cut obliquely and the machined trigger guard became a simple stamped strip.

1973: new Models 1434 D (single trigger) and 1434 St (double set trigger) were similar to the Model 1432, but their butts had more typically European cheek pieces and lower combs than the Monte Carlo roll-over pattern. The pistol grip was shortened and had a differing style of cap.

1974: Model 1432E ('D' or 'St' subvarieties) was a competition rifle satisfying the Deutsche Jägerschafts-Verband (hunting association). It shared the basic action and trigger options of the ·22LR version introduced in 1971, but had a plain half-stock with a deep fore-end, a vertical pistol grip, a high straight comb, and a wooden butt plate with rubber spacers. The fore-end and the pistol grip were stippled to improve grip. No open sights were fitted, as optical types were used in competition.

1976: the 1433 St Luxus rifle was introduced, with a double set-trigger, a shortened barrel and a full-length 'Mannlicher' stock. The butt had a low European-style comb and a small rounded cheek piece. Skip-line chequering appeared on the fore-end and pistol grip, and the schnabel tip was rosewood.

1982: the stock of the Model 1432 Classic had a straight comb and a deep round-tip fore-end, hand-cut chequering appearing on the pistol grip and fore-end. In common with most of the better models in the Anschütz range, the 1432 Classic trigger guard was a machined forging (a casting on later guns); rifles could be obtained with single or double triggers. The 1432 EK St, intended for DJV-style competition shooting, had a distinctive butt and extensive stippling on the under-surface of the deep fore-end. A ventilated rubber butt plate was standard and the unique trigger system had a reverse-curve setting lever.

1988: all the 1430-series guns were abandoned, excepting Models 1432 E (standard, D and St patterns), 1432 EK St and 1433 St.

1530 series

1530 A, 1530 D, 1530 St, 1531 A, 1531 AD, 1532 Bavarian, 1532 Classic, 1532 D, 1532 E D, 1532 E St, 1532 St, 1533 St Luxus, 1534 D and 1534 St patterns.
Made by J.G. Anschütz GmbH, Ulm/Donau.
·222 Remington only.
Action: as Model 1430, above.
DATA FOR MODEL 1533 ST LUXUS
1,000mm overall, 2·95kg unladen.
500mm barrel, 4-groove rifling; RH, concentric.
Detachable box magazine, 3 rounds.
Folding-leaf sight.
975 m/sec with 3·2-gram bullet.

☆

1965: the earliest ·222 rifles were the Models 1530 A and 1531 A, comparable with the 1430 series ·22 Hornet patterns described above.

1973: the range had been altered to comprise Model 1530 with a plain stock; 1532, with a roll-over Monte Carlo butt and a large pistol grip; 1532E with the DJV-style competition stock; and 1534, with a rounded cheek piece and a small pistol grip. All guns could be obtained in single- ('D') or double-trigger ('St') subvarieties.

1976: the Model 1533 St Luxus appeared with a full-length stock and a double set-trigger.

1982: the 1532 Classic was introduced, with a straight-comb butt and a rounded fore-end tip.

1988: all 1530-series guns were abandoned on the introduction of the 1700 series.

1700 series

1700 Classic, 1700, 1730, 1732, 1734, 1736, 1740, 1742, 1744 and 1746 patterns.
Made by J.G. Anschütz GmbH, Ulm/Donau.
·22 Hornet or ·222 Remington only.
Action: as Model 1430, above.
DATA FOR A TYPICAL MODEL 1742
·222 Remington only.
1,105mm overall, 3·45kg unladen.
610mm barrel, 4-groove rifling; RH, concentric.
Detachable box magazine, 3 rounds.
Folding-leaf sight.
975 m/sec with 3·2-gram bullet.

☆

1988: the Model 1700 was little more than an improved 1532 with a heavyweight barrel and an improved action. The standard ·222 Model 1700 had a plain walnut-finish beech stock with a straight-comb butt and a simple round-tip fore-end. Chequering was pressed into the pistol grip only. A single trigger was standard, but a double set pattern could be substituted on request.

The Model 1700 Classic was similar, but had a walnut stock with hand-cut chequering on the fore-end and pistol grip, a pistol-grip cap and a gold-plated trigger lever; it had a 590mm barrel and was about 1,080mm long. The Model 1700 Deluxe or 'Luxusmodell' had a walnut stock with a roll-over Monte Carlo comb, a contrasting

Anschütz

The Model 1434 St, with roll-over comb.
J.G. ANSCHÜTZ GMBH

The Model 1432 EK St rifle. J.G. ANSCHÜTZ GMBH

The ·22 Hornet Model 1434 D rifle. J.G. ANSCHÜTZ GMBH

rosewood pistol-grip cap, a schnabel-tip fore-end, and skip-line chequering.

1990: the series was refined and split into two groups—1730 patterns in ·22 Hornet and 1740 guns chambered for ·222 Remington. The 1730 and 1740 rifles, identical but for chambering, had the plain walnut-finish beech stock. The 1732 and 1742 were the Luxusmodelle, with roll-over Monte Carlo combs and schnabel fore-end tips; 1734 and 1744 types (sometimes sold as the 'Bavaria' in North America) had squared cheek pieces and hog's back combs; and the Models 1736 and 1746 were what had once been the Classics. The guns could all be obtained with single or double triggers, and with folding-(standard) or tangent-leaf (optional) sights.

ARISAKA

JAPAN

This sturdy turning-bolt action was designed and developed in Japan. The British, Chinese, Indonesian, Korean, Russian and Thai guns are described below; Finnish guns were taken from the Russians, while those used in Burma came from the Japanese.

When the Japanese became embroiled in war with China in 1894, they encountered the German Gew.88 (see 'Mannlicher') in combat. This showed that tube-magazine repeaters were less effectual than those with clip-loaded box magazines. A committee chaired by Colonel Nariake Arisaka was appointed to develop a new rifle, soon concluding that the Mauser action was preferable.

The perfected Meiji 38th Year Type rifle was distinguished by good-quality workmanship and excellent material. Excepting rifles made towards the end of the Second World War, which were often very poor, the Arisaka action was exceptionally strong and durable. It relied on a Mauser twin-lug lock, and had a Mauser-type trigger. However, the reciprocating bolt cover and distinctive method of stocking were uniquely Japanese.

Prior to 1930, the service weapons were designated according to the reign-period (nengo) of each emperor reckoned from the restoration of 1868; 1890 was the '23rd Year' of Emperor Meiji's reign. The system was maintained through the Taisho period (1912–26) and into the Showa era before being replaced by a calendar based on the mythical foundation of Japan in 660 BC. After 1929, therefore, terms such as 'Type 94' were used, 1934 being '2594' reckoned by the absolute calendar.

Receivers of pre-1945 Japanese small-arms displayed an imperial chrysanthemum and a mixture of pictographs derived from Chinese (kanji) and a phonetic alphabet used to assimilate foreign words into Japanese (katakana). Marks on a rifle read '38 Year Type'. Chrysanthemums were often defaced on guns due for surrender, to avoid shaming the emperor.

By about 1932, when the serial numbers of Meiji 38th Year rifles had exceeded two million, a cyclical numbering system was adopted. Individual blocks (1–99999) were identified by small encircled katakana prefixes, the sequence being taken from the traditional poem *Iroha*. Numerical values can be given to these symbols, but they should be regarded as letter-groups.

Arsenal identification marks were arbitrary; Tokyo and Kokura used a pile of cannon balls, while Nagoya had two stylised fighting fish. The principal navy mark was a large anchor.

Model 1896

Trials rifle: Meiji 29th Year Type.
Made by the Imperial artillery arsenal,
Koishikawa, Tokyo, 1896–7.
6·5 × 50mm, semi-rimmed.
Turning-bolt action, with two lugs on the bolt head
and the bolt handle turning down into the receiver.
1,271mm overall, 4·08kg unladen.
787mm barrel, 6-groove rifling; RH, polygonal.
Internal charger-loaded box magazine, 5 rounds.
Leaf sight graduated to 2,000 metres.
About 760 m/sec with ball cartridges.
Bayonet: not known.

☆

1896: made between July 1896 and April 1897, these guns had a modified Mauser action, chambered a 6·5mm semi-rim cartridge and had a most distinctive safety hook protruding from the cocking piece. Owing to a shortage of Western-style stock blanks in Japan, the two-piece butt was split horizontally along a line drawn backward from the base of the pistol grip, the toe being pinned and glued in place. Trials rifles lacked a hand guard.

Model 1897

Infantry rifle and cavalry carbine:
Meiji 30th Year Type.
Made by the Imperial artillery arsenal, Koishikawa,
Tokyo, 1899–1907.
Quantity: at least 550,000 rifles and 40,000 carbines.
6·5 × 50mm, semi-rimmed.
Action: as 29th Year Type rifle, above.
DATA FOR RIFLE
1,274mm overall, 4·01kg unladen.
789mm barrel, 4- or 6-groove rifling; RH, polygonal.
Internal charger-loaded box magazine, 5 rounds.
Leaf sight graduated to 2,000 metres.
775 m/sec with Meiji 30th Year Type ball cartridges.
Meiji 30th Year Type sword bayonet.

☆

1899: trials indicated that the experimental 29th Year Type rifle could be improved, the perfected version being adopted in February. The resulting 30th Year Type had a stock with a shallow pistol grip, a single spring-retained barrel band, and a plain nose cap carrying a bayonet lug on its underside.

A grasping groove was cut into the fore-end and a hand guard ran from the front of the back sight base to the barrel band. The swivels were placed conventionally under the butt and band. receivers were made with a distinctive bridge with an angular slot into which the bolt handle locked; a prominent hook on the bolt plug acted as a safety catch.

1900: the tangs of the receiver and trigger guard were extended to reinforce the stock-wrist. Most early guns were made with one-piece stocks, but an increasing shortage of suitable blanks led to

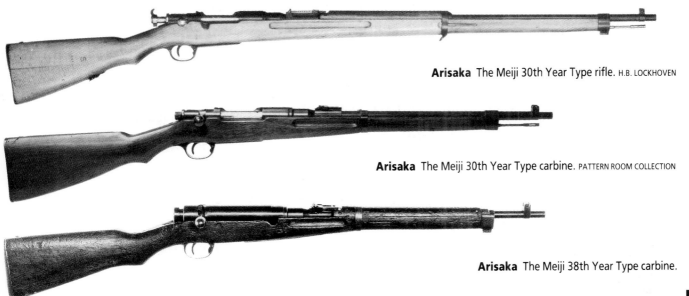

Arisaka The Meiji 30th Year Type rifle. H.B. LOCKHOVEN

Arisaka The Meiji 30th Year Type carbine. PATTERN ROOM COLLECTION

Arisaka The Meiji 38th Year Type carbine.

development of a two-piece butt with a separate toe pinned and glued in place.

A cavalry carbine was produced simply by shortening the standard rifle, omitting the hand guard and substituting a smaller back sight graduated to 1,500 metres. It was 962mm overall; had a 480mm barrel with six-groove polygonal rifling; weighed 3·39kg unladen; and was mechanically identical with the standard rifle. It also accepted the same bayonet.

1905: most of the original back-sight leaves were adapted for the 38th Year ball cartridge, which had a heavier bullet than the 30th Year pattern. New leaves could be identified by the 2,000-metre setting, which was a V-notch cut in the upper edge. Carbine sights do not seem to have been altered.

Model 1902

••

Infantry (navy?) rifle: Meiji 35th Year Type.
Made by the Imperial artillery arsenal,
Koishikawa, Tokyo, c.1903–6.
Quantity: 35,000?
6·5 × 50mm, semi-rimmed.
Action: as 29th Year Type rifle, above.
1,275mm overall, 4·07kg unladen.
790mm barrel, 6-groove rifling; RH, polygonal.
Internal charger-loaded box magazine, 5 rounds.
Tangent-leaf sight graduated to 2,000 metres.
775 m/sec with Meiji 30th Year Type ball cartridges.
Meiji 35th Year Type sword bayonet.

☆

1902: as the 30th Year system proved a disappointment—even though at least 600,000 guns had been made by 1905—this improved rifle was accepted in February. It had an enlarged cocking piece; a new gas-port on the bolt; an enlarged bolt knob; a better bolt head; an improved feed ramp; a sliding spring-loaded breech cover; a tangent back sight; and a hand guard extending back to the receiver ring.

Now widely regarded as naval issue, the gun may have been intended to substitute for the 1897 pattern until the Russo-Japanese War proved that more radical changes were required. If so, then 1902-pattern rifles would have been

issued to the navy only after the army had received the first of the perfected Meiji 38th Year Type rifles. Confirmation from Japanese sources is still lacking, however.

Model 1905

••

Infantry and sniper rifles: Meiji 38th Year Type and Type 97.
Made by the Imperial artillery arsenal, Koishikawa, Tokyo, 1907–32; the Imperial army arsenal, Kokura, 1932–3; the Imperial army arsenal, Nagoya, 1933–41; Heijo ordnance factory (Jinsen arsenal), Korea, c.1938–9; Mukden arsenal, Manchuria, 1940–4; Nanking and Tientsin arsenals, North China, c.1944 (mostly from sub-contracted parts).
Quantity: more than three million.
6·5 × 50mm, semi-rimmed.
Turning-bolt action with two locking lugs on the bolt head and the bolt handle turning down into its seat in the receiver.
1,275mm overall, 4·12kg unladen.
799mm barrel, 4- or 6-groove rifling; RH, polygonal.
Internal charger-loaded box magazine, 5 rounds.
Leaf sight graduated to 2,400 metres.
760 m/sec with Meiji 38th Year Type ball cartridges.
Meiji 30th Year Type or Type 97 sword bayonets.

☆

1905: experience in the Russo-Japanese War revealed several shortcomings in the standard Meiji 30th Year Type rifle, including the bolt-mounted extractor/ejector system, the separate bolt head, and the jamming by dust and mud.

1906: by mid May, a modified rifle had been developed with a simplified bolt, a non-rotating extractor, a reciprocating bolt cover and a large knurled safety shroud on the cocking piece. It was accepted immediately.

Production in Koishikawa continued until numbers in the original cumulative sequence exceeded 2,031,000. Work recommenced at *ne*·1, 'equivalent to number 2000000', a simplified notch safety head replacing the previous lug pattern in the *mu* series. Nagoya's first series had *no*-prefix characters. Production ran to the *ku* series, a sheet metal butt plate being substituted for the earlier forged type.

1937: the perfected Type 97 sniper rifle was adopted after trials that had lasted more than a decade. The bolt handle was lengthened and bent downward; a monopod was added beneath the fore-end; and an optical-sight mount on the left side of the receiver was pegged and screwed in place. About 19,500 guns were assembled in Kokura (5,500 in 1938–9) and Nagoya (14,000 in 1938–41). They weighed about 5·1kg.

The 2.5 × Type 97 sight was held in a base-plate dovetail by a radial latch. Mounting the sight on the left side of the gun facilitated charger loading, but made the gun-and-sight combination awkward to use. A rotary sleeve on the telescope body controlled elevation, though the sniper relied on a comparatively complicated graticle to estimate azimuth deflection.

1941: alteration of full-length 38th Year Type rifles was sanctioned to offset shortages of 7·7mm short rifles. The barrel was cut to about 640mm, increasing handiness but sharpening muzzle blast. District inspectors' stamps on the butt identified the converter as Nagoya arsenal.

Model 1905

••

Cavalry and artillery carbine: Meiji 38th Year Type.
Made by the Imperial artillery arsenal, Koishikawa, Tokyo, 1907–32 (about 235,000); the Imperial army arsenal, Nagoya, 1933–9 (25,000?); and Mukden arsenal, Manchuria (a few thousands?).
6·5 × 50mm, semi-rimmed.
Action: as M1905 rifle, above.
963mm overall, 3·35kg unladen.
487mm barrel, 4- or 6-groove rifling; RH, polygonal.
Internal charger-loaded box magazine, 5 rounds.
Leaf sight graduated to 2,000 metres.
730 m/sec with Meiji 38th Year Type ball cartridges.
Bayonet: as comparable rifle.

☆

1907: this was adopted for issue to cavalry, until the advent in 1911 of the Meiji 44th Year Type (q.v.). Production of the original design then continued for artillerymen and ancillary units. About 215,000 were made in Tokyo prior to the change to prefixed numbers, two blocks following before production transferred to

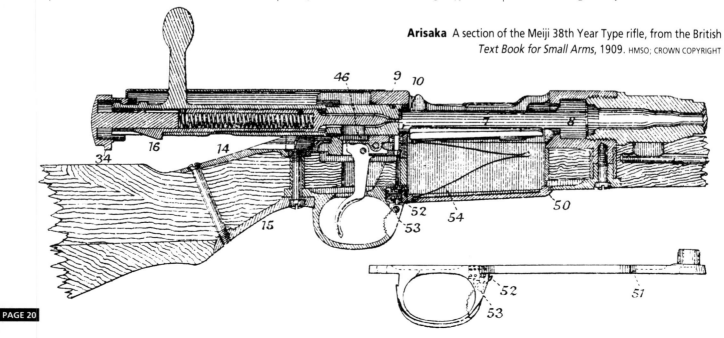

Arisaka A section of the Meiji 38th Year Type rifle, from the British *Text Book for Small Arms*, 1909. HMSO; CROWN COPYRIGHT

Nagoya and probably ultimately to Mukden. Apart from its reduced dimensions, the 1905 pattern carbine was essentially similar to the infantry rifle, with a hand guard running from the front of the back sight base to the nose cap.

Model 1911

Cavalry carbine: Meiji 44th Year Type.
Made by the Imperial artillery arsenal, Koishikawa, Tokyo, 1912–37; the Imperial army arsenal, Nagoya, c.1933–8; and Mukden arsenal, Manchuria, c.1939-42.
6·5 × 50mm, semi-rimmed.
Otherwise as 1905-type carbine excepting dimensions (965mm overall, 4·06kg unladen) and bayonet (integral folding pattern).

☆

1911: this cavalry carbine superseded the 1905 pattern described above. It had a unique folding bayonet attached to the nose cap. Originally confined exclusively to Koishikawa, work was eventually transferred to Nagoya.

The earliest bayonet-mounting block was very short, with the two lateral retaining bolts close together; the uncommon second pattern, dating from the mid 1920s, was greatly extended rearward and had a quillon on the right side of the muzzle block; the third was similar, but the rear bolt, moved back even farther, lay on a semicircular extension of the side plate. There were also two differing patterns of cleaning-rod chamber in the butt, the later type containing a sheet-steel liner.

Model 1939

Long and short rifles: Type 99 standard, sniper and substitute patterns.
Made by the Toriimatsu factory of the Imperial army arsenal, Nagoya, 1940–5; Dai-Nippon Heiki Kogyo, Notobe, c.1940–2; Kayaba Kogyo, Tokyo, c.1940–2; the Imperial army arsenal, Kokura, 1940–5; Toyo Juki, Hiroshima, 1941–5; Tokyo Juki, Tokyo, c.1943–4; and Jinsen arsenal, Korea, c.1942–5.
Quantity: at least 3·5 million.
7·7 × 58mm, rimless.
Turning-bolt action with two locking lugs on the bolt head and the bolt handle turning down into its seat in the receiver.
DATA FOR TYPE 99 SHORT RIFLE
1,150mm overall, 3·80kg unladen.
657mm barrel, 4-groove rifling; RH, polygonal.
Internal charger-loaded box magazine, 5 rounds.
Leaf sight graduated to 1,500 metres.
730 m/sec with Type 99 ball cartridges.
Type 97 sword bayonet.

☆

1938: the 38th Year rifle remained the standard infantry weapon until combat experience in the Sino-Japanese war, against troops armed with 7·9mm-calibre rifles, emphasised the poor short range performance of the Japanese 6·5mm rifle cartridge. Kokura arsenal subsequently modified three hundred guns for an experimental 7·7mm semi-rim round; tests at Futsu proving ground showed the conversion to be effectual, allowing specifications for a new rifle to be finalised in April. Two rifles based on the standard 38th Year

Type were then tested against modified 38th Year and 44th Year Type carbines.
1939: as the carbines had an unacceptably severe muzzle blast and Kokura's simplified breech action failed its endurance tests, the Nagoya 'Rifle Plan No.1' was developed into the long Type 99 rifle by May. A few thousand Type 99 long rifles without prefixed numbers were made in the Toriimatsu factory, but were judged too clumsy. They were 1,270mm overall, had 797mm barrels and weighed about 4·15kg. The back sight was graduated to 1,700 metres.
1940: rejection of the long rifle in favour of a shortened pattern, removing the need for separate carbines, allowed production to be undertaken in several factories simultaneously. As this was long before any major military reverses had been suffered, quality was good. For example, the Type 99 short rifles made in the Toriimatsu factory under Nagoya arsenal supervision showed all the regular production features—including the anti-aircraft lead bars on the back sight—for at least six number blocks.
1942: the improved Type 99 sniper rifle retained the basic features of the preceding Type 97, including the mount, bolt and monopod. The earliest Kokura-assembled guns featured 2·5 × sights, but the 10,000 or so Nagoya-made guns used the improved 4 × Type 2. Apart from a few Type 4 made towards the end of the war, with adjusting bolts in the front mounting ring, Japanese sights lacked external adjustments.
1943: attempts to conserve raw material led to the Substitute Type 99, also known as Type 99

Arisaka The Meiji 38th Year Type rifle. PATTERN ROOM COLLECTION

ARISAKA
THE LESSER MODELS

BRITAIN

1914: the authorities ordered at least 150,000 guns, a mixed batch of 30th and 38th Year Type rifles—plus some carbines—being delivered in 1914–15. Most were old guns with Japanese markings, but a few seem to have been newly made.
1915: suitably refurbished, the weapons were issued to the army from 24 February onward as the 'Rifle, Magazine, ·256-inch, Pattern 1900' (30th Year Type) and 'Pattern 1907' (38th Year Type). The designations were based on the date of issue in the Japanese army instead of approval. Arisaka rifles were also used by the Royal Navy—from 15 June onward—to free Lee-Enfields for land service. Others served the Royal Flying Corps and its 1918-vintage successor, the Royal Air Force.
1916: 128,000 Arisakas were sent to Russia.
1921: survivors were declared obsolete.

CHINA

1946*: large quantities of ex-Japanese Type 99 rifles were altered for the 7·9 × 57mm

cartridge, which was similar in size and shape to the rimless 7·7 × 58mm Type 99. Work was allegedly undertaken for the 'Nationalist North China Army'. The original barrel was shortened and re-chambered, then replaced in the receiver; the magazine was altered slightly, but little else was done apart from grinding the chamber markings away and refinishing most of the parts.

INDONESIA

1947: 38th Year Type and Type 99 rifles, taken from the Japanese occupation forces, were used by insurgents fighting against Dutch rule—and then by the newly-formed army once Indonesia had gained independence in 1949. Most rifles remained in their original state, though some will be found with crude replacement stocks and others with a bluish enamel finish. The army property mark was a small five-point star.

KOREA

1951: the conversion of selected weapons for the ·30–06 cartridge began under American supervision in Tokyo artillery arsenal. By the middle of 1952, about 126,500 short and 6,650 long Type 99 rifles had been altered. They were apparently

intended for South Korean gendarmerie—though possibly only a handful had been issued by the end of the Korean War in 1953. In addition to the new chambering, the magazine box was lengthened for the new cartridge and a groove was cut across the face of the breech to facilitate charger-loading. Japanese chamber marks were removed and the receivers were given a grey phosphated finish.

MEXICO

1910: faced with revolution, the government ordered about forty thousand 38th Year Type Arisakas to supplement the existing Mausers. The rifles—and a few carbines—were made in Koishikawa. They were practically identical with the standard Japanese service patterns, but chambered 7 × 57mm (necessitating a different back sight leaf) and the nose caps were altered to accept the standard Mexican bayonets. Eagle-and-cactus chamber motifs accompanied REPÚBLICA MEXICANA, a liberty cap and 'R M' being struck into the barrel near the breech.
1911: the overthrow of the president, Porfirio Diaz, cancelled orders after less than 5,000 guns had been delivered. The

remainder were stored in Japan until 1914.

RUSSIA

1914–15: the authorities, desperately short of effectual weapons, managed to obtain 600,000 6·5mm Arisaka rifles. Virtually all of these were old 30th Year Type guns, stored since improved patterns had been issued in 1907–9. The Japanese also seized the opportunity to dispose of 35,400 7 × 57mm 38th Year Type rifles held since the Mexican revolution of 1911.
1916: about 128,000 30th Year and 38th Year Type rifles were supplied from Britain. Most had British and Japanese markings; as some subsequently passed to Finland, the marks of four countries may be found.

THAILAND

The Thai army received ex-Japanese rifles of all types after 1945, some Type 99 short rifles being altered for the US ·30–06 cartridge. Undertaken in the government ordnance depot in Bangkok in the early 1950s, the conversion was essentially similar to that undertaken for the Koreans (q.v.). Thai guns often bore Sanskrit numbers and a disc-like Chakra, but the Japanese marks were left untouched.

Model 2 or Type 3 rifle. This was characterised by use of low grade steel, omission of bolt cover and sling swivels, and the deletion of chrome from the bolt-face and the bore. Nagoya-made guns, for example, soon exhibited a two-screw nose cap; the bolt knob became cylindrical; the back sight ultimately became a fixed block; the grasping groove in the fore-end was eliminated, and the butt plate changed from metal to wood. Solid barrel bands and welded safety shrouds appeared towards the end of 1944. The last guns were truly awful; that they worked at all was a tribute to the exceptional strength of the action.

Paratroop rifles

Types 0, 1 and 2.
ALL DATA FOR TYPE 2
Made by the Imperial army arsenal, Nagoya, 1943–4.
7·7 × 58mm, rimless.
Action: as Type 99, above.
1,150mm overall, 4·05kg unladen.
645mm barrel, 4-groove rifling; RH, polygonal.
Internal charger-loaded box magazine, 5 rounds.
Leaf sight graduated to 2,400 metres.
722 m/sec with Type 99 ball cartridges.
Type 97 sword bayonet.
☆

1940: the Japanese were very slow to develop effectual submachine-guns. Consequently, the paratroops had to rely on comparatively clumsy infantry rifles until the 1st Army Technical Research Institute developed the Type 0 (or 'Type 100') rifle, with an interrupted-thread joint between the barrel and receiver to allow rapid dismantling into two major components. Nagoya arsenal converted 500 standard Type 99 short rifles to permit field trials.
1941: the Type 1 paratroop rifle—no more than a 38th Year Type carbine with a folding butt—was developed to safeguard against the failure of the interrupted-screw system. Surviving guns were pressed into service at the end of the war.
1942: as the interrupted-thread lock of the Type 0 proved to be ineffectual, so a sliding wedge was substituted in October.
1943: the Type 2 was standardised in May,

production of 25,000 beginning immediately. The omission of a monopod and the rough surface finish betrayed late-war origins.

Other patterns

Training, Substitute 35th Year Type and Special Navy rifles.
☆

Prior to 1942, the Japanese made reduced-scale 38th Year Type rifles to train juvenile cadets. Excepting smooth-bored 38th Year and Type 99 rifles, the trainers had a simplified receiver with integrally-cast tangs and a detachable smooth-bore barrel. Niggardly proportioned one-piece stocks were ideally suited to rejected wood blanks. However, as pressures generated by regular ball ammunition would have wrecked training rifles, 'for blank ammunition only' was usually marked on receiver or butt.

Late in 1944, when the quality of rifle production had declined appreciably, emergency weapons were produced. The most effectual combined old 1902-pattern actions with barrels originally destined for training rifles. The '35th Year Type Substitute Rifles' could be recognised by the design of the back sight (graduated to 1,600 metres with an aperture on the slider), a flat sheet metal butt plate and, unusually, a one piece stock with an almost straight wrist. A very distinctive screw thread was found on the barrel surface ahead of the receiver ring. Some guns saw front-line service on Okinawa.

Made by Yokosuka navy arsenal in 1945, the Special Navy Rifle amalgamated a cast-iron training rifle receiver with a barrel modified to receive the locking lugs directly in the enlarged chamber—allowing ball ammunition to be fired without blowing the gun apart. About 12,500 rifles were made, initially with adjustable sights but later with fixed notches. Butt plates and barrel bands were generally crudely cast, and the finish was black stove-enamel. The earliest guns were marked 'Special' and often displayed a large anchor mark; later guns were marked 'Special Type 99', but the last bore nothing but an anchor on their receivers.

ARMALITE

UNITED STATES OF AMERICA
Stoner and other designs

The story of this interesting, controversial rifle began with the ArmaLite Division of Fairchild Engine & Airplane Corporation, formed in the autumn of 1954 to promote guns embodying aluminium alloy parts and foam-filled synthetic furniture. The auto-loading ·308 AR-3, designed by ArmaLite's chief engineer Eugene Stoner, was locked by a variation of the rotating bolt patented in the 1930s by Melvin Johnson (q.v.).

A small tube ran along the left side of the breech to direct propellant gas through the receiver wall into a chamber formed between the bolt and the bolt carrier. The bolt carrier was forced backward on firing, rotating the bolt to disengage the lock; when the carrier had moved back a short distance, it closed the port on the receiver side and cut off the gas supply. Though only a few AR-3 rifles were ever made, they led to the AR-10 and, ultimately, to the AR-15.

ArmaLite AR-10

Made by Artillerie-Inrichtingen, Zaandam, under licence from ArmaLite, Hollywood, California.
Quantity: about 5,500.
7·62 × 51mm NATO, rimless.
Gas-operated auto-loader, locked by multiple lugs on the bolt head rotating into the barrel extension.
DATA FOR TYPICAL RIFLE
41·30in overall, 6·85lb without magazine.
20in barrel, 4-groove rifling; RH, concentric.
Detachable box magazine, 20 rounds.
Pivoting-leaf sight.
2,700 ft/sec with M59 ball cartridges:
Optional knife bayonet.
☆

1955: the ·30–06 prototype showed enough promise for a ·308 version to be made in the summer. Successfully tested at Fort Benning, a third experimental rifle ('AR-10A') had a plastic butt filled with foam, a large cylindrical muzzle-

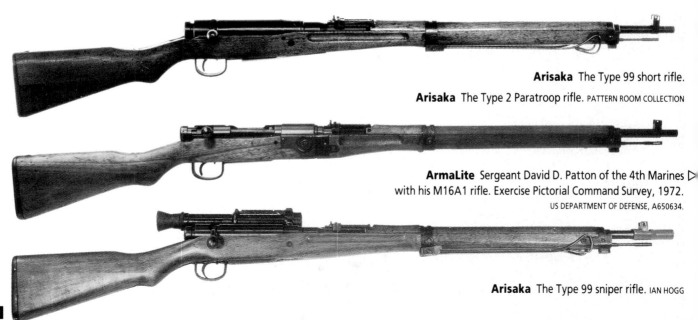

Arisaka The Type 99 short rifle.

Arisaka The Type 2 Paratroop rifle. PATTERN ROOM COLLECTION

ArmaLite Sergeant David D. Patton of the 4th Marines ▷ with his M16A1 rifle. Exercise Pictorial Command Survey, 1972.
US DEPARTMENT OF DEFENSE, A650634.

Arisaka The Type 99 sniper rifle. IAN HOGG

brake/compensator and a cocking handle on the receiver-side.

1956: about fifty semi-production AR-10B rifles were made. Modified by James Sullivan, they had a new gas tube above the barrel and an improved bolt carrier. A rifled steel liner lay inside an alloy barrel casing, and the charging handle was moved to the top of the receiver beneath the carrying handle. Trials held in Springfield in the winter revealed that the ArmaLite was in need of further development.

1957: trials of an improved rifle, in January, ended disastrously when a bullet came out of the side of the barrel and narrowly missed the firer's hand. Metallurgical analysis revealed flaws in the composite barrel concept and a conventional steel pattern was substituted.

ArmaLite had granted manufacturing rights to the state-owned Artillerie-Inrichtingen in the hope that a Dutch government order would follow. ArmaLite retained the North American sales agency; Sidem International SA of Brussels was granted Europe and North Africa; Cooper-Macdonald, Inc., of Baltimore took charge of Australasia and the Far East; and, belatedly, Interarms of Alexandria, Virginia, assumed responsibility for southern Africa, plus Central and South America.

1958: some AR-10 derivatives appeared, among them a carbine/submachine-gun, a sniper rifle and a light machine-gun.

The earliest AI-made rifles had perforated full length hand guards. The ejection-port cover was held by a plunger instead of the previous spring-clip, and the original compensator was replaced by an open 'prong-type' suppressor capable of handling rifle grenades. However, the suppressor seriously compromised the ability of the AR-10 to fire fully automatically.

Later guns had a new barrel, with a slotted suppressor and circumferential ribs to support a grenade tail. A fluted wooden hand guard appeared behind an abbreviated sheet-metal fitting, and the selector was altered so that the safety position was forward instead of upward. Most rifles were marked 'Patents Pending' over **ARMALITE AR10** on the left side of the magazine

housing, above **MFD. BY** ahead of the 'AI-in-a-triangle' trademark and **NEDERLAND**. The serial number usually lay beneath the trademark.

1959: AR-10 rifles were optimistically touted worldwide. The design finished a creditable second to the FAL in South African trials of 1960, but failure during an endurance test aborted a 7,500-gun order for the Nicaraguan national guard.

When the Dutch also rejected the ArmaLite in favour of the FAL, Artillerie-Inrichtingen lost interest. All work in Zaandam stopped, though guns were available from stock for some months thereafter. Interarms sold about 350 to Guatemala and perhaps 1,750 to the Sudan, while Sidem had sold Portugal about a thousand South African-style guns—with a telescoping charging handle and an improved trigger—and Cooper-Macdonald had disposed of limited numbers in Burma.

ArmaLite AR-15

AR-15, M16, M16A1, M16A1E1, M16A2, XM16 and XM16E1.
Made by Colt's Patent Fire Arms Mfg. Co., Hartford, Connecticut; Harrington & Richardson, Worcester, Massachusetts; Hydra-Matic Division, General Motors Corporation, Ypsilanti, Michigan.
5·56 × 45mm, rimless.
Action: as AR-10, above.
DATA FOR M16
39·00in overall, 6·31lb without magazine.
20·00in barrel (excluding flash supprpressor), 6-groove rifling; RH, concentric.
Detachable box magazine, 20 or 30 rounds.
Pivoting-leaf sight.
3,250 ft/sec with M193 ball cartridges; 750 ± 50 rpm.
M7 knife bayonet.
☆

1952–3: tests of an M2 Carbine chambered for a shortened ·222 Remington cartridge had shown that small-calibre high velocity bullets and light automatic rifles had important military applications...but incurred official disfavour.

1957: army authorities prepared a specification for a small-calibre selective fire rifle with a

magazine capacity of at least twenty rounds but a laden weight no greater than 6lb. At distances out to 300 yards, accuracy and trajectory were to be at least equal to the M1 Garand and the wounding power equal to (preferably, bettering) the M1 Carbine. The weapon was to chamber any suitable ·22 cartridge.

ArmaLite engineers Robert Fremont and James Sullivan altered the AR-10 to fire a modified ·222 Remington round, circumventing lengthy ammunition development but accepting a small-capacity cartridge case from which high velocity could be achieved only through high chamber pressures.

The first rifles weighed 6·12lb with a loaded 25-round magazine and were 37·5in overall. They had steel barrels and hollow fibreglass-reinforced plastic butts. Muzzles were plain cylindrical, the selector lever rotated up to the safety position, the charging handle still lay beneath the carrying handle, and a simple back sight was used.

About twenty of these early guns were made. They bore the 'encircled Pegasus' ArmaLite trademark on the left side of the magazine housing, above **AR-15**, the Hollywood address, a 'Patents Pending' mark and the serial number.

Differences of opinion amongst army experts had, meanwhile, increased the performance requirements from 300 to 500 yards. ArmaLite solved this by substituting ·222 Remington Special (known as ·223 Remington from 1959) for the original ·222 round, propellant capacity being increased by lengthening the case and moving the shoulder forward.

The AR-15 now gained a serious rival—the Winchester ·224 Light-Weight Military Rifle (or WLAR), created by Ralph Clarkson largely by amalgamating the best features of the company's previous auto-loaders.

1958: ten AR-15 rifles were delivered in March. Tests undertaken at Fort Benning, Aberdeen Proving Ground and Fort Greely were highly successful. Though doubts about the lethality of small-diameter bullets persisted, the AR-15 and the WLAR performed well—better, indeed, than the T44E4. The ArmaLite was most reliable,

ARMALITE
THE LESSER MODELS

Note: *The Black Rifle. M16 Retrospective* by R. Blake Stevens and Edward C. Ezell (Collector Grade Publications, Inc., Toronto, 1987) is highly recommended as a source of information about the AR-15/M16 series.

CANADA

The army has replaced the 7·62mm C1 rifle (FN FAL, q.v.) with the 5·56mm C7 rifle and C8 carbine, known to Colt as the models 715 and 725 respectively. Developed from a government contract given to Diemaco in the Spring of 1983, the C7 and C8 are essentially variations of the M16A2 with a simpler pivoting-leaf back sight, a thirty-round nylon magazine and a Colt-pattern butt trap. The C8 has a short barrel and a telescoping XM177E2-type butt. The three-round burst-fire mechanism was discarded in favour of the standard fully-automatic setting.

¶ Orders for nearly 80,000 C7 rifles and 1,570 C8 carbines were approved in 1984. Batches of C7 rifles were delivered in the summer of 1985, the first of the all-Canadian made guns appearing at the end of 1987. Though some of the earliest guns were marked differently, C7 rifles display 'CANADA/FORCES/CANADIENNES' under a stylised maple leaf on the left side of the magazine housing, above the designation, calibre and serial number. The left side of the receiver ahead of the selector displays 'MADE IN CANADA' and 'FABRIQUE AU CANADA' above Diemaco's trademark.

¶ The Royal Canadian Mounted Police has used commercial-pattern Colt AR-15 sporting rifles and carbines in small numbers.

CHINA

The China North Industries Corporation (Norinco) has made a few M16A1 copies as the 'Type CQ' or Model 311, the latter being a semi-automatic sporter. The guns are immediately recognisable by their curved pistol grip, with moulded-in decoration, and the humped under-edge of the grey butt.

KOREA

A licensed copy of the M16A1 (Colt Model 603-K) has been built in what was once the government-owned Pusan arsenal, after the US Military Aid Program had provided nearly 27,000 M16A1 rifles from US Army stores. The indigenous rifles bore 'MADE IN KOREA' above an acknowledgement of the licence on the right side of the magazine, the designation and K-prefix serial number appearing on the left. Production is said to have approached 600,000 before work finished c.1985. The selector was marked in Korean. In 1983, the Pusan facilities were sold to Daewoo Precision Industries (q.v.) and used to develop new rifles.

PHILIPPINES

About fifty thousand Model 613 (XM16E1) rifles were purchased from Colt in 1965–70, and 27,000 M16A1 rifles were provided under the US Military Aid Program in 1975–6. In 1967, however, a licence was granted to Elisco Tool Company of Manila.

¶ Elisco has since made Model 613-P rifles, in addition to a Model 653-P carbine with a

14·5in barrel and a telescoping tubular butt. The left side of the magazine housing displays suitable marks ('Made by Elisco Tool for the Republic of the Philippines') above a P-prefix serial number; an acknowledgement of the licence appears on the right. Selector marks are in English.

SINGAPORE

An order was placed with Colt in 1966 for 18,000 standard and 2,300 heavy-barrel CAR-15 rifles. Only a little over three thousand had been delivered before February 1967, when the authorities negotiated a licence to make 150,000 rifles.

¶ Production was entrusted to Chartered Industries Ltd (CIS), with technical assistance from Colt. The first guns were made in 1970, work continuing for about a decade; about 30,000 of a total approaching 185,000 rifles were shipped to Thailand. The SAR-80 was then derived from the AR-18 by way of the Sterling Automatic Rifle.

¶ Singapore-made rifles bore the 'CiS' trademark on the left side of the magazine housing, above an acknowledgement of the licensing agreement. The left side of the receiver ahead of the selector was marked ''COLT'S GOVT. MODEL'' over 'M16' over 'CAL. 5.56MM'.

TAIWAN

The government, which had been making the M14 under licence in the Hsing-Ho factory in Kao-Hsiung, proceeded in the mid 1970s to the 5.56mm Rifle Type 65 (i.e., 'M1976'). This mated an M16-type frame with a modified receiver/barrel assembly and a gas-piston system adapted from the AR-18. A pivoting back sight lay on top of the raised rear of the receiver.

USA

CAR-15 The original M16-type guns were offered commercially as the 'Colt Automatic Rifle', alternatively known as the Model 601. Later rifles, built on the M16A1-pattern action and known as 'AR-15A2 Sporter II' (Model 711), were usually accompanied by five-round magazines

CAR-15 HB M1 Also known as the Model 606, this heavy-barrel assault rifle weighed 7·5lb without its magazine or accessories and fed from a detachable box magazine. A Colt, modified BAR or standard M2 rifle-type bipod could be attached.

¶ The Model 606B was similar, but had a four-position selector and an additional burst facility. Several hundred were made for US Army SAWS trials.

¶ The commercial semi-automatic AR-15A2 H-Bar (Model 741), introduced at the end of 1985, was essentially similar to the M16A2—sharing the adjustable back sight and case deflector, but the barrel diameter is maintained throughout its length (unlike that of the military M16A2). It was joined in 1987 by the AR-15A2 Delta H-Bar, distinguished by a rubber-armoured 3–9 × optical sight on a special mount and an ambidexterous cheek piece with an under-cut to allow the charging handle to be retracted. The Delta H-Bar weighs about 10lb with its sight.

CAR-15 HB M2 Only about twenty of these belt-feed assault rifles were made in 1964. The basic gun weighed 8·3lb and fed from a detachable box holding a 50- or 120-rd belt.

CAR-15 Carbine Several prototypes of these were made, the earliest having a 16in barrel and a special short handguard. It could also fire two-shot bursts, necessitating a four-position selector. The finalised commercial semi-automatic pattern had a 16in barrel, a short (but otherwise standard) hand guard and a collapsible butt. It was 35in overall (31·75in with the butt retracted) and weighed about 5lb with a loaded magazine. Guns made after 1984 incorporated a bolt-closing plunger and were re-designated 'AR-15A2 Carbines' (Model 723).

¶ The Model 605B retained the burst-firing mechanism, but had a full-length hand guard from which only the muzzle of the 15in barrel protruded. It was 34·3in overall, weighed 5·75lb and accepted the standard magazines. It was not successful.

CAR-15 Sub-machine Gun This was an abbreviated version of the standard rifle, with a 10in barrel. The butt and pistol grip were shortened, though some of the earliest examples were fitted with a telescoping version of the conventional butt instead of the later tubular pattern.

¶ The submachine-gun attracted the interest of the US Army, which ordered 2,815 in June 1966 as the 'Commando' (Colt Model 609). The first examples retained the 10in barrel and had a long flash-hider with a small-diameter exit port. However, the muzzle blast and flash was such that the project was suspended while a more effectual muzzle attachment was developed. This was satisfactorily accomplished, whereupon the CAR-15 was reclassified in January 1967 as 'XM177' (Colt Model 649), or 'XM177E1' with the bolt-closing device. First deliveries had been made in November 1966.

¶ The perfected XM177E2 was an 'E1' with an 11·5in barrel. Colt also made some Model 610B guns, similar to the Model 609 Commando but with a burst-firing system.

¶ Though the XM177E2 was popular with the special forces, it suffered continual accuracy problems. Changes were suggested to make the suppressor more effectual, but the entire project was dropped in 1970. Colt subsequently offered fully automatic versions for police use, with barrels of 11·5–16in, in addition to a semi-automatic Sporter Carbine. In the 1980s, however, renewed interest created an improved XM177E2 known as 'XM4'.

CAR-15 Survival Rifle Also known as the Model 608, this shared the 10in barrel of the submachine-gun, but had a fixed tubular butt, a truncated pistol grip and a cylindrical hand guard. It was 29in overall and weighed 4·8lb without its magazine. Only ten were made before the project was abandoned.

M231 Port Firing Weapon Standardised in 1979, this hardly classifies as a rifle. Made without sights and capable only of automatic fire, it is easily distinguished by the absence of a butt—only the buffer protrudes from the rear of the receiver—and by a rapid-pitch screw thread on the front of the barrel casing. The screw mates with a suitable ball mount in the US Army M2 Bradley Fighting Vehicle. Known during development as the XM231, the gun can be dismounted in an emergency and fired by using the carrying handle as a rudimentary sight. The earliest prototypes had sliding butts, but these were soon abandoned.

OTHER USERS

Note: it is often difficult to assess whether rifles were acquired directly from Colt on a commercial basis, through US military aid programmes, or from intermediaries. In the list that follows, 'M16' or 'M16A1' infers US military surplus; guns supplied by Colt are given their commercial designations—Model 603 is the original XM16E1/M16A1; Model 604 is an XM16/M16; Models 613 and 614 are the 'export' versions of the 603 and 604 respectively; Model 616 was a heavy-barrel M16A1; Model 653 is the standard M16A1-type carbine; Model 701 is the commercial version of the M16A2; Model 703 is the standard military-type M16A2; Model 723 is the standard M16A2-type carbine; and Model 727 is a special XM4-type carbine.

¶ Australia (2,500 assorted Models 613, 614 and 653, 1965–73); Barbados (US Army surplus); Belize (ex-British M16 and some Colt Model 613, 1978–86); Bolivia (M16A1, US Army surplus?); Brazil (Model 614 for air force, M16A1 for police and M16A2 for special anti-terrorist forces); Britain (several thousand Model 614, plus a few Models 613 and 653, c.1967–80); Brunei (Models 613 and 653); Burma (M16A1, US Army surplus?); Cameroons (Model 613); Chile (5,500 M16A1 and Model 613, 1974–7); Costa Rica (US Army surplus?); Denmark (acquired for police in the early 1970s); Dominican Republic (at least 6,000 M16A1 and Model 613); Ecuador (10,000–12,000 M16A1, Model 613 and Model 653); El Salvador (32,600 M16A1, 1981–4); Fiji (M16A1, M16A2 and Model 701); Gabon (Model 613); Ghana (5,000–6,500 M16A1 and Model 613); Greece (about 500 Models 701 and 723 for the special forces); Grenada (about 250 US Army surplus M16A1); Guatemala (US Army surplus M16A1); Haiti (500 Model 613); Honduras (10,000 M16A1 and Model 613, 1977–83); Indonesia (at least 78,500 M16A1 and Model 613, 1971–81); Israel (97,000 M16A1, 65,000 Model 613 and 45,000 Model 653, 1970–85); Jamaica (about 500 Model 613 and 100 Model 653); Jordan (68,000 M16A1, 1967–75); Kampuchea (ex-US M16A1); Lebanon (50,000 ex-US Army M16A1, and 20,000 new Model 613 rifles distinguished by 'AL'-prefix numbers); Lesotho (Models 613 and 653); Liberia (Models 613 and 701); Malaysia (about 200,000 Model 613 and 5,000 Model 653); Morocco (M16A1, Model 613 and Model 653); New Zealand (Model 613); Nicaragua (M16A1 and Model 613); Nigeria (Korean-made); Oman (Model 613); Panama (M16A1 and Model 613); Papua New Guinea (US Army surplus); Peru (US Army surplus); Qatar (about 4,000 Model 613 and 2,500 Model 653, 1981–3); Somalia (US Army surplus?); South Africa (security police); Sri Lanka (M16A1 and Model 723); Thailand (89,000 US Army-surplus M16A1 in 1972–81, 55,000 Model 613 in 1975–85, and about 30,000 CIS Model 614-S in 1973–4); Trinidad & Tobago (Model 613?); Tunisia; Turkey (Models 711 and 723 for security forces); Uganda (Model 616?); United Arab Emirates (Models 613, 653, 703 and 727, from 1979 to date); Uruguay (US Army surplus); Vietnam [South](6,000 M16 and 938,000 M16A1, 1966–75); and Zaire (military surplus).

although it had been adversely affected by the use of ·224E2 cartridges; the Winchester rifle could not chamber ·222 Remington Special.

As a result of army trials, the AR-15 charging handle was moved to the rear of the receiver, as it could not be grasped through an arctic mitten and became too hot to hold during rapid fire. The safety position on the selector pointed forward instead of upright, barrel weight was increased, and a flash suppressor was added. Magazine capacity became twenty rounds to compensate for weight added elsewhere.

By this time, however, the small-calibre high velocity concept was encountering such fierce opposition from the Office of the Chief of Ordnance that problems were being magnified out of proportion.

An examination of optimal calibres then led to rejection of ·222 in favour of ·258. Rifle trials recommenced on 1 December, but the Army Chief of Staff reaffirmed that the M14 was the only rifle suitable for military use. Fairchild lost interest in the ArmaLite and licensed it to Colt in February 1959.

The first Colt-made rifles ('AR-15 Model 01', Colt Model 601) were completed in December; by this time, small-scale military sales had been made to Malaysia and India. The butts and hand guards of the earliest guns had a mottled brown finish, later painted green. They bore a rampant Colt trademark ahead of COLT on the left side of the magazine housing, above ARMALITE (plus 'AR15' on later examples), 'Patents Pending', the designation '01' and the serial number; the full Colt's Patent Fire Arms Mfg. Co. mark lay above the address on the left side of the receiver above the selector.

1960: Colt advertised that, among other things, the AR-15 could fire far more shots without cleaning than any rival. By this time, the USAF was actively seeking to replace obsolescent M2 Carbines and had requested that the AR-15 be reviewed. Trials confirmed accuracy and reliability, the failure rate being less than three rounds per thousand, and the 5·56mm rifle was grudgingly cleared for USAF scrutiny.

1961: ArmaLite, Inc., was formed under the presidency of Charles Dorchester after Fairchild had withdrawn its support entirely. However, Eugene Stoner and his design team joined the Cadillac Gage Company (see below).

USAF trials of the AR-15 were so encouraging that the air force asked for 8,500 guns. Congress rejected the request, but growing interest in Vietnam could not be ignored.

1962: the 5·56mm Rifle AR-15 (later XM16, then M16) was classified as USAF standard in January; on 15 May, purchase of 20,000 guns was approved by Congress for the USAF, Navy SEALs and American advisers in Vietnam. The guns were soon being hailed as a suitable replacement for virtually all the existing service small-arms.

Owing to the lack of progress with the SPIW project, the US Army renewed interest in the AR-15, acquiring 338 'XM-16' rifles in the autumn for trials against the M14 and the Kalashnikov.

1963: after many tribulations, the Secretary of the Army recommended the purchase of up to 100,000 AR-15 rifles for army airborne units and special forces. Major faults were blamed, with justification, on poor quality control of guns and ammunition. Minor problems continued to arise with exasperating frequency; however, as the Secretary of Defense had ordered that only unavoidable changes should be made, much correctional work was left undone.

Rifling making one complete turn in twelve inches (instead of 1-in-14) was accepted on 26 July to safeguard bullet performance in sub-zero conditions. The army then insisted that the breech should be capable of manual closure if a cartridge failed to chamber correctly, though neither airmen nor marines concurred. A plunger designed by Foster Sturtevant was added to the rear right side of the receiver above the pistol grip, but added needless complexity.

Eventually, on 4 November, Colt received the first large government contract—85,000 XM16E1 rifles for the army and 19,000 M16 for the air force.

1964: the first M16 and XM16E1 rifles were delivered in the Spring. They were similar to the preceding AR-15, excepting that the butt and hand guard were blacked, the charging handle was changed to a T-bar, the firing pin was altered to minimise slam-firing tendencies, the flash suppressor was strengthened, and magazine bodies became alloy instead of steel. Marks included a rampant Colt on the left side of the magazine housing ahead of COLT over AR-15. Then—in four lines—came the property mark, the calibre, MODEL 02 and the serial number.

1965: reports of severe problems soon filtered back from Vietnam. Though many were traced to lack of maintenance, persistent extraction failures and misfires due to the bolt carrier rebounding from the breech-face were much more serious. The original buffer, composed of compressible ring springs, was apt to seize solid; it was eventually replaced in December 1966 by a multi-weight buffer designed by Sturtevant, which not only cured the rebound problem but also reduced the cyclic rate and partly corrected the tendency of the bolt to run forward again after the last round had been fired.

Trouble stemmed partly from attempting to standardise the 1958-vintage AR-15, which had advanced no further than the pre-production stage; from rivalry in the upper echelons of command; and, particularly, from selecting too small a cartridge case. Trials undertaken in Frankford Arsenal in December showed that the supposedly perfected service rounds jammed five times more frequently than those used throughout the original trials!

1966: though better propellant was adopted in May, fouling continued to plague the rifles for some months. However, Colt was given a second contract, signed on 16 June and later extended to 836,810 guns valued at $91·7 million. The future of the AR-15 was assured.

On 29 June, Colt received a contract for nearly twenty thousand XM148 (Colt CGL-4) 40mm grenade launchers for the XM16E1, the first shipment leaving for Vietnam in December. The XM148 proved to be a disaster, and was abandoned in 1967 after about 34,000 had been made. It was replaced by the AAI XM203 launcher adopted in the summer of 1968.

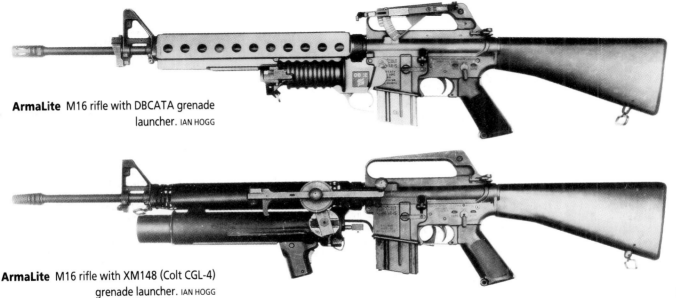

ArmaLite M16 rifle with DBCATA grenade launcher. IAN HOGG

ArmaLite M16 rifle with XM148 (Colt CGL-4) grenade launcher. IAN HOGG

Ironically, all post-1969 M203 launchers have been made by Colt.

A new slotted compensator was approved in September, as the open-prong pattern caught in undergrowth and encouraged entry of rainwater into the bore. In December, the Secretary of the Army reported that the XM16E1 was 'generally superior' for army use. As the Stoner Model 63 was not showing sufficient improvement over the ArmaLite, so the latter was recommended for adoption.

1967: the XM16E1 was reclassified as 'M16A1' on 28 February. On 3 May, however, the Ichord Congressional Sub-Committee began its first deliberations into the controversy surrounding the rifle, reporting in October—oblivious of important details—that the entire programme had been mishandled by the army.

A chrome-plated chamber was approved to minimise extraction failures on 26 May; on 30 June, the US government bought manufacturing rights from Colt for $4·5 million, plus a royalty on all guns made under government licence.

1968: reluctant to rely on Colt as the only supplier of ArmaLite rifles, the Department of Defense sought alternative contractors. On 19 April, provisional contracts (eventually totalling 240,000 guns apiece) were agreed with the Hydra-Matic Division of General Motors and Harrington & Richardson—in circumstances that raised more eyebrows in Congress. Each new contractor delivered rifles from 1969 onward, easily distinguished by HYDRA-MATIC DIV. over G.M. CORP. on the left side of the magazine housing or HARRINGTON & RICHARDSON on the left side of the receiver ahead of the selector, accompanied by all or part of the address. The Harrington & Richardson guns bore an encircled lion over H&R on the magazine housing.

By the end of the year, Colt reported that sales had amounted to 183,950 M16 (including forty thousand export and commercial guns) and 830,630 XM16E1/M16A1.

1969: thirty-round magazines became available, though the requirement had arisen in 1966. In November, Colt accepted a 'definitized' contract (an amalgamation of two smaller orders

provisonally awarded in 1968) for 740,800 M16A1 and 1,000 M16 rifles.

1970: Colt and GM Hydra-Matic received new contracts for 458,440 and 229,620 M16A1 rifles respectively. The GM-made rifles, in spite of doubts expressed in Congress about the suitability of the additional manufacturers, were highly regarded.

1980: heedless of US Army apathy, the marines embarked on a programme of improvements, eventually persuading the managers of the Joint Services Small Arms Program to acquire fifty Colt-made M16A1E1 rifles in November 1981.

1982: the M16A1E1, having demonstrated its superiority, was officially designated M16A2 in September though adoption was delayed until November 1983. The major changes concerned the new back sight and a heavy barrel rifled with 1-in-7 twist. The suppressor was redesigned to act as an effectual muzzle brake, the shape of the pistol grip was improved, and the stock was filled with nylon foam. The fully automatic capability was replaced with a quirky three-shot burst mechanism.

The US Army was initially scathing about the USMC improvements, especially the change in rifling pitch (preventing the use of M193 ball ammunition) and the advent of the burst-fire system, arguing that fully-automatic capability had offset the lack of confidence expressed by many individual soldiers in small-calibre bullets. From 1985, however, the army also began to purchase small quantities of M16A2 rifles.

Colt has made a selection of similar guns for commercial purposes (see panel), but not all have featured the 800-yard sight. The most important has been the Delta H-Bar sniper rifle, which has proved popular with SWAT squads.

A typical rifle bears the rampant colt trademark on the left side of the magazine housing, above the COLT logotype, designation, calibre and serial number. Numbers began at 8000001. Marks of Colt's Firearms Division, Colt Industries, appeared on the left side of the receiver ahead of the selector; selector marks were repeated beside the spindle-base on the right side of the receiver.

ArmaLite AR-18

Made by or for the ArmaLite Corporation, Costa Mesa, California, 1969-82; by Howa Machinery Ltd, Nagoya, 1972-3; and the Sterling Engineering Co. Ltd, Dagenham, 1976-8.
5·56 × 45mm, rimless.
Action: as AR-10, above.
DATA FOR AR-18 RIFLE
38·00in overall, 7·18lb with loaded magazine.
18·25in barrel, 6-groove rifling; RH, concentric.
Detachable box magazine, 20 or 30 rounds.
Pivoting-leaf sight.
3,185 ft/sec with M193 ball cartridges; 750 ± 50 rpm.
Optional knife bayonet.

☆

1961: designed by Eugene Stoner specifically for tank and armoured-vehicle crewmen, the 7·62mm AR-16 rifle was seen as an inexpensive alternative to the M14. Composed largely of stampings and parts that could be turned on a lathe, the rifle had a wooden butt that hinged to the left. It weighed about 8·75lb and had a 15in barrel. Only three were made.

1963: after the defection of Stoner and his design team to the Cadillac Cage Corporation, the basic principles of the AR-16 were scaled-down for the 5·56mm cartridge by Arthur Miller. The result was the AR-18, made largely of pressings and reliant on a tappet-type piston system in a tube above the barrel. The bolt carrier reciprocated on two guiding rods in the simplified receiver, the integral charging handle doubling as a bolt-closure device if required. The gas system could not be adjusted, but the selector could be set for safety, semi-automatic or fully automatic fire. Like most of the 5·56mm Stoner-inspired rifles, the AR-18 had seven lugs on the rotating bolt; the position of the eighth was occupied by the extractor claw.

1964: the AR-18 was tested by the US Army, but rejected as still in the prototype stage. More were purchased in 1965, but generated little additional interest.

1969*: a licence was granted to Howa in Japan, but production was small. A few ·223 AR-180 sporters had distinctive wood stocks.

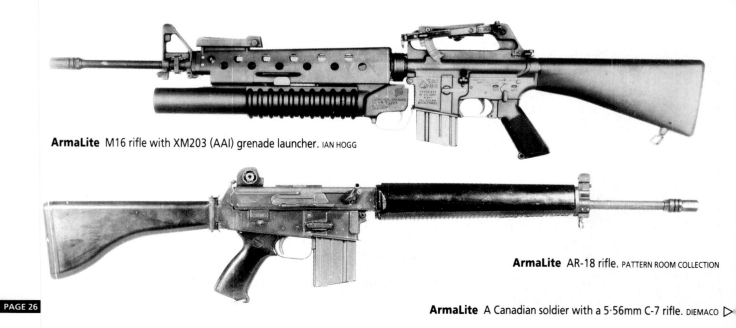

ArmaLite M16 rifle with XM203 (AAI) grenade launcher. IAN HOGG

ArmaLite AR-18 rifle. PATTERN ROOM COLLECTION

ArmaLite A Canadian soldier with a 5·56mm C-7 rifle. DIEMACO ▷

1976*: Sterling Engineering briefly participated in the AR-18 programme, before developing an automatic rifle of its own. This was credited to Frank Waters, but was little more than a modified AR-18. It was also closely related to the Singapore-made SAR-80 (q.v.).

Stoner Models 62 and 63

Made by the Cadillac Gage Corporation, 1963–9.
Quantity: 3,500 guns of all types.
Action: generally as AR-10, above.
DATA FOR MODEL 63
5·56 × 45mm, rimless.
40·25in overall, 9·65lb with loaded magazine.
20·00in barrel (excluding flash suppressor),
6-groove rifling; RH, concentric.
Detachable box magazine, 30 rounds.
Pivoting-leaf sight.
3,250 ft/sec with M193 ball cartridges; 650 ± 30 rpm.
Optional knife bayonet.

☆

1961: Gene Stoner, disaffected with ArmaLite, Inc., persuaded the Cadillac Gage Company to enter the arms industry.

1962: the 7·62mm Model 62 was a rotating-bolt auto-loader, though a gas piston replaced the direct-impingement system. Stoner's original patents had been assigned to Colt. The piston lay in a tube above the barrel, the charging slide and handle rode on rails on the left side of the receiver, and the furniture was wooden. The rifle was 42in overall, had a 20in barrel and weighed 8·9lb without its magazine. Most prototypes were semi-automatic, though some were adapted experimentally to fire at 600rpm. Though optimistically advertised as part of a multi-weapon system, the Model 62 offered too little advancement over guns such as the FAL.

1963*: the upsurge of interest in small calibres and high velocity persuaded Cadillac Gage to revise the Model 62 for the ·223 Remington (5·56 × 45mm) round, work being entrusted to James Sullivan and Robert Fremont.

The Model 63, also seen as an integral part of a weapons system, was potentially excellent. It was heavier than the AR-15, but the long-

stroke gas-piston system avoided most of the fouling problems of the ArmaLite while retaining adequate power to lift an ammunition belt in the machine-gun derivatives.

The rifle and accompanying carbine presented a neat, if very conventional appearance; they had charging handles on a non-reciprocating slide. Wooden butts were fitted to the earliest guns, but later examples were synthetic.

1964: the Stoner multi-weapon project was licensed to Mauser–IWK AG, but transferred to Nederlansche Wapen- en Munitiefabriek 'de Kruithoorn' NV (a Mauser subsidiary) in 1965.

1967: US Army trials had revealed sufficient flaws for the 5·56mm Stoner guns to be upgraded to '63A' standards. An ejection-port cover was added, the magazine housing was extended, improvements were made in the gas system, and a reciprocating charging handle on the receiver-top doubled as a bolt closing device. The selector had only two positions, as a separate safety catch had been added. The folding butt of Stoner 63A carbines was normally a skeletal tube instead of the earlier synthetic pattern.

The perfected Model 63A Stoner carbine (XM23), rifle (XM22E1) and light machine-gun (XM207) were tested enthusiastically by the US Marine Corps. However, only the XM207E1 was ever classified as limited standard—for issue to Marine SEALs as the Mk 23 Mod. 0.

A-SQUARE

UNITED STATES OF AMERICA

The products of this company—semi-custom rifles and proprietary ammunition, including some powerful big-game cartridges—gained nationwide acceptance only in the late 1980s.

A-Square Rifle

Caesar and Hannibal patterns.
Made by A-Square Co., Inc, Bedford, Kentucky, 1983 to date.

Chambering: see notes.
Turning-bolt action, with two lugs on the bolt head engaging the receiver.
DATA FOR A TYPICAL HANNIBAL RIFLE
9·3 × 62mm, rimless.
About 45·50in overall, 9·42lb unladen.
26·00in barrel, 4-groove rifling; RH, concentric?
Integral box magazine, 5 rounds.
Express sight.
2,330 ft/sec with 285-grain bullet.

☆

1983: the Hannibal was a conventional bolt-action design, with a claw extractor and a staggered-row magazine. It had an adjustable target-type trigger and a manual safety catch on the bolt shroud. Most guns offered hand chequered oil-finished Claro walnut stocks, with the company's patented Coil-Chek recoil suppressor, a straight comb and a deep pistol grip with a notably tight radius; excellent bedding was achieved with a composite steel and fibreglass insert. Some synthetic stocks (apparently Du Pont Rynite) have also been made. Two sturdy bolts ran laterally through the stock to dissipate recoil effects. Three-leaf Express sights were fitted to order, but most guns exhibited sight bases.

As the guns have been made to order, barrel lengths (20–26in), stock details and finish may vary. In addition to proprietary A-Square Magnums (·338, ·375, ·460 Short, ·495 and ·500), the Hannibal has been offered in an awesome variety of production, semi-production and wildcat chamberings. These include 7mm Remington Magnum, ·30–06, ·375 H&H Magnum, ·378 Weatherby Magnum, ·404 Jeffrey, ·416 Rigby, ·425 Westley Richards Express, ·458 Winchester Magnum and ·470 Capstick. The largest guns weigh up to 11·75lb.

1984: the A-Square Caesar Model appeared, essentially similar to the Hannibal but slightly lighter and available only in a wood stock. Unlike the earlier guns, a left-hand version has been made in small numbers. Caesar rifles have not been offered with the company's proprietary magnum cartridges and are generally about 8oz lighter than comparable Hannibals.

AYDT

GERMANY

Aydt-Haenel, Aydt-Ideal and Aydt-Reform

This swinging-block action, unique to Europe, was patented by Carl Wilhelm Aydt in 1884. It was successful commercially, though not strong enough for high-pressure cartridges.

Its essence was a block, hollowed to contain the hammer, which pivoted under the barrel and was locked in place by a shoulder on the operating lever. When the lever was depressed, the mechanism unlocked and the block rotated down until its upper edge lay level with the base of the chamber. As the block reached the end of its travel, the extractor pulled the spent case from the chamber. Most Haenel-made guns had an external extractor on the side of the receiver, but others were internal. The hammer was held on the sear and cocked as the action closed.

Aydt-type guns will be found in great diversity, owing to a production life of fifty years and stocking/finishing of actions by gunsmiths throughout Germany. More research is needed before classification is practicable.

Set triggers and good-quality aperture sights were standard fittings, operating levers were plain or eleborately shaped, and the butts came in a wide range of shapes and styles. The most popular were the Schützen patterns, with high combs and adjustable hook-style butt plates.

Haenel-Aydt

Made by C.G. Haenel, Suhl, c.1885–1925.
Chambered for many European cartridges, with
8·15 × 46·5mm predominating.
Swinging-block action, operated by a lever.
DATA FOR A TYPICAL EXAMPLE.
8·15 × 46·5mm, rimmed.
1,195mm overall, 5·02kg unladen.
790mm barrel, 4-groove rifling; RH, concentric.
Aperture sight on rear tang.
550 m/sec with 9·8-gram bullet.

☆

1885*: the Haenel-made 'Original-Aydt' had an external extractor and, in most cases, a lever that locked the barrel in place. The entire action could be dismantled without tools. An elaborately looped operating lever/trigger guard simply sprung into place over a stud integral with the lower tang. The tang was retained by a small spring catch behind the lever-retaining stud. Double set triggers were regarded as essential fittings, instead of an optional extra. Barrels were usually octagonal, though round versions could be supplied and some special fluted examples are known; the half-length fore-end, often with a schnabel tip, was usually keyed to the barrel. The standard butt displayed a dished Tyrolean cheek piece, though Bavarian, Swiss and other regional variations were made to order. Elaborate engraving was popular, while an aperture sight on the tang often replaced the quadrant back sight on the barrel.

Aydt-Reform

Made by August Schüler, Suhl, c.1910–35.
Chambered for a variety of European cartridges.
Action: as Haenel-Aydt, above.
DATA FOR A TYPICAL EXAMPLE
6·5x27mm, rimmed.
1,142mm overall, 4·88kg unladen.
740mm barrel, 4-groove rifling; RH, concentric.
Aperture sight on rear tang.
475 m/sec with 5·3-gram bullet.

☆

1910*: this was an improved version of the Original-Aydt, with an internal extractor and a radial-lever locking catch on the lower tang behind the triggers. Apart from the changes in the action, the modified Aydt was similar to the 1884 pattern; most rifles were made for Schützen purposes, with elaborate operating levers, high-comb butts and ultra-sophisticated sights, but plainer sporters were also produced.

Other guns

A simpler version of the Aydt-Reform, known as the 'Aydt-Ideal' or simply 'Ideal', may also have been made by Schüler. The Original Zentrum—widely credited to 'Neumann', but of uncertain provenance—was built on a modified Martini action instead of an Aydt.

BALLARD

UNITED STATES OF AMERICA

This dropping-block action, patented by Charles Ballard in November 1861, was very successful in its post-Civil War sporting guise. The essence of the action was a breech block containing the hammer, trigger mechanism and springs. When the operating lever was pushed down, the front of the block—loosely pivoted in the rear of the receiver or frame—dropped radially down and away from the chamber, disengaging the back of the breech block from shoulders in the receiver behind the hammer.

The pre-1873 extractor bar, under the barrel, was actuated by a large stud projecting from the underside of the fore-end. The stud was slid backward manually. Most Ballards made by Marlin after 1875, however, had an automatic extractor controlled by the operating lever.

The rifles were made by Ball & Williams (1861–4) and R. Ball & Company (1864–6) of Worcester, Massachusetts, though a few had been made in 1862–3 by Dwight Chapin & Company of Bridgeport, Connecticut, under contract to Merwin & Bray. Postwar production passed to Merrimack Arms & Mfg Co. (1867–9) and thence to the Brown Mfg Co. (1869–73), both of Newburyport, Massachusetts.

1873: rights to the Ballard were acquired by Schoverling & Daly of New York.

1875: manufacture was licensed to John Marlin of New Haven, Connecticut. Marlin-made rifles show many detail improvements on pre-1873 examples, though the earliest often incorporated Brown-made parts. The butt was attached by a bolt running up through the wrist into the back of the receiver; an automatic extractor replaced the previous manually-operated pattern; and the breech block was made in two halves.

COLLECTOR'S COMPENDIUM

Aydt Two typical swinging-block rifles, from the 1911 sales catalogue of A.L. Frank ('ALFA') , Hamburg.

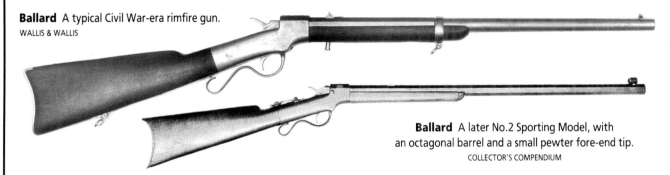

Ballard A typical Civil War-era rimfire gun.
WALLIS & WALLIS

Ballard A later No.2 Sporting Model, with
an octagonal barrel and a small pewter fore-end tip.
COLLECTOR'S COMPENDIUM

BALLARD
MARLIN-MADE PATTERNS, 1876–90, AND MODERN RE-CREATIONS

The original guns were made by John M. Marlin, New Haven, Connecticut (1879–81) or the Marlin Fire Arms Company, New Haven, Connecticut (1881–9). They shared the same dropping-block action; barrels were generally rifled with six concentric grooves twisting to the right.

MARLIN GUNS

No. 1 Hunter's Model Typically about 45·25in overall, weighing 8·05lb and fitted with a standing-block sight, this was introduced in 1876 in .44 rim- and centre-fire only, the first Marlin-made Ballard rifles were advertised with a round barrel (26–30in), a blued frame, a Marlin-patent automatic extractor, and a special reversible firing pin for rim- or centre-fire ammunition. The original rifle was renamed 'No.1' when additional patterns appeared, and a ·45–70 chambering was used in addition to ·44 Ballard Long and Extra-Long.

No. 1½ Hunter's Model Chambered for ·40–63 Ballard or ·45–70 Government cartridges, the 1879-vintage No. 1½ was a No. 1 with an extra-heavy wrought iron frame. A typical rifle was 47·30in overall, with a 32in round barrel, and weighed 10·07lb. A rifle-type butt plate and Rocky Mountain sights were standard. The No. 1½ lasted until 1883.

No. 1¾ Hunter's Model Introduced in 1879, for ·40–65 Ballard Everlasting or ·45–70 Government rounds only, this was a minor variant of the No. 1½ distinguished externally only by its double set trigger.

No. 2 Sporting Model Introduced in 1876 for ·32, ·38, ·41 or ·44 rim- and centre-fire cartridges, this had an octagonal barrel, a reversible firing pin, and a blued frame. A variant chambering '44 Colt and Winchester Center-Fire' chambering (·44–40 WCF) was added in 1882, but ·41 and ·44 Extra Long were abandoned. The ·32 version was sold with a 28in barrel, with which it weighed 8·25lb; ·38 patterns had 30in barrels and weighed about 8·75lb; ·44 examples, also generally made with 30in barrels, were about 45·25in overall and weighed 9lb unladen. Most had Rocky Mountain sights. The last guns were made about 1889.

No. 4 Perfection Model Dating from 1876, this—subsequently known as the 'Perfection'—was intended for hunting in ·38, ·40, ·44, ·45 and ·50 centre-fire, and usually had open Rocky Mountain sights.

So-called 'Everlasting Shells', specifically intended for reloading, were recommended for the No. 4. It had an octagonal barrel (26–32in) and an extra-heavy heavy case-hardened receiver.

¶ By 1881–2, guns had been chambered for the proprietary ·32–40, ·38–50, ·38–55, ·40–63, ·40–65, ·40–70 and ·44–75 Ballard cartridges, plus ·44–77 Sharps and ·45–70 or ·50–70 Government patterns. In 1883, however, Marlin had reduced the options to ·32–40, ·38–55 or ·40–63 only.

¶ A typical ·40–63 example, with a 30in round barrel, was about 45·35in overall and weighed 9·95lb unladen.

No. 4½ Mid-Range Model (4½ and 4½ A.1 patterns). Announced in 1878, No. 4½ had a pistol-grip butt and a half-length fore-end, woodwork being extensively chequered. The barrels were half- or fully octagonal, and an improved peep-and-globe sight system was fitted. A typical ·40–90 example was about 45·50in overall, had a 30in barrel and weighed 10·25lb. Chamberings included ·38–50 Ballard, ·40–70 Sharps, ·40–90 Ballard, ·40–90 Sharps, ·44–75 Ballard, ·44–77 Sharps, ·44–90 Sharps (2·63 and 2·88in cases) or ·44–100 Ballard, plus ·45–70 and ·50–70 Government.

¶ The No 4 A.1 rifle of 1879 was a minor variant with a fine English walnut half stock, Marlin's improved vernier back sight (graduated to 800 yards), and a wind-gauge front sight with bead and aperture discs. The frame was engraved, the optional shotgun- or rifle-type butt plate was rubber, and every part was 'finished in the best manner'. The frames usually displayed ᵐⁱᵈ-ᴿᵃⁿᵍᵉ ᴬ.1 in an engraved panel. Production continued into the mid 1880s.

No. 5 Pacific Model This 1876-vintage rifle was a modified No.4 (q.v.), with an extra-heavy iron frame, a heavy octagonal barrel (30–32in), double set triggers, and—unlike other Ballards—a cleaning rod beneath the muzzle. Rocky Mountain sights were standard.

¶ New ·40–85 and ·45–100 options were announced in 1882. Weights ranged from 10lb for the ·38–55 version to 12lb for the ·45–100 type. A typical 32in-barrelled ·45 example was 47·30in overall.

¶ Production continued until 1889, by which time rifles had been chambered for ·38–50 Ballard, ·38–55 Ballard, ·40–63 Ballard, ·40–65 Ballard, ·40–70 Sharps, ·40–90 Ballard, ·44–40 Winchester, ·44–75 Ballard, ·44–77 Sharps, ·45–70 Government or ·45–100 Ballard.

No. 5½ Montana Model Made only in 1882–3, this was essentially a heavier No. 5,

generally found with a ring-tip breech lever instead of the normal spur patterns and chambered for the ·45 Sharps cartridge (2·88in case). Rifle- or shotgun-style butt plates were supplied to order. A typical gun was 47·15in long, had a 30in barrel and weighed about 13·6lb.

No. 6 Schuetzen Model Known as the 'Off-Hand Model' when introduced in 1876, this was intended for European-style target shooting popular in the eastern USA. Originally chambered only for ·40–65 and ·44–75 cartridges, it had a half-octagonal barrel and weighed up to 15lb. A double set-trigger system was standard. Most guns were fitted with Marlin's short or mid-range vernier peep back sights, graduated to 800 yards. Hand-made straight-wrist 'German' (Swiss) style butts, with a cheek piece and a nickel plated hook-pattern shoulder plate, were standard fittings.

¶ By 1883, the chambering options—which had included ·32–40 Ballard, ·38–50 Ballard, ·38–55 Ballard, ·40–65 Ballard or ·44–75 Ballard—were restricted to ·32–40 or ·38–50. A typical ·38–50 example, with a 30in barrel, was 48·05in overall (including the butt-plate hook) and weighed 14·11lb.

No. 6½ Off Hand Model Also known as the 'No. 6½ Rigby', this was introduced in 1876. It was similar to the standard No. 6, but had a modified 'German'-pattern walnut butt with a chequered pistol grip and a Farrow shoulder plate. The barrels, measuring 28in or 30in, were bought from John Rigby & Company of London. Marlin mid-range (800-yard) vernier back sights were standard and a wind-gauge pattern front sight was fitted. The receivers of most rifles were engraved with scrollwork, though differences in pattern are known. A typical 28in-barrelled rifle measured 44·50in overall and weighed 10·12lb.

Long-Range Models (No. 7, No. 7 A.1, No. 7 A.1 Extra, No. 8 [old] and No. 9 [old] patterns). About 50·5in overall with a 34in barrel and a weight of 10·25lb, the 1876-vintage No. 7 Long-Range model—chambered only for the ·45–100 Ballard cartridge—had a half-octagon barrel and an improved vernier back sight graduated to 1,300 yards. The wind-gauge front sight was supplied with bead and aperture discs, plus a spirit level. Hand made pistol-grip butts were standard, with scroll engraving on the action, chequering on the pistol grip, and a schnabel-tipped fore-end.

¶ The No. 8 also had a pistol-grip butt, though much plainer; No. 9 was simply No. 8 with a straight-wrist butt. Production ended in about 1882.

¶ Announced in 1877 and made until 1880, No. 7 A.1 rifles were deluxe variants of the No.7, with Rigby barrels, special 'extra handsome English walnut stocks', rubber shoulder plates, and vernier sights of the finest pattern.

¶ Some No. 7 A.1 Extra rifles were made in 1879 with high-quality engraving and wood selected for its outstanding figuring. And finally, in 1885–6, a few rifles were assembled as the 'No. 7 Creedmoor Model'.

Union Hill Models (No. 8 [new] and No. 9 [new] patterns). Introduced in 1884, to compete in the medium-price target rifle market, these were offered with half-octagon barrels (28in or 30in), and pistol-grip butts with cheek pieces. A nickelled Farrow 'Off Hand' butt plate was usually supplied. Double set triggers and peep-and-globe sights were standard on the No. 8, the otherwise similar No. 9 being made with a single trigger. Looped finger levers were common on rifles sold after 1887. A typical gun with a 30in barrel, chambering the ·32–40 Ballard round, was 46·50in overall and weighed 9·65lb.

No. 10 Schuetzen Junior Model Offered only for the ·32–40 or ·38–55 Ballard cartridges, this 1884-vintage target rifle—often fitted with a short butt—was essentially the same as the No. 8 Union Hill pattern described previously. However, it was fitted with a heavy octagonal barrel and had a vernier-type Mid Range (800 yard) back sight. A typical ·32 example was 48·50in overall and weighed 11·85lb. Its barrel measured 32·00in.

MODERN GUNS

Red Willow models These re-creations of the Marlin-made Ballard were announced by the Red Willow Tool & Armory, Inc., of Stevensville, Montana, in 1992.

¶ All Red Willow guns chambered ·32–40 Winchester, ·38–55 Winchester, ·40–65 Winchester, ·40–70 Ballard, ·40–85 Ballard or ·45–70 cartridges, though others could be made to order. Options have included tang sights, set triggers, and selected woodwork.

¶ The Red Willow No. 1½ had a 30in barrel, an S-type lever and a single trigger.

¶ The Red Willow No. 5 Pacific rifle had a 30in octagonal barrel and a ring-pattern operating lever. A double trigger system was a standard fitting, and a typical rifle could weigh as much as 11·5lb.

¶ The Red Willow No. 8 rifle had a 30in half-octagonal barrel, and a double set trigger mechanism. The walnut butt had a cheek piece, a pistol grip, and a nickel-plated 'Off Hand' shoulder plate. It weighed 10lb.

The layout of the operating springs was changed, but not for the better: the original coil-pattern trigger spring was undoubtedly more reliable than the folded leaf pattern that replaced it.

1881: the Marlin Fire Arms Company was incorporated, Charles Daly of Schoverling, Daly & Gales becoming its president.

Note: the many differing patterns are listed in the accompanying panel (previous page). However, owing to its strength and availability, the Ballard action was used as the basis for many custom guns—prior to 1890, even Marlin made non-standard examples to order.

BARRETT

UNITED STATES OF AMERICA
✑

The original Light Fifty rifle was the subject of adverse comment from those who scoffed at its potential as a long-range sniper rifle. It was designed to strike 'compressor sections of jet engines or the transmissions of helicopters' and to 'destroy multi-million dollar aircraft with a single hit delivered to a vital area'.

Model 82A1

Also known as the 'Light Fifty'.
Made by the Barrett Firearms Manufacturing, Inc., Murfreesboro, Tennessee.
·50 Browning, rimless.
Gas-operated auto-loading action, locked by rotating lugs on the bolt into the barrel extension.
61·00in overall, 32·50lb unladen.
33·00in barrel, 4-groove rifling; RH, concentric?
Detachable box magazine, 11 rounds.
Optical sight.
2,910 ft/sec with M33 ball ammunition.
☆

1983: this huge rifle could not be confused with any other weapon. It had fashionable straight line construction with a skeletal butt, a bulky magazine, a fluted barrel with a muzzle brake, and a detachable bipod. The graticle of the 10 × optical sight was graduated for 500–1800 yards.

Model 90

Made by Barrett Firearms Manufacturing, Inc., Murfreesboro, Tennessee.
·50 Browning, rimless.
Turning-bolt action.
35·25in overall, 21·75lb unladen.
29·00in barrel, 4-groove rifling; RH, concentric?
Detachable box magazine, 5 rounds.
Optical sight.
About 2,750 ft/sec with M33 ball ammunition.

1990: this rifle offered a 'bull-pup' layout to reduce dimensions to an acceptable minimum while retaining the ·50 Browning machine-gun cartridge for optimal long-range performance. Recoil was still appreciable, the effect being lessened by an effectual muzzle brake and a sturdy shoulder pad. The Model 90 had a bipod with extending legs.

BEAUMONT

THE NETHERLANDS
✑

A turning-bolt mechanism developed by a well-established gunmaker, Beaumont of Maastricht, this was inspired by the Chassepot needle rifle. Principal among its unique features was the position of the striker spring, a V-type leaf being inserted in the hollow two-piece bolt handle instead of a conventional coil pattern in the annular space between the striker body and the inner surface of the bolt. The action was simple, with a separate bolt head retained by a screw through the rib. The extractor lay beneath the bolt head when the action was open, but no ejector was fitted.

Rigorous use showed the Beaumont rifle to be more fragile than many of its rivals, though an experimental Chassepot conversion pressed Gras prototypes hard in the French trials of 1873–4.

1869: the Beaumont was developed to replace Dutch Snider conversions. The strange striker-spring assembly was an Achilles heel. Not only was it more prone to breaking than the coil

patterns, but it also prevented development of Beaumont-type carbines with turned-down bolt handles. Articulated springs were not durable enough, so Remingtons were purchased instead.

Models 1871 and 1871–88

Infantry rifles: Infanterij-Geweer M1871 en M1871–88.
Made by Frans Beaumont, Maastricht.
11 × 50mm, rimmed.
Turning-bolt action, locked by the bolt-guide rib abutting the receiver bridge.
DATA FOR M1871
1,320mm overall, 4·38kg unladen.
830mm barrel, 4-groove rifling; RH, concentric.
Quadrant sight graduated to 1,100 paces.
405 m/sec with M1871 ball cartridges.
M1871 socket bayonet.
☆

1871: the basic Beaumont rifle was somewhat like the Chassepot or Gras rifles externally. However, it had a distinctive back sight, a safety button on the right side of the receiver bridge, and a concave rear face to the trigger guard (French designs were oval). Mounts comprised a single barrel band and a nose cap, swivels being fitted beneath the band and butt.

1876*: the safety system, which had originally locked the bolt in the half-rotated position, was finally abandoned.

1879: back sights were fitted with a new leaf graduated to 1,300 metres for the M1878 (Haarsveldt) cartridge, with a muzzle velocity of about 435 m/sec. Claims have been made that the cartridge case was lengthened by 2mm, but the evidence is contradictory. However, it does seem that the diameter of the bullet was reduced slightly to promote better performance in the existing barrels.

1888: the adaption of surviving rifles for the Italian-designed Vitali box magazine began. The work involved cutting away the lower part of the feed way to accept a case containing four rounds. The magazine follower was propelled by a coil spring around a guide-rod, the protruding housing for which gave the Vitali magazine its distinctive shape.

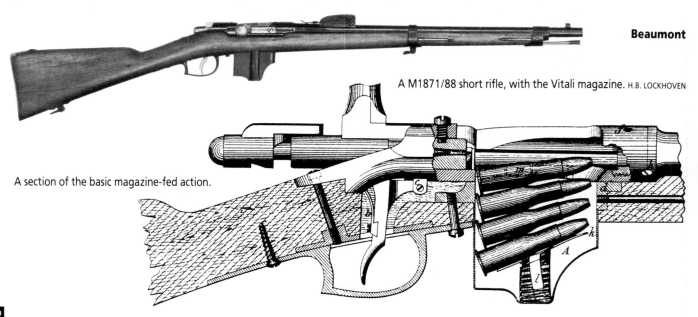

Beaumont

A M1871/88 short rifle, with the Vitali magazine. H.B. LOCKHOVEN

A section of the basic magazine-fed action.

1897: most surviving M1871–88 rifles were replaced in front-line service by the M1895 Mannlicher, though substantial numbers were still being held in reserve in 1914.

Sporting guns

Few sporters embody the Beaumont action, though some were doubtless made in the Netherlands toward the end of the nineteenth century. However, many obsolete rifles were converted into 20-bore shotguns prior to 1914.

BERDAN

UNITED STATES OF AMERICA

These guns were designed by General Hiram Berdan, who had achieved lasting fame in the American Civil War as the instigator of the Federal sharpshooters regiments.

1. THE BLOCK-ACTION PATTERNS

This breech system—similar to many of the breech-loading transformations made in the mid 1860s—was patented in the USA in February 1866. Its use was confined largely to Spain.

Berdan also developed an action relying on a straight-line striker instead of a clumsy external hammer; this was the subject of a US Patent granted in March 1869. Drawing back the striker allowed the breech block to be raised, extracting a spent case and gaining access to the chamber. A cartridge was then inserted, the

breech was shut and the gun could be fired; the mechanism was locked at the moment of discharge by the striker-nose running forward into the back of the breech block.

The individual guns, principally Spanish rifle-musket conversions are listed in relevant sections of Part Two. Though many served in Spain throughout the Carlist War period, the advent of the Remington Rolling Blocks rapidly rendered them obsolescent. Most survivors had disappeared into store by the late 1870s.

2. THE BOLT-ACTION PATTERNS

Patented in the USA in November 1870, this rifle served only in Russia and Bulgaria.

It was a straightforward design of no great originality, derived from the old Dreyse and Chassepot needle rifles. It had a sturdy split-bridge receiver and a short bolt body with a massive rib doubling as a locking shoulder. The most unusual feature was the cocking piece, prevented from rotating by a 'finger' projecting forward into the receiver.

A spring-loaded striker ran through the centre of the bolt to ignite the cartridge; an extractor was mounted in the guide rib; and—on the patent at least—the ejector lay in the bottom of the receiver beneath the bolt way. Some Russian-made rifles lacked the ejector, relying on the firer tipping spent cases out of the receiver.

BULGARIA

The Russian-pattern Berdan infantry rifle and cavalry carbine were apparently adopted by

the newly autonomous Bulgarian army as the 'M1880', serving until the adoption of the Austro-Hungarian Mannlicher. They were identical with Russian issue, but bore the 'crown A' cypher of Alexander I.

RUSSIA

1871: at the time of its adoption, the Berdan II bolt-action rifle was among the most powerful of all those being issued in European armies, the flatness of its trajectory causing worries in British and French ordnance circles in particular. However, production was slow; the Russians did not managed to re-equip even front-line infantrymen until the mid 1870s.

1914: on 1 July, the Berdan inventory still stood at 362,400 7·62mm and 10·67mm rifles plus a small number of 7·62mm carbines.

Model 1870

Infantry rifle: Pekhotniya vintovka Berdana, obr.1870g.
Made by the Birmingham Small Arms Co. Ltd, Small Heath, 1870–3 (30,000 only); and the Imperial arsenals in Tula and Izhevsk, c.1874–92.
Quantity: in excess of one million.
10·67 × 58mm, rimmed.
Turning-bolt action, locked by the bolt-handle rib abutting the receiver bridge.
1,355mm overall, 4·43kg unladen.
833mm barrel, 6-groove rifling; RH, concentric.
Ramp-and-leaf sight graduated to 1,500 arshin.
437 m/sec with obr.1870 ball cartridges.
Obr.1871g socket bayonet.
☆

1869: trials were completed with prototypes supplied from the USA. An order for 300,000

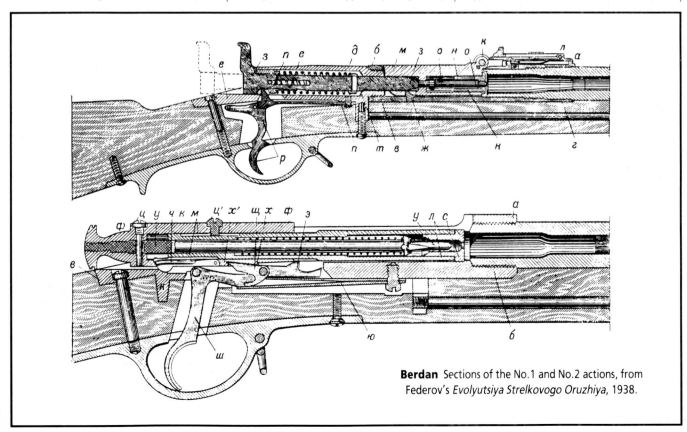

Berdan Sections of the No.1 and No.2 actions, from Federov's *Evolyutsiya Strelkovogo Oruzhiya*, 1938.

was placed with BSA on 24 October, delivery of 30,000 being requested by 1 February 1871.

1870: a hundred guns were supplied for trials.

1871: the authorities adopted the fourth-pattern experimental rifle on 1 February, approval of the bayonet following on 4 March. A decision was also taken to begin production in the Tula factory, machinery subsequently being ordered from Greenwood & Batley of Leeds. A few guns were made in Leeds to test the production line; these guns were then used for trials in Britain, France and elsewhere.

1874: production finally began in the Tula factory. Izhevsk began production about 1878. The standard rifle had two screw-clamping bands and a conventional trigger guard. The back sight had graduations for 200–500 arshin on the ramp and 600–1,500 on the leaf, which hinged at the front of the sight bed. Marks in Cyrillic lay on the barrel-top.

1877: some guns were fitted with a Krnka quick-loader, a ten-round canvas cartridge-box strapped to a plate on the left side of the fore-end ahead of the chamber.

1881: Russian authorities experimented with quick-loaders and magazine attachments for the Berdan. The six-round Lutkovskiy magazine, which hung on the left side of the breech, achieved limited service status—at least for extended troop trials—and several hundred guns may have been converted to the idiosyncratic Schulhof butt-magazine system for trials in the mid 1880s.

Model 1870

••
Cavalry and artillery carbine: Karabina Berdana, obr.1870g.
Made by the Imperial arsenal, Tula, c.1874–5.
10·67 × 58mm, rimmed.
Action: as M1870 rifle, above.
965mm overall, 2·80kg unladen.
475mm barrel, 6-groove rifling; RH, concentric.
Ramp-and-leaf sight graduated to 1,000 arshin?
362 m/sec with obr.1870 ball cartridges.
No bayonet.
☆

1875: little more than a shortened version of the infantry rifle with a single barrel band and a fore-end running almost to the muzzle, this does not seem to have been made in great numbers and is rarely encountered. It may have been confined to field trials and has not been widely recognised as a regulation pattern.

Model 1870

••
Dragoon rifle: Dragunskaya vintovka Berdana, obr.1870g.
Made by the Imperial arsenals in Tula and Izhevsk, 1875–92.
10·67 × 58mm, rimmed.
Action: as M1870 rifle, above.
1,237mm overall, 3·58kg unladen.
720mm barrel, 6-groove rifling; RH, concentric.
Ramp-and-leaf sight graduated to 1,400 arshin.
385 m/sec with obr.1870 ball cartridges.
No bayonet.
☆

1875: this modified version of the infantry rifle had a plain stock and sling-slots instead of swivels. The two slender bands were retained by springs. An auxiliary dismantling screw on the left side of the receiver mated with a groove cut into the left side of the bolt.

Model 1870

••
Cossack rifle: Kazachya vintovka Berdana, obr.1870g.
Details generally as dragoon rifle, above, excepting dimensions (1,219mm overall, 3·38kg unladen).
☆

1875: adopted at the same time as the dragoon rifle, this was easily distinguished by the absence of a trigger guard. Instead, there was a small reeded-drum or 'ball' trigger with a slotted underside. Three barrel bands were fitted, two being retained by friction and the other (nearest the muzzle) by a spring. Sling slots were cut through the butt and fore-end and the cleaning rod was carried almost completely internally. The back sight was set back on the barrel top to abut the receiver.

Note: several cossack rifles have been reported with barrels and overall lengths approximately 20mm greater than given by the Russian official figures in the data table. The discrepancies have yet to be resolved.

Three Line Model

••
Infantry rifle and carbine: Drelineinaya Pekhotniya vintovka i karabina Berdana.
Conversion was apparently undertaken in Liége.
7·62 × 54mm, rimmed.
Turning-bolt action, with two locking lugs on the bolt head and additional safety provided by the base of the bolt-handle rib abutting the receiver bridge.
DATA FOR RIFLE
1,322mm overall, 4·23kg unladen.
802mm barrel, 4-groove rifling; RH, concentric.
Ramp-and-leaf sight graduated to 2,700 arshin.
605 m/sec with obr.1891g ball cartridges.
Altered obr.1870 socket bayonet.
☆

1895*: approval for conversion of serviceable 10·67mm Berdan rifles to accept standard obr.1891 cartridges was apparently given. The work was entrusted to contractors in Liége; the rifles generally displayed Belgian proof marks, but rarely gave clues to the contractor. Auguste Francotte & Cie, Em. & L. Nagant and Anciens Établissements Pieper have all been suggested. More than 200,000 may have been altered.

Apparently confined to the infantry rifle and cavalry carbine, the changes were made by fitting a new barrel, greatly strengthened in the chamber area; milling a new locking-lug recess and raceway in the bottom of the receiver; and substituting a new bolt head with twin locking lugs to withstand the additional pressure. An obr.1891g back sight was fitted.

1905*: though conversion of Berdan-type rifles had been undertaken in the 1890s, some time elapsed before carbines were treated similarly— and then only as an expedient while the Mosin-Nagant magazine pattern was being perfected. The work is believed to have been undertaken in Tula, necessitating a new barrel and alterations to the bolt-head and receiver floor.

Berdan The Russian No.2 infantry rifle. PATTERN ROOM COLLECTION

Beretta A 5·56mm AR-70 rifle, c.1972. ARMI PIETRO BERETTA SPA

BERETTA

ITALY

Some guns were also known as
'Marengoni-Beretta'

The company's guns have all been gas-operated, and all but the Model 57 have relied on rotating-bolt locks. In spite of the efforts of Tullio Marengoni, little success was encountered prior to 1945; since the Second World War, however, far greater success has been achieved.

The BM-59, an adaption of the popular US ·30 M1 Garand, has been made in such vast numbers that many export orders were fulfilled in the 1960s. The Garand-based rifles were supplemented by the 5·56mm AR-70 and then, after protracted trials, replaced by the perfected AR-70/90 assault rifle in the mid 1980s.

1. THE AUTO-LOADING PATTERNS

NB: the BM-59 is covered in the Garand section.

MILITARY WEAPONS

ITALY

Model 1957

Also known as 'P-30'.
Made by Pietro Beretta SpA, Gardone Val Trompia (Brescia), 1957–62.
·30 M1 Carbine, rimless.
Gas-operated auto-loading action, locked by tilting the bolt downward into the receiver.
942mm overall, 2·95kg without magazine.
455mm barrel, 4-groove rifling; RH, concentric.
Detachable box magazine, 30 rounds.
Pivoting-'L' sight for 150 and 300 metres.
600 m/sec with ball cartridges; 500 ± 30 rpm.
US M4 knife bayonet.
☆

1955*: designed by Tullio Marengoni, this was inspired by the M1, M1A1 and M2 Carbines supplied to Italy by the US Government.
1958: the Mo.1957 carbine was introduced. Its action relied on a tilting-block lock adapted from the Soviet Tokarev; excepting the cocking handle and bolt carrier, no visible parts moved during the firing cycle. The carbine was usually supplied with a pistol-grip stock, with flutes in the fore-end and ventilating holes in the hand guard. However, folding-butt examples with a separate pistol grip were available to order, and a sheet-metal hand guard was often fitted. The most distinctive feature was the double-trigger system, the rear lever permitting fully automatic fire by disengaging the auxiliary sear.

Model 70

Fucile d'Assalto AR-70, SC-70 e SC-70 Versione Corta.
Made by Pietro Beretta SpA, Gardone Val Trompia (Brescia), 1970–83.
5·56 × 45mm, rimless.
Gas-operated auto-loading action, locked by rotating two lugs on the bolt into the receiver.
DATA FOR A PRE-1975 AR-70
990mm overall, 3·43kg without magazine.
450mm barrel, 4-groove rifling; RH, concentric.
Detachable box magazine, 30 rounds.
Tangent-leaf sight graduated to 500 metres.
930 m/sec with ball cartridges; 625 ± 25 rpm.
Optional knife bayonet.
☆

1970: announced after a lengthy development programme dating back to 1965, this presented a conventional appearance even though its receiver was made largely of pressings. The earliest AR-70 and its folding-butt derivative, the SC-70, had a ribbed synthetic fore-end. The pistol grip was originally chequered wood, but was soon changed to a synthetic pattern matching the fore-end.

The rotary selector lay above the pistol grip on the left side of the receiver (up for automatic fire, back for single shots, down to lock the trigger), the cocking handle was on the right, and conventional sights were accompanied by

folding grenade-launching patterns. Sling loops lay on the left side of the gas-port block and on the left side of the butt.

AR-70 and SC-70 rifles accepted optical or image-intensifying sights, and could fire grenades from a NATO-standard launcher. A bipod and carrying handle transformed them into light support weapons, and an American-style knife bayonet could be fitted when required.

1974: an ultra-short SC-70—'versione corta'—appeared. It measured 820mm overall with the stock extended (598mm when folded), had a 320mm barrel and weighed 3·21kg without the magazine. Grenade-launching sights and the muzzle-sleeve were omitted.

1983: substantial quantities of Beretta rifles had been purchased by the Italian airforce, and special counter-terrorist units such as the Nuclei Operativi Centrali di Sicurezza or Gruppi per Interventi Speciali. The perfected versions of the AR-70 and its derivatives offered a great many alterations in detail when compared with the earliest guns. The most obvious were the strengthened folding stock and the replacement of the original ribbed hand guard by a fluted pattern with ventilation slots. However, field trials and active paramilitary service showed that improvements could still be made.

Model 70-90

Fucile d'Assalto AR-70/90, SC-70/90 e SCS-70/90.
Made by P. Beretta SpA, Gardone Val Trompia (Brescia), 1985 to date.
5·56 × 45mm, rimless.
Action: as Mo.70, above.
DATA FOR A 1988-VINTAGE AR-70/90
995mm overall, 3·94kg without magazine.
450mm barrel, 6-groove rifling; RH, concentric.
Detachable box magazine, 30 rounds.
Tangent-leaf sight graduated to 500 metres.
930 m/sec with ball cartridges; 625 ± 25 rpm.
Optional knife bayonet.
☆

1983: rigorous service trials revealed minor flaws in the AR-70 and a light machine-gun derivative designated 'Mo.70/78'.

Beretta A 5·56mm SC-70 rifle, c.1983. ARMI PIETRO BERETTA SPA

Beretta A 5·56mm AR-70/90 rifle, 1992. ARMI PIETRO BERETTA SPA

1984: work began to revise the design so that guns could participate in Italian army trials.

1985: the first AR-70/90 rifles appeared. The major change was internal. The bolt of the AR-70 had reciprocated on rails pressed into the receiver; this method was not strong enough to satisfy the army, so hardened steel rails were inserted in the AR-70/90 frame.

The new straight-line layout was achieved by raising the heel of the butt, and a detachable carrying handle lay on top of the receiver. An ambidexterous selector/safety catch unit was fitted, while changes were made to the receiver and pistol grip. Bipods could be removed at will. Short-barrelled SCS-70/90 and SCP-70/90 had a folding butt, but the latter ('Tipo Paracudisti') would accept a grenade launcher and had a folding sight on the gas-port block.

1990: the Beretta rifle was finally selected to replace the 7·62mm BM-59 in Italian service.

MOROCCO

The Model 57 carbine was initially purchased from Beretta, with a licence to make guns in the government factory in Fez (Manufacture d'Armes de l'État de Fès). Moroccan-made guns seem to date from 1960-5, but the quantites involved were small.

OTHERS

5·56mm Beretta rifles, in varying guises, have been supplied in quantity to—among others—the forces of Jordan and Malaysia.

2. THE BOLT-ACTION PATTERNS

Model 500

• •
500, 500DL, 500S, 501, 501DL, 501S, 501 Sniper, 502, 502DL and 502S patterns.
Made by Pietro Beretta SpA, Gardone Val Trompia, 1984 to date.

Chambering: see notes.
Turning-bolt action, with two locking lugs rotating into the receiver wall.
DATA FOR A TYPICAL MODELLO 501
·243 Winchester, rimless.
About 1,095mm overall, 3.25kg unladen.
600mm barrel, 4-groove rifling; RH, concentric?
Internal box magazine, 5 rounds.
Open ramp sight.
1,020 m/sec with 5·2-gram bullet.
☆

1984: Beretta's bolt-action rifle was basically a Mauser. The extractor was a small claw let into the side of the bolt head; the plunger-type ejector was mounted in the recessed bolt face. The perfected post-1985 patterns—500, 501 and 502—had short, medium and long actions respectively. Chamberings have included ·222 or ·223 Remington (Modello 500); ·243 or ·308 Winchester (Modello 501); and ·270 Winchester, 7mm Remington Magnum, ·30–06 or ·375 H&H Magnum (Modello 502). Barrels measured 600mm or 620mm.

The standard rifles had a half-stock with a Monte Carlo comb, a North American-style cheek piece and a plain rounded fore-end tip; 'S'-patterns had a full-length Mannlicher stock and a short barrel. Custom Grade (DL) guns had a high-quality walnut half-stock with a low hog's back comb, a small oval cheek piece, a ventilated rubber butt plate, chequering on the pistol grip and fore-end. A schnabel tip was used.

1985: a sniper rifle appeared in 7·52 × 51mm NATO (·308 Winchester). It had a heavy barrel with a conical muzzle brake/flash-suppressor and an adjustable bipod attached to a bar projecting from the fore-end. A detachable box magazine was fitted, and the special thumb-hole stock had a removable cheek piece/comb unit.

BERTHIER

FRANCE
↭

This bolt-action system, unique to France at first, was also supplied to Russia and Greece during the First World War. Berthier weapons were used by the Kingdom of Serbs, Croats and Slovenes (later Yugoslavia) in the early 1920s; and also, more recently, throughout what was once the French colonial empire.

The Berthier action was a modified Lebel (q.v.), with the locking axis changed from horizontal to vertical and the substitution of a clip-loaded magazine for the fore-end tube. Though elegant and quite popular in France, the Berthier action was awkward, and a gap between the bolt and the right side of the magazine above the receiver allowed dirt to enter. Rigorous service during the First World War soon revealed the weakness of the slender rifle stock, and also that accuracy was generally inferior to that of the Lebel. Consequently, small numbers of the sturdier and more durable Mle.86/93 rifles were retained after 1918 for grenade-launching and sniping.

1887: attempts were being made to provide a suitable cavalry carbine when news reached the authorities of Adolphe Berthier's adaption of the Mle.86 (Lebel) action to accept an Austrian Mannlicher-style magazine. Approval to build a prototype Berthier rifle was withheld until May 1888, while the military experimented with Lebel-type guns. When these failed, about ten 8mm Berthier infantry rifles (see Part Two) were made by Ateliers de Puteaux. Trials held at Mont-Valérien soon showed the superiority of the Berthier over the Lebel in rapid fire.

1889: the first artillery musketoons and cavalry carbines were made for trials.

1890: trials began on 28 February with ten new Puteaux-made vertical-locking Berthiers and ten lightened Lebel short rifles—promoted by the École Normale de Tir—which were no more than a shortened Mle.86 with the magazine capacity reduced to six rounds.

Model 1890

• •
Carabines de Cavallerie, Mle.1890, Mle.90 T.15 et Mle.90 T.27.
Made by Manufacture d'Armes, Saint-Étienne, 1890-4.
8 × 51mm, rimmed.

Beretta A Model 501 sniper rifle.
ARMI PIETRO BERETTA SPA

Beretta An SCP-70/90 ('Tipo Paracudisti') carbine, 1992.
ARMI PIETRO BERETTA SPA

Turning-bolt action, with two lugs on the detachable bolt head locking into the receiver.
945mm overall, 3·02kg unladen.
453mm barrel, 4-groove rifling; LH, concentric.
Clip-loaded internal box magazine, 3 rounds.
Ramp-and-leaf sight graduated to 2,000 metres.
637 m/sec with Balle 1886 D.
No bayonet (see notes).

☆

1890: adopted in March and eventually issued to dragoons, hussars and mounted riflemen (Chasseurs)—together with colonial cavalrymen (Spahis)—this was a minor revision of the experimental 'Numéro 2.bis' trials gun. The original carbines had a conventional stock, a loose sling ring on the left side of the barrel band, and a swivel on the under edge of the butt. They were sighted for the Balle 1886 M, leaves being graduated to 1,800 metres with a 2,000-metre notch on the top edge.
1901: sights were revised for the Balle 1886 D, the 2,000-metre setting being moved to the body of the leaf.
1904: a sling bar appeared on the left side of the butt, with a fixed ring on the barrel band. These guns were sighted for Balles 1886 D.
1915: the 'Mle.90 T.15' was adapted to accept a standard Mle.92 sword bayonet, the modified nose cap being moved back far enough to admit the bayonet hilt beneath the muzzle. Sights were graduated for the Balle 1886 D.
1927: the 'Mle.90 T.27' had a modified nose cap with a rudimentary piling hook, and the clearing-rod channel on the left side of the fore-end was filled with a fillet of wood.

Model 1890

Carabines de Cuirassiers, Mle.1890 et Mle.90 T.15.
Made by Manufacture d'Armes, Saint-Étienne, 1890–4.
8 × 51mm, rimmed.
Otherwise as Mle.1890 cavalry carbine excepting weight (about 2·98kg unladen).

☆

1890: sharing the standard Mle.90 action, this carbine was introduced for the heavy cavalry. Its extraordinary stock had a quirky combless butt

suited to firers wearing a steel breast-plate. A leather butt plate replaced the cast-iron pattern, and sights were graduated for the original Balle 1886 M.
1901: sights were adapted for the Balle 1886 D, though still graduated to 2,000 metres.
1915: some guns were adapted for the standard Mle.92 sword bayonet, a new nose cap being moved back to receive the hilt.

Model 1890

Carabine de Gendarmerie, Mle.1890.
Made by Manufacture d'Armes, Saint-Étienne, 1890–4.
8 × 51mm, rimmed.
Otherwise as Mle.1890 cavalry carbine, excepting weight (3.10kg unladen) and bayonet (Mle.90 épée pattern).

☆

1890: similar to the cavalry carbine, this had a nose cap with a protruding stud to enter the pommel of the bayonet. Guns were originally sighted to 2,000 metres for the Balle 1886 M.
1901: sights were revised for the Balle 1886 D.

Model 1892

Artillery musketoons: Mousquetons d'Artillerie, Mle.1890 et Mle.92 T.27.
Made by Manufacture d'Armes, Saint-Étienne, 1892–1916.
8 × 51mm, rimmed.
Otherwise generally as Mle.1890, excepting bayonet (Mle.92 sword pattern).

☆

1892: adopted for issue to the artillery and, eventually, to the customs service, the Mle.92 musketoon was a derivative of the 1890-pattern cavalry carbine with the nose cap and barrel adapted for a different bayonet. A cleaning rod was carried in a channel hollowed out of the left side of the fore-end. A sling ring was fixed to the left side of the barrel band, and a barred sling indentation appeared in the left side of the butt.
1927: cleaning rods were removed from the 'Mle.92 T.27'. The cleaning-rod channel was filled with a glued-in wooden fillet, sanded

smooth and refinished. Despite the care with which the alterations were made, however, the line of the original channel was usually clearly discernible.

Model 1902

Colonial rifle: Fusil Mle.1902.
Made by Manufacture d'Armes, Saint-Étienne, 1902–14.
8 × 51mm, rimmed.
Turning-bolt action, with two lugs on the detachable bolt head locking into the receiver.
1,126mm overall, 3·62kg unladen.
633mm barrel, 4-groove rifling; LH, concentric.
Clip-loaded internal box magazine, 3 rounds.
Ramp-and-leaf sight graduated to 2,000 metres.
693 m/sec with Balle 1886 D.
Mle.02 épée bayonet.

☆

1902: this was introduced to arm colonial troops in Annam, Cambodia and Tonkin in French Indo-China—and, therefore, is often known as 'de Tirailleurs Indo-Chinois'. Lighter, handier and more effectual than the standard Mle.86 Lebel, it was the first Berthier rifle to be issued in the French services.
The action was essentially that of the Mle.90 cavalry carbine, but the rifle's life was short owing to the introduction of the Mle.07/15. Original guns were sighted for the Balle 1886 M, to expend existing supplies of ammunition. The back sight had a standing block for 250 metres, ramps for 400–800, and a folding leaf for 900–1,900. The 2,000 metre setting was a small V-notch in the top edge of the leaf body. Bolt handles were bent downward.
1909: the sights were changed for the Balle 1886 D. The original sight was retained, but the leaf was graduated to 2,400 metres and the sighting notch was deepened appreciably. Some sights were newly made—their bases are generally marked **N**—but many others were simply altered from the original pattern.
1937: a few surviving rifles were converted in the Saint-Étienne factory for 7·5mm rimless ammunition (see 'M1902/37').

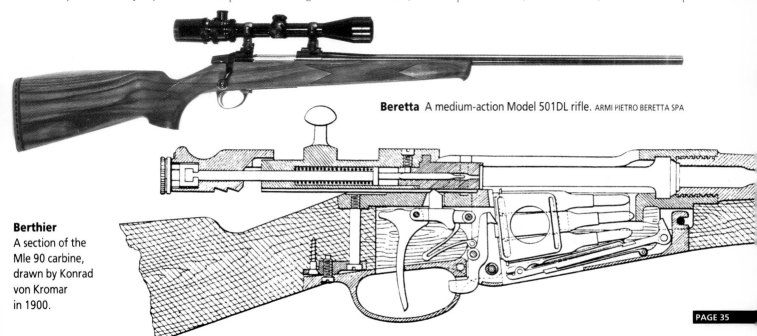

Beretta A medium-action Model 501DL rifle. ARMI PIETRO BERETTA SPA

Berthier
A section of the Mle 90 carbine, drawn by Konrad von Kromar in 1900.

Model 1907

Colonial rifle: Fusil Mle.1907.
Made by Manufacture d'Armes, Saint-Étienne,
1907–14.
8 × 51mm, rimmed.
Action: as Mle.1902, above.
1,306mm overall, 3·82kg unladen.
803mm barrel, 4-groove rifling; LH, concentric.
Clip-loaded internal box magazine, 3 rounds.
Ramp-and-leaf sight graduated to 2,000 metres.
701 m/sec with Balle 1886 D.
Mle.07 épée bayonet.

☆

1907: the success of the Mle.02 rifle, which was ideally suited to the small stature of the French colonial units raised in the Far East, persuaded the authorities to issue a modified full-size gun to the Senegalese sharpshooters (Tirailleurs Sénégalais). The Mle.07 lacked a cleaning rod, as the relevant equipment was carried separately. Sights were initially graduated to 2,000 metres for the Balle 1886 M, and the bolt handle was bent downward.

1910: sights were altered to 2,400 metres for the Balle 1886 D.

Model 1907/15

Infantry rifles: Fusils d'Infanterie, Mle.1907/15 et
Mle.07/15 T.16.
Made by Manufactures d'Armes, Châtellerault,
Saint-Étienne and Tulle, 1915–17; Manufacture
d'Armes de Paris, 1915–18 (components only);
Établissements Contin-Souza, Paris, 1915–18; Société
Française Delaunay-Belleville, 1915–18; and the
Remington Arms–Union Metallic Cartridge Company,
Ilion, New York, 1915–16 (9,440 only).
8 × 51mm, rimmed.
Action: as Mle.1902 rifle, above.
1,306mm overall, 3·81kg unladen.
803mm barrel, 4-groove rifling; LH, concentric.
Clip-loaded internal box magazine, 3 rounds.
Ramp-and-leaf graduated to 2,000 metres.
701 m/sec with Balle 1886 D.
Mle.15 épée bayonet.

☆

1915: the opening stages of the First World War soon showed the weaknesses of the Mle.86 Lebel rifle; the French were aware of them, but parsimony had prevented the introduction of a superior Berthier prior to 1914. Lengthening the Mle.92 artillery musketoon to infantry rifle proportions, even though the three-round clip was retained, bought time while a modified rifle was developed. The Mle.07/15 rifle was essentially similar to the 1907 colonial pattern (above), excepting for its straight bolt handle and a cleaning rod in the left side of the fore-end.

Fitted with the standard internal three-round clip-loaded magazine, Mle.07/15 guns fed from the Chargeur Mle.90 and were sighted to 2,400 metres for the Balle 1886 D. They were issued to some of the infantry units raised in 1916–18.

1917: small numbers of 'Mle.07/15 T.16' rifles were modified to accept the five-round Mle.16 clip. Though sheet metal magazine cases protruded beneath the stock, guns lacked the hand guard of the true Mle.16—and bore markings such as ST.-ETIENNE MLE.1907–15 on the left side of the receiver.

1934: the conversion of surviving rifles for the 7.5mm Balle 1929 C was approved (see 'Mle.07/15 M.34').

Model 1916

Infantry rifle: Fusil d'Infanterie, Mle.1916.
Manufacturers: generally as Mle.1907/15 (q.v.),
excepting Remington–UMC.
Quantity: 1.5 million?
8 × 51mm, rimmed.
Action: as Mle.1902 rifle, above.
1,306mm overall, 4·19kg unladen.
803mm barrel, 4-groove rifling; LH, concentric.
Clip-loaded box magazine, 5 rounds.
Ramp-and-leaf sight graduated to 2,400 metres.
701 m/sec with Balle 1886 D.
Mle.15 épée bayonet.

☆

1916: issued to many of the regiments raised in 1917–18, this was little more than an adaption of the Mle.07/15 to accept a five-round clip. The opportunity was also taken to provide a hinged cover for the spent-clip aperture, though the firer had to pull the cover downward when the gun was being used unless he wanted the spent clip to remain in the magazine. Guns were sighted to 2,400 metres for the Balle 1886 D and had a hand guard running from the receiver ring under the barrel band.

1920: the sight line was raised above the hand guard, necessitating replacement of the sight base, and a slider with a square notch replaced the original 'V'-type. New sights display A on their components.

1932: the adaption of guns for the Balle 1932 N was approved, necessitating changes in sights and chambering, though much of the work appears to have been delayed until 1945 or later. By 1939, the Mle.16 served much of the French army. It was also to be found on colonial service.

Model 1892–16

Mousquetons d'Artillerie, Mle.1892 M.16 et
Mle.92/16 T.27.
Manufacturer: generally as Mle.1916 rifle (q.v.).
8 × 51mm, rimmed.
Action: as Mle.1902 rifle, above.
945mm overall, 3·25kg unladen.
453mm barrel, 4-groove rifling; LH, concentric.
Clip-loaded box magazine, 5 rounds.
Ramp-and-leaf sight graduated to 2,000 metres.
637 m/sec with Balle 1886 D.
Mle.92 sword bayonet.

☆

1916: introduced to equip artillerymen and mounted troops, the ''Mousqueton d'Artillerie Mle.92 Modifié 1916'' served motorised and armoured units, infantry machine-gunners and some colonial units by 1939. It was retained by the gendarmerie, customs service and prison guards into the 1960s. Basically a newly-made variation of the Mle.92, with the magazine deepened to accept the Mle.16 clip, the gun had the sling ring fixed to the left side of the barrel band and a barred sling aperture cut into the left side of the butt. The earliest examples were made without the hand guard that was soon added above the barrel, and a clearing rod was

Berthier Pictured during the First World War, this French Hotchkiss machine-gun crew is accompanied by Britons with Lee-Enfields and Frenchmen carrying Mle 92 musketoons.

channelled into the left side of the fore-end. Sights were graduated to 2,000 metres for the Balle 1886 D.

1920: the sight line was raised, and the sight-block was given a deep squared notch instead of the original 'V'. New parts were marked A.

1927: the 'Mle.92/16 T.27' gained a stacking rod on the nose cap, and the rod channel was filled with a wooden fillet.

1932: the first batches of musketoons were re-sighted and re-chambered for the Balle 1932 N, though most of the work may have been undertaken after 1945.

Model 1907–15–34

Fusils d'Infanterie et de Cavallerie, Mle.07/15 M.34.
Made by Manufacture d'Armes, Saint-Étienne, 1934-9.
7·5 × 54mm, rimless.
Turning-bolt action, with two lugs on the detachable bolt head locking into the receiver.
1,080mm overall, 3·68kg unladen.
580mm barrel, 4-groove rifling; RH, concentric.
Charger-loaded internal box magazine, 5 rounds.
Tangent-leaf sight graduated to 900 metres.
815 m/sec with Balle 1929 C.
Mle.15 épée or Mle.15 sword bayonets.
☆

1925: something better than the Berthier was clearly needed—experiments eventually led to the MAS 36 (q.v.)—but, in the interim, the sharply tapering 8mm Lebel cartridge was replaced by the rimless 7·5mm Balle 1924 C. Some Lebel-type rifles were experimentally modified for this round (Mle.1886 M.27, q.v.), but had no long-term influence.

1929: the improved 7·5mm Balle 1929 C replaced the 1924 pattern, whereupon the first experiments to adapt the Berthier rifles to rimless cartridges were made.

1934: many existing Mle.07/15 rifles were modernised while development of the MAS 36 was completed. A hand guard was added above the barrel. The infantry pattern had a straight bolt handle, a swivel on the under-edge of the butt, and accepted the Mle.86/15 épée bayonet. Most metal parts were phosphated.

The cavalry pattern had a sling bar on the left side of the butt, a bent-down bolt handle, and accepted the Mle.92/15 sword bayonet. Issue was restricted to a few regiments in 1939.

Model 1902–37

Short rifle: Fusil Mle.1902/37.
Converted by Manufacture d'Armes, Saint-Étienne, 1938-9.
Quantity: a few hundred.
7·5 × 54mm, rimmed.
Turning-bolt action, with two lugs on the detachable bolt head locking into the receiver.
1,075mm overall, 3·65kg unladen.
570mm barrel, 4-groove rifling; RH, concentric.
Charger-loaded internal box magazine, 5 rounds.
Tangent-leaf sight graduated to 900 metres.
815 m/sec with Balle 1929 C.
Mle.02 épée bayonet.
☆

1937: this was a transformation of the old Mle.1902 colonial rifle (q.v.) to approximate to the new Mle.07/15 M.34. It retained the original turned-down bolt handle, but displayed a mark such as TYPE SE-MAS 1902 M 37 on the left side of the receiver.

BLASER

SWITZERLAND

This metalworking company turned to firearms in the late 1970s, and has since made a series of interesting designs—the falling-block BL-820, plus the bolt-system R-84/SR-850 series. The shotgun-type Blaser K-77A rifle is not included here. Guns are made largely to order.

BL-820

Made by Blaser-Jagdwaffen GmbH, Isny/Allgäu.
5·6 × 50mm R Magnum, 6·5 × 57mm R, 6·5 × 68mm R, 7 × 65mm R, ·222 Remington, ·243 Winchester, ·300 Winchester Magnum, ·30–06 or ·308 Winchester.
Dropping-block action, operated by a lever

combined with the trigger guard.
DATA FOR A TYPICAL EXAMPLE
6·5 × 68R, rimmed.
About 1,010mm overall, 3.00kg unladen.
600mm barrel, 4-groove rifling; RH, concentric?
Folding-leaf sight.
1,100 m/sec with 6-gram bullet.
☆

1982: this elegant rifle offered a compact action contained almost entirely within the receiver. Pushing the trigger-guard spur down opened the action around a pivot at the front of the action-plate, and dropped the locking block to expose the chamber. Once the breech had been closed, the hammer had to be cocked manually.

R-84 and SR-850

Made by Blaser-Jagdwaffen GmbH, Isny/Allgäu.
Chamberings: see text.
Turning-bolt action with three locking lugs rotating into the barrel.
DATA FOR A TYPICAL R-84
·280 Remington, rimless.
1,040mm overall, 3.20kg unladen.
585mm barrel, 4-groove rifling; RH, concentric?
Optical sight.
860 m/sec with 10·7-gram bullet.
☆

1984: the Blaser bolt lay in a non-rotating housing which slid back along rails on top of the receiver (cf., Certus). Lugs on the bolt head locked directly into the barrel, allowing the receiver to be made of special lightweight alloy. The safety pivoted on the rear of the mobile bolt-housing, could lock the bolt and the firing pin. Readily detachable free-floating barrels carried the optical-sight mount. Butts and fore-ends were made of Circassian walnut, quality of wood and metalwork being exemplary.

The standard R-84 has been offered in ·22-250, ·243 Winchester, 6mm Remington, ·25-06, ·270 Winchester, ·280 Remington or ·30-06; R-84 Magnums (1,065mm overall, 610mm barrel, 3·30kg) have been chambered for the ·257 Weatherby, ·264 Winchester, 7mm Remington, ·300 Weatherby, ·300 Winchester,

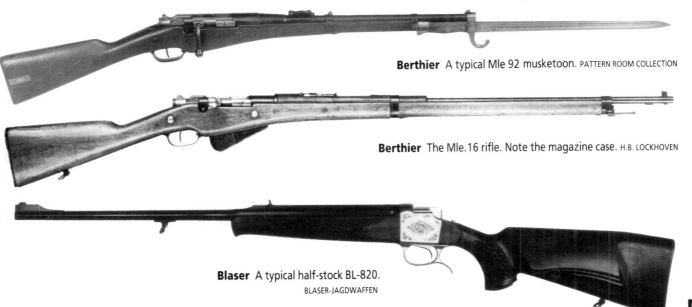

Berthier A typical Mle 92 musketoon. PATTERN ROOM COLLECTION

Berthier The Mle.16 rifle. Note the magazine case. H.B. LOCKHOVEN

Blaser A typical half-stock BL-820.
BLASER-JAGDWAFFEN

Borchardt A sporter, from an 1880-vintage Sharps catalogue.

SHARPS-BORCHARDT
SPORTING AND MILITARY

These rifles—which shared an identical dropping-block action—were all made by the Sharps Rifle Company of Bridgeport, Connecticut. Production totalled 10,000 military-style rifles and 12,500 sporters. The barrels invariably had six-groove concentric rifling twisting to the right. Unfortunately, Sharps was liquidated in September 1881.

SHARPS GUNS, 1878–81

New Model Military Rifle The first military-style rifles and carbines were introduced in 1878, chambered for the ·45–70 Government or ·45–75 Sharps cartridges only. Rifle barrels were usually held in the full-length fore-ends by two bands. Straight-wrist butts were standard. Swivels lay beneath the receiver ahead of the trigger guard and on the underside of the muzzle band. A typical ·45–70 example was 48·50in overall, had a 32·13in barrel and weighed 8·98lb. Its ramp-and-leaf sight was graduated to 1,100 yards and the M1873 socket bayonet could be fitted.

¶ Carbines were 40·6in overall, had 24in barrels and weighed about 7·65lb; their back sights were graduated to 900 yards. Half-length fore-ends were retained by a single band, and a sling ring lay on the left side of the receiver.

¶ An Officer's Model was stocked as a military pattern, but in wood selected for its figuring. It had chequering on the butt-wrist and diced rubber inserts in the receiver-side. According to catalogue testimonials, Borchardt rifles were bought by the National Guard in Michigan and North Carolina, while the Massachusetts militia acquired a few hundred to train marksmen.

New Model Sporting Rifle Introduced with a 30in round or octagonal barrel, chambered for the ·45–70 Government or ·45–120 Sharps (2·88in case) cartridges, the 1878-pattern or 'Hammerless' sporter had a half-stock with a straight-wrist butt and a plain rounded fore-end. Shotgun-style butts were standard. Double triggers and a selection of special finishes were optional. A typical example measured 46·38in overall and weighed 9·00lb. Its leaf sight was graduated to 1,000 yards.

New Model Hunter's Rifle Dating from 1879, this rifle featured a round barrel, a plain fore-end and a straight-wrist butt with a concave rifle-type butt plate. Chambered only for ·40–50 (1·88in case) or ·40–70 (2·5in case) Sharps cartridges, it had an open leaf sight graduated to 1,000 yards. Typically, the rifle was 42·38in overall—with a 26in barrel—and weighed about 8·55lb.

New Model Business Rifle Chambered only for the ·40–70 Sharps or ·40–90 Sharps rounds, this was 44·38in overall (28in barrel) and weighed 8·79lb. It had a blued octagonal barrel and a leaf sight graduated to 1,000 yards. The oil-finished straight-wrist butt was accompanied by an equally spartan fore-end.

New Model Target Rifle The ·40–50 Short Range target rifle, chambering a cartridge with a 1·5in case-length, was offered from 1878 with a vernier sight intended for distances up to 800 yards. A globe-pattern front sight with a wind gauge was standard, together with a chequered pistol-grip butt and fore-end. A rubber shotgun-style butt plate was fitted. A typical rifle fitted with a 28in round barrel was 44·38in overall and weighed about 9lb.

¶ The ·40–70 Short & Mid-Range Rifle (chambering cartridges with a 2·5in case) was similar, but had a 30in barrel and, apparently, a vernier sight suitable for ranges up to 1,000 yards. Conventional leaf sights were also fitted when requested.

New Model Target Rifle The Hammerless Long-Range pattern, chambered for the ·45–90 Sharps round (2·4in case), was 51·25in overall with a 34in round barrel and weighed 9·8lb without its sights. The deluxe chequered walnut pistol-grip butt had a rubber shotgun-type shoulder plate. The fore-end was also chequered, and a wood or rubber plate filled recesses milled out of the receiver sides. The rifles had Sharps' Long-Range Vernier Sight on the tang, graduated to 1,800 or 2,000 yards, and the globe-type front sight was accompanied by a wind gauge and a spirit level. The barrel-mounted back sight was usually omitted.

New Model Express Rifle Chambered for the ·45–100 or ·45–120 Sharps cartridges, this was made in small numbers for the African market. The octagonal barrel had a matted top, carrying a British-style Express sight with platinum centrelines and a front-sight bead. The pistol-grip butt and straight fore-end were both chequered, sling bars being driven through the woodwork, and the butt plate was a straight rubber shotgun pattern. A typical rifle, with a 26in barrel, was 42·38in overall and weighed 9·07lb.

THE MODERN GUNS

The advent in 1967 of the Sharps Arms Company, and a much-modernised action, held great promise, particularly when operations were acquired by Colt. Unfortunately, accuracy problems proved insurmountable and the project was abandoned in the mid 1970s after only about 450 actions had been made by the Bellmore-Johnson Tool Company in Hamden, Connecticut. Not all were assembled, though some were used in highly decorative presentation-grade guns in chamberings ranging from ·17 Remington to ·458 Winchester.

¶ A few modified Borchardt actions were made by Artistic Arms of Hoagland, Indiana, in 1972–5—but this enterprise also failed after a promising start.

Browning
The M1885 dropping-block rifle.

BROWNING
RE-CREATIONS OF THE BLOCK-ACTION PATTERN

Browning B–78 and M1885 Dating from 1973, the B–78 was a 'recreation' of the original 1878 pattern rifle, made for the Browning Arms Company by the Miroku Firearms Mfg Co. of Kochi, Japan. Chambered for ·22–250, 6mm Remington, ·270 Winchester or ·30–06, it had a straight receiver/butt joint and the receiver tangs were reduced to a minimum.

¶ A typical ·25–06 B–78 measured 42·00in overall and weighed 7·63lb with its 26in octagonal barrel. Rifling had six grooves, twisting to the right. Round barrels were optional. The chequered fore-end, with a shallow schnabel tip, was accompanied by a pistol-grip butt with a cheek piece, a Monte Carlo comb and a solid rubber butt plate.

¶ Work on a thousand special ·45–70 rifles celebrating the US Bicentennial began in 1975—a simplified version subsequently being offered commercially with a 24in octagonal barrel, a traditional straight-comb butt and a die-cast concave shoulder plate.

¶ Changes in the action led to suspension of work in 1983. When it resumed four years later, the rifle had been rechristened 'M1885'. Miroku delivered the first examples in the Spring of 1988. They were very similar externally to their predecessor, but the cartridge-case deflector (behind the breech block) could be adjusted to suit left or right-handed firers. M1885 guns were 43·5in overall, had 28in free-floating octagonal barrels and weighed about 8·75lb. The straight wrist butt had a plain solid-rubber plate, while the full-length fore-end had a schnabel tip. A classical spring-and-elevator back sight was offered as standard with the ·45–70 version, though the others—·22–250, 6mm Remington, ·25–06, ·270 Winchester, 7mm Remington Magnum or ·30–06—were tapped and drilled for optical-sight mounts.

Clerke High-Wall pattern Made by Clerke Recreation Products of Santa Monica, California, this modernised Winchester action was offered in ·222 Remington, ·223 Remington, ·22–250, ·243 Winchester, 6mm Remington, ·250 Savage, ·257 Roberts, ·25–06, ·264 Winchester, ·270 Winchester, 7mm Remington Magnum, ·300 Winchester Magnum, ·30–06, ·30–30 Winchester, ·375 H&H Magnum, ·45–70 or ·458 Winchester. A typical ·375 H&H Magnum version was 41·75in long, had a 26in barrel, and weighed about 8lb. Production was apparently confined to 1972–5.

¶ The standard rifle had a round barrel; a walnut pistol-grip butt; and a fore-end with a schnabel tip. The under-edge of the deepened fore-end lay below the base of the receiver. The receiver was generally colour case-hardened and the lever—unlike Winchester patterns—curved to follow the pistol grip. No open sights were fitted.

¶ A deluxe version of the Clerke rifle, with an adjustable trigger and half-octagon barrel, had chequered woodwork.

FBW pattern Announced in 1974 by the Falling Block Works of Troy, Michigan, this was a modernised High Wall. As the basic action was designed for completion elsewhere, FBW-type guns are not readily classifiable; the dimensions of the receiver were such that virtually any cartridge with a rim diameter less than that of the ·45–70 could be accommodated. Production seems to have continued until 1977–8.

Montana Armoury pattern A re-creation of the M1885 High Wall rifle was introduced in 1991 by the Montana Armory, Inc., of Big Timber. Chambered for ·30–40 Krag, ·32–40 Winchester, ·38–55 Winchester, ·40–65 Winchester or ·45–70 cartridges, it had a coil-spring action and a 28in octagonal barrel (26in on ·30–40 Krag only). The frame, breech block, operating lever and hammer were colour case-hardened. Rocky Mountain sights were fitted.

Serrifile pattern A modernised High Wall Schuetzen Rifle was introduced by Serrifile, Inc., of Littlerock, California, about 1983–4. Offered in ·32, ·33, ·38, ·41, ·44 or ·45 calibre, for virtually any suitable cartridge the purchaser cared to specify, production was never large. Work appears to have ceased by 1987. The Schuetzen Rifle had a round, half- or fully octagonal barrel—up to 32in long—and a walnut pistol-grip butt with a generous cheek piece and a Swiss-style hooked shoulder plate; the chequered walnut fore-end had a schnabel tip. Optical-sight mounts on the barrel were standard. In addition to the true Winchester types, with exposed hammers, some improved hammerless models were made and a selection of operating levers was encountered.

·338 Winchester and ·375 H&H magnum cartridges.

1986: the SR-850 was an improved R-84, with a similar single-shot action and an exchangeable barrel, but was styled more conventionally and had an exposed hammer.

BORCHARDT

UNITED STATES OF AMERICA
Also known as 'Sharps-Borchardt'

A hammerless dropping-block breech-loader based on a patent granted to Hugo Borchardt in December 1876, the Sharps-Borchardt rifle was a modernised version of the familiar Sharps dropping block system of 1848. Borchardt substituted a spring-loaded internal striker for the original external hammer, relying on cam-plates set in the frame sides and a transverse pin through the striker to cock the action as the breech block descended. The safety lever behind the trigger was applied automatically; when the action had been reloaded and closed, the firer could override the safety by pressing the projecting catch behind the trigger.

Lock-time was very short and the action was extremely strong; so strong, indeed, that modern re-creations are capable of handling virtually any sporting cartridge. However, unless carefully honed and adjusted, original Sharps-made rifles had comparatively poor trigger pulls.

The Sharps-made rifles existed in considerable variety, despite their short period in vogue. Details are summarised in the accompanying panel (opposite page).

BREDA

ITALY
Also known as 'Breda-Fiorini' or 'Fiorini'

This early assault rifle was developed in Italy in the 1930s by Sestilio Fiorini, head of the Breda technical department. Never particularly successful, the PG rifle was originally chambered for the 6·5mm rifle cartridge in the forlorn hope that it would interest the Italian army.

The rifle was very heavy, in spite of its compact dimensions. Gas was tapped from a port at the muzzle to strike an annular piston; this released the locking block and allowed the breech block and carrier to reciprocate. The gun fired single shots from a closed bolt, but relied on a complicated ratchet-type escapement to fire four-round bursts from an open-bolt position.

COSTA RICA
Model PG

....

Automatic rifle: Moschetto Automatico Breda Mo.PG.
Made by Società Italiana Costruzioni Meccaniche Ernesto Breda, Brescia, 1935–6.
Gas-operated auto-loading action, locked by a pivoting block.
7 × 57mm, rimless.
1,115mm overall, 5·25kg unladen.
455mm barrel, 4-groove rifling; LH, concentric?
Detachable box magazine, 20 rounds.
Quadrant sight graduated to 2,000 metres.
Bayonet: see notes.

☆

1935: the PG was a stubby gun with a magazine-case, not unlike that of the Italian Mannlicher-Carcano service rifle, from which the detachable magazine protruded. Feed lips were machined on the inside of the receiver instead of relying on a shaped magazine throat. The one-piece stock had a sling aperture and bar in the butt. A hand guard ran forward from the back-sight base. The double-band nose cap assembly, which surrounded the piston, had a swivel on the left side of the rear band and a bayonet lug on its underside; the bayonet was shared with Costa Rican Mauser rifles.

Receivers were invariably marked GOBIERNO DE COSTA RICA above the chamber, together with the gun designation, the serial number and a date (e.g., '1935-XIII', 'XIII' representing the thirteenth year of the Italian Fascist supremacy commencing in 1922).

BROWNING

UNITED STATES OF AMERICA

This section contains details of the rifles marketed under the Browning Arms Company name, and those marketed under others (usually Winchester's) prior to 1936, when the Model 94 lever-action rifle was abandoned in favour of the otherwise similar carbine. The original ·30 Browning Automatic Rifle has been omitted; though admittedly conceived as a shoulder weapon, almost all the variants of this weapon produced by Colt, FN and others after the end of the First World War—excepting the Colt-made 'Monitor'—were light machine-guns.

1. THE AUTO-LOADING PATTERNS

Locked by rotating the bolt, the current gas operated rifle—unrelated to the pre-1918 gun—is popular and effectual. Its design is usually credited to Val Browning, son of John Browning.

Browning Automatic Rifle

....

Affût, Battue, Magnum Standard and Deluxe patterns; also known as 'BAR'.
Made by FN Herstal SA, Herstal-lèz-Liège.
·270 Winchester, ·280 Remington, ·30–06;
·308 Winchester (Affût only);
7mm Remington Magnum, ·300 Winchester Magnum or ·338 Winchester Magnum.
Gas-operated auto-loading action, with seven lugs on the bolt locking into the receiver.
DATA FOR A TYPICAL AFFÛT
·270 Winchester, rimless.
1,097mm overall, 3·46kg unladen.
510mm barrel, 4-groove rifling; RH, concentric.
Detachable box magazine, 5 rounds.
Spring-leaf and elevator sight.
About 950 m/sec with 8·5-gram bullet.

☆

Browning
The Browning brothers pose in front of their gun shop in Ogden, Utah, in c.1882. From the left: Samuel, George, John M., Matthew and Edmund.
JOHN M. BROWNING MUSEUM

1967: the modern Browning Automatic Rifle was an elegant centre-fire design. The patented hinged floor-plate/detachable box magazine unit allowed the box to be replenished without removing it. The standard rifle (known from the mid 1980s as 'Modèle Affût') had an open back sight, and extensive chequering on the walnut pistol-grip butt and fore-end. The earliest deluxe examples had scroll engraving on the greyed receiver sides, gold-plated triggers and hand chequered woodwork chosen for its figuring.

1969: the first ·300 Magnums were introduced. They measured 1,146mm overall, with a four-round magazine, and had six-groove rifling.

1971: three new deluxe guns were introduced, differing in finish. Concurrently, the standard rifle was re-designated 'Grade I' and the original deluxe version became 'Grade II'. The new Grade III had a greyed steel receiver with trophy heads—deer and antelope on standard guns, elk and moose on magnums—set in fine English style scrollwork. Grade IV was similar, but had full-figure representations of the animals between reduced end-panels of heavier baroque scrollwork; Grade V had complete game scenes with gold animal inlays. Triggers were invariably gold plated and the woodwork was selected walnut, hand-chequered and carved.

1974: owing to limited demand, Grades II, III and V were abandoned. Grade IV remained as a stock item until the mid 1980s, but was then superseded by guns made individually to order.

1985*: the 'Battue' variant appeared with a small folding-leaf back sight let into a quarter rib. The standard rifle was renamed 'Affût' to distinguish it from the new pattern.

1988: ·280 Remington (standard) and ·338 Winchester (magnum) options were offered.

2. THE BLOCK-ACTION PATTERNS

The original dropping-block breech mechanism was patented by John Browning in October 1879, though commercial success awaited the introduction of a slightly modified pattern by Winchester in 1885.

The Browning breech was one of the sturdiest and most compact of its type ever to have been made. The block slid vertically in the massive receiver, the external hammer being pivoted in the block. As the operating lever was depressed, the pressure of the main spring was taken off the hammer and the breech block rose imperceptibly to release the toggle-type lock formed by the link-bar. Further movement pulled the breech block down into the receiver, lowering the hammer past the sear until the chamber was exposed for extraction, ejection and reloading. Returning the lever closed the breech and—by connecting the hammer and sear—cocked the trigger mechanism before rotating the link bar to its locked position. The gun could then be fired.

Alternatively, the hammer could be dropped under thumb control with the trigger pressed; just before the face of the hammer reached the breech block, the trigger could be released and the hammer retracted until the sear engaged a safety notch in the hammer body. To fire, the hammer had to be thumbed back to full-cock before pressing the trigger.

1878: John Browning began work on his dropping-block action, apparently seeking to improve on the popular Sharps pattern. After an application had been made in May, US Patent 220,271 was finally granted on 7 October 1879.

1880: J.M. Browning & Brother of Ogden, Utah, began to make rifles to special order. Doubt has been cast on the traditional estimate of 600 and the supposed purchase of partly completed rifles by Winchester; production may not have exceeded 150–200, but very few original rifles are known.

They were very similar to the later 'High Wall' Winchesters, but their receivers were less angular and the butt/receiver joint was straight instead of curved. Browning rifles also had heavier hammers than Winchester counterparts and were simpler internally.

1883: John and Matthew Browning sold rights vested in the design to the Winchester Repeating Arms Company, in return for $8,000.

Winchester Model 1885

Made by the Winchester Repeating Arms Company, New Haven, Connecticut, 1885–1920.
Quantity: 139,730.
Offered in a tremendous variety of chamberings, from ·22 Winchester and ·25–20 Single Shot to ·50–105 Winchester and ·50–140 Winchester Express (see notes).
Dropping-block action, operated by a lever combined with the trigger guard.
DATA FOR A TYPICAL SCHUETZEN PATTERN
·38–55 Winchester, rimmed.
50·50in overall, 12·41lb unladen.
30·00in barrel, 6-groove rifling; RH, concentric.
Vernier sight on tang, graduated to 1,200 yards.
1,320 ft/sec with 255-grain bullet.
☆

1883: Winchester bought manufacturing rights to the Browning dropping-block rifle, embarking on a series of minor changes that culminated in an improvement on the basic design.

1885: the Plain Sporting Rifle, Special Sporting Rifle, Special Target Rifle and Schuetzen Rifle were advertised. The sporters were identical but for finish, details and figuring in the woodwork; they had straight-wrist (standard) or pistol-grip (special) butts with concave iron butt plates, and short fore-ends with shallow schnabel tips. Back sights were open Rocky Mountain patterns, though aperture sights on the tang were used on the Special Target Rifle. The original Schuetzen Rifle offered a half-octagon barrel, a pistol-grip butt with a Swiss-style cheek piece, and a hooked shoulder plate. A vernier-pattern sight lay on the upper tang behind the receiver, but a conventional trigger was fitted. Sporting centre-fire chamberings included ·32–20, ·38–40 and ·44–40 Winchester, ·32–40 Ballard, ·38–55 Ballard, ·40–50 Sharps (straight and necked), ·40–70 Sharps (straight and necked), ·40–70 Ballard and ·45–70, but more were added as the years passed.

Alternative triggers were available at a later date, though their chronology is obscure. There was a single set trigger, with a small adjusting screw behind the trigger lever, and a unique

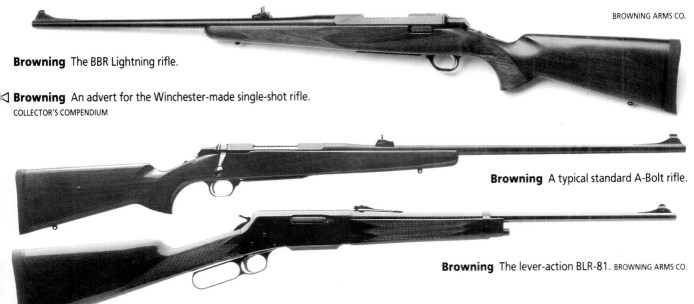

mechanism with two triggers set so closely that they appeared to touch.

1886: a thin-wall receiver was introduced, reducing the strength of the action compared with the original pattern but saving weight and material. The new receiver was apparently confined to medium-calibre cartridges.

Five differing types of barrel were offered. No.1 chambered the small rim- and centre-fire cartridges up to ·44–40 Winchester; No.2 was similar, but heavier. No.3 was intended for large-calibre sporting rounds; No.4 was a special heavy pattern; and No.5 was the heaviest that could be obtained.

A ·45–70 musket with a military-style stock was offered briefly in the autumn, but attracted little attention and was soon abandoned. New chamberings seem to have included several Winchester Central Fire cartridges—·40–82, ·45–90, ·45–125, ·50–105 and ·50–140.

1887: a 'Low Wall' receiver was introduced to facilitate loading small-calibre cartridges. Apart from a reduction in the height of metal alongside the breech block, the Low Wall was identical with the contemporaneous standard (thereafter known as 'High Wall') pattern, most of its parts being interchangeable. At least three new chamberings—·38–56, ·40–65 and ·50–110 Winchester—appeared at this time.

1894: ·38–70 and ·40–70 Winchester options appeared, together with a smaller flat-sided Low Wall action. This was the same length as its predecessors, but not as deep. Rifles intended for smokeless cartridges had nickel-steel barrels.

1895: ·25–20, ·25–35, ·30–30 and ·50–100 Winchester chamberings were introduced.

1897: an improved Schuetzen Rifle appeared. Offered with a 30in No.3 or No.4 barrel, it had chequered pistol-grip butt with a Swiss-pattern cheek piece, a nickelled butt plate and a double set-trigger mechanism. The extended spur-type finger lever was fitted, and a palm-rest lay beneath the fore-end. A vernier-type aperture sight was fitted to the upper tang.

1898: a special 'Baby Carbine' appeared in March, with a 15in barrel, a straight-wrist stock, and a sling ring on the left side of the receiver.

1901: colour case-hardening of the frames was replaced from August by a combination of heat treatment and blueing. Older actions could be returned to New Haven for refurbishment, however, blurring the distinction.

1903: ·33 WCF and ·35 WCF were added to the cartridge options.

1905: the ·405 Winchester chambering was offered for the first time.

1908: a change was made to the main-spring assembly. The old leaf anchored to the underside of the barrel became a coil looped under the hammer body, around each side of the hammer-pivot pin and up into the breech block. A small spring-and-plunger assembly in the receiver immediately beneath the chamber retained the operating lever in its closed position.

1910: a 'Take Down' pattern arrived in June, in accordance with a patent granted in May 1907, and a No.3½ barrel appeared. Specifically intended for ·35 WCF and ·405 WCF (though other chamberings are known), this combined the breech dimensions of the No.4 with the muzzle profile of the No.3.

1914: a 20-bore shotgun was introduced on the High Wall action, but lasted for only two years and was made in very small quantities.

1920: assembly ceased, though it is probable that little work had been done since 1917.

Note: the single-shot M1885 rifle has been chambered for a wide variety of non-Winchester and 'wildcat' cartridges, most of the latter group—e.g. ·22 R–2 Lovell, ·219 Wasp or ·219 Improved Zipper—originating long after the rifle had been discontinued. Typical of these non-Winchester chamberings were ·25–20 Single Shot, ·25–25 Stevens, ·303 (British), ·30–40 Krag, ·32 Ideal and ·50–90 Sharps.

3. THE BOLT-ACTION PATTERNS

Note: this part contains information about the Japanese-made guns promoted by the Browning Arms Company. Details of the FN-Mauser rifles,

which were built on a conventional turning-bolt action, will be found in the Mauser chapter.

BBR Lightning

Made for the Browning Arms Company, Morgan, Utah, by the Miroku Firearms Mfg Co., Kochi, 1979–84. ·25–06, ·270 Winchester, 7mm Remington Magnum, ·30–06 or ·300 Winchester Magnum. Turning-bolt action, with three lugs on the bolt locking into the receiver.
DATA FOR A TYPICAL RIFLE
·25–06, rimless.
44·70in overall, about 8lb unladen.
24·00in barrel, 4-groove rifling; RH, concentric.
Detachable box magazine, 4 rounds.
Spring-leaf and elevator sight.
About 3,100 ft/sec with 100-grain bullet.

☆

1979: this eschewed the Mauser two-lug lock and 90°-throw bolt for a three-lug 60° pattern. The plunger-type ejector was recessed in the shrouded bolt face and a small claw-pattern extractor was used. The box magazine/hinged floor plate system was shared with the BAR.

The standard rifle had a chequered pistol-grip butt with a low Monte Carlo comb and a plain synthetic shoulder plate. The chequered fore-end had a rounded rosewood tip.

1984: the BBR was replaced by the A-Bolt.

A-Bolt

Camo Stalker, Composite Stalker, Gold Medallion, Hunter, Medallion, Micro-Medallion and Stainless Stalker patterns.
Made for the Browning Arms Company, Morgan, Utah, by the Miroku Firearms Mfg Co., Kochi, 1986 to date. Chambering: see text.
Action: generally as BBR, above.
DATA FOR A TYPICAL A-BOLT HUNTER
·280 Remington, rimless.
42·75in overall, 6·65lb unladen.
22·00in barrel, 4-groove rifling; RH, concentric.
Detachable box magazine, 4 rounds.
About 2,900 ft/sec with 150-grain bullet.

☆

BROWNING ARMS CO.

Browning The BBR Lightning rifle.

◁ **Browning** An advert for the Winchester-made single-shot rifle.
COLLECTOR'S COMPENDIUM

Browning A typical standard A-Bolt rifle.

Browning The lever-action BLR-81. BROWNING ARMS CO.

1986: the A-Bolt rifle was an improved form of the Miroku-made BBR (q.v.), sharing the short-throw three-lug action. It had a fluted bolt with a short extractor set into one of the locking lugs, and an indicator protruded from the back of the bolt sleeve when the striker was cocked. A shotgun-style sliding safety catch lay on the upper tang behind the bolt. Williams ramp back sights were optional and the BAR magazine system was retained, with the addition of a patented scissors-type cartridge elevator.

The A-Bolt rifle was introduced in standard and short-action lengths, a strengthened version of the former sufficing for magnum chamberings. The standard rifle, called the Hunter, had a pistol-grip stock with a straight comb and a rounded fore-end tip. Chequering was standard and a plain rubber butt plate was fitted.

Short-action guns have chambered ·22–250, ·243 Winchester, ·257 Roberts, 7mm–08 Remington or ·308 Winchester. The standard Hunters have been made for ·25-06, ·270 Winchester, ·280 Remington or ·30–06; Magnums accepted 7mm Remington, ·300 Winchester or ·338 Winchester cartridges.

1987: introduced to satisfy more discerning clientele, the A-Bolt Medallion had high-gloss woodwork, darkened bolt flutes and scrollwork on the receiver flats. An otherwise identical left-hand action was made in ·270 Winchester, 7mm Remington Magnum, ·30–06 and ·300 Winchester Magnum only.

An A-Bolt Camo Stalker, which also made its debut in 1987, chambered the ·270 Winchester, ·30–06 or 7mm Remington Magnum rounds. It was easily distinguished from the standard Hunter by a laminated stock made from wood dyed alternately in shades of black and green. The metal parts had a matt blue finish.

1988: Browning introduced a ·375 H&H Magnum chambering for the A-Bolt Medallion.

The new A-Bolt Stainless Stalker (handling the same cartridges as the Camo Stalker) and Composite Stalker rifles (offered additionally in ·25–06 and ·280 Remington, plus ·300 and ·338 Winchester Magnum) embodied a textured grey-black stock of graphite-reinforced fibreglass.

Made in ·270 Winchester, 7mm Remington Magnum or ·30–06, the A-Bolt Gold Medallion offered a European-style stock with a palm-swell grip and a Monte Carlo comb. The butt plate, pistol-grip cap and contrasting fore-end tip were separated from the woodwork with thin brass spacers; the receiver flats were engraved with scrollwork and GOLD MEDALLION was inlaid in gold on the right side ahead of the bolt handle.

Available in short-action form only, handling the ·22-250, ·243 Winchester, ·257 Roberts, 7mm–08 Remington or ·308 Winchester rounds, the A-Bolt Micro-Medallion was a diminutive Medallion with a 20in barrel, a shorter butt and a three-round magazine. It was 39·56in long and weighed 6·1lb.

Note: special editions are included in Part Two.

4. THE LEVER-ACTION PATTERNS

This section contains details of rifles marketed under the Browning name, and, for the sake of continuity, pre-1936 guns made by Winchester in accordance with Browning patents.

MILITARY RIFLES

RUSSIA

Model 1915

Infantry rifle: Vintovka Vinchestya, obr.1915g.
Made by the Winchester Repeating Arms Company,
New Haven, Connecticut, 1915–17.
Quantity: about 295,000.
7·62 × 54mm, rimmed.
Lever action, locked by a vertically-sliding bar.
1,160mm overall, 4·10kg unladen.
712mm barrel, 4-groove rifling; RH, concentric.
Integral charger-loaded box magazine, 5 rounds.
Ramp-and-leaf sight graduated to 2,700 arshin.
About 820 m/sec with Type L ball cartridges.
Winchester export-pattern bayonets.

☆

1914: the beginning of the First World War found the Russian ordnance with far too few weapons to arm the many millions of men being mobilised. An approach to Winchester resulted in the production of Mosin-Nagants in North America, and also in an order for 300,000 M1895 lever-action rifles (known as 'obr.1915g' in Russia).

1915: production began. The guns followed the standard pattern, but chambered clumsy Russian rifle cartridges and were sighted accordingly. Charger guides lay above the receiver and a hand guard ran from the receiver ring to the band. The first five thousand rifles had bayonets with 10in blades, but later examples measured 16in.

1917: the fall of the Tsar and the ensuing unrest caused deliveries to cease. Winchester claimed to have despatched 293,816 rifles, while the Russians claimed to have received 299,000. The discrepancy may be due to purchases of 1895-type rifles in other chamberings, or simply to poor ordnance department record-keeping

SPORTING GUNS

Model 1886

Offered as a rifle or carbine.
Does not include the Browning B-71 re-creation
(see page 44).
Made in New Haven, Connecticut, by the
Winchester Repeating Arms Company (1886-1936,
owned by the Western Cartridge Company
from 1932 onward).
Quantity: 159,990 to 1936.
·33 Winchester, ·348 Winchester,
·38–56 Winchester, ·38–70 Winchester,
·40–65 Winchester, ·40–70 Winchester,
·40–75 Bullard (used in ·40–82 chamber),
·40–82 Winchester, ·45–70 Government,
·45–82 Winchester or ·45–85 Winchester (used in
·45–90 chamber), ·45–90 Winchester, ·50–100
or ·50–110 Express.
DATA FOR A TYPICAL EXAMPLE
Lever action, locked by a vertically-sliding bar.
·50–110 Express, rimmed.
45·75in overall, 8·77lb unladen.

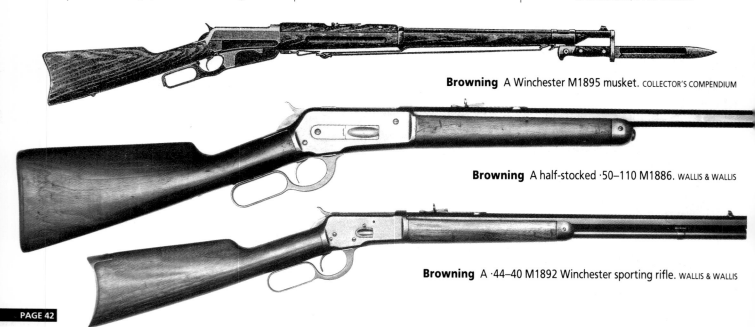

Browning A Winchester M1895 musket. COLLECTOR'S COMPENDIUM

Browning A half-stocked ·50–110 M1886. WALLIS & WALLIS

Browning A ·44–40 M1892 Winchester sporting rifle. WALLIS & WALLIS

26·00in barrel, 6-groove rifling; RH, concentric.
Tube magazine under barrel, 4 rounds.
Spring-leaf and elevator sight.
1,605 ft/sec with 300-grain bullet.

☆

1883: just as Marlin and other rivals began to exploit the inability of the 1876-pattern Winchester to handle high chamber pressures, the company management chanced upon the Browning brothers in Ogden, Utah. In addition to a promising single-shot dropping-block gun, the Brownings had also created a lever action locked by sturdy vertically-sliding bars (patented by John Browning in October 1884). Rights to the new rifles were immediately acquired and production began once the feed mechanism had been improved by William Mason.

1886: rifles were accepted into the New Haven warehouse in the late summer, the earliest chamberings being ·40–82, ·45–70 and ·45–90. The Sporting Rifle pattern had a straight-grip butt and a 26in round, octagon or half-octagon barrel; the Fancy Sporting Rifle was made with a pistol-grip butt and a 26in octagon barrel; the Half-Magazine Rifle had a 'shotgun butt' and the usual 26in barrel options. Identifying Winchesters of this period—unfortunately—is complicated by superior finishes, triggers and decoration applied to order.

1887: a full-stock carbine was described in the Winchester catalogue, but was made only until 1889 in pitifully small numbers. Rifles were offered in three new chamberings—·38–56 and ·40–65 Winchester, plus ·50–110 Express.

1889: the 1887-pattern carbine was replaced by a conventional version with a 22in round barrel, a straight-wrist butt, and a half-length fore-end.

1894: a Take-Down rifle appeared, but only about 350 were ever made. Rifles were first made in ·38–70 and ·40–72 Winchester.

1895: a ·50–100–450 option became available.

1897: the ·45–70 Extra Light-Weight Rifle appeared, with a 22in round barrel.

1903: a .33 Winchester chambering appeared.

1908: ultra-long (28in–36in) barrels, which had been made to special order, were abandoned.

1911: the ·38–56, ·38–70, ·40–65, ·40–72,

·40–82, ·45–90 and ·50–100–450 chamberings were all abandoned.

1920: the ·45–70 and, apparently, ·50–110 Express options were withdrawn.

1928: ·45–70 was reinstated, only to be finally abandoned three years later.

1935: ·33 WCF was abandoned shortly before the M1885 was superseded by the Model 71 (see 'Winchester').

Model 1892

Available as a rifle or carbine.
Made in New Haven, Connecticut, by the Winchester Repeating Arms Company (1892–1941, owned by the Western Cartridge Company from 1932 onward).
·218 Bee, ·25–20 Winchester, ·32–20 Winchester, ·357 Magnum, ·38–40 Winchester, ·44 Magnum or ·44–40 Winchester.
Action: as M1886, above.
DATA FOR A TYPICAL EXAMPLE
·32–20 Winchester, rimmed.
41·58in overall, 6·83lb unladen.
24·00in barrel, 6-groove rifling; RH, concentric.
Tube magazine under barrel, 5 rounds.
Spring-leaf and elevator sight.
1,290 ft/sec with 100-grain bullet.

☆

1892: this reduced-scale M1886 was developed partly to provide a cheaper rifle and partly to retain cartridges that had become popular with the original M1873—·38–40 and ·44–40. The Sporting Rifle had a straight-wrist butt and a 24in round, octagon or half-octagon barrel; the Fancy Sporting Rifle offered a pistol-grip butt, but any of the barrel styles. Magazines could be part- or full-length. The carbine usually had a straight-wrist butt and a round barrel of 14–20in.

1893: a Take-Down rifle was announced in the autumn, but few were ever made.

1895: a ·25–20 Winchester option was added.

1898: the short-lived 30in-barrelled Musket made its appearance, with a straight-wrist butt, barrel bands, a nose cap and swivels. It was withdrawn in 1903.

1932: the M1892 rifle was abandoned, having

been supplemented by the Models 53 and 65 (qq.v.), though production of carbines continued in ·25–20 and ·44–40. Most of these had raised back sights and ramp-type front sights. A few will be encountered with long Model 53-type barrels.

1936: the first of a few carbines were made for the ·218 Bee cartridge.

1941: production of carbines ceased.

Model 1894

Offered as a rifle or carbine.
Details of post-1936 guns will be found in the Winchester section.
Made in New Haven, Connecticut, by the Winchester Repeating Arms Company (1894-1936, owned by the Western Cartridge Company from 1932).
Quantity: several million.
·25–35 Winchester, ·30–30 Winchester, ·32 Winchester Special, ·32–40 Winchester or ·38–55 Winchester.
Action: as M1886, above.
DATA FOR A TYPICAL EXAMPLE
·30–30 Winchester, rimmed.
38·13in overall, 6·90lb unladen.
20·00in barrel, 6-groove rifling; RH, concentric.
Tube magazine under barrel, 6 rounds.
Spring-leaf and elevator sight.
2,220 ft/sec with 170-grain bullet.

☆

1894: this Browning, intended for smokeless cartridges, was patented in August. Chambered for the ·32–40, ·38–55 or ·44–40 Winchester cartridges, the Sporting Rifle (solid-frame or Take-Down) offered a 26in round, octagon or half-octagon barrel and straight-wrist or pistol-grip butts. The Fancy Sporting Rifle had a pistol-grip butt only. Most rifles had full-length eight-round magazines, though a four-cartridge half-length pattern was common on Take-Down guns. Carbines were simply shortened rifles, usually encountered with a 20in round barrel and a full-length (six-round) magazine, though a few four-cartridge magazines were made. Barrels, finish and accessories vary greatly.

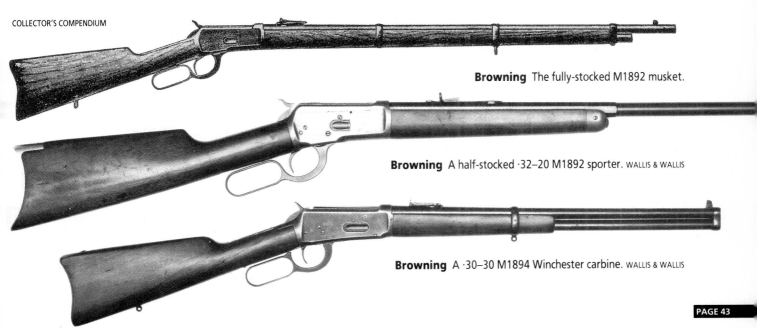

Browning The fully-stocked M1892 musket.

Browning A half-stocked ·32–20 M1892 sporter. WALLIS & WALLIS

Browning A ·30–30 M1894 Winchester carbine. WALLIS & WALLIS

1895: ·25–35 and ·30–30 chamberings were offered for the first time.

1897: a special Extra Light-Weight Rifle was introduced with a 22in or 26in round barrel and a shotgun-style butt. It was eventually discontinued in 1918, though none had been made for some time.

1902: rifles chambered for the ·32 Winchester Special cartridge appeared.

1924: the M1894 was supplemented by the Model 55 (see 'Winchester').

1925: saddle rings were omitted from carbines.

1927: the millionth M1894 was made.

1930: the ·32 Winchester Special option was withdrawn.

1931: a raised back-sight base and a ramp-type front sight were adopted in November.

1936: assembly of rifles ceased, though carbines continued to be made. All chamberings except ·44–40 were withdrawn. The history of the post-1936 M1894 carbines will be found in the Winchester section.

Model 1895

Offered as a rifle, carbine or musket.
Made by the Winchester Repeating Arms Company, New Haven, Connecticut, 1895–1931.
Quantity: 426,000 to 1931.
·30–03, ·30–06, ·303 British, ·30–40 Krag, ·35 Winchester, ·38–72 Winchester, ·40–72 Winchester or ·405 Winchester.
Action: as M1886, above.
DATA FOR A TYPICAL EXAMPLE
·40–72 Winchester, rimmed.
43·20in overall, 7·55lb unladen.
24·00in barrel, 6-groove rifling; RH, concentric.
Integral charger-loaded box magazine, 5 rounds.
Spring-leaf and elevator sight.
1,405 ft/sec with 330-grain bullet.
☆

1895: presenting a radical departure from the previous Winchesters, this rifle had a fixed box magazine beneath the receiver for high power small-calibre smokeless cartridges. The Sporting Rifle (·38–72 Winchester or ·40–72 Winchester) offered round, octagon or half-octagon barrels, and a straight-wrist rifle-style butt; the Fancy Sporting Rifle had a straight-wrist or pistol-grip shotgun-style butt.

Most half-length fore-ends had schnabel tips, and at least five thousand low-number guns had distinctive flat-side receivers. The carbine was a rifle with a straight-wrist butt and a 20in barrel. Its fore-end had a rounded tip.

1896: the 1895-type Muskets were invariably stocked to the muzzle, with a short upper hand guard, a grasping groove in the fore-end, a barrel band, and a nose cap with a bayonet lug. The original pattern (·30–40 Krag or ·303 British) was accompanied by a proprietary knife bayonet. Then came the six-shot ·30 'U.S. Army Pattern', with a 28in round barrel and the standard M1892 sword bayonet. Some of these guns saw service in the hands of militia and volunteers during the Spanish-American War.

1903: a ·35 Winchester version was introduced.

1904: an optional ·405 Winchester chambering was added.

1905: the 'N.R.A. Musket', essentially similar to the US Army model, was announced. It had a 30in barrel and a 1901-type Krag-Jørgensen back sight; chambered for the ·30 M1903 cartridge, the original version was superseded in 1908 by a ·30 M1906 gun with a 24in barrel.

1908: barrels measuring more than 28in, previously available to order, were abandoned.

1910: the first 'Take-Down' rifles were made.

1915: the Imperial Russian government ordered 300,000 7·62mm guns.

1918: ·303 chamberings were withdrawn.

1938: the last guns were sold from store, though assembly had ceased in 1931.

BLR and BLR-81

Made for the Browning Arms Company, Morgan, Utah, by the Miroku Firearms Mfg Co., Kochi, 1972 to date.
Chambering: see text.
Lever action, with seven lugs on the bolt locking into the receiver.
DATA FOR A TYPICAL BLR
·243 Winchester, rimless.
1,010mm overall, 3·15kg unladen.
510mm barrel, 4-groove rifling; RH, concentric.
Detachable box magazine, 4 rounds.
Spring-leaf and elevator sight.
About 3,000 ft/sec with 100-grain bullet.
☆

1971: this effectual lever-action rifle, designed by Val Browning in Belgium, was introduced commercially in ·243 and ·308 Winchester. Prototypes were made in Herstal.

The rotating-bolt action was amply strong enough to handle powerful sporting cartridges, giving the BLR an advantage over many other lever-action repeaters. Its trigger system was mounted on the operating lever, moving with the finger lever to prevent pinching.

The BLR had a chequered straight-wrist butt with a ventilated rubber recoil pad, and a short chequered fore-end. The back sight had a ramp, and a single barrel band was used. A half-cock position on the hammer and an inertia firing pin provided an element of safety.

1972: production was sub-contracted to Japan.

1982: the BLR was supplemented and then replaced by the BLR-81, similar externally but with an improved action. Chamberings have included ·22–250, ·243 Winchester, ·308 Winchester and ·358 Winchester. The butt wrist was lengthened, along with the chequering panel, and a white-line spacer usually accompanied the ventilated rubber butt plate. A gold-plated trigger lever was fitted and the magazine-release catch was improved. The original BLR magazine projected farther beneath the receiver than on the BLR-81.

1985: a .257 Roberts option was announced.

1987: three Remington chamberings—·222, ·223 and 7mm–08—were added. A plain solid rubber plate replaced the ventilated pattern, the accompanying spacer being discarded.

1991: a special long-action rifle was introduced to handle ·270 Winchester, 7mm Remington Magnum or ·30–06 rounds, barrels measuring 22in (24in in 7mm only). The rifles were about 42·5in long and weighed 8·5lb; their hammers folded down at half-cock to provide an additional safety feature.

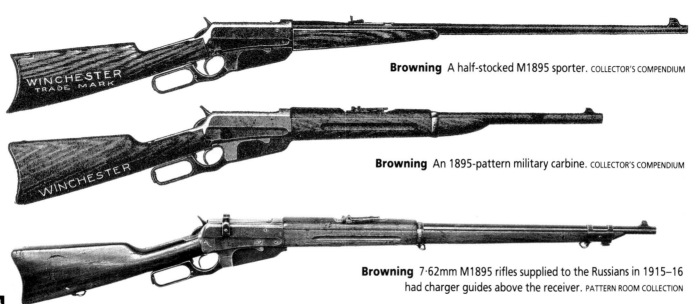

Browning A half-stocked M1895 sporter. COLLECTOR'S COMPENDIUM

Browning An 1895-pattern military carbine. COLLECTOR'S COMPENDIUM

Browning 7·62mm M1895 rifles supplied to the Russians in 1915–16 had charger guides above the receiver. PATTERN ROOM COLLECTION

BSA

BRITAIN

Developed in the period immediately after the end of the Second World War, and successfully exported to many countries, the BSA bolt relied on a standard Mauser two-lug locking system—though the third or safety lug was abandoned in favour of the bolt handle locking down into a seat in the receiver. A non-rotating collar-type extractor was retained until the late 1950s, but an entirely new firing mechanism then appeared (with a rotary safety catch on the right side of the bolt shroud) while an adjustable trigger was combined with the bolt stop and ejector.

Note: standard rifles were sold in the USA by Galef, Herter's and others, before a sole distributorship was granted to the Ithaca Gun Company in the mid 1970s. Herter's also sold barrelled Monarch actions as 'U9'.

Royal series

•••

Made by BSA Guns Ltd, Birmingham, 1954–9.
Short actions: ·22 Hornet or ·222 Remington.
Medium action: ·243 Winchester, ·257 Roberts,
7 × 57mm, ·300 Savage or ·308 Winchester.
Long action: ·270 Winchester, ·30–06 or
·458 Winchester.
Turning-bolt action, with two lugs on the bolt head locking into the receiver and a safety lug provided by the base of the bolt handle.
DATA FOR A TYPICAL EXAMPLE
·222 Remington, rimless.
43·88in overall, 7·55lb unladen.
24·00in barrel, 6-groove rifling; RH, concentric.
Internal box magazine, 4 rounds.
No sights.
3,200 ft/sec with 50-grain bullet.
☆

1954: the first of BSA's centre-fire sporting rifles appeared. The magazine floor-plate was released by a pivoting catch in the front of the trigger guard and dovetails for optical-sight mounts were milled into the top of the receiver.

The stock had a low Monte Carlo comb, a cheek piece, and a chequered pistol grip; the chequered fore-end had a plain rounded tip. Barrels were free-floating.

1956: a medium-length action was announced. A guide rib was added to the bolt, gas-escape ports were provided, and short blind holes were drilled down into the receiver-top dovetails to anchor optical sight mounts. The profile of the fore-end was changed to incorporate a schnabel tip but, excepting dimensions, the medium-action gun was practically identical with its shorter predecessor.

1957: the long-action rifle was essentially the same as the medium-action version, but had a modified chambering system. Instead of a Mauser 1898-type receiver ring, the BSA barrel was counter-bored to take the entire bolt head.

1958: the 'Featherweight' rifle amalgamated a 22in barrel with a lightened version of the medium (·222 or ·243) or long action (·270, ·30–06 and ·458). The thickness of the left receiver wall was greatly reduced to save weight and a 'Besa' recoil reducer was fitted. This consisted simply of counter-boring the barrel and cutting gas-escape ports through to the bore.

1959: the Royal rifle was superseded by the Majestic, though assembly continued until the end of 1960.

Majestic series

•••

Imperial, Majestic, Regent and Viscount patterns.
Made by BSA Guns Ltd, Birmingham, 1959–65.
Short action: ·22 Hornet or ·222 Remington.
Medium action: ·243 Winchester or ·308 Winchester.
Long action: ·270 Winchester, ·30–06 or
·458 Winchester.
Action: as Royal series, above.
DATA FOR A TYPICAL EXAMPLE
·243 Winchester, rimless.
41·75in overall, 7·55lb unladen.
22·00in barrel, 6-groove rifling; LH, concentric.
Internal box magazine, 4 rounds.
Folding-leaf sight graduated to 300 yards.
3,070 ft/sec with 100-grain bullet.
☆

1959: this was an improved BSA Royal, with a small extractor and a plunger-type ejector mounted on the bolt head, an enclosed cocking piece with a small red plastic indicator pin, and a few minor changes in the trigger mechanism. The safety catch remained on the right side of the bolt. A folding-leaf back sight and a hooded-ramp front sight were standard. The stock retained the low comb and cheek piece of its predecessors, chequering graced the pistol grip, and the chequered fore-end had a schnabel-type tip. The short action (Regent) was simply the medium-length (Viscount) pattern with a smaller magazine. The long action was known as the Imperial model.

Featherweight Majestic patterns were made in ·222 (short action), ·243 and ·308 (medium action), or ·270, ·30–06 and ·458 (long action). The principal distinguishing characteristic was the row of gas vents along the muzzle beneath the front sight ramp.

1961: the artificial distinction between the short and medium actions was abandoned.

1965: the Majestic series was replaced by the Monarch (q.v.).

Monarch series

•••

Made by BSA Guns Ltd, Birmingham, 1965–74.
Medium action; ·222 Remington, ·243 Winchester or
·308 Winchester.
Long action: ·270 Winchester, 7mm Remington
Magnum, ·300 Winchester Magnum or ·30–06.
Action: as Royal series, above.
DATA FOR A TYPICAL EXAMPLE
·243 Winchester, rimless.
43·75in overall, 7·15lb unladen.
22·00in barrel, 6-groove rifling; LH, concentric.
Internal box magazine, 4 rounds.
Folding-leaf sight graduated to 300 yards.
3,070 ft/sec with 100-grain bullet.
☆

1965: introduced to replace the Majestic, this had a rocking safety on the right side of the receiver behind the bolt handle. The trigger system was simplified and a few minor changes were made in the magazine, though the rifle

Browning A half-stocked M1886 rifle. COLLECTOR'S COMPENDIUM

BROWNING
RE-CREATIONS OF THE LEVER-ACTION GUNS

Model 1886 In 1986, the Browning Arms Company of Morgan, Utah, announced the manufacture of replica Model 1886 rifles, work being sub-contracted to Miroku in Japan. The Standard or Grade I rifle, offered in ·45–70 only, had a 26in octagonal barrel and an eight-round magazine; it was about 45in overall and weighed 9·4lb. The blued receiver was accompanied by a classically styled fore-end, and a straight-wrist butt with a rifle-type shoulder plate. Seven thousand guns were made.

¶ Miroku also made 3,000 M1886 Grade II rifles, with gloss instead of satin-finished woodwork and engraved scrollwork, elk

and bison on the receiver-side. A Montana Centennial gun was also made.

¶ Browning announced in 1992 that about 7,000 standard Grade I and 3,000 deluxe Grade II Miroku-made ·45–70 M1886 carbines would be made with 22in barrels and an overall length of 40·8in. Weight was to be about 8·3lb.

Model 71 The Browning B-71 was introduced in 1987 on the basis of the Miroku-made M1886 action. The half-length magazine held four ·348 Winchester cartridges and a round 24in barrel was fitted. Weight was about 8·15lb. The fore-end and pistol-grip butt were plain walnut, though a few guns were made with straight-wrist butts.

¶ The B-71 Carbine was identical, but had a 20in barrel and weighed about 7·8lb; the

High Grade rifle duplicated the standard pattern, but its woodwork had a glossy finish and the greyed steel receiver featured scroll engraving. The guns were not popular and were soon discontinued, though new guns were still available in the 1990s.

Model 92 A modern version of the original carbine was announced in 1979 as the 'Browning B-92', production being entrusted to Miroku. Offered only in ·357 and ·44 Magnum chamberings, the B-92 had a classically-styled straight-wrist butt and a half-length fore-end retained by a single band. It measured 37·5in overall and weighed about 6lb; the tube magazine held eleven rounds. An open spring-and-elevator back sight was fitted.

Model 1895 In 1984, the Browning Arms Company revealed a re-creation of the

M1895, made in Japan. The only important difference concerned the lower arm of the operating lever-trigger guard assembly, which was pivoted to lock the lever into the lower tang behind the trigger when the action was closed.

¶ Six thousand standard and a thousand 'High Grade' guns were made in ·30–06, with a straight-wrist butt and a half-length schnabel tip fore-end. Overall length was about 42in, the round barrel measuring 24in. The 8lb rifles had four-round magazines. High Grade rifles had scrollwork and an elk-and-bison scene on the greyed receiver, woodwork being selected walnut with hand-cut chequering.

¶ A ·30–40 Krag version was announced in 1985, production totalling 2,000. New guns were still being offered in 1990.

otherwise resembled its predecessors. Monarch actions were made in two patterns—long and short—and the Featherweight was abandoned.

1967: a 'Varmint Rifle' appeared, chambered only for ·222 Remington or ·243 Winchester. It had a 24in heavy barrel, lacked open sights and weighed about 9lb.

1968: the flat dovetailed rails were replaced by a round-top receiver drilled and tapped for conventional mounting bases.

1974: Monarch rifles were superseded by the improved CF-2 described below.

CF-2 series

Carbine, Classic, Regal Custom, Standard, Stutzen and
Varminter patterns.
Made by BSA Guns Ltd, Birmingham, 1974–86.
·222 Remington, ·22-250, ·243 Winchester,
6·5 × 55mm, 7 × 57mm, 7 × 64mm,
7mm Remington Magnum, ·270 Winchester,
·300 Winchester Magnum, ·30-06 or ·308 Winchester.
Action: as Royal series, above.
DATA FOR A TYPICAL CF-2
7 × 64mm, rimless.
44·40in overall, 8·05lb unladen.
23·60in barrel, 5-groove rifling; LH, concentric.
Internal box magazine, 4 rounds.
Williams ramp sight.
2,950 ft/sec with 160-grain bullet.
☆

1974: introduced to replace the Monarch, the first supplies of this rifle were not available until the summer of 1975. The basic CF-2 was a refinement of its predecessors, with a one-piece forged bolt and a shrouded bolt face. A plunger-type ejector and broad extractor claw were set into the bolt head so that full-size locking lugs could be retained. An indicator pin protruded from the top of the bolt plug and a rocking safety catch—part of the separate trigger unit—protruded from the stock behind the bolt handle. The guns originally had a roll-over Monte Carlo comb, with skip-line chequering on the pistol grip and fore-end; accompanied by a white spacer, the separate fore-end tip had an unusual 'wedge' joint with the stock. The

magazine floor plate was released by a catch on the front upper face of the trigger guard.

Williams sights were standard, among the options being a set trigger with an additional reverse-curved lever in the front of the trigger guard. A heavy 24in 'Varmint' barrel could be supplied in any of the standard chamberings, the resulting guns weighing up to 9·5lb.

1982: a 6·5 × 55mm chambering option was introduced for the standard CF-2, intended to boost sales in Scandinavia. The CF-2 Stutzen also appeared, in all the standard chamberings excepting 7mm Remington Magnum and ·300 Winchester Magnum. Mechanically identical with the rifle, it was 41·4in long, had a 20·6in barrel and weighed about 7·8lb; the principal distinguishing characteristic was a full-length stock with a separate schnabel fore-end tip.

The roll-over comb, white spacers and high gloss finish were abandoned on the Stutzen and standard CF-2, the original stock thereafter being restricted to the heavy-barrel rifle.

1984: a CF-2 Carbine amalgamated the barrel of the Stutzen and the stock of the standard rifle. Offered for all the chamberings excepting the two magnum types, it was not especially popular and was made only in small numbers.

1985: the new Custom, Varminter and Regal Classic models were built on the CF-2 action.

The Classic and Varminter rifles (the latter with a heavy barrel and no open sights) had distinctively angular bolt plugs, and oil-rubbed stocks with straight-comb butts. Their fore-end tips were rounded. Regal Custom rifles had a Monte Carlo comb, with ebonite caps on the pistol grip and fore-end. Bolt handles were spatulate and actions were engraved to order.

1986: production ceased when BSA Guns Ltd collapsed, the machinery and most of the parts apparently being sold to Pakistan. It is not known whether production ever began there.

CFT model

Made by BSA Guns Ltd, Birmingham, 1982–6.
7·62 × 51mm NATO/·308 Winchester only.
Action: as Royal series, above.

47·60in overall, 10·85lb with sights.
26·50in barrel, 4-groove rifling; RH, concentric.
Parker-Hale aperture sight.
2,860 ft/sec with 150-grain bullet.
☆

1982: this single-shot rifle was introduced to satisfy the target-shooting fraternity, with which it achieved a brief period in vogue. Built on a modified CF-2 action, with a solid-top receiver, it had a pistol-grip butt that could accept spacer plates to adjust its length. The fore-end was a broad plain-tipped pattern, with a rail for a hand-stop let into its underside. Micro-adjustable competition sights were usually fitted, though the mounting rail above the receiver could accept an optical sight when necessary.

Note: a CFT with a four-round box magazine, developed as a sniper rifle, was entered by the Sterling Engineering Co. Ltd of Dagenham in the British Army trials of the early 1980s before being offered commercially. The collapse of BSA in 1986 put an end to the project.

BÜCHEL

GERMANY

This swinging-block system, patented by Cuno Büchel in 1887, was unique. The breech block originally contained the entire lock mechanism, including the hammer and double set triggers. When the operating lever was depressed, the entire block moved radially down around a pivot at the lower front edge of the receiver. The lever was held in its closed position by a distinctive notched-nose catch set into its rearward spur.

By the turn of the century, however, the system had become more compact. Post-1900 rifles, therefore, embodied a shorter action with only the hammer contained within the block. Pivoted to the operating lever, the block moved vertically in the receiver; the trigger system was fitted into the stock behind the receiver and did not move when the lever was depressed.

Büchel rifles were often disguised by brand names 'Tell' or 'Luna'. Most had locking latches

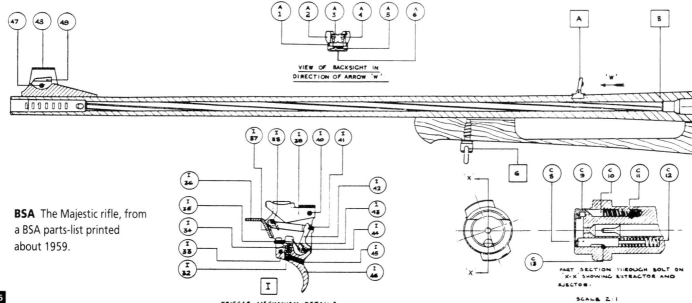

BSA The Majestic rifle, from a BSA parts-list printed about 1959.

VIEW OF BACKSIGHT IN
DIRECTION OF ARROW 'W'

TRIGGER MECHANISM DETAILS

PART SECTION THROUGH BOLT ON
'X-X' SHOWING EXTRACTOR AND
EJECTOR.

SCALE 2:1

on the rearward spur of the operating lever, but some of the largest had looped levers. Rifles may also bear other gunmakers' names.

Tell rifle

Made by Ernst Friedrich Büchel, Suhl, c.1890–1939. Chambered for a selection of European and American cartridges, with 8·15 × 46·5mm predominating.
DATA FOR A TYPICAL EXAMPLE, c.1910
Dropping-block action, with an operating lever doubling as the trigger guard.
5·6 × 35mm, rimmed.
1,075mm overall, 3·86kg unladen.
680mm barrel, 4-groove rifling; RH, concentric.
Block-and-leaf sight.
615 m/sec with 3-gram bullet.

☆

1910: the later rifle, with a vertically-moving block action, could be mistaken at a glance for an Aydt (q.v.). However, it had a characteristic locking latch on the operating lever spur and a raised wall on the left side of the receiver. The right wall was cut level with the base of the chamber to facilitate loading. A sliding safety catch lay on the tang, behind the cocking-indicator pin. A double set trigger mechanism was standard on these guns, particularly those destined for Schützen competitions. Barrels were invariably octagonal, though half-octagon, round and fluted patterns were also made.

BULLARD

UNITED STATES OF AMERICA
〜

These individualistic rifles were designed in the early 1880s by James Bullard to compete with the popular Winchesters and Marlins.

1. THE BLOCK-ACTION PATTERNS

These were simplifications of the lever-action rifles described below, locked by a very similar pivoting block but lacking the extended receiver.

Production was short-lived, owing to the failure of Bullard to compete with Winchester; the single-shot rifle offered little that rivals did not.

Target Rifle

Made by the Bullard Repeating Arms Company, Springfield, Massachusetts, c.1885–7.
Chambering: see notes.
Dropping-block action, operated by a lever.
DATA FOR A TYPICAL SPECIMEN
·38–45, semi-rimmed.
About 45·50in overall, 8·85lb unladen.
28·00in barrel, 4-groove rifling; RH, concentric?
Vernier aperture sight on rear tang.
1,385 ft/sec with 190-grain bullet.

☆

1885: these guns were made in rim- and centre-fire guise to satisfy the needs of target shooters, though a few ·45–70 examples were stocked as military-style muskets and carbines—the former with a full-length fore-end and two bands, the latter with a half-length fore-end and a single band.

The standard target and 'Hunting & Target' rifles were made with 28in round, half-octagonal or fully octagonal barrels, and could be obtained with straight-wrist or pistol-grip butts. Spring-leaf and elevator sights were usually fitted, though the target rifles often had vernier patterns. The finest single-shot Bullard was the Schuetzen Rifle, with a hooked Swiss-style butt plate and a spurred trigger guard. Made with a 30in barrel, it could weigh 12lb.

2. THE LEVER-ACTION PATTERNS

These were patented by Bullard in August 1881 and October 1883. Locked at the rear by a pivoting block—not unlike the Remington Rolling Block—the Bullard breech-bolt was moved by levers and rack-and-pinion gear. The operating stroke was extremely smooth, allowing Bullards to regularly win rapidity trials.

Lever Action Sporting Rifle

Offered as rifles, carbines and muskets.
Made by the Bullard Repeating Arms Company, Springfield, Massachusetts, c.1884–7.
·32–40, ·38–45, ·40–75, ·40–90, ·45–60, ·45–75, ·45–85 or ·50–115 Bullard, plus ·45–70 Government.
Lever action, operated by the trigger guard.
DATA FOR A TYPICAL EXAMPLE
·50–115 Bullard, semi-rimmed.
About 47·75in overall, 9·57lb unladen.
28·00in barrel, 4-groove rifling; RH, concentric?
Tube magazine under barrel, 11 rounds.
Spring-leaf and elevator sight.
1,535 ft/sec with 300-grain bullet.

1884: the standard or Medium Frame rifle—offered with 26in or 28in round, half-octagon or fully octagonal barrels—was chambered for ·40–90 rounds, though ·32–40 and ·38–45 options were added in 1885–6. A short 7-round magazine tube was usually fitted.

The Heavy Frame sporter accepted ·40–60, ·40–75, ·45–70 or ·45–85 cartridges, had a 28in barrel and offered a full-length eleven-round magazine. Bullard's Express Rifle, chambered only for ·50–115 ammunition, had a 28in round barrel and a full-length magazine.

Weights ranged from 7·55lb for the small '·32–40–105' sporter to a hefty 9·75lb for a '·50–115–300 Express Rifle' with an optional pistol-grip butt. Military-style muskets (30in barrel) and carbines (22in barrel) were made in small numbers. The musket had a full length fore-end retained by two barrel bands and accepted a socket bayonet; the carbine had a half-stock retained by a single band.

Bullards had a dated appearance. The absence of a conventional loading gate was also notable. Standard guns had straight-wrist stocks, though chequered butts or fore-ends could be ordered. Receivers were often colour case-hardened.

1890: unable to compete effectively against Winchester and Marlin, the Bullard company failed. Liquidation was concluded sometime in 1891—but whether volume production had been undertaken since c.1888 is questionable.

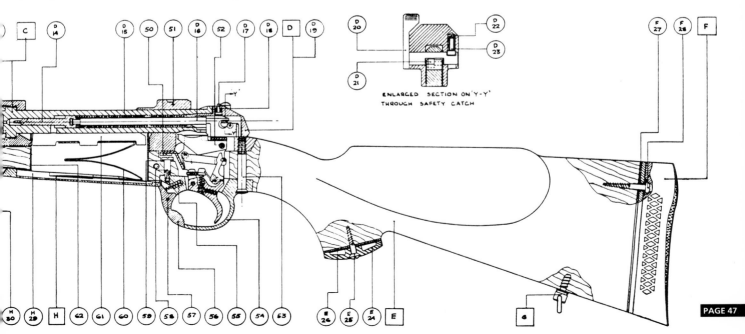

ENLARGED SECTION ON 'Y-Y' THROUGH SAFETY CATCH

BURGESS

UNITED STATES OF AMERICA

The action of these lever-action guns accorded with patents granted to prolific Andrew Burgess in 1873–82. Rifles made by Whitney and then Colt had a simple action. The operating lever—doubling as the trigger guard—extended up into the breech, where its short rear face rested against the rear of the receiver and an 'extension arm' ran forward along the top inner surface of the receiver. The breech block was pivoted to the tip of the extension arm. When the operating lever was pulled downward, the locking arm moved down and away from the rear face of the receiver; simultaneously, the extension arm retracted the breech block. The spent case was ejected as the elevator raised a new cartridge into the path of the returning breech block.

Burgess Repeating Rifle

••
'Whitney-Burgess' or 'Whitney-Kennedy'; also offered as a carbine.
Made by the Whitney Arms Company, Whitneyville, Connecticut, 1877–88.
·32–20 Winchester, ·38–40 Winchester, ·40–60 Winchester, ·44–40 Winchester, ·45–60 Winchester or ·45–70 Government.
Lever action, operated by an arm combined with the trigger guard.
DATA FOR RIFLE
·45–60 Winchester, rimmed.
46·50in overall, 8·72lb unladen.
28·00in barrel, 4-groove rifling; RH, concentric?
Tube magazine under barrel, 15 rounds.
Spring-leaf and elevator sight.
1,315 ft/sec with 300-grain bullet.
☆

1876: a lever-action rifle exhibited by Andrew Burgess at the Centennial Exposition attracted the attention of Eli Whitney, to whom it was licensed in 1877.
1878: two muskets were entered unsuccessfully in US Army trials.

1879: an improved cartridge elevator, patented in May by Samuel Kennedy, was added. The rifle subsequently—and misleadingly—became known as the 'Whitney-Kennedy'. It could be recognised by its large flat-side receiver and a small loading gate with an oval cartridge depression; it also had a niggardly proportioned open-loop operating lever. The rifle was made with a round, half-octagon or fully octagonal 24–28in barrel; carbines were also made in small numbers. Double set triggers, long barrels, selected woodwork, engraving and special sights were optional extras.
1886: a special small-action 'Light Model' was introduced, protected by additional patents issued in 1880 and 1883. It was offered only as a ·32–20 sporting rifle (with a 24in round, half-octagon or fully-octagonal barrel) or as a ·38–40 military-style musket. The sporter was 41·75in overall and weighed 8·75lb unladen.
1888: production ceased when Whitney was acquired by Winchester.

New Magazine Rifle

••
Alias 'Colt Burgess'; also offered in carbine form.
Made by Colt's Patent Fire Arms Mfg Co., Hartford, Connecticut, 1883–4.
Quantity: 6,400.
Lever action, operated by an arm combined with the trigger guard.
DATA FOR RIFLE
·44–40 Winchester, rimmed.
43·25in overall, 8·72lb unladen.
25·50in barrel, 4-groove rifling; RH, concentric?
Tube magazine under barrel, 15 rounds.
Spring-leaf and elevator sight.
1,310 ft/sec with 200-grain bullet.
☆

1883: the first ·44–40–200 centre-fire sporting rifles and a short-barrel carbine appeared in November. The Colt-made rifles offered round, half-octagon or fully octagonal barrels; carbines had a 20in round barrel, weighed 7·30lb and had twelve-round magazines. Decoration and specially selected woodwork were available to order, but guns of this type are very rare.

The Colts were similar externally to the Winchesters, but the receiver stopped only a short distance ahead of the loading gate.
1884: Winchester threatened to put its effectual revolvers into production to compete against the Single Action Army pattern, so Colt stopped making Burgess-type guns after only 3,810 rifles and 2,590 carbines had been made.

BURTON

UNITED STATES OF AMERICA
Lee-Burton and Ward-Burton patterns

These rifles originally combined a turning-bolt action derived from patents granted to Bethel Burton in December 1859 and August 1868 with an extractor/ejector credited to William Ward (patented in February 1871). Burton was also responsible for rifles with tube magazines in the fore-end, and the side-mounted hopper patented in Britain in the autumn of 1880.

BRITAIN

The first rifle was submitted to the Small Arms Committee in the early 1880s. A few guns were subsequently made with the effectual Lee bolt and an improved hopper magazine, but trials soon revealed their shortcomings.

Lee-Burton

••
Experimental infantry rifle, 1887 type.
Made by the Royal Small Arms Factory, Enfield, 1887.
·402, rimmed.
Turning-bolt action, with one lug on the bolt head locking into the receiver and an auxiliary lug opposite the bolt handle.
50·18in overall, 10·25lb unladen.
30·20in barrel, 7-groove rifling; LH, ratchet.
Detachable hopper magazine, 5 rounds.
Leaf sight graduated to 2,000 yards.
1,570 ft/sec with ball cartridges.
Experimental sword bayonet.
☆

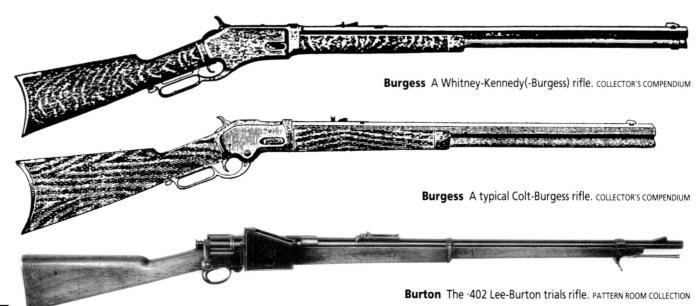

Burgess A Whitney-Kennedy(-Burgess) rifle. COLLECTOR'S COMPENDIUM

Burgess A typical Colt-Burgess rifle. COLLECTOR'S COMPENDIUM

Burton The ·402 Lee-Burton trials rifle. PATTERN ROOM COLLECTION

1883: an 'Improved Lee-Burton Magazine Rifle' was built at Enfield, with a modified Lee-type bolt and a Burton magazine. It had a very distinctive two-piece stock with the so-called Arbuthnot Pattern fore-end, cut down to expose almost all of the barrel—to promote cooling and prevent rust accumulating. The single nose band bore a swivel, and a short hand guard ran forward from the chamber to the back sight.

1886: approximately 25–27 of an order for 150 guns were made before trials against the Owen Jones were abandoned. They retained the odd Arbuthnot-type stock.

1887: about three hundred ·402 rifles were made for trials against the ·43 Remington-Lee. They were stocked conventionally, had two bands, and lacked a hand guard. The sear was moved from the receiver to the trigger-guard assembly and the hopper was simplified. An aperture on the outside of the magazine case allowed the contents to be seen at a glance.

USA

The Ward-Burton rifle deserved a better fate. One of its best features was the retraction of the firing pin into the bolt as the breech opened. Some units issued with trials rifles were enthusiastic, owing to effectual extraction and ejection, but the novelty soon palled and the Allin-type Springfield was preferred.

Model 1871

Rifle and carbine, Ward-Burton type.
Made by the National Armory, Springfield, Massachusetts, 1871–2.
·50–70, rimmed.
Turning-bolt action, with interrupted threads on the rear of the bolt body locking into the receiver.
DATA FOR RIFLE
51·88in overall, about 9lb unladen.
32·63in barrel, 3-groove rifling; RH; concentric.
Ramp-and-leaf sight graduated to 1,200 yards?
1,250 ft/sec with standard ball cartridges.
M1855 socket bayonet.
☆

1870: the Ward-Burton impressed the St Louis board sufficiently to be recommended for field trials. The action contained an extractor and ejector, mounted on the detachable bolt head; a bolt-lock catch lay on the right side of the receiver; and a spring-loaded firing pin ran through the bolt.

1871: General Alexander Dyer, the Chief of Ordnance, informed the Secretary of War on 31 May that a thousand rifles had been ordered.

1872: by March, when field trials began, 1,015 rifles and 317 carbines had been made. One gun was entered in the contemporaneous breech loading rifle trials as the 'Ward-Burton Musket, no. 26', but failed to challenge the supremacy of the Springfield-Allin. Survivors are now very rarely encountered.

A 'Ward-Burton Magazine Carbine, no. 97' was also tested. The tube magazine under the barrel, the cartridge elevator and the sliding cut-off had been developed by Burton and Ward in 1869–71. No. 97 was successful enough to be recommended for a trial with the cavalry, but the Chief of Ordnance disagreed. Nothing more was ever done.

CETME

SPAIN

This essence of this roller-delayed breech may be traced back to the German MG.42, and to experiments preceding the introduction of the MP.43—the first modern-style assault rifle.

1942: Mauser began work on a roller system credited to Wilhelm Stähle. Locked at the instant of firing, it tapped propellant gas from the bore to propel a piston backward. The piston moved the rear part of the breech block back until the locking rollers could move inward into the space thus created. A spring in a butt-tube returned the mechanism to re-load the chamber. The front part of the breech block stopped against the rear face of the barrel at the end of the loading stroke while the rear portion, still moving, forced the rollers out into the locking recesses.

1943: Mauser's technicians discovered that the mechanism worked satisfactorily without the piston assembly, using the backward thrust generated on firing through the base of the cartridge case to unlock the rollers.

1945: the military authorities were deeply suspicious of the delayed-blowback Gerät 06.H, which remained a privately-promoted project, and had only just commissioned thirty locked-breech assault rifles (Gerät 06 or StG.45 [M]) when the Second World War ended. After the Oberndorf factory had fallen into Allied hands, the French continued work until the Spring of 1946. Prototype assault rifles chambering ·30 M1 Carbine ammunition were subsequently made in Mulhouse under the supervision of ex-Mauser engineer Ludwig Vorgrimmler.

1951: the focus of attention shifted to Spain, whence Vorgrimmler had moved. As the Spanish army was in desperate need of modern weapons, the Instituto Nacional de Industrias formed the Centro de Estudios Técnicos de Materiales Especiales (CETME) in Madrid.

1952: prototype assault rifles were completed. They embodied the retarded-blowback roller lock and chambered a special 7·9 × 40mm cartridge in an effort to balance an ability to fire fully automatically with the need to keep a gun weighing less than 4kg under proper control. The original 6·8gm bullet had a copper jacket and a lightweight aluminium core, exposed at the tip; starting out at about 800 m/sec, the streamlined bullet was said to be capable of piercing most steel helmets at 1,000 metres.

1954: in March, impressed by the CETME rifles, the Spanish government invited Heckler & Koch to resolve mass-production problems.

MILITARY WEAPONS
SPAIN

7·62mm guns

A, B, C, D, E and R patterns.
Made in the Oviedo factory of Empresa Nacional de Militares 'Santa Barbara'.

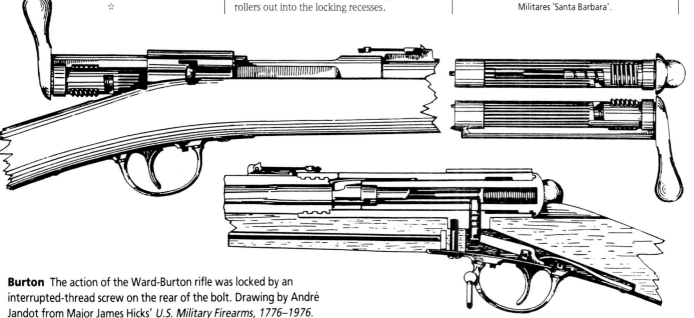

Burton The action of the Ward-Burton rifle was locked by an interrupted-thread screw on the rear of the bolt. Drawing by André Jandot from Major James Hicks' *U.S. Military Firearms, 1776–1976.*

7·62 × 51mm CETME or 7·62 × 51mm NATO. Auto-loading action, with a delayed-action breech system relying on rollers engaging the barrel-collar walls.

DATA FOR A TYPICAL MODELO C
7·62 × 51mm NATO, rimless.
1,015mm overall, 4·48kg with empty magazine (wooden hand-guard pattern).
450mm barrel, 4-groove rifling; RH, concentric.
Detachable box magazine, 20 rounds.
Drum sight graduated to 400 metres.
780 m/sec with NATO ball cartridges; 600 ± 50 rpm.
CETME knife bayonet.

☆

1954: pre-production guns were made for the 7·9mm CETME cartridge. Consisting largely of sheet-steel pressings, they had a straight-line layout with a tube containing the cocking handle above the barrel. The butt and pistol grip were wood, while a folded bipod provided a very uncomfortable forward hand grip. The straight base of the magazine housing was a prolongation of the receiver; the selector lever lay on the left side above the pistol grip; and a tangent-leaf back sight appeared on top of the action above the trigger aperture. A multi-port muzzle brake was standard, though a detachable grenade launcher could be fitted when required. Typical markings included FUSIL DE ASALTO above C.E.T.M.E. over the serial number (e.g., 'No. 433') on the left side of the magazine housing.

1955: promising trials were undertaken in Germany. After an abortive variant had been produced for a short 7·62mm round, the rifle was revised for the US ·30 T65 cartridge destined to become NATO standard.

Series 'A' 7·62 × 51mm rifles dated from this period. They were essentially similar to the pre-production examples, but had a straighter magazine, a rotating carrying handle on the bolt-tube, and an oblique-cut magazine housing. A typical marking read F.A. CETME over a number (e.g., 'A–356'). The guns fired automatically from an open-bolt position.

1956: the rifle was licensed to NWM in the Netherlands to take part in contemporary army trials that eventually resolved in favour

of the FAL. The Germans had also become very interested in the CETME and development subsequently passed to Heckler & Koch (q.v.).

1958: the Spanish government adopted the Modelo B for service. A grenade launcher and a sheet-metal fore-end had been added, and the mechanism was simplified by eliminating the open-bolt automatic firing capabilities.

1965: the CETME Modelo C was approved as a result of a decision taken in 1964 to standardise the 7·62mm NATO cartridge (loaded with the FN-designed SS77 bullet) instead of the lower-powered Spanish pattern. The rifle was strengthened to withstand additional chamber pressure and recoil impulse, and a combination flash-hider/grenade launcher was fitted to the muzzle.

A typical Modelo C rifle was marked with F.A.–CETME–C and the Santa Barbara logo (a sword transfixing a cogwheel) on the left side of the magazine housing ahead of 'cal. 7,62 mm.' and above a serial number such as ET☆68913☆. Selectors were marked T (top), S (middle) and R (bottom) for single shots, safety, and fully automatic fire respectively.

A few heavy-barrelled Modelo C sniper rifles have been made. Fitted with optical sights and restricted to semi-automatic fire, they were not especially successful; imported weapons and the Mauser-type Santa Barbara C-75 rifle have apparently been preferred in Spain—certainly in the hands of counter-terrorist and police units.

1978: development led to the abortive Modelo D and then, in 1981–2, to the Modelo E. This was little more than a C-pattern gun with improvements to the ejector, sights and hand guard. Greater use was made of synthetic parts, and some guns had burst-firing capabilities.

1982*: a short-barrelled Modelo R port-firing weapon was devised for armoured troops, the muzzle being adapted to fit a ball mount. The butt was replaced by synthetic cap and the cocking handle was moved backward to clear the short cylindrical fore-end.

1984: 7·62mm CETME rifles were superseded as the Spanish service rifle by the 5·56mm Modelo L rifle described below.

5·56mm guns

L, L1 and LC patterns.
Made in the Oviedo factory of Empresa Nacional de Militares 'Santa Barbara'.
5·56 × 45mm.
Action: as 7·62mm version, above.

DATA FOR A TYPICAL MODELO L1
925mm overall, 3·42kg with empty magazine.
400mm barrel, 6-groove rifling; RH, concentric.
Detachable box magazine, 30 rounds.
Pivoting-'L' sight for 200 and 400 metres.
970 m/sec with NATO ball cartridges; 750 ± 50 rpm.
Optional CETME knife bayonet.

☆

1980*: development of a small-calibre version of the 7·62mm CETME rifle began. The Modelo L shared the basic delayed blowback roller-lock system, but was designed with an eye to simplifying production. The pistol grip was moulded integrally with the butt and a synthetic hand guard was used.

The earliest guns had rotating four-position drum sights (100–400 metres), and used special 20-round magazines. Their selectors had an additional R position, giving a three-round burst, but this was subsequently reduced to the status of an optional extra.

1984: the Modelo L was adopted by the Spanish army to supplement and ultimately replace the 7·62mm rifles. An L1 variant accepted the NATO standard US M16-type thirty-round magazine, but was apparently destined more for export than Spanish service. L-type rifles have three-position selectors and a simplified two-position back sight; bipods and optical sights have been used, but are not in general service.

The first rifles were delivered to the army in 1987, by which time orders for about 60,000 had been placed. A typical marking read CETME 5,56 (·223) in three lines on the left side of the magazine housing. An 'L'-prefix serial number usually lay on the left side of the receiver above the trigger.

The Modelo LC had a 320mm barrel, with a short expansion chamber behind the flash suppressor, and was fitted with a retractable

butt. It was 860mm long—665mm with butt retracted—and weighed about 3·2kg.

OTHERS

Chad, the Congolese Republic, the Dominican Republic, Guatemala and Mauritania have all purchased substantial quantities of CETME-type rifles for front-line service. Several Scandinavian countries, Pakistan and Portugal have acquired sizeable numbers for trials.

SPORTING GUNS

The CETME Sport, derived from the Modelo C, differed from military-issue guns only in its trigger mechanism—limited to semi-automatic fire—and the addition of a recoil pad on the butt. A typical rifle imported into the USA in the mid 1960s was marked CETME "SPORT" on the left side of the magazine housing above the 'S'-prefix serial number; MADE IN SPAIN usually appeared on the right above the marks of the importer, Mars Equipment Corporation of Chicago, Illinois. Selectors were marked S (safe) above F (fire). Like all similar rifles, the CETME did not make an effectual sporter and sales were commensurately small.

CHAFFEE-REECE

UNITED STATES OF AMERICA

This bolt-action system was designed by Reuben Chaffee and General James Reece of Springfield, Illinois. It was patented in February 1879.

The feed mechanism relied on a special oscillating double-rack unit, operated by the bolt, instead of a conventional magazine spring. Retracting the bolt pushed the mobile rack down the magazine until special retainers slipped behind the cartridge rims; the fixed rack simply held the cartridges in place. Closing the bolt lifted the mobile rack, pulling the cartridges forward, until the bolt face caught the rim of the first cartridge and pushed it into the chamber.

Unlike the competing Hotchkiss rifle (q.v.), which had a conventional tube magazine, the Chaffee-Reece system separated the cartridge noses from the primers of the preceding rounds.
1882: a prototype rifle was submitted to the US Army trials, placing second behind the Lee and ahead of the Hotchkiss. The trial report recommended acquiring substantial numbers of each rifle for field trials, but the backers of the Chaffee-Reece—if not their rivals—lacked suitable facilities.
1883: after unsuccessfully approaching Colt, General Reece asked the Ordnance Department to make the rifles in Springfield Armory, costs being minimised by using machinery on which Ward-Burtons had been made in the 1870s.

Model 1882

Experimental infantry rifle.
Made by the National Armory, Springfield, Massachusetts, 1884.
Quantity: 750.
·45–70, rimmed.
Turning-bolt action, locked by the base of the bolt-handle rib abutting the receiver ahead of the bridge.
49·00in overall, about 9lb unladen.
27·88in barrel, 3-groove rifling; RH, concentric.
Tube magazine in butt, 5 rounds.
Ramp-and-leaf sight graduated to 1,200 yards.
About 1,300 ft/sec with standard ball cartridges.
M1873 socket bayonet.

☆

1884: readied for trials by midsummer, the rifles resembled the 1879-model Hotchkiss externally owing to the government-pattern stock.
1885: the rack mechanism proved unreliable and difficult to maintain. As the bolt had to be operated to load each cartridge through the butt-trap, the Chaffee-Reece was ranked below the Hotchkiss in the final analysis. Neither rifle challenged the Lee effectually.
1892: a single ·30-calibre gun appeared in the US Army magazine-rifle trials, with a lack of success comparable to that of its ·45-calibre predecessor.

1907: Francis Bannerman & Sons were still offering a hundred Chaffee-Reece rifles, acquired from US Army stores in the mid 1890s.

CHAMPLIN

UNITED STATES OF AMERICA

This interesting bolt-action system was designed by Jerry Haskins and patented in 1969. Rifles have been made since 1968, though only on a 'to order' basis; output has never been large. The essence of the action is a three-lug bolt, each lug being backed by a lengthy guide/safety rib. When the action is closed, the lugs rotate into their seats in the receiver and the guide ribs turn ahead of (but do not abut) the receiver bridge.

Sporting rifle

Made by Champlin-Haskins Firearms, Inc. (c.1968–70), and Champlin Firearms, Inc., Enid, Oklahoma (1971 to date).
Virtually any chambering can be made to order.
Turning-bolt action, locked by rotating lugs on the bolt head into the receiver.
DATA FOR A TYPICAL EXAMPLE
·340 Weatherby Magnum, belted rimless.
44·90in overall, 8·15lb unladen.
26·00in barrel, rifling pattern unknown.
Integral box magazine, 3 rounds.
Express sight.
2,850 ft/sec with 250-grain bullet.

☆

1968: the first Champlin rifles had receivers machined from steel forgings. They could be identified by their distinctive bolt and their elegant lines, which included an octagonal receiver and bolt shroud. The recessed bolt face accommodated a plunger-type ejector, the extractor claw being set into one of the locking lugs. Trigger guards were sometimes square backed, and often tapered from front to back.
1971: the forged-steel receivers were replaced with machined investment castings, almost contemporaneously with the change in company

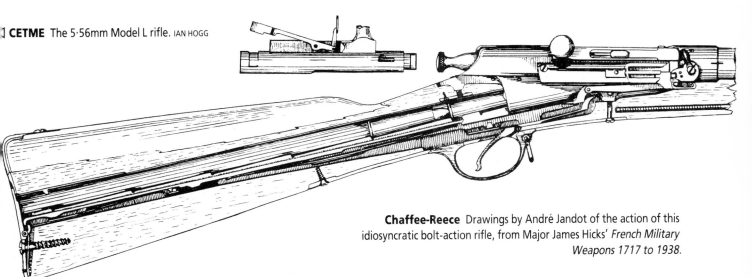

CETME The 5·56mm Model L rifle. IAN HOGG

Chaffee-Reece Drawings by André Jandot of the action of this idiosyncratic bolt-action rifle, from Major James Hicks' *French Military Weapons 1717 to 1938*.

structure, though the basic features remained unchanged. By 1990, the company was offering rifles of the highest quality, with round, octagonal, tapered octagon or ribbed octagon barrels; stocks were being made to individual specifications, with right or left-hand actions, but were usually Circassian walnut with steel pistol-grip caps and butt-plate traps. The tang safety—once optional—had become standard, with a bolt-shroud safety substituted to special order. Canjar triggers have always been fitted.

CHARTERED INDUSTRIES

SINGAPORE

This engineering company first became involved in the arms industry in the late 1960s, when a contract to produce M16-type rifles (see 'ArmaLite') was negotiated on behalf of the newly-independent Singapore state.

Making ArmaLites involved the payment of licensing fees; when work on the M16 came to an end, therefore, CIS produced the SA-80—an adaption of the ArmaLite AR-18 by way of the abortive Sterling Light Automatic Rifle.

The SA-80 and its successor, the SR-88, have been designed with a view to simplifying production. Their construction relies heavily on stampings and sheet-metal fabrication, reducing costs substantially compared with the M16.

SA-80

Made by Chartered Industries of Singapore Ltd, later Chartered Firearms Industries Pty Ltd, Singapore.
5·56 × 45mm, rimless.
Gas-operated auto-loading action, locked by rotating lugs on the bolt into the barrel extension.
970mm overall, 3·17kg without magazine.
460mm barrel, 6-groove rifling; RH, concentric.
Detachable box magazine, 20 or 30 rounds.
Rocking-leaf sight.
970 m/sec with standard ball cartridges, 700 ± 25 rpm.
Optional knife bayonet.
☆

SAR 80
5.56mm Law-Enforcement Rifle

A typical brochure promoting the SA-80. **Chartered Industries**

Chartered Industries The Sterling Light Automatic Rifle. IAN HOGG

Chartered Industries The 5·56mm SR-88A rifle is an improved form of the SR-88, differing largely in furniture. IAN HOGG

1978: the first prototypes of this assault rifle were revealed, most of the design studies being undertaken in England by Sterling Engineering Co. Ltd of Dagenham, work being credited to Frank Waters and L. James Sullivan.

1981: series production began in Singapore. The rifle was locked by a rotating Stoner-pattern bolt. It could be identified by 'crackle' finish on the receiver, and by a tapering synthetic fore-end with vertical ribs behind the front sight. Thinner finger grooves lay on the underside ahead of the magazine. An M16 magazine and a standard muzzle brake/grenade launcher were fitted, bipods and a folding butt being optional.

SR-88

Made by Chartered Firearms Industries, Singapore.
5·56 × 45mm, rimless.
Action: as SA-80, above.
972mm overall, 3·66kg without magazine.
460mm barrel, 6-groove rifling; RH, concentric.
Detachable box magazine, 20 or 30 rounds.
Adjustable aperture sight.
970 m/sec with standard ball cartridges; 750 ± 25 rpm.
Optional knife bayonet.

☆

1988: this improved SA-80 had a slotted hand guard to improve barrel ventilation, a folding carrying handle, and a new adjustable aperture pattern back sight. The US M203 grenade launcher could be attached to the underside of the fore-end when required. The butt, hand guard and pistol grip were made of fibreglass-reinforced nylon, and—profiting from US Army experiences in Vietnam—the bore and gas-tube were chromium plated to reduce the effects of fouling. Bipods and a folding skeletal butt could be supplied on request.

CHINESE STATE FACTORIES

PEOPLE'S REPUBLIC OF CHINA

Little is known about the genesis of this unusual rifle which, though sharing the lines of the SKS (Simonov) carbine, embodies a rotating bolt and a gas system adapted from the Kalashnikov. At least part of the design work has been credited to Tang Wen-Li, but several differing patterns have been reported and the information given below should be treated with a degree of caution.

Type 63 series

Types 63, 68, 73, 81 and 81–1.
Made by State Factory No. 90?
7·62 × 39mm, rimless.
Gas-operated auto-loading action, locked by rotating lugs on the bolt into the barrel extension.
1,035mm overall, 3·47kg without magazine.
520mm barrel, 4-groove rifling; RH, concentric.
Detachable box magazine, 15 rounds.
Tangent-leaf sight graduated to 1,000 metres.
735 m/sec with Soviet M43 cartridges; 750 ± 25 rpm.
Integral knife bayonet.

☆

1963: this rifle had a conventional appearance, with a crudely shaped hardwood stock and a bayonet that pivoted back on a block on the muzzle (behind the sight) to lie under the fore-end. Oddly, the magazine could be loaded through the top of the open action, suitable charger guides being milled into the rear edge of the ejection port.

1965: series production of the original Type 63 rifle began, several million being made. They were distinguished by machined-steel receivers. It is suspected, owing to the curious magazine arrangements and the absence of a grenade launching capability, that the Type 63 was intended for the people's militia rather than the regular forces for whom the 7·62mm Type 56 and 5·45mm Type 84 (Kalashnikov) assault rifles remained standard.

1969: an improved Type 68 rifle appeared, with a stamped receiver, minor changes in the action, and a synthetic hand guard.

1973: the new Type 73 rifle differed from its predecessors primarily in the addition of a fully automatic capability and the substitution of the standard AK-type thirty-round magazine for the smaller pattern of the earlier Types 63 and 68.

1983: the 'Type 81' variant of the Type 73 was introduced—apparently for commercial sale—with a three-round burst firing capability instead of the fully automatic setting. The Type 81–1 was identical, but had a folding butt. (Note: the 'Type 81' designation has also been applied to a modernised variant of the standard Type 56 carbine [SKS]. The confusion has probably arisen from the external affinity of the Type 63—and its successors—with the original Type 56.)

COGSWELL & HARRISON

BRITAIN

This well-established gunmaker exploited a unique turning-bolt action patented in 1900 by Edgar Harrison. It was applied to rimfire trainers and large-calibre Express Rifles alike, and also made as a shotgun. Production seems to have ceased in 1914; post-1918 Cogswell & Harrison sporters were built on standard Mauser actions.

Named after the company's telegraphic code-name, the Certus mechanism was built around a stubby rotating bolt set into a reciprocating block. When the handle was lifted, disengaging the locking lugs from the receiver, bolt and block could be slid backward along rails set into the stock. Most guns had readily detachable barrels.

Certus Sporting Rifle

Made by Cogswell & Harrison, London, c.1902–10.
·256 Mannlicher, ·303, ·375/·303 Axite, ·318 Accelerated Express, ·360 Nitro Express No.2, and many other British sporting rounds.
Turning-bolt action, with three lugs on the bolt head locking into the receiver.
DATA FOR TYPICAL EXAMPLE
·303, rimmed.
48·25in overall, 7·67lb unladen.
27·00in barrel, 5-groove rifling; LH, concentric.
Detachable box magazine, 4 rounds.
Express sight.
2,050 ft/sec with 210-grain bullet.

☆

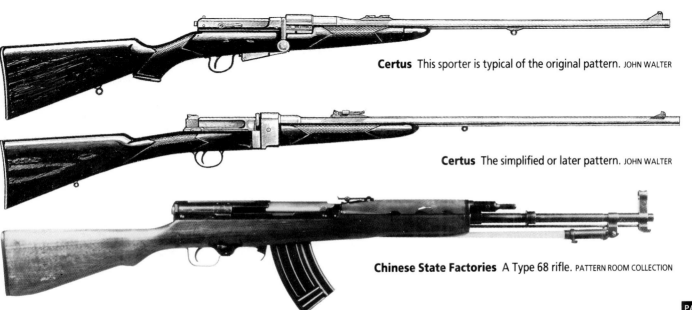

Certus This sporter is typical of the original pattern. JOHN WALTER

Certus The simplified or later pattern. JOHN WALTER

Chinese State Factories A Type 68 rifle. PATTERN ROOM COLLECTION

1902: the first rifles followed the 1900 patent specification drawings closely, with one-piece stocks and detachable box magazines. A radial safety lever lay on the right side of the breech block, and the tail of the striker acted as an indicator when the mechanism was cocked. The barrel, held by an effectual interrupted-thread screw, could be removed by turning it through 90° after a bolt running upward into the fore-end ahead of the magazine had been loosened.

Most guns of this pattern had impeccably chequered pistol grip half-stocks with an unusually short fore-end, sometimes retained by a transverse key set in oval escutcheons. The sights reflected the customer's specifications; though Express or Cape patterns predominated, they may range from simple open notches to military-style tangent-leaves.

Certus Sporting Rifle

Improved Pattern.
Made by Cogswell & Harrison, London, c.1906–14.
Chambered for many pre-1914 large-calibre British sporting rifle cartridges.
Action: as earlier type, above.
DATA FOR TYPICAL SINGLE-SHOT EXAMPLE
·450 No.2 Nitro Express, rimmed.
50·95in overall, 7·95lb unladen.
32·00in barrel, 7-groove rifling; LH, polygonal.
Ramp-and-leaf sight graduated to 1,000 yards.
2,175 ft/sec with 480-grain bullet.

☆

1906*: several of these guns have been reported with the name of Westley Richards & Co. Ltd, to whom Cogswell & Harrison may have granted a licence. Some rifles had magazines, but most were single-shot. The principal improvement concerned the detachable barrel, locked into the receiver by a lateral quick-release bolt. The breech mechanism was simplified—the bolt handle was sometimes no more than an open ring—and the striker-locking safety was usually replaced by a trigger-lock type. Owing to the slab-type barrel-lock housing, a two-piece stock was necessary. Butts had straight wrists or pistol grips; fore-ends were plain or horn tipped.

COMBLAIN

BELGIUM
∽

This dropping-block action was created by Hubert-Joseph Comblain of Liége. The standard Belgian-type Comblain was exported to Greece in 1873 (8,000 rifles and 500 musketoons) and then to Chile and Peru. A special pattern was made for Brazil.

Compact for its day and surprisingly durable, the basic action comprised a sturdy receiver with the breech lever (doubling as the trigger guard) pivoted at the lower front edge. Pulling the lever lowered the breech block—which contained the hammer, trigger and main spring—to disengage the locking shoulders and then moved it radially. The hammer cocked during the opening motion, at the end of which the extractor withdrew the spent case from the chamber.

MILITARY WEAPONS
BELGIUM
Models 1870 and 1882

Civil guard carbine and infantry rifle: Carabine de la
Garde Civique Mle.1870 et Fusil Mle.1882.
Made by the 'Petit Syndicat', Liége (Ancion & Co.,
Dresse-Laloux & Co., Auguste Francotte, and
Pirlot-Frésart & Co.).
11 × 51mm, rimmed.
Dropping-block action, with the operating lever
combined with the trigger guard.
DATA FOR MLE.1870
1,200mm overall, 4·46kg unladen.
808mm barrel, 4-groove rifling; RH, concentric.
Ramp-and-leaf sight graduated to 1,000 metres?
430 m/sec with Mle.1870 ball cartridges.
Mle.1868 sabre bayonet.

☆

1870: adopted on 26 March to supersede the Albini-Braendlin, supplies of which had not reached the Garde Civique, this 'carbine'—virtually a full-length rifle—was easily identified by its massive receiver and the housing immediately behind the trigger. It had a two-piece stock, the single band and simple nose cap being retained by springs. A cleaning rod was contained in the fore-end, projecting below the barrel, while swivels lay beneath the band and on the under-edge of the butt. Set in a distinctive washer, a retaining bolt ran laterally through the fore-end immediately below the back sight, the leaf of which hinged at the front of the bed. A bayonet lug and tenon lay on the right side of the muzzle.

1882: a modified gun, slightly longer than its predecessor but otherwise essentially similar, was adopted to cure faults in the original design. The breech lever was simplified; the hammer was altered so that the mechanism could be cocked or uncocked at will; and a half-cock safety notch appeared.

Models 1871 and 1871/83

Short rifles: Mousquetons Mle.1871 et Mle.1871/83.
Made by the 'Petit Syndicat' (see above).
Quantity: 7,500?
11 × 42mm, rimmed.
Action: as Mle.1870, above.
800mm overall, 3·03kg unladen.
455mm barrel, 4-groove rifling; RH, concentric.
Ramp-and-leaf sight graduated to 500 metres.
295 m/sec with ball cartridges.
No bayonet.

☆

1871: adopted on 15 July for the regular cavalry, this was little more than a shortened Mle.1870 Garde Civique carbine. The short fore-end was retained by a nose cap and a transverse bolt. Swivels lay beneath the nose cap and butt.
1883: many Mle.1871 guns were altered for the pioneers and Train to approximate to the Mle.1882 Garde Civique rifle (q.v.). As the musketoons were stocked to the muzzle, a new screw-retained barrel band and a new nose cap were required. A sling bar was fitted to the under-edge of the stock immediately behind the breech lever, and a cleaning rod lay beneath the

Double rifles of the type shown leaning on an ar hill behind 'A Good Head' (a Puku antelope), downed in what was then Northern Rhodesia, dominated the British African market in which t Certus and other bolt-action rifles struggled to make headway. COLLECTOR'S COMPENDIUM

muzzle. The new back sight was graduated to 1,070 metres.

1890*: a few guns were altered to accept the Mle.1867 bayonet. These had a new barrel band (fitted with a swivel) and a simple nose cap, sufficient of the muzzle being exposed to accept the bayonet socket. The second swivel lay on the under-edge of the stock.

BRAZIL
Model 1874

Manufacturer unknown—possibly Auguste Francotte & Co., Liége.
11·4 × 53mm, rimmed.
Action: as Belgian guns, above.
1,200mm overall, 4·65kg unladen.
803mm barrel, 4-groove rifling; RH, concentric.
Ramp-and-leaf sight graduated to 1,200 metres?
Performance: not known.
Socket bayonet?
☆

1874: this was a variant of the Belgian gun, lacking a cocking spur on the breech block as the hammer was carried inside a shroud. The rear swivel was mounted on a special plate screwed to the front of the receiver, and the lower tang—projecting backward from the receiver—was made separately rather than being forged integrally as in the Belgian prototype.

SPORTING GUNS

Sporters made in Liége in 1870–80 were soon overhauled by better designs; though the Comblain was strong enough to handle most of the medium-power sporting cartridges of its period, its unhandsome looks were a drawback. A few guns were stocked and completed in Britain, probably from components supplied by Francotte; usually displaying a 'small action' instead of the full-size military type, these often bear the marks of E.M. Reilly & Co. of Oxford Street, London. Edward Reilly had collaborated with the Belgian inventor in the Reilly-Comblain rifle of the mid 1860s.

DOMINICAN REPUBLIC
~

Unusually, for such an insignificant country, the Dominican Republic created an effectual arms factory in San Cristobal in the late 1940s—largely to use the talents of fugitive firearms designers from Hungary and Italy. The first weapon to be produced was a submachine-gun, copied from the Beretta Mo.1938, but work then concentrated on a light automatic rifle chambering the US ·30 M1 Carbine cartridge.

Cristobal carbines were popular in Central America, selling in quantity to Cuba in addition to service with the Dominican Republic armed forces. Production has been estimated in excess of 200,000, but details are lacking.

Cristobal Carbine

Models 2 and 3.
Made by Armeria San Cristobal.
·30 M1 Carbine, rimless.
Auto-loading action, delayed blowback.
945mm overall, 3·55kg without magazine.
412mm barrel, 4-groove rifling; RH, concentric.
Detachable box magazine, 30 rounds.
Spring-leaf and elevator sight.
570 m/sec with standard ball cartridges; 575 ± 25 rpm.
No bayonet.
☆

1953*: designed by the Hungarian Pal Kiraly, the Cristobal M2 had a Beretta-like appearance externally, relying on the mechanism of that submachine-gun to give single shots from the front trigger or fully automatic fire by pressing the rear trigger. Internally, however, a lever connected the lightweight bolt head and the heavy body. When the gun fired, the resistance of the lever had to be overcome before the bolt body began to move backward, delaying the opening of the breech until the chamber pressure had dropped to a safe level; much the same system had been used in Kiraly's Hungarian submachine-guns a decade earlier.

1961: service showed that the M2 overheated in automatic fire. The improved M3 (or 'Mk 3') discarded the original wooden hand guard for a perforated sheet-steel fore-end and could accept an FN export-pattern knife bayonet. A few guns were made with a tubular folding butt, but were only issued in limited quantities.

Model 62

Made by Armeria San Cristobal.
7·62 × 51mm, rimless.
Gas-operated auto-loading action, locked by displacing the rear of the breech block into the receiver floor.
1,080mm overall, 4·75kg with loaded magazine.
540mm barrel, 4-groove rifling; RH, concentric.
Detachable box magazine, 20 rounds.
Ramp sight graduated to 600 metres?
825 m/sec with standard ball cartridges.
No bayonet.
☆

1962*: this unexceptional gas-operated infantry rifle was created by combining the proven gas system of the US Garand/M14 rifle with the effectual locking system of the FN FAL. It had a conventional pistol-grip stock, ending well short of the muzzle, and a short sheet-steel hand guard above the fore-end.

By the time the rifle was ready for production (c.1966), the advent of better weapons and the movement of the USA towards a smaller calibre halted work after only a couple of hundred M62 rifles had been made.

Brno, Čermak, Galaš and other designs
~

Gaining independence after the collapse of the unloved Austro-Hungarian empire in 1918, Czechoslovakia rapidly created an effectual arms industry on the basis of the world-famous Skoda factory in Pilsen and machine-tools supplied as war reparations.

The Mauser-type bolt-action rifles—made in vast numbers between the wars—are covered

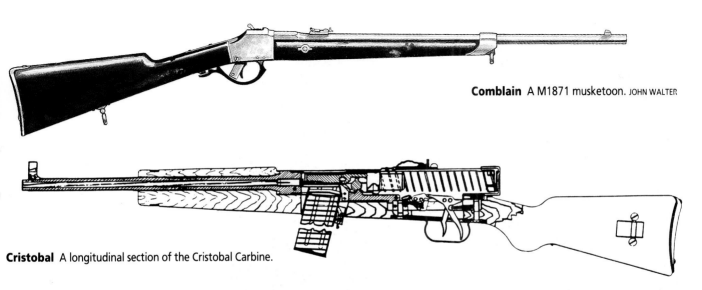

Comblain A M1871 musketoon. JOHN WALTER

Cristobal A longitudinal section of the Cristobal Carbine.

in the relevant section. Indigenous Holek and Koucky guns are also covered separately.

The earliest auto-loaders were developed by Karel Krnka from designs that had originated in the early twentieth century; the 'K' rifle of the mid 1920s became the ČZ HB, after work credited to Beneš, and then the 'Model S' rifle (indicating development in the Strakonice factory). Additional work by Vaclav Polanka and Jan Kratochvil created a ČZ 38 gas-operated rifle locked by a falling block. This weapon was extensively tested against the Holek (q.v.) designs, eventually becoming the vz.39; the rifle was provisionally adopted in 1939, but German invasion prevented further work.

After the end of the Second World War, the Czechoslovakian military authorities obtained substantial quantities of the German Gew.43 (Walther) auto-loader, whereupon development of indigenous designs was radically curtailed in favour of weapons chambering 7·5mm and—latterly—7·62mm intermediate cartridges.

Tests in 1949 with the ZK 472, ZJ 481 and ČZ 493 rifles, by Koucky, Kynčl and Kratochvil respectively, resolved in favour of the ČZ 493.

1. THE AUTO-LOADING PATTERNS

Model 52

vz.52 and vz.52–57.
Made by Československá Zbrojovka, Brno (code 'tgf').
7·62 × 45mm or 7·62 × 39mm.
Gas-operated auto-loading action, locked by displacing the bolt.
DATA FOR A TYPICAL VZ.52
7·62 × 45mm, rimless.
1,013mm overall, about 4·43kg laden.
525mm barrel, 4-groove rifling; RH, concentric.
Detachable box magazine, 10 rounds.
Tangent-leaf sight graduated to 800 metres.
About 745 m/sec with Czech vz.52 cartridges.
Folding bayonet.
☆

1951: the experimental ČZ 493 developed into the ČZ 502. Some of the trials guns had rod bayonets, but a side-mounted folding pattern was ultimately preferred.

1952: the rifle was formally adopted on 20 May as the '7·62mm samonabijecki puška vz.52'. However, problems with pre-production guns were not solved until a modified prototype (the ČZ 521) appeared. Series production began in 1953, the first guns entering service the following summer. They embodied a tilting-bolt locking system, powered by a conventional short-stroke piston; oddly, the locking lugs lay at the front of the bolt.

Though the box magazine was detachable, the rifle could also be reloaded through the open action, suitable charger guides being milled in the receiver-top behind the ejection cutaway. Unfortunately, despite its compact dimensions, the vz.52 was never popular; the cumbersome full-length stock and integral bayonet had an unbalancing effect, and the locking mechanism proved unsatisfactory in service.

1957: the vz.52 rifle was revised to accept the 7·62mm Soviet M43 intermediate cartridge, which had a shorter case than the standard Czechoslovakian round.

The modified gun was known as 'vz.52–57'; it seems that small quantities of the older pattern were also altered, but that the advent of the more effectual vz.58 (below) caused work to be abandoned.

Large numbers of vz.52 rifles—together with smaller batches of vz.52–57—were withdrawn from the armed forces once supplies of the vz.58 had been assured, and exported to many parts of the world. They were particularly common in Syria, Cuba and Nicaragua, and are still found throughout Africa.

Model 58

vz.58 P and vz.58 V patterns.
Apparently made by Československá Zbrojovka, Povaske Strjirny (code 'she').
7·62 × 39mm.
Action: generally as vz.52, above.

DATA FOR A TYPICAL VZ.58 P
838mm overall, about 3·97kg laden.
400mm barrel, 4-groove rifling; RH, concentric.
Detachable box magazine, 30 rounds.
Tangent-leaf sight graduated to 800 metres.
700 m/sec with Soviet M43 cartridges; 800 ± 50 rpm.
Knife bayonet.
☆

1953: this weapon arose from a competition to find a Kalashnikov-type assault rifle, field trials being undertaken with the ZK 503, ČZ 522 and ZB 530. The trials resolved in favour of the Holek design, but production of an improved version was deferred while the mechanism was adapted for the 7·62mm Soviet M43 cartridge. The relevant alterations have been credited to Josef Čermak.

1958: full-scale production of the Samopal vz.58 P (pěchotni, 'infantry') began. Though superficially resembling the Kalashnikov, the vz.58 had a tilting-block locking system and an axial striker instead of a swinging hammer. The selector lay on the right side of the receiver above the pistol grip.

Many of the earliest guns had wooden butts, pistol grips and fore-ends, but reddish-brown plastic/wood-fibre patterns had appeared by about 1960. Some of the newest guns had nylon polymer fittings. Most guns were phosphated externally, but some have been reported with a baked-on grey-green finish.

The vz.58 V, intended for armoured and airborne units, had a single-strut metal butt folding to the right alongside the receiver.

2. THE BOLT-ACTION PATTERNS

The first post-war sporters were conventional Brno-made Mausers (q.v.), but they were soon supplemented by the ZG 47, with a Mauser action modified by Otakar Galaš. This was adapted to provide two 7·92 × 64mm sniper rifles (ZG 49–Sn and ZG 51–Sn) and a single-shot 7·92 × 57mm ZK 474 target rifle—never

Czechoslovak factories The vz.52 rifle. IAN HOGG

Dae Woo The 5·56mm K2 assault rifle. IAN HOGG

Czechoslovak factories
The 7·62mm vz.58 V assault rifle; outwardly similar to the Kalashnikov, it is very different internally.
PATTERN ROOM COLLECTION

made in quantity. Most other Czechoslovakian bolt-action rifles have been Koucky designs.

ZG 47

47 A and 47 B patterns.
Made by Československá Zbrojovka, Brno.
Chambering: see text.
Turning-bolt action, locked by two lugs on the bolt head engaging the receiver and a safety lug on the bolt body.
DATA FOR A TYPICAL ZG 47 A
9·3 × 62mm, rimless.
About 1,110mm overall, about 3·15kg unladen.
600mm barrel, 4-groove rifling; RH, concentric.
Internal box magazine, 4 rounds.
Block-and-leaves sight.
720 m/sec with 18·5-gram bullet

☆

1947: this retained a Mauser bolt, with a collar-pattern extractor, but the safety catch was moved to the right side of the bolt shroud. The bolt handle was lowered, an adjustable single-stage trigger was fitted, and the sight rails were machined into the top of the receiver. Rifles chambered a wide variety of European sporting cartridges, from 7 × 57mm to 9·3 × 62mm, but could be adapted to order for special loads—e.g., 5·6 × 61mm Vom Hofe—provided that overall cartridge length was less than 85mm.
1960: the ZG 47 was superseded by the ZKK 600 (see 'Koucky', below).

DAE WOO

REPUBLIC OF KOREA
∽

Development of a series of weapons to replace the M16A1 in Korean service began when the government-owned arms factory in Pusan was transferred to private control in 1983, with the intention of freeing the country's small arms from US dominance. The prototype rifles appeared in 1984, series production beginning a year later.

'K' series

K1, K1A1 and K2 patterns.
Made by Dae Woo Precision Industries, Pusan.
5·56 × 45mm, rimless.
Gas-operated auto-loading action, locked by a rotating bolt.
DATA FOR A TYPICAL K2
988mm overall, 3·35kg unladen.
465mm barrel, 4-groove rifling; concentric, RH.
Detachable box magazine, 30 rounds.
Adjustable aperture sight.
970 m/sec with standard M193 bullet.

☆

1985: the K1 carbine, equivalent to the US Army XM177E2 (see ArmaLite), combined the direct-impingement gas system of the M16 with the bolt carrier and twin recoil-guide rod assembly of the AR-18. The lower part of the hinged receiver was very similar to that of the M16A1, though the upper section differed greatly; the integral carrying handle was replaced by a prominent sight protector and the butt had more of a drop at the wrist. One swivel lay on the barrel ahead of the hand guard, with the other on the back left side of the receiver.

The K1 was about 785mm long with its stock extended, had a 263mm barrel, weighed about 2·85kg and could fire single shots, three-round bursts or fully automatically. Selectors displayed markings in Korean or English.

The K2 rifle shared the basic construction of the K1 carbine, but had a full-length barrel and a solid polyamide butt swinging to the right instead of a retractable pattern. The gas system was changed to a long-stroke piston adapted from the Soviet Kalashnikov, and the muzzle-brake/compensator could accept standard rifle grenades. Like the K1, the K2 had a short fluted hand guard and chequering on the pistol grip.

The modified K1A1 carbine had a longer barrel than the K1 to minimise muzzle flash. It shared the construction of its predecessors, and has also been offered in semi-automatic 'Law Enforcement' form.

Note: guns were sold in the USA in the late 1980s by Stoeger Industries of Hackensack,

New Jersey, as the Max-1 and Max-2 Auto Carbines —the K1A1 and K2 respectively.

DAKOTA

UNITED STATES OF AMERICA
∽

Dakota Arms was formed by amalgamating two smaller companies with extensive gunmaking experience. The objective was to produce the Model 76 rifle, an improved Winchester Model 70 (q.v.) built to the high-quality manufacturing standards that had ruled prior to 1964.

Dakota 76

Classic, Rigby, Safari and Short Action patterns.
Made by Dakota Arms, Inc., Sturgis, South Dakota.
Chambering: see text.
Turning-bolt action, locked by rotating lugs on the bolt head into the receiver and by the bolt handle turning down into its seat.
DATA FOR A TYPICAL 76 CLASSIC
·338 Winchester Magnum, belted rimless.
About 42·50in overall, 7·50lb unladen.
23·00in barrel, 4-groove rifling; concentric, RH?
Internal box magazine, 3 rounds.
Williams ramp sight.
3,000 ft/sec with 200-grain bullet.

☆

1988: this effectual rifle had a Mauser collar-pattern extractor, a rugged adjustable trigger mechanism, and a Winchester three-position safety. The trigger-guard/floor-plate assembly was machined from a single piece of steel. A special combination bolt-stop, gas shield and bolt guide was the subject of a patent granted to Peter Grisel in 1985.

The standard Classic rifle had a straight-comb butt and a rounded fore-end tip, with hand-cut chequering and a solid rubber shoulder pad. The separate pistol-grip cap was usually steel. Chamberings have included ·257 Roberts, ·270 Winchester, ·280 Remington, 7mm Remington Magnum, ·300 Winchester Magnum, ·30—06, ·338 Winchester Magnum, ·375 H&H Magnum

or ·458 Winchester Magnum, but others have been made to order.

The Safari Grade rifle—in ·300 Winchester Magnum, ·338 Winchester Magnum, ·375 H&H Magnum or ·458 Winchester Magnum only—incorporated a one-piece magazine box unit and a specially selected gloss-finished walnut stock. The butt originally had a Monte Carlo comb and cheek piece, but this was changed to a straight comb pattern in 1990.

1989: a Short Action rifle appeared in ·22–250, ·243 Winchester, 6mm Remington, ·250–3000, 7mm–08 Remington or ·308 Winchester. It was little more than a scaled-down version of the standard action with a 21in barrel, offered in Classic and Alpine Grades; the latter had a slim stock and a blind magazine.

The Rigby rifle was an enlargement of the basic action, with a deepened stock to accept a four-round magazine, recoil bolts through the wrist and fore-end, and a 24in heavy barrel. A standing-block back sight was standard.

Chambered for ·404 Jeffrey, ·416 Rigby, ·416 Dakota or ·450 Dakota, the rifles weighed as much as 10lb.

DAUDETAU

FRANCE

A turning-bolt rifle, designed and patented by Commandant Louis Daudetau in 1889–92, this was chambered for cartridges ranging from 6 × 51mm to 8 × 60mm. No great success was encountered in France, though 6·5 × 53·5mm guns went to Portugal in 1899–1900; they were apparently used for field trials prior to the emergence of the Mannlicher-Schönauer and then the Vergueiro-Mauser. Daudetau rifles and carbines were sold to El Salvador and Paraguay in the late 1890s, while Uruguay selected the 6·5 × 53·5mm No.12 Daudetau cartridge for weapons converted from 1871-type Mausers in Saint-Denis. These are described in greater detail in the Mauser section. Production ended in the early 1900s, after about 5,000 had been made.

Model 1896

Experimental navy rifle.
Made by Compagnie des Forges et Aciéries de la Marine, Saint-Chamond, but marked as a product of Société Française des Armes Portatives, Saint-Denis, Paris.
6·5 × 53·5mm, semi-rimmed.
Turning-bolt action, with two lugs on the detachable bolt head locking into the receiver.
1,287mm overall, 3·95kg unladen.
825mm barrel, 4-groove rifling; LH, concentric.
Integral charger-loaded box magazine, 5 rounds.
Leaf sight graduated to 2,000 yards.
770 m/sec with Daudetau No.12 ball cartridges.
Special épée bayonet.
☆

1895: the first Daudetau rifles were purchased by the French navy at a time when calibres smaller than the regulation 8mm were being adopted throughout Europe.

They had split-bridge receivers and a two-lug bolt inspired by the Lebel. The charger was needlessly complex, and the box-magazine case was formed integrally with the small trigger guard. The trigger aperture was almost circular, giving the rifles an unmistakable appearance.

1896: several hundred 1896-pattern rifles were issued. They had a one-piece walnut stock with a hand guard running from the chamber under the broad retaining band, the band and nose cap being retained by springs. A stacking rod lay on the right side of the nose cap and a cleaning rod was set into a channel in the left side of the fore-end. Swivels lay beneath the band and the butt. The bayonet was essentially similar to the Mle.86 (Lebel) type, with the same type of spring-loaded locking collar, but the left side of the hilt had a longitudinal groove for the head of the cleaning rod.

1899: as Germany showed no inclination to accept a small-calibre cartridge, the French army elected to issue the improved 8mm Balle D instead and the navy soon followed suit.

1902: experiments with a selection of improved bolt-action rifles developed by Daudetau and the École Nationale de Tir (ENT) had finally ceased.

DEELEY & EDGE

BRITAIN

The Deeley & Edge rifle—developed for military use, but successful only for sporting purposes or match-shooting—was originally an underlever pattern, patented by John Deeley and James Edge of Birmingham in 1873 and improved in 1877. A hollow breech block contained the hammer, trigger lever and the relevant springs. Pulling down on the spur of the trigger guard (suitably offset to the right) lowered the breech block and cocked the hammer. The rifle was effectual enough, but the integration of the lever and the trigger guard was less acceptable militarily than the separate lever and trigger guard of the Martini-Henry. The modified (or 'Improved') pattern was somewhat like the earlier Field (q.v.), but had a compact solid block containing only a small inertia-pattern striker. The block was lowered by a projection on the thumb-lever boss directly engaging a finger on the underside of the breech block. The internal hammer cocked as the thumb-lever rotated. Though lacking the extracting qualities of long-lever actions, the 1881-type Deeley & Edge rifle was a simple and effectual design.

Virtually all of these guns were made by Westley Richards & Co. Ltd, John Deeley having succeeded Westley Richards in 1872. The rifles were made alongside proprietary Westley Richards pivoting-block rifles (q.v.) and a selection of Improved Martinis. Both types of Deeley & Edge rifle were made concurrently.

Breech-Loading Military Rifle

1877 pattern.
Made by Westley Richards & Co. Ltd, Birmingham.
·450 and other centre-fire chamberings.
Dropping-block action, operated by a lever combined with the trigger guard.
DATA FOR A TYPICAL EXAMPLE
·500/·450 No.2, rimmed.
49·80in overall, 9·04lb unladen.

Daudetau The French M1896 navy rifle. H.B. LOCKHOVEN

Deeley & Edge An 1877-pattern military style ·450 rifle. JOHN WALTER

Dragunov An SVD sniper rifle with a PSO-1 optical sight. IAN HOGG

33·00in barrel, 7-groove rifling; LH, composite.
Ramp-and-leaf sight graduated to 1,400 yards.
1,355 ft/sec with 480-grain bullet.
Sword or sabre bayonet, supplied to order.

☆

1877: this gun was immediately recognisable by its breech block, the top edge of which was dished to form a loading tray, and by the spur on the operating lever/trigger guard bent outward to the right. A straight-wrist butt and full-length fore-end were standard, the latter being hooked into the receiver and retained by a single band at the muzzle. The band carried the bayonet lug and a swivel, the other swivel appearing on the underside of the butt. A radial safety lever on the operating lever locked the trigger when the action was closed.

Improved Sporting Rifle

1881 pattern.
Made by Westley Richards & Co. Ltd, Birmingham.
Chambered for many large-calibre pre-1900
British sporting cartridges.
Dropping-block action, operated by a lever on the right side of the receiver.
DATA FOR A TYPICAL EXAMPLE
·500/·450 No.1 Express, rimmed.
43·13in overall, 8·10lb unladen.
26·00in barrel, 5-groove rifling; RH, concentric.
Multiple-leaf sight.
1,900 ft/sec with 270-grain bullet.

☆

1881: this rifle had a strong external affinity with the Farquharson (q.v.), excepting that the breech lever lay on the receiver-side instead of around the trigger guard. Internally, the Deeley & Edge pattern was much simpler.

A typical sporting rifle offered a pistol-grip butt and a half-length fore-end, woodwork being extensively chequered. Swivels appeared on the underside of the barrel ahead of the fore-end tip and under the butt.

A three-leaf Express back sight graduated for 100, 200 and 500 yards was fitted to the matted rib above the round barrel. The front sight was a small silvered bead.

DRAGUNOV

UNION OF SOVIET SOCIALIST REPUBLICS
〜

This was the standard Soviet bloc sniper rifle for nearly thirty years, being used in virtually all the constituent armies excepting Romania and independently-minded Yugoslavia. It has been credited to a design team led by Yevgeniy Dragunov and Ivan Samoylov.

Locked by a rotating three-lug bolt, similar to that of the Kalashnikov, the SVD gas system employs a short-stroke piston adapted from the pre-war Tokarev.

MILITARY WEAPONS
U S S R
SVD

Dragunov sniper rifle:
Snayperskaya Vintovka Dragunova.
Made by the State ordnance factory, Izhevsk, RSFSR.
7·62 × 54mm, rimmed.
Gas-operated auto-loading action, locked by rotating lugs on the bolt head into the receiver.
1,225mm overall
4·51kg with sight and empty magazine.
545mm barrel, 4-groove rifling; concentric, RH.
Detachable box magazine, 10 rounds.
Tangent-leaf sight graduated to 1,200 metres.
830 m/sec with standard Type L bullet.
AKM knife bayonet.

☆

1963: the outcome of a protracted design study, the Dragunov was accepted for service at the expense of prototypes submitted by—amongst others—Sergei Simonov. The first guns reached service in 1965.

Owing to the cutaway butt combined with the pistol grip, the Dragunov cannot easily be mistaken. Its slender barrel had a three-slot compensator/muzzle brake, and a two-position gas port could be adjusted with a cartridge-case

rim. The trigger was a simplified version of the AK mechanism, but the combined safety lever/selector restricted options to single shots.

The 4× PSO-1 optical sight was clamped onto a rail on the lower left side of the receiver. The long rubber eye cup was most distinctive, and a small battery carried in the integral mount illuminated the reticle. Optical performance was surprisingly good, whilst the sight doubled as an infra-red emission detector.

Ribs pressed into the sides of the box magazine facilitated feeding of the clumsy, but otherwise acceptable cartridge. It has been said that development of the magazine body was particularly protracted.

The SVD was light by modern sniper-rifle standards. However, it was issued far more widely in the Soviet army than any comparable Western design—a tradition dating back to the early 1930s. Western sources still proffer much conflicting data, but the Dragunov is pleasant to fire and capable of acceptable accuracy with good-quality ammunition.

OTHERS

SVD rifles have been used wherever Soviet influence was strong. Captured guns were used by the myriad warring factions in Afghanistan, while others have appeared in Iran. Production has been undertaken in Bulgaria, the People's Republic of China (variously reported as the Type 79 or Type 85), Egypt, Hungary and Poland. Most of the optical sights prove to have been made in the Soviet Union or the German Democratic Republic, but it is probable that the Chinese also make them. Markings usually determine the country of origin.

SPORTING GUNS
Medved

Made by the State ordnance factory, Izhevsk, RSFSR.
Chambering: see text.
Action: as military-pattern SVD, above.
1,110mm overall, 3·75kg unladen.

IAN HOGG

The Izhevsk-made Medved ('Bear') rifle, based on the Dragunov action.

Dragunov

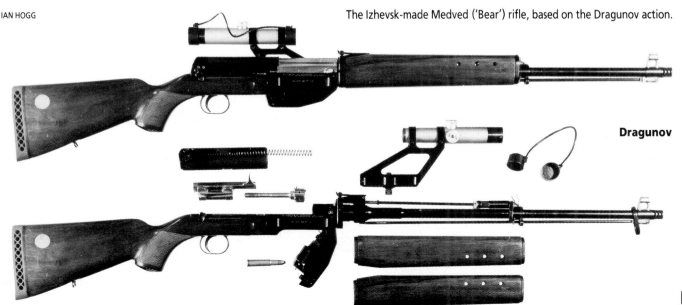

550mm barrel, 4-groove rifling; concentric, RH.
Integral box magazine, 5 rounds.
Tangent-leaf sight graduated to 1,200 metres.
710 m/sec with 16·6-gram 9mm bullet.

☆

1965*: among the most interesting sporting rifles made in the Soviet Union, the Medved ('Bear') shared the gas system and rotating-bolt lock of the SVD. The design of the receiver was refined and a conventional straight-comb butt was fitted. Chequering appeared on the pistol grip and the fore-end.

Among the rifle's strangest features were the military-style open sights and provision of a clearing rod beneath the barrel—more valuable than it may seem in sub-zero temperatures. A stubby 4× optical sight was carried in a trapezoidal mount that attached to the lower left side of the receiver above the protruding magazine housing.

Most rifles were chambered for adaptions of the standard Mosin-Nagant rifle cartridge, known in Finland, where they have been loaded by Sako, as '8·2 × 53mm R' or '9·3 × 53mm R'. Efforts were made to chamber the Medved for Western European cartridges of comparable dimensions, in an attempt to attract foreign currency, but it is suspected that production had ceased by the mid 1970s.

DUBIEL

UNITED STATES OF AMERICA

Created in 1975 by John Tyson and Joseph DuBiel, this company made rifles with a patented five-lug bolt system. This allowed the extractor to pass between two lugs rather than requiring one to be partially cut away, and gave a compact 36° throw. Work ceased in 1990.

DuBiel Sporting Rifle

DuBiel Arms Company, Sherman, Texas.
Chambering: virtually any from ·22–250 to ·458
Winchester Magnum.

Turning-bolt action, locked by rotating lugs on the bolt head into the receiver and by the bolt handle turning down into its seat.
DATA FOR A TYPICAL EXAMPLE
·300 Winchester Magnum, rimless.
About 43·50in overall, 7·50lb unladen.
24·00in barrel, rifling pattern not known.
Internal box magazine, 3 rounds.
Optical sight.
3,400 ft/sec with 150-grain bullet.

☆

1978: though made in large numbers, the DuBiel rifle was really a custom pattern and could be chambered for almost any cartridge the purchaser specified. Right- or left-hand actions were available from stock, their bolts being machine-jewelled and then chromed. Canjar triggers and Douglas barrels were used, though the length and profile of the latter varied.

The Classic stock had a straight comb; the Modern Classic was similar, but had contrasting ebonite pistol-grip caps and fore-end tips. The Rollover pattern had a distinctive Monte Carlo comb, while the design of the Thumbhole butt was self-explanatory. Thumbhole Mannlicher stocks extended to the muzzle, usually being confined to barrels measuring less than 22in. Most stocks prove to be walnut or maple, though some laminated examples were made.

The guns had a neat bolt shroud and a sliding tang safety (absent from thumbhole-stock guns), while the magazine floor-plate locking lever was reminiscent of pre-1939 Mauser sporters.

ELLIOTT

UNITED STATES OF AMERICA
Also known as 'Colt-Elliott'

Made exclusively by Colt, this slide-action repeater, patented by William Elliott in 1883, encountered modest commercial success. The mechanism was locked by a Burgess-type pivoting wedge beneath the breech bolt and could be fired merely by operating the slide with the trigger held back. The first

guns had troublesome ejectors, but problems were soon overcome and a reputation for reliability was acquired in the mid 1880s. Eventually, however, the Lightning Magazine Rifle succumbed to the simpler Winchesters and the high-pressure smokeless cartridge.

Lightning Magazine Rifle

Also offered as a carbine.
Made by Colt's Patent Fire Arms Mfg Co., Hartford, Connecticut, 1884–1900.
Quantity: 89,780.
·32–20 Winchester, ·38–40 Winchester or ·44–40 Winchester (·25–20 is said to have been offered, but no gun is known).
Slide action, locked by a pivoting wedge under the breech bolt engaging the receiver.
DATA FOR A TYPICAL EXAMPLE
·38–40 Winchester, rimmed.
43·60in overall, 8·15lb unladen.
26·00in barrel, 6-groove rifling; LH, concentric?
Tube magazine under barrel, 15 rounds.
Spring-leaf and elevator sight.
1,330 ft/sec with 180-grain bullet.

☆

1884: this unique rifle was introduced in the autumn. Standard medium-frame Lightnings were offered in rifle form, with a round or octagonal barrel, or as a twelve-shot carbine with a 20in round barrel. They resembled the contemporaneous lever-action Winchesters and Marlins externally, but lacked the finger lever; instead, a short wooden fore-end slid on tracks on the magazine tube. Straight-wrist butts were normal, but a selection of special sights, finishes and woodwork was available.

An auxiliary bolt-locking arm designed by Carl Ehbets and a set trigger mechanism credited to Frederick Knous (patented in April and December 1885 respectively) were used occasionally.

1885: a scarce Baby Carbine (chambered for ·44–40 and experimentally for ·32–20) appeared with a special 20in light barrel, a 12-round magazine and a weight of just 5·3lb.

1887: the first of the small-frame rimfire and

Enfield A prototype XL70E3 rifle. ROYAL ORDNANCE PLC ▷

Enfield A British 5·56mm L85A1 assault rifle, with a Pilkington image-intensifying sight. IAN HOGG

large-frame Express rifles appeared, barrels acknowledging additional patents granted in 1885–7. Apart from differences in size, the most obvious feature was the breech cover, added to the medium-frame guns at this time—pre-1887 examples had an exposed breech bolt.

1900: the Lightning was discontinued, though it is suspected that no production had been undertaken since the mid 1890s. Some had been purchased for the San Francisco Police Department, but orders of this type were few.

Lightning Express Rifle
Also offered as a carbine.
Made by Colt's Patent Fire Arms Mfg Co., Hartford, Connecticut, 1887–94.
Quantity: 6,500.
·38–56 Winchester, ·40–60 Winchester,
·45–60 Winchester, ·45–85 Winchester or ·50–95
Winchester Express.
Action: as Lightning Magazine Rifle, above.
DATA FOR A TYPICAL EXAMPLE
·45–85 Winchester, rimmed.
45·75in overall, 9·92lb unladen.
28·00in barrel, 6-groove rifling; LH, concentric?
Tube magazine under barrel, 10 rounds.
Spring-leaf and elevator sight.
1,510 ft/sec with 300-grain bullet.
☆

1887: designed for powerful black powder cartridges, Lightning Express Rifles were offered with round or octagonal barrels—though a 9lb carbine, with a 22in barrel, and an 8lb 'Baby Express Carbine' were made in small numbers.

1894: promotion was abandoned, owing to poor sales. It is likely that the largest cartridges tested the action to its limits, and that racking eventually afflicted the slide mechanism.

ENFIELD

BRITAIN

This title signifies participation in design by the Royal Small Arms Factory—founded in Enfield

Lock, Middlesex, but closed in the late 1980s when operations moved to Nottingham. The only truly Enfield-designed rifles to attain service status are the British Army's current auto-loader and the sturdy Mauser-type bolt-action Pattern 1914. Coverage here is restricted to these rifles and (in the case of the P/1914) their direct descendants. Details of the Lee-Enfield will be found in the 'Lee' section, while the British L1A1 is considered under 'Saive'.

1. THE AUTO-LOADING PATTERNS

Individual Weapon (IW)
XL64E5, XL68E2, XL70E3, L85A1 and L98A1 patterns.
Made by the Royal Small Arms Factories, Enfield Lock (to 1988) and Nottingham (1988 to date).
5·56 × 45mm, rimless.
Gas-operated auto-loading action, locked by a rotating bolt.
DATA FOR A TYPICAL L85A1
30·90in overall, 10·95lb with loaded magazine.
20·40in barrel, 6-groove rifling; concentric, RH.
Detachable box magazine, 30 rounds.
Optical sight.
3,085 ft/sec with SS109 bullet.
☆

1967*: trials with new small-calibre cartridges began, a 6·25 × 43mm pattern being tested in 1969–71. The 6·25mm round—a 92–95 grain bullet in a necked ·280 case—was a potentially effectual compromise between the 5·56mm and 7·62 × 51mm rounds; it promised to be very accurate, and had better hitting power (and a longer effective range) than the US 5·56mm M193 bullet. However, it was heavier than the 5·56mm pattern and thoughts turned instead to lightening the rifleman's burden.

1970: a 5 × 44mm cartridge appeared.

1972: the finalised 5mm pattern was renamed '4·85 × 44mm'. It was given a 49mm case in 1973, and more than a million rounds were expended during development trials. Once the

cartridge design had been stabilised, work began on a suitable rifle. The project team was initially led by the late John Weeks, co-author of *Military Small Arms of the 20th Century* and *Pistols of the World* but then a Lieutenant-Colonel in the British Army. The design of the rifle owed much to Sydney Hance, who had been involved with the abortive ·280 EM-2 (see Part Two).

The new 4·85mm Infantry Weapon ('IW') differed greatly from the EM-2 internally, though both guns favoured the bullpup layout. Its multi-lug bolt was adapted from the Stoner (ArmaLite) patterns, trial models being bullpup adaptions of AR-18 and Stoner 63 rifles.

1976: on 14 July, the British Army unveiled the new guns publicly. Four basic guns were demonstrated—XL64E5 and XL68E2 Infantry Weapons, with right- and left-hand ejection respectively, and the comparable XL65E4 and XL69E1 Light Support Weapons.

1977: the XL64 and XL65 were entered in NATO trials, which eventually standardised the thirty-round US M16A1 magazine, the French grenade launcher, and the Belgian FN SS109 5·56mm bullet. Agreement reached among the other participants left the British 4·85mm guns isolated even though they had performed acceptably enough.

1981: the receiver of the Infantry Weapon had been refined, gaining a straight under-edge. The gun had been re-chambered for the 5·56mm round, dimensionally similar to 4·85 × 49mm variety, to create the XL70E3.

1983: the first series-production guns were made in the Enfield factory for field trials. They were issued in the summer of 1984. The XL70 followed the fashionable straight-line bullpup layout, with the magazine protruding behind the pistol grip, and mounted the 4 × 'Sight, Unit, Small Arms, Trilux, L9A1' (SUSAT). The shoulder pad, hand guard and pistol grip were nylon and the construction relied heavily on stampings, pressings and spot-welding.

1984: a special Cadet Rifle derivative appeared, sharing the outline of the auto-loader but charged manually by retracting the handle on the right side of the breech. The optical sight

was replaced by a pivoting 'L' sight let into the fixed carrying handle. A ten-round magazine was developed specifically for this rifle, though the standard twenty- and thirty-round IW types would interchange if required. So, too, would the NATO-standard US M16A1 pattern.

1985: christened 'SA-80' for commercial sale, the XL70E3 was adopted as the 5·56mm Rifle L85A1 and the Cadet Rifle became the L98A1. The Cadet Rifle was about 29·75in long, had a 19·5in barrel and weighed about 9lb.

Compact dimensions and the universal issue of an optical sight have been welcomed, but the basic 5·56mm IW has been unsuccessful in competitive military trials—e.g., in Australia and Eire—and has encountered many unforeseen teething troubles. Field service in the Gulf War revealed serious problems attributed more to manufacturing deficiencies and poor-quality ammunition than design faults, but reports of widespread dissatisfaction throughout the British Army began to gain credence. The inability of the firer to choose the direction of ejection (cf., French FAMAS) was the target of much criticism, particularly as it also compromised the utility of the rifle in an urban environment.

2. THE BOLT-ACTION PATTERNS

This Mauser-based system was developed in Britain, but mass-produced in the USA. The original rifles were accurate and sturdy—apart from the flimsy ejector. Sights were excellent and a long sight radius promoted good shooting.

1910: increasingly worried that the German Gewehr 98 and the US M1903 Springfield developed considerably greater muzzle velocity than the short Lee-Enfield, the British Small Arms Committee was asked to list features to be incorporated in an entirely new rifle.

As much of the SMLE was to be retained as possible, but a Mauser-pattern action was to be used and an aperture back sight substituted for the open notch.

The first experiments were undertaken with a converted M1903 'Enfield-Springfield', a modified rifle and an experimental ·276 cartridge being recommended for field trials early in 1912.

MILITARY RIFLES
ARGENTINA

The Remington Arms Company is said to have supplied Model 40 rifles to the Argentine army in the mid 1930s, at about the time large numbers were sent to Honduras (q.v.). The guns are said to have chambered the 7·65 × 53mm rimless cartridge and to have borne the national arms above the chamber. However, the 'Argentine contract' has never been substantiated.

BRITAIN
Pattern 1913

Infantry rifle.
Made by the Royal Small Arms Factory, Enfield, Middlesex, 1913–14.
Quantity: at least 1,250.
·276, rimless.
Turning-bolt action, with two lugs on the bolt head locking into the receiver and the bolt handle turning down into its seat.
46·18in overall, 8·56lb unladen.
26·00in barrel, 5-groove rifling; LH, concentric.
Internal charger-loaded box magazine, 5 rounds.
Leaf sight graduated to 1,900 yards.
2,785 ft/sec with ·276 Ball Mk I.
P/1913 sword bayonet.

☆

1913: a thousand 'Rifles, Magazine, ·276-inch, Pattern 1913' were issued for trial. They had an aperture sight between prominent protectors above the rear of the receiver, ahead of the bolt handle. The leaf was graduated 400–1,900 yards, with a fixed aperture or 'battle sight' for 600 yards and an auxiliary long-range sight on the left side of the distinctively British-style one-piece stock. The magazine platform held

the action open when the last round had been fired and ejected. Four diagonal grasping grooves appeared on each side of the fore-end immediately ahead of the breech, but were unpopular with firers.

1914: the rifles undertook trials successfully, though there had been a tendency to misfire and trouble had been experienced with the charger guides. However, only poor magazine feed caused any real worry. Optimistically, the British authorities recommended the ·276 rifle as a replacement for the ·303 Lee-Enfield.

Pattern 1914

Infantry and sniper rifles: Mks I and I* (E), Mks I and I* (R), Mks I and I* (W), 'F', 'T' and 'T A' patterns.
Made by the Winchester Repeating Arms Company, New Haven, Connecticut, 1915–16 (235,530); Remington Arms–Union Metallic Cartridge Company, Ilion, New York, 1915–16; and the Remington Arms of Delaware Company, Eddystone, Pennsylvania, 1915–16 (about 450,000).
Quantity: 1,117,850.
·303, rimmed.
Action: as P/1913, above.
46·16in overall, 9·12lb unladen.
26·00in barrel, 5-groove rifling; LH, concentric.
Internal charger-loaded box magazine, 5 rounds.
Leaf sight graduated to 1,650 yards.
2,525 ft/sec with ·303 Ball Mk VII.
P/1913 sword bayonet.

☆

1914: when the First World War began, no production line for the ·276 P/1913 (see above) existed and the entire project was abandoned. To alleviate shortages caused by mobilisation, however, a contract for 200,000 'Rifles, Magazine, ·303-inch, Pattern 1914' was agreed with Winchester on 24 November. Similar contracts had previously been signed with Remington Arms–UMC.

1915: the perfected Winchester-adapted rifle was accepted on 22 March and ordered into immediate mass production. Test-firing of the first Ilion-made Remington rifles took place in October.

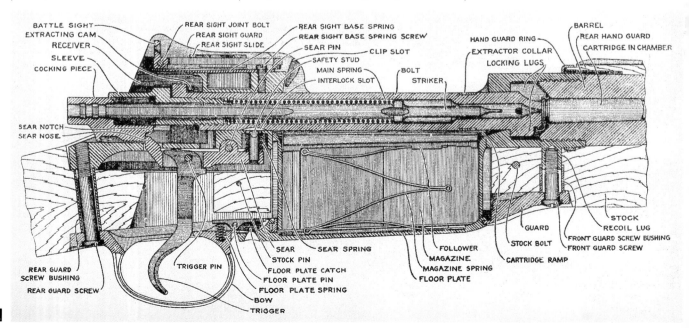

The P/1914 was similar to the experimental ·276 P/1913, but had a conventional grasping groove in the fore-end and the magazine was adapted for rimmed ·303 cartridges. Back sight graduations ranged from 200 to 1,650 yards, the battle-sight aperture being set for 400 and the long-range sights sufficing for distances up to 2,600 yards.

1916: final assembly in the Winchester factory in New Haven began in January. Sub-variants were introduced to British service on 21 June, designated Mks I (E), (R) or (W). The suffixes distinguished the rifles made by Eddystone, Remington–UMC and Winchester respectively, as parts were not always readily exchangeable from group to group.

Distinctive markings included 'ERA' on the Eddystone rifles, 'RA' on Remingtons made in Ilion, and 'W' on the Winchesters.

The Mark I* was approved in December. The most important changes were the lengthening of the left locking lug on the bolt and alterations to its seat in the receiver ring. These guns had additional five-point stars on the bolt handle, chamber, and right side of the butt. Rifles with finely-adjustable back sights had a pattern mark with an additional 'F' suffix.

In the autumn of 1916, the British greatly reduced their orders. Winchester ceased work in December, though assembly in the Ilion (Remington) factory continued into 1917.

1918: from 11 April, the P/14 Mk I* (W) was adopted as the official British Army sniper rifle, its designation becoming 'P/14 Mk I* (W) T'. Mounts for the P/1918 Aldis telescope sight (carried centrally above the bolt) were added on the left side of the breech and back sight protector, long-range sights being removed. About 2,000 rifle/sight combinations had been assembled prior to the Armistice.

1926: P/1914 rifles were recalled to store and re-classified, depending on pattern, as No.3 Mk I, Mk I*, Mk I* (F) or Mk I* (T).

1939: owing to ever-increasing certainty of war in Europe, survivors were hastily refurbished for reissue from 24 June onward, without the long range sight aperture bar and dial pointer.

At least 677,000 were so treated, mostly at Enfield or by Holland & Holland of London.

1940: the guns were initially used for training, and then issued to the Local Defence Volunteers (later known as the 'Home Guard'). A few 'No.3 Mk 1* (T) A' rifles were made by BSA in Birmingham (at least 79 examples) and Alex Martin & Company of Glasgow (at least 421). These had a wooden cheek piece and an Aldis sight in a low mount offset to the left of the bore.

1947: the No.3 was declared obsolete in July.

HONDURAS

The Remington Arms Company supplied about 3,000 modified M1917 Enfield rifles in the mid 1930s. Apparently issued as the Mo.1934, but known commercially as the 'Model 40', these chambered the 7 × 57mm cartridge and had new stepless-base tangent-leaf back sights protruding from the hand guard above the grasping groove. A new open barleycorn front sight was used. The sight on the bridge of the receiver was removed, but the Honduran rifles were otherwise similar to the US ·30 M1917 Enfield.

USA
Model 1917

....
Infantry rifle.
Made in 1917–19 by the Winchester Repeating Arms Company, New Haven, Connecticut; the Remington Arms–Union Metallic Cartridge Company, Ilion, New York; and the Remington Arms of Delaware Company, Eddystone, Pennsylvania.
Quantity: approximately 2·513 million.
·30–06, rimless.
Action: as British P/1914, above.
46·30in overall, 9·00lb unladen.
26·00in barrel, 5-groove rifling; RH, concentric.
Internal charger-loaded box magazine, 5 rounds.
Leaf sight graduated to 1,600 yards.
2,750 ft/sec with US ·30 M2 ball cartridges.
M1917 sword bayonet.
☆

1917: the entry of the USA into the First World War revealed a shortage of serviceable rifles. Only 740,000 Springfields and outmoded Krags were on hand. As production had already been radically curtailed and could not be accelerated quickly, a decision was taken to re-chamber the British P/1914 for the standard ·30–06 rimless cartridge. The ·30–06 case was longer than the ·303 pattern, though its body diameter was comparable; minor changes were needed in the magazine, but the action could be retained and Enfield-type rifling used merely by adjusting the bore diameter.

The 'Rifle, Caliber ·30, Model of 1917' was very similar externally to its British predecessor. Feed was improved by the rimless cartridge, and Enfield-type rifling unexpectedly resisted bore-wear better than the Springfield type.

1918: by Armistice Day, the Eddystone factory had made 1,181,910 rifles, Remington's Ilion plant had supplied 545,540, and Winchester had contributed 465,980. Springfield Armory and Rock Island Arsenal had made only 313,000 M1903 rifles in the same period.

1919: the US Army considered standardising the M1917 instead of the M1903, but it was unpopular with the rank-and-file—longer and heavier than the M1903, the Enfield also cocked on closing. As production facilities were in private rather than governmental hands, the plans were soon abandoned.

1920: almost a million refurbished rifles were placed in store.

1941: in accord with the terms of the Lend-Lease programme, some surviving M1917 rifles were sent to Britain. Official records reveal only an order for 50,000 placed on 31 January, but Ian Skennerton in *The US Enfield* notes the total to have been 119,000.

After a series of accidents, most of the guns used in Britain gained broad red stripes around the fore-end and butt to remind firers that they chambered the ·30–06 cartridge.

1942: the first batches of 143,000 new ·30-calibre M1917 barrels were made by the High Standard Manufacturing Company of New Haven, Connecticut (four-groove, right twist),

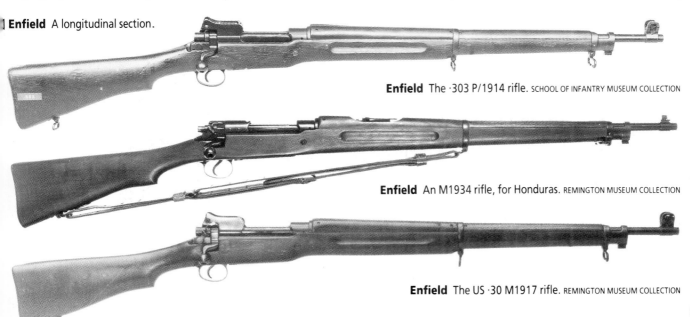

Enfield A longitudinal section.

Enfield The ·303 P/1914 rifle. SCHOOL OF INFANTRY MUSEUM COLLECTION

Enfield An M1934 rifle, for Honduras. REMINGTON MUSEUM COLLECTION

Enfield The US ·30 M1917 rifle. REMINGTON MUSEUM COLLECTION

and Johnson Automatics, Inc. of Providence, Rhode Island (two-groove, right twist).

SPORTING GUNS
BRITAIN

Though its strength was unquestioned, the P/1914 action was rarely used by gunmakers. Most preferred the 1898-pattern Mauser, which could be transformed into an elegant sporting gun with little trouble; the Enfield-designed rifle, conversely, had prominent back sight protectors on the receiver bridge and a particularly ugly bolt handle. In the 1920s, however, BSA introduced a range of rifles built on the Enfield system; the company is suspected to have manufactured many (if not all) of the actions incorporated in the P/1913 trials rifles, even though they were supposedly made at Enfield, and would have been a prime contractor had not the First World War intervened. It is highly likely that BSA had incomplete actions in store.

BSA High-Power Model

Made by BSA Guns Ltd, Birmingham, 1921–5.
·26 BSA, ·30–06, ·303, 8 × 56mm, ·33 BSA and ·40 BSA
Action: as British P/1914 rifle, above.
DATA FOR A TYPICAL EXAMPLE
·26 BSA, belted rimless.
48·00in overall, 8·00lb unladen.
26·00in barrel, 5-groove rifling; LH, concentric?
Internal charger-loaded box magazine, 5 rounds.
Back sight: see notes.
3,100 ft/sec with 110-grain bullet.

☆

1919: the Explosives Trades Ltd cartel, created from Kynoch, Eley and Nobel, formed a 'Rifle Committee' to perfect a range of sporting-rifle cartridges based on a pre-war Eley design.
1920: the project was unsuccessfully offered to Holland & Holland, and then, with greater success, to BSA.
1921: the ·26 and ·33 BSA sporters, based on the P/1913 action, offered an angular half-stock and had a short cylindrical bolt handle. The back

sight protectors on the receiver bridge were milled down around a compact twin-aperture sight. An additional folding-leaf sight (for 150 and 300 yards) lay on the barrel.
1925: BSA introduced a new sporting rifle based on the 1898-type Mauser, as most of the P/1913 actions had been used. The straight-tapered ·40 BSA belted cartridge appeared at the same time and could be chambered in either action. However, the Mauser was not successful and only a few were ever made.

USA

Remington had made such vast numbers of P/1914 and M1917 Enfield rifles during the First World War that an entire warehouse full of parts remained when military production finally ceased. The Model 30 rifle was conceived to make use of them.

Remington Model 30

Basic, A, Carbine, Express and R patterns.
Made by the Remington Arms Company, Inc., Ilion, New York, 1920–40.
Quantity: 22,730 (including Model 30S).
Chambering: see notes.
Action: as US M1917 rifle, above.
DATA FOR A TYPICAL 1938-VINTAGE EXAMPLE
·35 Remington, rimless.
42·75in overall, 7·25lb unladen.
22·00in barrel, 5-groove rifling; RH, concentric.
Internal charger-loaded box magazine, 5 rounds.
Spring-leaf and elevator sight.
2,210 ft/sec with 200-grain bullet.

☆

1920: the action of the ·30–06 Model 30 sporting rifle—credited to Crawford Loomis and Charles Barnes—was identical with the M1917, but the barrel was shortened and had a commercial-standard polish. A half stock with a pistol grip and a schnabel-tip fore-end was substituted for the plain military pattern, and an adjustable tangent-slide back sight graduated to 550 yards appeared on the receiver bridge.
1923*: the ·25, ·30, ·32 and ·35 Remington

chamberings were introduced. The back sight was replaced by a spring leaf and elevator pattern, the spring being dovetailed into the barrel band above the fore-end.
1924*: a 20in-barrelled carbine appeared.
1926: the action was modified to cock on opening by reducing striker travel. The bolt shroud was shortened and a coil-type ejector spring substituted for the original 'sliver' pattern. The butt comb was raised, the grasping groove was eliminated, and chequering was added to the pistol grip and fore-end. A recoil bolt appeared through the stock beneath the chamber at about the same time. The rifle then became the 'Model 30 Express'.
1930: a guide-rib was added to the bolt body, to make the operating stroke smoother, and the firing pin was lightened in an attempt to improve lock time. The bolt shroud was shortened again, and an additional gas-escape hole was bored into the bolt body level with the rear edge of the extractor spring.
1932: contact between the barrel and the band and fore-end was eliminated so that the barrel floated freely. The designations became Models 30A (standard rifle) and 30R (carbine).
1933: 7 × 57mm, 7·65 × 53mm and 8 × 57mm chamberings were announced at the beginning of the year, the range of proprietary Remington cartridges being dropped. All but ·30–06 had been discontinued by 1937.
1938: receivers were drilled and tapped for an optional back sight, though the spring-and-elevator pattern on the barrel was standard. The fore-end was broadened and had a rounded tip.

Remington Model 30S

S, S Special, SL, SR and SX patterns.
Made by the Remington Arms Company, Inc., Ilion, New York, 1930–40.
Chamberings: see notes.
Action: basically as US M1917, above.
DATA FOR A TYPICAL EXAMPLE
·257 Roberts, rimless.
44·88in overall, 7·95lb unladen.
24·00in barrel, 5-groove rifling; RH, concentric.

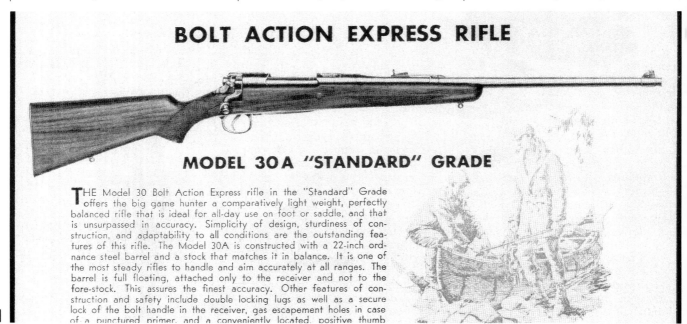

BOLT ACTION EXPRESS RIFLE

MODEL 30A "STANDARD" GRADE

THE Model 30 Bolt Action Express rifle in the "Standard" Grade offers the big game hunter a comparatively light weight, perfectly balanced rifle that is ideal for all-day use on foot or saddle, and that is unsurpassed in accuracy. Simplicity of design, sturdiness of construction, and adaptability to all conditions are the outstanding features of this rifle. The Model 30A is constructed with a 22-inch ordnance steel barrel and a stock that matches it in balance. It is one of the most steady rifles to handle and aim accurately at all ranges. The barrel is full floating, attached only to the receiver and not to the fore-stock. This assures the finest accuracy. Other features of construction and safety include double locking lugs as well as a secure lock of the bolt handle in the receiver, gas escapement holes in case of a punctured primer, and a conveniently located, positive thumb

Internal charger-loaded box magazine, 5 rounds.
Aperture sight on receiver.
2,650 ft/sec with 117-grain bullet.

☆

1930: this special Model 30 had an improved straight-comb stock with a pistol-grip cap and a shotgun-style butt plate. A Lyman No.48R sight was attached to the right side of the receiver and the gold-bead front sight lay on a ramp.

1932: changes in the stock and barrel bedding advanced the designation to '30S Special'.

1933: ·25 Remington and 7 × 57mm options were introduced, the former being available only with a 22in barrel.

1934: a ·257 Roberts version was announced.

1937*: a few rifles are said to have been made for the 7·65 × 53mm Mauser cartridge, popular in South America.

1938: the ·25 Remington chambering was abandoned. Models 30SL and 30SR appeared, with Lyman or Redfield back sights respectively. The Model 30SX, intended for use with optical sights, was sold with no fixed sights at all.

Remington Model 720

A, R and S patterns.
Made by the Remington Arms Company, Inc.,
Ilion, New York, 1941.
Quantity: 2,430.
·257 Roberts, ·270 Winchester or ·30–06.
Action: basically as US M1917, above.
DATA FOR A TYPICAL 720A
·30–06, rimless.
44·75in overall, 8·00lb unladen.
24·00in barrel, 5-groove rifling; RH, concentric.
Internal charger-loaded box magazine, 5 rounds.
Lyman No.48R aperture sight.
2,750 ft/sec with 180-grain bullet.

☆

1941: developed by the Loomis brothers and Aubrey Lowe to replace the Model 30, this offered a refined stock with a fluted tip to the comb, a better pistol grip and a broadened fore-end. A detachable magazine floor-plate was fitted, the lock mechanism was altered to reduce the already praiseworthy lock-time, and the bolt handle was streamlined to improve appearance. Numbered from 40000, the Models 720R, 720A and 720S were made with 20in, 22in and 24in barrels respectively. Each could be fitted with Lyman ('L'), Marble-Goss ('M') or Redfield ('R') receiver sights, suffixes being added to the designation wherever appropriate.

1944: the last guns were shipped from the Remington factory.

1947: the ill-starred Model 720 rifle—effectual excepting only for its military-style trigger—was still listed in Remington catalogues, though no guns had been made since war-work had been accorded priority.

EVANS

UNITED STATES OF AMERICA

This idiosyncratic gun was patented by Warren Evans of Thomaston, Maine, in 1868–71. Though all but ignored by the US Ordnance Department, it was apparently used by the Russian navy in the late 1870s. The action relied on a Spencer-like radial breech-block, fed from a capacious Archimedean screw magazine containing a four-fluted cylindrical cartridge carrier and a spiral-wire cartridge separator. The magazine tube doubled as the spine of the butt. The carrier made a quarter-turn each time the trigger guard/operating lever was thrown, ejecting the spent case before presenting a new round to the breech.

Patent Magazine Rifle

Also offered as a carbine.
Made by the Evans Rifle Manufacturing Company,
Mechanic Falls, Maine, 1871–7.
·44 Evans (short), rimmed.
Lever action, with a radial breech block operated by a lever doubling as the trigger guard.
DATA FOR MILITARY RIFLE
47·25in overall, 10·11lb unladen.
30·00in barrel, 4-groove rifling; RH, concentric?
Tube magazine in butt, 34 rounds.

Ramp-and-leaf sight graduated to 1,000 yards.
About 850 ft/sec with 215-grain bullet.
US M1873 socket bayonet?

☆

1871: the Evans rifle was promoted for its 'military potential' by Merwin & Hulbert. The greatest advantage was the huge magazine, but the mechanism was clumsy and delicate. The full-stock military rifles accepted a socket bayonet; half-stocked carbines had 22in barrels. Evans rifles could not be mistaken; they had massive receivers with an ejection port on the right side and the tube magazine running back through the split butt. The serpentine operating lever was locked by a small catch on its underside and the hammer was concealed. The mechanism could be fired as a single-loader merely by depressing the operating lever far enough to eject, but not far enough for the breech block to receive a new cartridge from the magazine. Among the biggest problem—of many—was the need to operate the action to turn the feed-cylinder for each and every cartridge inserted in the magazine.

1872: an Evans rifle was submitted to US Army trials, but predictably failed the dust and rust tests. Military-pattern rifles had full-length fore-ends held by two bands; carbines had a half-stock and a single band.

1874: despite the failure of Merwin & Hulbert to convince prospective purchasers of the merits of the Evans military musket, a sporting rifle appeared. These sporters had octagonal barrels measuring 26–30in and weighed about 10lb laden. The fore-end was generally a chequered half-stock type, often with a horn or pewter tip.

New Model Patent Rifle

Also offered as a carbine.
Made by the Evans Rifle Manufacturing Company,
Mechanic Falls, Maine, 1877–80.
·44 Evans (long), rimmed.
Action: as Patent Magazine Rifle, above.
DATA FOR SPORTING RIFLE
43·25in overall, 9·64lb unladen.
26·00in, 4-groove rifling; RH, concentric?

◄ Enfield Model 30 Remington rifles were adapted from the M1917.

Evans A typical new-model ·44-calibre carbine. JOHN WALTER

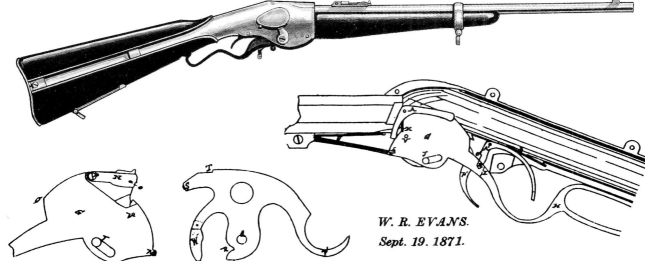

W. R. EVANS.
Sept. 19. 1871.

Tube in butt magazine, 26 rounds.
Ramp-and-leaf sight graduated to 1,000 yards.
About 1,200 ft/sec with 280-grain bullet.

☆

1877: the improved rifle was offered in the same varieties as its predecessor, but could be identified by its semi-external hammer and sliding ejection-port cover. A prominent locking catch lay on the underside of the operating lever, which had a recurved tip. Sporters had round, half-octagon or fully octagonal barrels measuring 26–30in, and weighed up to 10lb.
1878: about a thousand rifles were purchased during the Russo-Turkish War, apparently for the Imperial Russian navy.
1880: Evans went into liquidation.

FARQUHARSON

BRITAIN

Designed by John Farquharson and patented in Britain in May 1872, this is regarded as the classic English dropping-block action. Beloved by purists owing to its strength and elegance, the block is lowered by pulling the breech lever downward to expose the chamber through the intermediacy of a link. As the action opens, it cocks the hammer and pivots the extractor to clear the chamber of a spent case. An improved version designed by William Ruger (q.v.) in the 1960s has been very successful commercially.

The original Farquharsons were made by George Gibbs of Bristol, who supplied actions to other gunmakers in the period before the patents expired. Subsequently, guns were offered by gunmakers such as W.J. Jeffrey & Company. The ability to handle powerful cartridges in safety and a lengthy period in vogue—from the 1870s until the First World War—ensured that Farquharson has been made in a profusion of sizes and styles.

Military Rifle

Gibbs-Farquharson-Metford Pattern.
Made by George Gibbs & Company, Bristol.

·450 Government pattern, rimmed
Dropping-block action, operated by a lever beneath the receiver ahead of the trigger guard.
DATA FOR A TYPICAL EXAMPLE
49·88in overall, about 9lb unladen.
32·63in barrel, 7-groove rifling; RH, polygonal.
Ramp-and-leaf sight graduated to 1,400 yards.
1,315 ft/sec with rolled-case ball cartridges.
Sword bayonet.

☆

1877: the first of the Gibbs Farquharson rifles, distinguished by their Metford-pattern rifling, were introduced to the sporting rifle market to great acclaim. Work continued into the twentieth century, products ranging from plain military-style guns to the finest target rifles with heavy barrels and vernier sights.

Most of the military-style guns pre-date the introduction of the Lee-Metford in 1888; they had straight-wrist butts and full-length fore-ends retained by two screwed bands, the upper band usually carrying a standard bayonet lug on the right side. Swivels lay beneath the muzzle band and the butt.

Sporting Rifle

Jeffrey-Farquharson Improved or 1904 Pattern.
Made by W.J. Jeffrey & Company, London.
Chambered for many differing large-calibre British sporting cartridges.
Action: as Military Rifle, above.
DATA FOR A TYPICAL EXAMPLE
·450/·400 Nitro Express, rimmed.
43·75in overall, 8·45lb unladen.
26·00in barrel, 4-groove rifling; LH, concentric.
Express sight.
2,100 ft/sec with 400-grain bullet.

1895*: the first Jeffrey-made guns appeared towards the end of the nineteenth century, an assortment of differing patterns being introduced prior to 1914. A typical gun of the 'improved' or 1904 pattern, with a radial safety on the right side of the receiver, offered a chequered pistol-grip butt and a slender fore-end with a plain round tip. Sling eyes lay under the butt and on the barrel ahead of the fore-end; a five-leaf Express sight (100–500 yards) lay on a quarter rib and a vernier sight could be mounted on the tang behind the receiver.

FEDEROV

Russia

This assault rifle was designed in Russia prior to the revolution, but perfected only in Soviet days.

Vladimir Fedorov proposed a recoil-operated modification of the Mosin-Nagant in 1905, but it may never have been built. In 1907 he turned his attention to recoil operation, producing working prototypes in the Sestroretsk factory in 1908–9. The action relied on two blocks pivoted on the barrel extension. When the action recoiled, a projection on the standing frame pulled the rear of the locking blocks downward and released the bolt to reciprocate alone.

RUSSIA

Model 1913

Trials rifle: Avtomaticheskaya vintovka V. Fedorova, optnii obr.1913g.
Made by the Imperial ordnance factory, Sestroretsk, 1913–14.
Quantity: at least 150.
6·5 × 50mm, semi-rimmed.
Recoil-operated auto-loading action, locked by pivoting blocks on the barrel extension into the bolt.
About 1,255mm overall, 4·6kg unladen.
800mm barrel, 6-groove rifling; RH, polygonal.
Integral box magazine, 5 rounds.
Tangent-leaf sight graduated to 2,000 arshin?
730 m/sec with 38th Year Type ball cartridges.
Obr.1891g socket bayonet?

1910: trials undertaken at the Oranienbaum proving ground indicated the superiority of the Fedorov rifle over its Tokarev rival.
1912: the 7·62mm Fedorov was approved for field trials. It was long, very clumsy, and had

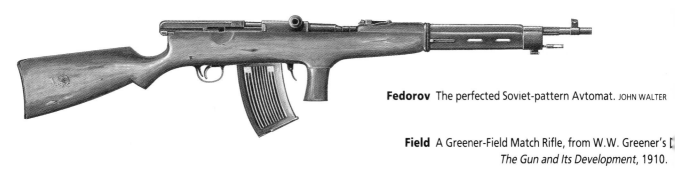

Fedorov The perfected Soviet-pattern Avtomat. JOHN WALTER

Field A Greener-Field Match Rifle, from W.W. Greener's [
The Gun and Its Development, 1910.

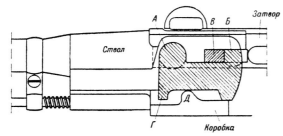

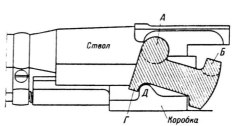

Fedorov The Avtomat locking system, from *Evolyutsiya Stelkovogo Oruzhiya*, 1938.

a butt with a distinctively shaped pistol grip. The box magazine protruded beneath the stock ahead of the trigger; a fire-selector lever lay on the top edge of the stock above the trigger; and a wooden hand guard ran from the back sight to the sheet-metal fore-end. However, the rimmed 7·62mm cartridge promoted misfeeds and jams.

1913: permission was granted to use the Japanese semi-rimmed 6·5mm cartridge and an improved 'obr.1913' rifle was produced. It was very similar externally to the 1912 (7·62mm) pattern, though the magazine differed slightly.

1914: trials against the Tokarev and a selection of foreign-made rivals, including the Sjøgren and the Bang, revealed the 1913-type Fedorov to be potentially the best—but still unreliable. Work ceased at the beginning of the First World War to concentrate on Mosin-Nagant infantry rifles.

Model 1916
••
Auto-loading rifle: Avtomaticheskaya vintovka V.
Fedorova obr.1916g.
Made by the Imperial ordnance factory,
Sestroretsk, 1916–17.
Quantity: about 350.
6·5 × 50mm, semi-rimmed.
Action: as 1913-pattern rifle, above.
975mm overall, 4·45kg without magazine.
520mm barrel, 6-groove rifling; RH, polygonal.
Detachable box magazine, 25 rounds.
Leaf sight graduated to 2,000 arshin?
705 m/sec with 38th Year Type ball cartridges.
Japanese 38th Year Type sword bayonet?
☆

1916: this was basically an improved 1913-type rifle, embodying the same short recoil action and locking system, but distinguished by its new detachable box magazine.

There was a rudimentary forward hand grip, and the sheet metal fore-end had been greatly shortened. Guns made in Tsarist days had plain-surface magazines and a back sight with three sighting notches. They lacked hold-opens or charger guides.

By October, sufficient rifles had been made to equip a company of the 189th infantry regiment.

1917: production in the Sestroretsk arms factory proceeded painfully slowly, even though many of the earlier 1913-type rifles were cannibalised to make Avtomats. The October Revolution stopped production altogether.

USSR
Automatic Rifle
••
Avtomata Federova.
Made by the State machine-gun factory,
Kovrov, 1920–5.
Quantity: about 3,200.
Otherwise generally as M1916, excepting back sight
(leaf graduated to 1,500 metres?).
☆

1919: production of the 1916-type Federov automatic rifle was optimistically scheduled to begin in February.

1920: the first guns were completed in mid September, but only about a hundred had been delivered by the end of the year. Niggling manufacturing problems had hindered progress.

1921: series production began in April.

1923: field service revealed serious faults. A hold-open and a disconnector were soon added; charger guides were machined in the receiver to allow the magazine to be refilled through the open action; a simpler back sight (with only one notch) was fitted; and the magazine-sides were ribbed to increase rigidity.

1924: a decision was taken to develop new rifles for the 7·62mm rimmed cartridge in the interests of standardisation.

1925: the Avtomat project was cancelled on 1 October. The guns had proved difficult to make, and tests with newer designs indicated greater long-term promise.

1928: surviving guns were placed in store. They had proved to be too delicate and unreliable, jammed easily when foul, and were difficult to control when firing automatically.

1939: remaining serviceable Avtomats were issued for 'active service' (possibly no more than propaganda pictures) during the Winter War against Finland.

BRITAIN

This dropping-block sporting rifle—another of the classic English systems—was designed by William Field of Birmingham and patented in Britain in May 1877.

Thumbing the operating lever forward moved the depressor-link past its locked position; projections on the tip of the depressor then ran along tracks cut diagonally into each side of the breech block, lowering the block into the receiver. The initial movement of the operating lever cocked the hammer; at the end of the stroke, the block struck the extractor and cleared the chamber. Pulling the lever back closed the breech, rotating the upper tip of the depressor behind the centre of the the axis pin to lock the breech block closed.

The Field action was compact, strong and simple, but extraction was inferior to rivals with extended operating levers (e.g., Farquharson).

The original rifles were marketed by the Field Rifle Company, formed in 1885 and active until 1898. The rifles are believed to have been made in Birmingham by W.W. Greener and Westley Richards. Most guns had external hammers and inertia strikers in the breech block, but a few hammerless versions were made.

Match Rifle
••
Greener-Field Pattern.
Made by W.W. Greener, Birmingham.
Chambered for a selection of large-calibre British
sporting cartridges.
Dropping-block action, operated by a lever on the right
side of the receiver.
DATA FOR A TYPICAL EXAMPLE
·303, rimmed.
45·00in overall, 9·92lb unladen.
28·25in barrel, 7-groove rifling; LH, polygonal.
Ramp-and-leaf sight graduated to 1,400 yards.
2,050 ft/sec with 215-grain bullet.
☆

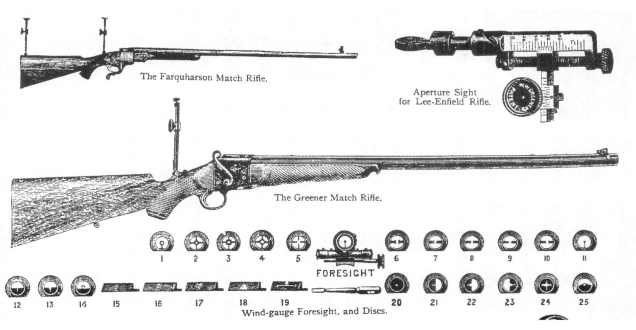

The Farquharson Match Rifle.

Aperture Sight
for Lee-Enfield Rifle.

The Greener Match Rifle.

FORESIGHT

Wind-gauge Foresight, and Discs.

1885: the Field rifle, like many comparable English designs, was made in styles ranging from ultra plain (for volunteers and military-style target shooting) to the finest match rifles. A typical example of the best pattern offered a heavy round barrel with a full-length matted rib, an exchangeable-element front sight with a spirit level, and a vernier aperture back sight on the tang. The butt had a chequered pistol grip with a horn cap, and the fore-end displayed chequering and a Henry-pattern tip.

FN

BELGIUM
Fabrique Nationale d'Armes de Guerre and
FN Herstal SA

Fabrique Nationale d'Armes de Guerre was founded in 1889 to make Mauser-type rifles, and has been involved in the production of firearms ever since. In addition to the guns described below, ascribed principally to the company's Bureau d'Études, products are covered in the Browning, Mauser, Saive and Sauer sections.

In 1988, FN announced the futuristic P90 'Personal Defence Weapon' (see *Military Small Arms of the 20th Century*, p.196). Chambered for a proprietary 5·7 × 28mm cartridge., this odd-looking weapon was still under evaluation when the manufacturer ran into severe financial difficulties in the 1990s. At the time of writing, its future remains in doubt.

BELGIUM

CAL

Carabine Automatique Légère.
Made by Fabrique Nationale d'Armes de Guerre,
Herstal-lèz-Liège, 1966–74?
5·56 × 45mm, rimless.
Gas-operated auto-loading action, locked by rotating
lugs on the bolt into engagement with the receiver.
DATA FOR A TYPICAL FIXED-BUTT EXAMPLE
980mm overall, 3·85kg laden.

467mm barrel, 6-groove rifling; RH, concentric.
Detachable box magazine, 20 or (later) 30 rounds.
Pivoting-'L' sight for 150/250 or 250/400 metres.
990 m/sec with M193 bullet; 850 ± 50 rpm.
'Flash-hider' tube bayonet.

☆

1963: the first attempts were made to adapt the FAL to 5·56mm, but the tilting-block locking system lacked the camming action to ease spent cases out of the chamber. Extraction was not reliable enough to satisfy potential users.

1967: prototypes of the Carabine Automatique Légère were demonstrated. The gun retained the proven gas system and trigger of the FAL, but a rotating bolt was substituted for the tilting block.

1969: series production began. Despite the different mechanism, the CAL was externally much like its 7·62mm predecessor, with a synthetic butt and pistol grip. A version with a folding tubular butt could also be supplied. Fore-ends were unnecessarily complex ventilated sheet-steel pressings; selectors lay on the left side of the receiver above the trigger, being marked S, 1, 3 and A—for safety, single shots, bursts, and fully automatic operation respectively.

1975: the CAL had been abandoned. Prone to extraction failures, it was too expensive...and had appeared at a time when many armies had either just re-equipped with 7·62mm NATO standard weapons or were still to be convinced of the efficacy of the 5·56mm bullet.

Guns had been tested extensively in Belgium and elsewhere, but had never challenged the 5·56mm AR-15/M16A1 and HK33. Gabon and Lebanon purchased a few in the early 1970s, but the CAL was then replaced by the sturdier FNC.

FNC

**'Fabrique Nationale, Carabine': Types 0000, 2000,
6000, 6040, 7000, 7030, 9000 and 9200.**
Made by FN Herstal SA, Herstal-lèz-Liège, 1982 to date.
5·56 × 45mm, rimless.
Gas-operated auto-loading action, locked by rotating
lugs on the bolt into engagement with the receiver.
DATA FOR A TYPICAL TYPE 2000
997mm overall with butt extended, 4·36kg laden.

450mm barrel, 6-groove rifling; RH, concentric.
Detachable box magazine, 30 rounds.
Pivoting-'L' sight for 250/400 metres.
915 m/sec with SS109 bullet; 650 ± 50 rpm.
Optional knife bayonet.

☆

1977: successor to the ill-starred CAL described above, the FNC was developed hurriedly to participate in NATO standardisation trials held at the end of the 1970s. However, development work had not been completed and the rifle was withdrawn from the competition; it had been entered at too early a stage, and did not perform as well as FN had hoped.

1980: protracted testing had revealed that problems centred mainly on the much simplified construction—pressings and welded seams being much in evidence—but also that the basic gas and rotating-bolt locking systems were effectual. Rifles were successfully entered in trials in Sweden in 1981–2 (see below), and performed well enough to convince the Belgian army of their merits. About ten thousand guns were sold to the Indonesian air force in 1982.

Originally known as the 'Model 90.00', the standard FNC Types 0000 and 2000 were identical, excepting that their rifling pitch was 1–in–12 and 1–in–7 respectively. These were suited to the Belgian SS109 and US M193 bullets. The guns were supplied with a folding skeleton butt of tubular steel, but a fixed polyamide butt was available on request; the bayonet, where used, was a variant of the US M7. Barrels and chambers were chromed to minimise the effects of propellant fouling, and a three round burst-fire mechanism could be supplied whenever required.

The standard short carbines, once known as 'Type 92.00' but now as Types 6000 (1–in–12 rifling) and 7000 (1–in–7), were 911mm long, had 360mm barrels, and weighed 3.7kg.

FNC Type 6040 had 1–in–12 rifling while the similar Type 7030 had the 1–in–7 pattern; they were semi-automatic 'Law Enforcement' variants, suited to security services but otherwise identical with the short-barrel carbine.

1989: after issuing the FNC to airborne forces

FN The 5·56mm CAL rifle. FN HERSTAL SA

FN A 5·56mm Type 2000 FNC, with an optical sight.

for some years, the Belgian government finally indicated that the 5·56mm gun would gradually replace the 7·62mm FAL in universal service. At the time of writing, however, progress is not clear. Though the FNC has been perfected too late to repeat the success of the FAL in a market-place dominated first by the M16 and latterly by the Steyr AUG, it still appeals to those who view bullpups without enthusiasm.

SWEDEN

Ak-5

Automatkarbin 5.
Made by FN Herstal SA (1984–6), and Forenade Fabriksverken AS, Eskilstuna (1986 to date).
5·56 × 45mm, rimless.
Generally as Belgian FNC (q.v.) excepting dimensions (1,007mm overall with butt extended, 3·90kg unladen).

☆

1982: trials undertaken with a variety of weapons resolved in favour of the FNC, which apparently performed acceptably in sub-zero. The Swedish government then purchased a licence allowing FFV to develop the design for Nordic service.
1984: the Ak-5 was adopted to replace the 7·62mm Ak-4 (Heckler & Koch G3, q.v.). Detail changes compared with the original Belgian FNC included enlargement of the trigger guard and cocking handle—facilitating use with arctic mittens—and a major change in the fore-end, which gained distinctive cross-hatching. The three-round burst-firing mechanism was sensibly discarded and the metal parts were given a green enamel protective finish.

The earliest Ak-5 were supplied by FN while tooling was undertaken in Eskilstuna; however, the first batches of an initial 80,000-gun order were delivered by FFV early in 1987.

OTHERS

In addition to service in Belgium and Sweden, the FNC is currently being made under licence in Indonesia. The Indonesian air force purchased 10,000 guns from FN in 1982 whereafter, in April 1984, the government signed a licensing agreement permitting manufacture in the state arsenal. Assembly is believed to have begun in 1987. The weapons presumably bear a Garuda mark on the receiver or magazine housing, but none has yet been examined.

No other large-scale purchases of FNC have yet been identified, though guns have been supplied for trials in many countries; small batches may also have found their way into Africa, the Middle East, South and Central America through dealers and intermediaries.

FRASER

BRITAIN

Made in small numbers for sporting use, this sturdy and effectual dropping-block action was patented in Britain in 1877. The mechanism had several interesting features, including a locking button beneath the head of the operating lever—though this was absent from some early guns, those with small actions (e.g., for so-called 'Rook Rifle' cartridges) or simply sometimes omitted on request. A toggle-type depressor-lever assembly opened the breech, and a main spring ran forward on a separate bracket beneath the barrel. The hammer pivoted on the same axis as the main depressor lever to strike a cut-away firing pin in the upper part of the breech block.

Improved Breech-Loading Rifle

Made by Daniel Fraser & Co., Edinburgh.
Chambered for a variety of pre-1914 cartridges.
Dropping-block action, operated by a lever.
DATA FOR A TYPICAL EXAMPLE
·303, rimmed.
42·00in overall, 7·05lb unladen.
25·75in barrel, 5-groove rifling; LH, concentric.
Screw-elevating tangent-leaf sight.
About 1,970 ft/sec with 210-grain bullet.

☆

1877: this distinctive single-shot sporting rifle was made to order by one of Scotland's leading gunmakers until 1914 or later. The elegant pistol-grip stock was retained by a massive bolt running up through the pistol grip into the back of the action, and the short fore-end usually had a hooked beak so characteristic of early British attempts to copy the original German schnabel pattern that it became established as a pattern of its own (now widely known as a 'Henry Tip'). Fraser rifles could be supplied with a variety of safety catches, including conventional shotgun-pattern tang buttons and a superfluous lever to hold the hammer at half cock. Cataloguing is difficult, as the rifles were made to order and vary greatly in size, finish, stock and decoration.

FRÜWIRTH

AUSTRIA-HUNGARY

This early bolt-action repeating mechanism is credited to a Viennese gunsmith. The basic Werndl-Holub drum breech was soon seen as cumbersome and incapable of transformation into a magazine-loader. Though experiments with quickloaders were undertaken throughout the 1870s, none was deemed acceptable; nor did the younger Krnka's experiments with 'Schnell-lader' rifles in the 1870s provide lasting results. Shortly after the first Werndls had been introduced, the Früwirth rifle appeared with a tubular magazine beneath the barrel. Though clearly based on the then-new Swiss Vetterli rifle, the Früwirth carbine had sufficient merit to be issued to gendarmerie units.

Model 1872

Gendarmerie carbine.
Made by Österreichische Waffenfabriks-Gesellschaft, Steyr, 1870–5.
Quantity: about 12,000.
11 × 42mm, rimmed.
Turning-bolt action, locked by the bolt-handle rib abutting the receiver ahead of the bridge.

FN The Type 2000 FNC with open sights. FN HERSTAL SA

FN HERSTAL SA

FN Derived from the FNC, the Ak-5 was adopted by Sweden to replace the G3 (Ak-4).

1,038mm overall, 3·69kg unladen.
570mm barrel, 6-groove rifling; RH, concentric.
Tube magazine under barrel, 8 rounds.
Ramp-and-leaf sight graduated to 600 schritt.
298 m/sec with M1867 carbine round.
M1854 socket bayonet.

☆

1869: the first carbines were issued for trials.

1872: on 23 May, the Früwirth was formally adopted for the Cisleithanischen Gendarmerie. The bolt-handle rib sufficed as a lock; no ejector was fitted; and the cocking piece had a prominent spur. The straight-wrist stock had a trigger guard with a spurred rearward extension, similar to that of the contemporaneous Werndl carbine. There was a small nose cap, a swivel on the under-edge of the butt, and a sling loop anchored laterally through the fore-end.

1873: the army briefly considered the gun as an Extra-Corps-Gewehr, but it proved too fragile even for the 1867-pattern carbine cartridge.

1874: issue of the Früwirth was extended to the Tiroler Landesschützen, but surviving guns had all been withdrawn into store by 1890.

GARAND

UNITED STATES OF AMERICA
M1 Garand and M14 series

These auto-loading rifles were developed by John C. Garand, who had been seconded to the National Armory, Springfield, in 1919. They were service issue only in the USA prior to 1945, but subsequently used by many armies; Rifles were also made in Taiwan and Italy.

After experimenting with primer actuation, John Garand finally perfected his gas-operated mechanism and applied for what became US Patent 1,892,541 on 12 April 1930. The Garand relied on gas tapped from a port under the muzzle to force back a spring-loaded operating rod. This acted on a roller on the right side of the bolt, rotating the lugs out of engagement with the receiver. The bolt and operating rod assembly retreated, ejecting a

spent case and re-cocking the hammer, then returned to reload the chamber and re-lock the bolt for another shot.

The action was effectual, though not without teething troubles. Its worst feature was the idiosyncratic magazine, which required a special clip and would not accept single cartridges. The clip ejected automatically after the last shot had been fired, which was at best a nuisance and at worst potentially fatal in situations where silence was required. In spite of these flaws, however, the M1 rifle gave the US soldier a great advantage over his opponents.

MILITARY RIFLES
ITALY

Italy received about 232,000 M1 Garand rifles from the USA in 1950–70, in addition to guns made by Beretta. War-surplus examples can be recognised by their original makers' marks and serial numbers in the US Army ranges.

1950: with the approval of the US authorities, Beretta began to tool to make the standard M1 Garand and delivered the first series-made gun to the Italian army in 1952. Small export orders were subsequently gained from Denmark and Indonesia.

1958: by the time nearly 100,000 guns had been made, Beretta realised that advances being made elsewhere—in particular, the adoption of the M14 by the US Army—were making the basic M1 obsolescent. A team led by Domenico Salza and later by Vittorio Valle shortened the original M1 Garand before revising it for a detachable magazine. The pre-production or prototype series included the M1 LS, a short rifle retaining the original clip-loaded magazine and the BM-58 with a detachable box pattern.

BM-59
....

CB, D, GL, Ital, Ital-A, Ital T A, Ital T P, Mks I–IV,
R and SL patterns.
Made by Armi Pietro Beretta SpA, Rome.
7·62 × 51mm, rimless.

Gas-operated auto-loading action, locked by rotating
lugs on the bolt head into the receiver.
DATA FOR BM-59 ITAL TIPO ALPINI
1,110mm overall, with butt extended
4·87kg with empty magazine.
491mm barrel, 4-groove rifling; RH, concentric.
Detachable box magazine, 20 rounds.
Tangent sight graduated to 2,000 metres.
812 m/sec with NATO SS77 ball cartridges; 800 rpm.
M7-type knife bayonet.

☆

1958: the first guns were simply shortened selective-fire 7·62 × 51mm M1 Garands with detachable box magazines.

1959: the BM-59D, BM-59R, and BM-59GL were fitted with a pistol grip behind the trigger, a rate-reducing device and a grenade launcher respectively.

The BM-59 Mk I had an improved trigger system and a 'tri-compensator'—a muzzle fitting serving as a muzzle brake, flash suppressor and compensator, but also capable of accepting a US-style M1 bayonet and Mecar rifle grenades.

The BM-59 Mk II was similar, but had a pistol grip behind the trigger guard to aid control when firing automatically, a winter trigger, a bipod attached to the gas tube and a hinged shoulder strap on the butt plate.

The BM-59 Mk III lacked the bipod, but had an additional pistol grip ahead of the magazine and a folding steel stock strong enough to withstand grenade launching. Intended as a light support weapon, the BM-59 Mk IV had a heavyweight barrel and a stock not unlike that of the later US M14A1 (q.v.).

1960: the BM-60 CB appeared, capable of firing three-round bursts instead of the usual fully automatic option.

1962: after extensive trials, the Italian army adopted the BM-59 Mk Ital. The service rifle had a conventional pistol-gripped wood stock, a bipod around the gas tube, and a grenade-launcher sight folding down behind the front-sight block. Marks on a typical army rifle included **BM-59** over **CAL. 7,62 NATO** above **BERETTA-ARMI** and **ROMA**, in four lines across the receiver behind the back sight.

Commercial and contract weapons generally bore P. BERETTA—BRESCIA—ITALIA and the date of manufacture above B M 59—CAL. 7,62 NATO and the serial number. These marks lay on the rear left side of the receiver below the back sight.

Series-production variants have included the BM-59 Ital Tipo Alpini (for Alpine troops), with a folding butt and a pistol grip behind the trigger, and the BM-59 Ital Tipo Paracudisti (for paratroops) with a short barrel and a detachable compensator. The BM-59 Ital A was a standard Ital with a folding butt. The BM-59 SL, restricted to semi-automatic fire, was an adapted M1 Garand with a detachable box magazine.

JAPAN

Experiments undertaken in the 1930s had no lasting results, so the war in China, which began in 1937, was fought with conventional Arisaka (q.v.) rifles. When the Pacific War began in 1941, Japanese troops soon found themselves at a severe disadvantage against US troops armed with Garands. The navy appears to have provisionally adopted the Type 4 recoil-operated rifle in 1944, based on contemporary Swiss practice, but the weapon was unsuccessful. The problems were eventually solved simply by adapting the Garand for the 7·7mm Japanese semi-rim rifle cartridge. No series production could be undertaken before the end of the war.

Type 5
....
Navy rifle.
Made by the Imperial navy arsenal, Yokosuka, 1945.
Quantity: about 250 sets of parts.
7·7 × 58mm, rimless.
Gas-operated auto-loading action, locked by rotating lugs on the bolt head into the receiver.
1,098mm overall, 4·14kg unladen.
588mm barrel, 4-groove rifling; RH, polygonal.
Integral charger-loaded box magazine, 10 rounds.
Tangent-leaf sight graduated to 1,200 metres.
730 m/sec with Type 99 ball cartridges.
Standard Type 99 sword bayonet?
☆

1945: unlike the M1 Garand, which required a special magazine clip, the Type 5 could be loaded with single rounds or from standard rifle chargers. Unfortunately, Japanese metallurgy had deteriorated so greatly that the Type 5 was never perfected. With widespread dislocation of Japanese industry by US bombing, only a few sets of components were found in Yokosuka when the war ended. There is no evidence to show that the 100–130 guns ever saw action.

TAIWAN

The US Military Aid Program supplied 173,730 M14 rifles prior to 1975, and the Springfield Armory production machinery had been sold to the Nationalist Chinese in 1967. Production of the 'Type 57' rifle began in 1968. Prior to gun number 048665, the ideographs across the rear of the receiver read 'Rifle 762' above '57 Type China' and the arsenal mark (a stylised encircled firewheel); later guns display ideographs reading 'Rifle 762 57 Type' above 'Made in Republic of China' over the arsenal mark. More than a million guns had been made by the end of the 1980s. They were identical with the last of the American-made rifles, though their stocks were generally cruder and a more noticeable flat appeared directly behind the receiver.

USA

The US Army's dormant interest in automatic rifles was rekindled by the submission of Bang and Murphy-Manning rifles in 1911. Though neither was particularly impressive, they inspired trials with a selection of guns in 1916–18.

Garand's first efforts—the patterns of 1920, 1921, 1922 and 1924—embodied the rarely encountered primer-actuation system, relying on the backward movement of a deep-seated primer to unlock the breech on firing. The guns worked well enough, but required special ammunition. They were tested against Thompson, Hatcher-Bang and Berthier rifles and then, from 1924 onward, against the highly promising delayed-blowback Pedersen. Primer-actuated Garands

were not made in quantity, though an order for 24 of the ·276 1922-type guns was completed in the summer of 1924.

1926: the Pedersen rifle impressed the Infantry Board during demonstrations at Fort Benning on 25–27 January, and was successfully tested by the Ordnance Board on 10 May. Within ten days, an order for twenty had been approved.

While work continued, extended trials were undertaken with ten modified Thompson Auto Rifles and ten improved or 1924-model Garands. An inconclusive report was submitted on 15 June. At the end of July, the Ordnance ordered construction of the first Garand chambered for standard ·30 ball ammunition.

Crimped-in primers forced John Garand to abandon his primer-actuated locking system in favour of gas operation, settling on a muzzle port with a piston and operating rod under the barrel after testing a Bang-type muzzle cup.

1927: in March, the Cavalry Board reported that the field trials of primer-actuated Garand, marginally delayed-blowback Thompson and recoil-operated Springfield rifles had failed to resolve the competition. By the end of the year, therefore, the first gas-operated ·276 Garand had also been sanctioned.

1928: throughout the Spring, the Infantry and Cavalry Boards experimented with 25 ·276 Tl Pedersen rifles, the highly favourable reports being submitted in April. In June, however, the 'Pig Board' had been appointed to consider the wounding power and lethality or various types of rifle ammunition, and, within a month, the Semi-Automatic Rifle Board (SRB) had been appointed to supervise trials on behalf of the US Army, Navy and Marine Corps. On 13 August, the SRB representatives met to test the ·276 primer-actuated M1924 Garand, the ·30 Thompson Auto Rifle, two versions of the ·276 Tl Pedersen and an improved ·256 Bang. Another inconclusive report was submitted on 21 September.

1929: experiments with the ·30 Garand ceased in February, as ·276 had been preferred. The second series of SRB rifle trials was programmed for 1 July but so few guns had been received that

ARMI PIETRO BERETTA SPA

Garand The 7·62mm BM59 Mk Ital rifle.

◁ **Garand** Italian parachutists on exercise, with BM59 Tipo Alpini rifles.
ARMI PIETRO BERETTA SPA

Garand One of the few Japanese Type 5 rifles ever assembled.

the committee postponed the acceptance date to 15 August. It made little difference, as the original guns—Brauning, Colt-Browning, Holek, T1 Pedersen, ·276 T3 Garand and Thompson—were joined only by a Rheinmetall rifle and an incomplete White. Submitted on 24 October, the trial board's report suggested that work on the ·30-calibre Garand should recommence. A prototype ·30 T3 was ordered from Springfield Armory on 14 November.

1930: the Ordnance Board tested two more rifles submitted by Joseph White of Boston but found them to be less rugged than either the Pedersen or the Garand.

1931: during the Spring, Springfield Armory completed twenty ·276 T3E2 Garands, which were despatched for trials against the ·276 T1 Pedersens. The third series of SRB trials lasted from 9 October 1931 to 4 January 1932.

Participants were the ·30 T1E1 Garand, the ·276 T1 Pedersen and ·276 T3E2 Garand, plus the renascent White Rifle.

M1 Garand

....
M1C, M1D, M1E5, M1E7, M1E8, T1E2, T3E2, T20, T20E1, T20E2, T22, T22E1 and T26.
Made by the National Armory, Springfield, Massachusetts (4·617 million, 1937–57); the Winchester Repeating Arms Company, New Haven, Connecticut (513,580, 1940–5); Harrington & Richardson, Inc., Worcester, Massachusetts (445,600, 1951–4); and the International Harvester Corporation, Chicago, Illinois (457,750, 1951–4).
Quantity: about 6·034 million.
·30–06, rimless.
Gas-operated auto-loading action, locked by rotating lugs on the bolt head into the receiver.
43·50in overall, 9·50lb unladen.
24·00in barrel, 4-groove rifling; RH, concentric.
Internal clip-loaded box magazine, 8 rounds.
Tangent sight graduated to 2,000 yards.
2,740 ft/sec with M2 ball cartridges.
M1 sword bayonet.
☆

1932: as the Federal government was spending thousands of dollars on rifle development, but

viewing progress with increasing anxiety, a meeting was held in Washington DC on 4 January. The retention of ·276-calibre was confirmed, production of 125 T3E2 Garands at Springfield Armory being authorised. However, as a result of General Douglas MacArthur's intervention, the reduction in calibre was officially rejected on 25 February. The ·30 T1E1 Garand was resurrected, tested in mid-February, and passed such an encouraging trial in March that eighty 'Semi-automatic Rifles, ·30, T1E2' were ordered immediately.

1933: on 3 August, the designation changed to 'Semi-Automatic Rifle, Caliber ·30, M1'. Two years were necessary to perfect the weapons; fifty had been sent to the Infantry Board and 25 to the cavalrymen in May 1934, but so many complaints had been received that the guns were withdrawn for modification and did not return for a year.

1935: trials were completed by October. The M1 was recommended for service and cleared for procurement by the Assistant Secretary of War on 7 November.

1936: the M1 Garand was standardised on 9 January. Severe problems with the design of individual parts delayed the first deliveries of machine-made guns until in September 1937. The M1 had a one-piece pistol-grip stock extending almost to the muzzle, though the last few inches of the gas tube and barrel protruded. A hand guard ran forward from the receiver ring and the solitary band carried a swivel; the other swivel lay beneath the butt. The magazine was contained entirely within the stock, while a distinctive tangent back sight was fitted to the receiver behind the feed-way.

1939: production in the Springfield factory reached a hundred a day by the beginning of September. Unfortunately, the early problems seriously damaged the M1's reputation long before samples were badly received at the 1939 National Matches, and a major redesign of the gas-cylinder assembly and barrel had to be authorised on 26 October.

1940: in February, the Ordnance Committee ruled that no further action be taken with the

promising Johnson rifle (q.v.) in case it affected remedial work on the Garand.

1941: by 10 January, Springfield Armory was making 600 M1 Garand rifles a day, and the first of Winchester's 65,000-gun 'educational' contract had also appeared.

1943: by September, Springfield Armory had reached a production total of 100,000 and was attaining a daily output of 4,000.

1944: the use of fully-automatic assault rifles by the Germans encouraged the Ordnance Department to develop selective-fire Garands. Springfield and Remington began work in the Spring and had virtually completed their guns (T20 and T22 respectively) by the end of August. In September, however, the Army Ground Forces headquarters revised the basic specification and the guns were withdrawn.

The folding-butt T26 rifle (or M1E5) was developed in Springfield in late summer. The most important occurrence, however, was the standardisation of the M1E7 and M1E8 sniper rifles in July and September, as the M1C and M1D respectively.

The M1C had an M73 (Lyman Alaskan) or M73B1 (Weaver 330) telescope sight in a Griffin & Howe side mount, while the M1D had an M81 or M82 sight. The M81 had a cross-hair graticule, whereas the M82 had a post pattern. Often found with the conical T37 flash-hider—later standardised as the M2—the rifles weighed 11·2–11·5lb with their sights.

1945: improved selective-fire T20E1 and T22E1 rifles were tested at Aberdeen Proving Ground in January/February, revealing that the T22E1 was still capable of improvement; the project dragged on into 1948. The T20E1 was judged to be almost acceptable and a hundred improved T20E2 rifles were successfully tested in May; 100,000 were to be ordered in 1945–6, but the war ended before the contract could be placed.

In July, Colonel William Alexander of the Pacific Warfare Board requested 15,000 short M1 rifles for jungle warfare. About 150 prototypes were subsequently converted in the ordnance workshops of the 6th Army in the Philippines, one being sent to Springfield Armory

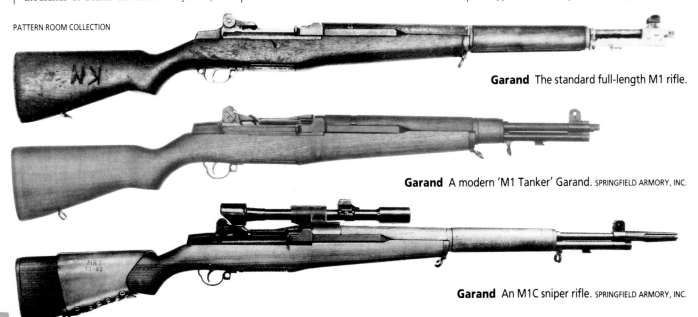

PATTERN ROOM COLLECTION

Garand The standard full-length M1 rifle.

Garand A modern 'M1 Tanker' Garand. SPRINGFIELD ARMORY, INC.

Garand An M1C sniper rifle. SPRINGFIELD ARMORY, INC.

for review. Springfield subsequently developed the T26 Wood Stock Garand from this sample, but the project was cancelled when fighting in the Pacific ended.

Garand production by VJ-Day amounted to about 4·028 million; 600,000 or more were made immediately after the war, and work began again during the Korean conflict.

1952: a production licence was granted to Beretta (q.v.) to make new guns to honour NATO/SEATO contracts.

1955: the M5 knife bayonet was approved. The conventional muzzle ring of the M1 pattern was replaced by a small rearward-facing spigot on the upper part of the guard, which locked into the gas-plug housing beneath the barrel.

1957: M1 rifle production ended on 17 May.

M1 conversions

M1E14 and Mk 2 Models 0–2

☆

A shortage of M14 and M16 rifles in the early 1960s prompted the US Navy to develop a special chamber insert to enable the ·30-06 M1 to fire 7·62 × 51mm cartridges. Patented by naval officer Richard Haley and civilian James O'Conner, then developed by H.P. White Laboratories, Inc., it consisted of a small sleeve in the front of the chamber to compensate for the shorter case-neck and different shoulder of the NATO round. The insert was retained in the gun simply by firing two eight-round clips to expand it against the existing chamber walls.

The first ten M1E14 rifles were successfully converted by the American Machine & Foundry Company of York, Pennsylvania, in the summer of 1964. Production of the 'Rifle, 7·62mm, Mk 2 Model 0' began in 1965, but insert-ejection problems were encountered immediately the modified rifles entered service.

An improved insert was hastily developed by the Navy Weapons Production Engineering Center in Crane, Indiana, to cure the faults.

Production was surprisingly large: AMF made 17,050 Model 0 guns with the first-pattern chamber insert and about 5,000 Model 1

with the modified type, while Harrington & Richardson made 12,050 Model 1 guns with the improved insert in addition to supplying 8,750 new barrels chambered for the 7·62 × 51mm cartridge. Guns with the new barrels were designated Mk 2 Model 2. The rifles were all marked 7·62 M.M. on the rear of the receiver.

M14

M14, M14A1, M14E1, M14E2, M15, M21, T44, T44E1, T44E4, T44E5 and XM21.

Made by the National Armory, Springfield, Massachusetts (167,100, 1958–62); Harrington & Richardson, Inc., Worcester, Massachusetts (537,580, 1959–64); Winchester Repeating Arms Company, New Haven, Connecticut (356,500 1959–64); and Thompson-Ramo-Wooldridge, Inc., Cleveland, Ohio (319,160, 1962–4).

Quantity: 1·380 million.

DATA FOR STANDARD M14

7·62 × 51mm NATO, rimless.

Action: as M1 Garand, above.

44·00in overall, 8·56lb unladen.

22·00in barrel, 4-groove rifling; RH, concentric.

Detachable box magazine, 20 rounds.

Tangent sight graduated to 1,500 yards?

2,750 ft/sec with M59 ball cartridges.

Cyclic rate 750 ± 25 rpm.

M6 knife bayonet.

☆

1951: suspended by the intervention of the Korean War, work on a modernised Garand created the T44 by amalgamating the action of the T20E2 with the gas cylinder of the T25 and the magazine of the abortive T31. Tested extensively against the T25 and the FN FAL ('T48' to the US Army), the T44, chambered for the ·30 T65 cartridge, performed so well for a rifle with such a short history that the Ordnance Department pressed strongly for improvement. A heavy-barrel T44E1 appeared in October.

1952: after procuring a few FAL rifles—3,200 were purchased in Belgium in 1950–6—testing was undertaken at Fort Benning in August. The FAL was preferred, ahead of the new T44, the T25 and the British EM-2. The T25 and EM-2

were eliminated, but the Ordnance Board was still impressed by the performance of the T44 and instructed Springfield to make 500 for trials against 500 T48 FAL-type rifles ordered from Harrington & Richardson.

1953: on 15 December, the ·30 (7·62mm) T65 cartridge was approved as a NATO standard, the perfected T65E3 being standardised by the Ordnance Committee in August 1954.

1954: arctic trials showed that the T44 rifle performed much better in sub-zero conditions than the T48. After remedial work on the latter, additional trials in 1954–5 were tied.

1955: the T48 rifle failed the Fort Benning 'Combat Course Test' so comprehensively that it was withdrawn so that British and Belgian representatives could supply their latest weapons for comparison. Surviving T48 rifles were then rebuilt in Springfield Armory to incorporate lessons learned in the Sudan by the British.

1956: a final test at Fort Benning in April showed that the T44 and T48 were equally suitable for adoption. The Ordnance Board recommended the indigenous T44 on the grounds that it was lighter and better suited to US production techniques.

1957: five years of trials with the T44 series (T44E2–T44E6) was finally resolved on 1 May, when the T44E4 and T44E5 were adopted as the 7·62mm Rifles M14 and M15 respectively. However, the heavy-barrel M15 was never successful; produced only in small numbers, it was declared obsolete on 17 December 1959.

The M14 was essentially similar to the Garand internally, though the detachable box magazine, shortened gas tube, and pistol-grip half-stock were most distinctive. The selector on many guns (unofficially known as 'M14 M[odified]') was plugged to restrict them to semi-automatic fire, though a standard three-position selector could be substituted when required.

The earliest M14 rifles were made with wooden stocks and hand guards, but the guard soon became ventilated fibreglass-reinforced plastic; finally, a durable synthetic stock was adopted and a ribbed non-ventilated hand guard was used.

GARAND LESSER PATTERNS

ARGENTINA

The US government supplied nearly 30,000 M1 Garand rifles prior to 1964, many being issued to the navy along with Beretta BM-59 rifles supplied directly from Italy. Some Garands were converted by Fabrica Militar de Armas Portatiles 'Domingo Matheu' in the 1960s to accept the standard Beretta-type 20-round box magazine.

BRAZIL

Like Argentina, Brazil received large numbers of M1 Garands in the early 1950s. Some were subsequently converted in Itajuba for the 7·62 × 51mm cartridge and accepted the 20-round FAL magazine.

INDONESIA

In addition to production of BM-59 rifles in the state factory in Bandung, Indonesia received 55,000–78,000 M1 Garands

(estimates vary) and a handful of M1C rifles from the USA prior to 1971. Substantial quantities of Italian-made M1 and BM-59 rifles were also supplied. A Garuda—a mythical half-human bird—lay across the receiver-back above the serial number.

MOROCCO

Beretta granted a licence to enable the BM-59 to be made in the government ordnance factory in Fez, but work was confined to the assembly of components imported from Italy; special markings, if any, have yet to be identified.

NIGERIA

The government purchased a licence to make the BM-59 in Kaduna. However, the Civil War interrupted plans and there is no evidence that guns were made. Nigerian

Garands invariably prove to be Italian.

OTHERS

The colossal numbers of M1 rifles made in 1936–57 enabled countless thousands to be distributed to friendly forces through the US Military Aid Programs. Virtually all of the rifles retained their American marks and numbers, unlike those newly made in Italy or Taiwan.

¶ Among major M1 users—in addition to those listed above—have been Turkey (312,430, 1953–70); South Korea (296,450, 1964–74); France (232,500, 1950–64); South Vietnam (220,300 M1 and 520 M1C/M1D, 1950–75); Greece (186,090 M1 and 1,880 M1C/M1D prior to 1975); Iran (165,490 prior to 1964); Pakistan (possibly 150,000 prior to 1975); Norway (72,800 prior to 1964); Denmark (69,810 'Gevær m/50' supplied

prior to 1964, some subsequently converted to 7·62 × 51mm); Israel (up to 60,000 prior to 1975); Venezuela (55,670 M1, prior to 1975); Federal Republic of Germany (46,750 prior to 1965); Thailand (about 40,000 prior to 1975); Philippines (34,300 M1 and 2,630 M1D in 1950–75); Laos (36,270, 1950–75); Saudi Arabia (34,530 prior to 1975); Paraguay (30,750 prior to 1975); Jordan (25,000–30,000 prior to 1974); and Ethiopia (20,700 M1 plus an unknown quantity of Beretta BM-59 rifles).

¶ In addition, the US armed forces abandoned nearly a million ·30-calibre M1/M2 Carbines, M1 Garand and M14 rifles in Vietnam in the mid 1970s.

¶ M14 rifles have been less widely distributed than the M1, large-scale users including Ethiopia (23,450 in 1971–4) and Israel (at least 22,500 prior to 1975).

Similar internally to the M14, the M15 had a heavy barrel, a fixed-leg bipod attached to the gas cylinder, a strengthened stock, and a folding shoulder strap on the butt plate.

1960: the M14E1 was a selective-fire M14 with a wood pistol grip behind the trigger, a bipod attached to the gas cylinder, a strap on the butt plate, and (on guns intended for use in support roles) a folding forward hand grip. Five differing butts were tested. Eventually, the M14E2 was standardised as the 'Rifle, 7·62mm, M14A1'.

Credited to Captain Durward Gosney of the US Army Infantry Board, the M14A1 employed the standard M14 action, but had a stabiliser over the compensator and would not accept a bayonet. A bipod with adjustable telescoping legs was fitted, a straight wooden stock with a pistol grip behind the trigger was developed, a folding forward hand grip was used, and the rubber butt plate had a folding shoulder strap. Hand guards were invariably synthetic.

1963: work ceased. The production machinery was sold to Taiwan (q.v.) in 1967.

1968: severe shortages of effectual sniper rifles, particularly in Vietnam, led to a demand for 1,800 specially selected M14-type rifles fitted with 3–9 × Leatherwood Adjustable Ranging Telescopes (ART). About three hundred M14 National Match rifles were fitted with M84 sights, sufficing until the projected XM21 rifle had been tested against the Marine Corps Remington 700, the MAS FR-F1 and the Steyr SSG-69. The XM21 proved to be as accurate as any of its rivals at long range when fired with M118 match ammunition.

1970: conversion of 1,435 NM-pattern M14 rifles to XM21 standards began immediately in Rock Island Arsenal.

1975: the XM21 was formally standardised in December as the M21, remaining the standard US Army sniper rifle until approval of the Remington Model 700 in 1987.

SPORTING GUNS

The M1 NM ('National Match') rifles mated specially-selected actions with barrels of proven accuracy, and had special attention paid to their triggers. The first were made in 1953—800 new guns—and the last in 1963, when 3,640 service rifles were rebuilt. Production totalled a little less than 45,000: 21,390 new guns and 23,460 rebuilds. Single-shot Ceremonial Pattern M1 rifles were made for the American Legion and the Veterans of Foreign Wars.

The first M14 National Match rifles appeared in 1963, with specially selected 'accurised' barrels and fibreglass-bedded barrels. The M14 proved effectual in its military-match shooting guise and generally outshot the FAL, ascribed by many to the superiority of a rotating bolt (which moves in a straight line) over a displaced block.

GOLDEN EAGLE

UNITED STATES OF AMERICA

A very well made, but short-lived product of Americano-Japanese co-operation, this rifle relied on a multi-lug bolt for its undoubted strength.

Model 7000

Made for Golden Eagle Rifles, Inc., Houston, Texas, by the Nikko Firearms Mfg Co., Tochigi, 1976–82.
·22–250, ·243 Winchester, ·25–06, ·270 Winchester, ·270 Weatherby Magnum, 7mm Remington Magnum, ·300 Weatherby Magnum, ·300 Winchester Magnum, ·30–06, ·338 Winchester Magnum, ·375 H&H Magnum or ·458 Winchester Magnum.
Turning-bolt action locked by five lugs on the head.
DATA FOR A TYPICAL EXAMPLE
·300 Weatherby Magnum, belted rimless.
About 44in overall, 8·55lb unladen.
26·00in barrel, 4-groove rifling; concentric, RH.
Internal box magazine, 3 rounds.
Optical sights.
3,245 ft/sec with 180-grain bullet.
☆

1976: this rifle was introduced in 'Grade I Big Game' or 'Grade I Magnum' patterns, in all chamberings listed above excepting ·375 and ·458. Barrels measured 24in or 26in. Excepting the lightweight ·22–250 variant, which held four, magazine capacity was always three rounds. A sliding safety lay on the tang. Walnut stocks had Monte Carlo butts and skip-line chequering on the pistol grip and fore-end. The separate pistol-grip cap had a gold eagle motif and the fore-end tip, generally rosewood, was accompanied by a white spacer. Grade II rifles had selected stocks and engraved metalwork.

The Grade I African rifle, chambered only for ·375 H&H and ·458 Winchester cartridges, was often stocked in bubinga; the pistol-grip cap and fore-end tip could be ebony or horn. Magazines held three ·375 or two ·458 rounds, the guns weighing about 8·8lb and 10·5lb respectively.

GRAS

FRANCE

This bolt-action rifle, perfected in the early 1870s, proved to be long-lived. It was also adopted in Greece in 1876.

1871: rapid progress being made in Germany frightened the French into reconsidering their Mle.1866 ('Chassepot') needle rifle. Though the French weapon was ballistically more effectual than the Dreyse needle guns, the annular india-rubber obturating washer on the Chassepot bolt head lost elasticity during prolonged fire.

1872: trials began in March with a Dutch Beaumont rifle, which performed well.

1873: on 8 May, army captain Basile Gras presented a Chassepot needle rifle converted to chamber a metal-case cartridge. The Gras bolt was comparatively simple, with a separate head carrying the extractor and a satisfactory lock being provided by the abutment of the bolt-handle rib against the receiver bridge. No ejector was fitted, spent cases being tipped from the bolt way by the head of a screw doubling as the bolt stop. Prototypes had a Chassepot-type safety system, in which the cocking piece could be retracted and rotated to rest on the back of the receiver. This prevented the firing pin reaching the chambered round, but also

PATTERN ROOM COLLECTION

Gras A French M1874 infantry rifle.

Garand A modern M21 sniper rifle clone, with an adjustable-comb butt and a commercial optical sight.
SPRINGFIELD ARMORY, INC.

prevented the bolt-handle being locked down and was abandoned on service rifles.

1874: a final elimination trial with Gras and Beaumont rifles began at the end of April.

FRANCE

Note: many minor and experimental adaptions of the Gras rifle have been made. In 1881, for example, substantial quantities of Mle.1866 Chassepot rifles were converted to fire reduced-charge ammunition for training. These displayed Gras-type bolts, but had a short chamber and the back sight was graduated to a mere 40 metres.

A few target rifles were built on modified Gras actions by a Parisian gunsmith, Arthur Nouvelle. Authorised for army shooting matches in the early 1880s, these had a micro-adjustable quadrant back sight, a special cheek-piece butt with a hooked wooden butt plate, and blued metalwork. They were marked NOUVELLE and BTÉ S.G.D.G. on the left side of the receiver.

Many guns were converted for experimental magazines in 1883–5—e.g., Gras-Vernet, Gras-Spitalski and Gras-Lee. Few of these were made in quantity, but substantial numbers of old Gras rifles were adapted in 1914–18 to provide the 'Bombarde DR' (a grenade thrower) and the 'Fusil-Signaleur'. The latter was patented by Louis Chobert of Paris, and is usually so marked.

Model 1874

Infantry rifles: Fusils d'Infanterie Mle.1866/74, Mle.1874 et Mle.1874 M.80.
Made by Manufactures d'Armes, Châtellerault, Saint-Étienne and Tulle, 1874–87; and Österreichische Waffenfabriks-Gesellschaft, Steyr, 1876–7 (bolts only).
11 × 59mm, rimmed.
Turning-bolt action, locked by the bolt handle rib abutting the receiver ahead of the bridge.
1,305mm overall, 4·19kg unladen.
821mm barrel, 4-groove rifling; LH, concentric.
Ramp-and-leaf sight graduated to 1,800 metres.
440 m/sec with Mle.1874 ball ammunition.
Mle.1874 épée bayonet.
☆

1874: adopted on 7 July, the Gras rifle was externally similar to the preceding Mle.1866 Chassepot needle gun. However, the detachable bolt head provided a visible distinction. The one-piece stock was accompanied by a single band and a simple nose cap, both mounts being retained by springs. Swivels lay on the underside of the band and on the under-edge of the butt, with a lug and tenon for the bayonet on the right side of the muzzle. The back-sight leaf, graduated to 1,400 metres, had an extending portion serving ranges up to 1,800 metres.

1875: the first deliveries were made from the state arsenals. Concurrently, conversion of old Chassepots began. They were changed simply by boring-out the breech to receive a short liner chambering the Gras cartridge. The receivers were modified, and a new Mle.1874 bolt was substituted. 'Mle.1866/74' conversions had smaller back-sight leaves graduated to 1,300 metres with the sliding extension to 1,700.

However, to complicate matters, conversions often received new barrels during their lives, these being distinguished by N on the upper surface near the breech.

The converted rifles initially retained their Mle.1866 sabre bayonets. Though they were gradually adapted to take the Mle.1874 épée, the programme, still incomplete, was abandoned in September 1880 and the Mle.1866 retained with unmodified guns.

1880: the addition of an annular channel and a longitudinal groove cut into the left side of the bolt way helped gas to escape should the primer rupture or the case-head fail—a worrying occurrence with pre-1879 ammunition, though strengthening the cartridge case-head reduced the problem to manageable proportions. Altered guns were designated 'Mle.1874 Modifié 1880' (Mle.1874 M.80), the distinction between Mle.1866/74 and Mle.1874 being abandoned.

1885: some guns were altered to approximate to the new Kropatschek infantry rifle (q.v.).

1887: the first large-scale withdrawals from line infantrymen were made with the advent of sufficient Mle.1886 Lebel rifles.

1914: surviving guns were issued for service in the First World War, many being modified for the 8mm cartridge in 1914–15.

Model 1874

Cavalry carbines: Carabines de Cavallerie Mle.1866/74, Mle.1874 et Mle.1874 M.80.
Made by Manufactures d'Armes, Châtellerault, Saint-Étienne and Tulle, 1874–87.
11 × 59mm, rimmed.
Action: as Mle.1874 rifle, above.
1,175mm overall, 3·56kg unladen.
702mm barrel, 4-groove rifling; LH, concentric.
Ramp-and-leaf sight graduated to 1,100 metres.
428 m/sec with Mle.1874 ball ammunition.
No bayonet.
☆

1874: adopted at the same time as the infantry rifle, this was simply a shortened gun with an additional spring-retained barrel band and the bolt handle turned down toward the stock. Swivels lay under the middle band and butt. Unlike similar mounted gendarmerie carbines (below), cavalry patterns were stocked almost to the muzzle and did not accept a bayonet. Some were converted Chassepots (Mle.1866/74), others were newly made (Mle.1874).

1880: most service weapons were modified to facilitate the escape of gas in the event of a case-head failure.

1890: replacement by the Mle.1890 began. Most Gras carbines had been sold by 1914.

Model 1874

Mounted gendarmerie carbines: Carabines de Gendarmerie à Cheval Mle.1866/74, Mle.1874 et Mle.1874 M.80.
Made by Manufactures d'Armes, Châtellerault, Saint-Étienne and Tulle, 1874–87.
11 × 59mm, rimmed.
Otherwise generally as cavalry carbine, excepting for bayonet (Mle.1874 socket pattern).
☆

1874: identical with the cavalry patterns, with an additional barrel band and a turned-down bolt handle, these accepted special bayonets.

Gras North African tribesmen with an M1874 artillery musketoon. Obsolescent guns of this type are still to be seen in isolated districts of North Africa.
COLLECTOR'S COMPENDIUM

1880: survivors were adapted to ease escape of gas from a failed case-head or a ruptured primer. Designations advanced to Mle.1874 M.80.

Model 1874

Foot-gendarmerie carbines: Carabines de Gendarmerie à Pied Mle.1866/74, Mle.1874 et Mle.1874 M.80.
Made by Manufactures d'Armes, Châtellerault, Saint-Étienne and Tulle, 1874–87.
11 × 59mm, rimmed.
Otherwise as cavalry carbine, above, excepting bayonet (Mle.1866 sabre pattern).

1874: this was little more than an infantry rifle shortened to carbine length. It had one band, bearing the swivel, and a plain nose cap. A lug and tenon for the bayonet lay on the right side of the muzzle. The cavalry-carbine back sight was used, and the bolt handle was turned down against the stock. Some guns were conversions; others were newly made.
1880: a channel and groove were cut inside the bolt way to protect the firer from gas escaping from a failed case-head, advancing the designation to Mle.1874 M.80.

Model 1874

Artillery musketoons: Mousquetons d'Artillerie Mle.1866/74, Mle.1874 et Mle.1874 M.80.
Made by Manufactures d'Armes, Châtellerault, Saint-Étienne and Tulle, 1874–87.
11 × 59mm, rimmed.
Action: as Mle.1874 rifle, above.
990mm overall, 3·26kg unladen.
510mm barrel, 4-groove rifling: LH, concentric.
Ramp-and-leaf sight graduated to 1,250 metres.
406 m/sec with Mle.1874 ball ammunition.
Mle.1866 sabre bayonet.

☆

1874: adopted to replace the earlier Mle.1866 (Chassepot) pattern, this was a much-shortened infantry rifle. It had the same band and nose cap, but the back sight differed and the bolt handle was turned down against the stock. The sabre

bayonet was retained, a suitable lug and tenon appearing on the right side of the muzzle.
1880: most surviving musketoons were adapted to protect the firer should gas escape from a failed cartridge ('Mle.74 M.80').

Model 1874/80/14

Fusil Mle.1874 M.80 M.14.
Converted by government- and privately-owned factories, 1914–15.
8 × 51mm, rimmed.
Action: as Mle.1874 rifle, above.
1,305mm overall, 4·08kg unladen.
820mm barrel, 4-groove rifling; LH, concentric.
Ramp-and-leaf sight graduated to 2,000 metres.
700 m/sec with Balle 1898 D.
Mle.1874 épée bayonet.

☆

1914: this was an emergency conversion of many surviving Gras rifles—Mle.1874 and Mle.1866/74—to fire 8mm Lebel cartridge. No changes were made in the basic action, as trials showed that the Gras was sturdy enough to handle the comparatively small increases in chamber pressure.
A minor change was made to the face of the detachable bolt head, to accept the different case-head shape, and the barrel and back-sight assembly were replaced. A short wooden hand guard ran from the receiver ring under the barrel band, but the original mounts were retained.
1920: many 8mm conversions were shipped to the colonies, where they remained until the end of the Second World War. Others were still being used in 1939 by airfield guards of the Armée de l'Air.

GREECE

Adopted in 1876 to replace the unsuccessful indigenous Mylona rifle, Greek Gras guns were made in Steyr by Österreichische Waffenfabriks-Gesellschaft: 57,000 rifles and 6,000 carbines had been delivered by the end of 1877. Many found their way to minor Balkan states (e.g., Montenegro) in the early twentieth century.

GRÜNIG & ELMIGER

SWITZERLAND

Once renowned for Lienhard-brand sub-calibre trainers, Grünig & Elmiger has also made target rifles based on the Swiss Kar.31 service rifle. Modern rifles embody a proprietary action, though the stocks and sights were originally purchased from Anschütz.

Sporting/target rifles

Matchkugelbüchsen: Standard and Luxusmodelle.
Made by Grünig & Elmiger AG, Jagd- und Sportwaffenfabrik, Malters.
·222 Remington, 5·6 × 50mm Magnum, ·243 Winchester, 6·5 × 55mm, 7 × 57mm, 7 × 64mm, 7·5 × 55mm, ·308 Winchester, 8 × 57mm, 8 × 68mm S and others.
Turning-bolt action, locked by lugs on the bolt head engaging the receiver.
DATA FOR A TYPICAL EXAMPLE
5·6 × 50mm Magnum, rimless.
1,135mm overall, 3·95kg unladen.
660mm barrel, 6-groove rifling; RH, concentric.
Optical sight.
1,095 m/sec with 3·2-gram bullet.

☆

1970*: these rifles, intended for sporting-style target shooting, usually had a special trigger mechanism. The rear lever was set by pushing the reversed lever in the front of the guard forward. Grünel rifles had free-floating barrels and solid beaver-tail fore-ends, and could weigh 3·8–5kg depending on calibre.

Target rifles

Matchgewehre 300, 300 LM, Super Target 200/40, Target 200, and UIT Standard.
Made by Grünig & Elmiger AG, Jagd- und Sportwaffenfabrik, Malters.
·222 Remington, ·243 Winchester, 6·5 × 55mm, 7·5 × 55mm or ·308 Winchester.
Action: as Matchkugelbüchse, above.

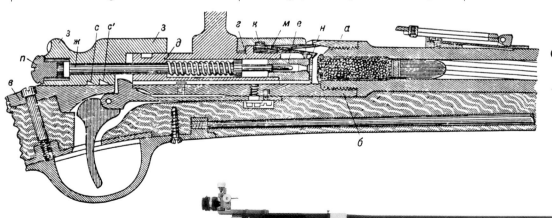

Gras A longitudinal section, from Federov's *Evolyutsiya Strelkovogo Oruzhiya*, 1938.

Grünig & Elmiger The 300m Grünel Matchgewehr (Free Rifle).

DATA FOR A TYPICAL MATCHGEWEHR 300
·308 Winchester, rimless.
1,150mm overall, 6·92kg without hand rest.
685mm barrel, 4-groove rifling; RH, concentric.
Micro-adjustable aperture sight.
820 m/sec with ball ammunition.

☆

1970*: Grünel target rifles shared the action of the Matchkugelbuchsen, but had a variety of differing triggers. The Matchgewehr UIT Standard had an Anschütz-pattern competition stock, with lateral slots in the fore-end of guns made after c.1983, and a direct-action trigger with a pull of 1,500gm. Most rifles also had a matted strap or 'mirage band' above the barrel.

The 300 LM (Liegendmodell) was similar, but designed for prone-position shooting. The fore-end was shallower than the UIT Standard version, and the butt-comb (adjustable on most post-1985 examples) sloped downward to the pistol grip. A direct-acting trigger was standard, though others could be supplied on request.

The Matchgewehr 300 had an adjustable trigger mechanism and a thumbhole stock. The comb, hooked shoulder plate and pistol-grip palm rest were also adjustable, and a hand rest could be fitted beneath the slotted fore-end.

1987: modernised guns with new stocks and optional electronic triggers were introduced. The Target 200 was generally similar to the earlier UIT Standard pattern, while the Super Target 200/40 Free Rifle replaced the Matchgewehr 300 (above).

GUEDES

PORTUGAL

This block-action rifle was developed for the Portuguese army in 1882–4, largely through the work of army lieutenant Luis Guedes Dias. About fifty 11m-calibre guns were made in Portugal in 1884, but the advent of smokeless propellant in France—accompanied by a small-calibre cartridge—caused the project to be revised for an 8mm rimmed cartridge before

production began. Owing to a lack of suitable facilities in the Lisbon arsenal, the contract was placed in Austria-Hungary.

The breech block of the rifle, containing the trigger, hammer and multi-purpose spring, was moved down and then slightly back from the face of the breech as the rear of the trigger guard was depressed. A spent case was thrown clear by a sturdy sliding extractor/ejector at the end of the opening stroke.

Model 1885

Infantry rifle.
Made by Österreichische
Waffenfabriks-Gesellschaft, Steyr, 1885–6.
8 × 60mm, rimmed.
Dropping-block action operated by a lever.
1,217mm overall, 4·10kg unladen.
845mm barrel, 4-groove rifling; concentric, RH.
Ramp-and-leaf sight graduated to 2,000 metres.
520 m/sec with 16·0-gram bullet.
Mo.1885 sword bayonet.

☆

1885: a contract for 40,000 rifles was placed with OEWG, the company being asked to alter the mechanism from 11mm to 8mm while tooling was underway. The rifle had a straight-wrist butt and a long fore-end retained by two bands, the bayonet lug appearing on the right side of the band nearest the muzzle. Among the most distinctive features were the breech lever combined with a trigger guard, a safety lever alongside the trigger, and a back sight—hinged at the front of its base—with a sliding long-range extension.

1886: the Mo.1885 was abandoned in March in favour of the Kropatschek (q.v.), though the Mo.1885 bayonets were accepted. The change is widely assumed to have been due to the preference for a magazine rifle, but it is probable that the 8mm Guedes was not as successful as the 11mm prototypes had been. The original cartridge had a sharply bevelled base to assist in seating a reluctant case in the chamber, but was too weak in the rim to extract reliably in adverse conditions. Greater pressure directed

back through the reduced-diameter chamfered base was apparently prone to bulging the hollow breech block.

1896: ownership of the remaining rifles had passed to OEWG in 1887, when the Portuguese contract had been cancelled. About 2,700 guns were purchased by the Transvaal in the mid 1890s, followed by 5,000 more in 1897, while several thousand went to the Orange Free State. The Transvaal contracts were arranged through Alfred Field & Co. of Birmingham by way of Stein & Hunter of Cape Town.

GUSTLOFF

GERMANY
Also known as 'Barnitske'

A delayed blowback credited to engineer Karl Barnitske, head of the Gustloff-Werke small arms development bureau, this dated from the end of the Second World War.

The action of the VG 1–5 was a sophisticated concept, though its value was reduced by poor construction. Gas was bled from multiple barrel ports into the bolt sleeve, to fill the annular gap between the surface of the barrel and the inside of the barrel casing. The gas then pressed against the bolt-sleeve to oppose the opening stroke of the breech until the residual pressure in the chamber had declined to a safe level.

VG 1–5

Gustloff-Werke, Weimar (code 'dfb')?
7·9 × 33mm, rimless.
Auto-loading action with a gas-delay system.
885mm overall, 4·41kg without magazine.
377mm barrel, 4-groove rifling; RH, concentric.
Detachable box magazine, 30 rounds.
Folded-strip sight for 100 metres.
About 645 m/sec with standard ball cartridges.
No bayonet.

☆

1944: very little is known about this interesting gun, usually known as Versuchs-Gerät 1–5 or

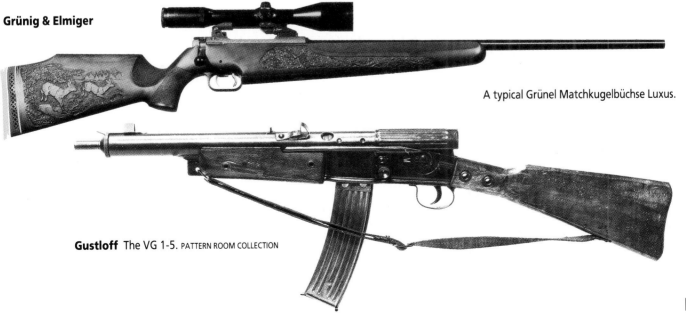

Grünig & Elmiger

A typical Grünel Matchkugelbüchse Luxus.

Gustloff The VG 1-5. PATTERN ROOM COLLECTION

Volksgewehr 1–5, excepting that development began in the late summer when it was clear that the Russians were menacing eastern Germany.

1945: the short rifle was very crudely made, with a sheet-steel barrel casing, and the badly shaped butt and fore-end were riveted to the frame. However, the mechanism worked well enough to handle the 7·9mm Kurz cartridge in reasonable safety—though prone to jamming from heat expansion or excessive fouling.

Small-scale production began in late January, apparently on the initiative of the Gauleiter of Thüringen. Survivors often have marks such as Th.1017 stamped or branded into the butt—but none displays the Waffenamt marks that would prove official recognition. Production lasted for no more than a few months.

HAENEL

GERMANY

An assault rifle developed in the late 1930s to chamber 'intermediate' short-case ammunition, this was originally unique to Germany—though survivors are still occasionally reported from the Third World.

1916: the Germans had realised that neither the standard 8mm rifle cartridge nor the 9mm Parabellum pistol pattern was suited to an 'all-purpose' role, but experimentation was stopped by Treaty of Versailles.

1930: drawings of experimental 7·65 × 27mm and 7·65 × 35mm Swiss cartridges, developed in 1919–21, reached German hands by way of Waffenfabrik Solothurn.

1933: Rheinisch-Westfälische Sprengstoff AG and Gustav Genschow & Co. AG produced intermediate cartridges on the basis of the rimmed 8·15 × 46mm sporting round. The case length was soon reduced from 45–46mm to 40mm, and a jacketed spitzer bullet weighing about 4·9gm appeared. Genschow was granted an army development contract in 1935.

1937: Genschow continued experiments with cases measuirng 37–46mm and bullets weighing

4·9–5·3gm; Rheinmetall-Borsig's cartridge had a 7mm-diameter bullet in a 36·5mm bottleneck case; and a BKIW/DWM pattern initially had a 39mm case. None was entirely successful.

1939: the army authorities recruited Polte-Werke of Magdeburg, and progress was made.

1943: the MP.43 (or StG.44) was the first weapon of its type to be mass-produced. Relying on an untried sub-contract system, production did not always proceed smoothly. Many of the components made by outworkers had to be hand-finished to fit and deliveries were erratic. Influence on post-war thinking was appreciably greater than the contribution to the campaign history of the Second World War.

MKb.42 (H)

Prototype assault rifle.
Made by C.G. Haenel AG, Suhl, 1942–3, with the assistance of sub-contractors.
Quantity: a few hundred.
7·9 × 33mm, rimless.
Gas-operated auto-loading action, locked by a tilting block engaging the receiver.
940mm overall, 4·87kg unladen.
365mm barrel, 4-groove rifling; RH, concentric.
Detachable box magazine, 30 rounds.
Tangent-leaf sight graduated to 800 metres.
640 m/sec with standard ball cartridges.
Cyclic rate 575 ± 50 rpm.
No bayonet (prototypes), or S.84/98
(finalised design).

☆

1938: by April, Wa-Prüf 2 (the research and development bureau of the Heereswaffenamt) had given Haenel a contract for a selective-fire Maschinenkarabiner chambering Polte's newest cartridge. The gun was designed largely by Hugo Schmeisser, basic work being complete by 1940.

1941: transforming the Haenel prototype for mass production was entrusted to Merz-Werke GmbH of Frankfurt am Main, whose experience with metal stamping, precision casting and spot-welding was unrivalled in Germany. The gas tube lay above the barrel, extending forward almost to the muzzle; and a curved 30-round

box magazine lay ahead of the trigger aperture. The rifles fired from an open breech.

1942: the Heereswaffenamt disrupted progress by altering the basic specifications to include a bayonet lug and provision for a grenade launcher; only 25 guns were delivered in November, and 91 in December.

1943: a total of 500 guns delivered in January represented a shortfall of only 200. The first full combat trials were apparently undertaken in the Spring by SS Division 'Wiking'. After seeking the troops' opinions personally, Hitler revised his low opinion of the assault rifle concept and ordered the Mkb.42 (H) into production at the expense of the FG.42 and Gew.43.

MP.43 and MP.44

Assault rifles: MP.43, MP.43/1, MP.44 und StG.44.
Made by C.G. Haenel Waffen- und Fahrradfabrik (code 'fxo'), Suhl, 1943–5; and Erfurter Maschinenfabrik B. Geipel GmbH 'Erma-Werk' ('ayf'), Erfurt, 1943–5. Mauser-Werke AG ('byf') of Oberndorf and an unidentified company using the code 'sup' made receivers. Lesser contractors included Merz-Werke Gebr. Merz ('cos'), Frankfurt am Main; Württembergische Metallwarenfabrik ('awt') of Geislingen-Steige; J.G. Anschütz Germania Waffenfabrik, Zella-Mehlis; Progress-Werke; Lux; J.P. Sauer & Sohn ('ce'), Suhl; Erste Nordböhmische Waffenfabrik Adolf Rossler ('fnh'), Niederinseidel; and Lothar Walther Zeug- und Metallwarenfabrik of Zella-Mehlis.
Quantity: 325,000?
7·9 × 33mm, rimless.
Action: as MKb.42 (H), above.
940mm overall, 4·92kg unladen.
365mm barrel, 4-groove rifling; RH, concentric.
Detachable box magazine, 30 rounds.
Tangent-leaf sight graduated to 800 metres.
640 m/sec with standard ball cartridges; 550 ± 50 rpm.
No bayonet.

☆

1943: though competing prototype Walther Maschinenkarabiner (MKb.42 [W], q.v.) were lighter, better balanced and more accurate, the simpler Haenel was easier to make in quantity. It

Heckler & Koch
A soldier of the Bundeswehr with a 7·62mm G3A3 rifle. Note the two magazines taped together to permit a rapid change.
GERMAN DEFENCE MINISTRY

Haenel
A senior British officer examines German weaponry captured after the invasion of Europe, 1944. He is holding an MP.43 assault rifle, chambered for the 7·9mm intermediate ('Kurz') cartridge.
COLLECTOR'S COMPENDIUM

was adopted once an adaption of the Walther hammer-fired trigger mechanism had replaced the original striker. The finalised rifle also fired from a closed breech.

The MP.43 had a ball-tipped rod projecting from the gas-port assembly instead of the original extended gas tube. MP.43/1 muzzles accepted a special grenade launcher (MP.GwGrGt.43); most other versions had a short muzzle for the Kar.98k-type launcher.

1944: the basic gun was renamed 'MP.44', though no modifications had been made. Most MP.43/1 and some MP.44 rifles had side-rails accepting the Zf.4 optical sight or the Zielgerät 1229 'Vampir' night sight. The MP.44 was eventually renamed 'Sturmgewehr 44' (StG.44) in recognition of its capabilities. A few guns were fitted with curved-barrel units (Krummläufe), originally designed for armoured-vehicle crews but ultimately developed to fire around street corners. They included the 30° 'Vorsatz J', the 40° 'Vorsatz J' and the 90° 'Vorsatz P'.

1945: trials of Mauser, Rheinmetall-Borsig and Grossfuss assault rifles, deferred from the previous November, began in January. The submissions apparently included the Haenel StG.45 (H)—a greatly simplified MP.43—but only one gun survived the war.

HÄMMERLI

SWITZERLAND

Now best known for its exemplary target pistols, Hämmerli has also made a substantial quantity of rifles—sporting guns based on the standard Mauser action, and target rifles based on the Martini or Schmidt-Rubin patterns. These are all noted in the relevant sections.

The last Schmidt-Rubin rifles (National and Olympia models) were made in 1959, but were not sold until the early 1960s. To fill the gap, therefore, improved turning-bolt Free Rifles made by Hans Tanner (q.v.) were sold under the Hämmerli name from 1965 until the early 1970s.

HARRINGTON & RICHARDSON

UNITED STATES OF AMERICA

Prior to its demise in 1987, Harrington & Richardson had enjoyed more than a century of unbroken production. Best known in the post-1945 era for unsophisticated revolvers and combination rifle-shotguns, the company also marketed a selection of centre-fire guns. Most were Mauser or Sako (qq.v.) rifles imported from Europe, though often stocked in North American style. However, H&R also made an auto-loading rifle of its own design.

Model 360

308, 360 and 361 patterns.
Made by Harrington & Richardson, Inc., Worcester, Massachusetts.
·243 Winchester or ·308 Winchester only.
Gas-operated auto-loading action, locked by rotating lugs on the bolt into the receiver wall.
DATA FOR A TYPICAL EXAMPLE
·243 Winchester, rimless.
43·38in overall, 7·43lb unladen.
22·00in barrel, 4-groove rifling; RH, concentric.
Detachable box magazine, 3 rounds.
Spring-leaf and elevator sight.
3,070 ft/sec with 100-grain bullet.
☆

1965: the Model 308 sporting auto-loader had a one-piece 'straight line' stock with a roll-over comb and minimal drop at the heel; white spacers accompanied the rosewood pistol-grip cap and the solid rubber butt plate. A cross-bolt safety ran through the front trigger-guard web.

1967: the ·308 rifle was joined by a ·243 version, whereupon the designation changed to Model 360.

1970: the Model 361 had an ambidexterous roll-over comb for left or right-handed firers alike. It lasted only until 1973.

1977: work on the Model 360 finally ceased, though it is suspected that none had been made for some years.

HECKLER & KOCH

GERMANY

Heckler & Koch was acquired by the British Royal Ordnance plc in 1991, after the German government had withdrawn support from the caseless-cartridge G11 project. The future of the H&K rifles, therefore, is currently uncertain.

1955: a promising trial of the CETME (q.v.) rifle was undertaken in Germany. After an abortive variant had been produced for a short 7·62mm round, the rifle was revised for the US ·30 T65 cartridge (later 7·62 × x51mm NATO).

1956: the German defence ministry ordered about four hundred CETME-type 7·62 × 51mm rifles for trials, apparently through Heckler & Koch though the guns were made in Spain. Tests were satisfactory, but so many changes were requested that the final German-made gun differed considerably from its Spanish prototype and fired from a closed bolt at all times.

1958: the licence granted by CETME to NWM was transferred to Heckler & Koch. After gaining extensive experience of the rifle by supplying machine tools to facilitate its production, H&K was keen to enter the arms-making industry.

1959: sufficient 'B'-type rifles were purchased in Spain to permit Bundeswehr field trials.

MILITARY WEAPONS

The Heckler & Koch-made versions of the CETME—the 7·62mm G3 and the 5·56mm HK33/G41 series—have been outstandingly successful. Though they lack the camming extraction action of a well-designed rotating-bolt lock, a fluted chamber reduces the problem to manageable proportions. As the roller-lock is symmetrical, and stresses in the action are balanced, the G3 is regarded as very accurate.

BRITAIN

G3-type rifles have been made by the Royal Small Arms Factory in Enfield, apparently to

utilise manufacturing capability that would otherwise have stood idle while the 5·56mm SA-80 rifle was being developed to replace the L1A1 (FAL). Guns have been exported in great quantity—mainly, but not exclusively, to British-orientated countries. However, the British Army has never adopted G3 or HK33 rifles as standard issue, though favour has been found with police marksmen and anti-terrorist groups. British-made guns generally exhibited the designation, usually G3A3, plus EN (for Enfield) on the left side of the magazine housing; the first two digits of the serial number sometimes gave a clue to the date of assembly.

FRANCE

Heckler & Koch rifles have been made by Manufacture Nationale d'Armes in Saint-Étienne (MAS, subsequently part of GIAT) and exported in quantity to countries within the French sphere of dominance—even though the army, satisfied with the 5·56mm FAMAS, never showed great interest in the G3 or HK33. A typical rifle made for the Lebanese army bore G3 CO and a serial number on the left side of the magazine housing, together with a MAS mark.

GERMANY
FEDERAL REPUBLIC

In addition to the many guns listed below, the Bundeswehr (and some police units) have used modified 7·62mm HK11 and HK11E 'rifles' under the designations G8 and G8A1. Though sometimes used in a sniping role, owing to their heavy barrels, they are regarded here as light machine-guns—the G8, indeed, can be belt fed.

Gewehr 3

Original, A1, A2, A3, A4, A5, A6, A7, INCAS, SG/1, TGS and Zf patterns.
Made by Heckler & Koch GmbH & Co.,
Oberndorf/Neckar, and contractors in many other countries.
Quantity: several millions.

7·62 × 51mm NATO, rimless.
Auto-loading action, with a delayed-action breech system relying on rollers engaging the barrel-collar walls.
DATA FOR A TYPICAL G3A3
1,020mm overall, 4·39kg with magazine.
450mm barrel, 4- or 6-groove rifling; RH, polygonal.
Detachable box magazine, 20 rounds.
Back sight: see notes.
790 m/sec with NATO ball cartridges; 550 ± 50 rpm.
G3 knife bayonet (optional).
☆

1960: the first-pattern rifle was approved, replacing the Gewehr 1 (FAL). It had a rocking-'L' back sight (Klappvisier), a bipod and a folding carrying handle.

1961: a modified G3 was approved, with a drum sight (Drehvisier) which rotated around its axis—markedly forward of vertical—to present a 100-metre notch or apertures for 200, 300 or 400 metres ahead of the firer's eye. The bipod and carrying handle were abandoned.

The G3 was standard until superseded in 1962 by the G3A2. Made largely of pressings and stampings, but sturdy and durable, it had a conventional fixed butt and a sheet-metal fore-end with ventilating slots. The folding cocking handle lay above the fore-end on the left side of the bolt-extension tube. A magazine protruded beneath the receiver, the release catch appearing between the back of the magazine and the front of the trigger guard bow; and a radial selector lever lay above the pistol grip. Most pre-1975 guns were marked S (top), E (middle) and F (bottom) for safety, single shots, and fully automatic fire respectively, the markings being repeated on the right side of the receiver where an engraved line on the selector spindle indicated the fire-state.

The designation and maker's mark lay on the left side of the magazine housing, ahead of the serial number—e.g., G3 HK 20472—and above the date of acceptance ('5/62' for May 1962). The right side of the housing displayed the dates on which the gun was rebuilt, generally at intervals of about five years. Most markings reveal the work to have been undertaken by

Heckler & Koch, though some was done by army ordnance depots.

1962: the G3A2 was approved in June. The principal change seems to have been the advent of a free-floating barrel, improving accuracy. Many older guns were rebuilt to G3A2 standards during overhaul and had an additional FS mark on the left side of the magazine housing beneath the original date of manufacture.

1963: the G3A1, delayed by prolonged trials, was finally approved in October. The retractable stock slid in grooves pressed into the sides of the receiver and was locked by a catch under the special receiver cap. The rifle measured about 800mm with the stock retracted, and weighed 4·64kg with an empty magazine.

1964: the G3A3, with a solid synthetic butt, and the retracting-butt G3A4 were approved for issue in December. Changes had been made in the design of the front sight, and a modified flash-suppressor/muzzle brake was approved to fire NATO standard grenades. Some otherwise standard rifles, selected for accuracy, have been sold as sniper's weapons under the designation 'G3 Zf.' (Zielfernrohr, 'telescope sight'). They are uncommon.

1968: a three-round burst mechanism was developed, though generally omitted from the German service rifles. The burst-fire capability was usually added to the selector levers, giving a fourth position, but was sometimes substituted for the auto-fire option.

1973: the G3 SG/1 sniper rifle supplemented the otherwise-standard G3 Zf. described above. SG/1 rifles were built on actions that had shown exemplary accuracy during test-firing, and had a special set-trigger system. This could only be used with the selector lever set to E, whereupon the small blade protruding ahead of the pistol grip was pressed to 'set' the front trigger. The adjustable pull could be set as low as 1,250gm, compared with 2·6kg if the setting mechanism was not used; the rifle could be fired simply by pressing the conventional trigger lever. If the selector lever was moved after the mechanism had been set, but before a shot was fired, the system reverted to normal operation. Most G3

Heckler & Koch A G3A3 rifle fitted with a silencer. IAN HOGG

Heckler & Koch
A variant of the 5·56mm G41 entered in Italian trials by Franchi.

LUIGI FRANCHI SPA

SG/1 rifles had a bipod, an auxiliary cheek piece, and a Zeiss 1·5–6 × optical sight.

1974: changes were been made to the pistol grip, the fore-end and the selector lever in search of simplicity.

1985: the G3 Tactical Group System (or 'TGS') was introduced, featuring an HK79 grenade launcher instead of the standard fore-end/hand guard assembly. Unladen gun weight rose to about 5·4kg. The auxiliary trigger lay on the left side of the HK79 frame above the barrel, and a ladder-pattern grenade-launching sight was fitted on the receiver-top—subsequently replaced by a radial drum on the fore-end. The breech of the single-shot launcher dropped open after it had been unlatched, though the striker had to be cocked manually.

1986: synthetic butt/pistol grip sub-frames and ambidexterous safety catches were adopted. The safety mark became a white diagonal cross superimposed on a white bullet in a rectangular border; single-shot fire was indicated by a red bullet, three-shot bursts by three red bullets, and fully automatic operation by seven red bullets.

Offered with fixed or retractable butts, the G3 INKAS rifles had an integral infra-red laser sighting system used in conjunction with Philips Elektro-Spezial BM·8028 image intensifying goggles. Built into the cocking handle tube, the laser projector was controlled by a switch behind the front sight.

Note: G3A5, G3A6 and G3A7 models were developed for the armies of Denmark, Iran and Turkey respectively. Guns made for the West Berlin police were marked 'MAS' to avoid infringing agreements preventing distribution of German-made guns in Berlin.

HK32

A2, A3 and KA1 patterns.
Made by Heckler & Koch GmbH & Co.,
Oberndorf/Neckar.
7·62 × 39mm M43, rimless.
Action: as G3, above.
DATA FOR A TYPICAL HK32A2
920mm overall, 3·64kg with magazine.

390mm, 6-groove rifling; RH, polygonal.
Detachable box magazine, 20, 30 or 40 rounds.
Drum sight graduated to 400 metres.
720 m/sec with Soviet PS ball cartridges; 600 ± 25 rpm.
H&K knife bayonet (optional).
☆

1965: though a few CETME rifles had been made for the Soviet 7·62mm M43 intermediate cartridge in the late 1950s, apparently for trials undertaken by NATO in Europe, some years passed before Heckler & Koch offered similar weapons. The HK32 was a diminutive G3 with a chequered plastic fore-end/hand guard. It was offered in fixed-butt or retractable-stock versions, designated HK32A2 and HK32A3 respectively. The latter was 940mm overall, or 730mm with the stock retracted. It weighed 3·99kg

1967: HK32KA1 was based on the HK32A3 but its barrel was shortened to 322mm. Fixed or retractable-butt guns were available to order. The latter measured 865mm overall—670mm with the butt retracted—and weighed about 3·94kg with an empty twenty-round magazine. It would not accept a bayonet, owing to minimal protrusion of the barrel from the fore-end, and muzzle velocity declined to about 695 m/sec.

1978: the 7·62 × 39mm guns were still being offered in Heckler & Koch catalogues, though no military sales are known to have been made.

HK33

Original, A2, A3, E, ECA2, ECA3, ESA2, ESA3, KA1, KC and KS patterns.
Made by Heckler & Koch GmbH & Co.,
Oberndorf/Neckar.
5·56 × 45mm, rimless.
Action: as G3, above.
DATA FOR A TYPICAL HK33A3
940mm overall (730mm with stock retracted)
3·96kg with empty 20-round magazine.
390mm barrel, 6-groove rifling; RH, polygonal.
Detachable box magazine, 20, 30 or 40 rounds.
Drum sight graduated to 400 metres.
960 m/sec with M193 ball cartridges; 600 ± 25 rpm.
H&K knife bayonet (optional).
☆

1963: inspired by the appearance of the AR-15 (M16) rifle, Heckler & Koch modified the G3 action to produce a small-calibre prototype.

1965: the first series-made HK33 rifles were released. Available in fixed-butt (HK33A2) or retractable-stock versions (HK33A3), they were externally similar to the HK32. The HK33A2 was 920mm overall and weighed 3·61kg with an empty magazine. An otherwise-standard rifle with an optical sight has been touted with limited success as the 'HK33 Zf.'.

1967: the short-barrelled HK33KA1 appeared, generally accompanied by a retractable butt. A fixed butt was optional, but compromised the compactness gained by shortening the barrel. The HK33KA1 shared the dimensions of the HK32KA1 (q.v.), but weighed 3·91kg with an empty magazine.

1983: the HK33, successful enough to attract military interest, developed into the HK33E.

1985: the HK33E gained a synthetic pistol-grip sub-frame. The improved ambidexterous safety catch/selector system incorporated a three-shot burst-fire mechanism. Special forest green or desert sand camouflage finish was introduced to minimise heat-absorption at high temperatures, guns receiving 'C' or 'S' suffixes whenever appropriate.

Variants included fixed-butt guns (HK33EC A2 and HK33ES A2); retractable-butt guns (HK33EC A3 and HK33ES A3); and guns with retractable stocks and short barrels (HK33KC and HK33KS).

HK36

Made by Heckler & Koch GmbH & Co.,
Oberndorf/Neckar.
4·56 × 36mm, rimless.
Action: as G3, above.
890mm overall, 2·87kg without magazine.
380mm barrel, 4-groove rifling; RH, polygonal?
Detachable box magazine, 30 rounds.
Collimator sight for 300 metres.
780 m/sec with ball cartridges; 1,100 ± 50 rpm.
No bayonet.
☆

HECKLER & KOCH GMBH

Heckler & Koch The 5·56mm HK33A2

Heckler & Koch A 5·56mm G41 Zf. HECKLER & KOCH GMBH

Heckler & Koch A 7·62mm G3A4, with the butt retracted. HECKLER & KOCH GMBH

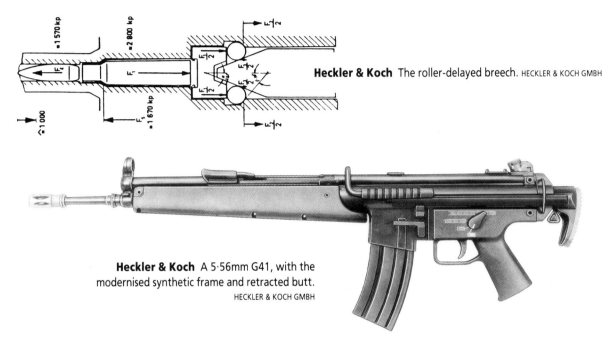

Heckler & Koch The roller-delayed breech. HECKLER & KOCH GMBH

Heckler & Koch A 5·56mm G41, with the modernised synthetic frame and retracted butt.
HECKLER & KOCH GMBH

HECKLER & KOCH
LESSER PATTERNS

Burma The first G3 were acquired from Heckler & Koch in 1963. By 1975, indigenous production of the G3A2 was under way. A modified heavy-barrel variation has also been made, apparently only after 1980. It had a special Burmese-designed bipod, but was otherwise similar to the standard G3-type service rifle.

Denmark The army received its first Rheinmetall or H&K-made Gevær M/66 (G3) in 1966–7, on lease from the Federal German government. The selector mechanism, normally set for single shots, could be altered with a special key to allow fully-automatic fire. In 1977, the G3A5-type Gevær M/75 superseded the earlier M/66 pattern. The guns were still in universal service in 1992.

Iran In the early 1970s, Iran placed an order with Heckler & Koch for sizeable quantities of German-type G3A3 and G3A4 rifles. Production of the modified G3A6 subsequently began in the state small arms factory at Mosalsalasi. Prior to the Islamic Revolution of 1979, this factory was said to be making 145,000 G3-type rifles annually, but output declined until only about 50,000

guns were being made by the mid 1980s.

Norway In 1964, the German-style Automatisk Gevær 3 (G3A3 type) was adopted for service with the army, tooling beginning immediately in Kongsberg Våpenfabrikk. The first Norwegian-made AG3 were assembled in 1966–7. However, production has always been slow and periodic shortages have been resolved by buying rifles from Germany.

Pakistan The army purchased the first of many G3, G3A2 and G3A3 rifles from Heckler & Koch about 1967, together with a licence to make the G3A2 sub-variant in the government ordnance factory in Wah. In 1986, the G3A3 was substituted for the G3A2 and production continued. The Pakistani-made version had a broad fore-end, the furniture being a speckled brown plastic; most metal parts were phosphated and then lacquered. Rifle bipods and the special knife bayonets were made by a local sub-contractor. The rifles were still regulation service issue in 1992.

Sweden The 7·62mm Automatkarabin 4 (Ak.4) was adopted in 1963, licences being acquired to permit production by Husqvarna Våpenfabrik as well as the government-owned Carl Gustafs Stads Gevärsfactori in Eskilstuna. The first Swedish-made rifles were delivered in 1965.

A reorganisation of the state-owned arms factories in 1971 created 'Forenade Fabriksverken' (FFV or FFV Ordnance), and production of the Ak.4 rifles was concentrated in the Eskilstuna factory. However, after trials spread over three years, the Ak.4 was superseded in 1984 by the Ak.5—a minor modification of the FN Herstal 5·56mm FNC. The first deliveries of the new rifle were made in 1986.

Others Heckler & Koch rifles—particularly those made in Germany, Britain and France—have achieved a truly worldwide distribution. In addition to the countries considered individually in earlier sections, the following have been identified:
¶ 7·62MM GUNS.
Bahrain, G3A3 (H&K); Bangladesh, G3A2 (Pakistani surplus) and G3A3 (H&K); Bolivia, G3A3 (H&K); Brunei, G3A3 (H&K); Chad, G3A3 (H&K); Colombia, 30,000 G3 delivered from Heckler & Koch in early 1970s; Dominican Republic, G3A3 (H&K); Gabon, G3A3 (MAS); Ghana, about 12,000 G3 and G3A1 rifles supplied by Heckler & Koch prior to 1965; Guyana, G3 (H&K); Haiti, G3A4 (H&K); Indonesia, G3 (H&K, Rheinmetall) and G3A1 (Heckler & Koch) prior to 1965, plus G3 SG/1 (H&K); Italy, G3 SG/1 (H&K) for police, carabinieri and special forces only; Ivory Coast, G3A3 (MAS); Kenya, 20,000

G3A3 supplied from Enfield in the 1970s; Lebanon, G3A3 (MAS); Liberia, a few G3 and G3A1 supplied by Heckler & Koch prior to 1965; Malawi, G3A3 (H&K); Malaysia, G3 SG/1 (H&K); Mauritania, G3A3 (MAS); Morocco, G3A3 (MAS); Niger, G3A3 (MAS); Nigeria, G3A3 and G3A4 (Enfield); North Yemen, G3A3 (Saudi Arabian); Paraguay, G3 and G3A3 (H&K); Qatar, G3A3 (Enfield); Senegal, G3A3 (MAS); Sudan, G3, G3A3 and G3A4 (H&K); Tanzania, G3A3 (Enfield?); Uganda, G3 and G3A3 (provenance unknown); United Arab Emirates, G3A3 (Enfield or Saudi Arabian) used in Sharjah, Dubai and Abu Dhabi; Upper Volta, G3A3 (MAS); Zaire, G3A3 (probably Enfield); and Zambia, G3A2 (Enfield).
¶ 5·56MM GUNS.
Chile, 500 HK33 from Heckler & Koch in 1975; Eire, HK33 (H&K): El Salvador, about 2,500 HK33 from Heckler & Koch in the early 1970s; Ghana, HK33 (Enfield?); Lebanon, HK33 from MAS and Enfield in the early 1970s, for police and the presidential guard; Malaysia, about 50,000 HK33 from Heckler & Koch in the early 1970s; Portugal, HK33 (assembled by FBP from H&K parts?); Senegal, HK33A1 (MAS); Tanzania, HK33 (Enfield?); and Thailand, about 30,000 HK33 assembled from German-made parts in the 1970s.

1971: this experimental lightweight rifle was introduced to fire a cartridge developed jointly by CETME and Heckler & Koch in 1967–8. An asymmetrical tungsten-carbide bullet core was intended to compensate for the reduction in hitting power. The rifle embodied the standard roller-locked delayed blowback action, but was much lighter than the HK33. The slender barrel protruded from the fore-end, all furniture being synthetic. A fixed-power collimator sight was contained within the carrying handle, a Betalight source providing illumination in poor light.

Many of the earliest guns had detachable box magazines, but later examples had fixed boxes with hinged covers. Fixed or telescoping butts were provided, most weapons having burst-firing capabilities (2–5 rounds, depending on pattern) in addition to normal selective fire.

1976*: the small-calibre trials were abandoned, owing to encouraging progress with the G11 and its consumable cartridge.

Gewehr 41

Standard, INKAS, K and TGS patterns.
Made by Heckler & Koch GmbH & Co.,
Oberndorf/Neckar.
5·56 × 45mm, rimless.
Action: as G3, above.
DATA FOR A TYPICAL G41
997mm overall, 4·10kg with magazine.
450mm barrel, 6-groove rifling; RH, polygonal.
Detachable box magazine, 30 rounds.
Drum sight graduated to 400 metres.
960 m/sec with M193 ball cartridges; 825 ± 50 rpm.
H&K knife bayonet (optional).

☆

1983*: this was an improved HK33, with a mechanical hold-open and a bolt-closing device on the right side of the action inspired by the M16A1. The ejection port was fitted with a hinged cover, the magazine attachment and optical-sight mounts were altered to conform with NATO standards, and Tritium sight inserts were fitted. The guns were designed for a minimum life of 20,000 rounds. Retractable-butt rifles were 985mm overall and weighed

4·3kg. Short-barrel G41K were 13cm shorter than the standard weapons.

1985: the G41 TGS and G41K TGS rifles were announced, fitted with 40mm HK79 grenade launchers. The oldest guns had a ladder-pattern auxiliary sight on top of the receiver, in front of the standard drum, but this was soon replaced by a radial sight on the right side of the fore-end.

1986: new synthetic butt/pistol grip sub-frames were adopted, together with an ambidexterous safety catch. The safety mark became a white diagonal cross superimposed on a white bullet; single-shot fire was indicated by a red bullet, three-shot bursts by three red bullets, and fully automatic operation by seven red bullets.

Similar to G3 INKAS (q.v.), G41 INKAS rifles had an integral infra-red laser projector in the cocking-handle tube. This was used in conjunction with Philips Elektro-Spezial BM 8028 goggles. Guns will be found with fixed or retractable butts, and in short 'G41K' form.

PSG-1

Sniper rifle: Präzisions-Scharfschützengewehr 1.
Made by Heckler & Koch GmbH & Co.,
Oberndorf/Neckar.
7·62 × 51 NATO, rimless.
Action: as G3, above.
1,208mm overall, 8·10kg without magazine.
650mm barrel, 4-groove rifling; RH, concentric.
Detachable box magazine, 5, 10 or 20 rounds.
Optical sight.
815 m/sec with SS77 ball cartridges.
No bayonet.

☆

1985: the PSG-1 had a butt with a detachable saddle-type cheek piece, similar to those found on H&K light machine-guns, and a butt-plate adjustable for length and rake. The separate anatomical walnut pistol grip had an adjustable palm rest.

A special heavyweight barrel was used, though the standard G3 action was limited to semi-automatic fire. Special attention to the trigger gave a smooth 1.5kg pull. Mounted and adjusted as an integral part of the weapon, the

6 × 42 optical sight had an illuminated range finding reticle graduated for 100–600 metres.

MSG3 and MSG90

Sniper rifles.
Made by Heckler & Koch GmbH & Co., Oberndorf.
7·62 × 51mm NATO, rimless.
Action: as G3, above.
DATA FOR A TYPICAL MSG3
1,100mm overall, 5.30kg without magazine.
500mm barrel, 4-groove rifling; RH, concentric.
Detachable box magazine, 5 or 20 rounds.
Drum sight graduated to 400 metres.
800 m/sec with NATO cartridges.
No bayonet.

☆

1988: built on G3 actions restricted to semi-automatic fire, these had specially honed (but otherwise standard) triggers. Bolt-closing devices were fitted to reduce cocking noise.

Developed specifically for the Bundeswehr and German police, the MSG3 had a standard barrel, an adjustable comb and butt plate, a fixed-leg bipod, and conventional open sights. The MSG90 was a variant of the MSG3 with a heavyweight barrel and a bipod with adjustable legs. About 1,165mm overall, it weighed 6·4kg. The drum sight was omitted.

GR3

CA2, CA3, KC, KS, SA2 and SA3 patterns.
Made by Heckler & Koch GmbH & Co.,
Oberndorf/Neckar.
5·56 × 45mm, rimless.
Action: as G3, above.
DATA FOR A TYPICAL GR3C A2
920mm overall, 3·92kg with empty magazine.
390mm barrel, 6-groove rifling; RH, polygonal.
Detachable box magazine, 20, 30 or 40 rounds.
Optical sight.
960 m/sec with M193 ball cartridges; 600 ± 25 rpm.
H&K knife bayonet (optional).

☆

1988: adapted from the HK33/G41 series, these guns had simple 1·5× optical sights—

HECKLER & KOCH GMBH

Heckler & Koch Intended for sniping, the PSG-1 is the company's most accurate military rifle.

Heckler & Koch The 7·62mm G3 SG/1 sniper rifle has been purchased in small quantities by security agencies.

HECKLER & KOCH GMBH

adjustable for elevation and azimuth—on a permanent receiver-top mount. Most of the dimensions paralleled HK33 equivalents, though GR3 patterns were all about 300gm heavier. GR3C A2 and GR3S A2 were fixed-butt rifles, with forest-green or desert sand camouflage respectively; GR3C A3 and GR3S A3 were similar retractable-butt models; while GR3KC and GR3KS amalgamated retractable stocks with short barrels.

GREECE

1974*: the army purchased G3A3 and G3A4 rifles for field trials. They were successful enough for a manufacturing licence to be acquired.
1979: the first of 200,000 guns ordered from Elleniki Biomichanica Oplon of Anjion was accepted. Greek-made weapons had a distinctive diamond-shape EBO trademark on the left side of the receiver, and selectors marked ΑΣ (top), **BB** (middle) and **BP** (bottom). The rifles were still in front-line service in 1992.

PORTUGAL

1961: in an effort to equip the Bundeswehr as quickly as possible, the German government ordered G3-type rifles from Fabrica Militar de Braco de Prata ('FBP'). The design was then adopted for Portugal's armed forces—as the 'Espingarda automatica Mo.961'—to make full use of the production run. The Mo.961 was identical with the G3, excepting markings.
1963: a modified Mo.963 was approved, made to G3A2 standards with a drum-pattern back sight instead of the rocking-'L' of the Mo.961. The Mo.963 remained the principal Portuguese service rifle in 1992, though small quantities of Israeli Galil and HK33 rifles have been acquired since the mid 1980s.

SAUDI ARABIA

1968: initially supplied from Germany and Britain, the Saudi authorities acquired a licence permitting guns to be made in the government

arms factory at al-Khardj. The rifles generally bore crossed scimitars beneath a palm tree on the left side of the receiver, above KINGDOM OF SAUDI ARABIA in Arabic and English. They bore their designation and serial number (in Arabic) on the left side of the magazine housing.
1980: the G3 was superseded by the Steyr AUG, though large numbers of the older rifles were still in service in 1992.

TURKEY

1972*: the army bought the first G3A3 and G3A4 rifles—'G3 Otomatic Piyade Tüfegi'—from Heckler & Koch, together with a licence to make guns in the government-sponsored Makina v Kimya Endustrisi (MKE) factory in the Kurumü suburb of Ankara. Indigenous production does not seem to have begun until 1977, the first guns being assembled in 1978. Turkish-made G3A7 guns had a distinctive retractable butt and bore the encircled MKE trademark on the right side of the magazine housing. They were generally phosphated and then lacquered.

SPORTING GUNS

The HK-91, derived from the HK33, was limited to semi-automatic fire and had a recoil pad on the butt. Optional small-capacity magazines were offered to non-military purchasers.

SL-6 and SL-7

Made by Heckler & Koch GmbH & Co., Oberndorf/Neckar.
5·56 × 45mm (SL-6) or 7·62 × 51mm NATO (SL-7).
Auto-loading action, delayed by rollers in the breech-block engaging the barrel-collar walls.
DATA FOR TYPICAL SL-6
5·56 × 45mm, rimless.
1,015mm overall, about 3·5kg unladen.
450mm barrel, 6-groove rifling; RH, polygonal.
Detachable box magazine (see notes).
Drum sight graduated to 400 metres.
975 m/sec with M193 ball cartridges.

☆

1975*: intended to fulfil a 25,000-gun order from police in Colombia (subsequently aborted), these guns had a three-quarter stock with a hand guard above the barrel. A barred plate was let into the left side of the butt to retain a sling; and radial safety levers appeared in the left side of the fore-end above the trigger guard. Magazines holding two rounds were intended for the West German sporting market, though ten-round patterns were available for export.

HK630, 770 and 940

Made by Heckler & Koch GmbH & Co., Oberndorf/Neckar.
Chambering: see notes.
Action: as SL-6, above.
DATA FOR TYPICAL HK770
·308 Winchester, rimless.
1,130mm overall, 3·65kg unladen.
450mm barrel, 6-groove rifling; RH, polygonal.
Detachable box magazine (see notes).
Folding-leaf sight.
815m/sec with ball cartridges.

☆

1978: these are all similar-looking guns, with squared trigger guard/magazine floor-plates, multi-slot muzzle brakes, and a folding cocking handle on the right side of the investment-cast receiver. Radial safety levers were set into the left side of the stock, the magazine catch appearing in the front of the trigger guard. The fine-quality walnut stocks had pistol grips, hog's back combs and squared cheek pieces. Cut chequering usually graced the pistol grip and fore-end, but some guns have been highly decorated. Swivels lay under the butt.

Chambered for ·223 Remington cartridges, the HK630 was 1,070mm overall and weighed 3.2kg; the HK940, available only in ·30–06, weighed 3·9kg and measured 1,200mm overall. Short-barrel HK770K and HK940K variants have also been offered.

Standard German-market magazines contain only two rounds, though three- and nine-round patterns (four and ten in ·223 only) have been fitted for export purposes.

Heckler & Koch A typical 7·62mm) SL-7 rifle. HECKLER & KOCH GMBH

Heckler & Koch The ·223 (5·56mm) HK 630 rifle. HECKLER & KOCH GMBH

Heckler & Koch The ·308 HK 770 sporter. HECKLER & KOCH GMBH

HEEREN

SWITZERLAND?

Heeren and Würthrich-Heeren

This dropping-block action was patented in 1880 by Christian Heeren, who gave his domicile as 'Paris' in patent applications but is believed to have been Swiss. The original patent was apparently filed in Austria-Hungary.

The Heeren system was unique in that its operating lever, combined with the trigger guard, was pulled downward at the front to lower the breech block—the opposite of most other systems. The result was a compact and surprisingly simple gun, but one in which the extraction leverage was comparatively poor. The modified Würthrich-Heeren has a special extractor to minimise this weakness.

The lever-locking catch pivoted in the front of the guard. Among other idiosyncratic features was the exposure of what was effectively the spur of the hammer in the guard behind the trigger lever. The hammer was cocked during the opening stroke, but could be uncocked or re-cocked manually at will.

Like many a European single-shot action, the Heeren was barrelled and stocked by many independent gunsmiths in Germany, Austria-Hungary, Switzerland, Britain and elsewhere. Examples have been noted with the marks of Carl Stiegle Hofgewehrfabrik of München, Thomas Bland of London, and Walter Glaser of Zürich. The popularity of the Heeren was due as much to its strength as compact design, as it was more durable than many of its rivals (e.g., Aydt or Büchel) and could chamber comparatively powerful cartridges. A modernised Heeren-type rifle is still available from Würthrich.

Heeren-Glaser pattern

Made by W. Glaser, Zürich, c.1925–50.
7 × 57mm, 7 × 65mm, 8 × 57mm,
8 × 60mm Magnum, 9·3 × 53mm R, 9·3 × 72mm R, or 9·3 × 74mm R.

Dropping-block action, locked by the operating lever engaging the receiver.
DATA FOR A TYPICAL EXAMPLE
8 × 60mm, rimmed.
960mm overall, 3·02kg unladen.
600mm barrel, 4-groove rifling; RH, concentric.
Block-and-leaf sight.
770 m/sec with 12·7-gram bullet.
☆

1932: a typical Glaser-made rifle had a walnut butt with a straight comb, a rounded cheek piece, and a chequered pistol grip with a horn cap. The full-length fore-end had chequering and a hand-stop swell at the mid point. Glaser-made actions were often highly decorative, and bases were sometimes provided on the half-octagonal barrel for sight mounts.

Würthrich-Heeren

Made by W. Würthrich Jagd- und Sportwaffen, Lützelflüh.
Chambering: see notes.
Action: generally as Heeren-Glaser, above.
DATA FOR A TYPICAL EXAMPLE
8 × 60mm S, rimless.
1,010mm overall, 3·16kg unladen.
650mm barrel, 4-groove rifling; RH, concentric.
No sights.
845 m/sec with 12·1-gram bullet.
☆

1977: this modernised Heeren was locked by a catch set into the trigger-guard web. The trigger mechanism, patented in Switzerland in 1978, was also derived from the original design. The hammer struck the firing pin through an intermediate 'firing piece' only when the breech was securely closed. A manual safety catch on the side of the receiver locked the firing piece.

1992: only about two hundred guns had been made. Round barrels have been regarded as standard, with half- or fully-octagonal versions supplied on special request. The half-length and Mannlicher-style pistol-grip stocks have squared cheek pieces with fluted under-edges. Receivers are usually engraved with deer, chamois or ibex, while the stocks may display foliate carving.

HENRY

BRITAIN

A sturdy and effectual dropping-block action, this was made in small numbers for sporting use. Henry patented the first of a series of improved rifles with internal hammers in 1870, but they were too delicate to have widespread appeal.

1865: a prototype was presented to the British breech-loading rifle trials. Its dropping block was controlled by a lever under the breech, and a conventional external hammer was fitted.

1867: a second series revealed the Henry to be effectual enough to be entered into the Prize Competition. Six more guns had been made by mid-October. They had 34in ·455-calibre barrels, rifled with seven grooves.

1868: in February, Henry was awarded £600 for the best breech mechanism entered in the government trials. The Peabody and Martini had been ranked sixth and seventh respectively, but a third series of trials ended with Martini, Henry and Westley Richards rifles being recommended.

1869: Westley Richards having withdrawn his rifle, the contest between the Enfield-modified Martini and an improved Henry resolved in favour of the former. Concurrently, ammunition trials approved of a ·450 Henry-rifled barrel—though its cartridge was considered to be too long—and the Martini-Henry (q.v.) was created.

Military Pattern

Made by Alexander Henry & Company, Edinburgh, 1870–5; and the National Arms & Ammunition Co. Ltd, Sparkbrook, Birmingham, 1872–5.
·450, rimmed.
Dropping-block action, operated by a lever.
DATA FOR A TYPICAL EXAMPLE
49·19in overall, 8·84lb unladen.
33·00in barrel, 7-groove rifling; LH, composite.
Ramp-and-leaf sight graduated to 1,400 yards.
1,315 ft/sec with rolled-case ball cartridges.
Socket or sabre bayonet.
☆

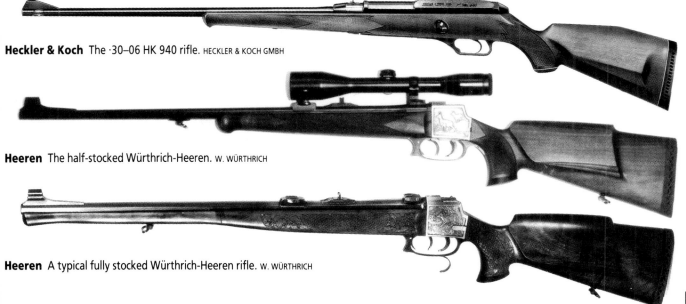

Heckler & Koch The ·30–06 HK 940 rifle. HECKLER & KOCH GMBH

Heeren The half-stocked Würthrich-Heeren. W. WÜRTHRICH

Heeren A typical fully stocked Würthrich-Heeren rifle. W. WÜRTHRICH

1870: small-scale production began for the volunteer units and officers who required rifles chambering service cartridges. A typical military-style Henry rifle had a two-piece stock and a short receiver. The hammer often lay on the left side of the receiver, to facilitate loading from the right, and an operating lever—pivoted at the lower front of the receiver—fitted around the stylish trigger guard. The lever was locked by a small sliding-plunger catch. The straight-wrist butt and the fore-end were essentially similar to those of the P/53 Enfield rifle-musket, with three (later two) screw-clamping bands.

1872: lacking suitable facilities of his own, Alexander Henry granted a licence to the National Arms & Ammunition Co. Ltd, which made a few rifles in an attempt to gain military orders. These were never forthcoming and the military rifles were abandoned c.1875..

Sporting Pattern

Made by Alexander Henry & Company, Edinburgh, c.1870–95.
Chambered for a selection of large-calibre British sporting-rifle cartridges.
Action: as Military Pattern, above.
DATA FOR A TYPICAL EXAMPLE
·303, rimmed.
42·00in overall, 7·05lb unladen.
25·75in barrel, 5-groove rifling; LH, concentric.
Screw-elevated block sight graduated to 500 yards.
About 1,970 ft/sec with 210-grain bullet.

☆

1870: the Henry rifle was usually chambered for the standard British service cartridges—·577 and then ·450—but lasted into the small-bore era. Excepting a very few 'improved' guns with internal hammers, the conventional external hammer was retained on the right side of the breech. Sporters usually had half stocks with rounded-tip fore-ends, though sights ranged from military ramp-and-leaf patterns to plain blocks. The most obvious feature was the plunger-type catch on the operating lever, which locked into the trigger guard. Quality was very good, the fit of wood to metal being exemplary. Delicate

scroll engraving often appeared on the hammer, lock and action.
Note: these guns were made to order, hindering accurate cataloguing as they varied so greatly in size, finish, stock, and decoration.

HEPBURN

UNITED STATES OF AMERICA
Also known as 'Remington-Hepburn'
~
A refinement of the famed Rolling Block it was designed to replace (see 'Rider'), the Remington-Hepburn rifle was introduced commercially in 1880. The action had been patented in October 1879 by Lewis Hepburn. Its dropping block was operated by a lever on the right side of the receiver, and a rebounding hammer was fitted. A minor variation patented by Linus Walker in December 1886 was operated by an underlever doubling as the trigger guard.

No. 3 Sporting Rifle

Made by E. Remington & Sons, Ilion, New York, 1880–6; and the Remington Arms Company, Ilion, New York, 1886–1907.
·22 Winchester, ·22 Maynard Extra Long, ·25–20 Stevens, ·25–21 Stevens, ·25–25 Stevens, ·32–20 Winchester, ·32–40 Ballard, ·38–40 Winchester, ·38–40 Remington, ·38–50 Remington, ·38–55 Ballard, ·40–50 Sharps (straight and necked), ·40–60 Ballard, ·40–65 Remington, ·40–70 Remington, ·40–82 Winchester, ·40–90 Sharps, ·44–77 Remington, ·44–90 Remington and Sharps, ·44–105, ·45–70 Government, ·45–90 Winchester, ·50–70 Government or ·50–90 Sharps.
Dropping-block action, operated by a lever.
DATA FOR A TYPICAL EXAMPLE
·38–55 Ballard, rimmed.
45·75in overall, 9·15lb unladen.
30·00in barrel, 5-groove rifling; RH, concentric.
Spring-leaf and elevator sight.
1,320 ft/sec with 255-grain bullet.

☆

1880: announced in the early part of the year, the standard No. 3 rifle was chambered for many differing cartridges. It had a half- or fully octagonal barrel measuring 26–30in, weight being 8–10lb. The pistol-grip butts were usually finely chequered, while the short fore-ends displayed pewter or German-silver tips.
Many other Remington-Hepburn rifles are described on the accompanying panel.

HEYM

GERMANY
Also contains brief details of the Mauser 2000–4000 series
~
Heym, founded in Suhl in 1865, made sporting guns—in particular, the three-barrel Drilling—until the end of the Second World War. The first post-war firearms were sporting rifles built on refurbished Mauser actions from 1952 onward.

Model 20

Heym SR 20 Alpine, SR 20 Classic, SR20 Classic Safari, SR 20 Classic Sportsman, SR 20D, SR 20F, SR20L, SR 20M, SR 20N, SR 20 Trophy and SR 40 patterns; Mauser 2000, 3000, 3000 Magnum and 4000 patterns.
Made by Friedr. Wilh. Heym GmbH & Co., Münnerstadt.
Chambering: see text.
Turning-bolt action, locked by two lugs on the bolt head engaging the receiver wall.
DATA FOR A TYPICAL SR 20N
7 × 57mm, rimless.
1,130mm overall, 3·18kg unladen.
610mm barrel, 4-groove rifling; RH, concentric.
Internal box magazine, 5 rounds.
Folding-leaf sight.
800 m/sec with 10·5-gram bullet.

☆

1968: apparently developed for sale by Mauser Jagwaffen GmbH of Oberndorf, as the 'Mauser 2000', this rifle had a bolt-mounted ejector and a short extractor claw let into the bolt body. The safety catch lay on the right side of the

---

REMINGTON-HEPBURN
LESSER PATTERNS

Note: guns made prior to 1886 (and most of those sold for much of 1887–8) were marked as the product of E. Remington & Sons; those dating later than 1888 were made by the Remington Arms Company.

No. 3 Improved Creedmoor Rifle The advent in 1880 of the No. 3 sporter created this target rifle, offered in chamberings ranging from ·38–40 to ·45-90. The guns had round or octagonal barrels, weighed 9–9.5lb and were invariably fitted with a set trigger. Vernier and wind-gauge sights were standard, often incorporating an optional spirit level. Their pistol-grip butts and schnabel-tip fore-ends were chequered, though cheek-piece butts and special nickel plated Schützen-style butt plates could be supplied on request.
¶ A typical ·40–70 Remington example, with

a 34in barrel, measured 49·75in overall and weighed 9·35lb. Production continued until the early 1890s.
No. 3 Long Range Military Creedmoor Rifle Made by from 1882 until c.1892, on the basis of the No.3 Sporting Rifle, this was confined to shooting matches in which military-style stocks were obligatory. Comparatively few were made. Offered in a single chambering, with a round barrel, it had a full-length chequered fore-end retained by two bands and a steel ramrod.
¶ A typical ·44–75–520 rifle measured 49·75in overall and weighed 10lb; it had a 34in barrel and a vernier sight on the tang behind the hammer.
No. 3 Match Rifle Dating from 1883–1907, this had a 28in or 30in half-octagonal barrel, chambering cartridges ranging from ·25–20 Single Shot to ·40–65. Plain butt plates, chequered walnut pistol-grip butts, and chequered fore-ends with pewter or German silver schnabel tips were standard, though cheek pieces and Schützen-style butt plates could be supplied to order.

¶ Typically, a 28in-barrelled ·40–65 WCF example was 45·75in overall and weighed 8·77lb. A vernier sight was fitted to the tang behind the hammer.
No. 3 Hunter's Rifle Introduced in 1885, and usually built on the Hepburn-Walker action, this chambered a selection of rim- and centre-fire cartridges from ·25–20 to ·50–70. A Hunter's Rifle had plain sights, a half-octagonal barrel (26–30in), and a chequered pistol-grip butt with a curved butt-plate.
¶ Tough and comparatively unsophisticated, it was regarded as the workhorse amongst contemporary Remington products and lasted until about 1907. A ·38–40 Remington example (28in barrel) was 43·75in overall, weighed 8·03lb and had open 'Rocky Mountain' sights.
New Model No. 3 Dating from 1893, this was specially strengthened to handle smokeless-powder ammunition and, as a result, chambered a variety of sporting cartridges—·30–30 Winchester, ·30–40 Krag, ·32 Winchester Special, ·32–40 Ballard,

·38–55 Ballard, or ·38–72 Winchester. It was made with an octagonal barrel measuring 26–30in, and may be found with the optional double set-trigger mechanism. A representative ·38–72 Winchester specimen (26in barrel) measured 41·72in overall and weighed 8·04lb.
No. 3 Schuetzen Match Rifle Made by the Remington Arms Company from 1904 until 1907, on the Hepburn or Hepburn-Walker action, this target rifle was offered with an impressively scrolled trigger-guard. A special vernier wind-gauge aperture sight lay on the tang—used in conjunction with a hooded or tunnel-type front sight—and a shallow cheek piece was fitted on the straight-wrist butt. Hooked Swiss-style butt plates and folding palm rests were standard.
¶ Chambered for ·32–40 Ballard, ·38–40 Remington, ·38–50 Remington or ·40–65 Remington, the half-octagon barrel measured 28in–32in. This gave the rifles a length of 49·5–53·5in (including the butt-plate hook) and a weight of 11·5–13lb. Less than two hundred were made.

bolt shroud: thumbed upward, it locked the firing pin, though the bolt could still be opened. The basic gun could be fitted with single-stage, adjustable or double set triggers. Standard stocks had a Monte Carlo comb and cheek piece, and a rubber shoulder plate. The rounded tip was separated from the obliquely cut fore-end by a white spacer. Chequering appeared on the pistol grip and fore-end.

Standard chamberings apparently included 5·6 × 57mm, ·243 Winchester, 6·5 × 57mm, ·270 Winchester, 7 × 57mm, 7 × 64mm, 7mm Remington Magnum, ·30–06, ·308 Winchester, 8 × 57mm, 8 × 60mm S, 9·3 × 64mm or ·375 H&H Magnum.

1971: the original rifle was replaced by the Mauser 3000, 3000 Magnum and 4000, with a full-length bolt-guide rib to prevent binding. The stocks gained skip-line chequering and squared fore-end tips.

Model 3000 was sold in similar chamberings to the original Model 2000, had a 22in or 24in barrel and weighed 6·75–7·25lb; the 3000 Magnum accepted 7mm Remington, ·300 Winchester or ·375 H&H magnum cartridges, had a 26in barrel, and weighed about 8lb unladen. Its magazine contained three rounds instead of the standard five.

Model 4000 was a short-action 'varmint' rifle in ·222 or ·223 Remington only, made with a solid rubber shoulder pad and a folding-block back sight.

1974: Mauser-Jagdwaffen ceased purchasing the Heym-made rifles, owing partly to the success of the Model 66 but also to the impending introduction of the Model 77 described in the Mauser section. Thereafter, Heym sold its rifles as the 'SR 20'. The safety catch was moved from the bolt shroud to the receiver immediately behind the bolt handle. It could be thumbed back to safe and pushed forward to fire; a third (central) position locked the bolt shut.

The standard SR 20N sporter (made in right- or left-hand actions) had a Monte Carlo half-stock with a rosewood pistol-grip cap and a schnabel pattern fore-end tip. It was offered in 5·6 × 57mm, ·243 Winchester, 6·5 × 55mm,

6·5 × 57mm, ·270 Winchester, 7 × 57mm, 7 × 64mm, ·30–06 Springfield, ·308 Winchester and 9·3 × 62mm.

SR 20G were chambered for 6·5 × 68mm S, 7mm Remington Magnum, 8 × 68mm S, ·300 Winchester Magnum and ·375 H&H Magnum. Their barrels measured 650mm, the guns being longer and slightly heavier than the SR 20N.

The SR 20L had a 510mm barrel and a full-length Mannlicher-style stock. It was available in all regular calibres excepting 9·3 × 62mm.

1984: made in the same chambering options as the 20N and 20G, the SR 20 Classic had a straight-comb butt, a rounded fore-end tip and a shallower pistol grip. Engraving was applied to order.

The SR 40 was a short-action version of the SR 20, chambered only for ·222 Remington, ·223 Remington or 5·6 × 50mm Magnum. Made with a 610mm barrel, it was about 1,115mm overall and weighed 2·95–3kg.

1988: the SR 20F ('Fiberglas') appeared with a classically-styled brown or black synthetic stock. Intended for snap-shooting, the SR 20D (Druckjagdbüchse) had a short barrel with a ventilated quarter-rib, while the single-shot SR 20M ('Match') rifle—destined for competition shooting—was offered only in 6·5 × 55mm or ·308 Winchester. The SR 20M had a near-vertical pistol grip and a beavertail fore-end; it weighed about 4·3kg without sights, and was about 1,130mm long.

1989: the Heym range was extensively revised, many of the older rifles being abandoned. The SR 20 Classic, renamed the 'Classic Sportsman', was joined by the SR 20 Trophy. This had a distinctive quarter rib on an octagonal barrel measuring 560mm for standard chamberings or 610mm for the magnums. The front swivel was attached to the barrel ahead of the fore-end tip.

The SR 20 Alpine was minor adaption of the Trophy pattern, with a 510mm barrel and a full-length Mannlicher stock with a steel fore-end cap. It was comparable with the old SR 20L.

The SR 20 Classic Safari rifle, built on the longest Heym action, has been chambered for ·404 Jeffrey, ·425 Express or ·458 Winchester

Magnum. It had a 610mm barrel and a three leaf Express back sight; recoil bolts appeared beneath the chamber and through the pistol grip. The fore-end tip was joined to the stock vertically, but lacked the accompanying spacer; the butt was a classically styled straight-comb pattern with little drop at the heel.

Magnum Express

....

Made by Friedr. Wilh. Heym GmbH & Co., Münnerstadt.

·338 Lapua Magnum, ·375 H&H Magnum, ·378 Weatherby Magnum, ·416 Rigby, ·450 Ackley, ·460 Weatherby Magnum, ·500 A-Square, ·500 Nitro Express or ·600 Nitro Express.

Turning-bolt action, locked by two lugs on the bolt head engaging the receiver wall and a third lug on the bolt body.

DATA FOR A TYPICAL EXAMPLE

·600 Nitro Express, rimless.

1,150mm overall, 4·46kg unladen.

610mm barrel, 4-groove rifling; RH, concentric?

Internal box magazine, 3 rounds.

Express sight.

600 m/sec with 58-gram bullet.

☆

1989: listed here in the interests of continuity, this could have been included in the Mauser section owing to the presence of a third or safety lug on the bolt and a full-length collar-pattern extractor. A Timney trigger was fitted and the safety catch was moved back to the bolt shroud. Twin lateral recoil lugs were used, though the stock was externally similar to the SR 20 Classic Safari described above.

HOLEK

CZECHOSLOVAKIA

Emanuel Holek first attained prominence in the late 1920s, when a ·276 version of his ZH 29 rifle was submitted for trials in the USA. This was the first of a lengthy series of gas-operated auto-loaders.

Heym The SR 20L Mannlicher, with a full-stock. F.W. HEYM GMBH & CO.

Heym The SR 20 Classic sporting rifle.

Heym SR 20 Match rifles had competition stocks. F.W. HEYM GMBH & CO.

Holek also developed simplified bolt-action rifles in the late 1940s for trial against a Kynčl-modified Mauser. The series culminated in the 7·5mm P-5 of 1949, tentatively approved in 1950 as the 7·62 × 45mm P-6. Owing to rapid progress with automatic weapons, however, the bolt-action project was abandoned in 1951.

Model 29

ZH 29, ZH 31 and ZH 39 patterns.
Made by Československá Zbrojovka, Brno.
·276, 7 × 57mm, ·30–06, 7·92 × 57mm and others.
Gas-operated auto-loading action, locked by displacing the bolt into the receiver wall.
DATA FOR A TYPICAL ZH 29
7·92 × 57mm, rimless.
1,150mm overall, 4·48kg unladen.
545mm barrel, 4-groove rifling; RH, concentric.
Detachable box magazine, 5, 10 or 25 rounds.
Tangent-leaf sight graduated to 1,400 metres.
820 m/sec with ball ammunition.
Knife or sword bayonet.

☆

1929: the ZH 29 is said to have been developed in response to a request from China for an auto-loading rifle. A ·276 gun was submitted to US Army trials, but did not perform well enough to challenge the Pedersen and Garand patterns. The earliest ZH 29 rifles had their conventional wooden fore-ends and hand guards retained by a single band. Some were semi-automatic, but others could also fire automatically. Later rifles had distinctive ribbed aluminium fore-ends to dissipate the additional heat generated on firing.

The ZH 29 was always beautifully made, but ill suited to mass production; the locking mechanism, particularly, was difficult to machine accurately and prone to jamming in adverse conditions. Most rifles also had a unique hold-open system; when the magazine had been replenished, pressing the trigger allowed the breech to close and chamber a fresh round. A second pull on the trigger then fired the gun. However, this attracted unfavourable comment.

The ZH 29 was promoted enthusiastically in 1930–2, being tested in South America, Europe

and the Far East. Only the Chinese acquired large numbers, beginning with 150 7·92mm rifles purchased in 1929. Limited sales were also made to Ethiopia and, allegedly, Siam.

1932: a modified rifle was tested unsuccessfully by Romania and Turkey as the 'ZH 32'. The published photographs reveal little difference externally from the perfected ZH 29, most of the improvements being internal.

1938: the Holek tilting-bolt mechanism was adapted so that the gas tube and piston system lay above the barrel. The resulting ZH 39 had a more modern appearance than its predecessors, with a short fore-end and a ventilated sheet-steel hand guard. The clearing rod was carried above the barrel. However, though the rifle was submitted for trials in Britain and elsewhere, the German invasion of Czechoslovakia in 1939 brought development to an end.

HOTCHKISS

UNITED STATES OF AMERICA
⤚

This bolt-action mechanism was designed by Benjamin Hotchkiss, an American living in Paris, and patented in the USA in August 1869.

Exhibited at the Centennial Exposition in Philadelphia in 1876, the potential of the rifle persuaded the Winchester Repeating Arms Company to purchase manufacturing rights in the hope of attracting US Army interest.

The tube magazine of the original guns ran up into the receiver above the trigger; five cartridges were loaded through a butt-trap, a sixth being inserted directly into the chamber if required. Each time the trigger was pressed, special cartridge stops allowed one round to move forward to the feed position.

When the Hotchkiss bolt was opened, the cartridge rim sprang upward until it could be caught by the lower edge of the bolt and pushed forward into the chamber on the closing stroke. Single shots could be fired when required by engaging the cut-off, which held the contents of the magazine in reserve.

MILITARY WEAPONS
Models 1878 and 1879

Rifles and carbines.
US Army guns were assembled at the National Armory, Springfield, Massachusetts, from parts supplied by the Winchester Repeating Arms Company, New Haven, Connecticut;
US Navy guns were supplied directly from Winchester.
Quantity: 513 1878-pattern guns for the army; 2,500 1879-pattern guns for the navy and about 1,000 for the army.
·45–70, rimmed.
Turning-bolt action, locked by the bolt guide rib abutting the receiver ahead of the bridge.
DATA FOR M1878 RIFLE
48·63in overall, about 9lb unladen.
28·63in barrel, 3-groove rifling; RH, concentric.
Tube magazine in butt, 5 rounds.
Ramp-and-leaf sight graduated to 1,200 yards.
About 1,280 ft/sec with standard ball rounds.
M1873 socket bayonet.

☆

1878: a special Board of Officers reported on 23 September that the 'Hotchkiss Magazine Gun no. 19', submitted by Winchester, had performed the best during magazine-rifle trials.
1879: some 1878-pattern guns were assembled from Winchester-made actions and government pattern one-piece stocks. The barrels were held in the elegant walnut stocks with two bands and an 1879-type buck-horn sight lay on the barrel ahead of the split-bridge receiver. A rotary safety/magazine cut-off unit was let into the right side of the stock above the trigger guard.

The first 1879-type Hotchkiss rifles were acquired by the US Navy in this era. They were similar to their army predecessors, but the cut-off lever projected above the right side of the stock, with a safety catch on the left.
1880: by the time work ceased, Winchester had made 6,420 first-pattern guns in musket (32in barrel) and carbine (24in barrel) forms.
1881: about a thousand 1879-type Winchester-made actions were stocked and completed in Springfield Armory for army trials.

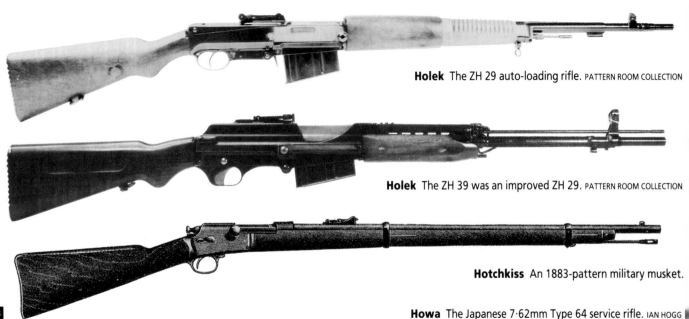

Holek The ZH 29 auto-loading rifle. PATTERN ROOM COLLECTION

Holek The ZH 39 was an improved ZH 29. PATTERN ROOM COLLECTION

Hotchkiss An 1883-pattern military musket.

Howa The Japanese 7·62mm Type 64 service rifle. IAN HOGG

1883: by the end of production, Winchester had made 16,100 second- or 1879-pattern Hotchkiss muskets and carbines, with 32in and 24in barrels respectively.

Model 1883

Made by the Winchester Repeating Arms Company, New Haven, Connecticut, 1883–4.
Quantity: about 750 (US Army guns only).
·45–70, rimmed.
Action: as M1878 rifle, above.
About 51·75in overall, 8·95lb unladen.
32·00in barrel, 3-groove rifling; RH, concentric.
Tube magazine in butt, 6 rounds.
Ramp-and-leaf sight graduated to 1,200 yards.
About 1,300 ft/sec with standard ball rounds.
M1873 socket bayonet.

☆

1882: on 29 September, the members of a Board of Officers convened to test magazine rifles reported that the Lee (q.v.) was preferred to the Chaffee-Reece and the Hotchkiss—largely owing to its detachable box magazine and an additional locking lug. However, as the margin of superiority was small, sufficient quantities of all three rifles were ordered for field trials.
1884: Springfield had completed its Chaffee-Reece rifles by midsummer, but late delivery of Lee and Hotchkiss guns—from Remington and Winchester respectively—delayed trials until the end of the year.

The improved Hotchkiss rifle had a two-piece stock and the magazine was loaded through the top of the open action instead of the butt trap. Cartridges were simply inserted into the feed way, then pressed back and down into the magazine tube. The bolt lock and the magazine cut-off appeared on the right side of the receiver.
1885: in December, the Chief of Ordnance reported that the Lee had performed best, but also that most of the officers charged with the trials favoured the Trapdoor Springfield. Winchester then attempted to sell the Hotchkiss elsewhere without ever encountering success. Most military-style rifles chambered the US regulation ·45–70–405 cartridge.

A few of the muskets were made with 32in barrels, but most measured 28in; similarly, the earlier 24in carbine barrel was replaced by a 22·5in pattern. Muskets were reasonably popular with privately-funded state militia units, and others were sold to warring factions in South and Central America.

Unfortunately, even the perfected Hotchkiss rifle was doomed by its reliance on a tube magazine—which proved to be a potentially dangerous liability once centre-fire primers and pointed-nose bullets became commonplace.

SPORTING GUNS

Model 1883

Made by the Winchester Repeating Arms Company, New Haven, Connecticut, 1883–99.
Quantity: 62,030 (including military weapons).
·45–70, rimmed.
Turning-bolt action, locked by the bolt guide rib abutting the receiver ahead of the bridge.
45·25in overall, 8·55lb unladen.
26·00in barrel, 3-groove rifling; RH, concentric.
Tube magazine in butt, 6 rounds.
Leaf sight graduated to 1,200 yards.
About 1,270 ft/sec with standard ball rounds.

☆

1884: Winchester announced the 'Hotchkiss Magazine Gun Model 1883' on 1 January for ·40–65 or ·45–70 cartridges, though there is no evidence that the smaller calibre was ever supplied. Made in standard or special Sporting Rifle grades, the guns had round, half-octagon or fully octagonal barrels; a plain straight-wrist or chequered pistol-grip butt could be obtained, butt plates being concave rifle or (more rarely) the straight shotgun pattern. The half-length fore-end usually had a schnabel tip. Some guns had set triggers and others were engraved.
1899: assembly finally ceased. The perfected Hotchkiss made a sturdy and effectual sporter, but few pre-1900 purchasers liked its bolt action and the butt magazine was patently inferior.
1913: all remaining parts were scrapped, as no guns had been sold for some years.

Other patterns

Once sufficient Krag-Jørgensen (army) or Lee Straight-Pull (navy) rifles had been obtained in the late 1890s, virtually all surviving Hotchkiss trials rifles were sold out of store and altered to sporting style. Most had their barrels cut to about 24in and the fore-ends trimmed to half-stock proportions. Work was undertaken professionally, but conversions usually retained original army or naval marks.

HOWA

JAPAN
Including Weatherby Vanguard rifles
~

Best known as a contractor to the Japanese defence forces, Howa made the Weatherby Vanguard actions from the early 1970s onward; once the exclusive licensing agreement had expired, however, these Sako-type bolt-action rifles also appeared in North America under the Howa brand.

1. THE AUTO-LOADING PATTERNS

Type 64

64-Shiki jidoju.
Made by Howa Machinery Company, Nagoya.
7·62 × 51mm, rimless.
Gas-operated auto-loading action, locked by tilting the breech block into the receiver.
990mm overall, 4·41kg unladen (with bipod).
450mm barrel, 4-groove rifling; RH, concentric.
Detachable box magazine, 20 rounds.
Folding aperture sight graduated to 400 metres.
700 m/sec with Type 64 ammunition; 500 ± 25 rpm.
Knife bayonet.

☆

1958: a search to find an auto-loader for the Japanese forces began in earnest when a team of

military personnel and Howa civilian technicans under the leadership of General Koni Iwashita began test-firing in April.

Experiments with R-1 and R-2 rifles—with decidedly ArmaLite exteriors, though differing internally—continued until the Howa-pattern R-6 appeared. This progressed through several stages until the R-6E (Modified) was approved for production; most of the minor variants differed in sights, charging facilities, fore-ends and muzzle brakes.

1964: adopted in April, the Type 64 was an amalgam of several European designs. However, the rifle was characterised by attention to detail to reduce length and weight to suit the stature of the average Japanese soldier. Special reduced-charge 7·62mm cartridges were fired, though conventional full-power rounds could be used if the gas regulator was adjusted accordingly.

The Type 64 had a short-stroke piston system and a distinctive straight-line layout, with a linear hammer running back into the butt housing. The hand guard was a ventilated metal pressing, a bipod was fitted, and a shoulder strap folded on the butt plate.

1985: production stopped after about 250,000 guns had been made, pending the investigation of 5·56mm designs.

2. THE BOLT-ACTION PATTERNS

Model 1500

Howa Deluxe, Hunter, Lightning, Short, Standard and Trophy patterns; Weatherby Classic II, Fiberguard, Vanguard, VGF, VGL, VGS, VGW, VGX and Weatherguard types.
Made by Howa Machinery Company, Nagoya.
Chambering: see text.
Turning-bolt action, locked by lugs on the bolt head rotating into the receiver wall and by the bolt handle turning down into its seat.
DATA FOR A TYPICAL WEATHERBY VGS
·270 Winchester, rimless

44·50in overall, 7·80lb unladen.
24·00in barrel, 4-groove rifling; RH, concentric?
Internal box magazine, 5 rounds.
Williams ramp sight.
3,140 ft/sec with 130-grain bullet.

☆

1973*: known in Japan as the Howa 1500 and in America as the Weatherby Vanguard Standard (VGS), this had a distinctive angular web ahead of the trigger guard to house the release catch for the detachable magazine floor-plate. The 1500 Deluxe or Vanguard Extra (VGX) had a selected stock, skip-line chequering and a ventilated rubber butt plate. The fore-end usually exhibited a squared oblique-cut tip, whilst the tapered barrel was drilled and tapped for optical sight mounts.

Standard guns have been chambered for the ·22–250 Remington, ·243 Winchester, ·25–06, ·270 Winchester or ·30–06 cartridges. The magnum versions, with three-round magazines, have handled 7mm Remington Magnum or ·300 Winchester Magnum.

1984: made for ·22–250, ·223 Remington, ·243 and ·308 Winchester, the Model 1500 Short (or Weatherby VGL) rifles had short actions. ·22–250 and ·223 'varmint' versions also had heavyweight cylindrical barrels.

1985: the Vanguard Fiberguard rifle (VGF) was introduced, with a matt-blued action set in a textured Forest Green synthetic stock. The rifle has been built around short (·223, ·243 or ·308) or standard actions (·270, 7mm Remington Magnum or ·30–06). A 20in barrel was used, overall length being 40–40·5in.

1989: the Vanguard Weathermark (VGW), alias Howa 1500 Lightning, appeared with a black or green CarboLite stock. Offered in ·223 Remington, ·243 Winchester, ·308 Winchester (short action) and ·270 Winchester, 7mm–08, 7mm Remington Magnum or ·30–06 (standard action), it was identical mechanically with the regular guns.

The VGX Deluxe, with a heavier barrel and minor improvements in the action, was introduced for the cartridges chambered by the VGS and VGL—the short action being restricted

to ·22–250 Remington or ·243 Winchester. It could also be supplied for the ·300 Weatherby and ·338 Winchester Magnums.

The Weatherby Vanguard Classic II (Howa 1500 Hunter) had a straight-comb stock lacking a fore-end tip. These rifles had the proprietary Weatherby pistol-grip cap, whereas Japanese examples were plain. Howa's 1500 Trophy model had a Monte Carlo comb and cheek piece, the pistol grip-cap being separated from the butt-wood by a white spacer.

HUSQVARNA

SWEDEN
Including the later Carl Gustaf patterns

The earliest sporting rifles made by Husqvarna Våpenfabriks AB embodied the standard 1896-pattern Swedish Mauser action, though a near-facsimile of the pre-war Belgian FN Mle.24 pattern was substituted in 1946. Changes were made in the mid 1950s and early 1960s, but the bolt retained the full-length collar-type extractor and the safety lug until the end of production. Consequently, these guns are considered in the Mauser section, as they retained virtually all of the original mechanical characteristics.

A redesigned action was announced in 1969 but, in 1971, the private Husqvarna and government-owned Carl Gustafs Stads Gevärsfactori were amalgamated under the Forenade Fabriksverken (FFV) banner.

Operations were concentrated in Eskilstuna and Husqvarna sporting rifles were marketed thereafter by Viking Sport Arms AB. However, they were often sold under the 'Carl Gustaf' or 'Carl Gustav' (sic) brandnames, particularly in North America. The perfected guns were sold by Smith & Wesson from 1970 onward and will be encountered with the distinctive S&W trademark instead of Swedish markings. The agency then passed for a few years to Stoeger Industries. Rifles were offered by Harrington & Richardson during the early 1980s, but these embodied original Mauser-type actions.

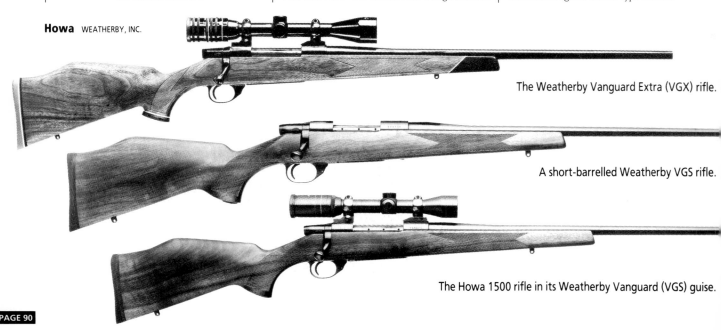

Howa WEATHERBY, INC.

The Weatherby Vanguard Extra (VGX) rifle.

A short-barrelled Weatherby VGS rifle.

The Howa 1500 rifle in its Weatherby Vanguard (VGS) guise.

HVA series

Husqvarna Crown, Imperial, 8000 and 9000 patterns; Carl Gustaf Deluxe, Grade II, Grade III, Special, Sporter, Standard, Trofé and V–T patterns.
Made by Husqvarna Våpenfabriks AB, Huskvarna, 1968–71; and Forenade Fabriksverken, Eskilstuna, 1971–83.
Chamberings: see notes.
Turning-bolt action, locked by rotating two lugs on the bolt head into the receiver and by the bolt handle turning down into its seat.
DATA FOR A TYPICAL CARL GUSTAF SPORTER
6·5 × 55mm, rimless.
1,205mm overall, 4·30kg without sights.
685mm barrel, 4-groove rifling; RH, concentric.
Internal box magazine, 5 rounds.
Optical sight.
780 m/sec with 9·3-gram bullet.

☆

1969: this much-modified Mauser retained the twin bolt-head lugs, but they were changed to fan-tail shape and the right-hand lug was given an additional guide rib to perfect an ultra-smooth operating stroke. The recessed bolt face contained the plunger-type ejector, and a short extractor claw was let into the bolt body above the right lug.

The conventional Mauser third (safety) lug was abandoned, the bolt-handle base sufficing, and the bolt shroud was neatly streamlined. The hinged magazine floor-plate was controlled by a catch let into the front web of the trigger guard.

The Model 8000, or Imperial Grade rifle continued a numerical sequence begun by the standard Mausers. Offered in 6·5 × 55mm, ·270 Winchester, 7mm Remington Magnum, ·300 Winchester Magnum, ·30–06 or 9·3 × 62mm, it had a selected walnut stock with a rosewood fore-end tip, a machine-jewelled bolt and an engraved magazine floor plate. The receiver was drilled and tapped for optical sight mounts, open sights being customarily omitted.

The Model 9000, or Crown Grade, was a simpler form of the 8000 with a standard Monte Carlo-type butt and a folding open back sight.
1971: the markings on the rifles changed from

Husqvarna (often simply a crowned 'H') to Viking Arms or FFV. The Model 8000 and Model 9000 were renamed 'Grade III' (Trofé, or Deluxe) and 'Grade II' (Special) respectively. They were joined by a sporting rifle—known in the USA as the 'Swede'—with a plain European-style stock. This standard sporter was made with a Monte Carlo butt and rounded fore-end tip, or with a straight-comb butt and schnabel-tipped fore-end.

Carl Gustaf rifles invariably had 610mm barrels and were chambered for ·22–250, ·243 Winchester, ·25–06, 6·5 × 55mm Mauser, ·270 Winchester, 7mm Remington Magnum, 7 × 64mm, ·300 Winchester Magnum, ·30–06, ·308 Winchester or 9·3 × 62mm; magazines held five rounds, excepting 9·3mm (four) and 7mm Remington Magnum (three). Magnum rifles had a ventilated butt plate instead of a solid rubber pattern.

The Sporter or Varmint-Target ('V–T') rifle appeared in ·222 Remington, ·22–250, ·243 Winchester, or 6·5 × 55mm only. Magazines held five rounds in all chamberings excepting ·222, which contained six. The plain walnut stock had a Wundhammer pistol grip, and the heavyweight barrel was allowed to float freely. The bolt handle was enlarged and the trigger could be adjusted without removing the stock.
1972: the agreement with Smith & Wesson lapsed, Carl Gustaf rifles thereafter being sold by Stoeger Industries until the mid 1970s.
1977: apart from the Sporter, which lasted into the 1980s, the rifles were all discontinued—though new guns were available for some years.

Model 2000

Made by Forenade Fabriksverken, Eskilstuna, 1991 to date.
·243 Winchester, 6·5 × 55mm, ·270 Winchester, 7mm Remington Magnum, 7 × 64mm, ·300 Winchester Magnum, ·30–06 or ·308 Winchester.
Turning-bolt action, locked by rotating three lugs on the bolt head into the receiver and by the bolt handle turning down into its seat.

DATA FOR A TYPICAL EXAMPLE
7 × 64mm, rimless.
1,115mm overall, 3·40kg unladen.
610mm barrel, 4-groove rifling; RH, concentric.
Internal box magazine, 3 rounds.
Optical sight.
880 m/sec with 11-gram bullet.

☆

1991: uncommon outside Europe, this is a departure from the previous FFV-made rifles. The original two-lug bolt was replaced with a short-throw three-lug pattern and an adjustable roller-bearing trigger was developed. The three-position safety catch was retained on the right side of the receiver behind the bolt handle. The barrel was allowed to float freely, though the rifle was stocked similarly to the preceding Model 8000.

JÄGER

GERMANY

These simple bolt-action rifles were sold in the USA by A.F. Stoeger & Co. and Charles Daly prior to 1939, but production was never large. Little is known of their history.

Herold-Repetierbüchse

Made by Franz Jäger & Co., Suhl.
5·6 × 35mm R or ·22 Hornet.
Turning-bolt action, locked by rotating a lug on the bolt body into the receiver and by the bolt handle turning down into its seat.
DATA FOR A TYPICAL EXAMPLE
·22 Hornet, rimless.
1,110mm overall, 3·52kg unladen.
610mm barrel, 4-groove rifling; RH, concentric.
Internal box magazine, 5 rounds.
Folding-leaf sight.
2,690 ft/sec with 45-grain bullet.

☆

1935*: this rifle, built on an action that was euphemistically advertised as a 'miniature Mauser', existed in grades ranging from plain-

Husqvarna A drawing of the perfected HVA action. COLLECTOR'S COMPENDIUM

Bolt locking lug

Setting surface for firing pin nut

Setting cam

Bolt sleeve

Firing pin nut

Firing pin

Safety spring

Trigger mechanism

Safety catch

Firing pin spring

Cut-out for guide rib

Receiver

Bolt

Locking arm.

Magazine follower

Extractor

Guide rib.

Recoil lug

Magazine well

Magazine spring

stock sporters to deluxe guns with selected woodwork and engraved actions. The cylindrical receiver had a large ejection port, the bolt handle was turned downward, and a double set trigger mechanism was common. The most distinctive feature was the magazine, which consisted of a light sheet-steel box attached to the floor plate.

JARMANN

NORWAY

The mechanism of this distinctive infantry rifle relied on a turning bolt and a tube magazine in the fore-end beneath the barrel that could be loaded through the top of the open action. Like virtually all similar rifles, the Jarmann could carry a ninth cartridge on the elevator and tenth in the chamber.

Model 1884

Infantry rifle: Jarmann Repetergevær M/1884.
Made by Kongsberg Våpenfabrikk, 1884–9.
10·15mm, rimmed.
Turning-bolt action, with a single lug on the bolt locking into the receiver.
1,345mm overall, 4·43kg unladen.
828mm barrel, 4-groove rifling; LH, concentric.
Tube magazine under barrel, 8 rounds.
Ramp-and-leaf sight (see notes).
About 415 m/sec with M/86 ball cartridges.
M/84 épée (army) or knife (navy) bayonets.
☆

1884: this indigenous design was adopted for the Norwegian army and navy. The bolt handle was set well forward above the trigger guard even though the receiver had a solid bridge. The one-piece walnut or birch stock had a single spring-retained band and a pinned nose cap with a bayonet bar on its right side. The original back sight was graduated to 1,500 metres with an auxiliary 'long range' sight on the left side of the fore-end for distances up to 2,400 metres.
1886: after a minor change in the ammunition, the back sight was re-graduated to 1,600 metres

and the long range sight on the fore-end was adjusted accordingly.

JOHNSON

UNITED STATES OF AMERICA

The prototype Johnson Automatic Rifle was tested in 1936, the relevant US patent being granted in September 1937. More than twenty experimental examples were made by Marlin and Taft-Pierce before the design was settled. As the original intention had been to develop a sporting rifle in parallel with the military version, some guns had chequered walnut half-stocks, box magazines and Lyman aperture back sights. However, only 5–6 of these were made.

The action was a novel combination of short recoil and an eight-lug bolt rotating through a mere 20°. Melvin Johnson, an officer in the Marine Corps Reserve, was a highly vocal (and often controversial) champion of his rifle and had powerful friends; only the intervention of the Secretary for War prevented the US Senate debating the adoption of the 'Semi-Automatic Rifle, ·30 M2' in the summer of 1940.

Interestingly, the Johnson-patent multi-lug bolt subsequently reappeared on the ArmaLite AR-10 and its derivatives (q.v.).

Model 1941

Made by Johnson Automatics Mfg. Co., Cranston, Rhode Island.
7 × 57mm or ·30–06.
Recoil-operated auto-loader, locked by rotating lugs on the bolt head into the receiver.
DATA FOR A TYPICAL EXAMPLE
·30–06, rimless.
45·50in overall, 9·50lb unladen.
22·00in barrel, 4-groove rifling; RH, concentric.
Detachable rotary magazine, 11 rounds.
Spring-leaf and ramp sight graduated to 1,000 yards.
About 2,700 ft/sec with US M2 ball ammunition.
Special knife bayonet.
☆

1938: a prototype was tested at Fort Benning in March and June, and then at Aberdeen Proving Ground from August onward.
1939: trials of an improved ·30 rifle, held in December, persuaded the Ordnance Board to take the Johnson rifle seriously.
1940: in February, the Ordnance Committee ordered interest in the Johnson to cease in case work being undertaken to rectify teething troubles with the Garand was adversely affected. Demonstrations revealed that the Garand was compact and more durable, but the Johnson magazine could be reloaded even with the bolt closed. In addition, the Johnson feed lips were machined in the receiver, reducing jamming tendencies, and the barrel was easily detached when required.

Trials undertaken by the US Marine Corps in San Diego, in mid November, favoured the M1903 Springfield at the expense of new M1 Garands with the post-1939 gas assembly, two well-worn Taft-Pierce Johnson rifles, and four differing Winchesters. As the Johnsons had each fired more than 10,000 rounds before trials began, and as the Winchesters were hardly out of the development stage, the conclusions were not altogether unexpected.

Spurned by the US Government, Johnson sold a substantial number of rifles to the Netherlands government-in-exile in the autumn of 1940. Destined for service with the Royal Netherlands Indies Army (KNIL), the perfected weapon was most distinctive, with a two-piece stock separated by the magazine housing. A pierced sheet-steel jacket surrounded the barrel, which moved back on firing to unlock the rotating multi-lug bolt by way of a locking-cam block. The wrist was noticeably shallow, as the return spring lay in a tube in the butt.
1942: the KNIL contract was cancelled by the capitulation of the East Indies to the Japanese, apparently before any large-scale deliveries had been made. Production was thereafter diverted to the US Marines. Johnson rifles saw active service with Raider Battalions in the Pacific and, in small numbers, with USMC forces in Europe. However, the mechanism was more likely to jam

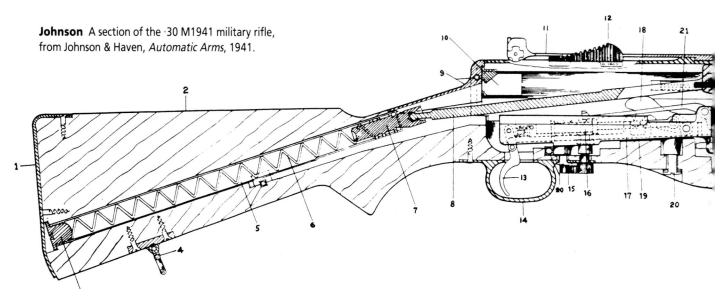

Johnson A section of the ·30 M1941 military rifle, from Johnson & Haven, *Automatic Arms*, 1941.

than the Garand under combat conditions, and the slender barrel proved susceptible to damage.

1944: production stopped in the Spring, after about 70,000 rifles had been made.

Note: a few hundred rifles apparently went to Chile, chambered for the 7 × 57mm rimless cartridge. However, it is not clear whether delivery was contemporaneous with the KNIL order or occurred after 1945.

KALASHNIKOV

UNION OF SOVIET SOCIALIST REPUBLICS

Including Galil, Valmet and other variants

The Kalashnikov has become one of the world's most favoured weapons—serving not only regular forces with pro-Communist leanings, but also countless insurgent and terrorist groups. Production has been undertaken in many former Soviet bloc countries, weapons being supplied to many armies in the Middle East and Africa. Modified guns have emanated from Finland, Israel and South Africa.

However, the recent political changes in Europe have thrown the future of the whole Kalashnikov genre into question. The former Soviet manufacturing facilities were largely confined to Russia and it will be interesting to see what the armed forces of newly independent states such as Latvia and the Ukraine procure over the next decade.

The Kalashnikov action taps propellant gas at the mid-point of the bore to strike a piston attached to the bolt carrier. This drives the piston/bolt carrier assembly backward and rotates the bolt out of engagement. Widely criticised for its clumsiness, low muzzle velocity and a poor-performing cartridge (from the purely technical standpoint, a criticism with validity), the Kalashnikov is simple, solid, reliable, and surprisingly effectual when firing automatically.

1943: capture of German assault rifles enabled development of intermediate cartridges, begun in the 1930s, to continue until a 7·62 × 39mm

pattern was perfected by Elizarov and Semin.

1944: a new Simonov carbine was produced, guns being sent for field trials in the summer. The weapon was ordered into mass production in 1945, but none had been made by the end of the Second World War. The first competition to find a suitable Avtomat—in Russian parlance, a hybrid of rifle and submachine-gun—favoured two Sudayev designs.

1945: a few Sudayev Avtomats were made for trials, but proved to be unreliable and too heavy.

1946: the first Kalashnikov Avtomat was readied in a factory in Alma-Ata, with assistance from a designers' collective.

Note: military and sporting guns are considered together, as the standard Kalashnikov—though touted commercially by the Chinese and (until recently) the Yugoslavs—cannot be considered as a real sporter. Excepting the Finnish-made Petra and the Israeli Hadar, which have much-modified stocks, few supposedly non-military variants offer much more than improved finish.

CHINA
PEOPLE'S REPUBLIC

Type 56

56, 56–1, 56–2 and 56–5, 81, 81–1, 84, 84–1, 86 and NM patterns.
Made by State Factory 66, 1956–73; and an unknown factory under Norinco control, 1973 to date.
Quantity: 15–20 million?
7·62 × 39mm, rimless.
Gas-operated auto-loading action, locked by rotating lugs on the bolt head into engagement with the receiver.
DATA FOR TYPE 56
870mm overall, 4·45kg with empty magazine.
415mm barrel, 4-groove rifling; RH, concentric.
Detachable box magazine, 30 rounds.
Tangent-leaf sight graduated to 800 metres.
710 m/sec with M43 ball cartridges; 775 ± 50rpm.
Type 56 folding bayonet.

☆

1956: the People's Republic was an early convert to the Kalashnikov. The standard Type

56 originally had wooden furniture and a machined steel receiver, with a knife-blade bayonet attached to a block beneath the muzzle. Type 56–1 had a squared 'U'-section butt, with an open 'U'-shape shoulder piece and two rivets each side. The selector markings 杀 and 连 were most distinctive, as was the '66-in-triangle' factory mark on the left side of the receiver ahead of the designation (e.g., 56–1式) and the serial number.

1959*: a triangular-blade bayonet replaced the shorter knife pattern, though the method of attachment remained the same.

1965*: production was switched to a stamped-sheet AKM-type receiver, without altering the basic designation. Bolt covers were usually plain-surface AK-pattern instead of the ribbed version associated with the Soviet-made AKM. Chinese rifles still bore standard ideographs on the selector, though export patterns were usually marked L and D. Furniture remained wooden, pistol grips being plain, and the triangular bayonet was retained.

The folding butt of the Type 56–1 displayed two spot welds on each side, behind the pivot. A swivel was often found on the top edge of the butt, instead of the left side. Machining marks were usually very evident, some of the minor parts were very crudely made, fitting was sloppy, and a curious semi-matt finish was adopted.

1973*: production apparently switched from Factory 66 to a plant run under the supervision of the North China Industries Corporation; these guns are often marked 'M22' and have N-prefix serial numbers. Those restricted to semi-automatic fire were apparently designated 'Type 56–5'; a heavy-barrel version has been sold in the USA as the 'NM-47', but the status of this designation is uncertain. Quality of Norinco Kalashnikovs is noticeably better than Factory 66's military output.

1975*: Type 56–2 introduced a metal skeleton stock folding to the right against the receiver-side. A reddish-brown plastic cheek piece was the principal distinguishing characteristic. Some guns of this type have been seen with a tubular butt, apparently inspired by the FNC; it is

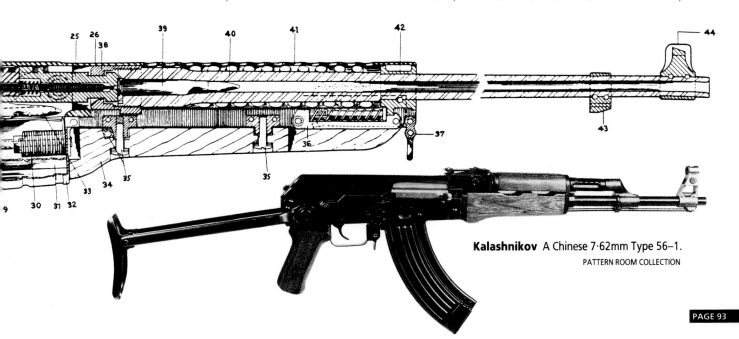

Kalashnikov A Chinese 7·62mm Type 56–1.
PATTERN ROOM COLLECTION

assumed that these date from the 1980s, but information is lacking.

1981*: a Chinese-made AK-74 appeared as the 'Type 81', chambered for the 5·45 × 39mm cartridge. Made with fixed or folding butts, the guns were otherwise very similar to the then-current Types 56 and 56–1. (Note: a version of the SKS [Simonov] seems to have been offered as the Type 81 *semi-automatic carbine*. The Kalashnikov is regarded as the Type 81 *sub-machine-gun*, a distinction carried over from the Type 56 series.)

1985: Type 84 was introduced commercially for the 5·56 × 45mm cartridge, rifled with six grooves though otherwise essentially similar to the Type 81. Fixed and folding-butt guns have been reported, apparently designated Type 84 and Type 84–1 respectively.

1986: a bullpup adaption of the Type 81/Type 84 series was announced as the 'Type 86'. It is not known whether series production has been undertaken: few have been seen in the West.

FINLAND

In addition to Sako- and Valmet-made guns, Finland has used the standard Soviet AK (as the Rynakkovivääri m/54). The folding-stock version was used by paratroops and police, but all Soviet-made weapons were withdrawn into store in the mid 1980s.

Model 1960

Assault rifle: Rynnakkokivääri m/60.
Made by Valmet Oy, Jyväskylä, 1960–1.
Quantity: a few thousands.
7·62 × 39mm, rimless.
Gas-operated auto-loading action, locked by rotating lugs on the bolt head into the receiver.
915mm overall, 4.09kg with empty magazine.
420mm barrel, 4-groove rifling; RH, concentric.
Detachable box magazine, 30 rounds.
Tangent-leaf sight graduated to 1,000 metres.
710 m/sec with M43 ball cartridges; 750 ± 25rpm.
m/60 knife bayonet.
☆

1960: based on the Kalashnikov internally, these rifles were very different externally. The plastic fore-end, tubular steel butt, and back sight on the receiver cover were distinctive. Two basic patterns were made for field trials.

'Type A' rifles lacked a trigger guard, relying on a vertical post between the trigger lever and the magazine, and had a fluted fore-end pierced with ventilation holes. The receiver was a machined forging, selectors were marked S and Y, and a bar in the butt was a sling-anchor point.

'Type B' guns were similar, but had trigger guards released by a spring-catch on the back of the pistol grip. A selection of bayonets was developed, often with Beretta-inspired folding blades, and the butt-tubes were usually covered with rubberised insulation. The Valmet mark appeared on the left side of the receiver.

Model 1962

Assault rifles: Rynnakkokiväärit m/62 i m/62 PT.
Made by Valmet Oy, Jyväskylä, 1963–75; and
Oy Sako Ab, Riihimäki, 1963–6.
7·62 × 39mm, rimless.
Otherwise generally similar to m/60, above, excepting bayonet (m/62 knife pattern).
☆

1963: adopted to replace the semi-experimental m/60, this embodied detail improvements. The receiver was simplified, and the ribbed plastic hand guard and pistol grip took different forms. The furniture was a dark greenish hue on the original Sako-made weapons, but black on the later Valmet examples. The gas tube of the original guns generally lay in a stamped liner, with the top exposed, while later ones were often enclosed. The back sight attachment was improved in the late 1960s, and a solid-top hood replaced the previous open pattern which had allowed easy access to the adjustable-height sight element. Selectors were marked ● and ●●●, for single shots and automatic fire respectively; the dots were impressed on early guns but raised on later examples.

1972*: tritium night sights were fitted to new guns, and the rounded back sight protectors

were replaced by taller square versions. Rifles with the original sights were reclassified as 'm/62 PT'. Small numbers of semi-automatic m/62-type rifles were sold commercially under the designation m/62 S; these were to be seen with fixed or folding tubular butts, though guns touted in the USA often had conventional fixed wooden butts and a wooden pistol grip.

1985: after purchasing small numbers of the m/62/76 (see below), the Finns returned to the folding-butt m/62 on the grounds that the machined-steel receiver was more durable than the stamped version.

Orders for about 40,000 new guns had been placed with the Sako-Valmet combine by the end of 1988. Apart from dated markings and minor improvements in the action and sights, they are identical with the original m/62 patterns.

Model 1971

Assault rifle: Rynnakkokivääri m/71.
Made by Valmet Oy, Jyväskylä, 1971–3.
5·56 × 45mm or 7·62 × 39mm, rimless.
Action: as m/60, above.
928mm overall, 3.59kg with empty magazine.
420mm barrel, 4-groove rifling; RH, concentric.
Detachable box magazine, 30 rounds.
Tangent-leaf sight graduated to 1,000 metres.
960 m/sec with M193 ball cartridges; 650 ± 25rpm.
m/60 knife bayonet (optional).
☆

1971: this was a short-lived variant of the m/62, with a stamped receiver and a front sight assembly much more like the Soviet AKM than the Finnish m/62 service rifle. The synthetic butt, shaped not unlike that of the Fabrique Nationale CAL (q.v.), was accompanied by a parallel-side fore-end enveloping the gas cylinder. Most guns had mechanical hold-opens and the back sight ahead of the ejection port. 5·56mm guns were offered commercially—some semi-automatic examples being sold as 'm/71 S'—while most of the 7·62mm guns were supplied to the Finnish army. The m/71 was soon withdrawn in favour of the improved m/62/76; survivors are apparently still held in store.

Model 1976

Assault rifles: Rynnakkokiväari m/62/76, 76B, 76F, 76P, 76T, 76W, 82, 90 and Law Enforcement patterns.
Made by Valmet Oy, Jyväskylä, 1976–88, and
Sako-Valmet, 1988–90.
5·56 × 45mm or 7·62 × 39mm, rimless.
Action: as m/60, above.
DATA FOR M76W
5·56 × 45mm, rimless.
913mm overall, 3·67kg with empty magazine.
420mm barrel, 4-groove rifling; RH, concentric.
Detachable box magazine, 15, 20 or 30 rounds.
Tangent-leaf graduated to 1,000 metres.
960 m/sec with M193 ball cartridges; 650 ± 25rpm.
m/62 knife bayonet (optional).
☆

1976: after producing a series of prototypes, Valmet introduced the m/76 rifle with a sheet-steel receiver. This was purchased by the Finnish armed forces in small numbers, as the m/62/76 and m/62/76 TP (folding butt version), but did not prove durable enough to displace the m/62.

This rifle has been made in several variants; Models 76F, 76P, 76T and 76W had folding tubular, fixed plastic, fixed tubular, or fixed wooden butts respectively. In addition to limited sales to the Finnish army, some have been sold to Qatar and Indonesia. Guns limited to semi-automatic fire have been advertised as the 'Law Enforcement' series.

1981: Valmet produced a bullpup version of the Model 76, known variously as 'M76B' or, later, 'Model 82'. The standard action was inserted in a one-piece synthetic stock, reducing overall length to about 710mm and weight to about 3·3kg. The trigger and pistol grip were moved forward ahead of the magazine, and a special raised back sight lay ahead of the ejection port. Like most guns of its type, the Model 82 handled oddly. It has not been made in quantity.

1989: a modified version of the m/76 was advertised as the 'Sako m/90'. The current production status of this rifle, which exhibits detail differences in the stock and hand guard arrangements, is not known. It is apparently being considered by the Finnish army.

Petra

Made by Valmet Oy, Jyväskylä, 1982–6.
·243 Winchester or ·308 Winchester.
Action: as m/60, above.
DATA FOR A TYPICAL EXAMPLE
·308 Winchester, rimless.
995mm overall, 3·85kg with empty magazine
450mm barrel, 4-groove rifling; RH, concentric.
Detachable box magazine, 10 rounds.
Tangent-leaf sight graduated to 1,000 metres
(optional).
800 m/sec with FN Match ammunition.
☆

1982: this was one of the few attempts to adapt the Kalashnikov for the sporting fraternity. An enlarged Model 76—restricted to semi-automatic fire—was fitted with a good quality wood butt featuring a straight comb, chequering on the pistol grip and a ventilated rubber recoil pad. The chequered open-top fore-end was also wood. Swivels lay on the barrel and under the butt, and a mount for an optical sight appeared to the receiver. Finish was excellent.

ISRAEL

The Israeli authorities, keen to establish an arms industry but dissatisfied with the FAL, elected to produce a modified Kalashnikov in the late 1960s. Known as the Galil, in honour of the engineer responsible for the transformation, the Israeli rifle approximates to the Finnish m/62—indeed, the earliest guns are said to have incorporated unmarked Valmet-made receivers.

Galil

AR, ARM, SAR and SARM patterns.
Made by Israeli Military Industries, Ramat ha-Sharon.
5·56 × 45mm or 7·62 × 51mm, rimless.
Gas-operated auto-loading action, locked by rotating lugs on the bolt head into the receiver.
DATA FOR ARM
5·56 × 45mm, rimless.
979mm overall (742mm with stock folded),
4·20kg with bipod.

460mm barrel, 6-groove rifling; RH, concentric.
Detachable box magazine, 12, 25 or 50 rounds.
Pivoting aperture sight for 300 and 500 metres.
975 m/sec with M193 ball cartridges; 650 ± 50 rpm.
Knife bayonet (optional).
☆

1969: the performance of AKM rifles in the Six-Day War of 1967 impressed the Israelis greatly. Work began immediately to amalgamate the basic Kalashnikov action, improved in detail, with a simpler gas system lacking a regulator.
1972*: the basic ARM rifle had a tubular plastic pistol grip and a tubular skeletal butt folding to the right to lie alongside the receiver. A radial selector lay on the right side, closing the ejection port when set to its uppermost (safe) position. The cocking handle was bent upward so that the rifle could be cocked with either hand, and a folding carrying handle lay above the chamber. The earliest rifles had fluted wooden fore-ends, but later examples usually had synthetic components

The standard 5·56mm ARM had a bipod, hinged to the gas block to double as a wire cutter. A short flash-suppressor/compensator was fitted to the muzzle and a short US-type bayonet could be attached. Among the most obvious features of the Galil was the back sight at the rear of the breech cover, accompanied by projecting ears and a folding 100-metre night sight with luminescent tritium dots.

In addition to the basic 5·56mm ARM, Galils have been offered in long barrel (AR) or short barrel (SAR) rifle patterns. The AR was basically an ARM without the bipod and carrying handle, and had a simplified synthetic fore-end. The SAR was 851mm long, folded to 615mm, had a 330mm barrel and weighed about 3·65kg.

The 7·62mm patterns were noticeably larger and heavier than the 5·56mm guns and had bulkier magazines with virtually no curve. The 7·62mm AR and ARM were 1,050mm long, had 533mm barrels, and weighed 3·95kg and 4·3kg respectively; relevant data for the 7·62mm SAR were 915mm, 400mm and 3·75kg. The rifles fired SS77 ball ammunition at about 850 m/sec. A typical example was marked A.R. GALIL above

Kalashnikov Finnish soldiers on manoeuvres, armed with 7·62mm m/62 assault rifles.
FINNISH DEFENCE MINISTRY

Kalashnikov
The Israeli Galil 5·56mm AR.
IAN HOGG

Kalashnikov A short-barrelled Galil 5·56mm SAR rifle. IAN HOGG

Kalashnikov
The Finnish m/62 assault rifle.
SAKO–VALMET OY

KALASHNIKOV
THE LESSER MODELS

BULGARIA

The People's Army was initially armed with rifles made in Poland (q.v.). A typical example—made by Factory 11 in 1963—had a machined-steel receiver, a wooden fore-end, a plain wood pistol grip, and a cleaning rod beneath the barrel. The solid 'C'-section folding butt, actuated by a press-stud on the left side, had an open 'U'-shape shoulder piece and no visible rivets. The selector bore 'C' over 'P'.

¶ Production of AK rifles began in State Factory 10 in c.1965. Plastic furniture was fitted, the pistol grip being crudely chequered, and selectors were marked 'AB' and 'ЕД'. A cleaning rod was carried under the barrel, but the gun did not accept a bayonet. Production switched to the AKM in the early 1970s, and then to a facsimile of the AK-74 in the mid 1980s.

EGYPT

The armed forces have used Soviet-made AK and AKM rifles in addition to several million AKM-type rifles made by 'Factory 54' of Maadi Military & Civil Industries Company. The factory was equipped with Soviet assistance in the late 1950s. The Misr has a laminated wood butt and fore-end, and a chequered plastic pistol grip.

GERMANY

The Democratic Republic used Soviet-made AK rifles from 1957 until indigenous production commenced in Suhl two years later. These may have Russian and East German marks, but the quantities involved seem to have been small and surviving guns are rarely seen.

¶ Production of a minor variant of the Soviet rifle began in 1959 in the former Sauer factory ('VEB Ernst-Thälmann-Werke') as the 'Maschinenpistole Kalashnikov' or MPi-K. About 1·3–1·5 million were made in c.1959–66. The guns had wood butts, fore-end and hand guards, but lacked the cleaning rod and butt-trap of their prototype and did not accept bayonets. Selectors were marked 'D' and 'E'. A curious night sight, comprising a luminous slider on rails, could be clipped onto the aperture in the front sight mounting block.

¶ The MPi-KS had a plain-sided folding butt, but was otherwise similar to the basic MPi-K. East German guns may be identified by marks such as '64 R 4925' on the left side of the receiver. The first two digits represent the date of manufacture—e.g., '64' is 1964. The guns also display a principal inspector's mark in the form of a letter inside a circle of dots.

¶ The first MPi-KM, based on the AKM, appeared in 1965. They had a wood butt, though later examples were fitted with a plastic hand guard, a wood fore-end and a blue-grey plastic butt with a distinctive stippled finish. Most guns had a cleaning rod. 1·8–2·2 million were made prior to the mid 1980s. The otherwise similar MPi-KMS had a distinctive butt, swinging to the right and locked by a latch protruding from the receiver beneath the butt-rod. The pressed-steel shoulder piece was retained by two rivets. Selectors bore 'D' above 'E', and date/serial marks such as '71 H 7472'.

¶ A copy of the AK-74 was introduced about 1983. Production does not seem to have been large, being stopped by reunification.

HUNGARY

The original AK-55, made by FÉG of Budapest in c.1955–65, had a cleaning rod but lacked a bayonet lug. Manufacturing quality was surprisingly good, with the stock, chequered pistol grip and fore-end all being solid wood. Selectors were marked '1' and '∞'. The serial number was usually stamped into a panel milled out of the left side of the receiver, but manufacturer's marks were rarely present.

¶ Introduced in 1963, the FÉG-made AKM-63, initially with a wood butt, had a unique metal fore-end formed integrally with the receiver. A supplementary pistol grip lay ahead of the magazine. The butt and pistol grip became grey-blue or dark-green polypropylene. Selectors still bore '1' and '∞'.

¶ The AMD-65 of 1966 was a shortened derivative of the AKM with a simple tubular butt and a rubber butt plate. The butt could be folded by pressing a slotted-head catch under the receiver behind the rear pistol grip. The short barrel had a distinctive two-port muzzle brake/compensator. Both pistol grips were greyish-green plastic, serial numbers appeared on the left side of the receiver, and selectors were marked in their customary Hungarian manner. Some guns were subsequently converted for grenade firing, acquiring a launcher on the muzzle, a special optical sight above the receiver on a mounting plate, and a shock-absorbing tubular butt.

¶ Production of an indigenous variant of the 5·45mm AK-74 began in c.1981 under the designation NGM (or NGM-81). Made only with a fixed butt and a wooden fore-end, the NGM had a chromium-lined bore. A good-quality variant chambered for the 5·56 × 45mm round has been offered for export.

KOREA

Production of the Type 58 began in the People's Republic of Korea in 1959. A straightforward copy of the AK, the guns had cleaning rods but lacked bayonet lugs. They were made with solid wooden butts and smooth-tapering fore-ends instead of the Soviet beaver-tail type. Pistol grips may be solid or (apparently later) laminated wood. Selector markings— ʀ̠ɫ above ʔ̠ʟ —were most distinctive, and the serial number on the left side of the receiver was generally prefixed by a large encircled star.

¶ The Type 68 of 1970 was basically an AKM with an AK-type trigger mechanism. The standards of manufacture were poor. However, sufficient production (at an annual rate of 150,000 in the early 1980s) has been undertaken in Factories 61 and 65 to allow substantial numbers of AK and AKM-type rifles to be exported.

THE NETHERLANDS

In the late 1970s, Nederlansche Waapen- en Munitiefabriek (NWM) negotiated a licence to make a modified form of the Israeli Galil known as the MN-1. This was touted as a replacement for the FAL rifle; at the time of writing, however, the latter is still in service—though soon to be substituted by the Belgian FNC.

POLAND

Production of the Pistolet Maszynowy Kalasznikow (PMK), alternatively known as the Karabinek Awtomata Kalasznikow (Kbk-AK), began in the principal state firearms factory in Radom in the early 1960s. The PMK was essentially similar to the original Soviet gun, with wooden furniture, but had a chequered pistol grip and a selector marked 'C' and 'P'. The rifles had cleaning rods, but were not issued with bayonets. The PMK-S had a folding butt—a 'C'-section pressing—with a 'U'-type shoulder piece. Polish Kalashnikovs will usually display an '11-in-oval' factory mark, the date and a prefixed serial number (e.g., '1964' and 'MK12891').

¶ A PMK-DGN (or Kbk.g wz/60) grenade-launching variant, apparently made in a former Perkun factory in Warsaw, could fire F1/N60 anti-personnel and PGN-60 anti-tank grenades from the LON-1 launcher. It had a special leaf sight, a special small-capacity magazine, and a gas-cylinder cut-off valve marked 'O' and 'Z'. Distinctive trapezoidal metal plates were added to each side of the butt.

¶ Production of an AKM-type rifle began in Factory 11 in 1966–7. It had a laminated fore-end and hand guard, in addition to a chequered plastic pistol grip. Manufacturing quality was quite good, the stamped receiver and bolt cover, together with most of the minor external parts, being well blacked. Selectors bore 'C' and 'P', and a cleaning rod lay beneath the muzzle. The

base of the short muzzle attachment was extended to serve as a rudimentary compensator. The otherwise identical PMK-MS had a folding stock, with three rivets, three spot-welds and two short flutes on each side of the pressed-steel strut. It rotated upward.

ROMANIA

Made in the arms factory in Çugir from 1960 onward, the AI (AK) rifle was little more than a copy of the Soviet pattern, with a selector marked 'S', 'FA' and 'FF'.

¶ The improved AIM (AKM)—introduced in the mid 1960s—had a plastic pistol grip, a laminated butt, a laminated hand guard, and a laminated fore-end with an integral pistol grip. It also had a stamped bolt cover, a 1,000-metre back sight, a cleaning rod and a bayonet lug. The rear sling swivel lay on the under-edge of the butt, though many guns have been reported with it removed to the left side of the butt-wrist. Romanian Kalashnikovs generally bore an arrowhead-in-triangle mark on the left side of the receiver, ahead of the date (e.g., '1967') and a serial number.

SOUTH AFRICA

After protracted trials, the South African government adopted the '5·56mm Rifle 4' (R4) in 1982, to replace the 7·62mm R1 (FAL) as well as some G3 weapons seized in the Angolan borderland. Made by the Lyttleton Engineering Works Pty. of Pretoria, the R4 was a minor adaption of the Israeli Galil (q.v.). The fore-end and pistol grip were made of fibreglass-reinforced plastic; the butt, steel on the original IMI guns, was similarly synthetic to reduce the effects of the hot South African climate. The butt was lengthened, giving an overall dimension of about 1,005mm, and changes were made in the bipod, gas system, receiver and rifling to suit SADF requirements. The rifles weighed about 4·3kg without the standard 35-round magazine.

¶ Adopted in 1987 to supplement and eventually replace the R4, the 5·56mm R5 was similar to its predecessor excepting for the omission of the bipod and a 13cm reduction in barrel length. A typical R5 is about 875mm long and weighs about 3·9kg.

SWEDEN

FFV Ordnance acquired a licence to make modified Israeli Galil rifles in the late 1970s, small quantities of the resulting Model 890C rifle being supplied for government trials. They could be distinguished by deeply ribbed fore-ends and trigger guards large enough to admit a gloved finger. The trials resolved in favour of the Belgian FNC—adopted in Sweden as the Ak.5—and the FFV rifle was abandoned.

7.62 x 51, IMI and ISRAEL on the left side of the receiver. Safety catches under the thumb on the left side of the pistol grip were marked S, A and R. Export patterns were generally marked in English; Israeli Defence Force rifles, stamped in Hebrew, also displayed a sword and olive branch inside a six-point star on the left side of the receiver above the pistol grip.

Many guns made after about 1980 may bear the Israeli Military Industries trademark of a sword and an olive branch superimposed on a cogwheel; serial numbers usually run vertically upward on the front left side of the receiver immediately behind the fore-end.

Sniper rifles

Galil and Hadar II patterns.
Made by Israeli Military Industries, Ramat ha-Sharon.
7·62 × 51mm NATO, rimless.
Action: as ARM, above.
DATA FOR GALIL SNIPER
1,115mm overall (840mm with stock folded), 6.40kg with bipod.
508mm barrel, 4-groove rifling; RH, concentric.
Detachable box magazine, 20 rounds.
Pivoting aperture sight for 300 and 500 metres.
815 m/sec with FN Match cartridges.

☆

1983*: developed for Israeli army snipers, the special 7·62mm AR-type Galil, restricted to semi-automatic fire, had a heavyweight barrel and a large tubular muzzle brake/compensator. A two-stage trigger was fitted, while the bipod was moved forward to pivot on the receiver instead of the gas block, relieving the barrel of unnecessary stress that could reduce accuracy. A folding wood butt was fitted, with a cheek piece and a ventilated rubber recoil pad. A bracket attached to the left side of the receiver accepted a 6 × 40 Nimrod sight or any NATO-standard infra-red and image-intensifying night-vision patterns.
1987*: intended for police use, and also occasionally sold as a sporting rifle, the Hadar II had a standard 7·62mm AR action set into a three-quarter length wooden stock with an unmistakable thumb-hole butt and a radial safety

lever set into the left side of the pistol grip. The rifles were about 980mm overall and weighed 4·35kg unladen.

U S S R
AK

Assault rifles: AK and AKS patterns.
Made in the state ordnance factories in Izhevsk, Tula and elsewhere, 1949–59.
Quantity: at least five million.
7·62 × 39mm, rimless.
Gas-operated auto-loading action, locked by rotating lugs on the bolt head into the receiver.
869mm overall, 4·30kg with empty magazine.
414mm barrel, 4-groove rifling; RH, concentric.
Detachable box magazine, 30 rounds.
Tangent-leaf sight graduated to 800 metres.
710 m/sec with M43 ball cartridges; 775 ± 50rpm.
No bayonet initially (see notes).

☆

1946: the 'Avtomaty sistemy Kalashnikova, optny obr.1946g' showed great promise, and a process of continuous refinement began in the Tula factory.
1949: series production began. The earliest guns incorporated extensive welding, stamping and pressed-metal parts, embodying the popular philosophy that excellent surface finish and slavish adherence to minuscule tolerances were secondary to efficiency and durability.
1951: an enforced change from stamped to machined components was made when Soviet industry proved incapable of mastering sheet-metal fabrication techniques gleaned from the Germans. The rifles had wood butts and fore-ends, pistol grips originally being laminated wood (often replaced with coarsely chequered or ribbed plastic varieties). Butt plates were steel, with a hinged trap, and a cleaning rod was carried beneath the barrel. No bayonets were issued. The rear swivel originally lay on the under-edge of the butt, but many guns will now be found with the swivel let into the left side of the wrist. Selectors were crudely marked AB and ОД with an electric pencil, the constructional

standards being adequate but not outstanding.
1953*: a change was made to the rear of the receiver, where an extension received the tip of the butt to strengthen the attachment. Laminated woodwork was standard. Selector markings were generally stamped, and shallow panels were milled in the sides of the receiver. There was no bayonet-attachment lug, but the Russians subsequently developed a knife bayonet locking around the front-sight block. Magazines were originally plain sided.

The AKS was a standard Kalashnikov with a pressed-steel butt folding down and forward under the receiver.

AKM

Assault rifles: AKM and AKMS patterns.
Made by the state ordnance factory, Izhevsk, 1959–75.
Quantity: at least ten million.
7·62 × 39mm, rimless.
Action: as AK rifle, above.
876mm overall, 3·82kg with empty magazine.
415mm barrel, 4-groove rifling; RH, concentric.
Detachable box magazine, 30 rounds.
Tangent-leaf sight graduated to 1,000 metres.
710 m/sec with M43 ball cartridges; 650 ± 30rpm.
AKM knife bayonet.

☆

1959: once Soviet industry had mastered new production techniques, a modified Kalashnikov Avtomat was introduced. The stamped-steel receiver—a sturdy 'U'-shape pressing—reduced weight appreciably compared with the original machined forging. The bolt-lock recesses were riveted in place, and the stamped receiver cover had prominent lateral ribs. The gas-piston tube of the AKM had semi-circular vents immediately behind the gas-port assembly rather than the eight circular holes (four on each side) on the AK; and the bolt carrier was parkerised. The butt and fore-end were usually laminated wood; pistol grips were usually plastic. Magazines were ribbed sheet-metal, then orange-red plastic.

The AKMS had a conventional folding butt, with three rivets and a long flute on each side of the strut. It swung down and forward.

An early Soviet-made **Kalashnikov** gun, with the butt retained by rivets and a sling ring on the left side of the receiver. IAN HOGG

Kalashnikov The standard Soviet 5·45mm AK-74. IAN HOGG

1961*: a short oblique-cut compensator was added to prevent the gun climbing to the right when firing automatically. This was largely due to reduced weight. Bayonet lugs appeared, and an additional mechanical safety in the trigger system held back the hammer after the bolt-carrier had depressed the safety sear; this merely added complexity to a simple design, though it also restricted cylic rate. Fore-ends were broadened in this era.

AKM SU

Made by the state ordnance factories, 1975–8.
7·62 × 39mm, rimless.
Action: as AK rifle, above.
722mm overall, 3·35kg with empty magazine.
225mm barrel, 4-groove rifling; RH, concentric.
Detachable box magazine, 30 rounds.
Rocking-'L' sight for 100 and 500 metres.
645 m/sec with M43 ball cartridges;
cyclic rate not known.
No bayonet.

☆

1975: introduced for armoured troops, notably for use as a port-firing weapon in armoured personnel carriers, this was basically an AKM shortened to submachine-gun length. It has also been called 'AKR' or 'Krinkov', apparently after the leader of the design team. Fitted with a folding butt, the AKMSU lacked the cleaning rod and bayonet lug of the full-length gun; instead, it had a short finned expansion chamber with a conical flash-hider, and the front sight block (with a sling bar on the left side) was moved back to abut the laminated wood hand guard. The back sight base was combined with the receiver-cover pivot, and a chequered plastic pistol grip was accompanied by a short wooden fore-end with a thumb hole to facilitate control during automatic fire.

AK-74

AK-74, AK-74S and AK-74N patterns.
Made by the state ordnance factories, 1975 to date.
Quantity: at least five million.

5·45 × 39mm, rimless.
Action: as AK rifle, above.
928mm overall, 3·86kg with empty magazine.
400mm barrel, four-groove rifling; RH, concentric.
Detachable box magazine, 30 or 40 rounds.
Tangent-leaf sight graduated to 1,000 metres.
900 m/sec with B-74 ball cartridges; 650 ± 30rpm.
AK-74 knife bayonet.

☆

1969: 5·56mm M16 rifles supplied from Vietnam indicated that the 7·62mm obr.1943g cartridge was less effectual than its American rival. Experiments continued until 1973. The new Russian 5·45mm cartridge had a two-piece bullet with a hollow tip within the jacket to improve lethality by deforming against a target.

1974: the new AK-74 appeared, chambering a new small-calibre round based on the 7·62mm case. Its muzzle-brake/compensator had a larger cut-out on the left than the right, and ports angled to counteract tendencies to climb to the right when firing automatically. Longitudinal grooves were cut into both sides of the butt to identify the calibre in the dark. A cleaning rod, carried beneath the muzzle, could only be removed after the muzzle brake had been detached. There were also two bayonet lugs for an improved wirecutter/tool bayonet. The so-called AK-74N (AK-74H in Cyrillic) had a mount for the infra-red NSP-2 or image-intensifying NSP-3 night-vision sights.

AK-74 SU

Made by the state ordnance factories, 1981 to date.
5·45 × 39mm, rimless.
Action: as AK rifle, above.
675mm overall (422mm with butt folded),
about 2·7kg with empty magazine.
200mm barrel, 4-groove rifling; RH, concentric.
Detachable box magazine, 30 rounds.
Rocking-'L' sight for 100 or 500 metres.
800 m/sec with ball cartridges; 800 ± 50 rpm.
No bayonet.

☆

1980*: this compact Kalashnikov derivative was developed to replace the AKM SU described

above. It shared many of the features of the older gun, including the pivoting breech cover/back-sight base unit, but pressing a catch on the left side of the receiver behind the pistol grip allowed the skeletal butt to fold back along the receiver. A small sliding retainer on the lower left side of the receiver ahead of the magazine well held the folded butt in place. The AK-74 SU also had a short cylindrical barrel extension, apparently to act as an expansion chamber and reduce the violence of the muzzle blast.

YUGOSLAVIA

A selection of Kalashnikov-type guns is still offered commercially. Most bear the ZCZ trademark ahead of the company name and country of origin on the left side of the receiver.

Model 64

64, 64A and 64B patterns.
Made by the state firearms factory (Zavodi Crvena Zastava), Kraguyevač.
7·62 × 39mm, rimless.
Gas-operated auto-loading action, locked by rotating lugs on the bolt head into the receiver.
Otherwise generally as Soviet AK (above), excepting for a 1,000-metre sight and a different bayonet.

☆

1964: the M64 introduced a wooden pistol grip with prominent finger grooves, and an integral grenade-launching sight attached to the gas-port housing (a suitable launcher replaced the muzzle brake/compensator when required). A mechanical hold-open was added internally.

Selectors were generally marked U, R and J, and the 1,000-metre back sight was used. However, some of the rifles made for export had selectors marked in English.

1967*: the advent of the improved M64A rifle brought a shorter barrel—375mm instead of 414mm—and, eventually, a ribbed black plastic pistol grip. The otherwise similar M64B Kalashnikov variant had a folding stock with three rivets and a prominent longitudinal flute on each side.

Kalashnikov
An East German MPi-KM,
showing the distinctive stippled
finish on the synthetic butt.
PATTERN ROOM COLLECTION

Kalashnikov The Finnish Sako-Valmet m/90 assault rifle.
IAN HOGG

Kalashnikov
A Romanian AIM (AKM copy),
with a forward pistol grip.
PATTERN ROOM COLLECTION

Kalashnikov The Swedish FFV-890C rifle, based
on the Galil, was entered unsuccessfully in the army rifle trials of
the early 1980s. The FNC was preferred.
FFV PHOTOGRAPH, IAN HOGG

Kalashnikov A Polish infantryman with
a PMK-S rifle emerges from a pipe obstacle.
POLISH DEFENCE MINISTRY, VIA IAN HOGG

Kalashnikov Hungarian AMD-65.
The metal fore-end and the tubular
hand grips are most distinctive.
PATTERN ROOM COLLECTION

Model 70

70, 70A, 70AB2, 70B1, 77B1, 80 and 80A patterns.
Made by the state firearms factory (Zavodi Crvena Zastava), Kraguyevač.
5·56 × 45mm, 7·62 × 39mm or 7·62 × 51mm NATO.
Action: as Model 64, above.
Otherwise generally as Soviet AK, excepting for the 1,000-metre sight and a different bayonet. 5·56mm guns usually have six-groove rifling.

☆

1972*: the Models 70 and 70A (7·62 × 39mm) were modelled on the Soviet AKM, generally with stamped-sheet breech covers, ribbed plastic pistol grips and an improved muzzle compensator. Continual improvement led to the current models with Soviet style spatulate compensators. The selector lever and receiver designs have also been modified.

1974*: Models 70B1 and 70AB2 appeared, with fixed and folding butts respectively. The principal change was the addition of a ladder-type grenade launching sight above the gas tube, used in conjunction with a detachable muzzle tube. Raising the sight automatically sealed the gas port to allow the entire gas volume generated on firing to propel the grenade.

1977: the Model 77B1 chambered the 7·62mm NATO cartridge. The receiver was suitably enlarged to accept the bulkier cartridge and a slotted muzzle brake/compensator was fitted. A grenade launcher tube and auxiliary ladder-type sights were optional extras.

1980: M80 and M80A rifles were adaptions of the Kalashnikov design for the 5·56 × 45mm cartridge. The gas system was modified to improve performance and the longitudinally slotted compensator was used. Some guns were rifled for the US M193 bullet and others for the Belgian SS109 type, the grooves making a turn in 180mm or 305mm respectively. The M80A had a fixed wooden butt and a synthetic pistol grip, while the M80A had a stamped-strip butt folding down and forward beneath the receiver. The guns could be distinguished from the 7·62 × 39mm versions by their muzzle fittings and short straight staggered-column magazines.

Model 76

Sniper rifle.
Made by the state firearms factory (Zavodi Crvena Zastava), Kraguyevač.
7·62 × 54mm, 7·62 × 51mm NATO or 7·9 × 57mm.
Action: as Model 64, above.
DATA FOR A TYPICAL EXAMPLE
7·9 × 57mm, rimless.
1,135mm overall, 4·25kg without sights.
550mm barrel, 4-groove rifling; RH, concentric.
Detachable box magazine, 10 rounds.
Tangent-leaf sight graduated to 1,000 metres.
850 m/sec with ball cartridges.
No bayonet.

☆

1976*: adopted as the official sniper rifle of the Yugoslav state army, and exported in small numbers, this was little more than a standard Kalashnikov action enlarged to handle full-power cartridges. It was restricted to semi-automatic fire. The straight-comb butt, ventilated fore-end and hand-filling pistol grip were all wood. Barrel length and the shallow magazine distinguished the Model 76 instantly.

A mount on the receiver accepted an indigenous copy of the Soviet PSO-1 optical sight, in addition to the standard NSP-2 or NSP-3 night-vision types.

Model 85

Made by the state firearms factory (Zavodi Crvena Zastava), Kraguyevač.
5·56x45mm
790mm overall (570mm with butt folded),
3·25kg without magazine.
315mm barrel, six-groove rifling; RH, concentric.
Detachable box magazine, 20 or 30 rounds
Rocking-'L' sight for 100 and 500 metres.
790 m/sec with SS109 ball cartridges; 700 ± 50 rpm.
No bayonet.

☆

1986: inspired by the Soviet AK-74 SU (q.v.), this compact weapon was introduced principally for use in armoured personnel carriers. It had a standard Yugoslavian-pattern butt, folding down and forward beneath the receiver, and a hinged breech cover doubling as the back sight base. The cylindrical expansion chamber fitted to the muzzle was simply copied from its Soviet counterpart.

KEENE

UNITED STATES OF AMERICA
Also known as 'Remington-Keene'

⌖

Patented by James Keene of Newark, New Jersey in 1874–7, this bolt-action rifle was tested by the US Army but never adopted in quantity by any military agency.

The bolt relied on a prominent rib turning down into the receiver to provide a satisfactory lock. The loading port lay on the underside of the stock ahead of the trigger, though the magazine could also be loaded from the top through the open action. As the cartridges were securely retained in the elevator during the loading stroke, the Remington-Keene—unlike many tube-magazine rivals—could be loaded and fired upside-down.

Model 1880

Made by E. Remington & Sons, Ilion, New York, 1877–80.
Quantity: about 5,000.
·40–70 Remington, ·43 Spanish or ·45–70 Government.
Turning-bolt action locked by the bolt-guide rib abutting the receiver ahead of the bridge.
DATA FOR MUSKET
·45–70, rimmed.
48·50in overall, 9·00lb unladen.
30·00in barrel, 5-groove rifling; RH, concentric.
Tube magazine beneath barrel, 8 rounds.
Ramp-and-leaf sight graduated to 1,200 yards.
About 1,275 ft/sec with standard ball cartridges.
M1873 socket bayonet.

☆

1878: developed as a sporter, generally with a 25in barrel, the rifle was difficult to mistake. It had a straight-wrist half stock with a notably

Kalashnikov A 7·9mm Yugoslavian M76 sniper rifle. ZCZ, VIA IAN HOGG

Kalashnikov Distinguished by the grenade-launcher sight behind the gas-port housing, this is a Model 70B1 Kalashnikov. ZCZ, VIA IAN HOGG

concave under-surface, and a prominent spur on the cocking piece which had to be cocked manually before firing—a safety feature deemed necessary on horseback.

1880: the US Navy acquired 250 rifles for shipboard trials. They apparently had nine-round magazines.

1881: the US Army acquired 250 guns for trials against the Hotchkiss and Remington-Lee. They had 30in barrels, full-length stocks, two bands, a cut-off on the left side of the breech, and a cleaning rod set in a channel on the left side of the stock. However, they were not successful and no additional purchases were made.

1884*: 200–250 half-stock rifles with full-length magazines were purchased on behalf of the US Indian Bureau and issued to reservation police. (Note: it has been suggested that these were the guns acquired by the US Army three year previously, but the case is not proven.)

1887: Remington disposed of the remaining stocks of unsold rifles at cut-price rates.

KIMBER

UNITED STATES OF AMERICA

Model 82 Sporter

Made by Kimber of Oregon, Inc., Clackamas, Oregon.
·218 Bee, ·22 Hornet, ·25–20 Winchester.
Turning-bolt action, locked by rotating lugs on the bolt body into the receiver.
DATA FOR A TYPICAL EXAMPLE
·218 Bee, rimless.
40·50in overall, 6·38lb unladen.
22·50in barrel, 6-groove rifling; RH, concentric.
Folding-leaf sight.
2,690 ft/sec with 45-grain bullet.
☆

1982: this was a modified version of the ·22 rimfire Model 82 rifle, sharing the same rear-locking action and straight-comb stock. The ·22 Hornet version had a three-round magazine, but the others were single-shot only. In addition to Classic and Custom Classic grades (see Model

84, below), the Model 82 was also made in 'Cascade' pattern, with a Monte Carlo cheek-piece and comb. However, the rifle lost popularity once the Model 84 appeared, and was discontinued in 1985–6.

Model 84 Sporter

Also known as the Model 84 Mini-Mauser.
Made by Kimber of Oregon, Inc., Clackamas, Oregon.
·17 Remington, ·22 Hornet, ·222 Remington, or ·223 Remington.
Turning-bolt action, locked by rotating lugs on the bolt head into the receiver and by the bolt handle turning down into its seat.
DATA FOR A TYPICAL SUPER VARMINTER
·222 Remington, rimless.
42·50in overall, 7·25lb unladen.
24·00in barrel, 6-groove rifling; RH, concentric.
Internal box magazine, 5 rounds.
Optical sight.
3,200 ft/sec with 50-grain bullet.
☆

1984: developed specifically for ·222 cartridges, this rifle amalgamated features of the pre-1964 Winchester Model 70—e.g., the distinctive safety on the bolt shroud and the spring-loaded ejector—with others provided by the proven 1898-type Mauser.

The standard or 'Classic' rifles had a 22in barrel and weighed about 6·3lb. They were also offered in a 'Classic Custom' or Deluxe Grade, with Claro walnut stocks and ebony fore-end tips. Borderless 20-line chequering was used and the steel shoulder plate was diced. A Super America pattern had special attention paid to the finish, a Claro or straight-grain English walnut stock selected for its figuring, beaded cheek-piece edges and borderless 22-line chequering. Niedner chequered-steel butt plates were standard, but skeletal pistol-grip caps or butt plates were available to order. Additional options included ebony fore-end tips, a quarter-rib with Express sights and chequering on the bolt-handle knob.

1986: a round-top receiver was adopted. The Super and Ultra Varminter models appeared,

distinguished by their heavyweight 24in barrels. The Ultra pattern had a laminated birch stock, with a plain butt and a rubber shoulder pad; the Super version had a selected Claro walnut stock with a beaded-edge cheek piece and inletted swivel eyes.

1987: a three-position safety replaced the earlier two-position type. Additional ·17 Mach IV, ·221 Remington Fireball, 5·6 × 50mm, 6 × 45mm and 6 × 47mm chamberings were offered, though these had all been discontinued by 1989.

Model 89 Big-Game Rifle

Made by Kimber of Oregon, Inc., Clackamas, Oregon.
Chambering: see notes.
Action: as Model 84, above.
DATA FOR A TYPICAL M89 MEDIUM MAGNUM
·300 H&H Magnum, belted rimless.
44·00in overall, 8·00lb unladen.
24·00in barrel, 6-groove rifling; RH, concentric.
Internal box magazine, 3 rounds.
Folding-leaf sight.
2,980 ft/sec with 180-grain bullet.
☆

1988: somewhat similar to the Model 84 and preceded by a series of pre-production guns made in 1987, this combined Winchester and Mauser practice. The Mauser provided the locking/breeching system, with an inner collar in the receiver ring; the collar-type extractor; the internal box magazine; and the pivoting bolt-stop on the left side of the receiver. The trigger, the safety and the ejector (which rode under the left locking lug) were inspired by the Winchester Model 70.

The Model 89 Big-Game Rifle was offered in ·257 Roberts, ·25–06, ·270 Winchester, ·280 Remington, 7 × 57mm Mauser or ·30–06 (with a 'Featherweight Profile'), and 7mm Remington Magnum, ·300 H&H Magnum, ·300 Winchester Magnum, ·338 Winchester Magnum, ·35 Whelen or ·375 H&H Magnum (with 'Medium Magnum' barrels). The stock was a classically styled Claro or European walnut pattern with a straight comb.

1990: the bolt-guide and the corresponding

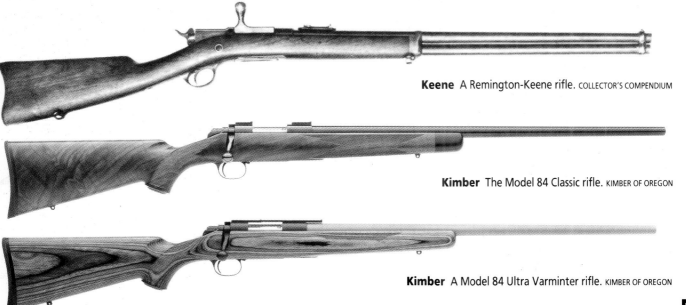

Keene A Remington-Keene rifle. COLLECTOR'S COMPENDIUM

Kimber The Model 84 Classic rifle. KIMBER OF OREGON

Kimber A Model 84 Ultra Varminter rifle. KIMBER OF OREGON

receiver rail were improved to smooth the bolt stroke. A new Model 89 African action was introduced to handle even the largest sporting cartridges—·375 H&H, ·404 Jeffrey, ·416 Rigby, ·460 Weatherby Magnum or ·505 Gibbs. The overall length was 47in; weight was 10–10·5lb.

Most Kimber African rifles were stocked in Classic or Custom Classic styles, the former being Claro walnut with 18-line chequering and the latter being figured walnut with 22-line chequering. There was very little drop at the heel, an Express sight was fitted on a quarter rib, the front sling-swivel eye lay on the barrel, and two lateral recoil bolts were fitted. Chequered steel butt plates and polished pistol-grip caps were standard on both, though the Custom Classic stock had an additional ebony fore-end tip. A full-length 'Continental' stock and a 'Super America' grade were also available.

KOUCKY

CZECHOSLOVAKIA

The products of Josef and František Koucky have included a wide range of auto-loading and bolt-action guns. The centre-fire sporters have been particularly successful, being widely distributed in the West since the late 1950s.

1. THE AUTO-LOADING PATTERNS

The ZK 371 of 1937 was quickly followed by the 7·92mm ZK 381. Locked by a tilting breech block, the 7·62mm ZK 381 Au II successfully underwent a 10,000-round endurance trial in the Soviet Union in August 1938. The ZK 391—the first of the series to embody a rotating bolt—is said to have been adopted by the Italians, production in Cremona being stopped only by the surrender of Italy in 1943. The ZK 420 and ZK 425 rifles were developed under German supervision in 1942–3.

ZK 420

420, 420–S and 472 patterns.
Made by Československá Zbrojovka, Brno.
Chamberings: see text.
Gas-operated auto-loading action, locked by lugs on a rotating bolt engaging the receiver.
DATA FOR A TYPICAL EXAMPLE
7·92 × 57mm, rimless.
1,058mm overall, 4·78kg laden.
550mm barrel, 4-groove rifling; RH, concentric.
Detachable box magazine, 10 rounds.
Tangent-leaf sight graduated to 1,000 metres.
820 m/sec with ball ammunition.
No bayonet.
☆

1945: a revised prototype ZK 420 appeared shortly after the Second World War had ended. Numbered '002', it had a conventional fore-end and nose cap assembly, a rifle-type tangent-leaf back sight set into the hand guard, and a curious integral magazine charger-loaded through the top of the action.

1946: a few semi-production guns were made for trials, the perfected ZK 420S featuring a detachable box magazine, a half-stock, and a sight with protective wings on top of the receiver.

At least 150 rifles were made in 7mm, ·30–06 or 7·92mm, for tests in countries as disparate as Britain, Ethiopia, Israel and Switzerland. The ZK 420 was effectual enough, but expensive to mass produce and offering no real advantages over existing guns. Owing to progress with smaller intermediate-cartridge guns, the project was abandoned in 1949.

The ZK 472 was a variant of the ZK 420, chambered for a 7·5mm intermediate cartridge. It had a detachable box magazine, for ten or fifteen rounds, but could be charger-loaded through the open action. A typical rifle was about 1,000mm overall, had a 500mm barrel and weighed 2·95kg without its magazine. At least fifty were made for trials in 1949–50 against the Kynčl-designed ZJ 481 and the Kratochvil CZ 493. The CZ 493 subsequently developed into the Model 52.

2. THE BOLT-ACTION PATTERNS

ZKW 465

Made by Československá Zbrojovka, Brno.
·22 Hornet only.
Turning-bolt action, locked by one lug on the bolt body and the bolt handle turning down into its seat.
About 1,075mm overall, 2·83kg unladen.
585mm barrel, 6-groove rifling; RH, concentric.
Detachable box magazine, 5 rounds.
Block-and-leaves sight.
740 m/sec with 3-gram bullet.
☆

1946: design of this Koucky 'miniature Mauser' was completed. The perfected rifle had a straight-comb half-stock, originally with a slender schnabel-tip fore-end. The pistol grip and fore-end were chequered, a flag-pattern safety catch was mounted on the bolt shroud, and a double set trigger mechanism was a popular optional extra.

ZKK 600

600, 601 and 602 patterns.
Made by Československá Zbrojovka, Brno.
Chamberings: see notes.
Turning-bolt action, locked by two lugs on the bolt head engaging the receiver and a safety lug on the bolt body.
DATA FOR A TYPICAL ZKK 600
8 × 60mm S, rimless.
1,110mm overall, 3·13kg without magazine.
600mm barrel, 4-groove rifling; RH, concentric.
Internal box magazine, 5 rounds.
Folding-leaf sight.
845 m/sec with 12·1-gram bullet.
☆

1960: unquestionably the most successful sporting rifle made in eastern Europe since 1945, this interesting Koucky design was basically a Mauser, with a safety lug opposing the bolt handle base and a full-length collar pattern extractor. It also retained the undercut

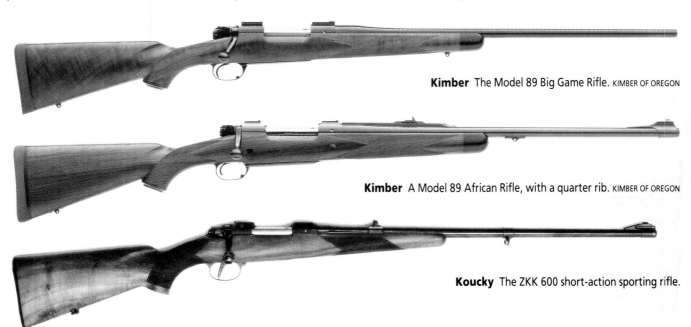

Kimber The Model 89 Big Game Rifle. KIMBER OF OREGON

Kimber A Model 89 African Rifle, with a quarter rib. KIMBER OF OREGON

Koucky The ZKK 600 short-action sporting rifle.

bolt face, preventing double loading. The standard trigger mechanism was an excellent single pattern, though a special set design could be obtained for the ZKK 600 and ZKK 601. This could be recognised by an auxiliary blade set into the main trigger lever.

The mechanism was set simply by pushing the lever forward, after which a light pressure on the auxiliary blade fired the gun. A small open back sight was set into the receiver bridge, where it could be raised when required, though a folding-leaf sight was often also mounted on the barrel. A rotary safety lay on the right side of the bolt shroud.

Designed for cartridges with an overall length of 80mm and a maximum case diameter of 12mm, the ZKK 600 has been chambered for ·270 Winchester, 7 × 57mm, 7 × 64mm, ·30–06 Springfield, 8 × 57mm, 8 × 60mm, 8 × 64mm (all with five-round magazines) and 10·75 × 68mm (four rounds).

The standard half-stock originally offered a niggardly proportioned fore-end; most butts have had straight combs, but Monte Carlo patterns have occasionally been offered for use with high-mounted optical sights. The pistol grip and the rounded-tip fore-end were chequered, the receiver was usually phosphated, and most of the other metal parts were blued. Most rifles displayed the Zbrojovka Brno trademark, MADE IN CZECHOSLOVAKIA, the designation, and dated proof marks (e.g., '68' for 1968).

The ZKK 601, designed for cartridges with a 70mm overall length, has chambered the ·222 Remington, ·222 Remington Magnum, ·243 Winchester or ·308 Winchester rounds. Magazines held five rounds, or six in ·222 only. A typical gun was 1,095mm overall, had a 600mm barrel and weighed 2·95lb.

Developed for cartridges with a maximum overall length of 95mm and a body diameter no greater than 14mm, the ZKK 602 has chambered the ·358 Norma Magnum, ·375 H&H Magnum, ·404 Jeffrey or ·458 Winchester rounds. A typical rifle had a 635mm barrel, measured 1,150mm overall and weighed about 4·20kg. The depth of the fore-end was increased

to accommodate a five-round magazine and recoil bolts were fitted through the stock.

ZKB 680

Made by Československá Zbrojovka, Brno.
·222 Remington only.
Action: as ZKK 600, above.
1,077mm overall, 2·62kg without magazine.
600mm barrel, 6-groove rifling; RH, concentric.
Detachable box magazine, 5 rounds.
Ramp-pattern sight.
950 m/sec with 3·2-gram bullet.

☆

1968: this rifle was little more than a ZKW 465 with a short Mauser action instead of the simplified 'miniature' pattern. A wing-type safety lay on the bolt shroud and a box magazine was used. The half-stock generally offered a low Monte Carlo comb, chequering on the pistol grip and fore-end, and a contrasting fore-end tip. A double set trigger was often fitted.

KRAG-JØRGENSEN

NORWAY

The Krag bolt-action rifle has a distinctive 'case' magazine in the receiver beneath the bolt, feeding cartridges laterally. The Danish loading gate hinges forward; US and Norwegian patterns hinge down. The comparatively weak one-lug action, which precluded the adoption of high power cartridges, caused the rapid replacement of the US Krag-Jørgensen by the ·30 Springfield magazine rifle (q.v.), which was a modified Mauser. Most of the Danish and Norwegian guns, however, lasted into the 1950s.

MILITARY RIFLES

DENMARK

1887: aware that their standard Remington rolling-block infantry rifles were obsolescent, the Danes sought an alternative. Five hundred

Lee-type Førsøgsrepetergevær m/1 ('Model 1 repeating trials rifle') were issued in April but, though reports indicated great superiority over the Remingtons, the rifle commission was not convinced.

1889: after tests had been undertaken with the latest weapons, including the Lebel and some Mannlichers, the Krag-Jørgensen was adopted.

Model 1889

Infantry rifle: Geværer m/89, m/89–08 og m/89–10.
Made by Geværfabriken Kjobenhavn and Københavns Tøjhus, Copenhagen, 1890–1915; and Hærens Tøjhus, Copenhagen, 1915–21.
Quantity: about 118,000.
8 × 58mm, rimmed.
Turning-bolt action, with a single lug on the bolt head locking into the receiver and the guide rib abutting the receiver bridge.
1,328mm overall, 4·58kg unladen.
950mm barrel, 6-groove rifling; RH, polygonal.
Integral pan magazine, 5 rounds.
Leaf sight graduated to 2,000 metres (see notes).
600 m/sec with m/89 ball cartridges.
m/89 knife or m/15 sword bayonets.

☆

1889: accepted in June, the original rifle was sighted for the 8mm m/89 cartridge, with a 250-metre standing block and a leaf graduated to 1,800 metres. A notch in the leaf-top sufficed for 2,000 metres. The gun lacked any safety features other than the potentially dangerous half-cock notch. It had a barrel jacket inspired by the Gew.88, a straight-gripped stock, two barrel bands, and a hooked cocking piece spur.

1890: the first series-made guns were accepted on 19 January, bulk deliveries commencing in the summer.

1908: on 19 September, the Danes adopted the pointed-bullet m/08 cartridge (muzzle velocity: 750 m/sec) and the sights were modified to give a maximum range of 2,100 metres. The auxiliary sights for the m/89 cartridge on the left side of the barrel band and the back-sight notch plate were discarded.

1910: a cocking-piece safety catch credited to

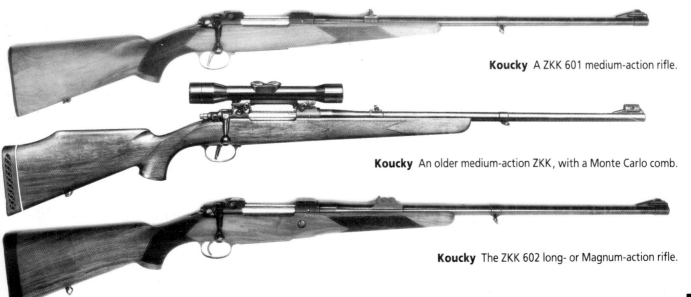

Koucky A ZKK 601 medium-action rifle.

Koucky An older medium-action ZKK, with a Monte Carlo comb.

Koucky The ZKK 602 long- or Magnum-action rifle.

C.C.G. Barry, an armourer attached to the Royal Danish Life Guards, was added to the right side of the receiver behind the bolt handle with effect from 23 June; most pre-1910 survivors were adapted when returning for repair.

1915: guns made or thoroughly overhauled after February were given new barrels with a modified chamber.

1916: the m/15 sword bayonet superseded the m/89 knife type on 22 August.

1917: a few m/16 periscope sights were issued.

1925: six-groove Rasmussen rifling was replaced by a four-groove concentric type on new barrels.

1939: some surviving m/89–10 rifles were issued to the Royal Danish Navy to replace venerable m/67–96 and m/67–97 Remingtons.

1942: the Germans sequestered roughly 60,000 assorted Krag rifles and carbines, then an extra 50,000 after finally disarming the Danish forces on 29 August 1943.

Model 1889

Cavalry carbine: Ryttergevær or Ryttekarabin m/89.
Made by Københavns Tøjhus, Copenhagen, 1912–13.
Quantity: about 2,600.
8 × 58mm, rimmed.
Action: as m/89 rifle, above.
1,100mm overall, 4·04kg unladen.
600mm barrel, 6-groove rifling; RH, polygonal.
Internal pan magazine, 5 rounds.
Tangent-leaf sight graduated to 2,000 metres.
About 620 m/sec with m/08 ball cartridges.
No bayonet.
☆

1912: the standard Danish cavalry carbine or Ryttergevær m/89 (renamed 'Ryttekarabin' in 1924), little more than a shortened version of the infantry rifle, was adopted after experiments that had lasted for years. The barrel jacket of the rifle was substituted by a conventional wooden hand guard, the butt plate was omitted, and a new back sight was developed. A large grooved stud was screwed laterally into the left side of the stock-wrist, level with the back of the trigger guard, to accept the m/05 leather suspender carried over the cavalryman's back.

1913: work in Copenhagen ceased after a short run of guns with 'R' prefixed numbers.

Model 1889

Engineer carbine: Ingeniørkarabin m/89.
Made by Hærens Tøjhus, Copenhagen, 1917–18.
Quantity: approximately 4,000.
8 × 58mm, rimmed.
Details generally similar to m/1889 cavalry carbine, excepting that the m/15 sword bayonet was used.

1917: approved as a rifle. Though resembling the contemporary cavalry carbine, it had barrel bands closer to the muzzle and accepted a bayonet. There was only a single production run, gun-numbers being prefixed by 'I'. The earliest issues were made in May 1918.

1924: the rifle was reclassified as a carbine.

Model 1889–23

Cavalry carbine: Ryttekarabin m/89–23.
Made by Hærens Rustkammer, Copenhagen, 1923–6.
Quantity: about 4,600.
8 × 58mm, rimmed.
Details generally similar to m/1889 cavalry carbine, excepting that the m/15 sword bayonet was used.
☆

1922: experimental short Krag-Jørgensens were made for the border guards and customs service.

1923: additional trials led to the approval of the m/89–23 on 28 June. Most were converted from old m/89–10 rifles. It is believed that only a few hundred of the m/89–23 carbines were newly made. They all exhibit Rasmussen polygonal rifling, abandoned in 1925.

Model 1889–24

Infantry carbine: Fodfolkskarabin m/89–24.
Made by Hærens Rustkammer, Copenhagen, 1923–32; and Hærens Vaabenarsenal, Copenhagen, 1932–40.
Quantity: see notes.
8 × 58mm, rimmed.
Turning-bolt action, with a single lug on the bolt head locking into the receiver.

1,105mm overall, 3·96kg unladen.
610mm barrel, 6-groove rifling; RH, polygonal.
Internal pan magazine, 5 rounds.
Tangent-leaf sight graduated to 2,000 metres.
About 620 m/sec with m/08 ball cartridges.
m/15 sword bayonet.
☆

1923: the first examples of this short rifle were converted from old infantry patterns. Back sights were replaced, but the barrel jacket and the original band arrangements were retained. Converted weapons were given an 'F' prefix to their serial numbers and can be distinguished by old marks on the receiver: e.g., GEVÆRFABRIKEN KJOBENHAVN 1893 M.89.

1925: the Rasmussen polygonal rifling was abandoned in favour of a more conventional four-groove concentric pattern.

1928: the chambering was revised in January. Issue was extended to the infantry machine-gun companies during the year.

1929: production of a few new guns began in the Copenhagen factory. Their receivers bear the correct designation—e.g., HÆRENS RUSTKAMMER 1931 M.89–24—to distinguish them from the conversions. Serial numbers have an 'F' prefix.

1930: important modifications in the trigger mechanism were introduced in September.

1931: issue of the m/89–24 was extended to mortar units, and then to the crews of anti-tank guns in 1937.

1944: shortages caused production to resume. Poor condition of the machinery and constant sabotage restricted output to less than 3,500 guns (April 1944–May 1945). Most were m/89–24 infantry carbines.

Model 1889–24

Artillery carbine: Artillerikarabin m/89–24.
Made by Hærens Rustkammer, Copenhagen, 1925–30.
Quantity: approximately 5,000, including the conversions.
8 × 58mm, rimmed.
Otherwise similar to the m/89–23 cavalry carbine; no bayonet.
☆

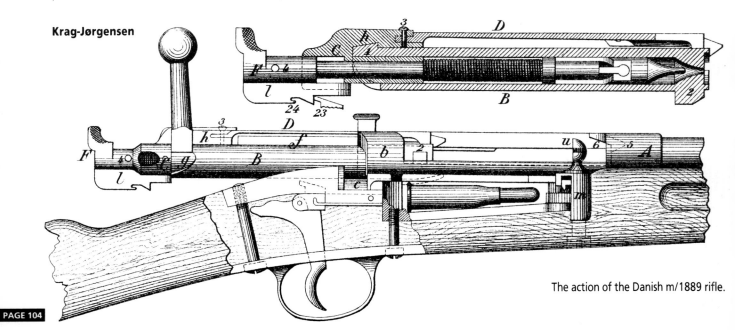

Krag-Jørgensen

The action of the Danish m/1889 rifle.

1925: the first batches of these guns were converted from m/89 infantry rifles. Otherwise essentially similar to the 1924-pattern infantry carbine, they retained the original leaf sight. A large triangular sling swivel lay on the second barrel band—the infantry type had been rectangular—and a large stud protruded from the left side of the straight stock-wrist behind the trigger guard. The bolt handle turned down towards the stock, a grasping groove was let into the fore-end, and a brass marking disc appeared on the right side of the butt.

NORWAY

1887: Ole Krag, director of the government small-arms factory in Kongsberg, reported that progress in Denmark would soon make the then-new Norwegian Jarmann rifle obsolete. In January 1888, therefore, the Defence Ministry sanctioned trials to find a new small-calibre service rifle.
1892: extensive trials had narrowed the choice to guns submitted by Mauser, Mannlicher and Krag & Jørgensen.
1893: the commission made its final report on 3 May. A Krag-Jørgensen was unanimously approved, fifty hand-made experimental guns being ordered from Kongsberg to facilitate troop trials in the late summer.
1894: the rifle was adopted on 21 April.

Model 1894

Infantry rifles: Krag-Jørgensengevær M/1894 og M/1894–43.
Made by Österreichische Waffenfabriks-Gesellschaft, Steyr, 1895–8 (29,000 guns); Fabrique Nationale d'Armes de Guerre, Herstal-lèz-Liége, 1895 (a few); and Kongsberg Våpenfabrikk, 1896–1935 (125,000).
Quantity: about 155,000.
6·5 × 55mm, rimless.
Turning-bolt action, with a single lug on the bolt head locking into the receiver and the bolt-guide rib abutting the bridge.
1,260mm overall, 4·05kg unladen.
760mm barrel, 4-groove rifling; LH, concentric.
Internal pan magazine, 5 rounds.
Tangent-leaf sight graduated to 2,000 metres.
730 m/sec with M/97 ball cartridges.
M/1894 knife or M/1912 sword bayonets.

1894: the Norwegian Krag was a considerable improvement on the Danish m/1889 (q.v.). Its rimless cartridge minimised feed troubles, while the downward-hinged magazine gate doubled as a loading platform.

Like all Krags, the M/1894 magazine could be replenished even when the action was cocked and locked, though a rotary cut-off isolated the magazine when required. The locking lug turned down into the receiver immediately behind the chamber, additional security being provided by the abutment of the bolt guide rib on the front of the receiver bridge and by the bolt handle seating in the receiver.

The rifles had an elegant pistol-grip walnut stock (later birch) with a grasping groove beneath the back sight. A hand guard ran from the receiver ring to the rear barrel band. The bands were retained by springs let into the left side of the stock, and did not touch the 'floating' barrel. Swivels usually lay on the upper band and on the underside of the butt, while a stacking swivel was fitted on the fore-band. A half-length cleaning rod was carried under the barrel. Sights were graduated for the M/94 cartridge, and a Mauser-type safety lay on the cocking piece. The later navy guns lacked the butt-trap.
1897: the combination bolt-stop/hold-open was abandoned. Whether changes were made for the improved cartridge is not known, as the trajectory of the M/94 and M/97 seems to have been similar.
1901: the navy received rifles taken from the commercial series (numbered 2511–3010, and apparently 3011–5906).
1905: Kongsberg began the adaption of a thousand standard rifles (89601–90600) to accept German Ajack 4 × optical sights for issue to marksmen, work being completed in 1907. The sights proved to be unreliable in sub-zero conditions and so the guns reverted to standard form after the introduction of the m/23.

1923: experiments with pointed bullets, begun in 1905, culminated in the adoption of the M/1923 spitzer. Revisions to the back sight—which was graduated to 2,200 metres—were not completed until 1938!
1943: some M/1894 rifles were modified to M/1912 short-rifle length in 1943, during the German occupation. Fitted with front sight protectors, these 'M/94/43' Krag-Jørgensens displayed German ordnance marks.

Model 1895

Cavalry carbine: Krag-Jørgensenkarabin for Kavaleriet, M/1895.
Made by Kongsberg Våpenfabrikk, 1896–1912.
Quantity: 5,000.
6·5 × 55mm, rimless.
Action: as M/1894 rifle, above.
1,015mm overall, 3·40kg unladen.
520mm barrel, 4-groove rifling; LH, concentric.
Internal pan magazine, 5 rounds.
Tangent-leaf sight graduated to 2,000 metres.
640 m/sec with M/1923 ball cartridges.
No bayonet.

☆

1895: this neat half-stock carbine had a short hand guard running from the receiver ring to the back sight base. Its action was identical with the M/1894 rifle. The fore-end, narrowing abruptly to save weight, was retained by a single sprung barrel band. Swivels lay on the left side of the band and under the butt behind the pistol grip.
1897: the hold-open/bolt-stop was abandoned.
1908: carbines made until production ceased had the rear swivel on the left side of the guard.

Model 1897

Mountain artillery and engineer carbine: Krag-Jørgensenkarabin for bergartilleriet og ingeniørvåpnet, M/1897.
Made by Kongsberg Våpenfabrikk, 1897–1911.
Quantity: less than 2,000.
6·5 × 55mm, rimless.
Otherwise generally as M/95.

☆

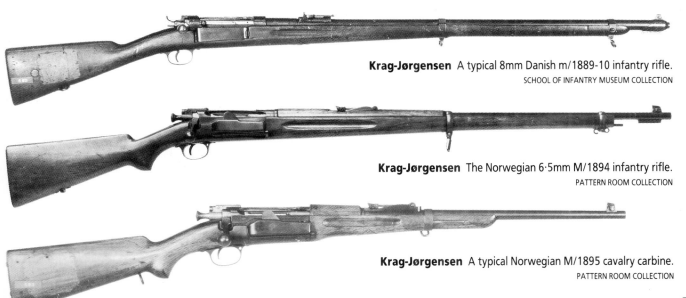

Krag-Jørgensen A typical 8mm Danish m/1889-10 infantry rifle.
SCHOOL OF INFANTRY MUSEUM COLLECTION

Krag-Jørgensen The Norwegian 6·5mm M/1894 infantry rifle.
PATTERN ROOM COLLECTION

Krag-Jørgensen A typical Norwegian M/1895 cavalry carbine.
PATTERN ROOM COLLECTION

1897: this was practically identical with the cavalry carbine described previously, excepting that the rear swivel lay 10cm from the toe of the butt instead of behind the pistol grip.

Model 1904

Engineer carbine: Krag-Jørgensenkarabin for ingeniørvåpnet, M/1904.
Made by Kongsberg Våpenfabrikk, 1904–15.
Quantity: a few thousands.
6·5 × 55mm, rimless.
Action: as M/1894 rifle, above.
1,015mm overall, 3·81kg unladen.
520mm barrel, 4-groove rifling; LH, concentric.
Internal pan magazine, 5 rounds.
Tangent-leaf sight graduated to 2,000 metres.
640 m/sec with M/1923 ball cartridges.
M/1894 knife or M/1912 sword bayonets.

☆

1904: similar to the M/1897, this was stocked to the muzzle and had two spring-retained barrel bands. The full-length hand guard and half-length cleaning rod increased the overall weight, while swivels lay under the front barrel band and on the left side of the trigger guard.

Model 1907

Field-artillery carbine: Krag-Jørgensenkarabin for feltartilleriet, M/1907.
Made by Kongsberg Våpenfabrikk, 1907–15.
Quantity: perhaps 2,000.
6·5 × 55mm, rimless.
Action: as M/1894 rifle, above.
1,015mm overall, 3·81kg unladen.
520mm barrel, 4-groove rifling; LH, concentric.
Internal pan magazine, 5 rounds.
Tangent-leaf sight graduated to 2,000 metres.
640 m/sec with M/1923 ball cartridges.
M/1894 knife or M/1912 sword bayonets.

☆

1907: this was introduced to replace the M/1895 cavalry carbine in the field artillery. It was identical with the M/1904 pattern described above, apart from the position of the swivels—one on the left side of the rear barrel band and the other on the under-edge of the butt about 10cm from the toe.

Model 1912

Short rifle: Krag-Jørgensenkarabin, M/1912.
Made by Kongsberg Våpenfabrikk, 1912–35.
Quantity: 30,120.
6·5 × 55mm, rimless.
Action: as M/1894 rifle, above.
1,106mm overall, 4·02kg unladen.
610mm barrel, 4-groove rifling; LH, concentric.
Internal pan magazine, 5 rounds.
710 m/sec with M/1923 ball cartridges.
M/1912 sword bayonet.

☆

1909: trials began with a shortened Krag-Jørgensen for universal issue. Prototypes had an assortment of pivoting or rod bayonets.

1912: adoption of the M/1912 was approved. The walnut pistol-gripped stock—birch in later examples—had a full-length hand guard with a grasping groove beneath the M/1894 tangent sight, which virtually abutted the receiver ring. The guard extended to a nose cap from which only a small portion of the muzzle protruded. The bayonet lug lay under the nose cap, while the single barrel band carried a sling swivel on the left side. The short cleaning rod could be pushed through an eye on the nose cap during stacking. The second swivel lay on the under-edge of the butt, an auxiliary sling-hole being bored through the trigger-guard bow.

1916: field service revealed a weakness in the stock where it joined the nose cap. A steel collar integral with the nose cap was added to guns made after 1916, older guns receiving an auxiliary bolted-on band when returning for repair. Army guns numbered below 21678 had bent-down bolt handles, but subsequent ones were straight.

1923: the back sight was revised for the M/1923 cartridge, and graduated to 2,200 metres. The alterations were made over a period of years. However, the M/1912 was not as successful as had been hoped and never entirely replaced the M/94 in Norwegian service.

USA

1890: worried by advances in Europe, the US Army decided to hold a competition to find a suitable small-bore magazine rifle.

1892: trials with more than fifty guns were concluded in August. Among the submissions had been several Krag-Jørgensen rifles. Krag no.1 was the 8mm Danish m/89; Krag no.2 was a similar gun in ·30-calibre with a Mauser-type safety, a pivoting ejector and a different cocking piece; Krag no.3 was identical to no.2, but had greater head-space; Krag no.4 was no.2 with a dust cover over the bolt and a downward-opening loading gate; Krag no.5 was the same as no.4, without the dust cover; and Krag no.6 was a variant of no.5 for a rimless .30 cartridge.

The trials resolved in favour of Lee no.3, Belgian-type Mauser no.5 and Krag no.5; the Krag was preferred simply because fresh cartridges could be inserted in the magazine when the bolt was shut on a loaded chamber.

Model 1892

Infantry rifle.
Made by the National Armory, Springfield, Massachusetts, 1894–7.
Quantity: 24,560.
·30–40, rimmed.
Turning-bolt action, with a single lug on the bolt head locking into the receiver.
49·01in overall, 9·38lb unladen.
30·00in barrel, 4-groove rifling; RH, concentric.
Internal pan magazine, 5 rounds.
Tangent-leaf sight graduated to 1,900 yards.
2,000 ft/sec with M1895 ball cartridges.
M1892 sword bayonet.

☆

1892: the 'US Magazine Rifle, Caliber ·30, Model of 1892' was officially adopted on 15 September, though production was deferred while trials were undertaken with additional indigenous rifles.

The straight-grip walnut stock had a grasping groove in the fore-end and a hand guard from the breech to the barrel band. An open stacking

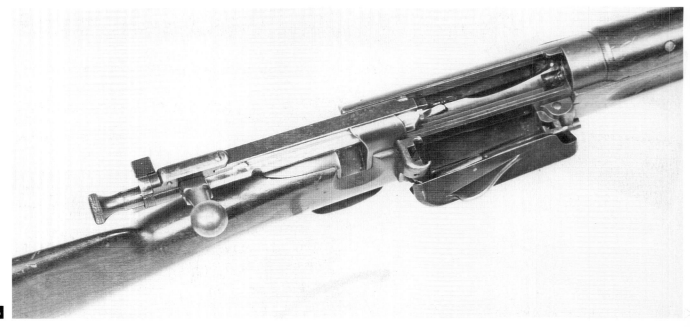

swivel was attached to the the nose cap, and a lug beneath the nose cap accepted a short sword bayonet of Swiss pattern. A full-length cleaning rod protruded below the muzzle. The original M1892 back sight was a tangent leaf pattern, graduated 300–600 yards on its stepped base and 700–1900 yards on the leaf. No azimuth adjustment was provided.

1894: the first M1892 rifles were assembled in Springfield Armory on 1 January, but issues were delayed until 6 October.

1895: the original flat butt-plate was replaced by a rounded pattern from 23 December.

1896: by the end of the year, forty changes had been made to the M1892. However, few guns received all the minor modifications owing to the adoption of the M1896.

1897: M1892 rifles altered to 1896 standards after March can be identified by filled rod channels in the fore-end, butts that accept the three-piece rod, the substitution of the M1896 back sight for the M1892 type—often later replaced by the M1901—and the addition of a bolt hold-open notch in the receiver for the extractor pin. Modified rifles do not bear MODEL 1896 on the side plate; marks read '1892'.

Model 1896

Infantry rifle.
Made by the National Armory, Springfield, Massachusetts, 1896–9.
Quantity: about 62,000.
·30–40, rimmed.
Action: as M1892, above.
49·10in overall, 8·94lb unladen.
30·00in barrel, 4-groove rifling; RH, concentric.
Internal pan magazine, 5 rounds.
Tangent-leaf sight graduated to 1,800 yards.
2,000 ft/sec with M1895 ball cartridges.
M1892 sword bayonet.

☆

1896: there was little difference between this rifle, standardised on 19 February, and the last of the preceding (and much modified) 1892-type guns. However, it had a radically different back sight and the three-piece cleaning rod

was carried in a butt-trap. The M1896 sight had a 'stepless' or continuously curved base, graduated from 275 to 650 yards; the leaf sufficed for 700–1,800 yards, though azimuth adjustments were still absent.

Model 1896

Cavalry carbine.
Made by the National Armory, Springfield, Massachusetts, 1896–9.
Quantity: about 22,500.
·30–40, rimmed.
Action: as M1892, above.
41·15in overall, 7·75lb unladen.
22·00in barrel, 4-groove rifling; RH, concentric.
Internal pan magazine, 5 rounds.
Tangent-leaf sight graduated to 2,000 yards.
About 1,750 ft/sec with M1895 ball cartridges.
No bayonet.

☆

1893: the first Krag carbines were made for trials by shortening M1892 rifles by about eight inches. A cleaning rod was carried in the stock, a saddle ring appeared on the left side of the wrist and the nose cap lacked a bayonet lug.

1895: a perfected carbine was approved on 17 May. It had a thin-wrist stock, and a saddle ring and bar assembly on the left side of the stock above the trigger guard. A two-piece cleaning rod and an oiler were carried in a butt-trap. Carbine sights were practically identical with those of the rifles, but the leaves bore a large C.

1900: cut-offs were reversed.

1901: 1896-type carbines were withdrawn for militia use, most being fitted with the 1899-type stock before issue. Survivors were among 9,000 assorted Krags sold to Cuba in 1912.

Model 1898

Infantry rifle.
Made by the National Armory, Springfield, Massachusetts, 1898–1904.
Quantity: 324,280.
·30–40, rimmed.
Action: as M1892, above.

49·13in overall, 9·00lb unladen.
30·00in barrel, 4-groove rifling; RH, concentric.
Internal pan magazine, 5 rounds.
Tangent-leaf sight graduated to 2,000 yards.
2,200 ft/sec with high-velocity ball cartridges.
M1892 sword bayonet.

☆

1898: approved on 14 March, this was the first major revision of the basic US Krag service rifle. The machining of the bolt mechanism, receiver and the magazine loading gate was simplified, the bolt-handle seat being milled flush with the receiver. The first M1898 rifles were delivered from Springfield in July. They had the M1898 or Dickson-pattern sight with an azimuth adjustment and a binding screw on the slider. The sight was graduated to 2,000 yards for a new high-velocity cartridge.

1899: the first M1898 rifles and the new high-power cartridge reached service in October. Some of the guns made in this period were distinguished by a short-lived headless cocking piece, which was abandoned in 1900. This was intended to reduce lock time, but prevented the mechanism being re-cocked after a misfire.

1900: the magazine cut-off mechanism had been experimentally reversed in 1897, when a few rifles had been modified for trials, but nothing was done until the change was applied to service weapons made after February 1900. In mid-summer, 100 rifles were converted to the Parkhurst & Warren charger system; tests were favourable, but better progress was being made with the M1900 trials rifle (see 'Springfield').

1901: the disappearance of the high velocity ·30 cartridge, which had been withdrawn in March 1900 once broken locking-lugs had been reported, heralded the M1901 (Buffington) sight. This was identified by a stepless base graduated for 100–500 yards. The elongated leaf was graduated to 2,300 yards, the slider could be fitted with an aperture, and azimuth adjustments were made by pivoting the entire sight before locking it with a clamp screw.

1902: the M1902 Dickson-type tangent sight, graduated for 200–2,000 yards, was similar to the 1898 pattern. However, it had one sight

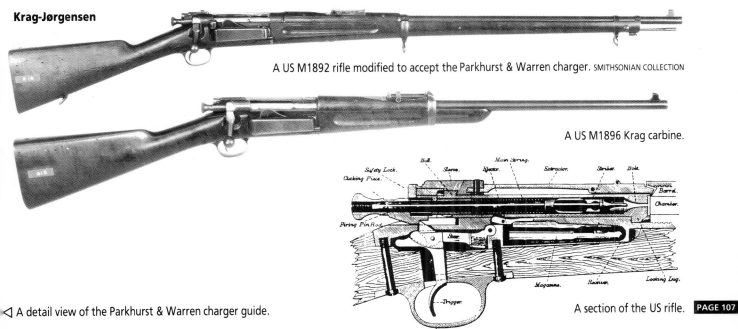

Krag-Jørgensen

A US M1892 rifle modified to accept the Parkhurst & Warren charger. SMITHSONIAN COLLECTION

A US M1896 Krag carbine.

◁ A detail view of the Parkhurst & Warren charger guide.

A section of the US rifle.

notch instead of three, and a spring plunger in the slider engaged the leaf-edge serrations.

Model 1898

Cavalry carbine.
Made by the National Armory, Springfield, Massachusetts, 1898–9.
Quantity: about 5,000.
·30–40, rimmed.
Action: as M1892, above.
41·15in overall, 7·80lb unladen.
22·00in barrel, 4-groove rifling; RH, concentric.
Internal pan magazine, 5 rounds.
Tangent-leaf sight graduated to 2,000 yards.
About 1,970 ft/sec with M1898 ball cartridges.
No bayonet.

☆

1898: this carbine was essentially similar to the M1896, but had the improved 1898-pattern rifle action. Few were made, as the high velocity cartridges for which the back sight had been graduated proved troublesome. Many of these guns were recalled in the early 1900s to receive 1899-type stocks and new sights.

Model 1899

Cavalry carbine.
Made by the National Armory, Springfield, Massachusetts, 1899–1904.
Quantity: 36,050.
·30–40, rimmed.
Otherwise generally as M1898 carbine excepting weight (about 7·87lb).

☆

1899: derived from the M1898, this Krag carbine had a plain stock with the fore-end lengthened by about three inches. It was initially fitted with the 1896-pattern back sight.
1900: about a hundred guns, and a similar quantity of M1898 rifles (q.v.), were adapted for the Parkhurst & Warren Device. This quick-loading system was soon abandoned, as the contemporaneous Mauser-type trials rifle (see 'Springfield') showed greater promise.
1902: a new hand guard was approved, with a special faired projection at the front of the sight base to protect the sight leaf when the carbine was thrust in its saddle scabbard, and the 1901-type Buffington sight replaced the 1896 type.

Philippine Constabulary Model

Carbine-type short rifle.
Converted by the National Armory, Springfield, Massachusetts, 1906–10; Rock Island Arsenal, Illinois, 1908–10; and the Manila ordnance depot, 1910–14.
Quantity: about 9,800.
·30–40, rimmed.
Action: as M1892, above.
41·15in overall, 8·03lb unladen.
22·00in barrel, 4-groove rifling; RH, concentric.
Internal pan magazine, 5 rounds.
Tangent-leaf sight graduated to 2,000 yards.
About 1,750 ft/sec with M1892 ball cartridges.
M1892 sword bayonet.

☆

1906: many old Krag-Jørgensen rifles were transformed into a 'Carbine M1899, altered for Knife Bayonet and Rifle Sling', originally authorised when Springfield modified 350 for Girard College in Philadelphia; 9,450 others were converted in 1907–14 to provide native troops in the Philippines with 'rifles' befitting their small stature. Some work was undertaken in the USA, but much was done in Manila.

Krag-Jørgensen The Danish m/1889 magazine.

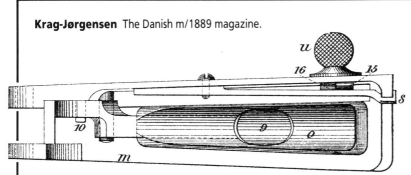
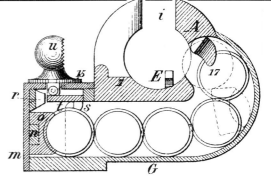

KRAG-JØRGENSEN
THE LESSER PATTERNS

DENMARK

m/1928 rifle Adopted in February 1928, a few hundred of these marksmen's rifles (Finskydningsgevær) were made by Hærens Rustkammer of Copenhagen prior to 1931. The rifle was little more than an infantry weapon with a large-diameter parallel-side free floating barrel. Though a hand guard stretched to the tip of the fore-end of the walnut half-stock, the woodwork was kept from direct contact with the barrel surface. A hooded-blade or globe front sight replaced the open barleycorn found on other Danish Krags, while a micro-adjustable aperture back sight on the left side of the receiver replaced the standard tangent pattern. Virtually all m/28 rifles chambered the 8mm m/08 cartridge; a typical gun was 1,170mm long and weighed 5·36kg. The 585mm barrel was rifled with four grooves twisting towards the right. They were numbered in the same series as m/89–24 infantry carbines, but their actions displayed 'fsk' and 'm/1928'.

¶ A new lightweight spurless cocking piece was introduced in 1929 to reduce lock time. Older guns were modified while under repair. Bolt handles were turned downward on newly made rifles from 1930 onward.

m/1928–31 rifle In 1932, a few of these marksman's rifles were made for the rimless 6·5 × 55mm Norwegian rifle cartridge. Apparently intended for military style 300-metre target-shooting, they are rarely encountered outside Scandinavian collections.

NORWAY

M/1906 cadet carbine The 6·5mm Krag-Jørgensenkarabin for Skoler was identical with the M/95 cavalry carbine excepting for the omission of the hand guard to save weight. These cadet carbines—colloquially known as 'gutte karabin' or "boys' carbines"—were used for marksmanship training in the Norwegian secondary schools, where shooting at 100 metres with reduced-charge ammunition was regularly practised. About 3,320 were made by Kongsberg Våpenfabrikk in 1906–12.

M/1923 rifle This marksman's rifle (Skarpskyttegevær) replaced the M/1894 pattern as the latter's Ajack optical sight had proved unreliable in sub-zero conditions. The M/23 rifle had an open micro-adjustable aperture sight ('Dioptersikte M/23'), graduated to 1,000 metres, and a full-length stock with a hand guard, two barrel bands, and a M/1912-type nose cap. The radius of the pistol grip was rather sharper than the standard M/1894

pattern and chequering improved grip. The special heavy 'floating' 665mm barrel had a muzzle diameter of 17mm rather than the standard 15mm. Sling swivels lay on the underside of the second barrel band and on the under-edge of the butt. About 320 M/1923 rifles were made by Kongsberg Våpenfabrikk in 1923–5, but virtually all were subsequently converted to M/1930 standards.

M/1925 rifle This marksman's rifle was little more than an infantry rifle with the aperture sight. However, the new rifle also had a large-diameter heavy barrel and a front sight with eared protectors. The guns were apparently numbered in the standard M/94 series, but their receivers displayed 'M.25' in addition to 'M/1894'. About 110 were made at Kongsberg Våpenfabrikk in 1926–7.

M/1930 The perfected 6·5mm Krag-Jørgensen marksman's rifle had a half-stock and a free-floating super-heavy 760mm barrel with a muzzle diameter of 21mm. A single broad band retained the barrel and the hand guard. The blade-type front sight had a tubular protector; swivels lay on the under-edge of the butt and under the fore-end behind the band; and receivers bore additional 'M/30' marks. About 150 guns were made in the Kongsberg factory in 1931–4, and about ninety M/23 rifles were converted to 1930 standards. These can be

recognised by the older marks on the receiver.

USA

M1896 cadet rifle. Adopted in December 1895, this is rarely encountered. It was similar to the standard 1896-type infantry rifle, but had a full length cleaning rod and a barrel-band spring. Cadet rifles originally lacked swivels. About 400 were made in Springfield Armory in 1896–7. They weighed 9·08lb and had tangent-leaf back sights graduated to 1,900 yards.

¶ In November 1900, all but a handful of guns were returned for the installation of swivels, and 1901-pattern back sights were fitted in 1902–3.

Board of Ordnance and Fortification rifle. A hundred of these experimental ·30–40 guns were made by the National Armory, Springfield, and issued for trials in the autumn of 1902. They shared the standard Krag action, but were 45·10in overall, had 26in barrels, and weighed 8·46lb. A special tangent-leaf sight was fitted and the M1892 sword bayonet could be attached at the muzzle. Muzzle velocity was about 1,910 ft/sec with M1892 ball cartridges. The short barrel increased muzzle blast and reduced accuracy, but the guns were well liked. However, progress being made with modified Mauser-type rifles was more encouraging.

SPORTING GUNS

Denmark Substantial numbers of Krag-type Salongevær and Salonkarabin m/89 were made for reduced-calibre training. They fired Flobert primer-propelled ammunition by means of a special chamber insert.

Single-shot target rifles were also made in a number of calibres, and actions were supplied to individual gunsmiths. These sporting rifles are uncommon, owing to the superiority of guns based on the Mannlicher and Mauser actions.

Norway About 33,900 army-type M/1894 rifles—numbered from 1—were made in the Kongsberg factory for private use, plus a further 4,500 (numbered 3001–7500) by Österreichische Waffenfabriks-Gesellschaft. Guns sold privately, or to the Norwegian rifle association, lacked the butt-trap found on army issue. Service-issue guns usually bore the 'OII' or 'H7' monograms of Oscar II and his successor, Haakon VII, but the bolts of commercial guns had an axe-carrying rampant lion.

Kongsberg also made approximately 1,590 commercial M/1912 short rifles. Sniper rifles were sold in this way—including 310 M/23 (2001–2310), 1,080 M/25 and a few M/30. After the end of the Second World War, 'new' Krag-Jørgensens were assembled from M/1912 carbine actions and surplus Colt machine-gun barrels. Their chambers were suitably strengthened for the 7·9mm German service cartridge. Sold commercially for target shooting, the M/48/51 had an aperture sight in front of the chamber whereas the M/48/53 had a folding open sight for 100–300 metres.

USA The issue of sufficient M1903 rifles (Springfields) allowed the first large-scale withdrawal of Krags. In March 1905, therefore, an Act of Congress allowed members of the National Rifle Association to buy Krag rifles. Sales were very poor prior to 1917, but war familiarised so many Americans with the bolt action that the situation changed dramatically in the early 1920s. Many Krags were cut to carbine length and given rounded fore-ends (the 'NRA Carbine'), but others were properly re-modelled.

Though the Krag action was not especially strong, its smooth operating stroke and the renowned accuracy of the perfected rifles—appreciably better than the pre-1914 M1903 Springfields at all but long ranges—prompted gunsmiths to transform military-surplus actions into effectual sporters. Many were fitted with high-quality Stevens-Pope barrels, while R.F. Sedgley, Inc. of Philadelphia marketed large numbers of Krag sporting rifles between the wars. Some retained their original ·30–40 chambering, while others were converted for ·25–35 WCF and a few for ·250–3000 Savage.

The Winchester cartridge was popular, as it had a light recoil and was more than adequate for small game, but the Savage pattern proved to be too powerful for the single locking lug of the Krag action. Sedgley seems to have withdrawn it in the early 1930s. By 1933, *The Rifleman*, the NRA journal, was already carrying warnings about the undesirablity of re-chambering Krags for the ·250–3000 cartridge.

KRAG-PETERSSON

NORWAY/SWEDEN

This quirky block-action magazine rifle, credited to Norwegian Ole Krag and Swedish engineer Axel Petersson, was inspired by the block-action Lee rifle of the early 1870s.

NORWAY

The basis of the Krag-Petersson mechanism was a hammer-like actuating lever above the breech. Pulling the lever back dropped the breech block to receive a cartridge from the magazine beneath the barrel, extracting the spent case as it did so. At the end of the stroke, the block halted and a new cartridge was pushed into the breech manually until it entered the chamber, riding over the extractor as it did so.

Pushing the operating lever half-forward until it was held on the trigger lever then closed the breech; pressing the trigger fired the gun.

Model 1876

Navy rifle: Marinen Repetergevær M/1876.
Made by Kongsberg Våpenfabrikk, 1876–7.
12·17mm, rimfire.
Pivoting-block action, operated by a hammer-lever.
1,250mm overall, 4·42kg unladen.
808mm barrel, 6-groove rifling; RH, polygonal.
Tube magazine under barrel, 9 rounds.
Ramp-and-leaf sight graduated to 2,200 alen?
About 365 m/sec with ball cartridges.
Sword bayonet.

☆

1876: the rifle had a two-piece stock, with a straight-wrist butt and three screwed barrel bands. One swivel lay under the middle band, with the other on the under-edge of the butt.

1878: a committee of Swedish and Norwegian officers, aware of its serious shortcomings, understandably rejected the Krag-Petersson in favour of the Jarmann (q.v.). The spurned rifle subsequently competed in Spain in 1881, with an equal lack of success.

DENMARK

Model 1877

Navy carbine: Flådens magasin-karabin m/1877.
Made by Geværfabrik Kjobenhavn, 1877–80.
Quantity: 1,500?
11·35mm, rimfire.
Action: as Norwegian M/1876, above.
952mm overall, 4·05kg unladen.
510mm barrel, 5-groove rifling; RH, concentric.
Tube magazine under barrel, 7 rounds.
Ramp-and-leaf sight graduated to 1,500 alen?
About 330 m/sec with standard ball rounds.
No bayonet.

☆

1877: the royal navy's magazine carbine was very similar to the Norwegian rifle, excepting in dimensions and magazine capacity. It lasted in front-line Danish service until the issue of Krag-Jørgensen rifles in the early 1890s.

The m/1877 had a two-piece stock and a barrel band with a swivel. The second swivel lay

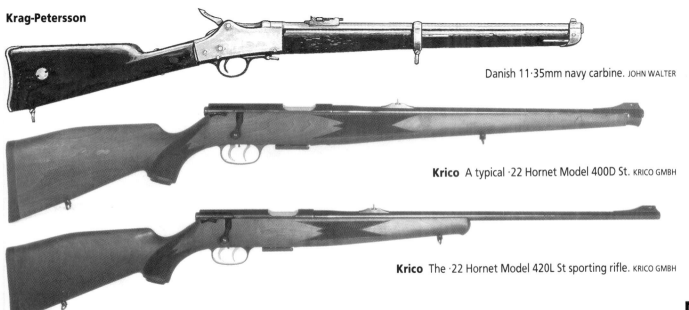

Krag-Petersson

Danish 11·35mm navy carbine. JOHN WALTER

Krico A typical ·22 Hornet Model 400D St. KRICO GMBH

Krico The ·22 Hornet Model 420L St sporting rifle. KRICO GMBH

on the under-edge of the butt. The fore-end ran to the muzzle, where the nose cap was retained by a sturdy cross-pin.

KRICO

GERMANY

Kriegeskorte & Co. ('Krico') began making sporting rifles on the basis of refurbished wartime Mauser (q.v.) actions, but then introduced a reduced-scale derivative in 1956. The first of the modern rifles appeared in 1962, distinguished by its streamlined bolt shroud and a radial safety catch above the stock behind the bolt handle.

Notes: Krico rifles have been offered in the USA under many names (e.g., 'Tradewinds Husky 5000'). The original importer was Tradewinds, Inc., of Tacoma, Washington (1968–82). After a short interregnum, the agency then passed to Beeman Precision Arms of Santa Rosa, California (1983–90), but is now in the hands of Mandall Shooting Supplies, Inc., of Scottsdale, Arizona. The Wolverine, sold by O&L Guns, Inc., of Seminole, Texas, was little more than a barrelled 700 Magnum action in a US-made stock; it was distinguished by a quarter rib on the barrel.

A few rifles were offered in the early 1980s as the '600EAC' or '700EAC', with straight-comb butts, rounded fore-ends and single-stage triggers. Production was very small. In addition, many designations have been seen with 'St' (Stecher) or 'E' (Einzelabzug) suffixes indicating the trigger design.

Model 400

400D, 400E, 420L, 430S and 440S patterns.
Made by Krico GmbH, Jagd- und Sportwaffenfabrik, Stuttgart.
·22 Hornet only.
Turning-bolt action, locked by a single lug and the bolt handle seating in the receiver.
DATA FOR A TYPICAL 400D
1,090mm overall, 3·23kg unladen.

600mm barrel, 4-groove rifling; RH, concentric.
Detachable box magazine, 5 rounds.
Ramp sight.
820 m/sec with 2·9-gram bullet.

☆

1983: these guns were based on the company's proven 300-series rimfires, with an extra locking lug behind the bolt-handle base.

The basic 400E rifle had a plain half-stock with a low Monte Carlo comb and a thin plastic or rubber shoulder plate. Simple chequering panels appeared on the pistol grip and fore-end, while swivels lay under the fore-end and butt. Williams ramp-type back sights were standard. The 400D was identical mechanically, but had a hog's back comb, a low squared cheek piece, and an imperceptibly schnabel-tipped fore-end; a thick rubber shoulder pad was used and the pistol grip had a separate cap. The 420L had a full-length Mannlicher stock and a 500mm barrel instead of 550mm.

The Krico 430S and 440S were target rifles; the former had a deep beavertail fore-end, whereas the latter had a slender fore-end with seven longitudinal slots. A double set trigger or a conventional match pattern was available, the latter being supplied to order.

Model 600

600A, 600D, 600DL, 601, 601K, 602, 602K, 603, 603K, 605, 605K, 606, 606K, 607, 607K, 620L, 620DL, 621, 622, 623, 625, 626, 630S, 640L, 640S, 640S Sniper, 641, 643 and 650S patterns.
Made by Krico GmbH, Jagd- und Sportwaffenfabrik, Stuttgart.
Chambering: see notes.
Turning-bolt action, locked by two lugs on the bolt head and the bolt handle seating in the receiver.
DATA FOR A TYPICAL 620L
5·6 × 50mm Magnum, rimless.
1,109mm overall, 3·42kg unladen.
550mm barrel, 4-groove rifling; RH, concentric.
Detachable box magazine, 3 rounds.
Ramp sight.
1,095 m/sec with 3·2-gram bullet.

☆

1962: the first of these guns was introduced to replace the previous Mauser-pattern rifle. The 600 series was built on a modified Mauser action, with dual opposed lugs on the bolt head and a simplified bolt shroud—black plastic on most guns. A small extractor claw was let into the side of the bolt head and a plunger-type ejector lay in the shrouded bolt face.

1964: chronology of the early rifles is difficult to unravel. By this date, however, a wide selection was being offered.

The original 600 series (Models 601–606) were similar short-action guns. They were about 1,110mm long, had 60cm barrels and weighed an average of 3·1kg. The back-sight block was usually regulated for 100 metres, with folding leaves for 200 and 300. The half-stocks had hog's back ('Bavarian') combs, low squared cheek pieces, and schnabel-tip fore-ends.

Chequered panels graced the pistol grip and fore-end. Dark plastic butt plates and pistol-grip caps were accompanied by white spacer plates, while swivels lay beneath the fore-end and butt. Detachable box magazines were standard, capacity being dependent on chambering. Guns in the 'K' series (601K–606K) were identical with the basic 600 pattern excepting that they had Monte Carlo butts and angular squared-tip fore-ends. Barrels were 600mm long, apart from ·222 (550mm) and 5·6 × 57mm (610mm).

The 620 series (621–626) was similar, but had 55cm barrels and were about 1,060mm overall. They had the full-length 'Mannlicher' fore-ends with sling loops and steel nose caps.

Intended for use under Deutsche Jägerschafts-Verband or Deutsche Schützenbund rules, the Models 641 and 643 competition rifles (·222 Remington and ·243 Winchester respectively) had high-comb Monte Carlo butts suited to optical sights. Their rounded fore-ends had oblique-cut rosewood fore-end tips. Double set triggers were standard, though single-trigger units could be supplied to order. A typical Model 643 was 1,110mm overall, had a 600mm barrel and weighed 3·5kg.

The basic Krico guns were all offered in the same five chamberings, the last digit of

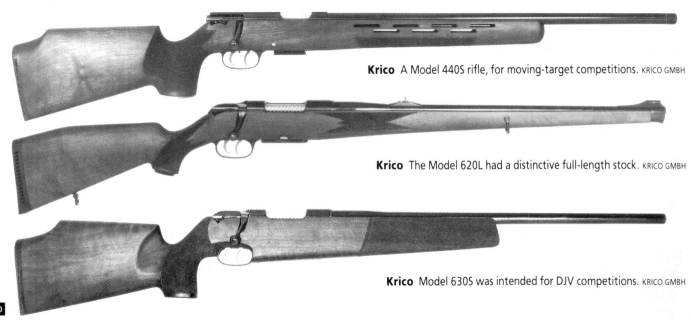

Krico A Model 440S rifle, for moving-target competitions. KRICO GMBH

Krico The Model 620L had a distinctive full-length stock. KRICO GMBH

Krico Model 630S was intended for DJV competitions. KRICO GMBH

the designation acting as an indicator—'1' for ·222 Remington; '2' for ·222 Remington Magnum; '3' for ·243 Winchester; '5' for ·308 Winchester; and '6' for 5·6 × 57mm. Thus the Model 602K accepted ·222 Remington Magnum cartridges, while Model 626 was chambered for 5·6 × 57mm. Most rifles sold in Europe were fitted with double set triggers, though many exported to North America had the simpler single-stage mechanism.

1966: a Model 607 appeared, chambered for the ·22–250 Remington round. It does not seem to have been popular and had been discontinued by 1969; however, the 607K rifle appears to have lasted into the early 1980s.

1983: the range was extensively redesigned, use of identifying suffixes being abandoned. The new basic models were the Krico 600 and 620, available in a selection of chamberings. The guns all had walnut stocks, with a distinctive hog's back comb and the Bavarian-type cheek piece, though there were appreciable differences in the fore-ends.

The half-stock of the plainly finished Model 600A ended in a shallow schnabel-tipped fore-end. A thin rubber shoulder plate was standard. Swivel eyes were fitted, but not open sights. The 600mm barrels were chambered only for ·222 Remington, ·243 Winchester or ·308 Winchester.

Krico 600D rifles had better-quality stocks than the 600A pattern, though comparable mechanically. Ventilated rubber shoulder plates were used, together with neater schnabel tips, attractively machine-jewelled bolts and Williams ramp-pattern back sights.

The Krico 620L had a 550mm barrel and a full-length Mannlicher stock. Double set triggers and an alternative single-trigger mechanism have been offered.

Deluxe guns (600DL, 620DL) had specially selected stocks with separate rosewood schnabel tips, and a spatulate handle on the machine-jewelled bolt. Sights comprised an open Williams ramp and a gold-plated blade. Triggers could be a single or double set pattern, a single-stage unit, or a match design.

Standard 600-series chamberings—for all except Model 600A—were ·222 Remington, 5·6 × 50mm Magnum, ·243 Winchester or ·308 Winchester; in addition, ·17 Remington, ·222 Remington Magnum, ·22–250, ·223 Remington and 5·6 × 57mm have been supplied to order.

The single-shot 630S (·222 Remington, ·243 and ·308 Winchester, plus ·223 Remington to order) was intended for the DJV 'hunting' competitions. Consequently, it had a half-stock with a deep fore-end, a massive butt with a low Monte Carlo comb and a fixed ventilated rubber butt plate. The fore-end and pistol-grip were extensively stippled. Available additionally in ·22–250, the Model 650S Benchrest was similar to the 630S, but had a heavier barrel and a more conventional stock.

The dual purpose target/sporting Model 640L—available in the same chamberings as the 650S—amalgamated the heavy-barrelled 640S action and a sporting style half-stock with a rounded rosewood fore-end tip. Chequering lay on the pistol-grip and fore-end, and a solid rubber butt plate was fitted.

The 640S and 640S Sniper rifles shared the normal detachable box magazine and the standard match stock with seven longitudinal slots through the fore-end. Chambered for ·222 Remington, ·223 Remington, ·22–250, ·243 Winchester or ·308 Winchester rounds, the Krico 640S had a fixed cheek piece and a solid rubber shoulder plate; the 640S Sniper (·222 and ·223 Remington, ·243 and ·308 Winchester only) had a butt plate adjustable for height and rake, plus a comb that could be elevated with a special key. A muzzle brake appeared on the phosphated barrel, a single set-trigger was standard, and the bolt-handle knob was enlarged to facilitate grip.

Model 700

700A, 700D, 700D Magnum, 700DL, 700DL Magnum, 701, 720L, 720DL, 740S and 740S Magnum patterns.
Made by Krico GmbH, Jagd- und Sportwaffenfabrik, Stuttgart.

Chambering: see notes.
Action: as 600 series, above.
DATA FOR A TYPICAL 700DL
7 × 64mm, rimless.
1,122mm overall, 3·38kg unladen.
600mm barrel, 4-groove rifling; RH, concentric.
Detachable box magazine, 3 rounds.
Ramp sight.
800 m/sec with 11·2-gram bullet.
☆

1962: the Model 701 was a long-action 601 chambered for ·270 Winchester, 7 × 57mm, 7 × 64mm or ·30–06 cartridges. Fitted with a 600mm barrel, it was about 1,120mm overall—10mm longer than the short-action guns.

1983: the basic manufacturing patterns were refined, though the action was unchanged. The new guns were identical with corresponding variants in the 600 group, apart from the longer bolt and receiver. The plain 700A chambered 7 × 64mm or ·30–06 rounds only. The Krico 700D—'700E' with a single-stage trigger—handled 6·5 × 57mm, 7 × 64mm or ·30–06 as standard, options including 6·5 × 55mm, 7 × 57mm, ·270 Winchester and 9·3 × 62mm. The 700DL and full-stocked 720L/720DL rifles were chambered similarly.

Krico's 700D Magnum and 700DL Magnum shared the standard long action, but had barrels of 650mm instead of the standard 600mm. Usually chambering ·300 Winchester Magnum or 8 × 68mm S, they have also been supplied to order in 6·5 × 68mm, 7mm Remington Magnum, 7·5 × 55mm or 9·3 × 64mm.

Krico's 740S (6·5 × 55mm, with a 600mm heavy barrel) and 740S Magnum (7·5 × 55mm, 650mm barrel) were identical with the Model 640S target rifle, excepting for the length of the action and chambering.

KROPATSCHEK

AUSTRIA-HUNGARY

The failure of the ineffectual Früwirth carbine (q.v.) to interest the Austro-Hungarian army

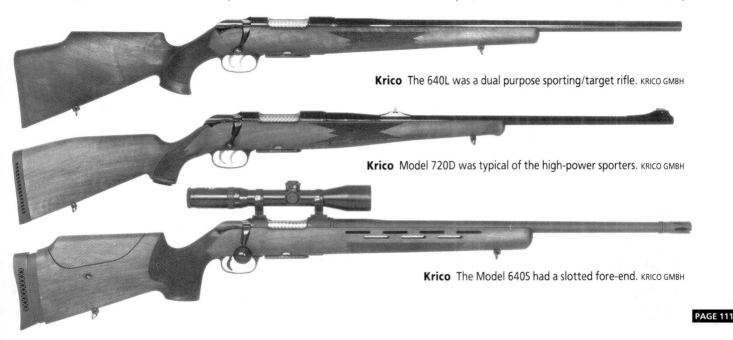

Krico The 640L was a dual purpose sporting/target rifle. KRICO GMBH

Krico Model 720D was typical of the high-power sporters. KRICO GMBH

Krico The Model 640S had a slotted fore-end. KRICO GMBH

cleared the way for a rifle designed by Alfred von Kropatschek.

1874: the first guns were submitted to the Minister of War on 24 September. They had a conventional action inspired by the German Mauser, using the bolt rib to lock against the receiver, and had a Vetterli-type tube magazine in the fore-end.

1876: the Kropatschek was declared 'suitable for adoption'—which simply allowed a lengthy programme of minor improvements to drag on into the 1880s.

1879: Leopold Gasser of Vienna patented a spring-loaded loading gate for the Kropatschek, adapted from the then-current Winchester pattern. The gate was used on some of the 'Gasser-Kropatschek' rifles tested in Austria-Hungary in the early 1880s.

1885*: the rise of the box magazine restricted distribution and influence of the Kropatschek—excepting in France, where its popularity in Indo-China and Equatorial Africa eventually created the Lebel (q.v.).

AUSTRIA-HUNGARY

Model 1881

Gendarmerie carbine.
Made by Österreichische
Waffenfabriks-Gesellschaft, Steyr, 1881–3.
Quantity: 3,500?
11 × 58mm, rimmed.
Turning-bolt action, locked by the bolt rib abutting the receiver ahead of the bridge.
About 1,040mm overall, 3·80kg unladen.
570mm barrel, 6-groove rifling; RH, concentric.
Tube magazine in fore-end, 5 rounds.
Ramp-and-leaf sight graduated to 600 schritt?
307 m/sec with M1877 (carbine) cartridges.
Socket bayonet?
☆

1881: a diminution of the army trials rifles, with a single barrel band and the bolt handle turned downward, the 'Repetier-Karabiner für königlich Ungarnische Landesvertheidigung' was adopted on 19 June. The gun was somewhat similar to

the earlier Früwirth (q.v.), but the striker had an integral cocking piece instead of an external hammer. Issue of the M1881 was extended in the late summer to the Bosnian gendarmerie.

1882: from 17 March, the carbine was also issued to the Austrian Landesgendarmerie.

1900*: surviving guns were replaced by 1890-pattern Mannlichers discarded by the army.

Model 1893

Navy rifle: Torpedo-Boots Gewehr M1893.
☆

1893: on 28 October, a Kropatschek rifle was adopted by the imperial navy for issue to the crews of torpedo-boats. It is believed that the guns were converted from the trials rifles issued in the early 1880s, which had been in store for many years. The principal change may have been a new barrel, chambering the 8 × 50mm rimmed rifle cartridge, but details are lacking.

1900*: surviving M1893 rifles were replaced by Mannlichers. The Kropatschek action was only marginally strong enough to withstand the pressures generated by smokeless cartridges.

FRANCE

The Kropatschek was more popular in France than Austria-Hungary, 50,000 being purchased from Steyr or made in the French ordnance factories. However, their service life was greatly curtailed by development of 8mm smokeless-propellant cartridges. Chamber pressures rose too far for the Gras-type Kropatschek bolt to handle safely, owing to the simple bolt-handle rib lock, and a symmetrical two-lug pattern was developed in 1885–6. This soon became known as the Lebel (q.v.).

Model 1878

Navy rifle: Fusil de Marine Mle.1878.
Made by Österreichische
Waffenfabriks-Gesellschaft, Steyr, 1878–9.
Quantity: 25,000.
11 × 59mm, rimmed.

Turning-bolt action, locked by the bolt rib abutting the receiver ahead of the bridge.
1,244mm overall, 4·50kg unladen.
743mm barrel, 4-groove rifling; RH, concentric.
Tube magazine in fore-end, 7 rounds.
Ramp-and-leaf sight graduated to 1,800 metres.
455 m/sec with Mle.74 ball cartridges.
Mle.78 épée bayonet.
☆

1877: tests undertaken by the French Navy in midsummer—with Hotchkiss, Krag-Petersson and Kropatschek rifles—resolved in September in favour of the Kropatschek.

1878: after approval of a cartridge-stop or cut-off mechanism, the trials rifle was adopted on 28 June to replace the Mle.66 (Chassepot), then still in naval service. The first Kropatschek rifle to encounter real success, it amalgamated the action of the single-shot French Mle.74 (Gras) with a tube magazine in the fore-end inspired by the Swiss Vetterli. The rifle had two screw-clamped barrel bands and a full-width nose cap with a bayonet lug on the right side. This accepted a special bayonet with a flat-backed hilt. Swivels lay under the rear band and butt.

Model 1884

Infantry rifles:
Fusils d'Infanterie Mle.1874/80 M.84 et Mle.1884.
Made by Manufactures d'Armes, Châtellerault and Saint-Étienne, 1884–5.
11 × 59mm, rimmed.
Action: as Mle.1878, above.
1,244mm overall, 4·26kg unladen.
743mm barrel, 4-groove rifling; RH, concentric.
Tube magazine in fore-end, 8 rounds.
Ramp-and-leaf sight graduated to 1,900 metres.
455 m/sec with Mle.74 ball cartridges.
Mle.74 épée bayonet.
☆

1883: developed by two employees of the Châtellerault arms factory, arms inspector Close and Commandant Lespinasse, this was little more than a French-made Mle.1878.

1884: some guns were converted from Mle.74 M.80 rifles, being distinguished by a new

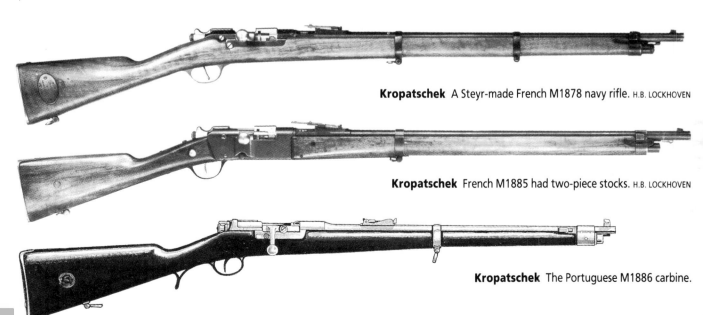

Kropatschek A Steyr-made French M1878 navy rifle. H.B. LOCKHOVEN

Kropatschek French M1885 had two-piece stocks. H.B. LOCKHOVEN

Kropatschek The Portuguese M1886 carbine.

one-piece stock with a prominent grasping groove in the fore-end. They had a single barrel band and a nose cap, retained by springs, but the bayonet bar lay on the right side of the muzzle. The cut-off lever rotated in a depression in the stock behind the bolt handle. Newly-made Mle.1884 rifles had a cleaning rod let into the left side of the stock; and the nose cap was clinched inward beneath the muzzle so that the lug would accept the raised pommel of the standard Mle.1874 bayonet. In addition, the magazine tube protruded a short distance forward beneath the muzzle. Most metal parts were browned, whereas naval Mle.1878 rifles were polished to resist corrosion.

Model 1885

Infantry rifles:
Fusils d'Infanterie Mle.1874/85 et Mle.1885.
Made by Manufacture d'Armes, Saint-Étienne, 1885–7.
11 × 59mm, rimmed.
Action: as Mle.1878 rifle, above.
1,244mm overall, 4·20kg unladen.
751mm barrel, 4-groove rifling; RH, concentric.
Tube magazine in fore-end, 8 rounds.
Ramp-and-leaf sight graduated to 1,900 metres.
455 m/sec with Mle.74 ball cartridges.
Mle.74 épée bayonet.

☆

1885: the perfected version of the French Kropatschek was easily distinguished by the separation of butt and fore-end by a deep metal receiver. The rifle was otherwise very similar to the Mle.1884, with the same clinched nose cap, but had only one band. Swivels lay under the band and on the under-edge of the butt. The bolt-handle rib was plain: Mle.78 and Mle.84 rifles had two blind holes in the right side of the rib beneath the bolt handle to receive the cut-off button. The Mle.1885 cut-off protruded from the bottom of a prominent housing on the right side of the receiver ahead of the trigger.

Some guns were converted from Mle.74 M.80 (Gras) rifles, but the changes were so extensive that the identity of the original guns was all but lost. However, they bore their

original markings on the barrel and other major components.

1886: a few guns made towards the end of production had the Lebel-type cut-off set into the receiver, which allowed the entire side panel to be milled flush. Though the rifle was soon replaced by the Lebel, it remained in service long enough to serve French forces in Indo-China.

PORTUGAL

The Portuguese adopted a Kropatschek to replace the single-shot Guedes (q.v.). Marks on the left side of the receiver included OE.W.F.G. STEYR, above the date of manufacture; the cypher of Luis I, a crowned 'LIº'; and the designation 'M 1886'.

Models 1886 and 1886/89

Infantry rifles:
Espingarda Mo.1886 e Mo.1886/89.
Made by Österreichische
Waffenfabriks-Gesellschaft, Steyr, 1885–8.
Quantity: 49,000.
8 × 60mm, rimmed.
Turning-bolt action, locked by the bolt rib abutting the receiver ahead of the bridge.
1,320mm overall, 4·57kg unladen.
802mm barrel, 4-groove rifling; RH, concentric.
Tube magazine in fore-end, 8 rounds.
Ramp-and-leaf sight graduated to 2,000 metres.
About 535 m/sec with Mo.1886 ball cartridges.
Mo.1886 sword bayonet.

☆

1885: worried by the obsolescence of the Mo.1885 Guedes rifle, which had only just been approved, the Portuguese ordered 6,000 Kropatschek rifles on 30 October. The standard infantry rifle was an improved version of the French Mle.1878, with a bolt patterned closely on that of the Gew.71/84 and an elevator/cut off mechanism credited to an ordnance officer named Dechambès.

The straight-grip walnut stock had two screw-clamping barrel bands, with swivels on the butt and middle band. The nose cap had a bayonet

lug on its right, and the cleaning rod was set into the left side of the fore-end. The trigger guard had a distinctive spurred rearward extension.

1886: a 40,000-rifle order was signed in July.

1887: three thousand additional rifles were ordered from Austria-Hungary.

1889: some guns were fitted with hand guards in the Arsenal do Exército in Lisbon. These were known as 'Mo.86/89', but not all were so treated; it is suspected that they were issued to colonial troops, to reduce the adverse effect of radiated barrel-heat on the sight picture.

1896*: a smokeless cartridge was approved, increasing muzzle velocity to about 690 m/sec. The back sights were altered to give a maximum range-setting of 2,200 metres.

1961: the last colonial guns were withdrawn.

Model 1886

Short rifle: Mosqueton Mo.1886.
Made by Österreichische
Waffenfabriks-Gesellschaft, Steyr, 1888.
Quantity: 4,800.
8 × 60mm, rimmed.
Action: as Mo.1886 rifle, above.
1,165mm overall, 4·25kg unladen.
657mm barrel, 4-groove rifling; RH, concentric.
Tube magazine in fore-end, 6 rounds.
Ramp-and-leaf sight graduated to 2,000 metres.
About 475 m/sec with Mo.1886 ball cartridges.
Mo.1886 sword bayonet.

☆

1888: ordered in March, specifically for the use of Treasury guards, this was simply a short version of the Mo.1886 rifle with the same fittings and fixtures.

1896*: most short rifles were altered for more powerful ammunition, receiving 2,200-metre back sights. Muzzle velocity rose to 625 m/sec.

Model 1886

Cavalry carbine.
Made by Österreichische
Waffenfabriks-Gesellschaft, Steyr, 1885–94.
Quantity: 4,000.

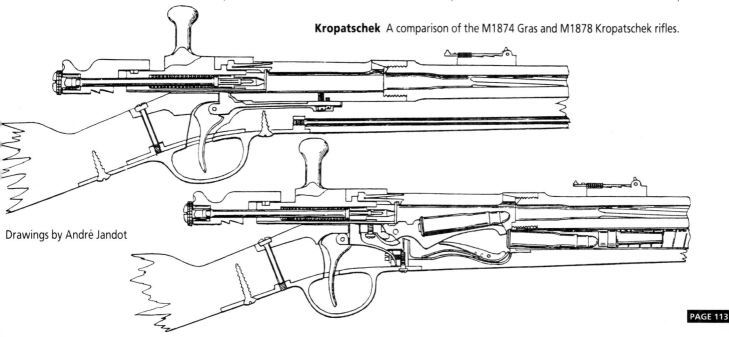

Kropatschek A comparison of the M1874 Gras and M1878 Kropatschek rifles.

Drawings by André Jandot

8 × 60mm, rimmed.
Action: as Mo.1886 rifle, above.
1,025mm overall, 4·00kg unladen.
521mm barrel, 4-groove rifling; RH, concentric.
Tube magazine in fore-end, 5 rounds.
Ramp-and-leaf sight graduated to 1,500 metres.
About 390 m/sec with Mo.1886 ball cartridges.
Mo.1886 sword bayonet.

☆

1885: 3,000 carbines were ordered on 30 October. They were similar to the infantry rifles purchased at the same time, but had a short fore-end and only a single barrel band. The carbines were stocked closer to the muzzle than rifles, the bayonet lug being set back on the side of the barrel behind the nose cap to compensate for reduced muzzle protrusion.

1894: 1,000 more carbines were purchased.

1896*: the Portuguese adopted a cartridge loaded with smokeless propellant purchased in Austria-Hungary. A few Kropatschek carbines are said to have been re-chambered in this period for a semi-experimental 6·5mm round—for issue to mounted units—but the guns were probably purpose-built French Daudetau patterns (q.v.).

LAIDLEY-EMERY

UNITED STATES OF AMERICA
Also known as 'Whitney'

This radial-block action, greatly resembling the Remington externally, was based on a patent granted to Theodore Laidley and C.A. Emery in May 1866. The Laidley-Emery rifle was safer than the Remington, but more complicated. A prototype took part in trials with the US Army—alongside the Allin transformation—but failed with over-load charges.

The Whitney version of the Laidley-Emery system had an auxiliary cam which locked as the breech was closed; the hammer simply struck the firing pin and played no other part in the operating cycle. The action loaded at half-cock.

The rifle was hard to distinguish from a Remington at a glance, but had an extra lateral

screw through the action. What appeared to be a retainer-plate on the left side of the breech for the major axis pins was two elongated lipped pin-heads locked by a central screw.

Whitney then produced a blatant copy of the Remington rolling-block action (see 'Rider'). A special Light Carbine, usually chambered for rimfire ammunition may also be occasionally encountered in ·44 S&W centre-fire.

MEXICO
Military Model

Rifle and carbine patterns.
Made by the Whitney Arms Company, Whitneyville, Connecticut, 1872–80.
11 × 58mm (·433), rimmed.
Radial-block action, locked by an auxiliary cam.
DATA FOR A TYPICAL RIFLE
50·48in overall, 9·50lb unladen.
35·00in barrel, 4-groove rifling; RH, concentric?
Ramp-and-leaf sight graduated to 1,200 yards.
1,440 ft/sec with 375-grain bullet.
Socket bayonet.

☆

1872: the standard Whitney military rifle—available in ·433 Spanish, ·45–70 or ·50–70—had a full-length fore-end retained by three bands; swivels lay on the band nearest the muzzle and through the front web of the trigger-guard bow. A half-stocked carbine was offered with a sling ring and bar anchored in the left side of the receiver; it was about 36in long, had a 20·5in barrel and weighed about 7·2lb. The ramp-and-leaf back sight was usually graduated to 600 yards.

1877: about 2,000 rifles and perhaps 500 carbines were purchased directly from Whitney on behalf of the Mexican government. They are usually distinguished by a liberty-cap-on-sunburst above R M for 'República Mexicana'.

The rifles accepted socket bayonets with conventional locking rings. These could fit the carbines in an emergency, but were never issued to mounted troops. Whitney could supply sabre patterns to order when required to do so.

LEBEL

FRANCE

This bolt-action rifle was designed and perfected in France in the mid 1880s. The Mle.1886/93 was used by several European countries during the First World War—it armed some of the Belgian troops fighting alongside the French on the Western Front, for example—and about 86,000 were shipped to Russia in 1915–16. Others served Greece and Czechoslovakia into the early 1920s.

1883: worried by the experiments then being undertaken in Germany with semi-experimental 1882-type Mauser rifles, which had a tube magazine, the French sought an effectual rival by modifying the Mle.1878 Kropatschek (q.v.).

1885: the Commission d'Étude des Armes à Répétition produced an improved Kropatschek (q.v.), but work had hardly begun when Paul Vieille produced an effectual smokeless powder. This allowed a reduction in the calibre of the service rifle to 8mm, but increased chamber pressures appreciably.

1886: as the margins of safety in the single-lug Gras-Kropatschek bolt action were not great enough for the Mle.1885 rifle to be adapted directly, modified rifles were completed with a symmetrical two-lug bolt head proposed by Colonel Bonnet.

The poorest feature of the new rifle was the retention of a tube magazine, credited to Colonel Gras but probably owing more to government insistence that a new rifle should hold at least as many cartridges as the German M71/84 Mauser. The perfected French gun was adopted in 1887. It had a Kropatschek-type tube magazine in the fore-end and a modified cartridge elevator. The bolt was basically that of the Mle.1874 (Gras), but the separate bolt head had two lugs that locked horizontally behind the chamber. The sturdy receiver and two-piece stock of the Mle.1885 were retained.

The new gun soon became known as the 'Lebel' after the commandant of the École

---

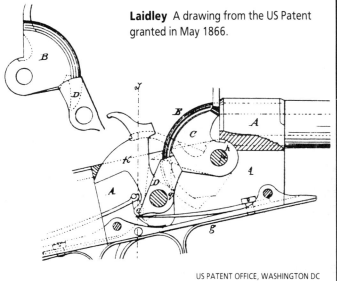

LAIDLEY-EMERY
SPORTING GUNS, 1872–80

Sporting Model Made from 1872–3 by the Whitney Arms Company of Whitneyville, Connecticut, this was offered as a rifle or carbine for a wide range of cartridges—·38 Long, ·38–40 Winchester, ·40–50 Sharps (necked), ·40–70 Sharps (necked), ·44–40 Winchester, ·44–60 Sharps (necked), ·44–77 Sharps (necked), ·44–90 Sharps (necked), ·44–100 Remington, ·45–100 Sharps (straight), ·45–70 Government, ·50–70 Government and others. The round, half-octagon or fully-octagonal barrels measured 24–30in. Straight grip butts and short slender fore-ends were regarded as standard, but schnabel tips and chequering were occasionally supplied to order.

¶ A typical rifle chambered for the ·44–77 Sharps cartridge was 42·50in overall (with a 26·50in barrel) and weighed 7·80lb. It had a folding-leaf sight graduated to 1,000 yards. **Creedmoor Model** Introduced in 1875 to compete with Remington, these rifles had specially selected butts with chequered pistol grips, and chequered half-length fore-ends. A vernier peep sight was fitted to the upper tang behind the action; the front sight was usually a globe type, often with an additional spirit level. The No. 1, chambered for ·44–90 Sharps (necked) or ·44–100 Remington cartridges, was offered with half- or fully-octagonal barrels (32in or 34in); the lighter No. 2, confined to ·40–50 Sharps (necked) or ·40–70 Sharps (necked), had barrels of 30in or 32in. A typical 32in-barrelled No.1 was about 48·25in overall and weighed 10lb.

Laidley A drawing from the US Patent granted in May 1866.

US PATENT OFFICE, WASHINGTON DC

Normale de Tir, who had personally directed most of the trials undertaken in the Camp de Châlons. Colonel Lebel protested, but the name soon gained common currency.

MILITARY WEAPONS
FRANCE
Models 1886 and 1886/93

Infantry rifles: Fusils d'Infanterie Mle.1886 et Mle.1886 M.93.
Made by Manufactures d'Armes, Châtellerault, Saint-Étienne and Tulle, 1886–1919; and Manufacture d'Armes de Paris, Saint-Denis, 1915–18.
Quantity: 3·5–4 million.
8 × 51mm, rimmed.
Turning-bolt action with two lugs on a detachable bolt head locking into the receiver.
1,307mm overall, 4·18kg unladen.
815mm barrel, 4-groove rifling; LH, concentric.
Tube magazine under barrel, 8 rounds.
Ramp-and-leaf sight graduated to 2,000 metres.
632 m/sec with Balle 1886 M.
Mle.1886 épée bayonet.
☆

1887: the Mle.1886 rifle was adopted on 22 April. It had a distinctive two-piece stock, separated by a massive machined-steel receiver; typically French, this can only be confused with the semi-experimental Mle.1885 (see 'Kropatschek'). The butt was bolted to the tangs and the fore-end was retained by a single spring-retained band. Swivels lay on the underside of the band and butt, whilst a radial cut-off lever was set in the right side of the receiver above the front of the trigger guard. The nose cap, retained by a spring let into the right side of the fore-end, had a boss that entered the bayonet pommel. Two distinctive tenons under the muzzle mated with the channelled back of the bayonet hilt. The original back-sight base was simply tin-soldered onto the barrel.
1892: no sooner had the new rifles entered service than problems were reported. The worst concerned the back sight base, which often loosened during rapid fire, so the original pattern was replaced by one with claws extending down around the barrel.
1893: the improved Mle.1886 M.93 rifle was adopted, with a lighter striker retainer in the cocking piece and a stacking rod on the right side of the nose cap. A special non-rotating obturator ('tampon-masque') on the bolt head behind the locking lugs deflected gas escaping from a case-head failure. The claw-type back-sight base was altered at about this time, but does not seem to have been a cornerstone of the improvements.
1900: work began to adapt back sights for the Balle 1898 D, which had a muzzle velocity of 701 m/sec. This required a new back-sight leaf graduated to 2,400 metres. The first modified guns were issued in 1901.
1902: the useless 'safety notch' on the cocking piece was abandoned. This left the Lebel rifle with no form of applied safety whatsoever.
1914: the Mle.86 M.93 rifle equipped virtually all front-line infantrymen, though colonial troops carried Mle.1902 or Mle.1907 Berthiers (q.v.). Only during 1917 did the Mle.1886 M.93 begin to give way to the Mle.1907/15 and Mle.1916 (Berthier) rifles—and even then Lebels were retained for marksmen. Sniper rifles were fitted with a 3 × Mle.1916 telescope sight on the left side of the receiver.
1920: Mle.1886 M.93 rifles were retained on a scale of four to each infantry-regiment section. Three were used to fire Vivens-Bessières rifle grenades, being stronger than the Berthiers; the fourth was retained as a sniper's weapon and mounted a 3 × Mle.1916 or, subsequently, 3 × Mle.1921 optical sight.
1927: some rifles were adapted to fire the 7·5mm Balle 1924 C.
1935: a programme to shorten the surviving Mle.1886 M.93 rifles began, but had not been completed by 1939.
1945: the decision was taken to modify Mle.1886 M.93 and Mle.1886 M.93 R.35 rifles for the Balle 1932 N before passing them to the reserve. This involved re-cutting the chamber to accept a longer bullet, and the opportunity was taken to strengthen the striker-spring. Modified guns bore N on the barrel near the breech.

Model 1886/35

Short rifle: Fusil Mle.1886 R.35.
Apparently converted in Châtellerault, 1936–9.
8 × 51mm, rimmed.
Action: as Mle.1886 rifle, above.
958mm overall, 3·77kg unladen.
450mm barrel, 4-groove rifling; LH, concentric.
Tube magazine under barrel, 3 rounds.
Ramp-and-leaf sight graduated to 2,000 metres.
605 m/sec with 1886 Balle D.
Mle.1935 épée bayonet.
☆

1935: the decision was taken to shorten many of the Mle.1886 M.93 rifles held in reserve, providing a handy weapon for cavalrymen and motorised units while tooling for the MAS 36 was undertaken. The barrel, fore-end and magazine tube were greatly shortened, though little else was necessary. The new barrel band had a fixed sling ring on the left side, a bar being added to the left side of the butt; the rear swivel on the butt-edge was retained. In common with most other tube-magazine designs, the cartridge capacity could be improved when necessary by placing a fourth round on the elevator and a fifth in the chamber.
1939: a few Mle.1886 R.35 rifles were issued to men on home service, but most had been sent to Africa before hostilities commenced.
1945: survivors were modified to chamber the 8mm Balle 1932 N and stored for the reserve.

LEE

UNITED STATES OF AMERICA
☞

1. THE STRAIGHT-PULL BOLT PATTERNS

James Lee was granted the first of a series of patents for straight-pull bolt-action rifles,

Lebel M1886/93 rifle.

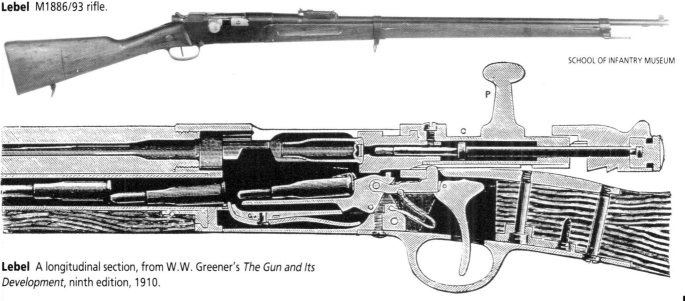

SCHOOL OF INFANTRY MUSEUM

Lebel A longitudinal section, from W.W. Greener's *The Gun and Its Development*, ninth edition, 1910.

improved clip-loaded magazines and a special cartridge-lifter arm in 1894. Trials undertaken in October, at the US Navy's Torpedo Station in Newport, Rhode Island, convinced the US Navy of the merits of the ·236 straight-pull Lee. It was subsequently adopted as the M1895, a production contract being given to Winchester.

The inclined bolt was locked by a wedge-type block, which disengaged when the bolt handle was retracted. A five-round clip could be inserted in the magazine with the bolt open. Tension on the cartridge rims was released automatically as the bolt closed, allowing the clip to fall out of the bottom of the magazine after a couple of rounds had been fired.

MILITARY RIFLES
Model 1895

Navy rifle.
Made by the Winchester Repeating Arms Company,
New Haven, Connecticut, 1896–8.
Quantity: about 18,000.
·236, rimmed.
Straight-pull action, locked by a retractable wedge
beneath the bolt handle.
47·60in overall, 8·13lb unladen.
28·00in barrel, 5-groove rifling; RH, concentric.
Integral clip-loaded box magazine, 5 rounds.
Ramp-and-leaf sight graduated to 2,000 yards.
2,560 ft/sec with M1895 ball cartridges.
M1895 knife bayonet.

☆

1895: the Lee rifle was adopted in May, ten thousand being ordered from Winchester. It had a conventional one-piece pistol-grip walnut stock, a single barrel band and a special nose band with a bayonet lug on the right side. The fixed magazine case, which protruded from the stock ahead of the trigger guard, had a distinctively concave lower edge. However, the extractor/ejector, the firing-pin lock and the bolt-lock actuator all gave constant trouble.
1899: production ceased. Most of the US Navy service rifles were replaced by Krag-Jørgensen patterns shortly after 1900.

SPORTING GUNS
Winchester-Lee

Made by the Winchester Repeating Arms Company,
New Haven, Connecticut, 1897–1904
Quantity: about 1,550.
Action: as M1895 rifle, above.
·236, rimmed.
43·50in overall, 7·56lb unladen.
24·00in barrel, 5-groove rifling; RH, concentric.
Integral clip-loaded box magazine, 5 rounds.
Spring-leaf and elevator sight.
About 2,450 ft/sec with 112-grain bullet.

☆

1897: encouraged by the adoption of the ·236 Lee rifle for naval service, Winchester announced a sporting version in its autumn catalogue, noting that guns would be available once navy contracts had been fulfilled.
1899: small batches of sporting rifles were released. They had good-quality half-stocks with a pistol grip and a shotgun-style butt plate. The fore-end had a lengthy grasping groove and a shallow schnabel tip. However, though the tiny bullet attained a high velocity for its day, its poor 'knock-down' capabilities did not commend themselves to hunters used to large and heavy (if slow-moving) projectiles. As the bolt action was rarely favoured by sportsmen—this Winchester must have known from experience with the Hotchkiss (q.v.)—commercial sales fell a long way short of expectations.
1904: the universal apathy with which the Winchester-Lee was received contributed to its rapid withdrawal.
1916: remaining components were scrapped.

2. THE TURNING-BOLT PATTERNS

This section contains details of the Lee-Enfield, Lee-Metford and Remington-Lee rifles. The Lee-Burtons are covered in the 'Burton' section. Developed in the USA, then perfected in the

USA and Britain, these guns were service issue in Britain and the British Empire—and in many former colonies after independence had been gained (e.g., India and Pakistan). Lee-Enfields were also used in Iraq and the Irish Free State (Eire) prior to 1939; many others were sold to Belgium, Denmark, Egypt, Greece, the Netherlands, Norway, Thailand, and Turkey in the post-1945 era.

The first turning-bolt design, with a single locking lug, sold in small numbers to warring factions in South and Central America while encountering continual apathy in the US Army. An improved two-lug mechanism was then perfected in Britain, where the ·303 Magazine Rifle Mk I (Lee-Metford) was adopted for military service in 1888.

Though the perfected British-type Lee served with honour through world wars and many lesser conflicts, criticism has always been made of its design. Placing the locking lugs behind the magazine put much of the bolt body under stress during firing. However, few problems arose when ·303 cartridges were used, and though occasional bolt failures were reported when conversions to 7·62 × 51mm were made in the 1960s, the deficiencies were exaggerated. Judged from a purely military standpoint, the Lee-Enfield has been a great success.

MILITARY RIFLES
AUSTRALIA

Prior to 1939, the Australian forces were armed with standard SMLE Mks III and III* (No. 1 Mk III and No. 1 Mk III*) rifles made in a government factory that had been established in Lithgow, New South Wales, in 1912. The guns dated from 1913–29, 1938–45 and 1953–6.

The Australian Lee-Enfields were virtually identical with British prototypes; however, apart from a few made immediately prior to the First World War with walnut stock blanks supplied from Britain, they were stocked in a selection of native woods. As these were softer than walnut, insignificant changes were made to the bedding,

Lee The ·236 M1895 US Navy rifle. COLLECTOR'S COMPENDIUM

Lee A ·303 Magazine Rifle (Lee-Metford), 1888. H.B. LOCKHOVEN

Lee A Winchester-Lee sporting rifle. JOHN WALTER

Lee Off to War. Men of the London Division, Territorial Army, on their way—ultimately—to the Western Front in 1914. They carry Charger-Loading Lee-Enfield rifles. COLLECTOR'S COMPANION.

Minor changes in the machining of components were also to be found, and rectangular apertures were cut through the front-sight protectors of many rifles during the Second World War to facilitate removal of the sight blade without detaching the nose cap assembly.

The Australians also made a heavy-barrelled model for military target shooting. Distinguished by a large 'H' on the knox-form and on the right side of the butt, many were impressed into military service in 1940–5.

Australian guns may be distinguished by their markings, which included the Lithgow factory mark in various guises; MA originally represented 'Made in Australia', but came to signify Lithgow when a chain of sub-contractors was established during the Second World War. These included government-owned factories in Bathurst (BA), Forbes (FA), Orange (OA) and Wellington (WA). Most of the stocks and hand guards came from the Slazenger factory in Sydney and displayed SLAZ. Property marks have included D∧D and Đ, or state markings such as TAS. and W.A. for Tasmania and Western Australia.

Rifle No. 1
•••
Sniper rifle: Mk 3* H (T) (Aust.) pattern.
Made by the Royal Australian Small Arms Factory,
Lithgow, New South Wales, 1944–6.
Quantity: see notes.
·303, rimmed.
Action: as No. 1 Mk 3, above.
44·56in overall, 10·30lb with sight.
25·19in barrel, 5-groove rifling; LH, concentric.
Detachable box magazine, 10 rounds.
Tangent-leaf sight graduated to 2,000 yards.
2,440 ft/sec with Mk VII ball cartridges.
No. 1 Mk 1 sword bayonet.
☆

1944: 2,500 of these heavy-barrel SMLEs were ordered to supplement the No. 3 Mk I* (T) sniper rifles on 10 November. They had Aldis telescope sights, offset to the left; cheek pieces were occasionally fitted, as were additional sling swivels on the front trigger guard screw.
1946: 1,612 rifles had been completed when

the project was terminated. They were made from old actions, and may be misleadingly dated as early as 1915. All but four hundred had P/1918 (Aust.) sights in special high mounts, the exceptions having Pattern 1918 (Aust.)/1 sights in low mounts. Very few of these weapons were ever used, though a few were issued in the 1970s pending the introduction of a new gun.

BRITAIN

British Lee rifles may display V.R. ('Victoria Regina') on the butt sockets of guns made between 1888 and 1901; alternatives include E.R. ('Edwardius Rex'), 1901–10 or 1936; G.R. ('Georgius Rex'), 1910–36 or 1936–52; and E.R. ('Elizabeth Regina') from 1952 to date.

Guns made by the Royal Small Arms Factory at Enfield Lock were usually marked ENFIELD or EFD. Guns made in BSA's Small Heath factory bore B.S.A. & M. CO. (Birmingham Small Arms & Munitions Company) until 1897, when the company reverted to original B.S.A. marks. Those made by the London Small Arms Co. Ltd were marked L.S.A. CO. or, alternatively, L.S.A. CO. LD. Rarer marks include V.S.M. for Vickers, Sons & Maxim Ltd (on charger-loading conversions only, 1911–12), S.S.A. for the Standard Small Arms Company, Birmingham (1916–18), and N.R.F. for its short-lived successor, the National Rifle Factory No. 1 (1918–19 only).

During the Second World War, No. 4 rifles were made by Enfield, the BSA factories in Small Heath (M47A) and Shirley (M85B and M47C), together with the Royal Ordnance 'shadow' factories in Fazakerley (ROF [F], FY, or F) and Maltby (ROF [M] or RM). No. 4 rifles were also supplied to Britain from Small Arms Ltd of Long Branch, Toronto (an 'LB' monogram), and by the Stevens Arms Company of Chicopee Falls, Massachusetts (a distinctive squared 'S', often in a box-border).

Designation marks take the form 'I' or 'II*' for Marks I and II* respectively, the 'star' being the standard method of indicating an improved pattern. The prefixes A.C. and C.C. represented artillery and cavalry carbines.

When the Lee-Enfield appeared, it was so similar to the Lee-Metford that the prefix L.E. was used to distinguish it. Thereafter, a series of descriptive prefixes had to be used: C.L.L.E. for 'Charger-loading Lee-Enfield'; COND.L.E. for 'Converted Lee-Enfield'; or SHT.L.E. for 'Short Lee Enfield'. After the First World War, with the adoption of a new system of designations, the butt-shoe marks read NO. 1 MK.VI or NO. 4 MK.1. By 1940, marks had been transferred from the butt-shoe to the left side of the receiver, a typical example reading No4 Mk1 ROF (F) over '2/45' for February 1945. Lee-Enfields converted to 7.62mm NATO ammunition bore marks such as RIFLE 7.62MM L8A3 over (CR 62 GA).

1880: the Lee appeared in Britain at the end of March, when three 1879-pattern rifles and two carbines chambering the ·45 drawn-case Gatling cartridge were amongst a selection of guns tried by the Small Arms Committee.
1881: a final report made on 21 March noted that, despite niggling extraction problems, the ·45 Lee had performed best of the submissions.
1883: a new Lee chambering the ·45–70 US Army cartridge was tested at Enfield in April, impressing the authorities sufficiently for a solitary 'Improved Lee' rifle to be built.
1887: a ·43 1885-pattern Remington-Lee rifle passed an outstanding test, three hundred being ordered for trials against the ·402 Lee-Burton. However, development of an 8mm smokeless cartridge in France persuaded the British to abandon the ineffectual ·402, trials revealing that a ·298 Rubin bullet offered flatter trajectory, better accuracy and greater penetration.
1888: a rifle chambering a straight-case cartridge was approved early in the year. It had a distinctive butt with a continuous comb and a straight wrist. A bolt-head release catch lay on the right side of the receiver and a long ejector was let into the left side of the bolt-way. The design of the box magazine, the cut-off and the long-range dial sight was credited to Joseph Speed of the Enfield factory. A Martini-style upper band accepted a special sword bayonet. Production amounted to at least 437 rifles and

51 carbines before the design of what became the Lee-Metford was settled. However, as the design was subjected to continual modification, these trials guns often exhibit variations in detail, chambering or construction.

Lee-Metford

Infantry rifles: Mks I and I*.
Made by the Royal Small Arms Factory,
Enfield Lock, Middlesex; the Birmingham Small Arms &
Munitions Co. Ltd, Small Heath; and the London
Small Arms Co. Ltd, Bow.
·303, rimmed
Turning-bolt action, with a single lug on the bolt body locking into the receiver and the rear of the bolt guide rib abutting the receiver bridge.
49·50in overall, 9·50lb unladen.
30·22in barrel, 7-groove rifling; LH, polygonal.
Detachable box magazine, 8 rounds.
Ramp-and-leaf sight graduated to 1,800 yards.
1,830 ft/sec with Mk I (black powder) ball rounds.
Pattern 1888 sword bayonet.

☆

1888: sealed on 12 December, the perfected 'Rifle, Magazine, ·303-inch (Mark I)' had a modified back sight and a long-range dial plate (for 1,800–3,500 yards) on the left side of the fore-end.
1889: first issues were made in December, but problems soon arose with the Lewes sights.
1890: the fore-end groove was abandoned; changes were made to prevent hand guards breaking; and a disc for regimental markings was added to the butt after 30 September. Omitting the safety catch from 31 December advanced the designation to 'Mark I*'.
1891: a combined front-sight protector and muzzle-stop was adopted in January. The rifles were redesignated 'Lee-Metford Mk I (or Mk I*) on 8 April.
1892: a reversion to V-and-barleycorn sights was made. Sights had been graduated on the basis that smokeless propellant would be available immediately, but the appearance of a satisfactory cordite load had been delayed by unforeseen manufacturing problems.

Lee-Metford

Infantry rifle: Mk II.
Made by the Royal Small Arms Factory,
Enfield Lock, Middlesex; the Birmingham Small Arms &
Munitions Co. Ltd, Small Heath; and the London
Small Arms Co. Ltd, Bow.
·303, rimmed.
Action: as Lee-Metford Mk I, above.
49·50in overall, 9·50lb unladen.
30·22in barrel, 7-groove rifling; LH, polygonal.
Detachable box magazine, 10 rounds.
Ramp-and-leaf sight graduated to 1,600 yards.
1,830 ft/sec with Mk I (black powder) cartridges.
Pattern 1888 sword bayonet.

☆

1890: a prototype rifle with a lightened barrel and a staggered-row box magazine appeared in September. The barrel band and safety catch had been omitted; changes were made in the bolt head, the bolt cover and the cut-off mechanism. The dial sight ranged to 2,800 yards.
A hundred trials rifles appeared in October, ten with sights calibrated for cordite and the remainder for black powder.
1891: trials finished in April, but changes were soon made. They included the approval of a new bolt head, designed by Deeley & Penn, and the reappearance of the lower band.
1893: the 'Rifle, Magazine, Lee-Metford, ·303-inch (Mark II)' was finally sealed on 12 April, though production had begun in October 1892.

Lee-Metford

Carbine: Mk I.
Made by the Royal Small Arms Factory, Enfield Lock,
Middlesex, 1894–6.
·303, rimmed
Action: as Lee-Metford Mk I, above.
39·88in overall, 7·43lb unladen.
20·75in barrel, 7-groove rifling; LH, polygonal.
Detachable box magazine, 6 rounds.
Ramp-and-leaf sight graduated to 2,000 yards.
About 1,680 ft/sec with Mk I (black powder) rounds.
No bayonet.

☆

1892: at least 150 trials carbines were made in the 1892–3 and 1893–4 financial years (i.e., between 1 April 1892 and 31 March 1894).
1894: sealed for cavalry use in June and again in September, the Mk I carbine was a short infantry rifle with a safety catch on the right side of the cocking piece. The bolt-handle knob was flattened and bent forward to facilitate inserting the carbine into a saddle bucket, and the magazine faired neatly into the underside of the fore-end. The guns had a sling bar and a marking disc on the right side of the butt, and a D-ring on the left side of the butt socket.
1896: the D-ring was abandoned with effect from 6 March. A leather back-sight cover, held to the fore-end by two protruding-head screws, was approved during the year.

Lee-Enfield

Infantry rifles: Mks I and I*.
Made by the Royal Small Arms Factory,
Enfield Lock, Middlesex; the Birmingham Small Arms &
Munitions Co. Ltd, Small Heath; and the London
Small Arms Co. Ltd, Bow.
·303, rimmed.
Action: as Lee-Metford Mk I, above.
49·50in overall, 9·50lb unladen.
30·22in barrel, 5-groove rifling; LH, concentric.
Detachable box magazine, 10 rounds.
Ramp-and-leaf sight graduated to 1,600 yards.
2,060 ft/sec with Mk II ball cartridges.
Pattern 1888 sword bayonet.

☆

1895: no sooner had the perfected Lee-Metford rifle entered service in quantity than the Mk I Cordite ·303 cartridge (approved in November 1890 but not made for some time) proved to wear out Metford-rifled barrels very quickly. Trials undertaken by the authorities led to the approval of new concentric 'Enfield' rifling with five square-shouldered grooves.

Sealed on 11 November 1895, the 'Rifle, Magazine, Lee-Enfield, ·303-inch (Mark I)' had new rifling and the front sight moved to the left. The marking on the butt socket read L.E. ('Lee-Enfield') instead of L.M. for 'Lee-Metford'.

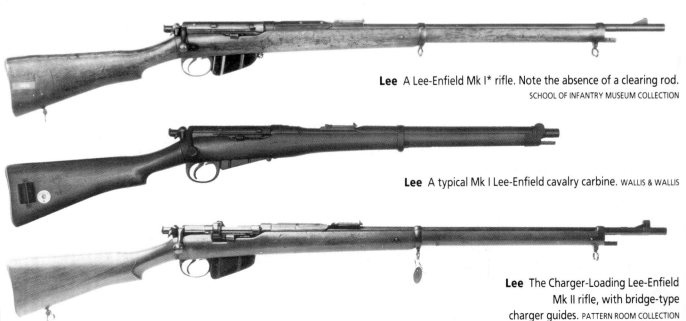

Lee A Lee-Enfield Mk I* rifle. Note the absence of a clearing rod.
SCHOOL OF INFANTRY MUSEUM COLLECTION

Lee A typical Mk I Lee-Enfield cavalry carbine. WALLIS & WALLIS

Lee The Charger-Loading Lee-Enfield Mk II rifle, with bridge-type charger guides. PATTERN ROOM COLLECTION

1899: sealed on 7 August, the Mark I* Lee-Enfield lacked a clearing rod and the associated rod-groove in the underside of the fore-end; Mk I rifles modified to Mk I* standards have a fillet of wood in the groove.

1906: with effect from February, the pull-off was lightened to 5–7lb to match the SMLE.

1907: conversion of many Lee-Enfields to the ·22 rimfire Aiming Tube system began, guns being marked **A.T.** Survivors were changed back to ·303 in 1939–40.

Lee-Enfield

Carbines: Mks I and I*.
Made by the Royal Small Arms Factory, Enfield Lock.
·303, rimmed.
Action: as Lee-Enfield Mk I, above.
39·31in overall, 7·44lb unladen.
20·75in barrel, 5-groove rifling; LH, concentric.
Detachable box magazine, 6 rounds.
Ramp-and-leaf sight graduated to 2,000 yards.
1,940 ft/sec with Mk II ball cartridges.
No bayonet.

☆

1896: approved on 17 August, the 'Carbine, Magazine, Lee-Enfield, ·303-inch (Mark I)' resembled the Lee-Metford equivalent, but lacked the sling bar. An **L.E.C.** mark ('Lee-Enfield Carbine') appeared on the butt socket.

1899: sealed on 7 August 1899, the Mk I* was identical with its predecessor excepting for the omission of the clearing rod.

Lee-Enfield

Short rifles: Mks I and I*.
Made by the Royal Small Arms Factory,
Enfield Lock, Middlesex; and the Birmingham Small
Arms Co. Ltd, Small Heath.
·303, rimmed.
Turning-bolt action, with a single lug on the bolt body
locking into the receiver and the rear of the bolt
guide rib abutting the receiver bridge.
44·56in overall, 8·15lb unladen.
25·19in barrel, 5-groove rifling; LH, concentric.
Detachable charger-loaded box magazine, 10 rounds.

Tangent-leaf sight graduated to 2,000 yards.
2,230 ft/sec with Mk VI ball cartridges.
Pattern 1903 sword bayonet.

☆

1902: by the end of the year, a perfected trials rifle had been forthcoming. Changes included provision of an 'eared' front sight, and a modified hand guard. It subsequently became the 'Rifle, Short, Magazine, Lee-Enfield, ·303-inch (Mark I)' on 23 December. Production began immediately, but many minor alterations were soon required.

1903: guns made for naval service were fitted with cut-offs from August 1903 onward, and the manufacturing pattern was re-sealed on 14 September.

1906: approved on 27 March, the Mk I* SMLE had a trap in the butt plate for the oiler and pull-through, a swivel on the butt, and a modified magazine. The basic Mk I pattern was sealed again in September. The use of the cut-off was extended to land service from October, and a shortened lead from the chamber to the bore was approved during the year.

1907: an improved U-notch replaced the 'V' on the back-sight leaf.

Lee-Enfield

Short rifles: [No. 1] Mks III, III*, sniper and emergency patterns.
Made by the Royal Small Arms Factory, Enfield Lock,
Middlesex (1907–22); the Birmingham Small Arms
Co. Ltd, Small Heath (1907–43); the Standard Small
Arms Company, Birmingham (1916–18); National Rifle
Factory No. 1 (1918–19); and many other
contractors (see notes).
Quantity: about 3 million.
·303, rimmed.
Action: as Lee-Enfield short rifle Mk I, above.
44·56in overall, 8·66lb unladen.
25·19in barrel, 5-groove rifling; LH, concentric.
Detachable charger-loaded box magazine, 10 rounds.
Tangent-leaf sight graduated to 2,000 yards.
2,440 ft/sec with Mk VII ball cartridges.
Pattern 1907 sword bayonet.

☆

1906: the ineffectual bolt-head charger guide loosened in service, so monoblock bridge-type guides were developed experimentally. Trials occupied several months.

1907: Enfield-pattern charger guides and an improved Watkin & Speed sight were adopted for a new Mk III SMLE on 26 January. The nose cap was lightened and the back sight protectors were altered.

1910: the adoption of the Mk VII cartridge, raising velocity from 2,230 ft/sec, required the sights to be adapted for the differing trajectory of the new lightweight projectile; changes to the original dial sight were made either by altering the existing graduations or replacing the dial plate entirely.

1911: the magazine and the receiver body were modified in the summer to ensure that the pointed Mk VII bullet fed properly.

1915: the earliest SMLE sniper rifles were fitted with fragile Galilean sights consisting simply of two widely separated lenses, but telescope sights were popular by mid-year. A typical Periscopic Prism Company sight was 12in long, with a 9° field of view and range drums graduated for 100–600 yards. Male dovetails on the sight rings fitted into a bar brazed to the left side of the SMLE action.

By 1918, the sturdy and effectual 2·5 × sights made by Aldis Brothers of Birmingham were preferred. A typical example had a 19mm objective lens and a range drum calibrated '1' to '6' (100–600 yards). Figures published in the 1920s revealed that 9,790 Mk III and Mk III* SMLE sniper rifles had been made during the First World War.

1916: approved on 2 January, the Mk III* SMLE embodied changes to raise production to levels demanded by the First World War. The most obvious external change was the omission of long-range sights. BSA had also discarded the cut-off plate from a few Mk III rifles made in the autumn of 1915, but the component was soon reinstated; however, the authorities subsequently relented, making the cut-off mechanism optional until the end of the First World War in November 1918. A simplified

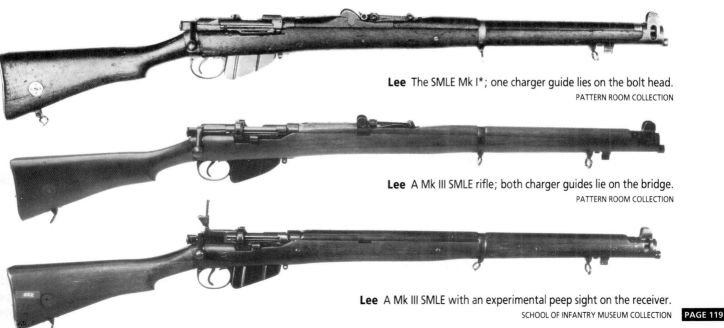

Lee The SMLE Mk I*; one charger guide lies on the bolt head.
PATTERN ROOM COLLECTION

Lee A Mk III SMLE rifle; both charger guides lie on the bridge.
PATTERN ROOM COLLECTION

Lee A Mk III SMLE with an experimental peep sight on the receiver.

cocking piece with grooved flat sides was introduced in August 1916.

1918: announced 'for the record' in December, though in use since mid 1916, ·303 Emergency Pattern Lee-Enfields were old, worn or damaged weapons with their fore-ends lashed with cable or copper wire to minimise splintering should the barrel burst.

1926: guns remaining in service after May were re-designated 'No. 1 Mk III' (or 'III*').

1943: production of No. 1 Mk III rifles ended in the BSA Small Heath, Redditch and Shirley factories (**M47A**, **M47B** and **M47C** respectively). Extensive use had been made of sub-contractors but, apart from insignificant changes to parts such as the cocking piece, few alterations had been made.

Lee-Enfield

Short rifles: Mks V and VI.
Made by the Royal Small Arms Factory, Enfield Lock, Middlesex, 1922–4.
Quantity: 20,000.
·303, rimmed.
Action: as Lee-Enfield short rifle Mk I, above.
DATA FOR SMLE MK V
44·53in overall, 8·65lb unladen.
25·15in barrel, 5-groove rifling; LH, concentric.
Magazine: detachable charger-loaded box, 10 rounds.
Aperture sight graduated to 1,400 yards.
2,440 ft/sec with Mk VII ball cartridges.
Pattern 1907 sword bayonet.

☆

1922: the 'Rifle, Short, Magazine, Lee-Enfield, ·303-inch Mark V' was approved, with aperture sights on the body behind the charger guides, and an additional 'battle sight' for use when the sight was folded down. A reinforcing band appeared behind the nose cap, while the hand guard reached back to the chamber-ring.

1924: extensive trials revealed that the Mk V was far from ideal, so its introduction was cancelled in favour of experiments with the Mk VI. The new gun, which appeared during the summer, had a heavy barrel, a modified body and an improved back sight with distinctive protecting wings. Only a few inches of the muzzle protruded from the fore-end.

Rifle No. 4

Short rifles: No. 1 Mk VI, No. 4 Mks I, I*, 1/2, 1/3, II.
Made by BSA Guns Ltd, Redditch and Shirley, 1940–5 (1·3 million?); the Royal Ordnance Factories, Fazakerley and Maltby, 1942–5 (700,000?); Small Arms Ltd, Long Branch, Toronto, 1942–5 (330,000 for Britain); and the Savage Arms Company, Chicopee Falls, Massachusetts, 1942–5 (1,196,710).
Quantity: about 3·53 million for Britain.
·303, rimmed.
Turning-bolt action, with a single lug on the bolt body locking into the receiver and the rear of the bolt guide rib abutting the receiver bridge.
DATA FOR NO. 4 MK I
44·43in overall, 9·06lb unladen.
25·19in barrel, 2- or 5-groove rifling; LH, concentric.
Detachable charger-loaded box magazine, 10 rounds.
Leaf sight graduated to 2,000 yards.
2,440 ft/sec with Mk VII ball.
No. 4 spike bayonet.

☆

1929: the earliest No. 1 Mk VI rifle was very similar to its mass-produced successor—the No. 4 Mk I—but had a different nose cap, dicing on the fore-end, and a low left body wall.

1930: the modified No. 1 Mk VI Model B lacked butt-plate chequering. At least 1,025 were made in 1930–1.

1933: two thousand additional 'Model B' trials rifles were made with raised left body walls and plain fore-ends. Tests were also undertaken during the mid-1930s with more than fifty examples of the Model C, but the final Model D was abandoned after only a handful had been made. Most surviving Model B rifles were converted to No. 4 standards and issued to the British Army in 1940, shortly after the withdrawal from Dunkirk. Diced fore-ends and fluted hand guards distinguished them.

1939: approved on 15 November on the basis of the Model B trials rifle, the No. 4 Mk I was not issued until the Spring of 1942. Rough machining and the six-inch spike bayonet soon received adverse comments. The rifle's real advantages initially passed unnoticed.

1941: many changes were made to fittings during the Second World War to simplify mass production. There were, for example, several No. 4 back sights, ranging from the Mk 1, graduated from 200 to 1,300 yards in 50-yard increments, to the Mk 2 rocking 'L' for 300 and 600 yards. Two-groove rifling was approved in 1941, and used until declared obsolete in July 1945. The early flared-rim cocking piece was replaced first with a flat three-groove pattern and then an entirely plain type. Butt plates on wartime guns were often mazak alloy instead of gunmetal, while stock wood was often inferior and sling swivels were reduced to bent wire.

The No. 4 Mk I* was approved in June 1941, but made only in Canada and the USA. The action body was modified and the 'catch head, breech bolt' was omitted.

1949: the No 4 Mk 2 was approved on 4 December 1947 to replace the unsuccessful No. 5, but was not introduced until 1949. The trigger pivoted on the underside of the body instead of on the trigger guard, so the revised Mk 2 fore-end could not be exchanged with the earlier type. No. 4 Mk 1 back sights were used. Revision of original Mk 1 and 1* rifles to Mk 2 standards began at this time; Mk 1/2 and Mk 1/3 had been British-made Mk 1 and North American-made Mk I* rifles respectively.

No. 4 Mk I (T)

Sniper rifle.
Most were assembled by Holland & Holland, London, 1942–5 (see notes).
·303, rimmed.
Otherwise as No. 4 Mk I, excepting 11·25lb with sight.

☆

1940: shortages of suitable equipment in the early stages of the Second World War were solved by fitting Aldis sights to P/14 rifles and by converting about 1,400 No. 1 Mk VI trials rifles to No. 4 standards. Auxiliary cheek pieces were authorised in September 1940.

1942: the perfected No. 4 Mk I (T) rifles,

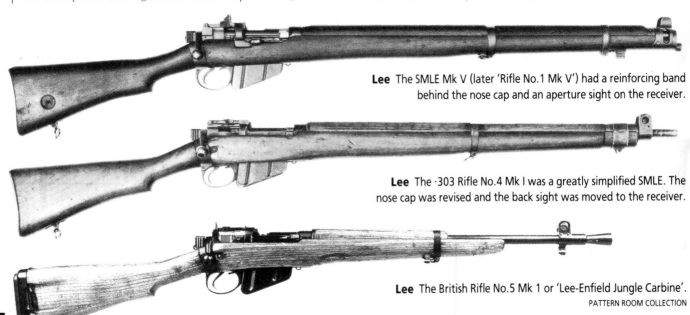

Lee The SMLE Mk V (later 'Rifle No.1 Mk V') had a reinforcing band behind the nose cap and an aperture sight on the receiver.

Lee The ·303 Rifle No.4 Mk I was a greatly simplified SMLE. The nose cap was revised and the back sight was moved to the receiver.

Lee The British Rifle No.5 Mk 1 or 'Lee-Enfield Jungle Carbine'.

PATTERN ROOM COLLECTION

approved on 12 February, were issued with No. 32 telescope sights. The No. 32 Mk I sight weighed 2lb 3oz, had a 19mm objective lens, a 9° field of view, and a range drum graduated 100–1,000 yards. Much conversion work was sub-contracted to Holland & Holland (S51), who completed 26,442 of about 28,500 sniper rifles. BSA-made guns were preferred, though a few Stevens-Savage examples were used in 1942.

No. 5 Mk 1

'Lee-Enfield Jungle Carbine'.
Made by BSA Guns Ltd, Shirley (81,330); and the Royal Ordnance Factory, Fazakerley (169,810).
·303, rimmed
Action: as No. 4 Mk 1, above.
39·50in overall, 7·16lb unladen.
18·70in barrel (excluding flash hider), 5-groove rifling; LH, concentric.
Detachable charger-loaded box magazine, 10 rounds.
Leaf sight graduated to 800 yards.
About 2,100 ft/sec with Mk VII ball cartridges.
No. 5 knife bayonet.

☆

1944: the Lee-Enfield 'Jungle Carbine' arose from a 1943-vintage request for a lighter weapon for use in the Far East. Trials undertaken in 1944 with shortened rifles proved that accuracy was acceptable, but that recoil increased.
1945: the No. 5 Mk 1 was approved on 23 May. Made with the three standard butts, it had a half-length fore-end, and a modified No. 4 Mk 1-type back sight. Guns were ordered from the BSA and Fazakerley factories, where work on the No. 4 stopped. However, the popularity of the Jungle Carbine was temporary: accuracy was poor. As experiments failed to pinpoint the cause, the No. 5 was declared obsolete in 1947.

L8 series

Short rifles: L8A1, L8A2, L8A3, L8A4, L8A5, L39A1 and L42A1.
Made by the Royal Small Arms Factory, Enfield Lock, Middlesex (Royal Ordnance plc).
7·62 × 51mm, rimless.

Action: as No. 4 Mk I, above.
DATA FOR L39A1
46·50in overall, 9·72lb unladen.
27·56in barrel, 4-groove rifling; RH, concentric.
Detachable charger-loaded box magazine, 10 rounds.
Micro-adjustable aperture sight.
2,770 ft/sec with standard ball cartridges.

☆

1960*: 7·62mm conversions of the ·303 No. 4 Lee-Enfield formed the L8 series. The L8A1 was based on the No. 4 Mk 2; the L8A2 on the No. 4 Mk 1/2; the L8A3 on the No. 4 Mk 1/3; the L8A4 on the No. 4 Mk 1; and the L8A5 on the No. 4 Mk 1*. Conversion kits comprising a new barrel, a modified extractor, a new magazine and a charger-guide insert were made in the Royal Small Arms Factory, Enfield (marked UE), and by the Sterling Engineering Co. Ltd of Dagenham (US).
1970: adopted on 24 August for issue to British snipers, prior to the introduction of the L96A1 in the mid 1980s, the L42A1 was converted from existing No. 4 Mk 1 (T) rifles and had the trigger lever pivoted on the trigger guard. It has been issued with the 'Telescope, Straight, Sighting, L1A1' (the old No. 32 Mk 3).

Touted commercially as the 'Enfield Envoy', the essentially similar L39A1 had a sporting-style half stock and aperture sights. Used by the British armed forces for competitive shooting, it was invariably built on a Mk 2 action with the trigger pivoted on the underside of the body.

USA

James Lee formed the Lee Arms Company in Bridgeport, Connecticut, in 1879. The earliest bolt-action prototypes had their bolt handles behind the receiver bridge.

Model 1879

Rifle and carbine: Remington-Lee.
Made by E. Remington & Sons, Ilion, 1880–4.
·45-70, rimmed (see notes).
Turning-bolt action, locked by the bolt-guide rib abutting the receiver ahead of the bridge.

DATA FOR US ARMY TRIALS RIFLE
48·50in overall, 8·50lb unladen.
29·50in barrel, 3-groove rifling; RH, concentric.
Detachable box magazine, 5 rounds.
Ramp-and-leaf sight graduated to 1,200 yards.
1,320 ft/sec with ball cartridges.
US M1873 socket bayonet.

☆

1879: a US patent granted to Lee in November protected a rifle with a simple turning-bolt action. The extractor rotated with the bolt, a detachable box magazine was fitted, and a cut-off permitted single-loading.
1881: the US Navy purchased the first of about 250 Lee rifles to arm newly-commissioning warships and facilitate long-term assessment. Made in Ilion by Remington, but marked as products of the Lee Arms Company, almost all 1879-type guns purchased by the navy bore distinctive inspectors' marks (e.g., WWK) plus an anchor above U.S.. The one-piece walnut stock, lacking a hand guard, had two barrel bands. Swivels lay on the magazine and on the nose-band. The half-cock notch sufficed as a safety.

Navy guns chambered the standard ·45–70 government cartridges, but ·44–77 Necked and ·43 Spanish were available to order. They were successful enough to convince the US Navy of their merits—the Bureau of Ordnance was less conservative than its army counterpart.

Model 1882

Rifle and carbine: Remington-Lee.
Made by E. Remington & Sons, Ilion, 1882–4.
·45–70, rimmed.
Turning-bolt action, locked by the bolt-guide rib abutting the receiver bridge and a lug opposing the bolt handle.
DATA FOR US ARMY TRIALS RIFLE
48·50in overall, 8·50lb unladen.
29·50in barrel, 3-groove rifling; RH, concentric.
Detachable box magazine, 5 rounds.
Ramp-and-leaf sight graduated to 1,200 yards.
1,320 ft/sec with ball cartridges.
US M1873 socket bayonet.

☆

Lee A ·433 M1885 Remington-Lee, tested in Britain in 1887.
PATTERN ROOM COLLECTION

Lee An 1899-model Remington-Lee carbine, with a leaf-type sight. This specimen lacks the cocking piece. REMINGTON MUSEUM COLLECTION

Lee An 1899-model Remington-Lee rifle, with a quadrant-type sight. This gun is cocked. REMINGTON MUSEUM COLLECTION

1882: the rifles tested during army trials in September chambered regulation government cartridges. One gun was a standard M1879, but there was also an M1882 with an 'improved bolt'. On 29 September, the board reported that the latter was preferred to the Chaffee-Reece and the Hotchkiss—owing to the detachable box magazine and an additional locking lug.

1884: E. Remington & Sons delivered 750 1882-pattern Lee rifles in the late autumn to facilitate trials against the Springfield-made Chaffee-Reece and the Winchester-Hotchkiss. Work was completed late in 1885, when the Chief of Ordnance informed the Secretary of War that the Lee had performed better than its rivals. However, most officers still preferred the single-shot ·45–70 service rifle.

The US Navy also favoured the Lee, acquiring 700 guns in 1884, but it is not known whether these were of 1879 or 1882 pattern.

Model 1885

Rifle and carbine: Remington-Lee.
Made by E. Remington & Sons, Ilion, New York, 1886–7; and the Remington Arms Company, Ilion, New York, 1888–92.
·45–70, rimmed.
Action: as M1882, above.
DATA FOR US NAVY TRIALS RIFLE
52·00in overall, 8·50lb unladen.
33·50in barrel, 3-groove rifling; RH, concentric.
Detachable box magazine, 5 rounds.
Ramp-and-leaf sight graduated to 1,200 yards.
1,350 ft/sec with ball cartridges.
US M1873 socket bayonet.

☆

1884: Lee and his employee Louis Diss received a US Patent in March to protect a magazine that retained cartridges when detached from the gun. Assigned to Remington, this feature was incorporated in an improved rifle, together with a separate bolt-head, a non-rotating extractor and an enlarged cocking-piece. Stocks and sights duplicated those of the M1882.

1887: 500 guns were supplied to Denmark as 'Førsøgsrepetergeværer m/1' (experimental repeating rifles), and 350 guns in ·43 (11mm Spanish) went to Britain.

1888: owing to the collapse of E. Remington & Sons, two years previously, newly made rifles were marked REMINGTON ARMS COMPANY. Guns marked U.S. beneath an anchor, with inventory numbers and inspectors' initials, were used by the US Navy: 1,500 were delivered in 1888–9.

Model 1899

Rifle and carbine: Remington-Lee.
Made by the Remington Arms Company, Ilion, New York, 1899–1906.
Quantity: 40,000?
6mm Lee, 7 × 57mm, 7·65 × 53mm, ·303, ·30–30 Winchester or ·30–40 Krag.
Action: as M1885, above.
DATA FOR A TYPICAL RIFLE
·30–40, rimmed.
47·60in overall, 8·50lb unladen.
29·00in barrel, 4-groove rifling; RH, concentric.
Detachable box magazine, 10 rounds.
Ramp-and-leaf sight graduated to 2,000 yards.
About 2,000 ft/sec with ball cartridges.
M1899 knife or sword bayonet.

☆

1899: chambered for a variety of cartridges, Lee-type turning-bolt rifles sold in substantial numbers in South and Central America prior to 1900. Gradually, however, the American design lost ground to rivals in the New World—particularly to Mauser. Even during the crisis of the Spanish-American War, only the Michigan State Militia purchased Remington-Lee rifles.

SPORTING GUNS

The Lee action, owing to its alleged weaknesses, has never been popular among sportsmen excepting in areas of British dominance. But even British gunsmiths promoted it apathetically; supplying good-quality sporting rifles built on Mauser actions, which commanded far higher prices, was more to their taste.

The Lee system has had two principal periods in vogue. It was reasonably popular prior to

1914, and again after the Second World War when colossal numbers of military surplus No. 1 and No. 4 rifles became available.

BRITAIN

Lee-Metford and Lee-Enfield

BSA 'Trade Pattern' rifles.

☆

1892: the Birmingham Small Arms & Munitions Co. Ltd ('BSA&M Co.') offered its first Lee-type rifles commercially, utilising actions taken from regular production runs. A change to Enfield rifling was made about 1896, though the guns were outwardly similar to Metford-barrelled predecessors. Details paralleled those of the contemporary army rifles (q.v.), excepting that the commercial proof marks were used and LEE-SPEED PATENTS replaced British government marks. Among the most desirable of these military-style rifles were many that had been made for volunteer units, until the great British Army reforms of 1908, and several thousands sold to the British South Africa Company prior to the abortive Jameson Raid into the Transvaal in 1896. Others went to India and Afghanistan.

Lee-Enfield

BSA High-Velocity Sporting Rifles: No. 1, No. 2 and No. 3 Patterns.
Made by the Birmingham Small Arms Co. Ltd, Small Heath, c.1902–14.
7 × 57mm, ·303, 8 × 51mm (rimmed), ·32–40 Winchester or ·375.
Turning-bolt action, with a single lug on the bolt body locking into the receiver and the rear of the bolt-guide rib abutting the receiver bridge.
DATA FOR A TYPICAL No. 2
·303, rimmed.
43·50in overall, 7·55lb unladen.
24·00in barrel, five-groove rifling; RH, concentric.
Detachable box magazine, 5 rounds.
Block-and-leaves sight.
About 2,140 ft/sec with 190-grain bullet.

☆

LEE-TYPE RIFLES
LESSER PATTERNS

AUSTRALIA

No. 1 Mk 3 This experimental short rifle was made in the Royal Australian Small Arms Factory, Lithgow, in 1944. Prototypes were given 18in (short) and 20in (intermediate) barrels in search of a handier weapon for jungle fighting. The intermediate barrel was preferred, and a hundred additional guns were made for trials in March. Measuring 39·56in overall, with 20·19in barrels and a weight of 7·8lb, they had a pivoting back sight regulated for 200 and 500 yards. However, the prototype No. 6 held greater potential and the No. 1 was abandoned. Its bayonet was adopted for the Owen sub-machine gun.

Rifle No. 6 Four batches of about fifty near-identical guns were made in the Lithgow factory in 1945, differing only in the butt plates (brass or rubber) and sights. Half the guns had No. 1 tangent-leaf back

sights (No. 6 Mk 1) while the remainder had pivoting aperture sights on the rear of the receiver (No. 6 Mk 1/1). The rifles were similar to the British No. 5 jungle carbine, but were built on the older No. 1 action. They had half-stocks and hand guards, retained by a single band, and multiple grasping grooves were cut in the fore-end. The guns were 39·50in overall, weighed 7·50lb and had 19·00in barrels with standard five-groove rifling; their tangent-leaf sights were graduated to 2,000 yards.

¶ The pattern was approved in the autumn, but the Australian No. 6 was declared obsolete before production began. A few survivors were altered in 1954 for the 7·62 × 51mm NATO cartridge and given detachable 20-round box magazines to satisfy a Royal Australian Air Force specification. Margins of safety in the action proved insufficient, however.

BRITAIN

Trials patterns A ·303 rifle chambering a straight-case cartridge was approved early

in 1888. It had a distinctive butt with a continuous comb and a straight wrist. A bolt-head release catch lay on the right side of the receiver and a long ejector was let into the left side of the bolt-way. The design of the box magazine, the cut-off and the long-range dial sight was credited to Joseph Speed of the Enfield factory. A Martini-style upper band accepted a special sword bayonet. Production amounted to at least 437 rifles and 51 carbines. A typical rifle was 49·88in overall and weighed 9·09lb. Its 29·50in barrel had seven-groove polygonal rifling. A detachable box magazine held seven rounds and the ramp-and-leaf sight was graduated to 1,600 yards.

¶ Experiments were continued throughout the autumn of 1888 with a selection of rimmed, rimless and semi-rim necked cartridge cases. Many minor changes were also made to the rifle, which gained Rigby's patented nose-cap, Lewes-pattern sights and an eight-round single-row magazine. The ejector was simplified, a new safety catch appeared on the left side of the receiver,

and a hand guard was added behind the back sight. The result was the Lee-Metford.

Lee-Metford, Charger Loading Mk II Though the pattern was sealed in 1907, replacement Metford-rifled barrels were in such short supply that work stopped in 1909. Most of the limited quantities of transformations were subsequently fitted with Enfield-type barrels before receiving charger guides and SMLE-type sights in 1913–14.

Lee-Enfield, Converted Mk I Sealed on 2 November 1903, this was such a complex adaption of the Lee-Metford Mk I* that few guns were altered before the design was declared obsolete in 1906.

Lee-Enfield, Charger Loading Mk I (N) Approved in 1914, the 'Rifle, Magazine, Charger-Loading, Lee-Enfield, Naval Service, ·303-inch (Mark I)' resembled the Charger Loading Mk I* (q.v.) and had an identical charger bridge. The original long rifle sights were altered for Mk VII ammunition, the leaf being graduated to 1,900 yards and marked 'C.L.' in the bottom left corner.

Lee-Enfield, Charger Loading Mk I* (N) This was simply a Mk I* Lee-Enfield adapted to Mk I (N) standards; it was approved on 2 October 1914.

Lee-Enfield, Charger Loading Mk II Approval of the bridge-type charger-guides allowed this rifle to be sealed on 1 July 1907. More than 300,000 Mk I and I* rifles had been adapted by Enfield, Vickers, BSA and LSA by 1913.

No. 1 Improved Rifle This was produced by the Royal Small Arms Factory in 1901, in response to complaints made during the Second South African War—for example, that the Lee-Enfield was too complicated and contained too many springs. The No. 1 Improved pattern had a lightened barrel and butt, a full-length hand guard, and an improved nose cap to remove the strain of a fixed bayonet from the barrel. The sights were changed and the safety catch was revised. The most important advance, however, was the advent of a Watkin & Speed charger-loading system. A typical rifle measured 44·56in overall and weighed 8·38lb unladen. Its 25·19in barrel had five-groove concentric rifling, the detachable charger-loaded box magazine held ten rounds, and the tangent-leaf back sight was graduated to 2,000 yards. Muzzle velocity was about 2,030 ft/sec with Mk II ball cartridges and the standard Pattern 1888 sword bayonet could be fitted.

Modified (Shortened) Rifle Made by the Royal Small Arms Factory and issued for trials in the autumn of 1901, this was basically a No. 1 Improved rifle, with additional refinements and a special sword bayonet. About 1,060 were made. The Pattern A (Watkin & Speed) back sight had a front-hinged leaf graduated from 200 to 2,000 yards; the competing Pattern B was hinged at the rear. The safety was changed and an internal barrel band was used. Short, normal and long butts were tested, as well as differing bayonets.

¶ The shortened rifles were popular, despite minor problems, and comparative trials with a selection of standard full-length rifles revealed little change in accuracy.

¶ Almost all surviving trial rifles were altered to SMLE standards in about 1903–4—and then converted for Aiming Tube use in 1906–7 before being discarded.

Short Lee-Enfield, Converted Mk I** Accepted for naval service in January 1908, this SMLE was transformed by Royal Navy ordnance depots in Chatham, Plymouth and Portsmouth. Despite being fitted with Mk III sights, the guns all retained the original two-piece charger guides on the bridge and bolt head. A large 'N' appeared on the left side of the receiver shoe. In 1912, surviving guns were re-sighted for Mk VII ball ammunition and given bridge-type charger guides. Complementary changes were made in the stock and the incurving front sight protectors were straightened.

Short Lee-Enfield, Converted Mk I*** This rifle was sealed on 22 August 1914 to guide adaption of the earlier Mk I* (q.v.) for Mk VII cartridges.

Short Lee-Enfield, Converted Mk II Sealed on 16 January 1903, though final approval was withheld until November, the Converted Mk II was adapted from the Mk I or Mk I* Lee-Enfields and a few Mks II or II* Lee-Metfords. New short barrels were fitted; charger guides appeared on the receiver and bolt head; there were new sights; and the original stock was greatly modified. Owing to improvements made in the Converted Mk II*, the pattern for the preceding Converted Mk II was re-sealed in September 1906.

Short Lee-Enfield, Converted Mk II* Approved on 15 March 1906 and adapted from old Lee-Metfords (Mks II, II*) or Lee-Enfields (Mks I, I*), this was comparable with the standard SMLE Mk I* (q.v.).

Short Lee-Enfield, Converted Mk II** Modified by the navy ordnance depots in Chatham, Plymouth and Portsmouth, these short rifles were accepted for naval service in July 1908. They were similar to the Converted Mk I** (q.v.), originally retaining two-piece charger guides. As described above, surviving guns were re-sighted for Mk VII ball ammunition in 1912 and fitted with bridge-type charger guides. Changes to the stock and sight protectors were made at the same time.

Short Lee-Enfield, Converted Mk II*** Introduced in 1909, this was practically identical with the Converted Mk II**. Two-piece charger guides were used. Most of the remaining rifles were re-sighted for Mk VII ball ammunition in 1912. They received bridge-type charger guides, minor changes were made in the stock, and the front sight protectors were straightened.

Short Lee-Enfield, Converted Mk IV Sealed on 17 June 1907, this was little more than the Converted Mk II (q.v.) improved to SMLE Mk III standards. It weighed 8·9lb.

Short Lee-Enfield, Mk I A.T. This centre-fire training rifle embodied the ·23 Mk I 'Aiming Tube' (a sub-calibre barrel insert). It was approved in November 1903, though a satisfactory pattern was not sealed until 1906. The guns were generally rebuilt from SMLE trials rifles and classified as 'Non-Interchangeable'. Specimens displayed 'A.T.' and 'N.I.' on the body, bolt, barrel and butt. On 13 December 1907, however, the ·22 rimfire SMLE Mk I trainer was substituted.

CANADA

After using Martini-Henry and Lee-Metford rifles, the Canadians elected to follow independent lines by adopting the Ross (q.v.) in 1903. The spectacular failure of the Ross in the First World War led to the belated standardisation of the SMLE in 1916, though no manufacture occurred until the Long Branch factory operated by the government owned Small Arms Ltd tooled for No. 4 rifles in 1940.

¶ Canadian-made rifles used by the British Army are described in the main text. They followed the improved No. 4 Mk I* pattern, unique to North American production, and had a distinctively shaped safety catch. Some had C Mk 2 and C Mk 3 back sights; fabricated from stampings, these were broadly similar to the British Mks 3 and 4 respectively. Canadian guns were regarded as very well made, had serial numbers such as '12L1926' and bore an 'LB' monogram maker's mark. By 31 December 1945, Long Branch had made about 905,730 No. 4 Mk I and I* rifles for the British and Canadian forces. Canadian rifles normally displayed 'DᴧC' ('Dominion of Canada') or '𝕮'.

¶ Substantial quantities of No. 4 Mk I* (T) sniper rifles had also been assembled, the total by the end of 1945 standing in the region of 1,140—some for Britain and the remainder for Canada. The actions were selected for accuracy and carefully stocked in the manner of the standard British No. 4 Mk I (T) (q.v.), though a few, intended for trials, have been found with pistol-grip butts and a roll-over Monte Carlo comb.

¶ A selection of optical sights was used, including the standard C No. 32, the No. 32 Trade Pattern (a commercial Lyman Alaskan sight in a Griffin & Howe mount), and the C No. 32 Mk 4. Made by Research Enterprises Ltd of Montreal, the Mk 4 was subsequently redesignated 'C No. 67'.

Lightweight No.4 rifle The only other indigenous development of note was this weapon, with a one-piece stock and every conceivable attempt to save weight. The gun measured 42·10in overall, had a 22·75in barrel and weighed less than 6lb. About fifty were made in 1944.

CHINA

At least 40,000 Stevens-Savage No. 4 Mk I* rifles were supplied under aid programmes agreed between China and the USA early in the Second World War. It is assumed that they bore appropriate markings.

INDIA

The army, part of British Establishment until independence was gained in 1947, was initially armed from Britain. Early in the present century, however, powder mills in the town of Ishapore (now Ishapur) were converted to an arms factory, the first guns being made in 1905. Gradually, a series of 'India Pattern' weapons was approved. Though they followed British prototypes, changes were authorised to suit local conditions. Differing butt plates were fitted, often to allow pull-throughs and cleaning material to be carried in the butts of rifles that were not similarly fitted in Britain; changes to stocks accounted for climate or unskilled labour.

¶ Indian-made rifles were distinguished by butt-socket marks such as 'ISHAPORE' or 'R.F.I.' ('Rifle Factory, Ishapur', post-1950) and 'I.P.' for 'India Pattern'. SMLE rifles made after 1950 substituted an *Asoka* for a crowned 'E.R.I.' cypher (1905–10, 1936) or 'G.R.I.' (1910–47). The *Asoka* comprised four lions on top of a column—not tigers, as has been claimed—though only three animals are visible. Property marks included ↑I, while stock roundels displayed names such as Ferozepore or Allahabad.

India Pattern Lee-Enfield carbine Approved on 8 January 1904, this was issued to the Sappers & Miners with the P/1888 sword bayonet. A standard rifle-type nose cap was fitted with a Martini-pattern swivel, a second swivel being added on the under-edge of the butt.

¶ In 1924, survivors were re-chambered for ·303 Mk VII cartridges and the back-sight graduations were altered. The maximum sighting distance was 1,000 yards.

India Pattern Lee-Enfield, Mk I* This was simply a Mk I* Long Lee-Enfield with a short-rifle butt, which had a trap for cleaning materials and the pull-through.

India Pattern Lee-Enfield, Charger Loading Mk I This was simply a Mk I long Lee-Enfield with one charger guide attached to the receiver bridge; the other was brazed to the bolt head and milled to size. Transformation was underway well before similar work began in Britain. Many were converted for bridge-type charger guides after 1912, and re-classified 'Mk II I.P.'.

India Pattern Lee-Enfield, Charger Loading Mk I* This was created by fitting charger guides to Mk I* long Lee-Enfield rifles. Rifles converted for bridge-type charger guides after 1912 were re-classified as 'Mk II I.P.'.

India Pattern Lee-Enfield, Charger Loading Mk II This conversion of British-made Mks I and I* long rifles was approved on 8 September 1909, the original weapons gaining SMLE Mk III bridge-type charger guides instead of the less effectual bolt-and-bridge design.

India Pattern Lee-Enfield, Charger Loading, Mk II* Approved in 1910, this was the Mk II rifle (described above) fitted with a Mk I* SMLE-type butt, shoulder plate and inletted butt swivel.

India Pattern Short Lee-Enfield, Mk I* Sealed on 30 August 1910, this was simply the standard British Mk I SMLE fitted with a Mk I* butt, shoulder plate, and inletted swivel.

India Pattern single-shot Lee-Enfield Approved by the Secretary of State for India in December 1909, 2,000 full-length guns were made at Enfield in 1911–12 for Frontier Levies. The magazine well was filled with a wood block and a special trigger guard/magazine plate was fitted.

¶ Beginning in 1913, most guns were altered to accept a Martini-type swivel through the front of the trigger guard, the butt swivel being removed.

India Pattern single-shot short Lee-Enfield This was approved on 21 August 1923. The magazine aperture was filled with a wood block and a special trigger-guard/magazine plate was fitted. Single-shot rifles were made at Ishapore into the 1930s, for issue to troops whose loyalty was not above suspicion.

7·62mm Rifles No. 1 Mk 3* These were made in the late 1950s for the 7·62 × 51mm cartridge—an interim measure while tooling for the 1-A SL rifle (an FAL variant) was undertaken. Distinguished by their squared box magazines, the guns were made of better-grade steel than their ·303 predecessors to perform reliably.

IRAQ

The government purchased new No. 1 Mk III Lee-Enfield short rifles from Britain in the mid 1930s, an order for 16,000 guns being passed to BSA Guns Ltd in 1935. As these guns were newly made, they lacked British markings; instead, they bore a reversed angular 'S' in a triangle.

IRELAND

This was integral with the United Kingdom prior to 1922, when the Irish Free State (Eire) gained independence from the six counties ('Northern Ireland') remaining loyal to the British.

Irish Constabulary Carbine Work began in Enfield in 1905 to create ten thousand of these guns from obsolescent rifles. They had a very distinctive nose cap, and feathers of wood were generally let into the fore-end channel. Butt discs were marked 'R.I.C.'

1902*: inspired by a rise of interest in the magazine sporting rifle, and particularly by some of the guns produced by enterprising gunsmiths on the basis of the Trade Pattern action, BSA introduced its own sporters.

Built on the action of the Lee-Enfield Mk I, with a plain Lee-Metford type cocking piece, the Pattern No. 1 BSA had its bolt handle turned down and slightly forward in the manner of the standard military carbines. The two-piece stock offered a pistol-grip butt, and a half-length fore-end with a rounded rosewood, horn or ebonite tip. The barrel had a full-length top rib mounting a Cape-pattern back sight graduated to 1,000 yards; the front sight was usually a bead with protecting wings.

No. 2 was a cheaper version of No. 1, with a plain barrel; No. 3 had a plainer stock and a safety catch mounted on the cocking piece. Cape-pattern back sights and protected front-sight beads were standard, though BSA No. 9 aperture sights could be fitted.

A special variant of the No. 1 sporter was made for the ·375 'Flanged' (rimmed) Nitro Express cartridge; it was identical with the standard No. 1, but had a heavyweight barrel, a four-round magazine and an Express back sight comprising a standing block and two small folding leaves. The front sight was usually a blade or barleycorn with a sheet-steel hood.

1914: production was apparently stopped by the First World War, and concentration on military production. Though it is believed that a few sporting rifles and carbines were sold in the early 1920s from store, none has yet been seen with the post-1919 trading style 'BSA Guns Ltd'.

Lee-Enfield

BSA Magazine Sporting Carbines.
Made by the Birmingham Small Arms Co. Ltd, Small Heath, c.1902-14
7 × 57mm, ·303 or 8 × 51mm.
Action: as BSA sporting rifle, above.
DATA FOR A TYPICAL NO. 3
·303, rimmed.
40·50in overall, 7·35lb unladen.

21·00in barrel, 5-groove rifling; LH, concentric.
Detachable box magazine, 5 rounds.
Leaf sight graduated to 2,000 yards.
About 1,900 ft/sec with 215-grain bullet.

☆

1902*: introduced concurrently with the BSA Lee-Enfield sporting rifle, these were also offered in four differing patterns.

Numbers 1 and 2, ''for officers' use'', very similar to each other and chambered only for ·303 cartridges, could be distinguished by their military-style butts with the unique semi-pistol grip. Chequering on the butt and fore-end distinguished the No. 1, which accepted the P/1888 bayonet, from many otherwise similar service-issue carbines. The No. 2, however, was stocked virtually to the muzzle and had a horn or ebonite fore-end tip.

The No. 3 'Trade Pattern' carbine was a plain version of No. 1. It lacked chequering on the stock, but had a military-type back sight and a safety catch on the cocking piece. No. 4 seems to have been a hybrid with a 22in barrel, a cocking-piece safety, the military-style butt and a half-length fore-end. Cape-type back sights were popular. Unlike the others, the No. 4 could chamber 7 × 57mm Mauser rimless or 8 × 51mm French rimmed cartridges.

Lee-Enfield

Parker-Hale No. 1 and No. 4 Sporting Rifles, Standard, De Luxe, Supreme and Custom models.
Made by Parker-Hale Ltd, Birmingham, c.1953–75.
·303, rimmed.
Action: as BSA sporting rifle, above.
DATA FOR A TYPICAL SUPREME NO. 1
41·50in overall, 8·00lb unladen.
22·00in barrel, 5-groove rifling; RH, concentric rifling.
Detachable box magazine, 5 rounds.
Tangent-leaf sight graduated to 2,000 yards.
About 2,080 ft/sec with 190-grain bullet.

☆

1953*: the first of these rifles, later known as the Standard and De Luxe No. 1, were converted from military surplus Mk III SMLE.

They retained their charger guides, but had a half-length fore-end and the original back sight protectors were removed. The standard pattern had a 10-round magazine and an open front sight; the De Luxe verson had its front sight on a special ramp and a five-round magazine.

1958*: the Supreme No. 1 was introduced to satisfy increasingly discerning clientele. Though retaining the original military-pattern action, complete with charger guides, it had a new pistol-grip butt with a sculpted Monte Carlo comb, and a chequered round-tipped fore-end.

1965*: the Custom No. 1 pattern embodied a refurbished SMLE action with the unsightly charger guides removed and the left wall of the receiver adapted so that an adjustable side mount for an optical sight could be fitted.

The butt had a ventilated recoil pad, and was separated by white spacers from the pistol-grip cap and obliquely-cut fore-end tip. A simple spring and elevator back sight was standard on these guns.

The Custom No. 4 Lee-Enfield was practically identical to the Custom No. 1, but built on the newer action; however, though this was stronger than the No. 1, there is no evidence that Parker-Hale ever offered chamberings other than ·303.

Note: rifles of this general type (though differing in detail) will also be found with the marks of A.G. Parker & Co. Ltd, one of Parker-Hale's forerunners. These date prior to 1936.

USA

Remington-Lee

Magazine Sporting Rifle.
Made by the Remington Arms Company, Ilion, New York, c.1899–1906.
6mm (Lee), 7 × 57mm, 7·65 × 53mm, ·303, ·30–30 Winchester, ·30–40 Krag, ·32–40 Winchester, ·35 Remington, ·38–72 Winchester, ·43 Spanish, ·44–77 Necked or ·45–70 Government.
Turning-bolt action, with a single lug on the bolt body locking into the receiver and the rear of the guide rib abutting the receiver bridge.

('Royal Irish Constabulary'); the last guns were dispatched to Ireland in 1906.

NEW ZEALAND

Lacking production facilities, New Zealand relied on British and Australian weapons. In response to requests, Enfield made the first of about 1,500 'Carbine, Magazine, Lee-Enfield, fitted to receive P/88 Sword-bayonet' in 1901. Work was completed in 1903. The diameter of the muzzle was increased, and the sights duplicated those of the Martini-Enfield Artillery Carbine Mk III. The guns were 40·31in overall, had 21in barrels and weighed about 7·5lb; 'N↑Z' usually appeared on the butt.

SOUTH AFRICA

Formed in 1900 during the Second South African (Boer) War, the Union of South Africa was armed with Lee-Enfield rifles until the approval of the R1 (FN FAL) in the early 1960s. The guns were usually distinguished by a ⌐↑⌐ property mark. No

substantial manufacturing has ever been undertaken, apart from replacement barrels marked 'U' over crossed pennants over 'P'.

USA

·30 M1885 rifle Breech-loading rifle trials undertaken by the US Army in 1890-2 included this ten-shot pattern submitted on behalf of the Lee Arms Company of South Windham, Connecticut. However, the small-calibre Lee rifles did not prove acceptable, even though one—No. 5—reached the final elimination stage. The Krag-Jørgensen was preferred largely owing to the design of its magazine.

SPORTING GUNS

Many British gunmakers handled Lee-type sporters, usually bought wholesale from BSA. These will usually bear a discreet Piled Arms mark on the action. **Century International Arms** of St Albans, Vermont, introduced the '·303 Century Enfield Sporter No. 4' in 1987. Built on a No. 4 Lee-Enfield action, this had beech

woodwork. The butt had a cheek piece and a Monte Carlo comb.
W.W. Greener Ltd of Birmingham offered Lee-Enfield sporting and military rifles prior to 1914. These were rarely anything other than standard BSA-made guns with Greener marks, the No. 1 sporting rifle being most popular; according to *The Gun and Its Development* (1910), ·303 or ·375 Magazine Action Rifles were being offered with 'sporting finish, and well engraved'; with a plain finish; or with a short barrel. Long Lee-Enfield rifles, 'specially sighted and tested for Match shooting', were also to be found. Other guns incorporated BSA actions with Greener's own stocks and fittings.
Alfred G. Parker & Co. Ltd of Birmingham, a part of Parker-Hale (q.v.) after 1936, offered Lee-Enfield sporters built on the SMLE Mk III or No. 1 action. Most of these prove to have been refurbished military weapons, though a few may have been purchased, new, from BSA.
Westley Richards & Co. Ltd of Birmingham, one of the few provincial

gunmakers to challenge 'Best London' work for quality, was another of many to offer BSA-made rifles. A few No. 1-type sporting rifles were chambered for the proprietary ·303/375 Axite cartridge introduced about 1906. The 215-grain bullet developed a muzzle velocity of 2,500 ft/sec, making it more powerful than the regular service-type ·303. It is suspected that the Axite cartridge tested the original Lee-Enfield action to its limits, as survivors are rare.

"THE MUSKETEERS"

Lee 'The Musketeers'. Taken in France in July 1918, this picture shows a fine array of bandoliers and SMLE Mk III rifle—note the long-range sights in the fore-end.

Lee A section of the Lee-Enfield rifle, from ▷ W.W. Greener's *The Gun and Its Development*, ninth edition, 1910.

Lee The King of the Belgians inspects Anzac troops stationed on the Belgian section of the Western Front, 1916.

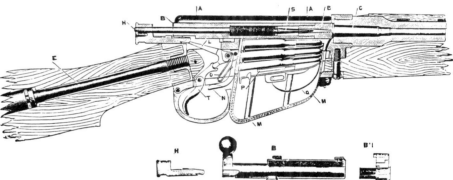

DATA FOR A TYPICAL EXAMPLE
·38–72 Winchester, rimmed.
46·25in overall, 8·53lb unladen.
28·00in barrel, 4-groove rifling; RH, concentric.
Detachable box magazine, 5 rounds.
Ramp-and-leaf sight graduated to 2,000 yards.
About 1,475 ft/sec with 275-grain bullet.

☆

1899: as the export markets that had once accepted Remington-Lee military rifles slowly disappeared, sporters were offered in an attempt to use existing actions.

Their round barrels measured 24–28in, and the high quality walnut stocks had generously proportioned and chequered pistol grips; the half length fore-ends were also chequered, but tapered rapidly to a very slender tip.

Although the Remington-Lee sporters were offered in a wide variety of chamberings, and despite the efforts made by Marcellus Hartley & Company and others to sell them throughout the Americas, the bolt action was still greeted apathetically by huntsmen.

Only after the end of the First World War—with the return to civilian life of so many conscripted servicemen—did the situation change sufficiently for bolt-action guns to challenge the traditional lever-operated varieties.

LJUNGMANN

SWEDEN
Also known as 'Eklund-Ljungmann'.

This gas-operated rifle owed its adoption to the enlargement of the Swedish armed forces during the Second World War, at a time when Mauser rifles were in short supply. As the principal suppliers in Belgium and Czechoslovakia were under German control, and unable to simply accelerate production of m/38 rifles in the state arms factory, the Swedish authorities decided to introduce an untried auto-loader made by a private contractor. A prototype Ljungmann rifle—said to have been based on Soviet Tokarevs captured in Finland—was given to an

experienced production engineer, Erik Eklund, progressing so speedily that series production commenced within a year. That the rifle worked at all was a considerable feat; field service subsequently revealed flaws, but they concerned constructional details rather than the basic direct-impingement gas system and the locking mechanism.

DENMARK
Madsen-Ljungmann

Made by Dansk Industri Syndikat A/S 'Madsen', Herlev.
7·9 × 57mm and others.
Gas-operated auto-loading action, locked by a tilting bolt.
Otherwise generally as Swedish and Egyptian rifles (see below), excepting that a Danish-type knife bayonet was used.

☆

1942: impressed by the success of the Swedish Ag-42, the Madsen company negotiated a licence with the inventor in the hope of persuading the Danish army to adopt the rifle to replace the Krag-Jørgensen once the German occupation had ceased.

1945: Madsen prototypes were chambered for—amongst others—the 7 × 57mm and 7·9 × 57mm cartridges, which were larger and more powerful than the 6·5mm Swedish pattern. Consequently, the Danish rifle had a more robust breech mechanism than the Ag-42. As the earliest Madsen prototypes had been prone to extraction failures and case-head separations, the gas tube was coiled around the barrel to lengthen the distance from the barrel-port to the bolt carrier face. This extended the delay before the breech opened, but made the rifles much more difficult to clean than their Swedish antecedents.

Work on the Madsen-Ljungmann dragged on into the early 1950s, with little tangible result. The rifles could be recognised by their nose caps, with an attachment bar for a conventional bayonet, and by the ventilated sheet-steel hand guard above the fore-end.

EGYPT
Hakim

Made by the State Factory 54, Port Said (later Maadi Military & Civil Industries Company).
7·9 × 57mm, rimless.
Action: as Danish Madsen rifle, above.
1,209mm overall, 4·82kg unladen.
590mm barrel, 4-groove rifling; concentric, RH.
Detachable box magazine, 10 rounds.
Tangent-leaf sight graduated to 1,000 metres.
870 m/sec with standard ammunition.
No bayonet.

☆

1954: a combination of the overthrow of King Farouk and the comparative failure of the SAFN rifle in service created the need to establish an indigenous small arms industry. This was undertaken with the machine-tools purchased from Husqvarna in Sweden.

1955: production of the Hakim rifle began. It was essentially similar to the Swedish Ag-42.B, sharing the straight-tube gas system and aberrant cocking system, but was appreciably heavier and its gas port could be adjusted to allow for variations in ammunition pressure. It was stocked to the muzzle, with a single retaining band, and had a wooden hand guard from the chamber to the nose cap. A perforated muzzle brake/compensator appeared ahead of the front sight block. In addition to Arabic markings on the back-sight leaf, the rifle was usually dated on the front left side of the receiver above its serial number.

The Hakim was acceptably accurate, but heavy and unwieldy. As it was also susceptible to jamming in sandy conditions, the Egyptians eventually substituted the lighter and more effectual Kalashnikov.

Rashid

Made by the State Factory 54, Port Said (later Maadi Military & Civil Industries Company).
7·62 × 39mm, rimless.
Action: as Danish Madsen rifle, above.

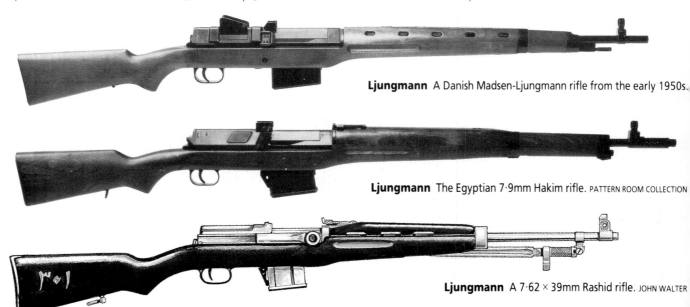

Ljungmann A Danish Madsen-Ljungmann rifle from the early 1950s.

Ljungmann The Egyptian 7·9mm Hakim rifle. PATTERN ROOM COLLECTION

Ljungmann A 7·62 × 39mm Rashid rifle. JOHN WALTER

1,077mm overall, about 3·75kg unladen. 570mm barrel, 4-groove rifling; concentric, RH. Detachable box magazine, 10 rounds. Tangent-leaf sight graduated to 1,000 metres. 730 m/sec with standard ammunition. Integral folding bayonet.

☆

1959*: apparently dating from the period in which tooling for the Kalashnikov was being undertaken, perhaps to provide the Egyptian reserve with weapons chambered for the new intermediate cartridge, this was an improved Hakim. It retained the direct-impingement gas system, but the charging handle was attached directly to the bolt carrier and an SKS-type bayonet pivoted on an attachment block behind the front sight.

SWEDEN

Ag-42

Automatic rifle: Automatiskgevär 42 and 42.B.
Made by Husqvarna Våpenfabriks AB, Huskvarna.
6·5 × 55mm, rimless.
Action: as Danish Madsen pattern, above.
1,205mm overall, 4·65kg unladen.
622mm barrel, 4-groove rifling; concentric, RH.
Detachable box magazine, 10 rounds.
Drum-type sight graduated to 800 metres.
750 m/sec with standard ammunition.
m/96 knife bayonet.

☆

1942: production began in the privately owned Husqvarna factory in an attempt to boost Swedish rifle production without interrupting work on standard m/38 Mauser rifles in the government's Eskilstuna plant.

The bolt of the Ag-42 rested in a carrier, being cammed upward to disengage the receiver floor as propellant gas forced the carrier backward. Though the rifle had a conventional full-length stock, with a hand guard from the chamber to a short distance ahead of the barrel band, it also had an unusual charging action: the sliding breech cover—carrying charger guides—was pushed forward to connect with the bolt mechanism, then retracted to open the breech. The cover disengaged at the end of its rearward stroke, allowing the bolt components to close automatically.

Unlike most other pre-1945 rifles, gas was taken from the bore to impinge directly on the bolt-carrier face without intermediate pistons or rods. This had the merit of simplicity, but was prone to fouling; consequently, the rifle never became universal issue in the Swedish army, being issued on the basis of a few guns per squad to provide additional firepower.

A typical example bore the date on the left side of the breech, split into groups of two digits by the crowned 'C' royal cypher (e.g., 19 [cypher] 43). The serial number lay below the date, and was generally repeated on the left side of the bolt carrier to facilitate assembly.

1947*: a few batches of rifles were made with a large-diameter chamber mid-way along the gas tube to minimise the effects of fouling, reduce the violence of the action and allow for variations in ammunition. However, most Swedish cartridges were loaded consistently enough to operate standard rifles effectually and the modifications were abandoned.

1953: the improved Ag-42.B was adopted. The extractor and the trigger mechanism were strengthened, a stainless-steel gas tube reduced fouling, and a rubber roller on the right side of the breech cover prevented cartridge cases being damaged during ejection. Minor changes were also made to the sights and magazine.

Work ceased in the mid 1950s, whereupon the machinery may have been sold to Egypt.

LJUTIC

UNITED STATES OF AMERICA

◠

The products of this manufacturing company, in addition to individualistic shotguns, have included one of the most bizarre-looking rifles of recent years; production apparently ceased at the end of the 1980s, but could easily be resumed if necessary.

Space Rifle

Made by Ljutic Industries, Inc., Yakima, Washington.
·22-250, ·30-30 WCF, ·30-06 or ·308 Winchester.
DATA FOR A TYPICAL EXAMPLE
·22-250, rimless.
44·00in overall, 8·75lb unladen.
24·00in barrel, rifling pattern not known.
Optical sight.
3,725 ft/sec with 55-grain bullet.

☆

1981: this extraordinary rifle, resembling a straight tube, cannot be mistaken. Often built to the requirements of individual customers, the Space Rifle loaded by twisting the fore-end to release the barrel. A striker was cocked by a handle protruding beneath the receiver, the adjustable trigger often being a thumb button. A recoil-absorbing mechanism was built into the butt and the sights were carried in a high mount.

McMILLAN

UNITED STATES OF AMERICA

◠

McMillan makes small numbers of good quality, but expensive rifles embodying variations on a Mauser-type twin-lug action. The latest guns also incorporate many lessons learned from the original Winchester Model 70.

Signature and Talon series

Alaskan, Classic, Mountain Rifle, Safari, Sporter and Super Varminter.
Made by McMillan Gunworks, Inc., Phoenix, Arizona.
Chambering: see notes.
Turning-bolt action, locked by lugs on the bolt and the bolt handle turning down into its seat.
DATA FOR A TYPICAL SIGNATURE ALASKAN
·358 Winchester, rimless.
44·38in overall, 8·25lb unladen.
24·00in barrel, rifling pattern not known.
Folding-leaf sight.
2,250 ft/sec with 250-grain bullet.

☆

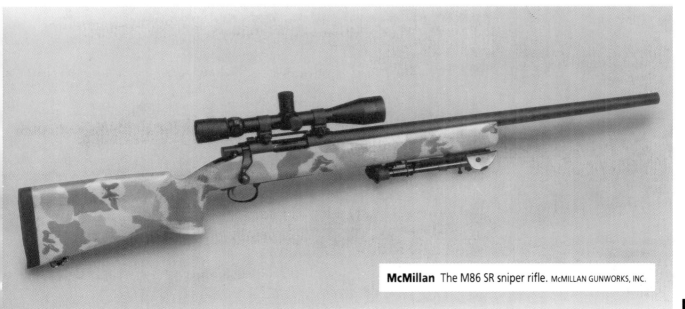

McMillan The M86 SR sniper rifle. McMILLAN GUNWORKS, INC.

1987: these rifles were introduced in right or left-hand versions. Short-action Signature Classic Sporters were offered—with fixed telescope sight rings—in ·22–250, ·243 Winchester, 6mm Remington, 7mm–08, ·284 Winchester, or ·308 Winchester; long-action patterns were chambered for ·25–06, ·270 Winchester, ·280 Remington, 7mm Remington Magnum, ·300 Weatherby Magnum, ·300 Winchester Magnum or ·30–06; and the Magnum action was made for ·338 Winchester Magnum, ·340 Weatherby Magnum or ·375 H&H Magnum.

The barrels measured 22–26in, magazines held three magnum or four standard cartridges, and the trigger pressure was set at 3lb. The fibreglass stocks were finished in beige, black, brown or green; synthetic Fibergrain and walnut patterns were optional extras.

1989: the Signature Super Varminter appeared in ·220 Swift, ·22–250, ·223 Remington, ·243 Winchester, 6mm Remington, ·25–06, 7mm–08 or ·308 Winchester. It was distinguished by a heavy barrel, an adjustable trigger and a specially bedded fibreglass or Fibergrain stock.

The Alaskan model, based on the Classic Sporter, had a folding-leaf back sight, a barrel band bearing a sling eye, and a walnut Monte Carlo-style stock with a Wundhammer-type pistol grip. Metalwork was generally nickel plated. Chamberings included ·270 Winchester, ·280 Remington, 7mm Remington Magnum, ·300 Weatherby Magnum, ·300 Winchester Magnum, ·30–06, ·340 Weatherby Magnum, ·358 Winchester or ·375 H&H Magnum.

The McMillan Signature Mountain Rifle was a Classic Sporter with a titanium alloy receiver. The stock was usually grey-black fibreglass reinforced with graphite, giving an unladen weight of only 5·5lb. Chamberings were ·270 Winchester, ·280 Remington, 7mm Remington Magnum, ·30–06 or ·300 Winchester Magnum.

The Talon Safari embodied a strengthened or 'Safari' action to handle a wide range of magnum cartridges—including ·300 H&H, ·300 Weatherby, ·300 Winchester, ·338 Winchester, ·340 Weatherby, ·375 H&H, ·416 Remington, ·458 Winchester—plus ·404 Jeffrey. The Safari

Super Magnum has been chambered for ·378, ·416 or ·460 Weatherby Magnums, plus ·416 Rigby. Made with a 24in barrel and a fibreglass stock, the rifles were about 43in overall and weighed up to 10lb. Express back sights were usually fitted, with a sling eye on a barrel band. Finish was customarily matt black.

1990: a version of the Classic Sporter appeared with the action and barrel of stainless steel, in a fibreglass stock. The finish was usually natural or black chrome.

1991: the Talon Sporter appeared with a modified action based on the best features of the Model 70 Winchester and the M1903 Springfield. A Winchester-type three-position safety was used. Offered with a choice of walnut or fibreglass stocks, with optional open sights, long-action rifles have been chambered for ·25–06, ·270 Winchester, ·280 Remington or ·30–06. Strengthened actions have been supplied for 7mm Remington Magnum, ·300 H&H, ·300 Winchester, ·300 Weatherby, ·338 Winchester, ·340 Weatherby, ·375 H&H or ·416 Remington Magnum rounds.

Target rifles

Long Range, M-86 Sniper, M-87, M-87R, M-89 Sniper and National Match patterns.
Made by McMillan Gun Works, Inc., Phoenix, Arizona.
Chambering: see notes.
Action: as sporting guns, above.
DATA FOR A TYPICAL M-89 SNIPER
·308 Winchester, rimless.
48·00in overall, 15·25lb unladen.
28·00in barrel (including muzzle brake), 4-groove rifling, RH, concentric.
Optical sight.
2,850 ft/sec with 150-grain bullet.

☆

1986: the M-86 Sniper rifle was introduced in 7mm Remington Magnum, ·300 Winchester Magnum or ·30–06, a special ·300 Phoenix alternative being added in about 1989. The magazines held three or four rounds, depending on chambering. Weighing 11–11·5lb, the M-86 offered a 24in match-quality heavy barrel, plus a

fibreglass stock with textured surfaces on the pistol grip and fore-end to improve grip. Most stocks had a camouflage finish. Fixed recoil pads and detachable bipods were standard.

1987: the ·50 M-87 was offered in single-shot form (M-87) or with a detachable five-round box magazine (M-87R). The gun was 53in long, had a 29in stainless-steel barrel and weighed about 21·75lb. A fibreglass stock was fitted. Detail improvements were made to the mechanism in 1988, advancing the designation to M-88.

1989: built on the detachable-box magazine action, the National Match Rifle appeared in 7mm–08 or ·308 Winchester. It could be identified by its 24in stainless steel barrel and fibreglass ISU-type stock with an adjustable butt plate. An adjustable Canjar trigger was standard, though others were available to order. A replaceable-element front sight was supplied, the choice of back sight generally being left to the purchaser. Weight with sights was 11lb.

The single-shot 14lb Long Range Rifle—in 7mm Remington Magnum, ·300 Phoenix, ·300 Winchester Magnum or ·338 Lapua—was very similar to the National Match pattern, but had a solid-base receiver, a 26in barrel and an adjustable cheek piece. The butt plate could be moved vertically, canted, or fitted with spacers.

1990: the M-89 Sniper Rifle was an improved form of the M-86, with a five-round magazine and a flash suppressor. The fibreglass butt could be lengthened with spacers, the butt plate was adjustable, and a bipod graced the fore-end.

MADSEN

DENMARK

Formed in 1896, Dansk Rekyriffel Syndikat sought to exploit a recoil-operated rifle patented by Julius Rasmussen. This had been developed from an unsuccessful prototype created in the 1880s by Lieutenant Madsen, later Minister of War. It was only moderately effectual, but a light machine-gun derivation proved to be extremely successful.

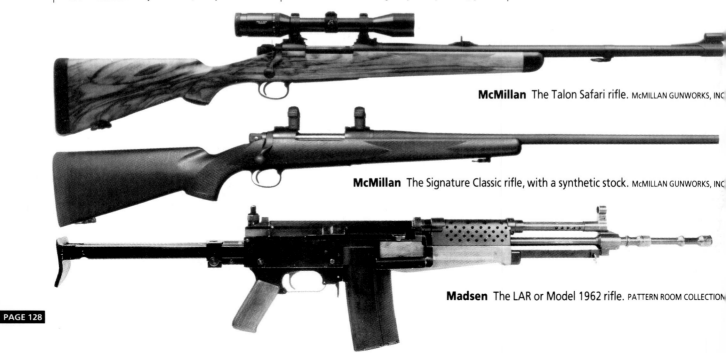

McMillan The Talon Safari rifle. McMILLAN GUNWORKS, INC

McMillan The Signature Classic rifle, with a synthetic stock. McMILLAN GUNWORKS, INC

Madsen The LAR or Model 1962 rifle. PATTERN ROOM COLLECTION

After the end of the Second World War, the Madsen machine-gun had been overtaken by more modern designs. Its manufacturer then attempted to diversify, with minimal success.

1. THE AUTO-LOADING PATTERNS

LAR

Also known as the Madsen A-Carbine, or Light Automatic Rifle.
Made by Dansk Industri Syndikat AS 'Madsen', Copenhagen.
7·62 × 51mm only.
Gas-operated auto-loading action, locked by rotating lugs on the bolt head into the barrel extension.
DATA FOR A SLIDING-BUTT EXAMPLE
1,100mm overall with butt extended,
4·64kg with empty magazine.
523mm barrel (rifled portion only), 4-groove rifling; RH, concentric.
Detachable box magazine, 20 rounds.
Aperture sight graduated to 600 metres.
825 m/sec with ball ammunition; 575 ± 25 rpm.
Optional knife bayonet.
☆

1957: DISA designer Gunnegaard Poulsen began development of this rifle, a handful of 7·62 × 39mm examples being made for trials in Finland in 1958. The piston rod had a spherical head entering a recess in the tubular bolt carrier; after the gun had been fired, the piston struck the carrier backward, rotating the bolt through 37° to disengage the locking lugs.
1960: the prototype rifles, which had one-piece wood stocks and short tubular compensators, were not successful enough to persuade the Finns to abandon a Kalashnikov copy.
1962: the 7·62mm LAR appeared. Many of the major parts were made of high-tensile aluminium alloy, including the receiver, while the bore and parts of the gas system were chromium plated to minimise fouling. The perfected rifles could be recognised by the floating barrel, protruding

from the ventilated sheet-steel upper hand guard between the gas-piston tube and a support rail. A short wooden fore-end was fitted, though the butt could be fixed wooden, sliding-bar or fixed-tube patterns. Most guns were accompanied by a detachable bipod, which clipped to the bayonet scabbard when not required.
1965: though the LAR would undoubtedly have made an effectual weapon had development continued, it could not challenge established market leaders such as the FN FAL and Heckler & Koch G3. As the project looked unlikely to repay much of the effort that had been invested in it, the rifle was abandoned.

2. THE BOLT-ACTION PATTERNS

Model 47

Also known as Madsen Light Military Rifle.
Made by Dansk Industri Syndikat AS 'Madsen', Copenhagen.
Chambering: see notes.
Turning-bolt action, locked by rotating lugs on the bolt head into the receiver.
DATA FOR A TYPICAL COLOMBIAN EXAMPLE
7·62 × 63mm (US ·30-06), rimless.
1,100mm overall, 3·85kg unladen.
595mm barrel, 4-groove rifling; concentric.
Internal box magazine, 5 rounds.
Tangent-leaf sight graduated to 900 metres.
825 m/sec with ball ammunition.
Knife bayonet.
☆

1948: specifically intended for sale in areas where soldiers were of small stature, this most distinctive rifle had a split-bridge receiver with the bolt handle acting as a safety lug. The pistol-grip stock had a short hand guard running from the chamber to the barrel band. Guns were also fitted with rudimentary muzzle brakes and rubber butt plates.
Touted in chamberings ranging from 6·5mm to 8mm—including 7 × 57mm, 7·65 × 53mm,

7·9 × 57mm or ·30-06—the Madsen was not especially successful. Too many military-surplus weapons were available at modest prices, and the only order known to have been fulfilled was for about 5,000 guns placed by the government of Colombia in c.1957. Chambered for the US ·30 rimless cartridge, these rifles bore the national Arms on a circular medallion let into the left side of the stock. They were apparently used by the navy as the 'Modelo 58'.

MANNLICHER

AUSTRIA-HUNGARY

This section contains details of the many straight-pull and turn-bolt rifles developed in Austria-Hungary, but also used in Romania, the Netherlands and elsewhere. The 1895-type Mannlichers found limited success in the export markets, selling to Bulgaria and Siam, but were soon overshadowed by guns derived from the Gew.88 and later Mannlicher-Schönauers.

This section includes not only those guns with Mannlicher actions and Mannlicher or Mannlicher-Schönauer magazines, but also the German Gew.88. This amalgamated a modified Mannlicher-type clip-loaded magazine with a bolt adapted from the M1871/84 Mauser rifle. A patent infringement suit ensued over the use of a clip system in the German magazine and Österreichische Waffenfabriks-Gesellschaft was subsequently allowed to incorporate the Gew.88-type bolt in export rifles. Consequently, the Gew.88 is considered here as an improved Mannlicher. The Haenel bolt-action rifle is also included, being little more than a Gew.88 with an improved magazine.

MILITARY RIFLES
AUSTRIA-HUNGARY

The shortcomings of the Austro-Hungarian Werndl were so evident by the end of the 1870s that a commission was charged with the

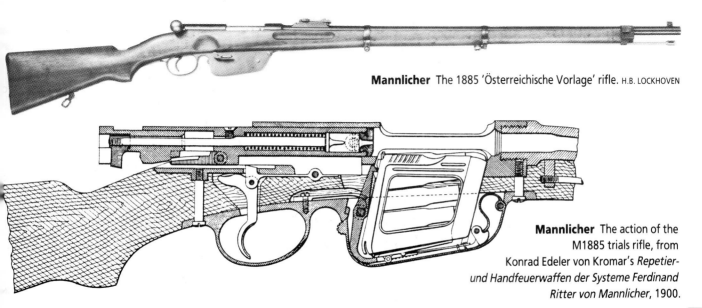

Mannlicher The 1885 'Österreichische Vorlage' rifle. H.B. LOCKHOVEN

Mannlicher The action of the M1885 trials rifle, from Konrad Edeler von Kromar's *Repetier-und Handfeuerwaffen der Systeme Ferdinand Ritter von Mannlicher*, 1900.

development of a magazine rifle. The trialists are known to have included two Spitalsky designs, a Winchester, four Mannlichers, the Spencer, a Kropatschek modified by the Viennese gunsmith Gasser, a Kropatschek-Kromar, two modified Werndls, various Schulhofs, an Odkolek, two Schönauers and a Lee.

Brief details of some of these guns—including the 1884-pattern Mannlicher, which was issued for field trials in some quantity—will be found in Part Two.

Model 1885

Trials rifle: Repetier-Gewehr 'Österreichische Vorlage', 1885.
Made by Österreichische Waffenfabriks-Gesellschaft, Steyr, 1885.
Quantity: about 1,520.
11 × 58mm, rimmed.
Straight-pull bolt action, with a locking bar under the back of the bolt engaging in the bolt-way floor.
1,328mm overall, about 4·75kg unladen.
808mm barrel, 6-groove rifling; RH, concentric.
Integral clip-loaded box magazine, 5 rounds.
Ramp-and-leaf sight graduated to 1,600 schritt.
440 m/sec with M1877 ball cartridges.
Special épée bayonet.

☆

1885: the 1884-pattern rifle (see Part Two) was replaced by this gun, issued for troop trials in 1885–6. The complexity of the earlier helical-channel bolt head was replaced by a simple bar cammed into engagement with the receiver immediately behind the bolt well. Unlike its predecessor, the M1885 accepted a clip through the top of the open action, cartridges being forced up by a driver arm until the last one had been chambered, fired and extracted. The rifle had a one-piece stock with a pointed pistol grip, the two bands and the nose cap being pinned in place. A bayonet lug lay on the right side of the nose cap. The M1885 was similar to the succeeding M1886 externally, but had a cleaning rod beneath the muzzle, a Werndl-type back sight, and a large radial catch on the right side of the magazine casing to eject spent clips.

Model 1886

Infantry rifles: Infanterie-Repetier-Gewehre M1886 und M1886–90.
Made by Österreichische Waffenfabriks-Gesellschaft, Steyr, 1886–8.
Quantity: about 90,000.
11 × 58mm, rimmed.
Action: very similar to the 1885-type trials rifle described above.
1,326mm overall, 4·52kg unladen.
806mm barrel, 6-groove rifling; RH, concentric.
Integral clip-loaded box magazine, 5 rounds.
Quadrant sight graduated to 1,500 schritt.
440 m/sec with M1877 ball cartridges.
M1886 knife bayonet.

☆

1886: trials of the 1885-pattern Mannlicher indicated that changes could be made. The clip-catch was greatly simplified and moved to the lower back of the magazine casing; the leaf-type back sight was replaced by a tangent pattern; the stock was refined and lightened; the cleaning rod under the muzzle was deleted; and the nose cap was redesigned to accept a stacking rod. Finally, the Repetier-Gewehr M1886 was officially approved on 20 June.

Production began immediately—even though concurrent trials had shown an 8mm cartridge to have greater potential.

The M1886 was an elegant rifle with a straight-pull bolt and a prominent flat-sided magazine case protruding ahead of the trigger guard bow. It had a conventional sight, though the slider could be extended laterally to the left and used in conjunction with a pin on the left side of the front band for distances up to 2,300 schritt. There were two screw-retained barrel bands, and a third doubling as a nose cap to carry the stacking rod beneath the muzzle. A lug on the left side of the nose-cap band received the pommel of the short-bladed M1886 knife bayonet. Sling swivels lay beneath the middle band and on the under-edge of the butt.

1892: most of the surviving 1886-type rifles were converted to 8mm under the designation 'M1886–90'.

Model 1888

Infantry rifles: Infanterie-Repetier-Gewehre M1888 und M1888–90.
Made by Österreichische Waffenfabriks-Gesellschaft, Steyr, 1888–96.
Quantity: 350,000?
8 × 50mm, rimmed.
Action: as M1886 rifle, above.
DATA FOR M1888 RIFLE
1,281mm overall, 4·41kg unladen.
765mm barrel, 4-groove rifling; RH, concentric.
integral clip-loaded box magazine, 5 rounds.
Quadrant sight graduated to 1,700 schritt.
615 m/sec with M1888 ball cartridges.
M1888 knife bayonet.

☆

1886: no sooner had mass-production of the M1886 began than the results of the small-calibre trials drew attention to the grave mistake in accepting the obsolescent 11mm pattern. Archduke Rudolf, the Inspector of Infantry, was made scapegoat for the embarrassment.

1887: work on the M1886 ceased, and trials began again. Major contenders were a Belgian-made Schulhof, an 1887-pattern Mannlicher with a drum magazine (soon withdrawn), the M1887/88 Mannlicher-Schönauer, and a new small-calibre M1886.

1888: concerned by the complexity of the Schulhof and Mannlicher-Schönauer, the trials board recommended the simplest solution—the 8mm variant of the M1886 rifle, production tooling for most of which already existed.

The Repetier-Gewehr M1888 was identical with its predecessor, apart from chambering a smaller cartridge and having a differently graduated back sight. The auxiliary long-range sighting system sufficed for 1,800–2,500 schritt. Owing to the reduced diameter of the cartridge base, the magazine case of the M1888 is noticeably shallower than the M1886.

1890: the adoption of smokeless powder forced changes to the sights. Most existing guns were modified by attaching new plates, suitably graduated for the M90 cartridge, over the old M1888 black-powder graduations on the side of

Mannlicher An 11mm M1886 infantry rifle. H.B. LOCKHOVEN

Mannlicher Men of k.u.k. Infanterie-Regiment Freiherr von Hess Nr.49, in Brünn (Brno, Czechoslovakia) prior to 1914. The 1886-type Mannlichers were probably converted to 8mm.
COLLECTOR'S COMPENDIUM

Mannlicher The 1886-type rifles had a locking wedge beneath the bolt. Drawing from von Kromar, 1900.

the quadrant-base. Rifles made after 1890–1, generally known as 'M1888–90', had newly made sights graduated to 1,800 schritt. Long-range sights on the left side of the gun—an extension to the back sight slider and a protruding pin on the front band—were used for distances up to 3,000 schritt.

Model 1890

••

Cavalry and gendarmerie carbines: Kavallerie- und Gendarmerie-Repetier-Karabiner, M1890.
Made by Österreichische Waffenfabriks-Gesellschaft, Steyr, 1891–6.
8 × 50mm, rimmed.
Straight-pull bolt action, with two lugs on a detachable bolt head engaging the receiver.
DATA FOR CAVALRY CARBINE
1,005mm overall, 3·30kg unladen.
498mm barrel, 4-groove rifling; RH, concentric.
Integral clip-loaded box magazine, 5 rounds.
Quadrant sight graduated to 2,400 schritt.
About 545 m/sec with M1888 ball cartridges.
No bayonet.

☆

1889: perfection of the M1888 rifle turned thoughts toward a carbine. The experimental guns were simply cut-down rifles, with the weak dropping-bar lock, but only a few were made.
1890: the new action reverted to the helically-grooved bolt head system of Mannlicher's first straight-pull action, patented in 1884, as this had proved much stronger than the bar-lock.

The M1890 cavalry carbine embodied a much shorter action than its predecessors, allowing the trigger guard to flow straight into the magazine casing, and the cocking piece lay almost directly above the trigger. The gun had a one-piece walnut stock with a simple nose cap without a stacking rod; sling swivels lay on the left side of the fore-end and stock-wrist.
1892: the gendarmerie carbine, a variant of the cavalry gun, accepted the standard bayonet and had a stacking rod on the nose cap.

Model 1895

••

Infantry rifle: Repetier-Gewehr M1895.
Made by Österreichische Waffenfabriks-Gesellschaft, Steyr, 1895–1918; and Fémáru Fegyver és Gépgyár, Budapest, 1897–1918.
8 × 50mm, rimmed.
Action: as M1890, above.
1,272mm overall, 3·78kg unladen.
765mm barrel, 4-groove rifling; RH, concentric.
Integral clip-loaded box magazine, 5 rounds.
Leaf sight graduated to 2,600 schritt.
620 m/sec with M1893 ball cartridges.
M1895 knife bayonet.

☆

1892: trials failed to convince the authorities that ultra-small calibres were effectual enough to change from 8mm. However, it was equally clear that even the new 1888-pattern rifles were ineffectual compared with the latest European advances, and that their weak bar-locks could not withstand the pressures generated by high velocity cartridges.
1895: an improved infantry rifle was adopted, incorporating a straight-pull action adapted directly from that of the 1890-vintage cavalry carbine. The M1895 differed in several important respects from the earlier service rifles; for example, it had a full-length hand guard and a leaf-pattern back sight. Sling swivels lay on the under-edge of the butt and under the barrel-band, while the nose cap (which carried the stacking rod) had the bayonet lug on its underside. The magazine clip could be ejected by opening the bolt and pressing the catch in the front edge of the trigger guard.

The slender barrel was prone to warping during rapid fire. Though the straight-pull action was effectual enough in peacetime and even acceptable under the stress of battle, the authorities would have issued a Mauser in 1914 had not the First World War begun.

Model 1895

••

Cavalry carbine and short rifle: Repetier-Karabiner und Repetier-Stutzer M1895.
Made by Österreichische Waffenfabriks-Gesellschaft, Steyr, 1895–1918; and Fémáru Fegyver és Gépgyár, Budapest, 1897–1918.
8 × 50mm, rimmed.
Otherwise generally as M1895 rifle, above, excepting dimensions (1,003mm overall, 3·09kg unladen), barrel length (500mm), back sight (to 2,400 schritt), muzzle velocity (580 m/sec) and bayonet fittings.

☆

1896: the M1895 rifle was successful enough to inspire a cavalry carbine, two patterns of which were made. They had full-length stocks and hand guards. Swivels appeared on the left side of the barrel band and on the left side of the butt-wrist.

The M1895 Stutzen or Extra-Corps-Gewehr, otherwise similar to the 1895-type cavalry carbine, had swivels on the under side of the butt and barrel band. It accepted a variant of the standard 1895-type knife bayonet with an auxiliary front sight on top of the muzzle ring. This compensated for the change in point-of-

impact caused by firing the rifle with the bayonet fixed; the effect was much more marked in the short-barrel carbines than the full-length rifles.

1907: some guns were given additional swivels so that they could be used interchangeably for mounted or foot use.

Model 1904

Made by Österreichische
Waffenfabriks-Gesellschaft, Steyr.
8 × 57mm and others.
Turning-bolt action, locked by rotating lugs on the
detachable bolt head into the receiver.
DATA FOR A TYPICAL EXAMPLE
8 × 57mm, rimless.
1,225mm overall, 4·00kg unladen.
725mm barrel, 4-groove rifling; RH, concentric.
Clip-loaded integral magazine, 5 rounds.
Leaf sight graduated to 2,000 metres.
685 m/sec with ball ammunition.
☆

1904: this was a large-calibre version of the series that had included the Romanian and Dutch Mannlichers. It had a straight-grip stock, and a hand guard ran from the receiver ring to the barrel band. The magazine case resembled that of the Gew.88, but the barrel jacket of the German gun was absent; a bayonet lug lay on the right side of the nose cap.

Sales of 1904-pattern Mannlichers were few, largely owing to the near-universal success of the Mauser. Österreichische Waffenfabrik had tooled to make the latter as part of a cartel encompassing itself, DWM, Fabrique Nationale and Mauser. However, substantial quantities went to China (perhaps being the basis for the Hanyang pattern) and nearly eleven thousand were purchased by the Ulster Volunteer Force in c.1913–14 together with a little over nine thousand Gewehre 88. It is suspected that they came from A.L. Frank of Hamburg. UVF guns often bore FOR GOD AND ULSTER in a cartouche around the Red Hand of the O'Neills, the provincial badge. Many were seized by the British before entering Ireland, and were used for home defence during the First World War.

Other guns

A few Austro-Hungarian units—particularly the Landwehr—used Gewehre 88 as the 'Repetier-Gewehre M 13'. These chambered the standard 8 × 57mm cartridge. It is assumed that they were supplied in the early days of the First World War, when Austria-Hungary lacked serviceable weapons; it is not known whether they came from Germany or had been stored by the Steyr factory since the termination of German orders in the mid 1890s.

AUSTRIA

Conversions of earlier Austro-Hungarian guns are listed on the accompanying table.

Model 69 Sniper Rifle

Scharfschützengewehre (SSG) 69, P–I, P–II, P–III, P–IV
and Match patterns.
Made by Steyr-Daimler-Puch AG, Steyr.
·243 Winchester or ·308 Winchester only.
Turning-bolt action, locked by rotating lugs on the bolt
into the receiver behind the magazine.
DATA FOR A TYPICAL SSG P–I
7·62 × 51mm NATO (·308 Winchester), rimless
1,130mm overall, 3·95kg without sights.
650mm barrel, 4-groove rifling; RH, concentric.
Detachable spool magazine, 5 rounds.
Optical sight.
820 m/sec with SS77 ball ammunition.
☆

1969: adopted by the Austrian army, and then by military and police forces throughout the world, this was built on a heavy version of the standard short action in which the receiver extended forward to enclose the chamber. A spool magazine was standard, though a ten-round detachable box could be substituted if requested.

The original SSG-69—sold commercially in North America as the 'SSG Marksman'—had a walnut or Cycolac stock, the latter being brown or olive green; spacers adjusted the butt length when necessary. Most military-issue rifles had

optical sights, though 'Match Target' guns sold commercially had a micro-adjustable aperture back sight and a replaceable-element tunnel at the muzzle. Major metal parts were usually phosphated to eliminate reflections.

1988: the SSG P–II had a heavy barrel and a large bolt-handle knob instead of the slender spatulate type, the original 1969-type rifle being retrospectively designated 'P–I'. A ·243 option for the SSG series appeared at the same time.

1992: the SSG P–III was simply a P–I with aperture-sight bases, a heavyweight 600mm barrel, and an American-made synthetic H-S Precision stock. The P–IV (·308 only) had an unusually short 425mm barrel with a flash-hider and a stock of black or green Cycolac.

CHINA

The Chinese were enthusiastic purchasers of the Gewehr 88, sufficient guns being acquired from Loewe and Österreichische Waffenfabriks-Gesellschaft to equip front-line troops in the Sino-Japanese War of 1894. Additional examples were purchased in 1907, once Gewehre 98 had been issued to the German armies.

The Chinese apparently held a competition in the early 1900s to find a new rifle, testing a Mauser, a Mannlicher-Schönauer and a Haenel; the guns chambered a 6·8mm round and were marked accordingly. Mauser was victorious.

Hanyang model

Infantry rifle.
Made by Hanyang arsenal, perhaps with the
assistance of other contractors.
8 × 57mm, rimless.
Turning-bolt action, with two lugs on a detachable bolt
head locking into the receiver.
1,251mm overall, 3·87kg unladen.
743mm barrel, 4-groove rifling; RH, concentric.
Integral clip-loaded box magazine, 5 rounds.
Tangent-leaf sight graduated to 2,000 metres.
About 630 m/sec with ball cartridges.
Sword bayonet.
☆

STEYR-DAIMLER-PUCH AG

Mannlicher The SSG-69, with a selection of butt spacers.

Mannlicher
Men of the Bavarian 6.Landwehr-Infanterie-Bataillon, 1915.
Several Gew.88 have covers over the clip-ejection port.
COLLECTOR'S COMPENDIUM

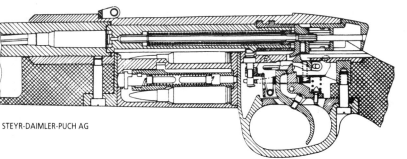

STEYR-DAIMLER-PUCH AG

Mannlicher A sectional drawing of the SSG-69 action.

1916*: the history of these guns, sometimes erroneously known as the Type 88, is far from clear. It is assumed that production began after the 1911 revolution, or, more probably, after the beginning of the First World War cut supplies from Germany. The Hanyang used a copy of the Gew.88 action, with a clip-loaded magazine, but lacked the barrel jacket. The fore-end and hand guard had much more in common with pre-1914 export Mannlichers, and the bayonet lug lay beneath the nose cap. Swivels usually lay on the rear band, held by a spring. Hanyangs may also be found with a semi-pistol grip stock with little drop at the toe. Like the original straight-wrist patterns, these guns have 8·08mm (·318) bores and chamber M1888 cartridges.

Model 1907

Experimental infantry rifle.
Made by C.G. Haenel, Waffenfabrik, Suhl, 1907–10.
6·8 × 57mm, rimless.
Action: as Hanyang rifle, above.
1,218mm overall, 3·87kg unladen.
710mm barrel, 4-groove rifling; RH, concentric.
Internal charger-loaded box magazine, 5 rounds.
Tangent-leaf sight graduated to 2,000 metres.
Special Haenel sword bayonet.

☆

1907: these guns bore few marks other than 𝔐𝔬𝔡. 𝔒7. 𝔠𝔞𝔩. 6.8𝔪𝔪. on the left side of the action ahead of the clearance cutaway. The Haenel, serviceable enough, was less effectual than its Mauser rival and is presumed to have been rejected after field trials.

GERMANY

1887: the authorities decided to improve the Gewehr 71/84 by adding a second locking lug. Suitable machinery was ordered in December.
1888: mindful of the introduction of the Mle.86 (Lebel) rifle in France, the Germans sought a more effectual weapon than a converted Gew.71/84. The resulting 'commission rifle' had a bolt developed by Louis Schlegelmilch, a clip-loaded magazine inspired by Mannlicher

(modified by the GPK so that the clip would load either way up) and a barrel jacket designed by Armand Mieg. To save time, the rifling was simply copied from the French pattern.

Experiments with pre-production guns made in Spandau in April–May 1888 resolved the question of calibre in favour of 8mm; production began in October to permit field trials.

Model 1888

Infantry rifles: Gewehre 88/●, 88/Z und 88/S.
Made by the Königliche Gewehrfabriken in Danzig, Erfurt and Spandau (750,000?); Königlich bayerische Gewehrfabrik, Amberg (100,000?); Ludwig Loewe & Co., Berlin-Charlottenburg (425,000); Österreichische Waffenfabriks-Gesellschaft, Steyr (300,000); and private contractors in Suhl (100,000?).
Quantity: in excess of 1·68 million in 1888–97.
8 × 57mm, rimless.
Turning-bolt action, with two lugs on a detachable bolt head locking into the receiver.
DATA FOR GEW.88
1,245mm overall, 3·90kg unladen.
740mm barrel, 4-groove rifling; RH, concentric.
Integral clip-loaded box magazine, 5 rounds.
Leaf sight graduated to 2,050 metres.
630 m/sec with Patrone 88.
S.71 sword bayonet (S.71/84 in Bavaria).

☆

1888: the rifle was adopted in Prussia, Saxony and Württemberg on 12 November.
1889: issue began in the autumn to XV. and XVI.Armeekorps, stationed in Alsace-Lorraine.
1890: by the beginning of the year, sufficient guns had been delivered to allow most Prussian, Saxon and Württemberg line infantry regiments to re-equip by 1 August.
1891: rifles received a strengthened barrel from January onward. A large dot was struck into the receiver and barrel-side.
1894: excessive gas leakage from the ruptured primers of defective cartridges was minimised by fitting striker heads with gas deflection flanges.
1896: new rifling was introduced on 7 July. The guns fitted with altered or newly made barrels—some had been re-rifled satisfactorily—

usually displayed a 3mm letter z on top of the chamber and a 7mm z on the butt.
1900: Gew.88 were gradually replaced by the Gewehr 98 and relegated to the Reserve, Landwehr and Landsturm.
1905: the approval of the S-Patrone on 3 April 1903 caused a change in bore-diameter and chambering. Only guns with new Z-pattern barrels were altered, receiver-tops gaining a 3mm s. A 7mm-high version was often repeated on the side of the butt. A new sight leaf was graduated to 2,000 metres, the supplementary leaf on the original sight being abandoned.
1906: the first batches were converted to 88/05 standards.
1907: many Gewehre 88 were sold to China.
1911: most survivors passed to the Landwehr.
1914: when hostilities began, Gew.88/05 and surviving Gew.88/S were being stored for Landwehr and Landsturm respectively. The wholesale conversion of rifles to upward clip-ejection commenced, and the first Gew.88/S were converted to 88/14 standards.
1915: 88/S, 88/05 and 88/14 rifles were retrieved from the Landwehr and issued to front-line units to overcome a shortage of serviceable Mauser-type weapons. They were withdrawn again at the end of the year.
1918: about 120,000 88/05 and 88/14 rifles remained nominally on the army inventory, though many were serving in Turkey.

Models 1888/05 and 1888/14

Infantry rifles: Gewehre 88/05 und 88/14.
The 88/05-type rifles were converted by the Prussian government factory in Spandau, 1906–7; 88/14 conversions date from 1914–15.
Quantity: about 370,000 Gew.88/05 and 75,000 Gew.88/14.
8 × 57mm, rimless.
Otherwise similar to the Gew.88, excepting that the back sight was graduated to 2,000 metres.

☆

1907: adopted on 3 January, the 88/05 rifle was converted from standard Gew.88 and may be found with 'Z' and 'S' marks above the

chamber. It was loaded from a pressed-tin charger, blocks containing the charger guides being screwed to the top of the receiver bridge. The left side of the receiver wall was ground out to enable the thumb to press the cartridges fully down into the magazine well, and a channel was milled across the breech face so that the pointed-nose S-Patrone could be used. As the comparatively bulky clip was no longer used, the magazine was narrowed and shortened internally; a spring-loaded cartridge retainer was added, and the opening in the bottom of the magazine was closed by a pressed-steel cover.

1914: the first Gew.88/14, approximating to the 88/05, were hastily altered from Gew.88/S from December on into the summer of 1915. The charger guides were formed by protrusions welded onto the front of the receiver bridge. The left wall of the receiver was cut away and a groove was milled across the face of the chamber. The opening in the bottom of the magazine was blocked by a sheet-steel cover, the magazine well being shortened and narrowed for the S-Patrone. Work was rushed, finish being inferior to the peacetime 88/05 conversions.

Model 1888

Cavalry carbine: Karabiner 88.
Made by C.G. Haenel, Suhl, 1889–95; V.C. Schilling,
Suhl, 1890–5; and the Königlich Gewehrfabrik,
Erfurt, 1891–6.
8 × 57mm, rimless.
Action: as Gew.88, above.
953mm overall, 3·12kg unladen.
435mm barrel, 4-groove rifling; RH, concentric.
Integral clip-loaded box magazine, 5 rounds.
Leaf sight graduated to 1,200 metres.
About 575 m/sec with Patrone 88.
No bayonet.
☆

1890: adopted for the armies of Prussia, Saxony and Württemberg on 19 January, after protracted trials, this was a short version of the Gewehr 88. It had a turned-down bolt handle, a full-length stock, and a plain nose-cap with 'ears' around the front sight. There was a single

spring-retained barrel band, with a fixed sling bar on the left side, and a sling-anchor point was cut through the butt.

By March 1890, sufficient carbines had been delivered to permit issue to each Prussian cavalry squadron to begin.

1891: the incidence of ruptured barrels was reduced by modifying barrel contours. Chamber tops thereafter bore a large dot.

1894: new striker heads with gas deflection flanges were fitted.

1896: excessive bore-wear was answered by deepening the grooves in barrels made after July (chambers were marked z).

1905: the first Karabiner 88 converted for S-Munition were issued, bearing an additional chamber-top s. Owing to its short barrel, the carbine had always had an unpleasant muzzle blast: S-Munition simply made problems worse.

1908: the Kar.88 was superseded by the Karabiner 98 AZ (q.v.) with effect from January.

1910: the last survivors were withdrawn from regular units into store, or to be sold.

1914: surviving Kar.88 were re-issued in the autumn to ancillary units.

Model 1891

Artillery carbine: Gewehr 91.
Made by C.G. Haenel, Suhl, 1891–5; V.C. Schilling, Suhl,
1891–5; and Königlich Gewehrfabrik, Erfurt, 1891–6.
8 × 57mm, rimless.
Otherwise similar to Kar.88 (above), except
3·23kg unladen.
☆

1891: this carbine length 'rifle' was adopted for the foot artillerymen of Prussia, Saxony and Württemberg on 25 March. It was simply a Kar.88 with an additional stacking rod integral with a steel plate let into the underside of the fore-end immediately behind the nose-cap.

1894: striker heads with gas deflection flanges were fitted to minimise gas-leakage in the event of a primer rupture or case-head failure.

1896: after July, when barrels with modified rifling were used, chambers bore z.

1905: conversion of surviving guns for the new

S-Munition began, altered guns gaining a large **s** on top of the chamber.

1910: the last survivors were withdrawn from regular units into store, or to be sold.

1914: surviving Gew.91 were re-issued when the First World War began. Many will be found with markings applied on behalf of munitions columns and similar minor formations.

1915: some guns were apparently fitted with auxiliary bayonet-attachment bars, though it is not yet known why.

Model 1907

Infantry rifle: Aptierte Haenel-Gewehr M1907.
Made by C.G. Haenel, Waffenfabrik, Suhl, 1907–10.
8 × 57mm, rimless.
Action: as Gew.88, above.
1,218mm overall, 3·87kg unladen.
710mm barrel, 4-groove rifling; RH, concentric.
Internal charger-loaded box magazine, 5 rounds.
Tangent-leaf sight graduated to 2,000 metres.
About 855 m/sec with S-Patrone.
No bayonet in German service?
☆

1907: apparently developed for sale to China (q.v.), this gun had an 1888-type bolt, modified by the addition of a bolt-guide rib and a gas-escape port bored into the bolt body ahead of the rib. The lugs locked vertically into the receiver behind the chamber. Charger guides were machined into the receiver, a clearance cutaway was milled out of the left receiver wall, and the bolt handle was turned down against the stock. The Mannlicher-style clip-loaded magazine was replaced by an internal box with Haenel's 1906-patent pivoting floor plate.

The bayonet fitting comprised a T-lug on an extension of the nose cap and a boss surrounding the clearing rod.

1914: small quantities remained in store when the First World War began. Some were issued for service in their original 6·8mm chambering, but others were modified for the standard 8mm service cartridge. They were probably issued to Landsturm troops or recruiting depots to free Gew.88 for front-line service.

Mannlicher Drawing of the Gew.88 from Konrad Edeler von Kromar's *Repetier- und Handfeuerwaffen der Systeme Ferdinand Ritter von Mannlicher*, 1900.

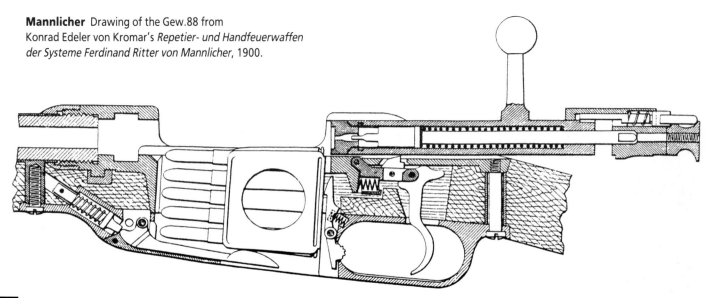

Model 1898/40

Short rifle: Gewehr 98/40.
Made by Fémáru Fegyver és Gépgyár,
Budapest, 1941–4.
7·9 × 57mm, rimless.
Action: as Gew.88, above.
1,097mm overall, 4·08kg unladen.
600mm barrel, 4-groove rifling; RH, concentric.
Internal charger-loaded box magazine, 5 rounds.
Tangent-leaf sight graduated to 2,000 metres.
755 m/sec with sS-Patrone.
S.84/98 bayonet.

☆

1941: the first of these guns, adapted from the Hungarian 35.M pattern, was delivered from 'Metallwaren-, Waffen- und Maschinenfabrik'— the Hungarian state firearms factory in Budapest, code 'jhv'—in the Spring. Unlike its Hungarian predecessors, the Gew.98/40 had a German-style charger-loaded magazine, a 4cm bayonet bar, sights for the sS-Patrone, a bolt handle turned downward, and a sling-slot in the butt. Its British-type butt was held in the action-body socket by a sturdy bolt running up through the butt-body and pistol grip.

1944: production ended in the autumn, when the advance of the Red Army made further work impossible. The Gew.98/40 was sturdy and reliable, though the butts occasionally worked loose. It provided the basis for the Hungarian 43.M service rifle (q.v.).

GREECE

The Greeks were originally armed with 1888- and 1895-pattern Mannlichers, supplied in small numbers by Österreichische Waffenfabriks-Gesellschaft prior to 1900. A desire for a gun of their own led the authorities to consider the Mannlicher-Schönauer rifle then being tested in Portugal. Its spool magazine appeared to feed more precisely than box patterns. Chamber-tops of Greek rifles normally displayed a crowned shield bearing a cross above the designation Υ.1903 or Υ.1903/14, with the maker's mark (e.g., STEYR 1909) on the left side of the receiver.

Model 1903

Rifle and carbine.
Made by Österreichische
Waffenfabriks-Gesellschaft, Steyr, 1902–14.
6·5 × 54mm, rimless.
Turning-bolt action, with two lugs on a detachable bolt head locking into the receiver.
DATA FOR RIFLE
1,226mm overall, 3·77kg unladen.
725mm barrel, 4-groove rifling; RH, concentric.
Internal charger-loaded spool magazine, 5 rounds.
Tangent-leaf graduated to 2,000 metres.
680 m/sec with M1903 ball cartridges.
M1903 knife bayonet.

☆

1903: after extensive testing, the Mannlicher-Schönauer was officially adopted. The rifle was essentially similar to the experimental 1900 Portuguese pattern (q.v.), its action being all but identical. The one-piece stock, with a semi-pistol grip, had a half-length hand guard and two bands. Grasping grooves in the side of the fore-end turned upward at the breech to facilitate removing the hand guard. The band nearest the muzzle—with a bayonet lug on its underside—acted as a nose cap, while a half-length cleaning rod was carried in the fore-end. The magazine floor plate could be removed by depressing its retaining spring and turning through 90°; alternatively, the magazine could be emptied by opening the bolt and pressing a catch on the right side of the receiver alongside the feed way.

The cavalry and artillery carbine, which accepted the standard bayonet, was simply a shortened rifle with a sling ring on the left side of the barrel band and a swivel on the side of the butt. It was about 1,025mm overall, had a 525mm barrel and weighed 3·53kg unladen. The back sight was graduated to about 1,600 metres and muzzle velocity fell to 627 m/sec.

These weapons rapidly gained a reputation for smooth operation, generally reckoned as better than any military magazine rifle with the possible exception of the US and Norwegian Krag-Jørgensens.

Model 1903/14

Rifle and carbine.
Made by Österreichische
Waffenfabriks-Gesellschaft, Steyr, 1914; and Società Italiana Ernesto Breda, Brescia, 1926–9.
6·5 × 54mm, rimless.
Otherwise generally as M1903 rifle, above, excepting weight (about 3·83kg unladen).

☆

1914: the basic Mannlicher-Schönauer action was retained, but the hand guard ran the full length of the barrel, the grasping grooves no longer had the distinctive rearward upturn, and a stacking rod was added to the left side of the nose cap. Few guns emanated from Steyr before the beginning of hostilities stopped work.

Excepting for the shortened barrel and fore-end, and the appearance of the swivels on the left side of the barrel band and butt, M1903/14 carbines were identical with the corresponding rifle. Bolt handles are occasionally found bent downward, but this was not universal. Carbines were 1,025mm overall, with 525mm barrels, and had an unladen weight of 3·58kg.

1925*: with stocks of M1903 and M1903/14 rifles declining, the government placed an order for 100,000 rifles and about 10,000 carbines in Italy. Apart from marks (e.g., BREDA 1927), they were identical with Steyr-made weapons.

HUNGARY

Model 1935

Short rifle: Huzagol 35.M.
Made by Fémáru Fegyver és Gépgyár,
Budapest, 1936–42.
8 × 56mm, rimmed.
Action: as M1931, above.
1,110mm overall, 4·03kg unladen.
600mm barrel, 4-groove rifling; RH, concentric.
Integral clip-loaded box magazine, 5 rounds.
Tangent-leaf sight graduated to 2,000 metres?
730 m/sec with 31.M ball cartridge.
35.M sword bayonet.

☆

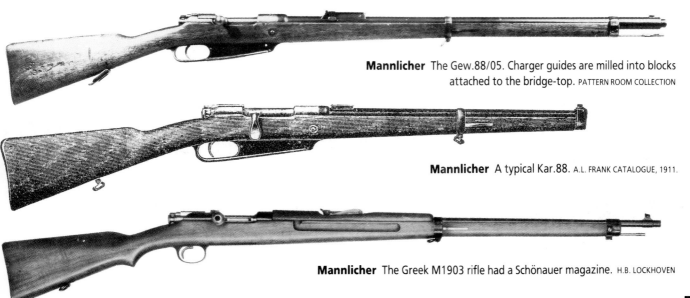

Mannlicher The Gew.88/05. Charger guides are milled into blocks attached to the bridge-top. PATTERN ROOM COLLECTION

Mannlicher A typical Kar.88. A.L. FRANK CATALOGUE, 1911.

Mannlicher The Greek M1903 rifle had a Schönauer magazine. H.B. LOCKHOVEN

1933: work began on a new infantry rifle with a turning bolt action, retaining the best features of the 1895-pattern Mannlicher but designed specifically around the 31.M cartridge and thus more durable than its predecessors.

1935: the 35.M rifle had a split-bridge receiver and a British-style two-piece stock, the butt being held in the receiver by a sturdy bolt. A turning-bolt action was preferred, though the spur-type cocking piece of the 1895-model rifle was retained. The rifle was clip-loaded and had a projecting magazine case. Swivels lay beneath the butt and the barrel band, and the front face of the nose cap carried a small projecting stud to enter the bayonet pommel.

Model 1943

Short rifle: Huzagol 43.M.
Made by Fémáru Fegyver és Gépgyár,
Budapest, 1944–50.
8 × 56mm, rimmed.
Otherwise as 35.M rifle, above, excepting dimensions
(1,092mm overall, 3·92kg unladen), magazine (internal
charger-loaded 5-round box) and bayonet
(43.M sword pattern).

☆

1943: the unexpected success of the German Gew.98/40—a modification of the 35.M being made in Budapest under contract—persuaded the Hungarians to adopt a new rifle. The 43.M, which had a Mauser-type magazine, was little more than a Gew.98/40 with Hungarian-style barrel band, nose cap and sling swivels.

1945: production was interrupted by the end of the Second World War after only a few thousand had been made. Work began again about 1947, but apparently ceased in the early 1950s.

ITALY

1887: the Italians realised that the 10·35mm Vetterli-Vitali rifles were obsolescent even on the day of their approval. The introduction of the Lebel in France and—most importantly—the adoption of the 8mm M1888 Mannlicher by arch-rival Austria-Hungary forced the authorities

to form an infantry-weapon commission. This commenced work in the school of musketry, Parma, at the end of 1888. The president was Generale Gustavo Parravicino.

1889: in December, the committee reported on trials with more than fifty rifles submitted by (among others) Vitali, Bertoldo, Mauser and Lee. None had proved ideal.

1890: in March, the decision was taken to adopt a 6·5mm cartridge and ten differing breech systems were tested for suitability. Eventually, manufacturing problems were referred to the government arsenals; progressive rifling was adopted, and the cartridge was perfected in the Bologna munitions factory.

1891: a report recommending the Mannlicher magazine in preference to Lee, Mauser and other patterns was made on 23 April. The major contestants in subsequent trials were the 'Mauser-Mannlicher Terni Tipo 2'—essentially similar to the Gcw.88, with Italian-pattern sights but no barrel jacket—and 'Fucile italiano No.1', a modified Mannlicher developed in Fabbrica Nazionale d'Armi de Torino (Turin) by a team headed by Salvatore Carcano.

Model 1891

Infantry rifle: Fucile di Fanteria Mo.1891.
Most were made by Fabbrica Nazionale d'Armi, Terni,
1892–1937; some were also produced—generally prior
to 1912—in Brescia, Turin and Torre Annuziata.
Quantity: 3·5–4 million?
6·5 × 52mm, rimmed.
Turning-bolt action, with two lugs on a detachable bolt
head locking into the receiver.
1,282mm overall, 3·78kg unladen.
780mm barrel, 4-groove rifling; RH, concentric.
Integral clip-loaded box magazine, 6 rounds.
Quadrant sight graduated to 2,000 metres.
700 m/sec with Mo.91–95 ball cartridges.
Mo.1891 sword bayonet.

☆

1892: on 5 March, the army infantry-weapons commission recommended adoption of 'Fucile No.1 ter', a modified form of Turin's Fucile italiano No.1. The war ministry concurred on

29 March, when the M1891 or Mannlicher-Carcano rifle was approved. It had a one-piece straight-wrist stock and a protruding magazine case. Unlike Austro-Hungarian service rifles, the Italian gun accepted reversible clips; adopting a small-calibre cartridge also allowed one extra round to be carried.

The M1891 had a split-bridge receiver, but its bolt was simpler than the Mannlichers based on the Gew.88 and the safety was nothing more than a projecting plate between the rear of the bolt body and the cocking piece. A typically Italian quadrant sight lay on the barrel ahead of the chamber, while swivels appeared under the butt and rear band. A conventional bayonet lug lay beneath the nose cap. The bolt could be removed simply by holding the trigger back.

Maker's marks—e.g., a crown above R.E. TERNI—lay on the barrel ahead of the receiver and on the right side of the butt.

1894: the first rifles were issued in the Spring.

1895: the bolt-head was strengthened, pending the introduction of the smokeless Mo.91–95 cartridge (approved in February 1896).

1905: trials undertaken from August 1904 with a thousand modified rifles brought a change in the hand guard.

1907: a modified extractor was adopted

1913: by April, monthly production of rifles in the Terni factory had risen to about 2,500. At this time, production of carbines was centred on Brescia, the factories in Turin and Torre Annuziata being partially closed.

1914: when hostilities commenced, the army inventory stood at 700,000 Mo.1891 rifles.

1918: by the Armistice, the Terni factory alone had made 2,063,750 rifles since the outbreak of the First World War.

Model 1891

Cavalry carbine: Moschetto Mo.1891.
Mostly made by Fabbrica Nazionale d'Armi, Brescia;
some were also made in Terni.
Quantity: 750,000–1,000,000 moschetti of all types.
6·5 × 52mm, rimless.
Action: as Mo.1891 rifle, above.

Mannlicher The Italian M1891 'Mannlicher-Carcano'. H.B. LOCKHOVEN

Mannlicher A cut-away version of the Italian M1891 infantry rifle, showing the clip-loaded magazine. IAN HOGG

Mannlicher
Austro-Hungarian alpine troops with
the 1895-pattern Mannlicher short rifles.
COLLECTOR'S COMPENDIUM

MANNLICHER
LESSER PATTERNS

Austria The earliest Mannlicher conversions for the 8mm German service cartridge seem to date from 1918; most M1895/24 guns, however, served Bulgaria and Yugoslavia.

¶ Possibly converted in the Steyr factory, the M1895/24 short rifle was an adaption of the standard 1895-pattern Mannlicher (see Part One) for the German 8mm service cartridge, huge quantities of which had become available after1918. The barrels were shortened to 600mm, giving an overall length of 1,100mm and a weight of about 3·5kg, and charger guides were added to the front of the receiver bridge. The modified magazines, into which a clip was welded to hold the cartridges, could be loaded from the standard German-style charger; the clip-ejection port in the base of the magazine body had a sheet-metal cover. The back sights were usually graduated to 2,000 metres, muzzle velocity being about 825 m/sec with German S-Patrone.

¶ The M1930 short rifle, converted in the Steyr factory, chambered a new 8 × 56mm rimmed cartridge standardised in collusion with Hungary to replace the venerable 8 × 50mm pattern. Converted guns were difficult to distinguish externally from 1895-type short rifles, excepting for back sight graduations extending to 2,000 metres. They were 1,000mm overall, had 500mm barrels and weighed 3·12kg. Muzzle velocity was 730 m/sec and the Austro-Hungarian M1895 knife bayonet with an auxiliary front sight was used.

Bulgaria The army used M1888 and M1895 rifles, supplied by Österreichische Waffenfabriks-Gesellschaft in 1890–2 and 1897–1901 respectively. They were identical with Austro-Hungarian weapons, excepting that they bore Bulgarian arms over the chamber, rampant lion inspectors' marks, and the 'crowned F' cypher of Prince Ferdinand.

¶ Several thousand 8mm M1895 rifles were converted in the early 1920s to 'M95/24' short rifles, chambering the German 8mm service cartridge. Most of the work appears to have been undertaken at Steyr.

Finland Many Italian-type Mo.1891–38 Mannlicher-Carcano rifles and carbines were supplied to Finland during the Winter and Continuation Wars of 1939–40 and 1941–4. These can usually be identified by the army property mark, 'SA' in a square.

Germany A few Austro-Hungarian Mannlicher bayonets have been found with standard German property and inspectors' marks. They include M1888 examples usually dated 1910-2 and a few of 1895 type dating from 1917. Their history is still obscure. It has been suggested that Mannlicher rifles were acquired to offset a temporary shortage of Mausers prior to 1914 or, alternatively, during the war to offset a temporary shortage of weapons. Neither case is proven, though Bavaria did purchase Steyr-made handguns in 1916–18.

Hungary In 1931, the authorities adopted a rimmed 8mm cartridge to replace the old Austro-Hungarian 8 × 50mm design. The new round, known as the 31.M in Hungary, was initially used in modified 1895-type straight-pull Mannlichers—rifles, short rifles and carbines alike. These were essentially similar to the Austro-Hungarian patterns (q.v.), but had new back sights and new front-sight protectors. A large 'H' was stamped into the chamber. Service life was brief, as the adoption of the 35.M rifle caused the conversions (which suffered perpetual extraction difficulties) to be withdrawn into store. Survivors were reissued for service in 1940.

Italy Adopted officially but never made in quantity, the Fucile Mo.1940 was an improved Mo.1891 with a distinctive back sight with a rotary elevator. A few hundred were made by Fabbrica Nazionale d'Armi, Terni, but the Second World War prevented progress. Chambered for the 6·5 × 52mm rimless cartridge, the rifle was 1,175mm overall and weighed 3·71kg. Its 690mm barrel had concentric four-groove rifling and the magazine accepted the standard six-round clip. Muzzle velocity was 685 m/sec with Mo.91–95 ball cartridges and the Mo.1891 sword bayonet could be attached to the muzzle.

¶ The Mo.1941, credited to Major Roberto Boragine, was recognisable by its shortened barrel and reduced-scale 1,000-metre quadrant sight. Constant-twist rifling replaced the original progressive variety, but few guns were made before the major part of the Italian armed forces surrendered to the Allies in 1943. Perhaps 1,000 were made in the Terni factory. Chambered for the 6·5 × 52mm rimless cartridge, they were 1,172mm overall, had 690mm barrels and weighed 3·72kg unladen.

The Netherlands The army acquired substantial numbers of rifles for field trials in the 1890s. They were virtually identical with the M1892 Romanian Mannlicher (Part One, q.v.) excepting for detail differences—a special back sight, an enlarged bolt handle, and an additional guide rib on the bolt body. The bayonet lug lay under the nose cap. Unlike the Romanian gun, which would accept a bolt in the unlikely event of the head being omitted during reassembly, the Dutch rifle could not receive a wrongly assembled bolt unless the bolt stop was depressed manually.

¶ Made by Österreichische Waffenfabriks-Gesellschaft for the 6·5 × 53mm rimmed cartridge, they were 1,290mm overall and weighed 4·14kg. The 790mm barrel had four-groove rifling twisting to the right, the internal magazine accepted a five-round clip, and the quadrant sight was graduated to 2,100 metres.

Portugal The army acquired about 1,000 OEWG-made 6·5mm Mannlicher-Schönauer trials rifles—essentially similar to the Greek M1903 (Part One, q.v.)—after two had successfully undertaken trials in 1900. The rifles had one-piece stocks with a shallow pistol grip, and a hand guard ran forward from the receiver ring to the spring-retained barrel band. The bayonet lug lay on the underside of the nose cap and a half-length cleaning rod was carried beneath the muzzle. Sling swivels were to be found on the under-edge of the butt and barrel band. Unlike contemporaneous box-feed Mannlichers, the M1900 had its Schönauer magazine entirely within the stock. The magazine floor plate could be detached by pivoting it laterally through 90°. The rifle had a standard Mannlicher-type bolt, essentially similar to that of the M1895 Dutch rifle, but the centre of the guide rib was milled away to save weight; the bolt-knob was also hollowed out.

¶ Trials failed to convince the Portuguese that the many merits of the rotary magazine outweighed its complexity and, ultimately, the Vergueiro rifle was developed instead.

Siam (Thailand) Substantial numbers of 1888 and 1888-90 Mannlichers were supplied to the Siamese army in the 1890s. They did not prove successful enough to have long-lasting influences on the country's ordnance affairs, as a Japanese-made Mauser rifle was adopted in 1902. Siamese Mannlichers bore Sanskrit serial numbers and the *Chakra* or war-quoit symbol.

Others Captured and war-surplus ex-Italian guns equipped some Albanian, Ethiopian, Greek and Yugoslavian troops during and immediately after the Second World War. Most of these were soon replaced by more effectual weapons—particularly British Lee-Enfields and German Kar.98k Mausers.

953mm overall, 3·16kg unladen (walnut stock).
451mm barrel, 4-groove rifling; RH, concentric.
Integral clip-loaded box magazine, 6 rounds.
Quadrant sight graduated to 1,500 metres.
635 m/sec with Mo.91–95 ball cartridges.
Integral folding bayonet.

☆

1893: this was adopted on 9 June for cavalry, carabineri (mounted gendarmerie) and cyclists. The original carbine had a straight-wrist half-stock, a recoil bolt laterally through the stock beneath the receiver ring, a turned-down bolt handle, and a folding bayonet attached to a special muzzle block. The bayonet was locked by a sliding catch on the blade.
1897*: the bayonet lock became a radial lever on the right side of the muzzle block.
1900*: the recoil bolt was abandoned, and a hand guard ran from the back sight to the combined barrel band/nose cap. At about this time, the bayonet attachment became a push-button on the muzzle block. A variant of the carbine was adopted for the royal bodyguard— 'Squadrone Reali Carabinieri Guardie del Re'— and, subsequently, for the guard of the president of the Italian republic. It had a hand guard, a turned-down bolt handle, and a special nose cap into which the socket bayonet could be reversed. The bolt, nose cap, magazine body and parts of the back sight were gilded, the remaining metal parts being blued.
1940: a few cavalry carbines were made with barrels strengthened in the chamber area, the back sight being moved farther forward.

Model 1891

Carbine for special units: Moschetto Mo.1891 per Truppe Speciali.
Most were made by Fabbrica Nazionale d'Armi, Brescia; though some emanated from Terni.
Quantity: 750,000–1,000,000 moschetti of all types.
6·5 × 52mm, rimless.
Action: as Mo.1891 rifle, above. Otherwise as Mo.1891 carbine except for weight (3·22kg unladen) and bayonet (Mo.1891 TS pattern—see text).

☆

1897: this carbine was adopted for the Truppe Speciali. The original nose cap was similar to that of the rifle, with a bayonet lug, but carried a swivel on its rear edge. The second swivel lay on the underside of the butt. A recoil bolt ran through the stock beneath the receiver ring and the bolt handle was straight.
1900*: the recoil bolt was abandoned, the bolt handle was turned down, and a modified nose cap was approved. This had a prominent rearward extension for the front swivel and the attachment lug for the bayonet ran laterally. The press-stud on the special bayonet protruded from the end of the pommel.
1908*: the first guns were modified so that the swivels lay on the left side of the stock. Work was not completed until 1913.
1923*: surviving Mo.91 TS carbines were recalled for modification. The old nose cap was replaced by a shortened version—accepting the standard sword bayonet—and a new swivel-bearing band was added, accompanied by its retaining spring.
1930*: some TS carbines were fitted with a grenade launcher (Annesso trombonico Mo.28) on the right side of the fore-end.

Grenades were fired by removing the bolt from the carbine and inserting it in the bolt-way of the launcher.

Model 1891–24

Carbine: Moschetto Mo.1891–24.
Converted by Fabbrica Nazionale d'Armi, Terni.
6·5 × 52mm, rimless.
Otherwise generally as Mo.1891 carbine, excepting bayonet (Mo.91 sword pattern).

☆

1924: this was created simply by converting full-length infantry rifles, particularly those returning for major repairs to the barrel or fore-end.

The Mo.91–24 had the modified nose cap and barrel-band assembly of the modified Mo.91 TS carbine, but retained the full-size back sight of the rifle—though the graduations were suitably altered to allow for the reduction in muzzle velocity.

Model 1891–38

Short rifle: Fucile Mo.1891–38.
Made by Fabbrica Nazionale d'Armi, Terni.
6·5 × 52mm, rimless.
Action: as Mo.1891 rifle, above.
1,075mm overall, 3·46kg unladen.
562mm barrel, 4-groove rifling; RH, concentric.
Integral clip-loaded box magazine, 6 rounds.
Fixed-notch sight for 300 metres.
655 m/sec with Mo.91–95 ball cartridges.
Mo.1938 knife bayonet.

☆

1938: this modified Mo.1891 was intended to expend 6·5mm ammunition before all service rifles were converted to 7·35mm. Mo.91–38 was identical with the 7·35mm Mo.38 rifle (q.v.), but retained the original barrel and bolt.
1940: a barrel band with a swivel on the left side was approved, the nose cap receiving distinctive extensions.

Model 1891–38

Carbines: Moschetti Mo.1891–38 e Mo.1891–38 TS.
Converted by Fabbrica Nazionale d'Armi, Terni.
6·5 × 52mm, rimless.
Otherwise as Mo.1891 carbine, above, apart from back sight (fixed notch for 200 metres) and bayonet (see notes).

☆

1938: these conversions of the 6.5mm cavalry and Truppe Speciali carbines retained their original barrels and bolts. The back sight was modified, but transformations were uncommon. Cavalry carbines had a folding bayonet; the TS patterns accepted a Mo.91 sword bayonet.

Model 1938

Short rifle: Fucile Mo.1938.
Converted by Fabbrica Nazionale d'Armi, Terni, 1939–40.
7·35 × 52mm, rimless.
Action: as Mo.1891 rifle, above.
1,020mm overall, 3·68kg unladen.
562mm barrel, 4-groove rifling; RH, concentric.

H.B. LOCKHOVEN

Mannlicher An Italian M1891 cavalry carbine. This is the perfected pattern, with a hand guard ahead of the back sight.

PATTERN ROOM COLLECTION

Mannlicher An Italian M1891 'Truppe Speciali' musketoon, with the M1928 grenade launcher ('Tromboncino lanciabombe').

Integral clip-loaded box magazine, 6 rounds.
Fixed-notch sight for 300 metres.
755 m/sec with Mo.38 ball cartridges.
Mo.1938 knife bayonet.

☆

1935: experience with the 6·5mm round in the First World War suggested that it lacked power. Troubles in the Italian colonies in North Africa highlighted the shortcomings of the original cartridge. In the mid 1930s, therefore, experiments to improve it began at Terni under the supervision of Colonel Giuseppe Mainardi. With the co-operation of Bombrini Parodi Delfino and Società Metallurgica Italiana, a satisfactory 7·35mm bullet was created. This could be loaded in the 6·5mm cartridge case with minimal alterations.

1938: the new weapon was initially made by converting Mo.1891 rifles. A selection of new parts was needed—from the barrel and bolt to the bands and stock—and a new folding-blade knife bayonet appeared. The guns could be recognised by a simple back sight and, initially, by absence of intermediate barrel bands. They had a swivel on the left side of the nose cap and a fixed bar on the left side of the butt.

1939: weaknesses in the fore-end and nose-cap assembly led to the reappearance of a barrel band with a swivel on the left side. The modified nose cap had small rearward extensions let into the fore-end sides and held by two lateral pins.

1940: the decision was taken to withdraw all 7·35mm-calibre guns from the armed forces and re-issue 6·5mm versions, as the commencement of the Second World War would complicate wholesale rearmament too greatly. Large-calibre rifles were apparently given to the militia.

Model 1938

Carbines: Moschetti Mo.1938 e Mo.1938 TS.
Converted by Fabbrica Nazionale d'Armi, Terni.
7·35 × 52mm, rimless.
Otherwise as Mo.1891 carbine, excepting for back sight (fixed notch for 200 metres), performance (725 m/sec with Mo.1938 ball cartridges) and bayonet.

☆

1938: mostly converted from the Mo.91 cavalry carbines, retaining the folding bayonet, the Mo.38 had a new 7·35mm barrel and bolt. The otherwise similar Mo.38 TS carbine had a barrel band and a nose cap accepting the Mo.91 sword bayonet. Adjustable back sights were replaced by fixed notches.

1940: surviving guns were passed to the militia.

Model 1938–43

Short rifle: Moschetto Mo.1938–43.
7·9 × 57mm, rimless.
Otherwise generally as Mo.1891 carbine, above, excepting magazine (integral 5-round box), back sight (fixed notch for 300 metres) and performance (about 625 m/sec with sS-Patrone). The Mo.1891 sword bayonet was used.

☆

1944: small quantities of these weapons were made in Cremona in northern Italy for the Co-Belligerent forces, fighting alongside the Germans. The barrel was bored for the standard 7·9mm German service cartridge, suitable adjustments being made to the bolt-head face, and a semi-circular channel was milled vertically across the chamber to allow the rounds to be pushed down into the magazine. A modified clip was welded into the magazine to retain the cartridges, which had to be loaded singly owing to the absence of charger guides. A large s was struck into the chamber-top, with 7.9 ahead of the back sight. The quality of the alterations was very poor; and the action was only marginally strong enough for such a powerful cartridge.

JAPAN

I-Type

Infantry rifle.
Assembled by Fabbrica Nazionale d'Armi, Terni, 1938–9; major sub-contractors included the Italian government factories in Gardone (RSFAE) and Brescia (FNAB), plus Pietro Beretta SpA.
Quantity: 60,000.
6·5 × 50mm, semi-rimmed.

Turning-bolt action, with two lugs on a detachable bolt head locking into the receiver.
1,262mm overall, 4·07kg unladen.
778mm barrel, 4-groove rifling; RH, concentric?
Internal charger-loaded box magazine, 5 rounds.
Leaf sight graduated to 2,400 metres.
755 m/sec with Meiji 38th Year Type ball cartridges.
Meiji 38th Year Type sword bayonet.

☆

1937: embroilment in a war with China caught the Japanese authorities with too few rifles to satisfy mobilisation. However, a mutual trade agreement allowed large numbers of hybrid rifles to be ordered in Italy. These combined Japanese-style barrels, sights, bayonets and stocks with the Mannlicher-type split-bridge actions.

1940: the butts of some rifles were shortened by 20mm, suiting them to troops of small stature.

1941: the rifles were replaced by the Type 99, survivors being relegated to training duties.

THE NETHERLANDS

The adoption of small-calibre magazine rifles throughout Europe placed the army of the Netherlands at a disadvantage in the early 1890s. The Dutch maintained a small colonial empire and did not wish to be outgunned by potential aggressors. A Mannlicher was adopted to replace the M1871/88 (Beaumont-Vitali).

Model 1895

Infantry rifle: Infanterij-Geweer M1895.
Made by Österreichische Waffenfabriks-Gesellschaft, Steyr, 1895–1902; and Koninklijk Geweerfabrik, Hembrug, 1901–40?
6·5 × 53mm, rimmed.
Turning-bolt action, with two lugs on a detachable bolt head locking into the receiver.
1,295mm overall, 4·30kg unladen.
790mm barrel, 4-groove rifling; RH, concentric.
Integral clip-loaded box magazine, 5 rounds.
Quadrant sight graduated to 2,000 metres.
740 m/sec with M1895 ball cartridges.
M1895 épée bayonet.

☆

Mannlicher The M1891 'Mannlicher-Carcano' rifle in the hands of Italian 52nd infantry regiment. The picture was taken during the colonial campaign that led to the annexation of Libya in 1911–12.

COLLECTOR'S COMPENDIUM

1895: this was an adaption of the preceding 1892-pattern trials rifle, sharing a split-bridge receiver. The magazine projected beneath the stock. The butt had a straight wrist, a hand guard ran forward from the receiver ring to the spring-retained barrel band, and the nose cap carried a projecting bayonet bar similar to that found on the British Lee-Metford.

1917: a few guns were converted to 8mm.

1930★: some guns were cut down to produce No.5 carbines for the Dutch air force.

Model 1895

Carbines No.1 (cavalry), No.2 (gendarmerie), No.3 (artillery and engineers) and No.4 (cyclists and machine gunners): Karabijner M1895 A.1–A.4.
Made by Österreichische Waffenfabriks-Gesellschaft, Steyr, 1897–1904; and Koninklijk Geweerfabrik, Hembrug, 1902–40?
6·5 × 53mm, rimmed.
Action: as M1895 rifle, above.
DATA FOR NO.1 (CAVALRY) CARBINE
952mm overall, 3·10kg unladen.
450mm barrel, 4-groove rifling; RH, concentric.
Integral clip-loaded box magazine, 5 rounds.
Quadrant sight graduated to 2,000 metres.
About 625 m/sec with M1895 ball cartridges.
M1871 socket bayonet.
☆

1897★: a half-stocked carbine was issued to the cavalry and horse artillery. A hand guard was omitted, and the fore-end narrowed perceptibly ahead of the single barrel band. Fixed sling bars lay on the left side of the barrel band and on the left side of the butt close to the butt plate.

1899★: adopted for the Korps Marechaussee (military gendarmerie), the No.2 was a variant of the No.1 or cavalry pattern with a conventional full-length stock. There were two bands, the front one doubling as a nose cap, and a special bayonet—locked by a spring—could be rotated into place on the right side of the muzzle. When reversed, the tip of bayonet blade abutted a shoulder on the right side of the rear band. Swivels lay beneath the barrel band and butt. Details were generally similar to No.1, excepting

an unladen weight of 3·22kg and the attachment of a folding bayonet.

1904★: believed to have been adopted for the fortress artillery, engineers and sappers, the No.3 carbine had a distinctive hand guard running forward past the nose cap and over the top of the muzzle. It was issued with a long-bladed bayonet to compensate for the lack of reach. The swivels lay on the underside of the barrel band and the under-edge of the butt. The gun weighed 3·14kg and accepted the long M1895 épée.

1908★: the No.4 carbine was a minor variant of the No.3, for cyclists and machine gunners, with a conventional hand guard assembly ending at the nose cap. The swivels lay on the left side of the fore-end—owing to the lack of a barrel band—and on the side of the butt.

1915★: most carbines were improved to the 'New Model' (Nieuw Model) standards, which included pinning and gluing a wooden fairing to the left side of the magazine to stop the uniform being abraded when the gun was slung over the shoulder. Surviving guns of original pattern were reclassified as 'Old Model' (Oude Model) to distinguish them.

The cavalry carbine stock was adapted in this era to receive a conventional nose cap, and a short M1895 cavalry-pattern bayonet was adopted. Some No.4 guns apparently received new swivels on the side of fore-end and butt, the barrel band being discarded.

Model 1917

Machine-gunners' rifle: Geweer M1917.
Made by Koninklijk Geweerfabrik, Hembrug, 1917–19.
8 × 57mm, rimmed.
Action: as M1895 rifle, above.
1,295mm overall, 4·22kg unladen.
792mm barrel, 4-groove rifling; RH, concentric.
Integral clip-loaded box magazine, 5 rounds.
Quadrant sight graduated to 2,000 metres.
About 880 m/sec with German S-Patrone.
M1895 épée bayonet.
☆

1917: this was approved during the First World War to ensure common ammunition supply with Dutch Lewis and Schwarzlose machine-guns. M1917 rifles were issued primarily to machine-gunners and ancillary troops, but were discarded rapidly once hostilities had finished.

Model 1895

Carbine No.5: Karabijn M1895 A.5.
6·5 × 53mm, rimmed.
Action: as M1895 rifle, above.
960mm overall, 3·56kg unladen.
455mm barrel, 4-groove rifling; RH, concentric.
Integral clip-loaded box magazine, 5 rounds.
Quadrant sight graduated 2,000 metres.
625 m/sec with M1895 ball cartridges.
M1895 sword bayonet.
☆

1930★: the No.5 carbine, issued to the Dutch air force, was made by cutting down full-length rifles. It lacked the wood fillet on the magazine side, had a rifle-type nose cap, and could be identified by original manufacturing marks.

Other guns

A M1911 colonial-pattern carbine was made in small numbers for the Royal Netherlands Indies Army (KNIL); its bolt handle was turned down, and it accepted a strange knife-bladed bayonet with a bar hilt. There was also a practice rifle (Geweer tot kamerschietoefeningen) of very uncertain vintage. Low-powered 5·5mm (·22) centre-fire cartridges were loaded in a special five-round clip; the rifle was basically an M1895 infantry pattern, but weighed 4·7kg.

ROMANIA
Model 1892

Made by Österreichische Waffenfabriks-Gesellschaft, Steyr, 1892.
6·5 × 53mm, rimmed.
Turning-bolt action, with two lugs on a detachable bolt head locking into the receiver.

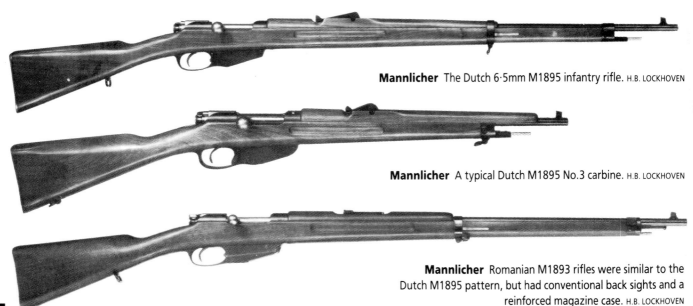

Mannlicher The Dutch 6·5mm M1895 infantry rifle. H.B. LOCKHOVEN

Mannlicher A typical Dutch M1895 No.3 carbine. H.B. LOCKHOVEN

Mannlicher Romanian M1893 rifles were similar to the Dutch M1895 pattern, but had conventional back sights and a reinforced magazine case. H.B. LOCKHOVEN

1,227mm overall, 4·06kg unladen.
725mm barrel, 4-groove rifling; RH, concentric.
Integral clip-loaded box magazine, 5 rounds.
Tangent-leaf sight graduated to 2,000 metres.
680 m/sec with ball cartridges.

☆

1892: acquired for field trials, these were the first Mannlicher-type rifles to embody lessons learned from the Gew.88. They had straight-grip stocks and two barrel bands, the front band doubling as a nose cap and carrying the bayonet lug on the right side. The hand guard ran from the receiver ring to the rear band. There were swivels under the rear band and the butt-edge, whilst a half-length cleaning rod lay beneath the muzzle. Chamber-tops were marked ARMA MD. 1892 below a crown, with STEYR 1892 on the left side of the receiver. The guns were readily distinguishable by their plain-sided magazines.

Model 1893

Infantry rifle and carbine.
Made by Österreichische
Waffenfabriks-Gesellschaft, Steyr, 1893–1914.
Quantity: 100,000 by 1907.
6·5 × 53mm, rimmed.
Action: as M1892, above.
1,227mm overall, 4·11kg unladen.
725mm barrel, 4-groove rifling; RH, concentric.
Integral clip-loaded box magazine, 5 rounds.
Tangent-leaf sight graduated to 2,100 metres.
731 m/sec with M1893 ball cartridges.
M1893 knife bayonet.

☆

1893: an improved form of the 1892 trials rifle described above, this had an additional stacking rod on the left side of the nose cap and prominent reinforcing ribs on the lower sides of the magazine housing. Internally, a change was made to the left locking lug and the bolt stop so that the bolt could be re-inserted only if properly assembled; otherwise, the bolt stop had to lifted manually. Like the earlier gun, the M1893 had a gas-escape port in the bolt and a secondary cocking-piece notch on the rear of the bolt to assist dismantling. The chamber-top

marking read simply Md.1893 beneath a crown.
1903*: a carbine was adopted for cavalry and artillerymen. 953mm overall, with a 450mm barrel and a weight of 3·29kg, it was identical with the rifle apart from the turned-down bolt handle and the omission of the barrel band. A swivel lay on the left side of the butt, with a loop on the left side of the nose cap.

SWITZERLAND

Model 1893

Carbine: Repetier-Karabiner M1893.
Made by Schweizerische Industrie-Gesellschaft,
Neuhausen, 1895–1900; and Eidgenössische
Waffenfabrik, Bern, 1898–1905.
Quantity: 7,750
7·5 × 53·5mm, rimmed.
Straight-pull action, with two lugs on a detachable bolt
head locking into the receiver.
1,016mm overall, 3·08kg unladen.
550mm barrel, 4-groove rifling; RH, concentric.
Detachable box magazine, 6 rounds.
Quadrant sight graduated to 1,200 metres.
560 m/sec with M1890 ball cartridges.
No bayonet.

☆

1893: the 1889-pattern Schmidt action was too clumsy to be incorporated in a carbine and so, on 29 June, trials began with two Neuhausen turning-bolt designs, turn-bolt and straight-pull Mannlichers, a Mauser turn-bolt with Rubin's modifications, and straight-pull actions designed by Vogelsang and Krauser.
1895: the compactness of the straight-pull Mannlicher action, 8cm shorter than Schmidt's, allowed the adoption of the M1893 carbine on 1 March. These guns had a straight-wrist stock with a German-style sling-anchor slot in the butt, a full-length hand guard and a single barrel band. They were stocked to the muzzle.

SPORTING GUNS

Prior to the perfection of the Schönauer rotary magazine, the Mannlicher rifle had had little

commercial success; few sportsmen liked the clip loaded magazine, excepting possibly in Germany where thousands of Gew.88 actions had been converted. The advent of an effectual magazine that could be loaded with loose cartridges changed the situation appreciably, as the Mannlicher was sturdy; furthermore, owing to the split-bridge receiver design, its bolt stroke was easy to use.

In addition to the guns made in central Europe, the Mannlicher was also popular in Britain early in the twentieth century. Sporting rifles were built on military 1895-pattern actions imported from the Netherlands by W.J. Jeffrey, Thomas Bland and many other well-known gunsmiths. Stocks customarily followed the slender typically British variety, with straight combs, small oval cheek pieces and delicately contoured pistol grips.

Some guns were made in 'Take-Down' form, locked by interrupted threads or screws through the breech, while others—intended for long range target shooting—had vernier sights on the heel of the butt. Cocking-piece aperture sights, patented triggers and adapted magazines were commonly encountered, together with Henry-type fore-end tips and Express or Cape back sights. The most popular chambering was the original 6·5 × 53mm rimmed Dutch cartridge, but rifles converted for ·303 and others have been catalogued.

AUSTRIA-HUNGARY

The first sporters were identical mechanically with the Greek M1903 service rifle, though greater care was taken over surface finish and greatly improved stocks were fitted.

Repetier-Pirschbüchse

Offered in rifle or carbine patterns.
Made by Österreichische Waffenfabriks-Gesellschaft,
Steyr, c.1903–16.
Chambering: see notes.
Turning-bolt action, locked by rotating lugs on the
detachable bolt head into the receiver.

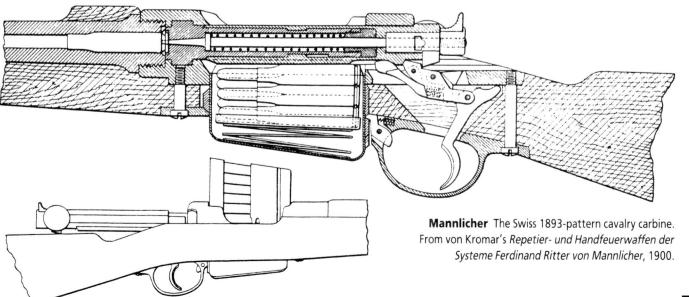

Mannlicher The Swiss 1893-pattern cavalry carbine. From von Kromar's *Repetier- und Handfeuerwaffen der Systeme Ferdinand Ritter von Mannlicher*, 1900.

DATA FOR A TYPICAL SHORT RIFLE
6·5mm × 54mm, rimless.
993mm overall, 3·02kg unladen.
450mm barrel, 4-groove rifling; RH, concentric.
Internal rotary magazine, 5 rounds.
Block-and-leaf sight.
685 m/sec with 8·2-gram bullet.

☆

1904: the 1903-pattern rifle was offered only in 6·5 × 54mm rimless chambering. Most were made as short rifles (Repetier-Pirschstutzen), with full-length stocks, but long-barrelled half-stock examples were also available. The military-style action could be loaded from a charger, a safety catch lay on top of the cocking piece, and the bolt handle was a flattened spatulate form inspired by the German Karabiner 88.

Butts had a straight comb, a small oval cheek piece and a rounded pistol grip. The grip and fore-end were chequered, a steel nose cap was fitted, and a sling ring was held by a bolt through the stock and a small collar on the barrel. A trap in the butt plate housed a four-piece cleaning rod, and sometimes also two spare cartridges. The back sight (Klappvisier) had a standing block for 100 metres, with folding leaves for 200 metres or—alternatively—200 and 300 metres. A double set trigger mechanism was customary, but single-trigger guns were also made.

1905: a variant chambered for the 9 × 56mm cartridge appeared, identical with the 6·5mm gun excepting for a 500mm barrel.

1908: an 8 × 56mm (Austrian) and, apparently, an 8 × 57mm (German) chambering appeared.

1910: a 9·5 × 56mm version was introduced.

1912*: a special 10·75 × 63mm version was announced, but few were made before the First World War began.

Note: cartridges were widely designated by bullet diameter in pre-1918 Austria-Hungary, causing much confusion as the standard 6·5mm varieties were classified as '6·7mm'.

AUSTRIA

Production began again in the early 1920s, guns being identical to pre-1918 patterns.

Repetier-Pirschbüchse

Offered in rifle or carbine patterns.
Made in Steyr by Österreichische
Waffenfabriks-Gesellschaft (c.1921-34) and
Steyr-Daimer-Puch AG (1934–40, 1950–71).
Chambering: see notes.
Action: as Austro-Hungarian guns, above.
DATA FOR A TYPICAL 1932-VINTAGE RIFLE
6·5mm × 54mm, rimless.
1,145mm overall, 3·38kg unladen.
600mm barrel, 4-groove rifling; RH, concentric.
Internal rotary magazine, 5 rounds.
Block-and-leaf sight.
685 m/sec with 8·2-gram bullet.

☆

1921*: production resumed with permission from the Allied authorities. The first guns were assembled from pre-war parts, the first entirely new examples dating from 1923–4—though the manufacturing pattern remained unchanged. The first guns chambering the 7·62 × 63mm cartridge (·30–06) originated in this era for sale in North America.

The rifles retained the block-and-leaf back sight or Klappvisier, though the popularity of optical patterns soon increased. Short-barrelled Repetier-Pirschbüchsen were chambered for 6·5mm, 8mm, 9mm or 9·5mm cartridges; long-barrelled half-stocked guns ('Hochrasanz-Modelle') were usually supplied for 7 × 64mm, 7·62 × 63mm or 8 × 60mm. Other chamberings could be supplied to order: e.g., a 9·3 × 53mm pattern was particularly popular in Switzerland. Longer barrels than normal, multi-leaf Express sights, optical- or aperture-sight mounts, sling eyes on barrel collars, engraving and stock carving were also available.

1940*: production ceased in favour of war-work, the Steyr factory being re-tooled for the Kar.98k under German supervision. Assembly of sporting rifles is believed to have continued on a small scale until 1942.

1950: work finally resumed in the Steyr factory. The first sporters were based on the pre-war patterns, though the bolt handle was refined and the safety catch moved from the cocking piece to

the rear right side of the bridge. This had the important effect of reducing the comparatively slow lock time of pre-1950 rifles. Chambered for ·257 Roberts, ·270 Winchester or ·30–06 in the hope of attracting orders from North America, the rifle had a 610mm barrel, a walnut half-stock with a straight-comb butt, a capped pistol grip, and a rounded rosewood fore-end tip. The short rifle, with a full-length 'Mannlicher' stock, had a 510mm barrel. A 6·5 × 54mm carbine was made in small numbers with a 465mm barrel.

Many of the guns sold in the USA had single triggers, though the double set pattern retained much of its popularity in Europe.

1952: in an attempt to modernise the design, the bolt handle was swept backward and the stock detailing improved. Chamberings remained unchanged from 1950.

1956: a revised stock was introduced, with a Monte Carlo comb and spacers accompanying the fore-end-tip, pistol-grip cap and butt plate. Additional ·243 Winchester, 7 × 57mm and ·308 Winchester chamberings appeared in this period.

1961: a universal stock, with a Monte Carlo comb but lacking a cheek piece, was introduced.

1971: production ceased in favour of the improved Model 72 (q.v.).

Model 1969

Alternatively known as 'Model 67'.
Made by Steyr-Daimler-Puch AG, Steyr.
Chambering: see notes.
Turning-bolt action, locked by rotating lugs on the bolt
into the receiver behind the magazine.
DATA FOR A TYPICAL FULL-STOCK MODEL L
·243 Winchester, rimless.
995mm overall, 3·12kg unladen.
510mm barrel, 4-groove rifling; RH, concentric.
Detachable box magazine, 3 rounds.
Folding-leaf sight.
3,070 ft/sec with 100-grain bullet.

☆

1967: developed to replace the obsolescent Mannlicher-Schönauer rifle, these guns had six lugs (in two rings of three) on the bolt to

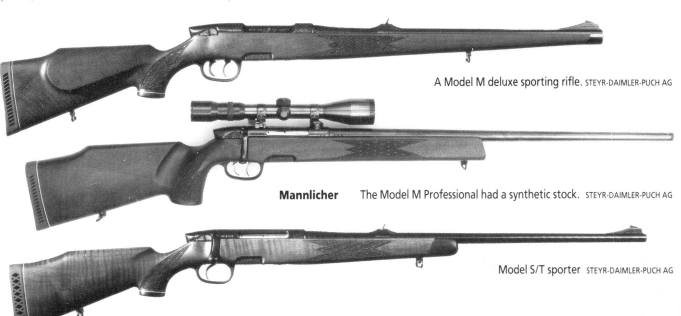

A Model M deluxe sporting rifle. STEYR-DAIMLER-PUCH AG

Mannlicher The Model M Professional had a synthetic stock. STEYR-DAIMLER-PUCH AG

Model S/T sporter STEYR-DAIMLER-PUCH AG

lock into the receiver behind the magazine well. A substantial part of the bolt is placed under compressive stress during firing (cf., Lee-Enfield), but the system has proved sturdy enough in practice. One substantial gain from construction of this type is that cartridges feed directly into the chamber instead of crossing the space left for locking lugs. As the perfected detachable spool magazine positions cartridges more consistently than a thin-lipped box, feed is practically flawless.

1968: the first sporting rifles had a neat spatulate bolt handle and a safety catch on the right side of the solid-bridge receiver immediately behind the bolt handle. The ''monk's cowl'' bolt shroud was unmistakable.

Most magazines had a skeletal spool inside a transparent case, though box magazines could be fitted to order.

Made with the shortest of the three basic actions, the SL ('Super Light') has been offered in ·222 Remington, ·222 Remington Magnum, ·223 Remington and 5·2 × 50 Magnum. The double set trigger was standard, though a single-trigger system could be substituted to order. A folding-leaf back sight was used in conjunction with a ramp-mouted blade.

SL rifles had a half- or full-length stocks with skip-line chequering on fore-ends and pistol grips, low Monte Carlo combs, plastic pistol-grip caps and rubber shoulder plates.

Model L ('Light') rifles, also built on the short action, chambered the 5·6 × 57mm, ·243 Winchester and ·308 Winchester rounds. They were made in the same three basic variants as the SL.

1969: the Varmint patterns of the Models SL and L were introduced, with heavy barrels, and a half-stock with a stippled pistol grip. Seven short slots were cut through the fore-end.

1970: offered in 6·5 × 68mm, 7mm Remington Magnum, ·300 Winchester Magnum, ·375 H&H Magnum or 8 × 68mm S, Model S ('Standard') rifles were built on the largest of the new actions. The receiver was strengthened to withstand pressures generated by high-power cartridges. Conventional pistol-grip stocks with low Monte Carlo combs and ventilated rubber butt plates were retained; rosewood fore-end tips and pistol-grip caps had thin white spacers.

1971: heavy-barrel ·222 options appeared for the standard Model L and SL rifles.

1973: the Model M ('Medium') rifle was built on a similar action to the Model L, enlarged to accept cartridges such as 6·5 × 57mm, ·270 Winchester, 7 × 57mm, 7 × 64mm, ·30–06, 8 × 57mm and 9·3 × 62mm. The rubber recoil pad was ventilated and a contrasting rosewood fore-end tip was fitted. Model M Professional had a warp-proof Cycolac synthetic stock.

1974: the S/T ('Standard/Tropical') rifle shared the S-pattern action. Supplied only for the 9·3 × 64mm, ·375 H&H Magnum or ·458 Winchester Magnum cartridges, the guns had 650mm barrels (600mm option in ·458 only), weighed up to 4·2kg and were fitted with four-round magazines. Their Express-type or multi-leaf back sights were mounted on very distinctive squared blocks.

1977: 6·5 × 55mm and 7·5 × 55mm options were introduced for the Model M.

1984: the Match-UIT rifle, made in single-shot or magazine-feed versions in ·243 or ·308 Winchester only, had the fore-end of the stock cut away to allow the barrel to float freely. The straight bolt handle had a large synthetic knob, and the trigger could be adjusted longitudinally. Aperture sights were standard and a woven 'mirage band' ran from the receiver ring to the front-sight block. The rifle was about 1,130mm overall, had a 650mm barrel, and weighed about 4·95kg with its sights.

Note: deluxe guns (Luxusmodelle) have also been made in large numbers. The spool magazines were generally replaced by three-round boxes and steel floor plates, whilst the safety catch was moved to the upper tang. A single trigger, set by pushing the trigger-lever forward, was regarded as standard instead of optional. The stock lacked the hunched appearance of the standard patterns, the pistol grip being lengthened. Bavarian-style cheek pieces and hog's back combs were customary. Excepting the Model S, half-stocked guns had a delicate rosewood schnabel tip and the front sling swivel lay on a barrel collar. Metalwork and stock wood were decorated to order.

Model 1972

Made by Steyr-Daimler-Puch AG, Steyr.
Chambering: see notes.
Turning-bolt action, locked by rotating lugs on the bolt head into the receiver.
DATA FOR A TYPICAL MODEL S
8 × 68mm S, rimless.
1,165mm overall, 3·97kg unladen.
610mm barrel, 4-groove rifling; RH, concentric.
Detachable spool magazine, 4 rounds.
Block-and-leaf sight.
990 m/sec with 11·7-gram bullet.

☆

1972: made only for a few years (c.1972–7), this rifle was apparently introduced to guard against the failure of the rear-locking action to handle high pressures effectually. The Model 72 lugs lay on the bolt head, though construction was otherwise similar to the Model 69.

The short action, embodied in the L ('Light') and M ('Medium') variants, was chambered for ·22–250 Remington, 5·6 × 57mm, 6mm Remington, ·243 Winchester, 6·5 × 57mm, ·270 Winchester, 7 × 57mm, 7 × 64mm, ·308 Winchester or ·30–06. Barrels were 560mm long; stocks and fittings were similar to the Model 69.

A long S ('Standard') action was chambered for 6·5 × 68mm, 7mm Remington Magnum, 8 × 68mm S, 9·3 × 64mm or ·375 H&H Magnum rounds. A 610mm medium-weight barrel was standard, rifles weighing 3·7–3·9kg.

1974: an S/T version was introduced in ·300 Winchester Magnum, 9·3 × 64mm, ·375 H&H Magnum or ·458 Winchester Magnum, identical with the Model S excepting for its heavy 610mm barrel and a weight in excess of 4kg.

GERMANY

Sporting rifles based on the 'Mannlicher' action embodied in the Gew.88 enjoyed a period in

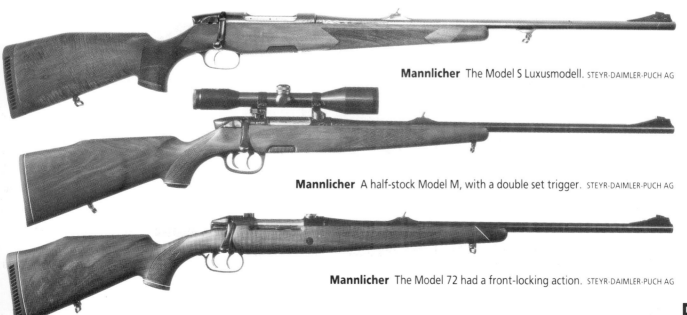

Mannlicher The Model S Luxusmodell. STEYR-DAIMLER-PUCH AG

Mannlicher A half-stock Model M, with a double set trigger. STEYR-DAIMLER-PUCH AG

Mannlicher The Model 72 had a front-locking action. STEYR-DAIMLER-PUCH AG

vogue prior to 1914. Though many were stocked and finished by independent gunsmiths on the basis of military-surplus actions, new patterns almost always prove to have been made in Suhl by Haenel or Schilling. Both manufacturers continued production long after the Gew.88 had been displaced in the German army by the perfected Mauser.

Classifying these guns is often very difficult, as they may bear nothing but a retailer's name; stocks, barrels and fittings offered such great diversity that dating is also problematical.

Model 1888

Made in Suhl by C.G. Haenel & Co. or
V.C. Schilling & Co.
Chambering: see notes.
Turning-bolt action, locked by rotating lugs on the detachable bolt head into the receiver.
DATA FOR A TYPICAL RIFLE
9 × 63mm, rimless
1,062mm overall, 3·35kg unladen.
550mm barrel, 4-groove rifling; RH, concentric.
Integral clip-loaded box magazine, 5 rounds.
Block-and-leaves sight.
745 m/sec with 11·9-gram bullet.

☆

1894*: the first sporting rifles were essentially similar to the military Gewehr 88 (q.v.). They lacked the superfluous barrel jacket, had better stocks, and were often fitted with set triggers.

1900*: as time passed, more effectual guns appeared. Most accepted 8 × 57mm German service cartridges, though some examples were chambered for the 9 × 57mm or 9·3 × 57mm rounds. By 1911, 6·6 × 57mm and 9 × 63mm were also among the options. Military-style Wehrmannbüchsen fired the 8·15 × 46·5mm rimmed cartridge.

A typical gun made by Haenel at the turn of the century had a good quality pistol-grip half stock, with extensive chequering on the grip and the horn tipped fore-end. A sling eye was brazed to the underside of the barrel, a block-and-leaf back sight was fitted, and the front sight was a silvered bead. A double set trigger was fitted.

A differing Schilling gun had an octagonal barrel and a full-length fore-end held to the barrel by two transverse keys set in escutcheons. It had a spring-loaded ejection port cover under the magazine case and a hinged aperture sight on the wrist. The action was lightly engraved.

1915: the German authorities ordered Haenel and Schilling to tool for the Gew.98, whereupon production of the older actions ceased. Though most 1888-type sporters were made before the First World War, a few were assembled in the early 1920s from surplus rifles and old parts.

Model 1909

Made by C.G. Haenel, Waffen- und Fahrradfabrik, Suhl.
7 × 57mm, 8 × 57mm or 9 × 57mm.
Action: as 1888 pattern, above.
DATA FOR A TYPICAL EXAMPLE
9 × 57mm, rimless
1,120mm overall, 3·15kg unladen.
580mm barrel, 4-groove rifling; RH, concentric.
Internal box magazine, 5 rounds.
Block-and-leaves sight.
565 m/sec with 18·2-gram bullet.

☆

1909: this was simply the 1907-type military rifle in sporting guise ('Haenel-Jagdbüchse'). The basic 'Grade I' pattern amalgamated a modified 1888-type action with an internal box magazine, distinguished by a patented detachable floor plate. It had a walnut pistol-grip half stock, a barleycorn front sight on a matted saddle, and a simple back sight with a standing block plus a small folding leaf. The metal parts were blacked. The basic rifle cost about 20 per cent less than a comparable Mauser prior to the First World War.

A 'Grade II' rifle offered better finish, flat side plates on the stock alongside the action, a cheek piece on the butt and an additional set-trigger; 'Grade III' guns had a silver-bead front sight on a long matted-top saddle, and a tangent-leaf sight graduated to 1,000 metres.

Though Haenel-Mannlichers were effectual enough—the best of true Gew.88 derivatives—they were not made in sufficient numbers to challenge the supremacy of Mauser.

MARLIN

UNITED STATES OF AMERICA
〜

For more detailed information, see William S. Brophy's standard history *Marlin Firearms. A History of the Guns and the Company that made them* (Stackpole Books, 1989).

1. THE LEVER-ACTION PATTERNS

The earliest guns were based on patents granted to Andrew Burgess in 1873–9, allied with an improved cartridge elevator designed by Burgess and John Marlin in December 1881. Later ones were largely the work of Lewis Hepburn, whose first relevant patent dated from 1886.

The original Marlin rifle was very simple. The breech-lever extension served as a prop for the longitudinally sliding breech block. When the gun fired, the strain was taken by the breech-lever pivot pin—theoretically unsound, but in practice more than able to withstand the pressure. Later guns relied on a sliding block or bolt locked by a rising bar. This proved to be most effectual; consequently, the Marlins have been extremely successful, with production of the 1893/1936/336 series reaching three million guns in 1979.

Model 1881

Known prior to 1888 simply as the 'Marlin Repeating Rifle'; available in standard, medium and small-frame patterns, plus a carbine.
Made by the Marlin Fire Arms Company, New Haven, Connecticut, 1881–91.
Quantity: about 20,540.
·32–40 Ballard, ·38–55 Ballard, ·40–60 Marlin,
·45–70 Government or ·45–85 Marlin.
Lever action, locked by propping the bolt in place.
DATA FOR A TYPICAL EXAMPLE
·40–60 Marlin, rimmed.

ENGRAVINGS FROM THE 1911 A.L. FRANK CATALOGUE

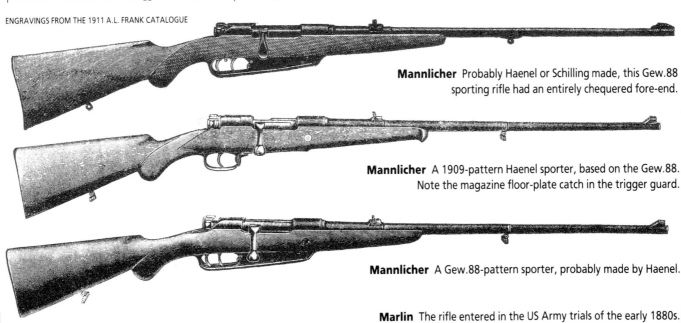

Mannlicher Probably Haenel or Schilling made, this Gew.88 sporting rifle had an entirely chequered fore-end.

Mannlicher A 1909-pattern Haenel sporter, based on the Gew.88. Note the magazine floor-plate catch in the trigger guard.

Mannlicher A Gew.88-pattern sporter, probably made by Haenel.

Marlin The rifle entered in the US Army trials of the early 1880s.

44·00in overall, 9·88lb unladen.
26·00in barrel, 6-groove rifling; RH, concentric.
Tube magazine in fore-end, 8 rounds.
Spring-leaf and elevator sight.
About 1,385 ft/sec with 260-grain bullet.

☆

1881: the first top-ejecting prototypes were distributed to Schoverling, Daly & Gales of New York. They had 28in octagonal barrels chambering ·40–60 or ·45–70, and ten-round magazines. They could be identified by the distinctively-shaped operating lever combined with the trigger guard. The front section of the trigger guard had less of a curve than on contemporary Winchesters, while the loading gate—with a sliding spring-loaded cover—lay on the lower front right side of the receiver.

1882: production began, all but the first sixty guns being made with a stirrup-top ejector instead of the original blade. The improved ejector was patented in January 1883. A selection of barrel options (24–30in) was accompanied by magazines whose contents depended on the length of the barrel. Select woodwork, pistol-grip butts, engraving, and special sights were available to order. The original heavyweight receiver was soon replaced by a revised pattern without the rebated or stepped underside at the joint with the fore-end. However, the guns still weighed 9–11lb. A ·45–70 M1881 performed surprisingly well in the US Army repeating rifle trials.

1883: two fingers were added to the cartridge elevator ('carrier' in Marlin terminology) to improve feed. A comparable wedge was used in small-frame ·32 and ·38 rifles, where space was limited. Double set triggers were introduced; a popular accessory, these were subsequently fitted to roughly one in every six guns.

1885: a medium-frame rifle was introduced, 'specially for export'. Chambered for ·40–60 or ·45–70, it had a barrel of 24in or 28in and weighed 8·3–8·8lb. A small-frame adaption of the M1881 suitable for ·32–40 Ballard cartridges was introduced at the end of the year. Offered with standard-weight barrels (24in or 28in), it weighed 7·3–7·5lb.

1886: a ·38–55 Ballard option was added, and a heavy barrel appeared for the small-frame guns.

1891: production ceased in October. The guns had been made in series with the other Marlins; consequently, numbers ran into the 50000s.

Model 1888

Made by the Marlin Fire Arms Company, New Haven, Connecticut, 1888–9.
Quantity: about 4,820.
·32–40 Ballard, ·38–40 Winchester or ·44–40 Winchester.
Lever action, locked by a vertically-sliding bolt.
DATA FOR A TYPICAL EXAMPLE
·38–40 Winchester, rimmed.
40·75in overall, 6·72lb unladen.
24·00in barrel, 6-groove rifling; RH, concentric.
Tube magazine in fore-end, 10 rounds.
Spring-leaf and elevator sight.
About 1,330 ft/sec with 180-grain bullet.

☆

1888: this improved small-action rifle, similar to the M1881 externally, loaded from the side and ejected upward. It was initially offered for ·38–40 and ·44–40 cartridges, but a ·32–40 option had been added by the end of the year. Octagonal barrels of 24in, 26in and 28in were available until August, whereafter many alternative half-octagon or round patterns could be acquired. The half-octagon was particularly unpopular; only 23 such guns are known to have been made. Frames were normally blued, with the hammer and operating levers colour case-hardened. The M1888 embodied changes patented by Lewis Hepburn in December 1886 and October 1887. Its locking mechanism was similar to the Browning-designed Winchesters, which may not have been entirely coincidental.

Model 1889

Also known as 'Marlin New Safety Repeater'; available in carbine, rifle and musket patterns.
Made by the Marlin Fire Arms Company,
New Haven, Connecticut, 1889–1903
Quantity: about 55,120.

·25–20 Winchester, ·32–20 Winchester, ·38–40 Winchester or ·44–40 Winchester.
Lever action, locked by a vertically-sliding bolt.
DATA FOR A TYPICAL EXAMPLE
·25–20 Winchester, rimmed.
40·75in overall, 6·80lb unladen.
24·00in barrel, 6-groove rifling; RH, concentric.
Tube magazine in fore-end, 10 rounds.
Spring-leaf and elevator sight.
About 1,450 ft/sec with 85-grain bullet.

☆

1889: the principal improvement in this rifle, patented by Lewis Hepburn in April 1889, was lateral ejection. Though requiring a different bolt and elevator mechanism, the change allowed a solid-top receiver to be offered. The gun was introduced in September in ·32–40, ·38–40 and ·44–40 chamberings, the round or octagonal barrels measuring 24in, 26in or 28in; the 24in octagonal type was most popular. The receivers were blued, with colour case-hardened levers and hammers, and a distinctive locking catch lay in the rear of the operating-lever bow.

1889-type rifles could not fire until the lever was fully closed. Half-length magazines were optional, but were uncommonly requested. Plain straight-wrist butts were fitted as standard, pistol grips and chequering being obtainable on special request.

1890: a carbine was introduced with a 20in round barrel, though a few hundred were made with 15in barrels towards the end of the century. There were also seventy fully-stocked muskets with 30in barrels, military ramp-and-leaf back sights and provision for a bayonet.

1903: work ceased, though guns continued to be available for years. Excepting ·25–20—only 34 guns are known to have been made—the chamberings had proved equally popular.

Model 1891

Also known as 'Marlin Safety Rifle, Model 1891'.
Made by the Marlin Fire Arms Company, New Haven, Connecticut, 1891–1905.
Quantity: see notes.
·32 Short or Long CF only.

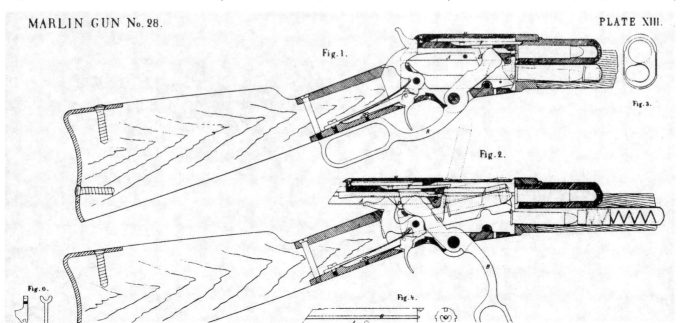

MARLIN GUN No. 28.   PLATE XIII.

Fig. 1.
Fig. 3.
Fig. 2.
Fig. 6.
Fig. 4.

Lever action, locked by a vertically-sliding bolt.
DATA FOR A TYPICAL EXAMPLE
·32 Long CF, rimmed.
40·65in overall, 6·50lb unladen.
24·00in barrel, 6-groove rifling; RH, concentric.
Tube magazine in fore-end, 15 rounds.
Spring-leaf and elevator sight.
About 850 ft/sec with an 85-grain bullet.

☆

1891: introduced in accordance with a patent granted to Lewis Hepburn in August 1890, this was a diminutive version of the side-loading side-ejecting Marlin. The first guns were made with 24in round or octagonal barrels, and short or full-length magazine tubes. They all chambered rimfire cartridges.
1892: a revised model with 26in and 28in barrel options was introduced, featuring a tube-loading system patented by John Marlin in March. These lacked the gate that had previously appeared on the right side of the receiver; magazines accepted fifteen long or seventeen short centre-fire rounds.
1905: the M1891 was discontinued, though few had been made since 1896. Production totalled about 18,650, but only about 6,270 were ·32-calibre; round barrels had been fitted to about one gun in six.

Model 1892

Rifle and carbine.
Made by the Marlin Fire Arms Company, New Haven, Connecticut, 1895–1915.
·32 Long or ·32 Extra Long CF only.
Lever action, locked by a vertically-sliding bolt.
DATA FOR A TYPICAL EXAMPLE
·32 Long CF, rimmed.
42·75in overall, 5·82lb unladen.
26·00in barrel, 6-groove rifling; RH, concentric.
Tube magazine in fore-end, 15 rounds.
Spring-leaf and elevator sight.
About 850 ft/sec with 85-grain bullet.

☆

1896: announced at the beginning of the year, though production had begun late in 1895, this succeeded the 1891 pattern. It ejected laterally from the 'closed-side' receiver, retained the loading-tube system, but lacked the lever-operated trigger safety system; instead, the action was altered so that the firing pin could not reach the chambered round unless the lever was completely closed. The M1892 usually chambered rimfire ammunition, but the ·32 version was also offered in centre-fire simply by changing the firing pin. An octagonal or round 24in barrel was standard, though others were available to order. Butts were generally straight-wristed and a full-length magazine was fitted.
1897: a new spring-retained ejector appeared.
1898: a half-length magazine was introduced.
1899: the addition of a cut-off mechanism allowed cartridges of differing length to feed satisfactorily, permitting the firer to mix long and short ammunition if desired.
1903: a 16in carbine barrel was introduced.
1904: a cartridge guide appeared in the receiver-top. It was abandoned on ·32 guns in 1906.
1907: the ejector was improved, the change being signified by two retaining screws on the left side of the receiver.
1908: a serpentine butt plate replaced the original rifle pattern, rubber being optional.
1915: the M1892 was abandoned owing to the rise of war-work. Production is believed to have reached about 60,000, about a quarter of this total being ·32-calibre.

Model 1893

Renamed 'Model 93' in 1905; available in standard, lightweight, carbine and musket patterns.
Made by the Marlin Fire Arms Company, New Haven, Connecticut, 1893–1915; the Marlin Firearms Corporation, New Haven, Connecticut, 1922–4; and the Marlin Firearms Company, New Haven, Connecticut, 1926–35.
·25–36 Marlin, ·30–30 Winchester, ·32 Winchester Special, ·32–40 Ballard or ·38–55 Ballard.
Lever action, locked by a vertically-sliding bolt.
DATA FOR A TYPICAL EXAMPLE
·25–36 Marlin, rimmed.
44·25in overall, 7·58lb unladen.

26·00in barrel, 6-groove rifling; RH, concentric.
Tube magazine in fore-end, 10 rounds
Spring-leaf and elevator sight
About 1,855 ft/sec with 117-grain bullet.

☆

1893: produced in accordance with a patent granted to Lewis Hepburn in August 1893 to compete with the Winchesters of 1886 and 1892, this incorporated a new locking-bolt system, a two-piece firing pin and an improved elevator mechanism. Originally chambered for ·32–40–165 and ·38–55–255 cartridges, offered in solid frame or 'Take Down' versions, the M1893 was an instantaneous success. Round, half- or fully-octagonal barrels of 20–32in could be obtained; the 26in pattern was regarded as standard, accompanied by a full-length magazine and a straight-wrist butt. Pistol-grip butts and engraving could be supplied to order. A 'Light-Weight Rifle' was made in small numbers, with a half-length magazine and a slim fore-end. It had a round 18in or 20in barrel. An 1893-pattern carbine, generally chambering ·30–30 or ·32–40 cartridges, had a 20in round barrel, a full-length magazine, a 'carbine' (leaf) back sight, and an unladen weight of about 6·75lb. A few carbines were made with 15in barrels towards the end of the century. An 8lb musket derivation, offered with a sword or socket bayonet until about 1905, had a 30in barrel and a full-length fore-end retained by two bands.
1905: a 'Grade B' rifle was introduced for black powder ammunition (·32–40 and ·38–55 only), the barrels of regular guns thereafter being marked SPECIAL SMOKELESS STEEL.
1906: total production had reached 69,100 rifles and 4,090 carbines. Work stopped about 1915 to concentrate on war-work.
1922: production of the standard 'Model No.93' recommenced. The rifle was made with a 26in round or octagonal barrel, had a ten-round magazine and weighed about 7·3lb. The receiver was colour case-hardened and the butt plate was blued steel. Rocky Mountain sights were fitted, chamberings being restricted to ·30–30 Winchester, ·32 Winchester Special,

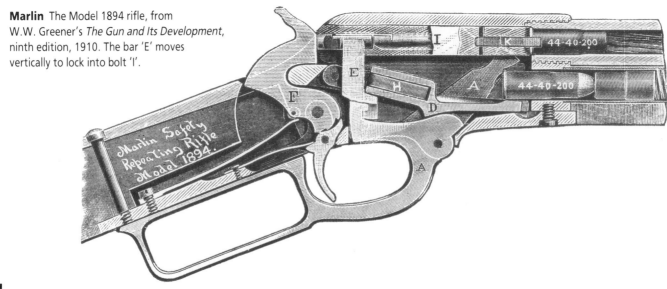

Marlin The Model 1894 rifle, from W.W. Greener's *The Gun and Its Development*, ninth edition, 1910. The bar 'E' moves vertically to lock into bolt 'I'.

·32–40 and ·38–55 Ballard. The carbine (·30–30 and ·32 only) had a 20in barrel, a seven-round magazine and weighed about 6·8lb. Its leaf-and-slider back sight was graduated to 900 yards and the fore-end was held by a band.

1923: Model No. 93CS 'Sporting Carbine' appeared. It was essentially similar to its predecessors, but had an abbreviated five-round magazine, a rubber butt plate, and an open spring-leaf back sight. Advertised 'for big game hunting', it weighed 6·5lb.

1935: the last guns were sold with the serpentine butt plate, regardless of pattern; the rifle had previously had a crecent plate while sporting carbines displayed a rubber type. The two Ballard cartridges—·32–40 and ·38–55—were abandoned, together with the octagonal barrel option.

1936: work on the Model 1893 ceased.

Model 1894

Renamed 'Model 94' in 1906; available in rifle, carbine, baby carbine and musket patterns.
Made by the Marlin Fire Arms Company, New Haven, Connecticut, 1894–1915; the Marlin Firearms Corporation, New Haven, Connecticut, 1922–4; and the Marlin Firearms Company, New Haven, Connecticut, 1926–33.
·25–20 Winchester, ·32–20 Winchester, ·38–40 Winchester or ·44–40 Winchester.
Lever action, locked by a vertically-sliding bolt.
DATA FOR A TYPICAL EXAMPLE
·44–40 Winchester, rimmed.
41·50in overall, 7·05lb unladen.
24·00in barrel, 6-groove rifling; RH, concentric.
Tube magazine in fore-end, 14 rounds?
Spring-leaf and elevator sight.
About 1,310 ft/sec with 200-grain bullet.
☆

1894: an improvement of the 1889-pattern Marlin, incorporating features patented by Lewis Hepburn in August 1893, this side-ejector had the new locking bolt and two-piece firing pin. It chambered standard Winchester cartridges, the most popular barrel being a 24in round or octagonal pattern accompanied by a full-length magazine; 20–32in versions were available to order. Other options included pistol-grip butts, short magazines, extra barrels (for the Take Down model), nickel plating and engraving.

Available until about 1908, the original M1894 carbine had a 20in round barrel or, more rarely, a 15in pattern; the full-length magazines held twelve and nine rounds respectively. The receiver, hammer, butt plate, and fore-end cap were colour case-hardened, though carbine receivers were generally blued. The Baby Carbine had a 20in barrel and a short six-round magazine; chambering the ·38–40 or ·44–40 cartridges, it weighed a mere 5·5lb.

1895: a ·25–20 option was introduced.

1897: an M1894 musket was offered, with a 30in barrel and a full-length fore-end retained by bands. Some examples had nose caps adapted for surplus British P/1888 sword bayonets. The musket was advertised until 1907, but very few were made.

1901: a half-octagonal barrel appeared, but was rarely requested and lasted for only six years.

1903: rifle receivers were drilled and tapped for a Hepburn-patent tangent back sight.

1906: production approached 60,000 guns, one in five of which had been carbines.

1915: assembly ceased, owing to war-work.

1922: production began again. However, the quantities involved were small and it is suspected that work stopped again about 1924.

1929: small batches of M1894 rifles were assembled from old parts, to be carried in the company's catalogues until 1933.

Model 1895

Standard rifle, lightweight rifle and carbine patterns.
Made by the Marlin Fire Arms Company, New Haven, Connecticut, 1895–1915.
·33 Winchester, ·38–56 Winchester, ·40–60 Marlin, ·40–65 Winchester, ·40–70 Winchester, ·40–82 Winchester, ·45–70 Government or ·45–90 Winchester.
Lever action, locked by a vertically-sliding bolt.
DATA FOR A TYPICAL EXAMPLE
·40–82 Winchester, rimmed.
42·50in overall, 8·00lb unladen.
24·00in barrel, 6-groove rifling; RH, concentric.
Tube magazine in fore-end, 8 rounds.
Spring-leaf and elevator sight.
About 1,490 ft/sec with 260-grain bullet.
☆

1895: the success of the M1894 Winchester forced Marlin to adapt the 1893-model rifle for the new ·30–30 Winchester cartridge, and then introduce ·25–36 Marlin to compete with Winchester's ·25–35.

The M1895 rifle was specifically created to handle cartridges as large and powerful as ·45–90. Based on Hepburn patents and first listed commercially in 1896, the earliest guns chambered ·38–56, ·40–65, ·40–82, ·45–70 or ·45–90 cartridges. The standard barrel was a 26in round or octagonal pattern, though alternatives—20–32in—could be supplied on request. The 'maximum length' (30in) magazine tube held ten rounds, though there was a special short three-round magazine, and the conventional half-length design held five rounds (four in ·40–82 and ·45–90). M1895 carbines had a 22in round barrel, a full-length seven-round magazine, and a sling ring on the left side of the receiver.

Rifle receivers were colour case-hardened; carbine examples, however, were invariably blued. Straight-wrist or pistol-grip butts were fitted, with half-length magazines, tang-mounted sights and several grades of decoration among the many options.

1897: a ·40–70 chambering and a 15in carbine barrel were introduced.

1903: holes were drilled and tapped in the receiver for the Hepburn tangent back-sight.

1906: production had reached 5,300, only 200 of which had been carbines.

1912: a lightweight rifle was introduced to accompany the ·33 Winchester cartridge. It had a 24in round barrel, a five-shot half magazine, a shotgun-style butt plate, and weighed 7·8lb.

1915: only the ·33 Winchester and ·45–70 chamberings were being offered. Assembly then ceased owing to war-work and did not resume after the end of the First World War.

Marlin The Model 1893, from a company catalogue.

Marlin A Model 1894 'Take Down' rifle, with an interrupted-thread screw on the barrel locking into the receiver. From Greener's *The Gun and Its Development*, 1910.

Model 36

••
Rifle, carbine, sporting carbine and
deluxe rifle patterns.
Made by the Marlin Firearms Company, New Haven,
Connecticut, 1936–48.
·30–30 Winchester or ·32 Winchester Special.
Lever action, locked by a vertically-sliding bolt.
DATA FOR A TYPICAL MODEL 36A
·30–30 Winchester, rimmed.
42·38in overall, 6·95lb unladen.
24·00in barrel, 6-groove rifling; RH, concentric.
Tube magazine in fore-end, 5 rounds.
Spring-leaf and elevator sight.
About 2,220 ft/sec with 170-grain bullet.

☆

1936: introduced as the 'M1936' to replace
the Model 1893 (q.v.), this exhibited many
detail improvements in the action—e.g., a new
rounded operating lever and, after the first
few guns, a coil-type main spring. The stock
comprised a pistol-grip butt with a fluted comb,
and a broad fore-end with a slightly convex belly
plus a steel cap.

The standard rifle had a 24in round barrel
with a ramped 'Huntsman' front sight, and a
short six-round magazine.

1937: the rifle was renamed 'Model 36'.
The Model 36 carbine appeared with a 20in
round barrel and a full-length magazine holding
seven rounds; it measured 38in overall and
weighed about 6·5lb. Bands appeared around
the muzzle and fore-end. The Sporting Carbine
amalgamated the general characteristics of the
rifle—short magazine, no bands—within the
overall dimensions of the carbine.

1938: the receiver was tapped and drilled for a
back sight.

1940: the deluxe ADL rifle was announced,
with chequered woodwork. Detachable swivels
lay on the magazine tube and butt.

1942: work was suspended for the duration of
the Second World War.

1945*: the top of the receiver was sand-blasted
to give a matted finish.

1948: the Model 36 was superseded by the
Model 336 (q.v.).

Model 336

••
A, ADL, C, CS, ER, LTS, Marauder, Octagon, SC, SD, T,
TDL, TS, Zipper and 44 Magnum patterns.
Made by the Marlin Firearms Company, New Haven,
Connecticut (1948–69), and North Haven, Connecticut
(1969 to date).
Quantity: hundreds of thousands (see notes).
·219 Zipper, ·30–30 Winchester,
·32 Winchester Special, ·35 Remington or
·44 Magnum.
Lever action, locked by a vertically-sliding bolt.
DATA FOR A TYPICAL POST-1955 336A
·32 Winchester Special, rimmed.
43·25in overall, 6·88lb unladen.
24·00in barrel, 16-groove rifling; RH, concentric.
Tube magazine in fore-end, 5 rounds.
Spring-leaf and elevator sight.
About 2,280 ft/sec with 170-grain bullet.

☆

1948: this was an improved form of the
Model 36, with a round breech-bolt, a refined
extractor, and a conventional ejection port on
the right side of the receiver.

1949: chambered for ·30–30 Winchester and
·32 Winchester Special only, the basic 336A rifle
had a 24in round barrel rifled with four grooves;
a short five-round magazine; a plain pistol-grip
butt; and a hooded front sight on a ramp. The
deluxe 336ADL rifle had chequered woodwork
and detachable swivels. The 336 Carbine was
similar to the rifle, but had a 20in barrel, a full-
length six-round magazine, and bands on the
muzzle and fore-end. The 336 Sporting Carbine
was little more than a 336A with a 20in barrel.

1951: designations of the Models 336 Carbine
and 336 Sporting Carbine were shortened to
336C and 336SC respectively. A pistol-grip cap
and spacer were added in this period.

1953: a ·35 Remington chambering was
introduced, barrels having seven-groove rifling.
The pistol-grip cap and spacer were abandoned.

1954: the Model 336SD (a deluxe 336SC)
appeared with a Monte Carlo-type Bishop stock
and detachable swivels. It was offered until
1962, production totalling about 4,390. The
336T ('Texan Carbine') was announced in

·30–30 Winchester and ·35 Remingtons. It
was little more than a 336C with a 20in
round barrel, a full-length six-round magazine, a
straight-wrist butt, and a slim fore-end.

1955: the first 336 Zipper rifles were advertised,
chambered for the ·219 cartridge. The guns
were similar to the 336SC and weighed about
6·8lb. Barrel-weight was increased by 1lb in
1956 in an abortive attempt to improve
accuracy, but the sixteen-groove rifling wore
out too quickly; the Zipper variant—never
popular—was abandoned in 1959 after 3,230
had been made. Only about a dozen deluxe guns
had been included in the total.

1956: receiver-tops were drilled and tapped for
sight mounts, and Marlin Micro-Groove rifling
replaced the conventional Ballard patterns on
the standard guns. Sixteen grooves were used
until 1958, when the ·30–30 pattern changed to
22; 12-groove ·30–30 and ·35 patterns were
adopted in 1968.

1957: the pistol-grip cap and spacer were
reinstated, and a new hooded-ramp front sight
was adopted. The 336ADL gained a Monte
Carlo stock, swivels and a Lyman back sight.

1959: a gold-plated trigger was standardised,
and a ramp-mounted front sight was added to
the 336T.

1960: the receiver top was sand-blasted to
minimise glare.

1962: the 336A and 336ADL rifles were
abandoned, having proved less popular than
carbines. Total production of the ADL version
had amounted to a mere 5,220 since 1952. The
336T was offered in ·44 Magnum, and a deluxe
version ('336TDL') featured a Texas Longhorn
steer superimposed on a map of Texas carved
into the right side of the walnut butt. Typical of
the gimmickry of its period, the TDL lasted less
than a year.

1963: the Model 336SC was abandoned,
production since 1952 amounting to 74,220. A
·44 Magnum version of the standard 336C
(Model 336/44 Magnum) was introduced, with
a 20in barrel and a ten-round magazine. It was
joined by the 336 Marauder—in ·30–30 and ·35
only—with a 16·25in barrel and a weight of

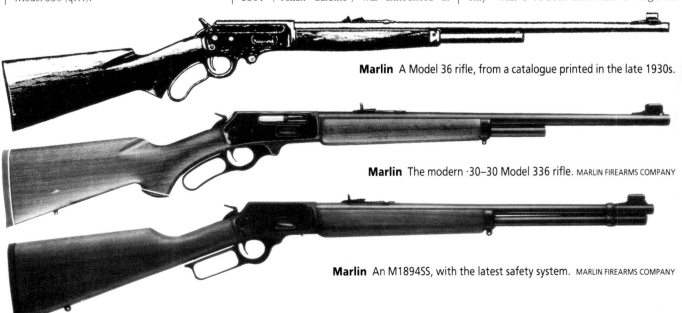

Marlin A Model 36 rifle, from a catalogue printed in the late 1930s.

Marlin The modern ·30–30 Model 336 rifle. MARLIN FIREARMS COMPANY

Marlin An M1894SS, with the latest safety system. MARLIN FIREARMS COMPANY

about 6·3lb. However, the 'Marauder' name was unacceptable commercially and the model merged with the Texan in 1964.

1964: the ·32 Winchester Special chambering was finally dropped from the 336C series. The ·44 336T and the 336/44 Magnum were also discarded.

1965: the ·35-calibre 336T was abandoned, a brass saddle ring being added on the left side of the receiver of remaining variants.

1970: a centenary medallion was let into the butt of all Marlins made in this year. (Medallions were sold separately and, therefore, may be found on older guns.)

1971: a folding-leaf back sight replaced the original Rocky Mountain pattern. The 336T operating lever was squared, the saddle ring on the receiver-side disappearing in the same era.

1972: a 'Wide Scan' hooded ramp-mounted front sight was added to the 336T. Marlin made nominally ten thousand ·30–30 WCF Zane Grey Centenary Rifles in this period (see Part Two).

1973: the Model 336A reappeared in answer to public demand, with a straight-wrist butt and a new 'Wide Scan' hooded front sight. About 2,420 Model 336 Octagon rifles were made in ·30–30. They had 22in octagonal barrels, full-length six-round magazines, and straight-wrist butts with rubber butt plates. The squared operating lever was used and the front sight was a gold bead.

1976: the fluted comb on the 336C and 336T butts was replaced by a plain design.

1979: gun no.3000000—suitably engraved—was presented by Marlin to the NRA Museum.

1980: the Model 336A rifle was abandoned once again. Total production since 1952 had amounted to a little under 40,000.

1982: a blued trigger replaced the gold-plated pattern.

1983: the barrel of the 336T was reduced to 18·5in. The first 336ER ('Extra Range') rifles were made for the ·356 Winchester cartridge, but sold so poorly that the project was abandoned after only 2,440 had been made. The guns had 20in round barrels and five-round magazines; they weighed about 6·8lb.

1984: the addition of a cross-bolt safety catch advanced the basic 336C and 336T designations to '336CS' and '336TS'.

1988: the 336LTS replaced the Texan (336TS) pattern. It had a 16·25in barrel, a straight-wrist butt, a squared operating lever and a five-round full length magazine.

Model 62

Made by the Marlin Firearms Company, New Haven, Connecticut, 1963–9.
Quantity: about 15,720.
·256 Winchester Magnum or ·30 M1 Carbine.
Lever action, locked by a vertically-sliding bolt.
DATA FOR A TYPICAL EXAMPLE
·30 M1 Carbine, rimless.
41·88in overall, 6·95lb unladen.
23·25in barrel, 12-groove rifling; RH, concentric.
Detachable box magazine, 4 rounds.
Spring-leaf and elevator sight.
About 1,870 ft/sec with 110-grain bullet.

☆

1963: designed by Bandell and Neal of Chicago, then perfected by Marlin engineers Nichol and Robinson, this action relied on a short-throw lever with a radial movement of just 25° to operate the bolt through a cam-and-roller accelerator. Chambered for ·256 Winchester Magnum ammunition, fired from a barrel rifled with 22 grooves, the Model 62 was the only centre-fire version of a series that had begun in 1955 with the rimfire Model 56 Levermatic. Its one-piece stock—with a Monte Carlo comb and a round-tip fore-end—presented a departure among Marlin lever-action rifles. The hammer was enclosed in the curved-top receiver and the mechanism fed from a detachable box magazine, 'clip' in Marlin terminology. Most examples also had receiver-top mounts for an optical sight.

1964: readily detachable swivels were added.

1966: the ·256 cartridge proved such an inhibition to sales that an alternative ·30 M1 Carbine chambering was offered.

1969: the Model 62 was discontinued, ·256 and ·30 patterns having been made in roughly equal numbers.

Model 444

Standard and Sporter patterns.
Made by the Marlin Firearms Company, New Haven, Connecticut (1965–9), and North Haven, Connecticut (1969 to date).
·444 Marlin only.
Lever action, locked by a vertically-sliding bolt.
DATA FOR A TYPICAL PRE-1971 EXAMPLE
42·44in overall, 7·53lb unladen.
24·00in barrel, 12-groove rifling; RH, conentric.
Tube magazine in fore-end, 4 rounds.
Spring-leaf and elevator sight.
About 2,400 ft/sec with 240-grain bullet.

☆

1964: the advent of the semi-rimmed ·444 cartridge—little more than an elongated ·44 Magnum—was heralded in the summer.

1965: adapted from the proven 336 action, the first Model 444 rifles were offered for sale. They had a straight-wrist butt with a high Monte Carlo comb, a ventilated recoil pad, and a short fore-end with a swivel-bearing band. A second band appeared behind the muzzle and a Lyman Model 16B back sight lay on top of the barrel.

1971: the original pattern was superseded at the end of the year by the modified 444S ('Sporter'), with a handier 22in barrel and a straight-comb pistol-grip butt/semi-beavertail fore-end assembly adapted from the Model 336A. Quick-detachable swivels were fitted.

1974: a simplified back sight replaced the Lyman pattern.

1976: the muzzle and fore-end bands were eliminated.

1984: the addition of a cross-bolt safety catch advanced the designation to '444SS'.

1988: eyes replaced detachable swivels.

Glenfield models

30A, 30GT, 30AS and 36G patterns.
Made by the Marlin Firearms Company, New Haven, Connecticut (1964–9), and North Haven, Connecticut (1969 to date).
Quantity: see notes.
·30–30 Winchester only.

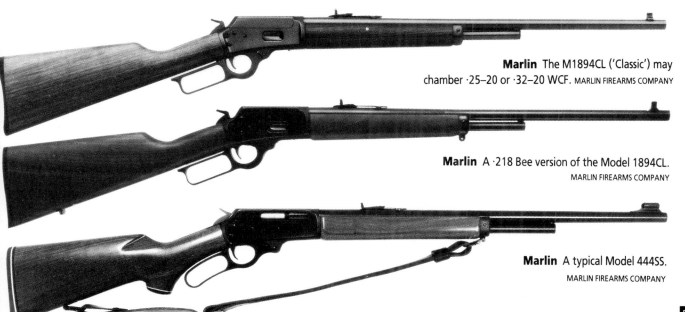

Marlin The M1894CL ('Classic') may chamber ·25–20 or ·32–20 WCF. MARLIN FIREARMS COMPANY

Marlin A ·218 Bee version of the Model 1894CL. MARLIN FIREARMS COMPANY

Marlin A typical Model 444SS. MARLIN FIREARMS COMPANY

Lever action, locked by a vertically-sliding bolt.
DATA FOR A TYPICAL MODEL 30AS
38·25in overall, 7·00lb unladen.
20·00in barrel, 12-groove rifling; RH, concentric.
Tube magazine in fore-end, 6 rounds.
Spring-leaf and elevator sight.
2,390 ft/sec with 150-grain bullet.

☆

1964: the first of these rifles, basically a simplified Model 336 (q.v.), appeared under Marlin's Glenfield brand. About 5,930 guns with 20in round barrels, birch pistol-grip butts and birch fore-ends were made in 1964–5.
1966: the Model 30 replaced the 36G, but was identical except for designation.
1969: decorative chequering panels, the design of which included a stag's head and oakleaves, were pressed into the pistol grip and fore-end. About 80,000 Model 30 rifles had been made by the end of 1972.
1973: the Model 30A replaced the Model 30, differing principally in the adoption of a full-length six-round magazine.
1979: a Model 30GT appeared with a straight-wrist butt, an 18·5in barrel, a full-length magazine and a squared operating lever. Production was confined to 1979–80, about 7,740 being made.
1982: impressed chequering on the Model 30A was abandoned.
1983: the Model 30A was abandoned after something in excess of 300,000 had been made. It was replaced by the Model 30AS, identical excepting for markings and the addition of a cross-bolt safety. As the Glenfield name had been dropped, the 30AS was marketed as a Marlin.

New Model 1894

C, CL, CS, Octagon, S and Sporter patterns.
Made by the Marlin Firearms Company, North Haven, Connecticut, 1969 to date.
·218 Bee, ·25–20 Winchester, ·32–20 Winchester, ·357 Magnum, ·38 Special, ·41 Magnum, ·44 Magnum, ·44 Remington Magnum, ·44 Smith & Wesson Special or ·45 Colt.
Lever action, locked by a vertically-sliding bolt.

DATA FOR A STANDARD MODEL 1894CL
·218 Bee, rimmed.
38·75in overall, 6·25lb unladen.
22·00in barrel, 6-groove rifling; RH, concentric.
Tube magazine in fore-end, 6 rounds.
Spring-leaf and elevator sight.
About 2,760 ft/sec with 46-grain bullet.

☆

1969: this was introduced after the failure of the 336/44 Magnum, its shorter action being better suited to a handgun cartridge. The M1894 had a straight-grip butt, a barrel with Micro-Groove rifling, and a band around the fore-end. The blued receiver, drilled and tapped for sight mounts, had a saddle ring on the left side and a sand-blasted top to minimise glare.
1970: guns made during the year had a centenary medallion let into the right side of their butts.
1971: the saddle ring was abandoned.
1973: the elevator was modified to feed cartridges with slightly longer cases than the ·44 Magnum. About 2,960 examples of the M1894 Octagon were made in ·44 Remington Magnum, with 20in octagonal barrels, straight-grip walnut butts and rubber butt plates. In addition, 1,400 M1894 Sporters were made with six-round half-length magazines and metal butt plates. Neither of the 1973 patterns proved popular enough to survive the year.
1974: the 'Wide Scan' front sight was adopted.
1975: the band around the fore-end and barrel was abandoned.
1979: the Model 1894C ('Carbine') appeared in ·357 Magnum/·38 Special, generally similar to the M1894 but with an 18·5in barrel, a nine-round magazine, a straight-wrist butt, and bands around the fore-end and muzzle. The carbine proved extremely popular, more than 90,000 being made before the 1894CS was substituted at the beginning of 1985.
1980: a blued-steel trigger lever replaced the gold-plated pattern.
1984: addition of a cross-bolt safety catch advanced the designation to M1894S (rifle).
1985: the safety catch was added to the basic 1894C, creating the M1894CS variant. A batch

of 1894S guns was chambered for ·41 Magnum, a second group made in 1989 bringing the total to 3,540.
1988: a ·45 Long Colt chambering was introduced for the M1894S, and the M1894CL ('Classic') variant appeared in ·25–20 or ·32–20. Made with a straight-wrist butt, a 22in barrel and a half-length six-round magazine, the 'CL' also had a spring-leaf back sight.
1990: a ·218 Bee chambering was added to the Model 1894CL options.

New Model 1895

Standard, S and SS patterns.
Made by the Marlin Firearms Company, North Haven, Connecticut, 1972 to date.
·45–70 Government only.
Lever action, locked by a vertically-sliding bolt.
DATA FOR A TYPICAL 1895SS
40·50in overall, 7·50lb unladen.
22·00in barrel, 12-groove rifling; RH, concentric.
Tube magazine in fore-end, 4 rounds.
Spring-leaf and elevator sight.
About 1,810 ft/sec with 300-grain bullet.

☆

1972: built on the 336-pattern receiver, this was introduced to handle the venerable ·45–70 cartridge. It had a straight-wrist butt with a curved rubber butt plate, a squared operating lever and a half-length magazine. The receiver was drilled and tapped for sight mounts, the top being sand-blasted to provide a non-reflecting surface. Early guns had eight-groove rifling.
1980: a pistol-grip butt appeared, with white spacers for the pistol-grip cap and butt plate. A hooded 'Wide Scan' front sight was fitted and the designation advanced to M1895S.
1984: addition of a cross-bolt safety catch created the Model 1895SS.
1988: swivels were replaced by eyes.

Model 375

Made by the Marlin Firearms Company, North Haven, Connecticut, 1980–2.
Quantity: about 16,320.

MARLIN
OTHER PATTERNS

In addition to the rifles marketed under its own and Glenfield names, Marlin has supplied substantial quantities of lever-action rifles to distributors. These have included Coast to Coast Stores of Minneapolis, Minnesota; Cotter & Company of Chicago, Illinois ('West Point' brand); the Firestone Tire & Rubber Company; Montgomery Ward, Inc. ('Western Field'); the Oklahoma Tire & Supply Company ('Otasco'); the J.C. Penney Company of New York ('Formost'); Sears, Roebuck & Company ('Ranger' prior to the Second World War, 'J.C. Higgins' thereafter); United Merchandising, Inc. ('Big 5'); and the Western Auto Supply Company ('Revelation').

¶ Virtually all the centre-fire guns have been Marlin Models 30 or 336, in a variety of patterns. These have often been sold under the distributors' own designations. For example, Montgomery Ward promoted an otherwise standard Marlin 336C with a special recoil pad as the 'EMN-70A'. Otasco's Model 3081—dating from 1981—was a Glenfield 30A with an Alamo medallion let into the butt-side, while the Model 3084 (1984) was a Marlin 30AS with a Mountain Man medallion.

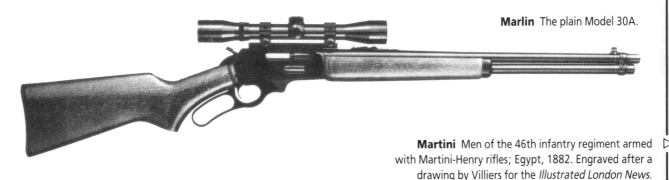

Marlin The plain Model 30A.

Martini Men of the 46th infantry regiment armed with Martini-Henry rifles; Egypt, 1882. Engraved after a drawing by Villiers for the *Illustrated London News*.

·375 Winchester only.
Data generally as Model 336C, excepting a muzzle velocity of 2,200 ft/sec with 200-grain bullet.

☆

1980: this was simply a minor variant of the 336C chambered for a specific cartridge. Slow sales caused the project to be abandoned in 1982, though new guns were available for some years thereafter.

2. THE SLIDE-ACTION PATTERNS

Inspired by the activities of Winchester, Marlin offered a series of rimfire slide-action rifles in the early years of the present century. However, they did not share the success of the company's lever-action patterns and only a few centre-fire examples were made.

Models 27 and 27S

Made by the Marlin Fire Arms Company, New Haven, Connecticut, 1910–15; the Marlin Firearms Corporation, New Haven, Connecticut, 1922–4; and the Marlin Firearms Company, New Haven, Connecticut, 1926–32.
·25–20 Winchester, ·25–35 Stevens or ·32–20 Winchester.
Slide action, operated by a fore-end handle.
DATA FOR A TYPICAL MODEL 27
·32–20 Winchester, rimmed.
42·20in overall, 5·86lb unladen.
24·00in barrel, 6-groove rifling; RH, concentric.
Tube magazine in fore-end, 6 rounds.
Spring-leaf and elevator sight.
About 2,100 ft/sec with 80-grain bullet.

☆

1909: built around patents granted to James Wheeler, George Beck and Melvin Hepburn in July 1911 on the basis of guns designed by John Marlin and Lewis Hepburn, this derived from the rimfire Model 20 of 1907. Introduced in ·25–20 or ·32–20, in 'Take Down' form, it was an exposed-hammer slide-action rifle typical of

the decade prior to the First World War. The barrel was octagonal; a short magazine tube was fitted; the straight-wrist butt had a crescent butt plate; and a short sliding fore-end (generally with nine grooves) doubled as the operating handle.
1910: the Model 27S was substituted for the original pattern, the principal improvement being a button on the right side of the receiver which allowed the action to be opened without dropping the hammer onto the firing pin.
1913: a round-barrel option was introduced, together with a ·25 rimfire chambering.
1916: production was stopped by war-work.
1922: work began again, concentrating on the round-barrel pattern. Available in a ·25–35 Stevens chambering in addition to the original Winchester options, the post-war 27S was abandoned in 1932.

MARTINI

SWITZERLAND

Enfield-Martini, Martini-Enfield, Martini-Henry, Martini-Metford, Peabody-Martini and Westley Richards Martini

↶

Perfected in Switzerland in the 1860s, these rifles saw service in Britain (Martini-Henry, Martini-Metford and Martini-Enfield), Portugal (Martini-Henry), the South African Republic (Westley Richards Martini), Romania (Peabody-Martini) and Turkey (Peabody-Martini). They were briefly adopted in Serbia (Martini-Henry), and ex-British rifles were used in Japan.

Swiss-born Friedrich Martini offered a prototype to rifle trials held in Aarau in 1866. The mechanism was patented in Britain in July 1868, where, after extensive improvements by technicians in the government small-arms factory in Enfield, it was approved for service.

The Martini is widely believed to have been an adaption of patents filed in the USA by Henry Peabody (q.v.); Martini himself acknowledged his rifle to be 'an improvement on the Peabody'. However, as dropping-block rifles were scarcely new, Peabody and Martini agreed mutually

beneficial terms prior to 1873: Peabody-Martini rifles emanated from the USA even as the Martini-Henry was being made in Britain.

The true Martini breech contained a sturdy block with a transverse pivot through the rear upper tip, inserted in a hollow box-type receiver. Pushing the breech lever downward dropped the front of the breech block to reveal the chamber, extracting the cartridge as it did so. If the movement was swift enough, the spent case flew clear of the gun and a new round could be pushed into the chamber manually. Returning the breech lever raised the front of the block and cocked the internal striker.

The action was very strong but, like all guns in its class, did not extract particularly well in adverse conditions. Some versions also had an inferior trigger pull, though this was rarely true of the effectual target rifles made in Europe.

MILITARY RIFLES
AUSTRALIA
Cadet rifles

Made by Auguste Francotte & Co., Liége, c.1900–3 (25,000?); the Birmingham Small Arms Co. Ltd, Small Heath, c.1907–14 (75,000?); and W.W. Greener Ltd, Birmingham, c.1907–14 (50,000?).
·297/·230 or ·310.
Pivoting-block action, operated by a lever.
DATA FOR A TYPICAL EXAMPLE
·310, rimmed.
44·75in overall, 8·98lb unladen.
29·00in barrel, 4-groove rifling; RH, concentric?
Ramp-and-leaf sight (see notes).
About 1,200 ft/sec with 120-grain bullet.
Special reduced-scale P/53 socket bayonet.

☆

1900: substantial quantities of these small-action trainers were acquired by the governments of Victoria and Western Australia. The first batches were apparently ordered from Francotte as the British manufacturers were struggling to satisfy demands of the Second South African (Boer) War, after which purchases continued on behalf

PHILIP HAYTHORNTHWAITE

of the Commonwealth of Australia. The original guns had military-style stocks with one (·230) or two (·310) barrel bands, a cocking indicator on the right side of the receiver, and ramp and leaf back sights similar to the Martini-Enfields.

1907*: additional guns were ordered from BSA and Greener in Britain. They were similar to the original Belgian pattern, but the back sights had SMLE-type protecting wings.

Writing in 1910, William Greener suggested that ·310 'Sharpshooter Cadet Rifles' and ·297/·230 'Miniature Patterns' were bought for adults and juniors respectively. They may be distinguished from commercial guns by VIC., W.A. or COMMONWEALTH OF AUSTRALIA marks.

BRITAIN

The inherently poor extracting qualities of the Martini breech were particularly evident when firing coiled-case ·450 cartridges in hot and dusty conditions, or when the chamber was foul. The original British version of the self-cocking striker also promoted a very poor trigger pull, which modifications did little to cure. This allowed enterprising gunmakers such as Swinburn or Westley Richards to amalgamate the basic breech mechanism with a simple hammer-type trigger.

However, despite problems, Martini-Enfields remained in yeomanry and then Territorial Army hands until the First World War. Some were still serving colonial police in 1939.

1867: competitions were held in the Spring to find suitable single-shot and magazine rifles. Though the Henry (q.v.) rifle almost managed to satisfy the War Office criteria, its cartridge was too poor; similarly, the Burton No.2, which had much to commend it, failed at long range.

However, trials with a variety of breech systems began again almost immediately. Only three rifles remained after an endurance trial—Martini, Henry and Westley Richards.

1868: a modified Martini was made at Enfield under supervision of the inventor. Final trials showed little superiority over the Henry, though the Martini was simpler and more compact.

1869: the Royal Small Arms Factory made four prototype Martini-Henry rifles, differing from each other only in detail. Apart from a weakness in the cartridge indicator, the rifles worked well.

Martini-Henry

••

Infantry rifle: Mk I.
Royal Small Arms Factory, Enfield, 1871–6.
·450, rimmed
Pivoting-block action, operated by a lever protruding from the receiver behind the trigger guard.
DATA FOR PATTERN NO.3 RIFLE
49·00in overall (with short butt), 8·75lb unladen.
33·22in barrel, 7-groove rifling; LH, composite.
Ramp-and-leaf sight graduated to 1,400 yards.
1,315 ft/sec with rolled-case ball cartridges.
Elcho-type sword bayonet (originally).

☆

1871: the long butt 'Rifle, Breech-Loading, Martini-Henry (Mk I)' was sealed on 3 June, with a sword bayonet and a selection of accessories. An improved trigger was approved on 21 November, though the pattern was sealed only in September 1872.

1872: the 'Bayonet, Sword, Martini-Henry Mk I' (Elcho pattern) was superseded in November by a bushed P/53 socket type.

1874: the Pattern No.3 or 'Approved Mk I' rifle was accepted on 17 July. It had a split-steel block axis pin, a modified cleaning rod, a longer butt than its predecessors, and a plain butt plate. The edges of the trigger guard had been rounded and the safety catch was discarded. Issues of the new rifle were made towards the end of the year.

1875: the swivel on the butt was eliminated on 20 January, though rifles issued to the Rifle Brigade and the 60th Rifles were exempted.

Martini-Henry

••

Infantry rifle: Mk II.
Made by the Royal Small Arms Factory, Enfield, 1877–81; the Birmingham Small Arms & Munitions Co. Ltd, Small Heath, 1880–90; and the London Small Arms Co. Ltd, Bow, 1880–7.
·450, rimmed.
Action as Mk I, above.

49·50in overall (with long butt), 8·66lb unladen.
33·19in barrel, 7-groove rifling; LH, composite.
Ramp-and-leaf sight graduated to 1,400 yards.
1,350 ft/sec with solid-case ball cartridges.
P/76 socket bayonet.

☆

1877: trouble with the Mk I trigger led to cancellation of the original Sealed Pattern while trials of modified weapons were undertaken. Formally approved on 25 April, the 'Arm, Interchangeable, Rifle, Breech-loading, Martini-Henry, with cleaning rod (Mark II)' lacked the tumbler rest and tumbler-rest axis screw. The upper surface of the breech block was browned, the back-sight V-notches were deepened, and changes to the trigger ensured that the trigger-guard plate shrouded the trigger lever well enough to reduce jamming caused by debris. The trigger screw and trigger spring were modified, and the pull-off was improved. Changes in the trigger and the lengthened butts—14in and 14·5in—reduced complaints of excessive recoil. Guns were only made by the Royal Small Arms Factory, Enfield, until the approval of the Mark III in August 1879. However, the trade then began to make Mark II Martini-Henrys: the last Mk II ordered from BSA was not forthcoming until June 1890.

Martini-Henry rifles had a nose cap with a bayonet lug on the right side. The original converted P/53 or later P/76 socket bayonets were issued to rank and file, a bushed P/58 or P/60 sabre pattern being issued to engineers, marine artillery and Serjeants of the Line.

Martini-Henry

••

Carbine: Cavalry Mk I.
Royal Small Arms Factory, Enfield, 1877–82.
·450, rimmed.
Action: as Mk I rifle, above.
37·69in overall, 7·50lb unladen.
21·38in barrel, 7-groove rifling; LH, composite.
Ramp-and-leaf sight graduated to 1,000 yards.
About 1,100 ft/sec with ball cartridges.
No bayonet.

☆

Martini A ·310 'Cadet Pattern' rifle, made for the government of Victoria (Australia) by Francotte. H.B. LOCKHOVEN

Martini The British ·450 Mark I Martini-Henry. PATTERN ROOM COLLECTION

Martini The first-pattern ·402 Enfield-Martini rifle, with quick-loader and Arbuthnot fore-end. PATTERN ROOM COLLECTION

-871: carbines were tested at Enfield in June.

-873: a Martini-type carbine tested in May had strong recoil and a badly shaped stock. Cartridge loading and bullet weight were subsequently reduced, but recoil and accuracy declined correspondingly.

-875: fifty guns were issued to the hussars.

-876: the Pattern No.6 carbine was approved on 15 June. The weapon was fully stocked, with two bands, a special nose cap, and a distinctive half-cock thumb-piece on the right side of the body above the scaled-down cocking indicator.

-877: the half-cock was abandoned before the Carbine, Breech-loading, Martini-Henry (Mark ?' was sealed on 24 September. The fore-end was retained by a hook, rather than the stud-and-pin of the Mk II rifle; the size of the cocking indicator was greatly reduced; two reinforces appeared on the breech instead of one; and breakages were minimised by altering the striker and breech-block assembly.

-879: a back-sight cover was adopted in April, anchored over two screws in the fore-end.

-880: the fore-end retaining hook was re-shaped in August, requiring changes in the Pattern Arm.

-882: swivels were reinstated in August.

Martini-Henry

Carbine: Artillery Mk I.
Made by the Royal Small Arms Factory,
Enfield, 1888–9.
Quantity: approximately 57,210.

·450, rimmed.
Action: as Mk I rifle, above.
37·69in overall, 7·66lb unladen.
21·38in barrel, 7-groove rifling; LH, composite.
Ramp-and-leaf sight graduated to 1,000 yards.
About 1,100 ft/sec with ball cartridges.
P/58 sabre bayonet.

☆

1878: 'Carbines, Breech-loading, Rifled, with Cleaning Rod, Martini-Henry, Interchangeable, Artillery (Mark I)' were sealed on 21 July to replace the abortive Garrison Artillery Carbine (see panel). They carried their swivels under the butt and upper band.

Martini-Henry

Infantry rifle: Mk III.
Made by the Royal Small Arms Factory,
Enfield, 1881–8.
·450, rimmed.
Action: as Mk I rifle, above.
DATA FOR LONG-BUTT PATTERN
49·50in overall (long butt), 9·06lb unladen.
33.19in barrel, 7-groove rifling; LH, composite.
Ramp-and-leaf sight graduated to 1,400 yards.
1,350 ft/sec with solid-case ball cartridges.
P/76 socket bayonet.

☆

1879: sealed on 22 August, this refinement of the Mark II had a fore-end that hooked into the front of the receiver ('body'). Changes were made to the breech block and sights, in addition to the striker and the striker hole in the front face of the breech block. The Mk III rifle was almost identical externally with its predecessor, with a two-piece stock and two screw-clamped barrel bands. The most obvious feature was the greatly reduced size of the cocking indicator.

1881: the first rifles were delivered into store.

1882: the advent of the Mk III was announced in the official *List of Changes* on 1 March.

Martini-Henry

Infantry rifle: Mk IV, later pattern.
Made by the Royal Small Arms Factory,
Enfield, 1888–9.
Quantity: about 21,750 Pattern A, 42,900 Pattern B
and 34,330 Pattern C.
·450, rimmed.
Action: as Mk I rifle, above.
DATA FOR PATTERN B
49·38in overall (long butt), 9·13lb unladen.
33·06in barrel, 7-groove rifling; LH, composite.
Ramp-and-leaf sight graduated to 1,400 yards.
1,350 ft/sec with solid-case ball cartridges.
P/76 socket bayonet.

☆

1887: the advent of the ·303 cartridge left 65,000 ·402 Enfield-Martini (q.v.) rifles in varying stages of completion. Re-boring to ·45—without altering the external barrel profile—was sanctioned on 15 September.

The Pattern A was a major reconstruction, salvaging only the butt, furniture, hand guard,

Martini The ·303 Martini-Metford Mk I rifle. PATTERN ROOM COLLECTION

MARTINI
LESSER PATTERNS

British trials rifles Sealed on 1 October 1869, this had swivels on the fore-end, trigger guard and butt. A cocking indicator pivoted on the right side of the action and the safety catch protruded from the trigger guard ahead of the trigger lever, where it could be pushed forward to fire. The most obvious features were the short-wrist butt and an unusually long action body. About 200 rifles were made in the Enfield factory in 1869. Chambered for a rimmed ·450 cartridge, they were 51·00in overall, weighed 9·34lb and had a 35·00in barrel with seven-groove composite rifling.

¶ Even as the long-chamber rifles were being issued for trials, William Eley successfully necked a cartridge case to give the powder capacity of the original straight Martini-Henry round in appreciably less overall length. Ten rifles were prepared to test it, eight sharing the long action of the 200 trials guns and the remaining two being specially shortened. Two new short-action guns were made to solve production problems; 24 more were then made for ammunition trials.

¶ By February 1871, the rifle committee reported that the short-chamber gun should be adopted for service immediately, an opinion endorsed by the Council of Ordnance on 30 March.

British Martini-Henry Garrison Artillery carbine Less than 100 of these ·450 guns were made in the Royal Small Arms Factory, Enfield, once the pattern had been approved on 9 April 1878. The Garrison Artillery carbine was similar to the Martini-Henry cavalry carbine, but took a sword bayonet.

British Martini-Henry Mk IV rifle, first pattern. In 1881, to simplify logistics, the army authorities decided to adapt the Martini-Henry for the ·45 Gatling machine-gun cartridge, which was preferable to adapting the Martini-Henry pattern for machine-guns. At least forty rifles were altered by inserting an annular bush in a reamed-out chamber.

¶ Trials at the School of Musketry showed that the accuracy of the original and converted guns had been comparable. Gatling cartridges raised muzzle velocity by 60–70 ft/sec, but recoil had also risen perceptibly. The performance of the improved ammunition being used in the then-experimental Gardner Guns was so satisfactory that the Mk IV was sealed on 1 October. However, issuing similar but non-interchangeable cartridges made no sense: in mid-January 1882, therefore, the

Mk IV was abandoned. About 100 had been made in the Enfield factory. They were 49·50in overall and weighed 9·06lb. Their 33.19in barrels had composite seven-groove rifling, the ramp-and-leaf sight was graduated to 1,400 yards, and muzzle velocity was about about 1,400 ft/sec.

British Martini-Metford Mk I rifle Approved by the Secretary of State for War on 30 July 1889, the 'Rifle, Martini-Henry, ·303-inch (Mark V)' was converted from the ·45 Mark III rifle. The barrel, breech block, striker, extractor, sights and many minor components were exchanged; Lewes sights were standard, the back sight being graduated for black powder ammunition. Only prototypes seem to have been made, doubtless owing to their comparative complexity. They were 49·75in overall, weighed 8·78lb, and had 33·25in barrels with polygonal seven-groove rifling. The ramp-and-leaf sight graduated to 1,900 yards, muzzle velocity was about 1,850 ft/sec (with ·303 Mk I ball cartridges) and the P/1888 bayonet could be mounted.

¶ In August 1891, to prevent unnecessary confusion with existing ·45 Martini-Henry guns, the pattern was renamed 'Rifle, Martini-Metford, ·303-inch (Mark II)'.

Colonial pattern guns The first of five hundred ·303 Martini-Metford rifles with iron butt traps ordered by South Australia was despatched in 1891, the last gun following in 1893. Sights were adjusted for black powder cartridges.

¶ Seven hundred similar rifles were sent to Western Australia in 1894, sighted for black powder ammunition and fitted with brass traps. A thousand near-identical rifles went to Canada in the same era.

¶ 760–800 rifles sighted for the ·303 Mk I (Cordite) cartridge were prepared for the government of Natal in 1895, despatch being completed in 1896. These had a short hand guard running to the back sight base.

¶ The first of 965 ·303 Martini-Enfield Mk II cavalry carbines was made for New South Wales in 1903, work being completed within a year. They were converted from Mk I Martini-Henry artillery carbines.

Serbian guns The government ordered 100,000 ·450 Martini-Henry rifles from 'an English company' in 1880. It is suspected that this was the National Arms & Ammunition Co. Ltd of Birmingham, but that only a few hundred guns were supplied owing to disputes between NA&Co. and the principal manufacturers of Martini-Henry rifles for the British government. In 1881, owing to lack of progress, the Mauser-Milanović was substituted for the Martini-Henry.

barrel and block of the original ·402 rifle. The body was a new second-pattern from store.

Pattern B rifles (converted from ·402 Pattern No.2) shared a similar body, but their front sights lay on a short ramp. Pattern C rifles were made from stored parts and had a longer knoxform. Barrels measured 33·19in, increasing overall length to 49·50in with the long butt.

Martini-Henry

Carbines: artillery, Mks II and III.
Made by the Royal Small Arms Factory, Enfield,
1893–6.
Quantity: 38,410 Mk II.
·450, rimmed
Action: as Mk I rifle, above.
DATA FOR MARK II
37·69in overall, 7·56lb unladen.
21·38in barrel, 7-groove rifling; LH, composite.
Ramp-and-leaf sight.
About 1,100 ft/sec with ball cartridges.
Converted P/58 sabre bayonet.

☆

1892: the Mk II artillery carbine, sealed on 16 June, was converted from the Mk II rifle. The barrel was shortened, the muzzle being turned down to receive the guard ring of the bayonet. The fore-end finished about 1in from the muzzle (distinguishing Mks II and III); a new upper band carried the bayonet lug. Back sight, swivels, butt disc and cleaning rod were new.
1894: supposedly converted from Mk III rifles, the Mk III carbine was approved but never sealed. It had a special cleaning rod, retained the original rifle front sight, and had a fore-end terminating about 2in from the muzzle.
1902: Mk II carbines were reduced to Drill Purpose status.

Enfield-Martini

Infantry rifle: Mk I.
Made by the Royal Small Arms Factory,
Enfield, 1887–8.
Quantity: 21,730 Pattern No.1 and
43,000 Pattern No.2.

·402, rimmed.
Pivoting-block action, operated by a lever protruding
from the receiver behind the trigger guard.
DATA FOR PATTERN NO.1
49·50in overall, 9·13lb unladen.
33·00in barrel, 7-groove rifling; LH, ratchet.
Ramp-and-leaf sight graduated to 2,000 yards.
1,570 ft/sec with ball cartridges.
Enfield-Martini sword bayonet.

☆

1886: derived from the experimental ·40 P/82 and P/83 rifles, the 'Rifle, Enfield-Martini, ·402-inch (Mark I), with cleaning rod' was sealed on 17 April to guide manufacture of a thousand guns for troop trials. It was similar to the P/83, but the long-range sights were replaced by an elevating leaf. The safety bolt, narrowed butt and curious fore-end were all retained.
1887: production was approved before the final trial reports had been submitted. Complaints were soon being voiced; no-one liked the quick-loader, and there had been extraction troubles.

Though production of Pattern No.1 rifles had started, Pattern No.2 was substituted on 13 May. This reverted to the standard Martini-Henry fore-end and bayonet bar, but the unpopular safety bolt had been superseded by a small cocking indicator and the quick-loader attachment plate was abandoned. The operating lever was lengthened to give more power to the extractor. Production continued until 1888, but most rifles were subsequently converted to ·450.

Martini-Metford

Infantry rifle: Mk II.
Made by the Birmingham Small Arms & Munitions
Co. Ltd, Small Heath, 1890–1.
Quantity: 9,600.
·303, rimmed.
Action: as Mk I Martini-Metford rifle, above.
49·75in overall, 9·69lb unladen.
33·25in barrel, 7-groove rifling; LH, polygonal.
Ramp-and-leaf sight graduated to 1,900 yards.
About 1,850 ft/sec with Mk I ball cartridges.
P/1887 sword bayonet.

☆

1890: this conversion of Mk II Martini-Henry rifles was approved on 10 January.
1891: the pattern was formally sealed on 18 June and renamed 'Rifle, Martini-Metford, ·303-inch (Mark II)' in August. The ·303 barrel shared the external contours of the ·45 version it replaced, allowing the existing bands, furniture and bayonet to be retained.
1892: Lewes sights were replaced by V-and-barleycorn patterns. The new back sights were graduated to 1,600 yards for black powder loads and subsequently to 1,800 yards for cordite.

Martini-Metford

Carbines: Cavalry, Mks I, I*, II, II* and III.
Made by the Henry Rifled Barrel Co. Ltd, Hoxton
(Mk I, I*, 1893–4); and the Royal Small Arms Factory,
Enfield, 1892–6.
Quantity: 11,150 Mk I and I*, 850 Mk II (1892–3), and
about 4,800 Mk III (1892–6).
·303, rimmed.
Action: as Mk I Martini-Metford rifle, above.
DATA FOR MK I CARBINE
37·63in overall, 8·09lb unladen.
21·00in barrel, 7-groove rifling; LH, polygonal.
Ramp-and-leaf sight graduated to 1,000 yards.
About 1,650 ft/sec with Mk I ball cartridges.
No bayonet.

☆

1892: formally approved in May, the 'Carbine, Martini-Metford, Cavalry, ·303-inch (Mark I)' was converted from the Martini-Henry Cavalry Carbine Mk I. Its new barrel shared the profile of the original, but the nose-cap was shortened and the cleaning rod was replaced.

The Mk II cavalry carbine was converted from Mk I Martini-Henry artillery examples, apparently for issue to horse and field artillery. The original bayonet bar disappeared, and the rear swivel was removed from the under-edge of the butt. Sight-cover retaining screws appeared on the fore-end beneath the back sight. Guns were 37·63in overall, had 21in barrels and weighed 8·25lb.

The Mk III, converted from Mk II Martini-Henry rifles, was approved in July and re-sealed

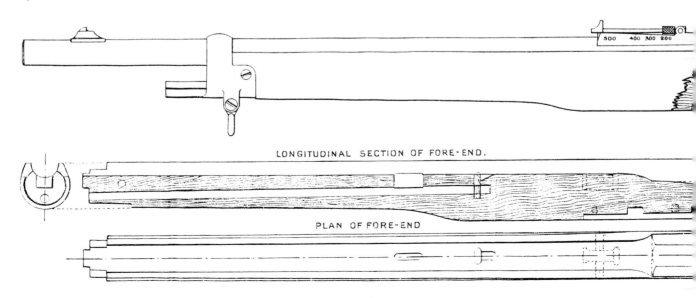

LONGITUDINAL SECTION OF FORE-END.

PLAN OF FORE-END

in December with front sight protectors. It had a new breech block and a 21in barrel, overall length being 37·31in and weight about 7·69lb. The front edge of the body was ground down to enable the rifle-type sights to be seen at low elevations, and a brass marking disc appeared on the butt. 4,300 were made for the British Army.

1893: most Lewes sights were replaced with standard V-and-barleycorn patterns, back sight graduations initially remaining unchanged but eventually altered substantially for cordite ammunition. Many guns converted after mid October received front sight protectors, their designation advancing to 'Mark I*' (or 'II*'). Earlier examples were often upgraded when returning for repair.

1894: most guns were given new back sights suited to ammunition loaded with cordite and graduated to 1,400 yards (Mk I, I*, II, II*) or an improbable 2,000 yards (Mk III).

1895: a small quantity of Mk III carbines, fitted with abbreviated wooden hand guards, was shipped to Natal. The deliveries were completed the following year.

1896: guns with replacement Enfield-rifled barrels became 'Martini-Enfield Mark I'.

Martini-Metford

Carbines: Artillery, Mks I, II, II* and III.
Made by the Royal Small Arms Factory, Enfield (Mks I and II, 1893–6); the Birmingham Small Arms & Munitions Co. Ltd, Small Heath (Mk III, 1895–8); and the London Small Arms Co., Ltd, Bow (Mk III, 1896–8).
Quantity: Mk I unknown (1893–4), 2,750 Mk II (1894–6) and about 47,000 Mk III.
·303, rimmed.
Action: as Mk I Martini-Metford rifle, above.
DATA FOR MK I CARBINE
37·63in overall, 7·77lb unladen.
21·38in barrel, 7-groove rifling; LH, polygonal.
Ramp-and-leaf sight graduated to 1,000 yards.
About 1,650 ft/sec with Mk I ball cartridges.
P/1888 sword bayonet.

☆

1892: approved in May, but re-sealed in June 1893 once front sight protectors had been added, Martini-Metford Mk I artillery carbines were transformations of Mk I Martini-Henry artillery patterns. New barrels, new bands, and a nose-cap taking a bayonet were fitted.

1893: original Lewes sights were replaced by V-and-barleycorn fittings, though graduations remained unchanged. Approved on 11 October, the Mk II (37·31in overall, 7·06lb) was similar to the Mk III Martini-Metford cavalry carbine, but accepted a sword bayonet. The Mk II* was little more than a Mk II with a newly-made breech block. Experiments showed that the original ·45 pattern could be retained, whereupon the Mk II* was abandoned.

1894: back sights graduated to 1,400 yards for cordite were fitted. The Mk III Martini-Metford artillery carbine was approved on 8 March, but re-sealed in December. A conversion of a Mk III Martini-Henry rifle, its fore-end was retained by a hook rather than a pin. It had 2,000-yard sights and a 21·00in barrel, measured 37·31in overall, and weighed 7·19lb.

1896: Mk I Martini-Metford artillery carbines with replacement Enfield-pattern barrels were renamed 'Martini-Enfield Mk III'. Mk II carbines with new barrels became Mk II Martini-Enfield.

Martini-Enfield

Infantry rifles: Mks I, I*, II and II*.
Made by the Royal Small Arms Factory, Enfield, 1896–1903 (48,610 Mk I, 33,020 Mk II); and Beardmore Engineering Co. Ltd, 1900–1 (7,000 Mk II).
Quantity: 88,630.
·303, rimmed.
Pivoting-block action, operated by a lever protruding from the receiver behind the trigger guard.
46·50in overall, 8·31lb unladen.
30·19in barrel, 5-groove rifling; LH, concentric.
Ramp-and-leaf sight graduated to 1,800 yards.
About 1,970 ft/sec with Mk I (Cordite) ball cartridges.
P/1895 socket bayonet.

☆

1895: formally approved on 4 October, the 'Rifle, Martini-Enfield, ·303-inch (Mark I)' was converted from the Mk III Martini-Henry. Its new barrel had Enfield rifling, accepted a socket bayonet and had a back sight graduated for cordite ammunition. The hand guard ran to the back-sight base, swivels lay on the butt and lower band, and an open piling swivel graced the upper band.

1896: approved on 11 February, the Mk II Martini-Enfield was a conversion of Mark II ·45 Martini-Henry rifles. It had a larger cocking indicator than the Mk I, but was otherwise similar. Beardmore guns, dating from the Second South African War, were marked B.E.CO..

1901: contact between the barrel and the fore-end or nose-cap of Martini-Enfield guns of all types was relieved from October onward in search of improved accuracy.

1903: approved in February after complaints emananating from South Africa, the Mk I* and Mk II* were simply standard Mks I and II Martini-Enfields with the new laterally-adjustable front sights (high, normal and low).

Martini-Enfield

Carbines: Cavalry, Mks I and II.
Made by the Royal Small Arms Factory, Enfield, 1898–1904.
Quantity: about 6,870.
·303, rimmed.
Action: as Martini-Enfield rifle, above.
37·31in overall, 6·56lb unladen.
21·38in barrel, 5-groove rifling; LH, concentric.
Ramp-and-leaf sight graduated to 2,000 yards.
About 1,690 ft/sec with Mk I (Cordite) ball cartridges.
No bayonet.

☆

1896: approved on 20 August, these differed from the comparable Martini-Metford patterns only in rifling and sights. About 5,900 were converted from Mk II Martini-Henry rifles.

1899: guns converted after the abolition of the clearing rod on 11 May had solid fore-ends.

Martini-Enfield

Carbines: Artillery, Mks I, II and III.
Made by the Henry Rifled Barrel Co. Ltd, Hoxton (Mk I, 1896–7; Mk II, 1898–1900); the Royal Small

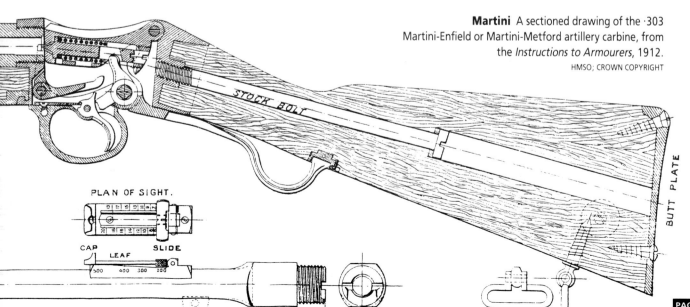

Martini A sectioned drawing of the ·303 Martini-Enfield or Martini-Metford artillery carbine, from the *Instructions to Armourers*, 1912.
HMSO; CROWN COPYRIGHT

Arms Factory, Enfield (Mk I, 1898–9; Mk II, 1898–1900; Mk III, 1900–4); and Beardmore Engineering Co. Ltd (Mk III, 1900–1).

Quantity: 44,720 Mk I, 26,000 Mk II and 32,540 Mk III.

·303, rimmed.

Action: as Martini-Enfield rifle, above.

DATA FOR MK I CARBINE

37·31in overall, 7·28lb unladen.

21·00in barrel, 5-groove rifling; LH, concentric.

Ramp-and-leaf sight graduated to 2,000 yards.

About 1,690 ft/sec with Mk I (Cordite) ball cartridges.

P/1888 sword bayonet.

☆

1895: the 'Carbine, Martini-Enfield, Artillery, ·303-inch (Mark I)'—converted from a Mark III Martini-Henry rifle—was approved for issue on 6 November.

1897: sealed on 6 December, the Mk II Martini-Enfield artillery carbine was converted from Mk I and Mk III Martini-Henry artillery patterns. The fore-end was retained by a pin instead of a hook.

1899: converted from the Mark II Martini-Henry rifle, the Mk III Martini-Enfield artillery carbine was sealed in July. However, the original pattern was speedily re-sealed with an offset front sight in wing-type protectors. The Mk III was similar to the Mark II Martini-Metford artillery carbine, but had an Enfield barrel and modified sights. It also had a solid fore-end.

ROMANIA

Model 1879

Infantry rifle and cavalry carbine.
Maker unknown, Witten an der Ruhr, 1878–80.
Quantity: perhaps 125,000.
·45, rimmed.
Pivoting-block action, operated by a lever protruding from the receiver behind the trigger guard.
DATA FOR RIFLE PATTERN
1,246mm overall, 4·36kg unladen.
845mm barrel, 5-groove rifling; RH, concentric.
Ramp-and-leaf apparently graduated to 1,600 metres.
About 455 m/sec with ball cartridges.
Socket bayonet.

☆

1879: this Peabody-Martini—the first rifle to be adopted after independence had been gained—was practically identical with the Turkish M1874. Differences were purely minor. The rifle was stocked almost to the muzzle, had two barrel bands, and the back sight leaf was hinged at the rear. Sling swivels appeared on the front band, ahead of the trigger guard, and on the underside of the butt.

The Romanians also acquired a few carbines for issue to cavalrymen. These had a half-length fore-end retained by a single band and did not accept a bayonet.

SOUTH AFRICAN REPUBLIC

Owing to the supply of 'monkey tail' breech loaders converted for centre-fire cartridges, Westley Richards & Co. Ltd had established a relationship with the two independent Dutch orientated states in southern Africa—the Orange Free State (OVS, 'Oranje Vrij Staat') and the South African Republic (ZAR, 'Zuid Afikaansche Republiek'). The Martini rifles were ordered before relations with Britain deteriorated.

Richards-Martini

Rifle and carbine.
Made by Westley Richards & Co. Ltd, Birmingham, 1896–7.
Quantity: see notes.
·450, rimmed.
Pivoting-block action, operated by a lever.
DATA FOR RIFLE
49·53in overall, 9·00lb unladen.
33·25in barrel, 7-groove rifling; RH, composite.
Ramp-and-leaf sight graduated to 1,200 yards.
1,350 ft/sec with solid-case ball cartridges.
No bayonet issued?

☆

1895: these rifles had already been ordered when the Jameson Raid (in January 1896) revealed a desperate need for modern firearms.

1897: no more than ten thousand Westley Richards Martini guns had been delivered against orders said to have totalled 36,000, owing to growing political unrest and impending deliveries of Mausers. Created from unfinished Mark IV actions made by the National Arms & Ammunition Company factory in Sparkbrook, Birmingham, in the early 1880s, the guns had a distinctive Francotte-type cocking indicator protruding above the right receiver wall. A patented knurled-head catch on the lower front right of the receiver allowed the entire breech mechanism to be taken out of the receiver.

The rifles displayed MADE SPECIALLY FOR Z.A.R. on the right side of the receiver, with the manufacturer's mark on the left and a date in a triangle—e.g., '1897'—on top of the barrel.

TURKEY

Model 1874

Infantry rifle and cavalry carbine.
Made by the Providence Tool Company, Providence, Rhode Island, 1874–9.
Quantity: about 600,000 rifles and 50,000 carbines.
·45, rimmed.
Pivoting-block action, operated by a lever.
DATA FOR RIFLE
1,245mm overall, 4·33kg unladen.
842mm barrel, 5-groove rifling; RH, concentric.
Ramp-and-leaf sight.
455 m/sec with ball cartridges.
Bayonet: see notes.

☆

1874: the Turks were among the first to buy sizeable quantities of the Peabody-Martini rifle, ordering 400,000. It has been suggested that they unsuccessfully approached the British before turning to the Providence Tool Company, but the case is not proven.

1875: the Turkish Peabody-Martini was almost impossible to distinguish at a glance from British Martini-Henry, apart from an 1869-type safety lever ahead of the trigger guard. Rifles were fully stocked, with two barrel bands; infantry rifles apparently accepted a standard socket bayonet, but others, possibly for riflemen and elite units, were issued with a distinctive

leather-gripped sword pattern. Sling swivels generally lay under the front barrel band, immediately ahead of the trigger guard, and on the under-edge of the butt. A large radial cocking indicator lay on the right side of the receiver above the rear of the trigger guard.

The Turks also ordered 25,000 carbines for their cavalry and placed other (smaller) orders into the late 1870s. They had half-length fore-ends, retained by a single band, and would not accept a bayonet.

SPORTING GUNS

An effectual combination of strength and simplicity has suited the Martini breech to many differing applications.

BRITAIN

The adoption of the Martini-Henry for service, and ready availability of government-pattern 'large' actions, persuaded many gunsmiths to create military-pattern rifles for volunteers and target shooting. These were distinguished from the official patterns only by superior finish, better woodwork, chequering on the wrist and fore-end, adjustable sights, and flat-faced or carefully counter-bored muzzles.

Sporters came in far greater variety. The most popular chambering was initially the government ·450 cartridge though, after the Martini-Henry had been superseded in the late 1880s by the Lee-Metford, emphasis shifted to cartridges such as ·500/·450 No.1 Express, ·461 Gibbs and ·500 No.2 Express.

The marks of many leading British gunmakers will be encountered on rifles of this pattern—e.g., John Rigby, Cogswell & Harrison, Daniel Fraser and John Blanch—together with lesser lights such as Alfred Field or Silver & Son. However, actions often prove to have been 'Trade Patterns' made by the major military contractors, BSA and the London Armoury Company. Others were acquired from Westley Richards, who made a series of government-type actions and a modified pattern embodying a

Francotte-patent cocking indicator protruding above the right receiver wall.

Many 'small action' guns were also made, often on the basis of the so-called Cadet Martini (or BSA No.12) action introduced early in the twentieth century. Though these guns were usually chambered for ·310 cartridges, a whole series of options from ·297/·230 Short and ·297/·250 to ·360 No.5 could be encountered; these were often known as 'Rook Rifles' owing to their role in controlling vermin.

Countless thousands of ·22 rimfire Martini rifles have been made in Britain, including conversions of substantial quantities of military-surplus actions by Greener, Bonehill and others for the Society of Miniature Rifle Clubs and, subsequently, the National Rifle Association. BSA was still making excellent ·22 Martini-International target rifles in the mid 1980s.

Field-Martini Sporting Rifle
••
Made by or for Alfred Field & Co., London.
·500/·450 No.1 Express, rimmed.
Pivoting-block action, operated by an underlever behind the trigger guard.
45·00in overall, 7·85lb unladen.
28·50in barrel, 7-groove rifling; LH, composite.
Cape sight.
1,900 ft/sec with 270-grain bullet.
☆

1892*: this interesting rifle offered several departures from the classical British Martini-Henry. It had a high-back or 'Mark IV' action (possibly purchased from Westley Richards) with an additional radial safety lever on the right side, and a pistol-grip butt. The grip and fore-end were extensively chequered, and a barrel-key was set in German silver escutcheons. The operating lever had a pierced-ring terminal.

A sturdy brass-tipped wooden clearing rod was carried in pipes attached to a rib beneath the octagonal barrel, sling eyes appearing on the rearmost pipe and the under-edge of the butt. The Cape-type back sight had four small folding leaves (100, 200, 300 and 400 yards) plus a large leaf for 500–1,000 yards.

BELGIUM

The British-pattern Martini was extensively copied in Liége in 1880–1910, principally by Auguste Francotte. Many guns incorporated Francotte's patented cocking indicator, whose blade protruded above the right receiver wall, and also had safety catches.

Belgian-made guns can usually be identified by their proof marks, even though marked as a product of another company; the Braendlin Armoury Co. Ltd of Birmingham, active until 1888, purchased many of its rifles in Liége and Francotte maintained an agency in London for about twenty years from 1873 onward.

CENTRAL EUROPE

The products of south Germany, northern Austria and Switzerland are often difficult to separate, unless their provenance is clearly marked.

The first guns were made by Friedrich [von] Martini in Frauenfeld, almost always featuring a cocking indicator protruding above the rear right side of the receiver and a pivoting safety lever immediately ahead of the trigger guard. The chambering customarily proves to be 10·4mm rim- or centre-fire.

Once the true Martini action had become established, other gunsmiths copied it; however, as many of the actions were hand-made, great variety in construction could be found. For example, guns made by F.W. Kessler & Co. of Suhl invariably had an unusually narrow action set in a one-piece stock. Swiss Martini rifles often had locking catches on the breech-block axis pin, facilitating dismantling, while their detachable floor plates contained the entire trigger mechanism. The lock work usually lay behind the receiver, unlike the British guns, allowing the trigger guard to be combined wih the elaborately looped breech lever. Butts, fore-ends and sights were all subject to variety.

Many rifle actions emanating from central Europe were cut down behind the breech so that the barrel could be cleaned from the

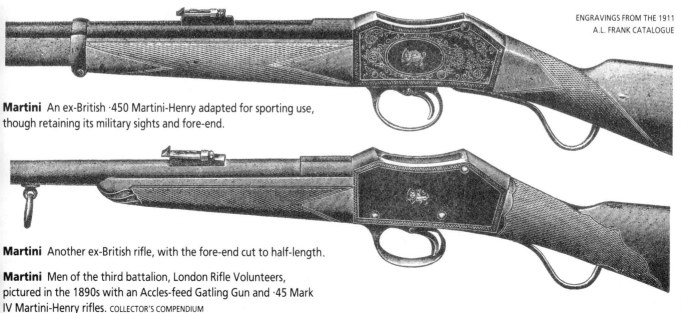

ENGRAVINGS FROM THE 1911
A.L. FRANK CATALOGUE

Martini An ex-British ·450 Martini-Henry adapted for sporting use, though retaining its military sights and fore-end.

Martini Another ex-British rifle, with the fore-end cut to half-length.

Martini Men of the third battalion, London Rifle Volunteers, pictured in the 1890s with an Accles-feed Gatling Gun and ·45 Mark IV Martini-Henry rifles. COLLECTOR'S COMPENDIUM

rear. Though this did not in itself compromise strength, the strain of firing was often taken on the breech-block axis pin instead of the rear inner face of the receiver. Consequently, some guns lack the strength of the true Martini-Henry or Peabody-Martini actions.

This is reflected in low-power chamberings: 6·5 × 27mm, 8·15 × 46·5mm or 9·5 × 47mm. Sturdier guns accepted such proven hunting cartridges as 9·3 × 72 or 11·15 × 65mm.

Hämmerli-Martini

Made by Rudolf Hämmerli & Co., Lenzburg.
7·5 × 55mm, rimless.
Pivoting-block action, operated by a lever combined with the trigger guard.
DATA FOR A TYPICAL 1930-VINTAGE EXAMPLE
1,415mm overall (including butt-plate hook),
5·13kg without the palm-ball.
855mm barrel, 4-groove rifling; RH, concentric.
Quadrant sight graduated to 1,200 metres.
625 m/sec with 12·3-gram bullet.

☆

1887: the first rifles made by Johann Ulrich Hämmerli rapidly attained a reputation for strength and outstanding accuracy, gaining a gold medal from the inaugural world shooting championships held in Lyon in 1897.
1921: the business passed to Rudolf Hämmerli, guns being marked appropriately. Rifles were even purchased for US Free Rifle teams.
1932: target rifles were being made for sale under the Hämmerli name, alongside actions to be stocked and completed elsewhere. Many leading Swiss gunmakers (e.g., Waffen-Glaser of Zürich) purchased them.

A typical Martini-Match-Stutzer offered a butt with a Tyrolean cheek piece and a ram's horn terminal. A forked shoulder plate, adjustable for height and cant, also had a hook. The underside of the wrist and the fore-end were extensively chequered, whilst the breech lever—combined with the trigger guard—had a looped rear spur and an open forward hand-grip. An adjustable palm-ball was fitted to a threaded socket under the front of the receiver.

1940*: production of Martini rifles ceased, owing to mobilisation in Switzerland and an impending concentration on war-work.

USA

Friedrich Martini and Henry Peabody reached an agreement over patent licences in the early 1870s, whereupon Peabody-Martini sporting rifles were substituted for the original Peabody (q.v.) external-hammer pattern. The Providence Tool Company made Peabody-Martini guns for some years. However, the sporters were too expensive to sell in quantity and production seems to have ended in the early 1880s.

Improved Sporting Rifle

Standard, Kill Deer, No.1 Mid Range Target, No.2 Creedmoor and No.3 What Cheer patterns.
Made by the Providence Tool Company, Providence, Rhode Island.
·40, ·44 or ·45—see notes.
Pivoting-block action, operated by a lever behind the trigger guard.
DATA FOR A TYPICAL NO.2 CREEDMOOR EXAMPLE
·44–95, rimmed.
About 49in overall, 9·25lb unladen.
32·00in barrel, 4-groove rifling; RH, concentric.
Vernier sight on tang.
1,310 ft/sec with 550-grain bullet.

☆

1875: the first rifles apparently included a half-stocked sporter chambered for a necked ·45–50 cartridge. A 'Kill Deer' model had a plain butt and a round 26in barrel chambered for the government ·45–70 cartridge. Open Rocky Mountain sights were fitted.
1876: the No.1 Mid Range Target Model appeared, with a 32in or 30in barrel chambered for ·40–70 or ·40–90 cartridges. The back sight was generally an 800-yard vernier-adjustable aperture pattern, used in conjunction with a bead front sight and spirit level.

The No.2 Long Range Creedmoor Rifle had a 32in half-octagon barrel, and a long-range (generally 1,200-yard) aperture sight that could be fitted interchangeably to mounts on the tang or butt heel. The breech lever was extended to curve around a shallow pistol grip on the underside of the butt wrist. It chambered a ·44–60 or ·44–100 cartridge.
1877: named after a well-known rifle range near Providence, the ·40–70 or ·40–90 No.3 'What Cheer' pattern was essentially similar to the Creedmoor but had a straight-wrist butt and a smaller-calibre 30in barrel.

MAS

FRANCE

These rifles, developed in France, were confined largely to the French army and the forces of former French colonies.

1. THE AUTO-LOADING PATTERNS

The introduction of a rimless 7·5mm cartridge in 1924, followed by the appearance of a new pattern in 1929, encouraged experimentation with semi-automatic rifles. The government factory in Saint-Étienne produced a series of prototypes between the wars, the earliest being based on the Mle.1918 RSC (q.v.) and the last sharing the basic action of the Russian Tokarev. MAS rifles proved to be sturdy and reliable, though they handled clumsily. The action relied on gas tapped from the top of the barrel, from where it bled back to impinge directly on the bolt carrier; as the carrier began to move back, it lifted the rear of the breech block above the locking shoulder in the receiver and the whole mechanism reciprocated to reload the chamber.

MAS 44 and MAS 49

Semi-automatic rifles: Fusils automatiques
MAS 44, MAS 44-A, MAS 49.
Manufacture d'Armes de Saint-Étienne, 1946–70.

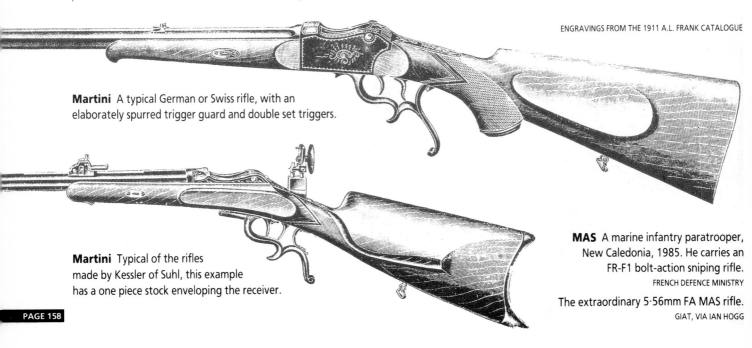

ENGRAVINGS FROM THE 1911 A.L. FRANK CATALOGUE

Martini A typical German or Swiss rifle, with an elaborately spurred trigger guard and double set triggers.

Martini Typical of the rifles made by Kessler of Suhl, this example has a one piece stock enveloping the receiver.

MAS A marine infantry paratrooper, New Caledonia, 1985. He carries an FR-F1 bolt-action sniping rifle.
FRENCH DEFENCE MINISTRY

The extraordinary 5·56mm FA MAS rifle.
GIAT, VIA IAN HOGG

7·5 × 54mm, rimless.
Gas-operated auto-loading action, locked by a tilting block engaging the receiver.
DATA FOR MAS 44
1,076mm overall, 4·07kg unladen.
580mm barrel, 4-groove rifling; LH, concentric.
Detachable box magazine, 10 rounds.
Tangent-leaf sight graduated to 1,200 metres.
850 m/sec with Balle 1929 C.
MAS 36 rod bayonet.

☆

1944: work began in the autumn to perfect the pre-war MAS 39 semi-automatic rifle for series production.

1946: the first batches of about a thousand MAS 44 rifles were delivered for field trials with marine commandos serving in Indo-China. The rifle shared the two-piece stock, fittings, rod bayonet and sights of the bolt-action MAS 36, but had a deep receiver containing the breech block and carrier assembly. The cocking handle protruded from the front right side of the feed way and the back sight lay immediately in front of the firer's eye.

1948: a modified MAS 44-A was developed to fire grenades, a suitable muzzle and sight being fitted. Bayonets were abandoned on these guns.

1949: experiments began with modified rifles, some chambered for the US ·30–06 service cartridge and others fitted with an assortment of grenade launchers or folding stocks.

1951: production of the finalised MAS 49 began in Saint-Étienne. It was practically identical with the MAS 44, but lacked the bayonet and had a differing charger. The gas tube, shorter than the MAS 44 version, was bent to follow the contours of the barrel. This allowed the fore-end and hand guard to be modified, reducing unladen weight to about 3·93kg.

1952: the first guns were issued to selected marksmen, virtually all being fitted with the Mle.1953 telescope sight and an auxiliary hard rubber cheek piece on the butt.

1957: production of the MAS 49 ceased in favour of the improved MAS 49/56, though the two guns co-existed in the army before being relegated to the reserve in the 1970s.

MAS 49/56

Semi-automatic rifles: Fusils automatiques MAS 49/56, MAS 49/56 de la Sûreté Nationale et MAS 49/56 M–SE.
Manufacture d'Armes de Saint-Étienne, 1957–70.
7·5 × 54mm, rimless.
Action: as MAS 44, above.
1,022mm overall, 3·88kg unladen.
580mm barrel, 4-groove rifling; LH, concentric.
Detachable box magazine, 10 rounds.
Tangent-leaf sight graduated to 1,200 metres.
838 m/sec with Balle 1929 C.
MAS 56 knife bayonet.

☆

1956: this was developed to replace the MAS 49, production beginning in 1957. The rifle was equipped to fire NATO-standard rifle grenades; a special sight was pivoted to the back of the front-sight mounting block, and the launcher collar/muzzle brake had a diameter of 22mm. The special bayonet, which locked behind the muzzle brake, had two attachment rings.

The butt duplicated the MAS 49 pattern, but the half-length fore-end and hand guard—retained by a single band—created space for the grenade-launcher sight. Accessories included the Mle.1953 telescope sight, a rubber cheek piece, and two types of sponge-rubber butt plate.

1965*: about 250 rifles destined for security police (Sûreté Nationale) were converted to fire 7·62 × 51mm NATO ammunition, the grenade launcher being modified to fire tear-gas and other specialised ammunition.

1971: a special competition-shooting version, known as the 'MAS 49/56 M–SE' ('modifié Saint-Étienne'), was formally approved on 10 July. Converted from new or reconditioned guns by ERM, Poitiers, it had an improved trigger with a shorter hammer fall and a pistol-grip stock based on that of the bolt-action FR F–1.

MAS 62

Automatic rifle: Fusil d'Assaut MAS 62.
Manufacture d'Armes de Saint-Étienne, 1963–5.
Quantity: about 1,000.

7·62 × 51mm NATO, rimless.
Action: as MAS 44 rifle, above.
1,035mm overall, 4·22kg without magazine.
500mm barrel, 4-groove rifling; LH, concentric.
Detachable box magazine, 20 rounds.
Drum sight graduated to 600 metres.
840 m/sec with ball ammunition.
MAS 56 knife bayonet.

☆

1956: prototype locked-breech assault rifles replaced unsuccessful delayed-blowback MAS 54 and MAS 55. The 1956 pattern had a distinctive wooden butt and a circular-section pistol grip. Its gas system and Tokarev-type tilting-block lock were adapted from the MAS 49/56, though direct impingement of gas on the face of the bolt carrier was replaced by a short-stroke piston. The half length wooden fore-end led to a ventilated sheet-steel guard, and the muzzle had a 49/56-type grenade launcher.

1958: the revised MAS 58 had a modified receiver, a new back sight, a carrying handle, and plastic furniture.

1959: the 'Fusil Automatique MAS Type AP 59', derived from the 1958-pattern gun, had a supplementary pistol grip ahead of the magazine. The back sight lay directly above the front grip.

1962: the perfected MAS 62 was little more than a MAS 58 simplified for series production. It had a more conventional pistol grip than its predecessors, and the shaping of the plastic butt and fore-end was refined. The metal parts were phosphated, the back sight was moved rearward, and a selector appeared above the pistol grip on the left side of the receiver. It was marked M, C and S for fully-automatic fire, single shots, and safety respectively.

The gun was issued with a special detachable bipod, which could be carried on the bayonet scabbard. The bipod fitted at the muzzle or under the fore-end.

1967: the French tentatively adopted the MAS 62 after protracted trials. However, the trend towards small calibres led to a reassessment of requirements and the gun was abandoned in favour of the 5·56mm FA MAS—the prototype of which was displayed in the summer of 1973.

FA MAS

Made by Manufacture d'Armes, Saint-Étienne (subsequently part of Groupement Industriel des Armements Terrestres [GIAT], Saint-Cloud).

5·56 × 45mm, rimless.
Auto-loading action, delayed blowback.
757mm overall, 3·93kg with bipod and empty magazine.
488mm barrel, 3-groove rifling; RH, concentric.
Detachable box magazine, 25 rounds.
Aperture sight regulated for 300 metres.
960 m/sec with M193 ball ammunition; 950 ± 50 rpm.
Knife bayonet.

☆

1973: the first prototypes of this idiosyncratic bullpup rifle were exhibited at Satory in June, though design work had hardly been completed.
1976: the perfected A6 prototypes were issued for field trials.
1979: series production began, the first issues being made to the French army early in 1980. Known to the soldiery as 'Le Clairon' ('The Bugle'), the FA MAS had an extraordinary appearance owing to ultra-compact dimensions and the unusually long carrying handle. The back sight was let into the rear of the handle. The bipod folded back along the sides of the receiver, above the pistol grip, and the direction of ejection could be changed simply by altering the position of the extractor on the bolt before reversing the cheek piece.

The action was charged by a handle on top of the receiver, beneath the carrying handle. No positive lock was fitted, as a transverse lever connecting the bolt and bolt carrier delayed the opening of the breech until chamber pressure dropped to a safe level.

Packaged in a replaceable synthetic box, the trigger system relied on a ratchet escapement to fire three-shot bursts. The selector in the trigger guard could be moved from s ('sûr', safe) to 1 or R—for single- or multiple shots respectively. With the main selector set to R and the burst-fire selector under the trigger on 0, the FA MAS fired fully automatically; if the settings were R and 3, a burst ensued.

The rifle has been successful enough to satisfy the authorities, though it is suspected that the delayed blowback system is only marginally effectual enough for the high-pressure 5·56mm cartridge and that extraction failures occur even though the chamber is fluted. At the time of writing, however, it is still the principal service weapon.

Small numbers of the Modèle de Police have been made, with a 360mm barrel and an overall length of just 590mm. Destined to replace the MAT 49 submachine-gun, the police rifle lacked the bipod and had a simplified fore-end with a short carrying handle.

2. THE BOLT-ACTION PATTERNS

Developed in France in the 1930s, these rifles have been confined largely to the French army and the forces of former French colonies in Africa and the Far East.

The MAS 36 and its derivatives were sturdy and durable, though safety features were poor and the bolt was more awkward to manipulate than some more conventional rivals. However, they gave excellent service for many years.
1924: the introduction of a rimless 7·5mm cartridge, which was far better ballistically than the venerable 8mm rimmed pattern, forced the French to re-examine their infantry weapons. The rifles had originally been developed in the 1880s and were in need of improvement.
1929: prototype rifles were offered from Tulle and Saint-Étienne. Virtually all had charger-loaded magazines, and socket or spike bayonets that could be reversed into the fore-end when not required.
1932: the MAT 1932 rifle had a two-piece stock and a simple bolt. The operating handle was bent forward so that its ball lay immediately above the trigger guard.

Development of the MAT 1932 produced the MAS 34, the 'B1' version being accepted for service in 1935.

MAS 36

Short rifles: Fusil MAS 36, MAS 36 CR 39, MAS 36 LG 48 et MAS 36 M.51.
Made by Manufacture d'Armes de Saint-Étienne, 1937–40 and 1945–53.

7·5 × 54mm, rimless.
Turning-bolt action, with two lugs on the bolt body locking into the receiver behind the magazine well.
DATA FOR MAS 36
1,022mm overall, 3·75kg unladen.
575mm barrel, 4-groove rifling; LH, concentric.
Internal charger-loaded box magazine, 5 rounds.
Tangent-leaf sight graduated to 1,200 metres.
850 m/sec with Balle 1929 C.
MAS 36 rod bayonet.

☆

1935: approval of the MAS 34 B1 rifle allowed a production line to be readied for the MAS 36 rifle. The pistol-grip butt was separated from the fore-end and hand guard by a massive forged receiver containing the one-piece bolt. No safety catch was provided, and the bolt handle was bent forward so that it came easily into the hand. The back sight lay on the rear of the receiver, immediately ahead of the firer's eye. The single barrel band, which carried a swivel, was accompanied by a machined nose cap carrying the front sight. The spike-type bayonet lay in a channel in the fore-end and a stacking rod protruded from the right side of the nose cap.
1939: adopted for airborne infantry and alpine ski-troops, the MAS 36 CR 39 was simply a short MAS 36 with a bifurcated aluminium butt which could be folded forward around the trigger and lower part of the receiver. It was 885mm long, had a 450mm barrel, and weighed 3·85kg. Muzzle velocity was 780 m/sec.
1940: though the first deliveries had been made in 1937, comparatively few MAS 36 rifles had reached French infantrymen when the Germans invaded. The principal metal parts of pre-war guns were generally phosphated, though some were painted black—perhaps those made hurriedly in 1939–40—and others were browned for the navy and marines.
1941: production of modified 5·6mm rifles

MAS A 7·5mm MAS 49.

MAS The folded MAS 36 CR 39.
PATTERN ROOM COLLECTION

MAS The FR-F1 sniping rifle. GIAT

began under German supervision. These had barrel liners, but retained the original chamber so that adaptors in the shape of the 7·5mm round could be used. The adaptors contained a firing pin allowing the centre-fire striker to ignite rimfire ammunition.

1945: production of MAS 36 and MAS 36 CR 39 rifles began again, post-war guns embodying a tunnel-pattern front-sight protector and sheet-metal mounts. The back sight was modified so that the adjustment rack lay on the sight base instead of the leaf. A sling bar lay on the left side of the butt and a fixed ring appeared on the left side of the barrel band.

1947: the first of about fifty long-barrelled single-shot competition rifles chambering the 8mm Balle 1932 N appeared. It was 1,200mm overall, weighed a little under 5kg, and had an aperture sight on the receiver. A ramp-mounted front sight appeared on the barrel, the band was omitted, and the nose cap was greatly simplified. Swivels lay under fore-end and butt.

1949: some guns were modified for the 1948-type grenade launcher. These MAS 36 LG 48 had a folding sight-arm on the left side of the new machined-steel nose cap, which also had an eared front sight protector. Grenade range was varied by rotating a collar around the muzzle.

1951: a NATO-standard grenade launcher was approved. Rifles modified in 1952-5 (MAS 36 LG 51) had an elongated ribbed muzzle and the pivoting grenade-sight arm was set into the top upper part of the hand guard. A few guns were chambered for ·30-06 and 7·62mm NATO cartridges, but 7·5 × 54mm remained standard.

FR F series

Sniper rifles: Fusils à Répétition, Modèles F–1 et F–2.
Made by Manufacture d'Armes, Saint-Étienne (subsequently part of Groupement Industriel des Armements Terrestres [GIAT], Saint-Cloud).
7·5 × 54mm or 7·62 × 51mm.
Action: as MAS 36, above.
DATA FOR A TYPICAL FR F–1
7·62 × 51mm, rimless.
1,137mm overall, 5·44kg with bipod and magazine.

552mm barrel (excluding muzzle brake), 4-groove rifling; RH, concentric.
Detachable box magazine, 10 rounds.
Folding leaf sight.
850 m/sec with SS77 ball ammunition.
No bayonet.

☆

1964: this sniper rifle was developed from the obsolescent but effectual MAS pattern described above. The work was credited to the factory design bureau and a leading French rifleman, Jean Fournier.

The military FR F–1 'Type A' or "Tireur d'Élite" had a distinctive wood butt with an all but imperceptible pistol grip, a separate hand grip immediately behind the trigger, and an enveloping fore-end from which the slender floating barrel protruded. A bipod and a muzzle brake were usually fitted. Wooden spacers could be used to lengthen the butt, and two differing detachable synthetic cheek pieces could be obtained.

A lever-pattern magazine catch lay on the right side of the receiver, and the magazine was generally fitted with a detachable rubber cover; when the magazine was inserted into the feed way, the cover was simply pushed over the magazine base. Service rifles were usually fitted with the 3·8 × Mle.1953 L.806 optical sight, though guns issued by the police and anti-terrorist agencies exhibit 1·5–6 × Zeiss Diavari patterns.

A FR F–1 'Type B' or 'Tir Sportif' target rifle lacked the bipod and had a micro-adjustable aperture sight attached to a bar mount above the receiver. It weighed about 4·5kg without its magazine. A 'Grande Chasse' sporting rifle was also made in small numbers with an APX L.804 sight and a simplified trigger mechanism.

1984: an improved F–2 pattern was introduced, made only in 7·62 × 51mm. The strengthened bipod was mounted on a yoke around the barrel, immediately ahead of the receiver, and the wooden fore-end was replaced by a plastic-coated metal frame. The barrel was enclosed in a plastic sleeve in an attempt to reduce the effect of radiated heat on the sight picture, and possibly also to reduce the risk of infra-red detection.

MAUSER

GERMANY

This section contains details of the principal Mauser-made rifles, and also of the many sporting rifles built on substantially unaltered actions—which are defined as having two lugs on a solid bolt head, a full-length collar-type extractor and, where appropriate, a third or safety lug on the bolt. Guns embodying modified Mauser actions are covered separately.

1. THE AUTO-LOADING PATTERNS

Many differing rifles were developed prior to 1914, but trials had invariably shown them to be complicated and unreliable. Virtually all were recoil-operated.

Ironically, the only lasting contribution made by the Mauser organisation to auto-loading rifle design was the gas-operated roller-locked breech system. Originated by Wilhelm Stähle, then perfected by a research team led by Ernst Altenburger and Ludwig Vorgrimmler, this has been the basis for the CETME and Heckler & Koch rifles (qq.v.).

Model 1915

Aviators' rifles: Mauser Flieger-Gewehr und Flieger-Karabiner.
Made by Waffenfabrik Mauser AG, Oberndorf.
8 × 57mm.
Auto-loading action, delayed blowback.
DATA FOR A TYPICAL RIFLE
1,248mm overall, 4·74kg unladen.
675mm barrel, 4-groove rifling; RH, concentric.
Detachable box magazine, 10 or 20 rounds.
Tangent sight graduated to 2,000 metres.
765 m/sec with S-Patrone.
S.98, S.98/05 or S.84/98 bayonet.

☆

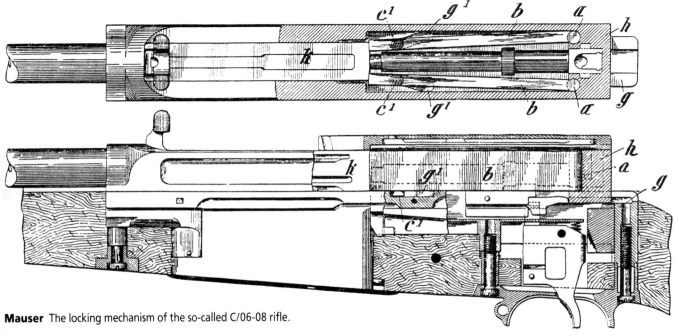

Mauser The locking mechanism of the so-called C/06-08 rifle.

1907: based on a patent granted in October 1906, the C.06/08 rifle was made in small numbers for field trials. Some rifles had leaf sights instead of the Lange tangent pattern, while a selection of internal or detachable magazines was tried. Most guns were stocked similarly to the Gew.98 and accepted bayonets without muzzle rings.

When the gun fired, the barrel and receiver slid backward for about 15mm. During this time, locking bars were cammed into the sides of the receiver to release the breech block to reciprocate. The action was long, cumbersome and unreliable; the slender locking bars were particularly prone to breakage. However, instead of abandoning the action in pursuit of simplicity, Mauser designers were doggedly persisting with the flap-lock when the First World War began.

1915: owing to an ever-increasing need for fire-power, possibly 200–250 fixed-barrel half- and full-stocked guns (similar in concept to the C.12/14 pistol) were issued, each costing six times as much as gas-operated Mondragons that had been purchased in Switzerland.

The fully-stocked rifles had standard Gew.98 pattern nose caps, accepted bayonets, and were tested in the trenches of the Western Front. Most of the half-stock patterns were initially used for air service. Experience showed that the imperfect Mondragon (q.v.) was preferable and the Mausers were rapidly withdrawn. Surviving guns seem to have been reissued to the navy.

Model 41

Infantry rifle: Gewehr 41 (M).
Made by Mauser-Werke AG, Oberndorf (code 'byf').
7·9 × 57mm.
Gas-operated auto-loading action, locked by rotating lugs on the bolt into the receiver.
1,172mm overall, 5·02kg unladen.
550mm barrel, 4-groove rifling; RH, concentric.
Detachable box magazine, 10 rounds.
Tangent-leaf sight graduated to 1,200 metres.
740 m/sec with sS-Patrone.
S.84/98 bayonet.
☆

1941: the army weapons office (Heereswaffenamt) issued specifications for a semi-automatic rifle to Mauser, Walther and others.

The resulting 'Gewehr 41' used an operating system developed by Søren Bang prior to 1914, in which propellant gases were trapped in a muzzle cup. Their expansive properties were used to drive an actuating rod back beneath the barrel to unlock a two-piece 'straight-pull' bolt that had been patented by Mauser engineers in 1935–6. The Gew.41 (M) was stocked in the manner of the Kar.98k, accepted the standard bayonet and could be loaded from chargers or with loose rounds; the main identifying feature was the bolt-type charging handle protruding from the lower right rear of the receiver.

2. THE BOLT-ACTION PATTERNS

These were widely used throughout the world. Estimates of total production run as high as a hundred million—depending on what is categorised as a Mauser. The 'modified Mausers' such as the Japanese Arisaka, the US Springfield and the British Enfield are covered separately. See also Ludwig Olson's authorititative *Mauser Bolt Rifles* (F. Brownell & Son, 1976).

MILITARY RIFLES

The steady improvement in design began with the single-shot M1871, progressing through the Serbian M78/80 and the German M71/84 to the Turkish rifle of 1887 and then the Belgian Mle.89—the first of the box-magazine guns. Major advances were made with the Spanish Mauser of 1893, the first to have its magazine contained in the stock, and then the German rifle of 1898. Virtually all Mausers made since the Gew.98 have embodied similar actions.

Prior to 1914, most rifles were supplied by Gebrüder Mauser and Waffenfabrik Mauser AG, Ludwig Loewe & Co. (only until the end of 1896) and then by Deutsche Waffen-

und Munitionsfabriken (from 1 January 1897), Österreichische Waffenfabriks-Gesellschaft and Fabrique Nationale d'Armes de Guerre. Indeed, in 1897, a cartel had been formed to divide production among the major participants: the agreement lasted until 1914.

The collapse of Germany in 1918 broke the domination of the pre-war supply ring. Alone among the pre-1914 participants, Fabrique Nationale managed to re-establish a flourishing export market under the growing challenge of Československá Zbrojovka. However, as purchases were generally smaller than they had been in the heady days prior to the First World War, weapons were often supplied from stock instead of tailored to specific requirements of individual governments.

ARGENTINA

The government purchased Mausers to replace Remington single-shot rifles and, apparently, Lee bolt-action rifles chambered for the 11mm Spanish cartridge. Argentinian Mausers usually had a chamber-mark of two hands clasping a Liberty Cap on a pole within an enwreathed oval border; MAUSER ARGENTINO was also usually present on the left side of the receiver. However, owing to a law promulgated during the 1930s, guns will be found with the marks ground away.

Model 1891

Infantry rifle: Fusil Mauser Argentino Mo.1891.
Made by Ludwig Loewe & Co., Berlin, 1891–6; and Deutsche Waffen- und Munitionsfabriken, Berlin, 1897–1900.
7·65 × 53mm, rimless.
Turning-bolt action, with two lugs on the bolt head locking into the receiver ring behind the chamber.
1,235mm overall, 3·99kg unladen.
740mm barrel, 4-groove rifling: RH, concentric.
Fixed charger-loaded box magazine, 5 rounds.
Ramp-and-leaf sight graduated to 2,000 metres.
650 m/sec with Mo.1891 ball cartridges.
Mo.1891 sword bayonet.
☆

Mauser A half-stocked Flieger-Karabiner. ROLF GMINDER

Mauser The Gewehr 41 (M).

Mauser Belgian machine-gunners on manoeuvres. Note the M1889 rifle and short-blade bayonet. COLLECTOR'S COMPENDIUM

1891: this was adopted after extensive trials, an order for 180,000 rifles being passed to Loewe. The rifle was an improved Turkish M1890, though the changes were comparatively few: a rotating lock-bolt was added to retain the magazine, guide ribs were added to the bolt sleeve, and the hand guard extended forward as far as the barrel band.

1909: most 1891-type rifles were altered for the spitzer-bulletted 'Bala S' cartridge.

Model 1891

Cavalry and artillery carbine:
Carabina Mauser Argentina Mo.1891.
Made by Ludwig Loewe & Co., Berlin, 1891–6; and Deutsche Waffen- und Munitionsfabriken, Berlin, 1897–1900.
7·65 × 53mm, rimless.
Action: as Mo.1891 rifle, above.
940mm overall, 3·28kg unladen.
448mm barrel, 4-groove rifling; RH, concentric.
Fixed charger-loaded box magazine, 5 rounds.
Ramp-and-leaf sight graduated to 1,200 metres.
577 m/sec with Mo.1891 ball cartridges.
No bayonet.

☆

1893: this was basically a shortened rifle. It was stocked to the muzzle, had a plain nose cap and barrel band, and the bolt handle was turned down against the stock. A sling bar and ring assembly was fitted beneath the wrist. The size of the back sight was greatly reduced, but a hand guard still ran from the front of its base to the band. The first order for 30,000 guns had been given to Loewe in 1891, but the guns were not delivered for some time. Rifles were presumably accorded priority.

1925*: some surviving guns were adapted to receive a sword bayonet.

Model 1909

Infantry rifle: **Fusil Mauser Argentino Mo.1909.**
Made by Deutsche Waffen- und Munitionsfabriken, Berlin, 1909–14; and Fabrica Militar de Armas Portatiles, Rosario, c.1942–59.

An unknown quantity was made in Germany, plus possibly 85,000 in Argentina.
7·65 × 53mm, rimless.
Turning-bolt action, with two lugs on the bolt head locking into the receiver ring behind the chamber and a safety lug opposing the bolt handle.
1,249mm overall, 4·07kg unladen.
740mm barrel, 4-groove rifling; RH, concentric.
Internal charger-loaded box magazine, 5 rounds.
Tangent-leaf sight graduated to 2,000 metres.
825 m/sec with Mo.1909 'S' ball cartridges.
Mo.1909 sword bayonet.

☆

1909: ordered in Germany, this was a standard 1898-type Mauser with a tangent-leaf sight and a hinged magazine floor plate, released by a small catch set into the trigger guard. The left charger guide, however, was provided by an upward extension of the spring-loaded bolt stop. The hand guard ran from the receiver ring to the narrow spring-retained barrel band, and the nose cap was a German 'H' type.

Though the first deliveries of rifles were apparently accompanied by German S.98-type épée bayonets, these broke too easily and had a short service career; most rifles, therefore, were subsequently fitted with adaptors for the sturdier Mo.1891 sword bayonet.

1940: the advent of the Second World War in Europe stemmed the flow of small arms from Belgium and Czechoslovakia. Consequently, the Argentine government decided to begin work in the Rosario factory, the first Mauser rifles being delivered in 1942.

Other guns

Argentina is said to have issued small numbers of the Mo.1909 engineer and mountain carbines; the former apparently had a nose cap with a bayonet lug on the right side, while the latter had an 'H' rifle-type fitting.

After the First World War, large quantities of Mle.24 and Mle.30 short rifles were purchased from Fabrique Nationale of Herstal. Additional FN Mausers were purchased in the late 1940s, though the numbers involved were small.

BELGIUM

1886: the army began testing rifles submitted by Francotte, Jarmann, Kropatschek, Lee, Mauser, Nagant and Schulhof.

1888: new tests began with small-calibre rifles. They included the Mauser C/88 and C/89; a Liége-made Schulhof; 'Engh' rifles made by SA Manufacture Liégeoise d'Armes à Feu; a Pieper; and several Lee designs.

1889: on 12 July, Alard Bormans and Henri Pieper signed a contract on behalf of Fabrique Nationale d'Armes de Guerre to produce 150,000 of whatever pattern of repeating rifle the Belgian government ultimately accepted. On 22 October, the Minister of War obtained a licence to allow Mauser rifles to be made in accredited private factories.

1891: in June, Loewe proposed to licence FN's Mauser production directly. The offer was quickly accepted, a revised contract being signed in Berlin on 26 November.

Model 1889

Infantry, civil guard and marksman's rifles: **Fusils d'Infanterie, de Corps Spéciaux de la Garde Civique, et pour Tireur d'Élite, Mle.1889.**
Made by Fabrique Nationale d'Armes de Guerre, Herstal-lèz-Liége, 1891–1914 and 1919–25 (275,000?); Fabrique d'Armes de l'État, Liége, c.1895–1914; Anciens Établissements Pieper, Herstal-lèz-Liége; and Hopkins & Allen, Norwich, Connecticut, 1914–16 (about 8,000); a few were also made in Britain during the First World War.
7·65 × 53mm, rimless.
Turning-bolt action, with two lugs on the bolt head locking into the receiver ring behind the chamber.
1,275mm overall, 4·03kg unladen.
780mm barrel, 4-groove rifling; RH, concentric.
Fixed charger-loaded box magazine, 5 rounds.
Ramp-and-leaf sight graduated to 1,900 metres.
625 m/sec with Mle.89 ball cartridges.
Mle.89 knife bayonet.

☆

1891: after extensive testing, the authorities decided to adopt a much-improved Mauser rifle.

Tooling had begun by the end of January and, on 31 December, Fabrique Nationale delivered the first four rifles to the Ministry of War.

1892: the 'Fusil à Répétition, système Mauser, Modèle de 1889' was adopted on 6 February. It was the first true small-calibre Mauser. The one-piece bolt was derived from that of the Gew.88, with two symmetrical locking lugs, but the handle turned down behind the solid bridge of the receiver. A cocking-piece housing or bolt-shroud was screwed into the rear of the perfected bolt (C/89 prototypes used a lug attachment system). The charger-loaded magazine was an improvement on Mannlicher clip patterns, as the charger was not essential to the action. Consequently, the magazine was simpler, less prone to mis-feed, and could be replenished with single rounds. A suitable guide was milled into the leading edge of the receiver bridge, its companion being formed by an extension of the spring-loaded bolt stop to hold the charger in place. Spent chargers were thrown clear as the bolt closed.

The rifle had a straight wristed one-piece stock; a housing for the follower-arm pivot projected from the lower front edge of the magazine case. A single spring-retained barrel band and a nose cap with a bayonet lug on its underside were used, but the barrel had a full-length annular jacket inspired by the Gew.88. Sling swivels lay beneath the barrel band and on the under-edge of the butt.

1893: by 30 June, 42,000 Mle.89 rifles had been delivered to the army; daily production had stabilised at 250 rifles, 25,000 bullets and 25,000 cartridge cases. The last of the 150,000 rifles was delivered on 31 December 1894.

1896: on 11 February, issue was extended to the Corps Spéciaux de la Garde Civique, accompanied by a bayonet with a blade of 30cm instead of the standard 25cm.

1903: Fabrique Nationale received another Belgian government contract for 1889-type rifles in June, an additional government contract following in November 1906.

1914: large numbers of Mle.89 rifles were seized by the Germans. Many were issued without alteration, but some were converted to fire the standard German 8 × 57mm cartridge. The remnants of the Belgian army fighting alongside the French placed production contracts with Hopkins & Allen after the fall of Belgium. In addition, a syndicate of exiles acquired facilities to make Mle.89 rifles in England. These are marked simply ÉTAT BELGE and BIRMINGHAM above the chamber.

1916: the Fusil d'Infanterie Mle.89 pour Tireur d'Élite was introduced in small numbers. It was little more than a standard infantry rifle with an offset mount for a suitable telescope sight on the left side of the receiver. The action could still be charger-loaded. Winchester sights were most common, but others were to be encountered.

1924: the knife bayonet was replaced by the Mle.24 épée pattern.

1935: conversion to Mle.89/36 (q.v.) began.

Model 1889

**Cavalry carbine:
Carabine de Cavallerie, Mle.1889.**
Made by Fabrique d'Armes de l'État, Liége,
c.1892–1914.
7·65 × 53mm, rimless.
Action: as Mle.1889 rifle, above.
885mm overall, 3·02kg unladen.
400mm barrel, 4-groove rifling; RH, concentric.
Fixed charger-loaded box magazine, 5 rounds.
Ramp-and-leaf sight graduated to 1,900 metres.
About 560 m/sec with Mle.89 ball cartridges.
No bayonet.

☆

1892: this was simply a much shortened form of the infantry rifle. The bolt handle was turned downward, the back sight was mounted on the chamber reinforce, and the fore-end extended only to the barrel band. This exposed a considerable length of the barrel jacket and cleaning rod.

A slotted plate was screwed to the left side of the butt to accept a stud on the carrying harness. Early carbines had a distinctive pivoting cover to protect the stud-slot, but this was eventually abandoned.

Model 1889

**Cadet carbine: Carabine des Enfants
de Troupe, Mle.1889.**
Made by Fabrique d'Armes de l'État, Liége,
c.1899–1914.
7·65 × 53mm, rimless.
Action: as Mle.1889 rifle, above.
1,045mm overall, 3·53kg unladen.
550mm barrel, 4-groove rifling; RH, concentric.
Fixed charger-loaded box magazine, 5 rounds.
Ramp-and-leaf sight graduated to 1,900 metres.
About 585 m/sec with Mle.89 ball cartridges.
Mle.89 knife bayonet.

☆

1899: this was similar to the carbine issued to dismounted gendarmerie and fortress artillery, but had a straight bolt handle and the barrel band lay midway between the back sight base and the nose cap. Few were made.

Model 1889

**Dismounted gendarmerie and fortress artillery
carbine: Carabine pour le Gendarmerie à Pied et de
l'Artillerie de Fortresse, Mle.1889.**
Made by Fabrique d'Armes de l'État, Liége,
c.1899–1914.
7·65 × 53mm, rimless.
Action: as Mle.1889 rifle, above.
1,045mm overall, 3·53kg unladen.
550mm barrel, 4-groove rifling; RH, concentric.
Fixed charger-loaded box magazine, 5 rounds.
Ramp-and-leaf sight graduated to 1,900 metres.
About 585 m/sec with Mle.89 ball cartridges.
Mle.89 sword bayonet.

☆

1904: issued from 9 May, this shared the action, stock, and barrel band/nose cap of the infantry rifle. The barrel band lay closer to the nose cap than back sight base, distinguishing it from the otherwise similar cadet carbine. The bolt handle was generally turned downward. Described as 'avec yatagan', the gun took a long-bladed bayonet.

1916: bayonets in the hands of the gendarmerie were replaced by the Mle.16 épée type.

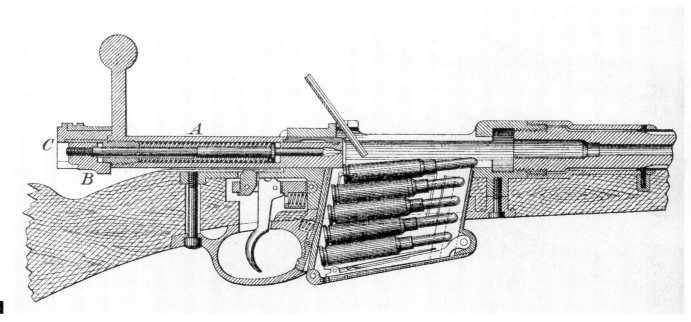

Model 1889

Mounted gendarmerie carbine: Carabine pour Gendarmerie à Cheval, Mle.1889.
Made by Fabrique d'Armes de l'État, Liége, c.1904–14.
7·65 × 53mm, rimless.
Action: as Mle.1889 rifle, above.
885mm overall, 3·05kg unladen.
400mm barrel, 4-groove rifling; RH, concentric.
Fixed charger-loaded box magazine, 5 rounds.
Ramp-and-leaf sight graduated to 1,900 metres.
About 560 m/sec with Mle.89 ball cartridges.
Mle.89 sword bayonet.

☆

1904: basically a shortened version of the Mle.89 cavalry carbine, this had a conventional length stock—though the barrel band was almost directly behind the nose cap. A sling swivel on the band was used in conjunction with a bracket screwed to the right side of the butt. It was issued with a long-blade ('yatagan') version of the Mle.89 knife bayonet.
1916: the sword bayonet was replaced by the Mle.16 épée pattern, which used a shortened Mle.82 (Comblain) blade.

Model 1889

Civil guard cyclists' carbine: Carabine pour les Cyclistes de la Garde Civique, Mle.1889.

☆

1907: made by Fabrique d'Armes de l'État until about 1912, this 7·65mm carbine apparently had a modified safety that could not be applied when the gun was cocked.
The back sight was graduated to 1,200 metres, a sling bar lay on the left side of the band, and a swivel was attached to the left side of the butt.

Model 1916

Carbine for machine-gunners, infantry-gun crews and despatch riders: Carabine pour Mitrailleurs, Batteries d'Infanterie et Agents de Transmission, Mle.1916.

☆

1916: this was adopted for a selection of special and ancillary troops during the First World War. It was similar to the 1889-type carbine issued to dismounted gendarmerie and fortress artillery, but had a 60cm barrel.

Model 1935

Short rifle: Fusil Mle.1935.
Made by Fabrique Nationale d'Armes de Guerre, Herstal-lèz-Liége, 1935–40,
7·65 × 53mm, rimless.
Turning-bolt action, with two lugs on the bolt head locking into the receiver ring behind the chamber and a safety lug opposing the bolt handle
1,107mm overall, 4·08kg unladen.
595mm barrel, 4-groove rifling; RH, concentric.
Internal charger-loaded box magazine, 5 rounds.
Tangent-leaf sight graduated to 2,000 metres.
715 m/sec with Mle.35 ball cartridges.
Mle.24 épée bayonet.

☆

1935: this was a standard 1898-pattern Mauser, with a non-rotating extractor, a safety lug on the bolt and most of the refinements found on the Gew.98. The barrel jacket was abandoned and the magazine lay within the stock. The barrel band and the nose cap both hinged open for removal, an open stacking swivel was fitted, and the bayonet lug projected beneath the nose cap.
1940: production had hardly begun in the FN rifle factory when the Germans invaded once again. Work stopped immediately. A few guns made for snipers were distinguished by ring mounts above the chamber and on the receiver bridge. A special rubber cheek piece was fitted in a metal cradle on the comb of the butt.

Model 1889/36

Short rifle: Fusil Mle.1889/36.
Apparently converted by Anciens Établissements Pieper, Herstal-lèz-Liége, 1936–40.
7·65 × 53mm, rimless.
Action: as Mle.1889 rifle, above.
1,094mm overall, 3·77kg unladen.
600mm barrel; 4-groove rifling; RH, concentric.

Fixed charger-loaded box magazine, 5 rounds.
Tangent-leaf sight graduated to 2,000 metres.
715 m/sec with Mle.35 ball cartridges.
Mle.24 épée bayonet.

☆

1936: the conversion of Mle.89 rifles to Mle.35 standards began in the Pieper factory. The resulting weapon combined the action and shortened stock of the Mle.89 with the barrel, sight, fore-end and hinged nose cap of the Mle.35. A recoil bolt was added through the stock beneath the chamber.
1940: the German invasion of Belgium brought operations to a halt after only a few thousand rifles had been transformed. Work does not seem to have been resumed after 1945.

Models 35/46 and 50

Short rifles: Fusils Mle.36/46 et Mle.50.
Made by Fabrique Nationale, Herstal, 1946–53.
Quantity: possibly 5,000 conversions and about 10,000 new guns.
·30–06, rimless.
Action: as Mle.1935 rifle, above.
1,105mm overall, 4·06kg unladen.
590mm barrel, 4-groove rifling; RH, concentric.
Internal charger-loaded box magazine, 5 rounds.
Tangent-leaf sight graduated to 2,000 metres.
About 835 m/sec with US M2 ball cartridges.
Mle.24 épée bayonet.

☆

1946: conversion of surviving Mle.35 rifles for the US service cartridge began, owing to the tremendous quantities of war-surplus guns and ammunition provided to re-equip the Belgian armed forces. Alterations included a groove cut across the face of the chamber to accommodate the longer American cartridge, and the guides on the receiver re-cut to accept US chargers.
1950: production of new Mle.30-type guns began in FN's Herstal factory. The magazine well was lengthened, though the grooved chamber face was retained. The guides accepted the standard American charger. Internally, the race-way for the left locking lug was milled through the shoulder in the receiver ring in

Mauser The action of the Belgian M1889 rifle.

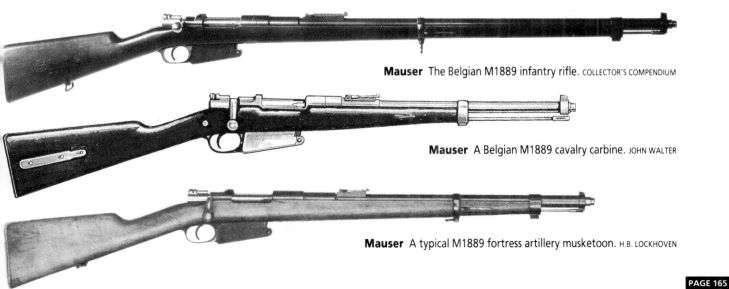

Mauser The Belgian M1889 infantry rifle. COLLECTOR'S COMPENDIUM

Mauser A Belgian M1889 cavalry carbine. JOHN WALTER

Mauser A typical M1889 fortress artillery musketoon. H.B. LOCKHOVEN

typical post-1946 FN fashion. Receiver-tops bore a crowned B above ABL and the date of manufacture.

FN CONTRACT PATTERNS

1894: by the middle of the year, Fabrique Nationale had supplied rifles and cartridges to the Netherlands, Spain, Serbia, Brazil, Chile, Brazil, China, Norway and Costa Rica. In December, Chile approached the company to place an order for 60,000 Mauser-system rifles, but Mauser objected to the fulfilment of non Belgian orders and the irritated Chileans placed the order with Loewe. In December, Mauser asked Fabrique Nationale to cease using the patents covering the 1893 or Spanish-pattern Mauser on the grounds that these were not part of the original 1891-vintage agreement.

1895: backed by a campaign in the Belgian Press and parliament, Fabrique Nationale tried to fight the injunction, but it was eventually decided at a high level in the government that there were no real grounds for objection. FN conceded the case.

1896: in February, FN and Loewe amicably negotiated a new contract with Mauser.

1897: in January, a production agreement was signed by the principal manufacturers of Mauser rifles—FN, Mauser, DWM and OEWG—under which each was allocated a specific quota.

1914: contract work ceased for the duration of the First World War, resuming in 1919.

1940: total FN Mauser rifle production since 1899, excluding Belgian orders, amounted to at least 517,000. In addition to the guns considered here individually, the company had made at least 143,000 'unattributed' examples for France, Greece, Lithuania, Paraguay, Peru, Venezuela and Yemen.

Model 1922

Rifle and short rifle.
Made by Fabrique Nationale d'Armes de Guerre,
Herstal-lèz-Liége, 1922–5.
Quantity: 50,000?

7 × 57mm, 7·65 × 53mm or 7·9 × 57mm.
Turning-bolt action, with two lugs on the bolt head locking into the receiver ring behind the chamber and a safety lug opposing the bolt handle.
DATA FOR A TYPICAL EXAMPLE
7 × 57mm, rimless.
About 1,237mm overall, 4·00kg unladen.
740mm barrel, 4-groove rifling; RH, concentric.
Internal charger-loaded box magazine, 5 rounds.
Tangent-leaf sight graduated to 2,000 metres.
785 m/sec with FN ball cartridges.
FN export-pattern bayonet.

☆

1922: these were the first post-war Mausers to be made in the reconditioned and re-equipped Herstal factory. The Mle.22 was mechanically similar to the Gew.98, but had the standard export fittings—a tangent-leaf back sight, a hand guard running forward from the receiver ring, and a conventional bayonet attachment incorporating a muzzle ring. The barrel band was particularly narrow and the nose cap was as simple as it could be. Though Mle.22 FN Mausers went to Brazil, the market for full-length rifles was declining fast. The Mle.24 short rifle soon proved to be much more popular.

Models 1924 and 1930

**Rifles and short rifles: Fusils et carabines
Mle.24, Mle.24/30 et Mle.30.**
Made by Fabrique Nationale d'Armes de Guerre,
Herstal-lèz-Liége, 1924–40 and 1946–54.
Quantity: 650,000?
7 × 57mm, 7·65 × 53mm or 7·9 × 57mm.
Action: as Mle.22 rifle, above.
DATA FOR A TYPICAL MLE.24
7·65 × 53mm, rimless.
1,090mm overall, 3·81kg unladen.
591mm barrel, 4-groove rifling; RH, concentric.
Internal charger-loaded box magazine, 5 rounds.
Tangent-leaf sight graduated to 2,000 metres.
725 m/sec with FN ball cartridges.
FN export-pattern bayonet.

☆

1924: a short rifle appeared to supplement, then replace the Mle.1922. It had a conventional

1898-pattern Mauser action and a non-rotating extractor. Though a straight-wrist stock was offered for a short period, virtually all known guns have a pistol-grip pattern with a single band and either a simple nose cap or a German 'H' pattern. The mounts were retained by springs let into the right side of the fore-end. A hand guard generally ran either from the receiver ring to the fore-end, or only as far as the barrel band. Swivels invariably lay under the band and beneath the butt, though alterations were sometimes specified by the purchasers.

A Mle.24 carbine was also made in small numbers, being shorter and lighter than the rifle. The bolt handle was generally turned down towards the stock.

1930: modifications were made to the basic Mauser action, advancing the designation. It is believed that they were largely changes of dimension, and that, externally at least, the weapons were similar to their predecessors. Attempts have been made to link the changes to matters of nose cap, hand guard and stock design, but these were largely controlled by the purchaser and may not have been the arbiters. There are also some 'Mle.24/30' rifles, but whether these are Mle.24 brought up to Mle.30 standards or simply an alternative designation for the true Mle.30 has not been resolved.

1940: production ceased when the Germans invaded Belgium in May, though the factory subsequently made parts for the Kar.98k.

1946: production of Mle.30-type rifles began again, though demand was never great. Too many war-surplus weapons were available for the pre-war markets to be re-established.

CZECHOSLOVAKIA

Guns used by the Czechoslovakian forces were distinguished by a crowned twin-tailed Lion of Bohemia with a shield on its breast. They may also show ČSK or ČSZ for Československá ('Czechoslovakia') and Československá Státni Zbrojovky ('Czechoslovakian state factory'). The export weapons usually bore the marks of Československá Zbrojovka, Brno.

Mauser Fabrique Nationale's Model 1922 rifle and short rifle were soon superseded by the M1924. FN HERSTAL SA

Mauser A 7·9mm FN-Mauser Type 30-11 sniping rifle. FN HERSTAL SA

Czechoslovakia seized independence from Austria-Hungary at the end of the First World War, gaining the nucleus of an effectual arms industry—in the form of the Skoda factory—and many Austro-Hungarian, German and Russian rifles. A factory was created in Brno to make Mausers, equipped with Austro-Hungarian or German machinery supplied as war reparations.

Mauser-Jelen

Short rifle: Puška Mauser-Jelena.

☆

1919: chambered for the 7 × 57mm cartridge, the first rifles were standard 1898-type Mausers with non-rotating extractors and special sword bayonets. Most guns had a distinctive pistol-grip stock and a hand guard running from the receiver ring to the muzzle. The magazine floor plate was often fitted with a quick-release lever similar to those found on Mauser sporters.

The most distinctive feature was the nose cap assembly inspired by the British SMLE, which ran back under the fore-end to an intermediate screw-clamped band. The ring on the bayonet cross-guard fitted around a boss on the nose cap beneath the muzzle. Sling swivels appeared on the underside of the true barrel band—which lay some way behind the auxiliary nose-cap fitting—and on the under-edge of the butt.

1921: several hundred rifles were manufactured by Československá Státni Závody na Vyrobu Zbrani, including at least 150 in 7 × 57mm and a roughly comparable quantity in 7·92 × 57mm. Most were issued to the Czechoslovakian army, but some went to Yugoslavia.

1922: the Jelen-type Mauser was abandoned in favour of a copy of the pre-war Mo.1912 Mexican rifle made in Steyr.

Model 1898/22

Rifle and short rifle: Puška a krátká puška vz.98/22.

Made by Československá Státni Závody na Vyrobu Zbrani, Brno, 1923–4; and Československá Zbrojovka AS, Brno, 1924–30.

7·92 × 57mm, rimless.
Turning-bolt action, with two lugs on the bolt head locking into the receiver ring behind the chamber and a safety lug opposing the bolt handle.
DATA FOR TYPICAL RIFLE
1,240mm overall, 4·22kg unladen.
740mm barrel, 4-groove rifling; RH, concentric.
Internal charger-loaded box magazine, 5 rounds.
Tangent-leaf sight graduated to 2,000 metres.
870 m/sec with standard ball cartridges.
Standard vz.23 knife or sword bayonets

☆

1922: this was adopted for service with the Czech army. It was little more than a slightly improved Mo.1912 Steyr-made Mexican Mauser, with a pistol-grip stock and a hand guard running from the receiver ring to the barrel band. A German 'H'-pattern nose cap was used, a front sight hood was fitted, and the swivels lay in conventional positions beneath the band and butt.

1924: the state-owned factory was reorganised as a private company to encourage exports. The 98/22-pattern long rifles were initially popular with purchasers, but vz.24 short rifles soon attained greater renown.

Models 1923, 1923A and 1924

Short rifles: Krátká puška vz.23, vz.23A a vz.24.

Made by Československá Státni Závody na Vyrobu Zbrani, Brno, 1923–4; and Československá Zbrojovka AS, Brno, 1924–40.
Quantity: hundreds of thousands.
7 × 57mm, 7·65 × 53mm or 7·92 × 57mm.
Action: as vz.98/22 rifle, above.
DATA FOR VZ.24
7·92 × 57mm, rimless.
1,098mm overall, 4·14kg unladen.
590mm barrel, 4-groove rifling; RH, concentric.
Internal charger-loaded box magazine, 5 rounds.
Tangent-leaf sight graduated to 2,000 metres.
840 m/sec with standard cartridges.
Standard vz.23 or vz.24
sword bayonets.

☆

1923: the first of these short rifles was based on the German Kar.98AZ, but stocked more in the manner of the Gew.98. The action was essentially that of the vz.98/22 rifle, but minor improvements were made internally, the barrel was shortened, and the hand guard extended to the nose cap.

Swivels lay on the under-edge of the butt and on the underside of the barrel band. Most vz.23 short rifles incorporated old or cannibalised parts, whilst vz.23A examples were entirely newly made. The barrel band was noticeably closer to the German 'H'-type nose cap than the receiver ring.

1924: the perfected short rifle appeared at a time when the government rifle factory was being reorganised. It was very similar to the vz.23, but the design of the fore-end had been improved and the band—retained by a lateral bolt in Austrian fashion—was moved back until it was approximately mid-way between the nose cap and the receiver ring. An additional bolt was placed laterally through the pistol grip and a grasping groove was invariably present on the fore-end beneath the back sight. Some (but by no means all) guns had their bolt handles turned down into a recess in the side of the stock.

1925: the first large export orders were attracted, and sufficient guns had been delivered to the Czechoslovakian army—about 80,000 vz.23/vz.23A, plus 40,000 vz.24—for issue to infantry, cavalry and armoured divisions.

1939: the Brno factory was seized by the Germans. Most existing vz.24 short rifles were sequestered, serving the Wehrmacht as the 'Gew.24 (t)', and production continued. Rifles made under HWaA supervision had German-style butts with sling slots and hollow washers to assist dismantling the firing pin. The first of the stamped 'bucket'-type butt plates appeared in the summer of 1942.

1942: production of the Kar.98k-type version of the vz.24 began, distinguished from the German prototype largely by its markings ('dot' code). Work ceased in the face of the Russian advance at the end of 1944, after about 1·25 million guns had been made.

Mauser Prior to the adoption of the Československá Zbrojovka-made Mausers, the Czechoslovakian army was armed with a selection of old weapons. These included M1895 Mannlichers, seen here in the hands of Czechs serving the Austro-Hungarian army. The photograph was taken in Leitmeritz an der Elbe (now Litoměřice).
COLLECTOR'S COMPENDIUM

Model 1933

Gendarmerie carbine: Krátká puška vz.33 pro četnictvo a financi straz.
Made by Československá Zbrojovka AS, Brno, 1933–9.
7·92 × 57mm, rimless.
Action: as vz.98/22 rifle, above.
996mm overall, 3·48kg unladen.
490mm barrel, 4-groove rifling; RH, concentric.
Internal charger-loaded box magazine, 5 rounds.
Tangent-leaf sight graduated to 1,000 metres.
780 m/sec with standard ball cartridges.
Standard vz.24 sword bayonet.

☆

1933: the military version of the vz.16/33 export carbine was bought in small quantities. It was essentially a diminutive vz.24, but had a small-diameter receiver ring and flutes were milled out of the receiver sides below the line of the stock to save weight. The bolt-handle knob was hollowed and a sling bar was fixed to the left side of the barrel band. Swivels lay beneath the band and butt.
1934: 12,740 guns were acquired for the gendarmerie and 5,300 for the treasury guards.
1938: 2,730 additional gendarmerie and 2,270 treasury-guard guns were ordered.
1939: work continued under German auspices.
1940: the modified Gew.33/40 (q.v.) was adopted by the Wehrmacht. Assembly continued until late in 1941.

ČZ CONTRACT PATTERNS

Huge quantities of Mauser-type weapons were exported prior to 1939. They included the vz.98/22 rifle, vz.23 and 23A short rifles, and vz.24 short rifle (above), as well as the 'JC' short rifle, 'L' short rifle and carbine described below.

Model 1898/29

Rifle and short rifle: Puška a krátká puška vz.98/29.
Made by Československá Zbrojovka AS, Brno, 1933–9.

7 × 57mm or 7·92 × 57mm.
Action: as vz.98/22 rifle, above.
DATA FOR TYPICAL VZ.98/29 SHORT RIFLE
7·92 × 57mm, rimless.
965mm overall, 3·77kg unladen.
455mm barrel, 4-groove rifling; RH, concentric.
Internal charger-loaded box magazine, 5 rounds.
Tangent-leaf sight graduated to 2,000 metres.
765 m/sec with standard ball cartridges.
Standard vz.23 sword bayonet.

☆

1929: these were minor adaptions of the vz.98/22 rifle and vz.24 short rifle respectively. The rifle generally had a much broader barrel band than the vz.98/22 pattern (which was unusually narrow), the front sight block was extended upward to protect the sight blade, and an open piling swivel was added on the under side of the nose cap. A third swivel was generally fitted through the front of the trigger-guard web, in addition to those under the band and on the under-edge of the butt. The additional bolt through the pistol grip, characteristic of the vz.24, was lacking from the vz.98/29.

The 98/29 short rifle was a shortened rifle, with the same band, nose cap and front-sight guard, but the bolt handle was turned down into a recess in the side of the stock and a fixed sling bar was added to the left side of the band to supplement the conventional swivel.

Models 08/33, 12/33 and 16/33

Short rifles and carbines: Krátká puška vz.08/33, vz.12/33 a vz.16/33.

☆

Excepting the vz.08/33 pattern, which was made for Brazil in 7 × 57mm and may also have accepted the Brazilian Mo.1908 bayonet, these generally chambered 7·92mm cartridges and were accompanied by vz.23 bayonets.

The 12/33 carbine was a lightened vz.24 intended for use in hot climates; consequently, it was particularly popular in Central and South America. It was derived from the 'vz.12 mex.' pattern supplied to Mexico in the late 1920s. The vz.16/33 was the shortest of the group, providing the basis for the Czech vz.33 service weapon described above.

Other guns

The 'JC' short rifles were lightened versions of the standard vz.24; 'L'-pattern short rifles and carbines, believed to have been developed at the request of the Lithuanians, chambered the British ·303 rimmed cartridge and accepted surplus Austro-Hungarian 1895-pattern knife bayonets. They were easily recognised by the magazine, which protruded slightly from the underside of the stock ahead of the trigger guard, and by the bayonet lug on the underside of the nose cap.

Guns described as 'vz.32' or vz.35' usually prove to have been minor variations of the vz.24—e.g., the Peruvian Mo.32 short rifle had a small-diameter receiver ring and a reversed safety lever.

GERMANY

Prior to 1914, Mauser, Loewe and DWM made vast quantities of rifles for export; Mauser continued to export rifles in the 1930–9 era.
1867: Mauser developed a self-cocking bolt-action rifle on the basis of the Dreyse needle gun, the prototypes being built on old Württemberg rifle-muskets. The 'C/67' is now sometimes known as the 'Mauser-Norris' rifle, owing to participation of Remington salesman Samuel Norris in its development. It had been rejected by the Württemberg state army at the beginning of the year, and then also by Austria-Hungary.
1870: Paul and Wilhelm Mauser submitted an improved 'C/70' rifle to the Prussian army, the gun being tested at the school of musketry in Spandau in midsummer.
1871: trials with many differing rifles continued throughout the period of the Franco-Prussian war, until only the Mauser and the Bavarian Werder (q.v.) remained. On 9 December, the Mauser was provisionally adopted, pending the development of a satisfactory safety mechanism.

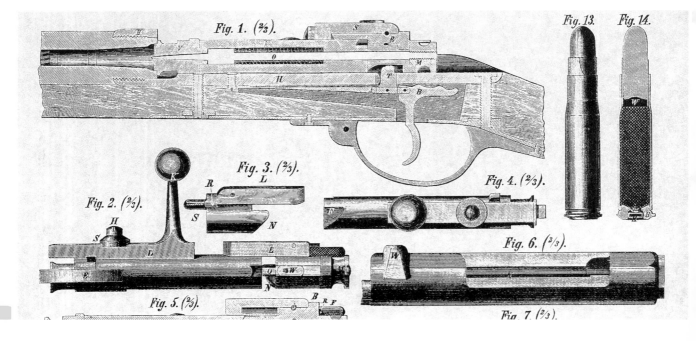

Fig. 1. (⅔). Fig. 13. Fig. 14.
Fig. 2. (⅔). Fig. 3. (⅔). Fig. 4. (⅔).
Fig. 5. (⅔). Fig. 6. (⅔).
Fig. 7. (⅔).

Model 1871

Infantry rifle: Infanterie-Gewehr M1871.
Made by Königlich Gewehrfabrik, Spandau, 1872–84;
Österreichische Waffenfabriks-Gesellschaft, Steyr,
1873–8; Gebr. Mauser & Co., Oberndorf, 1873–84;
Productionsgenossenschaft, Suhl, 1876–82; and the
National Arms & Ammunition Co. Ltd,
Birmingham, 1876–8.
11×60mm, rimmed.
Turning-bolt action, locked by the bolt-guide rib
abutting the receiver ahead of the bridge.
1,345mm overall, 4·58kg unladen.
855mm barrel, 4-groove rifling; RH, concentric.
Leaf sight graduated to 1,600 metres.
430 m/sec with Reichspatrone M1871.
M1871 sword bayonet.

☆

1872: on 14 February, Mauser demonstrated a wing-type safety catch, and the perfected rifle was adopted on 22 March. It presented a dated appearance, with a straight-wrist stock, two spring-retained barrel bands, and a nose cap with a bayonet lug on the right side. Swivels lay on the trigger guard and under the middle band. The back sight had a small leaf for 400 metres, and a large one, with a sliding extension, for 500–1,600 metres. The standard brass-hilted sword bayonet had a muzzle ring and an attachment groove in the pommel.

The Bavarian government ordered 100,000 rifles from the factory in Amberg in May, but the facilities were occupied converting Werders and no Mausers were made there until 1877.
1873: in December, the Württemberg army ordered 100,000 guns from the Mausers.
1875: the first series-made Spandau rifle was presented to the Kaiser on 22 March.
1876: Prussia ordered 180,000 additional guns from the 'Productionsgenossenschaft Suhl' in February, 100,000 from OEWG in July, and 75,000 from the National Arms & Ammunition Co. Ltd in Birmingham at about the same time. British-made guns were marked N.A. & A. CO. in a triangle. About 26,000 Mauser-made rifles were sold to China in this period.
1877: tests were undertaken with five hundred

guns modified in the Spandau factory in the autumn of 1876 to receive a modular striker, retaining nut and cocking-piece assembly. The new component was not adopted; though it improved the certainty of ignition, lock-time was also increased greatly. By 31 December, OEWG had delivered more than 474,000 rifles to the armies of Prussia and Saxony alone.
1882: a coil spring was added to the small back-sight leaf hinge, a hardened insert was pinned into the locking shoulder (the rear of the bolt guide rib) to reduce wear, and the bolt-stop screw was also given a retaining pin to prevent it falling out. An ejector was added at this time.
1884: on 28 January, the Kaiser signed an order suspending production of 1871-type rifles.
1886: rifles were gradually withdrawn from regular units as supplies of the Gew.71/84 (q.v.) became available, passing down through the active reserve, the Landwehr and Landsturm until—by about 1900—they had either been sold or placed in store. Catalogues such as that of A.L. Frank of Hamburg ('Alfa') advertised large numbers of them commercially.
1914: surviving rifles were re-issued to free better weapons for active service. Some were subsequently re-bored to 13mm-calibre to fire incendiary anti-balloon ammunition.

Model 1871

Short rifle: Jägerbüchse M1871.
Made by Königlich Gewehrfabrik, Danzig, 1876–84;
Österreichische Waffenfabriks-Gesellschaft, Steyr,
1876–7; and Gebr. Mauser & Co.,
Oberndorf, 1876–81.
11×60mm, rimmed.
Action: as M1871 rifle, above.
1,240mm overall, 4·48kg unladen.
750mm barrel, 4-groove rifling; RH, concentric.
Leaf sight graduated to 1,600 metres.
418 m/sec with Reichspatrone M1871.
M1871 Hirschfänger (sword) bayonet.

☆

1876: adopted on 18 January, this was similar to the infantry rifle apart from overall length, the sight graduations and a spurred trigger-guard.

The Jägerbüchse had only one barrel band, though the rifle-type nose cap was retained. The rear sling swivel lay beneath the butt instead of the trigger guard. A turned-down muzzle crown accepted the bayonet.
1882: changes were made to the back sight, the bolt-guide rib and the bolt-stop screw. Also applied to the 1871-pattern infantry rifle, these are described above.
1886: the rifles were displaced by Gew.71/84, and passed to lesser formations. Eventually, many seem to have been given to the navy or sent to the colonies. Marks applied by the Schutztruppe Deutsche Ost-Afrika (SCH.D.O.A...) are particularly common.
1914: surviving guns were brought out of store, though most were discarded during the First World War.

Models 1871 and 1879

**Carbine and border-guard rifle:
Karabiner M1871 und Grenz-Aufsichts-Gewehr M1879.**
DATA FOR M1871 CARBINE
Made by Österreichische Waffenfabriks-Gesellschaft,
Steyr, 1876–7; Arbeitsgemeinschaft Haenel, Suhl,
1877–85 ; V.C. Schilling, Suhl, 1877–85; and
Gebr. Mauser & Co., Oberndorf, 1876–81.
Quantity: 150,000?
11×60mm, rimmed.
Action: as M1871 rifle, above.
995mm overall, 3·42kg unladen.
505mm barrel, 4-groove rifling; RH, concentric.
Leaf sight graduated to 1,200 metres.
390 m/sec with Karabiner-Patrone M1871.
No bayonet.

☆

1875: development of an experimental carbine commenced in January, a workable prototype being tested at Spandau in May.
1876: adopted on 31 August, the Karabiner M1871 was issued to dragoons, hussars and lancers to replace Chassepot carbines altered to fire metal-case ammunition. The carbine had a single spring-retained barrel band; a full-length stock; a nose cap from the which the muzzle

Mauser Drawings of the 1871-pattern Mauser, from Schott's *Grundriss der Waffenlehre*, 1876.

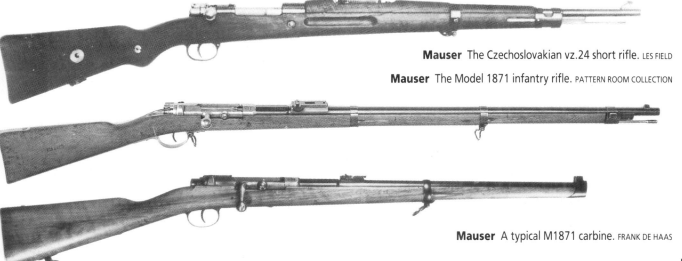

Mauser The Czechoslovakian vz.24 short rifle. LES FIELD

Mauser The Model 1871 infantry rifle. PATTERN ROOM COLLECTION

Mauser A typical M1871 carbine. FRANK DE HAAS

scarcely protruded; a turned-down bolt handle; a small back sight; and the sling-swivel under the foot of the butt. The Prussian carbines were made in Steyr and Suhl, Württemberg issue coming from Mauser.

1877: by 31 December, Steyr had delivered 60,000 carbines to Prussia and Saxony.

1880: about a thousand special carbine-length rifles were made by Schilling of Suhl for the Grenz-Aufsichts-Beamten, border guards under the control of the customs service instead of the army. The guns had simple two-position rocking back sights, Dreyse-style stock fittings, and could accept sword bayonets.

1884: issue of carbines was extended to the cuirassiers from 12 April.

1890: replacement of Karabiner M1871 began.

1906: a thousand carbines were sold out of store to China.

Model 1871/84

Infantry rifle:
Infanterie-Gewehr M1871/84.
Made by Königliche Gewehrfabriken, Danzig, Erfurt and Spandau, 1900–18; Königlich bayerische Gewehrfabrik, Amberg, 1886–90; and Waffenfabrik Mauser AG, Oberndorf, 1885–7.
Quantity: 950,000?
11 × 60mm, rimmed.
Turning-bolt action, locked by the bolt-guide rib abutting the receiver ahead of the bridge.
1,297mm overall, 4·61kg unladen.
800mm barrel, 4-groove rifling; RH, concentric.
Tube magazine in fore-end, 8 rounds.
Leaf sight graduated to 1,600 metres.
430 m/sec with Reichspatrone 71/84.
M71/84 sword bayonet.

☆

1884: basically an improved version of the C/82 rifle (see panel), this was adopted everywhere except in Bavaria on 31 January. Bavarian adoption occured in May.

The Gew.71/84 was similar externally to the single-shot M1871, but the standards of manufacture were higher. An elevator mechanism was added beneath the bolt way and

a conventional tube magazine ran forward beneath the barrel. The magazine was loaded through the top of the open action. The short-blade bayonet had a muzzle ring.

Prussian guns were made in the principal government arsenals; Bavarian guns came from Amberg; and Württemberg's were supplied by Waffenfabrik Mauser.

1885: the first rifles were delivered from Spandau, Erfurt and Danzig. The depth of the rifling grooves was halved (to 0·15mm) with effect from 14 November, though the change was not made in Bavaria until the end of 1886.

1886: the first Amberg-made guns were delivered into store in January. Though the advent of the French Lebel (q.v.) made the Gew.71/84 obsolescent overnight, issues were made to the army corps in Elsass-Lothringen (Alsace-Lorraine) in July. A thousand sectioned actions had been distributed to facilitate training.

1888: the Germans nearly adopted an 8mm Gew.71/84 with an extra locking lug, mooted in 1887. Sense prevailed, however, and the Gew.88 (see 'Mannlicher') was taken instead.

1890: issue of Gewehre 88 allowed the first 71/84-type rifles to be withdrawn, serving the active reserve, the Landwehr and then the Landsturm before being stored or sold. A few guns appear to have been modified for the 8mm service cartridge in this period, but are rarely encountered.

1914: surviving guns, and those retrieved from wholesalers such as A.L. Frank, were issued to free better weapons for active service.

Note: 71/84-type carbines exist, as do some Jägerbüchsen with a single barrel band and a swivel on the butt midway between the toe and the trigger guard. Their history is not yet known in detail.

Model 1888/97

Infantry rifle: Infanterie-Gewehr M1888/97
('Gew.88/97').
Made by Waffenfabrik Mauser AG, Oberndorf, 1895.
Quantity: about 2,000.

8 × 57mm, rimless.
Turning-bolt action with two lugs on the bolt head locking into the receiver behind the chamber and a safety lug opposing the bolt handle.
1,240mm overall, 3·98kg unladen.
740mm barrel, 4-groove rifling; RH, concentric.
Internal charger-loaded box magazine, 5 rounds.
Tangent sight graduated to 2,000 metres.
630 m/sec with Patrone 88.
Special sword and épée bayonets.

☆

1895: delivered in the summer, this was an adaption of the contemporary Mauser rifles—made in Oberndorf but incorporating features requested by the army. It had the 1895-patent third or 'safety' locking lug, a cocking-piece housing with an integral gas-deflector flange, and gas-escape holes in the bolt body. The action cocked on opening.

1897: formally accepted in Prussia, Saxony and Württemberg on 11 March (21 April in Bavaria), after trials against 6mm-calibre Mausers, the Gew.88/97 had a uniquely squared Lange tangent-pattern back sight and a full-length barrel jacket. The straight-wrist stock had a single barrel band, carrying the front swivel, and there were two unmistakably closely spaced nose bands. The tubular-steel hilts of the bayonets slid over (and locked onto) the cleaning-rod housing beneath the barrel jacket, the basic idea of isolating the bayonet from the barrel having been patented by Mauser in October 1895.

1898: before the Erfurt factory could begin production, the authorities reconsidered design details and the Gewehr 88/97 was abandoned.

Model 1898

Infantry rifles: Gewehre 98, 98/17 und 98/18,
Karabiner 98b.
Made by Königliche Gewehrfabriken, Danzig, Erfurt and Spandau, 1885–9; Königlich bayerische Gewehrfabrik, Amberg, 1903–7; Waffenfabrik Mauser AG, Oberndorf am Neckar, Württemberg, 1904–18; Deutsche Waffen- und Munitionsfabriken, Berlin, 1904–18; Simson & Co., Suhl, 1915–18; C.G. Haenel, Suhl, 1915–18; V.C. Schilling & Co., Suhl,

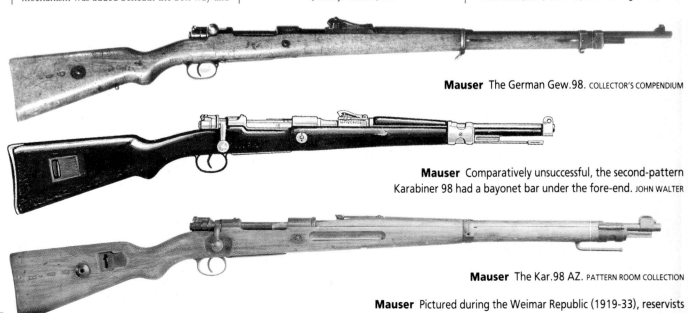

Mauser The German Gew.98. COLLECTOR'S COMPENDIUM

Mauser Comparatively unsuccessful, the second-pattern Karabiner 98 had a bayonet bar under the fore-end. JOHN WALTER

Mauser The Kar.98 AZ. PATTERN ROOM COLLECTION

Mauser Pictured during the Weimar Republic (1919-33), reservists pose with unaltered Gewehre 98. COLLECTOR'S COMPENDIUM

1915–18; and Waffenwerk Oberspree, Kornbusch & Co., Niederschönweide bei Berlin, 1915–18 (acquired by DWM in 1916).

Quantity: in excess of five million.

8 × 57mm, rimless.

Turning-bolt action with two lugs on the bolt head locking into the receiver behind the chamber and a safety lug opposing the bolt handle.

DATA FOR GEW.98

1,250mm overall, 4·09kg unladen.

740mm barrel, 4-groove rifling; RH, concentric.

Internal charger-loaded box magazine, 5 rounds.

Tangent sight graduated to 2,000 metres.

870 m/sec with S-Patrone.

S.98 sword bayonet.

☆

1898: adopted in the armies of Prussia, Saxony and Württemberg on 5 April, to replace the Gew.88/97, this was a standard Mauser with a third (safety) lug, a guide rib, an under-cut extractor and a shrouded bolt face. The bolt-sleeve lock was introduced, the travel of the firing pin was reduced to accelerate lock time, and a large-diameter receiver ring enhanced strength. The mechanism cocked as the bolt was opened and the internal box magazine could be loaded from a charger or with loose rounds.

Gew.98 were originally accompanied by the Seitengewehr 98, with a 'pipe back' or strengthening rib along the back of the blade and a very distinctive hilt. The sturdy twin-band nose cap had an unusually long attachment bar, appropriate bayonets having a commensurately long attachment slot to give rigidity to the mount without the assistance of a muzzle ring.

1899: sufficient rifles had been made to allow large-scale troop trials to commence on 9 February. As few important faults were revealed, tooling for mass production began immediately.

1901: the first issues were made to the navy, the East Asian Expeditionary Force, and the three premier Prussian army corps. The rifle was adopted in Bavaria on 2 May.

1902: lugs were added to the firing pin, in accordance with a patent granted to Mauser in May 1901. They aligned with shoulders in the unlocked bolt to prevent accidental firing.

1904: the first 'private' contracts were placed with Waffenfabrik Mauser AG and Deutsche Waffen- und Munitionsfabriken, for 290,000 and 210,000 rifles respectively. A perfected self-sprung brass-body charger was introduced in October, remaining standard issue until the end of the First World War. A Radfahrer-Gewehr 98 was introduced for cyclists, but was no more than a Gew.98 with the bolt-handle turned down into a depression in the stock-side.

1905: the change from the Patrone 88 to the improved S-Patrone, first mooted in 1903, was made with effect from 1 October. A change of sights was approved owing to the increase in velocity. The modified Lange sight was much taller than its predecessor, and its slider was greatly modified. Converted guns received a 2·5mm s above the chamber and on the barrel behind the back sight base.

1907: rearmament of virtually all regular units was completed. Most of the Reserve and active Landwehr had been re-equipped with Gewehre 98 by 1912.

1915: the Scharfschützen-Gewehr 98 was adopted to regularise the equipment of the snipers, who had previously been armed with an assortment of sporting rifles. It was mechanically identical with the standard Gew.98, but the bolt handle was bent down against a special stock recess, and two ring mounts held a 4 × Goerz or Zeiss telescope sight. The sight was offset to the left so that the magazine could still be loaded from a charger. The sight drums were graduated to 1,000 metres in 100-metre increments, except in Bavaria where they were graduated for 200, 400 and 600 metres only.

An auxiliary front sight (or 'Hilfskorn') was developed to allow accurate shooting at 100 metres, as the graduations on the post-1905 Lange sight began at 400. From 19 November, the marking disc on the butt of all rifles—infantry, sniper or otherwise—was replaced by two washers with a central hole connected by a short metal tube. The tip of the firing pin was inserted in the hole while the bolt was being dismantled, preventing damage that could promote a misfire.

1916: an emergency production programme began. Parts made by the many sub-contractors were assembled in the government factories by experienced armourers. Unfortunately, these guns required too much hand fitting for the system to be effectual.

Rifles that were successfully test-fired bore a large ☆ above the chamber, and are known as 'Stern-Gewehre'. Parts were rarely completely interchangeable.

1917: minor changes were made to simplify Gew.98 components to accelerate production, and the standards of finish began to deteriorate perceptibly. Bolts were browned, and differing stock woods were used.

The refined (but semi-experimental) Gewehr 98/17 appeared, with a tangent-leaf back sight, a cylindrical barrel, a stamped-steel bolt-cover and a hold-open. Five thousand were ordered from Simson of Suhl for trials, but the first batch was not forthcoming until March 1918.

1918: the Gewehr 98/18 (or 'Gewehr 18'), developed privately by Waffenfabrik Mauser, had a detachable box magazine, a bolt stop included in the trigger system, an improved stock and a new mechanical hold-open. It was too late to see war service. A few hundred were made for field trials, but never issued; they were apparently destroyed after the Armistice.

1920: rifles retained by the Reichswehr were given simple tangent-leaf back sights. The swivel-bearing barrel band was replaced; the 'Klammerfuss' under the butt was superseded by a lateral sling slot; and the bolt handles were turned down into a stock recess. Known as 'Karabiner 98b' to distinguish them from the former Kar.98 AZ, which had been renamed 'Karabiner 98a', these guns usually display 1920 or 1921 permission marks in addition to (or instead of) their original date-marks.

Model 1898

Carbine, first pattern: Karabiner 98.

Made by Königlich Gewehrfabrik, Erfurt, 1900–1.

Quantity: perhaps 3,000.

8 × 57mm, rimless.

Action: as Gew.98, above.
945mm overall, 3·33kg unladen.
435mm barrel, 4-groove rifling; RH, concentric.
Internal charger-loaded box magazine, 5 rounds.
Tangent sight graduated to 1,200 metres.
565 m/sec with Patrone 88.
No bayonet.

☆

1900: apparently adopted in June, this was a diminutive of the standard infantry rifle with a small Lange-pattern back sight, a spatulate bolt handle turned down against the stock, and a plain nose cap from which only the muzzle crown protruded. A hand guard ran from the back sight to the muzzle.

1902: owing to the lack of a bayonet lug, inhibiting use by the artillery and Train, the first Karabiner 98 was abandoned. Most of the surviving guns were converted in 1902–3 to form Zielkarabiner, chambering special 5mm primer-propelled practice ammunition.

Model 1898A

Carbine, second pattern: Karabiner 98A.
Made by Königlich Gewehrfabrik, Erfurt, 1902–5.
Quantity: perhaps 7,500.
8 × 57mm, rimless.
Action: as Gew.98, above.
945mm overall, 3·42kg unladen.
435mm barrel, 4-groove rifling; RH, concentric.
Internal charger-loaded box magazine, 5 rounds.
Tangent sight graduated to 1,200 metres.
795 m/sec with S-Patrone.
S.98 sword bayonet.

☆

1902: adopted to replace the Karabiner 98 on 26 February, this had a Gew.98-type nose cap assembly placed—curiously—well back from the muzzle. Consequently, the Kar.98A had a short wooden fore-end ahead of the nose cap. The nose cap was retained by a transverse slotted-head bolt instead of the customary spring, and carried the standard 4cm bayonet bar.

1904: experiments began to adapt the Kar.98A for the S-Patrone.

1905: the flash and excessive muzzle-blast of

the new cartridge in such a short-barrelled gun led to substitution by the Kar.98 AZ.

Models 1898 AZ and 98a

Carbine, third pattern: Karabiner 98 AZ und 98a.
Made by Königlich Gewehrfabrik, Danzig, 1912-4;
Königlich Gewehrfabrik, Erfurt, 1908–18; and Königlich bayerische Gewehrfabrik, Amberg, 1909–12.
Quantity: perhaps 1·5 million.
8 × 57mm, rimless.
Action: as Gew.98, above.
1,090mm overall, 3·71kg unladen.
590mm barrel, 4-groove rifling; RH, concentric.
Internal charger-loaded box magazine, 5 rounds.
Tangent-leaf sight graduated to 2,000 metres.
840 m/sec with S-Patrone.
S.98/05 sword bayonet.

☆

1906: trials began in June with about eight hundred long-barrel carbines, all but a hundred fitted with stacking rods.

1907: by midsummer, work had shown that recoil and muzzle-blast were more acceptable in the long-barrel guns than the short Kar.98A. However, a bayonet lug was demanded and changes were required in the stock.

1908: official adoption of the 'Karabiner 98 mit Aufplanz- und Zusammensetzvorrichtung' (Kar.98 AZ) occurred on 16 January. Its action was comparable to that of the Gew.98, but the external diameter of the receiver ring was noticeably smaller.

A full-length hand guard lay above the barrel, a simple tangent-leaf back sight was used, and a unique hinged nose cap appeared behind an ultra-short muzzle. The front sight had prominent protectors; a stacking rod protruded beneath the nose cap; and a hemispherical bolt handle turned down into the stock, its back face being chequered. The curve of the pistol grip was tightened to combat additional recoil. The standard bayonet had a 40cm fullered blade tapering gradually outwards towards the tip. Some were saw-backed for NCOs in standard German fashion.

1909: first issues were made to Prussian cavalry.

1910: issue was extended to the foot artillery.

1914: when war began, the Kar.98 AZ was being carried by cavalry; by foot artillerymen; by cyclists attached to infantry regiments, riflemen, sharpshooters and pioneers; by the independent machine-gunners; by the telegraphists and the field-telephonists; by airship and motor-transport units; and in parts of the Train.

1915: flash from the S-Patrone charred the back of the bayonet grips if the Kar.98 AZ was fired with the bayonet fixed, as was common in war. To prevent unnecessary damage, a modified bayonet with a sheet-steel flash guard along the back of the hilt was approved in the summer.

1920: no changes were made to the guns retained during the Reichswehr, though they were renamed 'Karabiner 98a' to distinguish them from the Kar.98b—a minor adaption of the full-length Gewehr 98.

Model 1898k

Short rifle: Karabiner 98k.
Made by Mauser-Werke AG, Oberndorf am Neckar, Württemberg (code 'S/42', '42', 'byf' or 'svw');
Mauser-Werke AG, Berlin-Borsigwalde ('S/243', '243' or 'ar'); Sauer & Sohn, Suhl ('S/147', '147' or 'ce'); Berlin-Lübecker Maschinenfabrik, Lübeck ('S/237' or '237'); Waffenwerk Brünn AG, Brno ('dot'); Fabrique Nationale d'Armes de Guerre, Herstal-lèz-Liége ('ch'); Feinmechanische Werke GmbH, Erfurt ('S/27', '27' and 'ax'); Gustloff-Werke, Weimar ('bcd'); and Steyr-Daimler-Puch AG, Steyr/Oberdonau ('660', 'bnz').
Quantity: about 11·5 million.
7·9 × 57mm, rimless.
Action: as Gew.98, above.
1,110mm overall, 3·92kg unladen.
600mm barrel, 4-groove rifling; RH, concentric.
Internal charger-loaded box magazine, 5 rounds.
Tangent-leaf sight graduated to 2,000 metres.
755 m/sec with sS-Patrone.
S.84/98 sword bayonet.

☆

1935: superficially resembling the full-length Kar.98b, the Karabiner 98k was recognisable by its reduced dimensions.

1940: standard apart from optical sights, the

Zielfernrohr-Karabiner 98 (or Zf.-Kar. 98) were selected for their accuracy. Early combinations used 4× Zf.39 sights made by Zeiss, Leitz, Goerz, Hensoldt and others; during the war, however, smaller 1·5× Zf.40, Zf.41, Zf.41/1 and Zf.41/2 sights became common.

Zf.39 had separate 'turret' mounts, on top of the receiver bridge and the chamber, or—more rarely—a one-piece twin ring mount clamped onto a rail on the left side of the receiver; 1·5× sights slid into a rail on the back sight, where they were held by a spring loaded catch.

A Gebirgsjäger-Karabiner 98k, with a steel plate on the left side of the butt, was made in small numbers in this period.

1941: Fallschirmjäger-Karabiner 98k (paratroop rifles) were developed for trials, work spilling over into 1942. One pattern had a hinged butt; another used a detachable barrel with an interrupted-screw joint ahead of the receiver. After the costly invasion of Crete, however, the faith of the military hierarchy in mass airborne assaults diminished greatly.

1942: manufacturing standards fell as the war progressed, creating the so-called Kriegsmodell. Distinguishing characteristics included stamped nose caps, barrel bands and butt-plates, crudely finished trigger-guards and thinly varnished stocks. Most guns—but by no means all—had laminated stocks, the result of trials that had stretched through the 1930s. Plywood laminates resisted warping better than the conventional one-piece patterns, did not require lengthy maturing, and were less wasteful.

1944: a few guns were fitted with the Zf.4 sight, developed for the Gew.43 (q.v.), in a rearward-slanting twin-ring monoblock. The Zf.4 was shorter and stubbier than the Zf.39.

Model 29/40

Short rifle: Gewehr 29/40.
Made by Steyr-Daimler-Puch AG, Steyr/Oberdonau
(code '660' or 'bnz').
Otherwise similar to Kar.98k—q.v.

☆

1940: this was a variation of the Steyr-made 'export Mauser', apparently issued largely to the Luftwaffe. The rifles were assembled from a combination of old parts, destined for the Steyr (or 'Steyr-Solothurn') 1929 and 1931-pattern export rifles, and cannibalised Polish Karabinek wz.29. The Gew.29/40 was identical with the Kar.98k apart from its distinctive nose cap, a hand guard stretching from the receiver ring to the nose cap, and a pointed Austrian-style pistol grip. Unlike the Austrian guns made prior to 1939, the 29/40 accepted the German bayonet.

Model 33/40

Short rifle: Gewehr 33/40.
Made by Waffenwerk Brünn AG, Brno
(code 'dot'), 1941–3.
Quantity: perhaps 50,000.
7·9 × 57mm, rimless.
Action: generally as Gew.98, above.
990mm overall, 3·78kg unladen.
490mm barrel, 4-groove rifling; RH, concentric.
Internal charger-loaded box magazine, 5 rounds.
Tangent-leaf sight graduated to 1,000 metres.
685 m/sec with sS-Patrone.
S.84/98 sword bayonet.

☆

1939: the invasion of Czechoslovakia provided the Germans with large numbers of the Gewehr 24(t), a designation that covered a selection of Kar.98k-type vz.24 and vz.24/30 short rifles made by Československá Zbrojovka in Brno. There were also a few vz.98/22 and vz.98/29 long rifles, approximating to the Karabiner 98b.

1940: officially adopted by the Wehrmacht on 16 October, the Gewehr 33/40 had originally been introduced as the 'Krátká četniká puška vz.33' for the Czechoslovakian police and the gendarmerie responsible for protecting the country's financial institutions. Production of the minuscule carbine continued under German supervision until emphasis switched to the Kar.98k; most Gew.33/40 were issued to the mountain troops (Gebirgsjäger) and had special reinforcing plates on the left side of the butt. There was a German-style nose cap, but a full-length hand guard ran forward from the front of the back sight. Unlike the original vz.33, the 33/40 accepted the S.84/98.

Model 1898 VK

The ultimate deterioration of the bolt-action rifles was the crude Volksgewehr or ''People's Rifle''. The earliest apparently dates from the autumn of 1944, though specifications had been circulated some months previously. The goal was a simplified weapon that could be made with a minimum of machine-time or raw material; the results included simplified Kar.98k developed by Mauser-Werke; Volkskarabiner 98 (VK.98) made by Steyr-Daimler-Puch (code 'bnz'), Walther ('qve') and others; and the Volksgewehre contributed by many anonymous machine-shops. VK.98 chambered the standard sS-Patrone and, excepting the final patterns, had conventional Mauser bolt actions.

Most VK.98 had half-stocks, fixed-notch back sights and roughly stepped or cylindrical barrels. However, though their finish was rough, they were not as poorly made as the Volksgewehre. Chambering full-power 7·9mm S-Patrone or the intermediate Pist.Patr.43, Volksgewehre have been credited to 'Erma-Werke', Erfurter Maschinenfabrik B. Geipel GmbH (code 'ayf'), but it is suspected that many other contractors were to have been involved had not the Second World War ended.

Most had stamped and welded receivers, and simple bolts with one or two locking lugs. They had plain cylindrical bolt handles made from bar-stock, roughly planed woodwork (often with separate butts and fore-ends), and could accept neither bayonets nor grenade launchers. Though Gew.43-pattern magazines were usually fitted, some of the last and crudest Volksgewehre were single-shot only.

No official orders governing the introduction of these Volkswaffen have ever been found. The HWaA was ordered to develop an effectual weapon, which is assumed to have been the Volkskarabiner 98, but it seems much more likely that the cruder guns were procured on a purely local basis.

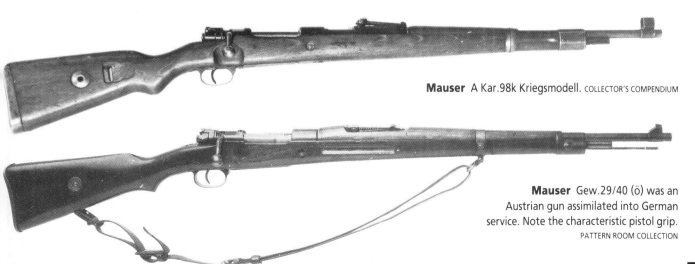

Mauser Musketry training during the Third Reich. A junior officer checks sight slignment. COLLECTOR'S COMPENDIUM

Mauser A Kar.98k Kriegsmodell. COLLECTOR'S COMPENDIUM

Mauser Gew.29/40 (ö) was an Austrian gun assimilated into German service. Note the characteristic pistol grip. PATTERN ROOM COLLECTION

MAUSER
LESSER PATTERNS: A–G

AUSTRIA-HUNGARY

By the early twentieth century, the performance of the arms industry was declining in the face of state-underwritten German exports and the success of the Mausers. Consequently, Österreichische Waffenfabriks-Gesellschaft was forced into a DWM-controlled cartel to assure a share of Mauser production; a new factory was built in Steyr in 1912–14, though no new orders for the army had been forthcoming.

M1914 rifle The army had decided to replace the Mannlichers with a Mauser rifle. Made by OEWG in Steyr, the Infanterie-Repetir-Gewehr M1914 was a standard 1898-type Mauser chambered for the rimmed 8 × 50mm cartridge. Distinguished by an Austrian-style stock with a sharply pointed pistol grip, the rifle was about 1,275mm overall, weighed 4·00kg, and had a 780mm barrel rifled with four grooves twisting to the right. Muzzle velocity was 620 m/sec with M1893 ball cartridges. The internal charger-loaded box magazine held five rounds and the leaf sight was graduated to about 2,000 metres. The M1895 bayonet was to be retained, as the barrel band and nose cap duplicated those of the Mannlicher.

¶ Only a few pilot models had been made when the First World War began. The project was immediately abandoned and the Mannlicher reinstated. Apart from ordering the new Steyr factory into full production, all that could be done was to sequester 1912-model Mauser rifles awaiting delivery to Colombia, Mexico and elsewhere, and to rehabilitate as many old guns as possible.

BOLIVIA

The receiver-top crest was a pastoral scene—including a llama and a wheatsheaf—within a circlet containing 'BOLIVIA' and nine stars. It was surmounted by a condor and backed by a trophy of arms and flags. Later guns were often simply marked 'EJERCITO DE BOLIVIA'.

M1895 rifle The earliest small-calibre Mauser was identical with the Mo.1891 Argentine rifle, except for markings, and was made by Ludwig Loewe & Co. in Berlin.

M1907 rifle and short rifle These were standard German 1904- or export-pattern guns, believed to have been supplied by Deutsche Waffen- und Munitionsfabriken.

M1950 rifle Made by Československá Zbrojovka of Brno in 1950–2, the 7·65 × 53mm 'Fusil Mauser Boliviano Serie B-50' was essentially a vz.24 short rifle, though the stock and stamped-sheet bands were those of the wartime Kar.98k. A single spring let into the right side of the fore-end sufficed to hold the band and the nose cap. The butt plate was a stamped 'bucket' pattern and the trigger guard and magazine floor-plate assembly were stamped from a single strip. Swivels lay under the band and butt. The B–50 was 1,100mm overall, weighed 3·89kg and had a 600mm barrel. Its tangent-leaf sight was graduated to 2,000 metres and a Czechoslovakian export-pattern bayonet was used.

Other guns Czech 7·65mm vz.24/26 short rifles were purchased in the late 1920s, and 7·65mm Standard-Modell guns were supplied from Mauser-Werke in the 1930s.

BRAZIL

These guns invariably had an enwreathed star-and-sword above their chambers, while 'ESTADOS UNIDOS DO BRASIL' often appeared on the receiver.

M1894 rifle Adopted after extensive tests, the 7 × 57mm Fusil Mo.1894 was virtually identical with the Spanish Mo.1893 (q.v.) excepting for a cylindrical bolt head. The magazine-follower tail was rounded so that the bolt shut on an empty chamber after the last round had been ejected. The guns were made by Ludwig Loewe & Co. of Berlin (1894–6), Deutsche Waffen- und Munitionsfabriken, Berlin, (1897-9?), and Fabrique Nationale d'Armes de Guerre, Herstal (1894–9). They were 1,235mm overall and weighed 4·03kg unladen. The 738mm barrels had four-groove rifling twisting to the right. The charger-loaded magazine held five rounds, the leaf sight was graduated to 2,000 metres, and the Mo.1894 knife bayonet could be mounted.

M1904 rifle Supplied by Deutsche Waffen- und Munitionsfabriken of Berlin in 1904–6, the 7 × 57mm Fusil Mo.1904 measured 1,249mm overall and weighed 4·00kg unladen. It embodied an 1898-type Mauser action and had a pistol-grip stock, but shared the nose cap of the M1894 so that the same bayonet could be used. Swivels lay under the barrel band and butt. Sights were originally identical with the Mo.1894 type.

M1907 carbine This 7 × 57mm weapon (Carabina Mo.1907), issued to cavalry and artillerymen, was supplied from Deutsche Waffen- und Munitionsfabriken in 1907–12. Little is known about the gun, which embodied the 1898-pattern action and has often been mistakenly identified as the 'Mo.1908'. The short pistol-grip stock had a hand guard running from the chamber ring to the single screw-clamping barrel band. The nose cap was basically that of the Mo.1894 rifle, with a bayonet lug on its underside. One swivel lay on the left side of the band, with the other on a short bar attached to the under-edge of the butt behind the pistol grip. A tangent-leaf sight graduated to 2,000 metres was used.

M1908 rifle The Fusil Mo.1908 was made by Deutsche Waffen- und Munitionsfabriken of Berlin in 1908–14, and by Fabryka Bronie w Radomu in 1935–8. 1,248mm overall and weighing 4·03kg, the rifle had a standard 1898-type action and a pistol-grip stock with a hand guard running from the chamber ring to the solitary barrel band; the German 'H' type nose cap accepted a bayonet with a muzzle ring. The tangent-leaf sight was graduated to 2,000 metres. Swivels lay under the band and butt, and a washer was held in the right side of the butt by a slotted-head screw. Some guns have been seen with the DWM name and the Oberndorf address, which may suggest that work was sub-contracted to Mauser.

M1908 short rifle Virtually identical with the full-length gun, apart from dimensions, this was generally found with the bolt handle turned down toward the stock.

Other patterns Substantial numbers of FN-made Mle.1922 7mm short rifles were supplied in 1923–4. They were followed by 15,000 Czech vz.24 short rifles in 1931, then by an order for 100,500 Czech-made 7mm vz.08/33 and vz.12/33 guns in 1938. The last order had not been completed when the Germans entered Czechoslovakia in 1939.

CHILE

Adopted to replace a selection of obsolescent Comblain, Winchester and Mannlicher rifles, these Mausers may be identified by chamber crests of a star on a horizontally divided shield supported by a huemal (Andes deer) and a condor. They were also marked 'MAUSER CHILENO' on the left side of the receiver.

M1895 rifle The first examples of the 'Fusil Mauser Chileno Mo.1895' were supplied by Ludwig Loewe, though others came from Deutsche Waffen- und Munitionsfabriken in 1897–1900. They were 1,232mm overall, weighed 3·92kg, and had 738mm barrels rifled with four grooves twisting to the right. Muzzle velocity was 823 m/sec with standard ball cartridges. The internal charger-loaded box magazine held five rounds and the tangent-leaf sight was graduated to 2,000 metres. The rifles were identical with the Mo.1893 Spanish Mauser rifle excepting for conventional cylindrical-head bolts, and the tail of the magazine follower was rounded so that the action closed automatically on an empty chamber. An auxiliary shoulder on the receiver behind the bolt handle was intended to act as a last-ditch safety should the action fail on firing. The stock had a straight wrist, a hand guard ran forward from the receiver ring to the barrel band, and the nose cap bore a lug for the Mo.1895 bayonet. Swivels lay on the band and butt.

M1895 short rifle The Mosqueton Mauser Chileno Mo.1895 was identical with the rifle, excepting for length, but the bolt handle turned down toward the stock.

M1895 carbine The Carabina Mauser Chilena Mo.1895 was only 940mm long, with a 465mm barrel, and weighed about 3·4kg. It had a standard nose cap and could accept a bayonet. The swivels lay on the left side of the band and on the left side of the butt behind the wrist.

M1904 rifle The Fusil Mauser Chileno Mo.1904 was supplied only in small numbers by Deutsche Waffen- und Munitionsfabriken in 1904–6. It is believed to have been a standard 1898-pattern export Mauser with a pistol-grip stock and a nose cap adapted to take the standard knife bayonet. Markings would distinguish it from a Brazilian rifle.

M1935 short rifle These were 7·65mm standard Mausers purchased in the 1930s.

CHINA

M1895 rifle An unknown quantity of 7 × 57mm guns is said to have been ordered by the government from Waffenfabrik Mauser AG about 1896, though the period of delivery is no longer known. The guns seem to have duplicated the Chilean rifle described above, but may have borne ideographs on the receiver. They were 1,232mm overall, weighed 3·92kg unladen, and had 738mm barrels. Their tangent-leaf sights were graduated to 2,000 metres and a variant of the Spanish Mo.1893-type sword bayonet is said to have been used.

M1906 rifle A few 7mm-calibre rifles were purchased from Germany for field trials. They were standard 1898-pattern guns (1,250mm overall, 3·88kg) with the 1904-type heavyweight cocking piece, a tangent-leaf back sight, and a hand guard stretching forward from the receiver ring to the barrel band. Sling swivels lay beneath the band and on the under-edge of the butt behind the pistol grip. The simple nose cap anchored a short attachment bar, requiring a bayonet with a conventional muzzle ring.

M1907 rifle The Chinese acquired a selection of rifles—including a Mauser, a Haenel and a Mannlicher-Schönauer—chambered for a unique 6·8 × 57mm cartridge, similar to the 7mm pattern but with a shallower neck taper. The guns were all clearly marked '6,8MM MOD.07'. However, the experiments had not resolved when the 1911 revolution intervened. Rifles issued in China after 1920 almost always chambered 7·9 × 57mm ammunition.

Model 21 short rifle This 7·9 × 57mm Mauser is enigmatic, said to have been made by Kwantung arsenal in 1932–7 for the Kuomintang (North China Army). Copied from the FN Mle.30, it was identifiable by poor quality workmanship and Chinese markings on the receiver. The hand guard from the receiver ring to the nose cap distinguished it from the Chiang Kai-Shek rifle. A typical example was 1,108mm long, had a 600mm barrel, and weighed 3·92kg. Its back sight elevated to 2,000 metres.

Chiang Kai-Shek short rifle Several million of these copies of the Standard Modell Mauser were made by state arsenals prior to 1949. Work is believed to have begun shortly before the Sino-Japanese war, as some guns have been seen dated '25-11'—November 1936, counting from the revolution of 1911. Though displaying a German-style back sight and hand guard, quality was far poorer than a genuine Mauser; stocks were roughly shaped, and a crude groove was cut into the fore-end.

Other patterns FN supplied 24,220 Mle.24 and Mle.30 7·9mm short rifles in 1930–4, followed by 164,500 more Mle.30 in 1937–9. The Chinese also acquired Czech-made vz.98/22 rifles in the 1920s, and then about 100,000 7·92mm vz.24 (mostly) short rifles in the mid 1930s. Mauser 'Standard Modell' guns followed in 1935–7, with banner marks over the chamber and B-prefix numbers.

CONGO FREE STATE

According to Korn's book *Mauser-Gewehre und Mauser-Patente* (1908), Mauser supplied 7·65 × 53mm 1894-type rifles to arm the European elements of the army of this Belgian-sponsored state. It is not yet known if distinctive markings were applied.

COLOMBIA

These bore either 'Ejercito de Colombia' or the national crest on the chamber top. Surmounted by a condor and set on two pairs of national flags, the shield contained a pomegranate and two cornucopiae above a Liberty Cap, two sailing ships and a depiction of the isthmus of Panama.

Pre-1914 patterns Small numbers of Loewe-made Mo.1891 (Argentine pattern) and DWM-made 'Mo.1904' rifles were acquired, the latter being identical with the Brazilian guns of the same year. Ordered from Österreichische Waffenfabriks-Gesellschaft shortly before the outbreak of the First World War, the Mo.1912 was identical with the Mexican pattern (q.v.). Hostilities began before work was completed, the guns being diverted to the Austro-Hungarian army.

Later patterns About five thousand Czech 'vz/12 mex.' 7mm short rifles with 556mm barrels were acquired in 1929, followed by a few 7mm Mo.1929 short rifles from Steyr-Solothurn AG. Sizeable quantities of Mle.24/30 short rifles came from Fabrique Nationale in the early 1930s, plus some similar vz.24 guns from Československá Zbrojovka. Many of the Herstal- and Brno-made weapons were converted to ·30–06 in the early 1950s, when FN supplied an unknown number of new rifles chambered for the American cartridge. A typical ·30–06 rifle displayed a large '·30' on top of the chamber, with 'R. FAMAGUE' and the date (e.g., '1953') on the left side of the receiver. The marks showed that it was converted ('Reformado') by Fabrica de Material de Guerra in Bogota.

COSTA RICA

The chamber-crest was a shield depicting nine stars, above an isthmus of three volcanoes separating two sailing ships.

M1895 rifle This virtual duplicate of the 1895-type Chilean rifle was purchased from Ludwig Loewe & Co. (1895–6) and then Deutsche Waffen- und Munitionsfabriken (c.1897–1900). The quantities involved were small—perhaps no more than 10,000—and survivors are rarely encountered.

M1910 rifle Made by Waffenfabrik Mauser AG of Oberndorf am Neckar in 1911–14 and chambered for the 7 × 57mm rimless cartridge, it was 1,240mm overall, had a 740mm barrel and weighed about 3·97kg. Virtually identical with the Gew.98, the guns had 2,000-metre tangent-leaf sights and standard 'export' stock arrangements with a hand guard running forward from the receiver ring to the band. The simple nose cap had a bayonet lug on its underside. The most obvious feature, however, was the shrouded bolt-face enveloping the case rim, patented in Germany in February 1898 but rarely used on service weapons. The face of the chamber had a recess for the extractor, necessitating precise machining and reassembly after repair. Altering the bolt forced Mauser to omit the small lug on the bolt-edge that supported the cartridge case during the feed stroke and extraction.

Other patterns FN supplied 7mm Mle.24 short rifles in the 1930s.

DOMINICAN REPUBLIC

Some ex-Brazilian Mo.1908 rifles and short rifles were acquired by the Dominicans in

the early 1950s. They were refinished in the government arms factory in San Cristobal, but were soon displaced by surplus US weapons and sold on the commercial market. Brazilian markings were ground away and a new identifier added to the left side of the receiver—'ARMERIA F.A. REP. DOM.' with a date and a new serial number.

ECUADOR

These guns were generally marked 'EJERCITO DEL EQUATOR' or 'EJERCITO EQUATORIANO' on the receiver. The chamber-top crest comprised an oval landscape featuring the Chimborazo volcano rising, below a shining sun, out of a sea on which a steamer rode. The device was surmounted by the obligatory condor, had a fasces at its base, and was backed by two pairs of national flags plus a wreath.

Pre-1914 patterns The earliest Mausers were Argentine-type 7·65 × 53mm Mo.1891 (q.v.), followed by 7·65mm 'Mo.1907' (1904 Brazilian-type) rifles and a handful of carbines of unknown designation.

Later patterns Substantial quantities of Czechoslovakian 7·65mm vz.24 short rifles and vz.12/33 carbines were purchased during the 1930s, while Fabrique Nationale supplied additional short rifles in the 1940s.

EL SALVADOR

These guns bore a chamber crest of a triangular seascape with five volcanoes, beneath a staff supporting a Liberty Cap on a sunburst. The device was backed by five national flags and usually lay on a wreath. The legend 'REPÚBLICA DE EL SALVADOR' was also to be found.

Pre-1914 patterns The earliest Mausers were Chilean-style Mo.1895 rifles in 7 × 57mm, apparently purchased from DWM in about 1900.

Later patterns Some 7mm vz.12/33 short rifles were acquired from Československá Zbrojovka in the early 1930s.

ESTONIA

Czechoslovakian 'L'-model short rifles were purchased in 1931, the guns apparently being supplied with Austrian-style M1895 knife bayonets. Their chambering may have been for the British ·303 rimmed round, substantial quantities of which had been sold to Estonia in the early 1920s.

ETHIOPIA

Most of these Mausers will be found with the crowned cypher of Haile Selassie I in Amharic letters on the chamber-top, surrounded by a wreath of a grape-vine and an ear of wheat. They may also display a

Lion of Judah property mark. FN supplied 25,000 Mle.24 Mauser short rifles and carbines in 1933–5, and similar quantities of 'Standard-Modell' Mausers—all used as the 'M1933'—were purchased in the same era.

¶ Three contracts were placed with Mauser-Werke in 1933, 1934 and 1935. The earliest, perhaps for a few hundred rifles only, was identified by A-prefix serial numbers and the elaborate chamber crest. The second order was larger, but the pattern of the numbers is not known; the third order, however, was taken from the B-prefix commercial series, displayed five-digit numbers, and bore the Mauser banner trademark on the receiver ring. The Lion of Judah lay on the barrel between the back-sight base and the receiver.

FRANCE

A few Mle.30 short rifles were purchased from Fabrique Nationale in the mid 1930s, apparently to undertake trials against the experimental MAS 36 (q.v.).

M1898 short rifle Production of a slightly modified Kar.98k (see 'Germany' in the main directory) continued in the Mauser factory after the end of the Second World War, guns being destined for French police units but subsequently returned to West German border guards. They were similar to the so-called Kriegsmodell, with bucket-shape butt plates and crude sheet-steel bands/nose caps held to the fore-end with wood screws. The most recognisable feature was the stacking rod beneath the muzzle, where the cleaning rod would normally lie; the unique hexagonal extension of the rod was threaded to screw into the fore-end face.

¶ In 1946, the French bowed to international pressure and ceased production altogether at the beginning of May. However, many ex-German Kar.98k served in Indo-China into the early 1950s.

GERMANY

M1882 rifle The experimental Infanterie-Repetier-Gewehr C/1882 was developed from the Serbian M78/80 and patented in March 1882. It was 1,345mm overall, weighed 4·58kg unladen, and had an 855mm barrel rifled with four grooves. A tube magazine lay under the barrel, the leaf sight was graduated to 1,600 metres and the 1871-type bayonet could be mounted.

¶ Mauser delivered 2,000 C/82 rifles in the summer of 1882 for trials with garrison battalions in Darmstadt, Königsberg and Spandau. The guns incorporated many 1871-pattern components, but had new receivers. Testing revealed that changes were required to ensure the rifle was

durable enough for service. Premature magazine ignition was cured by developing a new flat-nose bullet and seating the primers more deeply. The result was the Gew.71/84 (q.v.).

M1896 rifle This experimental Mauser seems to have been ordered to enable trials to be undertaken with small-calibre ammunition, as its action bore more resemblance to the 1894-pattern Swedish Mauser rifle than the Gew.88/97. At least 2,185 were made in Oberndorf in 1896–7.

¶ The guns had a non-rotating extractor, a shrouded bolt head, an auxiliary locking lug on the underside of the bolt body, and an under-cut extractor to prevent double loading. The straight-wrist stocks were retained by a single sprung band, and a small nose cap had a bayonet lug on its right side. A half-length cleaning rod was normally carried in the fore-end; swivels lay under the band and on the under-edge of the butt; and a hand guard ran from the receiver ring to the band. The back sight was carried above the hand guard on a short sleeve around the barrel.

¶ A typical 6 × 58mm example measured 1,250mm overall and weighed 3·63kg unladen. Its 740mm barrel had six-groove concentric rifling and the tangent-leaf sight was graduated to 2,000 metres.

¶ The earliest guns cocked as the bolt was closed, but later examples cocked on opening. The effort was eased by increasing the diameter of the bolt behind the handle to lengthen the cocking-cam track.

¶ Trials eventually resolved in favour of the existing 8mm cartridge. As Mauser had improved the basic rifle, and as the German army wanted refinements of its own, the 1896-type gun was abandoned. It is highly likely that some were rebarrelled and re-stocked, as specimens have been reported in 7·65 × 53mm and 8 × 57mm.

GREECE

These Mausers generally have a chamber mark in the form of a crowned shield bearing a short-armed cross. This appears above the designation, e.g., 'ϒΠ 1930'. Though normally reliant on Mannlicher-Schönauers, the Greek army bought a few 7·9mm Mle.30 FN short rifles in the 1930s.

GUATEMALA

Guatemalan rifles usually displayed a chamber-top crest comprising a quetzal bird perched on a scroll reading 'Libertad de 15 de Set. de 1821' (liberation day), with crossed swords and rifles within a laurel wreath. It was used on Czech 7mm vz.12/33 short rifles acquired in the 1930s.

pre 1909

post 1909

TRADEMARKS

MAUSER CONTRACT PATTERNS

Waffenfabrik Mauser made large quantities of rifles for export prior to 1914, but most of these are considered in the country-by-country registers; their history was intertwined with the guns made by the other participants in the original 1897-vintage cartel.

During the 1920s, however, aware of the export successes of Fabrique Nationale and Československá Zbrojovka, Mauser-Werke AG began development of a comparable short rifle. The work was completed in the late 1920s and assembly of components made secretly in Oberndorf began in a factory in Kreuzlingen, Switzerland, in 1929–30. Overt production did not begin until the last restrictions of the Treaty of Versailles had been repudiated in 1933. By this time, Mauser's rivals had established an unassailable dominance on the export markets.

The earliest orders seem to have been placed by China, though Paraguay and Ethiopia were also keen. The most important variation was the so-called 'Postal Rifle' (Reichspost-Gewehr), purchased by the German mail service. This was practically a Kar.98k, but had a narrow band and the nose cap was pinned to the fore-end instead of being held by a spring. Genuine Reichspost guns were marked appropriately on the side of the butt, but the term was also used to camouflage sales of rifles to paramilitary formations of the SA and SS.

A few small-scale orders were forthcoming throughout the 1930s from Ethiopia, China and Portugal, but, after 1934, the bulk of Mauser rifles went to the Wehrmacht. So important were the early military deliveries that supplies to the paramilitary ceased, forcing the SA, so it is said, to acquire rifles from Fabrique Nationale.

Model 1933

Offered as a short rifle or carbine:
Mauser Standard-Modell.
Made by Mauser-Werke AG, Oberndorf am Neckar, 1932–44.
Quantity: 235,000?

7·9 × 57mm, rimless.
Turning-bolt action with two lugs on the bolt head locking into the receiver behind the chamber and a safety lug opposing the bolt handle.
DATA FOR A REPRESENTATIVE CARBINE
1,056mm overall, 3·85kg unladen.
550mm barrel, 4-groove rifling; RH, concentric.
Internal charger-loaded box magazine, 5 rounds.
Tangent-leaf sight graduated to 2,000 metres.
855 m/sec with standard ball ammunition.
Standard export-pattern
sword bayonet.

☆

1933: export-pattern Mausers were essentially similar to the 1924-model short rifles offered by Fabrique Nationale and Československá Zbrojovka. However, unless otherwise specified by the customer, they had a German-type exchangeable-bed back sight and a hand guard running from the front of the back sight base only as far as the barrel band. A German 'H' type nose cap was fitted. Most short rifles had a grasping groove on the stock, but this was customarily omitted from the carbines. The bolt handles of the latter were generally turned downwards: most rifle examples were straight.

1940: manufacture stopped for the duration of the war though, curiously, guns were still assembled for commercial sale. The postwar Allied CIOS report indicates that 8,800 'sporting rifles' were produced in 1940–4.

MEXICO

These rifles invariably bear the national arms above the chamber. Inspired by Aztec legend, these show an eagle—perched on a cactus—with a snake in its beak. The marks were usually accompanied by REPÚBLICA MEXICANA or R M.

Model 1895

Infantry rifle and cavalry carbine: Fusil Mauser Mexicano y Carabina Mauser Mexicana Mo.1895.
Made by Ludwig Loewe & Co., Berlin (1895–6); and Deutsche Waffen- und Munitionsfabriken, Berlin (1897–1901).

Quantity: 50,000 rifles and 10,000 carbines?
7 × 57mm, rimless.
Turning-bolt action with two lugs on the bolt head locking into the receiver behind the chamber.
DATA FOR RIFLE
1,234mm overall, 3·97kg unladen.
738mm barrel, 4-groove rifling; RH, concentric.
Internal charger-loaded box magazine, 5 rounds.
Leaf sight graduated to 2,000 metres.
730 m/sec with standard ball cartridges.
Mo.1895 sword bayonet.

☆

1895: this rifle was adopted after extensive tests, proving to be simpler and more durable than the 1893-model Mondragon. The contract was placed with Ludwig Loewe & Co., but only a few guns were made before work was passed to DWM at the beginning of 1897. The rifle was virtually identical with the Spanish Mo.1893 (q.v.), but had a normal cylindrical bolt head.

Adopted at the same time as the Mo.1895 rifle—for cavalry and artillerymen—the carbine was simply a shortened gun with a small back sight graduated to 1,400 metres, the bolt handle turned down against the stock, and the sling mounts on the left side of the butt and barrel band. It was 953mm overall, had a 465mm barrel, and weighed 3·40kg unladen.

Model 1902

Infantry rifle: Fusil Mauser Mexicano Mo.1902.
Made by Deutsche Waffen- und Munitionsfabriken, Berlin, 1902–4; and Österreichische Waffenfabriks-Gesellschaft, Steyr, 1906–7.
Quantity: 80,000?
7 × 57mm, rimless.
Turning-bolt action with two lugs on the bolt head locking into the receiver behind the chamber and a safety lug opposing the bolt handle.
1,234mm overall, 4·01kg unladen.
738mm barrel, 4-groove rifling; RH, concentric.
Internal charger-loaded box magazine, 5 rounds.
Leaf sight graduated to 2,000 metres.
730 m/sec with standard ball cartridges.
Mo.1895 sword bayonet.

☆

Mauser Pictured in Karlsruhe/Baden in October 1918, shortly before the end of the First World War these German soldiers—from Eisenbahn-Regiment Nr.4?—pose with standard Kar.98 AZ.
COLLECTOR'S COMPENDIUM

Mauser The breech of a typical Kar.98k, made by Gustloff-Werke in 1943.
PATTERN ROOM COLLECTION

Mauser Men of I. Ersatz-Bataillon, Füsilier-Regiment Prinz Heinrich von Preussen Nr.35, pictured in a studio in Brandenburg an der Havel in November 1915. They carry a mixture of Gew.88 and Gew.98.
COLLECTOR'S COMPENDIUM

Mauser Part of the Oberndorf factory, photographed in 1930.
ROLF GMINDER

1902: adopted to supersede the Mo.1895, this embodied an 1898-type action with a non-rotating extractor and a gas-shield on the bolt plug. The rifle was otherwise similar to its predecessors, with a straight-wrist stock and a simple nose cap with a lug for the standard Mo.1895 knife bayonet.

Model 1907

Infantry rifle: Fusil Mauser Mexicano Mo.1907.
Made by Österreichische
Waffenfabriks-Gesellschaft, Steyr, 1907–10.
7 × 57mm, rimless.
Otherwise generally as Mo.1902 (above) excepting:
1,239mm overall, 4·05kg unladen.
Mo.1907 sword bayonet.

☆

1907: ordered in Austria-Hungary, this was mechanically similar to the earlier Mo.1902. However, it had a pistol-grip stock and a German 'H'-style nose cap. The attachment bar lay beneath the barrel, forcing a change in bayonet.
1925*: the original back sight leaf was replaced by a 1,800 metre pattern after the introduction of heavy-ball ammunition suited to rifles and machine guns alike.

Model 1910

Infantry rifle: Fusil Mauser Mexicano Mo.1910.
Made by Fábrica Nacional de Armas,
Mexico City, c.1913–35.
Quantity: about 44,000.
Otherwise generally as Mo.1902 (above).

☆

1910: plans were readied to make the first indigenous Mauser-type rifle, though they were interrupted by revolution in 1911 and it is believed that the first series-production guns were not forthcoming until about 1913. The rifles duplicated the preceding Mo.1902, with 1898-type actions, straight-wrist stocks, and nose caps adapted for the original knife bayonet. They bore the factory name above an elaborate version of the national arms over the chamber, adding a wreath of laurel to the eagle-on-cactus

motif; MEXICO D.F. and the date of manufacture lay below the wreath.
1925*: introduction of heavy-ball ammunition for rifles and machine-guns caused back-sights to be revised to 1,800 metres.

Model 1912

Infantry rifle: Fusil Mauser Mexicano Mo.1912.
Made by Österreichische
Waffenfabriks-Gesellschaft, Steyr, 1913–14.
7 × 57mm, rimless.
Otherwise generally as Mo.1902 (above) excepting:
1,242mm overall, 4·11kg unladen.
Tangent-leaf sight graduated to 2,000 metres.
Mo.1907 sword bayonet.

☆

1912: tortuous progress with the FNA-made Mo.1910 forced the Mexican government to order another batch of rifles from Austria. The Mo.1912 had a large-ring receiver, a pistol-grip stock, a tangent-leaf back sight, and an 'H'-type nose cap taking a bayonet with the muzzle ring close to the hilt-back.
1914: deliveries had hardly started when the First World War cut supplies. Many Mexican rifles were issued to Austro-Hungarian units, survivors being altered to 7.9mm in 1919–20 for the Kingdom of Serbs, Croats and Slovenes.

Model 1924

Short rifle: Fusil Mauser Mexicano Mo.1924.

☆

This designation included about 25,000 Mle.24 short rifles purchased from Fabrique Nationale in 1926–7, and a few vz.12 carbines and vz.24 short rifles acquired from Československá Zbrojovka in the 1930s. The guns chambered standard Mexican 7 × 57mm ammunition.

Model 1936

Short rifle: Fusil Mauser Mexicano Mo.1936.
Made by Fábrica Nacional de Armas,
Mexico City, 1936–51.
7 × 57mm, rimless.

Turning-bolt action with two lugs on the bolt head locking into the receiver behind the chamber and a safety lug opposing the bolt handle.
1,090mm overall, 3·78kg unladen.
590mm barrel, 4-groove rifling; RH, concentric.
Internal charger-loaded box magazine, 5 rounds.
Tangent-leaf sight graduated to 1,500 metres.
About 715 m/sec with standard ball cartridges.
Mo.1936 sword bayonet.

☆

1936: adopted to replace the Mo.1910, this combined an 1898-type Mauser action with the bands, nose cap and cocking-piece of the US M1903 Springfield rifle. It had a pistol-grip stock with the fore-end swelling slightly ahead of the magazine floor plate, and the bolt handle was turned downward. American-style swivels lay on the butt and barrel band, with an open stacking swivel on the nose cap. The top of the chamber displayed an elaborate Mexican Arms.

Model 1954

Short rifle: Fusil Mauser Mexicano Mo.1954.
Made by Fábrica Nacional de Armas,
Mexico City, 1954–5.
Quantity: at least 7,500
·30–06, rimless.
Action: as Mo.1936, above.
About 1,120mm overall, 4·37kg unladen.
610mm barrel, 4-groove rifling; RH, concentric.
Internal charger-loaded box magazine, 5 rounds.
Tangent-ramp sight graduated to 1,000 metres?
About 845 m/sec with US M2 Ball cartridges.
Mo.1936 sword bayonet.

☆

1954: a sudden influx of war-surplus US weapons, particularly M1 Garands, persuaded the Mexicans to adapt the basic Mo.1936 to fire ·30–06 cartridges. Alterations to the face of the chamber allowed the longer cartridges to pass into the modified magazines. The resulting rifles, often using receivers salvaged from earlier guns (dated prior to 1950), had laminated stocks and the trigger guards and magazine floor plates made from a single continuous stamping. The back sight was an aperture pattern on the

Mauser The 7mm 'vz.12 Mex.' carbine. LES FIELD

Mauser Czechoslovakian-made vz.98/29 rifles were supplied to Persia in the 1930s. LES FIELD

Mauser The vz.98/29 musketoon, widely used in Persia. LES FIELD receiver bridge, inspired by the US M1903A4.

1955: faced with the increasing availability of semi-automatics, the Mexicans abandoned the ·30–06 Mauser after few had been assembled.

PERSIA (IRAN)

Persian guns had an elaborate chamber-top mark comprising a stylised scimitar-wielding lion on a sunburst, beneath the distinctive Pahlavi Crown, surrounded by a wreath of laurel and oak leaves. The earliest rifles seem to have been of Chilean Mo.1895 pattern, but pre-1914 Mauser records give no other details.

Models 1310 and 1317

Rifles and short rifles.
Made by Československá Zbrojovka, Brno, 1931–9.
7·9 × 57mm, rimless.
Turning-bolt action, with two lugs on the bolt head locking into the receiver behind the chamber and a safety lug opposing the bolt handle.
DATA FOR SHORT RIFLE
965mm overall, 3·78kg unladen.
455mm barrel, 4-groove rifling; RH, concentric.
Internal charger-loaded box magazine, 5 rounds.
Tangent-leaf sight graduated to 2,000 metres.
840 m/sec with standard ball cartridges.
Standard vz.23-type sword bayonet.

☆

1931: 80,000 vz.98/29 rifles and 10,000 vz.98/29 short rifles (carbines) were ordered. The guns chambered the 7·92mm cartridge and were apparently known as 'M1310', suitable Arabic marks appearing on the receiver.
1938: an order for about 100,000 vz.98/29 (or 'M1317') rifles—including some vz.24 short rifles—was agreed, but had not been completed when the Germans invaded Czechoslovakia.

Model 1328

Short rifle.
Made by the state rifle factory, Mosalsalsasi.
7·9 × 57mm, rimless.
Action: as M1310, above.

970mm overall, 3·90kg unladen.
460mm barrel, 4-groove rifling; RH, concentric.
Internal charger-loaded box magazine, 5 rounds.
Tangent-leaf sight graduated to 1,500 metres?
About 725 m/sec with standard ball cartridges.
Standard vz.23-type sword bayonet.

☆

1949: made in an arms factory erected with Czechoslovakian assistance, this was a modified vz.98/29 carbine. The barrel-band and nose cap were stamped from steel sheet, and retained by a single spring let into the fore-end. A sling slot, cut through the butt in German fashion, could be used in conjunction with a fixed bar on the left side of the barrel band. A sling ring was also fitted through the front web of the trigger guard.

Other guns

Approximately 10,000 vz.24 short rifles were acquired from Československá Zbrojovka in the early 1930s, together with some Mle.24 short rifles from Fabrique Nationale.

POLAND

The Poles, who inherited large numbers of ex-German guns, began production of 1898-type long and short rifles in the rifle factory in Warsaw after the end of the First World War. Production had moved to Radom by the late 1920s. Guns usually had a large displayed eagle on the chamber-top above the maker's marks.

Model 1898

Rifle and short rifle: Pusek a Karabinek wz.98.

☆

Made by the Polish government rifle factory (Panstwowa Fabryka Karabinow) in Warsaw, c.1923–9, these were simply copies of the German Gew.98 and Kar.98 AZ—apparently built on ex-German machinery from Danzig arsenal. The full-length rifle, made only in small numbers, was difficult to distinguish from the German pattern; the short rifle, however, had a sling bar on the left side of the stock in addition

to swivels under the band and on the under-edge of the butt. A distinctive stacking rod with a squared elbow protruded from the nose-cap extension beneath the fore-end. Production seems to have exceeded 125,000.

Model 1929

Short rifle: Karabinek wz.1929.
Made by Fabryka Broni w Polska, Radom, 1929–40.
7·9 × 57mm, rimless.
Turning-bolt action with two lugs on the bolt head locking into the receiver behind the chamber and a safety lug opposing the bolt handle.
1,102mm overall, 4·09kg unladen.
600mm barrel, 4-groove rifling; RH, concentric.
Internal charger-loaded box magazine, 5 rounds.
Tangent-leaf sights graduated to 2,000 metres.
755 m/sec with German sS-Patrone.
wz.29 sword bayonet

☆

1929: inspired by the FN Mle.24 and the Czechoslovakian vz.24 Mauser short rifles, this was adopted to supersede the wz.98.
1930: production began in the newly equipped Radom arms factory. The gun was very similar to the Brno-made vz.24, with the barrel band retained by a transverse bolt and a hand guard running from the elongated receiver ring to the nose cap. A cleaning rod lay under the muzzle the front-sight block was continued upward to protect the sight blade, and the bolt handle turned down into a recess cut in the side of the stock. Swivels lay on the underside of the butt and under the fore-end. A sling bar was let into the left side of the butt, where a hollow washer facilitated dismantling the firing mechanism.
1940: the wz.29 was the standard infantry weapon when the Germans invaded Poland. However, work stopped immediately and never resumed—unlike affairs in Czechoslovakia.

Very few ex-Polish rifles seem to have been issued to front-line Wehrmacht units, though some were doubtless held in reserve. However, many of the short rifles were subsequently converted in Austria to Gew.29/40 standards (see 'Germany').

This view of the Swiss arms factory in Bern, taken early in the twentieth century, is typical of the mass-production facilities of its period. COLLECTOR'S COMPENDIUM

SERBIA

1879: trials began to find a rifle for the army. It soon became clear that the 1871-type Mauser was likely to win once changes made by the trials commission had been made.

1880: the perfected trials rifle operated similarly to the German service rifle, but had a neater trigger guard and a rail extending back from the receiver above the wrist. This prevented the cocking piece from rotating, but also prevented the firer placing his thumb comfortably over the wrist. A small coil spring was added around the safety-catch spindle, allowing the cocking piece to be dismantled without tools, and an extractor/ejector was fitted to the bolt head.

Model 1878/80

Infantry rifle.
Made by Waffenfabrik Mauser, Oberndorf, 1881–7.
Quantity: 120,000.
10·15 × 63mm, rimmed
Turning-bolt action locked by the bolt-guide rib abutting the receiver ahead of the bridge.
1,288mm overall, 4·47kg unladen.
780mm barrel, 4-groove rifling; RH, concentric.
Leaf sight graduated to 2,025 metres.
510 m/sec with ball cartridges.
M1880 sword bayonet.

☆

1881: on 14 February, Mauser won a contract for the M78/80 rifle, colloquially known as the Mauser-Koká or Mauser-Milanovič. Major Koká Milanovič of the arsenal in Kragujevač had been responsible for a number of new features, the most important (but least obvious) being rifling grooves whose width reduced from breech to muzzle. This was apparently intended to improve obturation, but was a needless manufacturing complication.

The M78/80 was long and clumsy, typical of its era, and had a straight-wrist stock. There were two screw-clamped bands and a nose cap with a bayonet lug on the right side. Swivels lay on the underside of the butt and on the rear band. A cleaning rod lay under the barrel.

1907: the first of many surviving guns was converted to chamber the standard 7mm round and renamed 'M80/7C'.

Model 1885

Cavalry carbine.
Made by Waffenfabrik Mauser,
Oberndorf am Neckar, 1885–7.
Quantity: 4,000
10·15 × 63mm, rimmed.
Action: as M1878/80, above.
955mm overall, 3·75kg unladen.
465mm barrel, 4-groove rifling; RH, concentric.
Tube magazine in fore-end, 5 rounds.
Leaf sight graduated to 1,200 metres?
465 m/sec with ball cartridges.
No bayonet.

☆

1885*: the first modern magazine carbines were purchased from Mauser. Mechanically similar to the contemporaneous M1871/84 German infantry rifle, they had the extended cocking-piece rail at the back of the receiver. The Milanovič decreasing-width rifling was abandoned. One-piece stocks, extending to the muzzle, had an unusually long wrist; a single sprung band and a simple nose cap were used.

Models 1880/6C and 1880/7C

Infantry rifles.
Converted in the state arsenal, Kraguyevač, 1907–12.
7 × 57mm, rimless.
Action: see notes.
1,288mm overall, 4·52kg unladen.
780mm barrel, 4-groove rifling; RH, concentric.
Integral charger-loaded box magazine, 5 rounds.
Leaf sight graduated to 2,000 metres.
About 710 m/sec with ball cartridges.
M1880 sword bayonet.

☆

1906: the first of these rifles was adapted from the single-shot M78/80, a new barrel and a protruding single-row magazine being provided.
1907: early rifles, locked only by the abutment of the bolt-handle rib on the receiver, proved too weak. Later batches, therefore, had a special housing on the right side of the receiver for a locking lug cut in the front end of the bolt rib.

Model 1899

Infantry rifles: M1899, M1899/07 and M1899/08.
Made by Deutsche Waffen- und Munitionsfabriken,
Berlin, 1899–1906; and Österreichische
Waffenfabriks-Gesellschaft, Steyr, 1907–10.
7 × 57mm, rimless.
Turning-bolt action with two lugs on the bolt head locking into the receiver behind the chamber.
DATA FOR M99/08
1,230mm overall, 4·03kg unladen.
740mm barrel, 4-groove rifling; RH, concentric.
Internal charger-loaded box magazine, 5 rounds.
Leaf sight graduated to 2,000 metres.
About 710 m/sec with ball cartridges.
M1899 knife bayonet.

☆

1899: the first order for these rifles, similar mechanically to the Chilean Mo.1895 (q.v.), was placed with DWM. Deliveries continued until about 1903. They had straight-wrist stocks with hand guards running from the receiver ring to the band, and a simple nose cap with a bayonet lug on its underside. A cleaning rod was carried in the fore-end. Swivels lay on the under edge of the butt and beneath the band.
1907: more rifles were acquired from OEWG. They were stocked in the manner of the original DWM-made pattern, but may have had an improved action. A thumb-cut in the left wall of the receiver facilitated charger-loading and the bolt head enclosed the cartridge case-head.
1908: additional deliveries were made. Guns were marked '99/08C' instead of '99/07C', but the differences are not clearly understood and are believed to have been minor—possibly little more than a separate order-code or differing back sight graduations, though improvement in the action may have been made.

Purchased in small numbers for cavalry and artillerymen, the 99/08 carbine was simply a shortened version of the Steyr-made rifle. About 997mm overall, it had a 500mm barrel and an

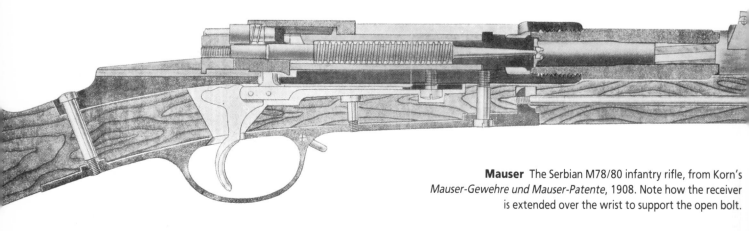

Mauser The Serbian M78/80 infantry rifle, from Korn's *Mauser-Gewehre und Mauser-Patente*, 1908. Note how the receiver is extended over the wrist to support the open bolt.

Mauser
Spanish soldiers greet visitors during the Mediterranean cruise of a German naval squadron, 1931.

unladen weight of 3·68kg. The stock extended to the muzzle and had a pointed Austrian-style pistol grip. The carbine did not accept a bayonet.

Model 1910

Infantry rifle.
Waffenfabrik Mauser AG, Oberndorf, 1910–12.
7 × 57mm, rimless.
Turning-bolt action with two lugs on the bolt head locking into the receiver behind the chamber and a safety lug opposing the bolt handle.
1,238mm overall, 4·11kg unladen.
740mm barrel, 4-groove rifling; RH, concentric.
Internal charger-loaded box magazine, 5 rounds.
Leaf sight graduated to 2,000 metres.
M1899 knife bayonet.

☆

1911: ordered during a period of unrest that culminated in the Second Balkan War, this was a Gew.98-type gun with the standard 'export' stock, a hand guard from the receiver ring to the band, and a simple nose cap with a bayonet lug.

SIAM (THAILAND)

These rifles had a chamber-top *Chakra* and Sanskrit markings. The earliest were of 1898 pattern, with the safety lug and a non-rotating extractor. Supplied by Waffenfabrik Mauser in small numbers, they were used for field trials..

Model 1902

Infantry rifle; also known as Type 45.
Made by the Imperial artillery arsenal, Koishikawa, Tokyo, c.1903–8.
8 × 50mm, rimmed.
Action: generally as German Gew.98 (q.v.).
1,247mm overall, 3·88kg unladen.
740mm barrel, 4-groove rifling; RH, concentric.
Internal charger-loaded box magazine, 5 rounds.
Tangent-leaf sight graduated to 2,000 metres.
About 625 m/sec with Type 45 ball cartridges.
Type 45 sword bayonet.

☆

1902: this was adopted to replace earlier Mannlichers. The guns had angular stocks with pointed Japanese-style pistol grips. A hand guard ran forward from the receiver ring to the barrel band, its rear surface being reduced so that the manually operated bolt cover could be slid forward when the gun was to be fired. Swivels lay under the spring-retained barrel band and on the under-edge of the butt, and a bayonet bar appeared beneath the muzzle. Internally, the magazine case was sloped so that the rims of the cartridges would not interlock.
1923: the rifles were adapted for the 8 × 52mm Type 66 cartridge, which had a pointed bullet and would not interchange with its predecessor. The principal external change concerned the back-sight ramps, which were much lower.
1952*: some surviving rifles were converted for the US ·30–06 cartridge, their barrels being shortened appreciably at the same time.

Model 1923

Short rifle; also known as Type 66.
Made by Imperial artillery arsenal, Koishikawa, Tokyo?
8 × 52mm, rimmed.
Action: as M1902, above.
About 1,065mm overall, 3·65kg unladen.
560mm barrel, 4-groove rifling; RH, concentric.
Internal charger-loaded box magazine, 5 rounds.
Tangent-leaf sight graduated to 1,200 metres?
About 640 m/sec with Type 66 ball cartridges.
Type 66 sword bayonet.

☆

1923*: these may have been converted from Type 45 long rifles, for cavalry or artillery use. They had a simplified barrel band, sling mounts on the left side, and a Japanese-type nose cap. The muzzle ring of the special bayonet lay well away from the back of the hilt.

SPAIN

1887: trials with a few Turkish 1887-pattern Mausers began, but were not successful. The appearance of smokeless propellant in France then shifted interest to smaller-calibre weapons.

Model 1891

Infantry rifle: Fusil Mauser Mo.1891.
Made by Waffenfabrik Mauser AG,
Oberndorf am Neckar, 1891.
Quantity: 1,200.
7·65 × 53mm, rimless.
Turning-bolt action, with two lugs on the bolt head locking into the receiver behind the chamber.
1,238mm overall, 4·11kg unladen.
740mm barrel, 4-groove rifling; RH, concentric.
Semi-fixed charger-loaded box magazine, 5 rounds.
Leaf sight graduated to 2,000 metres.
About 630 m/sec with ball cartridges.

☆

1891: in accordance with a royal decree of 2 December, Turkish-type Mausers were acquired for trials with the Regimiento de Infanteria Saboya No. 6 and the Batallón de Cazadores de Puerto Rico No. 19. Bolt heads were modified to eliminate double-loading, the face being partially under-cut and a spring-loaded plunger added in the right locking lug.

Model 1892

Infantry rifle: Fusil Mauser Español Mo.1892.
Made by Waffenfabrik Mauser,
Oberndorf am Neckar, 1893–4.
7 × 57mm, rimless.
Action: as Mo.1891, above.
1,235mm overall, 4·11kg unladen.
738mm barrel, 4-groove rifling; RH, concentric.
Fixed charger-loaded box magazine, 5 rounds.
Leaf sight graduated to 2,000 metres.
About 670 m/sec with ball cartridges.
Mo.1892 sword bayonet.

☆

1892: adopted on 30 November, this was basically a Turkish rifle in 7mm calibre, but with the improvements made in the 1891 troop trials rifle. It had a non-rotating 1892-patent extractor and a detachable floor plate and follower, a catch being set into the straight front magazine-edge. The trigger system was altered so that the sear could not release the striker unless the bolt was fully locked.

A guide rib was added in the left side of the receiver, the cocking piece was attached to the firing pin with interrupted lugs, and the safety catch had a third (vertical) position to assist dismantling. The hand guard ran from the front of the back sight base to the barrel band.

1893: the acquisition of 20,000 guns was authorised on 21 July, and then another 10,000 on 27 August. However, very few rifles were ever delivered owing to advent of the improved Mo.1893 (q.v.).

1907*: the survivors were given Mo.1893-type back sights, and hand guards running from the receiver ring to the barrel band.

Model 1892

Cavalry carbine: Carabina Mauser Española Mo.1892.
Made by Ludwig Loewe & Co., Berlin, 1893–5.
Quantity: 10,000.
7 × 57mm, rimless.
Action: as Mo.1891, above.
943mm overall, 3·30kg unladen.
445mm barrel, 4-groove rifling; RH, concentric.
Fixed charger-loaded box magazine, 5 rounds.
Leaf sight graduated to 1,200 metres.
About 560 m/sec with ball cartridges.
No bayonet.
☆

1892: stocked to the muzzle, this had a plain nose cap and barrel band, and its bolt handle was turned down against the stock. A sling bar and ring lay under the straight butt-wrist.

1893: the purchase of five thousand carbines was authorised on 21 July, followed by a similar supplementary order on 27 August.

Model 1893

Infantry rifle: Fusil Mauser Español Mo.1893.
Made by Ludwig Loewe & Co., Berlin, 1893–8; and Fábrica Nacional de Armas, Oviedo, 1896–1943.
Quantity: 206,830 in Germany (apparently including carbines) and more than two million in Spain.
7 × 57mm, rimless.
Action: as Mo.1891, above.
1,235mm overall, 3·95kg unladen.

738mm barrel, 4-groove rifling; RH, concentric.
Internal charger-loaded box magazine, 5 rounds.
Leaf sight graduated to 2,000 metres.
About 680 m/sec with Mo.1895 ball cartridges.
Mo.1893 sword bayonet.
☆

1893: adopted on 7 December, this was the first Mauser to feature a charger-loaded magazine contained entirely within the stock. The initial contract is said to have been for 251,800 rifles and 25,000 carbines, but may include the 40,000 1892-pattern guns described above.

The Mo.1893 was mechanically identical with its predecessor, though the safety catch was retained by a lug on the bolt plug engaging the safety-catch head. The safety could only be applied when the action was cocked. The lower portion of the bolt face was squared to improve cartridge feed (abandoned on later Mausers) and the development of an improved charger allowed both guides to be milled into the front of the receiver bridge.

Previous Spanish guns relied on an upward extension of the spring-loaded bolt stop to provide the left guide. Unlike some essentially similar guns (e.g., Brazilian Mo.1894), the Mo.1893 would not close on an empty chamber until the magazine follower had been depressed manually.

1895: the perfected Mo.1895 cartridge was approved on 1 October, issue commencing in earnest after this date.

1896: production began in Oviedo. All but a few of the guns made in Spain had the left side of the receiver cut to about half-depth to facilitate charger-loading.

1906: back-sight sliders were improved in May.

1907: strikers were strengthened in February.

1913: the approval of an improved cartridge, with a muzzle velocity of 850 m/sec, led to a modification of sight leaves.

1933: the basic action was improved by Antonio Ramirez de Arellano and José Garcia Menéndez. The cocking piece and safety mechanism were modified, changes were made to the striker and bolt face, and a new ejector was fitted to cure breakages.

Model 1895

Cavalry carbine: Carabina Mauser Española para Plazas Montadas Mo.1895.
Made by Ludwig Loewe & Co., Berlin, 1893–8; and Fábrica Nacional de Armas, Oviedo, 1896–1915.
Quantity: about 22,500 in Germany and an unknown number in Spain.
7 × 57mm, rimless.
Action: as Mo.1891, above.
943mm overall, 3·20kg unladen.
446mm barrel, 4-groove rifling; RH, concentric.
Internal charger-loaded box magazine, 5 rounds.
Leaf sight graduated to 1,400 metres.
About 665 m/sec with Mo.1895 ball cartridges.
No bayonet.
☆

1895: adopted on 7 May, this was a short Mo.1893, stocked to the muzzle, with a small back sight, and the bolt handle turned down.

1896: a change was made to the barrel band, which gained a sling ring on the left side, and a sling bar was fixed in the left side of the butt in addition to the bar-and-ring assembly beneath the wrist. A half-depth cut in the left side of the receiver was added to facilitate charger-loading.

Model 1913

Short rifle: Mosqueton Mauser Español Mo.1913.
Made by Fábrica Nacional de Armas, Oviedo, 1907.
7 × 57mm, rimless.
Action: as Mo.1891, above.
944mm overall, 3·23kg unladen.
446mm barrel, 4-groove rifling; RH, concentric.
Internal charger-loaded box magazine, 5 rounds.
Leaf sight graduated to 1,400 metres.
About 665 m/sec with Mo.1895 ball cartridges.
Mo.1893 sword bayonet.
☆

1907: these were made for trials, apparently with the artillery. Mechanically identical with the cavalry carbine, they had swivels under the barrel band and the butt.

1914: the guns were issued for field trials as the 'Mo.1913', presaging adoption of the Mo.1916 short rifle.

Mauser A longitudinal section of the Spanish (Argentine-type) M1891 rifle, purchased in small numbers in the early 1890s. From Korn's *Mauser-Gewehre und Mauser-Patente*, 1908.

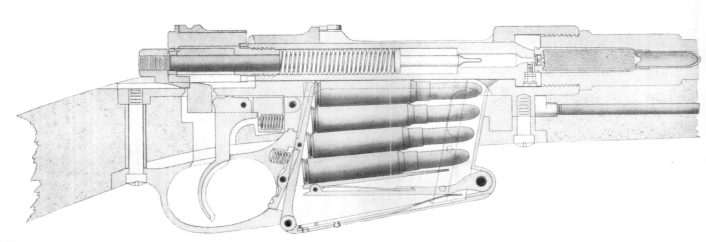

1918: from 2 April, the surviving musketoons were issued to buglers of the cavalry squadrons.

Model 1916

Short rifle: Mosqueton Mauser Español Mo.1916.
Made by Fábrica Nacional de Armas, Oviedo, 1916–51; and Industrias de Guerra de Cataluña, Tarrasa, c.1936–9.
7 × 57mm, rimless.
Action: as Mo.1891, above.
1,050mm overall, 3·75kg unladen.
551mm barrel, 4-groove rifling; RH, concentric.
Internal charger-loaded box magazine, 5 rounds.
Tangent sight graduated to 2,400 metres.
About 825 m/sec with Mo.1913 'S' ball cartridges.
Mo.1913 sword bayonet.
☆

1916: this was adopted on 14 November to replace the Mo.1895 carbine, the short barrel of which was not suited to the ballistics of the 1913-pattern cartridge.

The Mo.1916 had a full-depth cut-out on the left of the receiver to facilitate charger loading, and additional gas-escape holes in the bolt body and chamber-side. The original back sight was a Lange-style tangent pattern. The short rifle had a single barrel band and a standard nose cap, retained by springs let into the underside of the fore-end; the bolt handle turned down toward the stock. A pivoting swivel on the left side of the band was used in conjunction with a bar on the left side of the butt.
1918: prominent protectors appeared on the front-sight block.
1933: the basic design was upgraded in much the same way as the Mo.1893 rifle (q.v.).
1936: to accelerate production during the Civil War, the Lange sight was substituted by a more conventional tangent-leaf graduated to 2,000 metres. The hinged magazine floor-plate and the release catch pivoted in the front of the trigger guard were replaced by a detachable floor-plate. These guns also had a recoil bolt through the fore-end beneath the chamber.
1943: some surviving Mo.1916 short rifles

were converted for the standard German 7.9mm cartridge, owing to the adoption of the Mo.943.

Model 1943

Short rifle: Fusil Mauser Español Mo.1943.
Made by Fábricas Nacionales de Armas, Oviedo and La Coruña, 1943–59.
7·9 × 57mm, rimless.
Turning-bolt action, with two lugs on the bolt head locking into the receiver behind the chamber and a safety lug opposing the bolt handle.
1,105mm overall, 3·91kg unladen.
600mm barrel, 4-groove rifling; RH, concentric.
Internal charger-loaded box magazine, 5 rounds.
Tangent-leaf sight graduated to 2,000 metres.
750 m/sec with Mo.1943 ball cartridges?
Mo.1943 knife bayonet.
☆

1943: this was adopted to replace the 7mm Mo.1916 short rifle, owing to the widespread issue of machine-guns chambering the German-pattern service cartridge. The Mo.1943 was a conventional 1898-pattern weapon, essentially similar in size and mechanical characteristics to the Kar.98k, but had a straight bolt handle and a short grasping groove in the fore-end. A hand guard ran from the receiver ring to the band. Sling swivels lay under the butt, and on the left side and under the barrel band; a sling bar appeared on the left side of the butt. The nose cap was very similar to the 'H' pattern of German guns, but accepted a bayonet with a muzzle ring. An adaptor enabled any of the earlier Mo.1893 and Mo.1913 bayonets to be used when required.

Other guns

Immediately prior to adoption of the Mo.1893 rifle, the Spanish purchased 10,000 7·65mm Mo.1891 rifles and 5,000 Mo.1891 carbines from the Argentine government. These appear to have been delivered directly from the Loewe factory, but already had Argentine marks on the left side of the receiver; however, chamber-tops were plain. The guns were issued to Spanish

colonial troops in Africa and the Ejército de Ultramar in Cuba. About four thousand 7mm Mexican Mausers with an 1898-type bolt were acquired for trials in the early 1900s.

SWEDEN

Sweden accepted the Mauser after trials had been undertaken with Mauser, Mannlicher, Lee, Krag-Jørgensen and other patterns.

Model 1894

Cavalry and artillery carbines: Karabin M/1894 och M/1894/17.
Made by Waffenfabrik Mauser AG, Oberndorf am Neckar, 1894–6; and Carl Gustafs Stads Gevärsfactori, Eskilstuna, c.1900–30.
6·5 × 55mm, rimless.
Turning-bolt action with two lugs on the bolt head locking into the receiver behind the chamber.
DATA FOR M1894
950mm overall, 3·31kg unladen.
440mm barrel, 4-groove rifling; RH, concentric.
Internal charger-loaded box magazine, 5 rounds.
Leaf sight graduated to 1,600 metres.
About 650 m/sec with M1894 ball cartridges.
No bayonet.
☆

1894: an order for 5,000 guns was authorised in August. The carbine was mechanically similar to the Mo.1893 Spanish rifle (q.v.), but the safety could be engaged with the striker almost fully forward and a distinctive angular extension appeared on the cocking piece. The M/1894 had a straight-wrist full length stock and a hand guard running forward from the receiver ring to the band. The edges of the nose cap carried upward to protect the sight blade, while a sling bar on the left side of the band was used in conjunction with a slot cut through the butt.
1895: 7,185 guns were ordered from Mauser.
1899: after the adoption of the M/1896 rifle, the carbine was revised. A cut-out on the left side of the receiver facilitated charger loading, but most other changes were internal.
1900: production began in the state factory.

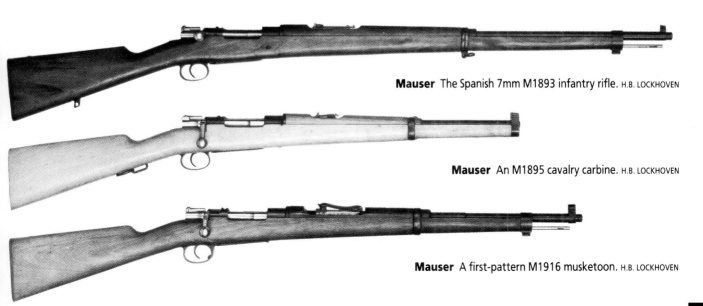

Mauser The Spanish 7mm M1893 infantry rifle. H.B. LOCKHOVEN

Mauser An M1895 cavalry carbine. H.B. LOCKHOVEN

Mauser A first-pattern M1916 musketoon. H.B. LOCKHOVEN

1917: the nose cap was altered so that a sword bayonet could be attached. The new design, inspired by the British SMLE, comprised a boss beneath the muzzle and a long rearward extension with an attachment lug.

1941: introduction of the improved M/1941 cartridge, with a trajectory differing from the M/1894 pattern for which the sights had been calibrated, was solved by adding sight-setting information on the right side of the butt.

Model 1896

Infantry and sniper rifles: Gevär M/1896, M/1938 och M/1941.
Made by Waffenfabrik Mauser AG, Oberndorf am Neckar, 1899–1904; Carl Gustafs Stads Gevärsfactori, Eskilstuna, c.1900–30; and Husqvarna Våpenfabrik, Huskvarna.
6·5 × 55mm, rimless.
Action: as M1894, above.
DATA FOR M/1896
1,256mm overall, 4·07kg unladen.
739mm barrel, 4-groove rifling; RH, concentric.
Internal charger-loaded box magazine, 5 rounds.
Leaf sight graduated to 1,600 metres.
725 m/sec with M/1894 ball cartridges.
M/1896 knife bayonet.
☆

1896: this improved M/1894 carbine was very similar to its predecessor, but part of the left side of the receiver was cut away to facilitate charger loading and the guide rib was moved from the receiver-wall to the bolt body. A gas-escape hole was added in the receiver ring.

The rifle had a straight-wrist stock, with a hand guard from the receiver ring to a simple barrel band. A monopod could be fitted to the nose-cap eye, while the tube-hilted bayonet locked onto the angled lug beneath the cleaning-rod boss. The back-sight leaf pivoted at the front of the bed; swivels lay under the band and butt.

1899: a contract for 45,000 rifles was given to Mauser, tooling in the Swedish state rifle factory beginning at much the same time.

1938: the M/1938 short rifle was practically identical with the M/1896, but the bolt handle was turned down, the barrel was cut to 600mm and overall length reduced to 1,120mm.

1941: the advent of an improved cartridge, with a velocity of 800 m/sec, required a sight-setting plate on the butt. The M/1941 sniper rifle was a selected M/1896 with its bolt handle bent down and a telescope-sight mount clamped in a dovetail plate on the side of the receiver. German Ajack 4 × 90 or Swedish 3 × 65 AGA M/1942 or M/1944 sights were fitted to virtually all the M/41 sniper rifles.

Models 1939 and 1940

Short rifles: Gevär M/1939 och M/1940.
☆

1939: likelihood of war in Europe persuaded the Swedish authorities to create a special rifle for the machine-gun units, chambered for the 8mm M/1932 cartridge to simplify ammunition supply. A few altered Kar.98k were issued for field trials, as the M/1939, but these predictably revealed that the recoil of the 8mm round—firing a 14·3-gram bullet at 770 m/sec—was unmanageable in a shoulder weapon.

A few thousand M/1940 rifles with special muzzle brakes were assembled by Carl Gustafs Stads Gevärsfactori in 1940, using Kar.98k-type actions supplied by Mauser. Never successful, they were rapidly replaced by 6·5mm versions when it became clear that Swedish neutrality would be respected.

Note: most types of Swedish service rifle may be encountered with Finnish property marks (generally 'SA' within a square), showing that they were supplied during the Winter War before neutrality prevailed.

A Danish coin replacing the marking disc in the butt denotes guns supplied in 1946–8 to replace Krags sequestered by the Germans.

Mauser The Swedish M1894 carbine. H.B. LOCKHOVEN

MAUSER
LESSER PATTERNS: H-Y

HONDURAS
These guns are rarely encountered in collections, though 7 × 57mm Mo.1895 (Chilean type) rifles are said to have been purchased prior to 1914, and some Standard-Modell Mausers followed in the mid 1930s. The arms comprised a triangular volcano, flanked by two towers, set in front of a pyramid on a grassed field. The device was set inside an oval border bearing the date of independence (15 September 1821).

ISRAEL
Immediately after the Israeli state was formed in 1947, many thousands of ex-German Kar.98k rifles were refurbished and re-issued. These guns almost always display their old marks in addition to new Israeli ones. In 1949, the authorities decided to purchase an entire Kar.98k production line from Switzerland—at enormous cost—and installed it in a new factory in Ramat ha-Sharon (now Israeli Military Industries, IMI). However, the advent of effectual semi-automatic rifles caused the Mauser to be abandoned in favour of the FN FAL after only a few new guns had been made. Manufacture then concentrated on old German actions, and others purchased from Fabrique Nationale in the 1950s.

Survivors have been rebarrelled for the 7·62 × 51mm NATO round since the 1960s.

JAPAN
The Arisaka rifle, widely regarded as a much-modified Mauser, is covered separately. The Japanese made 8mm Mauser rifles for Siam prior to 1914, and also apparently supervised work on 7·9mm rifles in the Mukden factory in the puppet state of Manchukuo (Manchuria, q.v.) in the 1930s. Substantial numbers of these Manchurian guns were apparently used during the Second World War, alongside many conventional Mausers captured in China from 1937 onward. Some Chinese guns are said to have been rebarrelled to fire Japanese 6·5 or 7·7mm cartridges.

LATVIA
About 15,000 vz.24 short rifles were purchased from Československá Zbrojovka in 1935. It is not known whether they bore any distinctive markings.

LIBERIA
Fabrique Nationale Mle.24 short rifles were purchased in the early 1930s, but details are lacking. The arms consisted of a shield bearing a star above eleven vertical bars.

LITHUANIA
In 1931, the army apparently bought small quantities of Czechoslovakian-made

'L'-model short rifles chambering the British rimmed ·303 cartridge. Whether these were issued to the army or to a gendarmerie has not been determined, as 7·92mm vz.24 short rifles had been purchased from Československá Zbrojovka in 1926–7 and some 7·9mm Fabrique Nationale Mle.30 short rifles followed in 1935–8. These were all used as 'Model 24.L'. The chamber mark was a highly stylised crown beneath 'GINKLU FONDAS' ('arms fund') and the date of manufacture.

LUXEMBOURG
A few Mausers were supplied prior to 1900 to equip the tiny state army. The guns are believed to have been similar to the 1895 Chilean pattern (q.v.), but special markings—if any—have not been identified.

MANCHURIA
Mukden arsenal made curious rifles, apparently in the period of the Japanese inspired Manchukuo state (1932–45). **'Manchurian Mauser'** Apparently made by Mukden arsenal in c.1933–9, this interesting 7·9 × 57mm weapon appears to have been created with Japanese technical assistance. It had an 1898-type Mauser action, with the third (safety) lug and a non-rotating extractor, but changes were made to the firing pin assembly and the bolt plug had an elongated housing for the main spring. There were two gas-escape holes in

the receiver ring, the bolt handle was a typically Japanese oviform type, and a reciprocating sheet-steel cover could be attached over the receiver. A typical rifle was 1,240mm overall, with a 740mm barrel. Its internal charger-loaded box magazine held five rounds and the tangent-leaf sight was graduated to 2,000 metres.
¶ In about 1938, Mukden arsenal re-tooled to make the 7·7mm Type 99 Japanese Arisaka short rifle. However—towards the end of the second World War—some Mausers were modified for the Japanese 6·5mm semi-rim round, gaining an auxiliary block in the back of the magazine well to compensate for the appreciable reduction in the length of the cartridge.

NICARAGUA
Some 7 × 57mm vz.12/33 short rifles were ordered from Československá Zbrojovka in the 1930s. They are believed to have borne their maker's name in Spanish and a version of the National Arms above the chamber. This comprised five volcanoes and a Liberty Cap on a staff, rising out of a seascape beneath a sunrise and a rainbow.

ORANGE FREE STATE
The ordnance affairs of the Oranje Vrij Staat (OVS), a short-lived independent republic in southern Africa, remain mysterious. However, shortly after the Jameson Raid into neighbouring Transvaal in January

1896, an order was placed in Germany.
M1896 rifle The first of these weapons was purchased from Deutsche Waffen- und Munitionsfabriken in 1897. True OVS rifles followed the 1893 (Spanish) pattern, but had cylindrical-head bolts. They chambered a 7×53mm cartridge with a short neck and had an 'O.V.S.' mark on the receiver ring, usually accompanied by the DWM monogram and 'MOD.MAUSER'. A few guns dated 1896 used Loewe-made receivers, though apparently delivered after 1 January 1897. Work was halted in 1899 by the Second South African War after about 18,000 had been delivered. They were 1,235mm overall, weighed 3·96kg unladen, and had 738mm barrels rifled with four grooves twisting to the right. The internal charger-loaded box magazine held five rounds and the leaf sight was graduated to 2,000 metres. A Spanish-type sword bayonet was acquired in small numbers.
¶ About 2,000 half-complete guns were re-chambered for the 7×57mm cartridge and sold to Chile. They bore the Chilean arms as well as OVS markings.

PARAGUAY

These guns can usually be identified by the chamber-top crest of a star on a stylised sunburst within a wreath, usually encircled by 'REPÚBLICA DEL PARAGUAY'.
Pre-1900 patterns Small quantities of Mo.1895 (Chilean type) rifles were purchased from DWM in the late 1890s.
M1907 rifle The Fusil Mauser Paraguayano was made by Deutsche Waffen- und Munitionsfabriken in 1907–12. Chambered for the the 7·65×53mm rimless cartridge, they were very similar to the then current Gew.98, with safety lugs and non-rotating extractors, and even had Lange-pattern back sights. However, the heavy 1904-type cocking piece was used and the 'H'-type nose cap accepted a standard German export-model bayonet with a muzzle ring. Swivels lay on the underside of the butt and barrel band. A typical example measured 1,247mm overall, weighed 4·11kg, and had a 740mm barrel with concentric four-groove rifling. The tangent sight was graduated to 2,000 metres and the Mo.1907 knife bayonet was used.
M1907 carbine The Carabina Mauser Paraguayana Mo.1907 was similar to the infantry rifle, but its stock extended to the muzzle and the plain nose cap protruded upward to protect the front sight. Bayonets could not be mounted. A sling mount lay on the left side of the spring-retained barrel band and a sling slot was cut through the butt. The back sight was changed to a Mauser-type tangent-leaf pattern and the bolt handle was turned down against the stock.
M1927 rifle The Fusil Mo.1927 was ordered in Spain, being made by Fábrica Nacional de Armas, Oviedo, in c.1927–32. Though mechanically similar to the guns supplied in 1907, it had a combination bolt stop/charger guide. Rifles required a bayonet with the muzzle ring set close to the back of the hilt, but were usually fitted with an auxiliary-lug attachment so that 1895-type bayonets could be used. Full-length rifles were similar to the Gew.98, with a pistol-grip stock and an 'H' nose cap.
¶ Conversion to 7·9×57mm began in the early 1950s.

M1927 short rifle The Mosqueton Mo.1927 shared the action of the full-length rifle, but had a straight-wrist stock. The bolt handle was often (but not invariably) bent downward. It was about 1,100mm overall, weighed 3·93kg and had a 595mm barrel rifled with four grooves turning to the right. The tangent-leaf sight was graduated to 2,000 metres.
M1927 carbine Stocked virtually to the muzzle, where a simplified nose cap was fitted, the Carabina Mo.1927 could not accept a bayonet. The action was identical with the rifle; however, the bolt handle was turned down against the stock and a sling loop lay on the left side of the barrel band.
Other patterns Standard-Modell Mausers were bought in the mid 1930s, and FN-made Mle.24 'Mo.1935' short rifles in the late 1930s. More FN rifles were acquired after the end of the Second World War. Many surviving Mle.24-type guns were converted to 7.9 × 57mm in the 1950s.

PERU

These guns are invariably distinguishable by the chamber-top mark. The national arms comprised a shield divided into three, with a llama and a cinchona tree (in the upper compartments) above a cornucopia. The shield was usually superimposed on two pairs of national flags, surmounted by a sunburst and surrounded by a wreath. The legends 'REPÚBLICA DEL PERU' or, latterly, 'REPÚBLICA PERUANA' may also appear.
M1891 rifle The Fusil Mauser Peruano Mo.1891, about 30,000 of which were made by Ludwig Loewe & Co. in 1892–5, chambered the 7·65×53mm cartridge. It was identical with then-current Argentine gun (q.v.) excepting markings. The rifle was 1,235mm overall, weighed 4·10kg, and had a 738mm barrel. The leaf sight was graduated to 2,000 metres and an Argentine-type sword bayonet was used.
¶ A programme began in 1912 to convert most surviving Mo.1891 rifles to handle improved pointed-bullet ammunition. These guns can be recognised by a Lange-type tangent back sight replacing the original leaf design.
M1909 rifle Made by Waffenfabrik Mauser AG in Oberndorf am Neckar, about 50,000 of the 7.65mm Fusil Mauser Peruano Mo.1909 were delivered in 1910–14. An 1898-pattern Mauser, with an auxiliary lug on the bolt and a non-rotating extractor, the rifle used the heavy 1904-type cocking piece. However, the 'H'-type nose cap accepted a standard German S.98 bayonet. The Peruvian gun—1,248mm overall, 4·23kg unladen—was mechanically similar to the Argentine Mo.1909, but had a Lange tangent back sight graduated to 2,000 metres and lacked the special magazine floor-plate release catch in the front of the trigger guard.
Other patterns Peru purchased some six hundred 7·65×53mm vz.24-pattern short rifles from Československá Zbrojovka in 1930, and then 5,000 'vz.32' short rifles in 1934; these were apparently used as 'Mo.1932'. Subsequent guns—Mo.1935 short rifles and a few carbines—seem to have been acquired from Fabrique Nationale, a few being delivered after 1945. Pre-1939 guns usually had the action of the safety catch reversed.

¶ Many surviving guns were converted to chamber the ·30–06 cartridge in the early 1950s, owing to the ready availability of US war-surplus ammunition.

PORTUGAL

Portuguese guns used after the revolution of 1910 generally bore the national arms above the chamber. These consisted of a shield inside a shield, containing five small shields each charged with five discs; seven castles lay around the edge of the outer shield, the whole being placed on an armillary sphere (a navigating instrument) and surrounded by a wreath of laurel leaves. Prior to 1937, however, the Mauser had not been popular in Portugal.
M1937 short rifle The original Espingarda Mo.937 was a 'Standard Modell' Mauser, similar to the Kar.98k with German-style slot-and-bar sling mounts. In 1938, however, a modified 'Mo.937-A' was substituted, with swivels under the butt and barrel band. The front sight could be adjusted laterally in a diagonal slot, and the mounting-block edges extended upward to protect the sight blade. The last deliveries were made in 1943. A typical 937-A was 1,103mm overall and weighed 3·96kg. Its 600mm barrel was rifled with four grooves turning to the right, the charger-loaded box magazine held five rounds and the tangent-leaf sight was graduated to 2,000 metres. The Mo.937 sword bayonet was used.
¶ Guns remaining in store in Oberndorf in 1944 were issued to the Wehrmacht, after a sling slot had been cut in the butt and the barrel band had been changed.

ROMANIA

7·92mm vz.24 short rifles were purchased from Československá Zbrojovka to supplement the issue Mannlichers. These had a chamber-mark comprising the cypher of Michael I (four crowned letters 'M' forming a cross) or Carol II (a crowned encircled 'CC' monogram in a laurel wreath). Confusion exists over the dating of these guns, owing to the fact that Carol II—most unusually—interrupted Michael's reign. It is suspected that they date from 1929–33.

SAUDI ARABIA

FN-Mauser short rifles were acquired in the late 1930s (the kingdom in its present form dates from 1932). The guns were apparently chambered for 7·9×57mm cartridges, but it is not known how they were marked.

SOUTH AFRICAN REPUBLIC

The Mausers used by the Zuid Afrikaansche Republiek (ZAR), alternatively known as the Transvaal, were ordered from DWM through the intermediacy of Krupp after the Jameson Raid of January 1896 showed the inadequacy of the country's arsenal. They supplemented orders for obsolescent Westley Richards Martini-Henry rifles and Steyr-made Portuguese Guedes rifles.
M1896 rifle Purchase of as many as 50,000 of these DWM-made rifles was authorised in 1896 though only about 37,000 had been delivered by the start of the Second South African War in 1899. The rifles were all but identical with the Chilean Mo.1895 (q.v.), though whether they chambered 7×53mm or 7×57mm cartridges has not been determined. A typical example was

1,235mm overall, had a 738mm barrel and weighed 3·99kg. Its leaf sight was graduated to 2,000 metres and a typical German export-pattern sword pattern could be fitted when required.
¶ Oddly, though many OVS guns survive in collections, few ZAR examples exist. The reason for this is not clear.

URUGUAY

These rifles will usually be found with the national arms over the chamber. These comprised a quartered oval displaying the scales of justice, the citadel of Montevideo, a horse and a bull, beneath a rising sun. The mark lay within a laurel wreath; 'REPÚBLICA ORIENTAL DEL URUGUAY' or 'REPÚBLICA ORIENTAL' also appeared.
Daudetau-Mauser Ordered c.1897, these were 1871-pattern Mauser rifles and carbines, originally purchased in the 1880s, converted by Société Française des Armes Portatives de Saint-Denis, Paris.
¶ The guns were rebarrelled for the distinctive 6·5×53·5mm Daudetau No.12 semi-rim cartridge, the bands and nose caps being replaced by typically Daudetau patterns. The mark 'ST.-DENIS' was struck into the top surface of the barrels.
¶ Converted rifles were issued with a special bayonet combining a French-style épée blade with a cast-brass hilt; their nose caps had a bayonet lug. The bolt and receiver may have been altered to allow an additional locking lug to be used. The work was supervised by a Uruguayan engineer named Dovitiis; his name has often been attached to the guns.
Pre-1914 patterns Little is known about the early ordnance history of Uruguay, though many Remington Rolling Block rifles had been issued. Mo.1895 and Mo.1904 Mausers—apparently identical with the Chilean guns—were acquired prior to 1914 from Ludwig Loewe and then DWM.
Post-1914 patterns About six thousand Czechoslovakian vz.32 7·65mm short rifles were delivered in 1937, to serve as the 'Mo.1934'; some 7mm Mle.24-type short rifles were also purchased from Fabrique Nationale in the same era.

VENEZUELA

These Mausers are usually distinguished by the national arms above the chamber. These comprised a shield divided into three, with a wheatsheaf and a trophy of arms and flags above a white horse. The mark was surmounted by two entwined cornucopiae, and usually surrounded by a wreath.
M1910 rifle The 7mm Mo.1910 rifle was essentially similar to the Costa Rican gun (q.v.) of the same date, but had a conventional bolt-face.
Other patterns The army also purchased substantial quantities of 7 × 57mm vz.24/26 short rifles from Československá Zbrojovka in the early 1930s. Fabrique Nationale Mle.24/30 short rifles were acquired in the 1930s, beginning with 16,500 in 1934–5, and small quantities of FN-Mausers followed after the end of the Second World War.

YEMEN

A substantial quantity of Mle.30 short rifles was purchased from Fabrique Nationale in the late 1930s, but it is not known how (or even if) they were specially marked.

TURKEY

Turkish rifles made prior to about 1926 can usually be identified by marks in Arabic; in addition, many of the more modern Mausers have a *Toughra* (a calligraphic symbol unique to each ruler) on the chamber top. The Turks were among the first to order Mauser-type magazine rifles in quantity. A feature of the initial contract was a clause forcing the substitution of a better rifle should one be adopted elsewhere.

Model 1887

Infantry rifle.
Made by Waffenfabrik Mauser, Oberndorf am Neckar, 1888–90.
9·5 × 60mm, rimmed.
Turning-bolt action locked by one lug on the bolt and the bolt-guide rib abutting the receiver ahead of the bridge.
1,251mm overall, 4·19kg unladen.
760mm barrel, 4-groove rifling; RH, concentric.
Tube magazine in fore-end, 8 rounds.
Leaf sight graduated to 1,600 metres.
535 m/sec with ball cartridges.
M1887 sword bayonet.
☆

1886: trials began to find a magazine rifle to replace the Peabody-Martini.
1887: an order for 500,000 rifles and 50,000 carbines was shared by Waffenfabrik Mauser and Ludwig Loewe & Co. Before work began, however, the contractors decided that Mauser should make all the Turkish guns while Loewe made the German Gew.88.

The new rifle chambered a powerful black-powder cartridge, necessitating an additional locking lug, but was externally similar to the Gew.71/84. It had a straight-wrist stock, a single spring-retained barrel band, and a nose cap with a bayonet lug on the right side. The swivels lay on the underside of the nose cap and in the front web of the trigger guard, and a German-type back sight was attached to the barrel ahead of the octagonal chamber reinforce.
1890: owing to progress with the 1889-type

Mauser in Belgium, the Turkish authorities invoked the substitution clause in the original contract. Production of M1887 rifles stopped in the Oberndorf factory after about 225,000 had been made. Whether any carbines were among them is not known; none could be found.

Model 1890

Infantry rifle and cavalry carbine.
Made by Waffenfabrik Mauser, Oberndorf am Neckar, 1891–3.
Quantity: 245,000 rifles and possibly 30,000 carbines.
7·65 × 53mm, rimless.
Turning-bolt action, with two lugs on the bolt head locking into the receiver behind the chamber.
DATA FOR RIFLE
1,237mm overall, 4·00kg unladen.
740mm barrel, 4-groove rifling; RH, concentric.
Semi-fixed charger-loaded box magazine, 5 rounds.
Leaf sight graduated to 2,050 metres.
650 m/sec with ball cartridges.
M1890 sword bayonet.
☆

1890: a variant of the Belgian Mle.1889 rifle, this was adopted to replace the obsolescent M1887. It had a plain barrel, stepped to allow for expansion during rapid fire without upsetting the stock bedding and reducing accuracy. This was particularly important in hot climates. A one-piece sear was fitted and the magazine—though intended to be permanently emplaced—could be removed by pressing a catch set into the front face of the trigger-guard. The back sight was carried on a sleeve around the barrel, while a curiously abbreviated hand guard ran forward from the sight base. The guard did not reach the solitary spring-retained band. The nose cap assembly was simpler than that of the M1887, carrying its bayonet lug on the underside. Swivels lay on the band and butt.
1892*: the first carbines were supplied for cavalry and artillerymen. About 995mm overall, with 500mm barrels and a weight of 3·5kg, they were similar mechanically to the rifles. However, the stock extended to the muzzle—preventing bayonets being used—and bolt

handles were turned down. The back sight was apparently graduated to a mere 1,200 metres.

Model 1893

Infantry rifle.
Made by Waffenfabrik Mauser, Oberndorf am Neckar, 1894–9.
Quantity: 201,100.
7·65 × 53mm, rimless.
Action: as M1890, above.
1,235mm overall, 4·06kg unladen.
738mm barrel, 4-groove rifling; RH, concentric.
Fixed charger-loaded box magazine, 5 rounds.
Leaf sight graduated to 2,000 metres.
650 m/sec with ball cartridges.
M1890 sword bayonet.
☆

1894: the approval of the Spanish Mo.1893 caused the Turks to substitute a modified version for their M1890.

The new gun was a virtual duplicate of the Spanish weapon, but had a conventional cylindrical bolt and a unique cut-off lever in a housing on the right side of the receiver beneath the bolt-way. An extension of the bolt stop doubled as the left charger guide and Arabic markings lay on the receiver.

Model 1903

Infantry rifle.
Made by Waffenfabrik Mauser, Oberndorf am Neckar, 1903–6.
7·65 × 53mm, rimless.
Turning-bolt action, with two lugs on the bolt head locking into the receiver behind the chamber and a safety lug opposing the bolt handle.
1,235mm overall, 4·06kg unladen.
738mm barrel, 4-groove rifling ; RH, concentric.
Integral charger-loaded box magazine, 5 rounds.
Tangent-leaf sight graduated to 2,000 metres.
650 m/sec with ball cartridges.
M1903 sword bayonet.
☆

1903: true to their policy of keeping up with developments in Germany, doubtless influenced

Mauser Turkish troops armed with Gew.98 rifles supplied to Turkey during the First World War. The Turkish M1903 was very similar to the Gew.98, excepting for its leaf-type back sight and simple nose cap.
IMPERIAL WAR MUSEUM; NEGATIVE NO. Q60321

by the restrictive clauses in the original 1887-vintage contract, the Turks purchased large quantities of this Gew.98-like rifle prior to 1914.

The M1903 resembled the contemporary German service rifle externally, though it had a standard back sight, a hand guard extending from the receiver ring to the band, and a simple nose cap with the bayonet lug underneath. The cocking-piece was longer and heavier than the German pattern, and the bolt stop was extended upward to form the left charger guide. The stock had a pistol grip, while the swivels lay under the band and butt.

1925*: the first batches of M1903 rifles were converted to chamber the 7·9 × 57mm rimless cartridge, large quantities of which had been supplied to assist pro-German Turkey repulse Allied invasion during the First World War.

Model 1905

Cavalry and artillery carbine.
Made by Waffenfabrik Mauser, Oberndorf
am Neckar, 1903–6.
7·65 × 53mm, rimless.
Action: as M1903, above.
1,045mm overall, about 3·75kg unladen.
550mm barrel, 4-groove rifling; RH, concentric.
Integral charger-loaded box magazine, 5 rounds.
Leaf sight graduated to 1,600 metres?
635 m/sec with ball cartridges.
No bayonet.
☆

1905: this gun, virtually a short rifle, was acquired to replace the earlier 1890 pattern. It had a pistol-grip stock, a spring-retained barrel band, and a simple nose cap carried upward to protect the front-sight blade. The bolt handle was turned down toward the stock, and sling mounts lay on the left side of the band and butt.
1925*: many surviving guns were converted for the standard 7·9 × 57mm cartridge.

Other guns

Turkey also purchased 7·92mm vz.98/22 rifles in the early 1920s. Many Gew.88 and Gew.98

were still in service in the mid 1920s, when replacement bolts were made in Czechoslovakia.

YUGOSLAVIA
KINGDOM OF SERBS, CROATS AND SLOVENES UNTIL 1929

These Mausers usually displayed markings in Cyrillic. The guns made before 1939 also had a chamber-top crest of a crowned shield bearing a double-headed eagle, placed on a pavilion of gathered cloth. Products of Voino Tekhniki Zavod—'state technical factory'—in Kraguyevac often bore a trademark comprising **BT3** (Cyrillic for 'VTZ') within a triangle. The chambers of post-1948 weapons had the state emblem of six torches within a circlet of wheat-ears.

Prior to 1923, the Kingdom of Serbs, Croats and Slovenes used a selection of Serbian M1899 and M1899/07 rifles converted to 7·9 × 57mm; 7·9mm 'M24B' rifles (ex-Mexican M1912), converted at Steyr in the 1920s; and shortened ex-Turkish 'M90T' 7·9mm conversions.

Post-1923 guns

1923: 50,000 Mle.22 rifles were ordered from Fabrique Nationale on 14 July, together with sufficient machinery to equip the Kraguyevac factory to make Mauser-type rifles.
1926: a second order for 40,000 rifles (Mle.24 short pattern?) was placed on 16 February. Forty thousand vz.24 short rifles were ordered from Československá Zbrojovka at the same time. Most guns were delivered in 1929–30.
1935: an order for Mle.30 short rifles and carbines was placed with Fabrique Nationale.

Model 1948

Short rifle.
Made by Zavodi Crvena Zastava, Kraguyevac, 1948–55.
7·9mm, rimless.
Turning-bolt action, with two lugs on the bolt head locking into the receiver behind the chamber and a safety lug opposing the bolt handle.
1,085mm overall, 4·02kg unladen.

590mm barrel, 4-groove rifling; RH, concentric.
Internal charger-loaded box, 5 rounds.
Tangent-leaf sight graduated to 2,000 metres.
About 835 m/sec with ball cartridges.
Czechoslovakian-type 'export' sword bayonet.
☆

1948: production of this Kar.98k variant began. The M48 shared the bucket-type butt plate and sling attachment of its German prototype, but had a forged barrel band and an 'H'-pattern nose cap. Essentially similar 'M24/47' conversions were made of old Mle.24 (Belgian) and vz.24 (Czechoslovakian) parts in this era.

SPORTING GUNS

The rise of big-game hunting, particularly in Africa and India, created a rapidly growing need for sporting rifles. This was initially satisfied by single-shot and shotgun-style double rifles, until the widespread issue of military magazine rifles caused hunters to question whether they should carry guns that gave them the chance of a speedy third, fourth or fifth shot.

The renowned military rifles—Lee-Enfield, Mannlicher and Mauser—attracted the greatest attention prior to 1914. However, owing to the rearward position of its locking lugs, the Lee was comparatively weak; and the magazine of most pre-1900 Mannlichers required a special clip, acceptable militarily but much less appropriate for sportsmen. Only the Mauser had impeccable credentials.

Though Mauser actions were supplied to individual gunsmiths prior to 1900—George Gibbs, for example, obtained Husqvarna-made examples from Sweden as early as 1899—commitment to huge military orders prevented Waffenfabrik Mauser participating with any real enthusiasm. About 1899, however, the Mauser Repetier-Pirschbüchse was introduced. This used the standard 1898-pattern action, usually fitted with the heavyweight cocking piece associated with the export-pattern rifle of 1904. The rifle was capable of withstanding high chamber pressures, encouraging ammunition makers in Germany and Britain to develop new cartridges.

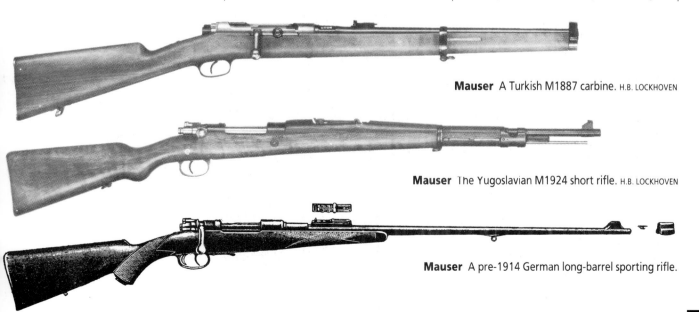

Mauser A Turkish M1887 carbine. H.B. LOCKHOVEN

Mauser The Yugoslavian M1924 short rifle. H.B. LOCKHOVEN

Mauser A pre-1914 German long-barrel sporting rifle.

BRITAIN

The home market was too small to justify production of indigenous Mausers, though BSA touted a modified P.14 (see 'Enfield') whilst Vickers briefly promoted rifles with actions made by DWM prior to 1918.

Prior to 1914, the magazine rifle struggled to gain a foothold in a market dominated by single-shot block-action rifles and the shotgun-like Double Rifles beloved by big-game hunters in Africa and India.

The inability of the Lee action to handle cartridges powerful enough to down rhino and elephant created a niche for the Mauser. Most British gunmakers bought actions in Germany or simply imported complete rifles; many marked by W.J. Jeffrey & Co. of London prior to 1914, for example, seem to have been made in Suhl by Sauer & Sohn.

Anglo-German sporters, though engraved and often stocked in somewhat minimal British style, rarely deviated from the tested 1898-pattern action. Minor components such as safety catches and magazine floor plates occasionally showed proprietary features, but the bolt mechanism was rarely altered. The most obvious differences concerned the sights, but even these blurred as the years passed.

German ammunition makers developed many cartridges powerful enough to satisfy British sportsmen, but poor bullet design—real or imagined—hindered the export success. Until 1939, therefore, most of the 'British Mausers' chambered special proprietary cartridges.

GERMANY

Mauser supplied enormous numbers of actions to custom gunmakers prior to 1914, most being identified only by trademarks on the underside of the receiver. Details of the most important agencies will be found in the accompanying tables. After about 1930, Mauser also finished many 7·9mm Standard-Modell (Kar.98k) rifles for commercial sale. These were offered to those who needed a military-style weapon.

MAUSER-ACTION PATTERNS

Model 1898

Sporting rifle: Pirschbüchse C.98.
Made by Waffenfabrik Mauser AG, Oberndorf am Neckar, 1899–1910.
6 × 57mm, 6·5 × 54mm, 6·5 × 57mm, 7 × 57mm, 8 × 51mm, 8 × 57mm, 9 × 57mm, 9·3 × 57mm or 10·75 × 57mm.
Turning-bolt action, with two lugs on the bolt head locking into the receiver behind the chamber and a safety lug opposing the bolt handle.
DATA FOR A TYPICAL EXAMPLE
9 × 57mm, rimless.
1,142mm overall, 3·25kg unladen.
598mm barrel, 4-groove rifling; RH, concentric.
Internal charger-loaded box magazine, 5 rounds.
Block-and-leaves sight graduated to 300 metres.
640 m/sec with 16·0-gram bullet.

☆

1899: this was introduced in a limited range of chamberings based on the standard military cartridge case—7 × 57mm, 8 × 57mm and 9 × 57mm. Rifles were offered in a selection of half- and full-stock patterns with 600mm barrels and a 1000-metre tangent-sight or simple block-and-leaf Jagdvisier. Mausers all had rounded pistol grips, extensively chequered, and slender stocks. Some of the ribbed rubber butt plates offered before 1909–10 bore 'WM' monograms ('Waffenfabrik Mauser'); later ones used the better-known banner trademark. A standard military-pattern magazine floor plate was used. Bolt handles were invariably turned down and front sights appeared on ramps forged integrally with the barrel. Swivels lay on the butt and barrel collar or band. Set-triggers were optional.

Militia Model

Militia and Universal Rifles:
Wehrmannbüchse und Einheitsgewehr.
Made by Waffenfabrik Mauser AG, Oberndorf am Neckar, c.1900–15.
8·15 × 46·5mm, rimmed.
Action: as Model 1898 sporter, above.

DATA FOR A TYPICAL SPECIMEN
1,250mm overall, 4·17kg unladen.
740mm barrel, 6-groove rifling; RH, concentric.
Sights: see notes.
550 m/sec with 9·7-gram bullet.

☆

1900*: this was little more than a single-shot version of the military Gew.98. A few rifles have been reported with magazines, but a wood block generally altered them to single-loaders; these are believed to be ex-military conversions. Virtually all the rifles chambered a low-power cartridge, credited to a Suhl gunmaker called Fröhn, which seems to have been standardised by the German hunting associations prior to the First World War.

The bolt way had a solid base on purpose-built guns, shaped into a loading tray, and the bolt head lacked the cutaway rim of the service weapon. The Einheitsgewehr ('universal rifle') could be supplied with exchangeable military or sporting-style triggers. An adjustable aperture sight could be fitted to the left rear of the receiver to facilitate target shooting.

Production continued into the post-war era, when a short-lived version with a sleeve-type receiver and an ejection port was offered.

Model 1908

Sporting rifle: Mauser-Pirschbüsche C.98–08.
Made by Waffenfabrik Mauser AG, Oberndorf am Neckar, 1908–15.
6 × 58mm, 6·5 × 54mm, 7 × 57mm, 8 × 57mm, 9 × 57mm, 9·3 × 62mm or 10·75 × 68mm.
Action: as M1898 sporter, above.
DATA FOR A TYPICAL SPECIMEN
6 × 58mm, rimless.
1,141mm overall, 3·02kg unladen.
600mm barrel, 4-groove rifling; RH, concentric.
Internal charger-loaded box magazine, 5 rounds.
Tangent-leaf sight graduated to 1,000 metres.
850 m/sec with 8·2-gram bullet.

☆

1908: very similar externally to the C.98, this was offered in half- and full-stock versions with 600mm barrels and a selection of sights. Most

MUZZLE VELOCITY, 3000 ft. per sec.   MUZZLE ENERGY, 2000 ft. lbs.

Very Flat Trajectory.   No Recoil.   Extremely Accurate.

Magazine Rifle, 5 shots : Weight, 7 lbs.

Diagram made before the Editor of the "FIELD."
Single Rifle.
5 Consecutive Shots at 100 Yards.

HOLLAND'S '240 SUPER EXPRESS

Hollands' " Apex " ·240 Super Express Cartridges,
Showing Belted Positive Stop.

Bullets Cut from Stags.

Actual size : group 1·3 in. by 1·45 in. ;

popular was the block-and-leaves Jagdvisier, but a 1,000-metre tangent-leaf pattern was widely favoured. A 500-metre tangent sight with azimuth adjustment was less common.

Model 1908

Sporting carbine: Mauser-Pirschbüsche C.98–08.
Made by Waffenfabrik Mauser AG, Oberndorf
am Neckar, 1908–15.
6·5 × 54mm, 6·5 × 58mm, 7 × 57mm, 8 × 57mm
or 9 × 57mm.
Action: as M1898 sporter, above.
DATA FOR A TYPICAL SPECIMEN
6·5 × 54mm, rimless.
1,039mm overall, 2·88kg unladen.
500mm barrel, 4-groove rifling; RH, concentric.
Internal charger-loaded box magazine, 5 rounds.
Block-and-leaves sight graduated to 300 metres.
720 m/sec with 7·7-gram bullet.
☆

1908: this carbine had a full stock with a slight swell or hand-stop under the fore-end behind the front sling swivel. The barrel band and the nose cap were carried internally, the Jagdvisier and radial lever floor-plate release were standard, and the trigger guard had a recurved front web.

Model 1908

Army Rifle: Mauser-Armee-Pirschbüsche C.98–08.
Made by Waffenfabrik Mauser AG, Oberndorf
am Neckar, 1908–15.
7 × 57mm, 8 × 57mm or 9 × 57mm.
Action: as M1898 sporter, above.
DATA FOR A TYPICAL SPECIMEN
8 × 57mm, rimless.
1,141mm overall, 2·99kg unladen.
600mm barrel, 4-groove rifling; RH, concentric.
Internal charger-loaded box magazine, 5 rounds.
Block-and-leaves sight graduated to 300 metres.
705 m/sec with 12·9-gram bullet.
☆

1908: this gun had a half-stock, a marking disc on the butt and a standing-block sight. Army type rifles had stepped-cylinder barrels instead of the continuously tapering sporting patterns, and

military-style magazine floor plates replaced the lever-locked unit associated with other Mausers.

Model 1908

Africa Rifle: Mauser-Afrika-Pirschbüsche C.98–08.
Made by Waffenfabrik Mauser AG, Oberndorf
am Neckar, 1909–14.
8 × 57mm, 9·3 × 62mm or 10·75 × 68mm.
Action: as M1898 sporter, above.
DATA FOR A TYPICAL SPECIMEN
9·3 × 62mm, rimless.
1,341mm overall, 3·78kg unladen.
800mm barrel, 4-groove rifling; RH, concentric.
Internal charger-loaded box magazine, 5 rounds.
Sights: see notes.
690 m/sec with 18·5-gram bullet.
☆

1910*: apparently derived from a long-barrelled 1908-type sporter, originally made with a three-quarter stock and a short hand guard running from the chamber to the barrel band, this was specifically intended for sale in India and southern Africa.

It was designed to compete with rifles offered by British gunmakers such as George Gibbs, Holland & Holland and others—many of which were built on actions supplied from Oberndorf.

German-made guns were usually appreciably cheaper than the custom-built English guns, and could be supplied from stock. They were fitted with long barrels 'of best Krupp Steel', and had a ramped silver-bead front sight. The Cape-type back sight, on a prominent base, had two small folding leaves and a large leaf-and-slider. The chequered pistol grip of the half stock had a horn cap; the fore-end had a rounded horn tip.

The bolt handle was turned down, eyes for detachable swivels lay under barrel and butt, and a double set trigger was available to order.

Model A

Made by Mauser-Werke AG, Oberndorf
am Neckar, 1922–41.
Small action: ·250–3000 Savage, 6·5 × 54mm
or 8 × 51mm.

Medium action: 7 × 57mm, ·30–06, 8 × 60mm,
9 × 57mm or 9·3 × 62mm.
Large action: ·280 Ross, ·318 Rimless Nitro Express,
10·75 × 68mm or ·404 Rimless Nitro Express.
Action: as M1898 sporter, above.
DATA FOR A TYPICAL MEDIUM-ACTION GUN
8 × 60mm, rimless.
1,141mm overall, 3·36kg unladen.
600mm barrel, 4-groove rifling; RH, concentric.
Internal charger-loaded box magazine, 5 rounds.
Tangent-leaf sight graduated to 1,000 metres.
775 m/sec with 12·7-gram bullet.
☆

1922: intended for the British market, this was made in three action lengths. These were mechanically identical, differing only in the length of the receiver and the depth of the magazine; the medium and large actions had large-ring receivers, while the smallest had the so-called 'small ring'. The back sight was carried on a distinctive base ahead of the chamber, the front sight being mounted on a ramp.

Pattern No.1 rifles had an Express back sight, with a block for 100 metres and four small folding leaves (200–500 metres); Pattern No.2 had a 1,000-metre tangent-leaf sight.

The magazine floor-plates were released by a pivoting catch inside the trigger guard. The stock had a chequered pistol grip, usually with a metal cap, and a hard rubber butt plate. A fore-end tip of rosewood or buffalo horn was usually fitted to German-made guns. Swivel eyes lay under the butt and on a collar around the barrel.

Though guns varied in detail, military-style two-stage triggers and Express back sights were standard. Optional extras included partly or fully octagonal barrels, set-triggers, or an additional sliding safety catch on the receiver-side or tang.
1941: manufacture ceased, though small-scale assembly continued until 1944.

Model B

Made by Mauser-Werke AG, Oberndorf
am Neckar, 1922–41.
Chambering: as Model A.
Action: as M1898 sporter, above.

Sales ephemera for the ·240 'Apex Super Express' Mauser

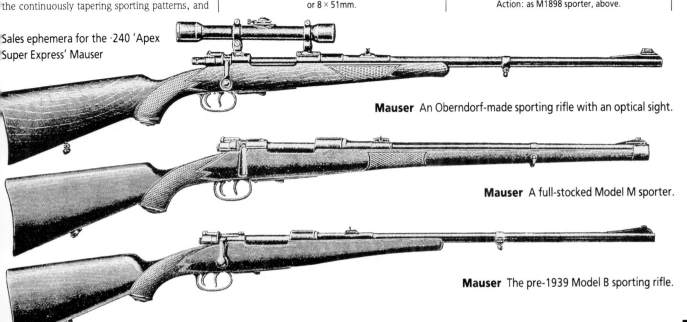

Mauser An Oberndorf-made sporting rifle with an optical sight.

Mauser A full-stocked Model M sporter.

Mauser The pre-1939 Model B sporting rifle.

DATA FOR A TYPICAL EXAMPLE
10·75 × 68mm, rimless.
1,141mm overall, 3·23kg unladen.
600mm barrel, 4-groove rifling; RH, concentric.
Internal charger-loaded box magazine, 5 rounds.
Block-and-leaves sight graduated to 300 metres.
715 m/sec with 18·2-gram bullet.

☆

1922: the standard post-war sporting rifle was essentially similar to the pre-1914 C.98–08. The radial-lever magazine floor-plate release was retained, while the half-stock had a cheek piece, a chequered pistol grip—generally with a metal cap—and a schnabel tip.

A small panel of chequering with distinctive concave borders lay beneath the back sight. A tapered-cylinder barrel was standard, but half- or full-octagon versions were available. Two-stage military, direct-action or double-set triggers could be supplied to order.

Model K

Made by Mauser-Werke AG, Oberndorf am Neckar, 1922–41.
·250–3000 Savage, 6·5 × 54mm or 8 × 51mm.
Action: as M1898 sporter, above.
DATA FOR A TYPICAL SPECIMEN
8 × 51mm, rimless.
1,077mm overall, 2·75kg unladen.
550mm barrel, 4-groove rifling; RH, concentric.
Internal charger-loaded box magazine, 5 rounds.
Block-and-leaves sight graduated to 300 metres.
705 m/sec with 10·2-gram bullet.

☆

1922: this was the small (Kleine) version of the sporting rifle, essentially similar to Model B, but with a short action, a small-diameter receiver ring, and a tapered-cylinder barrel.

Model M

Made by Mauser-Werke AG, Oberndorf am Neckar, 1922–41.
6·5 × 54mm, 7 × 57mm, ·30–06, 8 × 51mm, 8 × 60mm or 9 × 57mm.
Action: as M1898 sporter, above.

DATA FOR A TYPICAL EXAMPLE
6·5 × 54mm, rimless.
1,041mm overall, 3·15kg unladen.
500mm barrel, 4-groove rifling; RH, concentric.
Internal charger-loaded box magazine, 5 rounds.
Block-and-leaves sight graduated to 300 metres.
675 m/sec with 7·7-gram bullet.

☆

1922: this full-stocked Model B had a spatulate bolt handle and the magazine floor-plate released by a catch in the trigger guard. The nose cap was external and a ribbed steel butt plate contained a trap for cleaning equipment.

The usual options were available, though the three-leaf sight and the double set trigger seem to have been considered as standard fittings.

Model S

Made by Mauser-Werke AG, Oberndorf am Neckar, 1922–41.
6·5 × 54mm, 7 × 57mm, 8 × 51mm, 8 × 60mm or 9 × 57mm.
Action: as M1898 sporter, above.
DATA FOR A TYPICAL EXAMPLE
7 × 57mm, rimless.
1,038mm overall, 2·96kg unladen.
497mm barrel, 4-groove rifling; RH, concentric.
Internal charger-loaded box magazine, 5 rounds.
Block-and-leaves sight graduated to 300 metres.
670 m/sec with 10-gram bullet.

☆

1922: a lightweight Model M, this had the normal bolt handle instead of the spatulate form and a radial lever floor-plate release. The stock extended to the tip of the muzzle, the nose cap being fitted internally, and there was usually a slight hand-stop swell at the mid-point of the fore-end. A solid rubber butt plate was fitted.

Heym-made guns

From 1969 until c.1977 Mauser-Jagdwaffen marketed conventional Mauser-action rifles made by Heym (q.v.). The Modell 2000 was available in ·270 and ·308 Winchester, or ·30–06. In 1971, however, it was replaced by

the Model 3000S with skip-line chequering an a ventilated shoulder plate. The Model 3000M (7mm Remington Magnum, ·300 Wincheste Magnum or ·375 H&H Magnum) had a longe barrel and its magazine was restricted to thre rounds instead of five. The short-action Mode 4000 chambered ·222 or ·223 Remingto cartridges only, and had a solid butt plate.

Model 77

77S, 77SM, 77 Sportsman, 83 UIT and SR 86 patterns.
Made by Mauser-Werke Oberndorf GmbH, Oberndorf/Neckar, 1977 to date.
Chambering: see notes.
Action: turning bolt-action, locked by three lugs on th bolt engaging in the receiver bridge (Models 77 and 83) or two lugs on the bolt head engaging the receiver (Model 86).
DATA FOR A TYPICAL MODEL 77S
7 × 64mm, rimless.
About 1,100mm overall, 3·52kg unladen.
600mm barrel, 4-groove rifling; RH, concentric.
Detachable box magazine, 5 rounds.
Block and folding-leaf sight.
900 m/sec with 9-gram bullet.

1977: the Jagdrepetier 77S had a detachabl magazine with the release catch in the for end of the half stock. Hog's back combs an schnabel fore-end tips were standard. The safet catch lay on the right side of the bolt plu and a button controlling the action of the se trigger protruded from the stock behind th bolt handle. Opening the action automaticall returned the trigger to normal operating mode.

The standard chamberings included ·24 Winchester, ·270 Winchester, 6·5 × 57mm 7 × 64mm, ·30–06 Springfield and ·30 Winchester. The similar 77SM rifle—with special 650mm barrel—accepted high powe rounds such as 6 × 68mm, 7mm Remingto and ·300 Winchester Magnums, 8 × 68mm S 9·3 × 62mm, 9·3 × 64mm or 10·3 × 60mm. special heavy pattern, or 'Afrikamodell', wa made for ·375 H&H Magnum.

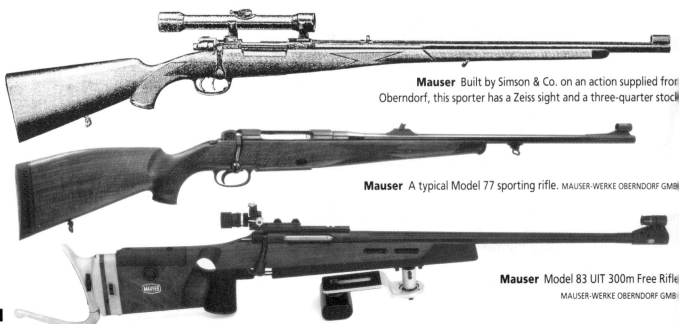

Mauser Built by Simson & Co. on an action supplied fror Oberndorf, this sporter has a Zeiss sight and a three-quarter stoc

Mauser A typical Model 77 sporting rifle. MAUSER-WERKE OBERNDORF GMB

Mauser Model 83 UIT 300m Free Rifl
MAUSER-WERKE OBERNDORF GMB

The M77 Sportsman, with a 600mm heavy barrel and no open sights, was offered in ·243 and ·308 Winchester only. It weighed 4·85kg with a Zeiss Diavari 2·5–10 × 52 optical sight. It had a Monte Carlo-type butt and an accessory rail was let into the underside of the fore-end.

1983: available in single-shot or magazine-fed versions, the Model 83 UIT Standardgewehr (in ·308 Winchester only) was specifically developed for 300-metre target-shooting. Built on an improved 77-type action, it had a match-quality trigger and a competition stock with an adjustable shoulder plate and butt-comb. The Freigewehr was similar, but had a hooked butt plate, a thumb-hole butt and an adjustable palm rest beneath the fore-end. It was destined for 300-metre Free Rifle competitions.

1986: the SR 86 appeared in ·308 Winchester only. Intended as a sniper's rifle, it retained the basic shape of the Model 83; however, the bolt had two lugs locking into the receiver ring instead of the bridge in a search for better accuracy. The sight-rail above the breech was lowered and a laminated stock was used. Fluted to save weight while retaining rigidity, the barrel had an effectual flash suppressor/muzzle brake. Nine-cartridge magazines were standard.

1989: synthetic/thumbhole-type stock options were announced.

GEHMANN-ACTION PATTERNS

Designed by Walter Gehmann of Karlsruhe in the early 1960s, this unique short action presents a complete departure from traditional Mausers. The reduction in length was due largely to the location of the magazine between the trigger and the bolt, and by telescoping the bolt and bolt carrier.

As the bolt retracted to open the breech, the handle struck the bolt-carrier bridge; bolt and carrier then ran back together over the wrist of the stock. The ejector and extractor were both carried in the bolt head; a safety catch lay on the right side of the cocking-piece shroud; and the bolt stop protruded from the right side of the stock above the trigger.

Model 66

66 Diplomat, 66S, 66SM, 66S Magnum, 66SM Magnum and 66ST patterns.
Made by Mauser-Werke Oberndorf GmbH, Oberndorf/Neckar, 1965 to date.
Group I: ·243 Winchester, 6·5 × 57mm, ·270 Winchester, 7 × 64mm, ·30–06 or ·308 Winchester.
Group II: 9·3 × 64mm only.
Group III: 6·5 × 68mm, 7 × 66mm vom Hofe or 8 × 68mm S.
Group IV: 7mm Remington Magnum, ·300 Winchester Magnum, ·375 H&H Magnum or ·458 Winchester.
Action: turning bolt-action, locked by lugs on the bolt head engaging in the barrel extension and by the bolt handle turning down into its seat.
DATA FOR A TYPICAL EXAMPLE
7 × 66mm vom Hofe, rimless.
992mm overall, 3·65kg unladen.
600mm barrel, 4-groove rifling; RH, concentric.
Internal box magazine, 3 rounds.
Block and folding-leaf sight.
1,005 m/sec with 11-gram bullet.
☆

1965: the prototype was exhibited at the international fair (IWA) in Nürnberg.

1966: guns were introduced commercially. Cap-head bolts retaining the receiver ring and the back sight block could be loosened, allowing the barrel/receiver ring assembly to be replaced after the bolt had been opened. Shutting the action automatically indexed the barrel, the retaining bolts were replaced and the gun was ready for use.

The Modell 66S had a walnut half-stock with a hog's back comb, a ventilated rubber butt plate, a rosewood or ebonite pistol-grip cap, and a rounded rosewood fore-end tip. Chequering lay on the pistol-grip and fore-end, swivels appearing under butt and barrel. A double set trigger was regarded as standard, though a single trigger (with a setting button on the upper tang) and a two-stage match trigger were optional.

Model 66ST ('Stutzen') shared the basic action and half-stock, but had a 530mm barrel. It has been marketed as the '660 Ultra' in the USA. The 66SM amalgamated the standard action and barrel with a Monte Carlo comb, modified pistol-grip contours and a schnabel fore-end tip. The Model 66SM Carbine was a short form of the 66SM, with a 530mm barrel, a full-length stock, a straight comb and a Bavarian cheek piece.

The 66S Magnum and 66SM Magnum were identical with the standard rifles, but had 650mm barrels, larger diameter bolt faces and deeper magazines.

Diplomat guns (66S, 66SM and magnums) displayed engraved game motifs—red and roe deer, or red deer and wild boar—and had selected stocks. 'Super deluxe' versions, made only to order, featured complex chequering, scroll engraving and baroque stock-carving.

Model SP 66

Sniper rifle.
Made by Mauser-Werke Oberndorf GmbH, Oberndorf/Neckar, 1976 to date.
·308 Winchester/7·62 × 51mm NATO only.
Action: as Model 66, above.
1,120mm overall, 6·25kg with sight.
680mm barrel, 4-groove rifling; RH, concentric.
Internal box magazine, 3 rounds.
Optical sight.
720 m/sec with 10·9-gram bullet.
☆

1976: this gun embodied a specially-selected action, a heavy barrel with an effectual flash-hider/muzzle brake, and a massive wood stock with a thumb-hole grip. The butt plate and cheek piece were adjustable and a Zeiss Diavari 1·5–6 × 42 optical sight was fitted.

The SP 66 offered advantages over most conventional bolt-action patterns, as it had an ultra-fast lock time and—owing to the position of the handle—the bolt could be operated with minimal disturbance of aim.

Mauser-Gehmann sniper rifles have been used in small numbers by military, paramilitary and police throughout the world. However, the lack of a high-capacity box magazine has been disadvantageous.

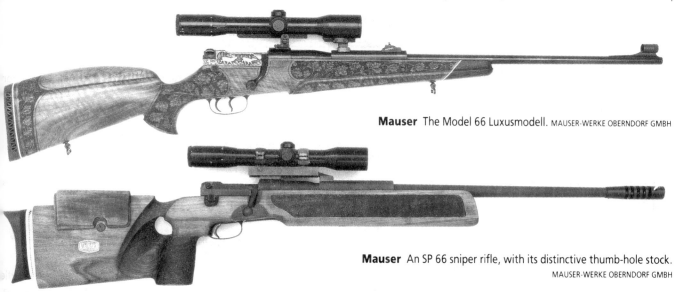

Mauser The Model 66 Luxusmodell. MAUSER-WERKE OBERNDORF GMBH

Mauser An SP 66 sniper rifle, with its distinctive thumb-hole stock.
MAUSER-WERKE OBERNDORF GMBH

MAUSER
SPORTING RIFLES: LESSER MAKERS, 1900–92

Very few Mauser-system sporters were made in Germany prior to 1918, other than those emanating from Waffenfabrik Mauser AG or created around Oberndorf-made actions. Effectual patent legislation, and the stranglehold of the production cartel, prevented any large-scale exploitation of the Mauser action virtually until the beginning of the First World War; Schilling and Haenel, for example, continued to offer guns based on the obsolescent Gew.88.

¶ After 1920, however, the scene changed dramatically; tens of thousands of war-surplus guns were available for customisation, and the major manufacturers still had huge stockpiles of unused parts. A few thousand actions could keep a moderate-size gunmaker busy for years.

¶ Consequently, the strength and availability of the Mauser action encouraged independent gunsmiths—particularly in and around Suhl—to stock or finish sporting rifles in their own name. The list that follows, therefore, can be little more than a guide to the most important customisers.

¶ In addition, substantial quantities of two-shot 12, 16 and 20-bore shotguns were made in Suhl from war-surplus Gew.98. The work of Gebrüder Heym ('Geha') and Gebrüder Rempt ('Remo'), these date from c.1925–33 and c.1932–3 respectively.

¶ Some of the special cartridges chambered in British-made Mauser sporters were extremely hard-hitting, Jeffrey's ·500 Rimless Nitro Express being the most powerful available prior to 1939. They were also often very large, necessitating deepened magazine cases to contain three, four or five rounds. However, excepting these modifications, the rifles were generally much the same as their German rivals. Folding-leaf Express sights were preferred to tangent-leaf types, and the use of folding aperture sights (usually attached to the cocking piece) was encouraged.

THE REGISTER

Atkin, Grant & Lang of St James's, London, was a 1960s amalgamation of the businesses of Henry Atkin, Stephen Grant & Sons, and Joseph Lang & Son. All three of these original London gunmakers made sporting rifles under their own names, apparently including a few Mausers created around actions purchased in Germany. Similar guns have been made in more recent times.

¶ In 1965, Atkin, Grant & Lang was offering the budget-price 'Charles Lancaster' rifle on the basis of a standard military-surplus 1898-pattern Mauser action. Chambered for ·243 Winchester, ·270 Winchester, ·30–06 or ·308 Winchester rounds, it had a 24in barrel, weighed about 7lb, and had a walnut stock with a Monte Carlo comb. A ventilated rubber shoulder plate was used, and the pistol grip had a separate cap (synthetic or ebonite). Chequering appeared on the pistol grip and fore-end, the rounded tip of the latter being rosewood or ebony on better-quality guns. Sights comprised a ramped blade and a 100-yard block with folding leaves for 200 or 300 yards.

Bighorn Rifle Company of Orem and (subsequently) American Fork, Utah, made sporting rifles on commercial Mauser actions in 1983–7—apparently FN or Spanish Santa Barbara types. Made to individual specifications in chamberings from ·22–250 to standard medium-length magnums, the Bighorn rifle usually had a good quality straight-comb half stock, with hand-cut chequering and a rounded ebony or rosewood fore-end tip. Two barrels were supplied with each gun.

Otto Bock of Berlin made sporting rifles embodying Oberndorf-made Mauser actions. Many chambered the then- proprietary 9·3 × 62mm cartridge, developed in c.1905.

Wilhelm Brenneke of Leipzig and Berlin was basically a developer of ammunition, his Mauser-type rifles embodying Oberndorf actions. The first guns, made about 1912, chambered a special 8 × 64mm round. A 7 × 64mm Brenneke cartridge was introduced during the First World War, followed by a 9·3 × 64mm pattern in 1924. This was chambered in conventional Mauser-type sporters. However, many guns were modified in Brenneke's workshops before being stocked. Typical of the improvements were a raised left receiver wall, an improved floor-plate release, and a ball-catch on the receiver to keep the bolt handle shut.

¶ The 8 × 64mm cartridge was reintroduced in the late 1950s by W. Brenneke GmbH of Berlin-Schöneberg, descended directly from the pre-1945 company. By 1965, Brenneke was offering an assortment of Mauser-action rifles, older versions embodying war-surplus Kar.98k actions while newer ones used newly-made FN-Mauser patterns. Most of the older guns had the thumb-cut on the left side of the receiver filled and the receiver-side refinished to hide their origins. Available in 7 × 64mm, 8 × 64mm S or ·30–06, the Model 1 offered a 660mm barrel and weighed about 3·3kg unladen. It had a slender stock with a slight hog's back comb, a small round cheek piece, and a ventilated butt pad. A pistol-grip cap and a contrasting fore-end tip were customary. Chequering was hand cut. The sights were usually a hooded ramped blade and a folding leaf, but optical-sight mounts could be encountered on the bridge and barrel. Models 1A and 1B had double and single triggers respectively.

¶ Model 2 was a 'carbine' version of the Model 1, with a 600mm barrel; the Model 3 big-game rifle had a 660 or 680mm barrel and weighed 4·1kg. It chambered 9·3 × 64mm rounds and had a single trigger.

Browning Arms Company of St Louis, Missouri (now Morgan, Utah), offered substantial numbers of rifles built on FN-Mauser actions from 1959 onward. They featured a simplified trigger—inspired by the Winchester Model 70—and a modified bolt stop that could be pressed inward to release the bolt. The safety was changed to a sliding catch on the tang behind the bolt shroud. The earliest guns were chambered for ·243 Winchester, ·264 Winchester Magnum, ·270 Winchester, ·300 H&H Magnum, ·30–06, ·308 Winchester, ·338 Winchester Magnum, ·375 H&H Magnum, or

·458 Winchester Magnum cartridges. Others (e.g., 7mm Remington Magnum and ·308 Norma Magnum) were added at a later date. The guns were offered until 1974; however, the ·243 and ·308 Winchester options were abandoned on the introduction of Sako medium-action sporters in 1965. Standard Mauser-pattern rifles had 22in barrels and weighed 7·1–7·2lb. Butt plates were solid rubber. The Magnums had 24in barrels, weight averaging 8·25lb. Their butt plates were ventilated.

¶ The basic Browning rifles were offered in Safari Grade, with folding-leaf back sights, good quality walnut stocks with Monte Carlo combs, and hand-cut chequering on the pistol grip and fore-end. The Medallion Grade version, introduced in 1961, had scroll engraving on the receiver and barrel. A ram's head was engraved on the floor plate, selected walnut was used for the stock; pistol-grip caps and fore-end tips were rosewood. The Olympian Grade had an engraved blued barrel, but the receiver and trigger guard/floor plate assembly were engraved satin chrome. A gold inlay distinguished the pistol-grip cap, whilst the stocks were selected for the beauty of their figuring.

H. Burgsmüller & Söhne of Kreiensen am Harz, Germany, manufactured a few combination guns prior to 1914. Usually built on Oberndorf-made 1898 type actions, the curious-looking weapons had a separate shotgun barrel beneath the rifle. The breech of the shotgun, locked by a lever running forward beneath the fore-end, swung outward to the left for loading. An auxiliary hammer protruded from the stock alongside the left side of the bolt shroud, and was generally fired by the front trigger.

Carl Gustafs Stads Gevärsfactori of Eskilstuna, the principal Swedish government rifle factory, made large numbers of Model 63 target rifles. Based on the proven 1896-pattern Swedish military action—lacking the third or safety lug associated with the 1898-type Mausers—the rifle cocked on closing, though changes had been made to reduce the lock time. Chambered for 6·5 × 55mm or 7·62 × 51mm NATO cartridges, the rifle had a distinctive half stock with a deep butt and an upright pistol grip. A hand guard ran from the receiver ring to the tip of the fore-end. A single band was used, and swivels lay under the fore-end and butt; competition-pattern aperture sights were customary. Bolt handles were straight, slightly bent, or turned down against the stock.

¶ The Carl Gustaf factory was amalgamated with the Husqvarna operations in 1970, forming Forenade Fabriksverken. Work on the Model 63-type Mausers had already ceased; subsequent interest centred on the Husqvarna-type sporting rifles.

Century International Arms, Inc. of St Albans, Vermont, have offered refurbished ex-Swedish Model 1896 or Kar.98k-type actions in good-quality beech half-stocks with Monte Carlo butts, chequered capped pistol grips, and round-tipped fore-ends. 1987-vintage No.38 (Swedish type) guns were chambered for 6·5 × 55mm cartridges only, while No.98—introduced in

1992—may be obtained in ·243 Winchester, ·270 Winchester, ·30–06 or ·308 Winchester.

Československá Zbrojovka of Brno made its first sporting rifles in the early 1930s, apparently to compete against the output of Oberndorf. They had military-style actions, with cut-outs milled in the left side of the receiver and classical wing-type safety catches. The Model A was a half-stock rifle; Model B was a fully stocked carbine. The bolt handles were generally turned downward and—on most carbines at least—spatulate. A double set trigger mechanism was standard, together with a delicate pierced-web trigger guard. Chambering options included 7 × 57mm, 8 × 57mm and 8 × 60mm S.

¶ The original guns were supplemented shortly before the German invasion of Czechoslovakia by the Models 21 (half-stock rifle) and 22 (fully stocked carbine). Most guns had 560mm (rifle) or 520mm (carbine) barrels, weights averaging 3–3·3kg. The bolt handles were generally spatulate, turned downward and shaped to clear an optical sight. The safety catch was moved to the left side of the bolt shroud, where it locked the firing pin, and the left receiver wall retained its full height. Chamberings included 6·5 × 57mm, 7 × 64mm, 8 × 57mm, 8 × 60mm S and 9 × 57mm. The magazines held five rounds, and folding back sights were standard.

¶ The Thalson Import Company of San Francisco sold some 7 × 57mm guns in the USA after the Second World War as the Models 721 and 722.

¶ The pre-war Mauser-pattern rifles were replaced after the 1948 revolution by the ZG 47, a modified Mauser credited to Galaš (see 'Czechoslovak factories', page 57).

Churchill (Gunmakers) Ltd of London, created from Robert Churchill & Company since the end of the Second World War, has made rifles embodying Mauser actions supplied by ZCZ in Yugoslavia. A special 'One of One Thousand' was made for Interarms, Churchill's parent, to celebrate the American company's twentieth anniversary in 1973. Offered in ·270 Winchester, 7mm Remington Magnum, ·300 Winchester Magnum, ·30–06, ·308 Winchester, ·375 H&H Magnum or ·458 Winchester Magnum, the rifle had a 24in barrel and weighed 8·0–8·5lb; the magazine held five standard or three magnum cartridges. The half-stock had a straight comb, chequering on the pistol grip and fore-end, and a rounded ebonite tip. Express-type sights and quick-detachable swivels were standard. (Note: the Churchill brand-name has also been associated with bolt-action rifles made in Italy by FIAS and sold in North America by Kassnar.)

Cogswell & Harrison of Piccadilly, London, incorporated with a limited liability in 1882, has also made Mauser-action sporting rifles. Most of these are believed to date from the post-1945 period; prior to 1939, Cogswell & Harrison had relied on Lee-type rifles and expended effort on the comparatively unsuccessful Certus (q.v.) before the First World War.

¶ In 1965, Cogswell & Harrison was offering a series of Mauser-action rifles, built on old

German or new FN actions. The Longford, available in ·30–06 or ·308 Winchester only, was the basic pattern; built on a war-surplus action, it had a 22in barrel and a plain pistol-grip stock with a straight comb. Swivels lay under butt and round tipped fore-end. The back sight was usually a tangent-leaf.

¶ Offered in 7 × 57mm Mauser, ·30–06, ·300 H&H Magnum, ·308 Winchester, 9·3 × 62mm Mauser, 9·5mm Nitro Express, ·375 H&H Magnum, ·404 Nitro Express or ·458 Winchester, the Special Model had a better-quality stock than the Longford and greater attention was paid to finish. Barrels measured 22–26in. The front swivel lay on the barrel, and a folding-leaf back sight was usually fitted. Rosewood or ebonite fore-end tips were customary. The Take Down model was similar to the Special, but had an interrupted-screw joint between the action/butt group and the barrel/fore-end.

¶ The De Luxe pattern was essentially similar to the Special Model, but had a select walnut stock (with a straight or Monte Carlo comb) and the action was engraved with scrollwork. A Cape or Express sight lay above the barrel on a quarter-rib, though a curious folding peep sight was also often attached to the bolt plug. De Luxe rifles were chambered to order.

Colt's Patent Fire Arms Mfg Co. (Colt Industries, Firearms Division) of Hartford, Connecticut, marketed rifles built on FN-Mauser actions in 1957–61. Embodying the improved Supreme action, with the safety catch on the receiver behind the bolt handle, they had conventional internal magazines.

¶ The Coltsman Standard had a 22in barrel and a plain straight-comb butt without a cheekpiece. The Coltsman Deluxe had a 24in barrel and better woodwork, with chequering on the pistol grip and fore-end; the Coltsman Custom had a selected walnut stock with a Monte Carlo comb and cheek piece. The guns were all available in ·300 H&H Magnum or ·30–06 only, had five-round magazines and weighed between 7 and 7·3lb.

Libero Daffini of Brescia, Italy, offered a sporting rifle built on surplus Kar.98k actions in 1955–70. Chambered for ·30–06 or 8 × 57mm cartridges, typical examples had 550mm barrels and pistol-grip stocks with Monte Carlo combs.

John Dickson & Sons of Edinburgh made a few Mauser-type sporting rifles on old German or new FN actions. A typical Caledonian Model—chambered for ·243, ·270 or ·308 Winchester cartridges—had a 22in barrel and a typically British Express back sight on a short rib. Walnut stocks with Monte Carlo combs and rounded fore-ends were standard.

G.C. Dornheim of Suhl—one of Germany's principal wholesalers of guns and hunting goods—marketed 'Gecado' brand Mauser sporters between the wars. They were invariably made elsewhere. The business was purchased by Albrecht Kind in 1940.

Karl Dschulnigg of Salzburg, basically a custom gunsmith, made sporting rifles on Mauser, Mannlicher and Sako actions in virtually any chambering the customer requested. The basic Mauser—in 1965, at least—was generally a refurbished Kar.98k action in a good-quality stock. The butt had a straight comb, a small round cheek piece, and a slender pistol grip with hand-cut chequering. The chequered fore-end had a shallow schnabel tip. Single or double triggers were fitted to order, within a typically European trigger-guard bow.

¶ The 'Top Hit' was similar to the standard pattern, but had a beech stock with a Monte Carlo comb and skip-line chequering. A radial magazine floor-plate latch was popular, with sights comprising a hooded ramped blade and an adjustable folding leaf. Most guns were supplied with extended safety catches and mounts for optical sights.

¶ The Grade I rifle offered a walnut stock, with a sharply curved pistol grip and a contrasting rosewood fore-end tip. A military-surplus action was often used, though the cut-out in the left receiver wall was generally filled and refinished.

¶ The Ibex Model had a modernistic stock, with a straight-cut fore-end tip, an exaggerated pistol-grip cap, and a broad beaver-tail fore-end. The standard guns had silver-inlaid engraving on the receiver and magazine floor plate, though gold inlay could be substituted on request. The Chamois was similar, though its butt had a Monte Carlo comb and a conventional pistol-grip cap; the slender fore-end had an oblique-cut tip. Chequering was often replaced by carved oakleaves.

¶ The Tiger Model was similar to the Chamois, excepting for its hog's back comb and squared Bavarian-style cheek piece. The ebonite fore-end was squared.

¶ Ram and Roebuck models had a schnabel-tip ebonite fore-end and a roll-over comb, plus oakleaves instead of chequering. They invariably had spatulate bolt handles.

¶ Excepting the Tiger, most rifles were supplied with double triggers unless the purchaser specified otherwise. Open sights, when fitted, comprised a hooded ramped blade (or bead) and a folding leaf.

Doumoulin & Fils of Milmort, near Liège, made Mauser-type sporters. The MR-2 was a standard rifle with a refurbished action, a straight-comb stock and a rounded fore-end tip of ebony, rosewood or horn. The pistol grip and the fore-end were chequered; swivels lay under the butt and on the barrel; and the leaf sight was graduated for 100–300 metres.

¶ The MR-5 was a deluxe version, with a block-and-leaves sight set into the front of a short rib stretching forward from the chamber. The receiver was invariably engraved with scroll or foliation.

¶ Type A rifles were built on new actions purchased from Fabrique Nationale. Chambered for ·375 H&H Magnum cartridges, they had Monte Carlo combs and tapering fore-ends with short rounded ebony or rosewood tips. Two- or three-leaf Express sights were let into quarter ribs, hinged magazine floor plates were fitted, and the front swivel was attached to the barrel ahead of the fore-end.

¶ Type DM rifles—chambered for 7 × 57mm,

7·65 × 53mm or 8 × 57mm ammunition— were also built on FN actions. Their stocks usually exhibited an exaggerated pistol-grip cap, a notch-back Monte Carlo comb, and a squared reverse-cut ebonite fore-end tip; chequering was skip-line or basket-weave. Williams sights were fitted.

Fabrique Nationale d'Armes de Guerre of Herstal-lèz-Liège, Belgium, made sporting rifles in small numbers prior to the First World War—apparently to use old 1893-pattern actions that had remained in stock since the 1890s. Chambered for 7 × 57mm or 7·65 × 53mm cartridges, they cocked on the closing stroke of the bolt and were stocked in minimal English fashion, with straight combs and slender round-tipped fore-ends.

¶ Guns made between the wars were based on the 1924-pattern military action. The most popular version had a straight-comb half-stock, though fully stocked examples are known. However, production does not seem to have been excessive.

¶ Work on 1924-type sporting rifles began again in 1947, the earliest being assembled from a selection of pre-war and wartime parts. Bolt handles were swept downward, though the first guns retained a simple military-style single-stage trigger. The chamberings were initially 7 × 57mm, 8 × 57mm and ·30–06 only, ·270 Winchester being added in 1948.

¶ Changes were soon made: the underside of the bolt-handle knob was chequered, the military-style trigger was altered to give a single pressure, the magazine floor-plate release was improved, and the left wall of the receiver retained its height where the thumb cut-away would normally lie. In the autumn of 1948, the safety was altered to limit its rotation (but remained on top of the bolt shroud) and the charger guides were deleted. Alternative ·220 Swift, ·257 Roberts, ·250–3000 Savage and ·300 Savage chamberings were available by the beginning of 1950; ·243 Winchester, ·244 Remington, ·308 Winchester, 8 × 60mm S, 9·3 × 62mm, 9·5 × 57mm and 10·75 × 68mm were subsequently added.

Mauser An RWS (Dynamit Nobel) sporter, built on a Spanish Santa Barbara action. KARL SCHÄFER

Mauser A Model 66 sporting rifle, with the short Gehmann-pattern action. MAUSER-WERKE OBERNDORF GMBH

Mauser A typical Model 77 sporting rifle. MAUSER-WERKE OBERNDORF GMBH

Mauser
The Oberndorf factory, from a painting dated 1909.
ROLF GMINDER

¶ Most of the rifles had straight combs and generously proportioned fore-ends with rounded tips. Their barrels were usually 610mm long, weights were 3·4–3·7kg, and the magazines held five rounds. Guns intended for sale in North America had Monte Carlo-type stocks and Tri-Range back sights; most European examples had straight combs and folding two-leaf sights. Presentation-grade guns were introduced in the mid 1950s, with selected stocks and engraved metalwork, but were discontinued in 1963.

¶ Known as the Deluxe or 'Serie·200' after the introduction of the 300-pattern guns in 1957, the standard FN-Mauser action was discontinued in the early 1960s—though new guns were available from dealers' stock for several years.

¶ A Magnum version appeared in 1953, sharing the standard action with the magazine box and the bolt head altered to accommodate the ·300 or ·375 H&H Magnum cartridges. The pattern was abandoned about 1963, having been offered for the ·264 Winchester, 7mm Remington, ·300 Winchester or ·458 Winchester magnum rounds in addition to the original Holland & Holland types. Magazine capacity was three cartridges instead of the standard five.

¶ The first single-shot 'Bench rest' action appeared in 1955, with a solid-base receiver. Three differing bolts accepted ·222 Remington, ·30–06 or the belted magnums.

¶ In the mid 1950s, Fabrique Nationale developed the 'Serie·300' action, announced in Europe in 1956 and later known as the 'Supreme'. Characterised by a radial safety on the right side of the action behind the bolt handle, it had a smooth-topped receiver bridge and a modified trigger mechanism. A hinged magazine floor plate was standard, the release catch being set into the front of the trigger-guard bow. The trigger itself

was a minor adaption of the Sako No.4.

¶ The actions were successful commercially, being used by Colt, Harrington & Richardson, High Standard and Marlin. In 1970, they were being made in several patterns, ranging from the No.1, for standard-length cartridges (e.g., ·270 Winchester and ·30–06), to the No.7 for magnums such as ·264 or ·338 Winchester; all versions shared the same receiver, alterations being made only to the magazine and the bolt where necessary. The No.6 Bench Rest pattern could be supplied with any of three differing bolts, depending on cartridge case-head diameter.

Reinhart Fajen Mfg Co., Inc. of Warsaw, Missouri, stocked and completed large numbers of Acra S-24 rifles on Santa Barbara actions. They were bedded with synthetic Acraglas in pursuit of consistent accuracy.

FAVS (Fabbrica Armi Valle Susa di Guglielminotti) of Villarfochardio/Torino, Italy, offered refurbished military-surplus actions in the mid 1960s in a slender three-quarter length stock. Monte Carlo combs, schnabel-tip fore-ends, and skip-line chequering were standard. Barrels measured 600mm or 650mm, and were chambered to order; double triggers were also supplied on request. Most guns had engraving on the receiver and magazine floor-plate.

Firearms Co. Ltd of Bridgwater, England, has been making the 'Alpine' Mauser-action sporting rifle for many years. The actions, once refurbished war surplus, have apparently been purchased from Belgium (FN) and Spain (Santa Barbara).

¶ The 1965-vintage pattern was made with a plastic-finished wood stock in ·243 Winchester, ·270 Winchester, ·30–06 or ·308 Winchester. It had a 24in barrel, weighed

about 7·5lb and had a five-round magazine. The sights comprised a hooded blade and an adjustable Williams ramp.

¶ By 1991, guns were being made in Custom and Supreme grades, chambered for ·22–250, 7mm Remington Magnum and 8mm Remington Magnum in addition to those previously listed. Standard guns had 23in barrels and five-round magazines; magnums had 24in barrels and three-round magazines. The walnut stock generally displayed skip-line chequering.

Firearms International Corporation of Washington, DC, sold sizeable numbers of the Musketeer rifle, built on an FN-Mauser action. Dating from 1963–69, these had comparatively plain pistol-grip half stocks with Monte Carlo combs. Bolt handles were generally turned downward, but open sights were customarily omitted. Standard chamberings included ·243 Winchester, ·25–06, ·270 Winchester, ·30–06 or ·308 Winchester (five-round magazines), plus ·264 Winchester Magnum, 7mm Remington Magnum or ·300 Winchester Magnum (three rounds). Barrels usually measured 24in, weights averaging 7·3lb.

Waffen-Frankonia of Würzburg has handled large numbers of Mauser-pattern sporting rifles, usually built on refurbished 1898-type military actions. The origins of these rifles remain unclear. In 1965, the company was advertising the Favorit, in a pistol-grip half-stock with a slight hog's back comb and a small round cheek piece. Available in ·243 Winchester, 6·5 × 57mm, 7 × 57mm, 7 × 64mm, ·270 Winchester, ·30–06, ·308 Winchester, 8 × 57mm, 8 × 68mm S, 9·3 × 62mm or 9·3 × 64mm, it had a double trigger system (within the cramped military-style trigger guard) and a folding-leaf back sight.

¶ The 'Favorit Safari' was similar to the standard gun, excepting for its single trigger, ventilated rubber shoulder pad and recoil bolt; it was chambered for 8 × 68mm S, ·375 H&H Magnum, 9·3 × 62mm, 9·3 × 64mm or ·458 Winchester.

¶ The Favorit De Luxe was offered as a 2·8kg 'Leichtmodell' (in ·243, 6·5 × 57mm, 7 × 57mm, 7 × 64mm or 8 × 57mm only) or as a 3·3kg Standardmodell in all the regular chamberings. The lightweight gun had a slender stock with a Monte Carlo comb, a ventilated rubber butt pad, a contrasting square-cut fore-end tip, and skip-line chequering. The standard rifle had a shallow hog's back comb, a small rounded cheek piece, a plain rounded fore-end, and conventional chequering.

Walter Gehmann of Karlsruhe (see Vom Hofe, below), has made Mauser-type 'Original Vom Hofe' rifles on the basis of actions purchased from Husqvarna. Offered with double triggers, twin lateral recoil bolts and sharply curved pistols grip, the rifles generally had 620mm or 680mm barrels and three-cartridge magazines. Chamberings were restricted in 1965 to 5·6 × 61 Vom Hofe, 7 × 66mm Vom Hofe and 6·5 × 68mm RWS.

Gustav Genschow & Co. AG (Berlin, Durlach bei Karlsruhe, Alstadt-Hachenburg) sold many Mauser-type sporters in 1920–39. Almost all were made elsewhere, even though Genschow maintained substantial gunsmithing facilities in its principal warehouses. Genschow Mausers often bore nothing but the well-known 'Geco' trademark. The business was eventually acquired by Dynamit Nobel in 1959.

George Gibbs of Bristol, England, chambered Mauser-type rifles for his ·256

Gibbs Magnum (introduced in 1913) and the ·505 Rimless Magnum of 1910–11. The actions were purchased directly from Oberndorf prior to 1914, though post-1920 guns showed greater variety.

Gibbs Rifle Company of Martinsburg, West Virginia, succeeded to the rifle-making operations of Parker-Hale (q.v.) in 1990. In addition to perpetuating many of the Parker-Hale Mauser patterns, Gibbs has introduced several new patterns. They are distributed by the Navy Arms Company (q.v.), Gibbs' parent.
¶ The Parker-Hale Model 1300C Scout was introduced in 1992 to use spare 1200-series components. Characterised by the old broad trigger guard, it had a 20in barrel with a muzzle brake, a laminated birch stock, and a detachable ten-round box magazine. Supplied only for ·243 or ·308 Winchester cartridges, it was about 41in overall and weighed 8·5lb.
¶ The Midland Model 2100, unlike the original gun of the same designation (see Midland Gun Company, below) embodied a modified 1898-pattern action instead of the 1893 Spanish version. Offered in ·22-250, ·243, 6mm Remington, 6·5 × 55mm, 7 × 57mm, 7 × 64mm, ·300 Winchester Magnum, ·30–06 or ·308 Winchester, it had a walnut stock with a low Monte Carlo comb. About 43in long with the standard 22in barrel, it weighed 7lb. The Model 2600 was similar, but had a plain hardwood stock; the Model 2800 simply had a laminated birch Monte Carlo-pattern stock.
¶ The Midland Model 2700 Lightweight, announced in 1992, had a slender barrel, an alloy trigger guard/magazine floor plate and a lighter stock. Available in all chamberings listed previously, excepting ·300 Winchester Magnum, it weighed a mere 6·5lb.

Golden State Arms Corporation of Pasadena, California, made the Centurion Model 100 (plain), 200 (deluxe) and other rifles on the basis of the Spanish Santa Barbara action. Dating from the mid 1960s, they ranged from plain guns with blind three-cartridge magazines to conventional patterns with hinged magazine floor plates.

Griffin & Howe, Inc. of New York City completed many European-made actions in the USA. Most prove to incorporate Oberndorf-made components.

C.G. Haenel of Suhl is said to have completed a few Mauser-action sporting rifles immediately after the end of the First World War. However, though Haenel had been making Gew.98 since 1915, no guns could be traced for examination. Haenel sporters usually prove to be pre-1920 variations on the Gew.88 or the similar 'Improved Model' rifle of the early 1900s.

Halbe & Gerlich (Halger-Waffenfabrik) of Kiel and later Hamburg, made their first Mauser-type rifles about 1923. These chambered the ·244 Halger Magnum round, though the range was later enlarged to include ·280 Halger Magnum, ·30–06, ·335 Halger Belted Magnum, ·375 H&H Magnum and ·404 Rimless Nitro Express.
¶ The rifles were essentially similar to the standard Oberndorf Mauser sporters of the

period between the wars, though they were often made with half-octagonal barrels and had a mount for an optical sight set forward on the barrel ahead of the receiver ring. Their claim to fame lay in chamberings.

Hämmerli Jagd- und Sportwaffenfabrik of Lenzburg, Switzerland, stocked ex-military Mauser actions until the late 1960s.
¶ The basic Model 700 was a standard Kar.98k— complete with cutaway receiver wall and charger guides—in a walnut half-stock with a straight comb, a small round cheek piece, a ventilated rubber shoulder pad, and a schnabel tip fore-end. The pistol grip and fore-end were chequered. Standard chamberings were 6·5 × 55mm, 6·5 × 57mm, ·270 Winchester, 7 × 64mm, 7·5 × 55mm, ·300 H&H Magnum, ·30–06, ·308 Winchester, 8 × 57mm, 8 × 60mm S, 9·3 × 62mm or 10·3 × 60mm, but others could be supplied on request.
¶ Model 701 was identical, but had a double set trigger instead of the military pattern.
¶ The Models 705 (single trigger) and 706 (double trigger) shared the Kar.98k-type action, but had finer stocks with a Monte Carlo cheek piece and comb; Models 710 and 711 shared the stock of the 705 and 706, but the receivers and magazine floor-plates were engraved. The deluxe Model 715 had extensively engraved metalwork and a carved select-grain stock. Hämmerli Mausers usually had swivels on the butt and barrel, and adjustable folding-leaf sights.

Harrington & Richardson of Worcester, Massachusetts, marketed substantial numbers of Mauser-pattern rifles.
¶ The Model 300 Ultra, built on an FN action, was available in 1967–82 in ·22-250, ·243 Winchester, ·25-06, ·270 Winchester, 7mm Remington Magnum, ·300 Winchester Magnum, ·30–06 or ·308 Winchester. It had a roll-over comb, a contrasting fore-end tip, and chequering on the pistol grip and fore-end. Williams ramp sights were standard. The standard barrel measured 22in, giving an overall length of about 42·5in and a weight of 7·7lb.
¶ The Model 301 Ultra Carbine had a full-length stock with a low Monte Carlo comb and a simple folding-leaf back sight. Available in all the '300' chamberings excepting ·22-250, it was 39in overall, had a 18in barrel and weighed about 7·25lb.
¶ The Model 370 Ultra Medalist (1968–73) varmint/target rifle was also built around an FN Supreme action. Its plain walnut stock had a roll-over comb and a sculpted pistol grip, together with a semi-beavertail fore-end. Offered only in ·22-250, 6mm Remington or ·243 Winchester, it had a heavy 24in barrel and weighed about 9·5lb. Open sights were not supplied.
¶ Introduced in 1982, the Model 340 was built on Husqvarna-Mauser actions imported from Sweden. It was chambered for ·243 Winchester, ·270 Winchester, 7 × 57mm, ·30–06 or ·308 Winchester rounds, had a 22in barrel and weighed about 7·3lb. The half-stock had a straight comb and a generously proportioned round tipped fore-end; the butt plate was a ventilated rubber pattern and the chequering was hand-cut. The rifle was abandoned in 1984.

Friedr. Wilh. Heym GmbH & Co. of

Münnerstadt, Bavaria, made classical Mauser-type sporters for many years. The oldest were based on refurbished wartime actions, though later examples used FN-Mauser actions. Heym then made modified rifles for Mauser (q.v.) before progressing to the SR-20 series described on pages 86–7. Recent large-calibre rifles have reverted to traditional Mauser actions.

High Standard Mfg. Co. of Hamden, Connecticut, made a few thousand High-Power rifles in 1962–6, embodying Mauser actions purchased from Fabrique Nationale.
¶ The Field Model, offered only in ·270 Winchester or ·30–06, had a 22in barrel and a four-cartridge magazine. Its plain hardwood stock had a straight comb and a rounded fore-end tip.
¶ The De Luxe pattern had a chequered walnut stock with a Monte Carlo comb, and quick-detachable swivels. Folding-leaf back sights were standard, though Redfield or Lyman peep sights were sometimes fitted to the receiver.

Hoffmann Arms Company of Cleveland, Ohio, and Ardmore, Oklahoma, marketed substantial numbers of Mauser-action rifles, often chambering proprietary ·276 or ·300 Hoffmann cartridges. A few guns were fitted with the Howe-Whelen aperture back sight, which replaced the bolt shroud; owing to its complexity and high cost, however, the sight was not popular.

Holland & Holland of London, a limited liability company from 1899, offered Mauser rifles chambering ·240 Belted Rimless Nitro Express cartridges (introduced c.1923); ·244 Belted Rimless Magnum (c.1955); ·275 Belted Rimless Magnum Nitro Express (date unknown); ·300 Holland's Super Thirty, subsequently known as the ·300 H&H Magnum (1925); ·375 Belted Rimless Magnum Nitro Express, subsequently known as ·375 H&H Magnum (1912); and the ·400/375 Belted Nitro Express (1905).
¶ The company has made small quantites of Best Quality Magazine Rifles and Deluxe Magazine Rifles in recent years, usually on the basis of FN Mauser actions. Available in ·240 Apex, ·300 H&H Magnum ('Super Thirty Model') and ·375 H&H Magnum only, with four-round magazines and 24in barrels, they usually displayed stocks of the finest quality. Straight combs were considered to be standard, with simple oval cheek pieces and round-tip fore-ends. The folding-leaf sights were often set on a short barrel rib, and a recoil bolt ran through the stock beneath the chamber.

Husqvarna Våpenfabriks of Huskvarna made small numbers of sporting rifles prior to 1940. Built on the 1896-pattern Swedish military Mauser action, most chambered 6·5 × 55mm or 9·3 × 57mm rounds. A typical rifle had a straight-comb half stock, with a shallow pistol grip and the hint of a schnabel tip to the fore-end.
¶ The first 1898-type Mauser sporting rifles were made in the late 1930s, the earliest being chambered for the 9·3 × 57mm cartridge though 6·5 × 55mm, 7 × 57mm, 9·3 × 62mm and others had been added by the end of the Second World War. The

actions were mostly German, supplied as part-payment for machine-tools, steel and roller bearings.
¶ The earliest post-war Husqvarna sporting rifles were built around actions purchased from Fabrique Nationale (q.v.) and had birch stocks. They chambered 6·5 × 55mm, 8 × 57mm or 9 × 57mm ammunition.
¶ They were supplemented by a 1950 model, intended for sale in North America and stocked in walnut. Most guns had straight-comb stocks, but Monte Carlo patterns became increasingly popular as the years passed. Chamberings usually prove to be ·220 Swift, ·270 Winchester or the ubiquitous ·30–06.
¶ The Model 1951 was very similar to the Model 1950, but the safety catch was altered so that it cleared an optical sight in low mounts.
¶ The FN-Husqvarna rifles were replaced by the HVA action, introduced about 1955. The new rifle embodied a small-ring action, lacking the reinforcing collar in the receiver, and the left wall retained its height throughout its length. The bolt shroud was streamlined, a radial safety was added to the right side of the receiver behind the bolt handle, and the ejector was moved to eliminate the slot cut through the relevant locking lug. Bolt handles were generally swept down and back.
¶ The Crown Grade rifles had walnut half-stocks with ebonite pistol-grip caps and fore-end tips; the Model 3000 had a Monte Carlo comb, whereas the otherwise-identical Model 3100 had a straight pattern. Chamberings included ·243 Winchester, ·270 Winchester, 7 × 57mm, ·30–06 or ·308 Winchester. Most rifles had five-round magazines and 600mm barrels; weight averaged 3·4kg.
¶ A few P-3000 'Presentation' rifles were made in the late 1960s, with specially selected walnut stocks and contrasting rosewood accessories. The actions were cursorily engraved.
¶ Lightweight rifles shared the action of the Crown Grade version, but had 520mm barrels and weighed about 2·85kg. The slender stock had a Monte Carlo (4000) or straight (4100) comb and a delicate schnabel tip on the tapering fore-end.
¶ Models 4500 and 4600, sometimes listed as '456', had the standard Lightweight action in a full-length Mannlicher stock. The 4500 pattern had a Monte Carlo comb, whereas its near-relation 4600 was straight.
¶ Made from 1968 until c.1971, the 6000 series (Imperial Custom Rifle) was a variation of the Model 3000 or 3100 with a walnut stock selected for its attractive figuring, an improved trigger and a three-leaf back sight.
¶ The Models 7000 and 7100 (Imperial Custom Lightweight Rifle) were variations of the 4000 series with better stock, trigger and sights. Production was apparently confined to 1968–70.
¶ Many Husqvarna-type rifles were sold in the USA under the Smith & Wesson banner (see below). The perfected Husqvarna rifle, modified in many respects, is considered in the relevant section (pages 90–1). The company's operations were eventually amalgamated with those of the Carl Gustaf factory and marketed under the FFV–Viking Sport Arms AB banner.

M

Paul Jaeger, Inc. of Grand Junction, Tennessee, introduced the Jaeger African, Alsakan and Hunter rifles in 1989. All three were built on commercial (most probably Spanish) Mauser actions.

¶ The African rifle was chambered for ·375 H&H, ·416 Taylor or ·458 Winchester Magnum cartridges, had a graphite-reinforced synthetic stock and weighed about 9lb. The hooded front sight, fitted on a muzzle band, was accompanied by a folding 'night sight'; the back sight was a fixed leaf adjusted for 50 yards.

¶ Alaskan-pattern rifles chambered the 7mm Remington, ·300 Winchester or ·338 Winchester magnum rounds. They had Douglas Premium barrels, Williams ramp back sights, silver bead front sights, and matt blue-black metalwork. Weight was 8lb.

¶ Hunter rifles had Bell & Carlson composite Kevlar-reinforced fibreglass stocks with a wrinkle finish. Offered in ·243 Winchester, ·257 Roberts, ·25–06, ·280 Remington, 7 × 57mm, 7mm–08, ·30–06 or ·308 Winchester chamberings, guns had 22in or 24in Douglas Premium barrels and weighed about 7lb. A laminated wood stock was available as an option.

Jager-Armi di Armando Piscetta of Milano, now better known as 'Armi-Jager', made a few sporting rifles in the 1960s on the basis of refurbished military 1898-type Mauser actions. Offered in ·220 Swift, ·243 Winchester, 6·5 × 57mm, ·270 Winchester, 7 × 57mm, 7 × 64mm, ·30–06, ·308 Winchester or 8 × 57mm, they had half-stocks with Monte Carlo combs and chequering on the pistol-grip and round-tipped fore-end; thin white spacers accompanied black plastic shoulder plates and pistol-grip caps. A folding-leaf back sight was often supplemented by a micro-adjustable peep-sight fitted to the receiver bridge.

W.J. Jeffrey & Company of London—formed from Jeffrey & Davies in 1891—developed the ·280 Rimless (c.1913), the ·303 Magnum (1919), ·333 Rimless Nitro Express (1911), ·404 Rimless Nitro Express (c.1909); and the devastating ·500 Rimless Nitro Express (c.1913).

Kassnar Imports, Inc. of Harrisburg, Pennsylvania, has sold Sabatti (q.v.) bolt-action rifles under the 'Churchill' name. The Highlander and Regent were standard and deluxe versions of the Carabina Modelo Rover. The Highlander Combo was fitted with a 3–9 × 32 Kassnar Vistascope. Highlander rifles had straight-comb butts; Regents had a Monte Carlo pattern.

Albrecht Kind AG ('Akah') of Nuremburg and Berlin was another of the wholesalers that sprang to prominence in the period between the wars. Mauser-action sporting guns have been reported with the company's trademarks—'Akah', 'Eichel', 'Schutzmann' and 'Tanne'—but were undoubtedly made elsewhere, and evidence of the actual manufacturer should be sought from a close inspection of the guns.

¶ Business was re-established in the 1950s from a new headquarters in Hunstig bei Dieringshausen. Among many sporting rifles offered under the Akah brand have been the

Mauser-pattern Merkur and Saturn rifles, often identified by the code-numbers 6939 and 6940 respectively.

¶ Built on refurbished Kar.98k-type actions, possibly by Kriegeskorte (q.v.), the guns had beech or walnut sporting half stocks with hog's back combs and small oval cheek pieces. Chequering appeared on the capped pistol-grip and the shallow schnabel-tipped fore-end. Folding-leaf back sights were fitted and the front swivel eye lay on the barrel ahead of the stock. Chamberings included ·243 Winchester, 6·5 × 57mm, ·270 Winchester, 7 × 57mm, 7 × 64mm, ·30–06, ·308 Winchester or 8 × 57mm. The guns were about 1,130mm long, had 600mm barrels and weighed 3·2kg; five-cartridge magazines were standard.

¶ The Merkur originally had a double set trigger system, while the Saturn had a conventional single trigger. About 1968, however, the categories were merged under the Merkur name and a Merkur-Super appeared with a Monte Carlo-pattern butt and a ventilated rubber shoulder pad. A contrasting fore-end tip was fitted. The standard barrel length remained 600mm, though a 6·5 × 58mm chambering option was added. A new 650mm barrel was introduced, chambered only for 7 × 64mm, 8 × 68mm S, 9·3 × 63mm or 9·3 × 64mm.

Kodiak Mfg Co. of North Haven, Connecticut, made rifles on the basis of refurbished 1898-pattern Mauser actions in c.1959–73. The Model 98—chambered for ·243 Winchester, ·30–06 or ·308 Winchester rounds—was made with a 20in or 24in barrel and a five-round magazine. It had a plain hardwood stock with a low Monte Carlo comb and impressed chequering on the pistol grip and fore-end sides.

¶ The Model 100 Deluxe was similar, but had a better quality stock, a ventilated shoulder plate, and a pistol-grip cap. Made only with a 24in barrel, it chambered, in addition to the three standard 'Model 98' options, an assortment of magnum cartridges—·264 Winchester, 7mm Remington, ·300 Winchester, ·308 Norma, ·338 Winchester, ·350 Remington or ·358

Winchester—and had a 3-round magazine.

¶ The Kodiak 101 Ultra was a variant of the Model 100 with a better walnut stock. The comb was a roll-over pattern and an ebonite fore-end tip was fitted. The pistol grip had an ebonite cap, and a ventilated rubber shoulder pad was used.

¶ Model 102 Varmint Ultra was similar to the '100' pattern, but had a heavy barrel and lacked open sights. It weighed 8·5lb.

Kriegeskorte & Co. of Stuttgart, now better known as Krico GmbH (q.v., Part One) converted standard military-action rifles to effectual sporters in the early 1950s. The company then proceeded to a short-action 'Miniature Mauser'—dating from 1956–62—before developing more modern designs.

Lecocq & Hoffmann of Brussels, Belgium, offered Mauser-type sporting rifles prior to 1940 and again in the 1955–70 period. Built on refurbished military-surplus actions, the post-war standard model had a half-stock with a straight comb. The shallowly curved pistol grip and tapering round-tipped fore-end were extensively chequered; a multi-leaf Express back sight appeared on a short rib and a detachable magazine floor-plate was used. Chamberings included 8 × 60mm, 9 × 57mm, 9·3 × 62mm, 9·5 × 57mm and 10·75 × 68mm.

¶ A big-game rifle was made for the ·375 H&H Magnum round. It had a tangent-leaf or Express back sight, a four-round magazine and a double set trigger system. Pre-war guns had flat panels alongside the action, rounded pistol grips and schnabel-tip fore-ends; post-war examples usually had ventilated rubber butt plates, capped pistol grips and rounded fore-ends.

Manufrance SA of Saint-Étienne, formerly Manufacture Française d'Armes et Cycles, offered Mauser-action sporting rifles into the late 1960s. Built around refurbished wartime actions, with the cutaway on the left side of the receiver filled and the charger guides removed, they included the Model 462 Rival (10·75 × 68mm) and Model 463 Rival (·375 H&H Magnum). The guns had

four-cartridge magazines, were 1,115mm overall, had 600mm barrels, and weighed 3·6kg. Their straight-comb stocks had rounded fore-ends; and three-leaf Express sights were common.

Marathon Products, Inc. of Wethersfield, Connecticut, introduced the Sportsman Bush & Field rifle in 1984. Marketed until about 1987–8, it was built on a Spanish Santa Barbara action and could be obtained in kit form. Chamberings included ·243 Winchester, ·270 Winchester, 7 × 57mm, 7mm Remington Magnum, ·300 Winchester Magnum, ·30–06 or ·308 Winchester. The standard rifle was about 45in overall, had a 24in barrel and weighed 8lb. It had a walnut stock with a low Monte Carlo comb and a heavy squared-tip fore-end.

Mre d'Armes de Chasse Masquelier of Liège offered AMD-1, AMD-2 (both in 8 × 68mm S) and AMD-3 (7 × 64mm) rifles on the basis of FN-Mauser actions. The AMD-2 was simply an AMD-1 with engraving on the receiver and better-quality woodwork. The rifles had slender pistol-grip stocks with Monte Carlo combs and rounded fore-ends with a contrasting rosewood or ebony tip. Thin white spacers generally accompanied the shoulder pad, pistol-grip cap and fore-end tip. (Note: Masquelier may have purchased the guns from Raick Frères [q.v.].)

Gebr. Merkel of Suhl, Germany, stocked and completed Mauser sporters prior to the Second World War—though best known for shotguns, double-rifles and combination guns (Drillinge) of impeccable quality. Merkel used genuine newly-made actions, purchased from Obendorf and acknowledged in the company's advertising literature. The rifles could be supplied in any of the standard Mauser chamberings. Typically, they had long barrels (usually about 710mm) and were stocked almost to the muzzle. The pistol grip was chequered, whilst the fore-end was usually made in two pieces with a diagonal joint behind the front sling loop. The barrels were half-octagonal with a matted top rib, and had a combined

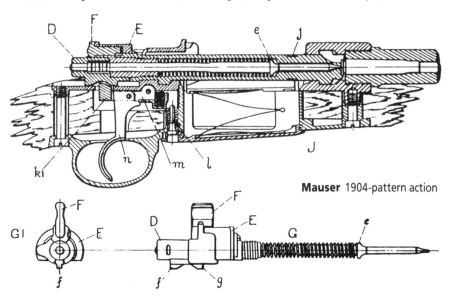

Mauser 1904-pattern action

block-and-leaf back sight (Jagdvisier). Set triggers were common, and the receiver was often engraved; the individual details, however, were left to the whims of the purchaser. By 1939, the company was owned by Adolf Schäde and trading as 'Suhler Waffenwerk Gebr. Merkel'.

Müller & Greiss of Munich, Germany, made a few Mauser-action rifles chambering a special 9·5 × 73mm Magnum cartridge shortly before the First World War. The cartridge was apparently created by necking the British ·404 Rimless Nitro Express.

Midland Gun Company This trading name was used by Parker-Hale (q.v.) to promote the 'Midland Model 2100' rifle, built on an 1893-type Spanish Mauser action. The trading style has been perpetuated by Parker-Hale's successor, the Gibbs Rifle Company (q.v.).

Navy Arms Company Best known for its reproduction firearms, Navy Arms promoted ·45–70 conversions of the military Thai ('Siamese') Mauser rifles in the mid 1970s.
¶ The rifle had a 24in or 26in barrel, weighed 8·2–8·5lb and had a three-round magazine. Its bolt handle was generally straight; the plain pistol-grip stock had a Monte Carlo comb; and a Williams ramp back sight was standard.
¶ The carbine had an 18in barrel, a straight-comb pistol grip half-stock, and the bolt handle turned downward. It weighed 7·5lb.

Parker-Hale Ltd of Birmingham, England, made its first Mauser rifles in the 1960s on the basis of actions purchased in Spain. Work continued until 1990, when interest in the guns passed to the Gibbs Rifle Company (q.v.). Excepting the Model 2100 Midland pattern, discussed separately, Parker-Hale Mausers featured a classic 1898 Mauser action with two locking lugs on the bolt head and a safety lug on the bolt body.
¶ Model 1000 Safari. Introduced about 1965, this had a Santa Barbara (q.v.) action, complete with a cut-away receiver and a conventional safety mechanism on top of the bolt shroud. A five-round magazine with a hinged floor-plate (Model 1000) or a detachable box magazine (1000C) could be obtained. Standard chamberings were ·243, ·270 or ·308 Winchester, plus ·30–06. The walnut half-stock had a Monte Carlo comb, a capped pistol grip, and a fore-end with a plain rounded tip. The chequering was conventional; swivels were fitted under the butt and fore-end. Sights comprised a simple folding leaf dovetailed into the barrel and a ramp-mounted bead with a tubular hood. A typical ·270 1000C was 43in overall, weighed 7·05lb unladen, and had a 22in barrel rifled with four grooves turning to the right. The detachable box magazine held four rounds.
¶ The Model 1000 Standard rifle (apparently dating from the mid 1980s) had a plain walnut stock with a low Monte Carlo comb, impressed chequering on pistol grip and fore-end, and a diced nylon butt plate. Obtainable in nine regular chamberings, the guns were 43in overall and weighed 7·25lb.
¶ The Model 1000 Safari Magnum, only made in ·375 H&H Magnum, had the back sight mounted on a short block and an additional recoil bolt through the stock beneath the chamber. A ventilated rubber butt plate was fitted, and the fore-end had a schnabel tip. The rifles were 44·5in overall, had 24in barrels and weighed 8·5lb.
¶ The Model 1100 (dating from 1968) had a safety catch on the right side of the receiver and the bolt handle swept downward. The magazine floor-plate was released by a catch in the front of the guard. Chamberings were restricted to ·243 Winchester, ·270 Winchester, 7mm Remington Magnum, ·30–06 or ·308 Norma Magnum.
¶ The Model 1100 De-Luxe Safari amalgamated the stock pattern of the ·375 Safari Magnum (above) with the new action.
¶ The Model 1200 Super Safari was originally made in two versions—Model 1200, with a traditional five-round magazine with a hinged floor-plate, and the 1200C with a detachable four-round box magazine ('clip' in Parker-Hale terminology). Standard chamberings were ·243 Winchester, ·270 Winchester and ·30–06. A typical ·243 rifle was 43in overall, weighed 6·8lb and had a 22in barrel with four-groove concentric rifling. The internal box magazine held five rounds and a folding-leaf sight was fitted. All Super Safari rifles had half-stocks with roll-over Monte Carlo combs; ventilated rubber butt plates; contrasting rosewood fore-end tips; white spacer-plates separating the stock from the butt plate, pistol grip and fore-end tip; and skip-line chequering.
¶ Characterised by a 24in barrel, Model 1200 Magnum (1200M) rifles were made only in conventional style for 7mm Remington or ·308 Norma magnum ammunition. Three-round magazines were standard.
¶ The Model 1200 TX was a target rifle, fitted with a PH5 aperture sight. It had a straight comb, a plain pistol grip and a half-length fore-end. Made only for the ·308 Winchester (7·62 × 51mm NATO) cartridge, it was 46·5in long, had a 26in barrel and weighed about 11lb with sights.
¶ The Model 1261 (1968–9) was chambered only for the ·222 Remington cartridge and offered with a detachable box magazine. It had the Safari De Luxe stock and weighed 7·3lb, but was replaced by the 1200V.
¶ From 1969 onward, presentation-grade (1200P) and Varmint (1200V) models were made, the former having quick-detachable swivels and a scroll-engraved action while the latter—chambered for ·22–250, 6mm Remington, ·243 Winchester or ·25–06—offered a 24in heavy barrel without sights. The 1200P was abandoned in 1975.
¶ Announced in 1983, the M81 Classic had a straight-comb walnut stock with hand-cut chequering on the pistol grip and fore-end. The rubber shoulder pad was accompanied by a black spacer, whilst quick-detachable swivels lay under the butt and fore-end. A Williams ramp-pattern back sight could be fitted, though optical sights were popular; set triggers were among the options. Chambered for ·22–250, ·243 Winchester, 6mm Remington, ·270 Winchester, 6·5 × 55mm, 7 × 57mm, 7 × 64mm, 7mm Remington Magnum, ·30–06, ·300 Winchester Magnum or ·308 Winchester rounds, the M81 Classic was about 44·5in overall and weighed 7·7lb.
¶ The M81 African rifles featured engraving on the actions, folding-leaf 'Express' back sights on a quarter rib, and an additional recoil lug. The front swivel lay on the barrel instead of the stock. Chamberings were restricted to ·300 H&H Magnum, ·308 Normag, ·375 H&H Magnum or 9·3 × 62mm. Overall length was about 45in, weight averaging 9lb without sights.
¶ The Model 1200 Super, sharing the action of the M81 series, had a gold-plated trigger. Its half-stock had a roll-over Monte Carlo comb, white spacers, and a ventilated rubber recoil pad. A contrasting rosewood fore-end tip was customary. The 1200 Super was 44·5in long, weighed 7·5lb, and was chambered similarly to the M81 Classic.
¶ Model 1200M Super Magnum rifles duplicated the 1200 Super type described previously, but were chambered for the 7mm Remington, ·300 Winchester and ·308 Norma magnum cartridges.
¶ Otherwise identical with the 1200 Super and Magnum rifles, the 1200C and 1200CM Super-Clip patterns had detachable box magazines restricted to three rounds only.
¶ Dating from 1984, the Model 1100L Lightweight chambered the same cartridges as the 1200 Super (above), but its 22in barrel gave an overall length of 43in. An unladen weight of just 6·5lb was obtained by hollowing the bolt handle, fitting an alloy trigger-guard/floor plate assembly, and slimming the schnabel-tip stock.
¶ Chambered only for ·375 H&H Magnum, ·404 Jeffrey and ·458 Winchester Magnum ammunition, Model 1100M African Magnums (46in long, 9·5lb) had a heavy barrel and a strengthened stock containing an additional recoil bolt. The Monte Carlo comb was shallower than normal, the fore-end had a rudimentary schnabel tip, and a ventilated shoulder pad was standard.
¶ The first of the company's sniper rifles was the Model 82, production of which continued only until the mid 1980s. The rifle was adopted by Australia, Canada (as the Rifle C3) and New Zealand. A typical example was 45·75in overall, had a 26in barrel and weighed about 10·6lb without the optional bipod. Small quantities of M82-type target rifles were also made, often fitted with vertically adjustable butts and Parker-Hale PH5E/TX sights.
¶ The success of the M82 encouraged Parker-Hale to enter a single-shot cadet rifle in British Ministry of Defence trials. A sturdy gun with a short butt and half-length fore-end, this was officially approved for issue as the L81A1 cadet rifle. Some were subsequently offered commerically as the 7·62mm M83 NATO Target Rifle. The action was specially bedded in epoxy resin, accuracy being claimed as a half-minute of angle at 100 yards. A folding leaf sight lay on top of the strengthened receiver, and a replaceable-element tubular front sight was fitted at the muzzle. The L81A1 was 46·73in long, had a 26in barrel, and weighed 10·9lb.
¶ The 7·62 × 51mm M84 Mk II Canberra target rifle had an ambidexterous walnut stock with stippling on the pistol grip and fore-end. It was 48–49·5in overall, depending on butt spacers, and weighed 11·5lb with sights and hand-stop. A full-length accessory rail lay under the fore-end; PH5E aperture sights were used.
¶ Similar mechanically to the Canberra, the M84 Mk II Bisley Model was made with plain right- or left-hand stocks.
¶ The Model 85 sniper rifle was entered in British Army trials in the mid 1980s. It had a detachable ten-round box magazine, measured 45·3in overall (without butt spacers) and weighed 13·75lb with a 6 × 44 optical sight and bipod. The M85 was assessed as 'fit for service', but the Accuracy International PM rifle (q.v.) was preferred; however, Parker-Hale managed to sell the Model 85 to police and paramilitary organisations worldwide.
¶ Derived from the M85, the 7·62mm M86 target rifle had a detachable five-round box magazine and could accept an optical sight. Stocks resembled the Canberra pattern.
¶ Model 87 rifles, adapted from the M86 for moving-target shooting, had distinctive heavy 26in barrels and squared fore-ends with restricted amounts of stippling. Optical sights were standard. A typical example was 45in long and weighed 10lb; chamberings included ·243 Winchester, 6·5 × 55mm, ·30–06, ·300 Winchester Magnum or 7·62 × 51mm NATO.

James Purdey & Sons Ltd of London has made some of the most desirable of all Mauser-type sporters, those dating prior to 1939 incorporating Oberndorf-made actions while the origin of post-war specimens generally proves to be Fabrique Nationale. Some of the rifles made in the 1950–65 period, however, were built around refurbished Kar.98k or similar actions; typically, they were chambered for 7 × 57mm Mauser, ·300 Nitro Express, ·375 Nitro Express (·375 H&H Magnum) or ·404 Nitro Express (·404 Jeffrey, 10·75 × 73mm). Barrels were usually about 22in long, while stocks took the classical English form with a straight comb and a plain rounded fore-end tip. Express sights were commonly fitted.

Rahn Gun Works of Grand Rapids and then Hastings, Michigan, has built sporting rifles around a conventional 1898-pattern Mauser, probably a Santa Barbara (q.v.) pattern. Rifles have been made in four groups.
¶ Deer Series examples had 24in barrels chambered for ·25–06, ·270 Winchester or ·308 Winchester cartridges. A deer's head motif, bordered by oak leaves, was engraved on the floor plate.
¶ The 26in-barrelled Elk Series rifles were offered in 6 × 57mm, 7mm Remington Magnum or ·30–06 and had an oakleaf-bordered elk's head.
¶ Himalayan Series guns had 24in barrels chambered for 5·6 × 57mm or 6·5 × 68mm S cartridges. The floor plate bore a yak-head motif within scroll engraving. A fibreglass stock was optional.
¶ 26in-barrelled Safari Series rifles offered the choice of an elephant, rhinoceros or Cape Buffalo head on the floor plate. Chamberings ranged from ·308 Norma Magnum to 9·3 × 64mm. The walnut pistol-grip half stock had a Monte Carlo cheek piece and a rubber recoil pad; the fore-end had a shallow schnabel tip.

Raick Frères of Liège made substantial quantities of Mauser-type sporting rifles, initially built around refurbished wartime actions and then on new examples purchased from Fabrique Nationale. There were two basic patterns in 1965—the Models 155 (standard) and 156 (Magnum) with conventional half-stocks, and the

Models 160 (standard) and 161 (Magnum) with full-length Mannlicher stocks. The half-stocked rifles had barrels of 550–610mm, while the 'carbines' had 520mm barrels. The standard chamberings were ·243 Winchester, 6·5 × 55mm, ·270 Winchester, ·280 Remington, 7 × 57mm, ·30–06, ·308 Winchester, 8 × 60mm, ·358 Winchester and 9·3 × 62mm; magazines held five rounds. The four-shot Models 156 and 161 were made for 7mm Remington Magnum, ·300 Winchester Magnum and ·375 H&H Magnum.

¶ Raick also made a Model 165 big-game rifle on the FN-Mauser action, with barrels of 550–650mm and a ventilated rubber butt pad. The rifles had folding-leaf Express sights on a quarter rib, and the front swivel eye lay on the barrel instead of fore-end.

Westley Richards & Co. Ltd of Birmingham and London chambered Mauser-action sporting rifles—from c.1909 onward—for (among others) the company's proprietary ·318 Nitro Express and ·425 Rimless Magnum cartridges.

John Rigby & Company of London offered Mauser-action rifles chambered for ·275 Rimless cartridges (1907); ·350 Rimless Magnum (1908); ·400/350 Nitro Express (1899); and ·416 Rigby (1911). Most of the actions were bought in Oberndorf prior to the First World War.

¶ Later examples showed greater diversity; in 1965, for example, the 'Rigby 243' was being built on a refurbished action. Chambering ·243 Winchester, with a barrel of 21in or 25in, it had a pistol-grip half-stock with a Monte Carlo comb. The 'Rigby 275', chambered for the 7x57mm Mauser cartridge, had a traditional straight-comb butt and a rounded half pistol-grip. The front swivel eye lay on the barrel and the back sight was a leaf pattern. The Rigby Big-Bore Magazine Rifle—available in ·375 H&H Magnum, ·404 Jeffrey or ·416 Rigby—customarily had a sturdy stock with a Monte Carlo comb and a rounded fore-end tip. A recoil bolt ran laterally through the fore-end beneath the chamber. The pistol grip had a shallow English-style cap, plus a cap of horn, ebony, rosewood or steel. One swivel eye was carried on a collar around the barrel, ahead of the fore-end. Magazines were deepened to accept four of the large-diameter cartridges. Sights comprised folding leaves (often set into a quarter rib) and a replaceable-element tunnel.

RWS-brand guns, perpetuating the pre-war trademark of Rheinsch-Westfälische Sprengstoff AG, have been marketed in recent years by Dynamit Nobel of Troisdorf/Oberlar. The most common centre-fire bolt-action cartridge rifles are made by Kriegeskorte, but some Mausers—apprently emanating from Spain—have also been offered.

Società Armi Bresciane Srl ('SAB') of Gardone Val Trompia, near Brescia, has marketed 'Linea Renato Gamba' firearms. The RGZ 1000 sporting rifle had a Mauser-pattern action with a pivoting safety catch on the right side of the action behind the bolt handle. In addition to the standard pattern, it has been offered in 'Battue' form

for snap-shooting at driven game. The standard gun had a 600mm barrel, conventional open sights and a double set trigger; the Battue model had a 520mm barrel, a fixed back sight at the front of a quarter-rib, and a single direct-acting trigger. The European-walnut Monte Carlo stocks had contrasting rosewood schnabel tips and pistol-grip caps.

Sabatti SpA (Fabbrica Italiana Armi Sabatti, or FIAS) of Gardone Val Trompia built the Carabina Rover 87 around a conventional modified Mauser action and an internal magazine with a detachable floor plate. The standard rifle offered a classic straight-comb stock, whereas the deluxe Rover 87DL had a Monte Carlo comb. Chamberings in the 22in barrel included ·243 Winchester, ·25–06, 7mm Remington Magnum, ·270 Winchester, ·300 Winchester Magnum, ·30–06 or ·308 Winchester.

Sako Prior to the development of the long L-61 proprietary action described on pages 240–1, Sako offered rifles on the FN-Mauser action (1950–7 only). Chambered for the ·270 Winchester or ·30–06 cartridges, the guns had 24in barrels and weighed about 7·5lb. They had Monte Carlo-pattern half stocks with plain rounded fore-end tips, and open folding-leaf back sights. A Magnum version, with a rubber recoil pad, accepted ·300 or ·375 H&H Magnum ammunition.

Santa Barbara Manufactured by the state-owned Empresa Nacional de Industrias Militares 'Santa Barbara' SA of La Coruña, these actions represent the classical modern version of the 1898-pattern Mauser—with a low swept-back bolt handle and a radial safety on the right side of the receiver behind the bolt handle. In addition to gracing the standard Spanish army sniping rifle, the Modelo 75, actions have been supplied in quantity to Fajen, Golden State, Parker-Hale and others.

Smith & Wesson of Springfield, Massachusetts, distributed Husqvarna-made rifles in 1969–72. The Model A was the Husqvarna 3000 pattern; Model B was the P-3000; Model C was the 4000 Lightweight; Models D (straight comb) and E (Monte Carlo comb) were short carbine-pattern guns with full-length Mannlicher stocks.

J.P. Sauer & Sohn of Suhl, Germany, was an early convert to the Mauser action, making a few high-class sporting rifles from c.1901 until the beginning of the First World War. The rifles were generally engraved, and often had ultra-slim fore-ends held to the barrel by a transverse key in oval escutcheons. Horn trigger guards and notable flats in the woodwork beneath the receiver were popular on Sauer products, though they should not be taken to indicate a Sauer sporter in the absence of the company's name or wild-man trademark.

V. Chr. Schilling of Suhl, Germany, completed Gew.98 actions left over from wartime production. They were offered in a variety of chamberings—e.g., 6 × 58mm Förster, 6·5 × 61mm or 8 × 75mm—but were often anonymous. Others bore a tiny 'V.C.S.' somewhere on the action. Operated by

Ludwig Bornhöft from c.1919, business failed about 1934.

E. Schmidt & Habermann of Suhl made a 'Model 21' short-action Mauser rifle in 6·5 × 54mm, 8 × 51mm and ·250–3000 Savage. This was basically a modified Gew.98 with a special knurled cocking-piece knob—not unlike that of the US M1903 Springfield—and a simplified safety system. ¶ Schmidt & Habermann also handled conventional Mauser-pattern sporting rifles, often identified only by a small 'S & H' mark (cf., Sempert & Krieghoff).

Richard Schüler, junior partner with his brother Oskar in the well-established Waffenfabrik August Schüler of Suhl, developed a 11·2 × 60mm cartridge from the old Reichspatrone 71 about 1913. This was chambered in a selection of sporting rifles, some single-shot and others embodying Mauser actions. Its distinctive 'rebated' case rim, smaller than the case head, was necessary to fit the recessed Mauser bolt face. The 11·2 × 72mm Magnum cartridge appeared in the early 1920s, suitable rifles being made for Schüler by Sempert & Krieghoff. In 1923, however, Schüler produced an awesome 12·7 × 70mm cartridge, similar to the ·500 Jeffrey Rimless, for use on the biggest game southern Africa had to offer. The rifle was very large and heavy, with a large diameter barrel befitting its calibre. The pistol-grip stock was similarly massive, but the magazine box still protruded beneath the line of the fore-end ahead of the trigger. The magazine floor-plate catch was usually a radial-lever pattern. The last proprietary Schüler round, 6·5 × 68mm, appeared in the early 1930s.

Sempert & Krieghoff of Suhl, Germany, was merged into Heinrich Krieghoff in 1924 though retaining its separate identity until the 1930s. Mauser-action sporting rifles were stocked for general sale, and also for supply to August Schüler of Suhl in the immediate post-1920 period. An 'S. & K.' mark was used (cf., Schmidt & Habermann).

Simson & Company of Suhl, appointed prime contractor to the German army in the immediate post-1919 period, is said to have completed some Gew.98 actions in sporting-rifle form. The company became 'Berlin-Suhler Waffen- und Fahrzeugwerke GmbH' in 1932, but was nationalised in the mid 1930s; by 1940, it had become a division of 'Gustloff-Werke'.

Franz Sodia of Ferlach, the renowned gunmaking centre in the Kärnten district of Austria, was best known in the 1950s for good-quality sporting rifles built on the Mannlicher-Schönauer action. In the 1960s, however, attention turned to the Mauser. ¶ The Model 1963—apparently built on refurbished actions, engraved to order—was offered in a sporting stock with a Bavarian-style cheek piece and an oddly humped comb. The drop at the comb was small and the pistol-grip radius was much tighter than that found on many British-style rifles. The fore-end had a short tip with an unusually sharp schnabel profile, the front swivel eye was fixed to the barrel, and a plain folding-leaf sight was used. A 600mm

barrel was standard, gun weight averaging 3·25kg. Chamberings included ·220 Swift, ·243 Winchester, 6·5 × 57mm, ·270 Winchester, 7 × 57mm, 7 × 64mm, ·30–06, ·308 Winchester, 8 × 57mm, ·338 Winchester, 9·3 × 62mm or 9·3 × 64mm. ¶ The Model 1964 Super Express was similar to the standard 1963 pattern, but accepted 5·6 × 61mm, 7 × 66mm Vom Hofe, 6·5 × 68mm or 8 × 68mm RWS cartridges.

Stiga AB of Tranås, Sweden, made sporting rifles based on refurbished M1896 military actions. The guns were offered in ·270 Winchester, ·30–06 or 8 × 57mm, had 600mm barrels and weighed about 3·25kg unladen. They had plain straight-comb half-stocks with pistol grips and slender fore-ends terminating in a schnabel tip. Single-trigger systems were standard, though a double set pattern could be fitted.

Stoeger Arms Corporation of New York City offered rifles built on Oberndorf- and FN-Mauser actions prior to 1939.

Voetter & Co., originally of Vöhrenbach in the Schwarzwald district of Germany, began to make Mauser-type firearms in the 1950s. ¶ The most basic rifle available in the mid 1980s was the Repetierbüchse 2155, with a Kar.98k-type action and a spatulate bolt handle. Model 2155/1 had a walnut stock with a Bavarian-style cheek piece and a hog's back comb; skip-line chequering lay on the pistol-grip and fore-end. The 2155/2 pattern had a walnut-finish stock with a Monte Carlo comb and cheek piece. The guns usually offered double set triggers, and weighed about 3·2kg with a 610mm barrel. Chamberings included 5·6 × 57mm, ·22–250 Remington, ·243 Winchester, ·25–06 Remington, 6·5 × 55mm Mauser, 6·5 × 57mm, ·270 Winchester, 7 × 57mm, 7 × 64mm, 7·5 × 55mm, ·30–06, ·308 Winchester, 8mm × 57S and 9·3 × 62mm. ¶ The Repetierbüchse 2165 was an improved 2155 with a double set-trigger, an elegant bolt shroud and a streamlined bolt handle. The safety catch lay on the upper tang. Detachable box or internal hinged floor-plate magazines were available; the walnut stock had a hog's back comb and a squared Bavarian cheek piece. Skip-line chequering appeared on the pistol grip and fore-end, whilst a rosewood schnabel tip was standard. Chamberings duplicated the 2155 model (excepting 7·5 × 55mm), with the addition of 6·5 × 68mm, 7mm Remington Magnum, ·300 Winchester Magnum, 8 × 68mm S and 9·3 × 64mm to order. ¶ Magnum rifles had 650mm barrels and were 1,175mm overall instead of 1,130mm; weight averaged 3·3kg. ¶ The Voere 2175—Light, Medium or Special—had a Bavarian-style walnut half-stock, but the bolt shroud was a short cylinder and a pivoting safety protruded from the stock behind the bolt handle. A selection of single and double triggers was offered. The 'L' action chambered ·222 and ·223 Remington, ·223 Remington Magnum or 5·6 × 50mm Magnum; 'M' guns were chambered similarly to the Voere 2165; and the 'S' version handled the same magnum cartridges as its immediate predecessor.

Vom Hofe & Scheinemann of Berlin,

Germany, made their first sporting rifles on the basis of 1898-pattern Mauser action in c.1927. From 1931, Ernst-August vom Hofe continued business after the withdrawal of his partner, developing the 6·2 × 73mm Super Express (Belted) cartridge soon afterward. A 7 × 73mm cartridge replaced the 6·2mm pattern in 1933 and business moved to Karlsruhe in 1936. Almost immediately, the 5·6 × 61mm Super Express cartridge was introduced commercially. The first Vom Hofe Super Express rifles date from this period, built on Oberndorf-made actions and barrels supplied by Christoph Funk and Triebel-Gewehrfabrik of Suhl.

¶ In 1955, Walter Gehmann (q.v.) of Karlsruhe succeeded to the business of vom Hofe (who had died some years earlier) and the 7 × 66mm Super Express was announced little more than a year later.

Carl Walther Sportwaffenfabrik of Ulm/Donau built sporting rifles on refurbished Mauser actions in 1955–74, before they were replaced by the JR pattern (see page 287). The guns had conventional stocks, with low Monte Carlo combs, and plain-tipped fore-ends. Hand cut chequering graced the pistol grip and fore-end. A unique safety bolt ran laterally through the stock above the trigger.

¶ The Model A rifle had a double set trigger mechanism; the Model B was similar, but had a simple single trigger. Sights comprised a pearl bead on a ramp at the muzzle and a folding two-leaf back sight. Standard 600mm barrels were chambered for the 6·5 × 57mm, ·270 Winchester, 7 × 57mm, 7 × 64mm, ·30–06, 8 × 57mm, , 9·3 × 62mm or ·375 H&H Magnum cartridges. The ·243 Winchester and 8 × 60mm options were added in the early 1960s.

¶ Walther also made small numbers of the Model A and Model B Carbines, with full-length Mannlicher stocks. They were normally chambered only for 6·5 × 57mm and 7 × 57mm rounds (550mm barrels), though 7 × 64mm and 8 × 57mm (600mm barrels) could be obtained on request.

Weatherby, Inc. of South Gate, California, offered sporting rifles on the basis of FN-Mauser actions (1949–58) prior to the appearance of the Weatherby Mark V rifle. Made for the ·220 Rocket and ·375 H&H Magnum in addition to the ·257, ·270, 7mm and ·300 Weatherby magnums, the Deluxe Magnum rifles had a Monte Carlo-style stock with contrasting pistol-grip caps and fore-end tips. Quick-detachable swivels and ventilated recoil pads were standard.

¶ The Deluxe patterns were similar, but chambered non-magnum cartridges—e.g., ·270 Winchester or ·30–06.

Benedikt Winkler of Ferlach, Austria, made sporting rifles on the basis of refurbished military Mauser actions. The Model 80N, made to order in virtually any calibre the purchaser cared to specify, had a 660mm barrel and weighed about 3·4kg. It was usually supplied with a straight-comb pistol-grip half stock with a small oval cheek piece, and had a plain fore-end with a rounded tip. The Model 80L ('Luxusmodell') was similar, but had an engraved action and, occasionally, carving on the stock instead of chequering. Most rifles were fitted with double set trigger systems and a magazine floor-plate latch.

Winslow Arms Company of Camden, South Carolina, made Mauser-type sporting rifles from 1962 until the late 1980s. The actions were purchased when required from Fabrique Nationale, Zavodi Crvena Zastava

and others; the guns were distinguished more by their extraordinary stocks. The Bushmaster and Plainsmaster were each orffered in eight grades of finish.

¶ At its most extreme, the Plainsmaster featured a bizarre combination of fully-curved pistol grip, exaggerated wedge-type pistol-grip cap, soaring flyaway comb, basket-weave chequering and contrasting inlays.

¶ Chamberings were supplied virtually to order, though most guns had 24in or 26in barrels; weight ranged from 7·2–7·5lb for standard cartridges to 8–9lb for the magnums.

Zastava or ZCZ These rifles were made by the Yugoslavian government factory in Kragujevač (Zavodi Crvena Zastava, 'Red Flag Works'). There have been many differing models, including the Churchill (q.v.) 'One of One Thousand' and Whitworth—stocked in English style in the Interarms factory.

¶ The basic rifles, sold in North America by Herter's of Waseca, Minnesota, prior to the involvement of Interarms in the early 1970s, relied on a conventional 1898-pattern Mauser action with some of the characteristics of the Belgian FN Model 1924—scarcely surprising, as the original Kraguyevač production machinery was installed by FN in the 1920s as part of an agreement to supply technical assistance. The bolt handle was swept backward, the safety appeared on the right side of the receiver behind the bolt, and the hinged magazine floor plate was activated by a catch set into the front of the trigger-guard bow. They have been sold as the Herter J9 or Zastava 67 (the latter confined largely to Europe) in addition to the Interarms 'Mark X' brand.

¶ Introduced in 1972, the standard Interarms Mark X rifle has been offered in ·22–250 Remington, ·243 Winchester, ·25–06, ·270 Winchester, 7 × 57mm, 7mm Remington Magnum, ·30–06, ·308 Winchester and ·300 Winchester Magnum. Offered with a 24in barrel, it weighed 7·5lb; magazines held three magnum or five standard cartridges. The European walnut stock had a Monte Carlo comb and an ebonite fore-end tip.

¶ The 1974-vintage Mark X Cavalier was simply a standard pattern with a roll-over comb. The pistol-grip cap and the fore-end tip were rosewood.

¶ Also dating from this era, the Whitworth Express Rifle African Model (·375 H&H or ·458 Winchester magnums only) had a three-leaf Express sight and an English-style stock of good-quality walnut. A black fore-end tip, a ventilated rubber shoulder pad and quick-detachable swivels were all standard.

¶ Mark X Viscount rifles had a plain stock with a low Monte Carlo comb, a white spacer accompanying the pistol-grip cap, and a plain round tipped fore-end.

¶ Dating from 1976, the Mark X Alaskan was made only in ·375 H&H Magnum or ·458 Winchester Magnum. It had a three-round magazine, weighed about 8·3lb with a 24in barrel, and had a ventilated rubber shoulder pad. A recoil bolt ran laterally through the stock beneath the chamber.

¶ Mark X Continental carbines had 20in barrels and straight-comb full-length Mannlicher stocks. Double set triggers were standard, together with a sculpted cheek piece and a spatulate bolt handle. The Mark X Marquis was similar, but had a Monte Carlo comb and a steel fore-end cap. Available in ·270 Winchester, 7 × 57mm, ·30–06 or ·308 Winchester, the guns date from 1976 onward.

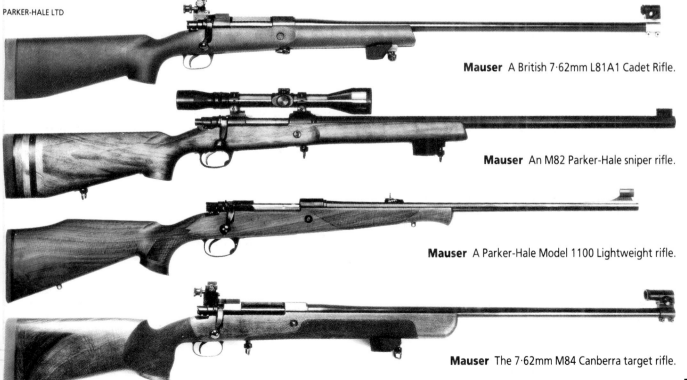

PARKER-HALE LTD

Mauser A British 7·62mm L81A1 Cadet Rifle.

Mauser An M82 Parker-Hale sniper rifle.

Mauser A Parker-Hale Model 1100 Lightweight rifle.

Mauser The 7·62mm M84 Canberra target rifle.

MAYNARD

UNITED STATES OF AMERICA

Based on a patent granted to Edward Maynard in December 1859, this Civil War relic originally fired a metal-case cartridge with a notably thick rim. It was operated by depressing the breech lever, doubling as the trigger guard, to allow the muzzle to tip downward so that the spent case could be extracted and then ejected manually. The best feature was the ease with which a barrel could be changed, allowing a 28-bore shotgun pattern to be substituted.

Maynards were distinguished by the absence of a fore-end from all but a few custom-made examples, among them some stocked in Britain. They were often fitted with ring-tip operating levers, though target rifles (particularly the Creedmoor versions) sometimes had wooden pistol grips attached to the lever.

Maynard sporting rifles were made until the late 1880s. The assets and liabilities were sold in 1890 to J. Stevens Arms & Tool Company.

Model 1873

Made by the Massachusetts Arms Company, Chicopee Falls, Massachusetts, c.1873–5; and the Maynard Gun Company, Chicopee Falls, Massachusetts, 1876–82 (probably sub-contracted).
·35–30, ·44–100 or ·50–100 'thick-rim' cartridges.
Tipping-barrel action, operated by a lever combined with the trigger guard.
DATA FOR A TYPICAL EXAMPLE
·35–30 Maynard, rimmed.
About 41·50in overall, 7·75lb unladen.
26·00in barrel, 6-groove rifling; RH, concentric.
Folding leaf sight on upper tang.
Performance: not known.
☆
1873: Maynard patented a new self-contained cartridge conversion for his original cap-lock guns, allowing many existing parts to be used. Concurrently, manufacture of centre-fire rifles began, but sales were never great. Reliance on idiosyncratic cartridges inhibited sales, as the ammunition was difficult to obtain.

Guns were made in a bewildering profusion of patterns, ranging from the plainest No. 7 Hunter's Rifle to the ·44–100–520 No. 14 Long Range Creedmoor of 1876. This had a 32in round barrel, a special two-piece half-stock with chequering on the pistol-grip and fore-end, and adjustable vernier peep-and-globe sights.

Model 1882

Made by the Maynard Gun Company, Chicopee Falls, Massachusetts, 1882–9 (probably sub-contracted).
·35–30, ·35–40, ·38–50, ·40–40, ·40–60,
·40–70, ·44–70, ·50–50 and ·55–100 (all proprietary cartridges), or ·32–35 Stevens.
Action: as M1873, above.
DATA FOR A TYPICAL EXAMPLE
·35–40 Maynard, rimmed.
37·50in overall, 7·50lb unladen.
22·00in barrel, 6-groove rifling; RH, concentric.
Spring-leaf and elevator sight.
1,355 ft/sec with 250-grain bullet.
☆
1882: the perfected Maynard-type sporters fired conventional centre-fire cartridges, but were not strong enough to withstand the most powerful sporting-rifle cartridges of their day. They were made in a variety of patterns, including the No. 7 Hunter's Rifle (·35–30, ·40–40), No. 9 Hunting & Target (·40–40); No. 10 Mid-Range Hunting & Target (·35–30, ·40–40 and ·40–60); Hunter's Rifles No. 11 (·44–70, ·50–50 and ·55–100), No. 12 and No. 13 (both ·40–60); Creedmoor Rifle No. 14 (·44–70); plus Target Rifles No. 15 (·40–60) and No. 16 (·35–30, ·40–60). Most of the gaps in this series were filled either by original cap-locks or small-calibre rimfires. 1882-pattern guns were often classed as 'Improved Models' to distinguish them from the otherwise similar 1873 types.
1890: interest in the odd-looking Maynard rifle, which had declined greatly in the face of strong competition, waned until the remnants of the business were sold to Stevens. It is unlikely that production had been undertaken for some years.

MEUNIER

FRANCE
Also known as 'STA'

This semi-automatic rifle was designed by Colonel Meunier of the Section Technique de l'Artillerie, outcome of experiments undertaken in 1897–1910 with a variety of gas- and recoil-operated CTV, ENT and STA rifles (see Part Two). The Meunier rifle apparently worked reliably enough in the hands of the well-trained specialists to whom it had been issued during the First World War, but was complicated and difficult to make; its brief success was due to a temporary absence of simpler RSC (q.v.) guns.

Fusil A6

Assembled in Manufacture d'Armes de Tulle, with parts from Châtellerault and Saint-Étienne, 1916–17.
Quantity: 1,010.
7 × 59mm, rimless.
Recoil-operated auto-loading action, locked by rotating lugs on the bolt head into the receiver.
1,293mm overall, 4·04kg unladen.
720mm barrel, 4-groove rifling; LH, concentric.
Integral charger-loaded box magazine, 6 rounds.
Leaf sight graduated to 2,300 metres.
795 m/sec with ball cartridges.
Special sword bayonet.
☆
1910: the rifle was provisionally adopted after successfully undergoing field trials.
1913: the construction of a production line began in Tulle. However, increasing likelihood of war delayed progress and nothing other than a few pre-production samples had been made by August 1914.
1916: limited series production began, owing to problems with the Mle.1917 RSC rifle. The one-piece stock had a small sharply-pointed pistol grip, with ventilation slots in the fore-end between the barrel band and the special nose cap. A short hand guard ran under the band. Sling swivels lay on the underside of the band

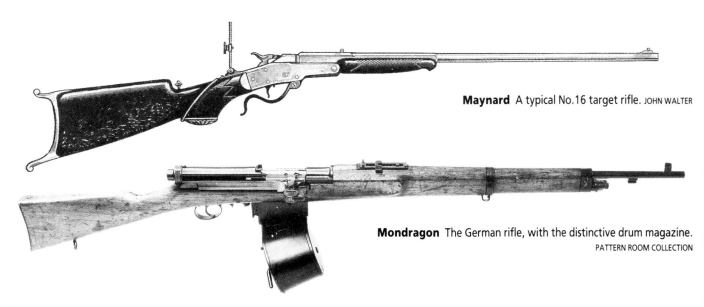

Maynard A typical No.16 target rifle. JOHN WALTER

Mondragon The German rifle, with the distinctive drum magazine.
PATTERN ROOM COLLECTION

and butt, and a lug under the nose cap accepted a modified Mle 1892-type sword bayonet.

The A6 rifle had a hollow-headed straight bolt handle and was loaded from a Mauser-type charger, suitable guides being milled in the receiver; a radial safety lever appeared on the right side of the trigger guard.

1917: about 750 rifles were issued to selected marksmen. Survivors had been replaced by March 1918 with the Mle.1917, owing to shortages of suitable ammunition.

MONDRAGON

MEXICO

The first auto-loading rifle to encounter real success was the work of a talented Mexican army officer, Manuel Mondragon.

After developing a unique straight-pull bolt action rifle (see Part Two), Mondragon began work on a gas-operated auto-loader in the mid 1890s. However, many years passed before a patent was sought in the USA in August 1904.

Gas was tapped from the bore into an expansion chamber under the barrel, forcing a piston back against the bolt actuator. As the actuator moved back, it rotated the locking lugs out of engagement with the receiver walls. Slight camming action helped to extract the spent cartridge case, then the mechanism ran back to eject and cock the hammer before returning to chamber a new round.

A pivoting claw on the bolt handle could disconnect the bolt assembly from the recoil spring during the cocking stroke, turning the rifle into a manually operated straight-pull pattern if the gas port had been closed—though the action was difficult to retract in this guise.

The finalised Mondragon was very prone to jamming and breakages. Though it was greatly superior to most pre-1914 designs, and has the distinction of being the first auto-loader to reach the status of official issue*, service with the German army in the First World War rapidly revealed its major shortcomings.

GERMANY
Model 1915

Airman's self-loading rifle:
Flieger-Selbstlade-Karabiner ('FSK') Modell 1915.
Made by Schweizerische Industrie-Gesellschaft, Neuhausen, 1909–11.
7 × 57mm, rimless.
Gas-operated auto-loading action, locked by a rotating bolt.
1,068mm overall, 4.25kg without magazine.
620mm barrel, 4-groove rifling; RH, concentric.
Detachable drum magazine, 30 rounds.
Leaf sight graduated to 2,000 metres.
625 m/sec with ball ammunition.
No bayonet.

☆

1915: about 3,000 Mexican guns (see below) stored in Switzerland since the revolution of 1911 were purchased for the German forces, as effectual automatic weapons were in short supply. Adopted on 2 December, Mondragons were to fire FN-made 7 × 57mm ammunition seized in Belgium.

1916: as the Germans did not wish to use the special Mexican clip-loaded magazines, about 25,000 Trommelmagazine (i.e., drum or 'snail' type) were made by Hamburg-Amerikanischen Uhrenfabrik of Schramberg for issue on a scale of six to each gun.

Mondragons were issued to the flying corps and the imperial navy, but were withdrawn from air service once enough machine-guns became available. However, many navy rifles remained in use throughout the war; the Baltic Station (Kiel) inventory alone stood at nearly five hundred in September 1918. Though most of the guns had been withdrawn to store, some were still held on board U-Boats.

1917: FSK were issued experimentally along the Western Front, publication of the official manual occurring in February. However, the mechanism was much too delicate; easily jammed by mud unless cleaned thoroughly after use, the rifles had been withdrawn from front-line service by the autumn.

MEXICO
Modelo 1908

Fusil Automatico de 7mm 'Porfirio Diaz', Modelo de 1908.
Made by Schweizerische Industrie-Gesellschaft, Neuhausen, 1909–11.
7 × 57mm, rimless.
Otherwise as German FSK.15, above, excepting magazine (clip-loaded 8-round box) and a special bayonet.

☆

1903: two 7mm prototypes were unsuccessfully tested in Britain in the summer, failing the sand test though effectual enough when clean.
1908: the rifle was officially adopted in Mexico, and a contract for four thousand guns was placed in Switzerland. The barrels were apparently to measure about 75cm, though this was soon reduced to 62cm on production guns. They were conventional-looking auto-loaders, with a one-piece straight-wrist stock (most of the prototypes had two-piece stocks) and a hand guard stretching forward from the chamber to a nose cap from which the gas regulator protruded. A lug for the unique trowel bayonet lay under the muzzle, one swivel lay on the barrel band and another lay beneath the butt.

Mexican-service rifles had an enwreathed eagle perched on a cactus, with a snake in its beak, above the chamber; RM ('Republica de Mexico') also appeared, whilst the Mo.1908 designation and the maker's mark FABRICA DE ARMAS NEUHAUSEN SUIZA lay on the top rear of the receiver.

1911: the first batch of 400 guns reached Mexico. Revolution in May then toppled Diaz. The new government seems to have seized on unreliability and excessive parts-breakage to cancel the order, leaving SIG with substantial quantities of unwanted guns.

Some modified 7·5 × 55mm examples were tested by the Swiss army—with detachable ten- or twenty-round box magazines—but had no lasting effects.
1915: remaining rifles were sold to Germany.

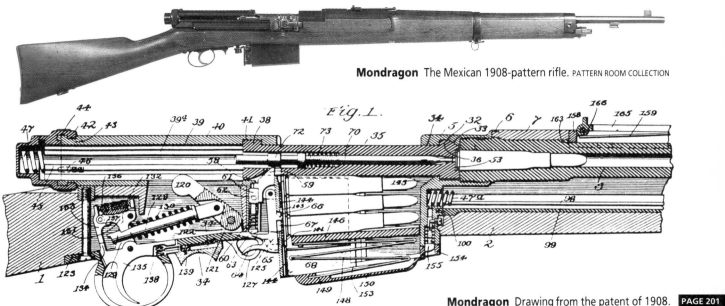

Mondragon The Mexican 1908-pattern rifle. PATTERN ROOM COLLECTION

Mondragon Drawing from the patent of 1908.

MOSIN-NAGANT

RUSSIA

This Russo-Belgian design was also used in Montenegro, Turkey and (after 1945) in many Soviet-aligned armies. Large quantities were also made in the People's Republic of China.

The action was based on a French-style bolt, inspired by the Lebel, with a detachable head and a cocking piece that could be retracted and turned to the left as a safety measure.

Though clumsy, the mechanism was durable and free of serious weaknesses; the interruptor ensured an unusually good feed with the badly shaped $7 \cdot 62 \times 54$ cartridge. Consequently, the rifle remained in service with some Russian satellite armies well into the 1960s; many guns are still held in reserve.

MILITARY WEAPONS

CZECHOSLOVAKIA

After the revolution of 1948, Czechoslovakia continued to produce Mauser-type rifles. A modified sniper rifle (ZG 49 Sn), submitted to trial by Otakar Galaš in the late 1940s, was developed into the ZG 51 Sn but a change of heart—perhaps influenced by the Soviet Union—led to the development of the similar ZG 51/91/30 on the Mosin-Nagant action.

Model 1954

Sniper rifle: Odstrelovaci puška vz.54.
Made by state factories, 1954–7.
$7 \cdot 62 \times 54$mm, rimmed.
Turning-bolt action, with two lugs on a detachable bolt
head locking into the receiver behind the chamber.
1,230mm overall, 5·20kg without sights.
730mm barrel, 4-groove rifling; RH, concentric.
Integral charger-loaded box, 5 rounds.
Tangent-leaf sight graduated to 2,000 metres.
805 m/sec with Type D ball cartridges.
☆

1954: built on specially finished, but otherwise standard obr.1891/30 actions, this sniper rifle was developed to share a special 7·62mm ball cartridge being made for the Goryunov machine-gun. It had a pistol-grip half stock and a hand guard running forward from the receiver ring. There was a single band at the tip of the fore-end and a grasping groove beneath the back sight. Owing to the free-floating barrel, the vz.54 was accurate and dependable. However, it was never made in large numbers.

FINLAND

The Finns seized the chance to free themselves from Russian shackles soon after the October Revolution and declared independence on 20 July 1919. By 1920, the Finnish army and Protective Corps (Suojeluskuntain Ylieskunnan, or Sk.Y) mustered a hundred thousand men under arms.

Owing to the capture of thousands of Russian rifles in Helsinki armoury, the Mosin-Nagant was selected as the standard infantry weapon—though 8,000 ex-German Kar.98 AZ obtained from the French served the cavalry until 1923.

The Finns soon began to make changes of their own, but the rifles were always built around original pre-1917 Mosin-Nagant actions repaired and refinished in Finland.

Model 1891

Infantry rifle: Kivääri M/91.
☆

Many ex-Russian rifles were used with little modification. However, some others—infantry and dragoon patterns alike—will now often be found with modified hand guards and sling rings through slots in the stock, replacing the original Russian swivels. Those that survived into the 1920s received back-sight leaves graduated in metres instead of arshin.

Some will be found with the barrel and fore-end cut to approximate to the later short rifles; most of these date from the Winter War, but it is not known whether the changes were official.

Model 1924

Infantry rifle: Kivääri m/24.
Converted by the Sk.Y workshops in Helsinki, 1924–7.
Quantity: about 38,000.
$7 \cdot 62 \times 54$mm, rimmed.
Turning-bolt action, with two lugs on a detachable bolt
head locking into the receiver behind
the chamber.
1,300mm overall, 4·20kg unladen.
818mm barrel, 4-groove rifling; RH, concentric.
Integral charger-loaded box magazine, 5 rounds.
Ramp-and-leaf sight (see notes).
880 m/sec with obr.1908g ball cartridges.
obr.1891g socket bayonet.

1923: the Finns ordered three thousand new 7·62mm barrels from Schweizerische Industrie-Gesellschaft. These displayed the maker's name on the right side ahead of the breech.
1924: the Swiss barrels—which had a step rather than a continuous taper—were fitted to reconditioned actions retrieved from scrapped weapons, creating the m/24 (or m/91–24) rifle. The stock-bedding was altered, requiring a new barrel channel, and the front band was pinned to the stock so that the barrel could float. The conversions were so successful that the Finns made a few small dimensional changes and ordered 10,000 more barrels. Work continued until the Sk.Y workshop moved to Riihimäki in 1927. Most of these rifles retained the original Russian back sight, though the graduations on the back-sight base—to 1,200 arshin—were replaced by metric near-equivalents running to 850 metres. Sight leaves were rarely altered.
1932: several hundred m/24 were shortened by the government rifle factory (VKT) in Jyväskylä, possibly for artillerymen. Work was apparently spread over two years.

Model 1927

Short rifle, army type: Kivääri m/27.
Made by Valtions Kivääritedhas, Jyväskylä, 1927–39.
$7 \cdot 62 \times 54$mm, rimmed.
Action: as m/1924 rifle, above.

Mosin-Nagant A group of Soviet women snipers with ▷
M1891/30 rifles; Second Baltic Front, 1944.
NOVOSTI PRESS AGENCY

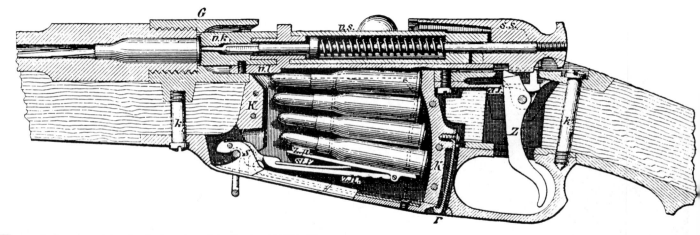

Mosin-Nagant A longitudinal section of the Russian M1891 rifle.

DATA FOR INFANTRY PATTERN
1,185mm overall, 4·11kg unladen.
685mm barrel, 4-groove rifling; RH, concentric.
Integral charger-loaded box magazine, 5 rounds.
Ramp-and-leaf sight (see notes).
740 m/sec with heavy ball cartridges.
m/27 or m/35 sword bayonet.
☆

1927: these were shortened versions of the m/24, though otherwise comparable. The nose cap, hinged in the manner of the German Kar.98 AZ, carried a bayonet lug. The back sight had an aperture instead of the original open notch and its base was re-graduated to 800 metres. The bolt handle was turned down, part of the stock-side being removed to receive it. Cavalry rifles, identical with the infantry type, were 1,110mm overall and weighed 3·98kg.
1930: problems with the nose cap, which tended to rotate laterally, were solved with extension plates. Anchored in a recess milled in the side of the nose cap, these ran back along the fore-end and were retained by transverse bolts.

Model 1928

Short rifle, Protective Corps: Sk.Y kivääri m/28.
Made by Suojeluskuntain Ase- ja Konepaja Osakeyhtiö ('Sako'), Riihimäki, 1927–30.
Quantity: 30,000?
7·62 × 54mm, rimmed.
Otherwise generally as m/1927 army rifle, above, excepting weight (4·18kg unladen) and bayonet (m/28 Sk.Y or m/35 sword patterns).
☆

1927: adopted in August, this refinement of the m/24 has been credited to Niilo Talvenheimo, the principal arms inspector of the Protective Corps. The barrel was shortened, the depth and pitch of the rifling were revised, the trigger was improved, and the stock was changed. The first rifles were assembled in the Sako factory in November using new SIG-made barrels and selected Russian actions. They had a single barrel band and a simple nose cap. The base of the back sight was re-graduated to 850 metres.
1928: issue of m/28 rifles began.

Model 1928–30

Short rifle, Protective Corps: Sk.Y. kivääri m/28–30.
Made by Suojeluskuntan Ase- ja Konepaja Osakeyhtiö ('Sako'), Riihimäki, 1931–40.
Quantity: 55,000–60,000?
7·62 × 54mm, rimmed.
Otherwise generally as m/1927 army rifle, above, excepting weight (4.36lb unladen), sight (tangent-leaf graduated to 2,000 metres) and bayonet (m/28 Sk.Y or m/35 sword patterns).
☆

1930: this improved m/28 rifle had a revised magazine and a greatly improved back sight. The barrels were made in the Sako factory, quality proving at least the equal of SIG products.

Model 1939

Short rifle: kivääri m/39.
Made by Suojeluskuntain Ase- ja Konepaja Osakeyhtiö ('Sako'), Riihimäki, 1939–44.
Quantity: 70,800?
7·62 × 54mm, rimmed.
Action: as m/1924 rifle, above.
1,185mm overall, 4·55lb unladen.
685mm barrel, 4-groove rifling; RH, concentric.
Integral charger-loaded box magazine, 5 rounds.
Tangent-leaf sight graduated to 2,000 metres.
700 m/sec with D166 ball cartridges.
m/35 sword or m/39 knife bayonet.
☆

1938: developed by a committee drawn from the Department of Defence, the army and the Sk.Y, the m/39 had the Mausner-pattern back sight of the m/28–30 Sk.Y rifle. Detail changes included an increase in bore diameter to handle a new ball cartridge, the development of a two-piece stock made in interlocking parts, and the adoption of a two-piece interruptor copied from the Soviet obr.1891/30 type. Army-type rifling was retained, along with a lightweight barrel to conserve weight.
1939: the rifle was formally approved, and production began.
1944: the Sk.Y disbanded with effect from 3 November and Sako was sold to the Finnish Red Cross. Ten thousand incomplete m/39 rifles were sold for conversion into sporters.

Other guns

Non-standard weapons assembled during the Winter and Continuation Wars (1939–44) were cannibalised from Finnish, Russian and Soviet parts. They are often difficult to categorise.

In the late 1980s, after protracted trials with Valmet, Sako and other rifles, the Finnish army adopted a new sniper rifle built on the *original* Imperial Russian actions. The guns have special heavy barrels, pistol-grip stocks with adjustable combs, and are fitted with modern optical sights. At the time of writing the specifications are not clear, though the process undoubtedly saves costs—and testifies to the outstanding durability of the basic Mosin-Nagant.

RUSSIA

By 1888, the authorities had realised that the Berdan rifle was obsolete. Though experimental rifles submitted by Mauser and Kropatschek were tested, the indigenous butt-magazine Mosin and the Lutkovskiy, based on the Berdan, were regarded as more promising.
1889: single- and five-shot Mosin rifles were submitted for trials, along with some five-shot Belgian Nagants (see Part Two).
1890: trials were undertaken in the summer with 300 Mosins, 100 Nagants and 100 single-shot Berdans lined down to 7·62mm. The best features of the magazine rifles were combined to form the Mosin-Nagant, though the participation of Nagant was widely overlooked.

Model 1891

Infantry rifle: Pekhotniya vintovka obr.1891g.
Made by the ordnance factories in Tula, Sestroretsk and Izhevsk, 1892–1922 (about 7·25 million); Manufacture d'Armes de Châtellerault, 1893–6 (503,540); the New England Westinghouse Company, 1915–17 (770,000); and Remington Arms–Union Metallic Cartridge Co., Bridgeport, Connecticut, 1915–17 (840,310).

M

Quantity: at least 9·36 million.
7·62 × 54mm, rimmed.
Turning-bolt action, with two lugs on a detachable bolt head locking into the receiver behind the chamber.
1,318mm overall, 4·06kg unladen.
820mm barrel, 4-groove rifling; RH, concentric.
Integral charger-loaded box magazine, 5 rounds.
Ramp-and-leaf sight graduated to 2,700 arshin.
605 m/sec with obr.1891g ball cartridges.
obr.1891g socket bayonet.

☆

1891: adopted in April, this was immediately recognisable by its length. The earliest examples had a finger rest extending backward from the trigger guard. The split-bridge receiver was octagonal and the wooden hand-guard ended level with the rearmost screw-clamping barrel band. Swivels lay ahead of the magazine and beneath the front band, though it is alleged that rifles intended for guard units had the back swivel on the underside of the butt. The flat back sight leaves were originally graduated from 1,300 to 2,700 arshin for the round-nose obr.1891g bullet.

1892: 3·29 million guns had been ordered from the principal Russian arsenals by the end of the 1891–2 financial year. Tula delivered the first rifles in the autumn, though only 1,440 had been made by the end of December.

1893: mass production began. By the end of 1896, Tula, Izhevsk and Sestroretsk had contributed 1·470 million combat-worthy rifles and 32,440 trainers to the total of a little over two million. As a shortage of machine-tools in Russia restricted production, the French arms factory in Châtellerault also contributed obr.1891g rifles.

1894: the finger-rest behind the trigger guard was deleted, and insignificant changes were made in the action.

1908: experience in the Russo-Japanese War of 1904–5 proved that rifles were very badly sighted at short range. As the old round-nose bullet performed poorly at long range, the pointed obr.1908g—subsequently designated 'Type L'—was introduced. Back sights were fitted with new curved leaves graduated from

1,300 to 3,200 arshins, but retained the original sight base. A recoil bolt was added through the fore-end above the front of the magazine.

1914: on 1 January, the inventory stood at 3·427 million obr.1891g—but more than five million men were mobilised in the summer and the rifle reserve fell woefully short of needs. In December, therefore, the Chief of Staff ordered the acquisition of weapons regardless of calibre.

1915: contracts for 1·5 million and 1·8 million guns were agreed with Remington–UMC and the New England Westinghouse Corporation.

1917: by 1 January, deliveries had amounted to only 131,440 Remington–UMC and 225,260 Westinghouse rifles. However, by 1 October, 3·286 million Mosin-Nagants (with full-length infantry guns predominating) had been made in the state ordnance factories since 1 July 1914.

1922: production of full-length infantry rifles ceased in favour of the dragoon rifle.

Model 1891

Dragoon and cossack rifles: Kazachya i dragunskaya vintovki obr.1891g.
Made in the ordnance factories in Tula, Sestroretsk and Izhevsk.
7·62 × 54mm, rimmed.
Otherwise generally as obr.1891g infantry rifle, above, excepting dimensions (1,235mm overall, 3·93kg unladen, 760mm barrel).

☆

1891: the cossack rifle was little more than a shortened infantry rifle with a hand guard extending as far as the back sight base. The barrel bands were retained by springs, sling slots were cut laterally through the butt and the fore-end (protected by oval blued steel washers) and a modified cleaning rod was provided. The serial numbers had a distinctive 'KA3' prefix.

The dragoon rifle was a near-duplicate of the cossack rifle with a different cleaning rod. It was issued without a bayonet, although the standard pattern would fit. Serial numbers were given no particular distinction.

1905: production of the cossack rifle was greatly reduced after Russian cavalry had been unable to

dominate well-trained machine-gunners during the Russo-Japanese War—a failure attributed in military circles to cowardice!

1908: the introduction of the obr.1908g ball cartridge led to the 3,200-arshin sights being fitted. The work continued until 1911 or later.

1914: the inventory on 1 January contained 204,390 cossack and 540,270 dragoon rifles.

1915: production of cossack rifles ceased in favour of the dragoon pattern.

1922: the Red Army standardised the dragoon rifle as a substitute for the full-length infantry pattern. Production continued into the early 1930s; consequently, guns will be found with imperial or post-Revolutionary marks.

Model 1907

Carbines: Karabin obr.1907g i obr.1910g.
Made by the ordnance factories in Tula, Sestroretsk and Izhevsk.
7·62 × 54mm, rimmed.
Action: as obr.1891g infantry rifle, above.
1,020mm overall, 7·51lb unladen.
510mm barrel, 4-groove rifling; RH, concentric.
Integral charger-loaded box magazine, 5 rounds.
Leaf sight graduated to 2,000 arshin.
550 m/sec with obr.1891g ball cartridges.
No bayonet.

☆

1907: the first Mosin-Nagant carbine pattern (obr.1907g or '1891/07') was issued to the Tsar's artillery and cavalrymen. It was much shorter than the infantry rifle and the stock extended so close to the muzzle that the standard socket bayonet could not be mounted. The diminutive ramp-and-leaf back sight was originally graduated to about 1,600 arshin.

1910: adoption of the obr.1908g cartridge caused a change in sights. It is believed that a few changes were made in the 1907-type carbine—perhaps in the stock—and that an improved pattern was substituted. However, it is not known whether the popular 'obr. 1910g' designation has an official standing.

1914: the inventory of carbines stood at 118,660, including 25,000 converted Berdans.

MOSIN-NAGANT
LESSER MODELS

AUSTRIA-HUNGARY

1915: Austro-Hungarian forces on the Eastern Front captured sizeable quantities of Russian rifles, and also received large numbers taken by the Germans.

1916: guns in Austro-Hungarian service were issued with Russian ammunition. When supplies began to run short, some guns were converted at the Wiener-Neustadt armoury for the standard rimmed 8 × 50mm Austrian round. The original Russian-style socket bayonets were retained wherever possible, but some crude Austro-Hungarian substitutes have been reported.

CHINA

The People's Republic made Mosin-Nagant Type 53 carbines. They are virtually identical with the Soviet obr.1944g, but were marked '53' on the receiver and often bore the encircled-triangle mark of factory 66.

Production ceased in favour of SKS and AK copies in the late 1950s.

GERMANY

1915: many Russian rifles were captured on the Eastern Front during the opening stages of the First World War. Some were retained by the German army, to serve recruiting depots and lines-of-communications troops until the end of hostilities. Others went to the navy. A few were converted to handle the standard 8mm service cartridge, but so much ammunition had been captured that most guns were simply issued unaltered. However, changes were often made so that German-style bayonets could be fitted. The revisions usually comprised a muzzle tube with a bayonet lug, requiring the original fore-end to be cut back.

HUNGARY

Substantial quantities of Mosin-Nagant guns were made by FÉG of Budapest in the early 1950s. Production seems to have been confined to good-quality copies of the

obr.1944g carbine and obr.1891/30g sniper rifle, known as 44.M and 48.M respectively.

NORTH KOREA

A poor-quality copy of the Soviet obr.1891/30g rifle was made in the 1950s, apparently as the 'Type 30'. It was distinguished by a large encircled five-point star, preceding the serial number on the left side of the receiver.

POLAND

The earliest Polish Mosin-Nagant, introduced in the late 1920s, was a converted Russian rifle with a new 7·9mm-calibre barrel and the magazine altered to feed rimless cartridges. The resulting wz.91/98/25 had a German-style nose cap and bayonet bar, a swivel on the side of the barrel band and another on the left side of the butt. The gun was about 1,100mm overall, had a 600mm barrel and weighed 3·7kg.
¶ Copies of Soviet obr.1944g carbines and obr.1891/30 rifles—the latter usually for snipers—were made in the 1950s. They

were identical with the original patterns, but bore Polish factory marks.

USA

1918: the US government purchased more than a million obr.1891 rifles from Remington–UMC and the New England Westinghouse Company after the Russian revolution had left the two American manufacturers with huge numbers of unwanted guns and potentially serious financial difficulties. Only 280,050 guns were retained for US Army service, most being used for basic training.

1919: substantial numbers of 7·62mm Russian-pattern rifles equipped the US divisions sent to Archangelsk with the Allied intervention forces, apparently to ease logistics by allowing captured ammunition to be used. The guns, which were accompanied by the Russian-style socket bayonets, were heartily disliked by men accustomed to the M1903 Springfield. Most of them were abandoned in Russia when the Allies finally withdrew in 1920.

USSR

1919: revolution and civil war drove the arms industry perilously close to collapse. In July, Trotsky warned that new rifles were in short supply, as White forces had captured Izhevsk; Sestroretsk had been evacuated. By September, however, the crisis had passed.

1922: 1·272 million obr.1891g rifles made in 1918–20 had been supplemented by 920,000 refurbished ex-Tsarist guns. The decision was then taken to standardise the dragoon rifle once existing infantry-rifle parts had been exhausted. The first new guns were to be made in Izhevsk in 1923, and in Tula a year later. Production continued until about 1930.

Model 1891–30

Infantry rifle: Vintovka obr.1891/30g.
Made by state ordnance factories in Tula, Izhevsk,
Sestroretsk and elsewhere.
Quantity: about 17·475 million in 1930–45 alone
(including 185,000 sniper rifles).
7·62 × 54mm, rimmed.
Turning-bolt action, with two lugs on a detachable bolt
head locking into the receiver behind the chamber.
1,230mm overall, 3·95kg unladen.
730mm barrel, 4-groove rifling; RH, concentric.
Integral charger-loaded box magazine, 5 rounds.
Tangent-leaf sight graduated to 2,000 metres.
805 m/sec with Type D ball cartridges.
obr.1891/30g socket bayonet.

☆

1930: adopted on 28 April, the perfected Soviet version of the Tsarist dragoon rifle had a simplified cylindrical receiver and a hooded front sight. Developed by Kabakov and Komaritskiy in 1928, its socket bayonet had a spring catch instead of an archaic locking ring. Finish on Soviet-made guns was notably poorer than on pre-1917 examples, but the obr.1891/30g was solid and reliable. It was also more accurate at short ranges than its predecessors owing to greater care taken in calibrating the sights.

1932: the need for an effectual sniper rifle (Snayperskaya Vintovka) arose from attempts to

develop marksmanship made during the First Five Year Plan. Guns selected for accuracy had their bolt handles turned downward to clear the telescope sights, the side of the stock being cut away to accept the handle.

Russian sights were made in factory equipped by Carl Zeiss of Jena. The 4× PE type had a 30mm objective lens, a field of view of 8° 30'; azimuth and elevation adjustments were internal. It gave good optical performance for its day, but was comparatively heavy. The earliest sights were mounted in a single-piece twin split ring mount held on the receiver ring above the chamber, but this was replaced by a twin split ring mount fitted to a dovetailed base-plate on the left of the receiver.

1940: use of the PU telescope ('U', universal), introduced for the Tokarev sniper rifle (q.v.), was extended to the obr.1891/30g. Shorter and lighter than the PE pattern, the 3·5× PU was carried in a twin-ring slab-side mount locking onto the left side of the Mosin-Nagant receiver.

A few rifles were used with 26mm-diameter rubber-baffle silencers weighing about 480gm. These combinations could only fire subsonic 'partisan' ammunition, with green marks on the bullet, case or primer; otherwise, baffles were wrecked after a few rounds.

Model 1938

Carbine: Karabina obr.1938g.
Made by state ordnance factories, 1939–44.
7·62 × 54mm, rimmed.
Action: as obr.1891/30g rifle, above.
1,020mm overall, 3.45kg unladen.
510mm barrel, 4-groove rifling; RH, concentric.
Integral charger-loaded box magazine, 5 rounds.
Tangent-leaf sight graduated to 2,000 metres.
785 m/sec with Type D ball cartridges.
obr.1891/30g socket bayonet.

☆

1939: this replaced obr.1891/30g rifles and surviving ex-Tsarist carbines in the hands of the cavalry, artillery, signals and motor-transport units. Unlike the 1910 pattern, the 1938-type carbine was basically a shortened infantry rifle

and would accept the standard socket bayonet. Production exceeded two million; 687,430 were made in 1942 alone.

Model 1944

Carbine: Karabina obr.1944g.
Made in state ordnance factories, 1944–9?
7·62 × 54mm, rimmed.
Otherwise generally as obr.1938g, excepting
dimensions (1,025mm, 4·03kg, 520mm barrel) and
bayonet (integral folding pattern).

☆

1943: eight differing bayonets were tried on obr.1938g carbines throughout May. The Semin system was preferred by November.
1944: the obr.1944g was standardised on 17 January. It was identical with the 1938 pattern excepting for the special cruciform-blade bayonet pivoting on a block attached to the right side of the muzzle.

SPORTING GUNS

Substantial quantities of sporting and target rifles have been made in the USSR, using actions either cannibalised from old military weapons or assembled from unused parts. Identification is still handicapped by lack of information; 7·62 × 54mm rifles have included the MTs-13, MTs-13·1, MTs-16, TsV-52, Zenit-2, Zenit-3 and Tallinn patterns, but only a few of these have been built on Mosin-Nagant receivers.

BI-7·62

Target rifle.
Made by the state ordnance factory, Izhevsk.
7·62 × 54mm, rimmed.
Action: as obr.1891/30g rifle, above.
1,300mm overall (including butt-plate hook),
4.60kg unladen.
750mm barrel, 4-groove rifling; RH, concentric.
Integral charger-loaded box magazine, 5 rounds.
Aperture sight.
About 800 m/sec with Type D ball cartridges.

☆

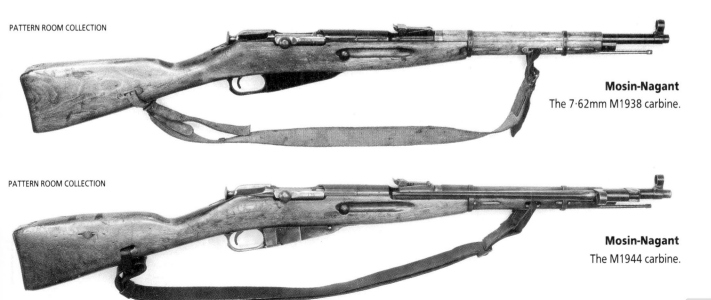

PATTERN ROOM COLLECTION

Mosin-Nagant
The 7·62mm M1938 carbine.

PATTERN ROOM COLLECTION

Mosin-Nagant
The M1944 carbine.

1962*: intended for biathlon competitions (an arduous mixture of cross-country skiing and target shooting), this amalgamated a standard Mosin-Nagant action—generally a reconditioned pre-1917 example—with a pistol-grip half stock. Chequering appeared on the fore-end and pistol grip of selected guns, though standard rifles were apparently plainly finished.

The greatly refined trigger had a lateral safety bolt through the stock. The bolt handle had a spatulate shank and a spherical grasping knob, while a lightweight cylindrical cocking piece reduced lock time appreciably. Swivels lay under the fore-end and butt, the latter being moved forward far enough to allow a hinged trap to be fitted. Two loaded chargers could be carried in the butt when required. The wooden shoulder plate slid vertically on its alloy mount, but could be locked by a large thumb-wheel in the lower right side of the butt.

A micro-adjustable aperture sight was fitted to the rear left side of the receiver, with a sturdy replaceable-element tunnel at the muzzle.

MOSSBERG

UNITED STATES OF AMERICA

These guns were made by O.F. Mossberg & Sons, now renowned as a leading shotgun manufacturer.

Though large numbers of rimfire rifles had been made prior to the Second World War, Mossberg was a late convert to the high-power centre-fire sporting rifle. The bolt-action types remained in production for nearly twenty years, but were never particularly successful. They were more expensive than the effectual Savage 110 and lacked the refinements found on Remington, Ruger and Winchester rivals. The bolt-stroke was often rough, the extractor was fragile, and the combination of sear and bolt-release catch was widely criticised.

Mossberg countered criticism with the Pedersen range, but the venture was short lived. The rifles—rim- and centre-fire alike—had all been abandoned by 1985. Thereafter, Mossberg promoted the Model 1500—Sako-action (q.v.) rifles purchased from Smith & Wesson.

1. THE BOLT-ACTION PATTERNS

Model 800

A, B, C, D, F, M, SM and V patterns.
Made by O.F. Mossberg & Sons, Inc., North Haven, Connecticut, 1966–78.
·222 Remington, ·22–250 Remington, 6·5mm Remington Magnum, ·243 Winchester, ·308 Winchester or ·350 Remington Magnum.
Turning-bolt action, with six lugs on the bolt head rotating into the receiver behind the chamber and the bolt handle turning down into its seat.
DATA FOR A TYPICAL EXAMPLE
·243 Winchester, rimless.
42·00in overall, 6·50lb unladen.
22·00in barrel, 6-groove rifling; RH, concentric.
Internal box magazine, 4 rounds.
Folding-leaf sight.
3,500 ft/sec with 80-grain bullet.
☆

1963: Louis Seecamp and Carl Benson began work on a centre-fire sporting rifle amalgamating the best of an unsuccessful Seecamp prototype with elements of the Mossberg Model 385 bolt-action shotgun. The project is said to have been undertaken to provide Montgomery, Ward & Co., Inc., with a centre-fire sporter to sell alongside Mossberg-made 'Western Field'-brand rimfires. Design work was completed in 1965.
1966: production of the Model 800 rifle began, initially in ·243 and ·308 Winchester only. An oddly shaped bolt handle—bent forward above the trigger—failed to mar the elegance of the action, the neat lines of which were achieved partly by using two rows of three lugs on a sub-diameter bolt head but also by relying on a shotgun-type sliding safety on the streamlined bolt shroud. The vestigial extractor blade was controlled by a sprung plunger in the bolt head,

and the hinged magazine floor plate was released by a catch ahead of the trigger guard.

The earliest guns had walnut pistol-grip stocks with Monte Carlo combs, the synthetic grip cap and butt plate being accompanied by white-line spacers. The impressed skip-line chequering featured a deer-head on the pistol grip and a running buck on the fore-end.
1967*: a ·22–250 Remington chambering was offered as the Model 800C, the earlier guns being retrospectively classified as 800A (·308) or 800B (·243). Rifles sold with optical sights had an additional 'SM' suffix.
1968: a Varmint pattern was introduced with a heavy 24in barrel and additional sight bases. This was identified by a 'V' suffix (later 'VT' for 'Varmint/Target'), which could be added to existing designations—e.g., Model 800BVT was a varmint rifle in ·243 Winchester. A few rifles were made in ·350 and 6·5mm Remington Magnum chamberings (the Models 800D and 800E?), but were unsuccessful. The design of the firing pin changed in this era from a two-part assembly joined by lugs to one connected by a splined lug and cross-pin.
1969: the 'M' variant was introduced with a 20in barrel, a straight spatulate bolt handle, and a full-length or 'Mannlicher style' stock. It was offered in ·22–250, ·243 and ·308, being designated 'CM', 'BM' and 'AM' respectively.
1970: the ·222 Remington Model 800F was introduced, but production was very small. A deluxe Super Grade ('D' suffix) pattern also appeared, with a select walnut stock, rollover comb, rosewood fore-end tip and pistol-grip cap, and damascened bolt.
1972: the Mannlicher stock and Super Grade rifles were abandoned, the latter being replaced by the Pedersen series described below.

Model 810

A, B, C, D, H and SM patterns.
Made by O.F. Mossberg & Sons, Inc., North Haven, Connecticut, 1972–8.
·270 Winchester, 7mm Remington Magnum, ·30–06 or ·338 Winchester Magnum.

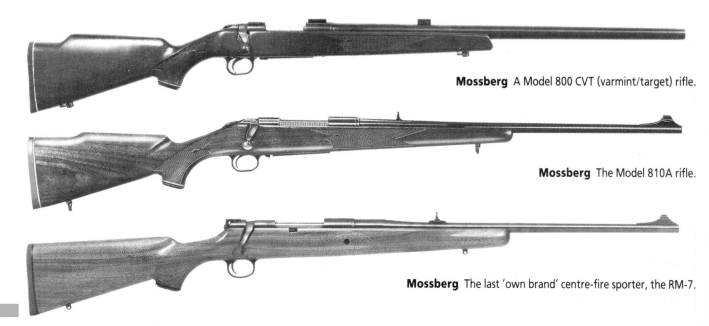

Mossberg A Model 800 CVT (varmint/target) rifle.

Mossberg The Model 810A rifle.

Mossberg The last 'own brand' centre-fire sporter, the RM-7.

Turning-bolt action, with four lugs on the bolt head rotating into the receiver behind the chamber.

DATA FOR A TYPICAL 810A
·30–06, rimless
42·00in overall, 7·75lb unladen.
22·00in barrel, 8-groove rifling; RH, concentric.
Detachable box magazine, 4 rounds.
Folding-leaf sight.
2,800 ft/sec with 165-grain bullet.

☆

1972: the Model 810 shared the elegant lines of the Model 800, but its bolt had twin lugs in tandem and a conventional firing pin assembly. The trigger, adjustable for engagement and pull weight, was contained in a steel housing and the trigger-guard bow/magazine floor plate assembly was steel instead of nylon.

The standard rifle was available in ·30–06 (810A) or 7mm Remington Magnum (810B); magazines held four standard or three magnum rounds. The Mossberg had an elegant half-stock with a low Monte Carlo comb and a plain rounded fore-end tip. Chequering appeared on the pistol-grip and fore-end, swivels being placed conventionally. The butt plate and pistol-grip cap were accompanied by white spacers. Rifles sold with factory-fitted optical sights were given additional 'SM' suffixes.

1973*: ·270 Winchester and ·338 Winchester Magnum chamberings were announced (810C and 810D), magazines holding four and three rounds respectively. The ·338 had a 24in barrel.

1975: a top-loading magazine with a hinged floor plate was introduced to accompany the box pattern, work on which was greatly reduced thereafter. The Model 810BSMH, therefore, chambered 7mm Remington Magnum rounds, had a factory-fitted optical sight, and an internal magazine with a hinged floor plate.

RM-7

A and B patterns.
Made by O.F. Mossberg & Sons, Inc., North Haven, Connecticut, 1978–84.
·30–06 (RM-7A) or 7mm Remington Magnum (RM-7B).
Action: generally as 810 series, above.

DATA FOR A TYPICAL RM-7B
7mm Remington Magnum, rimless
46·00in overall, 7·65lb unladen.
24·00in barrel, 8-groove rifling; RH, concentric.
Internal spool magazine, 4 rounds.
Folding-leaf sight.
3,020 ft/sec with 175-grain bullet.

☆

1978: introduced to replace the 800 and 810-series rifles, this was distinguished by its magazine. The action was basically a modified multi-lug type, but the bolt handle was re-shaped and the streamlined bolt shroud was replaced by a conventionally squared pattern.

A three-position safety was fitted, whilst the receiver was drilled and tapped for optical-sight mounts. The ·30–06 version had a 22in barrel and a five round magazine, details of the 7mm version being given above.

The classically styled walnut stock had a straight comb, chequering on the pistol grip and fore-end, a black plastic pistol-grip cap and a rubber butt plate. Swivel eyes appeared beneath the fore-end and the butt-edge.

1984: the RM-7 was abandoned, partly owing to lack of success in a market-place already crowded with more effectual rifles and partly to a decision to purchase substantial numbers of Sako-action rifles from Smith & Wesson.

2. THE LEVER-ACTION PATTERNS
Models 472 and 479

Brush Gun, carbine and rifle patterns.
Made by O.F. Mossberg & Sons, Inc., North Haven, Connecticut, 1974–9 (Model 472) and 1980–5 (Model 479).
·30–30 Winchester or ·35 Remington.
Lever-action, locked by a vertically sliding bolt.

DATA FOR A TYPICAL 479
·30–30 Winchester, rimmed
38·25in overall, 6·85lb unladen (straight-wrist butt).
20·00in barrel, 8-groove rifling; RH, concentric.

Tube magazine beneath barrel, 6 rounds.
Spring-leaf and elevator sight.
2,410 ft/sec with 150-grain bullet.

☆

1972: Mossberg's classical lever-action sporting rifle, apparently largely the work of Carl Benson, incorporated a locking bolt inspired by the Browning-designed Winchesters (q.v.). Unlike the Winchesters, however, the trigger mechanism was attached to the operating lever and a hammer-block safety lever was fitted to the rear left side of the receiver.

The side-ejecting Model 472 bore a superficial external resemblance to the Marlin 336, with a loading gate on the side of the receiver and a prominent operating-lever pivot. It was offered as a rifle (Model 472PR), with a pistol-grip butt, a 24in barrel and a short five-round magazine; as a carbine, with a pistol- or straight-grip butt (472PC and 472SC respectively), a 20in barrel and a full-length six-round magazine; and as a Brush Gun (472SB), with a straight-wrist butt, an 18in barrel and a full-length five round magazine. An 'A' suffix indicated a ·30–30 gun, 'B' examples chambering ·35 Remington.

1980: the Model 479 was little more than a 472 with an improved hammer-blocking cross-bolt safety, available in the same chamberings and with similar pistol-grip or straight-wrist butts. Production apparently ceased in 1981.

1983: the ·30–30 Model 479PCA reappeared, with a 20in barrel and a six-round magazine.

MURATA

JAPAN

Derived by combining features of the French Gras and German Mauser, supplies of which had been purchased in Europe, this rifle was developed in the period immediately after the Satsuma rebellion (1877) showed the poverty of the Japanese arms industry. Ordnance factories were established in Tokyo and Osaka, and Major Tsuneyoshi Murata was appointed not only to supervise development of an indigenous rifle but

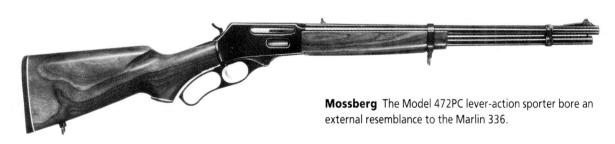

Mossberg The Model 472PC lever-action sporter bore an external resemblance to the Marlin 336.

MOSSBERG
THE LESSER PATTERNS

Pedersen series The Pedersen Custom Guns Division of Mossberg was created to market deluxe versions of the Model 810 (1973-5) and Model 472 (1975 only), the results being designated 'Model 3000' and 'Model 4700' respectively.

¶ The Model 3000 was offered in three grades. Grade I was the finest, with selected woodwork, engraving, silver inlays and a choice of butt plates; Grade II was similar, but lacked the inlays; and Grade III, the most basic, also lacked engraving.

¶ The Model 4700 was distinguished by selected woodwork and a broad or semi-beavertail fore-end.

Western Field series Sold by Montgomery, Ward & Co., Inc., of Chicago, these 'own brand' guns included a range of otherwise standard Mossberg rifles.

¶ The Western Field 765 was a ·30–06 Mossberg 810 with a walnut-stained beech stock. Chequering was omitted, the Monte Carlo comb was very shallow, and the butt plate was ribbed plastic.

¶ The Western Field 771, 772 and 778 were, respectively, a Mossberg Model 472 with straight-wrist butt, a 472 with pistol-grip butt, and a standard 479.

¶ The Western Field 775 (·243 Winchester) and 776 (·308 Winchester) were original 800-type bolt-action Mossbergs.

¶ The Western Field 782 (sometimes listed, apparently wrongly, as '732') was a Model 810 in ·30–06 or 7mm Remington Magnum, often with distinctive 'Mountain Top' skip-line chequering on the pistol-grip and fore-end.

¶ The Western Field 786 (·30-06) and 787 (7mm Remington Magnum) were minor variants of the Mossberg RM-7.

also to find a suitable conversion system for Chassepot needle rifles.

Models 1880, 1883 and 1885

Rifles, short rifles and carbines:
Meiji 13th, 16th and 18th Year Types.
Made by the Imperial ordnance factory,
Koishikawa, Tokyo, 1880–7.
11mm, rimmed.
Turning-bolt action, locked by the bolt-guide rib
abutting the reciever ahead of the bridge.
DATA FOR 18TH YEAR TYPE RIFLE
1,276mm overall, 4·09kg unladen.
813mm barrel, 4-groove rifling; RH, concentric.
Ramp-and-leaf sight graduated to 1,600 metres.
About 435 m/sec with 13th Year Type cartridges.
18th Year Type sword bayonet.

☆

1880: inspired by the French Gras rifle, the first or 13th Year Type Murata had a one-piece stock with a straight wrist. The front band doubled as a nose cap—with the bayonet bar on the right side—while the rear band carried a swivel. Another swivel lay on the under edge of the butt. The 13th Year Type bayonet was used.
1883: the 16th Year Type cavalry carbine apparently had a 510mm barrel and a stock extending to the muzzle. Weight was 3·24kg and the back sight ranged to 1,200 metres.
1885: an improved 18th Year Type bolt was adopted, and the stock was refined. The comb was lowered and a shoulder appeared at the rear of the receiver. The trigger-guard bow was simplified (the earlier pattern had a bulkier rear tang) and the protrusion of the barrel ahead of the fore-end tip was reduced. A small auxiliary bayonet-mounting tenon appeared on the left side of the muzzle; consequently, the 18th Year Type bayonet was not interchangeable with its 13th Year Type predecessor.

An 18th Year Type cavalry rifle was made in small numbers; it seems to have had a 640mm barrel—much longer than a carbine—and may have been stocked to the muzzle. However, very few guns were produced before the 22nd Year Type magazine rifle appeared.

Model 1889

Infantry rifle: Meiji 22nd Year Type.
Made by the Imperial artillery arsenal, Koishikawa,
Tokyo, 1888–97.
Quantity: more than 100,000.
8mm, rimmed.
Turning-bolt action, with two lugs on the bolt head
locking into the receiver behind the chamber.
1,207mm overall, 3·94kg unladen.
750mm barrel, 4-groove rifling; RH, concentric.
Tube magazine under barrel, 8 rounds.
Ramp-and-leaf sight graduated to 2,000 metres.
About 565 m/sec with 22nd Year Type cartridges.
22nd Year Type sword bayonet.

☆

1887: an experimental Meiji 20th Year Type magazine rifle was issued for field trials.
1889: after minor changes and improvements had been made, the Meiji 22nd Year rifle was approved. It had a distinctive straight-wrist one piece stock with a barrel band and a sturdy nose cap. The magazine tube protruded beyond the nose cap to receive the cross-guard ring of the strange little knife bayonet. A short hand guard ran forward from the back sight to the rear band, and dicing was usually found on the fore-end to improve grip. Swivels lay on the underside of the band and butt. A magazine cut-off lever lay behind the bolt handle.
1894: field service in the Sino-Japanese war highlighted the shortcomings of the Murata.

Model 1894

Cavalry and artillery carbine: Meiji 27th Year Type.
Made by the Imperial artillery arsenal,
Koishikawa, Tokyo, 1894–7.
8mm, rimmed.
Action: as 22nd Year Type rifle, above.
952mm overall, 3·11kg unladen.
490mm barrel, 4-groove rifling; RH, concentric.
Tube magazine under barrel, 6 rounds.
Ramp-and-leaf sight graduated to 1,600 metres?
About 520 m/sec with 22nd Year Type cartridges.
No bayonet.

☆

1894: this was mechanically similar to the 22nd Year Type rifle, but had a spring-retained barrel band; the shortened magazine tube did not protrude past the nose cap. Swivels appeared on the underside of the fore-end and butt for the artillery, or on the left side of the barrel band and butt for cavalrymen. The tube magazine was ill-suited to mounted units, but the 30th Year Type carbine did not appear for some years.

MUSGRAVE

REPUBLIC OF SOUTH AFRICA

Designed by members of a well-known South African gunmaking family, Musgrave rifles were based on the proven Mauser action. Though series production began in the early 1970s, the Mauser-type rifles were replaced in the late 1970s by modified Model 80 and Model 90 patterns—details of which are still lacking.

RSA NR-1

Made by Musgrave Manufacturers & Distributors
(Pty) Ltd, Bloemfentein, 1970–6.
·308 Winchester only.
Turning-bolt action, locked by lugs on the bolt-head
and the bolt handle turning down into its seat.
About 46·5in overall, 10·00lb without sights.
26·45in barrel, 4-groove rifling; RH, concentric?
Aperture sight.
2,625 ft/sec with 180-grain bullet.

☆

1970: this single-shot target rifle seems to have been developed for the South African Rifle Association, and possibly also as a military trainer. Built around a much-modified Mauser action, which cocked on closing, the NR-1 was distinguished by a massive tubular receiver, pierced only by an ejection port, and a plain straight-comb half stock with a hand guard running forward from the chamber. A band around the fore-end bore a swivel, though an accessory rail was often let into the underside of the fore-end. A rubber butt plate was standard,

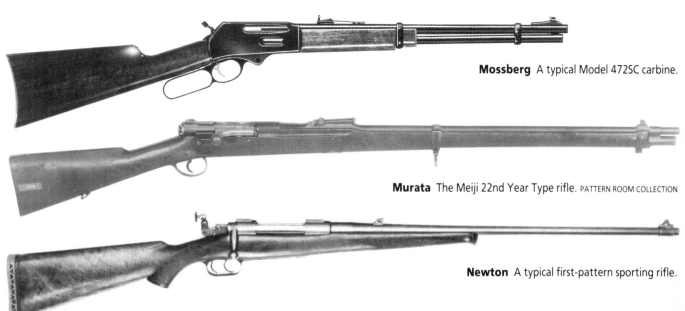

Mossberg A typical Model 472SC carbine.

Murata The Meiji 22nd Year Type rifle. PATTERN ROOM COLLECTION

Newton A typical first-pattern sporting rifle.

the barrel was a special heavyweight pattern, and micro-adjustable sights were used.

Sporting rifle

NR-5, NR-6, Premier and Valiant patterns.
Made by Musgrave Manufacturers & Distributors
(Pty) Ltd, Bloemfontein, 1971–6.
·243 Winchester, ·270 Winchester, 7mm Remington
Magnum, ·30–06 or ·308 Winchester, and ·458
Winchester Magnum to special order only.
Action: as NR-1, above.
DATA FOR A TYPICAL NR-5
·270 Winchester, rimless.
46·70in overall, 8·25lb unladen.
25·75in barrel, 4-groove rifling; RH, concentric?
Internal box magazine, 5 rounds.
Optical sight.
2,900 ft/sec with 150-grain bullet.
☆

1971: the NR-5 or Premier had a good-quality walnut stock with a low Monte Carlo comb and a slender pistol grip. Chequering appeared on the pistol grip and fore-end, the separate olivewood grip-cap and fore-end tip contrasting with the dark finish of the stock. A ventilated shoulder pad was fitted to the butt and studs for readily detachable swivels lay beneath the fore-end and butt-toe.

The NR-6, also sold as the 'Valiant', had a 24in barrel and a simpler stock with a straight comb. Skip-line chequering appeared on the pistol grip and fore-end, the grip cap and fore-end tip being abandoned. Sights usually comprised a folding leaf and a ramped blade.

NEWTON

UNITED STATES OF AMERICA

Charles Newton is best known for his cartridges, but deserves recognition as the father of the modern high-velocity sporting rifle. The essence of the first Newton action was a turning bolt with multiple locking lugs on the head and two auxiliary or safety lugs on the body ahead of the bolt handle. Careful design ensured that the lugs aligned when the breech was open, allowing an unusually slender receiver bridge to be used.

The first sporting rifle failed, partly owing to the advent of the First World War, but Newton proved to be a poor businessman. His second venture fared little better, and, by 1929, he had eschewed the turning-bolt action in favour of a straight-pull pattern. The LeverBolt Rifle Company had been formed in New Haven to exploit the new rifle, but Newton's death in 1932 brought work to an end.

Note: the earliest guns offered by the Newton Rifle Company were built around Mauser actions imported from Germany.

Sporting Rifle

Original pattern.
Made by the Newton Arms Company, Buffalo,
New York, 1916–18.
·256, ·30, ·33 or ·35 (proprietary designs).
Turning-bolt action, with seven lugs on the bolt head
and two on the body locking into the receiver.
DATA FOR A TYPICAL EXAMPLE
·30 Newton, rimless.
44·10in overall, 6·85lb unladen.
24·00in barrel, 5-groove rifling; RH, polygonal.
Charger-loaded internal box magazine, 5 rounds.
Standing block sight with folding leaves.
About 2,950 ft/sec with 172-grain bullet.
☆

1916: the ·256, ·30 and ·35 Newton rifles were announced in April. They had slender stocks with a schnabel-tip fore-end; the butts had a chequered pistol grip and a narrow straight comb. A three-position radial safety appeared on the right side of the bolt plug, while the detachable magazine floor-plate helped to retain the barrelled action. The first Newtons had an adjustable set-trigger with an auxiliary lever at the back of the trigger-guard aperture and were often fitted with an adjustable column-type sight on the cocking piece. Bolt handles were low enough to clear a telescope sight.

1918: its affairs ruined by the entry of the USA into the First World War, the Newton company was liquidated in April. Only about half the 4,000 fully-assembled rifles had been sold.

1919: about 350 rifles were completed and sold by the Newton Arms Company liquidators. The inventor, meanwhile, had formed the Charles Newton Rifle Corporation.

1920: rifles made from old parts, which had been sold to a machine-tool refurbisher, were advertised as products of a spurious 'Newton Arms Corporation' until an injunction was granted in July. The quality of these guns ranged from barely acceptable to abysmal.

Sporting Rifle

Second or 'Buffalo Newton' pattern.
Made by the Charles Newton Rifle Corporation,
Buffalo, New York, 1921–2; and the Buffalo Newton
Rifle Company, Buffalo, New York (c.1923–4),
or New Haven, Connecticut (1925–9).
Quantity: 2,500 in Buffalo and 400–500 in New Haven.
·256 Newton, ·30 Newton, ·35 Newton or ·30–06.
Turning-bolt action, with multiple lugs on the bolt
head and one lug on the body.
DATA FOR A TYPICAL EXAMPLE
·256 Newton, rimless.
44·05in overall, 7·42lb unladen.
24·00in barrel, 4-groove rifling; RH, concentric.
Internal box magazine, 5 rounds.
Standing block sight with folding leaves.
About 3,100 ft/sec with 123-grain bullet.
☆

1921: after the failure of his original company, Charles Newton tried again. The modified rifle was a simplified version of the 1916 sporter, with an interrupted-thread on the bolt head—easier to machine than the previous lugs—and a greatly simplified cocking piece. The sear doubled as a bolt stop, a prominent recoil bolt ran through the stock below the receiver bridge, and the bolt handle was a cranked pattern. A reversed set-trigger lever was also distinctive.

1922: the Buffalo Newton company was formed to promote the new rifle. However, good fortune was still elusive; the guns were rarely as well made as the previous pattern and sales suffered accordingly. Trading ceased in 1930.

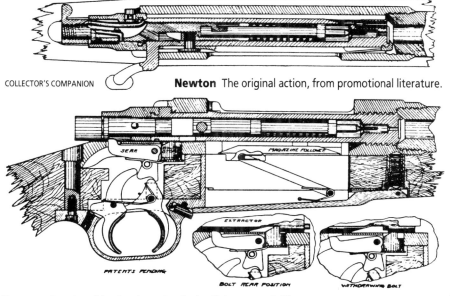

COLLECTOR'S COMPANION **Newton** The original action, from promotional literature.

Newton An advertising brochure for the 'Buffalo Newton' rifle.

PEABODY

UNITED STATES OF AMERICA

This pivoting-block action was developed in the USA, but proved to be more popular abroad before developing into the Peabody-Martini.

The original rifle was patented in July 1862 by Henry Peabody of Boston. A slot under the breech block opened the action in conjunction with pins on the breech lever. The mechanism was very strong, as it took much of the strain of firing on the rear inner face of the receiver and the position of the breech-block pivot pin prevented the action opening prematurely.

The patent was reissued in 1866, with a rider that pin-and-slot depressors were only one operating method. Peabody then added a lever-and-slot alternative and a pivoting extractor.

MILITARY WEAPONS

In an 1870-vintage broadsheet, the Providence Tool Company claimed to be making a standard ·45 side-hammer or 'Roumanian Model'; the similar ·43 'Spanish Model' with a spiral firing-pin retractor spring; a 'Self-Cocking Gun' with a top-lever depressor and a coil-pattern firing-pin spring; and the ·42 (Russian) Peabody-Wessely, a self-cocking design with an internal hammer.

ROMANIA

Prior to gaining independence in 1878, Romania was an autonomous province of the Turkish empire. About 30,000 Peabody rifles were purchased in 1867–9; superseded in the late 1870s by the Peabody-Martini (see 'Martini'), they had a leaf-type firing-pin retractor spring.

SPAIN

Colonial Model

••
Rifle and carbine: Fusil y Tercerola Peabody do Ejercito de Ultramar.

Made by the Providence Tool Company, Providence, Rhode Island, c.1868–9.
Quantity: perhaps 25,000 rifles and 5,000 carbines.
·56–50 Spencer ('13mm'), rimfire.
Pivoting-block action, operated by a lever combined with the trigger guard.
DATA FOR RIFLE
1,373mm overall, 4·52kg unladen.
912mm barrel, 3-groove rifling; RH, concentric?
Leaf sight for 200, 300 and 500 metres.
375 m/sec with ball cartridges.
Socket bayonet (US M1855 pattern?).

☆

1868: these were purchased for service with the Spanish colonial army (Ejercito de Ultramar) based in Cuba. They were conventional Peabody patterns, with back-action locks, and had three spring-retained bands. Swivels lay on the middle band and beneath the receiver ahead of the breech lever. Internally, the firing-pin retractor had a coil spring. The carbine was a shortened rifle, 970mm long with a 507mm barrel and an unladen weight of 3·86kg. It had a simpler sight and a half-length fore-end held by a single band. A sling ring was attached to the left side of the stock level with the hammer-pivot screw.

1870: some rifles are said to have been supplied chambering the standard 11mm (·43) Spanish Remington cartridge.

SWITZERLAND

Model 1867

••
Engineer rifle:
Genie-Gewehr system Peabody, M1867.
Made by the Providence Tool Company, Providence, Rhode Island, 1867–8.
Quantity: 15,000.
10·4 × 38mm, rimfire.
Action: as Spanish guns, above.
1,310mm overall, 4·40kg unladen.
833mm barrel, 3-groove rifling; RH, concentric.
Quadrant sight graduated to 800 metres.
435 m/sec with M1867 ball cartridges.
M1863 socket bayonet.

☆

1867: a large quantity of these rifles, adopted on 14 June, was ordered from America. About 5,000 were issued to riflemen (Scharfschützen) in 1868, pending perfection of the Vetterli magazine rifle; the others were stored.

1872: remaining guns were given to engineers.

1875: the rifles were modified by changing the extractor and altering the striker-block to a more conventional form. Altered guns had a narrow extractor blade with a tapering tip, protruding at the base of the chamber.

1877: survivors received Swiss-made barrels. These were about 820mm long, reducing overall length to 1,298mm, and had a distinctive 80mm octagonal section at the breech; the original American-made barrel was a tapering cylinder. Modified guns, often known as 'M1867/77' or 'M1877', served the Landwehr for ten years.

Note: it has been claimed that Swiss Peabody rifles were converted to centre-fire. None of those examined had been altered, however.

TURKEY

No mention was made in Peabody literature reliably dated to 1870, suggesting that the order dates from about 1871. The guns were standard external-hammer types with back-action locks and leaf type firing-pin retractor springs.

USA

Military Model

••
Offered as a musket or carbine.
Made by the Providence Tool Company, Providence, Rhode Island, 1867–73.
Chambering: see notes.
Action: as Spanish guns, above.
DATA FOR MUSKET
·45–70, rimmed.
51·50in overall, 8·95lb unladen.
33·00in barrel, 3-groove rifling; RH, concentric.
Leaf sight graduated to 1,200 yards.
1,275 ft/sec with ball cartridges.
M1855 socket bayonet.

☆

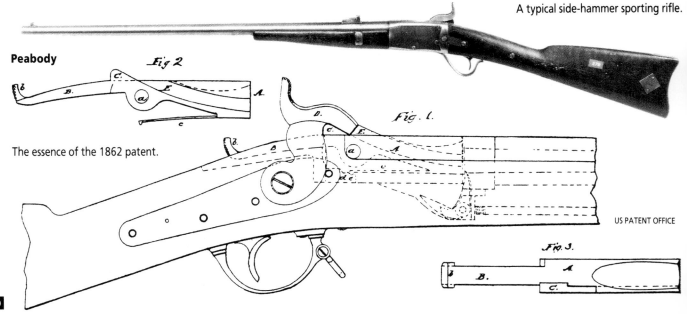

A typical side-hammer sporting rifle.

Peabody

Fig 2

Fig. 1.

The essence of the 1862 patent.

Fig. 3.

US PATENT OFFICE

1865: Peabody rifles received great praise from the US Army. However, though they were much more effectual than the Allin-type Springfield, they could not be created from existing rifle muskets. The deep receiver, two-piece stock and back-action lock required complete re-tooling.

1867: by the summer, the Peabody had been converted to centre-fire. According to catalogues printed in 1871, military-style muskets, stocked to the muzzle, were available in ·43 (11mm Spanish), ·45–70 and ·50–70 centre-fire, plus ·50–60 rimfire; military carbines were made in ·45 and ·50. The guns were never popular in the USA, though some were purchased on behalf of state militia in Connecticut and Massachusetts.

SPORTING GUNS

The original Peabody Sporting Gun of 1865 had a half-octagon barrel and a side-barred patch box in the butt. It was superseded in 1866 by a plainer gun chambering a variety of rimfire cartridges, a centre-fire version being available by the summer of 1867.

A catalogue produced in 1871 indicated that the sporter was available only in ·45–70, with a round barrel measuring 20–28in; the standard back sight was a leaf pattern, though a folding tang sight was optional.

Deluxe guns—with half-octagon or fully octagonal barrels—offered chequering on the stock-wrist and fore-end, and silver or nickelled escutcheons for the barrel-key. However, the Peabody sporters were too expensive to sell in large numbers and were speedily replaced by more effectual Peabody-Martini patterns (see 'Martini'); surviving examples are uncommon.

RANGER

UNITED STATES OF AMERICA

Designed by Homer Koon, this distinctive action was sold in considerable numbers—left and right-hand—often to be completed elsewhere. Excepting rifles made under the Bortmess brand,

a vast range of stocks and fittings will be encountered. Few prove to be 'factory original'.

Ranger Sporting Rifle

Maverick and Texas Magnum patterns.
Made by Ranger Arms Co., Inc., Gainesville, Texas.
Chambering: see text.
Turning-bolt action, locked by rotating lugs on the bolt head into the receiver wall.
DATA FOR A TYPICAL TEXAS MAGNUM
·308 Winchester, rimless.
45·00in overall, 7·28lb unladen.
24·00in barrel, 4-groove rifling; RH, concentric.
Internal box magazine, 5 rounds.
Optical sight.
2,610 ft/sec with 180-grain bullet.

☆

1967: the Ranger rifle relied on three sturdy locking lugs on the bolt head, giving a 60° throw. The plunger-type ejector and the short-claw extractor were also carried on the bolt head, the face of which was fully recessed.

The bolt handle unit screwed into the back of the bolt body and the streamlined bolt shroud screwed in turn onto the back of the bolt handle, the parts being locked by small Allen-head screws. The trigger mechanism was attached to the trigger guard bow, owing to the inclusion of a lateral safety bolt.

A typical rifle had an excellent walnut stock with a roll-over Monte Carlo comb, a contrasting fore-end tip and pistol-grip cap accompanied by thin white spacers, and a ventilated rubber butt plate. However, thumb-hole butts, full-length fore-ends, and a selection of stock woods (e.g., Claro walnut or a walnut/maple laminate) were also offered.

Texas Magnum actions accepted cartridges comparable in size to the ·30–06, while the shorter Maverick type—single-shot or magazine-fed—was intended for cartridges about the size of the ·308 Winchester pattern.

1972*: Ranger-made actions were sold under the banner of the Bortmess Gun Co., Inc., of Scenery Hill, Pennsylvania, fitted with Douglas Premium barrels and differing stock styles. The

Classic rifle had a conventional stock, whereas the Big Horn Rifle pattern, for example, had an exaggerated 'half curl' pistol-grip and the height of the cheek piece was emphasised by deeply scalloping the heel. The stock was walnut with rosewood accessories, the shoulder plate being a steel Niedner or rubber Pachmayr design.

1978*: work ceased. By 1980, the Bortmess organisation was using Voere actions for its Big Horn and Classic rifles.

REMINGTON

UNITED STATES OF AMERICA

This section contains details of post-1900 guns, excepting the many variations of the renowned Rolling Block (see 'Rider').

1. THE AUTO-LOADING PATTERNS

The original Model 8-type guns acknowledged US patents granted to John Browning on 9 and 16 October 1900 (659,507 and 659,786) and 3 June 1902 (701,289). Guns made after 1918 listed additional patents granted in May 1907 and February 1911.

Models 8 and 81

Made by the Remington Arms Company, Ilion, New York, 1906–36 (Model 8) and 1936–50 (Model 81).
Chambering: see text.
DATA FOR TYPICAL MODEL 8
Recoil-operated auto-loading action, locked by two lugs on the bolt engaging the barrel extension.
·32 Remington, rimless.
41·00in overall, 7·63lb unladen.
22·00in barrel, 6-groove rifling; RH, concentric.
Detachable box magazine, 5 rounds.
Spring-leaf and elevator sight.
2,220 ft/sec with 170-grain bullet.

☆

Automatische Rückstoss-lader-Waffen. Armes automatiques se chargent par la force du recul. Automatic recoil-loading arms. Armas automáticas que se cargan por la fuerza del retroceso.

Automatische Büchse System „Browning". Carabine automatique système Browning. Automatic rifle, system „Browning". Carabina automática sistema „Browning"

Browning. Browning.

Auf 50 Meter aufgelegt geschossen.
Diamètre de la cible 20 cm. Tiré à 50 mètres de distance.
diameter of target 20 cm. fired from a distance of 50 meters.
Diámetro del blanco 20 cm. Tirado a una distancia de 50 metros.
Durchmesser der Scheibe 20 ¾ m

Remington The Browning blowback auto-loader, seen here in the 1911 Alfa catalogue, was a European version of the Remington Model 8.

1906: this, the first centre-fire auto-loader to be made in North America, was a Browning design relying on the barrel sliding back within a sleeve to unlock the breech. Chambered for proprietary ·25, ·30, ·32 and ·35 cartridges and sold only with a round barrel and a box magazine, standard 'Take-Down' guns had two-piece stocks with a straight-wrist butt and a schnabel fore-end tip, though half pistol grips could be obtained on request. A radial safety lever lay on the right side of the receiver. The rifles were offered in five grades—A, C, D, E and F—each being a little more luxurious than its predecessor.

1936: the Model 8 was superseded by the improved Model 81 Woodsmaster, chambered for ·300 Savage in addition to ·30, ·32 and ·35 Remington. The rifles were made in four grades: A, B, D and F. Their action remained practically unchanged, but the half pistol-grip butt was standardised and the semi-beavertail fore-end had a plain round tip. Weight rose to 8·15lb, largely owing to the extra woodwork.

Model 740 Woodsmaster

••

4, 740A, 740ADL, 740BDL, 742A, 742ADL, 742BDL, 742 Carbine, 742CDL, 742D, 742F, 7400 and 7400 Carbine patterns.

Made by the Remington Arms Company, Ilion, New York, and Wilmington, Delaware, 1952 to date.
Chambering: see notes.
DATA FOR TYPICAL 742A
Gas-operated auto-loading action locked by rotating lugs on the bolt into the barrel extension.
·280 Remington, rimless.
42·06in overall, 7·22lb unladen.
22·00in barrel, 6-groove rifling; RH, concentric.
Detachable box magazine, 4 rounds.
Spring-leaf and elevator sight.
2,820 ft/sec with 165-grain bullet.
☆

1955: the Model 740 Woodsmaster, developed as a replacement for the ageing Model 81, was a conventional gas-operated sporting rifle relying on a rotating multi-lug bolt. The pistol-grip butt was separated from the fore-end by a machined

steel receiver. Chambered only for ·30–06 or ·308 Winchester, it could be distinguished from the externally similar slide-action Gamemaster—Model 760, q.v.—as the fore-end ran back as far as the receiver instead of exposing several inches of operating rods.

The standard rifle had a plain butt with a pistol grip and a straight comb; the broad fore-end was fluted to improve grip. The open back sight was usually accompanied by a ramped blade at the muzzle. The 740ADL, identical mechanically, had chequering on the pistol grip and fore-end, and was sometimes to be found with a Monte Carlo comb on the butt. Model 740BDL was simply an ADL with select-grade woodwork, the high comb being standard.

1957: a ·280 Remington option was added.
1960: the improved Model 742A Woodsmaster appeared in ·243 Winchester, ·280 Remington, ·30–06 and ·308 Winchester. Though a few alterations were made internally, the principal changes were cosmetic. The standard straight comb butt displayed impressed chequering with a fleur-de-lys border, while the beavertail fore-end had skip-line chequering with foliate edging. An ADL version seems to have been made in small numbers, with hand-cut chequering and better-quality woodwork.

1961: the 742D (Peerless) and 742F (Premier) variants were announced, distinguished by finish. Peerless rifles had scroll engraving on their receivers and hand-cut chequering on the pistol grip and fore-end; scrollwork on Premier examples enclosed game scenes inlaid in gold. The wood of the butt and fore-end was specially selected for its figuring.

The first 742-pattern guns were chambered for the ·244 (6mm) Remington cartridge, and a short-barrelled 742 Carbine soon appeared in ·30–06 or ·308 only. Its 18·5in barrel reduced overall length to 38·5in, weight being about 7lb.

1963: the last of the 740-pattern guns left Remington's warehouse.
1966: a modified BDL version of the Model 742 was introduced, with a Monte Carlo comb and a fashionably angular fore-end with a reverse-cut tip. Basket-weave chequering was used. The rear

upper surface of the receiver was raised, unique to the 740 BDL and 760 BDL patterns.
1980: all 742-pattern guns were discontinued.
1981: chambered for 6mm Remington, ·243 Winchester, ·270 Winchester, 7mm Remington Express (·280 Remington), ·30–06 or ·308 Winchester cartridges, the Model 4 had a high gloss polyurethane finish on the woodwork and a Monte Carlo comb on the butt. Chequering appeared on the pistol grip and fore-end. The Peerless and Premier Grade guns had selected woodwork and engraved receivers, gold inlay being confined to Premier examples.

The Model 7400 rifle (with a 22in barrel) was essentially similar to the Model 4 but, at least until the mid 1980s, had a much plainer finish. Model 7400 carbines have been made with 18·5in barrels in ·30–06 only.

2. THE BOLT-ACTION PATTERNS

Remington re-entered the post-1945 sporting rifle market with a new bolt action developed by a team led by Michael Walker. Markings on Models 721, 722 and 725 usually acknowledge patents granted to John Howell for the extractor (1949) and Michael Walker & Phillip Haskell (1950) for the safety and trigger mechanism.

Though effectual mechanically, the Models 721 and 722 lacked the mystique of the rival Winchester Model 70; sales declined after a promising start, until the advent of the Model 700 in 1962 reversed the trend.

The standard Remington-Mauser action had twin opposed locking lugs, additional security being provided by the bolt handle turning down into its seat. The extractor and ejector were mounted in the bolt head. The most interesting feature was recessing of the bolt head in a counter-bore in the barrel, a strong system that minimised problems should the case head fail during firing.

As the guns had an excellent trigger and offered exemplary accuracy, complaints were

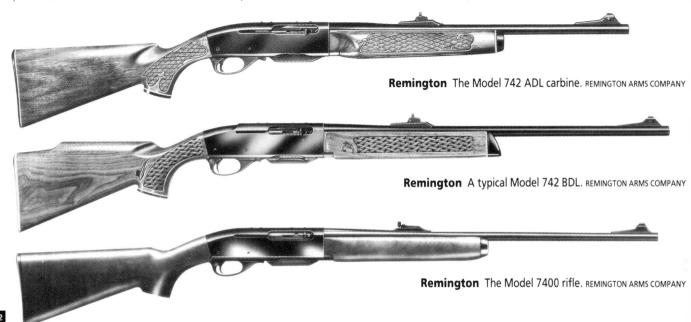

Remington The Model 742 ADL carbine. REMINGTON ARMS COMPANY

Remington A typical Model 742 BDL. REMINGTON ARMS COMPANY

Remington The Model 7400 rifle. REMINGTON ARMS COMPANY

aimed largely at magazine construction and the poor finish. These problems were progressively eradicated until the Model 700 became regarded as a classic design.

The Model 788, unique among bolt-action Remingtons, embodied a special bolt system with lugs locking into the receiver immediately behind the magazine well. This allowed the receiver to be made from high-grade tubing, multiple lugs keeping lug height to a minimum. Though extremely rigid, the Model 788 was not effectual enough to replace the 700 in public favour and was discontinued in the mid 1980s.

Note: Remingtons usually bear R.E.P. or REP in an oval, generally on the barrel near the breech. This is simply the company proof mark.

Model 721

A, A Magnum, AC, B and BDL patterns.
Made by the Remington Arms Company, Ilion,
New York, 1948–62.
Quantity: 125,000?
·264 Winchester Magnum, ·270 Winchester,
·280 Remington, ·300 H&H Magnum or ·30–06.
Turning-bolt action with two lugs on the bolt head
locking into the receiver behind the chamber.
DATA FOR TYPICAL MODEL 721A
·30–06, rimless.
44·25in overall, 7·31lb unladen.
24·00in barrel, 6-groove rifling; RH, concentric.
Internal box magazine, 4 rounds.
Spring-leaf and elevator sight.
2,700ft/sec with 180-grain bullet.

☆

1949: introduced in January, the Model 721A rifle chambered ·270 Winchester or ·30–06 cartridges. The standard gun had a round barrel, a straight bolt handle; and its straight-comb half stock had a pistol grip and a round tipped fore-end. The trigger guard was a stamped strip doubling as a floor plate, as a 'blind' magazine was fitted.

A small safety catch protruded on the right side of the action behind the bolt handle, and the bolt-stop catch projected into the trigger guard immediately ahead of the finger lever.

The 8·25lb 721A Magnum was made for ·300 H&H Magnum only, with a three-round magazine, a heavyweight 26in round barrel, and a recoil pad on the butt.

1953: Models 721AC and 721B appeared. The former is believed to have had chequering on the pistol grip and fore-end, but to have been otherwise standard; the latter apparently had a detachable magazine floor plate.

1955: the Model 721BDL had an improved deluxe stock with a low Monte Carlo comb and a constrasting fore-end tip. Sling swivels were standard and most guns had effectual Williams ramp-pattern back sights.

1959: a ·280 Remington option was added.

1960: a few guns were chambered for ·264 Winchester Magnum.

1962: the Model 721 was superseded by the significantly improved Model 700.

Model 722

A, AC, B and BDL patterns.
Made by the Remington Arms Company,
Ilion, New York, 1949–62.
·222 Remington, ·222 Remington Magnum,
·243 Winchester, ·244 Remington, ·257 Roberts,
·300 Savage or ·308 Winchester.
Action: as Model 721, above.
DATA FOR A TYPICAL MODEL 722A
·257 Roberts, rimless.
43·25in overall, 6·98lb unladen.
24·00in barrel, 6-groove rifling; RH, concentric.
Internal box magazine, 4 rounds.
Spring-leaf and elevator sight.
2,650 ft/sec with 117-grain bullet.

☆

1949: a short-action version of the Model 721, the Model 722A was offered in the customary Remington variety—though not in magnum chamberings. Construction paralleled the 721A.

1950: a ·222 Remington option was available, with a 26in round barrel and a five-cartridge magazine. The rifle weighed 7·85lb.

1953: 722AC and 722B rifles were introduced with chequered woodwork and a detachable magazine floor-plate respectively.

1955: the Model 722BDL offered a stock with a Monte Carlo comb, a contrasting fore-end tip, and sling swivels. A ·244 Remington chambering option (later known as '6mm Remington ') was introduced at the same time.

1957: the ·257 Roberts, ·300 Savage and ·308 Winchester rounds were added to the options.

1958: a ·222 Remington Magnum chambering became available.

1961: the ·243 Winchester cartridge was added to the range of chamberings.

1962: the Model 722 was superseded by the short-action version of the Model 700.

Model 725

ADL and Kodiak patterns.
Made by the Remington Arms Company,
Ilion, New York, 1958–61.
Quantity: 9,850.
·222 Remington, ·243 Winchester, ·244 Remington,
·270 Winchester, ·280 Remington, ·30–06,
·375 H&H Magnum or ·458 Winchester Magnum
(see notes).
Action: as Model 721, above.
DATA FOR A TYPICAL 725ADL
·244 Remington, rimless.
42·28in overall, 7·04lb unladen.
22·00in barrel, 6-groove rifling; RH, concentric.
Internal box magazine, 4 rounds.
Spring-leaf and elevator sight.
3,200 ft/sec with 90-grain bullet.

☆

1958: this was a short-lived improvement of the Model 721, introduced in ADL form. It was essentially the same as its predecessors, but had a detachable magazine floor plate and the safety system was modified to duplicate that of the original Model 30 ('Enfield') Remingtons. A third position on the safety allowed the bolt to be withdrawn from the receiver. The bolt handle was swept backward to improve its looks, and the shaping of the trigger lever was improved.

1961: as the decision to replace the 725-type rifle had already been taken, many actions were completed as 'Kodiak Models' in ·375 H&H Magnum or ·458 Winchester Magnum.

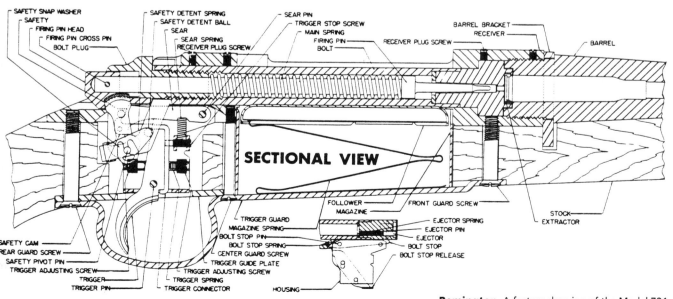

SECTIONAL VIEW

These guns had 26in round barrels with muzzle brakes, recoil bolts through the stock beneath the chamber, and special ventilated rubber recoil pads. They were otherwise standard DL grade, with Monte Carlo combs, hand-cut chequering on the pistol grip and fore-end, contrasting fore-end caps, white spacer plates, and swivels under the stock.

Model 40

X, XB, XBBR, XB Repeater, XB Varmint Special, XC, International Free Rifle and International Match Free Rifle patterns.
Made by the Remington Arms Company, Ilion, New York, and Wilmington, Delaware, 1961 to date.
Chambering: see notes.
Action: as Model 721, above.
DATA FOR TYPICAL MODEL 40-XB
·222 Remington Magnum, rimless.
46·75in overall, 10·62lb unladen (with standard barrel and competition sights).
28·00in barrel, 6-groove rifling; RH, concentric.
Micro-adjustable aperture sight.
3,300 ft/sec with 55-grain bullet.

☆

1955: the Model 40, utilising a modified Model 722 action, was introduced to handle ·22 rimfire ammunition.

1961: the Model 40-X and the International Match Free Rifle (both discontinued in 1964) were built on a single-shot 721- or 722-type action, rigidity being improved by the solid receiver floor. The 40-X was offered in ·222 Remington, ·222 Remington Magnum, ·30–06 and ·308 Winchester, though other chamberings were made to order. It had a half-stock with a straight comb and a plain pistol grip. Standard guns lacked chequering, but were supplied with sturdy rubber butt plates. Mounting blocks for optical sights and rails for aperture sights were standard, and a track for an adjustable hand stop was often let into the underside of the fore-end.

The International Match Free Rifle—offered in ·222 Remington, ·222 Remington Magnum, ·30–06 or ·308 Winchester, in addition to ·22 rimfire—shared the same basic action as the 40-X, but had a match-quality adjustable trigger and a thumb-hole stock with the leading edge of the pistol grip sculpted for the fingers of the trigger hand. Accessories included adjustable hooked or rubber butt plates, a palm rest and a special adjustable hand stop with a sling swivel. Micro-adjustable aperture sights were used, though the receiver was tapped and drilled for an optical-sight mount; a corresponding mounting block was fitted to the barrel. The guns weighed about 15·5lb with a 28in extra heavy barrel.

1964: the Model 40-XB Rangemaster and the International Free Rifle (discontinued in 1974) replaced the original 40-X and International Match Free Rifle respectively. The new guns were virtually identical with their predecessors, but incorporated a perfected 700-type action and could be identified by the rearward sweep of the bolt handle. The single-shot 40-XB also had a straight comb sloping downward to the pistol grip; without sights, it weighed 9·25lb with the standard barrel or about 11·25lb with the heavy pattern. Factory chamberings have included ·220 Swift, ·222 Remington, ·222 Remington Magnum, ·22–250, ·223 Remington, 6 × 47mm, 6mm Remington, ·243 Winchester, ·25–06, 7mm Remington BR, 7mm Remington Magnum, ·30–06, ·308 Winchester/7·62 × 51mm, ·30–338 and ·300 Winchester Magnum.

The basic heavy-barrel pattern was also made with a five-round magazine, in all the foregoing chamberings except ·25–06, ·30–06, ·30–338 and ·300 Winchester Magnum.

1969: a 40-XBBR ('Bench Rest') gun appeared. Offered during its life in ·22 Remington BR, ·222 Remington, ·222 Remington Magnum, ·223 Remington, 6 × 47mm, 6mm BR Remington or ·308 Winchester, with a 20in or 26in heavy round stainless-steel barrel, the 40-XBBR had a conventional plain half-stock with a straight comb and a rounded fore-end. It weighed 12lb with a 26in barrel.

1974: a Model 40-XC National Match Rifle made its début in ·308 Winchester, with charger guides on the front of the receiver bridge for military-match competitions. It weighed about 11lb and had a distinctive half-stock with a near-vertical thumb-groove pistol grip and a fore-end as deep as the underside of the trigger guard. An adjustable butt plate and hand stop were supplied, and there were the usual provisions on the receiver and barrel for an optical sight.

1987: the 40-XBBR KS (sometimes advertised as the '40-XB Varmint Special KS') appeared, based on the XBBR of 1969 but fitted in a Kevlar stock. The synthetic-stock option was extended in 1988–9 to XB Rangemaster and XC patterns, each gaining an extra KS ('Kevlar Stock') suffix.

Model 700

ADL, BDL, BDL Varmint Special, C, Camo Synthetic, Classic, D, F, FS, Kit Gun, KS, LS, Mountain, RS, Safari, Stainless Synthetic and Varmint Special Synthetic patterns.
Made by the Remington Arms Company, Ilion, New York, and Wilmington, Delaware, 1962 to date.
Chambering: see notes.
Action: as Model 721, above.
DATA FOR TYPICAL MODEL 700ADL
·25–06, rimless.
42·37in overall, 7·08lb unladen.
22·00in barrel, 6-groove rifling; RH, concentric.
Internal box magazine, 5 rounds.
Ramp-pattern sight.
3,120 ft/sec with 120-grain bullet.

☆

1962: a remodelled version of the 720 series described above, this has been made in long- and short-action patterns. The Model 700 ADL had a half-stock with a low Monte Carlo comb. A 'blind' magazine and a short nylon or alloy trigger guard were used on early guns. The butt had a cheek piece and a Monte Carlo comb, the butt plate was plain rubber, the pistol grip lacked a cap, and the fore-end tip was rounded. The pistol grip and fore-end were chequered, and sling-swivel eyes appeared beneath the butt and fore-end. Williams back sights were used.

Chamberings have included ·222 Remington, ·22–250, 6mm Remington, ·243 Winchester, ·25–06, ·270 Winchester, 7mm Remington

Remington The Model 40-XBBR rifle, with an extra-heavy barrel.
REMINGTON ARMS COMPANY

Remington A centre-fire
Model 40-XB. REMINGTON ARMS COMPANY

Remington The original Model 700 ADL rifle. REMINGTON ARMS COMPANY

Magnum, ·30–06 and ·308 Winchester; all rifles had five-round magazines excepting the ·222 (six) and 7mm Remington Magnum versions (four). Barrels measured 22in, or 24in in ·222, ·22–250, ·25–06 or 7mm Remington Magnum.

The Safari Grade guns were offered in 8mm Remington Magnum, ·358 Winchester Magnum, ·375 H&H Magnum, ·416 Remington Magnum, or ·458 Winchester Magnum. They had heavier barrels, reinforced stocks with two recoil bolts, and weighed 8.85lb. The earliest guns had Monte Carlo combs, but many made after the introduction of the Model 700 Classic in 1981 have had straight-comb butts.

The Model 700BDL—available in short or long actions, and in all regular ADL chamberings plus ·17 Remington, ·264 Winchester Magnum, ·300 Winchester Magnum or 8mm Remington Magnum—was essentially an ADL with a better stock and a detachable magazine floor plate. The butt plate, pistol-grip cap and contrasting rounded fore-end tip were all separated from the woodwork by thin white synthetic spacers, and the stock had a high-gloss finish.

1965: Models 700C (Custom), 700D Peerless and 700F Premier were announced. The 700C was a BDL with a selected stock, skip-line chequering and special high-quality blueing. Currently offered in four grades (I–IV), it has been chambered for ·22–250, ·222 Remington, 6mm Remington, ·243 Winchester, ·25–06, ·270 Winchester, 7mm Remington Magnum, ·300 Winchester Magnum, ·30–06 or ·308 Winchester.

1967: the 700BDL Varmint Special appeared, chambered for ·22–250, ·222 Remington, ·223 Remington, 6mm Remington, ·243 Winchester, ·25–06, or ·308 Winchester. It was basically a BDL with the short action and a 24in heavy barrel, lacked open sights and weighed 9lb.

1968: a one-piece sear replaced the previous two-piece fabrication, jewelling was added to the bolt, and the bolt plug was lengthened to enclose the cocking-piece head.

1973: a left-hand version of the Model 700BDL was introduced in ·270 Winchester, 7mm Remington Magnum or ·30–06 only. Guns were

subsequently made in ·22–250 Winchester, ·243 Winchester, 7mm Remington Magnum and ·338 Winchester Magnum.

1974: a bolt guide-rib system was added, the rearward sweep of the bolt handle was reduced to prevent the shank bruising the fingers during recoil, and a special cast stainless-steel magazine follower replaced the older folded stamping.

1981: the Model 700 Classic offered a high-quality walnut stock with a satin finish and a straight comb. Hand-cut chequering graced the pistol grip and fore-end. Most fore-ends have had rounded tips, though a few schnabel patterns have been made. The Classic Magnum was similar, but had a sturdier rubber butt plate.

1986: a Mountain Rifle appeared, with a 22in tapered lightweight barrel and a straight-comb stock with refined pistol grip contours. Offered in ·243 Winchester, ·25–06, ·257 Roberts, ·270 Winchester, 7mm–08, 7 × 57mm Mauser, ·280 Remington, ·30–06 or ·308 Winchester, it was about 42·5in long and weighed 6·7lb.

Introduced at the same time as the standard Mountain Rifle, the Custom KS Mountain Rifle had a Kevlar-reinforced stock with plain or wood-grain finish. Right- or left-hand actions could be supplied to order in satin-finish stainless steel. Chamberings included ·270 Winchester, ·280 Remington, 7mm Remington Magnum, ·300 Weatherby Magnum, ·300 Winchester Magnum, ·30–06, 8mm Remington Magnum, ·338 Winchester Magnum, ·35 Whelen or ·375 H&H Magnum. A typical gun weighed about 6·4lb with a 24in barrel.

1987: a laminated stock was introduced for the standard Model 700ADL. Readily distinguished by pattern and colour, the 700ADL LS has been made in ·243 Winchester, ·270 Winchester or ·30–06 only.

An FS variant with a straight-comb fibreglass stock was offered in ·243 Winchester, ·270 Winchester, 7mm Remington Magnum, ·30–06 or ·308 Winchester. It had a solid rubber recoil pad and weighed about 6·3lb.

A Kevlar Stock (KS) Model 700, made in left- or right-hand versions and weighing about 6·7lb, could be obtained in ·270 Winchester, ·280

Remington, 7mm Remington Magnum, ·300 Winchester Magnum, ·30–06, 8mm Remington Magnum, ·338 Winchester Magnum or ·375 H&H Magnum.

Stocked in synthetic Du Pont Rynite, the Model 700 RS chambered ·270 Winchester, ·280 Remington or ·30–06 ammunition. Made only with a 22in barrel, it weighed about 7·2lb.

1988: the short-lived Model 78 Sportsman combined a 700-type action, a plain hardwood stock and a plastic butt plate. Intended to compete in the lower-price market, it was made only in ·223 Remington, ·243 Winchester, 6mm Remington, 7mm–08, or ·308 Winchester.

The Model 700 Kit Gun was a standard '700' barrelled action accompanied by an inletted but otherwise unfinished ADL-pattern hardwood stock. It could be obtained in ·243 Winchester, ·270 Winchester, 7mm Remington Magnum, ·30–06 or ·308 Winchester.

1992: a ·220 Swift chambering was offered with the Model 700 Classic, and a synthetic version of the BDL Varmint Special was introduced in ·22–250, ·223 Remington or ·308 Winchester. It was distinguished by an aluminium bedding block running the length of the receiver, a floating barrel, and a straight-comb textured stock of Kevlar, fibreglass and graphite. The stock was dark grey and the metal was blacked.

Model 700 Camo Synthetic rifles appeared in ·22–250, ·243 Winchester, ·270 Winchester, ·280 Remington, 7mm–08, ·30–06 or ·308 Winchester (standard guns), in addition to the 7mm Remington and ·300 Weatherby Magnum rounds. Excepting the bolt, metalwork and the synthetic stock bore Mossy Oak Bottomland camouflage patterns.

The Model 700 Stainless Synthetic guns amalgamated a matt-finish stainless-steel barrel and action—similar to that of the Mountain Rifle—with a black textured composite stock. Standard 700SS rifles were chambered for ·25–06, ·270 Winchester, ·280 Remington or ·30–06 Springfield; magnums accepted the 7mm Remington Magnum, 7mm Weatherby Magnum, ·300 Winchester Magnum or ·338 Winchester Magnum cartridges.

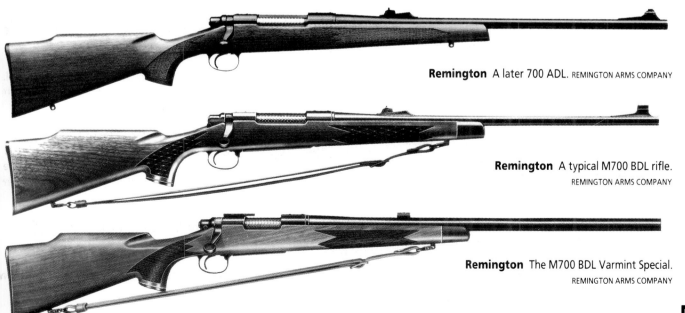

Remington A later 700 ADL. REMINGTON ARMS COMPANY

Remington A typical M700 BDL rifle.
REMINGTON ARMS COMPANY

Remington The M700 BDL Varmint Special.
REMINGTON ARMS COMPANY

Models 600 and 660

600, 600 Magnum, 660, 660 Magnum and Mohawk patterns.
Made by the Remington Arms Company, Ilion, New York, 1964–71.
·222 Remington, 6mm Remington, ·243 Winchester, ·308 Winchester or ·35 Remington.
Action: as Model 721, above.
DATA FOR A TYPICAL MODEL 600
6mm Remington, rimless.
37·25in overall, 5·99lb unladen.
18·45in barrel, 6-groove rifling; RH, concentric.
Internal box magazine, 5 rounds.
Spring-leaf and elevator sight.
3,190 ft/sec with 90-grain bullet.

☆

1964: these rifles were intended to compete in the market for cheap and compact 'Brush Guns'. They had an adapted 700-type short action with the bolt handle cranked forward above the wedge-shape synthetic trigger guard. Box magazines contained five rounds, excepting the six-round ·222.

The earliest guns had conventional pistol-grip half stocks and tapering fore-ends; they could be easily distinguished by the prominent ventilated barrel rib.

1965: a strengthened version was introduced for the 6·5mm Remington Magnum or ·350 Remington Magnum cartridges, but had been abandoned by 1967. It was essentially similar to the standard 600, but had a 20in barrel, a four-round magazine, and an integral recoil stop for the sight mounts. The stock was an interesting walnut/beech laminate, and quick-detachable swivels were fitted.

1968: the basic rifles were superseded by the improved Models 660 and 660 Magnum, having undergone similar changes to the Model 700. The unsightly barrel rib was eliminated, while a contrasting fore-end tip and spacer were added. The magnum stock retained its distinctive laminate pattern.

1971: production ceased, remaining guns being sold through wholesalers (as the 'Mohawk 600') for several years thereafter.

Model 788

Made by the Remington Arms Company, Ilion, New York, and Wilmington, Delaware, 1967–84.
Chambering: see notes.
Turning-bolt action with lugs on the rear of the bolt body engaging the receiver behind the magazine.
DATA FOR A TYPICAL EXAMPLE
·223 Remington, rimless.
41·37in overall, 7·19lb unladen.
22·00in barrel, 6-groove rifling; RH, concentric.
Detachable box magazine, 4 rounds.
Screw-and-leaf sight.
3,300 ft/sec with 55-grain bullet.

☆

1967: credited to Charles Morse and Wayne Leek, and chambered for ·222 Remington, ·22–250, ·30–30 and ·44 Magnum to compete in the low-price market, this was a complete departure from the Model 700. Only one action length was made, though the dimensions of the magazine well and the length of the bolt travel were specifically matched to the chambering. The most obvious feature was the tubular receiver and a bolt with nine small locking lugs in three rows of three. Standard barrels measured 22in, excepting ·222 and ·22–250 versions (24in apiece), while all the magazines offered three-round capacity excepting ·222 and ·223 (four apiece). The rifles had plain half stocks with low Monte Carlo combs and pistol grips. No cheek piece was fitted, and chequering was omitted to reduce costs to a minimum.

1968: 6mm Remington and ·308 Winchester options were added.

1969: a left-hand action was introduced in 6mm and ·308 only.

1979: the 788L was finally discontinued, to be followed in 1984 by the standard Model 788.

Model 7

Standard, FS and KS patterns.
Made by the Remington Arms Company, Wilmington, Delaware, 1983 to date.
Chambering: see notes.
Action: as Model 721 above.

DATA FOR A TYPICAL MODEL 7
7mm–08, rimless.
37·56in overall, 6·38lb unladen.
18·50in barrel, 6-groove rifling; RH, concentric.
Internal box magazine, 4 rounds.
Ramp-pattern sight.
2,860 ft/sec with 140-grain bullet.

☆

1983: this was originally designed to fill a need for an inexpensive short-barrelled brush gun. Introduced in ·222 Remington (5-round magazine), 6mm Remington, ·243 Winchester, 7mm–08 or ·308 Winchester (all four rounds), it was little more than a 700-pattern short action in a straight-comb stock with a prominent schnabel tip. A silent side-mounted safety was fitted and the barrel floated freely excepting for a single bearing point in the tip of the fore-end.

1984: a ·223 Remington option was added.

1987: fibreglass and Kevlar-reinforced stocks were introduced, producing the Model 7 FS and Model 7 Custom KS variants respectively. The FS gun—with Kevlar inserts at the stress points in the stock—was offered in ·243 Winchester, 7mm–08 or ·308 Winchester only. It weighed about 5·31lb. The Custom KS version, made to special order, could be obtained in ·223 Remington, 7mm–08, ·308 Winchester, ·35 Remington or ·350 Remington Magnum. It had a 20in barrel, increasing overall length to about 39in, and weighed 5·8lb.

3. THE SLIDE-ACTION PATTERNS

Models 14 and 141

14, 14 Carbine, 14½, 14½R and 141 patterns.
Made by the Remington Arms Company, Ilion, New York, 1912–36.
Chambering: see notes.
Slide action, locked by displacing the bolt-lug upward into the receiver.
DATA FOR A TYPICAL MODEL 141A
·30 Remington, rimless.

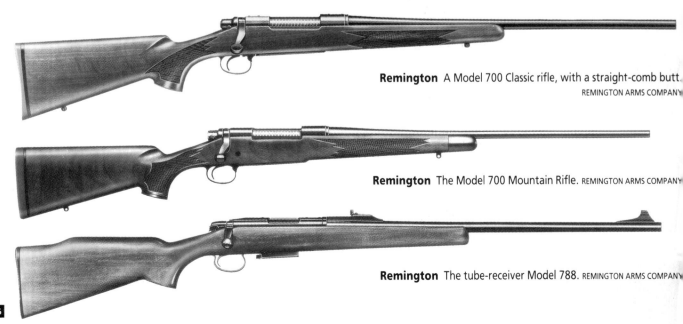

Remington A Model 700 Classic rifle, with a straight-comb butt. REMINGTON ARMS COMPANY

Remington The Model 700 Mountain Rifle. REMINGTON ARMS COMPANY

Remington The tube-receiver Model 788. REMINGTON ARMS COMPANY

42·78in overall, 7·15lb unladen.
24·00in barrel, 6-groove rifling; RH, concentric.
Tube magazine under barrel, 5 rounds.
Spring-leaf and elevator sight.
2,220 ft/sec with 160-grain bullet.

☆

1912: the success of the slide-action rimfire Model 12 inspired the introduction of the Model 14, an enlargement of the sturdy Pedersen tipping-bolt action for centre-fire ammunition. A special spiral magazine was used to prevent cartridge noses igniting the primer ahead of them. Made with a straight wrist butt and a ribbed slide, standard guns had round barrels.

Capable of handling Regular and High-Speed ammunition, the Model 14 was the first truly successful slide-action centre-fire sporting rifle. Optional extras included half pistol-grip butts and differing finishes. The carbine (1912–34) had an 18·5in barrel and a straight wrist stock.

1914*: the Models 14½ and 14½R were rifle and carbine-length derivatives handling ·38–40 and ·44–40 Winchester cartridges. Their action was substantially shorter than that of the guns chambering regular rifle rounds, but they were unpopular and had been discontinued by 1925.

1918: the Remington Arms–Union Metallic Cartridge Company markings were replaced with Remington Arms Company patterns. They also acknowledged John Pedersen's patents of 12 October 1909 and 5 July 1910.

1936: the Model 14 was replaced by the Model 141A Gamemaster (·30, ·32 or ·35 Remington). Available only in standard grade, with a 24in round barrel, the Gamemaster had a pistol-grip butt and a finely ribbed fore-end.

1950: the Model 141A as discontinued.

760 Gamemaster

Models 6, 760A, 760ADL, 760BDL, 760 Carbine, 760D, 760F, 7600 and 7600 Carbine.

Made by the Remington Arms Company, Ilion, New York, and Wilmington, Delaware, 1952 to date.
Chambering: see notes.
Slide action, locked by rotating lugs on the bolt into the barrel extension.

DATA FOR TYPICAL MODEL 760A
·270 Winchester, rimless.
42·00in overall, 7·45lb unladen.
22·00in barrel, 6-groove rifling; RH, concentric.
Detachable box, 4 rounds.
Spring-leaf and elevator sight.
2,900 ft/sec with 150-grain bullet.

☆

1952: introduced to replace the Model 141A, the Model 760A Gamemaster had a pistol-grip butt separated from the fore-end by a machined steel receiver. It relied on a rotating bolt instead of the previous tipping pattern, and had a detachable box magazine. It was distinguishable from the similar-looking 740 auto-loader by the fore-end, which exposed several inches of the barrel and operating rods instead of running back to the receiver.

1953: the basic 760A, which had impressed skip-line chequering on the pistol grip and fore-end, was joined by the ADL version. This had better-quality woodwork with hand-cut chequering, and was generally offered with a straight comb (though Monte Carlo versions were known). Standard and ADL guns have been chambered for ·223 Remington, 6mm Remington, ·243 Winchester, ·257 Roberts, ·270 Winchester, ·280 Remington, ·300 Savage, ·30–06, ·308 Winchester or ·35 Remington ammunition.

1961: the Peerless (D) and Premier (F) grades were distinguished by scroll-engraved receivers. The latter also had gold-inlaid game scenes.

Offered in ·270 Winchester, ·280 Remington, ·30–06 or ·308 Winchester, as well as in deluxe grades, the Model 760 Carbine had an 18·5in barrel and weighed about 7·3lb. A Williams ramp sight was usually fitted instead of the spring-leaf pattern.

1963: the 760ADL was discontinued.

1966: a modified BDL version appeared in ·270 Winchester, ·30–06 or ·308 Winchester only. It displayed high gloss polyurethane finish on the woodwork, and had basket-weave chequering on the pistol grip and fore-end.

1980: all the remaining 760-pattern guns were discontinued.

1981: the Models 6 and 7600 were introduced, the latter originally offering plain finish though the two were identical mechanically. By the late 1980s, however, the 'Model 6' designation had been dropped and the standard 7600 featured walnut woodwork with hand-cut chequering. Model 6 rifles have also been made in Peerless and Premier grades.

The 22in-barrelled Model 7600 rifles have been chambered for 6mm Remington, ·243 Winchester, ·270 Winchester, ·280 Remington, 7mm Remington Express, ·308 Winchester, ·30–06 or ·35 Whelen, weights averaging 7·5lb; they had cross-bolt safety catches, Williams ramp sights, and receivers drilled and tapped for optical-sight mounts. 7600 Carbines had 18·5in barrels and were available in ·30–06 only.

RICHARDS

BRITAIN
Also known as 'Westley Richards'

⤴

These pivoting-block action rifles were designed and developed in Britain. The first of Westley Richards' rifles was patented in Britain in 1868, but was withdrawn from army trials when likely to place third behind Martini and Henry rivals. Continual improvements culminated in British patents granted in 1870.

Essentially simple, though not as compact as the Martini, the action relied on a pivoting Peabody-type breech block tipped by the head of an operating lever pivoted transversely at the lower front of the receiver. A simple trigger and sear system released an internal hammer, which cocked automatically as the breech block descended. The hammer shared the operating-lever axis-pin, while the main spring ran forward beneath the barrel. The worst feature was the sear spring, bent downward at an odd angle.

Westley Richards retired in 1872, selling his operations to John Deeley (see 'Deeley-Edge'). Production seems to have been transferred to the National Arms & Ammunition Company, to which relevant patents had been licensed,

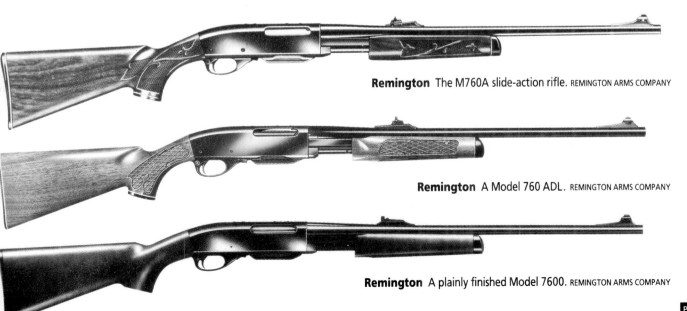

Remington The M760A slide-action rifle. REMINGTON ARMS COMPANY

Remington A Model 760 ADL. REMINGTON ARMS COMPANY

Remington A plainly finished Model 7600. REMINGTON ARMS COMPANY but reverted to Westley Richards & Co. in the 1880s. However, in later years, the company made extensive use of conventional Martini-type actions with special detachable triggers. Quality was good, as Richards had a reputation as the only Birmingham gunmaker of his era able to compete with the established 'Best London' makers as an equal.

Breech-Loading Rifle

Also known as the Patent Central-Fire Breech-Loading Military & Sporting Rifle.
Manufacturer: Westley Richards & Company, Birmingham, 1870–2; Westley Richards & Co., Ltd, Birmingham, c.1873–92.
Chambered for many large-calibre British black-powder sporting cartridges.
Pivoting-block action, with an operating lever ahead of the trigger guard.
DATA FOR A TYPICAL EXAMPLE
·500 No.2 Express, rimmed.
44·88in overall, 7·50lb unladen.
28·00in barrel, 5-groove rifling; LH, concentric?
Standing-block sight for 200 yards.
1,870 ft/sec with 300-grain bullet.
☆

1870: invariably distinguished by an operating lever with a ring tip beneath the trigger guard, these sporting rifles were generally built to individual requirements; each differed in detail, though the action remained the same.

Most had a two-piece stock with a straight-wrist butt curved to fit against the back of the receiver, owing to the use of butt-tangs instead of a Martini-type socket, but a few were made with one-piece stocks enveloping the action. A radial trigger-blocking safety lever appeared on the right side of the receiver and a detachable lock was usually fitted.

The finely chequered wrists and half-length fore-ends, the latter occasionally retained by a transverse key, often had plain rounded horn tips. Some rifles had sling eyes on the barrel and butt, while simple, Cape or Express sights could be fitted to order. Guns were made to individual specifications and vary greatly in detail.

RIDER

UNITED STATES OF AMERICA
'Remington Rolling Block' or 'Remington-Rider'; copied by Whitney and others.
↶

The rolling-block breech, developed from the earlier split-breech pattern credited to Leonard Geiger, was the subject of patents granted to Joseph Rider in the late 1860s. The essence of the system lay in an interlock between a sturdy hammer and the radial breech piece. Rolling blocks were opened by thumbing back the hammer to full-cock and pulling back on the finger spur of the breech piece to give access to the chamber, partially extracting a spent case. After the gun had been reloaded and the breech piece rotated forward to its closed position, a pull on the trigger dropped the hammer. As the hammer fell, shoulders ran forward under the breech piece in such a way that the thrust generated on firing back through the case base held the mechanism securely closed.

The rolling-block system was simple, strong and effectual, particularly judged by standards of its day. Remington made great capital of its durability, camouflaging comparatively poor extraction.

1867: though the US Army viewed rolling blocks without enthusiasm, foreign governments were more accommodating. Denmark ordered substantial numbers of rifles and carbines in a year in which the Rider breech received a silver medal from the Paris Exposition.

1873: Remington claimed sales of 16,500 rifles, carbines and pistols to the US Army; 23,000 to the US Navy; fifteen thousand Model 1871 Locking Rifles to New York State; and five thousand rifle-musket conversions to South Carolina. Among the export orders had been 75,000 rifles and carbines supplied to Spain for use in Cuba, beginning in 1867, and thirty thousand guns for Sweden from 1868 onward.

1876: sales of a million military-style rifles were claimed. Among the differing patterns advertised were the ·50-calibre US Model (1871); two converted ·58 Springfield rifle-muskets, long and short, which mated the original barrel, stock and furniture with a new action; the ·43 or 11mm-calibre Spanish Model with its socket bayonet; the ·43 Civil Guard Model, chambered for the 'Spanish or Russian Cartridge' and offered with a sabre bayonet; the ·43 French Model and sabre bayonet, chambered for the 'Egyptian Cartridge'; and a ·43 or ·50-calibre carbine.

MILITARY WEAPONS
DENMARK
Model 1867

Infantry rifles: Bagladeriffel m/1867 og m/1867/96.
Made by E. Remington & Sons, Ilion, New York, 1867–70 (40,540); and Gevaerfabrik Kjobenhaven, 1870–88.
Quantity, excluding conversions: 80,000?
11·7 × 51mm, rimfire (see notes).
Radial-block action with shoulders on the hammer body locking under the breech block.
1,280mm overall, 4·20kg unladen.
907mm barrel, 5-groove rifling; RH, concentric.
Ramp-and-leaf sight graduated to 2,000 alen.
About 375 m/sec with m/1867 ball cartridges.
m/1867 sabre bayonet.
☆

1867: chambered for a rimfire cartridge, this had a straight-wrist butt and a fore-end with three spring-retained bands. The bayonet lug and tenon appeared on the right side of the muzzle. Swivels lay under the middle band and the butt. The back sight lay close to the receiver, the leaf being hinged at the front.

1893: conversion of some surviving guns to m/67/93 standards began (see below).

1896: the advent of the m/89 Krag-Jørgensen rifle led to the withdrawal of the 11·7mm Remington rifles from the infantry. They were converted for centre-fire cartridges and issued to coast and fortress artillerymen as 'm/67/96'. The obvious feature was a greatly lengthened back-sight leaf graduated to 2,100 metres.

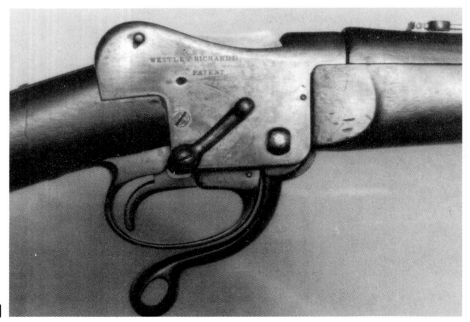

Richards A typical pivoting-block rifle, dating from the early 1870s.
PATTERN ROOM COLLECTION

Rider Typical military Remington Rolling Block rifles and carbines, from the 1911 catalogue of A.L. Frank, Hamburg. Note the similarity of the engravings!

Model 1867

Cavalry, artillery and engineer carbines: Karabinen for rytter, artilleri og ingeniør, m/1867.
Made by E. Remington & Sons, Ilion, New York, 1867–70 (1,800); and Geværfabrik Kjobenhaven (5,200), 1870–1908.
Quantity, excluding conversions: 7,000.
11·7 × 51mm, rimfire (see notes).
Action: as m/1867 rifle, above.
DATA FOR ENGINEER CARBINE
915mm overall, 3·15kg unladen.
535mm barrel, 5-groove rifling; RH, concentric.
Ramp-and-leaf sight graduated to 1,500 alen.
265 m/sec with m/1867 ball cartridges.
No bayonet.
☆

1867: these were little more than shortened m/67 infantry rifles, the single barrel band being retained by a spring under the half-length fore-end. The artillery and engineer carbines had swivels on the band and butt; the artillery carbine accepted a sword bayonet, while the engineer and cavalry carbines did not. The original cavalry carbine carried its sight on a muzzle band and is believed to have had a sling stud or ring on the left side of the breech. The back-sight leaves hinged at the back of the block.

Model 1867/93

Navy rifle: Flådens Bagladeriffel m/1867/93.
Converted by Geværfabriken Kjobenhaven, 1893–5.
8 × 58mm, rimmed.
Action: as m/1867 rifle, above.
1,022mm overall, 3·81kg unladen.
740mm barrel, 6-groove rifling; RH, polygonal.
Ramp-and-leaf sight graduated to 2,000 metres.
About 585 m/sec with m/1889 ball cartridges.
m/1893 sword bayonet.
☆

1893: these were made from m/1867 rifles. They had a new barrel and fore-end, and a full-length hand guard. Two bands and a special nose cap were fitted, the bayonet bar and lug appearing on the right side of the muzzle. The back sight lay immediately ahead of the receiver.

Model 1867/96

Cavalry carbine: Rytterkarabin m/1867/96.
Converted by Geværfabriken Kjobenhaven, 1897–1908.
Quantity: about 3,000.
11·7 × 51mm, rimmed.
Action: as m/1867 rifle, above.
Otherwise similar to unaltered m/1867 carbies excepting back sight (ramp-and-leaf pattern graduated to 1,200 metres) and muzzle velocity (285 m/sec).
☆

1897: this was a conversion of the m/1867 carbine for cavalry use, pending development of a Krag-type carbine. Chambering centre-fire ammunition, it originally had swivels on the underside of the butt and band. The back-sight leaf was apparently re-graduated, but was otherwise the same as the original 1,500-alen pattern and hinged at the back of the base.

1905: surviving carbines were recalled for modification. They were given a new butt, with a magazine replacing the comb and the swivel on the left side. The second swivel was fitted to a collar on the barrel. Distinguished by its hinged aluminium lid, the magazine could hold ten rounds vertically. Cartridges could be transferred if required to a quick-loader fixed to the right side of the fore-end ahead of the breech. The modified Remington carbine lasted until replaced by the Krag m/89 Rytterkarabin about 1914.

EGYPT

Model 1868

Rifle and carbine.
Made by E. Remington & Sons, Ilion, 1869–76.
11·43 × 50mm, rimmed.
Radial-block action with shoulders on the hammer body locking under the breech block.
DATA FOR RIFLE
1,278mm overall, 4·15kg unladen.
889mm barrel, 5-groove rifling; RH, concentric.
Ramp-and-leaf sight graduated to 1,000 metres.
390 m/sec with ball cartridges.
Sabre bayonet.
☆

1868: the government gave Remington an order for a substantial quantity of rifles.
1869: an additional order was forthcoming, but the original 'Egyptian' guns were sold to France during the Franco-Prussian War. M1868 rifles had standard American-type rolling blocks, with three spring-retained bands. Swivels appeared beneath the butt and the middle band, while the lug on the right side of the barrel accepted a brass-hilted bayonet made by Ames.
1876: the contractual obligations were finally fulfilled when the last of 60,000 rifles was delivered from Ilion. However, some Egyptian-type rifles and carbines have been seen with the marks of E. & L. Nagant of Liége, to whom a licence had been granted in the mid 1870s.

MEXICO

The government bought 10,000 11mm Spanish type rifles from Remington in the early 1870s, and then ordered 3,000 additional rifles in 1877. A thousand 'convertible carbines' could fire ·50–70 centre-fire or ·56–50 Spencer rimfire cartridges as required. They were 915mm long, had 520mm barrels and weighed about 3·06kg.

Mexican rifles were marked R. DE MEXICO or RM on the barrel, although those marked after 23 July 1894 displayed an additional Liberty Cap on a sunburst. The 1897-pattern guns bore the eagle-on-cactus above the receiver.

Model 1897

Rifle and carbine.
Made by the Remington Arms Company, Ilion, New York, 1897–1902.
7 × 57mm, rimless.
Radial-block action with shoulders on the hammer body locking under the breech block.
DATA FOR RIFLE
1,156mm overall, 3·86kg unladen.
762mm barrel, 5-groove rifling; RH, concentric.
Ramp-and-leaf sight graduated to 1,900 metres.
640 m/sec with Mo.1895 ball cartridges.
Remington 'export' knife or sword bayonets.
☆

MDF 21 a		Aeg. Remington Car.	Vorrat / Approvisionnement / Supply / Existencia 300

Aegyptischer Remington-Carabiner, hergestellt aus M. D. F. 21, Gewicht 3,250 kg, ganze Länge 96 cm. | Carabine Remington égyptienne, faite du fusil M. D. F. 21, poids 3,250 kg, longueur totale 96 cm. | Egyptian Remington carbine, made from rifle M. D. F. 21, weight 3,250kg, entire length 96 cm. | Carabina Remington egypcia, hecha del fusil M. D. F. 21, peso 3,250 kg, longitud total 96 cm.

MDF 21 b		Am. Remington.	Vorrat / Approvisionnement / Supply / Existencia 2000

Original amerik. Remington-Gewehr, Cal. 11/43 mm spanisch, ganze Länge 1,28 m, Gewicht 4 kg. | Fusil Remington américain original, Cal. 11/43 mm espagnol, longueur totale 1,28 m, poids 4 kg. | American original Remington rifle, Cal. 11/43 mm Spanish, entire length 1,28 m, weight 4 kg. | Fusil Remington americano original, Cal. 11/43 mm español, longitud total 1,28 m, peso 4 kg.

MDF 21 c		Span. Remington Car.	Vorrat / Approvisionnement / Supply / Existencia 800

1897: several thousand of these guns were purchased from Marcellus Hartley & Company, Remington's agents. They had straight-wrist butts, hand guards running from the receiver to the spring-retained barrel band, and a band-like nose cap with a bayonet lug and a swivel. The other swivel lay under the butt. Back sights had protecting wings and the barrels were marked 7 M.M.–S.M. ('7mm calibre, Spanish model').

The carbine was a short version of the rifle—915mm overall—with a half-stock and a rounded fore-end tip. It did not accept a bayonet. A sling ring lay on the left side of the receiver, while swivels were to be found on the right side of the butt and band. The back sight was graduated to 1,300 metres.

NORWAY
Model 1867

Infantry rifle: Remingtongevær M/1867.
Made by Husqvarna Våpenfabrik, 1867–8 and 1872–3
(5,000); Kongsberg Våpenfabrikk, 1869–90; and
Høvedarsenalet, Christiania, c.1875–6 (a few hundred, assembled from Kongsberg parts).
12·17mm, rimfire.
Radial-block action with shoulders on the hammer body locking under the breech block.
1,358mm overall, 4·50kg unladen.
948mm barrel, 6-groove rifling; RH, concentric.
Ramp-and-leaf sight (see notes).
380 m/sec with M/1867 ball cartridges.
M/1860 sabre bayonet.

☆

1867: this was a standard rolling-block rifle, chambering a rimfire copper-case cartridge. Norwegian-made guns usually had two-piece birch stocks, with iron furniture—including three screw-retained bands—and a brass butt plate, though the first 3,000, made in Sweden, were marked with an H (for 'Husqvarna') and had iron butt plates.
1869: the first Kongsberg-made guns appeared, marked with a crowned K (Høvedarsenalet weapons bore a crowned A). A Krag sight with distinctive protective wings, graduated to 1,500

alen, had been substituted for the original British Enfield tangent-leaf pattern.
1871: changes were made in the action, when a revised gun was approved. As most of the revisions were internal, the M/1867 designation was retained. The guns had a single lateral screw through the back of the receiver instead of two.
1879: the cartridge designation was changed to '12mm', without affecting chambering.

Model 1888

Cavalry and engineer carbines: Remingtonkarabinen for kavaleriet er ingeniørvåpnet, M/1888.
Converted by Kongsberg Våpenfabrikk, 1888–92.
8 × 58mm (?), rimmed.
Action: as M/1867 rifle, above.
1,025mm overall, 3·80kg unladen.
615mm barrel, rifling pattern unknown.
Ramp-and-leaf sight graduated to 1,600 metres.
About 545 m/sec with ball cartridges.
No bayonet.

☆

1887: issue of the Jarmann (q.v.) repeater freed substantial quantities of single-shot Remingtons.
1889: some rifles were converted to centre-fire and cut to carbine length for the cavalry. They had new half-stocks and a barrel band with a swivel on the left side. A sling bar was fixed to the left side of the the butt.

The M/1888 Royal Engineers carbine was similar, but had swivels on the underside of the band and butt. In addition, the engineer pattern often had a single extractor whereas virtually all cavalry guns possessed two.

Model 1891

Cavalry and engineer carbines: Remingtonkarabinen for kavalleriet er ingeniørvåpnet, M/1891.

☆

1891: converted by Kongsberg Våpenfabrikk (1891–5), these were modifications of the earlier 1888 models with a single extractor and a safety catch for the firing pin. The axis pins of the hammer and breech block were held by a pivoting retainer on the right side of the receiver.

The half-length fore-end was held by a single barrel band at its tip, and a short hand guard ran from the receiver to the back-sight base.

The cavalry carbine had its swivels on the side of the butt and band; the engineer carbine, however, had them under the butt and band.
1892: issue of the cavalry carbine was extended to the mountain artillery (Bergartilleriet).

SPAIN
American pattern, 1870

Infantry rifle: Fusil Remington Norteamericano.
Made by E. Remington & Sons, Ilion,
New York, 1870.
11 × 58mm, rimmed.
Radial-block action with shoulders on the hammer body locking under the breech block.
1,278mm overall, about 4·2kg unladen.
892mm barrel, 5-groove rifling; RH, concentric.
Ramp-and-leaf sight graduated to 1,000 yards.
416 m/sec with US-made ball cartridges.
Socket bayonet (two blade lengths).

☆

1871: the Remington Rolling Block was adopted in Spain on 24 February, though approximately 32,000 (of a 75,000-gun order) had already been delivered for service with the Ejército de Ultramar in Cuba. The rifle was a standard North American-pattern Remington, with three spring-retained barrel bands, a cleaning rod beneath the muzzle, and a concave butt plate. The sight leaf was hinged at the back of its block.
1874: two additional contracts were placed in the USA for a total of 60,000 guns, but were probably never completed.
1878: surviving American-type Remingtons were relegated to the Cuerpo de Carabineros once sufficient Oviedo-made Mo.1871 rifles were available to arm the regular troops.

Carbine, 1870

Carabina Remington para Carabineros, Mo.1870.
Made by Fábrica de Armas, Oviedo, 1870–1.
Quantity: 6,000.

IAN HOGG

11 × 58mm, rimmed.
Action: as American-pattern rifle, above.
1,070mm overall, about 3·9kg unladen.
690mm barrel, 6-groove rifling; RH, concentric.
Ramp-and-leaf sight graduated to 1,000 metres.
About 350 m/sec with ball cartridges.
Socket bayonet.
☆

1870: adopted by the provisional government during an interregnum, this was similar to the American rifle but had two bands. Swivels lay under the butt and the rear band. The curve of the butt comb was greater than on the later Spanish guns, and the butt plate was flatter.

Short rifle, 1870

Mosqueton Remington, fabricación Vascongada.
Made by Orbea Hermanos and others, 1870–1.
11 × 58mm, rimmed.
Action: as American-pattern rifle, above.
1,190mm overall, about 4kg unladen.
820mm barrel, 6-groove rifling; RH, concentric.
Back sight: as Mo.59 rifle (see 'Berdan' in Part Two).
About 395 m/sec with ball cartridges.
Socket bayonet.
☆

1870: made during the Carlist War, apparently in the Basque region of northern Spain, these guns often differ in detail. A typical example had two screw-clamping barrel bands, swivels beneath the butt and rear band, and a transverse barrel-retaining screw set in lugged washers. The back sight leaf hinged at the rear of its bed.

Royal Bodyguard rifle

Fusil Remington para Guardias del Rey.
Made by Fábrica de Armas de Oviedo, 1870–1.
11 × 58mm, rimmed.
Action: as American-pattern rifle, above.
1,315mm overall, about 4·25kg unladen.
940mm, 6-groove rifling; RH, concentric.
Ramp-and-leaf sight graduated to 1,000 metres.
400 m/sec with Mo.1871 ball cartridges.
Mo.1871 sword bayonet.
☆

1870: apparently authorised specifically to equip the bodyguard of the king, Amadeo I, this rifle was little more than a longer version of the Mo.1871 described below. It was introduced in advance of the infantry weapon, presumably owing to the demands of protocol but also as it was required in smaller numbers. The guns had three barrel bands, whilst a bayonet lug lay on the right side of the muzzle. The bayonet had an unusually long double-edged blade—700mm— and a reverse finial on top of the guard.

Model 1871

Infantry rifles: Fusils Remington Mo.1871 y 1871/89.
Made by Fábrica de Armas de Oviedo, 1871–92; and
Euscalduna, Planencia, c.1872–4.
11 × 58mm, rimmed.
Radial-block action with shoulders on the hammer
body locking under the breech block.
1,315mm overall, 4·08kg unladen.
940mm barrel, 6-groove rifling; RH, concentric.
Ramp-and-leaf sight graduated to 1,000 metres.
400 m/sec with Mo.1871 ball cartridges.
Mo.1871 socket bayonet.
☆

1871: adopted on 24 February, this was the standard Spanish infantry rifle for many years. It had three screw-clamping barrel bands, and a small back sight with the leaf hinged at the rear of the attachment block. There were three screws and the axis-pin retaining plate on the left side of the receiver, and a transverse bolt through the rear of the fore-end. Swivels lay under the butt and middle band. The cleaning rod protruded beneath the muzzle, and the bayonet locked around the front-sight base.

A minor variation of the basic rifle was made by Euscalduna. Instead of the firing-pin retractor found on the standard Oviedo guns, a spring-loaded inertia-type pin was used.
1875: by decree of 26 January, the rolling block was declared the only breech-pattern approved for the Spanish army.
1883: the original iron bands were substituted by new steel patterns from 30 April, their form being revised with effect from 8 November.

1889: from 22 May onward, many surviving guns were re-chambered for the new 11mm Mo.1889 cartridge developed by Lieutenant-Colonel Luis Freire y Góngora and Captain José Brull y Seoane. Muzzle velocity increased to 450 m/sec, maximum range-setting being increased to 1,200 metres by adding an auxiliary front sight on the left side of the front barrel band and an extended back-sight slider with an additional V-notch. Screw-clamping bands were adopted to replace the spring-retained type. Modified rifles were often known as 'Mo.71/89'.
1909: the Remington was declared obsolete on 26 March, guns subsequently passing to the Guardia Civil, gendarmerie and militia.

Model 1871

Short rifle: Mosqueton Remington Mo.1871.
Made by Euscalduna, Planencia, date unknown.
11 × 58mm, rimmed.
Action: as Mo.1871 infantry rifle, above.
1,080mm overall, about 4kg unladen.
710mm barrel, 6-groove rifling; RH, concentric.
Ramp-and-leaf sight graduated to 1,000 metres.
About 370 m/sec with Mo.1871 ball cartridges.
M1871 socket bayonet.
☆

1873*: this short rifle had two barrel bands, conventional swivels and accepted a standard socket bayonet. It may simply have been one of many non-standard weapons made at the time of the Carlist War; alternatively, it may represent a short-lived experimental pattern.

Model 1871

Carbine: Tercerola Remington Mo.1871.
Made by Fábrica de Armas de Oviedo.
11 × 58mm, rimmed.
Action: as Mo.1871 infantry rifle, above.
963mm overall, 3·28kg unladen.
588mm barrel, 6-groove rifling; RH, concentric.
Leaf sight graduated to 600 metres.
357 m/sec with Mo.1874 ball cartridges.
No bayonet.
☆

Rider US and Irish teams wrestle for supremacy at Creed's Farm, New York, 1873—the contest for which the 'Creedmoors' were developed.

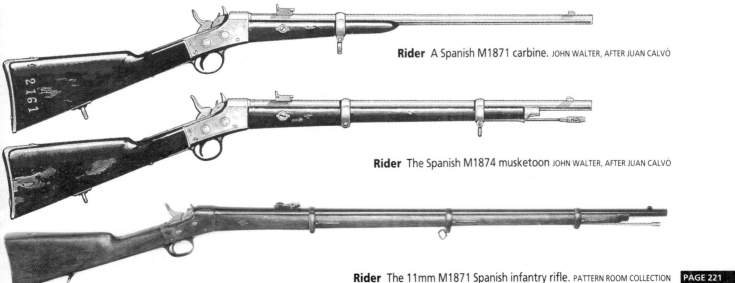

Rider A Spanish M1871 carbine. JOHN WALTER, AFTER JUAN CALVÓ

Rider The Spanish M1874 musketoon JOHN WALTER, AFTER JUAN CALVÓ

Rider The 11mm M1871 Spanish infantry rifle. PATTERN ROOM COLLECTION

REMINGTON
LESSER MILITARY PATTERNS

Argentina Large numbers of 11mm Spanish-pattern guns were purchased from E. Remington & Sons in 1875–86. Issued as Mo.1875 (rifle) and Mo.1879 (carbine), they were accompanied by Ames-made bayonets.

Chile About 10,000 Spanish-type Remington rifles were apparently purchased for the Chilean army in the late 1870s. It is assumed that they bore distinctive identifying marks.

France The initial purchases occurred in 1870, during the Franco-Prussian War, when many Remingtons were acquired by the Gouvernement de la Défense Nationale. They included 63,030 ·58 rimfire Springfield rifle-muskets with rolling-block breeches; about 21,120 ·56–50 rimfire Remington-Geiger carbines; 16,940 ·50–70 US Navy-type M1870 Remington rifles; 100,000 Egyptian-contract 11·43mm rifles; 49,960 additional Egyptian-pattern rifles, in accordance with French requests; 3,700 11mm Spanish-model rifles; and 9,200 'Greek' Remingtons of unknown pattern. ¶ In 1915, the authorities ordered 100,000 'Mle.1897/02' guns from the Remington Arms Company. The contract was largely complete by November 1918. The rifles and carbines were substantially the same as the Mo.1897 Mexican patterns (q.v.), but had an improved ejector patented in October 1901. They chambered the standard 8 × 51mm round and were sighted to 2,400 metres, though a few in 7 × 57mm (with 2,000-metre sights) were supplied from stock while adjustments were made for the French cartridge. The rifles were issued for the duration of the war as 'Fusils Remington Mle.1915' to non-combatants, lines-of-communication units and the heavy artillery. Survivors were sent to Indo-China in the 1920s.

Sweden The first M/1867 Remington rifles (30,000) and carbines (3,000) were purchased in America, though production soon began in Husqvarna Våpenfabrik. The guns were much the same as the Norwegian patterns (q.v.); indeed, the first three thousand Norwegian infantry rifles were made in Sweden before production began in the Kongsberg factory. It is assumed that the rifles and carbines were subject to alterations during their career, but, at the time of writing, details are not known. They probably duplicated progress in Norway, where conversion of rifles to 8mm centre-fire carbines began in 1888.

Uruguay The army acquired Spanish type three-band rifles and two-band short rifles in the late 1870s, apparently issuing them as 'Mo.1879'. The mark REPÚBLICA ORIENTAL lay on top of the barrel ahead of the receiver.

Rider A typical 1897-pattern military rifle. J.E. COOMBES

REMINGTON
THE SPORTING MODELS

Note: in 1886, the manufacturer's marks changed from the old 'E. REMINGTON & SONS, ILION, N.Y.' to the new 'REMINGTON ARMS CO.' after the failure of the original family business. Virtually all rifles had five-groove rifling twisting to the right.

No. 1 Sporting Rifle Introduced in 1867 and made until 1890, this was the earliest commercial Rider-pattern rolling block, eventually acknowledging patents granted in 1864–73. Standard guns were made with a 20in round barrel; a 26in round, half- or fully-octagonal barrel; or a 30in octagonal pattern. However, octagonal barrels ranging in length from 24in to 34in could be obtained to order. According to an 1876 Remington catalogue, weight ranged from 8·5 to 15lb, depending largely on barrel-length and design. Optional extras included pistol-grip butts, woodwork being varnished, oiled or polished. Sights ranged from open notches to vernier-adjustable peep-and-globe patterns. ¶ Chamberings included ·32–20 Winchester, ·32–40 Ballard, ·38–40 Remington, ·40–50 Sharps, ·40–70 Remington and Sharps, ·43 Spanish, ·44 Smith & Wesson, ·44–40 Winchester, ·44–77 Sharps, ·44–90 Creedmoor, and ·45–70 or ·50–70 Government. A typical ·44–77 Sharps rifle was 45·50in overall and weighed 9·15lb. It had a 30·00in barrel and a spring-leaf and elevator sight. ¶ The plain finish Hunter, Business and Black Hills rifles appeared in 1875 and remained available until c.1882. Minor variants of the No.1 with 28in round barrels, they weighed about 7·5lb and invariably chambered ·45–70 cartridges.

No. 1½ Sporting Rifle Dating from 1888, this was simply a lightened version of the No. 1, generally encountered with an octagonal barrel though round and half-octagonal patterns were made to order. It chambered a variety of rim- and centre-fire cartridges from ·22 to ·38 and lasted until about 1897. A typical ·32–20 Winchester rifle measured 41·50in overall, weighed 7·50lb, and had a 26·00in barrel. Spring-leaf and elevator sights were standard.

No. 2 Sporting Rifle Also known as the 'Gem' or 'New Model Light Rifle', this was made from 1872 to about 1910. It was an ultra-lightweight Rolling Block with as much weight saved in its action as practicable. Made for a selection of centre-fire cartridges and a few rimfires, it had an octagonal barrel, a straight-wrist butt, and a notably concave butt plate. The standard barrel-lengths included 24, 26, 28 and 30in, weight varying between about 5·5 and 8lb. ¶ Chamberings are known to have included ·25–20 Single Shot, ·25–20 Winchester, ·32–20 Winchester, ·32–40 Remington, ·38–40 Remington, ·38–40 Winchester, or ·44–40 Winchester. A representative ·38–40 Remington rifle was 41·15in overall, weighed 6·75lb, and had a 26·00in barrel.

Buffalo Rifle Announced in 1874, this was a variant of the basic rolling block with an octagonal or round barrel. It chambered cartridges ranging from ·40–50 Sharps to ·44–90 and ·50–70, and was made until about 1890. A typical ·44–90 Remington example measured 45·50in overall, weighed 10·13lb and had a 30·00in barrel. A spring-leaf and elevator sight was fitted.

Mid-Range Target Rifle Built on the No. 1 action, this 1875-vintage pattern Rolling Block had a 28in or 30in half-octagon barrel and chambered cartridges ranging from the ·40–50 Sharps to ·50–70. A pistol-grip butt was usually fitted, together with a globe-pattern front sight and a folding vernier-type aperture back sight on the tang behind the breech. It was offered until 1890, though it is unlikely that any manufacture took place under the Remington Arms Company regime. Typically, a Buffalo Rifle was 45·50in long, had a 30·00in barrel and weighed 9·80lb. Open 'Rocky Mountain' sights were popular, but some guns had sophisticated vernier sights on their tangs.

Short-Range Target Rifle Apparently dating from 1876, this was similar to the Mid-Range gun described above, but had a short half-octagon barrel. It chambered a wide range of rim- and centre-fire cartridges from ·38 Extra Long to ·46. Production continued until the collapse of E. Remington & Sons in 1886, and new guns were still being sold out of store in 1890. A typical ·38–50 version was 41·50in overall, weighed 9·18lb, and had a 26in barrel. An aperture sight lay on top of the barrel near the breech.

Creedmoor Target Rifle Built from 1874 onward on specially finished No. 1 actions, this was named after a rifle range at Creed's Farm, Long Island. It had a 32in octagonal barrel chambered for ·44–90, ·44–100 or ·44–105 Remington cartridges, was 48·38in overall and weighed about 10·5lb. Stocks were selected walnut, with chequered pistol grips, and matching fore-ends terminated in pewter or German silver finials. Vernier peep-and-globe sights were fitted on the tang behind the hammer, among the optional extras being special gun cases, a spirit level, and discs for the front sight. Earliest guns had a special brass faced 'horse-shoe' plate on the pistol-grip butt, but later examples usually had rubber shotgun-type plates. Creedmoors were regarded among the finest rifles of their day. Work continued until 1886, and new guns were still being sold five years later.

Light Model Sporting Carbine The renascent Remington Arms Company inherited thousands of incomplete rolling-block actions from the moribund Remington & Sons. From 1888 until about 1908, therefore, actions were completed as light or 'Baby' carbines in an attempt to reduce stocks of what had become an obsolescent mechanism. Carbines had round barrels, were finished in blue or nickel, and had traditional military-style sights, butt and fore-end. A sling ring often lay on a D-bar on the left side of the receiver. Typically, they were 35·13in overall, had 20in barrels and weighed 5·50lb unladen. The standard leaf sight was graduated to 500 yards.

No. 5 Sporting Rifle Introduced in 1897, apparently for sale to the Mexican army, this rolling-block rifle was specifically intended for smokeless ammunition. Barrels measured 30in, the rifles being stocked to the muzzle with hand guards from the breech to the back sight base. Half-stock carbines with 20in barrels were also made. ¶ A sporting version was offered from 1898. Its round barrel measured 24, 26in or 28in, giving an unladen weight of 7–7·5lb. Chamberings were extended to include 7mm Mauser (7 × 57mm), ·30 M1903, ·30–30 Winchester, ·30–40 Krag, ·303 British, ·32–40 Remington High Powered, ·32 Winchester Special and ·38–55 Remington High Powered. Butts had a straight wrist, and the rounded fore-ends had a schnabel-style tip. ¶ Eclipsed by its competitors and never popular in North America, the No. 5 sporter was abandoned in 1905—though new guns continued to be available through the retail trade until the beginning of the First World War. In 1914, however, many 7 × 57mm guns were supplied to France while work commenced on a large order for an 8 × 51mm version. It is also believed that a few 7·62 × 54mm guns were supplied to Tsarist Russia in 1915–17.

WHITNEY COPY

New System Sporting Rifle By 1880, the Whitney Arms Company of Whitneyville, Connecticut, had realised that the Laidley-Emery (q.v.) rolling-block was unnecessarily difficult to make, production ceasing in the early 1880s in favour of a blatant copy of the Rider-type Remington. ¶ The only cartridges chambered in New System Whitney guns, distinguished by a rounded receiver, appear to have been ·32–20, ·38–40 or ·44–40 Winchester; virtually all were made as sporting rifles, with 24–28in octagonal barrels, though a few short-barrelled carbines are known. Weights ranged from 5·25lb to 7·50lb. A typical ·38–40 Winchester example measured 43·75in overall, had a 28in barrel rifled with four grooves, and weighed 8·85lb. Open 'Rocky Mountain' sights were standard. ¶ The pivoting-lever extractor offered better performance than most of the Remington patterns. Much less desirable, however, was the omission of a Remington-type locking bar to prevent the hammer falling from full cock unless the breech piece was shut. ¶ A main-spring roller and a mechanical firing-pin retractor were added in 1886, but few of the perfected guns were made before Whitney was bought by Winchester in 1888.

1871: adopted on 24 February to replace the cap-lock of 1855, this was apparently considered as semi-experimental. Its half-stock was held by a single screw-clamping barrel band and a small back sight lay on the barrel. Swivels beneath the band and butt were accompanied by a ring on a bar attached to the left side of the receiver.

Model 1874

Artillery carbine: Mosqueton Remington Mo.1874.
Made by Fábrica de Armas de Oviedo, 1874–91.
11 × 58mm, rimmed.
Action: as Mo.1871 infantry rifle, above.
963mm overall, 3·47kg unladen.
588mm barrel, 6-groove rifling; RH, concentric.
Ramp-and-leaf sight graduated to 600 metres.
357 m/sec with Mo.1874 ball cartridges.
Mo.1874 socket bayonet.

☆

1874: adopted on 23 December to equip the engineer corps and garrison artillerymen (los Ingenieros y Artilleros de Plaza), this was a variant of the Mo.1871 rifle with two bands and the small carbine-type back sight.
1879: issue was extended to the military service corps (Brigada de Administración Militar).
1911: surviving guns were withdrawn, about 700 re-chambered for the Freire & Brull cartridge being issued to the security corps.

Model 1889

Dragoon carbine: Carabina Remington para Dragones, Mo.1889.
Made by Fábrica de Armas de Oviedo, 1888–90.
Quantity: 1,650?
11 × 58mm, rimmed.
Action: as Mo.1871 infantry rifle, above.
1,175mm overall, 3·95kg unladen.
802mm barrel, 6-groove rifling; RH, concentric.
Leaf sight graduated to 1,200 metres.
443 m/sec with Mo.1889 ball cartridges.
No bayonet.

☆

1889: adopted in May after fifty experimental guns had been issued in 1888 for trials with the

cavalry, this was the first new Remington to be introduced since the mid 1870s. It was also the first rolling-block carbine to be officially adopted for widespread service in the Spanish army. The Mo.1889 had two screw-clamping bands and a modified back sight, though its action was essentially that of the 1871-type rifle.

Other guns

In addition to the regulation patterns and recognisable guns from the Carlist War, Spanish Remingtons may be found with a variety of non-standard characteristics. Often assembled from cannibalised parts and of inferior quality, these 'Modelos de Recomposición' date from the 1870s. Incorporating old American- or Spanish-made components, they offer a wide variety of lengths, weights and fittings.

U S A

The Remington enjoyed a brief vogue in the US services, rather longer in the navy than in the army. Poor extraction with government-issue copper case cartridges in the trials of 1872–3 persuaded the Board of Ordnance to favour the Trapdoor Springfield. By the time drawn brass cases had been substituted, the US government was committed to the ·45–70 M1873 rifle.

Model 1870

Navy rifle.
Made by the National Armory, Springfield, Massachusetts, 1870–1.
·50–70, rimmed.
Radial-block action with shoulders on the hammer body locking under the breech block.
48·63in overall, about 9lb unladen.
32·63in barrel, 3-groove rifling; RH, concentric.
Ramp-and-leaf sight graduated to 1,000 yards.
1,275 ft/sec with standard ball cartridges.
M1870 sword bayonet.

☆

1869: trials began in March. As experimental rolling-block carbines had been purchased in

1867, there was little surprise when the navy adopted a ·50–70 rifle. The regulation Springfield barrel was used, chambered for a Martin cartridge. The Bureau of Ordnance escutcheon and a fish-scale pattern were cast into the hilt of the distinctive bayonet, made by the Ames Sword Company.
1870: an order for 10,000 guns was passed to Springfield Armory on 3 February. The guns were delivered into navy stores by late summer, but the back sights were positioned wrongly. The rifles were sold to Poultney & Trimble, then re-sold to France during the Franco-Prussian War at a considerable profit.
1871: on 27 January, the Chief of the Bureau of Navy Ordnance requested twelve thousand properly-sighted rifles.

Model 1871

Infantry rifle.
Made by the National Armory, Springfield, Massachusetts, 1870–1.
Quantity: see notes.
·50–70, rimmed.
Action: as M1870 navy rifle, above.
51·75in overall, about 9·25lb unladen.
36·00in barrel, 3-groove rifling; RH, concentric.
Ramp-and-leaf sight graduated to 1,000 yards.
1,315 ft/sec with ball cartridges.
Socket bayonet.

☆

1870: a Board of Officers convened in March at St Louis to investigate the latest rifle designs, eventually reporting that only six guns among many had proved to be acceptable—in declining order of preference, Remington, Springfield-Allin, Sharps, Morgenstern, Martini-Henry and Ward-Burton. As 504 rolling-block rifles had been made at Springfield two years earlier, their characteristics were well known.
1871: by March, Springfield had made 1,008 infantry-pattern Remington rifles, with 32·5in barrels, to compete against a similar quantity of 1870-pattern Springfield and Sharps guns. Trials began in midsummer; Remingtons performed best, though their ejection was often poor and

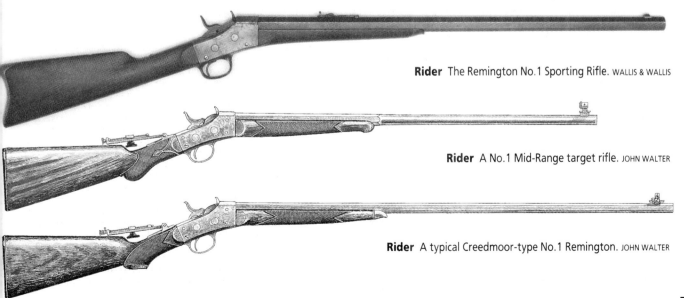

Rider The Remington No.1 Sporting Rifle. WALLIS & WALLIS

Rider A No.1 Mid-Range target rifle. JOHN WALTER

Rider A typical Creedmoor-type No.1 Remington. JOHN WALTER misgivings were expressed about dust jamming the mechanism.

1872: the 10,000 Model 1871 rifles made at Springfield Armory were similar to the 1870-pattern US navy rifles, but had an additional 'Locking Bolt' to allay fears that loading the standard rolling-block rifle at full-cock was potentially dangerous. The hammer of Locking Bolt guns dropped to half-cock when the breech piece was closed and had to be retracted manually before firing. Though these rifles were rejected by army trial boards in 1872–3, 21,000 were purchased by the New York state militia.

Model 1871

•••

Carbine.
Made by the National Armory, Springfield, Massachusetts, 1870–1.
Quantity: at least 315.
·50–70, rimmed.
Action: as M1870 navy rifle, above.
38·50in overall, about 7·8lb unladen.
23·25in barrel, 3-groove rifling; RH, concentric.
Ramp-and-leaf sight graduated to 600 yards?

About 1,100 ft/sec with ball cartridges.
No bayonet.

☆

1871: concurrently with field trials of the Remington army rifle described above, the US cavalry experimented with 313 Remington, 308 Sharps and 341 Model 1870 Springfield carbines. The St Louis board had recommended that no Remington carbines should be issued until a half-cock loading feature had been added, but this proviso went unheeded. However, a similar conclusion was reached by the end of the 1871 trials, introduction of a rolling-block carbine being rejected in favour of a variant of the Springfield-Allin pattern.

SPORTING GUNS

The simplicity, legendary strength and ready availability of the rolling-block action allowed many an individual gunsmith—and, indeed, Remington itself—to build guns to individual order. In addition to the standard patterns (see panel on page 223), tremendous variety will be found in chambering, stocks and sights.

Many modern versions of the rolling-block rifles have been made in Europe. Amongst th[e] best known are the products of Aldo Uberti o[f] Ponte Zanano, Brescia, Italy, and Star–Bonifaci[o] Echeverria y Cia of Eibar, Spain.

Uberti has made guns in ·22 Hornet, ·35[7] Magnum or ·44–40 WCF (on a modified sma[ll] or No.2 action), plus ·444 Marlin and ·45–7[0] (large or No.1 action). Some will be found wit[h] marks of the Navy Arms Company of Ridgefield New Jersey, the principal American distributor.

The Uberti rolling-block replicas have usuall[y] offered 26 or 30in octagon or half-octago[n] barrels. The Buffalo Rifle had a plain butt with [a] straight comb, whereas the Creedmoor had [a] chequered pistol-grip butt and a vernier sight o[n] the tang.

Distributed in the USA by Garcia Sportin[g] Arms Corporation of Teaneck, New Jersey, th[e] Star Rolling Block Carbine was offered in ·30–3[0] WCF, ·357 Magnum or ·44 Magnum. It wa[s] 35in long, had a 20in barrel and weighed 6lb. [A] rifle-pattern (curved) butt plate was fitted an[d] the fore-end was retained by a single band. The action was usually colour case-hardened.

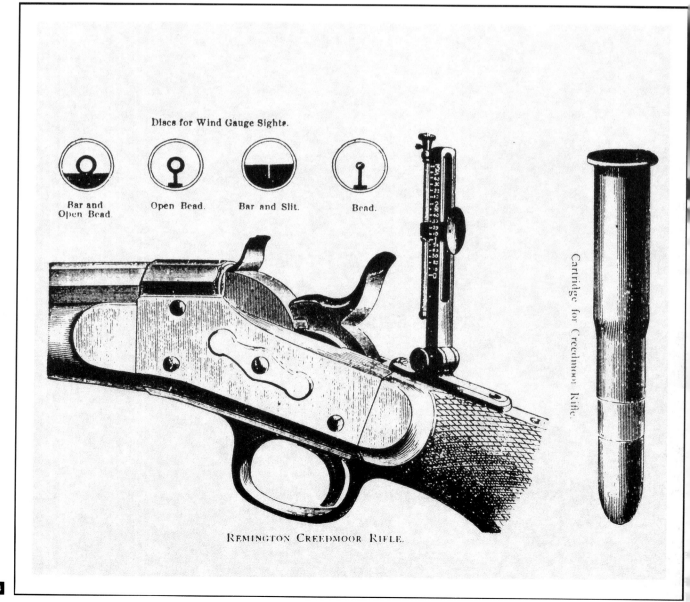

Discs for Wind Gauge Sights.

Bar and Open Bead.   Open Bead.   Bar and Slit.   Bead.

Cartridge for Creedmoor Rifle.

REMINGTON CREEDMOOR RIFLE.

R M & M

GERMANY
Including Dreyse

These sporting rifles owed their existence to the needle guns (Zündnadelgewehre) developed by Johann-Niklaus Dreyse in the 1830s. The needle guns had been very successful, but their day had all but passed by 1870. Franz von Dreyse, the son of Johann-Niklaus, patented a convertible needle-fire/centre-fire bolt mechanism in 1874. However, even the improved Dreyse cartridge rifles were markedly inferior to the Mauser; as the latter grew in importance, Dreyse company fortunes declined. Its assets were purchased by Rheinische Metallwaaren- und Maschinenfabrik in 1901, allowing curiously archaic pistols, light automatic carbines and sporting rifles to be produced under the 'Dreyse' brand until the end of the First World War. An auto-loading rifle designed by Karl Heinemann (see Part Two) were promoted unsuccessfully in the 1920s by what had become known as 'Rheinmetall'.

Dreyse Sporting Rifle

Made in Sömmerda by Waffenfabrik von Dreyse
(c.1875–1900) and Rheinische Metallwaaren und
Maschinenfabrik (1901–14).
Chambering: see text.
Turning-bolt action, locked by the abutment of the
bolt-handle base on the receiver ahead of the bridge.
DATA FOR A TYPICAL TARGET RIFLE
10·4 × 42mm, rimmed.
1,085mm overall, 3·92kg unladen.
700mm barrel, 5-groove rifling; RH, concentric.
Aperture sight on tang, and quadrant sight on barrel.
430 m/sec with 17-gram bullet.
☆

1875*: the first guns shared the general split-bridge 'Z slot' receiver of the perfected needle guns, but had a separate bolt head carrying an extractor claw and a conventional spring-loaded firing pin lay inside the bolt body. Excepting the earliest transitional models, which had to be cocked separately in the manner of their needle-gun predecessors, Dreyse cartridge rifles cocked automatically as the bolt closed. The handle was usually bent downward into a spatulate form.

A typical sporter had an octagonal barrel held in a straight-wrist half-stock by a transverse key set in small silver-plated escutcheons. The action was lightly engraved and, typical of southern German guns, the trigger guard had a separate horn finger rest instead of a pistol grip. A small quadrant sight appeared on the barrel.

1885: the perfected Dreyse rifles had a simplified action, often advertised by less discerning dealers as 'Mauser' or—marginally more realistically—'Mauser Type'. The resemblance was nothing more than superficial, and then only to the single shot 1871 pattern.

1910: a typical RM&M-made 'Dreyse' differed little from its pre-1900 equivalents. Barrels were usually octagonal, retained by transverse keys, and the bolt handle was bent downward ahead of the simplified split receiver bridge. The half-stock had a chequered wrist, prominent flats lay alongside the action, and the fore-end had a schnabel tip. Some guns had pistol grips, but the horn finger rest remained popular.

Double set triggers and light engraving were customary on better-grade examples, together with a small pillar-type aperture sight that folded into the elongated upper tang.

Owing to the comparatively weak locking system, the guns were restricted to black-powder ammunition or low pressure smokeless loads. Among the popular rimmed cartridges were 6·5 × 27mm, 8·15 × 46·5mm, 9·3 × 57mm, 9·3 × 72mm, 11 × 65mm or 11·15 × 52mm.

Target-shooting guns had heavier barrels and better sights. Trigger guards were elaborately spurred or scrolled; set triggers were standard. German-style rifles had straight-wrist butts and plain shoulder plates, whereas Swiss-style guns had squared cheek pieces and heavy hooked shoulder plates. Most rifles were chambered for the rimmed 8·15 × 46mm or 9·5 × 47mm rounds, though Swiss 10·4 × 38mm rimfire or 10·4 × 42mm (Vetterli) centre-fire cartridges enjoyed local success.

ROSS

CANADA

Perhaps the most misunderstood of twentieth-century rifles, the Ross owed its temporary military success to the refusal of the British to supply Canadian troops with Lee-Enfields during the Second South African War of 1899–1902. The invention of Sir Charles Ross, it relied on threaded helical ribs on the bolt engaging mating threads inside the bolt sleeve. When the bolt was pulled back, the ribs rotated the locking lugs out of the receiver wall. However, though the Ross was effectual when clean (and firing good-quality ammunition), war in the trenches emphasised the ease with which the action could be jammed by mud or heat generated during rapid fire.

A catalogue of serious accidents, including fatalities, soon arose. Those involving 1905-type actions may have been due to faulty engagement of the locking lugs, or the trigger releasing the striker before the breech was properly locked. In most of the later 1910-pattern guns, however, the bolt could be rotated under the extractor after the bolt-sleeve had been removed from the bolt-way. Though the bolt sleeve would re-enter the receiver, the bolt could not lock on the closing stroke and slammed back on firing. If the bolt-stop failed, the bolt flew back out of the gun with potentially disastrous consequences.

1901: Ross submitted a military version of his 1900-pattern sporting rifle to the Canadian militia. The prototype proved effectual enough in rapid fire, but comprehensively failed an endurance test negotiated by the competing Lee-Enfield without trouble. A Ross rifle was taken to Britain shortly afterwards, but was rejected by the Small Arms Committee in favour of the shortened Lee-Enfield.

1902: with the British still unwilling to supply rifles, the Canadians were forced into adopting the Ross. The first contract, for 12,000 rifles, was signed in March with the promise of others to follow. The 'Rifle, Ross, ·303-inch, Mark 1' was sealed in April, the Ross Rifle Company was

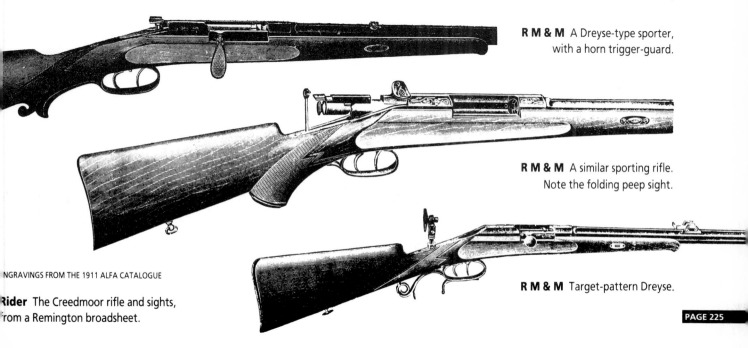

R M & M A Dreyse-type sporter, with a horn trigger-guard.

R M & M A similar sporting rifle. Note the folding peep sight.

R M & M Target-pattern Dreyse.

NGRAVINGS FROM THE 1911 ALFA CATALOGUE

Rider The Creedmoor rifle and sights, rom a Remington broadsheet.

formed in the autumn of 1903, and construction of a purpose-built factory began.

1905: the first guns were made in the Quebec factory, initially using many parts bought in from Billings & Spencer and Mossberg.

MILITARY RIFLES
Model 1905

Mks I, II, II**, II***, II*****, Short Mks I and II.
Made by the Ross Rifle Company, Quebec.
·303, rimmed.
Straight-pull bolt action, locked by two lugs on the bolt head engaging the receiver wall.
DATA FOR A TYPICAL MARK I
48·63in overall, 8·03lb unladen.
28·00in barrel, 4-groove rifling; RH, concentric.
Internal box magazine, 5 rounds.
Tangent sight graduated to 2,200 yards.
2,000 ft/sec with Mk II ball ammunition.
Sword bayonet.
☆

1905: the first 'Rifles, Ross, .303-inch, Mark I' were delivered to the Department of Militia and Defence in August. The Mk I had a pistol-grip stock and a barrel band. A nose cap carried the bayonet lug and a piling swivel; sling swivels lay on the band and under the butt. The Mk I back sight had a long leaf, graduated to 2,200 yards, but predictably proved to be too fragile.

The magazine featured the so-called 'Harris Controlled Platform', with a depressor behind the back sight on the right side of the fore-end. This could be actuated by the thumb to allow cartridges to be dropped into the magazine. The cut-off lay above the trigger guard.

There was little doubt that the Ross action was very fast in perfect conditions; in addition, when properly locked, it was unusually strong. However, quality control was poor and problems were soon apparent. After part of a bolt blew back into the face of a Royal North West Mounted Policeman during shooting practice in 1906, costing the firer an eye, RNWMP Ross rifles were recalled into store. Survivors were exchanged for improved Mk II rifles in 1909.

1906: a German-style tangent-pattern Mk II back sight was approved, with a rotating-collar micrometer system that permitted the sight to be elevated in 10-yard increments. The improved Mk II rifle retained the Harris magazine, but the hooked cut-off lay inside the trigger guard and the rear swivel lay ahead of the guard

1907: a strengthened Mk III back sight was introduced, distinguished by its flat-top elevator bar. After a tremendous number of minor changes had been made, the Mark II** rifle appeared with a 30·5in barrel, an improved 'flag' safety catch instead of a press-catch, a longer nose cap (not unlike that of the US Krag-Jørgensen) and a broader barrel band. The cut-off mechanism was omitted.

Most rifles had simpler hand guards and leaf-type back sights made by the Sutherland Sight Company (renamed Canada Tool & Specialty Company in c.1911). The sights lay mid-way between the receiver ring and the barrel band. Some Mk II** rifles were specially built in 1909 for military target shooting, with heavy barrels, modified fore-ends, and a Ross battle sight mounted on the receiver bridge.

1909: the Mark II*** rifle had a 28in barrel and a Sutherland sight ahead of a prominent steel housing abutting the receiver ring. The cut-off was reinstated and the safety reverted to the press-catch design.

1910: the Mark II***** was another of the 28in-barrelled guns, distinguished from the Mk II*** by a simpler housing immediately behind the Sutherland sight.

1912: to camouflage the steadily growing list of modifications, the Canadians re-designated the 30·5in-barrelled Mk II** as the 'Rifle, Ross Mk II', while the 28in-barrelled Mks II*** and Mk II***** became 'Rifles, Short, Ross Mk II'. All other short-barrel guns, regardless of sub-class, were to be known as 'Rifles, Short, Ross, Mk I'.

Model 1910

Military Match, Mks III and IIIB.
Made by the Ross Rifle Company, Quebec.
·303, rimmed.

Straight-pull bolt action, locked by multiple lugs on the bolt head engaging the receiver wall.
DATA FOR A TYPICAL MK III
50·56in overall, 9·85lb unladen.
30·25in barrel, 4-groove rifling; LH, concentric.
Integral box magazine, 5 rounds.
Folding leaf sight graduated to 1,550 yards.
2,520 ft/sec with Mk VII ball ammunition.
Sword bayonet.
☆

1911: approved in the summer, this was the principal weapon of the Canadian Expeditionary Force in 1914, though guns had only just reached the troops before hostilities began. The Mk III featured a 'triple-thread interrupted screw double-bearing cam bolt head', owing more to Ross's desire to create a suitable action for powerful sporting-rifle cartridges than military desirability. The substitution of a charger-loaded five-round in-line box magazine for the original Harris platform type could be seen as an advantage, though the new rifle lacked the elegance of its predecessor. The new bolt locked vertically instead of horizontally in an attempt to improve the feed stroke.

The unwieldy Mark III Ross was characterised by the protruding magazine housing, shallow pistol grip, and bridge-mounted back sight. The bolt-stop was combined with the cut-off on the left rear of the receiver.

1912: the ·280 Military Match rifle appeared for military-style target shooting. It was essentially similar to the Mark III, but had an internal box magazine and a 26in barrel. Guns of this pattern were unbelievably successful at Camp Perry and Bisley in 1913, US NRA rules being re-written to exclude them.

1914: the British government ordered 100,000 Mk III rifles in September, but deliveries were erratic. Under combat conditions, the Ross proved a disaster; it was much too cumbersome in hand-to-hand combat and was distressingly prone to jamming.

1915: the modified Mark IIIB was approved in October, with an SMLE-type cut off, but reports of bolts flying out of the Ross as it fired were multiplying.

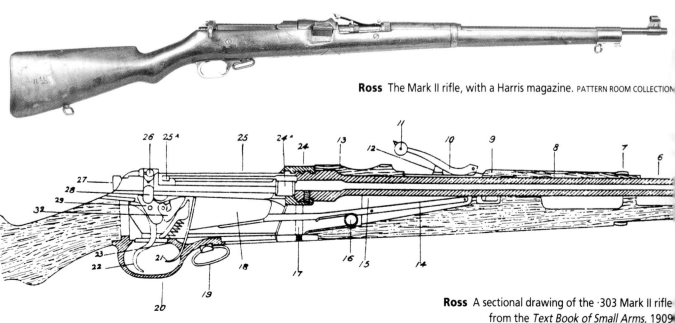

Ross The Mark II rifle, with a Harris magazine. PATTERN ROOM COLLECTION

Ross A sectional drawing of the ·303 Mark II rifle from the *Text Book of Small Arms*, 1909

1916: adjustment of the extractor groove, and the addition by armourers in France of a rivet or screw in the bolt sleeve, prevented bolts being wrongly assembled. However, the adjustments were too late to prevent the unpopular Ross being replaced by the short Lee-Enfield in the autumn. Tests showed that jamming often arose simply from the bolt-stop damaging the rearmost locking thread, but the Canadians had lost all confidence in their rifle.

1917: the British contract was cancelled in March, after 66,590 guns had been accepted, owing to the appropriation of the Ross Rifle Company's Quebec factory by the Canadian government.

Some rifles were retained for sniping, fitted with American 1908 or 1913-model Warner & Swazey sights offset to the left to clear the charger guides. Ironically, these were perhaps the most accurate of all pre-1918 sniper rifles.

1921: the Ross rifle were declared obsolete in British service in November.

1940: surviving guns were reissued to the Royal Canadian Navy, coastal artillery, militia units and training camps. A few thousand were sent to Britain for the Home Guard. Soon displaced by more effectual No.3 (P/14) and US M1917 Enfield rifles, most of the Ross guns ended their days aboard merchant ships.

Some rifles went to the Soviet Union in the early 1940s, sufficient examples surviving to be used—rebarrelled for the 7·62 × 54mm rimmed cartridge—to gain the Soviet running-boar team a gold medal from the 1954 world shooting championships.

SPORTING GUNS

1897: Ross developed his first Magazine Sporting Rifle. Distinguished by a small external hammer, this embodied a straight-pull bolt adapted from the Austro-Hungarian M1895 Mannlicher. A few guns were made in Hartford, Connecticut, under the supervision of Joseph Bennett (manufacturing was undertaken by Billings & Spencer and Mossberg), while others were made in London by Charles Lancaster.

1900: an improved sporting rifle was patented in Bennett's name, featuring a conventional striker-type firing mechanism inside the bolt.

1903: assembly of a minor modification of the 1900-pattern sporter began in the new Quebec factory, after a few ·370 Express examples had been made in Hartford. Most of the earliest 'Canadian' rifles were made from American-produced parts. Actions were also supplied to Charles Lancaster & Company to be barrelled, stocked and finished for the ·256 (6·5mm) Mannlicher, ·303 or ·370 Express cartridges.

1906: a few sporting rifles were built on military Mk II actions. Their walnut half stocks had short fore-ends with a single encircling barrel band.

Sporting Model

E, E-10, M-10, R, R-1910 and Scotch Deer Stalking patterns.
Made by the Ross Rifle Company, Quebec.
·280 Ross, ·303 or ·35 WCF (see notes).
Straight-pull bolt action, locked by lugs on the bolt head engaging the receiver wall.
DATA FOR A TYPICAL M-10
·280 Ross, rimless.
48·50in overall, 7·35lb unladen.
28·00in barrel, 4-groove rifling; LH, concentric.
Integral box magazine, 4 rounds.
Folding-leaf sight.
3,050 ft/sec with 140-grain bullet.

☆

1907: the Models E and R appeared, built on the 1905-pattern action with modified threaded locking lugs. The fabled ·280 Ross cartridge also appeared, creating the Scotch Deer Stalking Sporting Rifle (also known as the High Velocity Sporting Rifle) when chambered in the Model E.

Chambered for ·303 or ·35 WCF, with a 28in barrel, the standard Model E had a neatly proportioned half-stock, with chequering on the pistol grip and fore-end. An improved five-round internal magazine was fitted. ·303 Model R rifles were little more than military actions in half stocks. The Harris controlled-platform magazine was retained, though the back sight became an open spring-leaf and elevator pattern.

1913: the E-10 and R-1910 sporting rifles appeared, followed by the M-10. Incorporating the multi-lug action, they differed appreciably in details. The basic R-1910 (·303 only) was built on a conventional breech, with a protruding magazine case and a 26in barrel. It had a plain pistol-grip walnut half-stock and an adjustable spring-leaf and elevator back sight. The E-10 (·303 or ·35 WCF) was similar, but the pistol grip and fore-end were chequered; the back sight was a folding two-leaf Express type.

The ·280 M-10 had a 28in barrel and an elegant chequered half-stock with a schnabel-tipped fore-end. An internal magazine was fitted, resulting in a much smoother outline than its immediate predecessors. The sight was generally a folding leaf on the barrel, though an optional folding aperture pattern could be dovetailed into the receiver bridge. Most Ross sporters carried a sling eye on a barrel collar, protruding behind the fore-end tip.

1914: production of sporting rifles ceased on the outbreak of war, though assembly apparently continued into 1915. The perfected patterns had enjoyed a brief period in vogue, selling extremely well before the stopping power of their high-velocity lightweight bullets was questioned.

Match Target Rifle

Made by the Ross Rifle Company, Quebec.
·280, rimless.
Straight-pull bolt action, locked by lugs on the bolt head engaging the receiver wall.
DATA FOR A TYPICAL EXAMPLE
51·00in overall, 9·00lb unladen.
30·50in barrel, 4-groove rifling; RH, concentric.
Vernier sight on the butt-heel.
2,850 ft/sec with 180-grain bullet.

☆

1908: a Ross rifle fired by F.W. Jones created a sensation by winning major prizes at the Bisley meeting, including the Match Rifle Aggregate. The gun was found to have an overweight barrel, whereupon Jones disqualified himself, but the Ross name had been established even though the heights of 1908 were never regained

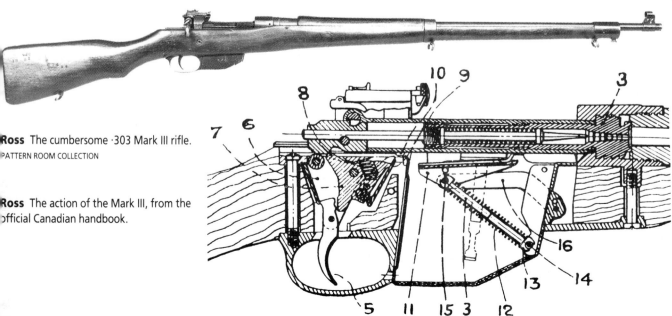

Ross The cumbersome ·303 Mark III rifle.
PATTERN ROOM COLLECTION

Ross The action of the Mark III, from the official Canadian handbook.

in this particular category—even in 1913, when the ·280 Military Match and other Ross rifles took first, second and third prize in every competition for which they were eligible.

The Match Target was a single-shot rifle embodying a modified 1905-type action (with threaded locking lugs), a pistol-grip half stock and a floating barrel. Sights comprised a vernier-adjustable folding leaf on a mount embedded in the heel of the butt, and a large cross-hair lens unit with a spirit level.

RSC

FRANCE
Also known as 'Saint-Étienne'

Designed in 1915–16 by Ribeyrolles, Sutter and Chauchat, the RSC rifle was created once it had been realised that the Fusil A6 (Meunier) was too complicated to mass-produce satisfactorily.

Gas was tapped from the underside of the RSC barrel to impinge on a piston and drive the operating rod—exposed on the right side of the breech—back to rotate and disengage the multiple interrupted-screw type lugs on the separate bolt head. Rigorous service showed the Mle.1917 rifle to be effectual, though continual refinements were made. These ultimately led to the Mle.1918, but series production did not commence until after the Armistice.

The RSC was undoubtedly among the best semi-automatic rifles produced during the First World War, but was handicapped by the clumsy rimmed French cartridge.

MILITARY WEAPONS

Model 1917

Rifles and short rifles: Fusils Mle.1917 et Mle.1917/35, Mousqueton Mle.1917.
Assembled by Manufacture d'Armes, Saint-Étienne, with parts supplied from the government factories in Tulle and Châtellerault plus the privately-owned Hotchkiss factory in Saint-Denis, 1917–18.
Quantity: 86,330.
8 × 51mm, rimmed.
Gas-operated auto-loading action, locked by rotating multiple lugs into the receiver.
1,328mm overall, 5·19kg unladen.
800mm barrel, 4-groove rifling; LH, concentric.
Integral charger-loaded box magazine, 5 rounds.
Leaf sight graduated to 2,000 metres.
700 m/sec with Balle 1898 D.
Mle.86/15 épée bayonet.

☆

1915: experiments began with prototypes, apparently adapted from Mle.86/93 Lebel rifles. They showed sufficient promise for work to continue throughout the year.

1916: the RSC rifle was provisionally adopted in May, and an assembly line was readied in Saint-Étienne. However, problems slowed progress so greatly that limited quantities of the Fusil A6 (Meunier, q.v.) were made as an expedient.

1917: the first batches of Mle.1917 rifles were assembled early in the year, issues being ordered (in March) on a scale of sixteen to each company of the line infantry regiments. The guns had distinctive two-piece stocks and a prominent rounded magazine case beneath the receiver. The band and nose cap were essentially similar to those of the Mle.1916 Berthier rifle, and the standard bayonet was retained. The hand guard ran from the front of the back sight base, over the top of the band to approximately half-way to the nose cap.

A prominent operating slide reciprocated on the right side of the receiver, a stubby retracting handle appearing on the bolt. A safety button protruded on the right side of the receiver between the trigger guard and the magazine, a manual hold-open lever being added shortly after series production commenced.

By the end of the year, sufficient quantities were available for general issue to begin; RSC rifles were usually given to the squad leaders and the best marksmen.

1918: active service showed the Mle.1917 to be reliable, but too clumsy for trench warfare. Small numbers of a shortened 'Mousqueton Mle.1917' were made, with a different nose cap moved back around the gas-port assembly and minor changes in the action.

1935: most survivors were converted to manual straight-pull operation simply by blocking the gas port. These 'Mle.1917/35' guns seem to have been held in reserve in 1939, though a few may have served the Gardes Mobiles.

Model 1918

Short rifles: Fusils Mle.1918 et Mle.1918/35.
Assembled by Manufacture d'Armes, Saint-Étienne, with parts supplied from the government factories in Tulle and Châtellerault, 1918–19.
Quantity: 9,500?
8 × 51mm, rimmed.
Action: as Mle.1917, above.
1,099mm overall, 4·75kg unladen.
580mm barrel, 4-groove rifling; LH, concentric.
Integral charger-loaded box magazine, 5 rounds.
Leaf sight graduated to 2,000 metres.
655 m/sec with Balle 1898 D.
Mle.86/15 épée bayonet.

☆

1918: this was an improved Mle.1917, shorter and lighter but otherwise similar. The hand guard ran from the front of the receiver to the nose cap; a lever on the right side of the receiver held the action open after the last case had been ejected; and a tubular sleeve prevented debris entering the cocking-lever slot. Production began in the late summer, but no guns had been issued by the Armistice.

1919: a few thousand rifles were made before the project was abandoned. Some were issued for service in Morocco in the early 1920s, but the introduction of a 7·5mm rimless cartridge rendered them obsolescent.

1935: surviving Mle.1918 rifles were converted to the manually-operated 'Mle.1918/35' by blocking the gas port. The charging stroke was appreciably stiffer than a conventional bolt-action rifle, making the conversions unpopular. They were brought out of store briefly in 1939, to arm Gardes Mobiles, and a few were converted to semi-automatic operation merely by unblocking the gas port.

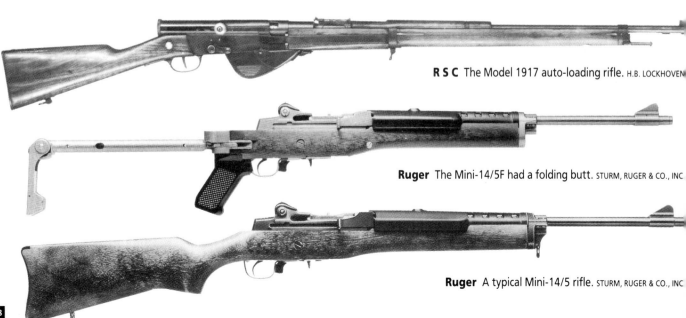

R S C The Model 1917 auto-loading rifle. H.B. LOCKHOVEN

Ruger The Mini-14/5F had a folding butt. STURM, RUGER & CO., INC.

Ruger A typical Mini-14/5 rifle. STURM, RUGER & CO., INC.

RUGER

UNITED STATES OF AMERICA

The success of Sturm, Ruger & Company was based on a ·22 rimfire pistol designed by Alexander Sturm and William Ruger, then introduced commercially in 1949. The company entered the rifle business in the early 1960s with the first of a series of highly successful auto-loaders, then progressed to effectual block- and bolt-action designs.

MILITARY WEAPONS
AC-556

AC-556, AC-556F, KAC-556 and KAC-556F patterns.
Made by Sturm, Ruger & Co., Inc., Southport,
Connecticut, 1975 to date.
5·56 × 45mm only.
Gas-operated auto-loading action, locked by rotating
lugs on the bolt into the receiver wall.
38·78in overall, 6·86lb with laden 20-round magazine.
18·50in barrel, 6-groove rifling; RH, concentric.
Detachable box magazine, 5, 20 or 30 rounds.
Adjustable aperture sight.
3,300 ft/sec with 55-grain bullet; 750 ± 50 rpm.
Optional US M7 knife bayonet.

☆

1982*: this was a selective-fire derivative of the commercial Mini-14, described below, which had been attracting considerable attention in military circles—and had even been offered (as the Mini-14/20GB) with a flash-hider and a bayonet lug. The action relied on a Garand-type rotating bolt, powered by a piston attached to the actuator. When the gun fired, propellant gas bled from the barrel into the cupped head of the piston surrounding the gas port. The piston was given a sharp backward thrust before clearing the port-cylinder and allowing the gas to vent to the atmosphere. Momentum then carried the moving parts back to the limit of their travel, cocking the hammer, until they were propelled forward by the return spring.

Externally, the rifle could be recognised by its half-stock and ventilated fibreglass hand guard covering the actuator slide on the right side of the fore-end. The safety catch lay in the front face of the trigger guard.

The major difference between the AC-556 and the Mini-14 concerned the trigger system, and the addition of a three-position selector at the right rear of the receiver for single shots, three-round bursts or fully automatic fire.

The AC-556F had a tubular butt folding to the right, 'K' prefix versions being made of stainless instead of blued steel. Owing to light weight and durability, Rugers have proved popular with police and anti-terrorist units, including the Royal Ulster Constabulary and the Compagnies Republicaines de Sécurité (CRS).

SPORTING GUNS
1. THE AUTO-LOADING PATTERNS

These blowback and gas-operated locked-breech designs have been very successful commercially.

Model 44

Carbine, International, Sporter and Standard
patterns.
Made by Sturm, Ruger & Co., Inc., Southport,
Connecticut, 1961 to date.
·44 Magnum only.
Gas-operated auto-loading action, locked by rotating
lugs on the bolt into the receiver wall.
DATA FOR A TYPICAL STANDARD EXAMPLE
36·75in overall, 5·75lb unladen.
18·50in barrel, 12-groove rifling; RH, concentric.
Tube magazine beneath barrel, 4 rounds.
Folding-leaf sight.
1,830 ft/sec with 180-grain bullet.

☆

1961: this gun—also made in ·22 rimfire from 1964—featured a hammer-type ignition system contained in the trigger housing, and a cross-bolt

safety through the front web of the trigger guard. The Model 44 Standard had a pistol-grip half-stock with a plain comb and concave butt plate. A barrel band lay toward the round fore-end tip. Open sights were standard, though the receiver was drilled and tapped for optical-sight mounts. A Model 44 Carbine version differed solely in the addition of an aperture back sight and swivels under the butt.

1963*: the Model 44 Sporter had a deluxe stock with a low Monte Carlo comb, a fluted fore-end, a folding-leaf back sight, and swivels beneath the stock. The International Model, whch is believed to have been a contemporary of the Sporter, had a full-length fore-end.

1967: a catch was added to facilitate detaching the magazine.

1971: the 44 Sporter and International patterns were discontinued, followed by the 44 Carbine in 1978 and 44 Standard in 1987.

Mini-14

K-Mini-14/5, K-Mini-14/5F, K-Mini-14/5R,
K-Mini-14/5RF, Mini-14/5, Mini-14/5F, Mini-14/5R and
Mini-14/5RF patterns.
Made by Sturm, Ruger & Co., Inc., Southport,
Connecticut, 1975 to date.
·223 Remington only.
Gas-operated auto-loading action, locked by rotating
lugs on the bolt into the receiver wall.
DATA FOR A TYPICAL MINI-14/5
37·25in overall, 6·40lb unladen.
18·50in barrel, 6-groove rifling; RH, concentric.
Detachable box magazine, 5 rounds.
Adjustable aperture sight.
3,300 ft/sec with 55-grain bullet.

☆

1973: announced at the end of the year, but not made in quantity until 1975, the action of the Mini-14 is described above (see AC-556). The pistol-grip half-stock had steel liners to protect the mechanism; a safety catch through the front web of the trigger guard locked the hammer and sear. A five-round magazine was standard, though twenty- and thirty-round alternatives could be obtained to order for police and security

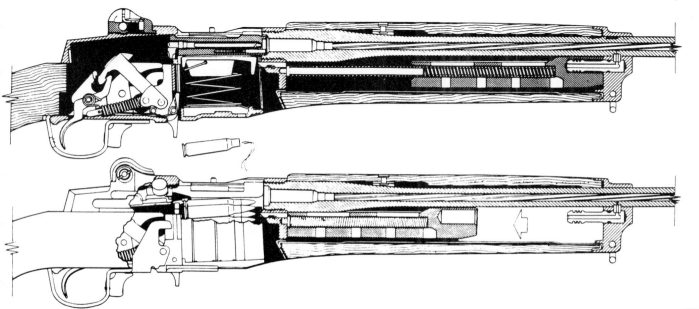

Ruger The action of the basic Mini-14 rifle.

services. The standard guns were blued, but a stainless steel version (K-Mini-14) was available.

1982: the original Mini-14 had a conventional wooden hand guard with the actuator sliding in an exposed channel on the right side of the fore-end. This was potentially dangerous, forcing Ruger to develop a fibreglass hand guard/actuator cover, introduced to accompany the Mini-14/5-R (later known as the Ranch Rifle). This gun also featured a modified receiver with a folding-leaf back sight, patented integral optical-sight mount dovetails, and an improved buffer between the actuator slide and the receiver. The bolt stop was modified to double as an ejector, eliminating the earlier spring-loaded ejector mechanism. Ranch Rifles originally had a straight shotgun-style butt plate, were 37·75in long and weighed about 6·8lb. Eventually, however, the standard rifle-type Mini-14 shoulder plate was substituted.

1985: variants of the basic Mini-14 and Ranch Rifle were introduced with separate chequered plastic pistol grips and tubular metal butts, folding to the right. The rifles folded to about 27·5in overall, weighed approximately 7·55lb, and were known to Ruger as Mini-14/5F or Mini-14/5RF respectively.

Mini-Thirty

Made by Sturm, Ruger & Co., Inc., Southport, Connecticut, 1987 to date.
7·62 × 39mm only.
Action: as Mini-14, above.
37·75in overall, 7·15lb unladen.
18·50in barrel, 6-groove rifling; RH, concentric.
Detachable box magazine, 5 rounds.
Pivoting-leaf sight.
2,330 ft/sec with 125-grain bullet.
☆

1987: this variant of the standard Mini-14 Ranch Rifle, with the patented optical-sight mount and a folding sight, was made for the Soviet-type 7·62mm intermediate cartridge. This had advantages over the 5·56mm (·223) pattern on medium-size game, being only marginally inferior to ·30-30 WCF at 150 yards.

2. THE BLOCK-ACTION PATTERNS

The Ruger block-action rifle was based on the best of British single-shot designs, particularly the Fraser, though with a greater external affinity with the Farquharson. A straight-line striker—struck by the hammer by way of a transfer block—was substituted for the original inclined pattern, and the butt-tang system was replaced by a socket to receive a large bolt running up through the butt. The Ruger is superior to its antecedents in strength and design.

GERMANY

No.1 actions have been used as the basis for guns engraved and stocked in European style.

Heym-Ruger

HR 30, HR 30L and HR 38 patterns.
Made by Sturm, Ruger & Co., Inc., Southport, Connecticut, but completed by Friedrich Wilh. Heym GmbH & Co., Münnerstadt.
Chambering: see notes.
Dropping-block action, locked by shoulders on the operating lever.
DATA FOR A TYPICAL HR 30
7 × 65mm, rimmed.
1,020mm overall, 3·05kg unladen.
600mm barrel, 6-groove rifling; RH, concentric.
Folding-leaf sight.
770 m/sec with 11·2-gram bullet.
☆

1978*: the first guns were built around US-made actions. The basic patterns differed only in their barrels—round (HR 30) or octagonal (HR 38). They usually had single set Canjar triggers and open sights, though claw-pattern optical-sight mounts have been popular. Most rifles were stocked in walnut; HR 30 and HR 38 had half-stocks, whereas the HR 30L Carbine had a full-length Mannlicher pattern. Bavarian cheek

pieces invariably had scalloped lower edges. Owing to its comparatively short barrel, the HR 30L was not available in magnum chamberings.

Standard actions offered game-and-oakleaf engraving, but 'Modell HR 38 Exclusiv' had side-plate extensions on the receiver.

HR 30 rifles have been chambered for ·243 Winchester, 6·5 × 57mm R, 6·5 × 68mm R, ·270 Winchester, 7 × 64mm, 7 × 65mm R, ·300 Winchester Magnum, ·30-06, ·308 Winchester, 8 × 68mm S, 9·3 × 72mm R or 10·3 × 60mm R. The HR 38 versions have chambered 6·5 × 57mm R, 6·5 × 68mm R, 8 × 68mm S or 10·3 × 60mm R.

USA

Number 1

Government, International, Light Sporter, Medium Sporter, Special Varminter, Standard, Standard/Light Sporter, Tropical, 1-A, 1-AB, 1-B, 1-H, 1-RSI, 1-S and 1-V patterns.
Made by Sturm, Ruger & Co., Inc., Southport, Connecticut, 1967 to date.
Chambering: see notes.
Dropping-block action, locked by shoulders on the operating lever.
DATA FOR STANDARD NO.1 RIFLE
·25-06 Remington, rimless.
42·50in overall, 7·95lb unladen.
26·00in barrel, 6-groove rifling; RH, concentric.
Folding-leaf sight.
3,500 ft/sec with 87-grain bullet.
☆

1967: the No.1 Standard Rifle, made with a 26in round barrel and often known by the Ruger catalogue number 1-B, had a chequered pistol-grip butt with a straight comb and a broad fore-end. A solid rubber shoulder plate was standard, swivels lay under butt and fore-end, and a sliding safety lay on the tang behind the breech block. The quarter-rib above the breech was tapped and drilled for optical-sight mounts.

The chamberings originally included ·220 Swift, ·22-250 Remington, 6mm Remington, ·243 Winchester, ·25-06, ·270 Winchester,

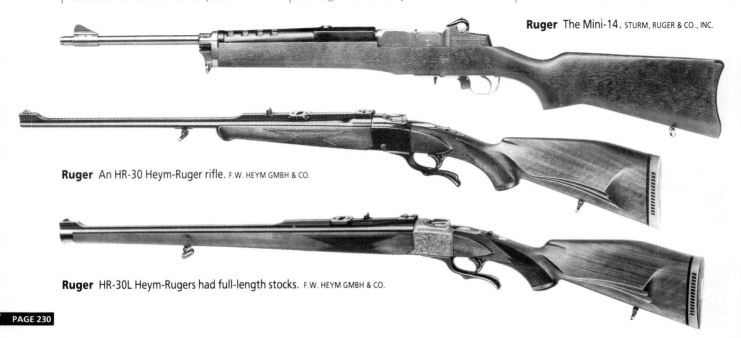

Ruger The Mini-14. STURM, RUGER & CO., INC.

Ruger An HR-30 Heym-Ruger rifle. F.W. HEYM GMBH & CO.

Ruger HR-30L Heym-Rugers had full-length stocks. F.W. HEYM GMBH & CO.

7mm Remington Magnum, ·300 Winchester Magnum or ·30–06.

The No.1 Medium Sporter (1-S) had a beaked Henry-type fore-end tip, an open back sight set into the rib, and a swivel on the barrel instead of the fore-end. The barrels measured 26in for 7mm Remington Magnum or ·300 Winchester Magnum cartridges.

Generally made with a quarter rib, the 7·25lb No.1 Light Sporter (1-A) had a slender 22in barrel chambering ·243 Winchester, ·270 Winchester or ·30–06. A few guns were also made in 7 × 57mm. The idiosyncratic Henry fore-end and a barrel-mounted front swivel were standard. A similar Standard/Light Sporter (or 1-AB) chambered the ·223 Remington, ·270 Winchester, 7 × 57mm or ·30–06 rounds. It had a plain fore-end and a mount for an optical sight on the quarter rib.

Ruger's No.1 Tropical Rifle (1-H), originally chambered only for ·375 H&H Magnum and ·458 Winchester Magnum, had a 24in heavy barrel and weighed 8·25–9lb. The Henry fore-end was standard, whilst the front swivel was generally carried on a band around the barrel. The open back sight was set into the quarter rib.

No.1 Special Varminter rifles (1-V) had heavy 24in barrels tapped for scope-mounting blocks and weighed 9lb; open sights were eliminated. They could be obtained in ·220 Swift and a clutch of proprietary Remington chamberings—·22–250, ·222, ·223, 6mm or ·25–06.

The No.1 Government Model, offered only in ·45–70, had a 22in barrel, a Henry fore-end, and a front swivel on the barrel. It weighed about 7·3lb. The separate designation was dropped after the introduction of the ·45–70 No.3 (q.v.).

1973: a ·338 Winchester Magnum option was added to the Standard (1-B) and Medium Sporter (1-S) chamberings. The ·45–70 1-B chambering was transferred to the Medium Sporter owing to the introduction of the No.3 described below.

1974: the ·222 Remington 1-V disappeared.

1979*: a ·280 Remington chambering was offered with the Standard 1-B rifle.

1983: the No.1 International Rifle (1-RSI) was

introduced. Distinguished by a full-length or 'Mannlicher' stock and a lightweight 20in barrel, it could be obtained in ·243 Winchester, ·270 Winchester, 7 × 57mm Mauser or ·30–06. Concurrently, the Standard Light Sporter (1-AB) was discontinued.

1987: ·270 Weatherby, ·300 Weatherby and ·300 Winchester Magnum chamberings were offered with the Standard 1-B rifle.

1990: the last Varmint rifles chambered for the 6mm Remington cartridge were sold. A ·416 Rigby Tropical (1-H) rifle appeared.

Number 3

Made by Sturm, Ruger & Co., Inc., Southport, Connecticut, 1972–87.
Chambering: see notes.
Action: as No.1 rifle, above.
DATA FOR A TYPICAL EXAMPLE
·45–70, rimmed.
38·50in overall, 6·00lb unladen.
22·00in barrel, 8-groove rifling; RH, concentric.
Folding-leaf sight.
About 1,250 ft/sec with modern ball cartridges.

☆

1972: introduced in ·22 Hornet and ·30–40 Krag, this modified No.1 had a traditional American-style breech lever with a plain tip. It also had a curved rifle-type shoulder plate, and the short rounded fore-end was retained by a single barrel band. The butt had a straight wrist.

1974: a ·45–70 version appeared.

1978*: the last ·30–40 guns were made.

1980*: ·223 Remington and ·375 Winchester options were added, though the latter was never popular and had been deleted by 1984.

1985: a ·44 Magnum option appeared.

1987: the No.3 rifle was finally discontinued.

3. THE BOLT-ACTION PATTERNS

The basic action was adapted from the original 1898-pattern Mauser, retaining the non-rotating

collar-type extractor. One of the best features—among many—was the front action-retaining bolt, which screwed diagonally upward into the underside of the receiver to give excellent bedding qualities.

Model 77

All Weather Stainless, Deluxe, International, Mark II, New Varmint, Round Top, Special, Standard, Tropical, Ultra Light, Ultra Light Carbine, Varmint, 77-EXP II, 77-LR II, 77-MAG II, 77-NV II, 77-R, 77-R II, 77-RL, 77-RL II, 77-RLS, 77-RP II, 77-RS, 77-RS II, 77-RSI, 77-ST, 77-T and 77-V patterns.
Made by Sturm, Ruger & Co., Inc., Southport, Connecticut, 1968 to date.
Chambering: see notes.
Turning-bolt action, locked by rotating two lugs on the bolt head into the receiver wall and by the bolt handle turning down into its seat.
DATA FOR A TYPICAL 77-R
·270 Winchester, rimless.
44·00in overall, 7·53lb unladen.
24·00in barrel, 6-groove rifling; RH, concentric.
Internal box magazine, 5 rounds.
Optical sight.
3,140 ft/sec with 130-grain bullet.

☆

1968: the Standard Rifle had a classically styled half-stock with a straight-comb butt and a rubber shoulder plate. The pistol grip and fore-end were chequered, but white-line spacers were omitted. Swivels lay beneath the stock, whilst a safety catch was set into the upper tang. The receivers of 77-R and 77-RS guns had integrally-machined bases for Ruger's own optical-sight mounts; 'RS' guns also had folding open back sights. A release catch for the alloy magazine floor plate was let into the trigger guard bow—steel trigger-guard/floor plates being optional extras only with the long (or Magnum) action.

The original short-action Standard Rifles were chambered for the ·22–250 Remington, ·220 Swift, 6mm Remington, ·243 Winchester or ·250–3000 Savage cartridges.

1971: the shape of the bolt handle was greatly refined. The earliest long-action rifles were

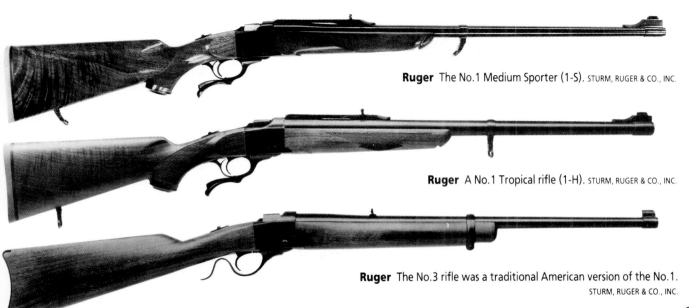

Ruger The No.1 Medium Sporter (1-S). STURM, RUGER & CO., INC.

Ruger A No.1 Tropical rifle (1-H). STURM, RUGER & CO., INC.

Ruger The No.3 rifle was a traditional American version of the No.1.
STURM, RUGER & CO., INC.

offered in ·25–06, ·270 Winchester, 7 × 57mm Mauser or ·30–06 (five-round magazines), and 7mm Remington Magnum, .300 Winchester Magnum, ·338 Winchester Magnum or ·458 Winchester Magnum (three-round magazines). No additional distinction was drawn between these and the standard guns, catalogue numbers remaining unchanged.

The receiver of the Special or 'Round Top' Rifle (77-ST), originally offered only in ·243 and ·308 Winchester, accepted non-Ruger sight mounts. Additional open sights were standard. Long-action rifles of this type were apparently restricted to ·25–06, ·270 Winchester or ·30–06 (22in barrels) and 7mm Remington Magnum, ·300 Winchester Magnum or ·338 Winchester Magnum (24in barrels).

1973: the short-action Varmint Rifle (77-V) was introduced for ·220 Swift (26in barrel) ·22–250, 6mm Remington, ·243 Winchester or ·25–06 (24in barrels). It lacked open sights and weighed about 9lb.

1978*: a ·280 Remington chambering was offered on the basis of the 77-R long action.

1979*: the ·250–3000 Standard or 77-R rifle was withdrawn, and the ·300 Winchester Magnum and ·338 Winchester Magnum 77-ST chamberings were also abandoned. However, as compensation, new ·308 and ·358 Winchester options were made available for the Model 77-R.

1982: a short-action International Model (or 77-RSI) appeared with an integral-base receiver and a full-length stock. The 18·5in barrel was chambered for ·22–250, ·243 Winchester, ·250–3000 Savage or ·308 Winchester rounds, unladen weight being about 7lb.

1983: a short-action Ultra Light version of the basic Model 77 (77-RL) was introduced in ·243 Winchester or ·308 Winchester. It had a 20in barrel and weighed a little over 6lb.

1985: the perfected Tropical Rifle (77-RT) was chambered exclusively for the ·458 Winchester Magnum. It had a steel trigger guard/floor plate assembly, a strengthened stock with transverse recoil bolts, and weighed about 8·75lb.

The ·358 Winchester and ·458 Winchester Model 77-R options were abandoned; a ·257

Roberts chambering was added to the Standard 77-R list, using the long action, and the last ·280 Remington Varmint rifles were sold. New ·22–250 and ·250–3000 Savage options were introduced for the short-action Ultra Light rifle, together with long-action ·257 Roberts and ·270 Winchester patterns; ·22–250 and ·250–3000 International-pattern rifles were also made for the first time.

1987: long-action ·270 Winchester and ·30–06 chamberings were introduced for International (77-RSI) rifles, and a ·30–06 Ultra Light also appeared. The last 6mm Remington Varmint guns were made.

The Ruger 77-RLS or Ultra Light Carbine was introduced in ·243 Winchester or ·308 Winchester (short action), and ·270 Winchester or ·30–06 (long action). It had an 18·5in barrel and weighed about 6lb. Folding-leaf sights were standard.

1988: a Desert Camo stock was introduced for the 77-R, 77-RL and 77-RLS rifles, initially in ·270 Winchester or ·30–06 only.

1989: the Mark II rifle heralded an improved trigger and a modified three-position safety system. The ejector became a fixed blade and a patented magazine floor-plate latch was set into the front face of the trigger guard. Standard 77-RL II short-action 'Light' rifles have been offered with 20in barrels in ·223 Remington, ·243 Winchester or ·308 Winchester; they weighed about 6lb.

Standard 77-R II guns, with 22in barrels and a weight of 7–7·25lb, were made additionally in 6mm Remington, ·270 Winchester, 7mm Remington Magnum, ·30–06, ·300 Winchester Magnum, or ·308 Winchester.

Open-sight 77-RS II guns were restricted to ·243 Winchester or ·308 Winchester, while a left-hand action (77-LR II) has been offered in ·270 Winchester, 7mm Remington Magnum, ·300 Winchester Magnum or ·30–06. A true Magnum (77-MAG II) was built on the basis of the previous Tropical Rifle, with an enlarged and strengthened action chambered for the ·375 H&H, ·416 Rigby or ·458 Winchester cartridges. The Mark II Magnum weighed as much as 10lb,

depending on chambering and the density of the stock-wood.

1990: a ·223 chambering option was added for the Model 77-R II, plus ·35 Whelen for the Model 77-RS II. The short-action Ultra Light Carbine was abandoned in this period.

The Model 77 Mk II All Weather Stainless (77-RP II) appeared in ·223 Remington, ·243 Winchester, ·270 Winchester, ·308 Winchester or ·30–06, plus 7mm Remington Magnum, ·300 Winchester Magnum or ·338 Winchester Magnum. The major metal parts were made of stainless steel and the straight-comb half-stock was fibreglass-reinforced DuPont Zytel.

1991: a deluxe rifle (77-EXP II) appeared, with a specially selected stock and a quarter-rib on the barrel. The barrel measured 22in and a four-round magazine was fitted. Chamberings were originally ·270 Winchester, 7mm Remington Magnum, ·300 Winchester Magnum or ·30–06.

1992: the Model 77 Mk II Varmint Rifle (or 77-NV) was introduced in ·220 Swift, ·22–250, ·243 Winchester or ·308 Winchester. It had a distinctive laminated stock, with a sharply angled pistol grip, and a flat-bellied fore-end. The guns had 26in matt-finish stainless steel barrels, measured 44in overall and weighed 9·25lb.

SAIVE

BELGIUM
Also known as 'FN' or 'FN-Saive'

The origins of these gas-operated auto-loading rifles, originally developed in the late 1930s, are obscure. Owing to the similarity of the breech-locks, it is suspected that Dieudonné Saive was familiar with the Tokarev—but it is not known whether this was due to supply of information from the Soviet Union, or if weapons captured by the Finns in the opening stages of the Winter War had been examined in Herstal.

Whatever the source of inspiration may have been, the SAFN and FAL rifles proved to be successful militarily—in the latter's case, almost unbelievably so.

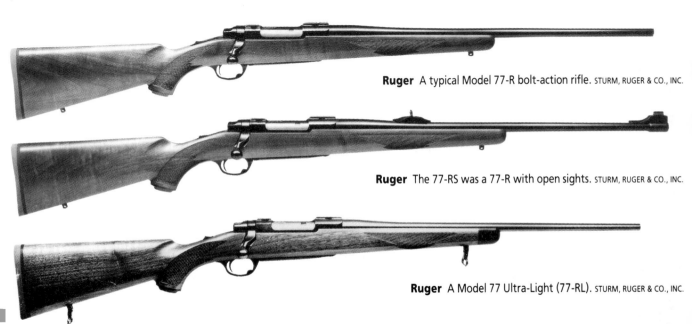

Ruger A typical Model 77-R bolt-action rifle. STURM, RUGER & CO., INC.

Ruger The 77-RS was a 77-R with open sights. STURM, RUGER & CO., INC.

Ruger A Model 77 Ultra-Light (77-RL). STURM, RUGER & CO., INC.

MILITARY WEAPONS

The Germans invaded Belgium before Saive and his team had completed preliminary work on the rifle. Many technicians subsequently escaped from Herstal (taking some blueprints with them) and eventually set to work in Britain, where the prototype SLEM—'Self-Loading, Experimental Model'—was made in about 1943.

The experimental rifles developed into the Mle 49 or SAFN rifle after the end of the Second World War; this in turn led to the Fusil Automatique Léger (or LAR, 'Light Automatic Rifle') in the early 1950s.

AUSTRALIA

L1A1

Made by the Lithgow Small Arms Factory,
New South Wales, c.1958–78.
7·62 × 51mm NATO, rimless.
Action: as Belgian FAL, below.
44·72in overall, 12·00lb laden.
20·97in barrel, 6-groove rifling; RH, concentric.
Detachable box magazine, 20 rounds.
Sliding aperture sight, graduated to 600 yards.
2,750 ft/sec with L2A2 ball cartridges.
L1A2 knife bayonet.

☆

1957: the Australian Army adopted the British 7·62mm L1A1 rifle on 1 March, preparing the government-owned factory immediately.
1959: the first Lithgow-made guns were delivered into store in March. Excepting markings, they were identical with British-issue weapons—with wood furniture and anti-fouling grooves cut in the side of the bolt carrier. The carrying handles were generally synthetic and had shallow finger grooves.
1973*: a shortened version of the basic L1A1, designated L1A1–F1, was introduced. It was about 41·95in overall, had an 18·22in barrel and weighed about 10·82lb laden.
1978: production stopped. The Steyr AUG, adopted in the mid 1980s, is superseding the L1A1 in Australian service.

L2A1

Made by the Lithgow Small Arms Factory,
New South Wales, c.1960–75.
7·62 × 51mm NATO, rimless.
Action: as Belgian FAL, below.
44·75in overall, 15·21lb laden.
20·97in barrel, 6-groove rifling; RH, concentric.
Detachable box magazine, 20 or 30 rounds.
Tangent-bar sight graduated to 1,000 yards.
2,750 ft/sec with L2A2 ball cartridges.
No bayonet.

☆

1960*: unlike Britain, the Australians have issued small quantities of a heavy-barrel FAL derivative capable of fully automatic fire. Known as the L2A1, this was originally intended for line infantry; however, operating problems caused it to be withdrawn from front-line units in favour of the heavier but much more effectual Bren Gun (L4). Surviving L2A1 rifles were re-issued to support second-line and ancillary units.

AUSTRIA

Model 58

Sturmgewehr 58 or StG.58.
Made by Steyr-Daimler-Puch AG, Steyr, 1959–75.
7·62 × 51mm NATO, rimless.
Action: as Belgian FAL, below.
1,135mm overall, 4·25kg unladen.
535mm barrel, 6-groove rifling; RH, concentric.
Detachable box magazine, 20 rounds.
Sliding aperture sight graduated to 600 metres.
838 m/sec with standard NATO ball rounds.
No bayonet.

☆

1958: the first Austrian service rifles were supplied from Fabrique Nationale, during the period in which tooling was being undertaken in Steyr. The perfected StG.58 was distinguished by a fluted sheet-metal fore-end. According to FN records, the guns originally had the muzzles threaded for a combination grenade launcher and muzzle brake/compensator, a two-piece extractor; a butt with a nose cap, and a trap in the butt plate for cleaning material. They lacked bipods and could not be loaded from chargers. Carrying handles were ribbed synthetic cylinders.
1975: production had been completed.
1981: the StG.58 was superseded by the StG.77 (Steyr AUG), the FAL-type weapons gradually passing to the reserve.

BELGIUM

Model 1949

Fusil Semi-automatique Mle.1949.
Made by Fabrique Nationale d'Armes de Guerre,
Herstal-lèz-Liège, c.1949–52.
Quantity: about 160,000.
7 × 57mm, 7·65 × 53mm, 7·9 × 57mm or ·30–06.
Gas-operated auto-loading action, locked by tilting the bolt into engagment with the receiver.
DATA FOR A BELGIAN MLE.49
·30–06, rimless.
1,110mm overall, 4·30kg unladen.
589mm barrel, 4-groove rifling; RH, concentric.
Charger-loaded integral box magazine, 10 rounds.
Tangent-leaf and aperture sight graduated to 1,500 metres.
905 m/sec with 9·7-gram bullet.
Mle.49 knife bayonet.

☆

1948: development work on the experimental British SLEM rifle (see below) was completed in Herstal and a production line had been readied.
1949: the rifle was adopted by the Belgian army as the ·30 Fusil Semi-automatique Mle.1949, though it has also been known as the SAFN ('Semi-Automatic, Fabrique Nationale'). The term ABL, often misleadingly applied, arose from the property mark—'Armée Belge Leger'—which was a combination of French ('Armée Belge') and Flemish ('Leger Belge').

The Mle.49 had a tall squared receiver, carrying the back sight and its prominent guards, and a conventional pistol-grip stock held by a single swivel-carrying band. The rear swivel lay on the under-edge of the butt. A hand guard ran from the chamber to the back sight/gas-port

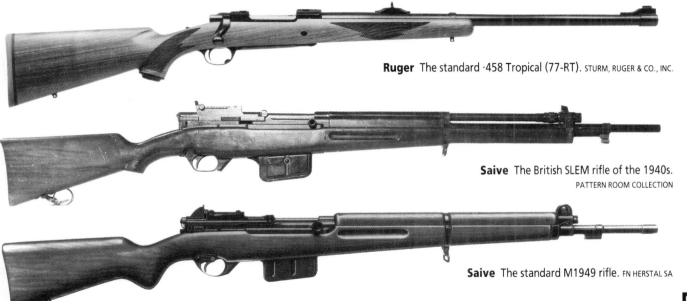

Ruger The standard ·458 Tropical (77-RT). STURM, RUGER & CO., INC.

Saive The British SLEM rifle of the 1940s.
PATTERN ROOM COLLECTION

Saive The standard M1949 rifle. FN HERSTAL SA

Carrying an L1A1 rifle with a SUIT sight,
a private of the 2nd Royal Anglian Regiment
patrols South Armagh, Northern Ireland,
in the summer of 1986.
MINISTRY OF DEFENCE

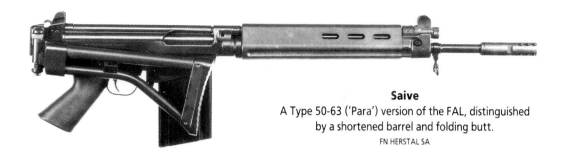

Saive
A Type 50-63 ('Para') version of the FAL, distinguished
by a shortened barrel and folding butt.
FN HERSTAL SA

SAIVE (FN) RIFLES
LESSER PATTERNS

ARGENTINA

A few thousand ·30–06 Mle 49 (SAFN) rifles were acquired in 1950, apparently for the navy. They were followed a decade later by the first FAL rifles. Substantial numbers of Types 50–00 FAL II, 50–61 Para and 50–63 Para rifles were provided from Belgium before the first licence-built guns emanated from Fábrica Militar de Armas Portatiles of Rosario, Santa Fé. A typical army rifle was marked 'FABRICA MILITAR DE ARMAS PORTATILES—ROSARIO' over 'INDUSTRIA ARGENTINA', behind the maker's encircled 'FM' on the right side of the receiver; 'F.S.L.–Cal.–7,62–002' lay on the left rear side. Argentine-made guns have been supplied to other countries in South and Central America.

¶ By 1981, about 129,680 standard and 8,460 heavy-barrel guns had been made when work in the Rosario factory ceased. The FALs have since been replaced in front-line service by the 5·56mm FARA 83.

BRAZIL

Fabrique Nationale supplied small numbers of ·30–06 SAFN in the early 1950s, apparently for the marines and navy. Small quantities of Belgian-made FAL rifles followed in the early 1960s, and a licence was granted to permit production in the government factory (Fábrica de Armas) in Itajubá under the supervision of Industria de Material Belico de Brasil ('Imbel'). FN-made rifles bore the company name on the right side of the frame above the pistol grip; 'EXERCITO BRASILEIRO' appeared in the panel milled out of the frame (on the right side above the magazine) together with the national arms, comprising a five-point star pierced by a sword.

¶ Standard FAL-type rifles were then made in Brazil as the M964 (fixed butt) and M969A1 (folding butt), the latter being issued largely to airborne forces and marines. Their markings were essentially similar to the Belgian-made originals, excepting that the maker's name on the receiver usually read 'FABRICA DE ITAJUBA—BRASIL' and 'FZ. 7.62 M 964' lay on the left above the selector lever. Brazilian guns had plain-sided receivers instead of the milled-panel FN type.

EGYPT

Fabrique Nationale supplied the Egyptian army with subtantial quantities of 7·9 × 57mm SAFN rifles in the days of King Farouk. They were later superseded by the Hakim, based on the Swedish Ljungmann rifle (q.v.). The Egyptian rifles may be recognised partly by the chambering, and also by Arabic numerals on the back sight.

GERMANY

In the late 1950s, the Federal German authorities acquired about 100,000 FN-made guns for the Bundesgrenzschutz in the days before the army (Bundesheer) was properly re-created. Known as the Gewehr 1, these served only until supplies of the Gewehr 3 (made by Rheinmetall and Heckler & Koch) became available in 1959. After a period in store, most of the German FAL-type rifles were sold to Turkey.

INDIA

About 1963, India adopted an L1A1 made under licence in the state owned Ishapur rifle factory. Known as the 'Rifle 1–A SL', it is distinguished by the *Asoka*—the national crest of four lions on a pillar-cap—on the right side of the receiver.

ISRAEL

The army acquired the first of many FAL rifles in the early 1960s, the guns remaining regulation issue until the advent of the 5·56mm M16A1 and Galil rifles. The earliest weapons were purchased directly from Fabrique Nationale, but later examples were assembled by Israeli Military Industries. These had FN-made receivers, but the remaining components were made locally. Guns emanating from IMI exhibited changes suggested by combat in desert conditions: the butt had a lower comb; the fore-end was pressed-metal, with a short finely-fluted wooden grip; the cocking handle was modified to double as a bolt-closing device; the front sight/gas plug assembly was improved; and the dismantling catch was recessed to reduce the chances of accidentally opening the receiver.

¶ Distinguishing marks included the Defence Force badge of a sword and an olive branch on a six-point Star of David above a scroll. Inspector's and property marks also appeared, the serial number commencing with the date of manufacture—e.g., '6312539' on a gun made in 1963.

MEXICO

The Belgian-pattern FAL was adopted as the standard service weapon in 1963, serving until superseded in the late 1970s by the

Heckler & Koch G3. The earliest guns were acquired from Belgium; later ones were assembled by the government factory (Fábrica de Armas) in Mexico City. They may be identified by the Mexican eagle-on-cactus badge on the side of the magazine housing, or by a 'REPÚBLICA MEXICANA' mark.

NIGERIA

The basic FAL was adopted in 1967. Most were made in Belgium, though some Enfield-made L1A1 rifles were supplied from Britain. A licence to make FALs in the Kaduna ordnance factory was purchased in the mid 1970s, superseding the Beretta BM-59 (q.v.), but no production was ever undertaken.

SOUTH AFRICA

The government obtained FAL-type rifles from Fabrique Nationale immediately after gaining independence in 1960. The earliest guns had plain muzzles without flash suppressors, and accepted a tube-hilt bayonet. They had two-piece extractors, butts with nose caps, and lacked the butt trap for cleaning equipment. The hand guard was synthetic. South African weapons were usually distinguished by a property mark comprising 'M' within 'U'.

¶ In 1963, under the terms of a licence granted by FN to the South African Armament Corporation, Pty ('Armscor'), the first indigenous rifles were delivered to the Defence Force from Lyttleton Engineering Co., Pty, of Pretoria. These were essentially similar to the Para FAL, with a tube-frame butt folding to the right. The 1974-vintage R2 was simply a shortened form of the original rifle, reducing weight by about 450gm. R1 and R2 rifles were superseded by the Galil-type R4 in the early 1980s.

USA

The US Army experimented with the perfected FAL or 'Rifle, ·30 T48' in the early 1950s. About fifteen guns were made by the High Standard Manufacturing Company of Hamden, Connecticut, in 1954; and a further 500—numbered from 4001 upward—by Harrington & Richardson of Worcester, Massachusetts, in 1955. Including the flash-hider, they measured about 44·5in overall and weighed 9·43lb with an empty magazine. The competing T44 rifle was preferred, eventually becoming the M14 (see 'Garand').

VENEZUELA

A substantial quantity of 7 × 57mm SAFN

rifles, believed to have been about 15,000, was acquired from Fabrique Nationale in 1950–1. In 1954, however, five thousand FAL rifles were acquired. They chambered a 7 × 49mm cartridge but were soon converted for 7·62 × 51mm NATO. Additional deliveries were made into the 1960s, and about 10,000 Type 50-63 Para rifles were acquired for the Guardia Nacional in 1974. These were assembled from Belgian-made components by Compaña Anonima Venezolana de Industrias Militares (CAVIM).

OTHERS

In addition to the countries listed above, the following used SAFN and FAL-type rifles—newly made or military surplus. Dates of adoption are given where known. R. Blake Stevens' trilogy of books devoted to the FAL is the indispensable source of detailed information.

¶ Argentinian FAL-type guns, from Rosario—Colombia; Honduras; Peru (FAL and FAL Para); and Uruguay (FAL and FAL Para).

¶ Australian L1A1-type guns, from Lithgow—Barbados; Fiji; Jamaica; Malaysia; New Zealand and Singapore.

¶ Belgian SAFN-type guns, from Herstal—Belgian Congo (Zaire), via the Belgian army; Colombia; Indonesia; and Luxembourg.

¶ Belgian FAL-type guns, from Herstal—Bahrain, 1968; Belgian Congo (Zaire), 1961; Burma, by way of Germany; Burundi; Cambodia (Kampuchea), 1960; Chad; Chile, 1960; Colombia; Congo People's Republic; Cuba; Dominican Republic; Dubai (United Arab Emirates); Eire; Ecuador; Ethiopia, possibly supplied by way of Chile or Colombia; Ghana; Greece (FAL and FAL Para); Haiti; Honduras; Indonesia, 1958; Kuwait (FAL and FAL Para), 1957; Lebanon, 1956; Liberia, 1962; Libya, 1955; Luxembourg; Malawi, 1974; Mauritania, apparently supplied by way of Cuba; Morocco, 1963; the Netherlands (FAL and FALO), 1961; Oman; Paraguay, 1956; Peru, FAL and FAL Para; Portugal, 1959; Qatar; Rwanda; Saudi Arabia; Syria, 1956; Tanzania; Thailand, 1961; Tunisia; Turkey, by way of Germany; and possibly Uganda.

¶ British L1A1-type guns, from Enfield—Bangladesh; Belize; Botswana; The Gambia; Ghana; Guyana; Kenya, 1966; Mauritius; Sierra Leone; Swaziland; Trinidad & Tobago; and Zambia.

¶ South African R1-type guns, from Lyttleton—Lesotho; Rhodesia (Zimbabwe); South West Africa (Namibia); Swaziland.

block, and a bayonet bar lay beneath the exposed muzzle. The magazine was loaded from chargers, suitable guides being milled in the receiver-top ahead of the back sight base. Muzzle brake/compensators were optional, and guns could be supplied to order in semi-automatic and selective-fire versions.

A sniper version with a telescope sight made by Société Belge d'Optique et d'Instruments de Précision was issued in small numbers, but was replaced first by optically-sighted FALs and then by FN-Mauser bolt-action rifles.

1952: though large-scale export orders had been fulfilled, the Mle.49 rifle proved to be unsuitable for prolonged arduous use. It was unbalanced by the height of the receiver, handled clumsily, and breakages in the trigger system sometimes led to unexpected automatic fire. Thus the Mle.49 was replaced by the FAL.

FAL

50–00, 50–63 Para and 50–64 Para patterns.
Made by Fabrique Nationale d'Armes de Guerre,
Herstal-lèz-Liège, 1953 onward.
7 × 49mm or 7·62 × 51mm.
Gas-operated auto-loading action, locked by tilting the bolt into engagment with the receiver.
DATA FOR A TYPICAL TYPE 50–64 PARA
7·62 × 51mm NATO, rimless.
1,095mm overall (845mm with stock folded),
3·90kg unladen.
533mm barrel, 6-groove rifling; RH, concentric.
Detachable box magazine, 20 rounds.
Pivoting 'L'-sight for 150 and 250 metres.
838 m/sec with standard NATO ball cartridges.
Bayonet: optional.

☆

1948: a prototype FN assault rifle, chambered for the German 7·9mm intermediate (Kurz) cartridge, was demonstrated at the company's Zutendael proving range.
1950: trials were undertaken with standard (No. 1) and 'bullpup' (No. 2) rifles, but neither was made in quantity. No. 2 was abandoned owing to its poor handling characteristics, bad balance, and concern that the firer's cheek was

too near the chamber should the case-head fail.
1951: the No.1 rifle was enlarged to chamber the semi-experimental British ·280 (7 × 49mm) cartridge. The resulting weapons had wood furniture with a ribbed fore-end, and a plain muzzle with no additional fittings. They were capable of fully-automatic fire, cyclic rate being 675 ± 25rpm.
1952: rejection of the ·280 round, principally by the US Army, persuaded FN to re-chamber the assault rifle for the ·30 T65 pattern proffered by the Americans. The work was undertaken in Liège by Dieudonné Saive and Ernest Vervier. Similar internally to the ·280 rifles, the 7·62mm (·30) pattern had a folding carrying handle and a swell-pattern wooden fore-end with a short ribbed section. The standard barrel had a six-slot compensator, and the magazine well was still cut higher on the left side than the right. Detachable bipods, flash-hiders and grenade launchers were optional; and a knife bayonet with a conventional hilt could be attached.
1953: small-scale series production began to provide guns for field trials in the principal NATO armies, and the first of a great many export orders—for Venezuela—was fulfilled. The earliest Venezuelan weapons chambered the British ·280 cartridge (7 × 49mm).
1956: the rifle was adopted by the Belgian army. It had charger guides on the receiver; a smooth muzzle with neither grenade launcher nor flash suppressor; a nose-cap butt; and a plain butt plate without a trap. A tubular bayonet doubled as a flash suppressor/compensator if necessary, and the hand guard was usually an injection-moulded plastic pattern.
1963: synthetic furniture replaced the wood pattern as standard. The fore-end generally had a groove along the lower edge to accept the legs of the bipod, even though this was rarely fitted to infantry-weight rifles. Three cooling slots were customary.
1985: a selection of FAL variants was still being offered. The standard Type 50–00 (infantry) pattern—1,090mm overall, 4·25kg empty—had nylon furniture, a fixed butt and a tubular flash suppressor. It was capable of firing fully

automatically. Finish was usually durable grey phosphating. Details of the Type 50–64 Para are given above. Apart from the folding cocking handle and a change in the position of the breech-block return spring, which was due to the folding tubular-frame butt, it was similar to the standard infantry rifle.

Type 50–63 Para (1,020mm overall or about 770mm with the butt folded) had a folding cocking handle and a 300-metre battle sight. It weighed about 3·75kg and had a 436mm barrel. The hold-open and carrying handle of the 50–64 Para were omitted.

FALO

HB or 50–41 pattern.
Made by Fabrique Nationale d'Armes de Guerre,
Herstal-lèz-Liège, 1958 onward.
7·62 × 51mm NATO, rimless.
Action: as FAL, above.
1,150mm overall, 6·00kg unladen.
533mm barrel, 6-groove rifling; RH, concentric.
Detachable box magazine, 20 or 30 rounds.
Sliding aperture sight graduated to 600 metres.
838 m/sec with standard NATO ball cartridges.
No bayonet.

☆

1958: this was a special heavy-barrel FAL, usually known as the Lourd ('heavy') pattern or—more simply—as the FALO, HB ('heavy barrel') or Type 50–41. Though it shared the action of the standard FAL series, the FALO had a sturdier hand guard, wood or synthetic furniture, and a combination flash suppressor/muzzle brake. A folding bipod was provided to suit a light support role, but the FALO has never been regarded as effectual. This has arisen partly from the lack of a readily exchangeable barrel, but largely owing to an inexplicable tendency to fire twice and then jam on the third round of automatic fire. Consequently, some users of FAL-type rifles (e.g., Britain) never purchased heavy barrel versions, while others such as Australia soon withdrew them from front-line service. Many have since seen use as sniper weapons, as their

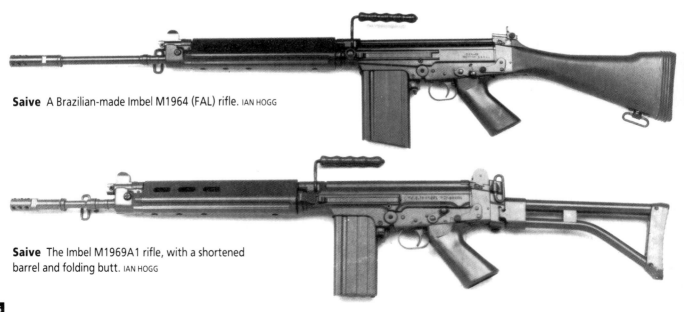

Saive A Brazilian-made Imbel M1964 (FAL) rifle. IAN HOGG

Saive The Imbel M1969A1 rifle, with a shortened barrel and folding butt. IAN HOGG weight was advantageous and fully automatic operation was unnecessary.

BRITAIN

1944: prototypes of the 'Rifle, 7·92mm, Self-Loading, Experimental Model No.1' (SLEM No. 1) were made at Enfield to a design prepared by Dieudonné Saive and emigré FN technicians attached to the Small Arms Group, Cheshunt.

1946: 2,000 SLEM-type 'Rifles, Automatic, 7·92mm' were ordered for field trials, though the order was soon rescinded. Very few rifles were ever made. They were very similar to the Mle.49 SAFN (see above), but the hand guard ran only to the barrel band, the pistol grip was much slimmer, and the back sight lacked protecting wings.

1951: the first comparative trials against the EM-2 ('Rifle No. 9 Mk 1'—see Part Two, 'Januszewski/Janson') favoured the ·280 FN rifle. Though field trials undertaken in the summer were inconclusive, progress being made in Herstal was sufficient for the adoption of the No. 9 rifle to be rescinded in October.

1953: failure of the 7·62mm EM-2 to challenge the Belgian rifle was resolved in December, when five thousand FALs were ordered from Fabrique Nationale.

L1A1

X8E1, X8E2, X8E3, X8E5, X14E1 and L1A1.
Made by the Royal Small Arms Factory, Enfield Lock, Middlesex, 1958–75 (a million?); and BSA Guns Ltd, Shirley, Warwickshire, 1958–64 (150,000).
7·62 × 51mm NATO, rimless.
Action: as Belgian FAL, above.
45·00in overall (standard butt),
11·19lb with full magazine.
21·00in barrel, 6-groove rifling; RH, concentric.
Detachable box magazine, 20 rounds.
Sliding aperture sight graduated to 600 yards.
2,750 ft/sec with L2A2 ball rounds.
L1A3 knife bayonet.
☆

1954: the first thousand rifles were delivered in two differing models. They were tested as the 'Rifle, 7·62mm, FN, BR X8E1' (open sights) and 'X8E2' (EM-2 optical sight); flash suppressors were absent. The X8E1 pattern was subsequently developed into the X8E3, which had an American-type flash suppressor; a folding cocking handle appeared on the X8E5.

1956: channels were cut in the bolt carrier to reduce the likelihood of accumulated fouling jamming the action. FN had supplied 14,530 trial guns since 1954.

1957: the X14E1 prototype was formally adopted as the 'Rifle, 7·62mm, FN, L1A1' on 1 March. Capable only of single-shot fire, the standard infantry rifle had wooden furniture and a folding cocking handle on the left side of the receiver. Charger guides were abandoned and a longitudinally slotted muzzle-brake/compensator was fitted. Four lengths of butt were made (short, standard, long and extra long) to suit individual soldiers. The thirty-round L4 (Bren Gun) magazine could be used with the L1A1 rifle if necessary.

CANADA

C1

CDN EX-1, CDN EX-2, C1, C1A1 and C1D patterns.
Made by Canadian Arsenals Ltd, Long Branch, Ontario, 1957–68.
7·62 × 51mm NATO, rimless.
Action: as Belgian FAL, above.
DATA FOR A TYPICAL C1A1
44·72in overall, 9·37lb without magazine.
21·00in barrel, 6-groove rifling; RH, concentric.
Detachable box magazine, 20 rounds.
Folding rotating aperture sight graduated to 600 yards.
2,750 ft/sec with standard NATO ball rounds.
C1 knife bayonet.
☆

1954: the first trials undertaken with the experimental EX-1 and EX-2 rifles—essentially similar to the British X8E1 and X8E2, with fixed and optical sights respectively—convinced the

Canadian authorities of their merits. About two thousand were acquired from Fabrique Nationale in 1954–5.

1955: the C1 rifle was adopted in June. It differed from the British X8E5 and X14E1 rifles (which became the L1A1) in the addition of charger guides to the receiver. It also had a unique rotating-disc back sight. The furniture was wood and a cylindrical flash suppressor was fitted. The first issues were made in 1956. A typical receiver mark—on the left side above the pistol grip—read RIFLE, 7.62MM FN (C1).

1958: a selective-fire C1, differing from the army rifle only in the selector and trigger mechanism, was adopted by the Royal Canadian Navy as the 'Rifle, 7.62mm, FN, C1D'.

1959: the rigours of service showed that the original firing pin could fail to retract into the breech block automatically if the tip was deformed, igniting the cartridge before the breech was properly locked. The adoption of a two-piece firing pin and a new plastic carrying handle advanced the designation to C1A1 (army) or C1A1D (navy, selective fire).

1984: the 7.62mm C1A1 was superseded by the 5.56mm C7 rifle (a modified M16A1).

C2

C2 and C2A1 patterns.
Made by Canadian Arsenals Ltd, Long Branch, Ontario, 1958–68.
7·62 × 51mm NATO, rimless.
Otherwise generally as C1 rifle, above, excepting dimensions (44·72in overall, 15·28lb with loaded magazine), back sight (sliding aperture graduated to 1,000 yards) and bayonet (none).
Cyclic rate was about 710rpm.
☆

1958: this was a heavyweight version of the C1, sharing the same basic characteristics but offering a unique combination fore-end/bipod with wood strips attached to the metal legs. The gas tube was exposed above the heavy barrel and a three-position selector lever appeared on the left side of the receiver above the pistol grip. The upper left side of the pistol grip was rebated to

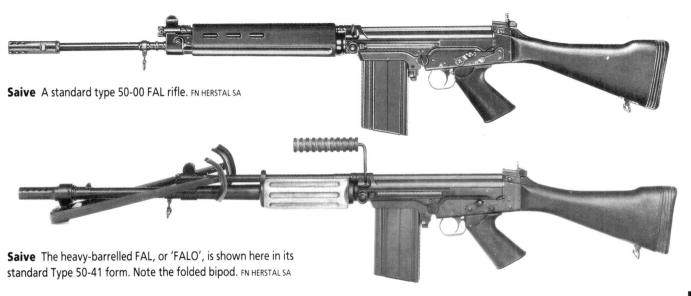

Saive A standard type 50-00 FAL rifle. FN HERSTAL SA

Saive The heavy-barrelled FAL, or 'FALO', is shown here in its standard Type 50-41 form. Note the folded bipod. FN HERSTAL SA

allow the selector to rotate. A mark such as RIFLE AUTO 7·62MM FN C2 was found on the left side of the receiver.

1960: the supersession of the original one-piece firing pin by a two-piece design, introduced with the C1A1 infantry rifle, was extended to the C2. The designation advanced to C2A1, though only the markings and the plastic carrying handle distinguished the two patterns externally.

SAKO

FINLAND

Sako was originally a government-owned repair shop, created in an old brewery in Helsinki but soon progressing to a purpose-built factory and the manufacture of new rifles. Owing to harsh conditions attached by the Soviet Union to the treaty ending the Continuation War, however, Sako was sold to the Finnish Red Cross in 1944. As production of war matériel was no longer possible, sporting rifles were substituted. The company made modified Kalashnikov (q.v.) assault rifles for the Finnish army in the 1960s, but was amalgamated with the state-owned Valmet organisation in 1987. Sako–Valmet has promoted a bolt-action TRG-21 sniper rifle, but the Finnish army has apparently preferred modified Mosin-Nagants—a cheaper solution. The TRG-21 is pictured in *Military Small Arms of the 20th Century*, p.90.

1. THE BOLT-ACTION PATTERNS

These much-modified Mausers are classified by action-length: L-461 (short), L-579 (medium) and L-61 (large). Development began in Riihimäki in 1942, work being credited to Niilo Talvenheimo. War with the USSR curtailed progress, though prototype L-42 sporters were made in 1942–4. The perfected L-46 appeared after the Second World War had ended.

The earliest Sako rifles had a spring-steel extractor dovetailed into the right side of the bolt body—originally patented by Mauser in 1890—and the bolt shroud was attached by a lug (once confined to the L-57 only).

L-46 series

Carbine, Classic Sporter, Deluxe, Heavy Barrel, Hunter, Hunter LS, L-46, L-461, L-469, M74, Standard, Super Deluxe, Super Sporter, Target, Varmint and Vixen patterns.
Made in Riihimäki by Oy Sako AB (1946–87) and Sako–Valmet Oy (1987 to date).
Chambering: see notes.
Turning-bolt action, locked by rotating two lugs on the bolt head into the receiver wall.
DATA FOR A TYPICAL L-461 VARMINT PATTERN
·222 Remington, rimless.
1,090mm overall, 3·70kg unladen.
603mm barrel; 6-groove rifling; RH, concentric.
Internal box magazine, 6 rounds.
Optical sight.
3,200 ft/sec with 50-grain bullet.

☆

1946: production began for the European market in ·22 Hornet and 7 × 33mm. The L-46 had a detachable single-column box magazine, a lugged firing pin and a trigger copied from the Winchester Model 70. Birch half stocks had low Monte Carlo combs. The bolt handle was straight, a safety lay on the left side of the bolt shroud, and the trigger guard/floor plate was a simple stamped strip.

1949: the first guns were made for the North American market in ·218 Bee and ·22 Hornet.

1951: a ·222 Remington option was added.

1952: a distinctive pivoting safety catch on the right side of the bolt shroud was substituted for the unpopular left-side pattern.

1956: a single-shot 'Bench-rest' version with a solid-bottom receiver appeared.

1958: a machined steel trigger guard/magazine floor-plate replaced the stamped-strip version.

1959: a ·222 Remington Magnum chambering was offered for the first time, but the basic short L-46 action was soon refined to become

the short-lived L-469—few of which were ever made before being abandoned in 1962.

1961: the perfected short-cartridge action was developed, work being credited to Eino Mäckinen. First produced in quantity in 1962 as the 'Vixen', the new rifle embodied many of the changes pioneered by the L-57 and L-579 described below. An internal staggered-column box magazine was fitted, the modified trigger had a vertically-moving sear, and a rocking safety lay on the right side of the receiver behind the bolt handle. The firing pin was threaded into the cocking piece, simplifying production.

1971: the original Vixen pattern was replaced by the 'Model 72'. A minor change had been made to prevent the bolt-guide rib rotating past the fully-open position behind the left locking lug, and then releasing the bolt-stop as the bolt was retracted. However, the manufacturing pattern was short-lived.

1974: a revised 'Model 74' was introduced in ·222 and ·223 Remington, as a result of attempts to rationalise the three types of action to simplify manufacture. Post-1974 L-461 rifles had the same spring-loaded extractor as the L-579 and L-61. The M74 Vixen had a 575mm barrel and weighed about 2·95kg. Monte Carlo-type butts were standard, with chequering on the pistol grip and the fore-end; the fore-end tip was a plain rounded pattern.

Super Sporters had deluxe stocks with skip-line chequering; contrasting rosewood pistol-grip caps and fore-end tips were accompanied by thin white spacers. Varmint rifles had heavy barrels and broad semi-beavertail fore-ends. They weighed about 3·85kg.

1977: the L-461 A I appeared in the ·17, ·222 and ·223 Remington chamberings, the Vixen name being dropped. The most obvious change was the adoption of a plunger-type ejector set into the bolt face. The A I PPC was made for two highly successful bench-rest rounds, initially only for the promoters of the cartridges.

The standard L-461 rifle (·17, ·222 or ·223 Remington) had a walnut half stock with a Monte Carlo comb and a solid rubber shoulder plate. Its pistol-grip and fore-end were hand-

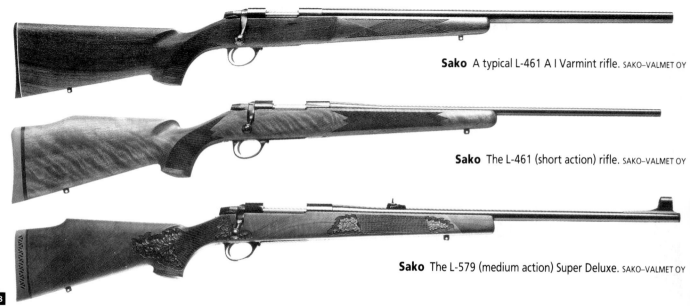

Sako A typical L-461 A I Varmint rifle. SAKO–VALMET OY

Sako The L-461 (short action) rifle. SAKO–VALMET OY

Sako The L-579 (medium action) Super Deluxe. SAKO–VALMET OY

chequered. The rifles were 1,065mm overall, had 573mm barrels and weighed 2·85kg.

The Deluxe pattern was similar, but had a selected stock with skip-line chequering and a contrasting rosewood fore-end tip. Super Deluxe guns had a hand-carved and chequered stock.

The Heavy Barrel or Varmint model lacked open sights; it was initially made only for the ·222 Remington and ·223 Remington rounds.

1983: a few fully stocked L-461 Carbines, of a pattern associated more with the L-579 and L-61 actions, were offered in ·222 Remington.

1985: a Classic Sporter was introduced in ·17, ·222 or ·223 Remington. It had disappeared two years later.

1987: the Standard rifle was renamed 'Hunter', and a Hunter LS (Laminated Stock) appeared in ·222 and ·223 Remington chamberings only. Made from 36-ply blanks, each stock had a colour and pattern of its own. A stainless-steel barrel option was added about the same time, and the ·222 L-461 Carbine was abandoned.

The Target rifle (initially in ·222 Remington only) had a heavy free-floating barrel in a deep competition-style stock, with a detachable cheek piece and four slots cut laterally through the fore-end. Unlike the outwardly similar L-579 type, L-461 Target rifles had internal six-round box magazines. They were 1,075mm long, had 603mm barrels and weighed 4·2kg.

1988: the ·17 Remington, ·22 PPC and 6mm PPC options, previously made to special order, became factory options on the Heavy Barrel and Target models, the latter handling PPC rounds only. The standard heavy-barrel PPC guns were generally special single-shot derivatives intended for bench-rest shooting. They had a stiffened solid-bottom receiver.

L-57 series

Carbine, Classic Sporter, Deluxe, Fiberclass, Forester, Handy, Heavy Barrel, Hunter, Hunter LS, L-57, L-579, M74, Standard, Super Deluxe, Super Match, Super Sporter, Target and Varmint patterns.
Made in Riihimäki by Oy Sako AB (1957–87) and Sako–Valmet Oy (1987 to date).

Chambering: see notes.
Action: as L-46, above.
DATA FOR A TYPICAL L-579 HUNTER RIFLE
7 × 64mm, rimless.
1,083mm overall, 3·10kg unladen.
573mm barrel, 4-groove rifling; RH, concentric.
Internal box magazine, 5 rounds.
Folding-leaf sight.
900 m/sec with 9-gram bullet.
☆

1957: the medium-length L-57 action was developed specifically to handle ·243 and ·308 Winchester cartridges, small quantities being made commercially in 1957–9 before teething troubles were encountered.

The L-57 was basically an L-46 lengthened to accommodate cartridges up to 70mm long. A fixed staggered-column box magazine was fitted, feed lips being machined in the underside of the receiver. The magazine floor-plate was hinged, the release catch appearing in the front of the machined-steel trigger guard bow. The catch initially protruded inside the guard, but was subsequently changed so that it could only be operated externally. A trigger with a vertically sliding sear was fitted, adapted from those used on contemporary Sako-Mausers (q.v.).

The first guns were made in standard, deluxe, fully-stocked Mannlicher and heavy barrel patterns. Most heavy-barrel examples had broad semi-beavertail fore-ends.

1961: the perfected L-579 action, developed two years previously, replaced the L-57. The initial chamberings were ·243 Winchester, ·244 Remington, 7·62 × 39mm or ·308 Winchester. The most obvious change was the addition of the Sako No.4 trigger mechanism, with an integral radial safety protruding from the receiver behind the bolt handle.

A new smooth-surface shroud was held to the the bolt by a small lug. The bolt-stop housing was retained by two short screws instead of sliding into a dovetailed mortise, and a sliding spring-loaded extractor replaced the earlier fixed claw pattern.

1964*: a Forester carbine appeared with a full length fore-end and a 510mm barrel.

1965*: a ·22–250 Remington chambering was introduced, and ·244 was abandoned.

1972: the original Foresters were replaced by the Model 72, changes being made to prevent the bolt-guide rib over-rotating. The resulting rifle did not last long.

1974: changes were made to the design of the L-579 so that all three Sako actions were essentially similar. The M74 L-579 Forester chambered ·22–250, ·243 Winchester or ·308 Winchester cartridges, had a 580mm barrel and weighed about 3·1kg. A Super Sporter was made with a deluxe stock (see L-461, above) and a heavy-barrel Varmint rifle, in the three standard chamberings, weighed about 4kg.

1977: a modernised L-579 A II action was introduced, with a streamlined bolt shroud and a plunger-type ejector in the bolt face, whereupon the Forester name disappeared. The A IIa rifles chambered ·220 Swift or ·22–250 Remington rounds; A IIb handled ·243 Winchester and ·308 Winchester patterns.

The Standard rifle (renamed 'Hunter' in 1987) had a hand-chequered Circassian walnut stock with a Monte Carlo comb, a pistol-grip and a solid rubber butt plate. The Deluxe version had a selected stock with skip-line chequering and a contrasting rosewood fore-end tip; Super Deluxe guns had a hand-carved stock.

The Carbine, 997mm overall, had a 493mm barrel and weighed about 3·1kg. A joint in the full-length Mannlicher fore-end was concealed by the barrel band. It was initially made only in ·243 Winchester.

The Heavy Barrel or Varmint rifle, with a special large-diameter barrel, was initially made only in ·220 Swift, ·22–250, ·243 Winchester or ·308 Winchester. The standard barrel measured 603mm, giving an overall length of 1,090mm and a weight averaging 3·7kg.

1980: the Classic Sporter appeared in ·243 Winchester, with a straight-comb butt.

1983: Target rifles (·308 Winchester) had a massive half-stock with a plain fore-end and a floating barrel. The guns were 1,137mm overall, had 660mm barrels, and weighed about 4·5kg. Detachable five-round magazines were standard.

Sako A long-action L-61 Finnbear from the early 1970s.

Sako An L-61 Carbine. SAKO–VALMET OY

Sako The L-61 Safari has a quarter rib on the barrel. SAKO–VALMET OY

1985: a ·308 Carbine was announced.

1986: half-stock L-579 Handy [Carbines] were made in ·22–250, ·243 Winchester, 7mm–08 or ·308 Winchester. They were 997mm overall, had 493mm barrels and weighed about 3·1kg. Handy, Hunter, Carbine and Varmint rifles could all be obtained to special order with five-round detachable box magazines.

1987: a Hunter LS (Laminated Stock) model was announced, with stocks made from 36-ply blanks. A stainless-steel barrel was introduced, plus a 7mm–08 chambering option for the Standard and Heavy Barrel rifles. The Classic Sporter was finally discontinued.

The Super Match rifle (·308 Winchester only) had a heavy competition-style half stock with a detachable cheek piece and four slots cut laterally through the fore-end. Its barrel floated freely. The special L-579 SM action had a strengthened receiver pierced only by the magazine feed-way and ejection port. A ten-round detachable box magazine was standard.

1988: the last of the Standard and Heavy Barrel rifles chambered for ·220 Swift were sold.

1989: L-579 Fiberclass rifles were introduced in ·22–250, ·243 Winchester, 7mm–08 and ·308 Winchester.

L-61 series

··

Carbine, Classic Sporter, Deluxe, Fiberclass, Finnbear, Handy, Handy Fiber, Hunter, Hunter LS, L-61, M74, Safari, Standard, Super Deluxe and Super Sporter patterns.

Made in Riihimäki by Oy Sako AB (1961–87) and Sako–Valmet Oy (1987 to date).

Chambering: see notes.

Action: as L-46, above, with an additional lug on the bolt.

DATA FOR A TYPICAL L-61R HANDY FIBER RIFLE

·30–06, rimless.

1,025mm overall, 3·25kg unladen.

490mm barrel, 4-groove rifling; RH, concentric.

Internal box magazine, 5 rounds.

Folding-leaf sight on ramp.

2,970 ft/sec with 150-grain bullet.

☆

1960: development of the L-61 began after demands for greater power emanated from North America. A third locking lug was added on the bolt body, ahead of the handle. Announced for ·30–06 and ·300 H&H Magnum only, it replaced the earlier 'Sako Mauser' or 'USA Mauser' rifles. The L-61 was made in standard, deluxe and Mannlicher patterns.

1963*: ·264 Winchester Magnum and ·338 Winchester Magnum options were introduced.

1964: a 7mm Remington Magnum version was introduced.

1965: ·300 Winchester Magnum chamberings were announced.

1970*: a few carbines were built on the L-61 action, with full-length Mannlicher stocks and 510mm barrels.

1972: a new (M72) version of the Finnbear was created to prevent the bolt-guide rib over-rotating as the bolt was operated. Open back sights were fitted to all but heavy-barrel guns.

1974: a rationalised manufacturing pattern was approved to simplify production. The changes were comparatively minor. M74 L-61 Finnbear rifles had 610mm barrels accepting ·25–06, ·270 Winchester, 7mm Remington Magnum, ·300 Winchester Magnum, ·30–06, ·338 Winchester Magnum or ·375 H&H Magnum ammunition. The standard stocks had Monte Carlo combs, chequering on the pistol grip and fore-end, and a plain rounded fore-end tip; Super Sporter stocks had Monte Carlo combs, skip-line chequering, and white spacers accompanying the pistol-grip cap and oblique-cut rosewood fore-end tip. A few heavy-barrel Varmint rifles,

SAKO
LESSER PATTERNS

Standard Sako rifles were imported by Firearms International Corporation of Washington, DC, and the Garcia Sporting Arms Corporation of Teaneck, New Jersey.

¶ The standard Sako No.4 trigger unit had a vertically sliding sear, which was more susceptible to binding than radial designs; consequently, few Sako actions stocked in the USA retained the original trigger.

Browning of Morgan, Utah, sold Sako L-461 and L-579 rifles in 1963–74, chambered at varying times for ·222 Remington, ·222 Remington Magnum, ·22–250, ·243 Winchester, ·264 Winchester Magnum, ·284 Winchester Magnum or ·308 Winchester.

Colt of Hartford, Connecticut, marketed the L-57 Coltsman rifle in the 1957–61 era. The Standard rifle had a straight-comb butt and a rounded fore-end. The Deluxe pattern was similar, but the wood offered better quality and a Monte Carlo butt was used. The Custom version had skip-line chequering and a ventilated shoulder pad; the separate pistol-grip cap and obliquely cut fore-end tip were rosewood. Chamberings were restricted to ·243 or ·308 Winchester.

¶ The L-461, L-579 or L-61 Coltsman (1963–5) were available in Standard or Custom patterns. Monte Carlo combs and cheek pieces were standard, but the Custom pattern had skip-line instead of plain chequering. It had a rosewood pistol-grip cap and fore-end tip; standard stocks simply had a plastic grip cap. Guns were available in ·222 Remington, ·222 Remington Magnum, ·223 Remington (L-461); ·243 Winchester or ·308 Winchester (L-579); and ·264 Winchester Magnum, ·270 Winchester, ·30–06 or ·300 H&H Magnum (L-61).

Harrington & Richardson of Worcester, Massachusetts, made extensive use of Sako actions. Chronologically, the series began with the Model 300, offered in 1965–82 on the L-469, L-579 or L-461 action.

Chamberings included ·22–250 (L-461), ·243 Winchester (L-579), ·270 Winchester (L-61), ·30–06 (L-61) or ·308 (L-579), plus 7mm Remington or ·300 Winchester Magnums (both L-61). A 1974-pattern gun was 42·5in overall, had a 22·0in barrel and weighed 7·75lb. It had a Williams ramp sight with a folding leaf, and an American-style stock with a roll-over comb. The fore-end tip and pistol-grip cap were usually rosewood.

¶ The Model 301 (1967–82) was similar to the M300, but had a full-length stock; it measured 39in overall, had an 18in barrel and weighed 7·25lb. The same cartridges were chambered, excepting ·22–250.

¶ The Model 317 Ultra Wildcat, introduced in 1968 on the L-461 action, was originally chambered for the ·17 Remington round—though ·17/223, ·222 and ·223 options were added before the model was discontinued in 1976. Standard rifles had Monte Carlo-pattern stocks with conventional chequering, plus rosewood pistol-grip caps and fore-end tips. The Model 317P had a better stock with basket-weave chequering.

¶ The Model 333 (1974 only) was built on the Sako L-61 action, chambering 7mm Remington Magnum or ·30–06 cartridges only. Its plain ambidexterous beech stock had neither chequering nor a cheek piece.

Howa Firearms Company of Nagoya has made a near-facsimile of the Sako action for some years, supplying actions to Weatherby to form the Vanguard series. The guns are listed in the Howa section. Some were sold in North America by the American Import Company of San Francisco, as the ·30–06 'Dickson Golden Bear FSD-43'.

Marlin of New Haven, Connecticut, offered the Model 322 rifle in the 1954–7 period. Built on a standard Sako L-46 action chambered for the ·222 Remington cartridge, it had a 24in Marlin barrel with Micro-Groove rifling and weighed 7·13lb. Its American-made stock had a straight comb and a rounded

fore-end tip. White spacers accompanied the plastic shoulder plates and pistol-grip caps, whilst the chequered panels on the pistol grip and fore-end had a double-line border. A two-position aperture sight (for 100 and 200 yards) appeared on the receiver bridge.

¶ Rifling in the 322-pattern barrel wore too quickly to be acceptable, so a Model 422 Varmint King—with a stainless-steel barrel—appeared in 1956. It could be identified by its Monte Carlo butt. Work ceased in 1958 after 5,860 M322 and a mere 350 M422 rifles had been made.

Mossberg of North Haven, Connecticut, purchased the remaining Smith & Wesson (q.v.) Model 1500 rifles in 1985, selling them for several years. The Model 1500 Mountaineer and Varmint Deluxe, plus the Model 1700LS, are described below.

¶ A Model 1550 was introduced in 1986, with a detachable box magazine; it chambered ·243 Winchester, ·270 Winchester or ·30–06 rounds only. Model 1500 Varmint rifles were offered with a parkerised finish in this period.

¶ The Model 1500 Mountaineer Grade I appeared in 1987 with a straight-comb hardwood stock, guns with walnut Monte Carlo stocks being classed as 'Grade II'. Open sights became optional on both grades.

Sears, Roebuck & Co., Inc. of Chicago, Illinois, sold a few 'Model 52' rifles in ·222 Remington in the mid 1950s. These were made by Marlin on the Sako L-46 action. Apart from markings, they were essentially similar to the Marlin Model 322.

Smith & Wesson of Springfield, Massachusetts, acquired substantial quantities of 1974-type Sako actions from 1979 onward, probably to allow Sako to introduce new patterns unencumbered by stocks of obsolescent parts. Built on the L-579 or L-61 action, the guns were stocked and finished in North America to be sold as the 'Model 1500' in ·243 (L-579), ·270, 7mm Remington Magnum or ·30–06 (all L-61). Standard rifles had straight-comb stocks

with rounded fore-ends. Conventional chequering graced the pistol grip and the sides of the fore-end. A 22in barrel was standard in all versions excepting 7mm Remington Magnum (24in), giving a length of 42–42·5in and a weight of 7·5–7·8lb. A Williams ramp back sight was customary.

¶ The Deluxe rifle had a jewelled bolt, a scroll on the magazine floor plate, an S&W pistol-grip cap inlay, and skip-line chequering. No sights were furnished.

¶ The range was enlarged in the early 1980s, by which time the standard Model 1500 was being chambered for ·222 or ·223 Remington (L-461 action); ·243 Winchester or ·308 Winchester (L-579); and ·25–06 Remington, ·270 Winchester, 7mm Remington Magnum, ·300 Winchester Magnum or ·30–06 (L-61). A walnut Monte Carlo stock was used. The Model 1500 Deluxe lacked open sights, but had a jewelled bolt, a scroll on the floor plate, an S&W pistol-grip cap, and skip-line chequering.

¶ Introduced in 1982 on the L-461 action, the Model 1500 Varmint Deluxe chambered ·222, ·22–250 or ·223 Remington ammunition. It shared the deluxe-pattern Monte Carlo stock and weighed about 9·3lb.

¶ The 1983-vintage Model 1500 Mountaineer was little more than a standard rifle with a satin finished stock and a straight-comb butt. It was offered in ·223 Remington (L-461 action), ·243 Winchester (L-579), ·270 Winchester, 7mm Remington Magnum or ·30–06 (all L-61).

¶ Another of the 1983 patterns, the Model 1700LS Classic Hunter was a version of the standard M1500 with a straight comb and a schnabel-tipped fore-end. The hand-cut chequering was divided into panels by sinuous ribands. A detachable five-round box magazine was fitted. Chamberings were restricted to ·243 Winchester (L-579 action), or ·270 Winchester and ·30–06 (L-61).

¶ In the mid 1980s, however, S&W decided to concentrate on handguns (q.v.) and sold the remaining rifles to Mossberg (q.v.).

with broad fore-ends, were made in ·25–06 and a thousand special 7mm Remington Magnum 'Golden Anniversary Model' rifles were created to celebrate Sako's fiftieth birthday.

1978: a new-pattern rifle appeared, with a streamlined bolt shroud and a bolt-mounted ejector. The Finnbear name was dropped. The new rifle was known to the factory as 'L-61 A V'—i.e., the fifth action—and existed in three actions: right-hand (L-61R), left-hand (L-61L, introduced in 1987) and magnum (L-61R Mag).

The earliest 'A V' rifles were chambered for ·25–06 Remington, ·270 Winchester, ·30–06 or 9·3 × 62mm; L-61 A V Mag accepted the 7mm Remington, ·300 Winchester, ·338 Winchester or ·375 H&H magnum rounds. The guns had 580mm barrels (620mm for Magnums) and measured 1,100mm (1,150mm) overall. Weight ranged from 3·3 to 3·7kg, depending on barrel length and stock-wood density.

The half stock had a Monte Carlo comb and a rubber butt plate, with hand-cut chequering on the pistol grip and fore-end. A recoil bolt ran through the stock beneath the chamber. Deluxe and Super Deluxe rifles were similar, but had selected stocks with skip-line chequering and a contrasting rosewood fore-end tip; Super Deluxe stocks usually exhibited hand-carved oak leaves.

The Carbine (L-61R only) was stocked to the muzzle and had a barrel band covering the joint in the fore-end. It was available in ·270 Winchester and ·30–06, was about 1,025mm long, had a 490mm barrel and weighed 3·3kg.

1980: the L-61 Classic Sporter appeared for the ·270 Winchester, 7mm Remington Magnum or ·30–06 rounds. A few Heavy Barrel rifles were chambered for ·25–06 or 7mm Remington Magnum, but had been discontinued by 1983. Substantial quantities of the 'Finnsport 2700' seem to have been made in this era to dispose of pre-1977 actions. Chambered for the ·270 Winchester, 7mm Remington Magnum, ·300 Winchester Magnum or ·30–06 cartridges, they had plain stocks and 610mm barrels. Weight averaged 3·65kg.

1981: the Safari model (L-61R Magnum) was chambered for several popular cartridges: 7mm Remington, ·300 Winchester, ·338 Winchester or ·375 H&H Magnums. The butt had a straight comb, two transverse recoil bolts ran through the stock, and an Express back sight lay above the barrel on a traditional quarter-rib. A typical rifle was 1,100mm overall, with a 520mm barrel and an unladen weight of about 4·2kg.

1984: the Fiberclass Sporter, in ordinary or magnum actions, had a charcoal-grey synthetic stock with a textured finish and a straight comb. It was initially offered in ·25–06, ·270 Winchester, 7mm Remington Magnum, ·300 Winchester Magnum, ·30–06, ·338 Winchester Magnum or ·375 H&H Magnum.

1985: ·338 Winchester and ·375 H&H magnum options were added to the Carbine chamberings.

1986: the half-stocked L-61R Handy (or 'Hunter Lightweight') carbine appeared, chambered for the ·25–06, 6·5 × 55mm, ·270 Winchester, 7 × 64mm, ·30–06 or 9·3 × 62mm rounds. A Handy Fiber version was also made. Synthetic stocks had a straight comb, whereas wooden examples had a Monte Carlo pattern.

1987: the Hunter LS (L-61R or L-61R Magnum) had a multi-layer stock blank. A stainless-steel barrel option was introduced, together with new 6·5 × 55mm or 7 × 64mm chamberings. The last L-61 Classic Sporters were sold in this era.

1989: a ·300 Weatherby Magnum option was added to the Hunter series, a ·280 Remington version of the Fiberclass rifle appeared, and the ·300 Winchester Magnum Safari was dropped.

1990: ·300 Winchester Magnum L-61 Carbines were introduced.

1991: ·416 Remington Magnum chamberings were offered for Fiberclass, Hunter and Safari.

Note: 'Hunter Lightweight' rifles were allegedly introduced in the mid 1980s. In the absence of confirmation from Sako literature, they are assumed to have been nothing other than refinements of the standard guns.

2. THE LEVER-ACTION PATTERNS

These were introduced to compete with the American rifles that had a stranglehold on the European market. They were never as successful as the Sako bolt-action guns, owing partly to robust competition and partly to high price.

VL-63

Finnwolf, VL-63 and VL-73 patterns.
Made by Oy Sako AB, Riihimäki (1962–75).
·243 Winchester or ·308 Winchester.
Lever action, locked by rotating lugs on the bolt into the receiver walls.
DATA FOR A TYPICAL RIFLE
·243 Winchester, rimless.
1,079mm overall, 3·06kg unladen.
583mm barrel, 4-groove rifling; RH, concentric.
Detachable box magazine, 4 rounds.
Optical sight.
3,070 ft/sec with 100-grain bullet.

☆

1962: developed in 1959–62, this lever-action rifle fed from a box to allow spitzer cartridges to be used. A rack-and-pinion mechanism revolved the bolt, and a lateral safety bolt ran through the breech-lever web behind the trigger.

Also known as the VL-63, after the year in which it was introduced, the Finnwolf had a one-piece half stock with a Monte Carlo comb and a right- or left-hand cheek piece. Hand-cut chequering graced the pistol grip and fore-end. The single-column magazine protruded slightly beneath the stock.

1973: the VL-73 was a modified gun with a four-round staggered-column magazine fitting flush with the stock.

1975: production ceased.

SAUER

GERMANY
Including 'SIG-Sauer'

Sauer & Sohn, after undertaking sub-contract work for Weatherby (q.v.), developed a unique bolt with three locking flaps retracting into the cylindrical body as the bolt handle rose. As the handle turned down into its seat on the return

SAKO–VALMET OY

Sako L-61 Target rifles have detachable box magazines. This is an early example.

Sako An L-61 Deluxe rifle, with select woodwork. SAKO–VALMET OY

Sauer A Model 90 Magnum rifle, with open sights. J.P. SAUER & SOHN

stroke, the flaps were cammed outward into the receiver wall. This allowed the surface of the bolt to be entirely smooth, greatly simplifying the machining of the receiver.

Owing to the position of the locking flaps behind the magazine well, placing much of the bolt under compressive stress at the moment of firing, head-space problems were predicted when the first guns appeared. The fears soon proved to be groundless.

BELGIUM

FN Herstal SA made a small quantity of FN-Sauer rifles in 1979–84. Based on the Sauer Model 80, the Belgian rifle was distinguished by a massive forged-steel receiver separating the fore-end from the hog's back butt. The pistol grip and fore-end were chequered, and a ventilated rubber butt plate was standard. The chamberings included ·270 Winchester, 7 × 64mm, 7mm Remington Magnum, ·30–06, ·300 Winchester Magnum and 8 × 68mm S.

GERMANY

Models 80 and 90

Junior, Magnum, Medium, Safari, Standard, Stutzen
and Stutzen Junior patterns.
Made by J.P. Sauer & Sohn, Eckenförde/Holstein.
Chambering: see notes.
Non-rotary bolt action, locked by three retractable lugs
engaging the receiver behind the magazine well.
DATA FOR A TYPICAL MODEL 90 MAGNUM
9·3 × 64mm Brenneke, rimless.
1,180mm overall, 3·62kg unladen.
660mm barrel, 4-groove twist; RH, concentric.
Detachable box magazine, 3 rounds.
Folding leaf sight.
820 m/sec with 18·5-gram bullet.
☆

1973: the rifles had the patented bolt, designed in 1970–2. A cocking indicator appeared in the bottom of the bolt-way, a loaded-chamber indicating pin lay on the left side of the breech, and a sliding shotgun-pattern safety could be

found on the upper tang behind the bolt shroud.

The standard medium-action Model 80 was made for ·25–06, ·270 Winchester or ·30–06. A similar Model 80 Magnum chambered 7mm Remington or ·300 Winchester rounds, a ·458 Winchester 'Super Magnum' also being built on the basic mechanism. A typical medium-action rifle was 1,110mm long, had a 610mm barrel, and weighed about 3·6kg.

1974: a short-action rifle was introduced for ·22–250, ·243 Winchester or ·308 Winchester.

1982: the new standard pattern—the 570mm-barrelled Model 90 Medium—chambered ·270 Winchester, 7 × 64mm or ·30–06 cartridges. It was about 1,100mm long and weighed 3·4kg. The selected walnut stock had a rosewood pistol-grip cap and fore-end tip. Comb and cheek piece followed classical German hog's back form, while a ventilated rubber shoulder plate was fitted. Swivels lay on the barrel ahead of the fore-end tip and under the butt.

Stutzen were Medium rifles with full-length Mannlicher stocks. They were 1,040mm long, had 510mm barrels and weighed 3·5kg.

The Model 90 Junior, available only in ·22–250 Remington, ·243 and ·308 Winchester, was about 20mm shorter in the butt than the standard medium-length pattern. It was 1,080mm long and weighed 3·3kg. A Stutzen Junior was also made, with a 510mm barrel and an overall length of 1,020mm.

Sauer 90 Magnum rifles were chambered for 6·5 × 68mm, 7mm Remington Magnum, ·300 Weatherby Magnum, ·300 Winchester Magnum, 8 × 68mm S, ·375 H&H Magnum or 9·3 × 64mm Brenneke. Barrels measured 660mm, excepting for the 600mm ·375 pattern.

Available only in ·458 Winchester Magnum, the Model 90 Safari had a strengthened stock and two transverse recoil bolts to handle recoil. A typical rifle was 1,140mm long, had a 600mm barrel and weighed 4·8kg.

1983*: ·222 Remington options appeared for the Models 90 Junior and Junior Stutzen, whilst 6·5 × 57mm and 9·3 × 62mm were added for all standard Medium-action guns.

1986*: ·222 and ·22–250 were abandoned.

SSG 2000

Sniper rifle: Scharfschützengewehr.
Made by J.P. Sauer & Sohn, Eckenförde/Holstein.
·223 Remington, 7·5 × 55mm, ·300 Weatherby
Magnum or ·308 Winchester.
Action: as Model 80, above.
DATA FOR A TYPICAL EXAMPLE
7·5 × 55mm, rimless.
1,210mm overall, 6·62kg with sight.
610mm barrel, 4-groove twist; RH, concentric.
Detachable box magazine, 4 rounds.
Optical sight.
805 m/sec with 11·6-gram bullet.

1983: introduced to provide SIG with a sniper rifle, this was built on a Model 90 action. Its heavy barrel ended in a slotted compensator. The competition-type thumb-hole half stock had a separate comb, controlled by a thumb wheel, and an adjustable shoulder plate. An accessory rail was let into the underside of the deep angular fore-end; the pistol grip and the sides of the fore-end were stippled to improve grip.

Guns were supplied with Zeiss Diatal ZA 8 × 56mm or Schmidt & Bender 1·5–6 × 42mm telescope sights. Among the accessories were butt-spacers, tripods and mirage bands.

Model 200

Europa, Lux, Lux E, Standard and USA patterns.
Made by J.P. Sauer & Sohn, Eckenförde/Holstein.
Chambering: see notes.
Turning-bolt action, locked by rotating multiple lugs
into the barrel extension.
DATA FOR A TYPICAL STEEL-RECEIVER MAGNUM
6·5 × 68mm, rimless.
1,180mm overall, 3·78kg unladen.
650mm barrel, 4-groove twist; RH, concentric.
Detachable box magazine, 4 rounds.
Folding leaf sight.
1,150 m/sec with 6-gram bullet.
☆

1986: the cylindrical bolt of this interesting rifle carried two banks of three lugs on a reduced-diameter head, locking directly into the barrel

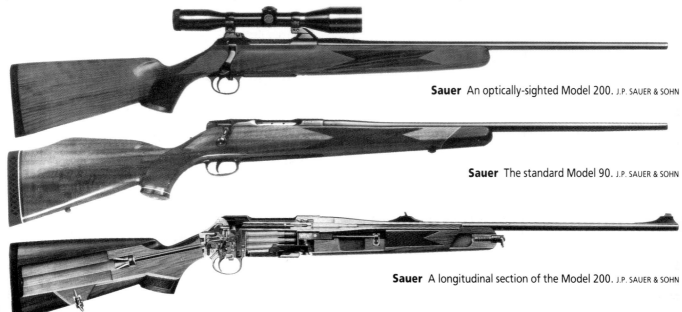

Sauer An optically-sighted Model 200. J.P. SAUER & SOHN

Sauer The standard Model 90. J.P. SAUER & SOHN

Sauer A longitudinal section of the Model 200. J.P. SAUER & SOHN

extension to isolate the receiver from stress. This allowed an optional alloy receiver to be offered. Three large cap-head bolts clamped the barrel into the receiver ring, facilitating a change of calibre. The magazine-release catch was recessed into the floor plate, the safety catch lay in the front web of the trigger guard, and an indicator protruded from the back of the bolt shroud when the striker was cocked. The trigger could be replaced by an optional 'set' system with a button substituting for an additional lever.

Butt and fore-end were separated by a sliver of receiver-metal beneath the bolt handle, tenons on the wood engaging under-cut edges in the receiver shoulder. The butt was retained by a bolt that ran up through the pistol grip and into the receiver. The spatulate bolt handle could be replaced with an optional rounded alternative, and the front sling swivel bush was screwed horizontally into the fore-end tip.

Assuming the relevant barrel, magazine and bolt were available, chamberings were easily exchanged. The Group I rifles handled ·243 Winchester, ·25–06 Remington, 6·5 × 55mm, 6·5 × 57mm, ·270 Winchester, 7 × 64mm, ·30–06, ·308 Winchester or 9·3 × 62mm. Bolts were common to all options excepting ·243; magazines, to all but ·243 and ·308 (which share case-head dimensions) plus 9·3 × 62mm.

The Group II magazine was common to all chamberings. However, bolt IIa handled 6·5 × 68mm and 8 × 68mm S, while bolt IIb was confined to the 7mm Remington, ·300 Winchester or ·300 Weatherby Magnum.

Standard rifles had a straight-comb walnut butt and a simple fore-end with a plain rounded tip, though synthetic carbon fibre patterns have also been made. The pistol grip and fore-end were chequered; the shoulder plate was solid rubber. The 200 Lux and Lux E patterns were identical with the standard guns, excepting for their selected woodwork. The Lux E was engraved in any of seven basic styles; Lux rifles also had gold-plated triggers and jewelled bolts.

Sauer's 200 Europa models (sometimes listed as 'Europe') had low hog's back combs and German-style cheek pieces; Europa Lux and Lux

E guns also had rosewood schnabel fore-end tips. The 200 USA was basically a Europa with a Monte Carlo comb and cheek piece. Its fore-end was a plain round-tip pattern.

USA

Sauer rifles were marketed exclusively by Colt in 1973–85. The Colt-Sauer Rifle (·25–06 Remington, ·270 Winchester, 7mm Remington Magnum, ·30–06 or ·300 Winchester Magnum) had an American-type walnut stock with a Monte Carlo comb. The rosewood pistol-grip cap and fore-end tip, plus the rubber shoulder pad, were accompanied by white spacers. A ·300 Weatherby Magnum option was added about 1979.

Colt-Sauer Short Action Rifles were similar, but chambered ·22–250 Remington, ·243 Winchester or ·308 Winchester ammunition. The Colt-Sauer Grand African Rifle, offered in ·458 Winchester only, had a stock of dense-grain bubinga wood. Though little larger than the standard guns, it weighed 4·75kg or more. Grand Alaskan rifles were otherwise-standard examples chambering ·375 H&H Magnum.

SAVAGE

UNITED STATES OF AMERICA

1887: Arthur Savage's first patent was granted in July to protect a Peabody-Martini rifle with a tube magazine in the butt. Prototypes were made in ·45–70 and ·44–40, but hinged-block actions were unsuited to magazine feed.
1889: Savage lodged a patent application to protect an improved lever-action mechanism.
1892: two rifles took part in US Army trials. They had 34in barrels, and nine-round rotary magazines with radial-arm followers. They were not good enough to beat the Krag-Jørgensen.
1893: in February, Savage received a patent protecting a refined magazine in which each cartridge was carried in a separate cradle.
1894: the inventor and his backers incorporated

the Savage Repeating Arms Company in Utica.
1897: the Savage Arms Company was formed, remaining independent until its assets were acquired by Driggs-Seabury Ordnance in 1915.

1. THE BOLT-ACTION PATTERNS

The first rifle suitable for powerful centre-fire cartridges was introduced soon after the First World War had ended. It was an adaption of the Mauser action, with two opposed lugs on the bolt head, but was not especially successful. The replacement was the Model 40, apparently designed by Nicholas Brewer—one of the many firearms designers whose contributions have passed largely unsung.

This rifle carried its locking lugs on a sleeve around the rear of the bolt body, simplifying manufacture though theoretically objectionable owing to the compression of the bolt body as the gun fired.

Centre-fire chamberings were also offered in the Models 19 and 23, which incorporated a sleeve with the lugs (and the bolt handle) at the mid point of the bolt body. This action was only suitable for short cartridges.

The first post-war rifles formed the Stevens 322/325/330 series, designed for inexpensive production. They incorporated a variation of the Krag-Jørgensen bolt with one lug on the head and a secondary lock at the rear of the body.

Savage's perfected high-power rifle, another Brewer design, appeared in 1958. Though its twin-lug bolt was an adapted Mauser, the Model 110 had special features of its own. Easily made, if complicated, the action operated smoothly and was inherently safe. The ready availability of barrelled actions contributed greatly to success.

Models 19 and 23
••
19H, 23B, 23C and 23D patterns.
Made by the Savage Arms Company, Utica, New York, 1923–4.

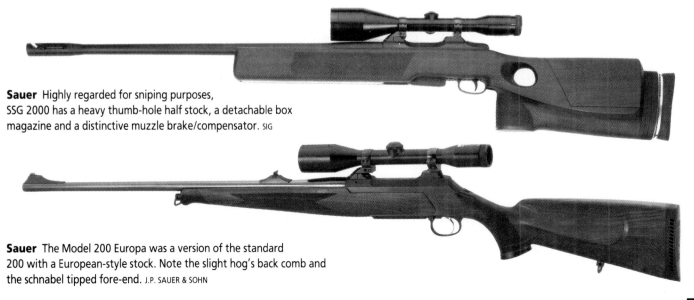

Sauer Highly regarded for sniping purposes, SSG 2000 has a heavy thumb-hole half stock, a detachable box magazine and a distinctive muzzle brake/compensator. SIG

Sauer The Model 200 Europa was a version of the standard 200 with a European-style stock. Note the slight hog's back comb and the schnabel tipped fore-end. J.P. SAUER & SOHN

·22 Hornet, ·25–20 Winchester or ·32–20 Winchester.
Turning-bolt action with two lugs on the bolt sleeve locking into the mid-point of the receiver.
DATA FOR A TYPICAL EXAMPLE
·22 Hornet, rimmed.
45·50in overall, 6·45lb unladen.
25·00in barrel, 6-groove rifling; RH, concentric.
Detachable box magazine, 5 rounds.
Spring-leaf and elevator sight.
2,690 ft/sec with 45-grain bullet.

☆

1919: locked by lugs on a sleeve mid-way along the bolt body, this action was originally intended to handle ·22 rimfire ammunition. The resulting target rifle could be distinguished by the tubular receiver with a port cut into the upper surface, ejection being upward and to the right.

1923: an improved sporting version of the Model 19 action was introduced to handle rimfire and low-power centre-fire ammunition. The Model 23A was a ·22 rimfire, 23B was expressly chambered for ·25–20 Winchester, and 23C fired ·32–20 Winchester cartridges. The guns had an oval port in the side of the tubular receiver (ejection being more lateral than upward); a safety on the receiver behind the bolt handle; and a plain-comb pistol-grip butt with a slender schnabel-tip fore-end.

1933: the handling qualities of the 1923-type guns were improved by chequering the pistol grip, deepening the round-tip fore-end, and adding swivels to the underside of the stock. The Models 19H and 23D were introduced in this period for the ·22 Hornet cartridge, apparently sharing the 1923-type action. The 19H had an adjustable aperture back sight, whereas the 23D had the open sporting pattern.

1941: production stopped at the end of the year, owing to the declaration of war on Japan immediately after the attack on Pearl Harbor.

1945: small-scale assembly began again, though only a few Model 23B and 23C rifles were made. Model 23D, the most popular '23'-type centre-fire, lasted until 1947—though it is unlikely that any major components had been made since the beginning of 1942.

Model 20

Made by the Savage Arms Company, Utica, New York, 1920–9.
·250 Savage or ·300 Savage only.
Turning-bolt action with two lugs on the bolt head locking into the receiver behind the chamber.
DATA FOR A TYPICAL PRE-1926 EXAMPLE
·300 Savage, rimless.
About 45·50in overall, 6·03lb unladen.
24·00in barrel, 6-groove rifling; RH, concentric.
Internal box magazine, 5 rounds.
Spring-leaf and elevator sight.
2,670 ft/sec with 150-grain bullet.

☆

1920: production of this Mauser-type sporter began. Offered only in ·250 (22in round barrel) and ·300 (24in barrel), it had a one-piece stock with a pistol-grip butt and a straight comb. The slender fore-end tapered to a schnabel tip. The bolt handle was angled slightly back to improve handling characteristics, but the rifle was not especially popular and did not sell well.

1926: the shorter barrel option was abandoned. The improved stock had a chequered pistol grip and a small chequered panel on the fore-end. Post-1926 rifles often had sling eyes under the stock and a Lyman sight on the bolt shroud.

1928: production ceased in favour of the Model 40, though assembly continued for a while.

Models 40 and 45

'Super Sporters'.
Made by the Savage Arms Company, Utica, New York, 1928–40.
·250 Savage, ·300 Savage, ·30–30 WCF or ·30–06.
Turning-bolt action with two lugs on a sleeve engaging the receiver behind the magazine well.
DATA FOR A TYPICAL EXAMPLE
·30–30 Winchester, rimmed.
About 43·25in overall, 7·40lb unladen.
22·00in barrel, 6-groove rifling; RH, concentric.
Detachable box magazine, 5 rounds.
Spring-leaf and elevator sight.
2,410 ft/sec with 150-grain bullet.

☆

1928: this enlargement of the sleeve-lock Model 23, with the lugs towards the back of the bolt body instead of centred, handled some of the most powerful medium-calibre sporting cartridges available in the late 1920s.

The Model 40 had a distinctively tubular receiver with the bolt-handle knob directly above the trigger. A small safety catch appeared on the right side of the action behind the bolt handle, and the magazine button protruded from the stock beneath the ejection port. The plain wooden stock had a straight comb, a pistol grip, and a tapering schnabel-tip fore-end. Barrels measured 22in for ·250 Savage and ·30–30 Winchester, or 24in for ·300 Savage and ·30–06 Springfield.

The Model 45 Super Sporter was a deluxe pattern with chequering on the pistol grip and fore-end. A Lyman No. 40 aperture sight on the receiver usually supplemented the open sights.

1940: as the Savage 'Super Sporters' were unprepossessing, lacking the refinement of rival designs such as the Remington Model 30S and Winchester Model 70, they were abandoned after a comparatively short and unsuccessful production life.

Model 340

322, 325, 330, 340, 340C, 340S, 342 and 342S patterns.
Made by the Savage Arms Company, Utica, New York, and Westfield, Massachusetts, 1957–85.
Quantity: 100,000?
·22 Hornet, ·222 Remington, ·223 Remington, ·225 Winchester or ·30–30 Winchester.
Turning-bolt action with one lug on the bolt head locking into the receiver behind the chamber, and an auxiliary lug at the rear of the bolt body.
DATA FOR A TYPICAL EXAMPLE
·222 Remington, rimless.
About 45·50in overall, 7·35lb unladen.
24·00in barrel, 6-groove rifling; RH, concentric.
Detachable box magazine, 4 rounds.
Spring-leaf and elevator sight.
3,200 ft/sec with 50-grain bullet.

☆

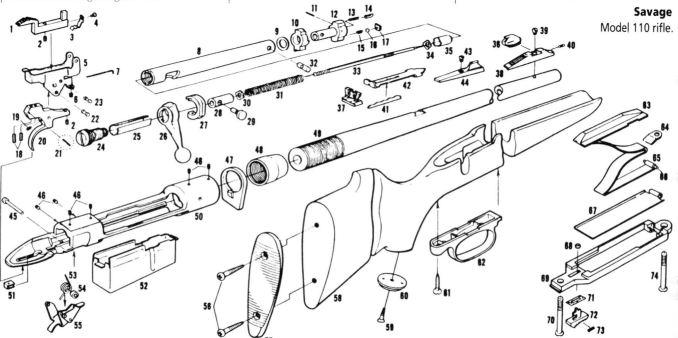

Savage
Model 110 rifle.

1947: introduced as the Stevens Models 322 (·22 Hornet), 325 (·250 Savage) and 330 (·30–30 WCF), this inexpensive rifle had a tubular receiver and a stamped-strip trigger guard/magazine floor-plate assembly. Apart from the ·30–30 guns, which were three-shot, magazines held four rounds. Among the most obvious identification features were a safety catch on the right rear of the action and a reinforcing rib on the left side of the receiver. The barrel was retained by a threaded collar.

Early guns had round 22in barrels—·30–30 examples generally measured 20in—while the plain pistol-grip stocks had straight combs and round-tip fore-ends.

1950: the rifles became the Savage Models 340 (·30–30) and 342 (·22 Hornet), the ·250 Savage option having proved to generate too much chamber pressure for safety. Deluxe versions of the basic rifles, known as 340S and 342S, had chequering on the pistol grips and fore-ends, aperture sights on the receiver, and sling eyes under the stock. They lasted until 1960.

1955: distinctions between Models 340 and 342 were abandoned when a ·222 Remington option became available, all guns being regarded thereafter as '340' (standard pattern) or '340S' (deluxe). A 22in round barrel was standard on the ·30–30 version, but a 24in type was supplied with the others.

1962: a 340C ('Carbine') made its debut. It was made in all then-standard calibres excepting ·30–30 and had an 18in barrel. Production continued only until 1964.

1965: the basic stock pattern was improved by the advent of a low Monte Carlo comb on the butt and skip-line chequering on the pistol grip and fore-end. Plastic butt plates and grip-caps were fitted, separated from the stock by thin white spacers. A folding-leaf back sight replaced the traditional elevator type. The ·223 Remington and ·225 Winchester chamberings date from this period.

1985: the Model 340 was finally abandoned. Most of the guns made in 1983–5 had a simplified stock without the skip-line chequering of their predecessors.

Model 110

·····································

B, BL, C, CL, CY, D, DL, E, EL, ES, F, FNS, FP, FXP3, G, GC, GLNS, GNS, GV, GX, GXP3, K, M, ML, P, PE, PEL, PL, S, V and WLE patterns.
Made by the Savage Arms Company, Utica, New York, and Westfield, Massachusetts, 1958 to date.
Turning-bolt action with two lugs on the bolt head locking into the receiver behind the chamber and the bolt handle turning down into its seat.
Chambering: see notes.
DATA FOR A TYPICAL MODEL 110C
·30–06, rimless.
About 44·00in overall, 6·85lb unladen.
22·00in barrel, 6-groove rifling; RH, concentric.
Detachable box magazine, 4 rounds.
Spring-leaf and elevator sight.
2,950 ft/sec with 150-grain bullet.
☆

1958: introduced in ·243, ·270 and ·308 Winchester chamberings plus the ubiquitous ·30–06, the Model 110 had many interesting features. Its barrel was retained by a locking collar; the tip of the sear/bolt stop unit protruded from the stock on the right side of the bridge when the trigger was cocked; and an unusually short cocking-piece head lay behind the bolt handle. A sliding safety catch lay on the upper tang, and the internal magazine was replenished through the open action.

The original stock had a straight comb and chequering on the pistol-grip and fore-end. The front sight was mounted on a ramp, though the receiver-top was drilled and tapped for optical sight mounts. The action was made in two styles (left and right hand) and two lengths—medium and long. A magnum was introduced in the 1960s, differing from the long pattern only in the diameter of the recess in the bolt face.

1962: actions were offered for sale separately.

1963: the Savage 110E replaced the original Model 110 Sporter. It has been chambered for ·22–250, ·223 Remington and 7mm Remington Magnum in addition to the three standard Winchester cartridges and ·30–06. The earliest guns had plain pistol grip stocks with Monte Carlo combs.

The 110M ('Magnum') appeared at the same time, to handle ·264, ·300 and ·358 Winchester or 7mm Remington Magnum ammunition. It was virtually the same as the standard rifle, but had a long action with a large bolt-face recess, a 24in barrel, and a recoil pad on the butt. Production ceased in 1973, together with a left-hand 110ML version.

1964: the Premier Grade rifles, 110P and 110PL, were introduced in ·243 Winchester, 7mm Remington Magnum and ·30–06. Barrels measured 22in or 24in for the 7mm version, magazine capacity being three (7mm) or four rounds (others). The most recognisable feature was the French walnut stock with a cheek piece and a roll-over Monte Carlo comb. The fore-end had a rosewood cap, separated from the wood by a thin spacer, and skip-line chequering was used. Rifles were available until 1970.

1966: offered in ·22–250, ·243 Winchester, ·25–06, ·270 Winchester, 7mm Winchester Magnum, ·300 Winchester Magnum, ·30–06 or ·308 Winchester, the Savage Model 110C had a detachable magazine containing three magnum or four ordinary cartridges. The magazine release catch lay on the right side of the stock beneath the receiver and a new extractor in the lower locking lug replaced the old C-spring type.

The Model 110CL was similar, but had a left-hand action and was chambered only for ·243 and ·270 Winchester, 7mm Remington Magnum or ·30–06.

Folding-leaf sights replaced the elevator in this era, and skip-line chequering was introduced.

1968: the first Presentation Grade (110PE and 110PEL) Savages were made. They were similar to the 110P pattern, being sold in the same chamberings, but had superbly figured stocks and engraving on the receiver, trigger guard and magazine floor plate. Sights were rarely fitted as most purchasers opted for optical patterns. Presentation Grade guns were too expensive to sustain sales, and work ceased in 1970.

1969: a left-hand version of the 110E, known as the 'EL', was made until 1973 in 7mm Remington Magnum and ·30–06 only.

1972: the Model 110D (right hand) and 110DL

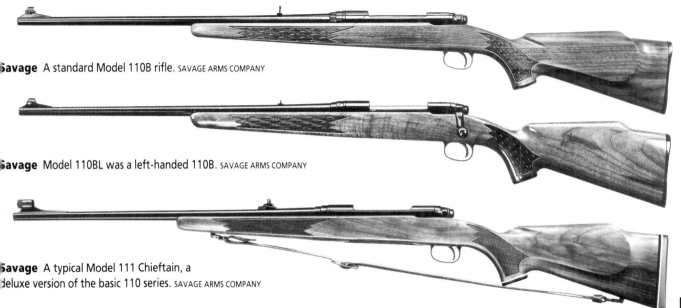

Savage A standard Model 110B rifle. SAVAGE ARMS COMPANY

Savage Model 110BL was a left-handed 110B. SAVAGE ARMS COMPANY

Savage A typical Model 111 Chieftain, a deluxe version of the basic 110 series. SAVAGE ARMS COMPANY

(left hand) were essentially similar to the standard 110 but had a detachable magazine floor plate with a pivoting locking latch. They chambered the three standard Winchester cartridges, plus 7mm Remington Magnum and ·300 Winchester Magnum.

1976: the original 110B (right hand) and 110BL (left hand) appeared in ·243 Winchester, ·270 Winchester, 7mm Remington Magnum, ·30–06 or ·338 Winchester Magnum. They were very similar to the standard 110E, but had selected walnut stocks with Monte Carlo combs.

1978: the ·308 Model 110S (Silhouette) rifle was introduced. It was distinguished by a heavy tapering 22in barrel, and a half-stock with a short rounded fore-end. The comb was higher than normal and the enlarged pistol grip was stippled instead of chequered.

1979: ·22–250 and ·25–06 Remington options were introduced for the Savage 110C. The rifles had 24in barrels (instead of the standard 22in pattern), but did not sell in large numbers. The ·22–250 was offered until 1984–5, but the last ·25–06 examples had gone by c.1982.

1981: the Stevens Model 110ES ('Super Value') was simply the Savage 110E under another name, with a 4× optical sight and mounts. Offered in ·243 or ·308 Winchester only, it had a hardwood stock and a 22in tapered barrel with a simple folding leaf sight. Impressed skip-line chequering was abandoned in this period in favour of a more conventional design.

1983: the Model 110V (Varmint) rifle shared the action of the 110D, but had a heavy 26in barrel, lacked sights, and its stock had stippling on the pistol grip. It chambered the ·22–250 round, though a short-lived ·223 Remington option appeared in 1986.

1985: the Stevens 110ES was discontinued.

1986: the Model 110K appeared in ·243, ·270, 7mm Remington Magnum, ·30–06 or ·338 Winchester Magnum. Based on the 110D, it had a special laminated camouflage-finish stock. The 110C was discontinued in this period, the last guns being chambered for the ·243 and ·270 Winchester, 7mm Remington Magnum or ·30–06 cartridges—with, apparently, a handful

of left-hand guns made for ·308 Winchester.

1987: new 110F and 110FNS ('No Sights') rifles were announced in ·22–250, ·223 Remington, ·243 Winchester, ·270 Winchester, 7mm Remington Magnum, ·300 Winchester Magnum, ·30–06 Springfield, ·308 Winchester or ·338 Winchester Magnum. The principal distinguishing characteristic was the straight-comb black DuPont Rynite stock. An 'FX' derivative, made only in small numbers, had Weaver-type mount bases machined integrally with the receiver.

1988: Models 110D and 110E were finally discontinued. By this time, 110D was being offered in ·223, ·243, ·270, 7mm Remington Magnum, ·30–06 (D and DL sub-classes) and ·338 Winchester Magnum (D only). The 110E pattern was available, in right-hand form only, in ·22–250, ·223 Remington, ·243 Winchester, ·270 Winchester, 7mm Remington Magnum, ·30–06 or ·308 Winchester.

1989: the 110G series appeared. The standard rifle had a 22in barrel (24in for magnums) and a Monte Carlo-pattern butt. The beech stock had a rubber shoulder plate. Chamberings have included the ·22–250, ·223 Remington, ·243 Winchester, ·250 Savage, ·25–06 Remington, ·270 Winchester, 7mm Remington Magnum, 7mm–08, ·300 Winchester Magnum, ·30–06, ·308 or ·338 Winchester Magnum cartridges. Standard rifles had five-round magazines, magnum patterns held four.

Variants have included 110GNS, supplied without sights; 110GLNS ('left-hand, no sights') in ·270 Winchester, 7mm Remington Magnum or ·30–06 only; 110GC in ·270 Winchester, 7mm Remington Magnum, ·300 Winchester Magnum or ·30–06, with a detachable box magazine; and 110GV, a ·22–250 or ·223 varmint rifle with a heavier barrel than normal. The short-lived 110GX had Weaver-pattern mount bases machined into the receiver.

Offered in all regular chamberings excepting ·250 Savage, ·25–06 and 7mm–08, the new or second-pattern Model 110B was a minor variant of the 110G with a brown-stained laminated stock and a brown rubber shoulder plate. Made

only in small quantities, it had been abandoned by 1991.

1990: the 110FP ('Police') model had a heavy 24in barrel and non-reflective finish on the metalwork. Chambered only for the ·243 or ·308 Winchester rounds, the gun was 45·5in overall and weighed about 9lb.

1991: the first ·243 Winchester or ·250 Savage 110CY ('Youth') rifles were made, distinguished by a short butt—with a 12·5in pull—though otherwise similar to the standard 110G.

New XP3 versions of Models 110F and 110G were supplied with 3–9× optical sights and accompanying ring mounts. XP3 rifles were available in ·22–250, ·223 Remington, ·243 Winchester, ·270 Winchester, 7mm Remington Magnum, ·300 Winchester Magnum, ·30–06 or ·308 Winchester. FXP3 had a straight-comb black DuPont Rynite stock, whereas GXP3 had a conventional walnut-finish beech pattern with Monte Carlo comb.

1992: Savage's Model 110WLE 'One of One Thousand' rifle appeared in 7×57mm Mauser, externally similar to the 110-G but with a select walnut stock and a laser-etched company logo on the bolt.

Model 111

Chieftain pattern.
Made by the Savage Arms Company, Westfield, Massachusetts, 1974–9.
·243 Winchester, ·270 Winchester, 7×57mm, 7mm Remington Magnum or ·30–06.
Action: as Model 110, above.
DATA FOR A TYPICAL EXAMPLE
7mm Remington Magnum, rimless.
About 44·00in overall, 8·22lb unladen.
24·00in barrel, 6-groove rifling; RH, concentric.
Detachable box magazine, 3 rounds.
Special ramp-pattern sight.
About 3,020 ft/sec with 175-grain bullet.

☆

1974: this was little more than a variant of the Model 110C with a detachable box magazine (holding four rounds in ordinary or non-magnum chamberings) and a modified stock with a plain

Savage The Model 110B sporter. SAVAGE ARMS COMPANY

Savage Model 110C was a 110B with a detachable box magazine. SAVAGE ARMS COMPANY

Savage Another view of the Model 111. SAVAGE ARMS COMPANY

heek piece and a conventional Monte Carlo omb. Heavyweight 22in barrels were standard n all but the magnum version. A Williams back ight and a front-sight hood were fitted.
979: the Chieftain pattern was abandoned.

Model 112

FV, FVS, R and V patterns.
Made by the Savage Arms Company, Westfield, Massachusetts, 1975–9 and 1991 to date.
Chambering: see notes.
Action: as Model 110, above.
DATA FOR A TYPICAL MODEL 112-FVS
·22–250, rimless.
46·75in overall, 9·00lb unladen.
26·00in barrel, 6-groove rifling; RH, concentric.
Optical sight.
About 3,730 ft/sec with 55-grain bullet.

☆

975: the original single-shot 112V varmint rifle vas offered in ·220 Swift, ·222 Remington, 22–250, ·223 Remington, ·243 Winchester or 25–06. It was about 47in long, had a 26in heavy barrel, and weighed 9·22lb. The stock had a straight comb, a deep pistol grip and a heavier fore-end than normal.
979: the 112V was replaced by the 112R pattern, with a conventional internal five-round magazine. Stippling replaced chequering on the pistol grip of guns made before the 112R was replaced by the Model 110V in 1983.
991: the 112-FV (five-round magazine) and 12-FVS (single shot) varmint rifles appeared, with 26in heavy barrels and black straight-comb DuPont Rynite stocks. Made in ·22–250 or ·223 Remington, they weighed 9lb without sights.

Model 114

Classic Ultra or CU pattern.
Made by the Savage Arms Company, Westfield, Massachusetts, 1991 to date.
·270 Winchester, 7mm Remington Magnum, ·300 Winchester Magnum or ·30–06.
Otherwise generally as Model 110, above.

☆

1991: this amalgamated the basic 110 action with an American walnut stock. The butt had a straight comb, a pistol-grip cap was fitted, and the shoulder plate was solid rubber. Chequering was cut rather than impressed, and a Williams ramp back sight was fitted. Standard rifles had five-round detachable box magazines; magnum magazines held a cartridge fewer.

Model 116

FCS and FSS patterns.
Made by the Savage Arms Company, Westfield, Massachusetts, 1991 to date.
·223 Remington, ·243 Winchester, ·270 Winchester, 7mm Remington Magnum, ·300 Winchester Magnum, ·30–06 or ·338 Winchester Magnum.
Otherwise generally as Model 110, above.

☆

1991: the Savage 116FSS was little more than a synthetic-stock Model 110F with a stainless steel barrel. The similar Model 116FCS (·270, 7mm, ·300 or ·30–06 only) had a detachable box magazine instead of the internal type.

2. THE LEVER-ACTION PATTERNS

The mechanism operated by depressing the finger lever to withdraw a long curved extension from under the rear of the breech block. The block dropped clear of the locking shoulder in the top of the receiver, to be drawn back clear of the magazine well as the lever was pushed farther down. The return stroke pushed a fresh cartridge into the chamber, and then tilted the breech block up into its locking recess.

Simple and sturdy, the action could handle all but the most powerful high-velocity cartridges available prior to 1917. The ·22 High Velocity round proved troublesome, as the Savage breech block compressed fractionally on firing and stretched the cases. However, as the Savage rotary magazine could handle ballistically effectual pointed-nose bullets in perfect safety,

handloaders accepted the need to re-size cases after they had been fired a few times. Fore-end tube magazines favoured by Winchester and Marlin were restricted to blunt-nose bullets in the interests of safety.

MILITARY WEAPONS

Note: the ·303 Savage cartridge has always been known in Britain as '·301 Savage', to prevent confusion with ·303 service rounds.
1895: the original military musket chambered ·30–40 Krag cartridges, had an eight-round magazine and weighed 8·69lb. The carbine was similar, excepting for its 22in barrel, half-stock and saddle ring. Very few guns were made.
1899: available until 1908, the M1899 military rifle and carbine were offered in ·303 Savage and, briefly, ·30–30 Winchester. The rifle is decribed below, as some served in Canada during the First World War. It was originally advertised with sword or socket bayonets, the former being the US M1892 (Krag) pattern and the latter—apparently—a bushed US M1873. The matching carbine had a 20in barrel, a leaf-type back sight, a sling ring on the right side of the receiver, and a half-length fore-end retained by a single band. It weighed 7·25lb.

CANADA
Model 1899

Made by the Savage Arms Company, Utica, New York, 1914–15.
·303 Savage, rimmed.
Lever action, locked by displacing the tail of the breech block upward into the receiver.
49·95in overall, 8·75lb unladen.
28·00in barrel, 6-groove rifling; RH, concentric.
Integral rotary box magazine, 5 rounds.
Ramp-and-leaf sight graduated to 2,000 yards.
2,180 ft/sec with 180-grain bullet.
Special knife bayonet.

☆

1914: the commencement of the First World War found Canada with insufficient rifles to

Savage 110HB was a heavy-barrel varmint rifle. SAVAGE ARMS COMPANY

Savage 110S was used for silhouette shooting. SAVAGE ARMS COMPANY

Savage Identifiable by its stock and heavy barrel, the 110V (Varmint) rifle replaced the 110HB pattern.

mobilise effectually. Among the many weapons acquired to free service-pattern Ross rifles for the Canadian Expeditionary Force were some 1899-pattern Savages, purchased by leading businessmen in Montreal to arm local militia. The rifles had a full-length fore-end, military-style sights, a barrel band, and a nose cap with a lug for a knife bayonet with a unique pivoting locking latch beneath the pommel. A cleaning rod protruded beneath the muzzle.

SPORTING GUNS

Model 1895

Rifle and carbine patterns.
Made by the Marlin Fire Arms Company, New Haven, Connecticut, for the Savage Arms Company, Utica, New York, 1895–9.
Quantity: about 5,000.
·30–40 Krag or ·303 Savage.
Lever action, locked by displacing the tail of the breech block upward into the receiver.
DATA FOR A TYPICAL RIFLE
·303 Savage, rimmed.
45·80in overall, 8·05lb unladen.
24·00in barrel, 6-groove rifling; RH, concentric.
Integral rotary box magazine, 8 rounds.
Spring-leaf and elevator sight.
2,140 ft/sec with 180-grain bullet.

1895: the first Savage sporter was made by Marlin in several styles. Chambered for a unique smokeless ·303 Savage 'High Velocity' cartridge and offered with round, half-octagon or fully octagonal barrels, the sporting rifle soon presented Winchester and Marlin with an effectual rival.

1970: a special 'M1895' was made to mark the Savage rifle's 75th anniversary. Mechanically, however, it was a Model 99 (q.v.).

Model 1899

Rifle, musket and carbine patterns.
Made by the Savage Arms Company, Utica, New York, 1899–1917.
Quantity: 250,000?
·22 High Velocity, ·250 Savage, ·25–35 Winchester, ·30–30 Winchester, ·303 Savage, ·32–40 Ballard (Winchester) or ·38–55 Winchester.
Action: as M1895, above.
DATA FOR A TYPICAL RIFLE
·32–40 Ballard, rimmed.
45·90in overall, 7·65lb unladen.
24·00in barrel, 6-groove rifling; RH, concentric?
Integral rotary box magazine, 5 rounds.
Spring-leaf and elevator sight.
1,440 ft/sec with 165-grain bullet.

☆

1899: though substantial numbers of M1895 sporters had been sold, improvements were soon made in the basic design. Production of a new rifle began in Savage's new factory in Utica.

The three 1895 variants were perpetuated, though magazine capacity was reduced (a sixth round could be carried in the breech if required). A cocking indicator lay in the top surface of the bolt and a firing-pin retractor was added.

The original pre-1917 sporter chambered an assortment of cartridges and could be obtained with round, half-octagon or fully octagonal 22–26in barrels. Butts originally had straight wrists, though pistol grips, once considered as optional, gradually became standard. Special sights, engraving and selected woodwork were obtainable to order.

1912: a ·22 high velocity round designed by Charles Newton (q.v.) was introduced.

1913: the famed ·250–3000 Savage appeared, offering a muzzle velocity of 3,000 ft/sec with an 87-grain jacketed bullet. This cartridge was also a Newton design.

1917: production ceased owing to war-work.

Model 99

Pre-1942 patterns: A, B, E, EG, F, G, H, K, R, RS and T.
Made by the Savage Arms Company, Utica, New York, 1920–42.
Quantity: 250,000?
·22 High Velocity, ·250 Savage, ·25–35 Winchester, ·300 Savage, ·30–30 Winchester, ·303 Savage, ·32–40 Ballard (Winchester) or ·38–55 Winchester.

Action: as M1895, above.
DATA FOR A TYPICAL MODEL 99E
·250 Savage, rimmed.
43·85in overall, 7·13lb unladen.
22·00in barrel, 6-groove rifling; RH, concentric.
Integral rotary box magazine, 5 rounds.
Spring-leaf and elevator sight.
About 2,950 ft/sec with 87-grain bullet.

☆

1920: work began again after the First World War, with the introduction of the Model 99A. The designation of the original pre-war rifle was correspondingly changed to 'Model 99'.

Made until 1936 in ·300 Savage, ·303 Savage or ·30–30 Winchester, the Model 99A was a minor variant of the pre-1917 gun. Like the others introduced in this period, it had a straight wrist butt, a slender schnabel-tip fore-end, and the front-sight bead on a short muzzle ramp.

The Model B was a 'Take Down' version, weighing about 7·5lb instead of 7·3lb; like the other guns with readily detachable barrels, it had an additional metal collar set into the front of the receiver and can be identified at a glance.

Model 99E was a carbine form of the 99A rifle, though the reduction in barrel length by a mere 2in was not especially notable. It could be obtained to fire ·250 Savage, ·300 Savage, ·303 Savage or ·30–30 Winchester cartridges.

Model 99F ('featherweight') was a lightened gun with a straight butt plate, made in 'Take Down' guise and weighing a mere 6·5lb with a 22in round barrel. It chambered the same cartridge as the contemporaneous 99E carbine. The 99G was mechanically identical with the other Savages introduced in 1920, but had chequered panels on the pistol grip and fore-end.

1931: the Model 99H carbine was introduced with a straight-wrist butt and a deep round-tip fore-end retained by a single band. It was chambered for ·250 Savage, ·303 Savage or ·30–30 cartridges and had a solid frame. Weight was about 6·5lb with a 20in round barrel. The Model 99K was a deluxe rifle with foliate engraving on the receiver-side, a chequered pistol-grip butt, and a chequered schnabel-tip fore-end. The woodwork was specially chosen

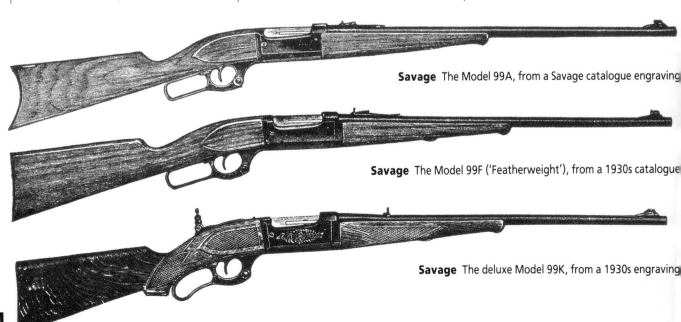

Savage The Model 99A, from a Savage catalogue engraving

Savage The Model 99F ('Featherweight'), from a 1930s catalogue

Savage The deluxe Model 99K, from a 1930s engraving

or its attractive figuring. A Lyman aperture sight appeared on the upper tang, while a small folding leaf replaced the spring-leaf and elevator on the barrel.

1936: Models 99A, 99B, 99C and 99E were replaced by the Model 99EG, a solid-frame rifle available in all standard calibres. Plain pistol-grip stocks and round-tip fore-ends were fitted.

The Models 99R and 99RS were introduced in ·250 Savage (22in barrel) or ·300 Savage (24in barrel). Weighing about 7·2lb, they could be distinguished by the pistol-grip butt and a short deep round-tip fore-end. Chequering appeared on the pistol-grip and the sides of the fore-end. The 'R' pattern had a conventional spring-leaf and elevator back sight, whereas the 'RS' had a Lyman aperture sight on the upper tang as well as a small folding leaf on the barrel.

Model 99T, a lightweight pattern with a solid frame, was made with a 20in barrel (in ·22 High Power, ·303 Savage and ·30–30 Winchester) or a 22in barrel for ·300 Savage. It had a chequered pistol-grip butt, a round-tip fore-end, and weighed about 7lb.

1941: production of Model 99 rifles ceased at the end of the year, owing to war with Japan.

1942: assembly of Models 99G, 99K, 99R, 99RS and 99T ceased.

Model 99

Post-1945 patterns: A, C, CD, DE, DL, E, EG, F,
PE, R, RS and 358.
Made by the Savage Arms Company, Utica, New York,
and Westfield, Massachusetts, 1946 to date.
Chambering: see notes.
Action: as M1895, above.
DATA FOR A TYPICAL MODEL 99C
·284 Winchester, rimless.
45·75in overall, 7·50lb unladen.
24·00in barrel, 6-groove rifling; RH, concentric?
Detachable box magazine, 3 rounds.
Spring-leaf and elevator sight.
2,900 ft/sec with 150-grain bullet.

☆

1946: the first Model 99EG rifles assembled in the Utica factory were essentially similar to

pre-1941 examples, excepting for the addition of chequering on the pistol grip and fore-end. The Models 99R and 99RS also reappeared, with 24in barrels and sling-swivel eyes on the underside of the fore-end and butt. Compared with the pre-war patterns, the chequering on the pistol grip was simplified, and the chequer panel on the fore-end—by then basically triangular—did not continue beneath the gun. In addition, the locking catch on the right side of the operating lever was soon abandoned and the Lyman sight of the pre-war 'RS' was replaced with a Redfield pattern. The 1946-type rifles were chambered for ·250 Savage or ·300 Savage cartridges only.

1955: ·243, ·308 and ·358 Winchester options were added. The pre-war Model 99F was reintroduced in ·243 Winchester, ·250 Savage or ·308 Winchester, with a chequered pistol grip and fore-end.

1960: the millionth Model 99 was presented to the National Rifle Association on 22 March. The Model 99EG was discarded during the year, but the 99E carbine reappeared with a 20in or 22in round barrel chambering ·243 Winchester, ·250 Savage, ·300 Savage or ·308 Winchester. Its pistol grip and notably bulky round-tip fore-end were skip-line chequered.

The deluxe Model 99DL was little more than a 99F (q.v.) with a Monte Carlo comb and a pistol-grip butt. It was abandoned in 1973.

1965: the Model 99C appeared, fitted with a detachable box magazine containing three (·284 Winchester) or four rounds (·243 and ·308 Winchester) instead of the traditional rotary pattern. The magazine-release button was set into the right side of the receiver. The butt of the '99CD' deluxe version had a Monte Carlo comb, a shallow cheek piece, and a pistol grip with skip-line chequering; the fore-end was a broad semi-beavertail type with a flute running back from the rounded tip. Chamberings seem to have been ·243 Winchester, ·250 Savage or ·308 Winchester, with four-round magazines.

1968: short-lived Models 99PE ('Presentation Grade') and the lesser 99DE ('Citation Grade') were announced, with elaborately engraved

receivers and superbly grained woodwork. Sales were so poor, however, that they were both abandoned in 1970.

1970: ten thousand ·308 'M1895' rifles were produced to mark the 75th anniversary of the Savage lever-action rifle (see Part Two).

1971: a modernised Model 99A appeared with a sliding safety catch on the upper tang, a folding-leaf back sight, and a straightened butt plate instead of the pre-1936 crescent form. The new 99A was offered with a 22in round barrel in ·243 Winchester, ·250 Savage, ·300 Savage and ·308 Winchester.

1973: the Model 99F was discontinued.

1977: the short-lived Model 99–358 appeared, chambered for the ·358 Winchester round. Apart from its straight-comb butt and ventilated shoulder pad, it was similar to the Model 99CD.

1981: the 99–358 and 99CD (·243 or ·308) patterns were abandoned.

1982: the last of the rotary-magazine Models 99A (·243 Winchester, ·250 Savage or ·308 Winchester) were sold.

1985: the Model 99E was abandoned, the final options including two Savage (·250, ·300) and two Winchester (·243, ·308) chamberings. This left only the box-magazine 99C in production.

3. THE SLIDE-ACTION PATTERNS

Only a single centre-fire slide action rifle has ever been made, though Savage's ·22 rimfires date back to 1903. The Model 170 rifle was based on the company's shotguns, using a similar rotating bolt. Though the project made economic sense, being based on proven components, the rifle did not sell especially well and had a short life.

Model 170

Rifle and carbine patterns.
Made by the Savage Arms Company, Westfield,
Massachusetts, 1970–81.
·30–30 Winchester or ·35 Remington.

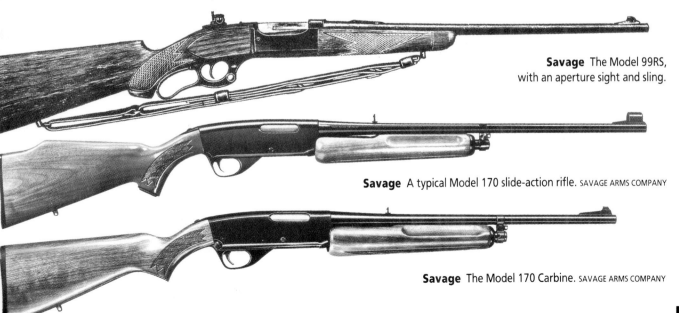

Savage The Model 99RS, with an aperture sight and sling.

Savage A typical Model 170 slide-action rifle. SAVAGE ARMS COMPANY

Savage The Model 170 Carbine. SAVAGE ARMS COMPANY

Slide action, locked by rotating lugs on the bolt into the receiver walls.

DATA FOR A TYPICAL EXAMPLE
·35 Remington, rimless.
About 43·50in overall, 6·80lb unladen.
22·00in barrel, 6-groove rifling; RH, concentric.
Tube magazine under barrel, 3 rounds.
Folding-leaf sight.
About 2,210 ft/sec with 200-grain bullet.

☆

1970: this was a typical shotgun-type rifle, with a short barrel and conventional open sights. Its Monte Carlo butt had a panel of chequering pressed into the pistol grip, and the broad fore-end had a short grasping groove running back from the tip. A safety catch lay on the upper tang behind the receiver, while swivel eyes appeared beneath the butt and on the front of the magazine support band under the muzzle.
1974: a 170C ('Carbine') appeared in ·30–30 Winchester only, with an 18·5in round barrel and a straight-comb butt.
1981: both patterns were abandoned.

SCHMIDT

SWITZERLAND
Also known as 'Schmidt-Rubin'

⌒

Eduard Rubin (1846–1920) developed the first small-calibre copper-jacketed bullets successful enough to withstand higher velocities than were normal in the 1880s. Rubin cartridges with a calibre of 8·1–9·6mm were tested against an 8·6mm Hebler pattern in Switzerland in 1882. The Hebler cartridge, which had a papier-mâché core, attained a prodigious velocity but the Rubin pattern was far more accurate.
1884: Schweizerische Industrie-Gesellschaft converted 130 Vetterli (q.v.) rifles to fire 7·5mm and 8mm Rubin cartridges. Most were adapted from obsolete infantry rifles, but a few had been trial guns of 1873–5: these had a distinctive bolt-support guide extending back above the wrist of the butt.
1885: Rudolf Schmidt's first straight-pull bolt

mechanism relied on an actuating rod, set in a channel on the right side of the breech, to rotate the bolt through a helical channel cut in the bolt sleeve. Twin lugs were provided midway along the bolt sleeve, locking into the receiver directly above the trigger.

Though the relevant patent was not granted until September 1889, the first rifles had been submitted for trials in December 1885. They had protruding box magazines, 1881-pattern quadrant sights, finger spurs behind the trigger guard, diced bolt-knobs and diced fore-ends.
1888: trials centered on eleven improved Schmidts and a similar number of 'Neuhausen' guns promoted by Schweizerische Industrie-Gesellschaft. The Schmidts, chambered for an experimental 1888-pattern Rubin cartridge, had a distinctive nose cap/bayonet lug assembly, quadrant sights, a lateral safety bolt on top of the receiver, and a selection of differing magazine release catches.

In the autumn of 1888, ninety more guns of each design were ordered for field trials. By this time, the Schmidt rifle had acquired a ring on the cocking piece, doubling as a safety catch. Ultimately, the Schmidt system, simpler and easier to use, was preferred to the SIG design.

MILITARY WEAPONS

Model 1889

Infantry rifle: Infanterie-Repetier-Gewehr M1889.
Made by Eidgenössische Waffenfabrik,
Bern, 1891–7.
Quantity: 211,930.
7·5 × 53·5mm, rimless.
Straight-pull action, with two lugs on the rear of the bolt sleeve locking into the receiver ahead of the trigger.
1,302mm overall, 4·85kg unladen.
780mm barrel, 3-groove rifling; RH, concentric.
detachable box magazine, 12 rounds.
Quadrant sight graduated to 2,000 metres.
590 m/sec with M1890 ball cartridges.
M1889 sword bayonet.

☆

1889: this rifle was officially adopted on 2 June. Tooling had already begun in the sta factory. The M1889 was a most unusual desig with a characteristic Swiss nose cap/bayon lug/stacking rod assembly, and a receiver with noticeable gap between the trigger guard and th magazine. The great length of the bolt weakene the Schmidt system greatly.
1897: production ceased after 211,890 rifl and 40–50 Exerzierwaffen had been delivered.

Model 1889/96

Infantry rifle: Infanterie-Repetier-Gewehr M1889/96
Made by Eidgenössische Waffenfabrik, Bern,
1897–1912.
Quantity: 127,070.
7·5 × 53·5mm, rimless.
Straight-pull action, with two lugs on the front of th bolt sleeve locking into the receiver behind
the magazine well.
1,300mm overall, 4·51kg unladen.
780mm barrel, 3-groove rifling; RH, concentric.
Detachable box magazine, 12 rounds.
Quadrant sight graduated to 2,000 metres.
590 m/sec with M1890 ball cartridges.
M1889 sword bayonet.

☆

1895: the inherent weaknesses of the 188 pattern Schmidt action were recognised aft protracted experience with the standard 7·5m 1890-pattern cartridge had been gained. As so as attempts were made to increase the muzz velocity, the problems intensified.
1897: testing of fifty modified rifles allowe the improved Vogelsang/Rebholz action to b adopted on 27 September. Though the 1889/9 rifle resembled its predecessor externally, th locking lugs had been moved to the front the bolt-sleeve. This strengthened the action, b placing less of the bolt sleeve under compressiv stress, and reduced the gap between the trigge and the magazine by 10mm.
1909: rifles were reclassified as '[Infanterie Gewehr 89/96'.
1912: by November, 127,050 service rifles an about twenty Exerzierwaffen had been made.

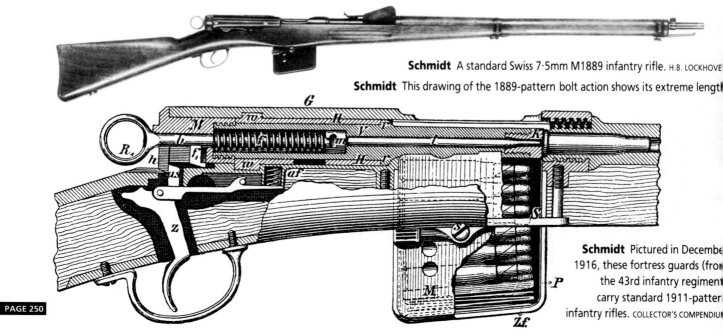

Schmidt A standard Swiss 7·5mm M1889 infantry rifle. H.B. LOCKHOVE

Schmidt This drawing of the 1889-pattern bolt action shows its extreme lengt

Schmidt Pictured in Decembe 1916, these fortress guards (fro the 43rd infantry regiment carry standard 1911-patter infantry rifles. COLLECTOR'S COMPENDIU

1913: as a result of a decree signed on 13 January 1911, the Eidgenössische Waffenfabrik began to convert 1896-type rifles to approximate to the 1911 pattern.

1920: 125,770 M1889/96 rifles had been altered by 1 March. They had four-groove rifling and chambered the Ordonnanz 11 cartridge.

Model 1897

Cadet rifle: Kadettengewehr M1897.
Made by Eidgenössische Waffenfabrik, Bern, 1898–1927.
Quantity: 7,900 rifles and 40 sub-calibre trainers.
7·5 × 53·5mm, rimless.
Action: as M1889/96 rifle, above.
1,105mm overall, 3·53kg unladen.
592mm barrel, 3-groove rifling; RH, concentric.
Quadrant sight graduated to 1,200 metres.
565 m/sec with M1890 ball cartridges.
M1892 socket bayonet.

☆

1898: the Kadettengewehr was adopted on 27 July after trials with guns derived from the Mannlicher cavalry carbine and Schmidt-system rifles. The single-shot M1897 had a special quadrant sight with differing sets of graduations for the Ordonnanzpatrone (to 1,200 metres, on the left side) or the reduced-charge Kadetten-Patrone (to 400 metres, right).

Model 1900

Short rifle: Kurzgewehr M1900.
Made by Eidgenössische Waffenfabrik, Bern, 1901–11.
Quantity: 18,750.
7·5 × 53·5mm, rimless.
Action: as M1889/96 rifle, above.
1,105mm overall, 3·79kg unladen.
592mm barrel, 3-groove rifling; RH, concentric.
Detachable box magazine, 6 rounds.
Quadrant sight graduated to 1,200 metres.
M1897 épée or saw-back M1906 sword bayonets.

☆

1901: adopted on 9 April, the Kurzgewehr was based on the 1896-pattern action; apart from its length, the smaller magazine and reduced-range sight, it was similar to the M89/96 infantry rifle.

1913: many surviving 1900-type guns were among the 26,340 carbines and short rifles converted to '1911' standards by Eidgenössische Waffenfabrik prior to 1920. Taking Ordonnanz 11 cartridges, they had four-groove rifling.

Model 1905

Cavalry carbine: Kavallerie-Karabiner M1905.
Made by Eidgenössische Waffenfabrik, Bern, 1906–11.
Quantity: 7,900.
7·5 × 53·5mm, rimless.
Action: as M1889/96 rifle, above.
1,070mm overall, 3·63kg unladen.
550mm barrel, 3-groove rifling; RH, concentric.
Detachable box magazine, 6 rounds.
Quadrant sight graduated to 1,500 metres.
550 m/sec with M1890 ball cartridges.
No bayonet.

☆

1905: preceded by a handful of experimental designs—including one with a folding stock and another with a three-piece cleaning rod carried beneath the fore-end—the Karabiner 05 was adopted to replace the 1893-type Mannlicher. Stocked virtually the muzzle, preventing the attachment of bayonets, it had a full-length hand guard and a sling-slot in the butt.

1913: A decree signed on 13 January 1911 ordered the Eidgenössische Waffenfabrik to modify 26,340 surviving M1900 short rifles and M1905 carbines to approximate to the 1911 pattern. The work was undertaken in Bern in 1913–20. The guns had four-groove rifling and chambered 7·5 × 55mm 1911-type cartridges.

Model 1911

Infantry rifle: Gewehr 11.
Made by Eidgenössische Waffenfabrik, Bern, 1913–19.
Quantity: 133,000.
7·5 × 55mm, rimless.
Staight-pull action, with two lugs on the front of the bolt sleeve locking into the receiver behind the magazine well.

1,308mm overall, 4·55kg unladen.
780mm, 4-groove rifling; RH, concentric.
Detachable box magazine, 6 rounds.
Tangent-leaf sight graduated to 2,000 metres.
805 m/sec with M1911 ball cartridges.
M1892 socket, M1889 sword or saw-backed M1906 bayonets.

☆

1908: a universal increase in muzzle velocity, arising from widespread adoption of pointed-bullet ammunition, caused further problems with the Swiss rifles.

Trials were undertaken in 1908–10 with modified bullets and rifles embodying a strengthened Vogelsang/Rebholz action. Apart from the tangent sight, these guns resembled their predecessors externally—though, once dismantled, three large lightening holes were to be found through the bolt sleeve.

1913: the perfected [Infanterie-]Gewehr 11 was formally approved on 10 January, together with adaptions of several previous weapons. The new guns had a strengthened action, a hold-open to signify an empty magazine, a pistol-grip stock and an improved back sight.

Model 1911

Carbine: Karabiner 11.
Made by Eidgenössische Waffenfabrik, Bern, 1914–33.
Quantity: 184,200.
7·5 × 55mm, rimless.
Action: as M1911 rifle, above.
1,103mm overall, 3·92kg unladen.
592mm barrel, 4-groove rifling; RH, concentric.
Detachable box magazine, 6 rounds.
Tangent-leaf sight graduated to 1,500 metres.
755 m/sec with M1911 ball cartridges.
Bayonet: as M1911 rifle.

☆

1913: adopted concurrently with the 1911-pattern infantry rifle in January, to replace the short rifle and cavalry carbine, this was readily distinguished by its short barrel and stock. It was mechanically identical with the rifle, embodying a similar breech mechanism.

Model 1931

Short rifle: Karabiner 31.
Made by Eidgenössische Waffenfabrik,
Bern, 1933–58.
Quantity: 582,230.
7·5 × 55mm, rimless.
Straight-pull action, with two lugs on the front of the
bolt sleeve locking into the receiver behind
the chamber.
1,107mm overall, 4·00kg unladen.
652mm barrel, 4-groove rifling; RH, concentric.
Detachable box magazine, 6 rounds.
Tangent-leaf sight graduated to 1,500 metres.
780 m/sec with M1911 ball cartridges.
M1889, M1889/18, M1918, M1889/55 or saw-backed
M1914 sword bayonets.

☆

1930: it was clear that important changes were required in the 1911-type Schmidt action to keep abreast of improved technology.

1932: on 22 January, the Bundesrat approved the manufacture of about twenty experimental short rifles.

1933: the Karabiner 31 was formally adopted on 16 June. Great changes had been made in the action which, though retaining the essence of the original Schmidt principle, locked into the receiver ring rather than behind the magazine well. In addition, the bolt did not project as far beyond the bolt carrier, reducing the length compared with the 1896-type action by 6cm.

The Karabiner 31 had a longer barrel than the Karabiner 11, which was of similar overall length. An improved sight was fitted, and the semi-pistol grip stock—with a sling bar let into the left side of the butt—was distinguished by a clamping nose cap accepting any of the standard Swiss sword bayonets.

1958: military production finished after more than half a million Karabiner 31 had been made in the Bern factory.

A hundred otherwise standard examples were supplied in the 1930s to equip the élite Swiss Guard (or 'Papstliche Schweizergarde') in the Vatican; these guns were apparently numbered 249047–249146.

Models 1931/42 and 1931/43

Sniper rifles: Zielfernrohr-Karabiner 31/42 und 31/43.
Made by Eidgenössische Waffenfabrik, Bern, 1944–6.
Quantity: 2,240.
7·5 × 55mm, rimless.
Otherwise as Kar.31, above, excepting weight
(4·28kg unladen).

☆

1935: experiments had been undertaken with optically-sighted Karabiner 11 as early as 1919, but the project had been shelved until Karabiner 31 with Zeiss, Wild, Gerber and Kern sights were tested in the Schiess-schule Walenstadt.

1944: though the low-power Kern sight was accepted in November 1940 and a hundred experimental carbines had been manufactured in 1943, the perfected Zf.-Kar. 31/42 was not approved until 1 July 1944. It had a 1·8 × sight, offset on the left side of the receiver alongside the bolt. Each sight had a small auxiliary tangent sight and a unique pivoting periscope head.

1945: the M31/43, otherwise identical with its predecessor, had an improved 2·8 × sight on the left side of the receiver.

1946: assembly ceased.

Model 1955

Sniper rifle: Zielfernrohr-Karabiner 55.
Made by Eidgenössische Waffenfabrik, Bern, 1957–9.
Quantity: 4,150.
7·5 × 55mm, rimless.
Otherwise as Kar.31, above, excepting overall length
(1,208mm) and weight (6·12kg with sight).

☆

1956: this conventional Zf.-Karabiner with a top-mounted Kern 3·5 × sight (graduated to 800 metres) was adopted in the mid 1950s to replace the M31/42 and M31/43. These guns had a special half-stock with a chequered pistol-grip, bipods and a muzzle brake.

SPORTING GUNS

In addition to regulation weapons and 13,260 commercial Karabiner 31 (the last being sold in 1972), the Swiss authorities accepted a short rifle with an aperture sight on 11 January 1963. Intended for use in military-style shooting matches, 'Präzisionskarabiner' models 70 and 74 were made for UIT full-bore (70-M and 74-M) and Biathlon (70-B, 74-B) competitions. The two '74' guns had a distinctive cut-away stock, whilst Biathlon guns were fitted with special shoulder harnesses.

Schmidt-type actions have been stocked and barrelled by Grünig & Elmiger, Hämmerli, Tanner and others in a wide selection of calibres and chamberings—mostly for target shooting. However, the excessive length of pre-1931 actions made them less suitable for sporting purposes than Mauser or Mannlicher designs.

SCHMIDT & HABERMANN

GERMANY

The attribution of this dropping-block action to one of the larger gunmaking establishments in the Suhl district rests entirely on the appearance of S. & H. marks on rifles bearing the names of two other makers. Guns have been reported by Franz Kettner of Suhl (to whom the design has also been attributed) or Theodor Kommer of Zella-Mehlis. All embody identical actions which were made in several sizes.

Walter Glaser of Zürich offered a series of excellent-quality sporters embodying this action in the period between the wars. Owing to the strength of the mechanism, they could chamber 'any sporting cartridges of between 6.5 and 11mm calibre'. The sturdy breech block, which contained the hammer and an inertia firing pin, moved vertically when the operating lever ahead of the trigger guard was pushed down and forward to break the lock.

Rifles from the 1920s were usually much less individualistic than pre-1914 equivalents, as the excesses of Schützen-style butts were replaced by straight-wrist or pistol-grip sporting patterns. Combs were invariably of hog's back type, cheek pieces either being rounded or the

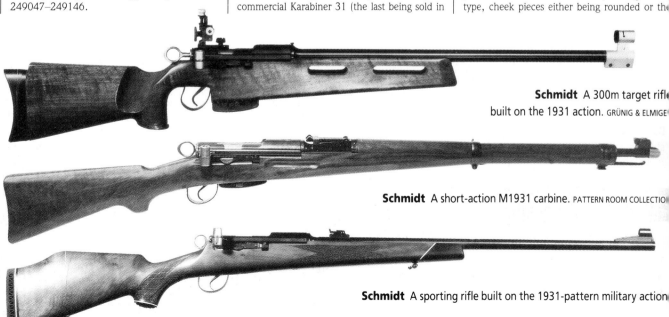

Schmidt A 300m target rifle built on the 1931 action. GRÜNIG & ELMIGER

Schmidt A short-action M1931 carbine. PATTERN ROOM COLLECTION

Schmidt A sporting rifle built on the 1931-pattern military action.

squared-edge patterns favoured in Germany and Switzerland. Barrels were usually partly or fully octagonal, though round examples are known.

Standard pattern

Made by E. Schmidt & Habermann, Suhl, c.1920–39.
Chambered for many European and American cartridges, with 8·15 × 46·5mm predominating.
Dropping-block action, locked by an intermediate block and the operating lever.
DATA FOR A TYPICAL EXAMPLE
8·15 × 46·5mm, rimmed.
1,140mm overall, 3·36kg unladen.
715mm barrel, 4-groove rifling; RH, concentric.
Quadrant sight graduated to 800 metres.
550 m/sec with 9·8-gram bullet.

☆

1925: a typical rifle had a colour case-hardened action with a lightly engraved breech-block. A set-trigger lever accompanied the conventional lever within the trigger guard, around which the operating lever curved in the fashion of many German-made break-action shotguns. The pistol-grip butt displayed a hog's back comb and a small rounded cheek piece; the fore-end, held to the barrel by a key set in oval silver escutcheons, had a shallow schnabel tip. The half-octagonal barrel carried a Swiss-style quadrant back sight at the breech, and a replaceable blade lay on a ramp at the muzzle.

SCHULZ & LARSEN

DENMARK

Best known for its custom gunsmithing work prior to 1939, Schulz & Larsen made a small number of carbines for the Danish police during the Second World War, progressing in the early 1950s to a modest range of improved rim- and centre-fire guns. In addition, large numbers of German Karabiner 98k were converted for the Danish rifle association in the 1950s. Details of these half-stocked target rifles will be found in the Mauser section.

MILITARY WEAPONS
Model 1942

State police rifle; Rigspolitikarabin m/42 (Rplt.42).
Made by Schulz & Larsen Geværfabrik,
Otterup, 1942–3.
8 × 58mm.
Turning-bolt action, locked by rotating four lugs on the bolt head into the receiver wall behind the magazine, and by the bolt handle turning down into its seat.
1,108mm overall, 3·93kg unladen.
575mm barrel, 4-groove rifling; RH, concentric.
Integral box magazine, 4 rounds.
Fixed sight regulated for 200 metres.
650 m/sec with ball ammunition.
No bayonet.

☆

1942: the first guns were delivered. Chambered for the standard 8mm rimmed Danish service cartridges, they had one piece pistol-grip stocks extending to the muzzle. A hand guard ran forward from the chamber under the single band. A simple nose cap was fitted, swivels appearing under the band and butt. The receiver was tubular, with a large oval ejection port, and the single-column magazine (integral with the trigger guard) protruded beneath the stock. Unlatching the floor plate allowed cartridges to be loaded singly into the magazine.

1943: persistently disrupted by sabotage, work finally finished after about six hundred guns had been completed.

SPORTING GUNS
Hunting and target rifles

54J, 54M, 62M, 65, 65DL, 68 and 68DL patterns.
Made by Schulz & Larsen Geværfabrik,
Otterup, c.1954–73.
Chambering: see notes.
Action: as M1942 police carbine, above.
DATA FOR A TYPICAL 68DL SPORTER
·308 Winchester, rimless.
1,130mm overall, 3·40kg unladen.
610mm barrel, 4-groove rifling; RH, concentric.

Internal box magazine, 4 rounds.
Optical sight.
870 m/sec with 9·7-gram bullet.

☆

1953: the first sporting rifles were made by adapting the 1942-pattern police carbine to accept an internal magazine, the ejection port being broadened to allow cartridges to be loaded through the open action.

1954: magazine-fed Model 54J sporting rifles were offered commercially in ·270 Winchester, 7 × 61 Sharpe & Hart or ·30–06 Springfield. Barrels measured 24in (·270 or ·30–06) and 26in (7 × 61). The half stocks had a Monte Carlo butt and cheek piece, with chequering on the pistol grip and fore-end.

The Model 54M ('Match') Free Rifle was built on a special single-shot action. Most guns chambered the Norwegian 6·5 × 55mm rimless service round, though some were made for ·30–06, ·308 Winchester or other American cartridges. Set triggers and 700mm heavy barrels were standard, weight totalling a little over 7kg with the hooked butt plate and a hand-rest beneath the fore-end. Thumb-hole stocks were customary.

1962: the 62M Free Rifle was distinguished by a refined stock with squared contours. Weight rose to about 7·5kg, sights were improved and most guns were chambered for ·308 Winchester (7·62 × 51mm NATO) ammunition. The pistol grips invariably had adjustable heel-rests.

1965: an improved sporting rifle appeared in standard (Model 65) and deluxe (65DL) forms. Chambered for ·270 Winchester, 7 × 61 Sharpe & Hart, ·30–06, ·308 Winchester, ·308 Norma Magnum or ·358 Norma Magnum, the standard rifle had an elegant Monte Carlo stock with white spacers accompanying the pistol-grip cap and the ventilated rubber shoulder pad. The fore-end tip was rounded. The deluxe gun was similar, excepting that fore-end tip and pistol-grip cap were rosewood. Bolt handles were swept backward in a curve until the grasping ball lay above the trigger.

1968: the 68 and 68DL sporters were similar to the 1965 patterns, but the curve of the bolt

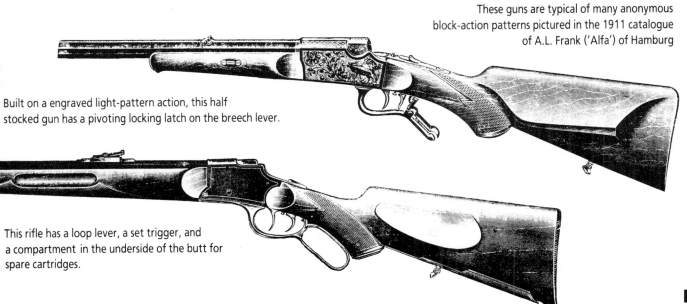

These guns are typical of many anonymous block-action patterns pictured in the 1911 catalogue of A.L. Frank ('Alfa') of Hamburg

Built on a engraved light-pattern action, this half stocked gun has a pivoting locking latch on the breech lever.

This rifle has a loop lever, a set trigger, and a compartment in the underside of the butt for spare cartridges.

SHARPS

SPORTING RIFLES

Improved Breech-Loading Sporting Rifle *1866 and 1869 patterns.* About 750–1,000 of these were made by the Sharps Rifle Mfg. Co. of Hartford, Connecticut, in 1866–71. Sharps' first metallic-cartridge rifle was a minor modification of the 1863-type cap-lock popularised during the Civil War. Based on existing components, it was made in such small numbers that it is now rarely encountered. An improved gun appeared in 1869, with a half-stock and a 26in octagonal barrel. Its breech block contained a cranked firing pin, enabling the side-mounted hammer to ignite a centre-fire cartridge, and a new extractor shared the axis pin of the operating lever. The earliest guns chambered ·52–70 rim- or centre fire cartridges, soon joined by ·44 Berdan Short and ·44 Berdan Long cartridges (subsequently known as ·44–60 and ·44–77 Sharps respectively).

¶ The adoption by the US Army of a ·50–70 cartridge—in 1870—persuaded Sharps to abandon the short-lived proprietary ·52–70, as it was preferable to re-tube old barrels to fire military-pattern ammunition. A typical post-1869 rifle, chambering the ·44 Berdan Long cartridge (·44–77), was 43·13in overall, weighed 8·04lb and had a 26in round barrel.

Sharps' New Model Sporting Rifle *1871 and 1874 patterns.* About 25,000 of these guns were made in Hartford, Connecticut, by the Sharps Rifle Mfg Co. (1871–4) and the Sharps Rifle Company (1874–6), then in Bridgeport, Connecticut until 1881.

¶ Announced at the beginning of 1871, the 1869-pattern sporter was improved to handle the most powerful sporting cartridges. The receiver was lengthened to form an effectual loading tray, whilst the design of the firing pin assembly was modified to improve ignition. The hammer nose was straightened to strike a firing-pin head, set into the rear right side of the breech block, and the breech lever spring-assembly was improved. Chamberings were initially the three established patterns—·44 Berdan Short and Long, ·50–70—plus the new ·40 Berdan Short (·40–50) and ·40–70 Berdan Long (·40–70). Excepting the straight ·50–70 pattern, these cartridges all had slightly necked cases.

¶ From 1872 onward, complaints about the effectiveness of the ·44 Berdan Long (·44–77) bullet on bison were answered with the ·50–90 'Big Fifty', in a 2·5in case. By 1873–4, Sharps cartridges were becoming known by their proprietary names. Designations based on case lengths also grew in popularity, as they prevented confusion arising from differing powder charges loaded in otherwise identical cases. For example, the ·40–50 cartridge had a 1·563in case, while the ·44–90 pattern measured 2·625in. The first guns appeared in 1873–4 chambered for ·45–70 government cartridges, which had replaced the ·50–70 type; two versions of the ·44–90—for hunting or target use—were also announced in this era.

¶ The 1871-type guns were made until the Sharps Rifle Manufacturing Company was succeeded by the Sharps Rifle Company. The 'Model 1874' rifle was identical with the 1871 type, but bore the new company name. Catalogues produced in the mid 1870s listed the Model 1874 with round, half-octagon or fully octagonal barrels (26–30in), and options such as double set triggers or peep-and-globe sights. A gun with an extra-heavy 34in barrel could weigh as much as 15lb, though most examples weighed 8–10lb. A pewter fore-end tip was characteristic.

¶ The original necked cartridge-cases were supplemented from 1875 onward by straight patterns, cheaper to make and easier to reload. The first to appear was the ·45–75 (2·1in case), which was announced at the beginning of the year. Business then moved to Bridgeport, Connecticut. Rifles leaving the Bridgeport factory after April 1876 bore an additional 'OLD RELIABLE' mark on their barrels. The straight ·40–70 (2·5in case) had appeared in March, followed by the first ·45–100 (2·875in case) in June. A modified ·45–100, in a shorter 2·6in case, was introduced in November.

¶ The ·45–90 cartridge was introduced in 1877, with a straight case measuring 2·4in, but the Sharps Rifle Company was liquidated in September 1881. Interested parties continued to sell the stock-in-hand until the middle of the decade, but the famous rifle then disappeared.

Sharps' Long Range or Creedmoor Rifle *1871 and 1874 No.1, No.2 or No.3 patterns.* The first guns were made in the middle of 1873, being announced simply as "Sharps' Long Range Rifles". The Creedmoor name had not then become fashionable. Chambered only for the ·44–90 cartridge, with a 2·6in case, they had octagonal barrels of 32in or 34in and chequered pistol-grip butts. Vernier sights lay on the upper tang behind the breech; globe-pattern front sights, with wind gauge and spirit level, were fitted at the muzzle. The three genuine 'Creedmoor' rifles were introduced in 1875 on the basis of the preceding Long Range pattern. The No.1 had a 32in half- or fully-octagonal barrel, a chequered pistol-grip butt, and a chequered fore-end. Straight shotgun-style shoulder plates were standard. A vernier sight lay on the tang, and a globe-pattern front sight (with wind gauge and spirit level) appeared at the muzzle. No.2 was similar, but had a plain straight-wrist butt and lacked chequering on the fore-end. No.3 had a 30in barrel, a straight-wrist butt and an aperture sight on the tang instead of the more sophisticated vernier type. A short-lived No.4 rifle, the plainest of the series, was similar to the No.3 but was stocked in poorer wood.

¶ Creedmoor Rifles chambered ·44–77 cartridges (2·250in or 2·438in cases) in addition to the popular ·44–90. The Creedmoor patterns were supplemented in 1876—perhaps actually superseded—by the Mid- and Long-Range Rifles.

Sharps' Hunter Rifle *1874 pattern.* Available from the Spring of 1875 onward, this is believed to have been a plain-finish sporting gun with a round barrel, a single trigger, and a straight wrist butt with a rifle-type butt plate.

Sharps' Business Rifle *1874 pattern.* This plain gun appeared in the summer of 1876. Offered only with a blued octagonal barrel, it had a double set trigger and open sights. The oil-finished straight wrist butt had a rifle-pattern (concave) butt plate. The Business Rifle was chambered only for the military ·45–70 cartridge, or for the proprietary long-case ·45–100 sometimes listed as '·45–120'.

Sharps' Mid-Range Rifle *1874 No.1, No.2 and No.3 patterns.* Introduced in the Spring of 1876, three differing Mid-Range Rifles were made. The No.1 (·40–70) had a 30in half- or fully-octagonal barrel, and a chequered pistol-grip butt with a nickelled rifle-type butt plate. It had a vernier back sight on the tang in addition to the conventional open back sight on the barrel, and the standard globe-pattern front sight—with wind gauge and spirit level—lay on the muzzle. No.2 was similar, but had a straight-wrist butt and a plainer finish; No.3 was identical to No.2, but chambered the smaller ·40–50 (1·875in case) cartridge.

Sharps' Long-Range Rifle *1874 No.1, No.2 and No.3 patterns.* Announced in the Autumn of 1876, this was really little more than a Mid-Range Rifle (q.v.) with a half-octagon or fully-octagonal barrel of 32 or 34in. Chamberings were ·44–90, ·45–90 or ·45–100, cases measuring 2·625in, 2·4in and 2·6in respectively. The Long Range Rifles lacked the barrel-mounted back sight, relying solely on vernier and globe fittings; the vernier sight could be mounted on the tang immediately behind the receiver or on the comb of the butt near the heel. The chequered woodwork of the No.1 pattern was selected for its decorative figuring, a sterling silver escutcheon—intended for the firer's name—being let into the fore-end. No.2 was similar, but had a plain fore-end without the escutcheon and lacked the spirit level on the front sight. No.3 was simply No.2 with a chequered straight-wrist butt.

Sharps' New or English Model *1875 No.1, No.2 and No.3 patterns.* Encouraged by sales in Europe, Sharps introduced this rifle, distinguished by a slender butt and fore-end and a lightweight action. The hammer was much more delicate than the sturdy patterns favoured in North America. The intention was apparently to provide as heavy a barrel as possible within the 10lb limit imposed in off-hand shooting competitions. Advertised from 1880 in three grades (cf., Mid-Range Rifle), the English Model proved to be very unpopular; less than 1,000 actions were made, many being completed as standard sporters for sale in John Lower's "Sportsman's Depot" in Denver, Colorado.

Other patterns Frank Freund of Cheyenne, Wyoming, patented a improved Sharps-type action in August 1876. The round-topped breech block, instead of moving vertically, was allowed to move backward as it dropped. When the breech lever was closed, the block moved up and forward to cam the cartridge-case forward into the breech. Sharps rifles modified by Freund—trading first as 'Freund & Bro.' and then as 'The Wyoming Armory'—often had patented 'More Light' sights, with a contrasting line on the back edge of the front-sight blade and an additional aperture in the back sight leaf beneath the notch. Guns may also be encountered with a patented detachable pistol grip. A few Wyoming Saddle Guns were made in the early 1880s, embodying hand-made Freund-Sharps actions with notably elongated flat-side receivers, but were too expensive to sell in quantity. It is suspected that no more than 10-15 were ever completed.

MODERN RE-CREATIONS

The strength and long-established reputation of the Sharps rifles led to a revival in popularity in the 1970s. The first guns were made in Italy, apparently by Pedersoli and others, but were followed in the 1980s by good-quality versions made in the USA.

¶ EMF Co., Inc., of Santa Ana, California, offered the first of its 'Old Reliable' Sharps in 1992. Made in sporting and military styles, as full-length rifles or half-stocked carbines, the guns originated in Italy.

¶ The Navy Arms Company of Ridgefield, New Jersey, began to import its ·45–70 Plains Rifles and Cavalry Carbines from Italy in the early 1990s. The rifle was about 45·8in long, had a 28·5in barrel and weighed 8·6lb. The straight-wrist butt and short round-tip fore-end were chequered. The carbine had a 22in barrel, giving an overall length of about 39in. Weight averaged 7·7lb.

¶ The C. Sharps Rifle Company of Big Timber, Montana, offered a range of Sharps-type rifles from 1987 onward. Since 1992, they have been distributed under the Montana Armory name. The Model 1874 was offered in ·40, ·44 or ·45 calibre, for virtually any suitable chambering. It has been made as a Military Rifle, Military Carbine, Business Rifle, Sporting Rifle No.1 and No.1, or Long Range Express Sporting Rifle. A typical sporter had a 30in octagonal barrel and weighed about 9·5lb. The Model 1875 was patterned on the improved Sharps rifle, with a greatly simplified slab-sided receiver and a shorter operating lever. The basic patterns included the Sporting Rifle (30in octagonal barrel), a Saddle Gun (26in octagonal barrel) or the Carbine (24in round barrel). A Business Rifle was added about 1990, with a 28in round barrel, and a Target & Long Range Model was announced at the beginning of in 1991.

¶ Shiloh Products, a division of Drovel Tool Company, began trading in Farmingdale, New York, in 1976. After expanding to become the Shiloh Rifle Manufacturing Company, Inc., business moved to Big Timber, Montana, in 1983. Shiloh Sharps rifles have been offered in cap-lock or metal cartridge versions, patterned after the original models of 1863 and 1874 respectively. Shiloh 'Model 1874' cartridge, offered in a wide range of chamberings, show great diversity. Virtually all sporting patterns, however, have double set-triggers.

¶ Sile Distributors of New York has distributed guns believed to have been made by Pedersoli. Chambered for ·45–70 or ·45–120 cartridges, they had colour case-hardened receivers, hammers and butt plates; the action was also fitted with an automatic safety. They were offered as the 'Old Reliable', with a 28in octagonal barrel, chequered walnut woodwork, and a weight of about 9·5lb; as a Sporting Rifle or Carbine; or as a Military Rifle. Vernier tang and globe sights were optional extras on the sporting rifles.

handle was reduced, an improved radial safety catch appeared on the right side of the bolt shroud, and a recessed bolt head was used. Rifles were made in about twenty chamberings, including several magnums, but work seems to have been abandoned about 1973.

SHARPS

UNITED STATES OF AMERICA

These dropping-block breech-loaders were based on a patent granted to Christian Sharps in September 1848, and improvements made by Richard Lawrence in the 1850s.

The essence of the Sharps rifle was a breech block sliding in a sturdy receiver. After thumbing the hammer back to half-cock, depressing the operating lever—which doubled as the trigger guard—dropped the breech block by way of an intermediate link, extracting a spent case as the block dropped below the bottom of the chamber. Returning the lever closed the block; if the chamber had been reloaded, thumbing the hammer back to full cock allowed the gun to be fired by pressure on the trigger.

Unlike many rival designs promoted prior to 1870, the Sharps action was reliable and could handle the most powerful sporting cartridges. Though the cumbersome external hammer and back-action lock were retained, Sharps rifles performed better with metal-case cartridges than combustible ammunition; even when fitted with the Conant or Lawrence gas-check systems, cap-locks had leaked gas. However, introduction of more effectual guns gradually eroded the superiority and even the improved Borchardt (q.v.) could not save the company.

MILITARY WEAPONS

The most important use of Sharps-type metallic cartridge guns was made by the US Army, which sanctioned the conversion of more than 30,000 in 1867–9. These served until displaced by the 1873-model Springfields in the mid 1870s.

Model 1870

Rifle and carbine patterns.
Made by the National Armory, Springfield, Massachusetts, 1870–1.
Quantity: see notes.
·50–70, rimmed.
Dropping-block action, operated by a lever forming the trigger guard.
DATA FOR A TYPICAL RIFLE
49·63in overall, 9·00lb unladen.
32·50in barrel, 3-groove rifling; RH, concentric.
Ramp-and-leaf sight graduated to 1,000 yards?
1,275 ft/sec with 425-grain bullet.
M1855 socket bayonet.

☆

1871: large numbers of these guns were issued for army trials, though the precise quantity remains in dispute. Springfield completed 501 rifles in March and an additional 500 in July; however, some reports suggest that 2,470 rifles and carbines were issued. The difference may have been the use of converted guns from store. The M1870 rifles amalgamated the fittings and barrels of M1863 rifle-muskets, lined down from ·58, and altered 1863-type actions taken from Civil War carbines. The guns had full-length fore-ends retained by two bands—a few three-band examples were also made—while the carbines had 22in barrels and half-length fore-ends retained by a single band. Carbine sights were graduated only to about 800 yards.

The guns were unpopular with the troops, as they jammed too frequently; and the carbines, chambering ·56–50 Spencer rimfire cartridges, misfired persistently. They were discarded after the trials had been completed.

Military Model

Rifle and carbine patterns.
Made by the Sharps Rifle Mfg Co., Hartford, Connecticut, 1870–4; and the Sharps Rifle Company, Hartford, Connecticut, 1874–6, and Bridgeport, Connecticut, 1876–8.
·45–70 Government or ·50–70 Government.
Action: as M1870 rifle, above.

DATA FOR A TYPICAL POST-1873 RIFLE
·45–70 Government, rimmed.
47·13in overall, 8·85lb unladen.
30·00in barrel, 3-groove rifling; RH, concentric.
Ramp-and-leaf sight graduated to 1,000 yards.
1,320 ft/sec with 405-grain bullet.
Sabre or socket bayonet.

☆

1870: military-style rifles and carbines, based on the original (1869) or perfected (1871) sporting rifles (see panel opposite) were offered until the advent of the Sharps-Borchardt rifle in 1878. Rifles generally had 30in barrels and full-length fore-ends retained by two bands. Carbines had 22in barrels, half-length fore-ends retained by a single band, and a sling ring on the left side of the receiver. A few sold to state militia units, but enthusiasm elsewhere was muted.

SPORTING GUNS

In addition to the post-1866 cartridge patterns, many pre-1865 cap-locks—made by Robbins & Lawrence for the Sharps Rifle Manufacturing Company—survived the American Civil War to be converted for sporting use. Major patterns are summarised in the panel on page 254.

SHILEN

UNITED STATES OF AMERICA

Founded by Ed Shilen in 1961, to make the high-quality barrels for which it is world famous, this company made its first complete guns in the 1970s. Five models share a turning bolt with dual-opposed locking lugs and a pin-type ejector. Excepting DGA/BP and DGA/BP-S patterns, the contours of the receivers are squared.

DGA

Made by Shilen Rifles, Inc., Ennis, Texas.
Chambering: see text.
Turning-bolt action, locked by rotating lugs on the bolt head into the receiver wall.

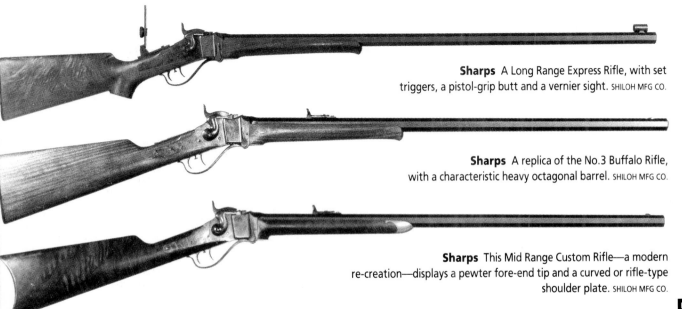

Sharps A Long Range Express Rifle, with set triggers, a pistol-grip butt and a vernier sight. SHILOH MFG CO.

Sharps A replica of the No.3 Buffalo Rifle, with a characteristic heavy octagonal barrel. SHILOH MFG CO.

Sharps This Mid Range Custom Rifle—a modern re-creation—displays a pewter fore-end tip and a curved or rifle-type shoulder plate. SHILOH MFG CO.

DATA FOR A TYPICAL DGA SPORTER
·284 Winchester, rimless.
44·50in overall, 7·55lb unladen.
24·00in barrel, 4-groove rifling; RH, concentric?
Internal box magazine, 3 rounds.
Optical sight.
2,900 ft/sec with 150-grain bullet.
☆

1975*: the standard DGA Sporter and DGA Magnum Sporter were introduced for cartridges with maximum overall lengths of 2·85in and 3·69in respectively.

Stocks were American walnut, or fibreglass finished in textured brown, silver, black, red, royal blue or green acrylic enamel. Sporter patterns had classic straight-comb butts and round-tip fore-ends; Bench-Rest guns offered unusually broad fore-ends; and the Silhouette versions had sharply-pitched high combs suited to optical sights mounted high above the bore. Varminters had broad fore-ends, sharply-curved pistol grips, and low roll-over combs.

Cylindrical or tapered barrels were standard, though octagonal patterns have often been made to order to complement the squared lines of the larger actions. The metalwork was either matt ('satin') blue or dulled nickel.

Triggers were sturdy adjustable multi-lever patterns with a pull of about 3lb, though Shilen Competition Triggers (with a pull of 2–6oz) and a comparable electronic version were supplied on request. Pivoting safety levers were usually fitted to the magazine rifles.

The rigid DGA Single-Shot action has proved popular for long-range silhouette shooting and 'Heavy Varmint' bench-rest competitions. The safety was customarily omitted from single-shot guns, which were often stocked in stable warp-resistant fibreglass. DGA/BP (lightweight) and DGA/BP-S (ultra light) actions were intended for single-shot rifles and silhouette pistols.

1980: Shilen listed 'All Caliber' chamberings for Sporter (24in No.2 barrel) and Varminter (25in No.5) rifles. The standard options for the Sporter were regarded as ·17 Remington, ·220 Swift, ·222 Remington, ·22–250, ·223 Remington, 6mm Remington, ·243 Winchester, ·250–3000

Savage, ·257 Roberts, ·284 Winchester, ·308 Winchester or ·358 Winchester.

The DGA Silhouette—in single-shot or magazine-fed forms—was offered in 7mm–08 or ·308 Winchester, with others available on request; DGA Benchrest Rifles accepted ·220 Swift, ·22–250, 6 × 47mm Remington or ·308 Winchester, though many others were supplied to order. The catalogue noted that choice of 'caliber, twist, chambering, [barrel] contour or [barrel] length' was left to the purchaser.

1988: Shilen listed more than seventy cartridge options ranging from ·17 Remington to ·458 Winchester Magnum.

SIG

SWITZERLAND
Also known as
Fabrique d'Armes de Neuhausen,
Schweizerische Industrie-Gesellschaft,
Société Industrielle Suisse or
Waffenfabrik Neuhausen
〜

The premier privately-owned Swiss gunmaking company, SIG has a history dating back to the middle of the nineteenth century. In addition to work on Vetterli and Schmidt(-Rubin) service rifles, semi-experimental Neuhausen straight-pull bolt actions were developed unsuccessfully in the late 1880s.

SIG made a wide variety of auto-loading rifles between the wars. A gas-operated 7·5mm KEG prototype, adapted from the promising KE-7 light machine-gun, was refined into the N-42 to compete in the mid 1940s with the AK-44 promoted by the Eidgenössische Waffenfabrik. Neither rifle was acceptable, even though a few hundred improved N-42 rifles, designated N-46 or SK46, were made for trials.

The state factory produced an 'AK-49', for intermediate and then full-power cartridges, while SIG attempted to perfect the AK-53—in which the barrel, once unlocked, was blown forward away from the standing breech. The authorities remained dissatisfied until the AM-55

was developed in Neuhausen in the mid 1950s under the supervision of Rudolf Amsler.

MILITARY WEAPONS
BOLIVIA

The army purchased about 5,000 SG 510-4 rifles in the 1960s, followed in 1980–5 by a substantial quantity of 5·56mm SG 540-type guns made in France by Manurhin.

CHILE

About 15,000 SG 510-4 rifles were purchased in the 1960s from SIG, by way of Beretta. A licence was also acquired to permit FAMAE of Santiago to begin production. Work had scarcely commenced, however, when the SG 540 was substituted in 1986. Guns are still being made for the Chilean armed forces. Military rifles apparently bear the national arms on the right side of the receiver—described in detail in the Mauser section—and EJERCITO DE CHILE.

FRANCE

The 540-series guns were licensed to Manurhin of Mulhouse in c.1975, not only so that they could enter trials with advantageous backing of a French manufacturer but also to permit export without contravening Swiss law. French-made 540-series rifles have been distributed more widely than SIG equivalents, especially among former French colonies in Africa. Large numbers have also been sold in Bolivia, Chile, Ecuador, Nicaragua and Paraguay. Some were supplied to Indonesia and others went to the Lebanon.

Substantial quantities of Manurhin SG 540 rifles—perhaps 20,000—were acquired by the French army in the late 1970s pending issue of the 5·56mm FAMAS. Though now displaced from front-line service, they were retained by the Foreign Legion and overseas units as late as 1990. The first issues were made to French contingents serving with United Nations forces in Lebanon in 1978–9.

SIG The 7·5mm SG 510-0 (Stgw.57), lacking its detachable box magazine; the sights are folded down. SIG

SIG Another view of the SG 510–0, with the sights raised and the magazine emplaced. SIG

SWITZERLAND
Model 510

AM-55, SG 510–1, SG 510–2, SG 510–3, SG 510–4
and Stgw.57.
Made by SIG, Neuhausen am Rheinfalls.
Chambering: see notes.
Auto-loading action, relying on rollers in the breech
block to delay the opening stroke.
DATA FOR A TYPICAL STGW.57
7·5 × 55mm, rimless.
1,105mm overall, 5·55kg with bipod and
empty magazine.
583mm barrel, 4-groove rifling; RH, concentric.
Detachable box magazine, 24 rounds.
Folding pillar sight graduated to 800 metres.
760 m/sec with ball ammunition; 475–500 rpm.
Stgw.57 knife bayonet.
☆

1954: inspiration for this rifle came from wartime German designs, specifically the StG.45 (M) (see 'CETME'). As the gun fired, generating pressure that tended to thrust the cartridge case backward, two short round-tip flaps anchored in the bolt-head were forced to retract into their housing. Resistance was provided partly by careful attention to the angled entry of the flaps into the receiver wall and partly by the inertia of the heavy bolt body. The whole mechanism then reciprocated to reload; as the bolt closed, the body forced the locking flaps outward into the receiver wall. Extraction was violent enough to demand a fluted chamber, but the weapon soon attained a reputation for reliability in untaxing Swiss service. Whether this could be sustained by less disciplined users, or in desert or arctic warfare, is another matter entirely.

1955: the prototype AM-55 rifle (subsequently renamed Selbstladegewehr [SG] 510–0), having passed army tests, was approved for service.

1957: the Sturmgewehr 57, also known as the "Fusil d'Assaut Mle.57", was easily identified by its straight-line construction and rubberised butt. A short ribbed plastic hand guard appeared beneath the barrel jacket ahead of the magazine, the sights could be folded, and the bipod could

be mounted at the muzzle or at the breech. The standard 24-round box magazine could be replaced when necessary by the 30-round type associated with the lMG.25 or by a special six-round version for grenade-launching blanks.

The Stgw.57 was very expensive to make, though quality was excellent. Weight was great enough to mask the effects of a rapid breech stroke, and accuracy was very good. However, firing automatically from a closed bolt meant that the effects of barrel heat had to be monitored to prevent 'cook off' ignitions.

1958: the improved SG 510–1 was introduced to encourage exports, though it was little more than a Stgw.57 chambering the 7·62 × 51mm NATO cartridge. The SG 510–2 was a lightened variant with a wooden butt and a slimmer barrel jacket; SG 510–3 chambered the 7·62 × 39mm Russian M43 round. All these guns had straight comb wood butts, but characteristics varied: the 510–3, for example, had a short barrel and its magazine had a sharper curve than the other versions. The bayonet stud lay on the barrel jacket behind the sight assembly to compensate for the shortened muzzle.

1963*: the SG 510–4 appeared, chambered for 7·62 × 51mm NATO ammunition. Made with a 505mm barrel, the gun was 1,015mm long; weight averaged 4·75kg with a bipod and an empty twenty-round magazine. Cyclic rate was about 600 rpm. A new wooden fore-end/hand guard assembly and curved-comb butt sacrificed some of the advantages of straight-line layout so that sturdier fixed sights could be used. A bipod could be fitted above the barrel jacket behind the front sight, whilst the muzzle was adapted to double as a grenade launcher. Changes to the woodwork and sights of the SG 510–3 were made in the same era.

The SG 510–4 sold comparatively well in South America, especially in Bolivia and Chile, but was too expensive to interest major armies. Swiss laws preventing the export of certain classes of weapon proved to be inhibiting.

1983: production of Stgw.57 ceased after about 585,000 had been made. Most of the work was undertaken by SIG, though some final assembly

work apparently occurred in the Eidgenössische Waffenfabrik in Bern.

Model 530

Made by SIG, Neuhausen am Rheinfalls.
5·56 × 45mm.
Gas-operated auto-loading action, locked by engaging
pivoting bolt-mounted struts in the receiver walls.
DATA FOR A TYPICAL SG 530–1
955mm overall, 3·27kg without magazine.
390mm barrel, 4-groove rifling; RH, concentric.
Detachable box magazine, 20 or 30 rounds.
Rotating aperture sight graduated to 400 metres.
875 m/sec with SS109 ball ammunition; 600 rpm.
Optional knife bayonet.
☆

1967*: committed to the Stgw.57, the Swiss army showed little interest in the improved SG 510–4. SIG then produced its first 5·56mm rifle, retaining the two-part bolt and pivoting locking flaps but adding a gas piston assembly above the barrel to operate what had become a positive lock. Gas was tapped from the barrel as the gun fired, impinging on the piston-head to force the rear part of the bolt carrier back far enough for the locking flaps to disengage the receiver wall. The action ran back until the return spring asserted itself, stripping a fresh round into the chamber and forcing the flaps back into their locked position as the breech closed.

1971: trials revealed that the breech system was not suited to the high pressure 5·56mm round. As the SG 530 was expensive to make, work concentrated thereafter on the simpler SG 540.

Model 540

540, 541, 542 and 543 patterns.
Made by SIG, Neuhausen am Rheinfalls.
5·56 × 45mm or 7·62 × 51mm.
Gas-operated auto-loading action, locked by rotating
lugs on the bolt head into the receiver walls.
DATA FOR A TYPICAL SG 542
7·62 × 51mm NATO, rimless.
1,000mm overall, 4·07kg with bipod and
empty magazine.

SIG A military version of the 7·5mm SG 510–4, with bipod, grenade launcher and bayonet lug. SIG

SIG Derived from the SG 510–4, the AMT Sporter was restricted to semi-automatic fire. It lacked the bipod, grenade launching attachments and bayonet fittings. SIG

465mm barrel, 4-groove rifling; RH, concentric.
Detachable box magazine, 20 rounds.
Drum sight graduated to 600 metres.
820 m/sec with SS77 ball ammunition; 625 ± 25 rpm.
Optional knife bayonet.

☆

1972: this replaced the unsuccessful SG 530. A rotating-bolt lock was used and the guns were simplified externally. Prototypes had wooden furniture, but synthetic versions were soon substituted. The gas regulator was adjustable and a selector lever lay on the left side of the receiver above the pistol grip; markings were displayed through a small circular aperture. Single shots and (optional) three-shot bursts could be fired, or the gun could be set to operate automatically. A Heckler & Koch-type back sight was used, a bipod folded under the fore-end, and special attention was paid to dismantling; pressing a catch on the left side of the receiver, above the magazine release, allowed the entire barrel/fore-end/breech assembly to swing open.

The standard SG 540 could be obtained in fixed or folding-butt patterns, as could the short-barrelled SG 543. The SG 541 formed the basis for the Stgw.90 described below. SG 540 rifles were 950mm long, had 460mm barrels and weighed 3·25kg without magazines or bipods; the alternative pattern was 720mm overall with the butt folded and weighed about 3·3kg.

The SG 543 was 805mm long, had a 300mm barrel and weighed 2·95kg without magazine. The bipod was omitted. Folding-butt examples collapsed to only 570mm overall.

1975: a manufacturing licence was sold to Manurhin (see 'France', above). The first guns were made in Mulhouse in 1977–8.

1979: a modified SG 540—known as the SG 541—was developed for trials against a rival Eidgenössische Waffenfabrik prototype.

The SG 541, made in two barrel lengths, had a synthetic skeleton butt, an integral bipod and a modified safety catch in which all the markings were stamped into the outside of the receiver.

1983: the Swiss army provisionally adopted the SG 541 to replace the ageing Stgw.57, but shortage of funds delayed final acceptance.

Model 550

SG 550, SG 551 and Stgw.90 patterns.
Made by SIG, Neuhausen am Rheinfalls.
5·56 × 45mm.
Action: as SG 540, above.
DATA FOR STGW.90
1,000mm overall (butt extended), 4·10kg with bipod and empty magazine.
528mm barrel, 6-groove rifling; RH, concentric.
Detachable box magazine, 20 or 30 rounds.
Drum sight graduated to 500 metres.
980 m/sec with US M193 ball ammunition.
Knife bayonet.

☆

1984: little more than an improved SG 541—practically indistinguishable externally—these guns were adopted by the Swiss Army as the Sturmgewehr Modell 90 (Stgw.90). They retained the operating system of the SG 540, but the previously optional three-round burst firing mechanism was standardised. The plastic butt had a distinctive central void, and a transparent plastic magazine was fitted. Bipods were fitted to the standard SG 550, but not on the SG 551 'headquarters weapon', the barrel length of which was reduced to 357mm. Heavy-barrel sniper rifles have been made for evaluation.

1986: the first of about 600,000 series-made Stgw.90 were issued for service, the intention being to issue each new recruit with a 5·56mm rifle while the ageing 7·5mm Stgw.57 is phased out—a process that will take many years.

SPORTING GUNS

In addition to military-surplus Stgw.57, limited to semi-automatic operation for sale in the USA as the 'PE-57', SG 510–3 and 510–4 rifles have also been advertised for sporting purposes. The most notable variant has been the ·308 AMT. Restricted to single shots and obtainable with five- or ten-round magazines (plus the standard military twenty-round pattern), this 'sporter' offered a folding winter trigger and a bipod. A combination of high price and ultra-military appearance kept sales to a minimum.

SIMONOV

UNION OF SOVIET SOCIALIST REPUBLICS

These gas-operated rifles originally served the Red Army, though some captured guns were used during the Winter War by the Finns and a few were impressed into the Wehrmacht after the German invasion of Russia. The SKS, introduced after the end of the Second World War, has been made in several satellite and Soviet Bloc countries.

Sergei Simonov began his design work in the mid 1920s. Stung by the failure of the AVS in the mid 1930s, he improved the basic action until an effectual prototype was tested against the Tokarev in 1939. Simonov always claimed that the adoption of the SVT-38 was politically motivated, and that his gun was actually better; this conclusion was partly supported by a Soviet technical commission, which reported that the improved Simonov was easier to produce and less wasteful of raw material. But the suspicion remains that the Tokarev shot better and had a more efficient locking mechanism.

Eventually, after extensive trials, Simonov perfected the SKS carbine at the end of the Second World War. Though supplemented and then superseded by the Kalashnikov, the SKS remained in production in the Soviet Union until the mid 1950s. Substantial quantities remain in store, and, owing to its good balance, the SKS is still preferred for ceremonial duties.

CHINA
PEOPLE'S REPUBLIC

Type 56

Carbine.
Made by Factory 26 and Factory 138.
Quantity: in excess of five million?
7·62 × 39mm, rimless.
Gas-operated auto-loading action, locked by tilting the tail of the bolt downward into the receiver.

SIG The unsuccessful 5·56mm SG 530–1 embodied a locked-breech version of the original pivoting strut mechanism. SIG

SIG Developed to replace the SG 530, the SG 540 incorporated a rotating-bolt lock. Machining was simplified where possible to reduce manufacturing costs. SIG

1,122mm overall, 3·86kg unladen. 520mm barrel, 4-groove rifling; RH, concentric. Integral charger-loaded box magazine, 10 rounds. Tangent-leaf sight graduated to 1,000 metres. 735 m/sec with Soviet Type PS ball cartridges. Integral folding bayonet.

☆

1956: though differing in detail, the Chinese SKS shared the general characteristics of its Soviet prototype (q.v.). The earliest guns were generally made of blued steel and had knife-bladed bayonets. Their safety heads were fluted or sometimes chequered. Later examples had triangular-blade bayonets, apparently to rationalise production with the Type 56–1 (Kalashnikov); guns made by Factory 26 were generally quite good quality, but the products of Factory 138 often had investment-cast receivers and presented a decidedly inferior appearance. Virtually all displayed the factory mark and designation on the left side of the receiver, accompanied by a serial number, seemingly sequential, that sometimes ran to seven digits.

Production in Factories 26 and 138 alone, on the basis of serial numbers, could have exceeded 22 million; given the enormous size of the Chinese militia, this is not beyond the realms of probability. However, it is suspected that other guns—e.g., the Type 56–1 Kalashnikov—were included in the same series.

1984: an improved 7·62mm 'Type 84' SKS with a twenty round Kalashnikov-type magazine was advertised, accompanied by a 5·56 × 45mm export version designated 'Type EM3611'.

GERMANY
DEMOCRATIC REPUBLIC

Karabiner-S

Made in the former Sauer & Sohn factory, Suhl. Quantity: perhaps 1·5 million. 7·62 × 39mm, rimless. Otherwise generally as Chinese Type 56 except back sight (graduated to 800 metres) and a knife-type folding bayonet.

☆

1955: production of the Karabiner-S appears to have begun in Suhl. The guns were closely patterned on the Soviet SKS, but had a sling slot through the butt and lacked the cleaning rod. A knife-type bayonet was fitted, the stock was generally a laminated pattern stained a yellowish shade, and the safety-catch head was ribbed. The carbines bore marks such as 60 K 1234 on the left side of the receiver, indicating the year of production ('60' = 1960) and the serial number.

KOREA
PEOPLE'S REPUBLIC

Type 63

Made by state factories. Quantity: at least a million. 7·62 × 39mm, rimless. Otherwise generally as Chinese Type 56 except back sight (graduated to 800 metres) and a knife-type folding bayonet.

☆

1963: production of this SKS variant began. It was generally similar to the Soviet pattern, but displayed lower standards of workmanship and finish. The bolt carrier was usually phosphated. A knife-blade bayonet and a cleaning rod were retained, but the stock and hand guard were generally laminated. A swivel lay on the under edge of the butt. The safety-catch head and bolt handle were ribbed; most other SKS derivatives have knurled bolt handles.

U S S R
Model 1931

Trials rifle: Avtomaticheskaya vintovka Sistemy Simonova, optny obr.1931g. Made by the state ordnance factory, Izhevsk, 1931–5. Quantity: at least 410 (see notes). 7·62 × 54mm, rimmed. Gas-operated auto-loading action, locked by displacing a hollow block downward into the receiver. Dimensionally similar to the 1936 pattern, below. Detachable box magazine, 20 rounds.

Tangent-leaf sight graduated to 1,500 metres. 835 m/sec with Type L cartridges, cyclic rate unknown. Integral folding bayonet.

☆

1931: the first of these guns was submitted for trials spread over several years. The Simonov is known to have been gas operated, but has proved difficult to identify. It is believed to have had a one-piece pistol-grip stock with the back sight on top of the distinctively squared receiver immediately behind the ejection port. A short sheet-metal guard appeared above the barrel, and an additional metal section lay ahead of the chamber. Both portions were drilled with holes to facilitate the circulation of air, and the two parts were connected by a wooden hand guard with three longitudinal slots. There were no barrel bands. Two transverse recoil bolts were used and fully-automatic fire was apparently achieved by pulling the trigger back far enough to depress a blade set into the rear of the trigger-guard bow.

1933: thirty more guns were made for trials.
1934: on 22 March, the authorities decided to adopt the Simonov automatic rifle, abandoning the obr.1930g Degtyarev. More than a hundred guns were made during the year, including a few 'AKSI' (Avtomaticheskaya karabina Simonova, 'Simonov automatic carbine') for trials against the 1935-type Tokarev. The AKSI was shorter and 400gm lighter than the 1931-pattern rifle, but was rejected in April 1935.
1935: 290 additional Simonov rifles were made for trials. It is assumed that they represented an improved form of the original obr.1931g, but the respects in which they differed are not known. Owing to the adoption of the AVS, which followed in 1936, it is suspected that they were much closer in design to the later gun than has been admitted.

Model 1936

Automatic rifle: Avtomaticheskaya vintovka Simonova (AVS), obr.1936g. Made by the state ordnance factory, Izhevsk, 1937–8. Quantity: about 32,000.

SIG The SG 540 with the optional folding butt. SIG

SIG A short-barrelled SG 543. SIG

SIG Adopted by the Swiss army, the short-barrelled version of the Stgw.90 (SG 551) has a distinctively voided butt. SIG

7·62 × 54mm, rimmed.
Action: as 1931 pattern, above.
1,259mm overall, 4·40kg with empty magazine.
627mm barrel, 4-groove rifling; RH, concentric.
Detachable box magazine, 20 rounds.
Tangent-leaf sight graduated to 1,500 metres.
835 m/sec with Type L ball cartridges; cyclic rate
600 ± 50 rpm.
AVS sword bayonet.

☆

1936: this improvement on the guns made in 1934–5 was ordered into full-scale production virtually before its trials had been completed.

The AVS had a one-piece pistol-grip stock with a short sheet-metal hand guard towards the muzzle. The cleaning rod was set into the right side of the stock alongside the barrel, whilst the distance from the pistol grip to the centre of the trigger lever was too great for comfort unless the firer had a large hand.

1937: series production began in the Izhevsk ordnance factory, but so many problems were encountered that only about 10,000 guns had been made by the end of the year.

Comparing an early undated rifle with a 1938-vintage weapon reveals that the original straight-top hand guard was soon replaced by a stepped pattern with an additional locking catch; the recoil-spring was strengthened; the receiver machining was simplified; the shape of the trigger guard was revised; the back-sight slider was improved; and the selector and safety catch were changed.

1938: experience revealed that the rifle had severe operating problems. It was much too light for effectual automatic fire, the standards of manufacture were poor, and the action jammed too often owing to variations in ammunition pressure. The AVS was controversially replaced by the simpler Tokarev (q.v.).

1939: the AVS served through the Winter War against Finland, but the campaigns emphasised structural weakness and constant susceptibility to jamming. Rifles captured by the Finns may be encountered with 'SA' property marks. Others were used by the Red Army and Soviet partisans in 1941–2; a few even served the Wehrmacht.

Model 1945

••

Semi-automatic carbine: Samozaryadnaya karabina sistemy Simonova ('SKS').
Made by the state ordnance factories in Izhevsk and elsewhere.
Quantity: several million.
7·62 × 39mm, rimless.
Gas-operated auto-loading action, locked by tilting the tail of the bolt downward into the receiver.
1,122mm overall, 3·86kg unladen.
520mm barrel, 4-groove rifling; RH, concentric.
Integral charger-loaded box magazine, 10 rounds.
Tangent-leaf sight graduated to 800 metres.
735 m/sec with Type PS ball cartridges.
Integral folding bayonet.

☆

1939: while the SVT-38 (Tokarev) was being mass-produced, Simonov, disappointed by the failure of the AVS and its successors, produced a short semi-automatic carbine with a fixed ten-round box magazine.

1940: tested, found wanting and rejected in October, the experimental Simonov was soon replaced by an improved version.

1941: encouraging tests were undertaken in April with two differing 'optny obr. 1941g' carbines, one with a ten-round magazine loaded from a special charger and the other loaded from two standard five-cartridge Mosin-Nagant chargers. The guns are said to have used special 7·62 × 25mm ammunition, but the project was abandoned when the Germans invaded the Soviet Union.

1943: once tests had been undertaken with captured German MP.43 (see 'Haenel'), Soviet designers recommended work on similar assault rifles. By the end of the year, a design team led by Semin and Elizarov had adapted the 7·9mm Kurz cartridge, but no effectual gun had been forthcoming apart from an improved version of the SKS41. The new SKS43 was smaller than its predecessor, lacked the muzzle brake and had a stronger folding bayonet. Charger guides were moved from the receiver to the bolt carrier.

1944: several hundred carbines were sent to the Byelorussian Front, where they were well

received. The SKS was promptly ordered into mass production, but the first series-built guns did not appear until after hostilities had ended.

1946: mass production of the SKS (or SKS45') began, apparently as a safeguard against the failure of the Kalashnikov (q.v.) assault rifle. It was a conventional weapon with a pistol-gripped wooden stock—laminated on some guns—and had a distinctive folding bayonet beneath the muzzle. It was easily dismantled and durable enough for arduous service.

The magazine could be loaded with single rounds or from rifle chargers, guides for the latter being machined on the bolt carrier face; unloading merely required the magazine housing to be unlatched and swung downward.

YUGOSLAVIA

Model 59

••

59, 59/66 and 59/66A1 patterns.
Made by Zavodi Crvena Zastava, Kraguyevač.
7·62 × 39mm, rimless.
Action: as Soviet SKS, above.
DATA FOR M59/66A1
1,120mm overall, 4·01kg unladen.
520mm barrel, 4-groove rifling; RH, concentric.
Integral charger-loaded box magazine, 10 rounds.
Tangent-leaf sight graduated to 800 metres.
735 m/sec with Soviet Type PS ball cartridges.
Integral folding bayonet.

☆

1959: production of an SKS copy began in the state arsenal, the guns being modelled closely on the Soviet version—excepting that they generally bore English-language marks and a distinctive ZCZ trademark.

1966: the basic design was modified to include a spigot-type grenade launcher and a grenade-launching sight which folded down behind the front-sight block when not required. The changes advanced the designation to 'Model 59/66' (subsequently '59/66A1'). Yugoslavian Simonov carbines were sold extensively on the export market, but were superseded in the 1970s by weapons based on the Kalashnikov.

Simonov The 7·62mm AVS auto-loader. PATTERN ROOM COLLECTION

Simonov A Chinese Type 56 rifle. PATTERN ROOM COLLECTION

Simonov A Yugoslavian Model 59/66, with an integral grenade launcher and a folding sight above the barrel. IAN HOGG

SNIDER

UNITED STATES OF AMERICA

This American design, best known for service in Britain, was also used in Denmark and Spain—and, in a modified form, by France. However, excepting those guns listed below, no new production was undertaken after 1875. Most of the lesser guns are listed in Part Two.

The essence of the Snider breech was a hinged block developed by Jacob Snider the Younger in association with François Eugene Schneider of Paris. Patents granted in Britain in 1864 protected an improved sideways-tipping block which could be retracted on its axis pin to extract the spent case.

The Snider was reliable once problems of premature opening had been overcome, solved in Britain with the Improved or Bolted breech of the Pattern III infantry rifle (q.v.). The short ·577 coiled-case cartridge proved to be more reliable in hot and arid conditions than the later ·450 design, and most British cavalrymen were sorry to receive Martini-Henry carbines instead of their Sniders.

Eventually, many British guns found their way abroad, particularly to Portugal and Japan. Several alleged 'proprietary' breech systems were very similar in principle to the Snider. They included the French Tabatière, submitted in questionable circumstances after a proper Snider conversion had been tentatively approved.

MILITARY WEAPONS

BRITAIN

1865: made by Potts & Hunt and chambered for French Pottet cartridges, the Snider trials rifle was susceptible to jamming. However, it was regarded as very strong; very little of the original stock needed to be cut away, unlike many of its rivals. The absence of the American Joslyn trials rifle promoted the Snider's cause appreciably, though the British Secretary of State preferred

the Storm conversion. This accepted standard combustible cartridges and could be loaded from the muzzle in an emergency.

Many inventors subsequently questioned the originality of the Snider breech, but only Thomas Wilson of Birmingham benefited by a grant of one tenth of the royalty payments.

Long Rifle

Infantry rifles: P/53 Converted and new Patterns I, I*, II, II*, II** and III.
Made by the Royal Small Arms Factory, Enfield (conversions and new guns, 1866–73); the Birmingham Small Arms Co. Ltd, Small Heath (conversions and new guns, 1867–73); and by the London Small Arms Co. Ltd, Bow (conversions and new guns, 1868–72).
Quantity: about 815,000.
·577, rimmed.
Laterally-swinging block, locked by an external hammer and (Pattern III breech only) a separate bolt.
DATA FOR PATTERN II** RIFLE
54·25in overall, 9·13lb unladen.
36·50in barrel, 3-groove rifling; RH, concentric.
Ramp-and-leaf sight graduated to 950 yards.
1,240 ft/sec with Mark IX ammunition.
P/53 socket bayonet.
☆

1865: an alteration of P/53 rifle-muskets with a Snider breech was sealed on 25 November as the "Musket, Rifled, Enfield P/53, converted on Snider's Principles". The first guns were delivered late in March 1866. They proved more accurate than the P/53 cap-lock and fired three times faster with practically no misfires or jamming. Results were so pleasing that the wholesale conversion of rifle-muskets began at Enfield immediately.

1866: a perfected 'Pattern I' was approved on 18 September, conversion contracts being placed with the Birmingham Small Arms Co. Ltd and the London Small Arms Co. Ltd to supplement the output of Enfield.

Based on the P/53 rifle-musket, the Snider had a new receiver and breech block unit ('shoe' in contemporary terminology). It was readily identified by its great length and three screwed

bands. Pattern I* was a conversion of Pattern I guns to Pattern II standards, with a partially squared counter-sink. The designation applied only to altered P/53 rifle muskets.

Approved in November 1866, the new long-base Mark II cartridge—with a squared case rim—necessitated a change in Snider breeches (P/53 and Lancaster patterns only). These were altered to Pattern II* standards by squaring the counter-sink for the case groove.

1867: Pattern II** was simply a Pattern II* with additional modifications to the extractor, and the underside of the breech block extended to cover the entire case-head; the receiver was revised and the nipple was shortened.

1869: existing actions showed a tendency to open prematurely as they began to wear. However, even though development of a ·450 Martini-Henry (q.v.) was proceeding steadily, large numbers of new Sniders were still needed to re-equip the standing army.

Trials with differing locking catches led to the approval of the Pattern III Snider breech, designed by Edward Bond of the London Small Arms Company and approved on 13 January. Guns embodying this 'Improved' or 'Bolted' action also had a steel barrel, a strengthened receiver and a squared-off hammer face. The knurled-head latch set into the left side of the breech block was most distinctive.

1870: the first rifles were issued in the summer. Military weapons displayed royal cyphers and government property/inspectors' marks, while commercial examples bore a large s transfixed by an arrow.

1874: the first issues of the Martini-Henry were made to infantry regiments on Home Service. Issue was completed at home and abroad by the end of 1875.

1879: about 5,000 Snider rifles were assembled in the Royal Small Arms Factory, Sparkbrook, Birmingham, from a mixture of old P/53 parts and new Pattern III actions.

1885: most Sniders serving the volunteers and militia had been replaced with the Martini-Henry. An inventory taken on 1 April revealed that 166,340 Sniders were in store.

Simonov Surviving AVS weapons were used during the Second World War. This famous picture, taken in Stalingrad in 1942, shows one such rifle in the foreground.
COLLECTOR'S COMPENDIUM

Cavalry Carbine

P/56 and P/61, converted; and Pattern III (newly made).
Made by the Royal Small Arms Factory, Enfield Lock, Middlesex (14,560 new guns and 14,390 conversions, 1866–72); the Royal Small Arms Factory, Sparkbrook, Birmingham (2,460 new guns from old parts, 1882–4); the Birmingham Small Arms & Munitions Co. Ltd, Small Heath (1,200, 1874); C.G. Bonehill, Birmingham (2,000, 1879).
Quantity: 34,610, excluding Trade, India and colonial patterns.
·577, rimmed.
Action: as P/53 infantry rifle, above.
DATA FOR PATTERN II** CARBINE
37·38in overall, 7·10lb unladen.
19·25in barrel, 5-groove rifling; RH, concentric.
Ramp-and-leaf sight graduated to 600 yards.
995 ft/sec with Mark IX ammunition.
No bayonet.
☆

1867: approved on 2 May, this conversion used the Pattern II** breech. It was applied to the original Pattern No. 1 (P/56) and Pattern No. 2 (P/61) carbines indiscriminately, the original 'P/56' designation being used for all the Sniders as the modified half-stock gave the cavalry carbine the appearance of a new design. The Baddeley-type (screwed) band was retained by a pin driven through the stock, a two-piece cleaning rod was carried in a butt-trap, and a snap-cap was secured by a chain attached to the trigger-guard bow. A ring slid on a bar anchored in the stock on the left side of the breech.
1869: approval of the Pattern III (Bolted) breech allowed the production of cavalry carbines to begin again. They had new stocks, and could be distinguished by the latch on the left side of the breech; in addition, III appeared on the receiver and STEEL lay on the left side of the barrel.
1878: replacement by the Martini-Henry began. It was complete by 1880.
1897: the first batches of at least 400 guns were smooth-bored for military guard purposes, being issued with buckshot cartridges. Work continued until 1900 or later.

Serjeant's Rifle

P/60 and P/61, Converted, and Pattern III (new).
Made by the Royal Small Arms Factory, Middlesex (31,710 conversions and 17,750 new guns, 1866–72); the Royal Small Arms Factory, Sparkbrook, Birmingham (5,000 new guns in 1873–4); the Birmingham Small Arms & Munitions Co. Ltd, Small Heath (at least 4,420 for the British Army, 1876); the London Small Arms Co. Ltd, Bow; and the National Arms & Ammunition Co. Ltd, Birmingham.
Quantity: about 80,000, including Trade, India and colonial patterns.
·577, rimmed.
Action: as P/53 infantry rifle, above.
DATA FOR PATTERN II** RIFLE
48·70in overall, 8·75lb unladen.
30·50in barrel, 5-groove rifling; RH, concentric.
Ramp-and-leaf sight graduated to 1,000 yards.
1,200 ft/sec with Mark IX ammunition.
P/60 sabre bayonet.
☆

1867: this transformation of the cap-lock P/60 short rifle to the Snider system was approved on 6 March. It had a Pattern II** breech. The rifle had two barrel bands and a bayonet lug on the right side of the muzzle; swivels appeared beneath the band and butt. Easily confused at a glance with the engineer carbine (see Part Two), the back sight leaf of the P/60 hinged at the back of the block instead of the front.
1869: the first guns were made at Enfield, with iron barrels and the Pattern III or Bolted Action. Obvious features were the locking latch on the left side of the breech, the new flat-face hammer and III on the receiver.
1874: replacement by the Martini-Henry began.

Artillery Carbine

P/61, converted; Pattern III (new) and Mk IV.
Made by the Royal Small Arms Factory, Enfield, Middlesex (37,560 conversions and 7,500 new guns, 1867–72); the Royal Small Arms Factory, Sparkbrook, Birmingham (17,000 conversions in 1871–3 and 460 new guns from old parts in 1882–4);

the Birmingham Small Arms Co. Ltd and the Birmingham Small Arms & Munitions Co. Ltd, Small Heath (at least 11,200 new guns in 1871–6); the London Small Arms Co. Ltd, Bow (6,000 new guns in 1871–4); and C.G. Bonehill, Birmingham (2,100 new guns in 1880).
Quantity: at least 81,820, excluding Trade, India and colonial patterns.
·577, rimmed.
Action: as P/53 infantry rifle, above.
DATA FOR PATTERN II** CARBINE
40·25in overall, 7·48lb unladen.
21·50in barrel, 5-groove rifling; RH, concentric.
Ramp-and-leaf sight graduated to 600 yards.
1,005 ft/sec with Mark IX ammunition.
P/61 sabre bayonet.
☆

1867: approved on 2 May and converted from the Pattern No. 3 (P/61) cap-lock, this also received the Pattern II** breech. Unlike the P/56 cavalry carbine, it had a full-length fore-end, a conventional cleaning rod, and brass furniture. The bayonet bar lay on the barrel.
1869: the adoption of the improved Bolted Action (Pattern III) on 13 January allowed the Snider artillery carbine to be revised, substantial quantities of new guns being made—though doubtless using many parts that had been in store. Furniture remained brass, but the barrels usually prove to be steel rather than iron.
1880: replacement by Martini-Henry carbines began. In April, however, 2,100 Sniders were ordered from Bonehill of Birmingham. Though otherwise identical with the standard Pattern III, they lacked bayonets and could be fitted with leather cavalry-type back sight protectors.
1885: a new Snider artillery carbine was sealed on 4 September for cadets. It was stocked to the muzzle, with a bar on the front band, and accepted a sabre bayonet. Barrels were rifled with three grooves instead of five and the back sight was a standard rifle pattern with altered graduations. Swivels lay under the front band and butt, while a snap-cap chain was attached to the front of the trigger-guard bow.
1891: the cadet-pattern artillery carbine was officially re-designated 'Mk IV'.

Snider A conversion of a P/53 rifle-musket, this gun has a 'TOWER' lock plate and sprung bands. It is accompanied by a P/1853 socket bayonet.

WALLIS & WALLIS

Snider A Pattern II** infantry rifle, converted from a P/53 rifle-musket. Note that this gun has a short-wrist butt and screwed Baddeley bands. PATTERN ROOM COLLECTION

Constabulary Carbine

Royal Irish Constabulary Pattern.
Converted in the government factory in Pimlico,
London (1869–71 and possibly later), and by the Royal
Small Arms Factory, Sparkbrook, Birmingham
(1869 and 1881–3).
Quantity: at least 16,910.
·577, rimmed.
Action: as P/53 infantry rifle, above.
DATA FOR PATTERN II** CARBINE
41·10in overall, about 7·30lb unladen.
22·50in barrel, 3-groove rifling; RH, concentric.
Ramp-and-leaf sight graduated to 900 yards.
1,020 ft/sec with Mark IX ammunition.
Bayonet: see notes.
☆

1867: accompanied by a saw-backed sword
bayonet designed by Colonel William Dixon, this
was approved on 16 July. Converted from old
two-band P/56 Short Rifles, it had iron furniture
and was stocked virtually to the muzzle. The
bayonet lug lay on the right side of the front
band. Swivels lay under the front band and butt.
Back sights were altered short-rifle patterns.
Most Pimlico guns had Pattern II** actions.
1869: some guns were made in Birmingham
with Pattern III (Bolted) breeches, though they
were still converted from P/56 short rifles and
had three-groove rifling.
1881: work began again in Birmingham, to
provide replacements for guns lost by attrition.

Yeomanry Carbine

Made by the Royal Small Arms Factory,
Sparkbrook, Birmingham, 1881–4.
Quantity: at least 4,500.
·577, rimmed.
Action: as P/53 infantry rifle, above.
DATA FOR PATTERN II** CARBINE
37·88in overall, 7·00lb unladen.
19·13in barrel, 3-groove rifling; RH, concentric.
Ramp-and-leaf sight graduated to 600 yards.
995 ft/sec with Mark IX ammunition.
No bayonet.
☆

1880: formally sealed on 19 July, the 'Carbine,
breech-loading, rifled, with cleaning rod, Snider,
Yeomanry, Interchangeable, with cover, leather,
back sight, Mk I' was the last service-pattern
Snider to be adopted in Britain. A conversion of
P/53 Snider long rifles, it was longer in the butt
than other carbines and lacked side-nail cups
for the sling bar. Most guns had Pattern II**
breeches and three-groove rifling.

India and Colonial Patterns

The principal private contractors—particularly
the Birmingham Small Arms & Munitions Co.
Ltd and the London Small Arms Co. Ltd—
continued to make Sniders long after work had
stopped at Enfield. Among the many orders were
2,000 short rifles with saw-back bayonets,
sought for New Zealand in 1871 and fulfilled by
BSA. The Agent-General for New Zealand also
ordered 1,000 short rifles and 400 artillery
carbines in May 1878; 2,000 short rifles in
August 1879; and 500 cavalry carbines in
December 1879. These were all fulfilled by
BSA&M Co., excepting 460 short rifles supplied
as part of the August 1879 contract by the
National Arms & Ammunition Co. Ltd.
India acquired 1,800 special short rifles,
accompanied by socket bayonets, in 1875; they
had two bands and barrels measuring 30·5in.
They were followed by 9,170 short rifles with
P/60 sabre bayonets (ordered in December
1876) and 2,130 cavalry carbines (1877–9).
Indian guns were almost always made by the
Birmingham Small Arms & Munitions Co. Ltd,
though the National Arms & Ammunition Co.
Ltd made 3,000 guns of the 1876 contract.

PORTUGAL

Traditionally allied with Britain, the Portuguese
government ordered 10,000 Snider long rifles
(with P/53 socket bayonets) and 1,200 cavalry
carbines from Britain. The War Office passed
the contract to the Birmingham Small Arms
& Munitions Co. Ltd in October 1874; guns
were delivered by the middle of 1875 to replace

altered Westley Richards 'Monkey Tail' weapons
in the line infantry and élite cavalry.

SPORTING GUNS

Though many French Tabatière-type guns (see
Part Two) were converted into rudimentary
hunting rifles in 1880–1900, the Snider was not
popular among discerning sportsmen. Its period
in vogue in Britain was comparatively short,
owing to the emergence of more effectual
breech-loading rifles within a few years of the
introduction of the perfected Bolted Action.
However, fine-quality rifles were proffered by the
principal military contractors—the Birmingham
and London Small Arms companies—and small
quantities of good-quality guns were made for
the volunteers by gunmakers such as Thomas
Turner of London and Birmingham; Parker,
Field & Company of London; Alexander Henry
of Edinburgh; or James Kerr & Company of
London. The actions were usually acquired from
BSA, whose marks will often be found on them.
An acknowledgement of Snider's patents, a large
s transfixed by an arrow, may also appear.
The Bolted Action was preferred. Woodwork
was often excellent, with chequering on the
wrist and fore-end; improvements were evident
in the locks, while the metalwork could be
lightly engraved. Furniture was generally iron
instead of brass and the service-pattern sights
were greatly refined. Most of the 'Volunteer
Sniders' were full-length rifles, though some
short patterns are also known.

SOPER

BRITAIN

This swinging-block rifle, designed by William
Soper of Reading, was patented in Britain in
1865 (the basic action) and 1867 (for the side-
mounted operating lever). It was renowned as
the gun that arrived too late for inclusion in the
British Army trials of the late 1860s. Pressing the
operating lever downward cocked the hammer,

PATTERN ROOM COLLECTION

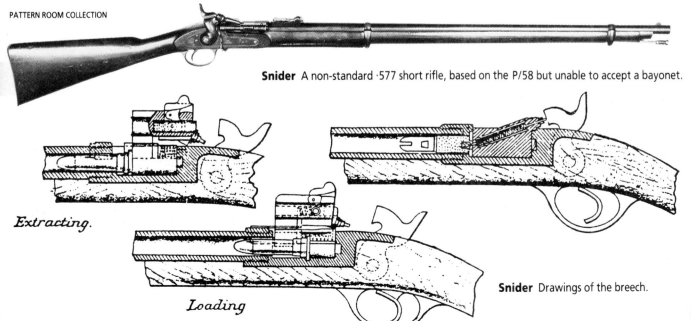

Snider A non-standard ·577 short rifle, based on the P/58 but unable to accept a bayonet.

Extracting.

Loading

Snider Drawings of the breech.

retracting the striker as it did so, and allowed the breech to spring open to the right. Spent cases were extracted and ejected automatically. The mechanism was simple and efficient, and proved capable of incredibly rapid fire; on one occasion, certified by many onlookers, sixty shots were fired in a minute. Why it failed to attract greater attention remains a mystery, as suggestions that extraction was capricious are rebutted by the contemporaneous rapid-fire trials.

Perhaps the gun was simply unlucky enough to be promoted by a provincial gunmaker with meagre manufacturing facilities. Most of the actions were made in Soper's own workshop, though a few guns may have been completed elsewhere during a very brief period in vogue. Their day had passed by 1890.

Improved Breech-Loader

Made by William Soper, Reading, Berkshire.
Chambered for many large-calibre pre-1885 British sporting cartridges.
Swinging-block action, operated by a lever on the right side of the stock.
DATA FOR A TYPICAL SPORTING PATTERN
·450, rimmed.
44·13in overall, 8·03lb unladen.
28·00in barrel, 7-groove rifling; LH, composite.
Standing block sight.
1,440 ft/sec with 370-grain bullet.

☆

1868: the style of Soper rifles ranged from ultra plain guns, for military-style target shooting or volunteers, to fine-grade sporters. The guns had one-piece stocks—rare among contemporary block-action guns—with the operating lever at the end of a serpentine plate let into the right side of the stock beneath the breech.

A typical sporter offered a pistol-grip butt and a short fore-end with a Henry-pattern tip. The round barrel had a full length top rib, suitably matted, and the rudimentary back sight was accompanied by a small silver-tipped blade at the muzzle. Swivels lay under the butt and barrel, while a small safety catch appeared behind the trigger lever.

SPRINGFIELD

UNITED STATES OF AMERICA

This bolt mechanism was unique to the USA—though many war-surplus rifles were used elsewhere after 1945 and others were supplied through Military Aid Programs into the 1960s.

Experience in the Spanish-American War showed that Spanish Mausers were superior to the Krag-Jørgensen. On 2 October 1900, therefore, a Board of Officers convened at Springfield Armory to test an experimental 'Model 1900' rifle combining the best features of both types of rifle. Its bolt had two locking lugs on the head plus a third (or safety) lug provided by the bolt handle base. A cut-off pivoted above the housing for the Mannlicher pattern clip-loaded magazine.

MILITARY RIFLES

Model 1901

Experimental infantry rifle.
Made by the National Armory, Springfield, Massachusetts, 1901.
Quantity: at least 100.
·30, rimless.
Turning-bolt action with two lugs on the bolt head locking into the receiver behind the chamber, and the bolt handle turning down into its seat.
49·25in overall, 9·47lb unladen (with bayonet).
30·00in barrel, 4-groove rifling; RH, concentric.
Integral charger-loaded box magazine, 5 rounds.
Tangent-leaf sight graduated to 2,000 yards.
2,300 ft/sec with 220-grain bullet.
M1901 rod bayonet.

☆

1901: this improvement on the experimental rifle of 1900 embodied changes suggested by the trials board. It had a straight-wrist butt, a new back sight, and a rod bayonet. Its magazine could only be loaded through the top of the open action—losing the one real advantage of the Krag, which could be replenished with the bolt

closed. Though much the same length as the M1898 Krag, it was appreciably lighter.

1902: approval was given for 5,000 M1901 rifles to be made at Springfield, by adapting existing machinery, until the folly of making M1901 and Krag rifles concurrently was realised. Consequently, only a hundred M1901 rifles were made—largely by hand—to prevent disrupting production of the Krag-Jørgensen. The rifling made a turn in 8in instead of 10in.

Model 1903

Short rifles: M1903 and M1903 (Modified).
Made by the National Armory, Springfield, Massachusetts, 1903–27 (about 1·275 million military M1903); Rock Island Arsenal, Illinois, 1904–19 (346,780 M1903); and the Remington Arms Co., Inc., Ilion, New York, 1941–3 (348,090 M1903 and M1903 [Modified]).
Quantity: about 1·97 million.
·30 M1903 or ·30–06, rimless.
Turning-bolt action with two lugs on the bolt head locking into the receiver behind the chamber, and the bolt handle seating in the receiver.
DATA FOR ORIGINAL PATTERN
·30 M1903, rimless.
43·41in overall, 8·50lb unladen.
24·21in barrel, 4-groove rifling; RH, concentric.
Integral charger-loaded box magazine, 5 rounds.
Tangent-leaf sight graduated to 2,000 yards.
2,300 ft/sec with M1903 ball cartridges.
M1903 rod bayonet.

☆

1902: series production of M1901 rifles had not begun when the advent of the Short Magazine Lee-Enfield rifle in Britain caused the US Army to reconsider. Trials undertaken at Springfield showed that the 1901-type barrel could be reduced to 24in without affecting performance adversely, so the back sight, hand guard, lower band and rod bayonet were suitably modified.

1903: the 'United States Magazine Rifle, Caliber ·30, Model of 1903' was approved on 19 June. A hand guard ran back to the receiver ring. Rifling reverted to a turn in 10in, as 1-in-8 had proved susceptible to wear.

1904: production at Rock Island Arsenal began

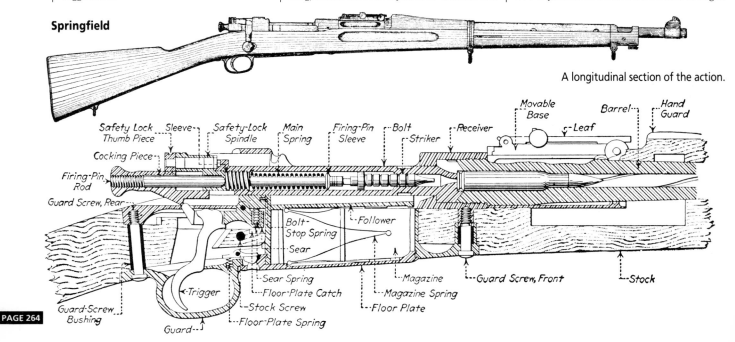

Springfield

A longitudinal section of the action.

in May and, by 30 June, Springfield had made thirty thousand rifles.

1905: manufacture was suspended on 11 January while criticisms of the bayonet and barrel-length were studied. On 1 April, the Chief of Staff reported that the barrel length was acceptable, but that the rod bayonet should be replaced by a conventional sword pattern. Existing rifles were recalled immediately. They were given new stocks and a nose cap with a bayonet lug.

On 24 May, an improved back sight was accepted. Graduated to 2,400 yards, it was based on that fitted to the experimental rifle of 1900. The hand guard, front sight and sight-cover were all modified in this period. The leaf of the M1905 sight was hinged at the rear of its base, which was carried on a sleeve.

1906: inspired by the development of the S-Patrone in Germany, the 'Cartridge, Ball, Caliber ·30, Model of 1906' (otherwise known as ·30–06) was approved on 15 October. Muzzle velocity rose to 2,700 ft/sec, and sight leaves were altered to a maximum range of 2,850yd. Re-chambering existing barrels was comparatively easy, though they were shortened to 24·01in; at the same time, a solid tubular back-sight mount replaced the skeletal pattern.

1907: tests were undertaken with optical sights developed by the Warner & Swasey Company of Cleveland, Ohio, in collusion with Frankford Arsenal staff.

1908: the experimental 1907-pattern sight was simplified and a thousand 'Telescopic Musket Sights, Model of 1908' were ordered from Warner & Swasey.

1909: issue of a few selected rifles to expert marksmen failed to reveal serious problems, though the sight was moved forward slightly and the rubber eye cup was softened. A general issue of rifles and 6× M1908 sights was made in .1910. The prismatic sights were initially greeted with enthusiasm, but they were very clumsy and uncomfortable. Short eye relief, for example, thrust the rubber eye cup back into the marksman's eye socket on firing. In addition, optical performance was poor.

1910: a flute was cut in the top surface of the hand guard to improve the sight line. The diameter of the azimuth adjustor on the back sight was increased perceptibly; a recoil bolt was added through the stock above the front of the trigger guard; the butt plate was chequered; and retaining clips were added in the hand guard.

1913: sufficient rifles had been made by the beginning of November to allow work to cease in Rock Island Arsenal until February 1917. An improved 5·2× M1913 prismatic optical sight was approved during the year. This could be identified by the elevation-dial lock nut, which had a cruciform head, and by an eye-piece lock screw ahead of the rubber eye cup. The flat cover plate on the top of the sight body was retained by a dozen screws, whereas the rounded 1908 pattern had been set into its base.

1915: from 30 March, a 'flaming bomb' above N.R.A. was applied to rifles sold to National Rifle Association members by the National Board for the Promotion of Rifle Practise.

1917: a parkerised finish replaced traditional browning to simplify production.

1918: a second recoil bolt appeared through the stock, beneath the chamber, and the bolt handle was bent slightly backward. Worryingly frequent receiver failures, which had been traced to poor heat treatment, were cured by improved manufacturing techniques. Springfield began the new 'double heat treatment' some time prior to receiver no.800,000 (20 February) while Rock Island Arsenal commenced with 285,507 (11 May). In early August, in the region of gun 320,000, Rock Island began making receivers of nickel steel alongside the carbon steel pattern. The situation continued until 1919. Nickel-steel receivers were marked **NS**, but the mark was rarely visible once the rifles had been assembled. Some guns were made in this era with blanks supplied by the Avis Rifle Barrel Company (marked **AV**).

The US authorities finally realised that the prismatic M1913 telescope sight was inferior to straight-tube patterns. A Frankford Arsenal sight, adapted from contemporaneous Winchester and Goerz designs, was adopted as the M1918 for

issue with a modified M1918 (Enfield type) sniper rifle. The war ended before Winchester could deliver any sights, and the project was abandoned. The unsatisfactory M1908 and M1913 Warner & Swasey sights were issued to the AEF in 1917, but saw little use.

1919: the last rifle was assembled in Rock Island Armory in June, though at least another 100,000 receivers were made (1919–20) and production of barrels continued until c.1922.

1927: military production at Springfield Armory virtually ceased, though ·30-calibre rifles were assembled for National Match target-shooting and the NRA.

1928: in late autumn, Springfield began to use nickel-steel receivers—apparently from no. 1,301,000 upward.

1942: the M1903 (Modified) rifle was approved on 10 March to accelerate production. It was basically an M1903 incorporating production expedients, made by Remington in 1941–2 on old machinery leased from Rock Island Armory. Among the major changes authorised between March and May 1942 were the deletion of the bolt stop and the advent of stamped bands and nose caps, simplified band-springs and a fabricated trigger guard/magazine floor-plate assembly. The last M1903 (Modified) guns were assembled in March 1943, as the basic pattern had been superseded by the M1903A3.

Model 1903 Mark 1

Short rifle and Pedersen Device.
Made by the National Armory, Springfield, Massachusetts.
Quantity: 101,780 rifles and 65,000 Pedersen Devices.
·30-06, rimless (rifle).
DATA FOR RIFLE AND PEDERSEN DEVICE
Auto-loading action, blowback.
·30 M1918, rimless.
43·21in overall, 10·31lb unladen.
Detachable box magazine, 40 rounds.
Back sight: as rifle.
1,300 ft/sec with 80-grain bullet.
M1905 sword bayonet.

☆

Springfield A typical ·30–06 M1903 rifle. REMINGTON MUSEUM COLLECTION

Springfield The breech of an M1903 rifle made in 1908. IAN HOGG

1916: developed by John Pedersen with the assistance of Remington's Oliver Loomis, this was designed in accordance with the doctrine of 'assault at the walk'—to deliver withering fire while advancing across no man's land.

1917: working prototypes for the French Lebel, Russian Mosin and US Springfield rifles were produced. Few changes were required in the M1903, apart from a minor alteration in the cut-off to lock the Pedersen Device in place. An auxiliary sear was added to the trigger mechanism, and an ejection port was cut through the left side of the receiver.

The firer only needed to replace the standard bolt with the Pedersen Device and insert the magazine to transform the M1903 Mk 1 (as the altered rifles were known) into a low powered semi-automatic. The Device was little more than a blowback pistol, with a 'slide' reciprocating behind the receiver bridge and a short barrel extending forward into the chamber.

1918: tests in the presence of General Pershing convinced the US Army that the Pedersen Device—its identity camouflaged as the '·30 Automatic Pistol, Model of 1918'—promised greatness. An order for 100,000 was given to Remington, to be made in the company's Bridgeport factory, and was almost immediately extended to 500,000. However, the war ended before any could be delivered.

1919: about 65,000 Pedersen Devices had been completed before work ceased, and more than 100,000 rifles were converted in Springfield Armory in 1919–20. Reappraisal in the calmer post-war conditions centred on the weaknesses of the plan instead of its strengths. The Devices were scrapped in the early 1930s, though the 'Mark 1' rifles served alongside the M1903 until they wore out. They could be identified by the ejection port in the receiver.

Model 1903A1

Short rifle.
Made by the National Armory, Springfield, Massachusetts.
Quantity: comparatively few.

·30-06, rimless.
Action: as M1903 rifle, above.
43·21in overall, 8·75lb unladen.
24·01in barrel, 4-groove rifling; RH, concentric.
Integral charger-loaded box magazine, 5 rounds.
Ramp-and-leaf sight graduated to 2,850 yards.
2,700 ft/sec with M1906 ball cartridges.
M1905 sword bayonet.

☆

1929: this was simply an M1903 fitted with a modified pistol-grip stock (Style C), which replaced the straight-wrist Style S with effect from 15 March. The change in designation was authorised on 5 December, but few M1903A1 guns were assembled; straight-wrist stocks were still being used in 1939.

1942: a 'scant pistol grip' was approved to enable under-size or flawed stock blanks to be used, but is rarely encountered.

Model 1903A3

Short rifle.
Made by the Remington Arms Co., Inc., Ilion, New York (about 707,630); L.C. Smith & Corona Typewriters, Inc., Pittsburgh, Pennsylvania (about 234,580); and the National Armory, Springfield, Massachusetts (about 850 in 1956).
Quantity: about 943,000.
·30–06, rimless.
Action: as M1903 rifle, above.
43·25in overall, 8·83lb unladen.
24·00in barrel, 2-, 4- or 6-groove rifling; RH, concentric.
Integral charger-loaded box magazine, 5 rounds.
Tangent sight graduated to 800 yards.
2,700 ft/sec with M1906 ball cartridges.
M1 sword bayonet.

☆

1942: this simplified M1903, with a profusion of stamped and fabricated parts, was approved on 21 May. The most obvious characteristic was a return to a straight-wrist stock—easier to make, and less wasteful of raw material than a pistol-grip pattern. The grasping groove was omitted and the recoil bolts were replaced with pins. These pins were unsatisfactory, however,

and M1903 (Modified) recoil bolts were soon substituted. An open aperture sight lay in an adjustable azimuth cradle on top of the receiver bridge behind the charger guides, and the hand guard extended rearward to the receiver ring.

The first M1903A3 rifles were assembled in the Smith & Corona factory in October and by Remington in December.

1943: the stamped trigger guard was deepened ahead of the trigger lever to allow a gloved finger better access. Some rifles had two-groove barrels made by Johnson Automatics, Inc., of Providence, Rhode Island (marked **JA**), or four-groove examples supplied by R.F. Sedgley, Inc., of Philadelphia (marked with an encircled **S**). A few early M1903A3 used six-groove barrels provided by Savage.

1944: contracts were cancelled in February, though assembly continued until the summer.

1956: about 850 'M1903A3 National Match' rifles were produced in Springfield Armory, using pre-war bolts and milled trigger guards. They had Redfield receiver sights, but were otherwise similar to pre-1945 service guns.

Model 1903A4

Sniper rifle.
Made by the Remington Arms Company, Inc., Ilion, New York, 1943–4.
Quantity: about 26,650.
·30–06, rimless.
Action: as M1903 rifle, above.
43·21in overall, 9·13lb without sights.
24·01in barrel, 2- or 4-groove rifling; RH, concentric.
Integral charger-loaded box magazine, 5 rounds.
No sights.
2,700 ft/sec with M1906 ball cartridges.
Bayonets were not normally issued.

☆

1943: standardised on 14 January, this was a modified M1903A3. Made exclusively in Ilion, sniper rifles were invariably fitted with Keystone (**K**) or Springfield (**S**) pistol-grip stocks. The earliest examples had two-groove cut rifling, but later barrels used a four-groove draw-formed pattern. The bolt handle was bent down to

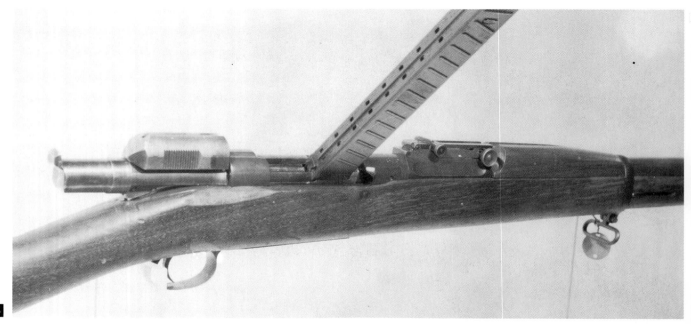

clear the 2·5 × Telescope M73B1, a militarised Model 330C made in El Paso by the W.R. Weaver Company. It was carried in a Redfield Junior mount.

On 18 January, twenty thousand receivers—numbered 3407088–3427087—were diverted from M1903A3 production for completion to M1903A4 standards. An additional order for 8,365 was placed in June.

1944: the final batches of M1903A4 rifles were delivered in June, owing to the approval of the M1C Garand with a Lyman Alaskan sight in a Griffin & Howe mount. The June 1943 contract was still apparently incomplete.

SPORTING GUNS

Excluding the output of custom gunsmiths and a few special-purpose rifles made in the National Armory—e.g., the Theodore Roosevelt gun of 1903—the M1903 had much less effect on the American sporting rifle scene than its cartridge. The only company to capitalise on its efficiency was R.F. Sedgley, Inc., of Philadelphia, which converted a selection of military surplus rifles.

Springfield also made ·30 International Match rifles with half-stocks, special set- or multi-lever triggers, palm rests, extended butt plates and a host of other special features. Less than fifty of each pattern were made in 1922–7.

In spite of refinements such as the Garand Super Speed Firing Mechanism, the modified Springfields were replaced by Martini-action guns. International Match rifles were offered for sale privately, or rebuilt to service pattern and reclassified as 'M1903 Special Target' (M1903A1 after 1928).

Model 1903 National Match

Short rifles, selected for accuracy.
Made by the National Armory, Springfield, Massachusetts, 1922–39.
Quantity: about 26,950.
·30–06, rimless.
Otherwise generally as M1903 rifle, above.
☆

1922: introduced specifically for military-style target shooting, which was being promoted enthusiastically by the Director of Civilian Marksmanship (DCM), these were little more than M1903 rifles with barrels selected for accuracy and actions honed for smoothness. The first pattern—Rifle, Caliber .30, 'Style NM Special'—had a standard service-pattern stock, band and nose cap. However, it lacked the grasping groove in the fore-end, and the butt had a pointed NRA-type pistol grip.

1928: a modified 'Style NB' National Match rifle was introduced with the ·30 M1922M1 stock, distinguished by a clumsy pistol grip. Tested a year previously, this had been rejected for field sevice. Standard service-grade rifles in this stock were designated 'Style SB'.

1929: a modified Type C stock, with a refined pointed-tip pistol grip, was adopted to create the 'Style NM 1929' National Match rifle. This remained in vogue until production ceased in 1933, though the original headless cocking piece was abandoned after 1930.

1936: assembly of the 'NM' rifles began again, continuing until parts were exhausted in 1939.

Model 1903 'Match Springfield'

Short rifle, selected for accuracy.
Made by the National Armory, Springfield, Massachusetts, 1922–7.
Quantity: about 2,000.
·30–06, rimless.
Otherwise as M1903 rifle, above, excepting weight (about 8·25lb without sights) and back sight (Lyman Model 48B aperture pattern).
☆

1922: this was a 1903 National Match (q.v.) action, with a headless cocking piece, fitted to a special heavyweight barrel. Blocks for optical-sight mounts appeared on the barrel and an aperture sight was fitted on the right side of the receiver bridge.

The rifle had a 1922-pattern half-stock, a grasping groove in the fore-end, and a single band carrying a swivel. The second swivel lay on the under-edge of the butt.

Model 1903 NRA Sporter

Military-style sporting rifle.
Made by the National Armory, Springfield, Massachusetts, 1924–38.
Quantity: about 7,140.
·30–06, rimless.
Otherwise generally as M1903 rifle, above, excepting weight (about 8·25lb without sights) and back sight (Lyman Model 48S aperture pattern).
☆

1924: announced in December by the Director of Civilian Marksmanship, this was produced to compensate for a dearth of adequate ·30–06 sporters. Made to National Match standards, 'Style NRA' guns had the barrels shaped so that they duplicated the standard ·22 pattern and could be fitted into a minor variation of the standard half-stock. They were distinguished by an additional cut-off cutaway and two transverse recoil bolts.

1926: a short-lived 'Style NBA' was introduced with the clumsy M1922M1 stock. This had a large pistol grip with a flat base, and an unsightly grasping groove in the fore-end. Only 590 guns were assembled before production reverted to the NRA pattern.

1933: production of NRA sporters ceased, perhaps as a result of complaints from the established sporting-gun manufacturers, though small-scale assembly apparently continued until the end of 1938.

Model 1903 Style T

Target rifle.
Made by the National Armory, Springfield, Massachusetts, 1929–30.
Quantity: about 100.
·30–06, rimless.
Action: as M1903 rifle, above.
47·20in overall, 10·55lb without sights.
28·00in barrel, 4-groove rifling; RH, concentric.
Integral charger-loaded box magazine, 5 rounds.
Lyman Model 48C aperture sight.
2,830 ft/sec with M1906 ball cartridges.
☆

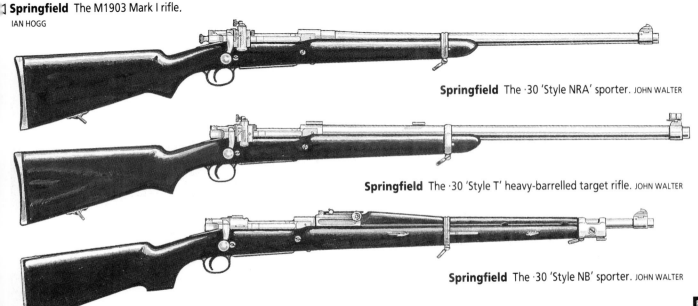

Springfield The M1903 Mark I rifle. IAN HOGG

Springfield The ·30 'Style NRA' sporter. JOHN WALTER

Springfield The ·30 'Style T' heavy-barrelled target rifle. JOHN WALTER

Springfield The ·30 'Style NB' sporter. JOHN WALTER

1929: this target rifle had a long and heavy barrel in a modified NRA-type half-stock. Made to National Match standards, it had blocks on the barrel for optical-sight mounts and a Lyman aperture sight on the receiver bridge. A Winchester globe-pattern front sight was used, but the 'Style T' rifle was not popular enough to justify more than a single short production run.

Sedgley Springfield
••
Sporting rifle.
Converted by R.F. Sedgley, Inc., Philadelphia, Pennsylvania, c.1925–41, from war-suplus rifles.
Quantity: several thousands.
·218 Bee, ·2R Lovell, ·22 Hornet, ·220 Swift, ·22–3000,
·22–4000, ·25–35, ·250–3000 Savage, ·257 Roberts,
·270 Winchester, 7 × 57mm or ·30–06.
Action: as M1903 rifle, above.
DATA FOR A TYPICAL EXAMPLE
·220 Swift, semi-rimmed.
43·35in overall, 7·27lb unladen.
24·00in barrel, 4-groove rifling; RH, concentric.
Integral charger-loaded box magazine, 5 rounds.
Lyman Model 48 aperture sight.
4,100 ft/sec with 48-grain bullet.
☆

1925*: the first batches of these guns were built around old Springfield Armory or Rock Island Arsenal actions. Offered as a 24in-barrelled half-stock rifle or a 20in-barrel carbine with a full length Mannlicher stock, Sedgley Springfields are rarely encountered today. Among the most interesting are adaptions with the bolt handle on the left side. Made of good quality walnut, butts usually had a straight comb, with a flute at the hand, while the pistol grip was chequered and capped; the fore-end was also chequered and often displayed a schnabel tip. Swivels were attached to the underside of the butt and on the internal barrel band. An aperture sight was attached to the receiver bridge and a hooded bead-type front sight lay on a ramp.

Other guns
••
Some 1903-type receivers were made in Japan

for the Santa Fé Arms Company of Pasadena, California (possibly 2,500 in c.1965–6), and National Ordnance, Inc., of Southern El Monte, California (about 23,500 in 1965–70).

Apparently produced by investment casting and then assembled in the USA with a variety of military-surplus parts, these had narrow receiver bridges without charger guides and offered neither the quality nor durability of the original machined forgings.

STANDARD

UNITED STATES OF AMERICA
✍

This short-lived repeater was patented by Morris Smith in 1906, a substantial part of the interest being assigned to W.D. Condit. Though offered commercially for a few years, the Model G was never successful. Like all gas-operated designs produced before the First World War, it was susceptible to the then-common variations in ammunition pressure and was much more prone to jamming than its recoil-operated Remington or Winchester rivals.

Standard Rifle
••
Models G and M.
Made by the Standard Arms Company, Wilmington, Delaware, 1910–12.
·25 Remington, ·25–35 Winchester, ·30 Remington,
·30–30 Winchester or ·35 Remington.
DATA FOR A TYPICAL MODEL G
Gas-operated auto-loading action, apparently locked by rotating lugs on the bolt into the receiver wall.
·30 Remington, rimless.
About 43·00in overall, 7·70lb unladen.
22·35in barrel, rifling pattern unknown.
Detachable box magazine, 5 rounds.
Spring-leaf and elevator sight.
2,220 ft/sec with 160-grain bullet.
☆

1909: the first gas-operated auto-loading rifle to be manufactured commercially in the USA, the short-lived Standard had few other claims to

fame. The rifle had a straight-wrist butt, a square-top receiver with an internal hammer, and a box-magazine housing ahead of the trigger. A hand-grip around the piston tube, cast from bronze, was decorated with a hunting scene; a catch on the grip disconnected the gas system, allowing the action to be operated manually merely by 'pumping' the grip.

1911*: the Model M was very similar to the auto-loader, but lacked the gas-port and piston mechanism. Operated by a sliding hand-grip, it may have been made to rid its manufacturer of unwanted Model G parts.

STANGE

GERMANY
Also known as 'Rheinmetall' or 'Rheinmetall-Stange'
✍

Developed for Rheinmetall by Louis Stange, this rifle relied on a long-stroke piston/bolt carrier rotating lugs on the bolt head into engagement with the receiver walls. When the mechanism was set to fire semi-automatically, the firing pin (mounted on the bolt carrier and released from the front sear notch) could reach the cartridge only after the trigger had been pressed; when firing fully automatically, the bolt and bolt carrier were released together from the rear position.

Once an empty magazine had been removed, the bolt remained open only if the selector was set for automatic fire; pulling the trigger then allowed the bolt to close, stripping a new round into the chamber. The bolt carrier immediately followed and the gun fired. If semi-automatic fire had been selected, the bolt closed on an empty chamber as the magazine was withdrawn and had to be retracted manually.

Not without faults—it was too light to control when firing automatically and had an oddly placed magazine—the FG.42 was a brave attempt to provide a full-power assault weapon.

1940: the Luftwaffe requested a special rifle for the paratroops (Fallschirmjäger). The gun was to be less than 1,000mm long and no heavier

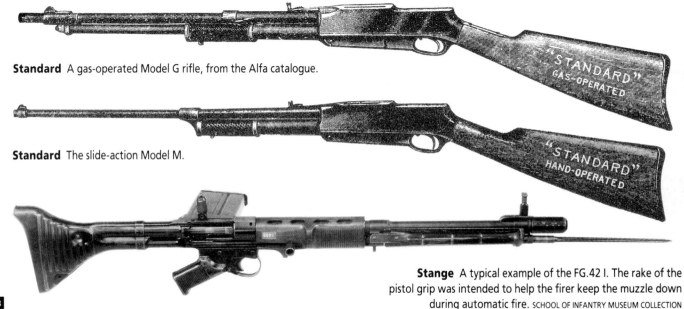

Standard A gas-operated Model G rifle, from the Alfa catalogue.

Standard The slide-action Model M.

Stange A typical example of the FG.42 I. The rake of the pistol grip was intended to help the firer keep the muzzle down during automatic fire. SCHOOL OF INFANTRY MUSEUM COLLECTION

than the Kar.98k, yet capable of firing standard full power 7·9mm cartridges automatically. The army rejected the goals as unattainable, so the Luftwaffe hierarchy simply contacted established arms-makers independently.

Model 42

**Paratroop rifle, first pattern:
Fallschirmjägergewehr 42 or FG.42 I.**
Made by Heinrich Krieghoff Waffenfabrik, Suhl ('fzs').
Quantity: 1,800–2,000?
7·9 × 57mm, rimless.
Gas-operated auto-loading action, locked by two lugs on the bolt engaging the receiver.
937mm overall, 4·38kg without magazine.
508mm barrel, 4-groove rifling; RH, concentric.
Detachable box magazine, 10 or 20 rounds.
Folding aperture sight graduated to 1,200 metres.
730 m/sec with sS ball cartridges; 800 ± 50 rpm.
Rod-type bayonet.

☆

1941: the Stange design was preferred to a rising-block Krieghoff prototype.
1942: series production of the FG.42 began in Suhl after development had been completed in the Rheinmetall-Borsig factory in Sömmerda. The paratroop rifle had a distinctive straight-line layout with folding sights, a pressed-steel butt, a sharply-angled pistol grip to improve control, a short wooden fore-end/hand guard, and a permanently attached bipod under the front of the receiver. The box magazine fed laterally from the left side and the reversible bayonet was carried beneath the barrel.

Model 42

**Paratroop rifle, second pattern:
Fallschirmjägergewehr 42 or FG.42 II.**
Made by Heinrich Krieghoff Waffenfabrik, Suhl ('fzs');
and Rheinmetall-Borsig AG, Sömmerda
('bmv', parts only?).
Quantity: 5,000–7,000.
7·9 × 57mm, rimless.
Action: as FG.42 I, above.
1,059mm overall, 5·05kg unladen.

525mm barrel, 4-groove rifling; RH, concentric.
Detachable box magazine, 20 rounds.
Folding aperture sight graduated to 1,200 metres.
730 m/sec with sS ball cartridges; 750 ± 30 rpm.
Simplified rod bayonet.

☆

1943: combat experience and a critical shortage of valuable manganese steel caused the FG.42 to be completely redesigned. The muzzle brake was improved; the bipod could be moved forward beneath the muzzle, improving stability in automatic fire; and a variable-orifice gas regulator was provided to handle fluctuating ammunition pressure or the effects of fouling. The trigger mechanism was detachable. The position of the safety catch was changed. A hinged cover kept débris out of the bolt way when the magazine was removed, and a deflector was fitted to ensure spent cases were ejected harmlessly.

The new rifle had a wooden butt and a conventional plastic pistol-grip, raked much less sharply than its predecessor. The flash-hider was a bulky ribbed pattern instead of the earlier pierced cylinder.

The bolt stroke was lengthened to reduce parts-breakage attributed to the violent action of the FG.42 I. Consequently, the second-pattern rifle was longer and heavier than its predecessor and had a lower cyclic rate.

STEVENS

UNITED STATES OF AMERICA

↶

Joshua Stevens's earliest rifles—introduced in 1871—were based on a simple tipping-barrel pistol patented in September 1864. Though the breech was not suited to high-power cartridges, Stevens longarms were popular in the eastern United States in the late nineteenth century.

The Stevens Arms & Tool Company made a wide range of sporting guns until the First World War. In 1920, however, the equity was acquired by the Savage Arms Company; Stevens finally merged with its parent in 1936.

'Side Plate Rifle'

Made in Chicopee Falls, Massachusetts, by J. Stevens & Company (1885–6) and J. Stevens Arms & Tool Company (1886–92).
Quantity: no more than 2,000.
Chambering: see notes.
Swinging-block action, locked by a toggle-link.
DATA FOR A TYPICAL SPORTING RIFLE
·25–20 Single Shot, rimmed.
45·00in overall, 8·25lb unladen.
30·00in barrel, 6-groove rifling; RH, concentric.
Fixed-notch sight.
1,410 ft/sec with 85-grain bullet.

☆

1885: patented in September 1884 and August 1885, this was the first Stevens rifle to feature the swinging-block action. An arm on the breech block, secured by a threaded bolt, ran forward under the chamber. Able to pivot loosely, it was connected with the sturdy breech lever—which doubled as the trigger guard—through a short intermediate toggle-link that held the breech closed during firing. A rocking-blade extractor was activated by the breech block.

Named for their construction, Side Plate rifles were short-lived; they were too complex to make cheaply, and removal of the right side of the frame to give access to the action reduced durability. In addition to plain sporters, target rifles were made in small numbers; a typical example had a straight-wrist stock with an 'Off Hand' shoulder plate, a heavy half-octagonal barrel, and adjustable vernier-and-globe sights.

Ideal Model

Numbers 44 to 54, 417–0, 417–1, 417–2, 417–3 and 417½.
Made in Chicopee Falls, Massachusetts, by J. Stevens Arms & Tool Company (1886–1916) and J. Stevens Arms Company (1916–47).
Chambering: see notes.
Action: generally as Side Plate pattern, above.
DATA FOR A TYPICAL NO.44
·32–20 Winchester, rimmed.
42·50in overall, 7·75lb unladen.

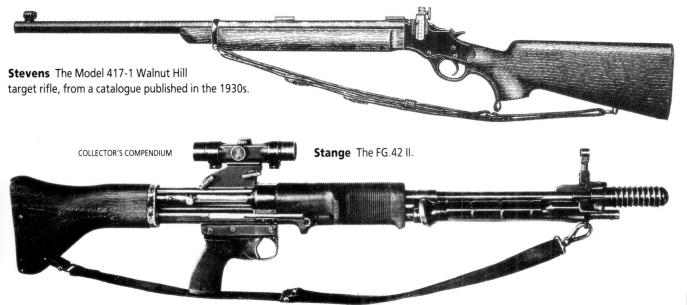

Stevens The Model 417-1 Walnut Hill target rifle, from a catalogue published in the 1930s.

COLLECTOR'S COMPENDIUM   **Stange** The FG.42 II.

26·00in barrel, 6-groove rifling; RH, concentric.
Spring-leaf and elevator sight.
1,290 ft/sec with 100-grain bullet.

☆

1891: alterations to the Side Plate action in the late 1880s created the 1889-pattern 'Favorite', though these rifles were generally confined to rimfire ammunition. In 1893, however, the mechanism was enlarged and strengthened to handle centre-fire rounds such as ·32–40 and ·38–55 Ballard.

1894: the Ideal No.44 rifle appeared at the beginning of the year. Production may have begun late in 1893, as the earliest rifles bear an October 1889 patent date instead of the April 1894 improvement.

Cheap, yet capable of outstanding accuracy and renowned for the quality of its barrel, the rifle was the mainstay of the Stevens line for many years. The most common variant of the No.44 had a 26in half-octagonal barrel, a straight-wrist butt and a short wooden fore-end with a schnabel tip. Nickel plating, engraving and specially finished woodwork were among the options; consequently, rifles are not always easily classifiable.

Barrels were generally half-octagonal, though round and fully octagonal patterns are known; those made by the renowned barrelsmith Harry Pope being especially desirable. Frames were originally colour case-hardened, and many of the better guns had set triggers.

Ideal rifles were popular, sturdy and very accurate. They were chambered for a wide variety of rim- and centre fire cartridges—e.g., ·25–20 Single Shot, ·32 Long and Extra Long Center Fire, ·32–20 Winchester, ·32–35 Stevens, ·32–40 Winchester, ·38 Long Center Fire, ·38–40 Winchester, ·38–55 Ballard or ·44–40 Winchester.

The basic No.44 had a plain fore-end, and a straight-wrist butt with a rifle-type shoulder plate. A rarely encountered 'Ladies' or 'English' pattern, listed as No.044, was made with a specially narrowed lightweight receiver. No.45 was very similar to No.44, but had a hooked 'Off Hand' butt plate.

No.48 usually had a spur-type breech lever, a shallow pistol grip, a cheek piece on its butt, and an Off Hand shoulder plate; No.49 was virtually identical, but had a pistol-grip butt. These guns were generally sold as 'Walnut Hill' models (named after a local rifle range) when fitted with 800-yard Mid-Range vernier sights.

No.52 was a light target rifle with a 28in barrel, Mid-Range sights, a Schuetzen-style pistol-grip butt, a sharply pitched comb, a cheek piece, and a hooked shoulder plate; the breech lever was usually spurred, but could be looped. No.53 and No.54 were similar, but had 30in or 32in barrels and 1,200-yard sights. No.54 had a hinged hand-rest beneath the fore-end and a Schuetzen breech lever with a small spur ahead of a distinctive wood-block inset in a loop.

1895: a straight-case ·25–25 cartridge, designed by Captain William Carpenter of the US Army, was introduced for the No.44 rifle. A ·25–21 version followed in 1897.

1897: cartridges as powerful as ·38–55 Ballard proved to strain the Ideal action excessively. Consequently, chamberings were reduced to nothing more potent than ·32–20 Winchester.

1900: a ·28–30–120 cartridge was introduced.

1901*: the extractor was moved from the left side of the action to a central position, and the pivot screws were replaced with heavier bolts to increase durability. A tension screw in the breech block (to keep the breech lever closed) was abandoned in this era.

1903*: the ·32 Stevens Ideal chambering option was added.

1906: Ideal rifles made after introduction of the improved No.44½ had a spring-and-plunger lever retainer.

1920*: production began again after the First World War, though only the No.44 reappeared.

1932: the improved No.417 Walnut Hill rifle was introduced. Most of the guns chambered rimfire cartridges, though some 417 and 417½ examples were chambered for the ·22 Hornet centre-fire round. Unfortunately, the additional pressure strained the action beyond its safety margins and the option was rapidly withdrawn. The 417 series usually featured 28in cylindrical

barrels. Weight averaged 10·5lb, owing to the heavy barrel, target-pattern butt and fore-end; No.417½, with a lighter sporting-style stock, weighed 2lb less. The guns all had pistol-grip butts with the ball-tipped breech lever curved to follow the underside of the grip.

No.417–0 had a Lyman No.52L back sight on the receiver; 417–1 had a Lyman 48L sight on the receiver; 417–2 had a Lyman No.144 vernier sight on the upper tang; and 417–3 was supplied without sights.

1935: the No.44 was discontinued.

1940: all surviving 417 and 417½ patterns were abandoned, excepting the basic 417–0.

1947: the last No.417 rifles were sold, either from store or after assembly from pre-war parts.

Improved Ideal Model

No.44½ only.
Made in Chicopee Falls, Massachusetts, by J. Stevens Arms & Tool Company (1904–16).
Chambering: see notes.
Dropping-block action, operated by a lever doubling as the trigger guard.
DATA FOR A TYPICAL SPORTING RIFLE
·38–40 Winchester, rimmed.
43·50in overall, 7·95lb unladen.
28·00in barrel, 6-groove rifling; RH, concentric.
Vernier sight on tang.
1,330 ft/sec with 180-grain bullet.

☆

1904*: this was the finest of all the Stevens target rifles. It shared the general lines of the Ideal series, but the action was a true dropping-block pattern. The breech block, canted back by the finger lever, dropped at a slight angle to the vertical until it was held against the rear of the receiver by a spring plunger beneath the barrel. As the breech was closed, the breech block was cammed forward sufficiently to seat recalcitrant cartridges in the chamber. As the receiver was a sturdy steel forging instead of a weaker malleable casting, No.44½ rifles were not confined to the same low-pressure ammunition as the No.44.

On the debit side, inclusion of a hammer-fly—intended to protect the tip of the trigger

Steyr The major component groups of the 5·56mm Armee-Universal-Gewehr. STEYR-DAIMLER-PUCH AG

if the hammer slipped during cocking—was a source of potential danger.

1908: a firing pin retractor was added.

1916: partly owing to limited demand (the gun was comparatively expensive for a Stevens product) and partly to war-work, the No.44½ was discontinued. Ironically, the weaker No.44 survived for another thirty years.

STEYR

AUSTRIA

The Mannlicher-pattern bolt action rifles are covered in their own section. Since the end of the Second World War, Steyr-Daimler-Puch has made a range of automatic weapons including the futuristic Armee-Universal-Gewehr (AUG). The company has now developed the Steyr ACR, chambered for a special flechette cartridge; this gun is described and illustrated in *Military Small Arms of the 20th Century*, p.135.

AUSTRIA

AUG

Armee-Universal-Gewehr or Sturmgewehr 77 (StG77).
Made by Steyr-Daimler-Puch AG, Steyr.
5·56 × 45mm, rimless.
Gas-operated auto-loading action, locked by rotating lugs on the bolt into the barrel extension.
DATA FOR A TYPICAL RIFLE
792mm overall, 4·09kg with loaded magazine.
508mm barrel, 6-goove rifling; RH, concentric.
Detachable box magazine, 30 or 42 rounds.
Integral 1·5 × optical sight.
970 m/sec with M193 ball ammunition; 650 ± 50 rpm.
☆

1977: this bullpup was developed specifically for the Austrian army. Gas was tapped from the barrel to strike one of the bolt-carrier guide rods, which rotated the bolt.

The AUG divided into six major component groups: barrel, receiver (cast integrally with the optical sight bracket), trigger, bolt, magazine and butt. Changing the barrel transformed the rifle into a light support weapon, a carbine or submachine-gun. The direction of ejection could be altered merely by changing the bolt and replacing the ejection-port cover.

The synthetic frame, in black or olive green, was common to all sub-variants. Barrels included 350mm, 407mm and 508mm patterns (without sights); 508mm with a front sight; 508mm with an integral M203 grenade launcher; and a heavy 621mm pattern carrying a bipod. The standard receiver had an integral optical sight mount, but alternative patterns offered an open back sight or ('N' pattern only) conventional optical sight mounts. Three differing trigger systems and three bolts allowed the purchaser to choose from a semi-automatic version, or selective-fire guns firing automatically from the open- or closed-bolt position. The contents of the transparent plastic magazines could be seen at a glance.

The futuristic lines of the AUG were difficult to mistake. Prong-type flash suppressors were used, and a pivoting hand grip lay immediately ahead of the trigger guard. Light pressure on the trigger fired single shots; strong pressure, where appropriate, allowed the mechanism to cycle automatically from the frame. A safety bolt ran laterally through the frame.

1978: the first series-made rifles were delivered.

1980: the standard selective-fire rifles were christened AUG-A1; the AUG-P (Polizei or Police) was a short-barrelled selective-fire or semi-automatic version, firing from a closed bolt.

AUSTRALIA

The AUG, effectual and sturdy, performed well in comparative trials. Consequently, the '5·56mm Rifle F8' was adopted in 1985. Initial orders for 85,000 rifles were given to the Lithgow small arms factory, 18,000 of which were destined for New Zealand. The first issues were made to the Australian Army in 1988.

Lithgow-made guns have also been offered commercially throughout Australasia; F88 was the standard rifle, F88C was a carbine with a 407mm barrel, the receiver of F88S was adapted for night-vision sights, and the heavy-barrelled F88–203 had a 40mm M203 grenade launcher.

OTHERS

Austrian-made AUG rifles have been tried in small numbers by many military and paramilitary organisations—about 500 went to Bolivia, for example, in the early 1980s.

Tunisia was an early convert to the Steyr design, purchasing sizeable numbers from 1978 onward. Saudi Arabia may have bought as many as 100,000 since 1980, and Oman purchased about 30,000 AUG rifles in 1982–3.

The AUG was adopted in Ecuador in 1987, deliveries apparently being complete by 1990. It is also the service rifle of the Irish Free State (Eire), adopted early in 1988 after trials against the Belgian FNC, British L85A1, French FAMAS, German G41, Israeli Galil, Italian AR 70/90, Swiss SG-550 and US M16A2.

SWINBURN

BRITAIN

Designed and developed by John Swinburn, this pivoting-block mechanism was the subject of several British patents granted in 1872–7...even though it was little more than a variant of the popular Martini.

The Model 1875 had a lever on the right side of the receiver to re-cock the striker should the gun misfire. The striker was hit by a hammer powered by a V-type main spring. The straight-wrist butt was attached by tangs, creating space for the trigger mechanism behind the receiver; consequently, though it had a more effectual trigger, the Swinburn was neither as compact nor as durable as the Martini-Henry when fired with comparable ammunition.

Guns with British Government-pattern ·450 Henry barrels were bought to arm militia and irregulars during the Zulu War of 1879 and the First South African War of 1881. They remained in service until the advent of Martini-Metfords.

Swinburn Carbines in the hands of the 90th Perthshire Light Infantry during the Zulu War, 1879. The guns can be identified by the shape and length of the breech lever and the 'hump' at the rear of the receiver.
AFRICANA MUSEUM COLLECTION

Model 1875

Offered as a rifle or carbine.

Marked as a product of Swinburn & Son, Birmingham, but probably made by Westley Richards & Co. Ltd.
Quantity: at least 1,200 rifles and 2,090 carbines.
·450, rimmed.
Pivoting-block action, with an operating lever behind the trigger guard.
DATA FOR RIFLE
49·50in overall, 9·31lb unladen.
33·00in barrel, 7-groove rifling; LH, composite.
Ramp-and-leaf sight graduated to 1,400 yards.
1,350 ft/sec with solid-case ball cartridges.
Special sword (rifle) or bowie-knife (carbine) bayonets were made, but were never general issue.

☆

1875: an order for 300 rifles and sixty carbines was placed on 15 July by way of V. & R. Blakemore of London, Crown Agents for Natal. The Swinburns resembled the Mk II Martini-Henry (q.v.) externally, but the shaping of the rear of the body differed and the shank of the operating lever was practically straight. The accompanying Swinburn carbine was similar, excepting for reduced dimensions (39·3in long, 7·5lb unladen). It had a plain fore-end with neither bands nor nose cap. All guns could take bayonets, though issue of leather back sight covers was apparently restricted to carbines.
1876: a hundred additional rifles and perhaps 1,250 carbines were ordered through the Crown Agents on 24 April. Like the earlier batches, they were viewed at the government small arms repair factory in Birmingham.
1878: volunteers in Natal ordered 1,500 rifles and carbines, apparently in equal proportions, directly from the manufacturer.
1886: about a hundred additional guns were sent to Natal. They are believed to have been assembled from old parts—possibly by Westley Richards, as Swinburn had ceased trading three years earlier.
1895: Swinburn-Henry rifles and carbines were finally withdrawn from service in favour of Martini-Metfords, though survivors remained in store for at least another decade.

Improved Sporting Rifle

Made by (or perhaps for) Swinburn & Son, Birmingham, c.1876–83.
Chambered for a variety of large-calibre British black-powder sporting cartridges.
Action: as Model 1875, above.
DATA FOR A TYPICAL EXAMPLE
·360 Express (black powder load), rimmed.
43·38in overall, 7·27lb unladen.
26·00in barrel, 3-groove rifling; LH, concentric.
Folding-leaf sight for 100, 200 and 300 yards.
1,500 ft/sec with 200-grain bullet.

☆

1876: the first sporters appeared. They are now rarely seen, as trading soon ceased. Surviving examples display typical English characteristics: slender pistol-gripped butts with straight combs, plain round-tipped fore-ends, Express-pattern back sights, simple trigger mechanisms, and—in some cases—restrained scroll engraving.
1883: Swinburn ceased trading, halting work on the dropping-block action. A few rifles may then have been completed by Westley Richards.

TANNER

SWITZERLAND

André Tanner began his gunmaking exploits in a converted garage in 1955, where the earliest target rifles were made. By 1960, a small factory had been opened in Neuenburg but a move to Fulenbach occurred in 1964. By this time, the rifles were attracting considerable attention. A distribution agreement with Hämmerli—signed in 1965—allowed the Free Rifles to enter series production. When Hämmerli participation ended in 1970, Tanner's operations were strong enough to survive on their own.

Free Rifle

Matchstutzer 300m.
Made by André Tanner, Werkstätte für Präzisionswaffe, Fulenbach.

7·5 × 55mm or ·308 Winchester.
Turning-bolt action, locked by rotating lugs on the bolt head into the receiver wall and the bolt handle turning down into its seat.
DATA FOR A TYPICAL 300M PATTERN
7·5 × 55mm, rimless.
1,160mm overall (with butt plate retracted), 6·75kg without hand rest.
734mm barrel, 4-groove rifling; RH, concentric.
Micro-adjustable diopter sight.
810 m/sec with 11·5-gram bullet.

☆

1962: the first rifles were made on the Tanner action, which had three symmetrically-spaced lugs on a separate bolt head. They had a massive receiver pierced only by the ejection port and a special trigger set by a lever protruding beneath the trigger guard.

The massive half-stock had a thumb-hole grip and a hooked butt plate, adjustable for height and length. The straight comb was fixed. An accessory rail was let into the underside of the stock, with aluminium finger-plates on either side of the fore-end. Many accessories have been offered, including a selection of competition-grade sights, hand rests and mirage bands.
1966: a distinctive aluminium bedding block was added between the barrel and receiver. Tests showed that this was effectual enough to become a Tanner hallmark.

UIT Short Rifle

UIT-Stutzer: Sniper, Standard and Modell 85.
Made by André Tanner, Werkstätte für Präzisionswaffe, Fulenbach.
7·5 × 55mm or ·308 Winchester.
Action: as Free Rifle, above.
DATA FOR A TYPICAL MAGAZINE-FEED MODELL 85
·308 Winchester, rimless.
1,135mm overall (with standard butt plate), 5·40kg with sights.
660mm barrel, 4-groove rifling; RH, concentric.
Detachable box magazine, 9 rounds.
Micro-adjustable diopter sight.
2,610 ft/sec with 180-grain bullet.

☆

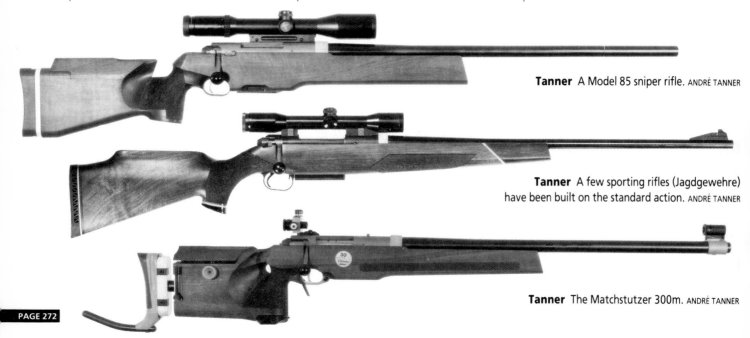

Tanner A Model 85 sniper rifle. ANDRÉ TANNER

Tanner A few sporting rifles (Jagdgewehre) have been built on the standard action. ANDRÉ TANNER

Tanner The Matchstutzer 300m. ANDRÉ TANNER

1980*: the first of the 300-metre Standard UIT rifles was based on the Tanner Free Rifle. The single-shot version had the original three-lug bolt, whereas the magazine-fed version had only two lugs. The trigger-pull could be adjusted between about 200gm and 3kg.

Competition-pattern dipoter back sights and replaceable-element 'tunnel' front sights were standard. A safety catch protruded above the stock behind the bolt handle.

Made of good quality walnut, the stock had an adjustable shoulder pad, a stippled pistol grip, a fixed straight comb, and a long slot through the fore-end. An accessory rail was also fitted.

1985: an improved UIT rifle was introduced to capitalise on an increase in the maximum permissible weight from 5 to 5·5kg. The Modell 85 could be identified by the stock, which had a revised pistol grip and a replaceable cheek piece; aluminium grasping plates were set in the sides of its fore-end. The trigger was altered to give an adjustment range of 100–2,000gm and the safety catch—which locked the bolt instead of the firing pin—moved forward to the right side of the receiver bridge ahead of the bolt handle.

1987*: a Modell 85 sniper rifle was offered with a shortened heavy barrel, a plain fore-end and a bipod. Optical sights were customary.

THOMPSON-CENTER

UNITED STATES OF AMERICA

This company, in addition to break-open guns, makes a solitary derivative of the Contender dropping-block pistol—a 1965-vintage design pictured in *Pistols of the World*, p.294.

Contender Carbine

Made by Thompson/Center Arms, Rochester, New Hampshire.
·22 Hornet, ·222 Remington, ·223 Remington, 7mm TCU, 7 × 30 Waters, ·30–30 Winchester, ·35 Remington, ·357 Magnum, ·357 Remington Maximum or ·44 Magnum.

Dropping-block action, operated by a lever doubling as the trigger guard.
DATA FOR A TYPICAL EXAMPLE
7 × 30mm Waters, rimless.
34·85in overall, 5·28lb unladen.
21·00in barrel, 4-groove rifling; RH, concentric.
Adjustable tangent-leaf sight.

☆

1985: this was made by attaching a long barrel, a round-tip fore-end and a pistol-grip walnut butt to the frame of the standard pistol. Barrels could be exchanged simply by removing the fore-end, tapping the hinge pin out of the frame, then lifting the barrel-block clear. Most guns were blued, with cougar motifs on the receiver-sides.

TIKKAKOSKI

FINLAND

Tikka sporters were originally derived from the 1898-pattern Mauser, omitting the safety lug in favour of the bolt handle turning down into its seat in the receiver. They were unremarkable mechanically, but sturdy and very dependable.

FINLAND

Model 55

Deluxe, Heavy Barrel, Master, Sniper, Sporter, SSP, Standard, Super Sporter and Varmint patterns.
Made by Oy Tikkakoski Ab, Tikkakoski.
·17 Remington, ·222 Remington, ·22–250, 6mm Remington, ·243 Winchester or ·308 Winchester.
Turning-bolt action, locked by rotating two lugs on the bolt head into the receiver wall and by the bolt handle turning down into its seat.
DATA FOR A TYPICAL EXAMPLE
·243 Winchester, rimless.
1,070mm overall, 3·25kg unladen.
580mm barrel, 4-groove rifling; RH, concentric.
Detachable box magazine, 3 rounds.
Folding leaf sight.
3,070 ft/sec with 100-grain bullet.

☆

1965*: the Tikka 55 Standard had a radial safety catch on the right side of the breech behind the bolt handle, and a magazine-release catch in the guard ahead of the trigger lever. The plain oil-finished hardwood stock had a pistol grip, a low Monte Carlo comb and a ventilated rubber shoulder pad. Chequering appeared on the pistol-grip and fore-end; swivels lay beneath the butt and the fore-end. The bolt handle was swept slightly backward. An optional large-diameter bolt-knob was popular—particularly in areas where gloves were used.

The 55 DL ('Deluxe') pattern had a walnut stock with a roll-over comb. The pistol-grip cap was rosewood, accompanied by a white-line spacer. The fore-end tip was also rosewood, cut obliquely and separated from the stock wood by another spacer. Chequering was conventional or a skip-line pattern.

1977*: chambered for the ·222 Remington, ·22–250 Remington, ·243 Winchester or ·308 Winchester cartridges, the Tikka 55 Sporter (also known as 'Heavy Barrel' or 'Varmint') had a 620mm barrel and a heavy stock. Overall length was about 1,100mm, and weight averaged 4·1kg. The robust pistol grip was almost vertical, and the fore-end was deeper than normal. Owing to the depth of the stock ahead of the trigger, a special extension was fitted to otherwise standard three-round magazines. Stippling ran from the fore-end to the pistol grip. One swivel lay on the right side of the straight-comb butt; its partner slid on a rail beneath the fore-end. Open sights were customarily omitted.

An essentially similar target-shooting version with micro-adjustable competition sights was promoted as the SSP.

1980: the rounded fore-end tips of standard and deluxe rifles were replaced by oblique-cut squared designs.

1983*: the Model 55 Super Sporter (alias Sniper or Master) had a Cycolac stock with a vertically sliding exchangeable cheek piece. The barrel was fluted, giving rigidity without increasing weight unnecessarily, and a muzzle weight was often attached by two cap-head bolts. Optical sights were retained by quick-release clamping

Tikka A standard Model 55 Deluxe rifle. OY TIKKAKOSKI

Tikka The Model 55 Sporter, with its curious stock. OY TIKKAKOSKI

Tikka The Model 55 Sport was a short-lived variation with a detachable box magazine and a large bolt-handle knob. OY TIKKAKOSKI

mounts, while a bipod could be attached to the rail beneath the fore-end.

1989: the basic Model 55 was superseded by the improved Tikka 558, described below.

Model 65

65A-308, Deluxe, Heavy Barrel, Sporter, Standard, Super Sporter, Trapper, Varmint and Wildboar patterns.
Made by Oy Tikkakoski Ab, Tikkakoski.
Chambering: see notes.
Action: as Model 55, above.
DATA FOR A TYPICAL STANDARD EXAMPLE
6·5 × 55mm, rimless.
1,080mm overall, 3·40kg unladen.
560mm barrel, 4-groove rifling; RH, concentric.
Detachable box magazine, 5 rounds.
Optical sight.
780 m/sec with 9·3-gram bullet.
☆

1970*: this was little more than a Model 55 enlarged to chamber magnum cartridges. The cocking-piece shroud was extended, owing to longer striker travel, and the bolt-handle base was smoothed. Free-floating barrels promoted excellent accuracy.

The stocks of the Tikka 65 Standard and Tikka 65 DL duplicated the corresponding '55' models. Five-round magazines were standard.

1977*: available in ·30–06 or ·308 Winchester, the Wildboar Model (sometimes known as the 'Trapper' in North America) had a 520mm barrel and a quarter-rib back sight. The pistol grip cap and fore-end tip were rosewood, but spacers were not used.

1978*: the Tikka 65 Sporters (6·5 × 55mm, ·270, ·30–06 or ·308 only) were introduced. Often known as 'Heavy Barrel' or 'Varmint' rifles—especially in North America—many were fitted with the wooden butt plates required in moving-target competitions. The Sporters were 1,110mm overall, had 600mm barrels and weighed 4·5kg. Magazines held seven rounds.

1979: 7 × 64mm, 7mm Remington Magnum and ·300 Winchester Magnum chamberings were added.

1983*: the Tikka 65 Super Sporter appeared. Apart from a longer receiver, it was identical with the Model 55 pattern described above.

1985*: the extraordinary M65A (or 65A-308) offered a special deep beavertail fore-end with a bipod attachment. The ten-round magazine was contained in an auxiliary wood housing and the anatomical plastic pistol grip anchored a tubular metal butt ending in an adjustable shoulder pad. A wooden comb-block could be slid along the butt-tube when required.

1989: the rifles were discontinued in favour of the improved Model 658.

Models 558 and 658

Battue, Continental, Premier, Standard, Varmint and Whitetail patterns.
Made by Oy Tikkakoski Ab, Tikkakoski.
Model 558: ·17 Remington, ·222 Remington, ·22–250, ·223 Remington, ·243 Winchester or ·308 Winchester
Model 658: 7mm Remington Magnum, 7 × 64mm, ·300 Winchester Magnum, ·30–06, ·338 Winchester Magnum or 9·3 × 62mm.
Action: generally as Model 55, above.
DATA FOR A TYPICAL STANDARD MODEL 658
·338 Winchester Magnum, rimless.
1,140mm overall, 3·35kg unladen.
620mm barrel, 4-groove rifling; RH, concentric.
Detachable box magazine, 3 rounds.
Folding leaf sight.
2,700 ft/sec with 250-grain bullet.
☆

1988: identical but for action-length, these were modernised versions of the earlier Tikka rifles with notably squarer contours and high walls on the left side of the receiver. The bolt shroud was streamlined, a radial safety catch lay on the right side of the action behind the bolt handle, and the receiver-top was grooved for optical sight mounts. The magazine-release catch was set into the side of the stock.

Short-action 558 guns had 560mm barrels, giving an overall length of about 1,095mm; weight averaged 3·2kg. Stocks were walnut, with a Monte Carlo comb, a rounded fore-end tip and a rubber shoulder pad.

1990: the first Premium or deluxe rifles were offered, distinguished by superior walnut stocks, roll-over combs, and rosewood accessories.

1991: the Battue and Continental patterns appeared, alternatively known as 'Whitetail' and 'Varmint' respectively in North America. The former (·270, 7mm Remington Magnum, ·300 Winchester Magnum, ·30–06, ·308 or ·338 Winchester Magnum) had a 520mm barrel with a quarter rib; the latter (·22–250, ·223, ·243 or ·308) had a heavy barrel and a broad fore-end.

USA

Ithaca-LSA models

The Ithaca Gun Company sold many Tikka rifles in 1969–77. The Ithaca-LSA 55 had squared stocks with reverse-cut fore-end tips. Standard and Deluxe patterns were available in ·222 Remington, ·22–250, 6mm Remington, ·243 Winchester, ·270 Winchester or ·308 Winchester. According to Ithaca catalogues, the guns were 42in long, had 22in barrels and weighed about 6·5lb. Three-round magazines were standard. The 55 HB ('Heavy Barrel') model, available only in ·222 or ·22–250, had a 23in barrel and weighed 8·25lb. The fore-end was a broadened semi-beavertail type, though the butt was a standard Monte Carlo design.

The Ithaca-LSA 65, offered in Standard or Deluxe options, was chambered for ·25–06 Remington, ·270 Winchester or ·30–06 rounds (·222 Remington versions were supplied to special order). Four-cartridge magazines were customary, standard guns weighing about 7lb.

TOKAREV

UNION OF SOVIET SOCIALIST REPUBLICS
~

These gas-operated guns were designed and developed by Fedor Tokarev in the 1920s, though the inventor had previously toyed with recoil-operated patterns dating back before the

Tikka The M55 Super Sporter.

Tikka A standard Model 65A sporting rifle. OY TIKKAKOSKI

Tikka The Model 65 Deluxe had better stock and white spacers. OY TIKKAKOSKI

Tikka Model 55 Sniper was a variant of the Super Sporter, with a muzzle brake and a fluted barrel. KARL SCHÄFER

Tokarev Soldiers of the Red Army man 83mm M1941 mortars during the Second World War. Note the rifle slung over the shoulder of the NCO alongside the nearest mortar. COLLECTOR'S COMPENDIUM

First World War. Tokarev rifles were unique to the USSR; however, captured weapons were used by the Finns and Germans prior to 1945.

Despite the poor reputation the guns enjoy in the West, the Tokarev was one of the most effectual auto-loading rifles to see widespread service during the Second World War, only the US M1 Garand being made in larger numbers. However, the SVT-40 was handicapped by poor manufacture—not surprisingly, in view of the unbelievable dislocation of Soviet industry after the German invasion—and also by the clumsy Russian 7·62mm rifle cartridge. The rifle would undoubtedly have performed better with the 6·5mm Japanese cartridge chambered in the Federov Avtomat (q.v.).

The SVT was difficult to field-strip, but had a better magazine than the US M1 Garand and its effectual locking system provided the basis for the post-war Belgian FN-Saive rifles.

1926: in January, two recoil-operated Tokarevs were tried against a selection of improved Federov Avtomats and several Degtyarev guns. One of the Avtomats returned the best results, the Tokarev patterns being rejected.

1928: modified recoil-operated Tokarevs were submitted to new trials, their major rivals being the so-called Co-operative ('Ko.') rifles derived from the Federov Avtomat. The 'Ko. No.3' rifle proved to be most effectual; Tokarev No.2, which had been showing promise, suffered a structural failure during the endurance trial.

1930: by March, five recoil-operated Tokarevs were being tried unsuccessfully against five Degtyarevs. The original Tokarev was then replaced by a gas-operated gun.

Model 1930

Semi-automatic trials rifle: Samozaryadnaya vintovka sistemy Tokareva ('SVT'), optny obr.1930g.
Made by the state ordnance factory, Tula, 1931–2?
Quantity: said to have been several hundred.
7·62 × 54mm, rimmed.
Gas-operated auto-loading action, locked by displacing the tail of the breech block down into the receiver.

1,185mm overall, about 4·00kg unladen.
605mm barrel, 4-groove rifling; RH, concentric.
Fixed box magazine, 10 rounds.
Leaf sight graduated to 1,500 or 2,000 metres.
755 m/sec with Type D ball cartridges.
Experimental bayonet.

☆

1930: the first of these rifles was submitted for trials against Degtyarev designs, a Simonov joining the competition in 1931. The basic 1930-type Tokarev had the piston assembly beneath the barrel, an open-top muzzle brake/compensator, and two barrel bands. The stock had a pistol grip, the magazine was a fixed protruding box with a distinctive rounded profile, and the leaf-pattern back sight lay on top of the receiver immediately in front of the firer's eye. As the guns were semi-experimental, it is suspected that there were many minor variations in dimensions and fittings.

Model 1935

Semi-automatic carbine: Samozaryadnaya karabina sistemy Tokareva, obr.1935g.
Made by the state ordnance factory, Tula, 1934–6.
Quantity: 450–500.
7·62 × 54mm, rimmed.
Action: as M1930 rifle, above.
1,050mm overall, about 3·70kg unladen.
450mm barrel, 4-groove rifling; RH, concentric.
Detachable box magazine, 20 rounds.
Tangent-leaf sight graduated to 1,500 metres.
715 m/sec with Type D ball cartridges.
Experimental sword bayonet.

☆

1934: this gun was developed from the earlier 1930 pattern, specifically to compete against a Simonov (presumably for cavalry or artillery use). It had a one-piece pistol gripped stock, with a wooden hand guard running to the barrel band and a perforated sheet-steel guard—five circular holes on each side—running forward to the muzzle shroud. The shroud contained the gas-port assembly and had an open-top muzzle brake/compensator adapted from the preceding type. Unlike the earlier Tokarev, the 1935-

pattern carbine had its piston and operating rod above the barrel to act directly on the bolt carrier. A cleaning rod was let into the right side of the stock, the back sight was moved forward until it was directly above the chamber, and a detachable box magazine was substituted for the older fixed housing.

1935: the Tokarev carbine was a considerable improvement on its prototypes, but was not initially successful enough to convince the Soviet authorities of its merits.

Model 1938

Semi-automatic rifle: Samozaryadnaya vintovka sistemy Tokareva ('SVT'), obr.1938g.
Made by the state ordnance factories, Tula and Izhevsk, 1939–40.
Quantity: 150,000?
7·62 × 54mm, rimmed.
Action: as M1930 rifle, above.
1,220mm overall, 3·95kg unladen.
635mm barrel, 4-groove rifling; RH, concentric.
Detachable box magazine, 20 rounds.
Tangent-leaf sight graduated to 1,500 metres.
770 m/sec with Type D ball cartridges.
SVT-38 sword bayonet.

☆

1938: in the late summer, trials were held with Tokarev, Simonov and Rukavishnikov guns. The Tokarev was an improvement of the preceding 1935-type carbine, but its barrel apparently had cooling fins. It was judged to be acceptable if the fins were discarded—they complicated manufacture—and if a hold-open and a better muzzle brake were added. A repeat of the trials in November confirmed the decision.

1939: the semi-automatic SVT rifle was adopted on 26 February. It was practically identical with the 1935-pattern carbine externally, with the cleaning rod let into the right side of the stock, but was longer and had two barrel bands. The stock was made in two parts, a vertical joint being found below ahead of the receiver. Four circular holes appeared in each side of the short sheet-metal hand guard, and five cooling slots were cut through the woodwork over the barrel.

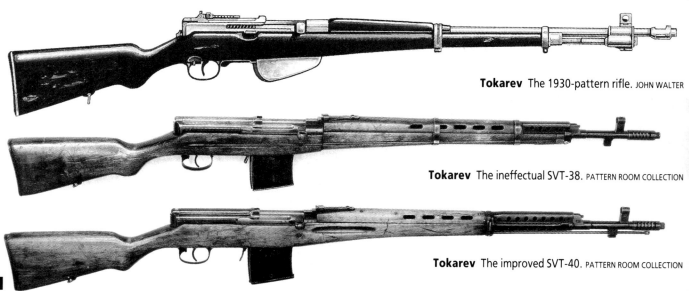

Tokarev The breech of the SVT-38. PATTERN ROOM COLLECTION

Tokarev The 1930-pattern rifle. JOHN WALTER

Tokarev The ineffectual SVT-38. PATTERN ROOM COLLECTION

Tokarev The improved SVT-40. PATTERN ROOM COLLECTION

The rear band usually ran over the rear of the fourth slot, counting back from the muzzle. The guns had swivels on the under edge of the butt and ahead of the nose cap, and a radial safety lever could be rotated down into the back of the trigger guard behind the trigger lever. Each side of the muzzle brake had six slender slots.

Before production could begin, however, Simonov claimed to have eliminated the faults of his AVS. A state commission, after considering the comparative merits of Tokarev and Simonov rifles, concluded that the latter was not only easier to make but also less wasteful of material. Its poor performance in the 1938 trials was blamed on poor manufacture.

However, mindful of the failure of the AVS, Joseph Stalin cancelled work on all other automatic rifles in July 1939 to concentrate on the SVT; 4·45 million guns were required by 1942, the first rifle being exhibited on 16 July. By October, mass production was underway.

1940: experience in the Winter War against Finland exposed the deficiencies of the SVT-38.

Model 1940

1940: this rifle was formally adopted on 13 April for the NCOs of the infantry and artillery, plus naval infantrymen and marines. Though many changes had been made compared with the SVT-38, the most obvious was the cleaning rod under the barrel instead of set in the stock-side.

The SVT had an improved one-piece stock with a lengthened sheet-steel hand guard/fore-end assembly. A recoil bolt ran through the stock beneath the cocking handle and a short grasping groove was cut into the sides of the stock below the back sight. The magazine catch, unlike the SVT-38 pattern, could be folded back against the stock to minimise the chances of releasing the magazine accidentally.

Production steadily gathered momentum in the autumn of 1940, the Snayperskaya vintovka sistemy Tokareva (SNT, 'Tokarev sniper rifle') being adopted early in October to replace the obr.1891/30 (Mosin-Nagant) pattern.

1941: output of 1·07 million SVT and SNT rifles compared favourably with 1·29 million obr.1891 rifles and obr.1938g carbines, but success was short lived. After the German invasion of the USSR in June, the Tokarev was regarded as too complicated to justify continuing production.

1942: a fluted chamber seems to have been introduced to improve extraction with the poor-quality wartime ammunition, and an improved muzzle brake with two large ports on each side replaced the earlier six-port pattern. Selective-fire rifles were made during 1942–3, when the Red Army was desperately short of machine-guns, but the Avtomatischeskaya vintovka Tokareva (AVT, 'Tokarev automatic rifle') was far too light to be successful. The guns generally had crudely shaped heavy stocks and lacked the optical sight grooves on the receiver-top.

1945: production of Tokarev rifles officially ceased on 3 January, but few had been made in the previous twelve months.

Model 1940

1940: a few purpose-built carbines were made in Tula, distinguishable from the emergency wartime conversions by the design of the full-length hand guard above the barrel; this had only five holes alongside the barrel (compared with seven on most rifle conversions) and only a single cooling slot was cut through the wooden hand guard. All known guns have the original six-port muzzle brake. Production seems to have stopped at the time of the German invasion.

Non-standard carbines

Some SVT-38 and SVT-40 rifles were cut to carbine length, probably after battle damage. They can usually be distinguished from the purpose-built obr.1940g carbine by the rifle-type sheet-metal fore-end, which either retains seven cooling holes alongside the barrel or will show evidence of hasty modification—e.g., the hole nearest the woodwork will be cut through. This may also be true of the cooling slots in the wooden hand guard.

A typical 'partisan carbine', originally a rifle made at Tula in 1941, had its barrel so greatly shortened that the sheet-steel fore-end was only about 40cm long. A sling swivel was crudely screwed to the left side of the butt. Standards of workmanship were very low, suggesting that the work was undertaken somewhere other than an ordnance factory.

ULTRA LIGHT

UNITED STATES OF AMERICA

Ultra-Light makes a series of rifles incorporating a conventional bolt with dual-opposed locking lugs. The guns are all made in right- ('R' suffix) or left-hand ('L') versions. A silhouette pistol has also been made on the Model 20 receiver.

Models 20, 24 and 28

Made by Ultra-Light Arms, Inc., Granville,
West Virginia.
Chambering: see notes.
Turning-bolt action, locked by rotating two lugs
on the bolt head into the receiver wall and by the bolt
handle turning down into its seat.
DATA FOR A TYPICAL MODEL 20
7mm–08 Remington, rimless.
41·50in overall, 4·75lb unladen.
22·00in barrel, 4-groove rifling; RH, concentric.
Detachable box magazine, 3 rounds.
Folding leaf sight.
2,850 ft/sec with 140-grain bullet.

☆

1987: the Model 20S was the smallest of the several otherwise identical actions. Fitted with a Douglas Premium No.1 barrel, it chambered ·17 Remington, ·22 Hornet, ·222 Remington or ·223 Remington rounds.

The similar short-action Model 20 rifle has been offered in ·22–250 Remington, 6mm Remington, ·243 Winchester, ·250–3000 Savage, ·257 Roberts, 7mm–08 Remington, 7 × 57mm, 7 × 57 Ackley, ·284 Winchester or ·300 Savage versions.

The intermediate or Model 24 action was intended for the ·25–06 Remington, ·270 Winchester, ·280 Remington or ·30–06 rounds.

The long-action Model 28 Magnum, offered with a 24in Douglas Premium No.2 barrel and a recoil arrestor (KDF or Ultra Light patterns), chambered ·264 Winchester, 7mm Remington Magnum, ·300 Winchester Magnum or ·338 Winchester Magnum cartridges. Model 28 rifles were about 45in overall and weighed a mere 5·75lb—somewhat light for even medium-power magnum ammunition.

Ultra Light rifles all had Timney triggers and patented sear-locking safety levers protruding from the stock behind the bolt handle. Graphite-reinforced Kevlar stocks had a straight comb and a rubber recoil pad; their matt ('suede') or glossy DuPont Imron epoxy finishes have included black, brown or green, plus Woodlands, Desert or Treebark Camo.

VERGUEIRO

PORTUGAL

〜

This rifle was developed after trials held in 1900–2 showed the Mannlicher-Schönauer to be effectual enough—but too expensive for the Portuguese treasury.

The best features of the contemporary 1898-pattern Mauser were simply combined with a split-bridge receiver and a simplified bolt based on the Mannlicher-Schönauer (i.e., a modified Gewehr 88 pattern). Ironically, the Vergueiro rifles were all made in Germany.

BRAZIL

DWM sold about 5,000 Vergueiro-type rifles to the federal police, probably in 1910–12 to use parts left over from the Portuguese contract. Guns were identical with the standard Mo.904, excepting that they were adapted for the 7 × 57mm cartridge; their chamber tops displayed the Brazilian 'enwreathed star' arms above F.P.D.F. (Força Policia Distrito Federal).

PORTUGAL

Model 1904

Infantry rifles; Espingardas 6·5 Mo.1904 e Mo.904/39.
Made by Deutsche Waffen- und Munitionsfabriken,
Charlottenburg, Berlin, c.1904–9.
6·5 × 58mm, rimless.
Turning-bolt action, locked by rotating two lugs on the
bolt head into the receiver wall.
DATA FOR MO.1904
1,223mm overall, 3·80lb unladen.
738mm barrel, 4-groove rifling; RH, concentric.
Internal charger-loaded box magazine, 5 rounds.
Tangent-leaf sight graduated to 2,000 metres.
715 m/sec with Mo.1904 ball ammunition.
M1904 sword bayonet.

☆

1904: the Vergueiro-Mauser rifle was easily recognised by the split-bridge receiver, with the

bolt handle turning down ahead of the bridge to act as a safety lug should the front lugs fail. A separate bolt head and a simplified cocking piece/safety mechanism eased manufacturing problems in an effort to reduce costs. Unlike some other rifles with detachable bolt heads, however, the Vergueiro could not be assembled unless the head was securely attached.

Rifles cocked partly during the opening stroke and partly as the action closed. The floor plate of the internal staggered-column magazine could be released by a catch inside the front of the trigger guard.

The one-piece walnut stock had a shallow pistol grip, whilst a hand guard ran from the chamber ring to the solitary sprung band. A bayonet bar lay ahead of the narrow nose cap, above the protruding half-length cleaning rod. Swivels lay under the band and butt.

A typical rifle bore its designation ESPINGARDA PORTUGUEZA 6,5 MOD. 1904 on the left side of the receiver above the DWM name. Chambers bore either the crowned 'CI' cypher of Carlos I (reigned 1889–1909) or, apparently, the 'M2' of his short-lived successor Manuel II (1909–10 only). Work may have been completed by the 1910 revolution; few, if any, deliveries were made thereafter. The original contract is believed to have been for about 100,000 guns.

1939: owing to the adoption of the 7·9mm Mo.937 (Mauser) rifle, substantial quantities of surviving Mo.1904 rifles were converted in Lisbon arsenal for the new cartridge. Known as 'Mo.904/39', they had 600mm barrels and front sights protected by prominent wings. A transverse bolt was added beneath the chamber to handle increased recoil.

VETTERLI

SWITZERLAND

〜

Designed by Friedrich Vetterli, this bolt-action rifle was used only in Switzerland and Italy.

Vetterli had joined Schweizerische Industrie-Gesellschaft's Waffen-Department in 1864, and

had soon developed a metallic-cartridge gun by combining a bolt inspired by the Dreyse with a Henry-type tube magazine. At the time the Vetterli was adopted by the Swiss army, it represented a significant advance: nowhere else in Europe had a magazine-feed rifle been accepted for universal military service. Its large-capacity magazine permitted an aimed fire-rate of 21 or more shots per minute, and, even if the bolt-lugs were not ideally positioned, the gun was sturdy enough for untaxing Swiss service.

MILITARY RIFLES

Note: even though the Swiss Vetterli fired rimfire ammunition, it remained in service until replaced by the Schmidt(-Rubin) in the 1890s.

ITALY

Unification created standardisation problems in ordnance circles. Rigorous trials undertaken in 1868-9 subsequently convinced the Italians of the merits of the Swiss Vetterli breech, but not of the tube magazine. Italy had a larger army than Switzerland and the cost of re-arming with magazine rifles was prohibitive. Italian weapons, therefore, were originally single-loaders.

Model 1870

Infantry rifles: Fucile di Fanteria, Mo.1870 e Mo.1870/87.
Made by Fabbrica d'Armi Pietro Beretta, Gardone Val Trompia; Reale Fabbrica d'Armi di Torino (Turin); Reale Fabbrica d'Armi, Torre Annunziata; and Officina Costruzione d'Artiglieria, Rome.
10·35 × 47mm, rimmed.
Turning-bolt action with two lugs on the bolt body locking into the receiver behind the elevator-well.
DATA FOR MO.1870
1,345mm overall, 4·12kg unladen.
860mm barrel, 4-groove rifling; RH, concentric.
Quadrant sight graduated to 1,000 metres.
430 m/sec with Mo.1870 ball cartridges.
Mo.1870 sword bayonet.
☆

1870: the standard infantry rifle was an elegant weapon, easily distinguished from the Swiss M1869 by the lack of a magazine and the slender stock ending well short of the muzzle. The Italian gun also had safety catch on the right side of the breech behind the bolt handle, and a rotating ejection-port cover with a knurled-head button. It also had a spurred trigger guard, two screw-clamping barrel bands and a small nose cap, all mounts being made of iron. A lug for the bayonet lay on the right side of the muzzle.
1881: an improved Vecchi-pattern quadrant sight was adopted, graduated to 1,200 metres.
1887: a magazine conversion proposed by Giuseppe Vitali was approved, many thousands of Mo.1870 rifles being converted in 1888-95. Though the action was practically unchanged, a new floor plate supported a detachable four-round box magazine loaded either singly or from a special charger; a central spiral spring gave the magazine its unique appearance. A support rail was added to the rear of the receiver to prevent the bolt rocking when open.
1890: the introduction of cartridges loaded with smokeless propellant, generating a muzzle velocity of about 610-615 m/sec, permitted 1,600-metre back sights to be fitted.
1912: substantial numbers of Mo.70/87 rifles were sold to the Ulster Volunteer Force, an ultra-Conservative paramilitary force raised in northern Ireland to fight—if necessary—against Home Rule. The guns were apparently military surplus bought in Germany, perhaps from A.L. Frank of Hamburg. In addition to original Italian ordnance marks, they often bore FOR GOD AND ULSTER, or U.V.F. and the Red Hand of the O'Neill family on a shield (taken from the provincial arms).
1916: survivors were converted to 6.5mm.

Model 1870

Short rifles: Moschetto per Truppe Speciali, Mo.1870 e Mo.1870/87.
Manufacturers: as Mo.1870 rifle (q.v.).
10·35 × 47mm, rimmed.
Action: as Mo.1870 rifle, above.

1,095mm overall, 4·22kg unladen.
610mm barrel, 4-groove rifling; RH, concentric.
Quadrant sight graduated to 500 metres.
410 m/sec with Mo.1870 ball cartridges.
Mo.1870 TS épée bayonet.
☆

1872: this was a shortened version of the infantry rifle, intended for special-service units (Truppe Speciali). It was distinguished by its short barrel, single barrel band, and plain trigger-guard bow. Its bayonet had a distinctive two-edged blade with a central rib.
1881: new guns were fitted with a Vecchi back sight graduated to 1,000 metres. Older weapons were adapted when returning for repair.
1887: the decision was taken to fit surviving guns with four-round Vitali box magazines ('Mo.1870/87'), work being undertaken over a period of several years.
1890: the introduction of cartridges loaded with smokeless propellant allowed sights to be graduated to 1,400 metres.
1916: some Mo.1870/87 TS short rifles were converted to accept 6·5mm ammunition.

Model 1870

Cavalry carbines: Moschetti Mo.1870 e Mo.1870/87.
Manufacturers: as Mo.1870 rifle (q.v.).
10·35 × 47mm, rimmed.
Action: as Mo.1870 rifle, above.
DATA FOR MO.1870
929mm overall, 3·53kg with bayonet.
450mm barrel, 4-groove rifling; RH, concentric.
Quadrant sight graduated to 500 metres.
375 m/sec with M1870 ball cartridges.
Mo.1870 socket bayonet.
☆

1872: adopted for the cavalry, this was little more than a rifle action in a short half-stock. The trigger guard had a plain bow, and the nose cap (which carried the front sling swivel) had a cranked appearance. The long-bladed bayonet, which locked round the front sight, could be reversed when not required; half the blade ran back inside the fore-end, a half-length cleaning rod being carried in a butt trap.

Tokarev Men of the Soviet army march past the Kremlin to celebrate the 31st anniversary of the October Revolution (1948). NOVOSTI PRESS AGENCY

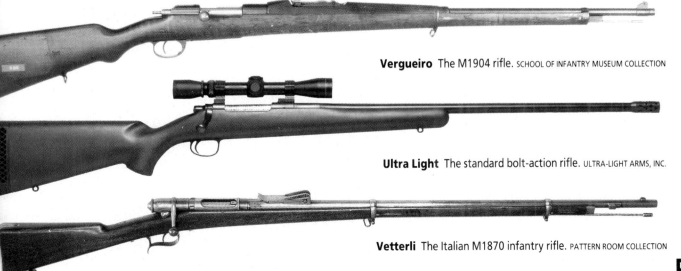

Vergueiro The M1904 rifle. SCHOOL OF INFANTRY MUSEUM COLLECTION

Ultra Light The standard bolt-action rifle. ULTRA-LIGHT ARMS, INC.

Vetterli The Italian M1870 infantry rifle. PATTERN ROOM COLLECTION

1875: a longer version of the cavalry carbine was adopted for the Carabineri, or gendarmerie. It shared the same general characteristics but was the same length as the Mo.1870 TS (q.v.). it weighed about 4·1kg with its socket bayonet.

1881: an improved Vecchi-pattern back sight was approved, extending the sight-range to 1,000 metres.

1887: surviving carbines were adapted for the four-round Vitali box magazine, being known as 'Mo.1870/87'. Work was undertaken from about 1890 onward.

1890: the approval of ammunition loaded with smokeless propellant allowed the sights on the Carabineri carbines to be altered to 1,400 metres. Though contemporary Italian manuals also show the short-barrel cavalry carbine with these extended sights, none could be found.

1916: a few survivors were converted for the 6·5mm cartridge.

Model 1882

Navy rifle: Fucile di Marina, Mo.1882.
Made by Reale Fabbrica d'Armi, Terni?
10·35 × 47mm, rimmed.
Action: as Mo.1870 rifle, above.
1,210mm overall, 4·05kg unladen.
730mm barrel, 4-groove rifling; RH, concentric.
Tube magazine under barrel, 8 rounds.
Quadrant sight graduated to 1,400 metres.
400 m/sec with Mo.1870 ball cartridges.
Mo.1870 sword bayonet?
☆

1882: this gun was adopted only by the Italian navy, principally for the use of the marine infantry. It was basically a standard Mo.70 rifle with a tube magazine beneath the barrel, giving the fore-end a much more massive appearance than the single-shot army rifles. Unlike the Swiss guns, which had a separate loading port on the right side of the receiver, the Mo.82 magazine loaded through the top of the open action.

Often known as the 'Vetterli-Bertoldo'— apparently honouring the president of the navy trials board—these guns had a plain stock, two spring-retained barrel bands and an exposed muzzle carrying a bayonet lug. Swivels lay on the underside of the butt and the rear barrel band, whilst the cleaning rod was carried in a channel cut into the left side of the fore-end.

1890: a few surviving Vetterli-Bertoldo rifles were adapted for the four-round Ferraciù box magazine, apparently for trials. An elongated triangular casing was fitted beneath the bolt way, relying on a spring-loaded lifter arm to raise the cartridges. Though the balance of the rifle improved perceptibly, improvements were purely temporary; Vetterli rifles were soon replaced in navy service by the Mo.1891 Mannlicher-Carcano.

Model 1870–87–15

Infantry rifle: Fucile di Fanteria, Mo.1870/87/15.
Believed to have been converted in the Terni arsenal, and possibly also by gunsmiths in the Gardone area.
6·5 × 52mm, rimless.
Turning-bolt action with two lugs on the bolt body locking into the receiver behind the elevator-well.
1,345mm overall, 4·62kg unladen.
860mm barrel, 4-groove rifling; RH, concentric.
Fixed clip-loaded box magazine, 6 rounds.
Quadrant sight graduated to 2,000 metres.
730 m/sec with Mo.1891/95 ball cartridges.
Mo.1870/15 sword bayonet.
☆

1916*: conversion of obsolescent Mo.1870/87 Vetterli-Vitali rifles was authorised, partly to offset losses of M1891 (Mannlicher-Carcano) guns and partly to arm newly-raised units. The work consisted of boring out the original barrel, inserting a rifled liner, changing the sights, and substituting a Mannlicher magazine for the old Vitali box type.

Owing to the position of the locking lugs, the Vetterli breech was only just strong enough to withstand the pressures generated by the 6·5mm cartridge. Consequently, the rifles were relegated to artillery, lines-of-communication and militia units wherever possible. However, some served colonial infantrymen in North Africa until the last of the Italian forces capitulated in 1941.

Model 1870–87–15

Carbines and short rifles.

In addition to the infantry rifles, the Italians converted quantities of the Mo.1870/87 T musketoons, the Mo.1870/87 cavalry carbine and the Mo.1870/87 Carabinieri carbine—the last pattern being adapted only in minuscule numbers. Their history parallels that of the rifles but most were discarded after 1918.

SWITZERLAND

1867: trials were undertaken with the 'Repetier Gewehr M1867'. This gun had an external rin hammer, hung centrally below the rear of th bolt, a pivoting loading cover on the right side receiver and a distinctively spurred trigge guard. The 1863-pattern quadrant sight wa retained, and the cleaning rod was channelled i the left side of the stock.

Model 1869

Infantry rifle: Repetier-Gewehr M1869.
Made by Schweizerische Industrie-Gesellschaft, Neuhausen, 1869–74 (59,000); Eidgenössische Montierwerkstätte, Bern, 1869–75 (8,900); Eidgenössische Waffenfabrik, Bern, 1875–8 (14,060); Cordier & Cie, Bellefontaine, 1869–73 (4,000); W. von Steiger, Thun, 1869–74 (15,200); Ost-Schweizerische Buchsenmacher, St Gallen, 1869–74 (8,700); Rychner & Keller, Aarau, 1869–73 (9,700); Valentin Sauerbrey, Basel, 1869–73 (7,000); and the Zürich Zeughaus, 1869–74 (1,500).
Quantity: 128,060.
10·4 × 38mm, rimfire.
Turning-bolt action with two lugs on the bolt body locking into the receiver behind the elevator-well.
1,320mm overall, 4·66kg unladen.
841mm barrel, 4-groove rifling; RH, concentric.
Tube magazine under barrel, 12 rounds.
Quadrant sight graduated to 1,000 schritt.
435 m/sec with M1867 ball cartridges.
M1863 socket bayonet.
☆

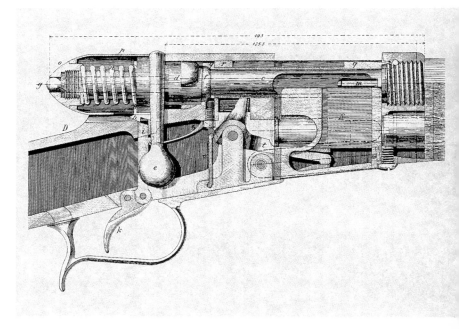

Vetterli The action of the Swiss M1869 rifle.

869: provisionally approved on 8 January, he first Swiss rifle (often known as the 'M1868/69') could be distinguished principally y its cleaning rod, which was set into the left ide of the stock. A thirteenth cartridge could be laced in the elevator.

Experience soon showed that the cleaning od was easily damaged. Changes were made, he improved 'M1869' being accepted by the ederal parliament on 1 August and declared egulation issue in December. The modified gun was 1,300mm overall, weighed 4·61kg and had n eleven-round magazine. Its cleaning rod was arried in the fore-end under the barrel; a nurled ring was added to the cocking-piece ead to facilitate re-cocking in the event of a nisfire; a gas-escape hole was added above he chamber; and the loading-gate cover was nodified so that the small transverse bolt on the ont of the action acted as a limit-stop.

870: changes were made, the most obvious eing the substitution (from 20 August) of a ansverse key through the fore-end—beneath he back sight—for a spring which had been set the right side of the fore-end at the joint with he receiver. The small threaded bolt that had reviously limited the rotation of the loading-gate over was also omitted.

871: the introduction of a new short rifle, escribed below, was accompanied by a change the rifle with effect from 31 December. The M1869/71' rifle (which accepted the new uadrangular-blade M1871 socket bayonet) was istinguished by an improved elevator system nd a simplified receiver, lacking the loading-gate over and the leaf spring that had previously ppeared on the left side. The two bands, nose ap and diced fore-end were all retained, though he back sight was graduated to 1,000 metres nd weight rose to about 4·7kg.

878: small numbers of M1869 rifles were nortened to offset shortages of true 1871-type arbines. A typical example was 945mm long, ith a 485mm barrel, and weighed 3·9kg. though the central barrel band and nose cap ere retained, shortening the muzzle prevented bayonet being used.

Model 1870

··

Cadet rifle: Kadetten-Gewehr M1870.
Made by Schweizerische Industrie-Gesellschaft,
Neuhausen, 1870–3.
10·4 × 38mm, rimfire.
Action: as M1869 rifle, above.
1,150mm overall, 3·25kg unladen.
680mm barrel, 4-groove rifling; RH, concentric.
Quadrant sight graduated to 600 metres.
About 400 m/sec with M1867 ball cartridges.

☆

1870: the single-shot cadet rifle was authorised by the Eidgenössische Militärdepartment on 22 November. Made exclusively by SIG, it had a one-piece stock resembling the Italian Vetterli rifles (q.v.) but did not take a bayonet.

Model 1871

··

Carbine: Repetier-Karabiner M1871.
Made by Eidgenössische Montierwerkstätte, Bern,
1871–2 (500?); and Rudolf Pfenninger, Stäfa, 1872–4
(about 2,500).
Quantity: about 3,000.
10·4 × 38mm, rimfire.
Action: as M1869 rifle, above.
932mm overall, 3·25kg unladen.
470mm barrel, 4-groove rifling; RH, concentric.
Tube magazine under barrel, 6 rounds.
Block-and-leaf sight graduated to 400 metres
(see notes).
375 m/sec with M1867 ball cartridges.
No bayonet.

☆

1871: adopted on 20 February, this had a rotating ejection-port cover, a straight-edge fore-end and a spatulate bolt handle. The back sight was a small standing block for 225 metres with folding leaves for 300 and 400 metres. Only about 200–250 carbines of this type were made. **1872**: a sliding Thury-pattern tangent back sight (225–300 metres) was approved on 14 May. At about the same time, the guns acquired a bolt handle with a conventional grasping knob, a fore-end with a notable step, and a modified receiver lacking the leaf spring on the left side.

1874: a Schmidt-pattern sight was accepted on 4 November and apparently fitted to carbines as they returned for repair—production had been completed in August.

Model 1871

··

Short rifle: Repetier-Stutzer M1871.
Made by Schweizerische Industrie-Gesellschaft,
Neuhausen, 1871–4 (1,000); Eidgenössische
Montierwerkstätte and Eidgenössische Waffenfabrik,
Bern, 1872–9 (about 15,000).
Quantity: about 16,000.
10·4 × 38mm, rimfire.
Action: as M1869 rifle, above.
1,260mm overall, 4·63kg unladen.
785mm barrel, 4-groove rifling; RH, concentric.
Tube magazine under barrel, 10 rounds.
Quadrant sight graduated to 1,000 metres.
430 m/sec with M1867 ball cartridges.
M1871 socket bayonet.

☆

1871: the infantry rifle was supplemented from 27 February by this gun, intended for the riflemen. A Thury double set-trigger was adopted in December. Stutzer were shorter than the contemporaneous infantry rifles; had only a single barrel band; and were fitted with special heavy butt-plates.

Model 1878

··

Infantry rifle: Repetier-Gewehr M1878.
Made by Eidgenössische Waffenfabrik, Bern, 1878–81.
Quantity: about 100,000.
10·4 × 38mm, rimfire.
Action: as M1869 rifle, above.
1,326mm overall, 4·58kg unladen.
841mm barrel, 4-groove rifling; RH, concentric.
Tube magazine under barrel, 12 rounds.
Quadrant sight graduated to 1,200 metres.
435 m/sec with M1867 ball cartridges.
M1878 sword bayonet.

☆

1872: experiments to improve the Vetterli rifle created a variation with a bolt guide above the wrist of the stock and another with a twin

Vetterli The M1870–87 ('Vetterli-Vitali'). PATTERN ROOM COLLECTION

Vetterli An Italian 6·5mm M1870–87–16 rifle. JOHN WALTER

Vetterli The Swiss M1878 infantry rifle. PATTERN ROOM COLLECTION

magazine containing more than twenty rounds. Trials rifles usually had one-piece stocks; at least one had an 1875-patent Pieri thumb-trigger on the upper tang behind the bolt, and a finger spur replacing the trigger guard.

1878: the improved Repetier-Gewehr M1878 was adopted on 30 April. The action was little more than that of the M1869/71, though a few detail improvements had been made internally; externally, the gun had only a single barrel band, lacked stock-dicing, and mounted a sword bayonet. The Schmidt quadrant sight had a much shorter leaf than its predecessor.

Model 1878

Short rifle: Repetier-Stutzer M1878.
Made by Eidgenössische Waffenfabrik, Bern, 1878–81.
Quantity: 5,410.
10·4 × 38mm, rimfire.
Action: as M1869 rifle, above.
1,326mm overall, 4·62kg unladen.
835mm barrel, 4-groove rifling; RH, concentric.
Tube magazine under barrel, 12 rounds.
Quadrant sight graduated to 1,200 metres.
435 m/sec with M1867 ball cartridges.
M1878 sword bayonet.

☆

1878: this was simply a minor variant of the M1878 infantry rifle fitted with a Schmidt-type set-trigger. Consequently, there are two trigger levers inside the spurred guard.

Model 1878

Carbine: Repetier-Karabiner M1878.
Made by Eidgenössische Waffenfabrik, Bern, 1879–85.
Quantity: 1,720.
10·4 × 38mm, rimfire.
Action: as M1869 rifle, above.
928mm overall, 3·30kg unladen.
470mm barrel, 4-groove rifling; RH, concentric.
Tube magazine under barrel, 6 rounds.
Quadrant sight graduated to 600 metres.
375 m/sec with M1867 ball cartridges.
No bayonet.

☆

1878: adopted on 30 April for dragoons, this shared the action of the rifle and Stutzer, but had a stepped fore-end. A pivoting loading-gate cover was retained, but the spur on the trigger guard was omitted, and the gun would not take a bayonet. Carbines often lacked the gas-escape holes found on rifle receivers.

1895: about 300 guns were modified for issue to the border guards (Grenzwächterkorps). These had an additional swivel on the nose cap.

Model 1878

Border-guard carbine: Repetier-Karabiner für Grenzwächterkorps, M1878.
Made by Eidgenössische Waffenfabrik, Bern, c.1880–1.
Quantity: 400.
10·4 × 38mm, rimfire.
Action: as M1869 rifle, above.
945mm overall, 3·34kg unladen.
485mm barrel, 4-groove rifling; RH, concentric.
Tube magazine under barrel, 6 rounds.
Quadrant sight graduated to 600 metres.
375 m/sec with M1867 ball cartridges.
Sword bayonet.

☆

1880*: approved for issue to the border guards, this was virtually an M1878 carbine with an additional barrel band (carrying the front swivel) and a rifle-type nose cap with a bayonet lug.

Model 1881

Short rifle: Repetier-Stutzer M1881.
Made by Eidgenössische Waffenfabrik, Bern, 1881–7.
10·4 × 38mm, rimfire.
Action: as M1869 rifle, above.
1,321mm overall, 4·62kg unladen.
840mm barrel, 4-groove rifling; RH, concentric.
Tube magazine under barrel, 12 rounds.
Quadrant sight graduated to 1,600 metres.
435 m/sec with M1867 ball cartridges.
M1878 sword bayonet.

☆

1881: adopted on 22 March, this gun had the modified Schmidt Quadrantenvisier, graduated 225–1,200 metres with an extending sight leaf

intended for 1600 metres; it also had an improved Schmidt set-trigger system, though the changes from the earlier (1878) pattern were not obvious externally.

Model 1881

Infantry rifle: Repetier-Gewehr M1881.
Made by Eidgenössische Waffenfabrik, Bern, 1881–7.
10·4 × 38mm, rimfire.
Action: as M1869 rifle, above.
1,326mm overall, 4·58kg unladen.
841mm barrel, 4-groove rifling; RH, concentric.
Tube magazine under barrel, 12 rounds.
Quadrant sight graduated to 1,600 metres.
435 m/sec with M1867 ball cartridges.
M1878 sword bayonet.

1881: the last Swiss Vetterli rifle, also known as 'M1878–81', was adopted on 1 November. It had an improved Schmidt Quadrantenvisier with an extending leaf (see M1881 Stutzer, above) but was otherwise difficult to distinguish from the 1878 infantry pattern.

Police carbines

Some seven shot 'carbines'—they were actually 1,145mm long compared with only 930mm for the Repetier-Karabiner M1871—were made for cantonal police in the early 1870s. They had single barrel bands and accepted the standard 1863-pattern socket bayonet.

SPORTING GUNS

The Vetterli was never very popular among the sporting fraternity, though many thousands of obsolescent single-shot Italian military rifles were converted either to rudimentary sporters or shotguns in the 1890–1914 era. Most of the former simply had the fore-end remodelled.

Some Swiss magazine rifles were converted for target shooting, though commercial versions are now scarce: the guns were clumsy and comparatively low powered. However, a few good quality sporting guns were made. Some

were made from new parts in the 1870s, but most prove to have been later adaptions of obsolescent military actions. The fore-end and magazine tube were shortened to half-length and set triggers were popular. Engraving sometimes graced the receiver, with carving on the stock.

A typical single-shot target rifle had an 850mm octagonal barrel with a quadrant sight. A double set trigger was fitted, the trigger guard was spurred, and the half-stock had a schnabel tip. The butt had a squared German-style cheek piece and a hooked shoulder plate.

VOERE

GERMANY

Voetter & Co. began to make rifles embodying Mauser actions in the 1950s. Business passed in 1978 to Tiroler Jagd- und Sportwaffenfabrik GmbH & Co. of Kufstein, and continued under a 'Voere–Austria' banner. In 1987, Voere–Austria sold rights to Mauser-Werke Oberndorf GmbH; the Titans are now being sold under the Mauser name. Guns that had no part in the new plans finally passed to Kufsteiner Gerätebau- und Handelsgesellschaft mbH ('KGH').

Titan

2130 E, 2130 F and 2130 St patterns.
Made by Voetter & Co., Schwarzwald (c.1967–76).
·243 Winchester, 6·5 × 57mm, ·270 Winchester,
7 × 57mm, 7 × 64mm, ·30–06, ·308 Winchester,
8 × 57mm or 9·3 × 62mm. See also notes.
Turning-bolt action, locked by rotating three lugs on the bolt head into the receiver wall and the bolt handle turning down into its seat.
DATA FOR A TYPICAL MODEL 2130 E
·30–06, rimless.
1,120mm overall, 3·2kg unladen.
600mm barrel, 4-groove rifling; RH, concentric.
Detachable box magazine, 5 rounds.
Folding leaf sight.
2,800 ft/sec with 165-grain bullet.
☆

1967: easily recognisable by its lofty angular receiver, this gun had a bolt head with three symmetrically-placed lugs. The bolt throw was about 60° and a safety catch protruded from the back of the angular bolt shroud. Lock time was claimed to be the fastest of all production rifles.

Most of the rifles had Monte Carlo half stocks, with skip-line chequering on the fore-end and pistol grip. A ventilated rubber shoulder pad was fitted. The pistol-grip caps and reverse-cut fore-end tips were rosewood, accompanied by thin white spacer plates. Most stocks had an oiled finish, though lacquered versions could be supplied on request.

A double set trigger (Doppelzüngelstecher, 'St') was regarded as standard, though a special single set system ('E', Einzelzüngelstecher) or a direct-acting shotgun-pattern ('F', Flintenabzug) could be substituted.

1973: options had been enlarged to include ·25–06, 7mm Remington Magnum, ·300 Winchester Magnum, ·308 Norma Magnum and ·375 H&H Magnum. Standard rifles had 600mm barrels; Magnum patterns measured 660mm. Magazine capacity was 3–5 rounds, depending on chambering.

1976*: the Model 2130 was replaced by the improved Titan II.

Titan II

225, 225 Luxus, 225 Match and 2145 Match patterns.
Made by Voetter & Co., Schwarzwald (c.1976–8);
Tiroler Jagd- und Sportwaffenfabrik GmbH & Co.,
Kufstein (1978–87); and Mauser-Werke Oberndorf
GmbH (1987 to date).
5·6 × 57mm, ·243 Winchester, ·25–06 Remington,
6·5 × 55mm, 6·5 × 57mm, 6·5 × 68mm,
·270 Winchester, 7 × 57mm, 7 × 64mm, 7mm
Remington Magnum, 7mm vom Hofe, 7·5 × 55mm,
·300 H&H Magnum, ·300 Winchester Magnum, ·30–06,
·308 Norma Magnum, ·308 Winchester, 8 × 57mm,
8 × 68mm S, 9·3 × 62mm, 9·3 × 64mm,
·375 H&H Magnum or, at extra cost, ·458 Winchester.
Action: as Model 2130, above.
DATA FOR A TYPICAL MODEL 225 LUXUSMODELL
7mm vom Hofe Super Express, rimless.

1,120mm overall, 3·2kg unladen.
600mm barrel, 4-groove rifling; RH, concentric.
Detachable box magazine, 5 rounds.
Folding leaf sight.
1,000 m/sec with 11-gram bullet.
☆

1976: changes were made, creating the Titan II, later known as the Model 225. The receiver was streamlined, a new safety (part of the trigger system) appeared above the right side of the stock behind the bolt handle, and the contours were refined.

Titan II and Titan II Luxus patterns could be fitted with the conventional single trigger, a double set trigger, or a single 'Rückstecher' set by pressing the solitary trigger lever forward. Both rifles had hog's back combs, and round tipped cheek pieces; the Luxusmodell featured selected woodwork, and a separate rosewood fore-end tip in addition to the otherwise standard rosewood pistol-grip cap. The fore-end tip, pistol grip cap and ventilated rubber butt pad were all accompanied by white spacers.

1977*: the Model 2145 Match was a moving-target rifle ('LS', Laufende Scheibe) built on the standard action. It had a heavier barrel than normal, a special stock with an upright pistol grip, and six ventilation slots through the fore-end. The pistol-grip and fore-end were stippled, open sights were omitted, and the shotgun type trigger was standard. The gun was about 1,180mm long and weighed 4·2kg; the standard chambering was ·308 Winchester, but other versions were made to order.

After the Titan II became known as the Model 225, the 2145 Match was apparently renamed '225 Match' without any change in the basic pattern.

1982*: as the Titan II had proved to be robust, three Weatherby Magnum chamberings (·257, ·270 and ·300) were added to satisfy the North American market.

1987: responsibility for the Model 225 Titan II passed to Mauser-Werke. Some have been sold in North America as the 'Mauser Model 99'. Chamberings were initially restricted to the ·257 Weatherby Magnum, ·270 Weatherby

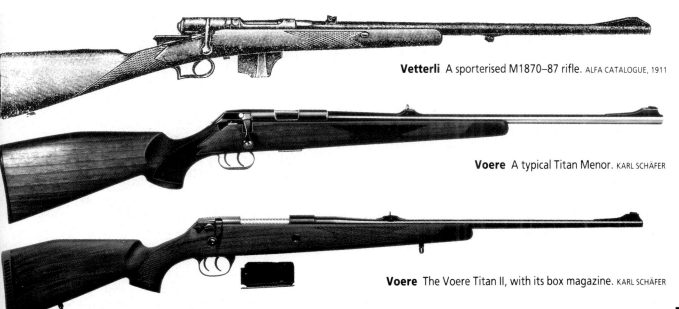

Vetterli A sporterised M1870–87 rifle. ALFA CATALOGUE, 1911

Voere A typical Titan Menor. KARL SCHÄFER

Voere The Voere Titan II, with its box magazine. KARL SCHÄFER

Magnum, 7mm Remington Magnum, ·300 H&H Magnum, ·300 Weatherby Magnum, ·300 Winchester Magnum, ·30–06 Springfield, ·308 Norma Magnum, 8 × 68mm S, ·338 Winchester Magnum, 9·3 × 64mm or ·375 H&H Magnum rounds. Others have been supplied to order.

Titan Menor

Standard, Luxus, 3145 DJV and 3145 Match patterns.
Made by Voetter & Co., Schwarzwald (c.1976–8); and Tiroler Jagd- und Sportwaffenfabrik GmbH & Co., Kufstein (1978–87).

·222 Remington, ·222 Remington Magnum, ·223 Remington or 5·6 × 50mm.
Turning-bolt action, locked by rotating two lugs on the bolt head into the receiver wall and the bolt handle turning down into its seat.
DATA FOR A TYPICAL TITAN MENOR
·222 Remington, rimless.
1,070mm overall, 2·85kg unladen.
600mm barrel, 6-groove rifling; RH, concentric.
Detachable box magazine, 3 rounds.
Folding leaf sight.
3,200 ft/sec with 50-grain bullet.

1976*: a version of the Titan II was introduced for ·22/5·6mm centre-fire cartridges. The Titan Menor had an ejection port rather than the entire upper surface of the receiver cut away. It accepted any of the standard triggers.

Stock options paralleled those of the Titan II (above), though an additional high-comb version was made for moving-target shooting.

Model 3145 Match (or 'LS') was simply a moving-target rifle built on the standard action. It had a heavy barrel and lacked open sights. Direct-action trigger systems (Flintenabzüge) were standard. The stock had a high comb, an upright pistol-grip and a fore-end with six lateral ventilating slots. Offered only in ·222 or ·223 Remington, the rifles were about 1,150mm overall and weighed 3·9kg.

The single-shot Model 3145 DJV rifle was intended for shooting under German national regulations. It could be distinguished externally from the 3145 Match pattern by the absence of a detachable magazine and by the deep fore-end. It weighed about 4·2kg.

Titan III

226 and 226 Luxus patterns.
Made by Tiroler Jagd- und Sportwaffenfabrik GmbH & Co., Kufstein (1985–7); and Mauser-Werke Oberndorf GmbH (1987 to date).

·22–250 Remington, ·243 Winchester, 6·5 × 55mm, 6·5 × 57mm, ·25–06 Remington, ·270 Winchester, 7 × 64mm, 7·5 × 55mm, ·30–06 or ·308 Winchester.
Action: generally as Titan II, above.
DATA FOR A TYPICAL MODEL 226 TITAN III
·22–250 Remington, rimless.
1,070mm overall, 2·85kg unladen.
600mm barrel, 6-groove rifling; RH, concentric.
Detachable box magazine, 5 rounds.
Fixed leaf sight.
3,725 ft/sec with 55-grain bullet.

1985: Modell 226 or Titan III rifles, available in standard and deluxe variants, utilised a small 225-type action. The rear of the receiver was noticeably more angular than the smooth diagonal of the Titan II and the bolt shroud was shorter. In addition, the trigger-guard was a light recurved-strip pattern and the recoil bolt associated with the Titan II stock was omitted.

The standard and deluxe Monte Carlo-pattern stocks duplicated the Titan II (q.v.) types.

1987: white spacers were omitted from the stocks of Mauser-marked guns, whilst a classical pattern with a straight comb and a schnabel fore-end tip became available as an option.

Model 2185

Made by Voetter & Co., Schwarzwald (c.1975–8); Tiroler Jagd- und Sportwaffenfabrik GmbH & Co., Kufstein (1978–87); and Kufsteiner Gerätebau- und Handelsgesellschaft mbH (1988–9).
5·6 × 50mm, 5·6 × 57mm, ·222 Remington, ·222 Remington Magnum, ·223 Remington, 6·5 × 57mm, ·243 Winchester, ·270 Winchester, 7 × 64mm, ·30–06, ·308 Winchester or 9·3 × 62mm.

Gas-operated auto-loading action, locked by rotating lugs on the bolt into the receiver wall.
DATA FOR A TYPICAL EXAMPLE
5·6 × 57mm, rimless.
About 1,165mm overall, 3·45kg unladen.
520mm barrel, 4-groove rifling; RH, concentric.
Detachable box magazine, 2 rounds.
Standing leaf sight.
1,040 m/sec with 4·8-gram bullet.

☆

1975*: this large auto-loader was introduced for sporting use, though sales have been relatively small. Its three-quarter pistol-grip stock had a hog's back comb and a schnabel fore-end tip. A ventilated shoulder pad and ports on the side of the muzzle beneath the front-sight block reduced the recoil sensation. The detachable box magazine was placed well forward of the trigger guard, which was a simple stamped strip.

1988: a few guns, excluded from the agreement with Mauser, were sold by KGH. It is suspected that they were actually several years old, and that only a single production run was ever made.

USA

Large numbers of Voere rifles were sold in North America by Kleinguenther's, Inc., of Seguin, Texas—originally without modification (as 'K-14 Insta-Fire' [Model 2130] and 'K-15 Insta-Fire' [Titan II]). However, the subsequent creation of KDF, Inc., allowed rifles to be stocked and completed in the USA. Special attention was paid to a patented pillar bedding system, with the result that KDF guaranteed the rifles to better ½-minute-of-angle accuracy at 100 yards.

In 1991, KDF introduced the K-15 American. Based on the Titan II, this contained sufficient US-made parts to be classed as an indigenous product. The K-15 American has been offered in ·25–06 Remington, ·257 Weatherby Magnum, ·270 Winchester, ·270 Weatherby Magnum, ·300 Weatherby Magnum, ·300 Winchester Magnum, ·30–06, ·338 Winchester Magnum, ·340 Weatherby Magnum, ·375 H&H Magnum, ·411 KDF Magnum, ·416 Remington Magnum or ·458 Winchester Magnum chamberings

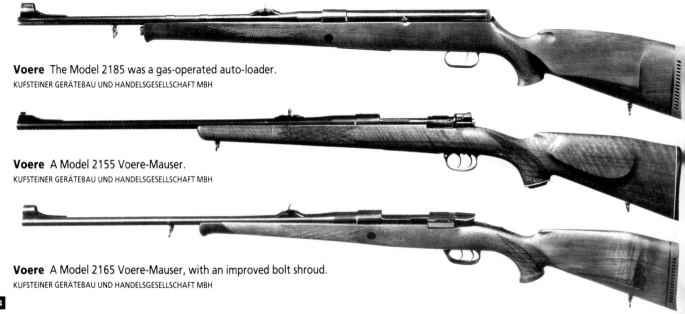

Voere The Model 2185 was a gas-operated auto-loader.
KUFSTEINER GERÄTEBAU UND HANDELSGESELLSCHAFT MBH

Voere A Model 2155 Voere-Mauser.
KUFSTEINER GERÄTEBAU UND HANDELSGESELLSCHAFT MBH

Voere A Model 2165 Voere-Mauser, with an improved bolt shroud.
KUFSTEINER GERÄTEBAU UND HANDELSGESELLSCHAFT MBH

Standard-option guns had four-round magazines; magnums held one cartridge less. Classic straight comb, Monte Carlo or thumb-hole type stocks were select walnut, walnut/maple laminate or Kevlar/carbon fibre composite patterns.

VOSTOK

UNION OF SOVIET SOCIALIST REPUBLICS
Also known as 'Izhevsk' or 'Ural'.

The firearms history of what, until recently, was the USSR remains shrouded in mystery. Though sporting guns of all types have been made in large numbers, very little is known about their background. Consequently, the centre-fire rifles have been listed under the export brand-name.

Los-4

Made by the state firearms factory, Izhevsk.
7·62 × 51mm and 9 × 54mm.
Turning-bolt action, locked by lugs on the bolt head rotating into the receiver wall and the bolt handle turning down into its seat.
7·62 × 51mm, rimless.
About 1,070mm overall, 3·30kg unladen.
600mm barrel, 4-groove rifling; RH, concentric.
Internal box magazine, 5 rounds.
Tangent-leaf sight graduated to 500 metres.
770 m/sec with 11-gram bullet.
☆

1965*: this sporting rifle, identified by its ugly stamped-and-folded trigger guard, introduced a quirky bolt action with the three lugs set back from the bolt face to lock in the receiver above the front of the magazine. The lugs were clearly visible towards the front of the ejection port when the mechanism was closed. Los rifles had a crudely shaped Monte Carlo-pattern half stock with a tapering fore-end. The plastic pistol-grip cap and ventilated rubber shoulder pad were accompanied by white spacers. Unusually for a sporter, the gun had a chromium-plated bore and a clearing rod beneath the barrel; in the

context of the harshness of a northern winter, both features were eminently practical.

SV-1

Made by the state firearms factory, Izhevsk.
7·62 × 51mm only.
Action: as Los rifle, above.
1,165mm overall (with butt plate retracted),
4·75kg without sights.
700mm barrel, 4-groove rifling; RH, concentric.
Micro-adjustable diopter sight.
785 m/sec with 11-gram bullet.
☆

1978*: the first of the modern Soviet 300-metre target rifles was based on the action of the Los hunting rifle (q.v.). Though the birch stock was crudely finished, the single-shot SV-1 performed very well. The butt plate could be adjusted for length and height; the anatomical pistol grip and fore-end were stippled; and the underside of the receiver was roughly chequered to improve bedding. The trigger was fully adjustable.

TsVR-1

Made by the state firearms factory, Izhevsk.
7·62 × 51mm only.
Action: as Los rifle, above.
1,335mm overall (with butt plate retracted),
8·00kg with hand rest.
760mm barrel, 4-groove rifling; RH, concentric.
Micro-adjustable diopter sight.
795 m/sec with 11-gram bullet.
☆

1978*: intended for use in 300-metre Free Rifle competitions, this had the standard three-lug bolt action in a massive thumb-hole half stock. An adjustable hooked butt plate and an elevating comb were fitted, together with a refined trigger giving a pull of 100–1,500gm.

Accessories included mirage bands, a hand rest, and a set of rod-mounted balance weights protruding from a block mounted in the rail under the fore-end. The TsVR-1 lacked the sophistication of Western rivals, but performed effectually enough on the range.

WALTHER

GERMANY

Little is known about the chronology of these rifles, though experiments undertaken by Fritz and Erich Walther dated back to the 1930s.

The unsuccessful flap-lock Gew.41 (W) was superseded by the perfected Gew.43, which shared the locking mechanism but had a greatly improved gas system. When the Gew.43 fired, gas was tapped from the bore into a hollow piston chamber and the actuating rod was forced back against the breech cover. The cover pulled the firing pin away from the breech as it retreated, camming the locking arms into the breech block, and then reciprocated to eject, cock the hammer, strip a fresh round into the chamber and re-lock the breech.

The perfected Walther rifle proved to be very efficient, though the workmanship and quality of material left much to be desired.

MILITARY WEAPONS
Model 41

Infantry rifle: Gewehr 41 (W).
Made by Carl Walther Waffenfabrik, Zella-Mehlis, Thüringen (code 'ac'); and Berlin-Lübecker Maschinenfabrik ('duv').
Quantity: 8,000.
7·9 × 57mm, rimless.
Gas-operated auto-loading action, locked by flaps in the bolt engaging the receiver.
1,128mm overall, 4·97kg unladen.
545mm barrel, 4-groove rifling; RH, concentric.
Charger-loaded integral box magazine, 10 rounds.
Tangent-leaf sight graduated to 2,000 metres.
745 m/sec with sS ball cartridges.
S.84/98 sword bayonet.
☆

1941: cocked by retracting the breech cover, this rifle shared the Bang-type muzzle cup system with the competing Mauser pattern (q.v.)—presumably in accordance with army

Walther The unsuccessful Gew.41 (W).

Vostok

The TsVR-1.

Walther An MKb.42 (W), lacking its detachable box magazine. COLLECTOR'S COMPENDIUM instructions. However, the Gew.41 (W) had its operating rod above the barrel instead of below, and the breech-locking system differed greatly from that of the Gew.41 (M).

1942: the Walther rifle, preferred to its Mauser rival, was officially adopted in December. The mechanical hold-open of the trials rifles was eliminated and the safety system was improved.

1943: the Gew.41 was abandoned in favour of the Gew.43 after experience in Russia showed that the muzzle cup soon corroded excessively. Though about 70,000 1941-pattern Walthers had been ordered, it is suspected that only a few were ever completed.

Model 42 (W)

Assault rifle: Maschinenkarabiner 42 (W).
Made by Carl Walther Waffenfabrik, Zella-Mehlis, Thüringen (code 'ac').
Quantity: 2,800?
7·9 × 33mm, rimless.
Gas-operated auto-loading action, locked by rotating lugs on the bolt into the receiver.
DATA FOR A 'PRODUCTION' GUN
933mm overall, 4·42kg with empty magazine.
405mm barrel, 4-groove rifling; RH, concentric.
Detachable box magazine, 30 rounds.
Tangent-leaf sight graduated to 800 metres.
645 m/sec with ball cartridges; 575 ± 50 rpm.
S.84/98 sword bayonet.

☆

1941: Walther produced a weapon to compete with the Haenel prototype (q.v.). The gun was successfully demonstrated to the authorities at the end of the year.

1942: a contract for 200 pre-production guns was approved in January, but only two guns had been made by July. Trials at the Schiessplatz Kummersdorf revealed that the Haenel and Walther carbines worked well enough to be issued for field trials. Both were ordered into production: Walther was to make five hundred guns in October, and attain 15,000 per month by March 1943. Changes to the specification then disrupted progress.

1943: in February, the combined efforts of

Walther and Haenel exceeded the thousand-gun production target by 217.

Made largely from pressings and stampings, the Mkb.42 (W) was superficially similar to the Mkb.42 (H), but fired from a closed breech at all times, had a more obvious 'straight-line' layout, and carried the back sight on a tall block. A cylindrical fore-end casing contained an annular gas piston/barrel construction.

Service trials showed that the Haenel gas system was easier to maintain and more reliable in adverse conditions—some testing had been undertaken in what had once been Soviet territory. The Walther was promptly abandoned.

Model 43

Short rifles: Gewehr und Karabiner 43.
Made by Carl Walther Waffenfabrik, Zella-Mehlis, Thüringen (codes 'ac', 'qve'); Berlin-Lübecker Maschinenfabrik ('duv'); and Gustloff-Werke, Weimar ('bcd').
Quantity: about 500,000.
7·9 × 57mm, rimless.
Action: as Gew.41 (W), above.
1,117mm overall, 4·18kg without magazine.
558mm barrel, 4-groove rifling; RH, concentric.
Detachable box magazine, 10 rounds.
Tangent-leaf sight graduated to 2,000 metres?
745 m/sec with sS ball cartridges.
No bayonet.

☆

1943: adopted on 30 April to replace the ineffectual Gew.41, retaining its breech-lock, this had a conventional port-and-piston gas system adapted from the Soviet Tokarev rifle. A detachable box magazine protruded beneath the stock ahead of the trigger-guard bow. The Gew.43 was an excellent design, but had been ordered into full-scale production too hastily—at a time when the German arms industry was in decline—and was prone to parts-breakage.

It had a laminated pistol-grip half stock with a full-length hand guard in wood or plastic. The gas-tube, piston and actuating rod lay above the barrel. A sling-slot was cut through the butt, a fixed bar appearing on the left side of the fore-

end band, and a rail for the Zf.4 telescope sight usually lay on the left side of the receiver.

1944: 324,300 guns were delivered during the year. Unfortunately, sub-contracting reduced the value of what was potentially among the best semi-automatic rifles of the Second World War.

The Kar.43 was simply a Gew.43 without the hold-open, cleaning rod and optical sight bracket. The breech cover was simplified, but few other changes were visible externally.

SPORTING GUNS
Model KKJ

KJS, KJS-II, KKJ-H, KKJ-HE, KKJ-HV, KKJ-HVE and SSV patterns.
Made by Carl Walther Sportwaffenfabrik, Ulm/Donau, 1959–87.
5·6 × 35mm R Vierling, ·22 Hornet or ·222 Remington. See notes.
Turning-bolt action, locked by two lugs on the rear of the bolt rotating into the receiver.
DATA FOR A TYPICAL KKJ-HV
5·6 × 35mm R Vierling, rimmed.
1,025mm overall, 2·65kg unladen.
560mm barrel, 4-groove rifling; RH, concentric.
Detachable box magazine, 5 rounds.
Tangent-leaf sight graduated to 200 metres.
615 m/sec with 3-gram bullet.

☆

1959: the first small-calibre centre-fire sporting rifles (Kleinkaliber-Jagdbüchsen) were based on rimfire pattern introduced in 1955. The bolt had two lugs, one of which was combined with the bolt handle base; a lateral safety catch, which could be applied only when the gun was cocked, ran through the stock above the rear web of the trigger guard. Conventional two-stage or double set triggers were used.

Stocks were generally pistol-grip half-length patterns, with a straight comb and a small oval cheek piece, but a few two-piece Mannlicher (full length) versions were made. Steel butt plates or rubber shoulder pads were optional. A 600mm barrel could be substituted for the standard 560mm pattern on request.

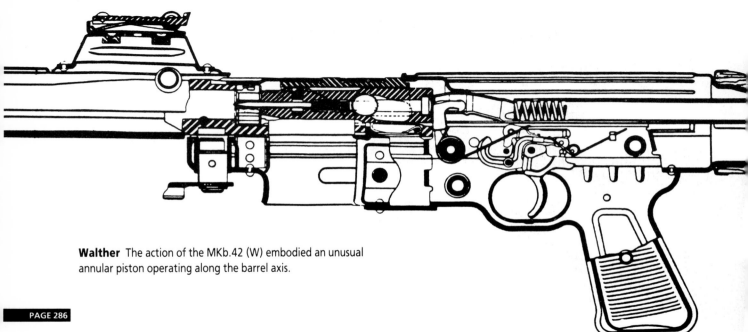

Walther The action of the MKb.42 (W) embodied an unusual annular piston operating along the barrel axis.

The ·22 Hornet rifles were designated KKJ-H and KKJ-HE, for magazine-fed and single-shot versions; those chambering the 5·6mm Vierling cartridge were KKJ-HV and KKJ-HVE. Vierling patterns soon lost their popularity, the last being sold in 1964, and the single-shot guns were never as popular as the repeating types.

1962: an adjustable cheek piece was introduced to satisfy users of optical sights, but failed to generate much enthusiasm.

1968*: rationalisation of the Walther small-bore rifles led to the KKJ being fitted with the action of the target rifles, which had a safety sleeve attached to the bolt and required part of the left side of the stock to be cut down behind the receiver. Until 1972, the guns also retained the original safety bolt through the stock. A shallow hog's back comb replaced the straight pattern.

1970: the first single-shot KJS rifles (Jagdliche Sportschiessen, 'Game Shooting') were made, chambered for ·22 Hornet or ·222 Remington cartridges in addition to ·22 rimfire. The double set trigger was customary, though a special match pattern could be supplied to order. The half-stock had a high comb and a squared cheek piece. Stippling covered the upright pistol grip and much of the deep round-tip fore-end. Open sights were omitted. Widely known in English-speaking markets as the SSV ('Single-shot, Varmint'), the guns weighed 3·5kg.

The ·222 Remington chambering proved to generate two much pressure for the rear-locking Walther action, and had been discontinued by 1973; very few guns had been made.

1981: the KKJ series was discontinued.

1982: Walther's KJS-II appeared, differing from the KJS largely in the form of the stock—which was more rounded—and the stippling on the fore-end, stopping short of the tip. A rubber shoulder pad was customary. The 600mm barrel had a small muzzle weight.

Model JR

JR, JR Jagd and JRM patterns.
Made by Carl Walther Sportwaffenfabrik,
Ulm/Donau, 1974–8.

7 × 64mm, 7·5 × 55mm, ·308 Winchester, 8 × 68mm S
or 9·3 × 64mm. See notes.
Turning-bolt action, locked by three lugs on the bolt
head rotating into the receiver.
DATA FOR A TYPICAL JRM
8 × 68mm S, rimless.
1,125mm overall, 3·77kg unladen.
650mm barrel, 4-groove rifling; RH, concentric.
Internal box magazine, 3 rounds.
Standing leaf sight.
930 m/sec with 12·7-gram bullets.

☆

1974: Walther's Jagd-Repetier-Gewehr replaced adaptions of the 1898-type Mauser. It had a three-lug bolt with a 60° throw and a conical plastic grasping knob. Unusual features included a pivoting firing-pin safety mechanism, a bolt lock, and a special 'silent' lateral magazine-release button—through the stock beneath the bolt way—that could be activated only when the safety catch was applied.

Standard rifles, available only in 7 × 64mm and ·308 Winchester, had 620mm barrels; magnum patterns (8 × 68mm S or 9·3 × 64mm) measured 650mm.

The Monte Carlo-type half stock had a plain round tipped fore-end, though a semi-beavertail fore-end could be supplied if required. Machine-cut chequering lay on the grip and fore-end sides, whilst the ventilated rubber shoulder pads were accompanied by plain dark spacers. Swivels lay under the butt and fore-end.

JR Jagd(-schiessen) rifles, specially designed for moving-target shooting, were chambered only for the 7·5 × 55mm Swiss ordnance or ·308 Winchester rounds. They were instantly recognisable: the stock had an upright pistol grip, the butt plate was adjustable, and the separate comb could be elevated by a knurled finger wheel.

A large spherical bolt-handle knob replaced the conical type and the quirky magazine-release system was discarded. The grip and fore-end were extensively stippled.

1978: owing to a marked lack of success in a market crammed with effectual rivals, the Walther JR was discontinued.

UNITED STATES OF AMERICA

Roy Weatherby was the first man to promote a matched range of powerful belted-case magnum cartridges in North America. Beginning in the early 1940s, Weatherby produced several new rounds by necking and re-forming Holland & Holland Magnum cartridge cases.

When hostilities ended, Weatherby began his own operations in earnest, offering rifles based on FN Mauser actions. Schulz & Larsen actions were purchased specially for the ·378 cartridge, introduced in 1953, and some left-hand guns were built on the Mathieu system.

Dissatisfied with these commercial actions, Weatherby and his chief engineer, Fred Jennie, began work on their own rifle in 1954. Patents were sought in 1958 and production began in San Francisco. The essence of the Mark V action was a counter-bored breech, enabling the barrel to shroud the bolt-head, and nine locking lugs disposed at 120° in three rows of three. This gave a 54° bolt-throw and allowed the lugs to share the external diameter of the bolt body. The extractor was set into the bolt head.

GERMANY

Sauer-Weatherby

Europa and Junior patterns.
Made by J.P. Sauer & Sohn, Eckenförde (1965–72).
Chambering: see notes.
Action: as Weatherby Mark V rifle, below.
DATA FOR A TYPICAL EUROPA
8 × 68mm S, rimless.
1,200mm overall, 4·10kg unladen.
660mm barrel, 4-groove rifling; RH, concentric.
Internal box magazine, 3 rounds.
Folding-leaf sight.
930 m/sec with 12·7-gram bullet.

☆

1965: introduced to capitalise on the great potential of the nine-lug action being made for

Walther The Gew.43 was the perfected wartime Walther auto-loader. COLLECTOR'S COMPENDIUM

Walther JR sporting rifle, showing the distinctive design of the bolt shroud. CARL WALTHER GMBH

Weatherby A Crown Custom example of the Mark V, embodying a Japanese-made action. WEATHERBY, INC.

Weatherby, the Europa rifle was stocked in European fashion. The Monte Carlo comb was shallower and the contours were much more rounded than the standard American stock. A double set trigger was regarded as standard, though conventional single-trigger options were also available.

The 610mm-barrelled rifle was available in three Weatherby Magnum chamberings—·270, 7mm and ·300—or ·30–06. The guns were 1,150mm overall and weighed about 3·6kg. The 660mm-barrelled versions were supplied in 6·5 × 68mm, 7 × 64mm, 8 × 68mm S or, occasionally, ·460 Weatherby Magnum.

Confined to ·224 Weatherby Magnum, with a short six-lug action, the Junior rifle had a four-round magazine and a plastic shoulder plate. It was 1,150mm long and weighed 3kg.

USA

Mark V

Classicmark I, Classicmark II, Crown Custom, Euromark, Fibermark, Fibermark Alaskan, Lazermark, Safari Classic, Safari Custom, Ultramark, Varmintmaster, Weathermark and Weathermark Alaskan patterns.
Made for Weatherby by Precision Founders, Inc., San Francisco (1958–9); J.P. Sauer & Sohn, Eckenförde (1959–72); and Howa Industries, Nagoya (1971 to date).
·224, ·240, ·257, ·270, 7mm, ·300, ·340, ·378, ·416 or ·460 Weatherby Magnums, plus ·22–250 Remington, ·30–06 and others. See notes.
DATA FOR A TYPICAL MARK V
·378 Weatherby Magnum, belted rimless.
46·25in overall, 8·38lb unladen.
26·00in barrel, rifling pattern not known.
Internal box magazine, 2 rounds.
Optical sight.
2,925 ft/sec with 300-grain bullet.
☆
1958: the first rifles were assembled in Weatherby's South Gate, California, workshops from Precision Industries actions. They had a plain bolt body, a chequered bolt knob, a safety on the right side behind the bolt handle, and (prototypes only) a two-piece bolt shroud. The awesome ·460 Weatherby Magnum cartridge was specifically intended for the new gun, though most of the other options had already been offered on the basis of FN Mausers.

1959: a one-piece bolt shroud was adopted before production started in earnest. Sauer rifles introduced the fluted bolts. The perfected Mark V was distinctive, owing to the unmistakable shape of the shroud. Barrels measured 24in or 26in, the latter being standard with ·340, ·378 or ·460 cartridges and optional with the others. Several forms of barrel have been fitted over the years—there have been four 26in types—but the lengths have rarely varied. A true left-hand action was also made.

The standard gloss-finish stock had a high Monte Carlo comb, skip-line chequering on the pistol grip and fore-end, and a separate ebony fore-end tip. White spacers accompanied the pistol-grip cap, the fore-end tip, and a ventilated rubber shoulder pad.

1960: the chequered bolt knob was abandoned.

1962: the old sear safety was replaced by an improved pattern mounted on the bolt shroud.

1963: work began on a short action with only six lugs (two rows of three), developed by Sauer largely by scaling-down the standard Mark V. The ·224 Weatherby Magnum cartridge was specifically introduced to accompany the new Mark V Varmintmaster. The first full-size ·340 guns also date from this period.

1964: production of Varmintmasters began in the Eckenförde factory.

1968: the ·240 Weatherby Magnum cartridge was introduced.

1969: owing to spiralling manufacturing costs in Germany, a contract was signed with Howa in Japan; the first Nagoya-made actions appeared in 1971. Changes were made so that the trigger could be adjusted externally, and the bolt stop—a separate component on Sauer-made rifles—became a spring-loaded plunger operated by an extension of the trigger lever.

1972: production finished in Germany.

1981: the Lazermark guns were similar to the standard deluxe Mark V, but intricate laser-cut carving appeared on the pistol grip, the fore-end, and also beneath the cheek piece. The standard chamberings listed above were all offered.

1983: Fibermark rifles had a textured matt black fibreglass stock with a black recoil pad and pistol grip cap. The receiver and magazine floor-plate had a matt sandblasted blue finish and the bolt was satin-chrome. Chamberings were initially all Weatherby Magnum cartridges up to ·340.

1986: introduced in all chamberings excepting ·22–250 and ·224, the Mark V Euromark was a minor variant of the standard rifle with a satin finish stock. It had conventional chequering, an ebony pistol-grip cap with a maplewood diamond inlay, an ebony fore-end tip, and a plain black spacer ahead of a solid rubber butt plate. White spacers were omitted.

1989: offered only in ·300, ·340, ·378, ·416 or ·460 Magnums, the Safari Custom rifle was a variant of the Mark V with a 24in barrel and a Euromark-style stock. A quarter rib on the barrel carried one fixed and one folding leaf. The front swivel was carried on a barrel band.

Crown Custom rifles, made in all regular Weatherby Magnum chamberings from ·240 to ·300 (plus ·30–06), had a selected walnut stock with inlays and carving. The bolt handle was chequered and the bolt was damascened. Right-hand actions and 24in barrels were standard. The floor plate bore WEATHERBY CUSTOM.

Available in all chamberings except ·22–250, ·224 and ·460, the Ultramark gun had a Claro walnut stock, basket-weave chequering and a jewelled bolt.

1991: initially available only in ·270, 7mm, ·300 or ·340 Weatherby Magnum chamberings, the Fibermark Alaskan rifle was nothing more than a Fibermark (described above) with nickel-plated metalwork.

1992: introduced in all regular chamberings excepting ·22–250 and ·224, the Classicmark I had a straight-comb butt, a rounded fore-end tip, and a 'presentation recoil pad'.

The Classicmark II had very fine wraparound chequering, a steel pistol-grip cap, and an 'Old English' shoulder pad. Metalwork had a matt

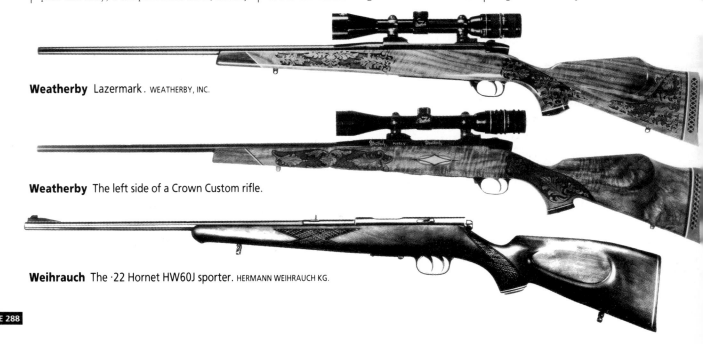

Weatherby Lazermark. WEATHERBY, INC.

Weatherby The left side of a Crown Custom rifle.

Weihrauch The ·22 Hornet HW60J sporter. HERMANN WEIHRAUCH KG.

finish. Safari Classic(-mark II) rifles were made for the ·375 H&H Magnum cartridge.

The Weathermark and Weathermark Alaskan patterns were similar to the Classicmark, but had composite stocks with raised chequering. They were offered in all regular chamberings from ·240 to ·300 Weatherby Magnum (24in or 26in barrels), plus ·270 Winchester (22in), 7mm Remington Magnum (24in), ·30–06 (22in) and ·340 Weatherby Magnum (26in).

WEIHRAUCH

GERMANY

The Weihrauch gunsmithing business was founded in Zella St Blasii in 1899, making large quantities of sporting guns—including Martini rifles—until 1939. Re-established in Bavaria after the Second World War, the company is now best known for Arminius-brand revolvers and high-quality sporting airguns.

HW 52

HW 52J and HW 55MM patterns.
Made by Hermann Weihrauch KG, Mellrichstadt, c.1952–88.
·22 Hornet, ·222 Remington or 5·6 × 50mm R.
Dropping-block action operated by a lever combined with the trigger guard.
DATA FOR A TYPICAL HW 52J
5·6 × 50mm, rimmed.
1,050mm overall, 3·30kg unladen.
650mm barrel, 4-groove rifling; RH, concentric.
Standing leaf sight.
1,000 m/sec with 3·6-gram bullet.
☆
1952: also made as a ·22 rimfire, this single-shot rifle was based on a pre-war FL (Langenhan) pattern. It had a lateral safety bolt and a finely adjustable trigger. Set triggers were available to order.

The earliest butt seems to have been a simple design with a shallow hog's back or straight comb and a small oval cheek piece. However,

a Monte Carlo type was standardised in the early 1970s. Deluxe patterns have been offered with skip-line chequering on the pistol grip; a ventilated rubber butt plate; and a rosewood fore-end tip. Thin white spacers separated the tip from the fore-end, the nylon pistol-grip cap from the butt, and the butt plate from the stock-wood. The action of Luxusmodelle often displayed scroll engraving.

The HW 52MM was a special match rifle, with a 700mm heavy barrel. The action was enclosed in a one-piece stock, with a squared Bavarian-style cheek piece and a hog's back comb. The butt plate was a rubber crescent design. A micro-adjustable diopter sight could be mounted on a block attached to the upper tang behind the breech; the front sight was a normal replaceable-element tunnel. Most MM rifles chambered rimfire ammunition, but a few were made for the ·22 Hornet cartridge.

HW 60

HW 60J and HW 66 patterns.
Made by Hermann Weihrauch KG, Mellrichstadt.
·22 Hornet or ·222 Remington. See notes.
Turning-bolt action, locked by two lugs rotating into the receiver above the trigger guard.
DATA FOR A TYPICAL HW 60J
·22 Hornet, rimmed.
1,060mm overall, 2·95kg unladen.
580mm barrel, 4-groove rifling; RH, concentric.
Detachable box magazine, 4 rounds.
Fixed leaf sight.
2,690 ft/sec with 45-grain bullet.
☆
1960: these rifles embodied a good-quality bolt action with a locking lug supplementing the bolt-handle base. A sliding safety appeared on the left side of the receiver. The half-stock of the HW 60J—the standard sporting version (Jagdbüchse)—had a hog's back comb and an oval cheek piece. Chequering appeared on the pistol grip and schnabel-tipped fore-end; a ventilated rubber butt pad was fitted, whilst swivels lay under the butt and fore-end. The receiver was grooved for optical sight mounts.

1982*: changes were made to the shape of the magazine base, projecting grooves facilitating removal, and a double set trigger option was added.
1985*: the HW 66 (in ·22 Hornet or ·222 Remington) was built on a single-shot version of the HW 60 action and could be fitted with conventional double-stage, single set or double set triggers. The heavy 560mm stainless steel barrel reduced overall length to about 1,045mm, though weight increased to 3·85kg without sights. Its competition-style stock had a squared cheek piece, a straight comb, and a broadened fore-end. Stippling covered the pistol grip and most of the underside of the fore-end.

WERDER

BAVARIA

The work of Johann-Ludwig Werder, director of the Cramer-Klett'schen Établissements in Nuremburg, this block-action mechanism was patented in Bavaria in June 1868.

As the Lindner conversion was a temporary solution, trials to find a new breech-loader began in Bavaria in the summer of 1868. The series resolved into a four-cornered contest between the Austrian Werndl, a Colt-made Berdan, a Mauser-Norris and the Bavarian Werder.

The indigenous Werder showed promise, though bad ammunition misfired continually. Once a new cartridge had been perfected in the Amberg manufactory, Werder and Werndl rifles were acquired for field trials. The Werndl was rejected after continual breech-jamming, and a straight fight developed between the Werder and the Colt-Berdan. Additional experiments failed to separate the contestants, so an example of each was shown to the king, Ludwig II; predictably, the Werder was adopted.

To load the Werder, the front trigger was pressed forward to release the block-prop, dropping the breech block automatically and kicking the spent case out of the breech. After a new cartridge had been inserted, pulling back on

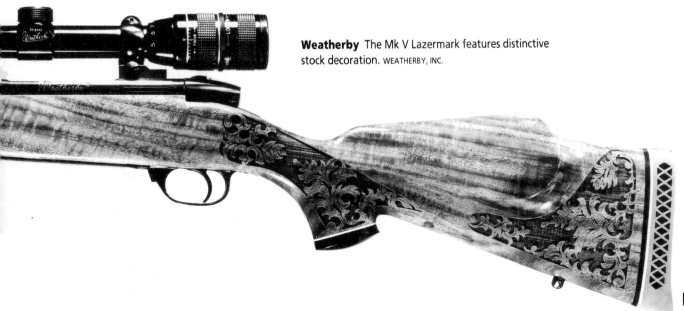

Weatherby The Mk V Lazermark features distinctive stock decoration. WEATHERBY, INC.

the spur of the operating lever (protruding upward from the rear right side of the action) raised and locked the block. The action could be worked extremely rapidly, earning the M/69 the sobriquet 'Blitzgewehr' ('Lightning Rifle') during the Franco-Prussian War—though only about half the Jäger-Bataillone and parts of three infantry regiments had been re-equipped by the end of hostilities.

Model 1869

Infantry rifles: Rückladungsgewehre M/1869 und aptierte M/1869, System Werder.
Made by the rifle factory in Amberg (125,000?), relying heavily on sub-contractors; and Handfeuerwaffen-Productionsgenossenschaft, Suhl (20,000).
Quantity: in the region of 150,000.
11 × 50mm, rimmed.
Pivoting-block action, operated by a lever protruding from the top of the breech.
1,300mm overall, 4·39kg unladen.
890mm barrel, 4-groove rifling; RH, concentric.
Ramp-and-leaf sight graduated to 1,000 schritt?
446 m/sec with M1869 ball cartridges.
M1869 sabre bayonet.

☆

1868: about a thousand Liége-made rifles were delivered for trials against Steyr-made Werndls. The experimental 1868-type rifle differed from the perfected M/1869 largely in the manner of stocking—it had one band instead of two—and accepted the French Mle.66 sabre bayonet. Most surviving trials guns were converted into M/69 carbines in 1870.
1869: the M/69 rifle was approved on 18 April. It was difficult to mistake for any other design, owing to the twin levers in the trigger guard and the position of the breech-lever spur.
1872: the ultimate fate of the Werder was sealed when the Bavarians were pressurised into accepting the Prussian Mauser infantry rifle on 23 March, though little was done until 1877.
1874: trials were undertaken with M/69 rifles chambering the 11mm Mauser cartridge, 200 converted rifles being issued in December.

1875: the authorities recommended adopting the Reichspatrone conversion despite evidence of continual breakages. The plans received royal assent on 5 June; by 1 November 1876, Amberg had produced 124,540 'aptierte M/69' rifles by rechambering the old barrels and fitting new 1871-pattern back sights.

Model 1869

Carbine.
Made by Maschinenfabrik 'Landes', Munich (4,000); and Auguste Francotte & Cie, Liége (4,000).
Quantity, including conversions: 8,600.
11mm, rimmed.
Action: as M/1869 infantry rifle, above.
About 960mm overall, 3·50kg unladen.
550mm barrel, 4-groove rifling; RH, concentric.
Ramp-and-leaf sight graduated to 500 schritt?
About 350 m/sec with M/1869 ball cartridges.
No bayonet.

☆

1869: adopted on 1 July, this was made only in small quantities. The first six hundred were converted from surviving 1868-type trials rifles, but new guns were subsequently made in Munich and Liége. Francotte also apparently made a Werder gendarmerie rifle, a variant of the standard carbine accepting a socket bayonet.

Model 1869 n.M.

Infantry rifle, new model: Rückladungsgewehr M/1869, neues Muster.

☆

1875: continual problems during trials showed that converted M1869 rifles were unlikely to be durable, and so the M/1869 n.M.—chambered for the standard 11 × 60mm 'Reichspatrone'—was substituted on 21 July. The extractor and receiver had been strengthened, the chamber, barrel, sights and nose cap being 1871-pattern Mauser designs to ensure partial conformity with the new imperial standards.

About 25,000 new actions were made by Maschinenfabrik Augsburg and assembled in Amberg with barrels and stocks made locally or

purchased from Österreichische Waffenfabriks-Gesellschaft of Steyr.
1877: the Bavarian army finally approved the Mauser in August, surviving Werder rifles being relegated to foot artillerymen. Re-issue had been completed by July 1882.

WERNDL

AUSTRIA-HUNGARY

These drum-action breech-loaders, developed in Austria-Hungary, were also used in Persia and Montenegro (23,000 and 20,000 respectively).

Experiments to find a new rifle, undertaken concurrently with the conversion trials (see 'Wänzl' in Part Two), created great interest. The Breech-loading Commission demanded that muzzle velocity should exceed 340 m/sec—eliminating the Spencer and the Winchester M1866—but more than a hundred designs were considered before the commission selected the Würzinger and Remington as the most desirable.

A Remington rolling block was recommended for adoption on 29 November 1866 and guns were readied for trials. However, rumours that this breech was unsafe allowed a rifle designed by Josef Werndl and Karl Holub to enter.

MILITARY WEAPONS

Model 1867

Infantry rifles: Infanterie- und Jägergewehre M1867 und M1867/77.
Made by Österreichische Waffenfabriks-Gesellschaft, Steyr, 1867–74.
Quantity: in excess of 611,000.
11 × 42mm, rimmed.
Rotary-block breech, with an external hammer.
1,278mm overall, 4·43kg unladen.
855mm barrel, 6-groove rifling; RH, concentric.
Ramp-and-leaf sight graduated to 1,400 paces.
436 m/sec with M1867 rifle cartridges.
M1867 sabre bayonet.

☆

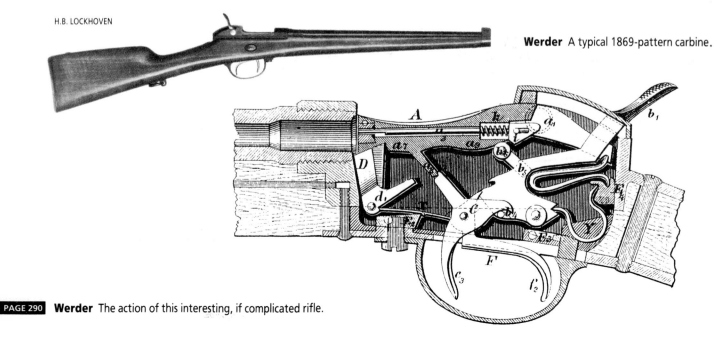

H.B. LOCKHOVEN

Werder A typical 1869-pattern carbine.

Werder The action of this interesting, if complicated rifle.

1867: the Werndl-Holub breech system was officially adopted on 28 July, the decision being widely acclaimed in Austria. The subsequent manufacture of guns in the new Steyr factory greatly contributed to its prosperity.

The principal feature of the M1867 was the drum-breech, which, while sturdy and secure, compromised extraction. The rifle had a one piece stock with a straight wrist, a back-action lock and an external hammer. There were two screwed barrel bands and a nose cap; swivels lay under the middle band and butt. A cleaning rod was carried beneath the muzzle.

The back-sight leaf was graduated to 1,200 paces with a 'V'-notch in the top edge for 1,400. A bayonet lug appeared on the right side of the muzzle. Standard infantry-pattern trigger guards were plain ovals, but a finger spur was substituted for Jäger units.

1878: with effect from 25 December, most surviving rifles were adapted to chamber a new 11 × 58mm long-body cartridge. They were known as 'M1867/77'.

Model 1867

Carbines: Karabiner M1867 und M1867/77.
Made by Österreichische Waffenfabriks-Gesellschaft,
Steyr, 1867–74.
11 × 42mm, rimmed.
Action: as M1867 infantry rifle, above.
991mm overall, 3·18kg unladen.
570mm barrel, 6-groove rifling; RH, concentric.
Ramp-and-leaf sight graduated to 600 paces.
298 m/sec with M1867 carbine cartridges.
M1867 sabre bayonet.

☆

1867: adopted at the same time as the infantry rifle, this had a nose cap but lacked barrel bands. A knob appeared on the hammer instead of a spur. Werndl carbines chambered a short-case necked 11mm cartridge developing appreciably less power than the rifle pattern.

1878: adoption of a more powerful cartridge, in December, led to a change in the chambering. The modified carbines were usually known as 'M1867/77'.

Model 1873

Infantry rifles: Infanterie- und Jägergewehre
M1873 und M1873/77.
Made by Österreichische Waffenfabriks-Gesellschaft,
Steyr, 1873–8.
11 × 42mm, rimmed.
Action: as M1867 infantry rifle, above.
1,265mm overall, 4·20kg unladen.
840mm barrel, 6-groove rifling; RH, concentric.
Ramp-and-leaf sight graduated to 1,400 paces.
About 445 m/sec with M1867/73 ball cartridges.
M1873 sabre bayonet.

☆

1872: the drum breech proved to be very susceptible to fouling, becoming increasingly difficult to rotate until it jammed altogether; constructional weaknesses were discovered in the receiver; and back-sight leaves regularly snapped. The action was extensively revised by Antonin Spitalsky, who had succeeded Josef Werndl as head of the technical section of the Steyr factory. The sight-base and the sight leaf were strengthened; the receiver sides were flattened; the lock-plate was redesigned with a central hammer; the bayonet attachment was improved by using an internal coil-spring and stud; and the standard cartridge was revised.

1873: the new rifle was formally approved on 10 February. It was similar to its predecessor, the central hammer and modified receiver casing being its most obvious features.

1874: troubles encountered with the original Wildburger-pattern rifle cartridge, in addition to jams and extraction failures, were solved only when a strengthened Roth-type case appeared.

1878: the 'M1873/77' was approved to allow 1873-type rifles to chamber a modified long-case cartridge approved in December. Outwardly all but identical with the unaltered guns, a revised example could be distinguished by its back sight.

Model 1873

Carbines and gendarmerie rifle:
Karabiner M1873, Karabiner M1873/77 und
Extra-Corps-Gewehr M1873.

Made by Österreichische Waffenfabriks-Gesellschaft,
Steyr, 1874–8.
11 × 42mm, rimmed.
Action: as M1867 infantry rifle, above.
DATA FOR CARBINE
1,004mm overall, 3·25kg unladen.
580mm barrel, 6-groove rifling; RH, concentric.
Ramp-and-leaf sight graduated to 600 paces.
Performance: as M1867 carbine, above.
M1873 sabre bayonet.

☆

1874: accepted on 6 November, the revised or 1873-pattern carbine had a low-profile hammer and a nose cap, but lacked barrel bands. One swivel was anchored through the fore-end and the other lay on the trigger-guard. Adopted contemporaneously, the gendarmerie rifle had a single barrel band and accepted the 1854-type socket bayonet. It weighed about 3·72kg.

1878: modifications were made to surviving 1873-type carbines to chamber the improved cartridge adopted in December.

Model 1877

Infantry rifle: Infanterie- und Jägergewehr M1877.
Made by Österreichische Waffenfabriks-Gesellschaft,
Steyr, 1878–85.
11 × 58mm, rimmed.
Otherwise generally as M1873, excepting back sight (graduated to 2,100 schritt) and a muzzle velocity of
455 m/sec with M1877 rifle cartridges.

☆

1877: trials of improved cartridges in 1875–7 led to a better rifle, adopted in December. The principal differences between the M1873 and M1877 rifles—and the assorted conversions— lay in the sights; rifles chambering the new long-case M1877 cartridge would not fire the short-case 1867 pattern, though unconverted guns were deliberately left in the Landwehr and Honved to expend existing supplies.

1878: the improved cartridge was issued from 25 December. It seems that no 1877-type rifles had been issued by this time, and thus that there was no need to re-graduate sights.

1881: adoption of a refined propellant raised

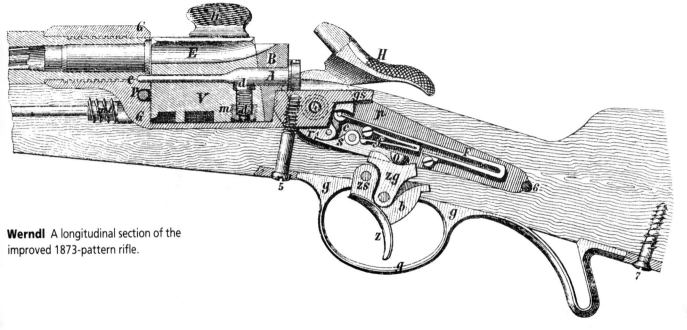

Werndl A longitudinal section of the improved 1873-pattern rifle.

velocity slightly (apparently to about 465 m/sec) and allowed the back sight graduations to be increased to 2,200 paces.

1888*: after the introduction of Mannlichers (q.v.), Werndls were passed down through second-line and lines-of-communication troops to the Landwehr and then into store. Survivors were reissued during the First World War.

Model 1877

Carbine: Karabiner M1877.
Made by Österreichische Waffenfabriks-Gesellschaft,
Steyr, 1878–85.
11 × 42mm, rimmed.
Otherwise generally as M1873 carbine, excepting
the back sight (graduated to 1,600 schritt) and a
muzzle velocity of 307 m/sec with M1877
carbine cartridges.

☆

1878: this was approved to replace the 1867 and 1873-pattern guns. The new cartridge was interchangeable with its predecessors, but much more powerful. Consequently, the 1877-pattern Kropatschek-designed sight was graduated to 1,600 paces compared with only 600 for the original carbine round.

Other guns

Werndl carbines were to be found with bronze barrels (so-called 'Alpine Models' but possibly naval) or cut to pistol proportions, generally chambering 11mm 'Zimmergewehr-Ladekonus' of 1871 and 1877 and intended for short range shooting practice. Some Zimmer-Karabiner may have been used by paramilitary units, but most were intended for civilian use.

SPORTING GUNS

Though the Werndl was never very popular commercially, a few sporters were made in the early 1870s. They were often distinguished by excellent quality and copious engraving on the action. Others—generally very plain—were adapted from military weapons in 1890–1910.

WHITNEY

UNITED STATES OF AMERICA
'Phoenix' or 'Whitney-Phoenix'

∽

A laterally-pivoting breech-block system patented by Eli Whitney III in May 1874, this enjoyed a short-lived popularity owing to competitive price, but was never able to challenge more effectual patterns (e.g., Ballard, Remington or Winchester) on the target range.

The Phoenix rifle had a side-hinged breech block lifting up and to the right for loading. The massive wrought-iron receiver was cut to accommodate the transverse breech block and the hammer was hung centrally. The block contained the firing pin and its coil spring.

Phoenix rifles had a mechanical extractor, but extraction was poor and constant modifications were made. The original breech-locking catch was let into the standing breech on the left side of the hammer, but was soon moved to the front right side of the receiver.

Military Model

Offered as a rifle or carbine.
Made by the Whitney Arms Company, Whitneyville,
Connecticut, c.1877–80.
·433 Spanish, ·45–70 Government or
·50–70 Government.
Laterally pivoting-block action, locked by
the hammer.
DATA FOR A TYPICAL RIFLE
·45–70 Government, rimmed.
50·63in overall, 9·00lb unladen.
35·00in barrel, 4-groove rifling; RH, concentric?
Ramp-and-leaf sight graduated to 1,200 yards.
1,320 ft/sec with 405-grain bullet.
M1873 socket bayonet.

☆

1877: the Phoenix was available as a rifle—with a full-length fore-end and three screw-clamped barrel bands—or as a 7lb cavalry carbine with a single band and a ring-and-bar assembly on the right side of the receiver. It was unpopular,

owing to a tendency for the breech to jam when hot, and never attracted the interest of a major army. Most rifles accepted standard socket bayonets, but Whitney advertised a brass-hilted sabre pattern as an optional accessory.

Sporting Model

Offered as a rifle or carbine.
Made by the Whitney Arms Company, Whitneyville,
Connecticut, c.1877–88.
·38 Long, ·38–40 Winchester, ·40–50 Sharps
(necked or straight), ·40–70 Sharps (necked or
straight), ·44–60 Sharps (necked), ·44–77 Sharps
(necked), ·44–90 Sharps (necked), ·44–100 Remington,
·45–70 Government or ·50–70 Government.
Action: as Military Model, above.
DATA FOR A TYPICAL RIFLE
·40–70 Sharps (straight), rimmed.
41·63in overall, 7·85lb unladen.
26·00in barrel, 4-groove rifling; RH, concentric?
Spring-leaf and elevator sight.
1,260 ft/sec with 330-grain bullet.

1880: the Phoenix sporter was made in many styles, ranging from a plain hunter's gun with a round barrel and open sights to decorative guns supplied to order. Barrels measured 26–32in, weights ranging from about 7·5lb to 10lb. A carbine with a 20in barrel was also available.

Schuetzen Model

Made by the Whitney Arms Company, Whitneyville,
Connecticut, c.1884–8.
·38 Ballard Extra Long or ·40–50 Sharps (straight).
Action: as Military Model, above.
DATA FOR A TYPICAL RIFLE
·38 Ballard Extra Long, rimmed.
48·50in overall (including the butt-plate hook),
about 11·50lb unladen.
30·00in barrel, four-groove rifling; RH, concentric?
Vernier sight.
1,275 ft/sec with 145-grain bullet.

☆

1884: this had adjustable vernier peep-and-globe sights, selected woodwork with chequering on

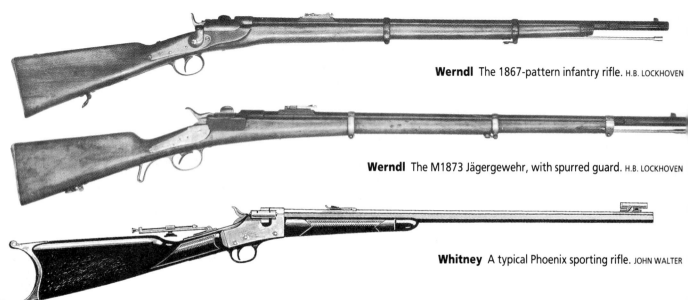

Werndl The 1867-pattern infantry rifle. H.B. LOCKHOVEN

Werndl The M1873 Jägergewehr, with spurred guard. H.B. LOCKHOVEN

Whitney A typical Phoenix sporting rifle. JOHN WALTER

the butt-wrist and fore-end, a cheek piece, and a hooked Swiss-style butt plate. Schuetzen rifles had 30in or 32in partly- or fully-octagonal barrels and weighed up to 12lb.

WICHITA

UNITED STATES OF AMERICA
‿

These rifles embody a bolt system with triple lugs and a 60° throw. Available separately, the action is neat, sturdy and effectual. All patterns were available in right- or left-hand versions.

Wichita Sporting Rifle
••

Classic, Silhouette and Varmint patterns.
Made by Wichita Arms, Wichita, Kansas.
Chambering: see notes.
Turning-bolt action, locked by lugs on the bolt rotating into the receiver wall and the bolt handle seating in the receiver.
DATA FOR A TYPICAL CLASSIC RIFLE
·243 Winchester, rimless.
41·00in overall, 8·15lb unladen.
21·20in barrel, 6-groove rifling; RH, concentric?
Internal box magazine, 2 rounds.
Optical sight.
3,070 ft/sec with 100-grain bullet.
☆

1977: Wichita Classic Rifles had an octagonal barrel, plus a select walnut stock with a shallow Monte Carlo comb and a slender pistol grip. The grip and fore-end had hand-cut chequering with spade bordering. A Niedner steel pistol-grip cap and a rubber Pachmayr shoulder pad were standard. Adjustable Canjar triggers were used and a safety catch lay behind the bolt handle.

Many guns were single-shot, but others had 'blind' magazines within the stock. The most distinctive feature was the action, with a high left side wall and three prominent gas-escape holes on the bolt.

The heavy-barrelled Wichita Varmint rifle had a 20·2in barrel and weighed about 9lb. Like the Classic, it could chamber any cartridge from ·17

Remington to ·308 Winchester, provided the overall length did not exceed 2·8in.
1980: Stainless Magnum rifles appeared in single shot or magazine-fed form, intended for cartridges from ·270 Winchester to ·458 Winchester Magnum. Made with 22in or 24in barrels, they were 44·8in overall and weighed 8–8·5lb. The guns were discontinued in c.1987.
1983: the grey Fiberthane stock of the Wichita Silhouette rifle had a high Monte Carlo comb and an upright pistol grip. The gun weighed about 9lb owing to its heavyweight 24in barrel. The bolt was fluted, whilst the Canjar trigger had a 2oz release.

WINCHESTER

UNITED STATES OF AMERICA
‿

Formed in New Haven, Connecticut, in 1866, the Winchester Repeating Arms Company succeeded to the business of the moribund New Haven Arms Company—and thus of the Volcanic Repeating Arms Company.

Volcanic had made a lever-action repeater firing primer-propellant ammunition, doomed by its low power. However, the Volcanic was refined into the Henry Rifle, chambering a more powerful rimfire cartridge; and then the Henry, suitably improved, became the Winchester Model 1866.

The Model 1873 and strengthened guns patented by John Browning (q.v.) in the 1880s brought Winchester tremendous success. Work continued after the First World War, creating the Model 54 and Model 70 bolt-action rifles, until war began again in 1941; the ·30 US M1 Carbine was a Winchester development.

Efforts were concentrated on sporting guns after 1945, but the company's fortunes declined appreciably in the 1960s in the face of an ill-judged change to the Model 70 and ever-increasing competition from Remington, Ruger and others. In the summer of 1981, Olin sold the Winchester gunmaking business to the US Repeating Rifle Company. Under more effectual

management, the Winchester reputation has been restored to much of its former glory.

1. THE AUTO-LOADING PATTERNS

Excepting the ·30 M1 Carbine and the hefty Browning Automatic Rifle (regarded here as a light machine-gun), most pre-1945 Winchester auto-loaders were blowbacks based on a design by Thomas Johnson. The M1 Carbine and the modern Model 100 featured a rotating bolt.

The success of the Browning-designed ·22 rimfire auto-loaders made by Fabrique Nationale persuaded Winchester to develop comparable guns. The M1903 was also a low powered ·22 rimfire, but inspired a series of centre-fire derivatives. However, owing to the retention of blowback operation, these guns could only chamber comparatively weak cartridges—too low powered, indeed, to commend expensive Winchesters to hunting fraternities.

The French purchased a few Winchester auto-loaders during the early stages of the First World War to arm aviators and balloonists, who appreciated their handiness and firepower; unfortunately, the magazine capacity was not large enough to be truly useful in combat. No other substantial military sales have ever been authenticated, though the ·351 M1907 rifle, in particular, was quite popular with North American police.

All Winchester centre-fire barrels made after July 1905 (October 1908 for rimfire patterns) bore the company proof mark, 'WP' in an oval; this was added to receivers from July 1908 onward. 'P' in an oval, used from June 1915, indicated that the guns had been sold through the company's mail order department.

Unqualified success awaited the appearance of the Winchester Light Rifle, which became the M1 Carbine. Though this was criticised for its short-range and poor hitting power compared with the M1 Garand, production of millions testified to the efficiency of the basic action.

Winchester By gaining its spurs in the Wild West, the lever-action rifle has entered international folklore. A detail from a 1909-vintage painting by Charles M. Russell, 'When Horse Flesh Comes High'.
AMON CARTER MUSEUM COLLECTION

The M1 Carbine amalgamated a rotating-bolt action adapted from an experimental Jonathan Browning rifle submitted to the US Marine Corps with a short-stroke piston credited to David 'Marsh' Williams.

Gas bled from the bore struck a tappet back about ·44in, transferring energy to a spring-loaded operating slide. The slide rotated the bolt, which continued back to eject the spent case, cock the hammer, and then return to strip a new cartridge into the chamber. The locking lugs were rotated back into engagement at the end of the return stroke and the gun could fire again.

MILITARY WEAPONS
USA

1937: the Chief of Infantry suggested in the autumn that the army needed a semi-automatic rifle with an effective range of 300 yards—more potent than a pistol, but light enough to be issued to men for whom the new M1 Garand was unsuitable.

1938: major criteria had been established—calibre greater than ·25, weight not more than 5lb, semi-automatic (preferable) or bolt-action, a magazine containing 5 or 7 rounds, and a fixed aperture sight.

1940: in June, the Chief of Ordnance was asked to expedite development of the light rifle as 500,000 were required immediately. Working with Winchester, the Ordnance Department staff proposed a new slightly-tapered rimless ·30 cartridge with a 110-grain bullet capable of attaining 2,000 ft/sec at the muzzle. The perfected 'Cartridge, Caliber ·30 SL, M1' was standardised on 30 September.

The 'Military Characteristics for Lightweight Semi-automatic Rifle, as Possible Replacement for Caliber ·45 Pistol and Submachine Gun' were circulated from 1 October.

1941: by the beginning of May, nine guns had been submitted. After preliminary trials had been undertaken, however, only the Garand-designed Springfield Light Rifle—with a top-mounted box magazine and downward ejection—and George

Hyde's distinctive pistol-gripped gas-operated gun (submitted by Bendix) showed any promise. No outstanding weapon had yet appeared.

M1 Carbine
....
Fixed-butt patterns: M1, M1A2 and M1E2.
Made by the Winchester Repeating Arms Company, New Haven, Connecticut (828,060, 1942–5); Inland Manufacturing Division of the General Motors Corporation, Dayton, Ohio (2·324–2·642 million, depending on estimates, 1942–5); the Rock-Ola Company, Chicago, Illinois (228,500, 1942–4); Quality Hardware & Machine Company, Chicago, Illinois (359,660, 1942–4); the Irwin-Pedersen Arms Company, Grand Rapids, Michigan (1,000, 1942, see notes); Underwood-Elliott-Fisher Company, Hartford, Connecticut (545,620, 1942–4); the Rochester Defense Corporation, Rochester, New York (see National Postal Meter); Standard Products Company, Port Clinton, Ohio (247,160, 1942–4); International Business Machines Corporation, Poughkeepsie, New York (346,500, 1943–4); Saginaw Steering Gear Division of the General Motors Corporation, Saginaw and Grand Rapids, Michigan (517,210, 1943–4); and the National Postal Meter Company, Rochester, New York (413,020, 1943–4).
Quantity: 6·010–6·225 million M1, M2 and M3 Carbines for the US armed forces.
·30 M1 Carbine, rimless.
Gas-operated auto-loading action, locked by lugs on the bolt engaging the receiver.
DATA FOR POST-1943 M1 CARBINE
35·65in overall, 5·42lb without magazine.
18·00in barrel, 4-groove rifling; RH, concentric.
Detachable box magazine, 15 or 30 rounds.
Back sight: see notes.
1,900 ft/sec with M1 Carbine ball cartridges.
M4 knife bayonet.
☆

1941: after the failure of other light rifles, a Winchester prototype reached Aberdeen Proving Ground on 9 August and performed most encouragingly. Work on an improved version began immediately.

Six differing guns entered the trials that began on 15 September. The modified Springfield Light

Rifle (Garand), with a conventional magazine and an improved action, would have prevailed had not the perfected Winchester passed all its tests with flying colours.

On 30 September, the Winchester Carbine was recommended for immediate adoption; formal approval was forthcoming on 22 October and the gun was standardised as the 'Carbine, Caliber ·30, M1'. The initial requirement was set—most precisely—at 886,698 guns and, in November, contracts were placed with Winchester and the Inland Manufacturing Division of General Motors.

The M1 Carbine had a pistol-grip half stock, with a single screwed band retained by a spring let into the fore-end. A hand guard ran from the receiver ring to the rear of the band. The box magazine protruded ahead of the trigger-guard web, through which a cross-bolt safety catch lay. One swivel appeared on the left side of the band, to be used in conjunction with a slot cut through the butt. The earliest guns had a two-position pivoting back sight and lacked the bayonet-lug assembly beneath the muzzle.

1942: on 25 March, Winchester licensed rights in the M1 Carbine to the US Government. By February, requirements had risen to 1·1 million and five additional contractors were recruited—Rock-Ola, the Quality Hardware & Machine Company, Irwin Brothers ('Irwin-Pedersen Arms Company'), Underwood-Elliott-Fisher, and the Rochester Defense Corporation.

By the beginning of June, only Inland had delivered guns—a paltry 382—but this did not prevent the Army Supply Program calculating the carbine requirements to December 1943 as an astonishing 4·47 million. In a third wave of expansion in August 1942, therefore, Standard Products Company was awarded a contract to make carbines at an unprecedented rate of 45,000 per month; 111,600 had been delivered by the end of 1942. Inland had supplied 97,920 and had even reached the desired 'thousand daily' by 31 December.

Winchester's 1942 contribution had been 10,310, which left 3,080 from Underwood and a handful from Rock-Ola and Quality Hardware.

1943: recruited in the Spring, the International Business Machines Corporation and the Saginaw Steering Gear Division of General Motors were expected to contribute 60,000 guns per month.

The problematical Irwin-Pedersen contract and the company's Grand Rapids factory were transferred to the General Motors Saginaw Division; consequently, all but about a thousand Irwin-Pedersen marked carbines were assembled under Saginaw control.

National Postal Meter, an original promoter of the Rochester Defence Corporation, began producing carbines in February 1943; Saginaw Steering Gear's first gun followed in May; then came Standard Products in June and, finally, IBM in August.

Experience soon showed the limitations of the rocking-'L' back sight, which provided two fixed range settings and had no provision for lateral adjustment. Standardised in January, the Carbine M1A2 (initially classified as 'M1E2') had an adjustable T21 back sight. However, as this required a modified receiver, adoption of the M1A2 was rescinded in November and the sight was adapted to fit the standard M1. The magazine-retaining plunger was modified and a new safety catch substituted for the original sliding pattern during this period.

By 31 December, with all nine facilities participating, nearly three million guns had been delivered. M1 Carbines were being made at a rate of more than 500,000 per month.

Experimental models had included M1E5, made largely from Arma-Steel castings; M1E6, a long-barrelled gun used by Frankford Arsenal for testing propellant; and the abortive M1E7 sniper's rifle, with a Weaver M73B1 sight.

1944: as production was rapidly outstripping predictions, the projected Army Supply Program requirement of 2·95 million was cut to 1·95 million. Accordingly, production at six factories was terminated with effect from 30 April and Rock-Ola completed work on 31 May. After 1 June, therefore, only Inland and Winchester continued to make carbines.

The Bayonet-Knife M4—known during its development as the T8E1—was approved on 10 May. It required a new front band assembly incorporating a bayonet lug, a modification soon made mandatory on guns returning for repair.

1945: carbine production exceeded six million. Most markings were self explanatory. However, Winchester barrels bore 'WRA' (early), 'W' or 'PW' (later), or sometimes nothing at all. Standard Products receivers displayed STD. PRO. while Saginaw Steering Gear guns were marked SAGINAW S.G. (Saginaw factory) or SAGINAW S'G' (Grand Rapids factory)—though a few early Grand Rapids guns displayed IRWIN-PEDERSEN.

The oldest National Postal Meter guns were marked ROCHESTER and a few hundred displayed 'CCC' for Commercial Controls Corporation. Barrels usually came from Underwood. Quality Hardware carbines sometimes incorporated receivers made by the Union Switch & Signal Company, marked UN-QUALITY; barrels usually came from Rock-Ola. Some IBM receivers were made by Auto-Ordnance and could bear 'AO'.

Note: government procurement figures show a total production for Inland between January 1942 and July 1944 of only 1,412,691. Though one source suggests that no fewer than 754,406 carbines were made in 1945, other estimates are much less generous.

M1 Carbine

Folding-butt patterns: A1, E1, A3, E3 and E4.
Made by the Inland Manufacturing Division of the General Motors Corporation, Dayton, Ohio, 1944–5.
Quantity: 150,000?
·30 M1 Carbine, rimless.
Action: as standard M1 Carbine, above.
DATA FOR M1A1 CARBINE
25·40in overall (folded), 6·20lb with empty magazine.
18·00in barrel, 4-groove rifling; RH, concentric.
Detachable box magazine, 15 or 30 rounds.
Ramp-mounted aperture sight graduated to 300 yards.
1,970 ft/sec with M1 Carbine ball cartridges.
M4 knife bayonet.
☆

1943: experimental collapsible-stock carbines were developed by Inland (known as M1E1) and Springfield Armory (M1E3 folding or M1E4 sliding), Springfield patterns being strengthened to withstand grenade launching. Though the M1E1 and M1E3 were standardised, only the former was made in quantity as the 'Carbine, Caliber ·30, M1A1'. It had a pistol grip and a skeletal butt with a reinforcing plate.

1944: made exclusively by Inland with the assistance of Royal Typewriters, Inc., 92,380 M1A1 Carbines had been delivered by July. Production is believed to have continued into 1945, though the final total is not known.

M2 Carbine

A selective-fire version of the M1.
Made by the Winchester Repeating Arms Company, New Haven, Connecticut (17,500, 1944–5); and the Inland Manufacturing Division of the General Motors Corporation, Dayton, Ohio (225,000, 1944–5?).
Quantity: about 242,500?
·30 M1 Carbine, rimless.
Action: as standard M1 Carbine, above.
35·65in overall, 5·65lb with empty magazine.
18·00in barrel, 4-groove rifling; RH, concentric.
Detachable box magazine, 30 rounds.
Ramp-mounted aperture sight graduated to 300 yards.
1,970 ft/sec with M1 Carbine ball cartridges.
750 ± 50 rpm.
M4 knife bayonet.
☆

1944: Inland evolved the selective-fire T4 to increase firepower. The perfected 'Carbine, Caliber ·30, M2' was standardised on 23 October with a new thirty-round box magazine and a selector on the left rear of the receiver to disengage the sear during automatic fire. The gun was made exclusively by Inland and Winchester. (Note: though all true M2 Carbines were newly made, a T17 kit permitted field conversion of M1 examples to M2 standards.)

M3 Carbine

Made by the Winchester Repeating Arms Company, New Haven, Connecticut (1,110 in 1945); and the Inland Manufacturing Division of the General Motors Corporation, Dayton, Ohio (810 in 1945).

Winchester Private Timothy Troast of 265 Field Artillery Battalion, Second Armored Division, tries his M1 Carbine; Germany, 1956.
US ARMY PHOTOGRAPH SC 474999

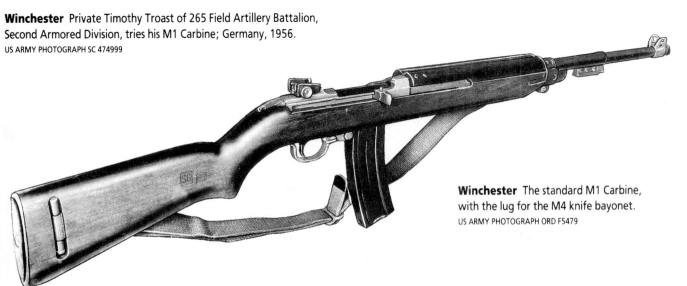

Winchester The standard M1 Carbine, with the lug for the M4 knife bayonet.
US ARMY PHOTOGRAPH ORD F5479

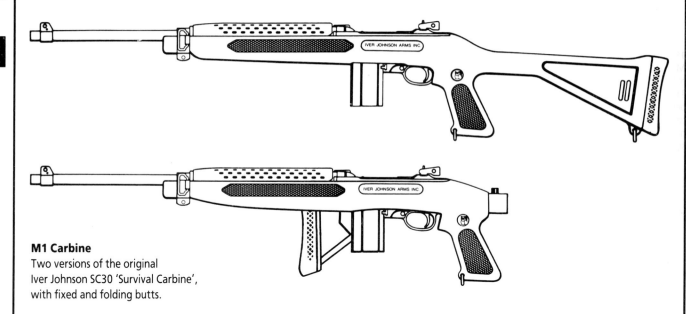

M1 Carbine
Two versions of the original
Iver Johnson SC30 'Survival Carbine',
with fixed and folding butts.

M1 CARBINE
OTHER USERS AND
COMMERCIAL VARIANTS

The tremendous quantities of M1 and M2 carbines made during the Second World War enabled weapons to be supplied to many foreign powers under the US Military Aid Programs. Virtually all of these guns were military surplus, and thus bore their original US military marks and numbers.

¶ The most important recipients were South Korea and South Vietnam, to whom 1·09 million and nearly 800,000 M1/M2 Carbines were supplied in 1950–75. The guns were ideally suited to men of small stature.

¶ Large numbers were also used in Taiwan (about 179,000); the Netherlands (170,000); Italy (159,000); France (155,000); Norway (98,000); Thailand (73,000); Federal Republic of Germany (34,000); Uruguay (about 33,000); Greece (30,000); Burma (29,000); and Indonesia (21,000). Austria and Belgium also issued substantial quantities; the precise figures are not known, but are believed to have run into tens of thousands.

COMMERCIAL GUNS

The outstanding success of the M1 Carbine, and the ready availability of spare parts, persuaded several manufacturers to offer similar guns commercially.

HOWA

The Howa Machinery Company of Nagoya, Japan, made substantial quantities of the ·30 Model 300 in the 1960s. Based on the M1 action, these carbines had Monte Carlo-pattern stocks and spring-and-elevator back sights. Most will be encountered with ports bored into the side of the muzzle alongside the front sight to reduce apparent recoil.

IVER JOHNSON

Iver Johnson's Arms, Inc., of Fitchburg, Massachusetts, entered the M1 Carbine-making business by purchasing the assets of the Plainfield Machine Company

(see below) and moving to Middlesex, New Jersey, in 1977. The business of Universal Sporting Goods was purchased in 1983, after a move to Jacksonville in Arkansas, but Iver Johnson was itself liquidated in 1986. The assets of the company were acquired by the American Military Arms Corporation and the 'Iver Johnson' name ceased to be associated with the M1 Carbine in 1987. Guns were marketed under the AMAC brand thereafter—at least until the end of 1992.

¶ The Iver Johnson PM30 was made in several versions; 'HB' was the standard blued gun, with a beech stock; 'WB' was blued, with a walnut stock; and 'WS' was a stainless-steel version. Most chambered the ·30 M1 cartridge, but others accepted the more potent 5·7mm MMJ.

¶ The standard guns were accompanied by the SC30 or Survival Carbine, introduced in 1983 and discontinued in 1986; the 'SS' model, made of stainless steel, had a black DuPont Xytel butt with a separate pistol grip behind the trigger. The 'FB' and 'FS' guns were essentially similar, but had folding butts; finish was blue or stainless steel respectively.

¶ After the demise of Iver Johnson, AMAC continued to sell the Models 3103, 3203 and 3200 Paratrooper models—the Iver Johnson PM30HB, PM30WB and SC30FB respectively—under its own name. However, the Iver Johnson name has since reappeared on 'fiftieth birthday' M1 Carbines. Appropriately roll-engraved, these have a figured walnut stock and an American flag medallion set into the butt.

JOHNSON

Johnson Automatics Associates, Inc., of Hope Valley, Rhode Island, marketed a series of modified M1 Carbines chambered for a potent 5·7mm MMJ cartridge—which may justifiably be regarded as the predecessor of the current 5·56 × 45mm round. Production ceased in the early 1960s.

NATIONAL ORDNANCE

Based in Southern El Monte, California, this

company advertised standard and folding-stock M1 Carbines (in ·30 or ·223 Remington) in the early 1970s. The major parts are belived to have been made in Japan, receivers being investment castings instead of the forged-steel versions favoured by Universal. Many of the other parts seem to have been refurbished war surplus. However, the quantities involved do not seem to have been large.

PLAINFIELD

The Plainfield Machine Company of Dunellen and then Middlesex, New Jersey, made a classical M1 Carbine replica (in ·22/·30, 5·7mm MMJ or ·30 M1 Carbine) from the early 1960s onward; most of examples made in the 1970s had ventilated sheet-steel hand guards and lacked the bayonet-lug assembly beneath the barrel. The Commando or Paratrooper Model had a forward pistol grip and a sliding skeletal butt; the M1 Sporter had a military-style butt without the sling bar; and the M1 Deluxe Sporter (later known as the 'Plainfielder') had a special half-stock with a Monte Carlo comb and a chequered pistol grip.

¶ The company was acquired by Iver Johnson (see above) in 1975, Iver Johnson moving its own headquarters from Fitchburg to Middlesex in 1977. Production continued thereafter under the Iver Johnson name, the entire enterprise moving to Arkansas in 1982.

UNIVERSAL

Universal Sporting Goods, Inc., of Hialeah and Miami, Florida, made a variety of M1 Carbine derivatives from c.1962 until the company was purchased by Iver Johnson (see above) in January 1983. The facilities were moved to Arkansas in the summer of 1984, consolidating Iver Johnson's M1 Carbine monopoly.

¶ The original Universal M1 Carbine was a straightforward copy of the military-pattern gun, though most reviewers agreed that it was not only better made but also shot much more reliably than the wartime

products. In 1965, the range comprised the standard sandblasted M1B (with a bayonet mounting); M1A, with a polished finish; the deluxe M1BB; M1BN, with nickel plating; M1BG, with 18-carat gold plating; M1OS, with a Monte Carlo-pattern stock; and the M1 Ferret, chambered for the ·256 Winchester cartridge instead of the standard ·30 M1 Carbine pattern.

¶ By mid 1970, the range had been refined; only the Model 1003, 1004 and 1941 were being offered—the M1A, M1A with an optical sight, and the M1B respectively. Excepting the Model 1941, the guns were fitted with ventilated sheet-steel hand guards. The nickel-plated Model 1011 (M1BN) and gold-plated Model 1016 (M1BG) had both been abandoned. By 1981, however, there had been a renewwal of interest; the '1003' designation reverted to the Model 1941 (wood hand guard), the standard sporting carbine becoming the Model 1002 (sheet-steel hand guard). The Model 5000PT appeared with a folding stock copied from the German MP.38 (Schmeisser) submachine-gun; the M1005SB offered 'Super Mirrored' finish and a walnut stock; M1010N was nickelled; M1015G featured gold plating; Model 1020TB had a DuPont 'Raven Black' Teflon-S finish; and Model 1025TCO had an olive drab/camouflage Teflon finish.

¶ A stainless steel version (Model 1006SS) was introduced in 1982, together with a stainless Ferret known as M2566 (the standard Ferret being redesignated '1256' accordingly). Two variants of the M5000PT were announced in 1983—M5016 with a 16in barrel instead of the standard 18in, and M5006 made of stainless steel. Model 1030 had a grey Teflon-S finish.

¶ A special commemorative version was made in 1981 to celebrate the fortieth anniversary of the wartime M1 Carbine. It had a bayonet lug and a special medallion in the side of the black walnut butt. Iver Johnson continued to sell Universal-branded Carbines as late as 1988, the Models 1003 and 5000PT lasting until the very end.

Quantity: 1,920
·30 M1 Carbine, rimless.
Otherwise generally as M2 Carbine, excepting the omission of a back sight.

☆

1945: known during development as 'T3', the M3 carbine was an M2 adapted for the infra-red Sniperscope M2 (standardised in August). The earliest M3 Carbines had an infra-red lamp beneath the stock—ahead of the lamp-actuating trigger—instead of above it. Owing to the end of hostilities and the cumbersome nature of the sight, production was small.

SPORTING GUNS

Model 1905

Made by the Winchester Repeating Arms Company, New Haven, Connecticut, 1905–19.
Quantity: 29,110.
Auto-loading action, blowback type.
·32 and ·35 WSL only.
DATA FOR A TYPICAL EXAMPLE
·32 WSL, semi-rimmed.
About 40in overall, 7·57lb unladen.
22·00in barrel, 6-groove rifling; RH, concentric.
Spring-leaf and elevator sight.
Detachable box magazine, 5 rounds.
1,400 ft/sec with 165-grain bullet.

☆

1905: delivered into stock in August, this Johnson design was made only in 'Take-Down' style. It was simply a more powerful centre-fire version of the ·22 rimfire M1903, retaining the general appearance of the earlier gun, with a straight-wrist butt and a half-length fore-end with the cocking rod protruding from its rounded tip. The receiver had an ejection port on the upper right side, directly above the box magazine, and a safety catch appeared on the trigger guard. Standard guns had plain woodwork, with a rubber butt plate, but special attractively figured butts could be obtained on order.
1908: a pistol-grip butt became standard.
1911: a ten-round magazine became an optional extra in October.

Model 1907

Standard and Police patterns.
Made by the Winchester Repeating Arms Company, New Haven, Connecticut, 1906–57 (see notes).
Quantity: 58,490.
·351 WSL only.
Action: as M1905, above.
About 39·5in overall, 7·81lb unladen.
20·00in barrel, 6-groove rifling; RH, concentric.
Spring-leaf and elevator back sight.
Detachable box magazine, 5 rounds.
1,850 ft/sec with 180-grain bullet.

☆

1906: delivered into factory stock in November, this improved M1905 also chambered a special WSL cartridge. The basic M1907 had a plain pistol-grip butt with a rubber plate, but was otherwise similar to the preceding rifle; the most obvious feature was the band around the barrel at the tip of the fore-end, which was plain on the M1905 but ribbed on the M1907.

Fancy Sporting Rifles were offered with selected woodwork and special finishes.
1911: an optional ten-round magazine was introduced in October.
1934: the 'Police Model', introduced at the end of the year, had a special pistol-grip butt and a broad or semi-beavertail fore-end. The butt plate was chequered steel and swivels were fitted. Available to order with a knife or sword bayonet, it was abandoned in 1937.
1937: the police-style butt and fore-end were approved for the standard rifle in December.
1948: a projection was added to the cocking rod in midsummer, and the magazine-release button was enlarged.
1957: the last guns were sold from store. It is unlikely that actions had been made since 1941.

Model 1910

Made by the Winchester Repeating Arms Company, New Haven, Connecticut, 1910–36.
Quantity: 20,790.
·401 WSL only.
Action: as M1905, above.

About 39·5in overall, 8·22lb unladen.
20·00in barrel, 6-groove rifling; RH, concentric.
Spring-leaf and elevator sight.
Detachable box magazine, 4 rounds.
2,135 ft/sec with 200-grain bullet.

☆

1910: introduced in the Spring, this was an improved M1907 chambered for an even more powerful WSL cartridge that explored the action to its limits. The gun was practically identical externally with its predecessor, but had a larger ejection port. The standard rifle had a plain pistol-grip butt with a rubber butt plate, and a half-length fore-end from which the cocking rod protruded. Selected stocks and butts, often finely chequered, could be supplied to order.

Model 100

Offered as a rifle and carbine.
Made by the Winchester Repeating Arms Company, New Haven, Connecticut, 1960–73.
·243 Winchester, ·284 Winchester or ·308 Winchester.
Gas-operated auto-loading action, locked by lugs on the bolt rotating into the barrel extension.
DATA FOR A TYPICAL EXAMPLE
·308 Winchester, rimless.
42·00in overall, 7·48lb unladen.
22·00in barrel, 6-groove rifling; RH, concentric.
Folding leaf sight.
Detachable box magazine, 4 rounds.
2,610 ft/sec with 180-grain bullet.

☆

1960: delivered into stock at the end of the year, this gas-operated semi-automatic sporter was a hammerless side-ejector sharing the general lines of the lever-action Model 88 (q.v.). It had a one-piece stock with basket-weave chequering on the pistol grip and round-tip fore-end. Synthetic butt plates and pistol-grip caps were fitted, and there were swivels beneath the fore-end and butt.

The front-sight lay on a hooded ramp. A detachable four-round box magazine (three rounds in ·284) lay directly under the ejection port and the safety bolt ran through the front trigger-guard web.

Winchester The ·401 Model 1910 rifle, from a company catalogue.

Winchester The M3 Carbine with the infra-red Sniperscope M2, but lacking the lamp assembly. PATTERN ROOM COLLECTION

1963: a carbine derivative appeared with a 19in barrel, a plain pistol-grip stock, and a band around the fore-end carrying the front swivel.

2. THE BLOCK-ACTION PATTERNS

The solitary Winchester dropping-block rifle was derived from the Browning single-shot rifle of 1878. As the two were essentially similar, and owing to the advent of modern re-creations of the Browning-Winchester rifle, they are covered in the Browning section.

3. THE BOLT-ACTION PATTERNS

Model 54

Carbine, National Match, NRA, Sniper's, Standard Super Grade and Target patterns.
Made by the Winchester Repeating Arms Company, New Haven, Connecticut, 1925–36.
·22 Hornet, ·220 Swift, ·250–3000 Savage, ·257 Roberts, ·270 Winchester, 7 × 57mm, 7·65 × 53mm, ·30–06, ·30–30 Winchester or 9 × 57mm.
Quantity: 50,150.
Turning-bolt action, locked by two lugs on the bolt head rotating into the receiver and a safety lug under the bolt handle turning down into its seat.
DATA FOR A TYPICAL STANDARD RIFLE
·270 Winchester, rimless.
44·00in overall, about 7·5lb unladen.
24·00in barrel, 6-groove rifling; RH, concentric.
Internal box magazine, 5 rounds.
Spring-leaf and elevator sight.
3,140 ft/sec with 130-grain bullet.
☆

1925: developed by a team headed by Thomas Johnson, around an experimental ·27 cartridge, the Model 54 was based on the US Army M1903 Springfield service rifle. It had twin opposed locking lugs, a Mauser collar-pattern extractor, and a special guide-lug—patented by Frank Burton in June 1927—to smooth the bolt stroke. A three-position safety appeared on the cocking-piece shroud and an internal box magazine was fitted.

The first rifles were chambered for ·270 Winchester and ·30–06 only and had 24in barrels. The walnut half-stocks had straight combs. Chequering graced the pistol grip and fore-end; shoulder plates were grooved steel, at least until 1930. The receiver ring (but not the bridge) was tapped for an optical-sight mount.

1927: a Model 54 Carbine was introduced with a 20in barrel. Chequering was omitted, though the fore-end had a grasping groove.

1928: a ·30–30 Winchester option was offered for the first time, but was never popular. Indeed, many rifles initially supplied in ·30–30 were rechambered by Griffin & Howe and others for the ballistically superior ·30–40 Krag.

1929: a Sniper's Rifle had a heavy 26in barrel. Its stock was plain walnut, without chequering, and the butt plate was chequered steel.

1930: three popular metric options—7mm, 7·65mm and 9mm—were added, and the old grooved butt plate was replaced with a revised chequered pattern.

1931: the front sight of the rifles and carbines was mounted on a forged base from March onward. An NRA Rifle was also made in small numbers, with the standard 24in barrel. Its select-grade walnut stock had a chequered butt plate and pistol grip, but the fore-end was plain. A ·250–3000 Savage version was advertised for the standard-pattern Model 54 in this period.

1932: the Speed Lock was adopted to reduce the lock-time. A one-piece firing pin replaced the original two-piece component and a modified striker spring halved the firing pin travel. This cut lock time from about ·0055 sec to ·0033 sec. Owners of older or 'Plain Lock' rifles could purchase replacement Speed Lock bolts; when the Model 54 was discontinued in 1936, modified Model 70-type bolts were supplied.

1933: a special ·22 Hornet version of the Model 54 was introduced. Owing to the small size of the cartridge compared with the length of the action, a special cartridge pusher, patented by Albert Laudensack in February 1933, was fitted in the bolt head. This feature was later perpetuated in the Model 70, together with a reduced-scale magazine inside the standard box.

1934: a second gas vent was added in the bolt, behind the extractor collar. A 20in barrel option was offered with the Standard Model rifle, and the Super Grade rifle appeared. Fitted with the standard 24in barrel, these guns had specially selected walnut stocks with chequering on the pistol grip and fore-end. An ebonite fore-end tip and a rubber pistol-grip cap were added, and a small oval cheek piece appeared on the right side of the butt. Weight rose to about 8lb.

1935: a Target Rifle (24in heavy barrel) and a National Match Rifle (24in standard barrel) were added, but production was very small. Standard-pattern stocks of the earliest Target rifles were changed in 1936 to a plain type specifically developed for target shooting. All National Match rifles and post-1936 Sniper's Rifles used this target-type stock, which had a deeper pistol grip with a sharper radius than the standard sporter. The fore-end was widened ahead of the magazine.

Though optical sight-mounting blocks were fitted on the chamber and barrel, Lyman vernier aperture and replaceable-element tunnel sights were also popular.

The 26in barrel of the Sniper's Rifle was changed from heavy to extra-heavy in this period, increasing weight from 11lb to 11·75lb.

1936: work ceased in favour of the Model 70, but not before a few Model 54 rifles had been chambered for ·220 Swift or ·257 Roberts cartridges. All ·220 rifles had 26in barrels.

Model 70

1936 TYPE
African, Alaskan, Bull Gun, Featherweight, National Match, Standard, Super Grade, Target, Varmint and Westerner patterns.
Made in New Haven by the Winchester Repeating Arms Company (1936–61) and the Winchester-Western Division of Olin Industries (1962–4).

Winchester A drawing of the Model 70 bolt-action rifle.

Until recent years, barrel straightening was undertaken by hand and eye. This picture was taken as recently as 1982. IAN HOGG

·22 Hornet, ·220 Swift, ·243 Winchester, ·250–3000 Savage, ·257 Roberts, ·264 Winchester Magnum, ·270 Winchester, 7 × 57mm, 7·65 × 53mm, ·300 H&H Magnum, ·300 Savage, ·300 Winchester Magnum, ·30–06, ·308 Winchester, ·338 Winchester Magnum, ·35 Remington, 9 × 57mm, ·358 Winchester, ·375 H&H Magnum or ·458 Winchester Magnum. See notes.
Quantity: about 525,000.
Action: generally as Model 54, above.
DATA FOR A TYPICAL AFRICAN RIFLE
·458 Winchester Magnum, belted rimless.
45·50in overall, 9·50lb unladen.
25·00in barrel, 6-groove rifling; RH, concentric.
Internal box magazine, 3 rounds.
Folding leaf sight.
2,130 ft/sec with 500-grain bullet.
☆

1933: the success of the Model 54 permitted Winchester to design its successor at leisure. Credited to a team led by Edwin Pugsley, in which Leroy Crockett and Albert Laudensack were prominent, the Model 70 retained the basic operating system of the older gun. It had a cone-breech, a partially shrouded bolt head and a modified bedding system with the front trigger guard bolt running up into the underside of the receiver instead of the recoil lug. The bolt handle was swept down and back, a graceful feature which allowed it to clear most optical sights. The safety catch on the cocking-piece shroud was changed to work laterally; it could be set to fire, to retract the firing-pin (yet allow the bolt to open), or to lock the bolt in the action. The bolt-stop was a separate part, independent of the sear. A hinged floor plate was fitted and the trigger guard became a machined steel forging.
1934: approval to manufacture the new gun in quantity was given on 29 December.
1936: the first rifles were delivered into store.
1937: the perfected Model 70 was added to the Winchester catalogue. Some of the earliest guns made for ·270 and ·30–06 had charger guides milled in the front edge of the receiver bridge. The top of the receiver ring and bridge were hatched to reduce reflections, and the receiver ring was tapped for an optical sight mount.

The standard Model 54-type stock was refined, with less drop at the heel and a broader fore-end. The chequering was improved. Barrels were 24in or 20in, the latter being discontinued shortly after the end of the Second World War. Barrels accompanying ·220 Swift and ·300 H&H Magnum chamberings were always 26in long; and the ·375 H&H Magnum pattern, originally a standard 24in, was soon substituted by a heavier version. In February 1937, the ·375 Magnum barrel was lengthened to 25in.

The ·30–06 National Match and Target rifles (7·8lb and 10·5lb respectively) had 24in barrels, the latter being a medium-heavy design, whilst the Bull Gun—which weighed 13lb—had an extra-heavy 28in barrel. All these guns used the Marksman stock, with a high straight comb, sharper pistol-grip radii and a broad fore-end.
1938: the safety catch was altered so that it operated on the right side of the bolt shroud rather than across it. A safety-catch thumb piece was added soon afterwards.
1946: production of the Model 70 resumed after the end of the Second World War.
1947: the upper tang was altered to lie on top of the stock behind the receiver. The original version had been let into the woodwork, but was prone to chipping.
1952: the Featherweight Rifle was introduced in standard and Super Grade versions. It had a slim 22in tapered barrel, a lightweight stock with an aluminium alloy butt plate, and an alloy trigger guard/magazine floor plate assembly. The ·308 Winchester cartridge appeared commercially.
1953: the bolt knob was hollowed.
1955: the first Varmint Rifle had a 26in barrel, a modified stock and optical-sight mounting bases. ·243 and ·358 options date from this period.
1956: the African Model big-game rifle was revealed, chambered specifically for the new ·458 Winchester Magnum cartridge. Its Monte Carlo stock had a sturdy rubber recoil pad; magazine capacity was three rounds.
1958: a ·338 Winchester Magnum option was announced at the beginning of the year.
1959: the first Model 70 rifles were made in ·264 Winchester Magnum.

1960: the first Westerner and Alaskan Rifles were made. Westerners were based on the standard Model 70, but chambered the ·264 Winchester Magnum cartridge and had three-round magazines. Barrels measured 26in.

Alaskan rifles were chambered exclusively for ·338 Winchester or ·375 H&H Magnum cartridges, magazines holding three and four rounds respectively. The guns had 25in barrels, rubber recoil pads and weighed 8–8·7lb.

The National Match, Super Grade and Super Grade Featherweight rifles were discontinued.
1961: Winchester was purchased by the giant Olin corporation. Work began to modernise the Model 70, with the primary goal of simplifying production.
1963: all surviving versions of the original or 1936-type Model 70 were abandoned at the end of the year, but not before a few Standard and Westerner rifles had been made for the new ·300 Winchester Magnum round.

Model 43

Standard and Special patterns.
Made by the Winchester Repeating Arms Company, New Haven, Connecticut, 1949–57.
·218 Bee, ·22 Hornet, ·25–20 Winchester or ·32–20 Winchester.
Quantity: 62,620.
Turning-bolt action, locked by two lugs on the bolt head rotating into the receiver.
DATA FOR A TYPICAL RIFLE
·218 Bee, rimmed.
43·50in overall, 7·05lb unladen.
24·00in barrel, 6-groove rifling; RH, concentric?
Detachable box magazine, 3 rounds.
Spring-leaf and elevator sight.
2,860 ft/sec with 46-grain bullet.
☆

1944: work on this 'Junior Model 70' began.
1949: the first guns were delivered into store. They had plain pistol-grip stocks with round tipped fore-ends and 24in tapered barrels. The Special Rifle had chequering on the pistol grip and fore-end, displayed a separate pistol-grip cap, and was often furnished with a Lyman No.57A

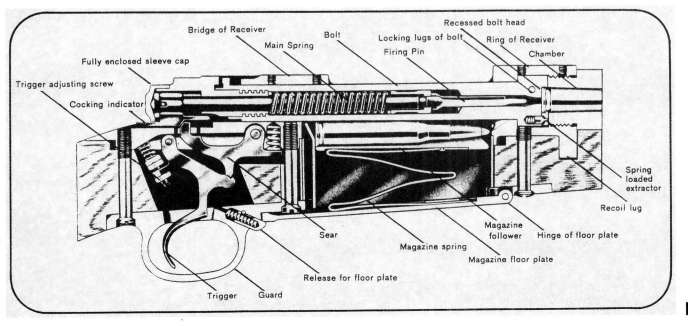

vernier back sight. Swivels lay under the butt and the tip of the fore-end. The safety catch lay on the right side of the action, whilst the bolt handle lay above the front of the trigger guard—farther forward than on other Winchesters.

Model 70

1964 TYPE
African, Custom, Deluxe, International Army Match, Magnum, Mannlicher, Sporter, Standard, Target and Varmint patterns.
Made by the Winchester-Western Division of Olin Industries, New Haven, Connecticut (1964–8).
Chambering: see text.
Quantity: about 166,000.
Action: generally as Model 54, above.
DATA FOR A TYPICAL VARMINT RIFLE
·243 Winchester, rimless.
44·50in overall, 9·70lb unladen.
24·00in barrel, 6-groove rifling; RH, concentric.
Internal box magazine, 5 rounds.
Optical sight.
3,500 ft/sec with 80-grain bullet.
☆

1962: work began on a major revision of the Model 70, to simplify machining and cut costs. The work was entrusted to Robert Creamer and John Walsh, though much of the detailed study was sub-contracted to the Pioneer Engineering & Manufacturing Company of Warren, Michigan. Among the most important changes was the reversion to a faced-off breech instead of the earlier coned pattern. The extractor and ejector were mounted in the bolt head, and the new bolt had a separate investment-cast handle. Barrels floated freely in the fore-ends, instead of being held by a threaded bolt.

1964: modified rifles, numbered from 700000 upward, were greeted with little enthusiasm. Though some changes were improvements, the new Model 70 was poorly finished and much less attractive than its predecessor. The omission of the bolt guide lost much of the smoothness for which the original action had been renowned.

The standard M70 Standard (or Sporter) had a 22in free-floating barrel chambered for the three major Winchester rounds—·243, ·270 or ·308—and the ubiquitous ·30–06. The glossy Monte Carlo-pattern stock had a short steep comb and impressed chequering on the pistol grip and fore-end. A recoil bolt ran through the stock above the front web of the trigger guard.

The Model 70 Magnum, with a 24in barrel, was offered in ·264, ·300 or ·338 Winchester Magnum options, plus ·375 H&H Magnum. It was stocked similarly to the standard Model 70, but usually exhibited a rubber recoil pad.

Custom (or Deluxe) versions of the Sporter and Magnum rifles were made only in small quantities. They had selected walnut stocks with ebony fore-end tips and hand-cut chequering. Quick-detachable swivels were standard, with a ramp-mounted Williams back sight.

The African Rifle, in ·458 only, offered a 22in barrel and a three-round magazine. It was much more heavily built than the standard M70 Sporter and had a recoil bolt through the fore-end beneath the chamber in addition to one ahead of the bolt handle. The stock had an ebony tip, a ventilated rubber recoil pad was fitted to the butt, and chequering was hand-cut. Special sights were fitted. One swivel lay under the butt with another on the barrel ahead of the fore-end tip.

Model 70 Target rifles offered a 24in heavy barrel chambered for ·30–06 or ·308 cartridges. Fitted with five-round box magazines, they had mounting blocks for optical sights on the receiver ring and barrel. The plain Marksman-style stock had a straight comb and a deep fore-end with an alloy hand stop. The guns weighed 10·2lb.

The Model 70 Varmint had a target-pattern barrel in the standard stock. It was introduced in ·243 only and had mounting blocks for optical sights on the receiver ring and barrel.

1965: barrelled actions were made available separately for the first time. The mainspring sleeve was replaced by a C-ring, to which a bearing cap was added in 1969.

1966: the Standard, Magnum and Varmint stocks were changed. The Monte Carlo comb was raised to improve its utility with optical sights, the cheek piece was re-shaped to reduce the effects of recoil, and a recoil bolt was added through the stock. A revised form of chequering was introduced, though still impressed, and a ·225 Winchester option was added.

1968: a 7mm Remington Magnum chambering was introduced for the M70 Magnum rifle.

1969: a Model 70 Mannlicher was introduced in ·243, ·270, ·30–06 or ·308. It had a 19in barrel and a Monte Carlo stock with a full length fore-end, but was never popular.

Contemporaneously, the ·222 and ·22–250 Remington chamberings were introduced for the Sporter and Varmint rifles.

1971: a few ·308 International Army Match rifles were made, easily distinguished by their 24in heavy barrels and massive wooden stocks with an adjustable butt plate. An accessory rail lay under the fore-end. The trigger could be adjusted externally and a five-round detachable box magazine was used. However, at the end of the year, all 1964-type rifles were discontinued.

Model 670

Carbine, Magnum and Standard patterns.
Made by the Winchester-Western Division of Olin Industries, New Haven, Connecticut, 1967–73.
·225 Winchester, ·243 Winchester,
·264 Winchester Magnum, ·270 Winchester, ·30–06
or ·300 Winchester Magnum.
Quantity: 20,000?
Action: generally as Model 54, above.
DATA FOR A TYPICAL RIFLE
·225 Winchester, rimmed.
42·50in overall, about 7lb unladen.
22·00in barrel, 6-groove rifling; RH, concentric.
Internal box magazine, 4 rounds.
Williams ramp sight.
3,570 ft/sec with 55-grain bullet.
☆

1966: introduced in Carbine (20in barrel), Standard (22in) and Magnum (24in) patterns, this was a budget-price Model 70. It had a walnut-finish beech stock, a 'blind' magazine contained entirely within the stock, and a sliding safety catch on the receiver side behind the bolt handle. Owing to the omission of a bolt shroud,

Winchester The Model 70 Magnum rifle.

Winchester A Model 70 Winlite rifle. US REPEATING ARMS COMPANY

Winchester The ·458 Model 70 African. US REPEATING ARMS COMPANY the cocking piece projected from the bolt sleeve when the action was cocked.

1971: chamberings had been reduced to ·243 Winchester and ·30–06 Springfield.

Model 770

Standard and Magnum patterns.
Made by the Winchester-Western Division of Olin Industries, New Haven, Connecticut, 1969–71.
·222 Remington, ·22–250, ·243 Winchester,
·264 Winchester Magnum, ·270 Winchester, 7mm Remington Magnum, ·30-06, ·300 Winchester Magnum or ·308 Winchester.
Action: generally as Model 54, above.
DATA FOR A TYPICAL RIFLE
·300 Winchester Magnum, belted rimless.
44·50in overall, 7·25lb unladen.
24·00in barrel, 6-groove rifling; RH, concentric.
Internal box magazine, 3 rounds.
Williams ramp sight.
3,070 ft/sec with 180-grain bullet.

☆

1969: introduced in Standard and Magnum form, with 22in and 24in barrels respectively, this occupied a niche in the market between the Models 70 and 670. Though it retained the blind magazine, the bolt was similar to the perfected Model 70—complete with guide rib, bolt shroud and the three-position safety.

Model 70

1968 TYPE
A, A Magnum, Custom, Custom Express, Custom Grade, Featherweight, Featherweight Classic, Featherweight Winlite, Featherweight Win-Tuff, International Army Match, Lightweight, Magnum, Mini-Carbine, Police, Sharpshooter, SHB, Sporter, Sporter DBM, Sporter SSM, Sporter Win-Tuff, Stainless, Standard, Super Express Magnum, Super Grade, Target, Ultra Match, Varmint, Winlite, Win-Cam, Win-Tuff, and XTR patterns.
Made in New Haven, Connecticut, by the Winchester-Western Division of Olin Industries (1968–81); and the US Repeating Arms Company (1981 to date)

Quantity: apparently in excess of 1·25 million.
Chambering: see text.
Action: generally as Model 54, above.
DATA FOR A TYPICAL FEATHERWEIGHT CLASSIC
·280 Remington, rimless.
42·50in overall, 7·25lb unladen.
22·00in barrel, 6-groove rifling; RH, concentric.
Internal box magazine, 5 rounds.
Spring-leaf and elevator sight.
2,970 ft/sec with 150-grain bullet.

☆

1968: another manufacturing pattern appeared, beginning with gun number 866000. A new guide slot in the bolt-head, patented by Robert Creamer in March 1969, engaged a narrow rib in the right side of the receiver to smooth the bolt stroke. All guns so fitted have a G-prefix number. The magazine follower was improved, no longer being riveted to the spring, and finish was improved. Knurling was added to the bolt handle knob.

1969: apart from the changes in the action, most of the new rifles duplicated their 1964-type equivalents. However, extensive revisions were made in the stocks.

The most basic patterns were Models 70A and 70A Magnum, which had Monte Carlo stocks with synthetic butt plates, and impressed chequering on the pistol grip and fore-end. The fore-end had a rounded tip. Standard Model 70A rifles lacked the floor plate assembly and had four-round 'blind' magazines. Their 22in barrels were chambered for ·222 Remington, ·22–250 Remington, ·243 Winchester, ·270 Winchester, ·30–06 or ·308 Winchester.

Magnum versions were offered for the ·264 Winchester or ·300 Winchester cartridges. They had 24in barrels, rubber recoil pads and three-round internal magazines.

The earliest Model 70 Standard rifles were similar to the 70A type, but had five-round staggered-column magazines and conventional magazine floor plates; chamberings duplicated the M70A list, with the addition of short-lived ·225 Winchester.

The Model 70 Magnum was similar to the M70 Standard rifle, but had a 24in barrel, an

additional recoil bolt beneath the chamber, and a ventilated rubber butt pad. Chamberings included a selection of most popular Magnum cartridges: ·264 Winchester, ·300 Winchester, ·338 Winchester or ·375 H&H. Excepting the ·375 version, which reached a hefty 8·8lb, the guns weighed 7·7–8lb.

The Model 70 Target rifle duplicated the original 1964 pattern, apart from the improved action. Model 70 Ultra Match was very similar, but had a counter-bored muzzle, a fibreglass bedded stock, and a trigger which could be adjusted externally.

Offered only in ·222 Remington, ·22–250 Remington or ·243 Winchester, M70 Varmint rifles were stocked identically with the M70 Standard variety apart from noticeably less drop at the heel. However, they had heavier barrels than normal and weighed 9·5–9·8lb.

The African Rifle was practically identical with the 1964 pattern, apart from the changes in its action. It was chambered only for the awesome ·458 Winchester Magnum round.

1972: machine-cut chequering replaced the impressed type and the contours of the butt—especially the Monte Carlo comb—were refined. The slab-sided fore-end, inspired by Weatherby patterns, had an ebonite tip and a white spacer.

A ·25–06 Remington option was introduced in this period for the Model 70A and Model 70 Standard (with 24in or 26in barrels), and the M70 Custom was renamed 'M70 Super Grade'.

1973: the International Army Match Rifle reappeared, identical with the 1964-type gun excepting for its improved action.

1974*: ·225 Winchester options were deleted.

1978: XTR ('Extra') rifles were introduced, distinguished by a high-polish blue finish and special walnut stocks with machine-cut wrap around chequering on the fore-end. The Monte Carlo combs were lower and appreciably longer than their predecessors.

Models 70, 70 Magnum, 70A, 70A Magnum could all be supplied in XTR guise, excepting the ·375 H&H version of the M70 Magnum.

1980*: the Model 70A Police was a short-lived version of the regular 70A pattern, offered with

Winchester Model 70 Lightweight. US REPEATING ARMS COMPANY

Winchester Featherweight Model 70. US REPEATING ARMS COMPANY

Winchester The standard M70 Sporter. US REPEATING ARMS COMPANY

an oil-finished stock in ·30–06 and ·308 only. It had been abandoned by 1983.

1981: the Model 70 XTR Featherweight was an M70 Standard rifle with a straight-comb walnut half-stock. Elegant schnabel fore-end tips were customary and the chequering included strap work. Weighing a mere 6·3–6·7lb, depending on chambering, the Featherweight rifle was introduced in ·243 Winchester, ·257 Roberts, ·270 Winchester, 7 × 57mm Mauser, ·30–06 Springfield or ·308 Winchester.

1982: the sale of Winchester's operations to the US Repeating Arms Company was accompanied by a change in the product range. Most of the older guns were discontinued, and the XTR stock became standard. XTR labels disappeared in the late 1980s, when supplies of the older-style guns had been exhausted. ·222 Remington chamberings were also abandoned, though the last Varmint rifles were not sold until 1985.

A Model 70 Westerner Rifle made a final, if brief appearance, chambered for the ·270 Winchester, 7mm Remington Magnum, ·300 Winchester Magnum, ·30–06 or ·308 rounds. It may simply have been the old Models 70 and 70 Magnum under a new name.

The Model 70 African Rifle was replaced by the Model 70 XTR Super Express Magnum, chambered for ·375 H&H or ·458 Winchester magnum rounds.

1984: a Model 70 Lightweight (·Carbine) was introduced in ·22–250, ·223 Remington, ·243 Winchester, ·270 Winchester, ·30–06 or ·308 Winchester. It had a 22in barrel, a light round tipped stock, and a weight of 6·3–6·5lb.

1985: a shorter version of the basic Model 70 action was introduced for cartridges shorter than ·308 Winchester. A few ·243 Model 70 Mini-Carbines dated from this period, one inch shorter in the butt than the XTR Sporter.

A ·22–250 option was added for the Model 70 XTR Sporter; ·223 Remington for the XTR Varmint pattern; and ·22–250, ·223 or ·25–06 for the XTR Featherweight.

1986: the Model 70 Winlite had a textured black McMillan fibreglass stock with a straight comb and conventional pistol grip. Chequering

was lacking. Stocks fitted to 22in-barrelled Featherweight actions had a shallow schnabel tip on the fore-end; 24in-barrelled Magnum patterns were rounded. Chamberings included ·270 Winchester, 7mm Remington Magnum, ·300 Weatherby Magnum, ·300 Winchester Magnum, ·30–06 or ·338 Winchester Magnum.

The walnut half-stocks fitted to Model 70 Lightweight guns had straight combs and tapering fore-ends with rounded tips. The rifles weighed 6–6·3lb, depending on type, and had 22in barrels. Magazines held five rounds (six in ·223 only), whilst the chamberings included ·22–250 Remington, ·223 Remington, ·243 Winchester, ·270 Winchester, ·280 Remington, ·30–06 or ·308 Winchester.

Model 70 Win-Cam rifles, available only in ·270 Winchester or ·30–06 Springfield, had a special warp-resistant laminated hardwood stock with a classic straight comb and green/brown camouflage finish. 24in barrels were standard, together with a rubber recoil pad. The receiver ring and bridge were drilled and tapped for optical-sight mounts.

Model 70 Win-Tuff rifles were similar, but had 22in barrels and brown laminated stocks. They were chambered for ·223 Remington, ·243 Winchester, ·270 Winchester, ·30–06 or ·308 Winchester.

Model 70 XTR Sporters had 24in barrels, three-round magazines, and walnut stocks with a longer and lower Monte Carlo comb than preceding Model 70 variants. Rubber butt plates were standard, together with drilled and tapped holes for optical-sight mounts on the receiver bridge and ring. Chamberings have included ·264 Winchester Magnum, 7mm Remington Magnum, ·300 Winchester Magnum and ·338 Winchester Magnum. The guns were about 44·5in overall and weighed 7·8lb.

1987: a ·25–06 option was introduced for the Model 70 XTR Sporter. The old ·257 Roberts and 7 × 57mm chamberings were deleted from the XTR Featherweight lists, but 6·5 × 55mm was added.

1988: Model 70 Featherweight Winlite (offered in ·270 Winchester, ·280 Remington or ·30–06)

had a textured McMillan fibreglass stock and weighed a mere 6·25lb.

New ·22–250, ·223 and ·280 Remington options were added for the Model 70 XTR Featherweight; ·280 Remington for the Model 70 Lightweight; ·22–250 Remington and ·243 Winchester for the Lightweight Win-Tuff; ·300 Weatherby Magnum for the standard Winlite sporter. Additional ·270 Weatherby, ·300 H&H and ·300 Weatherby magnum chamberings appeared for the 70 XTR Sporter Magnum.

Model 70 Super Express Walnut Magnum Winchesters had two steel recoil bolts in the stock, thermoplastic bedding, matt-black finish, open sights, and the front swivel eye on the barrel instead of the fore-end. Chambered only for ·375 H&H Magnum (24in barrel) and ·458 Winchester Magnum (22in), they weighed 8·5lb apiece and had three-round magazines.

1989: a revised Varmint Rifle had a standard Sporter stock—with Monte Carlo comb and cheek piece—plus a 26in heavyweight barrel with a counter-bored muzzle. The receiver was drilled and tapped for optical sight mounts. Weighing about 9lb, the Model 70 Varmint could be obtained in ·22–250, ·223 Remington, ·243 Winchester or ·308 Winchester.

1990: the Model 70 Super Grade was a deluxe version of the standard Sporter, made with a 24in barrel in ·270 Winchester, ·30–06, 7mm Remington Magnum, ·300 Winchester Magnum or ·338 Winchester Magnum. It weighed about 7·8lb unladen. The classic straight-comb stock had swivel eyes beneath butt and fore-end, but the hand-cut chequering lacked the strapwork of its Featherweight prototype. Super Grade rifles had a non-rotating collar-type extractor and were numbered in their own series.

·223 Remington and ·243 Winchester options were added for the standard 70 XTR Sporter.

1992: the Model 70 Stainless Rifle had a black fibreglass and graphite composite stock. The guns were available in ·270 Winchester and ·30–06 (22in barrels), or 7mm Remington Magnum, ·300 Winchester Magnum and ·338 Winchester Magnum (24in). Overall length was 43–45in, and weight averaged 6·75lb.

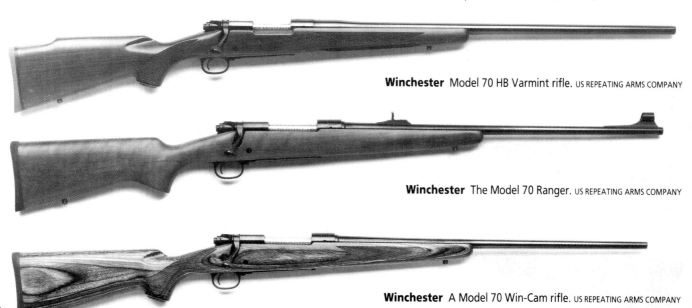

Winchester Model 70 HB Varmint rifle. US REPEATING ARMS COMPANY

Winchester The Model 70 Ranger. US REPEATING ARMS COMPANY

Winchester A Model 70 Win-Cam rifle. US REPEATING ARMS COMPANY

The Model 70 Featherweight Classic, with the non-rotating collar extractor, appeared in ·270 Winchester, ·280 Remington or ·30–06 Springfield. The gun had a standard straight comb Featherweight stock with a schnabel fore-end tip and riband chequering.

The Model 70 Win-Tuff Featherweight was also introduced, chambered for the ·22–250, ·223, ·243, ·270, ·30–06 or ·308 cartridges. Rifles had 22in barrels, were 42–42·5in overall, and weighed 6·75–7lb.

A Model 70 Sporter Win-Tuff had a brown laminated stock. The guns were 44·5in overall, with 24in barrels, and weighed 7·6–7·9lb. Chamberings included the ·270 Winchester, 7mm Remington Magnum, ·300 Weatherby Magnum, ·300 Winchester Magnum, ·30–06 Springfield or ·338 Winchester Magnum rounds.

The 24in-barrelled Model 70 SSM had a black composite fibreglass/graphite stock. Barrel and receiver had a non-reflective finish. Chamberings duplicated the Sporter Win-Tuff, apart from ·300 Weatherby Magnum.

The Model 70 Sporter DBM ('Detachable Box Magazine') was introduced for the ·270 Winchester, 7mm Remington Magnum, ·300 Winchester Magnum or ·30–06 rounds. The major identifying characteristic was the special three-round magazine. The guns were 44·5in long, had 24in barrels and weighed 7·8–7·9lb.

A ·308 Winchester Model 70 SHB ('synthetic [stock], heavy barrel') appeared. Measuring 46in overall, it shared the 26in heavy barrel of the Varmint rifles and weighed about 9lb.

A 7mm–08 Remington option was destined for the walnut stocked Model 70 Featherweight. **Note**: in addition to the patterns listed above, Winchester rifles have been made in a selection of deluxe versions. These have included the Model 70 Custom Grade, with selected wood-work and extensive engraving.

The Model 70 Custom Express chambered large cartridges such as ·375 H&H Magnum, ·375 JRS, ·416 Remington Magnum, ·458 Winchester Magnum or ·470 Capstick. It had a heavy 24in barrel (22in, ·458) and a three-leaf Express sight.

The Model 70 Sharpshooter, introduced in 1992, was made to order in ·300 Winchester Magnum or ·308 with a Schneider barrel and a synthetic McMillan A-2 target stock. A Harris bipod brought weight up to about 11lb.

Ranger

Standard and Youth patterns.
Made by the US Repeating Arms Company, New Haven, Connecticut, 1985 to date.
·223 Remington, ·243 Winchester, ·270 Winchester, 7mm Remington Magnum or ·30–06. See notes.
Action: generally as Model 54, above.
DATA FOR A TYPICAL RANGER
·243 Winchester, rimless.
42·00in overall, 6·75lb unladen.
22·00in barrel, 6-groove rifling; RH, concentric.
Internal box magazine, 5 rounds.
Folding leaf sight.
3,070 ft/sec with 100-grain bullet.

☆

1985: Ranger rifles (in ·270, 7mm Remington Magnum or ·30–06) were budget-price versions of the Model 70, with the standard action and a plain straight-comb hardwood stock. They lacked chequering, but were comparable with the Model 70 in most other respects.

The Ranger Youth Rifle was simply a Ranger with a short butt and the radius of the pistol grip tightened. Initially available only in ·223 Remington or ·243 Winchester, it was 41in long, had a 22in barrel and weighed 6·3lb.
1987: the ·223 (Youth) and 7mm Remington Magnum (Ranger) options were withdrawn.
1988: the ·243 chambering was extended to the Ranger, and ·308 to the Ranger Youth rifle.
1992: a ·223 Remington chambering was added to the list of Ranger patterns.

4. THE LEVER-ACTION PATTERNS

This section contains details only of the guns designed and manufactured in New Haven. The Browning designs—Models 1886, 1892, 1894 and 1895—are considered in detail in the 'Browning' section.
1860: Henry's Repeating Rifle, derived from the unsuccessful Volcanic repeater, was patented on 16 October.
1861: production began. The guns had 24in barrels with a bore diameter of ·420, and fired a rimfire cartridge containing 25 grains of black powder. Henry rifles had brass frames and hardwood butts, lacked fore-ends, and had tube magazines under the barrel.
1862: the first series-made Henrys became available in the summer, many selling to state and volunteer units in the face of official Federal Ordnance disapproval.
1865: only about 1,730 Henry Rifles had been acquired by Federal authorities by the end of the year. However, owing to many private sales, roughly ten thousand guns saw action during the American Civil War; total production amounted to about 11,500. The Henry was accurate and capable of high rates of fire—but complicated, delicate and surprisingly low powered.
1866: a new rifle was developed as soon as the Winchester Repeating Arms Company had succeeded to the assets of the moribund New Haven organisation. It was simply an improved Henry, with a hinged loading gate on the right side of the frame. Patented by Nelson King on 22 May, the gate permitted a fixed magazine and a sturdy wooden fore-end to be used.

The 1866-pattern Winchester remained low powered compared with many single-shot rivals. It was made as a rifle, with a 24in round or octagonal barrel; as a musket, with a 27in round barrel; and as a 20in-barrelled carbine. The tube magazines could hold a maximum of seventeen rounds for rifles or thirteen for carbines. The M1866 was finally dropped from the company catalogues in 1898, after about 170,100 had been made.
1873: a new centre-fire gun was introduced to supersede the M1866 and provide the basis for a series of similar guns. Its runaway success was due more to astute marketing and a high rate of fire than any great power.

Winchester The Ranger Youth Rifle. US REPEATING ARMS COMPANY

Winchester A Model 70 Featherweight Winlite rifle. US REPEATING ARMS COMPANY

Winchester The Model 1866 had a brass receiver. WALLIS & WALLIS

MILITARY RIFLES

The Models 1873 and 1876—together with the Browning-designed Model 1894—were offered as muskets or fully-stocked carbines, with military-style barrel bands and nose caps. They could also be fitted with bayonets. Authenticated sales are few, though 1,020 Model 1866 rifles chambering ·44 S&W centre-fire cartridges were sold to Brazil in 1891.

A few 1873-type guns were sold to interested parties in Central and South America, where they were favoured by rural gendarmerie and irregulars. Mexico, for example, had purchased about a thousand M1866 rifles for the forces of Benito Juarez (delivered in 1867) and an unknown quantity of M1894 carbines for the 'Rurales' (rural gendarmerie) about 1903.

The best-known purchaser, however, was Turkey. Sufficient M1873 muskets had been acquired to play a decisive role in the repulse of the Russians during the battle of Plevna (1878).

Large quantities of commercial-type M1894 rifles and carbines were purchased by the British and the French at the beginning of the First World War, but neither army used them for anything more than training.

SPAIN

The Spanish bought small numbers of 1873 type muskets and carbines from Winchester in 1878, the former having three barrel bands, and the latter a band and a nose cap. Muskets apparently had leaf-pattern back sights and could accept socket bayonets. The Winchester soon proved effectual enough to be copied.

Model 1873

Carbine: Tercerola Winchester Mo.1873.
Made by Fábrica de Artilleria, Oviedo, 1891–2.
Quantity: apparently 2,500.
Lever action, locked by a toggle joint.
10mm, rimmed (·44–40 WCF).
972mm overall, weight unknown.
507mm barrel, 4-groove rifling; RH, concentric?
Tube magazine under barrel, 10 rounds.
Leaf sight graduated to 800 metres.
About 385 m/sec with Spanish-made cartridges.
No bayonet.
☆

1891: production of these carbines began in the Oviedo factory, work being completed in 1892. They were to be issued to the royal bodyguard and the 14th troop of the Guardia Civil.
1893: by an order of 2 December, the guns were officially designated 'Tercerola Mo.1873'. They were essentially similar to American-made guns purchased in 1878–9, but quality was noticeably poorer. An encircled crown, OVIEDO and the date were stamped into the right side of the butt, together with the serial number (e.g., 'No. 1711').

SPORTING GUNS

The first of these developed from the Henry rifle by way of the rimfire Winchester Model 1866.

Model 1873

Offered as a rifle, carbine or musket.
Made by the Winchester Repeating Arms Company, New Haven, Connecticut, 1873–c.1924.
Quantity: 720,610.
·32–20 Winchester, ·38–40 Winchester or ·44–40 Winchester.
Lever action, locked by a toggle-joint.
DATA FOR TYPICAL EXAMPLE
·44–40 Winchester, rimmed.
43·75in overall, 8·87lb unladen.
24·00in barrel, 6-groove rifling; RH, concentric.
Tube magazine under barrel, 15 rounds.
Spring-leaf and elevator sight.
1,310 ft/sec with 200-grain bullet.
☆

1873: the 1866-type rifle, despite its success, was handicapped by its weak rimfire cartridge. The new centre-fire M1873 was similar to its predecessor externally, but had an iron receiver and mounts. Unlike the flush-sided M1866, but in common with the later M1876, the 1873 pattern gun had a prominent raised panel on the left side of the receiver. It was offered as a Sporting Rifle with a 20in octagonal barrel or a 24in round, half- or fully-octagonal pattern; as a Musket with a 30in round barrel; and as a 20in round-barrelled carbine. The rifle magazines held fifteen rounds, the carbines held twelve and the muskets could hold seventeen. Decoration, barrel length and details of finish were often left to the whim of the customer. Consequently, guns could be found with half-length (six round) magazine tubes, set triggers, unusually short or extraordinarily long barrels, or shotgun-pattern butts. Unusually accurate barrels were often finished as 'One of One Thousand' (best) or 'One of One Hundred' (second-best) guns.

Sights were customarily open spring-leaf and ramp patterns, though military-style leaf sights were favoured on muskets, and folding leaves or tang-mounted vernier sights could be provided on Special Sporting Rifles. Muskets and some military-contract carbines were provided with barrel bands and nose caps; socket bayonets predominated, though brass-hilted sword types were also available.
1876: the original screw-pattern lever retainer was replaced by a sliding catch.
1879: alterations were made to the finger lever so that the trigger could not operate until the action was completely closed. The breech cover was altered to slide on a rib held to the receiver with two screws, a solid-face bolt was fitted, and the standard butt—with a crescent-shape butt plate—was supplemented by an optional straight or 'shotgun' pattern. The ·38–40 chambering was developed during the year and announced at the beginning of 1880.
1882: ·32–20 Winchester was added to the cartridge options.
1884: the iron receiver was substituted by a forged-steel pattern with an integral breech-cover rib. A special rimfire M1873 rifle appeared, lacking the loading gate on the receiver-side. It was made until 1904.
1919: the centre-fire M1873 patterns were all discontinued, though guns assembled from a variety of parts were available in small numbers until the mid 1920s.

Winchester Capable of handling powerful cartridges, the M1876 was also offered as a musket.

WALLIS & WALLIS

Winchester The 1873-pattern sporting rifle was made in large numbers until the 1920s.

Winchester A typical fully stocked M1873 musket.

Model 1876

Offered as a rifle, carbine or musket.
Made by the Winchester Repeating Arms Company,
New Haven, Connecticut, 1876–97.
Quantity: 63,870.
·40–60 Winchester, ·45–60 Winchester, ·45–75
Winchester or ·50–95 Winchester.
Action: as M1873, above.
DATA FOR A TYPICAL EXAMPLE
·50–95 Winchester, rimmed.
47·88in overall, 9·15lb unladen.
26·00in barrel, 6-groove rifling; RH, concentric.
Tube magazine under barrel, 4 rounds.
Spring-leaf and elevator sight.
1,555 ft/sec with 300-grain bullet.

☆

1872: an experimental ·45–70–405 rifle,
patented by Luke Wheelock in January 1871,
was submitted unsuccessfully to the US Army.
1876: prototype rifles chambering a ·45–75
cartridge, powerful enough to down virtually
any North American game, were exhibited at
the Centennial Exposition in Philadelphia.
1877: the first series-made guns were shipped
from the New Haven factory in June. The
M1876 was offered as a Sporting Rifle with a
28in round, half- or fully-octagonal barrel; as an
Express Rifle, with a 26in barrel in each of three
standard patterns; as a fully stocked Musket,
with a 32in round barrel, bands and a bayonet;
and as a 22in barrelled carbine. Magazine tubes
held nine (carbine), twelve (rifle) or thirteen
(musket) rounds, though half-length six-round
magazines were available to order. Like all
Winchesters of this period, the M1876 rifles
could be fitted to the customer's requirements
and came in a bewildering profusion of styles
from 'One of One Thousand' grade downward.
The Special Sporting Rifle, for example, had a
pistol-grip stock and was often furnished with a
vernier sight on the tang behind the hammer.
1879: ·40–60 and ·50–95 Winchester were
added to the chambering options. A trigger-lock
was developed, and a breech-cover sliding on a
rib appeared. The rib was held to the receiver
with two screws.

1883: the first of about 750 full-stock Model
1876 carbines were purchased by the Royal
North-West Mounted Police of Canada.
1884: A change to a forged-steel receiver with
an integral breech-cover rib was made. The first
·40–60 Winchester rifles became available.

Note: for details of the Models 1886, 1892,
1894 and 1895 (excepting the modern Model
94), see 'Browning'.

Model 53

Made by the Winchester Repeating Arms Company,
New Haven, Connecticut, 1924–32.
Quantity: 24,920.
·25–20 Winchester, ·38–40 Winchester or
·44–40 Winchester.
Lever action, locked by a vertically-sliding bar.
DATA FOR A TYPICAL EXAMPLE
·38–40 Winchester, rimmed.
39·50in overall, 5·80lb unladen.
22·00in barrel, 6-groove rifling; RH, concentric.
Tube magazine under barrel, 6 rounds.
Spring-leaf and elevator sight.
1,330 ft/sec with 180-grain bullet.

☆

1924: this was an attempt to simplify the range
of options available with Winchester rifles. The
1892-pattern action was retained in a slightly
altered form, but only a single barrel option was
offered and standard guns all had a half-length
magazine contained in the fore-end. The butt
was usually straight wristed, though pistol-grip
patterns could be obtained on request.
1932: the Model 53 was replaced by the Model
65. The production total should be considered as
an approximation, as receivers were apparently
numbered in series with the Model 1892.

Model 55

Made by the Winchester Repeating Arms Company,
New Haven, Connecticut, 1924–32.
Quantity: 20,580.
·25–35 Winchester, ·30–30 Winchester or ·32
Winchester Special.

Action: as Model 53, above.
DATA FOR A TYPICAL EXAMPLE
·30–30 Winchester, rimmed.
42·10in overall, 6·81lb unladen.
24·00in barrel, 6-groove rifling; RH, concentric.
Tube magazine under barrel, 3 rounds.
Spring-leaf and elevator sight.
2,410 ft/sec with 150-grain bullet.

☆

1924: introduced to accompany the Model 53,
this simplification of the M1894 offered a more
limited range of options than purchasers had
previously been granted. The round barrel was
accompanied by a half-length magazine in the
fore-end, which restricted capacity too greatly to
have universal appeal. A straight-wrist butt was
regarded as standard, though a pistol-grip pattern
was available on order.
1932: the Model 55 was superseded by the
Model 64 (q.v.). The production total given
above is an approximation; after about 2,700
guns had been made, receivers were taken from
the same number series as M1894 carbines.

Model 64

Made by the Winchester Repeating Arms Company,
New Haven, Connecticut, 1933–57.
Quantity: 66,780.
·219 Zipper, ·25–35 Winchester, ·30–30 Winchester
or ·32 Winchester Special
Action: as Model 53, above.
DATA FOR A TYPICAL EXAMPLE
·25–35 Winchester, rimmed.
42·50in overall, 7·78lb unladen.
24·00in barrel, 6-groove rifling; RH, concentric.
Tube magazine under barrel, 5 rounds.
Spring-leaf and elevator sight.
2,300 ft/sec with 117-grain bullet.

☆

1933: the spartan lines of the Model 55, and
the limited options available to the purchaser,
restricted sales far more than Winchester had
predicted. The Model 64, announced in March,
had a longer magazine tube—protruding from
the fore-end—and a refined trigger mechanism.
Standard Rifles had a pistol-grip butt and a 20in

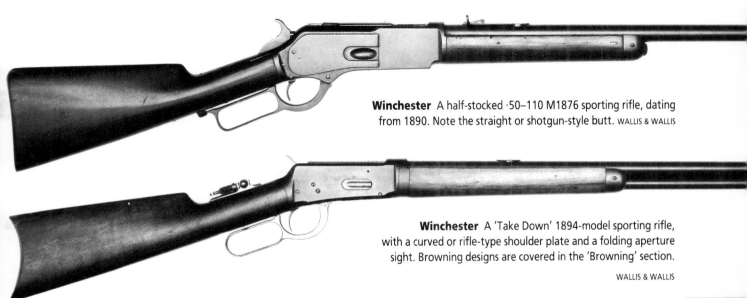

Winchester A half-stocked ·50–110 M1876 sporting rifle, dating
from 1890. Note the straight or shotgun-style butt. WALLIS & WALLIS

Winchester A 'Take Down' 1894-model sporting rifle,
with a curved or rifle-type shoulder plate and a folding aperture
sight. Browning designs are covered in the 'Browning' section.

WALLIS & WALLIS

or 24in round barrel. The guns all had a hooded front-sight blade on a forged ramp.

1934: the Deer Rifle was announced, with a rubber pistol-grip cap, a 20in or 24in round barrel, and detachable swivels.

1938: a ·219 Zipper variant of the Sporting Rifle appeared, but lasted a mere three years.

Model 65

Made by the Winchester Repeating Arms Company, New Haven, Connecticut, 1933–47.
Quantity: 5,700.
·218 Bee, ·25–20 Winchester or ·32–20 Winchester.
Action: as Model 53, above.
DATA FOR A TYPICAL EXAMPLE
·25–20 Winchester, rimmed.
39·63in overall, 6·47lb unladen.
22·00in barrel, 6-groove rifling; RH, concentric.
Tube magazine under barrel, 6 rounds.
Spring-leaf and elevator sight.
1,460 ft/sec with 86-grain bullet

☆

1933: announced on 1 March, this was an improved version of the Model 53 (M1892) with a refined trigger and an improved front sight on a forged ramp. It was offered with a 22in round barrel and a pistol-grip butt.

1939: a special 24in-barrelled ·218 Bee variant was announced, enjoying a brief period in vogue before the Second World War began.

Model 71

Made by the Winchester Repeating Arms Company, New Haven, Connecticut, 1935–57.
Quantity: 47,250.
·348 Winchester, rimmed.
Action: as Model 53, above.
44·58in overall, 7·95lb unladen.
24·00in barrel, 6-groove rifling; RH, concentric.
Tube magazine under barrel, 4 rounds.
Aperture sight on receiver.
2,530 ft/sec with 200-grain bullet.

☆

1936: announced on 1 January, this was an improved form of the M1886 specially adapted

for a powerful new cartridge suitable for game shooting. Made with a 24in barrel, the rifles had chequered pistol-grip butts, rubber pistol grip caps, beaver-tail fore-ends and detachable swivels. A plain-butt gun was authorised on 6 January. Some guns were sold with spring-leaf and elevator back sights, but most mounted the aperture pattern.

1937: a version with a 20in round barrel was announced in January. On 3 September, a long comb butt was substituted and a safety catch was added to the lower tang.

Model 94

Angle Eject, Antique, Big Bore, Classic, Deluxe, Long Barrel, Ranger, Side Eject, Standard, Trapper, Win-Tuff, Wrangler, Wrangler II and XTR patterns. For details of commemorative guns, see Part Two.
Made in New Haven, Connecticut, by the Winchester Repeating Arms Company (1894–1961), the Winchester-Western Division of Olin Industries (1961–81) and the US Repeating Arms Company (1981 to date),
Quantity: more than seven million.
Chambering: see notes.
Action: as Model 53, above.
DATA FOR A TYPICAL MODEL 94 STANDARD
7 × 30 Waters, rimmed.
37·25in overall, 6·65lb unladen.
20·00in barrel, 6-groove rifling; RH, concentric?
Tube magazine beneath barrel, 6 rounds.
Spring-leaf and elevator sight.
2,600 ft/sec with 139-grain bullet.

☆

1894: this Browning designed rifle, specifically intended for smokeless cartridges, was patented in August. Its history prior to 1936—when the sale of rifles ceased and all chamberings except ·44–40 were withdrawn—will be found in the Browning section.

1940: the ·25–35 Winchester chambering was reinstated, lasting for a decade.

1946: production began again after the end of the Second World War. The standard Model 1894 Carbine had a plain straight-wrist walnut

butt and a half-length fore-end held by a single band. The front sight had a detachable hood, a traditional spring-leaf and elevator back sight was fitted, and the receiver was drilled and tapped for optical sight mounts. Made with a 20in barrel, the guns were about 37·7in overall and weighed 6lb. A six-round magazine tube lay beneath the barrel.

1964: the Model 94 Antique Carbine appeared, chambered only for ·30–30 Winchester rounds. It had a colour case-hardened receiver with rolled-in scrollwork. The loading gate was brass plated and a saddle ring was fitted on the left rear side of the receiver.

1968: introduction of the Model 94 Classic rifle (with a 26in octagonal barrel) or carbine (20in barrel) was announced. Receivers and fore-end caps were black chrome, butt plates were blued and loading gates were gold plated. Classic patterns were not popular, however, and had been abandoned by 1971.

1978: the Model 94 XTR Big Bore carbine was specifically designed for the ·375 Winchester cartridge. The new reinforced receiver was machined from a solid billet of ordnance steel. Chequered walnut woodwork, a rubber butt plate and high-polish finish were standard.

XTR woodwork—better stock finish, cut chequering—and the high-polish blue finish were extended to standard gun, which became the 'Model 94 XTR Carbine'.

1980: Model 94 Trapper Carbines were made with 16in barrels, restricting magazine capacity to five ·30–30 WCF rounds instead of six. The front sight was moved back behind the barrel/magazine tube retaining collar. Overall length was 33·7in; weight averaged 6·2lb.

1983: the Model 94 Angle Eject carbine (·307, ·356 or ·375 Winchester) appeared in standard or XTR form, with an idiosyncratic Monte Carlo comb/straight wrist butt. Specifically designed for use with low-mounted optical sights, Angle Eject guns—later known as 'Side Eject'—were distinguished by the lowered right receiver wall. A lateral extension was added to the hammer spur to facilitate cocking with an optical sight above the receiver, and a transfer-bar safety

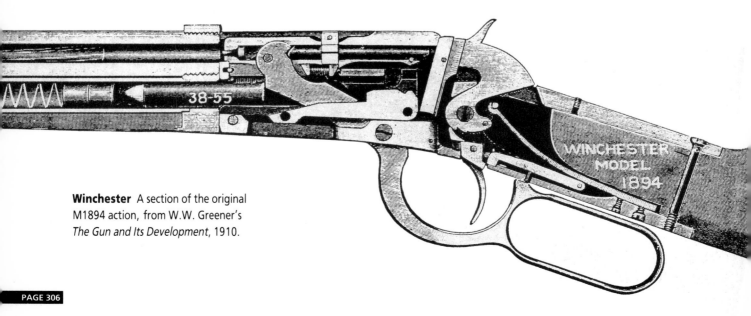

Winchester A section of the original M1894 action, from W.W. Greener's *The Gun and Its Development*, 1910.

system was added. Detachable swivels were usually fitted to the butt and magazine tube. The guns were 38·65in long, had 20in barrels and weighed 7lb; six-round magazines were used.

A Model 94 Wrangler Carbine appeared, chambered exclusively for the ·32 Winchester Special cartridge. Based on the Trapper, with the same 16in barrel, it had a roll-engraved Western scene on the receiver and an enlarged lever loop.

1984: the Model 94 Antique Carbine was discontinued and the Angle Eject feature was extended to the standard Model 94—offered in ·30–30 Winchester, ·38–55 Winchester, ·44 Remington Magnum/·44 S&W Special (fully interchangeable) or ·45 Colt. Magazines held six or eleven rounds, depending on whether the cartridge had been a rifle or handgun type.

A 7 × 30 Waters option was introduced for the XTR carbine and rifle, made with 20in and 24in barrels respectively. Overall length of the rifle was 41·7in, weight averaged 7lb, and a seven-round magazine was fitted; the carbine magazines contained one round fewer. Rifles lacked the front sight hood associated with most of the short-barrel guns.

Substantial quantities of ·38–55 Model 94 Wrangler II Angle Eject carbines were made in this period. They had 16in barrels, 'engraving' rolled into the receiver, and the characteristic ultra-large lever loop.

1985: the Model 94 Ranger (·30–30 only) had beech woodwork and a five-cartridge magazine. The front-sight hood was omitted, but the gun was identical mechanically with the standard Angle Eject Model 94.

1986: ·356 and ·375 Big Bore chamberings were discontinued.

1987: sales of Model 94 Winchesters of all types reached seven million, but the 20in heavy barrel and Monte Carlo butt options were abandoned.

1988: announced at the end of the preceding year, the Model 94 Win-Tuff (·30–30 only) had a laminated stock. The introduction of these special stocks has often led to the inclusion of 'Walnut' in standard designations.

A Model 94 XTR Deluxe was introduced in ·30–30, with a 20in barrel and the standard

high-polish finish. Its select woodwork had cut fleur-de-lys chequering, and the blued receiver displayed a roll-engraved cursive 'Deluxe'.

A Model 94 Long-Barrel Rifle had a 24in barrel chambered for the ·30–30 cartridge. The guns also had an open front sight, a long fore-end extending past the retaining band, and a seven-round magazine.

The ·356 Winchester Big Bore chambering reappeared after an absence of only two years.

1991: Model 94 guns were fitted with a safety bolt through the receiver ahead of the hammer.

1992: changes were made in the lever system to make its operation smoother and quieter, new-style guns being distinguished by an additional link pin and set screw in the mechanism. The ·32 Winchester Special chambering option was introduced for the standard Model 94; a ·357 Magnum option was announced for the Trapper; and the 94 Wrangler reappeared in ·30–30 or ·44 Remington Magnum/·44 S&W Special.

Model 88

Made by the Winchester Repeating Arms Company, New Haven, Connecticut, 1955–73.
·243 Winchester, ·284 Winchester, ·308 Winchester or ·358 Winchester.
Lever action, locked by three lugs on the bolt head rotating into the receiver.
DATA FOR A TYPICAL EXAMPLE
·284 Winchester, rimless.
42·10in overall, 6·53lb unladen.
22·00in barrel, 6-groove rifling; RH, concentric.
Detachable box magazine, 3 rounds.
Lyman No.16A folding-leaf sight.
2,900 ft/sec with 150-grain bullet.

☆

1955: this interesting rifle, introduced in ·308 and ·358, was developed to fire pointed-nose cartridges. The streamlined receiver contained a rotating bolt-type locking mechanism, operated by a special short-throw lever system. It also had a one-piece stock, with chequering on the pistol grip and fore-end; a nylon grip cap and butt plate; and swivels placed conventionally beneath the fore-end and butt. Magazine capacity was

listed as four rounds, increased to five in 1956; this seems to have strained the feed spring, as a reversion to four was made in 1957.

1956: a ·243 option was announced.

1962: the ·358 chambering was abandoned, as a new ·284 option was being developed.

1965: basket weave chequering appeared.

1968: a 19-in-barrelled carbine was introduced, with a plain stock and a swivel on a barrel band.

ZOLI

ITALY

Antonio Zoli makes a bolt-action rifle embodying a 'modified Mauser' action with twin opposed lugs on the bolt head and a recessed bolt-face.

AZ 1900

Made by Antonio Zoli SpA, Gardone Val Trompia.
·243 Winchester, 6·5 × 55mm Mauser, 6·5 × 57mm, ·270 Winchester, 7 × 64mm, ·30–06 or ·308 Winchester.
Turning-bolt action, locked by two lugs on the bolt head rotating into the receiver wall and the bolt handle turning down into its seat.
DATA FOR A TYPICAL MAGNUM
7mm Remington Magnum, belted rimless.
1,135mm overall, 3·40kg unladen.
610mm barrel, 4-groove rifling; RH, concentric.
Detachable box magazine, 4 rounds.
Folding leaf sight.
3,260 ft/sec with 150-grain bullet.

☆

1989: the rifle had a neatly contoured bolt shroud, and a rocking safety catch on the right side of the action behind the bolt handle. Its magazine floor-plate was released by a catch in the front of the trigger guard. Woodwork was generally European walnut. Swivels lay under the fore-end and the butt. The standard rifles were 1,060mm long, had 540mm barrels, and weighed about 3·25kg. Five-round magazines were customary.

1991: the AZ 1900M featured a Bell & Carlson composite synthetic stock.

ANTONIO ZOLI SPA

Zoli A typical AZ1900 bolt-action rifle.

Winchester A standard side-ejecting Model 1894 carbine, with a 4 × optical sight. US REPEATING RIFLE COMPANY

Winchester Model 1894 Big Bore guns have reinforced receivers.
US REPEATING RIFLE COMPANY

Index

The index contains details of significant pre-1875 cartridge rifles, and a limited number of experimental guns; however, those that were produced on a speculative basis for military trials have been omitted whilst additional research into their history is undertaken. It is hoped to expand coverage in the future, and readers wishing to help are encouraged to make contact by way of the publisher.
¶ Page references are given where a major entry is included in Part One; otherwise, a simple section reference suffices. A 't' suffix indicates that the reference occurs in an information panel.
¶ The system may require a search of several pages, but should be inconvenient only in lengthy entries (e.g., Lee, Mannlicher or Mauser). The nationality of manufacturers, inventors or patentees may limit the search.

AAI Corp.: ArmaLite (USA).
Accuracy International: 13.
Adjustable Ranging Telescope (ART): see 'Leatherwood'.
Akah brandname: see 'Albrecht Kind'.
Albini Augusto, and Albini-Braendlin rifles: 13, 14t.
Aldis Bros.: Lee (turning-bolt, military, Britain).
Allin Erskine S., and Trapdoor Springfields: 13–16, 14t.
Alpha Arms, Inc.: 17.
Altenburger Ernst: Mauser (auto-loading, Germany).
AMAC American Military Arms Corp.: 17.
Amberg Bavarian/German arms factory: Mannlicher (bolt-action, military, Germany), Werder.
American Legion: Garand.
American Machine & Foundry Co.: Garand.
American Military Arms Corp.: AMAC.
Amsler Rudolf: SIG.
Anciens Établissements: see 'Pieper'.
Ancion & Co.: Comblain (Belgium).
Anschütz J.G., GmbH: 17–18. See also Haenel.
APX Ateliers de Puteaux: see 'CTV'.
Arbeitsgemeinschaft Haenel: see 'C.G. Haenel'.
Arbuthnot Col. Henry: Burton (Britain).
Arellano Antonio Ramirez de: Mauser (Spain).
Arisaka Col. Nariake, and rifles: 18–22, 21t.
ArmaLite Division of Fairchild Engine & Airplane Corp.; ArmaLite, Inc.; and ArmaLite Corp.: 22–27, 24t. See also Chartered Industries, Dae Woo.
Armament Corporation Pty ('Armscor'): Saive (235t).
Armee-Universal-Gewehr ('AUG'): Steyr.
Armeria: 'Fabrica de Armas de Republica Dominicana'.
Armi-Jager: see 'Jager-Armi'.
Armscor: Saive (235t).
Artillerie-Inrichtingen: ArmaLite.
Artistic Arms: Borchardt (38t).
A-Square Co., Inc.: 27.
Atkin Henry: see 'Atkin, Grant & Lang'.
Atkin, Grant & Lang: Mauser, 192t.
Auto-Ordnance Corp.: Winchester (auto-loading patterns). See also 'Thompson', below.
Avtomat: Federov, Kalashnikov.
Avis Rifle Barrel Co.: Springfield.
Aydt Carl Wilhelm: 27.

Ball R., & Co.: Ballard.
Ball & Williams: Ballard.
Ballard Charles H., and rifles: 28–30, 29t.
Bandell & Neal: Marlin.
Bandung Indonesian arms factory: FN, Garand.
Bang See also Garand, Mauser, Walther. Credited to Søren H. Bang, this Danish rifle was tested by many armies in the early years of the twentieth century and is included in the current edition of *Military Small Arms of the 20th Century* (p.142). Though touted for some time, the muzzle-cup system was found wanting on trial. The German Gew.41 (Mauser and Walther) used a variation of the Bang system.

Bannerman Francis, & Sons: Chaffee-Reece.
Barnes Charles: Enfield (turning-bolt, sporting, USA).
Barnitske Karl: Gustloff.
Barrett Firearms Mfg., Inc.: 30.
Barry C.C.G., and safety catch: Krag-Jørgensen (military, Denmark).
Bathurst Australian arms factory: Lee (turning-bolt, military, Australia).
Beardmore Engineering Co.: Martini (military, Britain).
Beaumont Frans [de], and rifles: 30–1. See also Gras.
Beck George: Marlin.
Beeman Precision Arms: Krico.
Bellmore-Johnson Tool Co.: Borchardt (38t).
Bennett Joseph: Ross.
Benson Carl: Mossberg.

BERDAN See pp.30–2 for details of the bolt-action guns. The block-action rifles were made in two basic patterns—conversions of rifle-muskets, distinguished by an external hammer, and a simplified newly-made version with a linear striker system

SPAIN

Trials began in 1865 with more than a hundred breech systems, the authorities selecting the 'No.3' Berdan after minor changes had been made by a military commission.
M1867 infantry rifle Adopted on 14 December 1867, the Fusil para Infanteria Mo.1867 was converted by Ybarzabal of Eibar, Orbea Hermanos y Cia de Eibar, and Euscalduna of Planencia from Mo.59 rifle-muskets originally made in the government factory. Locks bore the original marks—a crown over an 'AR' monogram, above 'O' for 'Oviedo' and the date. The guns chambered a rimmed cartridge with a nominal calibre of 15mm. Once the hammer had been thumbed back to half cock, the breech block could be lifted up and forward by a small lever. The nose of the original hammer was bent up and back to strike the firing pin running through the breech block. The Mo.1867 rifle was 1,389mm overall, weighed 4·28kg, and had a 920mm barrel rifled with four concentric grooves. The ramp-and-leaf sight was graduated to 1,000 metres, muzzle velocity was about 364 m/sec with Mo.1867 ball cartridges, and the Mo.1857 socket bayonet could be fitted. The one-piece stock had three screw-clamping bands and a small nose cap. Swivels lay under the butt on the elongated trigger-guard tang, and on the middle band; the cramped trigger guard was characteristic of Spanish designs of the 1850s.
M1867 short rifle The Fusil para Cazadores Mo.1867 was similar to the infantry pattern. Converted from Mo.1857 and Mo.1857/59 cap-locks, two differing patterns were stocked similarly with two screw-clamping bands and identical ramrods. However, the Mo.57 had a generous trigger-guard bow and a round-edged butt plate; the Mo.57/59 had the cramped trigger guard and a much flatter butt plate. Similarly, though both were hinged at the rear, the Mo.57 sight ramp rose toward the muzzle while the Mo.57/59 type rose at the breech. The Mo.1857/67 was 1,230mm overall and weighed 3·83kg. It had a 770mm barrel, whilst the ramp-and-leaf sight was graduated to 900 metres. Muzzle velocity was about 335 m/sec and the Mo.1857 socket bayonet could be attached.
M1867 artillery and engineers carbine The Carabina para Artilleria e Ingenieros shared the action of the infantry rifle. It was adapted from the rifled engineer carbine of 1858, which was a variant of the Carabina Rayada para Cazadores Mo.57/59 (above) with the bands moved closer together to expose more of the muzzle. Artillerymen carried the Machete Bayoneta Mo.1858, which had a broad falchion-like blade and a cast-brass grip; unlike any other Spanish pattern, it also had a socket and locking ring on the guard. A typical 'Mo.58/67' was 1,230mm overall, weighed 3·77kg, and had a 770mm barrel.

The 1861-type engineer carbine was also altered to Mo.1867 standards, but only in small numbers. Its machete bayonet (Mo.1861) had a conventional guard and a spring-and-stud mechanism in the pommel. The carbine had less of the muzzle exposed than the otherwise similar Mo.58, the bayonet lug and tenon distinguishing it from the 'para Cazadores' Mo.59 adaption.
M1867 navy short rifle The Carabina para Infanteria de Marina was converted from Mo.1858 cap-lock naval short rifles that had been made by Juan Aldasoro of Eibar in 1860–1. They were similar to the infantry short rifle (above), with the back sight and butt plate of the Mo.57—the latter in brass—plus the Mo.59 trigger guard. The bayonet had a cast-brass hilt.

RUSSIA
M1868 infantry rifle About 30,000 of these guns (Pekhotniya vintovka Berdana, obr.1868g) were acquired from Colt in 1869–70. They chambered a 10·67 × 58mm rimmed cartridge, measured 1,346mm overall and weighed about 4·25kg. The 825mm barrel had six-groove concentric rifling with a right-hand twist. The leaf-type back sight was graduated to 1,400 arshin, muzzle velocity was about 442 m/sec and the obr.1868g socket bayonet was issued.
¶ The improved linear striker was used and the barrel top was marked in Cyrillic. There were two screw-clamped iron barrel bands and a trigger guard with a small spur on the rear tang. Swivels lay on the front band and trigger-guard bow; a cleaning rod was carried under the barrel. However, the rifle was soon replaced by the bolt-action Berdan No.2.
M1868 carbine Dating from about 1873, this was simply a shortened version of the infantry rifle, stocked to the muzzle and unable to accept a bayonet. The carbines are believed to have been converted from rifles, but may only have been used for field trials.

BERETTA The modern rifles are described on pp.33–4; see also Garand, Mannlicher, SIG (military, Chile), Vetterli (military, Italy). During the 1930s, under the supervision of Tullio Marengoni, auto-loading rifles were made. By 1939, however, the Beretta had been rejected in favour of the Revelli Armaguerra design.
1931-type rifle The Fucile automatico Beretta Mo.931 was subjected to Italian army trials in the early 1930s. It was an orthodox gas-operated weapon with a recoil-spring housing protruding back above the straight-wrist butt. The lower part of the integral clip-loaded magazine case pivoted forward when the catch on the side of the butt was released. Ventilating holes were cut through the fore-end and half-length hand guard. Chambered for the standard 6·5 × 52mm rimless cartridge, it was about 1,155mm overall and weighed 4·07kg unladen. The 600mm barrel had four-groove concentric rifling, twisting to the right, the magazine held six rounds, and the quadrant sight was graduated to 1,500 metres. The nose cap accepted the Mo.1891 sword bayonet.
1937-type rifle The improved 7·35mm Mo.1937 was 1,060mm overall, had a 485mm barrel and weighed 3·94kg. A notched block sufficed as a 300-metre sight and the Mo.91–38 knife bayonet could be attached when required. The Mo.1937 shared the rotating-bolt locking system of its predecessor,but chambered a more potent cartridge. The magazine was changed, eliminating the pivoting section, and charger guides were added to the front of the recoil-spring housing. The butt was given a shallow pistol grip; ventilating holes were cut through the half-length hand guard; and the fore-end between the barrel band and the nose cap was replaced by a fluted metal section.

Berlin-Lübecker Maschinenfabrik: Mauser (turning-bolt patterns, military, Germany), Walther.

Bang A 7·9mm gun tested in Britain in 1926–7. PATTERN ROOM COLLECTION

Beretta The 6·5mm M1931 rifle. PIETRO BERETTA SPA

Beretta The 7·35mm M1937 rifle. PIETRO BERETTA SPA

Engh A section of this unusual bolt-action rifle.

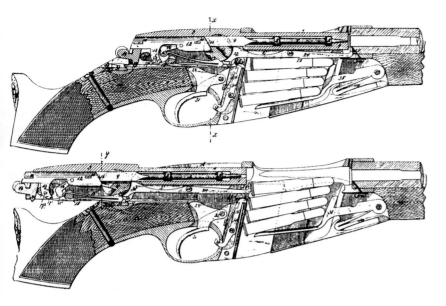

February 1929 in favour of ·276. However, after tests undertaken throughout the summer of 1929—with Brauning, Colt-Browning, Holek, T1 Pedersen, T3 Garand, Thompson, Rheinmetall and White rifles—work on the ·30-calibre Garand recommenced. A suitable prototype was ordered from Springfield Armory on 14 November.

·30 T1E1 rifle During the spring of 1931, Springfield Armory completed twenty ·276 T3E2 Garands for trials against the ·276 T1 Pedersens until a suitable ·30 rifle was available. The first ·30 T1E1 Garand appeared in the autumn of 1931, but broke its bolt on trial.

·30 T1E2 rifle Owing greatly to General Douglas MacArthur, ·276 was officially abandoned in February 1932 and an order for 125 ·276 T3E2 Garands was rescinded. The ·30 T1E1 Garand was successfully re-tested in March 1932 and 77 guns were ordered to facilitate field trials. Eighty 'Semi-automatic Rifles, ·30, T1E2' were ordered in March 1932 and the T1 Pedersen (q.v.) was abandoned.

T27 rifle Based on the M1, this chambered the ·30 T65 cartridge, but the project terminated in March 1948.

T35 rifle Fifty of these semi-automatics, based on the M1, were built before the project terminated in 1950—to be briefly revived in the mid 1950s without success.

T36 rifle This was a derivative of the T20E2 (Part One) with a lightweight barrel designed by Lloyd Corbett at Springfield Armory in November 1949; it chambered the ·30 T65 cartridge and was capable of selective fire. Suspended by the outbreak of the Korean War in 1950, the project was soon resurrected and the rifle became the T44.

Farrow Milton, and his butt plate: Ballard.
FAVS Fabbrica Armi Valle Susa: Mauser (194t).
Fazakerley arms factory: Lee (bolt-action, Britain).
Federov Vladimir G.: 66–7. Trials began in the USSR in January 1926 with two differing Degtyarev designs, a Tokarev and a modified Avtomat. However, even the best gun—one of the Fedorovs—jammed more than sixty times in 5,200 shots. The inventors were given six months to develop guns to a new specification: a barrel of 630mm, a 'needle bayonet', a five- or ten-round magazine and an aperture-type tangent back sight. The new or 1927-type 7·62mm trials rifle retained the recoil-operated pivoting-block lock of its Avtomat predecessors, but had a detachable box magazine and a large conical muzzle brake. A bayonet with a cruciform blade, which folded back along the underside of the fore-end, could be swung forward under the muzzle until it sprang back to lock around the front-sight block. The back sight lay on the receiver above the trigger guard, there were two recoil bolts through the stock, and cooling slots in the fore-end and hand guard. Small quantities of these rifles, sometimes wrongly identified as 1931-pattern Simonovs, were made for trials but proved to be inferior to gas-operated rivals. The Degtyarev (q.v.) was initially preferred.
FÉG: Kalashnikov (96t), Mosin-Nagant (204t).
Feinmechanische Werke GmbH: Mauser (turning-bolt patterns, military, Germany).
Fémáru Fegyver és Gépgyár: Mannlicher (bolt-action, military, Hungary).
Fez Moroccan arms factory: Beretta, Garand.
FFV Ordnance Forenade Fabriksverken AS: FN, Heckler & Koch (82t), Husqvarna, Kalashnikov.
FFV-Viking Sport Arms AB: Husqvarna.
FGGY: see 'Fémáru Fegyver és Gépgyár'.
FIAS: See 'Sabatti'.
Field Alfred A.: Guedes, Martini (sporting).
Field William, and rifles: 67–8.
Fiorini Sestilio: Breda.
Firearms Co. Ltd: Mauser (194t).
Firearms International Corp.: Mauser (194t) and Sako (240t).
Firestone Tire & Rubber Co.: Marlin (150t).
First Army Technical Research Institute: Arisaka (Japan).
FMAP: Garand, Mauser, Saive (235t).
FN Herstal SA: Browning.
Forbes arms factory: Lee (turning-bolt, military, Australia).
Forenade Fabriksverken AS: see 'FFV'.
Formost brandname: see 'J.C. Penney Co.'.
Fournier Jean: MAS (bolt-action patterns).

Franchi See Heckler & Koch. Luigi Franchi SpA of Fornaci, near Brescia, made small numbers of the 7·62mm LF-59 in the early 1960s. The gas-operated rifle bore a superficial resemblance to the FN FAL, and was also locked by tilting the tail of the breech block down against a transverse shoulder in the receiver. The piston was forged integrally with the bolt carrier, whilst the return spring was housed in a telescoping tube in the back of the receiver. Fixed and folding-butt versions were made, but the Italian army preferred the Beretta BM-59 and the LF-59 faded quietly into obscurity. A typical example was 1,030mm overall, had a 530mm barrel, and weighed about 4·3kg. A twenty-round detachable box magazine was used, cyclic rate being about 625 rpm.
Francotte Auguste, & Co.: Berdan, Comblain, Martini and Werder.
Frank A.L., & Co.: Mannlicher, Mauser, Vetterli (Italy).
Frankonia Waffen-: Mauser (194t).
Fraser Daniel, & Co., and rifles: 69. See also Martini (sporting, Britain), Ruger.
Freire y Góngora Col. Luis: Rider (military, Spain).
Fremont Robert: ArmaLite.
Frohn Wilhelm: Mauser.
Früwirth Ferdinand, and rifle: 69.
Funk Christoph: Mauser, 199t.

Galaš Otakar: Czechoslovak factories, Mosin-Nagant (military, Czechoslovakia).
Galef J.L., & Son, Inc.: BSA.
Galil: Kalashnikov (Israel).

GARAND John C., and rifles: 70–4, 73t. The original 1920-pattern primer-actuated rifle was withdrawn for improvement in May 1920, to be replaced in November 1921 by the improved 'M1921'. An order for 24 essentially similar 'M1922' rifles was approved in March 1922. Tests against the Thompson Auto Rifle PC (or 'M1922') in the summer of 1925 showed that the Garand had greater promise, but that there was still much work to do.
·30 M1924 rifle This was an improved M1922, tested at Fort Benning against ten Thompson Auto Rifles. The report of 15 June 1926 was inconclusive. Subsequently, however, the construction of the first ·30 Garand was authorised. Primer-actuation guns were still being tested in 1928, but were then abandoned.
·276 T3 rifle The first gas-operated ·30 Garand appeared by the end of 1927. Trials were undertaken throughout 1928 against M1924 primer-actuation Garands, ·30 Thompson Auto Rifles and ·276 T1 Pedersen rifles, plus a ·256 Bang. The ·30-calibre Garand was abandoned in

Garcia Sporting Arms Corp.: Rider (sporting), Sako (240t).
Gardone arms factory: Mannlicher (Italy).
Gasser Leopold: Kropatschek.
Gehmann Walter: Mauser (and 194t).
Geiger Leonard: Rider.
Geipel Berthold: see 'Erma-Werke'.
Genschow Gustav, & Co. AG: Haenel, Mauser (194t).
Germania-Waffenfabrik: see 'J.G. Anschütz'.
Geværfabrik Kjobenhaven: see 'Copenhagen'.
GIAT: MAS.
Gibbs George, & Co.: Farquharson, Mauser (194t).
Gibbs-Farquharson-Metford: Farquharson.
Gibbs Rifle Company: Mauser (195t).
Glaser Walter: Heeren, Schmidt & Habermann.
Glenfield brandname: Marlin.
Golden Eagle rifles: 74.
Golden State Arms Corp.: Mauser, 195t.
Gosney Capt. Durward: Garand.
Grant Stephen, & Son; see 'Atkin, Grant & Lang'.
Gras Basile, and rifles: 74–6. See also Lebel, Murata.
Greener William W., and W.W. Greener & Co.: Field, Lee (124t), Martini.
Greenwood & Batley: Berdan.
Griffin & Howe, Inc.: Mauser (195t).
Grisel Peter: Dakota.
Groupement Industriel des Armements Terrestres: GIAT.
Grünig & Elmiger: 76–7. See also Schmidt (sporting).
Grünel brandname: Grünig & Elmiger.
Gustloff-Werke 77–8. See also Mauser, Walther.

Hadar brandname: Kalashnikov (Israel).
Haenel C.G., AG; and rifles: 78–9. See also Aydt, Mannlicher, Mauser (sporting guns: 195t), Walther.
Haerens Rustkammer; Haerens Tøjhus; and Haerens Vaabenarsenal: see 'Copenhagen'.
Halbe & Gerlich: Mauser (195t).
Haley Richard, Cdr, USN: Garand.
Halger Waffenfabrik: see 'Halbe & Gerlich'.
Hamburg-Amerikanische Uhrenfabrik: Mondragon.
Hämmerli Johann Ulrich, Rudolf, and Hämmerli AG: 79. See also Martini, Mauser (195t), Schmidt (bolt-action, sporting), Tanner.
Hance Sydney: Enfield (auto-loading).
Handfeuerwaffen-Productionsgenossenschaft Suhl: Werder.
Hanyang arms factory: Mannlicher (China).
Harrington & Richardson Arms Co.; Harrington & Richardson, Inc.; and rifles: 79. See also ArmaLite, Garand, Husqvarna, Mauser (sporting guns: 195t), Saive (235t), Sako (240t).

BSA The unsuccessful Model 28-P auto-loading rifle, developed for British Army trials in the late 1940s. WELLER & DUFTY

Januszewski The abortive ·280 EM-2 rifle. IAN HOGG

Mannlicher The 1891-model automatic rifle.
From Greener's *The Gun and Its Development*, 1910.

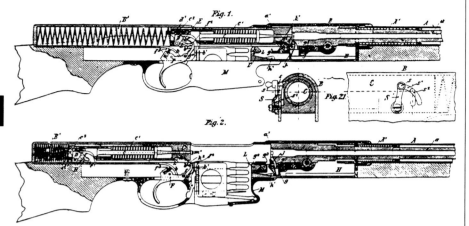

Index

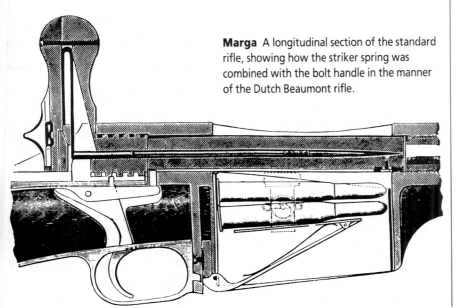

Marga A longitudinal section of the standard rifle, showing how the striker spring was combined with the bolt handle in the manner of the Dutch Beaumont rifle.

Index

Pieper A section of the bolt-action rifle.

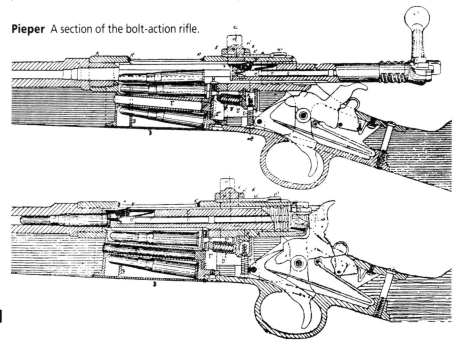

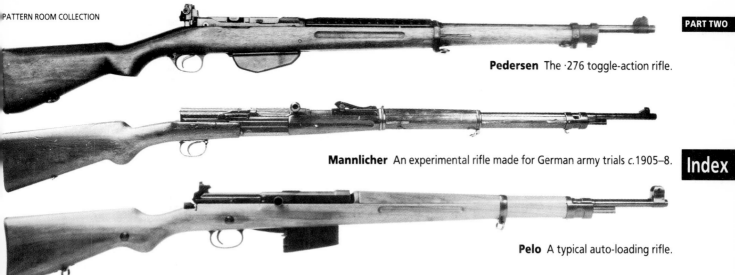

Pedersen The ·276 toggle-action rifle.

Mannlicher An experimental rifle made for German army trials c.1905–8.

Pelo A typical auto-loading rifle.

Excepting a handful made in 1869 with improved Bolted Actions, the guns all exhibit Pattern II** breeches. P/58 rifles were 48·75in overall, weighed 8·95lb, and had 30·5in barrels rifled with three grooves. Their ramp-and-leaf sights were graduated to 1,000 yards. In 1871, the first of at least 12,000 guns was altered for the yeomanry, work continuing until the 1880s. The rear swivel was moved to the underside of the butt and the P/59 cutlass bayonet was replaced with an altered P/60 sabre. Most Royal Navy guns were replaced after 1876 by Martini-Henry rifles.

Gaol, or Convict Civil Guard Carbine Approved on 25 September 1867, these ·577 guns were converted in the Pimlico factory; 330 had been adapted by March 1868 from P/53 rifle-muskets. They were 41in overall, weighed about 7·5lb, and had 21·5in barrels. Pattern II** breeches and three-groove rifling were standard; however, back sights and swivels were omitted. Fore-ends were rounded off ahead of the band and the special socket bayonet had a triangular-section blade.

DENMARK
The army adopted the Remington Rolling Block in 1867. However, sufficient funds could not be spared to re-equip completely—so a Snider conversion was also approved.

M1848–65 short rifle The breech-loading Bagladeriffel m/1848–65 was adapted from an old 1848-type pillar-breech rifle. The revisions were undertaken in the Copenhagen factory in 1866–8. The guns fired a 16·9mm rimfire cartridge with a muzzle velocity of 325 m/sec. The original barrels were fitted with a breech block swinging to the left, and the Dahlhoff sight was graduated for 300–900 Danish ells. Conversions were 1,325mm overall, had 865mm barrels, and weighed 4·41kg. They accepted the m/1848 socket bayonet. Some rifles also retained the patch-box in the right side of the butt, but many were re-stocked using the original bands and nose-cap. Trigger guards and side plates were brass, remaining mounts being iron. One swivel lay under the butt, the other being held by a screw through the middle band.

M1853–66 navy rifle The Flådens Bagladeriffel was originally a pillar-breech weapon, 5,000 of which had been bought in Liège—apparently from Malherbé—by the Schlewig-Holstein rebels. After the failure of the 1848 insurrection, 2,540 guns were adapted in the Kronborg factory for the navy (1853–5). The barrel was retained by keys, whilst a bayonet bar lay on the right side of the muzzle. Spurred brass trigger guards carried the back sling swivel, a Dahlhoff back sight was used, and the brass-hilted sword bayonet had a double-edged blade. About 2,250 rifles were adapted for the 16·9mm rimfire cartridge in the Copenhagen factory in 1866, their Snider-type breeches apparently opening to the right. Transformations were 1,200mm overall, had 725mm

barrels and weighed 4·05kg. The tangent sight was graduated to 600 ells.

FRANCE
Though Mle.66 Chassepot needle rifles served regular troops, the French needed to convert obsolescent cap-locks for second-line and militia units. Trials led to the adoption in 1867 of a Snider-type breech. Jacob Snider's executors protested, but the French cited the existence of earlier patents—notably Clairville's of 1853—to avoid licensing fees. By 1870, 342,120 converted guns were available to serve Gardes Nationales Mobiles, local militia and franc-tireurs. The French system was known colloquially as 'à Tabatière'—'like a snuff-box'—and opened to the right. Unlike the British Snider, it was cut down behind the breech to form a loading tray.

British-pattern Sniders The French purchased at least 20,000 breech-loading rifles in Birmingham in 1870, most of which were apparently standard Snider conversions of P/53 rifle-muskets. In addition, 21,400 Pattern III (Bolted) actions were ordered from BSA early in 1871 so that conversions could be made in France. There is no evidence that this contract was completed, but some work was undoubtedly undertaken before the end of hostilities.

M1867 infantry rifle The Tabatière-type Fusil d'Infanterie Mle.1867 was adapted by gunmakers in Paris, Versailles, Alsace and Liège from cap-lock Mle.57 rifle-muskets. It had two brass bands and an elaborate brass nose cap. A new iron receiver (often bronze on improved-pattern guns) was added to the existing barrel, suitably shortened to accommodate it. The hammer had a typically French straight spur. The guns chambered a rimmed 17·8 × 35mm centre-fire cartridge, were 1,423mm long and weighed 4·44kg; their 958mm barrels had four-groove concentric rifling. A pivoting-leaf back sight was graduated to 600 metres, muzzle velocity was 320 m/sec, and the Mle.1847 socket bayonet could be mounted.

¶ The breech-block of the original guns, lacking a method of locking it shut, was prone to open on firing if the parts had worn; consequently, a retaining catch (Bouton-Arrêt) was added in 1868. Improved-pattern guns had a broader shoulder behind the breech block than their predecessors.

M1867 dragoon rifle The Fusil de Dragon Mle.1867 was similar to the infantry pattern described previously—with two brass bands and the elaborate brass nose cap—but was only 1,322mm overall and weighed 4·25kg. The barrel was 851mm long, muzzle velocity was 312 m/sec and the Mle.1847 socket bayonet was retained. Only improved 'locking' actions seem to have been used.

M1867 cavalry carbine The rifle-length Carabine de Chasseurs, Mle.1867, was adapted from the Mle.1859 cap-lock. It could be distinguished from the other Tabatières by its dimensions, though the band and nose

cap were sprung instead of screwed. The carbine was 1,257mm overall, had an 808mm barrel and weighed 4·65kg. The leaf sight was graduated to 1,000 metres; a lug and tenon for the Mle.1842 M.59 sabre bayonet lay on the right side of the muzzle.

Conversions of obsolete weapons Many cap-lock muskets were altered for the Tabatière breech during the war of 1870–1. Most common was the Mle.1822 T.bis, but adaptions of Napoleonic 'An IX' flint-locks are known. Surviving Tabatière rifles were reduced to reserve status by the mid 1870s. Almost all had been discarded by 1885, many undergoing conversion to hunting rifles or shotguns.

SPAIN
The history of these Sniders is something of a mystery. They appear to have originated during the Carlist Wars (1873–5), probably made for one of the feuding factions.

La Azpeitiana short rifle These may have been made for use in Cuba (where the fighting was at its worst), but more probably emanate from one of the Spanish provinces favouring the royalist cause. The guns had back-action locks and the cramped trigger-guard bow characteristic of Spanish guns of the 1860s. The new Snider-type breeches swung to the right, while the back sights were similar to those of the 1871-model Spanish Remington rifle (q.v.). The mark 'LA AZPEITIANA', on top of the breech ahead of the new breech block, has defied interpretation. Two basic versions of the guns were made, individual examples differing in length and weight. The guns said to have been destined for riflemen (Versión Cazadores) accepted a socket bayonet, while the 'Versión Zouavos' had a brass-hilted sabre type with an unusually shallowly-curved blade. They all chamber the 11mm Remington cartridge. A typical example was 1,280mm overall, weighed about 4·2kg, and had a 900mm barrel rifled with four grooves. Its ramp-and-leaf sight was graduated to 1,000 metres.

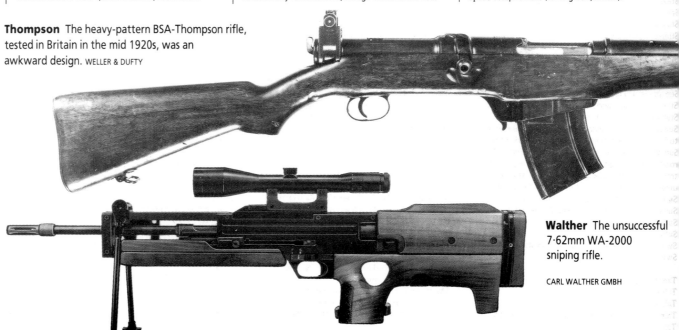

Thompson The heavy-pattern BSA-Thompson rifle, tested in Britain in the mid 1920s, was an awkward design. WELLER & DUFTY

Walther The unsuccessful 7·62mm WA-2000 sniping rifle.

CARL WALTHER GMBH

highlighted the conservatism of the Austrian ordnance and the quest for a suitable breech-loader began. Submissions included a selection of cap-locks and metallic-cartridge rifles, but, after extensive trials, a swinging block-action breech-loading transformation—developed by a Viennese gunsmith—was adopted on 28 January 1867.

M1866 infantry rifle This chambered 13·9 × 33mm rimfire cartridges, being converted from the cap-lock 'Lorenz' rifle-musket. Wrought-iron or steel barrels were used, depending on the manufacturing pattern (1854 or 1863 respectively); 1863-type guns also had smaller lock plates. The weapons had straight-wristed one-piece stocks, with two spring-retained bands and a heavy nose cap. A cleaning rod was carried beneath the barrel, whilst swivels lay on the middle band—unusually close to the nose cap—and under the butt. The rifle accepted the M1854 socket bayonet with a locking ring and a distinctive diagonal attachment slot. A typical M1863/66 was 1,329mm overall with an 885mm barrel. Weight averaged 4·27kg. Ramp-and-leaf sights were graduated to 1,100 paces, muzzle velocity being 390 m/sec. (Note: original rifle-muskets are often known by an '1862' pattern-date.)

M1866 short rifle These conversions of old Jäger-Stutzen had heavy octagonal barrels with the muzzle crowns turned down to accept a sword-bladed bayonet with a locking ring around the socket-base. The Ordinäre Stutzer of 1853 was originally rifled with four grooves and sighted to 1,000 paces, while the pillar-breech Dornstutzer of 1854 once had a heavy ramrod and sights graduated to 1,200 paces. The guns all had key-retained barrels, with swivels through the fore-end (above the cleaning-rod pipe) and on the under-edge of the butt. Trigger-guards ended in a finger-spur, while the back sights were curved-leaf 'grasshopper' patterns. Survivors had been converted to fire expanding-ball ammunition after 1863, when they had been assimilated in a single group. Virtually all of those remaining in service in 1866 were converted to the Wänzl system. A typical Stutzer M1853/63/66 was 1,105mm overall and weighed about 4·7kg. Its 661mm barrel had four-groove rifling, the ramp-and-leaf sight was graduated to 1,200 paces, and muzzle velocity was 378 m/sec. The 1853-pattern socket bayonet was used.

M1866 gendarmerie carbine Extra-Corps-Gewehre M1853/66 and M1863/66 were converted from the cap-locks of 1853 (iron barrel, large lock plate) and 1863 (steel barrel, small lock plate). Used by gendarmerie, sappers, pioneers and ancillary troops, they had a band in addition to a nose cap, accepted the M1854 socket bayonet, and had standard-weight barrels. Length was generally about 1,057mm, weight averaging 4·13kg. The barrel was 611mm long. Ramp-and-leaf sights were graduated to 500 paces, muzzle velocity being about 355 m/sec with M1866 ball cartridges.

COMMEMORATIVE GUNS

BROWNING

Big Game Limited Edition Six hundred of these ·30–06 Browning Automatic Rifles were made, their greyed receivers featuring whitetail and mule deer. An inlaid trophy head, in gold, appeared on each side of the receiver above the trigger.

Bicentennial Model Work on a thousand special ·45–70 B-78 single-shot rifles began in 1975. Sold in a wooden presentation case, accompanied by a medallion and an engraved hunting knife, the guns were numbered from 1776–1 to 1776–1000.

Big Horn Sheep Rifle This special ·270 A-Bolt had gold-plated trophy heads on the receiver sides and a buck, doe and calf group on the floor plate; 600 were made.

Pronghorn Antelope Rifle Five hundred of these ·243 A-Bolt rifles were made with appropriate gold-plated engravings—bucks on the receiver sides and a buck, doe and yearling group on the floor plate. The selected walnut stock had skip-line chequering.

Montana Centennial Two thousand of these Model 1886 lever-action rifles were offered with shotgun-style butt plates and distinctive receiver-side marks.

MARLIN

Zane Grey Centenary Rifle The company made these ·30–30 rifles to celebrate the birth in 1872 of Pearl 'Zane' Grey, best known for his Western novel *Riders of the Purple Sage* (1912). Numbered from ZG1, the rifles had 22in octagonal barrels and full-length magazines. A special medallion was set into the right side of the receiver above the trigger. Actual production amounted to 7,870.

SAVAGE

In 1970, Savage made about ten thousand special ·308 'M1895' rifles to mark the 75th anniversary of the Savage lever-action rifle. Built on the Model 99, they had 24in octagonal barrels and five-round rotary magazines. Engraving appeared on the receiver, and the operating lever was brass-plated. The straight-wrist butt had a brass shoulder plate and a medallion let into the right side. The slender fore-end had a traditional schnabel tip.

WINCHESTER

Winchester was renowned as the most prolific of the 'commemorative gunmakers', making variations of the lever-action M1894 in great quantity. Only a few typical examples are given below.

Alaskan Purchase Produced in 1967 to celebrate the centenary of the sale by the Russians of Alaska, purchased by the USA for $7·2 million, this ·30–30 M1894 carbine was identified by an appropriate medallion in the butt-side, a case-hardened receiver and a brass saddle ring; 1,500 were made in 1967.

Antlered Game A ·30–30 M1894 carbine, this had 'antiqued gold' receiver, lever and bands. Caribou, deer, elk and moose motifs were engraved on the butt-side medallion and receiver; 20,000 guns were made in 1978.

Bicentennial Carbine About 20,000 of these ·30–30 M1894 carbines were made in 1975–6, identical with the standard M1894 excepting their 'antique silver' engraved receiver, selected woodwork, chequered wrist and fore-end, and a medallion in the stock side.

Buffalo Bill Commemorative The first of these ·30–30 1894-type carbines (20in barrel) and rifles (26in octagonal barrel) were produced in 1968 to honour William F. 'Buffalo Bill' Cody (1846–1917). They had black-chrome receivers, nickel-plated furniture, a medallion in the butt side and a facsimile signature on the tang. Matched sets of rifle and carbine were offered, total production of all guns exceeding 120,000.

Canadian Centennial These ·30–30 M1894 carbines (20in round barrel) and rifles (26in octagonal barrel) dated from 1967. They offered black-chrome receivers, engraved with maple leaves, and a gold-filled inscription on the barrel and tang. Total production amounted to more than 90,000.

Canadian Pacific Railroad These ·32 M1894 rifles were offered in Standard, Members and Deluxe issues. Dating from 1981, they had a 24in barrel and a three-quarter length magazine; receivers were pewtered and 'CPR' branded into the butt.

Golden Spike Centennial Produced to celebrate the joining of the transcontinental railroads at Promontory Point, Utah, in 1869, this ·30–30 M1894 carbine had gold-plated furniture and a medallion in the butt-side; 64,760 were made in 1969.

Great Western Artists Engraved in Italy in 1982–3, the receivers of these ·30–30 M1894 carbines featured adaptions of Charles M. Russell's paintings *In Without Knocking* and *Wild Meat for Wild Men*, or, alternatively, Frederic Remington's *Cowboy* and *A Dash for the Timber*.

Illinois Sesquicentennial Typical of the many M1894 Winchesters produced to honour States of the Union, this ·30–30 carbine had gold-plated furniture and a butt medallion. The receiver was engraved with a portrait of Abraham Lincoln and a suitable inscription; more than 31,000 guns were made in 1967.

Louis Riel One of the most controversial of the Winchesters, this was produced in 1985 to mark the centenary of the execution of the Canadian nationalist, Louis Riel. It was basically a ·30–30 M1894 Trapper, offered in standard and deluxe grades.

NRA Centennial Honouring the centenary of the US National Rifle Association (1871–1971), these ·30–30 M1894 Winchesters were offered as 24in-barrelled half-stocked rifles or 26in-barrelled fully-stocked muskets. They were distinguished by folding-leaf back sights, black-chrome receivers, appropriate inscriptions, and medallions in the butt-side.

Oliver F. Winchester Marking the centenary of the famous entrepreneur's death, about 20,000 of these ·38–55 M1894 rifles were made in 1980 with pistol-grip butts and 24in octagonal barrels. The engraved receiver was finished in a gold plate, with a satin finish, whilst the chequering panels had spade-terminal borders.

Theodore Roosevelt Made as a rifle or carbine, these ·30–30 M1894 guns dated from 1969. The rifle had a 26in octagonal barrel, a half-length magazine and a pistol-grip butt; the carbine was similar, but had a 20in barrel and a short fore-end. The receiver, plated with a white gold, bore the American eagle, a facsimile Roosevelt signature, and '26TH PRESIDENT 1901–1909'. A medallion was set into the side of the butt and a saddle ring appeared on the left side of the receiver. Total production of rifles, carbines and matched sets amounted to 49,500.